A History of
International and
Comparative Education

A History of
International and
Comparative Education

Nineteenth-Century Documents

Stewart E. Fraser
George Peabody College for Teachers

William W. Brickman
University of Pennsylvania

Scott, Foresman and Company

The editors wish to express their gratitude to Professors George Z. F. Bereday and Harold Noah, editors of the *Comparative Education Review*, and to Professor R. L. Plancke, editor of *Paedagogica Historica*, for permission to reprint and otherwise utilize material originally published in their journals; to Miss Anna Leo Russell of the Peabody College Library and Dr. J. Isaac Copeland, Director of the Southern Historical Collection and Professor of History, the University of North Carolina at Chapel Hill, who have assisted immeasurably in the research for this work through their interest and professional library services; and to Mrs. Marie Williams and Miss Jeannette C. Weiss for their kind and extensive secretarial assistance.

Library of Congress Catalog No. 68-12941
Copyright © 1968 by Scott, Foresman and Company, Glenview, Illinois 60025
All Rights Reserved
Printed in the United States of America
Regional Offices of Scott, Foresman and Company are located in
Atlanta, Dallas, Glenview, Palo Alto, and Oakland, N. J.

This book is dedicated to

CLIFTON L. HALL
master teacher and educational historian
George Peabody College for Teachers

and to the memory of

ISAAC L. KANDEL
distinguished professor of international
and comparative education
Teachers College, Columbia University

Preface

This compilation of nineteenth-century documents on international and comparative education is concerned principally with the United States and Europe. It represents the transatlantic exchange of educational views of both European and American scholars and schoolmen. It also illustrates the diversity of educational interests and comparisons in the writings of innumerable visitors, many of whom were both commentators and critics. The main focus of attention is the nineteenth century, the century considered to be the principal crossroad in the systematic development of foreign and comparative educational studies. Yet, the editors recognize that there is now a growing awareness of the monumental comparative writings of previous centuries, and a historical introduction is included to give the reader an overview of these earlier contributions to the field. The editors are also interested in contemporary studies, and although this compilation terminates with documents at the beginning of the twentieth century, a conclusion summarizes major developments up to the present time.

A History of International and Comparative Education: Nineteenth-Century Documents is the result of the cooperative efforts of two editors. They have generally divided their responsibilities; Stewart E. Fraser has been primarily responsible for the initial selection, editing, and introduction of the documents in the collection, while William W. Brickman has been concerned with the historical introduction and concluding essay, as well as the bibliography. The whole compilation, however, is the joint concern, involvement, and responsibility of both editors. Editing of the material has necessitated that some footnotes be eliminated and some material be compressed. Spelling has been generally retained from the original documents with only occasional editing.

The editors, for the obvious reasons of space, time, and balance, were unable to include all the materials to which they have had access and which could have gone into a compilation such as this one. Certain important documents have been omitted which perhaps deserve a place in the historical record. For example, it seemed reasonable to exclude such widely known or readily available documents as Horace Mann's *Seventh Annual Report* on his European travels (1844), Jullien's *Plan for Comparative Education* of 1816–1817, or the well-known international studies of Victor Cousin of France. The works of other prominent historical figures in international education, such as Yung Wing of China, Arinori Mori of Japan, and Domingo F. Sarmiento of Argentina, have had to be excluded because this compilation focuses principally on the educational relations of the United States and Europe.

Since the concern for documentary histories of international and comparative education is growing, the editors have turned to many of their colleagues for assistance in developing this compilation to suit the various needs of both professors and students. Those who are interested in contemporary or developmental studies in international education may find materials that suggest new areas for research and study. Others will discover possibilities for further documentary histories. The bibliography will reveal a number of sources upon which the historian of international education can draw. This study should also contribute in part to overcoming the present hiatus between historical and contemporary studies, and it may lead to the compilation of works which include a judicious blend of historical and contemporary material. The editors believe that their work should become part of a continuum attracting further compilations and new analyses into the areas unable to be included in this book. It should further lead the way by indicating some of the material already available to the serious student of international education and illustrating the rich store of documents that still awaits garnering, translation, identification, and final dissemination.

Although this compilation has certain unique features, it is by no means the first published analysis of historical documents on international and comparative education. A pioneering work in the field is undoubtedly W. J. Osburn's almost forgotten *Foreign Criticisms of American Education* (1922). Edgar W. Knight's *Reports on European Education* (1930) is one of the earliest documentary collections on the subject and includes extracts from the works of Griscom, Stowe, and Cousin. A considerable debt is also owed to David Scanlon for putting together his concise and imaginative *International Education: A Documentary History* (1960).

A History of International and Comparative Education: Nineteenth-Century Documents aids American educators and students in understanding the considerable debt that is owed to their national forefathers for observing, borrowing, and comparing educational systems abroad. It is also important for the contemporary student of American educational history to realize what the thoughtful foreigner had to say about the educational system to which the American has now fallen heir. In this way, it is hoped that educational chauvinism at the international level can be challenged. Through books such as this the editors believe that they can contribute to teaching and research curricula in pedagogy, both in the United States and elsewhere, which will seek a better understanding of the international antecedents underlying America's educational and cultural heritage.

STEWART E. FRASER
Peabody International Center, George Peabody College for Teachers

WILLIAM W. BRICKMAN
Graduate School of Education, University of Pennsylvania

Contents

ON AMERICAN EDUCATION

Historical Introduction

The documents included in this book focus generally on the nineteenth century—the most formative period in international education. In order to place these documents in their proper historical perspective, this introduction presents an overview of the history of comparative and international education up to the nineteenth century. It touches briefly on many of the major highlights in the extensive history of education ranging from the classical period through the Middle Ages and the Renaissance to the eighteenth century. It illustrates some of the long-forgotten and virtually ignored contributions to the development of a scientific study of international and comparative education. The careful student of educational history will quickly note that certain historical periods appear to offer greater and perhaps more interesting examples of what we now refer to as international and comparative education and that other periods seem leaner and still need to be more fully and properly studied.

Terms and Definitions

The terms *international education* and *comparative education* are related, but they are different in emphasis. International education connotes the various kinds of relationships—intellectual, cultural, and educational—among individuals and groups from two or more nations. It is a dynamic concept in that it involves a movement across frontiers, whether by a person, book, or idea. International education refers to the various methods of international cooperation, understanding, and exchange. Thus, the exchange of teachers and students, aid to underdeveloped countries, and teaching about foreign educational systems fall within the scope of this term. On the negative side, international education also encompasses activities making for international misunderstanding, ill will, hatred, and even war. The expert in this field is interested in propaganda and the dissemination of different types of political ideas abroad. For example, the sociologist Charles E. Merriam, in his well-known study *The Making of Citizens: A Comparative Study of Civic Training* (1931), characterized Communist propaganda as "international education directed from Moscow."

Comparative education is, on the other hand, the analysis of educational systems and problems in two or more national environments in terms of socio-political, economic, cultural, ideological, and other contexts. Judgments are arrived at not to determine which system, idea, or method is superior but rather to understand the factors, underlying similarities and differences in education in the various nations. The study of comparative education does not necessarily aim at transplantation by one country of a school system prevailing in another, although this has been done repeatedly throughout history.[1]

For some time it has been customary to trace the beginnings of comparative education to the 1816—1817 publication of Marc Antoine Jullien's pamphlet on comparative education, which outlined a plan for analyzing educational questions in an international context.[2] As a matter of fact, the ultimate origins of comparative education are rather obscure and most

---

[1]Inasmuch as comparative education has an international character, it may be subsumed under international education. Indeed, some distinguished specialists, such as the late Professor I. L. Kandel, used the two terms interchangeably, as can be seen in his classic introductory work, *Comparative Education* (1933). Moreover, Carter V. Good's *Dictionary of Education* (1959) treats them synonymously. Nevertheless, one should be aware of the differences in meaning in order to make use in writing and discussion more clear and reliable. Comparative education and international education are two interconnected disciplines.

[2]See Stewart E. Fraser, *Jullien's Plan for Comparative Education, 1816—1817* (New York: Teachers College, Columbia University, 1964).

difficult to discover. Careful and persistent search, however, yields information which indicates that comparative education is much older than has hitherto been suspected.

One may certainly conjecture that comparative education is as old as the custom of visiting countries other than one's own. This practice—whether for purposes of commerce, religious conversion, war, or even curiosity—goes back to the early periods of human history. At various times travelers brought back facts, impressions, and ideas regarding the cultures of the peoples they visited. It is obvious, judging from some ancient writings, that these reports included comments on the upbringing of children and some remarks on the similarities and differences in the ways of educating children in different countries.

The Classical Period

We begin with the classical period, chiefly because most of us are more familiar with the sources of Western civilization than we are of those of the East. The celebrated Greek lyric poet Pindar (c. 522–438 B.C.) called attention to the fact that "different peoples have different customs, and each praise what is right as they see it." In his history of the Persian Wars, Herodotus (c. 484–425 B.C.) included some data about the culture of the foreign peoples with whom the Greeks came into contact. While he did not comment specifically about education, some of his remarks might be interpreted as having educational relevance. Thus, the Persians "look upon themselves as very greatly superior in all respects to the rest of mankind, regarding others as approaching to excellence in proportion as they dwell nearer to them."[3] Furthermore,

there is no nation which so readily adopts foreign customs as the Persians. Thus, they have taken the dress of the Medes, considering it superior to their own; and in war they wear the Egyptian breastplate. As soon as they hear of any luxury, they instantly make it their own; and hence, among other novelties, they have learnt unnatural lust from the Greeks. Each of them has several wives, and a still larger number of concubines.[4]

We might consider such observations as comparative ethnology, comparative culture, and possibly, by stretching the point somewhat, as the beginnings of comparative education. Herodotus' accounts of Egypt, Assyria, Persia, Babylon, and the various Greek states deserve careful attention. Consequently, even if we cannot claim Herodotus as a *bona fide* precursor of comparative education, he might qualify, at the very least, as a competent cultural comparativist of the ancient world.

Xenophon (c 430–355 B.C.), a Greek general and man of letters, included specific comments on education in Persia in *Cyropaedia* his biography of King Cyrus. After citing the "barbarians" to the effect that Cyrus was "most handsome in person, most generous of heart, most devoted to learning, the most ambitious,"[5] Xenophon testifies that:

he was educated in conformity with the laws of the Persians; and these laws appear in their care for the common weal not to start from the same point as they do in most states. For most states permit every one to train his own children just as he will, and the older people themselves to live as they please; and then they command them not to steal and not to rob, not to break into anybody's house, not to strike a person whom they have no right to strike, not to commit adultery, not to disobey an officer, and so forth; and if a man transgress any one of these laws, they punish him. The Persian laws, however, begin at the beginning and take care that from the first their citizens shall not be of such a character as ever to desire anything improper or immoral.[6]

Xenophon went on to describe the training of the Persian youth for citizenship and leadership. He did not shrink from comparative statements, as can be noted in the passage just quoted, nor did he overlook the opportunity of comparing Persia with his native land. "The boys go to school and spend their time in learning justice; and they say that they go for this purpose, just

---

[3]*The History of Herodotus*, Book I, Chapter 134, trans. George Rawlinson, *et al.* (New York: Appleton, 1859), p. 212.

[4]*Ibid.*, Chapter 135, pp. 213–214.

[5]Xenophon, *Cyropaedia*, trans. Walter Miller (London: Heinemann, 1925), I, 11.

[6]*Ibid.*

as in our country they say that they go to learn to read and write."[7] Obviously, Xenophon formulated a value judgment here, derived from the consideration of educational practices in two societies. In addition, he sought to interpret to some extent the system of education which he described as an integral part of Persian life and society. His writings include inklings of those educational issues which are still faced today by many nations: equality of educational opportunity, education of an elite, economic selectivity, character education, and educational qualifications as a prerequisite for civil service.

It is possible to argue with more assurance than in the case of Herodotus that Xenophon was a precursor of those who labor in the field of international and comparative education. Some restraint, however, is advisable. In the first place, it is not altogether certain that Xenophon was a purely detached objective observer. Some literary historians feel that he was not always circumspect with data. As a matter of fact, it seems that Xenophon was a social critic who wrote with admiration of the Persians so that the Athenians might learn a lesson and reform. Both Persian and Spartan societies were deeply concerned with military matters and objectives, and thus their systems of training can be presumed to have been similar in nature and scope. Since Xenophon was chiefly concerned with propagating a system of society and values of a particularly conservative kind, and since he understood the Spartan system of education, it was not at all difficult for him to describe Spartan training and to attribute its virtues to the Persians. It would seem easier to hold Athenian ears with praise for the Persians than with claims to the superiority of Sparta.

Clearly, then, we cannot make any unassailable claim for Xenophon as a practitioner of the art of comparative education. Nonetheless, we should not consign him to oblivion. After all, he did undertake what many today say they do—or try to do—in their research work in comparative education. He did try to make his own people rethink their educational values in terms of characteristics of another society.

The classical works of ancient Rome contain various writings which should be of interest to students of both international and comparative education. Cicero (106–43 B.C.) was aware of differences between Greece and Rome in culture and education, in part because of his studies of philosophy and oratory in Athens and Rhodes. In *De Oratore*, Cicero affirmed that Greece excelled every other nation in the practice of eloquence.[8] In the fragmentary *De Republica*, the Roman orator had Scipio Africanus Minor (*c.* 185–129) point out the differences in the approach to education by the Greeks and the Romans. The latter

did not desire that there should be a fixed system of education for free-born youth, defined by law or prescribed by the state or made identical for all citizens. The Greeks, on the other hand, expended much labor in vain upon the subject of education; and this is the only point with respect to which our guest Polybius charges our ancestral customs with neglect.[9]

The famous conqueror of Carthage was evidently critical of the educational situation of his time. Instead of a family-centered, tutorial, or private scheme of education, he called for a state-controlled school system. He suggested that the Greek experience was faulty and that the Romans might have more success in educational work.

Cicero criticized the gymnastic and military training of the Spartans as an encouragement to robbery and homosexuality. The extant text leaves room for the implication that Roman training was blessed with more virtue.[10] Cicero's displeasure, however, was not necessarily based on ethnocentric considerations, as can be seen in the fact that he studied in Athens and Rhodes, in his defense of Archias, and in his respectful references to Greek thought in his *De Senectute* and elsewhere. On the basis of the fragmentary comments in his *De Republica*, it is not unreasonable to regard Cicero as a contributor to comparative education.

Finally, in *Brutus*, Cicero repeatedly called attention to the cultural and educational achievements of Greece, particularly Athens, and to her contributions to the ancient world. He paid no higher tribute than his reference to the excellence of the Greek teachers of oratory

---

[7]*Ibid.*, p. 15.

[8]*Cicero on Oratory and Orators; with His Letters to Quintus and Brutus*, trans. J. S. Watson (London: Bell, 1891), p. 408. *M. Tullii Ciceronis Brutus de claris oratoribus*, ed. Martin Kellogg (Boston: Ginn, 1889), p. 13.

[9]Marcus Tullius Cicero, *On the Commonwealth*, trans. George Holland Sabine and Stanley Barney Smith (Columbus: Ohio University Press, 1929), pp. 231–232.

[10]*Ibid.*, pp. 232–233.

from whom he received his training. To him, the best teachers in the world were the Greeks.

Comparisons of cultural and educational conditions can also be found in the writings of Julius Caesar (*c.* 102–44 B.C.). In the very first sentence of his *Commentarii de bello Gallico*, the famous Roman general noted that the Belgians, Aquitanians, and Celts showed "fundamental differences both of language, customs, and political organization."[11] Caesar went on to state that "fortissimi sunt Belgae" and to present various reasons why the Belgians excelled the other groups in bravery.

Caesar was not content merely to call attention to the principle of comparison. He also made a specific analysis in the field of education. Thus, in Book VI he briefly sought to interpret the educational aims and procedures of the Druids. He mentioned the Druids' stress on memory training and their consequent unwillingness to commit their religious doctrine to writing. With regard to curriculum, Caesar noted

various lectures and discussions on astronomy, on the extent and geographical distribution of the globe, on the different branches of natural philosophy, and on the many problems connected with religion.[12]

On the basis of this type of content, Caesar could qualify at least as a gatherer of data on *Auslandspädagogik* (education in foreign lands), if not indeed as an ancient comparative educationist.

The Middle Ages

During the Middle Ages numerous European observers wrote accounts of the life and character of various peoples. Such writings resulted in part from expansion of trade, contacts made during the Crusades, missionary zeal, and curiosity. Rabbi Benjamin of Tudela of northern Spain reported on his travels throughout Europe, Asia, and Africa from 1165 to 1173 and referred to economic and political conditions in those areas. His report was not published, however, until 1543.[13] Niccolò and Maffeo Polo must have delivered an extensive report on Italian culture in 1266 to the Chinese ruler Kublai Khan, who commissioned them to bring back one hundred missionary educators on their next trip. Marco Polo (*c.* 1254–1324), Niccolò's son, wrote an enlightening account about the peoples of the Orient and was thus able to "open a new era in European knowledge of the Far East."[14]

Expeditions to Tartary and China were ordered by Louis IX of France (Saint Louis, 1214–1270), and the resulting reports shed light on the culture and learning of the inhabitants of these regions. Pope Innocent IV sent the Franciscan friar Giovanni de Piano Carpini (*c.* 1182–1252) to the Orient. Carpini's *Historia Mongolorum*, a description of the customs and institutions of the Mongols containing international comparisons, was written in about 1246–1247 and published in part in 1598 and in full in 1839.

Another Italian contribution to comparative cultural analysis is the report prepared in about 1490 by humanistic scholar Lippo Brandolini for King Matthias Corvinus of Hungary and Bohemia. Entitled *De comparatione rei publicae et regni*, this account is largely a comparative study of governmental and public institutions in Hungary and Florence, but it also contains accounts of common cultural ideals.[15]

An apparently forgotten precursor of the modern comparative educationists is the famous historian Abd-al-Rahman Ibn Khaldun (1332–1406), a Tunisian-born scholar of Spanish-Arab lineage. In *Muqaddimah* (*Prolegomena*), Ibn Khaldun showed his awareness of the significance of

---

[11]*Caesar's Gallic War*, trans. F. P. Long (Oxford: Clarendon, 1911), p. 1. *Caesar De Bello Gallico*, ed. St. George Stock (Oxford: Clarendon, 1898), pp. 8–9.

[12]*Caesar's Gallic War, ibid.*, p. 176. *Caesar De Bello Gallico, ibid.*, p. 217.

[13]Marcus N. Adler, ed. *Sefer Masaot shel R'Binyamin z'L* (The Itinerary of Benjamin of Tudela) (London, 1907).

[14]G. F. Hudson, *Europe and China* (London: Edward Arnold, 1931), p. 129.

[15]Lynn Thorndike, *Science and Thought in the Fifteenth Century* (New York: Columbia University Press, 1929), pp. 233–260. The text of the original report was published under the editorship of Jeno Abel by the Hungarian Academy of Sciences (Budapest, 1890).

the study of cultural and educational differences. Thus, he insisted that the scholar in historiography

needs to know the principles of politics, the [true] *nature of existent things, and the differences among nations, places, and periods with regard to ways of life, character qualities, customs, sects, schools, and everything else.*[16]

In addition, he must have "a comprehensive knowledge" of the contemporary situation of all these factors and

must compare similarities or differences between the present and the past (or distantly located) conditions. He must know the causes of the similarities in certain cases and of the differences in others.[17]

Since "schools" is one of the terms of reference of Ibn Khaldun, it can be fairly presumed that he had some grasp of the concept of comparative education. Certainly, he had a concrete notion of the methodology of studying a problem in a comparative context. Thus, he contrasted "the institution of scientific instruction" in Spain with that in the Arab East. He traced the decrease of interest in the sciences in Spain to the gradual decline of Moslem civilization there. Jurisprudence and the intellectual disciplines, he complained, had all but disappeared as studies. The sole reason for this lamentable situation

is that the tradition of scientific instruction has ceased (to be cultivated) in Spain, because civilization there has deteriorated and the enemy has gained control over most of it.[18]

The reference here to "the enemy," of course, was to the growing power of Catholic Castile.

On the other hand, observed Ibn Khaldun, "scientific instruction is very much in demand and greatly cultivated in the East, because of the continuity of the tradition (of scientific instruction) there,"[19] in spite of the fact that such cultural and scholarly centers as Baghdad and al-Basrah were in ruins. The Eastern Arabs, he noted, were "more firmly rooted in the craft of scientific instruction" and in all other skills than the Arabs of the West (the Maghribis). In fact, many Maghribis who had traveled to the East in quest of knowledge, were of the opinion that the intellect of the people of the East was, in general, more perfect than that of the Maghribis.[20] The superiority of the Eastern over the Western Moslems, however, was attributed by Ibn Khaldun not to a difference in native intellectual ability or in human nature but rather to environmental differences. The advantages of the Easterners lie "in the additional intelligence that accrues to the soul from the influence of sedentary culture."[21]

Ibn Khaldun, as a Westerner, appreciated the value of Eastern Moslem culture and education, and he may have sought to derive some lessons from his comparisons. Apparently, he equated the human and cultural heritage of the people of the two areas, but he found that differences arose in culture and education as a result of the Eastern policy of systematically teaching subjects and skills to young persons. By trying to avoid bias in determining cause-and-effect relationships in cultural and educational differentiation, Ibn Khaldun appears to qualify as an early researcher in comparative education.

The Renaissance

Travel reports and analyses were published with increasing frequency in the sixteenth century, probably as a concomitant of the age of discoveries and explorations. Boemus' *Repertorium librorum trium Ioannis Boemi de omnium gentium ritibus*, published in 1520, was a widely read report on the customs, characteristics, and life of many peoples in Europe, Asia,

---

[16]Ibn Khaldun, *The Muqaddimah: An Introduction to History,* trans. Franz Rosenthal (New York: Pantheon Books, 1958), I, 56.

[17]*Ibid.*

[18]*Ibid.,* p. 430.

[19]*Ibid.,* p. 431.

[20]*Ibid.*

[21]*Ibid.,* p. 432.

and Africa. In a sense, it can be termed a comparative ethnological treatise with decided implications for education.

In at least one instance, travel resulted in a more enlightened viewpoint about an area that was considered culturally and educationally underdeveloped. A visit to Poland in 1518 by Leonard Coxe, an English humanistic scholar, led to the discovery of competence in scholarship in a land that was dourly regarded as a *terra incognita* in Western Europe.

The Italian historian, Lodovico Guicciardini (*c.*1521–1589), nephew of the more famous Francesco, sojourned for a number of years in the Netherlands and published a study of the *Paesi Bassi* (Low Countries) in 1567. He paid tribute to the level of learning he found there.

Fond of learning and the arts, they [the Netherlanders] *could boast of a great number of learned and scientific men among them, and several authors of celebrity; most of the people were acquainted with the rudiments of grammar, and even the peasants were able to read and write well.*[22]

As a scholar who made field observations in a foreign country, Guicciardini was surely qualified to express educational judgments. While it is possible that he exaggerated somewhat about the peasants, it is likely that he gave his readers a substantial truth, as can be determined from a study of fifteenth- and sixteenth-century Dutch history. It is noteworthy that this Italian's appreciation of scholarship in the Netherlands was published a decade before the founding of the influential and internationally known University of Leyden. Guicciardini even implied that he was envious of Holland. Like other countries in Europe, Holland had drawn cultural and educational inspiration from Renaissance Italy, and its peasantry possessed a high educational *niveau* (level), which was lacking among the peasantry of Italy.

Two works published in 1560 testify to the growing international interest in the Middle East. The well-known French scholar Guillaume Postel (1510–1581), a professor of Hebrew, Arabic, and Greek at the Sorbonne, issued in Poitiers a study on the history of Turkey and the Middle East, *De la république des Turcs: . . . des meurs & loys de tous Muhamédistes.* Postel paid attention to the education, customs, life, and religion of the Turks, Persians, Arabs, and other Moslem peoples. This volume was the product of his trip, at the behest of King Francis I, to Turkey and Egypt in order to obtain manuscripts for the royal library. Postel was able to "spread knowledge of the Orient among his fellow Christians and to stimulate European interest in the outside world."[23] On a limited scale, Postel added to the meager knowledge Europeans then possessed on education in other countries.

The second important work published in 1560 was the *Libellus de Turcorum moribus*, issued in Wittenberg by Bartolomeo Georgiewicz, a Croatian soldier who had been a Turkish slave for some time. This book, with a preface by Philip Melanchthon, does not express admiration for the Turkish Empire or its people; however, it contains interesting data about Turkish customs, religious activities, life, and education. An appended glossary of conversational expressions and phrases enabled travelers to make themselves understood in Turkish, Arabic, and other languages.

The sixteenth century was also marked by the growth of interest in the life and culture of the Russians. Baron Sigismund von Herberstein, a German diplomat who served in Russia from 1517 to 1526, described "the more intimate habits of the Russians" but paid scant attention to education, ostensibly because there was very little formal schooling at the time. Education was mentioned in more detail later in the century by the British Ambassador, Dr. Giles Fletcher, who lived in Russia during 1588 and 1589. He analyzed Russian society, culture, and education in his *Of the Russe Common Wealth* (1591). According to Fletcher, the tyranny of the tsar was mainly responsible for the sad state of culture and education in Russia, and the ignorance of the priests was largely due to the lack of learning exhibited by their bishops. He testified that the Russian people were denied opportunities to study and were prohibited from travel so "that they may learn nothing, nor see the fashions of other countries abroad."[24] Dr.

---

[22]Lodovico Guicciardini, "Belgicae sive Inferioris Germaniae descriptio" (1660), in C. M. Davies, *History of Holland, from the Beginning of the Tenth to the End of the Eighteenth Century* (London: Parker, 1841), I, 487. The original publication was in Italian, *Descrittione di tutti Paesi Bassi Altrimenti detti Germania Inferiore* (Antwerp, 1567).

[23]William J. Bouwsma, *Concordia Mundi: The Career and Thought of Guillaume Postel* (Cambridge, Mass.: Harvard University Press, 1957), p. v.

[24]Giles Fletcher, *Russia at the Close of the Sixteenth Century: Comprising the Treatise "Of the Russe Common Wealth"* (London: Hakluyt Society, 1856), p. 63.

Fletcher's criticism must have hit home because the Muscovy Company, in order to maintain good relations with Russia, prevailed upon Queen Elizabeth to ban the book. Nonetheless, Fletcher's book appeared often in Russian translation, a fact leading one to believe that the Russians regarded it as a reliable work on their country's culture and education.

As other evidence of comparative education studies in the sixteenth century, the German scholar, Jacob Middendorp, in 1562 compiled data concerning the universities of France, Italy, Germany, Denmark, Bohemia, and Poland. He thus furnished many important and fundamental facts that would make some comparisons possible.[25]

Some of the leading scholars of the fifteenth and sixteenth centuries engaged in activities on the order of comparative education. In some of his letters, Erasmus (1469–1536) made statements about Oxford, Cambridge, and the state of learning in England. In a 1499 letter from London to an English friend and former student in Italy, Robert Fisher, Erasmus remarked about the excellence of scholarship in Italy. This attitude was shared by many Englishmen and other Europeans, and, in fact, Erasmus identified Italy as a land "where even the walls are both more learned and more eloquent than the men in our country."[26] However, he felt that there were also learned scholars in England, such as John Colet, William Grocyn, Thomas Linacre, and Thomas More. Writing to Johann Reuchlin in 1516 from Calais after a visit to England, Erasmus noted that England had made strides in learning and could be compared favorably with Italy.[27] It might be added that this letter was not written in England, and presumably Erasmus was under no obligation to make complimentary remarks to his hosts.

The writings of Michel de Montaigne (1533–1592) also reveal consciousness of cultural comparisons. In an essay "Of Cannibals" (*c*.1580), he was sharply critical of observers who lack objectivity in their descriptions of primitive peoples. The journal of his trip in 1580 and 1581 to Germany, Switzerland, and Italy, which was kept for the most part by his secretary, yields some insight into educational situations in other countries. In Rome, Montaigne noted that Pope Gregory XIII built and endowed colleges for the Greeks, English, Scots, French, Germans, and Poles "to call to the Church the children of those nations, corrupted by evil opinions against the Church; and there the boys are lodged, fed, dressed, instructed, and provided with everything."[28] Reports of such an educational experiment contributed much to a comprehension of foreign education at the time. Montaigne also attended a Jewish religious service in Rome and observed in the synagogue that "the children, even the very youngest, take part, and all without exception understand Hebrew."[29] Montaigne was deeply interested in all details of the life and customs of the peoples he visited, and he traveled "with the hope of coming to know people of other nations through their way of life."[30]

Toward the end of the sixteenth century a new type of literature emerged which contributed to the later development of a corpus of writings in comparative education. In 1589 an English translation of a German book, Albrecht Meier's *Certaine briefe, and speciall instructions for gentlemen, merchants, students, souldiers, marriners, etc. Employed in services abrode*, appeared in London. The aim of this work, which had first been published in German in 1587, was to aid travelers abroad in making systematic observations and to help them make the most of their foreign sojourns. Instruction number 11 was to observe "the industrie, studies, manners, honestie, humanitie, loue, and other morall vertues of the inhabitantes, and wherein they chiefly excell."[31] Here was an attempt at a check list for travelers which included the observation of educational and cultural activities in foreign countries.

A score or more books on the art of traveling were published in Germany and elsewhere in the late sixteenth and early seventeenth centuries. Francis Bacon (1561–1626), in his famous essay "Of Travel," noted the educational value of visiting a foreign country, but he stressed

---

[25]Jacob Middendorp, *Academiarum celebrium universi terrarum orbis Libri VIII* (Cologne: Cholin, 1562).

[26]P. S. Allen, *Selections from Erasmus, Principally from His Epistles*, second edition (Oxford: Clarendon, 1918), p. 31.

[27]*Ibid.*, p. 68.

[28]*The Complete Works of Montaigne*, trans. Donald M. Frame (Stanford: Stanford University Press, 1957), p. 939.

[29]*Ibid.*, p. 944.

[30]*Ibid.*, p. 861.

[31]Margaret T. Hodgen, *Early Anthropology in the Sixteenth and Seventeenth Centuries* (Philadelphia: University of Pennsylvania Press, 1964), p. 186.

the necessary qualifications, such as linguistic knowledge. He urged the traveler to visit libraries and colleges and to attend disputations and lectures. In addition, he warned that the traveler should not abandon his traditions for those observed in foreign countries but should "prick in some Flowers, of that he hath Learned abroad, into the Customes of his owne Country." Through such counsel, Bacon implied that a comparative study of different ways of life involved the study of many factors and that foreign ideas should not be transplanted on the basis of brief, glittering glimpses in other countries.

Bacon, no doubt, was distressed at the superficiality of the observations of some international travelers. A typical statement to which he would have reacted with extreme displeasure was made by Justus Zinzerling, a German author of the popular guidebook *Itinerarium Galliae* (Leiden, 1616). A Doctor of Law from the University of Basel, Zinzerling visited England around 1610 and made some remarks about higher education at Oxford. He said that Queen's College was

most hospitable; if students see strangers, they welcome them, and pledge their healths in college beer out of a large horn; this attentive politeness deserves another kind of praise than the unbridled insolence shown in other colleges by students who, by making attacks upon passengers, are rather deserving of the name of robbers.[32]

Zinzerling may have had a heartwarming experience drinking beer with the students; however, he had nothing to say about the academic situation at Oxford, a disappointing performance in reporting for an academic person.

The Seventeenth Century

The seventeenth century witnessed increasing and deeper international contacts in culture and education. The idea of comparative analysis, already begun in the field of philology in the previous century, was extended to other areas of learning. In 1617 John Selden (1584–1654) published *De diis Syris*, which used a comparative approach in the study of religion. A historical comparison of education in Sweden was undertaken in 1647 by Johan Loccenius (1598–1677), professor of history and law at the University of Uppsala. In this major work on the development of his country, he concluded that the status of learning in his own time was superior to that of the past.[33]

As in previous periods, foreign travel provided occasions for recording educational opinions of a comparative nature. However, travelers' observations concerning education sometimes turned out to be variable and unreliable. Sir William Brereton, who visited the University of Leyden in 1634, wrote about this young institution which had already earned an international reputation, but his report consisted of a mere listing of some of the professors and some random remarks of a rather superficial nature:

here is no face nor presence of a university. The scholars apparelled some as gallants, some like soldiers, some like citizens, some like serving-men; all in colours for most part.   The schools here are very poor, mean things in comparison of Oxford schools.[34]

We may take it for granted, on the basis of internal evidence, that this comparative judgment regarding Oxford and Leyden was derived from an examination of the physical resources rather than from an analysis of curriculum, instruction, qualifications of professors, and the like. Sir William mentioned the presence at Leyden of German students who were "not so safe" at the universities of their own country. The Thirty Years' War was then raging in Germany, and

[32]William B. Rye, *England as Seen by Foreigners in the Days of Elizabeth and James the First* (London: Smith, 1865), p. 135.

[33]Johan Loccenius, "De priscorum seculorum & nostri aevi studiis in Sveciae regno," *Antiquitatum Sveo-Gothicarum Libri tres; in quibus prisci Sveonum & Gothorum, mores, status regni atque instituta, cum hodiernis pro re nata moribus & institutis comparantur*, fourth edition (Frankfurt: Joachim Wild, 1674), pp. 73–78.   The first edition was published in 1647.

[34]Sir William Brereton, *Travels in Holland, the United Provinces, England, Scotland and Ireland* (London: Chetham Society, 1844), p. 39.   The writers acknowledge the assistance of Richard G. Durnin, School of Education, City College, City University of New York, for this reference.

his conjecture is understandable under the circumstances.

Let us consider the observations of two Dutchmen, Jasper Danckaerts and Peter Sluyter, who made a trip to New York in 1679–1680 and took some time off to visit Boston and its vicinity. In Roxbury, they called upon the Reverend John Eliot, the missionary who translated the Bible into Algonquian. They noted that although Eliot "could speak neither Dutch nor French, and we spoke but little English, and were unable to express ourselves in it always, we managed, by means of Latin and English, to understand each other."[35] After an exchange of religious and educational documents and information, the Dutchmen told Eliot about some of the leading personalities in the church in Holland, including Madam Schuurman. Anna Maria van Schuurman was the "Incomparable Virgin" whose knowledge of Greek, Hebrew, Arabic, and other languages was second to few in Europe. Danckaerts and Sluyter then went on to Cambridge to visit Harvard College.

We found there, eight or ten young fellows, sitting around, smoking tobacco, with the smoke of which the room was so full, that you could hardly see; and the whole house smelt so strong of it, that when I was going upstairs, I said, this is certainly a tavern. We excused ourselves, that we could speak English only a little, but understood Dutch or French, which they did not. However, we spoke as well as we could. We inquired how many professors there were, and they replied not one, that there was no money to support one. We asked how many students there were. They said at first, thirty, and then came down to twenty; I afterwards understood there are probably not ten. They took us to the library where there was nothing particular. We looked over it a little. They presented us with a glass of wine. This is all we ascertained there. The minister of the place goes there every morning and evening to make prayer and has charge over them. The students have tutors or masters. Our visit was soon over, and we left them to go and look at the land about there. . . . We passed by the printing office, but there was nobody in it; the paper sash however being broken we looked in; and saw two presses with six or eight cases of type. There is not much work done there. Our printing press is well worth two of it, and even more.[36]

These men also commented that "we have found the English the same everywhere, doing nothing but lying and cheating, when it serves their interest."[37] It does not require great perception to question the objectivity or the reliability of these judgments by the two Dutch visitors. What might have been an interesting and illuminating exercise in comparative education turned out to be, for the most part, a parade of prejudices. In any event, we can learn from this account that institutional visitation per se is not a guarantee of enlightenment in education.

It is a familiar fact that guidebooks in the late sixteenth century suggested that travelers should observe foreign schools. A century or so later, as the popularity of the grand tour for young gentlemen increased, such volumes began to appear with greater frequency. One by Edward Leigh (1671) urged these gentlemen to take note of "Libraries, Colleges, Disputations and Lectures where they are."[38] There was great concern at the time over the possibility that travelers might indulge in mere curiosity seeking or other time-consuming activities of little cultural or educational value or that they might fall prey to vice abroad. Some writers even opposed the practice of foreign travel by the very young because the lack of sufficient educational and cultural background often made it impossible for the traveler to understand, appreciate, and appraise what he observed in the foreign countries. As Dr. Joseph Priestley remarked:

How can . . . comparison be made, or any judgment formed of the constitution and laws of other countries with respect to our own, when that constitution, and those laws with which they are to be compared, are unknown?[39]

Priestley pointed up a principle which is not sufficiently stressed in comparative education circles—that to successfully learn about a foreign system of education, a student must first

---

[35]Jasper Danckaerts and Peter Sluyter, "Journal of a Voyage to New York to 1679–80," *Memoirs of the Long Island Historical Society*, I, 377–395; as reprinted in Peter G. Mode, *Source Book and Bibliographical Guide for American Church History* (Menasha, Wis.: George Banta, 1921), pp. 91–92.

[36]*Ibid.*, p. 92.

[37]*Ibid.*

[38]Edward Leigh, *Three Diatribes or Discourses First of Travel, or a Guide for Travellers into Foreign Parts* (London, 1671), pp. 7–8, as quoted in George C. Brauer, Jr., *The Education of a Gentleman: Theories of Gentlemanly Education in England, 1660–1775* (New York: Bookman Associates, 1959), p. 160.

understand his own system.

The growing number of accounts and reports on travels to various countries naturally included some comments on education. A beginning effort to gather basic data about society and education seems to have been made in the second half of the seventeenth century by Sir William Petty (1623–1687), a professor of anatomy at Oxford, a professor of music at Gresham College, and a founder of the Royal Society of London.

Petty . . . was the first to attempt the systematic collection of social facts and figures and to base upon them deductions both political and economical. He was thus the real founder and inventor of the science of Statistics, and in a more limited sense he may be said to have been the originator of that of Political Economy. [40]

In his ''The Method of Inquiring into the State of Any Country,'' Petty suggested the compilation of data indicating the proportion of clergy, physicians, and lawyers in the population; ''the games, recreations, exercises, studyes and pastimes; what are the bookes that do sell most, or whereof 3000 sell; and what arts, sciences and trades do most flourish.''[41] Presumably, the fundamental facts about England could be compared with similar data from other countries.

In another statement, Petty was even more specific about the kinds of information to be obtained in Great Britain and in the American colonies, suggesting the number of ''churches, houses, cottages, schooles, workhouses, harthes and families''[42] and ''the number of certaine select bookes yearely sold in England.''[43] Elsewhere, Petty urged the assembly of data about the number of students admitted to higher education, books published, university degrees conferred, as well as the number of existing college fellows, scholars, fellow commoners, pensioners, and servitors.

On the basis of his experience in education in England and on the continent, Petty felt confident about offering suggestions about education in colonial Pennsylvania. He studied educational developments in Pennsylvania and posed numerous questions, mainly of an ethnological nature, about the Indians. As a result, he must have obtained a clear notion of the frontier situation in the New World. His ''General Cautions Concerning Pennsylvania'' seems to reflect his conviction that the colonies required an education system designed for an underdeveloped area. Thus, he counseled:

Discourage the learning of lattine & greek, and of University learning; but promote arithmetic & measuring and drawing. [44]

In part, he anticipated the educational principles of Benjamin Franklin nearly a century later. If Petty discouraged universities, he at least called for ''common Nurseryes, Infirmaryes, hospitalls & schools.'' He recommended ''the Lattine and French tongues'' for young people who desired to study medicine but apparently not for others.[45] In his ''Political Observations'' he noted that in England ''2 million . . . are males, whereof $\frac{1}{4}$ are boyes between 7 & 17 years, whereof above 100,000 needlessly loose their tymes in learning lattine and greeke.''[46] The figure of 100,000 boys studying the classical languages may be an exaggeration, but it may not be inappropriate to characterize Petty as one of those seventeenth-century savants who had an awareness of cultural and educational differences and who suggested an approach toward the solution of problems by means of the accumulation of data.

A curious but interesting incident in the late seventeenth century illustrates a practical application of the comparative approach. In 1687 the iconoclastic scholar Christian Thomasius (1655–1728) horrified the academic world by publicly announcing in German that he would deliver a lecture in German at the University of Leipzig on Baltasar Gracian's *Oraculo manual*

---

[39]Joseph Priestley, *An Essay on a Course of Liberal Education for Civil and Active Life* (London, 1765), p. 91; as quoted in Brauer, *ibid.*, p. 171.

[40]Marquis of Lansdowne, ed. *The Petty Papers: Some Unpublished Writings of Sir William Petty* (London: Constable, 1927), I, xvii.

[41]*Ibid.*, pp. 175–176.

[42]*Ibid.*, p. 178.

[43]*Ibid.*, p. 179.

[44]*Ibid.*, II, 114.

[45]*Ibid.*, p. 168.

[46]*Ibid.*, p. 238.

o arte de prudencia. The use of German in the university was revolutionary enough, but he compounded the insult by suggesting the desirability of imitating the French in everyday living. He constantly emphasized, both at the University of Leipzig and later at the University of Halle, the excellence of the French language and of the French people, whom he characterized as "the cleverest people." In addition, he advocated the French educational ideal—"d'un honnete homme, d'un homme sçavant, d'un homme de bon goust et d'un homme galant—" and derived educational ideas from the textbooks used by the Jansenist educators in the "little schools" of Port Royal, near Paris. A veritable heretic on all fronts, Thomasius drew upon French ideas in his campaign to demolish what was left of Aristotelianism after the attacks by Pierre de la Ramée (Ramus) and Bacon.[47] The German scholar evidently derived his conclusions from a study of French writings rather than from a first-hand examination of French education, but he did make an attempt at comparative analysis. He was satisfied that the French system compared favorably to the systems in other countries and that his assumptions were logical. Perhaps Thomasius was playing the role of a crusading reformer rather than that of an academic analyst in his estimation of French education.

The Eighteenth Century

There is more information for the eighteenth century on education in foreign countries as recorded and analyzed by those who went abroad as travelers, students, observers, and professional workers. The famed Danish dramatist and essayist Ludvig Holberg (1684–1754) described in detail his reactions to foreign cultures and often contrasted them to his native land. Writing in about 1720, he noted that the southern Europeans were concerned with their own affairs and neglected foreign languages; whereas the northern Europeans, the Dano-Norwegians for example, neglected their native languages in favor of attaining proficiency in foreign idioms. Holberg himself was an exception to his own generalization, since he was a literary master of his native tongue and highly competent in English and other languages. He may have intended to prod his own people into a more careful study of their own language. He pointed out that the English see England first before going abroad, while "we, on the contrary, generally visit foreign countries before we know any thing of our own."[48]

Holberg went to Oxford as a student in 1706, and he described it as a place where only sound knowledge, not superficial learning, could ensure the success of a teacher. The brief account of his stay at Oxford yields some insights into education at the institution and reveals his appreciation:

. . . there is scarcely any institution for public instruction in which the authorities are more respected, and in which the conduct of the students is more uniformly correct and decorous, than the University of Oxford. Here the most trivial offences are noticed and corrected; and the benefit which the students derive from this salutary discipline, is as striking as is the mischief which results from an opposite system in some other seats of learning, which are at the same time schools for drinking, feasting, gaming, and every species of debauchery.[49]

In other parts of his memoirs Holberg repeatedly made observations and analyses, which were generally comparative, on education and culture in England, France, Germany, Spain, and Holland.[50] He was often incisive and usually subjective. If his writings on the topics in comparative culture lack systematic and objective treatment, they are, at least, full of insights and make an effort at analyses beyond the fact-gathering stage. In this sense, Ludvig Holberg might be regarded as a significant precursor of the scientific approach to comparative education.

Russia aroused the interest of European thinkers and attracted many first-hand observers all through the eighteenth century. John Perry, an English engineer in the service of Peter the Great from 1698 to 1712, evaluated Russian culture and education in his report *The State of*

---

[47]Theobald Ziegler, *Geschichte der Pädagogik mit besonderer Rücksicht auf das höhere Unterrichtswesen*, fourth edition (Munich: Beck, 1917), pp. 189−190. See Christian Thomasius, *Gedanken und Erinnerungen, 1723−1726.*

[48]Lewis Holberg, *Memoirs* (London: Hunt and Clarke, 1837), p. 18; from the unpublished manuscript by Stewart E. Fraser, "Ludvig Holberg's Memoirs: An Eighteenth Century Danish Contribution to International Education" (Nashville: Peabody International Center, 1965).

[49]*Ibid.*, p. 20.

[50]*Ibid.*, pp. 28, 219, and especially 228−254.

Russia Under the Present Czar (1716), and he called attention to the prevalence of ignorance. While Perry expressed admiration for Peter's reforms, such as the formation of a mathematical secondary school in Moscow and the dispatching of about one hundred young men to study naval science in England, Holland, and Italy, he felt it necessary to emphasize the extremely low state of learning among the clergy.[51]

A similarly sad portrait of the state of Russian culture was presented by the French historian and philosopher Abbé Guillaume-Thomas Raynal (1713–1796) in 1780. Although he appreciated the educational reforms of Catherine the Great, he was certain that they had scarcely made any dent in solving the problem of ignorance. He was interested enough to make positive suggestions for more effective and pervasive education in Russia and felt that until social reforms were accomplished, the educational measures by the government would be in vain.[52]

A somewhat different and more specific report was furnished by the English historian William Coxe (1747–1828), who visited Russia in the years 1768, 1778–1779, and 1784–1785. As a tutor to young Englishmen on the grand tour, Coxe visited several countries and took special note of schools and cultural institutions. While he observed the low state of Russian society and culture, he did notice "progress toward improvement" in St. Petersburg and Moscow. Like earlier visitors, he was especially critical of the parish priests, whom he called "the refuse of the people." He reasoned that if they were so ignorant that they could not read the Russian gospel, the ignorance of their parishioners must be even greater. Coxe praised the attempts of Catherine the Great to raise the level of learning among the priests and their children. He was certain, however, that no general cultural improvement could take place in Russia as long as a majority of the people were in a state of "absolute vassalage."

Coxe called specific attention to the Academy of Fine Arts, founded in 1758 in St. Petersburg by Count Ivan Shuvalov under the patronage of Empress Elizabeth. After a brief description of its organization and curriculum, Coxe remarked, "we observed several finished pieces of drawing, painting, and sculpture, which had much merit, and seemed to predict the future improvement of the arts in Russia."[53] Although he was convinced that "this institution is indeed admirably calculated for promoting the liberal arts, and is deserving of the highest encomiums . . . [and] the scholars, for the most part, make a considerable progress during the time they remain in the academy,"[54] he recognized that little would be contributed to the growth of culture because the people gave it little encouragement. Coxe suggested that the Russians, while by no means deficient in genius, did not as yet have that general zeal for the pursuit and cultivation of the arts which had developed in most other European countries. He believed that the Russians did not as yet have the "motives to animate and encourage a continuance of industry, or to gratify the pursuits of reputation and character."[55] His concluding observation was prophetic, for Coxe noted that as Russia gradually moved "towards a higher state of civilization and refinement," it would anticipate that its "institutions, still in their infancy, must infallibly be productive of more extensive and permanent effects."[56]

One of the features of Russian education which was attractive to Coxe was the attention given to pupils of special ability, and he took particular note of the careful selection of superior artists for foreign study at government expense. During his visit in November 1768 to the *Kadetskii Korpus* (Corps of Cadets), a school founded in 1731 to prepare nobility for military and civil service, he recorded the fact that "the boys, whose genius prompts them to such studies, are provided with masters in the Latin, English, and Tartar tongues."[57] He also praised the program of physical education in this school and testified that, because of the stress upon cleanliness, "the boys are remarkably healthy."[58] He was clearly impressed by the school,

---

[51]John Perry, *The State of Russia Under the Present Czar* (London: Tooke, 1716), pp. 209−212, 216−221; as reprinted in Peter Putnam, ed. *Seven Britons in Imperial Russia* (Princeton, N.J.: Princeton University Press, 1952), pp. 33−36.

[52]Guillaume-Thomas Raynal, *Histoire philosophique et politique des établissemens et du commerce des Européens dans les deux Indes* (Geneva: Pellet, 1780), III, 170−177; Abbé Raynal, *A Philosophical and Political History of the Settlements and Trade of the Europeans in the East and West Indies* (London: Strahan and Cadell, 1783), III, 132−137.

[53]William Coxe, *Travels into Poland, Russia, Sweden and Denmark* (London: Cadell, 1784), II, 149.

[54]*Ibid.*

[55]*Ibid.*, p. 150.

[56]*Ibid.*

[57]*Ibid.*, p. 155.

[58]*Ibid.*, p. 156.

and he may have meant to imply some criticism of the English public school system with which he was familiar.

Coxe also described the Smolny Institute, founded in 1764 by Catherine the Great for girls of the nobility and the middle class. He noticed "the designs, paintings, charts, genealogical tables, and other trophies of the ingenuity of the young ladies." [59] His simple mention of the linguistic course of study—"they obtain, beside a grammatical knowledge of their native tongue, the French, German, and Italian languages"—[60] may have been an implied comparative judgment. What particularly impressed him were the performances in "an elegant theatre" by sixteen- and seventeen-year-old girls of *La servante maitresse* and by ten- through twelve-year-olds of *L'oracle* in the original French. The pupils participating in both plays "acted with spirit, and displayed great propriety both in their gesture and elocution. I was greatly astonished at the surprising purity with which they pronounced the French tongue." [61]

Another traveler, a Danish entomologist, economist, and professor at the University of Kiel Johan Christian Fabricius (1745-1808), wrote a report on the Russian schools he visited during Catherine's reign. His attitude was more critical than that of Coxe, though his comments were less specific. The Dane stated that the existing schools were too expensive for the "common man" and that their quality was not of the best. The only way for the average Russian to have his children learn the rudiments of reading and writing, wrote Fabricius, was to pay "several rubles" to a retired soldier. He concluded that this was "the reason why no Christian nation other than the Russian knows so little even about the first principles of religion and can so scarcely read and write." [62]

His lack of precise knowledge about Russia did not prevent Diderot, when he visited the country in 1776, from presenting to Catherine II a plan to elevate the Russian educational standards. After describing a faculty of theology for the projected university, the French *philosophe* stated that:

it is thus that a good and learned ecclesiastical would be trained in Italy, in England, in Spain, and in Portugal. Is there any need of changing much in this education, either in regard to the scientific or the moral part, for another country, for Russia? I do not know. [63]

At least one commentator has interestingly remarked that Diderot's plan is as much a critique of French education as it is a proposal for a Russian system. [64] Diderot drew upon his knowledge of French schools for his proposal, and, in suggesting the transfer of a program of education from one country to another, without taking into account the different conditions, he committed one of the most common cardinal sins in comparative education proposals. However, Catherine II showed good sense by permitting the plan, which she had requested, to remain "many years undisturbed in the library of the Hermitage." [65] Moreover, there are no records to show if there were any attempts to carry out the plan in Russia.

With more apparent boldness than direct knowledge, La Chalotais judged in his "Essay on National Education" (1763) that:

in ten years, Russia has made more progress in physics and in the natural sciences than other nations would have made in a hundred. It suffices to examine the memorials of the Academy of Petersburg. Perhaps Portugal, which is entirely reforming its studies, will advance more rapidly in proportion than we shall if we do not think seriously of reforming ours. [66]

---

[59] *Ibid.*, p. 157.

[60] *Ibid.*

[61] *Ibid.*, p. 158.

[62] Document in S. Sugenheim, *Russlands Einfluss auf, und Beziehungen zu Deutschland* (Frankfurt am Main: Keller, 1856), I, 59−60.

[63] Denis Diderot, "Plan of a University for the Russian Government," in F. de la Fontainerie, trans. and ed. *French Liberalism and Education in the Eighteenth Century: The Writings of La Chalotais, Turgot, Diderot, and Condorcet on National Education* (New York: McGraw-Hill, 1932), p. 286. Used by permission of McGraw-Hill Book Company.

[64] *Ibid.*, pp. 2, 12, 197, 198.

[65] *Ibid.*, p. 190.

[66] Louis-René de Caradeuc de la Chalotais, "Essay on National Education," in De la Fontainerie, *op. cit.*, p. 63.

He did not seem to realize that the progress in Russia was primarily due to the writing, research, and teaching of Germans, Frenchmen, and other foreigners. It is clear, however, that La Chalotais was more concerned with the rapid improvement of education in France than he was with an objective appraisal of Russian learning. He argued that:

if we compare our colleges, of which the methods are defective, with those of Oxford, of Cambridge, of Leyden, of Göttingen, which have better elementary books than ours, we shall see that a German and an Englishman are necessarily better taught than a Frenchman.[67]

It is not what is taught in the universities which constitutes an index to "the knowledge diffused in the minds of the citizens," according to La Chalotais but it is the published writings of the academics and the good books which more truly indicate the knowledge of a nation. Consequently, the French educator believed, when the French literary achievements are compared to the literary achievements of other countries, it can be seen that the well-educated Frenchman is capable of superior knowledge, method, and taste. This is a fascinating point, but a reading of La Chalotais' essay affords no clues as to how he arrived at this interesting and provocative conclusion.

Another famous eighteenth-century French educator, Condorcet, also made use of comparative education in his work. In his 1792 report to the French National Assembly on behalf of the Committee on Public Instruction, of which he was a member, proposed the establishment of some nine lyceums (his term for universities).[68] Moreover, "the instruction which we propose to provide is more in accord with the present state of the sciences in Europe than in any establishment of learning in foreign countries."[69] Condorcet, it should be noted, was a serious scholar in mathematics and an associate editor involved actively in the publication of the *Encyclopédie*. In addition, he was permanent secretary of the French Academy of Sciences, a member of the French Academy, a member of the academies of Berlin and St. Petersburg, a biographer of Turgot and Voltaire, and a commentator on the problems and developments in America. With such qualifications, it is not unreasonable to suppose that Condorcet knew exactly what he was saying when he ventured to describe his program as second to none in Europe. Even if he seemed to be motivated to some extent by a feeling of nationalism, there is little doubt of his competence to appraise "the present state of the sciences in Europe."

A rather detailed analysis of foreign universities by an anonymous Englishman can be found in a treatise on Holland published in 1743. The author wrote some historical data and then critically described the various aspects of the University of Leyden. The professors' practice of holding classes at their homes and the lack of official lodging for students "very much diminishes the beautiful Order and Grandeur, that ought to adorn these noble Establishments."[70] No doubt, the Englishman was thinking of the stately towers and spacious green quadrangles of Oxford and Cambridge. "But the Want of external Pomp is well made amends for by the great Variety of useful and solid Learning taught in them."[71] The absence of impressive external structures, the academic dress of the faculty, and the students in the streets did not blind the visitor to what he regarded as the essential element in a university—academic excellence. Yet, one wonders how he arrived at his conclusions on the academic status of the Dutch universities, particularly concerning the English institutions:

All the Sciences and learned Languages are taught here [in the universities of Holland] *with extraordinary Care and Success. No Science has the Preference to another: they are all equally consid'd, encouraged, and cultivated; so that in respect to extensive learning these Universities far exceed those of* England, *which seem to be engrossed by Divinity.*[72]

---

[67]*Ibid.*, p. 64.

[68]*"The number of lyceums has been fixed at nine because, by comparing this number with that of England, of Italy, and of Germany, it seemed to correspond with the needs of the population of France."* Marie-Jean-Antoine-Nicholas Caritat de Condorcet, "Report on the General Organization of Public Instruction," in De la Fontainerie, *op. cit.*, p. 350.

[69]*Ibid.*

[70]*A Description of Holland: Or, the Present State of the United Provinces* (London: Knapton, 1743), p. 333. Richard G. Durnin called the writer's attention to this account.

[71]*Ibid.*

[72]*Ibid.*, pp. 334—335.

While few would question the judgment by this English writer, either with respect to the high academic level of the Dutch universities or to the lower level of Oxford and Cambridge in the eighteenth century, it would be interesting to know more about the man so that we might ascertain how he reached his conclusions.

This anonymous English traveler made a great variety of comparative statements, and in discussing the life of the students, he observed that:

they are left entirely to themselves. They live as they please, and study as much, or as little as they see fit; and yet perhaps there are no Universities in the World, where Sobriety and good Manners prevail so much, and where silly Frolicks and Levity are so little known.[73]

This description seems to fit the situation in continental universities generally, and we might suppose that the traveler was not familiar with the contemporary higher education in Europe. However, as a presumably educated man, he was in a position to testify that both natives and foreigners who were taught to speak and write Latin in the grammar schools of Holland "are generally better prepared, than those who come hither from Britain and Ireland."[74] The English observer paid another high tribute to higher education in Holland in the following words:

No Oaths are imposed here, and not a Syllable said about Religion. Roman Catholick, Greek, Jewish, &c. *Parents send their children hither with as little Scruple as* Protestants. *Degrees are not so much regarded here, nor in the other Protestant Universities of* Europe, *as in those of* Oxford *and* Cambridge, *where they are essential in all the learned Professions, except the Common Law.*[75]

One senses in this account a tendency toward sincerity in appreciation of Holland and toward moderation in criticism of England. Apparently, the anonymous English writer of *A Description of Holland* gave much thought to his observations and experiences and was thus able to compose a detailed, accurate, and objective account which may be fairly regarded as one of the highest points in the writing of comparative education in the eighteenth century.

An interesting development in this century was the emergence of the questionnaire as a technique of gathering data relevant to comparative education. In 1724 Reverend James Blair, on instructions from London, distributed to communities in Virginia a questionnaire concerning the status of education—particularly religious education.[76] Governor Sir William Berkeley of Virginia made his famous reply to the questionnaire of the Commission on Trade and Plantations in London in 1671. To the question "What course is taken about instructing the people, within your government in the Christian religion; and what provision is there made for the paying of your ministry?" the governor replied:

The same course that is taken in England out of towns; every man according to his ability instructing his children. We have forty-eight parishes, and our ministers are well paid, and by my consent should be better if they would pray oftener and preach less. *But of all other commodities, so of this,* the worst are sent us, *and we had few that we could boast of, since the persecution in* Cromwell's *tiranny drove divers worthy men hither. But I thank God,* there are no free schools *nor* printing, *and I hope we shall not have these hundred years, for* learning *has brought disobedience, and heresy, and sects into the world, and* printing *has divulged them, and libels against the best government. God keep us from both!*[77]

To some extent at least, these questionnaires can be considered preliminary exercises in data gathering for a systematic comparative education study.

More extensive use of the questionnaire for comparative education purposes was made by Count Leopold Berchtold in his manual for travelers (1789), which he based on Josiah Tucker's

---

[73]*Ibid.*, pp. 338–339.

[74]*Ibid.*, p. 341.

[75]*Ibid.*, p. 342.

[76]William S. Perry, *Historical Collections Relating to the American Colonial Church*, Vol. I, on Virginia (Hartford, 1870), pp. 257–348; as cited in Sadie Bell, *The Church, the State, and Education in Virginia* (Philadelphia: The Author, 1930), pp. 27, 101, 653–655.

[77]Henig, *Statutes at Large in Virginia*, II, 511–517; as given in Edgar W. Knight and Clifton L. Hall, *Readings in American Educational History* (New York: Appleton-Century-Crofts, 1951), p. 69.

1757 instructions for travelers. Both Tucker (1712–1799), a British churchman and economist, and Berchtold (1759–1809), a German philanthropist and medical writer, considered the questionnaire a suitable medium for the comparative analysis of socio-educational and other observations made while abroad. Surprisingly, both of these men greatly influenced those men who are now recognized as the founders of the formal study of comparative education in the early decades of the nineteenth century.

According to Berchtold, education was a most influential factor in the development of man and his society. Accordingly, it would be appropriate for the traveler "to inquire into the different methods of forming the bodies of children with powers of vigor, and activity, and of improving their hearts and understanding." [78] He felt that "a great many useful observations" could be obtained by a study of a foreign system of education and that these could be applied "to the benefit of our own country." [79]

Some four hundred pages of questions for the would-be traveler were proposed by Berchtold, including a reasonable number related to various aspects of education; nearly all were of a fact-finding nature, although some were directed at historical and contemporary comparisons. One question of a comparative nature was the following:

How far are the education and government calculated to make the inhabitants more or less vicious? and more or less virtuous than other nations? and what seems to contribute greatly toward the propagation of the national virtues and vices? [80]

Even if Berchtold did not show a significant awareness of the complexity of determining causal relations, he clearly had a conception of many of the significant matters and issues involved in a national educational system. Berchtold's *Essay* was widely circulated throughout Europe in the English text and in the French translation (1797), and it "was a standard travelling companion for those embarking on the 'grand tour of the continent' or completing their formal studies in education." [81] As a result, it may have been familiar to many serious travelers, and it is not difficult to suggest the strong possibility—even the probability—that it influenced the comparative educators of the following century.

Also of interest to students of intercultural and comparative education is the work by Benjamin Franklin on the North American Indians.

Savages we call them, because their manners differ from ours, which we think the perfection of civility; they think the same of theirs. Perhaps, if we could examine the manners of different nations with impartiality, we should find no people so rude as to be without rules of politeness; nor any so polite as not to have some remains of rudeness. [82]

Another work on comparative education in the eighteenth century was a study by Friedrich August Hecht, which aimed at a comparison of education in England and in Germany. [83] Although the author made use of the descriptive method to a large degree, he did show some evidence of comparative analysis.

One factor which tended to focus the minds of scholars on the idea of comparison was the critical reaction to the publication of Rousseau's *Émile* (1762). The dissemination of Rousseau's ideas and their implementation in schools by Johann Bernhard Basedow, Christian Gotthilf Salzmann, and others distressed the scholars in the traditional disciplines who were greatly concerned about the threat of the "new pedagogy" to the established order in education. Consequently, these traditionalists, particularly those professing the classical subjects, made an effort to discredit the new tendencies in education by vigorously calling attention to their deficiencies. They juxtaposed the education of Western Europe in the late eighteenth century

---

[78]Leopold Berchtold, *Essay to Direct and Extend the Inquiries of Patriotic Travellers* (London, 1789), p. 33; as quoted in Stewart E. Fraser, "Count Leopold Berchtold: Eighteenth Century Educational Travel Counselor," *Peabody Journal of Education*, XL (July 1962), 5.

[79]*Ibid.*

[80] "The Work of Berchtold," in Stewart E. Fraser, *Jullien's Plan for Comparative Education, 1816−1817* (New York: Teachers College, Columbia University, 1964), Appendix B, p. 143. This section contains other questions of comparative educational content.

[81]Fraser, "Count Leopold Berchtold . . . ," *op. cit.*, p. 6.

[82]Benjamin Franklin, "The Savages of North America," in *The Complete Works of Benjamin Franklin*, ed. John Bigelow (New York: Putnam, 1888), IX, 25.

[83]Friedrich August Hecht, *De re scholastica Anglica cum Germanica comparata* (Freiburg, 1795).

with that of ancient Greece and Rome, and, as a general rule, the new system proved to be grossly wanting. A specific example of this type of comparative education literature was issued in 1784 by the Lutheran theologian Johannes Peter Brinckmann.[84]

An interesting instance of international cooperation in the gathering and dissemination of comparative educational data resulted from the correspondence in 1795 between President Ezra Stiles (1727–1795) of Yale College and Christoph Daniel Ebeling (1741–1817), a German historian who edited the *Amerikanische Bibliothek* and the *Amerikanisches Magazin*. Ebeling made use of the information he received from Stiles on American colleges and other educational institutions, both in his periodicals and in his seven-volume study of United States history.[85] While Ebeling may not be considered a forerunner in the comparative education movement, he was, nonetheless, one of those who helped make popular the underlying principle of careful accumulation of data, a step which is essential before meaningful comparisons can be undertaken.

Conclusion

Some twenty centuries have passed in the preceding pages. This historical account of international and comparative education is but a sketch of a larger story which is yet to be fully told. It is evident that there exists a mass of historical material in the fields of education, literature, culture, economics, political science, sociology, and anthropology waiting to be exploited more fully by the historian. This material contains interesting and valuable observations and ideas on education in various countries at different times in man's long history. No doubt, some of these writings will reveal to us much about our predecessors, while others may indeed teach us something of significance for the present and future. We will, in all probability, gain more respect for the insights of the pedagogues and other scholars of earlier periods who paved the road for the later development of international and comparative education as a scientific field of thought, inquiry, and writing.

At the end of the eighteenth century, the development of a science for the comparative study of education was more clearly discernible than previously. There was, in addition, a growing consciousness of the dire need for educational reform. This impetus toward reform, coupled with the greater publicity accorded the works of traveling educators, satisfied to some extent the quest for information regarding education in various countries. At the beginning of the nineteenth century, however, a multitude of writings, especially in Europe and later in America, testify to the ever increasing interest shown in foreign educational systems and practices. The holocaust and upheaval caused by the French Revolution and the Napoleonic Wars in turn resulted in new political alignments and changing international relations, brought new states into being, and fostered the spirit of nascent nationalism with its eventual concomitant, new and nationalistic educational systems. The early nineteenth century is clearly a watershed in the development of a systematic and methodological study of both international and comparative education. Prior to the nineteenth century, the terms *cosmopolitanism* and *universalism* were accepted and understood, but the idea of *internationalism* was virtually unknown.

The divestment of the colonies in both North and South America, the convulsions and restructuring of the empires of Europe, either at the behest or because of Bonapartism, put the emergence of new national states into sharper focus. The growth of new states resulted in their desire to preserve or reawaken pride in their distinctive languages and cultures. The schools and universities of the nineteenth century were among the many agents for mirroring and perpetuating nationalistic tendencies. They became agents either for change or for conservation. Accordingly, they also became the pride or the despair of the newly emerging class of intellectuals and literati. The breakdown of old empires and the development of what would be later called European chauvinism led in turn to a better and perhaps more plagiaristic appraisal of the schools of neighboring countries.

The establishment by Napoleon of an embryonic national system of education stretching from the North Sea to the Aegean Sea at last forced Europeans to collect data and provide

---

[84]Johannes Peter Brinckmann, *Vergleichung der Erziehung der Alten mit der heutigen, und Untersuchung welche von beiden mit der Natur am meisten übereinstimme* (Dessau: Buchhandlung des Gelehrten, 1784).

[85]Christoph D. Ebeling, *Erdbeschreibung und Geschichte von Amerika: Die Vereinigten Staaten von Amerika*, 7 vols. (1793–1816).

comparative statistics for the imperial education inspectors. The deficiencies of the Empire and the differing quality of education between Holland and in Italy, for example, were high-lighted and documented more devastatingly than previously. They were eventually to provide fuel for the newly emerging practitioners of comparative education.

When Europe had been reconstituted into new empires and separate independent states after 1815 it was possible and perhaps even necessary to think in both collective and nationalistic terms. The need for independence was in part matched by the desire for limited union and per-mitted a new approach to educational cooperation. It might be suggested that the desire for some form of international collaboration in education had greater possibilities after the various European states had nationalized their systems of education.

Well before the end of the Napoleonic Empire—in fact, at the height of its power and glory in 1808—a learned and distinguished French professor, César Auguste Basset, suggested some cogent reasons for studying foreign education. In his *Essais sur l'organisation de quelques parties d'instruction publique* he devoted a section to "the usefulness of making observations in foreign countries about education and instruction in general." Basset called for the appoint-ment of a university official to travel in order to "make observations about education and in-struction in general." This man, he suggested:

must be free from national and methodological prejudices, a scholar, with literary ability, an administrator, familiar with all the aspects of liberal and popular education . . . , and surveyor of all the places likely to offer him useful researches. His work should be that of a historian: to observe, compare, and present the facts. . . . 'Moreover, this official should judge men and things in accordance with real and established facts, and not in terms of writ-ten systems or speculative plans.[86]

The second edition of Basset's work, issued in 1814 and distributed to a wider circle of read-ers, discussed more specifically, "the usefulness of making observations in foreign countries about their different procedures of education and instructions."[87]

In 1816 another essay appeared on a somewhat similar topic. This treatise by Marc-Antoine Jullien appeared first in Switzerland and later in Paris as *Sur l'éducation comparée* in 1816 and 1817, respectively. Jullien has been variously credited as being the "father of compara-tive education" and the "precursor of a systematic study of international education." His remarkable treatise offered, for the first time, a schematic and methodological plan for com-paring the educational systems of various countries. Moreover, it suggested the necessary and tangible steps required in establishing an international educational research and training center and a "UNESCO-type" educational institute.

The emergence of newly created European states and newly freed Latin American repub-lics, the greater awareness of Africa and Asia, and the discovery of the contributions of Hindu, Buddhist, and Moslem educators during the beginning of the nineteenth century all contributed to the emergence of comparative education as a new field of inquiry. This century has a definite right to be considered on its own as a distinctive and important period in the study of both in-ternational and comparative education. The preceding centuries obviously made their contri-butions as should be discernible from this historical overview. However, conditions in the nine-teenth century all led to greater travel opportunities and more active quests for better educational systems. The French scholars, Basset, Cuvier, and Jullien suggested a method and a reason for such an analysis. The Prussian and Swiss practitioners, specifically Pestalozzi and Fellenberg, attracted Americans and Englishmen alike to travel to the continent to see educational innovations. The era of the *grand tour* was certainly not over, but its complexion was changed from the eighteenth to the nineteenth century. The era of the traveling compara-tive educator and scholar intent on borrowing and adapting came into its own in the nineteenth century. The start of this century saw Jullien's exploratory treatise on *Comparative Education* exhort educators to travel and compare intelligently. By the end of the century, no self-respecting scholar, university president, or educational administrator from any European nation, the United States, or the British Empire could resist the urge to travel and make his own comparative analysis.

---

[86]César Auguste Basset, *Essais sur l'organisation de quelques parties d'instruction publique* (Paris: Hazard, 1808), pp. 85—87.

[87]*Ibid.*, second edition (1814), p. 100.

The meager literature at the beginning of the nineteenth century, highlighted with a few works on comparative methodology such as that of Jullien, was transformed into a flood of books on foreign education by the year 1900. The century saw the gradual development of an extensive body of literature which can today be conveniently categorized as *comparative*, *descriptive*, *analytical*, and *international*, or perhaps it can be looked upon as simple *foreign education*, or *Auslandspädagogik*. But the French, British, German, and Americans who traveled had no idea that their work would be so categorized, and they would not have admitted to following a methodological research pattern or to reading Jullien's modest treatise. The fact is that some of these travelers became better known than others, and the names of these men have been repeated and have perhaps been overemphasized in books on educational history while the contributions of many other writers have gone unnoticed. Although some of these unnoticed contributions may have been modest ones, there are certainly ample opportunities to rewrite the history of education, particularly in its international context, through the discovery of old manuscripts and the reappraisal of well-known volumes.

It is hoped that this extensive collection of documents will illustrate for students the immensely rich heritage of material which may have been overlooked or downgraded in the past by impetuous historians of education. It should illustrate that certain aspects of international and comparative educational history have not been always placed in clearest perspective. It is anticipated that further collections on the centuries preceding the nineteenth century can eventually be made, and that these would show that educational history has a long continuum which is broken up into irregular, though useful, segments often to suit the teaching inclinations of historians and teachers. The nineteenth century, however, has some very peculiar and distinct contributions to make in the methodological study of international and comparative education. Scientific studies of today's educational developments in other countries can find their origin in the careful, but perhaps rudimentary, works of such devoted scholars as Horace Mann of the United States, K. D. Ushinsky of Russia, Michael Sadler of England, Yung Wing of China, and D. Sarmiento of Argentina. These men traveled throughout the world seeking answers to educational problems and improvements to aid their own children. Their analyses were rarely intended to exacerbate international tensions, and their techniques were based on intellectual honesty and compassion for young people. They did not attempt "competitive analysis" or to formulate so-called "strategies for educational development." We have much to learn from them, and their works are now presented to illustrate the widening horizons that educators have made for themselves historically through both the international and comparative dimensions of education.

On European Education

Introduction

Our own national existence has been but brief, and although our progress in all that relates to exterior prosperity has been unexampled, we have not yet had time to organize a corps of literature, or to give to education the character of a science. . . . We have a few domestic materials in our hands on this subject, although we have carefully sought and urgently requested them, while an ample store of plans and methods and their results during a long course of experience are found in Europe. We are aware that there is much sensitiveness in our country in regard to foreign improvements—and have received some hints of the danger of exciting it. But we will not believe that our national vanity is so gross or our views so contracted that valuable lessons will be rejected because they did not originate on this side of the Atlantic.[1]

American educational and cultural relations with Europe during the nineteenth century can be divided into two rather indistinct periods. The first of these can be described as a borrowing and touring period during which educational tourists, schoolmasters, and some serious students visited Europe for a wide range of professional reasons. This period ran from the early days of the young American republic into the mid 1860's. These years before the Civil War saw the cautious blending of selected European educational ideas and a guarded respect for various continental pedagogic practices, some of which were ultimately incorporated into the public schools of the United States. The visiting American educator in Europe deserves credit for making his colleagues at home aware of the need for innovation and improvement.

When the Civil War ended, the second period of American educational and cultural relations with Europe began, and an even more important transatlantic pattern of exchange developed in the area of pedagogic training and higher education. Previously, the interests of professional American educators on tour in Europe had focused on particular aspects of elementary, secondary, and higher education; journalists and general tourists had contributed equally to the literature available to Americans on European educational and cultural developments. The post-Civil War decades saw a new generation of traveler manifest in the migration of thousands of American college-age students to obtain higher education in Europe, primarily in the German principalities. As a result, concepts of scholarship and serious graduate-study programs were installed throughout American universities before the end of the century. Secondary-school and college-preparatory programs still attracted increasing numbers of American educators to Britain, France, and Prussia; however, the broadening of interests of these travelers after the Civil War can be seen in the increased number of studies of European technical-, vocational-, and commercial-training establishments.

Although the latter part of the nineteenth century was perhaps the most exciting period in the international history of American education, the start of the nineteenth century saw a future President of the United States, John Quincy Adams, commenting cursorily on education in Silesia as he traveled through Eastern Europe in 1801. It also saw Thomas Jefferson, another future President who was once vehemently opposed to allowing American students to study overseas, asking Pierre DuPont de Nemours to draw upon his knowledge of European education to construct a plan for national education in the United States. Thus, both Adams and Jefferson, who represented the intellectual and political leadership of their country, had an interest in the international and comparative aspects of education as they related to the development and improvement of domestic education within the United States.

---

[1]William C. Woodbridge, an editorial, *The American Annals of Education and Instruction*, I (July, 1831), 243–244.

By the end of the nineteenth century the comparing and teaching of foreign educational philosophies and practices had become an accepted part of educational courses and various teacher-training programs at prominent universities and teachers colleges in the United States. In the 1894–1895 annual report of the United States Commissioner of Education, the universities of California (Berkeley), Stanford, Indiana, Kansas, Michigan, Missouri, Washington, and New York are all recorded as offering courses in comparative systems of education. Stanford University designated England, France, Germany, and Switzerland as the countries of special interest in the comparative study of European school systems. New York University, on the other hand, included the

historic development of the national systems of Germany, France, and England; relation of church and state to the problem of general education; principle of free and compulsory education; administration and supervision of schools; training of teachers; character and scope of elementary education; technical, commercial, and industrial education; female education; ancient and modern languages and sciences in secondary education; higher education.[2]

The end of the nineteenth century also saw young Americans visiting and studying in increasing numbers in Spain, France, Italy, England, and Scandinavia, as well as in Germany and Austria. Greater numbers of foreign students were enrolled at American colleges, and what would be called later American educational imperialism had manifested itself in various educational guises, mainly missionary and philanthropic. This was particularly evident in The Philippines, Puerto Rico, and Cuba, as well as throughout the rest of Latin America.

The full panorama of the century displayed American education as avidly seeking the best of Europe and vehemently rejecting that which was unsuitable after acrimonious debate and, at times, prolonged experimentation. It saw the importation from Europe of the teachings of two great nineteenth-century movements in American education—Pestalozzianism and Herbartianism—just as it saw the ideas of Bell and Lancaster manifested in the monitorial school and those of Fellenberg embodied in agricultural-manual training curriculums transported in part to America from Europe. The published reports of perhaps the most influential quintet of ideological importers—John Griscom, Calvin Stowe, Alexander Bache, Horace Mann, and Henry Barnard—are well enshrined in American educational history. These men played prominent roles in influencing the future direction of American education, particularly in educational provisions for public schools at the elementary level. Their reports of European educational programs and possible innovations for America are introductory and important studies in both comparative education and legitimate pedagogic plagiarism.

The early traveling schoolmen were keenly aware of the social and political backgrounds of their American constituents. They endeavored to compare, contrast, and transplant judiciously from Europe those practices which could be useful for America. They were not insensitive toward criticism regarding the importation of foreign or alien ideologies and warned succeeding generations of American educators traveling overseas not to be corrupted by continental practices and cultures which were inimical to the republican and democratic character of American society.

Shortly after the Civil War the presumed danger of European intellectual corruption and educational sabotage had so incensed certain American educators that many leading schoolmen and university presidents were persuaded to join together and denounce the indiscriminate education abroad of American youth. They suggested that the precollegiate and even some of the higher educational facilities of Europe were unsuited for American students, and that the loss of tuition fees to European institutes represented a severe drain on struggling domestic colleges, besides being flagrantly unpatriotic. Despite these critical comparisons, American youth and their elders searching for postgraduate education and specialized training flocked in increasing numbers to Europe. The cultural and educational enrichment afforded America by the returning scholar, as well as by the immigrant who came in larger numbers during the last quarter of the century, is attested to in the diversity of American colleges and universities by the turn of the century and in their higher scholarship levels.

While the very nature of certain principal characteristics of American education is historically British, the development of American education throughout the nineteenth century showed

---

[2]William T. Harris, *Report of the Commissioner of Education*, 1894–1895 (Washington, D.C.: U.S. Government Printing Office, 1896), I, 123.

not only an indigenous and nationalistic growth but a steady erosion of the purely British imprint on the American who traveled abroad to study and to do research. France, Italy, The Netherlands, even Spain and Scandinavia, and, of course, Prussia and the other German principalities, competed successfully for attention with the former mother country. The stagnation of English universities in the early part of the century and the concomitant steady rise of German higher scholarship and graduate training was to be the pride of the Americans, the dismay of the British, and, when they would admit it, the envy of the French.

The historic relationship of American education to the pedagogic products of Europe is richly illustrated with numerous, diverse, and pertinent sources of information to be found in the form of diaries, personal correspondence, and travel records of the myriad of Americans who visited Europe. There were many motives, including that of education and self-improvement, which took Americans to Europe immediately after the Revolutionary War, but perhaps 1812 or 1815 would be a more reasonable year to commence cataloging the educational tales of American travelers to Europe. After the "second" American war of independence and the demise of Bonapartism, it was safer for Americans to venture abroad to Europe. Prior to independence the American colonist was dependent on Britain as a prime and natural source of instruction for nearly all major branches of learning and knowledge. In the nineteenth century the nationalistic and practical desire to achieve cultural self-sufficiency was a major stimulus for Americans to travel to the continent for new ideas and led to a diffusion of their interests to all of Europe. It is important to remember, however, that England and Scotland still had a certain irrefutable attraction, for bonds of culture, language, and tradition could not be extinguished by the Declaration of Independence. British academics were generally sympathetic to the aspirations of the ex-colonials seeking education, and Americans were not discouraged from visiting and studying in the British Isles. In fact, few of the prominent American educators who visited Europe during the century failed to avail themselves of the opportunity to visit England and Scotland.

The cities of London, Oxford, Cambridge, and Edinburgh were of major importance for medical and scientific men, but these came principally as educated visitors or as professional practitioners rather than as students. In spite of the colonial veneration for such historic names as Oxford and Cambridge, few Americans attended these universities in the nineteenth century. Admittedly, Oxford was revered for its classics and Cambridge for science and theoretical mathematics, which may not have appealed greatly to practical American youth. Britain drew some Americans who wished to observe her industrial revolution and economic progress and to take advantage of her offerings in the fields of literature, religion, and the fine arts, but Oxford and Cambridge all too often rated only a tourist's visit, and few Americans looked upon them as suitable places to study as undergraduates. The situation regarding professional and postgraduate education was different, however. The Revolutionary War and the War of 1812 interfered with, but did not effectively curb, the practice of Americans attending English and Scottish institutes for scientific or specialized training in medicine, science, theology, and law. These professional men traveled to Britain throughout the nineteenth century and brought back their specially acquired knowledge to share with a carefully chosen and often preselected clientele. They attended courses of interest to their profession or they purchased book collections, whole libraries, or museums to be transplanted back to America.

Many Americans who made the trip to Britain were enchanted by Edinburgh, as can be seen in the diaries and letters of students such as James Jackson, John Shaw, John Warren, William Gibson, and Valentine Mott. A Yale professor of chemistry, Benjamin Silliman, wrote one of the more interesting pictures of student life at Edinburgh, where over thirty Americans were studying in 1806. Edinburgh attracted Americans for theological training, since the conservative theology of England was less popular with Americans, who enjoyed the greater intellectualism and liberality of the Scottish divinity courses. Edinburgh was also of interest to Americans as a center for advanced scientific training, and at the end of the nineteenth century it still ranked with London and Paris as a major center of medical education. A year of postgraduate study at the Scottish capital could be an important asset for an ambitious American physician and could give an American clergyman the added *savoir-faire* expected by his congregation.

The very limited intellectual scope of American colleges and universities in 1815 was such that it was difficult to keep the more ambitious students at home. The attempt to improve higher education in the United States and to prevent students from traveling to Europe, as recommended by many prominent Americans, was intended to encourage the development of better teachers, facilities, and libraries. The solution to the problem of encouraging American undergraduates to remain at home was certainly not comprehensively planned. Individual educators and university trustees who were alarmed at the academic gulf between Europe and the intellectually dormant young republic led the unconcerted attack which took on a threefold aspect. First, professors and selected educators skilled in science were dispatched overseas to collect books, scientific instruments, and museum artifacts for their college libraries and laboratories. Second, young and often recently appointed professors were given leave to attend universities in Europe for professional training. These were often men interested in the liberal arts who were expected to bring back knowledge from Europe and introduce it into their college curriculum in America. Third, professors and educational officials were sent abroad and given a specific commission to study and observe particular foreign pedagogical practices. In some cases these men were empowered to bring in immigrants as new faculty members. The first two practices were much in evidence during the early part of the nineteenth century, the latter developed as early as 1825, and all three continued unabated throughout the remainder of the century.

Benjamin Silliman was commissioned to go to Europe by the trustees of Yale College in an effort to improve the academic standards at that institution, and he explained the reason for his trip in 1805 by stating:

The trustees of Yale College, in the Autumn of 1804, appropriated a sum of money for the enlargement of their library and philosophical and chemical apparatus, and they determined on sending an agent to Europe for the purpose of making the contemplated collections. I was commissioned to execute this trust and was allowed to avail myself of such opportunities as might occur, for acquiring information, especially in chemistry, which it was my duty to teach. [3]

The American returning from Europe, whether his trip had been for the purpose of purchasing a library collection or securing an education, generally had an eagerness to put into practice his recently acquired intellectual wealth. While most were able to translate their new skills successfully, others met varying degrees of hostility or indifference and were frustrated in their attempts to readjust to American educational society.

The reports on education in Europe written by educators—such as John Griscom, *A Year in Europe . . . 1818 and 1819;* Henry Dwight, *Travels in the North of Germany, in the Years 1825 and 1826;* Calvin Stowe, *Report on Elementary Public Instruction in Europe* (1837); Alexander Dallas Bache, *Report on Education in Europe* (1839); and Horace Mann, *Seventh Annual Report* (1844)—are illustrative of the most important and influential studies made prior to the Civil War. To these individual studies must be added the names and works of educational journalists who were equally, if not more, important in persistently bringing to the attention of American educators news concerning educational developments in Europe. The first American educational journal, *The Academician,* published in 1818 by Albert Picket and his son John of New York, carried many newsworthy items including lengthy articles on famous European educators, reports on novel foreign educational practices, and statistics on school systems throughout the world. *The American Journal of Education,* edited by the Scottish immigrant William Russell from 1826 to 1829, faithfully recounted significant educational intelligence gathered from European sources. In fact, the first account from France of Marc Antoine Jullien's famous treatise on *Comparative Education* was translated in part and made known to American educators initially through Russell's *Journal* in 1826. The term and concept of "comparative education" was first put into English and introduced to American readers through the *Journal,* and the tenor of many of the articles showed an avid interest in comparative education and development throughout the world. School news from "Buenos Ayres, Hayti, Colombia, Greece, Armenia, Siberia, India, Cochin China, the Sandwich Islands" and even "Education among the Hottentots" were deemed noteworthy. Book reviews and lengthy extracts from overseas educational reports were regular features of Russell's *Journal* and its successor in 1829, *The American Annals of Education and Instruction,* which was edited by William Woodbridge, a widely traveled educator who resided in Europe from 1825 to 1829.

The importance of these early journals in disseminating news concerning education, and at times publishing the personal correspondence of foreign educators, cannot be minimized. A

---

[3]Benjamin Silliman, *A Journal of Travels in England, Holland, and Scotland, and of Two Passages over the Atlantic in the Years 1805 and 1806* (Boston: Howe and Deforest, and Increase Cook and Company, 1812), second edition, I, iii.

quick perusal of these journals would reveal a wide variety of suggestions from overseas for innovations in American education. In 1838 *The American Annals of Education and Instruction,* then edited by William Alcott, published an important but apparently neglected letter from Victor Cousin, French Minister of Public Instruction. Cousin's 1831 *Report on Public Instruction in Prussia* had been translated into English by Mrs. Sarah Austin in 1837 and was being widely distributed in the United States, when this letter revealed that Americans would be wiser to look at parts of the work still untranslated which "would be more appropriate models for a state of the American Union." Cousin specifically referred to his new work on Dutch education which he said "will perhaps be more useful to America than my work on Prussia, inasmuch as Holland is an ancient commercial and industrious republic whose manners and institutions bear a strong analogy to those of the United States." But his injunction went unheeded, and for a quarter of a century his work on Prussian education served as the starting point for predeparture reading of American educators destined for Europe.

International comparisons, reports of transatlantic educational exchanges, and studies of foreign education were regular features of the early educational journals. These journals did not offer, however, the extensive coverage that Henry Barnard later afforded his readers in his publications, particularly in *The American Journal of Education,* which he edited for over a quarter of a century. Barnard had visited Europe from 1835 to 1837, and many of his notes and reports on education were published in 1854 in his *National Education in Europe.* When he became the first United States Commissioner of Education in 1867, Barnard ensured that reports on foreign education would be a regular and important feature of the *Annual Reports* and other documents published under his auspices. His initial coverage of foreign and comparative educational topics set the pattern for his successors at the United States Office of Education.

Toward the end of the century American educators and laymen found that a wide range of literature was available to them concerning European education. The official publications of the United States Commissioner for Education augmented the increasing number of educational journals which carried news on educational developments in Europe and throughout the world. The number of books devoted exclusively to foreign education, many concentrating on a single country and several on a selected specialized aspect of that country's education, began to increase after 1880. A few of these works can be cited: Louis R. Klemm, *European Schools: Or What I Saw in the Schools of Germany, France, Austria, and Switzerland* (1888); James Parsons, Jr., twin studies, *Prussian Schools Through American Eyes* (1891) and *French Schools Through American Eyes* (1892); and John Prince, *Methods of Instruction and Organization of the Schools of Germany for the Use of American Teachers and Normal Schools* (1897).

The temptation was always strong for many American educators who traveled through Europe to describe their experiences and publish their impressions. These travelers can be grouped for convenience by *historic period,* such as pre- or post-Civil War; by *academic status,* such as student, teacher, professor, or appointed official functionary; by *professional interest,* such as education, law, medicine, science, or theology; and by country of *geographical emphasis,* such as England, Scotland, Prussia, France, or Switzerland. However, it is left to the reader to decide whether the travelers were essentially tourists, educational specialists, borrowers of ideas, or competent comparative observers.

These nineteenth-century American writings on international and comparative education or, to be more exact, the writings on foreign education often found a ready market in the United States among students and teachers in normal schools and universities. It is apparent from reading much of this literature that the authors were rarely content with merely "cataloging" the courses of a French university or "describing" the lesson plans of a Prussian teachers college. Instead, they made intra-European comparisons and attempted to directly relate, if not to compare, American education with European practices. The number of articles and books on European education published in the United States during the last quarter of the nineteenth century was much greater than the number made available to American educators during the whole preceding three quarters of a century. Until 1825 American literature on European education was scarce, and between 1825 and 1865 there was only a slow increase in its quantity and quality; but after 1875 it became possible and important to discriminate within the wide range of literature that was available. Throughout the remainder of the century the problem remained for American educators and interested laymen of what they should borrow, adopt, or adapt from Europe. What should they compare, criticize, or reject from the various reports that came to them across the Atlantic? The documentary selections which follow illustrate the continual interest by thoughtful Americans in the educational developments of Europe and indicate how American educators at home benefited from the experiences and reports of their traveling colleagues.

Thomas Jefferson   1785

The Comparative Advantages of an American Rather Than a European Education

Thomas Jefferson (1743–1826), the third President of the United States, had just succeeded Benjamin Franklin as resident minister in Paris, when he wrote the letter below to J. Bannister, Jr., in 1785. It is one of the more lucid pronouncements made at the turn of the century by a prominent American concerned with his country's educational independence. Jefferson's injunction to young Americans to remain at home for their education merely reflected a sentiment existing in the United States at the time. The legislature of Georgia, for example, in January of 1785, expressed its strong opposition to the education of American youth abroad, and shortly afterwards, in February of the same year, it threatened to regard any Georgians sent abroad for their education as aliens for three years. Jefferson's opposition to foreign studies for young Americans should be seen against a background of changing desires on the part of Americans to secure both political and cultural independence.

It should also be pointed out, however, that some years later, in 1880, Jefferson asked Dupont de Nemours to draw up a national education plan for the United States and specifically to draw upon his knowledge of the best of the European systems in formulating his plans. Jefferson valued the immense part that European culture and education could play in enriching the United States. But at the time he wrote this letter from France, he viewed somewhat critically the indiscriminate education of American youth in an alien environment.

I should never have answered the paragraph in your letter of Sep. 19 respecting the best seminary for the education of youth in Europe but that it was necessary for me to make inquiries on the subject, the result of these has been to consider the competition disputes as resting between Geneva and Rome. They are equally cheap and probably are equal in the course of education pursued. The advantage of Geneva is that students acquire there the habits of speaking French. The advantage of Rome are the acquiring a local knowledge of a spot so historical and so celebrated; the acquiring the true pronunciation of the Latin language; the acquiring a just taste in the fine arts, more particularly those of painting, sculpture, architecture and music; a familiarity with those objects and process of agriculture which experience has shown best adapted to a climate like ours and lastly the advantage of a fine climate for health. It is probable too that by being boarded in a French family the habit of speaking that language may be obtained. I do not (know of) any advantage to be derived in Geneva from a familiar acquaintance with the principles of that government. The late revolution has rendered it a tyrannical aristocracy more likely to give ill than good ideas to an American. I think the balance in favour of Rome. Pisa is sometimes spoken of as a place of education but it does not offer the 1st and 3rd of the advantages of Rome. But why send an American youth to Europe for education? What are the objects of an useful American education? Classical knowledge, modern languages, chiefly French, Spanish and Italian; Mathematics, Natural philosophy, Natural history, Civil history, (and) Ethics. In Natural philosophy, I mean to include Chemistry and Agriculture, and in Natural history, to include Botany, as well as the other branches of those departments. It is true that the habit of speaking the modern languages cannot be so well acquired in America, but every other article can be as well acquired at William and Mary College, as at any place in Europe. When college education is done with, and a young man is to prepare himself for public life, he must cast his eyes (for America) either on Law or Physic. For the former, where can he apply so advantageously as to Mr. Wythe? For the latter, he must come to Europe: the medical class of students, there-

---

A letter from Thomas Jefferson in Paris to J. Bannister, Jr., October 15, 1785.

fore, is the only one which need come to Europe. Let us view the disadvantages of sending a youth to Europe. To enumerate them all would require a volume. I will select a few. If he goes to England, he learns drinking, horse racing and boxing. These are the peculiarities of English education. The following circumstances are common to education in that and the other countries of Europe. He acquires a fondness for European luxury and dissipation, and a contempt for the simplicity of his own country; he is fascinated with the privileges of the European aristocrats, and sees, with abhorrence, the lovely equality which the poor enjoy with the rich, in his own country; he contracts a partiality for aristocracy or monarchy; he forms foreign friendships which will never be useful to him, and loses the reason of life for forming, in his own country, those friendships which, of all others, are the most faithful and permanent; he is led, by the strongest of all human passions, into a spirit for female intrigue, destructive of his own and others' happiness, or passion for whores, destructive of his health, and, in both cases, learns to consider fidelity to the marriage bed as an ungentlemanly practice, and inconsistent with happiness; he recollects the voluptuary dress and arts of the European women, and pities and despises the chaste affections and simplicity of those of his own country; he retains, thro' life, a fond recollection, and a hankering after those places, which were the scenes of his first pleasures and of his first connections; he returns to his own country, a foreigner, unacquainted with the practices of domestic economy, necessary to preserve him from ruin; speaking and writing his native tongue as a foreigner, and therefore, unqualified to obtain those distinctions, which eloquence of the pen and tongue ensures in a free country; for I would observe to you, that what is called style in writing or speaking is formed very early in life, while the imagination is warm, and impressions are permanent. I am of opinion, that there never was an instance of a man's writing or speaking his native tongue with elegance, who passed from nineteen to twenty years of age out of the country where it was spoken. Thus, no instance exists of a person's writing two languages perfectly. That will always appear to be his native language, which was most familiar to him in his youth. It appears to me, then, that an American, coming to Europe for education, loses in his knowledge, in his morals, in his health, in his habits, and in his happiness. I had entertained only doubts on this head before I came to Europe: what I see and hear, since I came here, proves more than I had even suspected. Cast your eye over America: who are the men of most learning, of most eloquence, most beloved by their country and most trusted and promoted by them? They are those who have been educated among them, and whose manners, morals, and habits are perfectly homogeneous with those of the country.

Did you expect by as short a question, to draw such a sermon on yourself? I dare say you did not. But the consequences of foreign education are alarming to me as an American. I sin, therefore, through zeal, whenever I enter on the subject. You are sufficiently American to pardon me for it. Let me hear of your health and be assured of the esteem with which I am Dear Sir your friend and servant.

John Mason 1791

A Father's Advice to a Son Leaving for Study Abroad

John Mitchell Mason (1770-1829) was sent to Edinburgh University in Scotland in 1791 by his father, the Reverend John Mason, minister of the Reformed Presbyterian Church, Cedar Street, New York. His father thought that Edinburgh University offered the best theological training for a Presbyterian minister and that it would lead his son to higher accomplishments in his profession, a wider range of general knowledge, and an acquaintance with cultured and Christian society abroad.

The letter below contained more than the usual personal and solicitous advice from a father to son setting out for graduate studies overseas. John Mitchell Mason was carefully instructed not to become involved in British politics and not to refer to the late unpleasantness between the United States and the former mother country. He was instructed to pay attention to female

A letter from John Mason in New York to his son, John Mitchell Mason, in Edinburgh, Scotland, April 27, 1791; in Jacob Van Vechten, editor, *Memoirs of John M. Mason, D.D., S.T.P., with Portions of His Correspondence* (New York: Robert Carter and Brothers, 1856), pp. 31–38.

society, to attend the best of theological lectures at the university, and to develop his pastoral training on the soundest Presbyterian models.

Upon his return home, John Mitchell Mason succeeded his father as pastor of the Cedar Street Church in New York and later distinguished himself by aiding in the establishment of the first theological seminary in the United States (Union Theological Seminary), where he served as a professor. In 1811 he became provost of Columbia College, and he was appointed president of Dickinson College, Carlisle, Pennsylvania, in 1821.

As you are about to leave your native land for some time, and perhaps I may never see your face again in this world, a sense of duty and tender regard for you, impel me to give you a few advices, which by the blessing of God will be useful to you in future life.

I wish you to have the air and address of a gentleman; not of an affected, but a real gentleman, in whose character, good sense, sincerity, discretion, affability, condescension, an obliging temper, and easy behaviour, are principal traits.

Go freely into every respectable company when you can be introduced with propriety, and esteem such an introduction into large and mixed companies a very great favour. Be modest and attentive in company. Equally avoid loquacity and silence. Beware of impertinent staring, but keep an open countenance. Do not flatly contradict any person present, nor be engaged in angry controversy. Never speak to the disadvantage of any absent person; this would be mean, ungenerous, impolite, wicked. Be very attentive to ladies, who will give a polish to your manners. Every part of your conversation towards them should be marked with the most refined delicacy. Do not repeat any little stories or anecdotes, but such as you have reason to think none present may be supposed to be acquainted with, but take notice of such as are mentioned by others, even of such as you know, without giving any hint that you have heard of them before. Respectfully turn your face to any person you speak to, or who speaks to you. Be fond of instructive conversation, but do not altogether disregard small-talk, some proportion of which is rendered necessary by the present state of society. Never give a decisive opinion about anything in the presence of your superiors, without pressing necessity; which will seldom happen. Say little about yourself, and never vex your friends with gloomy narratives about your little ailments. Be always cheerful, but be always grave. Avoid loud laughter and smile gracefully. Be careful not to hurt the feelings of any person present. If you begin to speak about anything, and the company do not take notice of you, do not make a second attempt unless you are desired.

While in Britain, say little about your own country. Speak respectfully of the British government, avoid controversy about the late contest between Britain and the United States, and do not directly or indirectly advise mechanics or farmers to leave the British dominions.

Accommodate yourself to the habits of people, and their way of living in any place you may visit. Do not discover any niceness of palate, but make the best of homely fare. Plain people do not study cookery, and you will hurt them much by showing any contempt of the provision they may set before you. Be not noisy when you stop at a tavern, be polite to the landlord and servants; a real gentleman gives little trouble; he is easily pleased.

Carefully observe the state of society, the customs and manners, the progress or decline of religion, or of the arts and sciences, in any place to which providence may lead you. Be very curious. Study mankind wherever you go.

I need not guard you against vulgar companions, but be very kind to pious poor people and converse familiarly with them. Have few intimate friends, and be nice in choosing them. Draw a narrow circle enclosing some about your own age, some of middle, and some of old age, and give the preference to those who are most eminent in piety, learning, and politeness. Depend most upon the advices which are the dictates of experience.

Have stated times for visiting your friends, unless they are in affliction. Let your complimental visits be always affectionate and short. Never suffer your presence to be painful to any person.

Be faithful to your friends. Be a punctual correspondent; keep secrets; be affable to all men. Be not overcome of evil, but overcome evil with good, praying for and seeking opportunities to promote the happiness of all who injure you.

Never give unnecessary trouble to any family where you may lodge. Be polite to children and servants. Observe family rules, and beware of being abroad at a late hour.

Consider manly exercise as an important duty in which you may serve God. This will contribute much to the preservation of your health, and will defend you against hypochondriac affections, which destroy the spring of animal spirits, and make one useless and ridiculous.

Let it be your principal care to be able to state the doctrines of religion in a simple and perspicuous manner; this you will find to be the most effectual means of enervating objections, and opposing error. Do not embarrass yourself with a great variety of systems, nor with speculations about things which cannot be understood in this world, and perhaps will remain mysteries in the world to come. Make as great progress as possible in your systematical reading during the first year after your arrival in Scotland, and review what you shall have read in the second. Study systems in a practical manner. Remember that you are deeply interested in every doctrine of Christianity, and that even Divinity will be useless to your own soul, and the souls of others, if it is considered only as an object of speculation.

In your first year at Edinburgh, prepare twelve short, practical sermons, twenty in the second.

Observe the method of the ablest, the most pious and accurate preachers. Write the substance of their discourses when you are at home; but beware of a servile imitation of any preacher.

Be very intent on the study of the Hebrew language, for three or four months, and make yourself well acquainted with its grammar. When you shall be able to understand the Hebrew Scriptures with some ease I wish you to attend as the professor directs to the Arabic, Syriac, and Chaldaic, especially the Arabic, as much at least as will enable you to make progress in the study of them, after you shall leave the University. While you are engaged in these exercises, it will be proper to read Leusdeni Philologus.

Do not, however, neglect the Latin, Greek, and French languages. Be a classical critic. Read some of Plato's works, and make notes on what you read. In a particular manner attend to the purity of your own language. Lay in a store of classical words, that you may be able to express your sentiments on any subject, and on any occasion, with propriety and ease. In order to do this, labour to have clear ideas of things. Endeavour to acquire the habit of speaking in a plain, neat, unaffected style. Avoid bombast and vulgarity. Seldom let the proud monosyllable I, have the place in your compositions or discourses. Accustom yourself to read aloud, as one of the best means to fit you for public speaking. Be accurate in all your compositions.

Read with great care the Fathers of the three first centuries, and the Apostolical Constitutions. In these you will find many jewels, mixed with much rubbish. Observe the exposition they give of the Scriptures and what views they had of the doctrine of the Trinity, and of the person and office of the Redeemer. Write your remarks upon them; this will save much time in the future periods of life.

Make much use of Prideaux Connections. Be very exact in reading the history of the Church, till you come to the destruction of the Exarchate of Ravenna. Read with attention, but not with explicit faith, the Ecclesiastical Histories of Eusebius, Socrates, Evagrius, Mosheim, and Spanheim, to which you may add Sigonius de regno Italiae, de Occidentali Imperio, and Ockley's History of the Saracens.

As a relief from severe study read some books of rational amusement, and make the tour of the world, in some short and well written General Geography.

That you may not fall into confusion, and give unnecessary fatigue to your mind, make a prudent distribution of your time. If you sleep only seven hours in one day, you will have seventeen hours for devotion, for study, and for exercise. Let me again recommend to you the strictest attention to exercise. It may sometimes be necessary to lay aside study for a week or two, and to make an excursion into the country on horseback.

Let it be your care to acquire authority over your own mind, that with ease you may be able to apply yourself to any branch of study.

If God shall be pleased to put you into the ministry, prepare your discourses with great accuracy. Let this be the principal business of the morning of every day. Do not put it off till the end of the week. This would be to trifle with the Gospel and the souls of men; persevere in accurate preparation till the 40th or 45th year of your age. Superficial study and writing, in youth, make a poor old man. Be not however a slave to your compositions; exercise, but do not overcharge your memory. Go to the pulpit so far possessed of your notes, as to be able to speak with dignity, propriety, and ease.

Fill your discourses with useful matter. A multitude of words without sentiments, or with sentiments not adapted to the pulpit, insult a grave worshipping assembly. Let the peculiar doctrines of the Gospel be your principal subjects. Do not however neglect morality, but see that you enforce it chiefly by arguments drawn from redeeming grace. Give faith and obedience their proper places. Reason closely, but with as little appearance of reasoning as is possible for you: give a practical turn to your arguments, and never abuse those who are of a contrary opinion.

Have short introductions. State the sense and connexion of the text with great precision. Let your method be natural, arising out of the subject. Be concise in the doctrinal part, that you may not be hurried in the application. Never depart wantonly from our translation, and if at any time you shall find it necessary to alter it, do it with great modesty, and without amusing the hearers with Latin, Greek, or Hebrew words. Do not meddle with the exposition of the Scriptures, which we commonly call lecturing, for two years at least after you have appeared in a public character. Meanwhile prepare yourself for it, by a diligent reading, and close attention to the connexions of Scripture. When you begin it, select such passages as have a peculiar fitness for fixing impressions upon the consciences of the hearers. Let this be your practice for one year. After that you may expound a chapter, or a book, as you shall think will be most for edification.

Endeavour to acquire the command of your voice. Never speak louder than is necessary, unless some Divine impulse lay a necessity upon you. Screaming and bawling disgrace the pulpit. Despise theatrical airs. Let your actions be easy and natural. Hate affectation.

Rise above the frowns and applause of men. Consider your hearers as your fellow sinners, and your fellow mortals, and realize the presence of the searcher of hearts. Be serious and pointed, and you will command attention. Preach to yourself, and you will preach well to others.

Often read the Epistles to Timothy and Titus. Travail as in birth till Christ be formed in souls.

When settled in a congregation, begin your ministry with great modesty, affection, and faithfulness. The first days of a man's ministry have frequently been found to be his best days. Endeavour to grow, that your profiting may appear to all.

Be very circumspect in your life. Let your conversation on all occasions proclaim the sincerity of your heart, and exemplify the salutary tendencies of the doctrine you deliver to others.

Be very solemn in speaking to persons who desire baptism for their children, or admission to the Lord's Supper; and never dispense those privileges to any, without the advice of your Session.

Consider that faithfulness in catechising young people, who are the hope of the Church, and visiting the poor and the afflicted are some of the most important duties that will be incumbent upon you.

Never attach yourself to any party in your congregation, nor suffer any differences among the people to come before the Session till every previous means of composing them shall fail. Whatever unfavourable opinion you may have of any of your hearers, keep it locked up in your own mind. If any of them shall treat you in an unbecoming manner, take no notice of it, but pray for them, and do your duty to them, as though they had not displeased you. Discourage tale bearers, and never point your discourses at individuals.

As the general interests of religion are much influenced by judicial proceedings, let it now be your care to prepare yourself for acting your part therein. Attend the meetings of the General Assembly, the Commission of the Assembly, Synods, and Presbyteries of the National Church, and also the Judicatories of the Seceders, as you shall have opportunity. Consider Church discipline as an important subject of study. Buy the Acts of the General Assembly and the Acts of the Synod of Dort; you have the Act of the National Synod of France in the Library. When you shall be called to act as a member of a Church Judicatory, do not speak often, nor make long speeches, but be decisive when you speak. When differences happen among ministers, be a peace-maker. Never be a party-man. Durham on Scandal will contribute much to make you a good disciplinarian.

Thus I have given you a few advices. I wish my time had permitted me to polish and extend them. Receive them as they are. They are an effusion of the heart of an affectionate parent. More will be occasionally sent to you, if life and health are preserved.

I commend you to God, and to the word of His grace; may His good spirit instruct you, and you will be happily directed. Your best interests are near the heart of your father.

JOHN MASON

Read these advices once a month, carefully preserve them as a memorial of me. They may be of use to you, even in old age. Don't be discouraged when so much work is cut out for you. Method, perseverance, due exercise, and, above all, Divine assistance, will enable you to do much more, with great ease.

John Quincy Adams 1801

Schools and Seminaries for the Instruction of Youth in Silesia

John Quincy Adams (1767–1848), sixth President of the United States, traveled abroad extensively as a youth. At the age of eleven he journeyed to Europe with his father, John Adams, the United States Commissioner to the French Court, and in 1780 he attended Leyden University in Holland. At the age of fourteen he was appointed private secretary to the American Minister to Russia in St. Petersburg. In 1782 he returned for further studies in The Hague and then went home to enroll at Harvard. He was appointed Minister to Holland in 1794 and Minister to Berlin in 1797.

While serving in Berlin, John Quincy Adams traveled throughout Eastern Europe, and in his private letters he described some of the schools that he visited. He often called special attention to the "public" schools so that the recipients of his letters, usually New Englanders, would appreciate the fact that Massachusetts was not the only state with some rudimentary provisions for universal and compulsory elementary education. The following description of education in Silesia was written in a letter to his brother, Thomas Adams, and, like many personal letters sent home by Americans abroad, it was later published in an account of his travels. The letter is typical of this genre of travelers who made interesting observations and, at times, useful comparisons.

I have promised in this letter to give you some account of the institutions in the province of Silesia, for the education of youth. The university at Breslau, and the academy of nobles at Liegnitz, I need not mention, having noticed them in my letters, at the time when we visited those places. Besides these, there are what we call grammar-schools, where Latin is taught in almost every town of the province, and usually in connexion with some church or convent. But the arrangements and regulations of the trivial schools, as they are here called, schools destined for that elementary instruction which ought to be diffused over the whole mass of the people, particularly deserve your attention; because you may perhaps, as a native of New-England, entertain the prejudice, that your own country is the only spot on earth where this object is rightly managed, and where the arts of reading and writing are accomplishments almost universally possessed.

Probably, no country in Europe could so strongly contest our pre-eminence in this respect as Germany; and she, for this honourable distinction, is indebted principally to Frederick II.; to the zeal with which he pursued the purpose of spreading useful knowledge among all classes of his subjects; and to the influence of his example, and of his success, even beyond the limits of his own dominions. To enter upon this topic, with the details of which it is susceptible, might, perhaps, not amuse you, and would lead me too far from my subject; I shall, therefore, confine myself to the measures he adopted, and the system he introduced, in this particular into Silesia.

At the time of his conquest, education had seldom made an object of the concern of governments, and Silesia, like the rest of Europe, was but wretchedly provided, either with schools or teachers. In the small towns and villages the schoolmasters were so poorly paid, that they could not subsist without practising some other trade, besides their occupation as instructors, and they usually united the character of the village-fiddler with that of the village-schoolmaster. Even of these there were so few, that the children of the peasants in general, throughout the province, were left untaught. This was especially the case in Upper Silesia. Frederick issued an ordinance, that a school should be kept in every village, and that a competent subsistence should be provided for the schoolmaster, by the joint contribution of the lord of the village, and of the tenants themselves. The superintendence of the schools was prescribed as the duty of the clergy.

But, in order that this ordinance might have its due execution, it was necessary to form the teachers themselves, properly qualified to give useful instruction. This was

---

A letter from John Quincy Adams in Berlin to his brother, Thomas Boylston Adams, in Philadelphia, March 7, 1801; in *Letters on Silesia, Written During a Tour Through That Country in the Years 1800, 1801* (London: J. Budd, 1804), pp. 361–372.

effected by the persevering intelligence and zeal of a man, by the name of Felbiger, an Augustine monk, belonging to a convent at Sagan; a man, says a Silesian historian, whom a great part of Germany must thank for a revolution, not less important, though of slower progress and milder character, than that which, two centuries and a half earlier, was accomplished by another monk of the same order—by Luther.

Felbiger, after spending some years at Berlin, to obtain a perfect knowledge of the best method of instruction practised in the schools there, returned to Sagan, and made the convent to which he belonged, a seminary for young ecclesiastics, and candidates as schoolmasters, to acquire the knowledge of the improved mode of teaching. Several other institutions of the same kind were, in due time, established at Breslau, Glatz, and other places, upon his principles, and conducted by persons whom he had formed. To defray the expenses necessary for the support of these seminaries, a fund is raised, consisting of one quarter's salary, which every Catholic curate is obliged to pay, upon being first settled in a parsonage.

With each of these seminaries are connected certain schools, where the young candidates for the clerical or teaching office are obliged to attend, and observe the practice of the method, the theory of which they learn at the seminaries themselves. The clergy are required, no less than the teachers, to go through this process, because the superintendence over the teachers is intrusted to them. No young man can be admitted to either of the offices, without an attestation of his qualification from one of the seminaries.

After all these preparatory measures had been carried into effect, an ordinance was published in the year 1765, prescribing the mode of teaching, as adopted in the seminaries, and the manner in which the clergy should superintend the efficacious establishment of the system. The regulations of this ordinance prove the earnestness with which the King of Prussia laboured to spread the benefits of useful knowledge among his subjects. The teachers are directed to give plain instruction, and upon objects applicable to the ordinary concerns of life; not merely to load the memory of their scholars with words, but to make things intelligible to their understanding; to habituate them to the use of their own reason, by explaining every object of the lesson, so that the children themselves may be able to explain it, upon examination. The candidates for school-keeping must give

specimens of their ability, by teaching at one of the schools connected with the seminary, in the presence of the professors at the seminary, that they may remark and correct any thing defective in the candidate's method. If one school suffices for more than one village, neither of them must be more than half a German mile distant from it, in the flat country; nor more than a quarter of a mile, in the mountainous parts. The school-tax must be paid by the lord and tenants, without distinction of religions. In the towns, the school must be kept the whole year round. It is expected that one month shall suffice to make a child know the letters of the alphabet; that in two it shall be able to join them; and in three, to read. The boys must all be sent to school, from their sixth to their thirteenth year, whether the parents are able to pay the school-tax or not. For the poor, the school-money must be raised by collections. Every parent or guardian who neglects to send his child or pupil to school, without sufficient cause, is obliged to pay a double school-tax, for which the guardians shall have no allowance. Every curate must examine, weekly, the children of the school in his parish. A general examination must be held annually, by the deans of the districts, of the schools within their respective precincts; and a report of the condition of the schools, the talents and attention of the schoolmasters, the state of the buildings, and of attendance by the children, made to the office of the vicar-general, who must transmit all these reports to the royal domain offices. From these, orders are issued to the respective landraths, to correct the abuses and supply the deficiencies indicated in the reports. This system was at first prepared only for the Catholic schools; but it was afterwards adopted, for the most part, by most of the Lutheran consistories. Its truly respectable author, Felbiger, was, in the sequel, with the consent of Frederick, invited to Vienna, by the Empress Maria Theresa, and her son Joseph II. who appointed him director of the normal schools, or seminaries, in all the Austrian dominions. His regulations have been introduced, and are acted upon, in almost all the Catholic countries of Germany.

In Silesia they had, at first, many old prejudices to contend with. The indolence of the Catholic clergy was averse to the new and troublesome duty imposed on them. Their zeal was alarmed at the danger arising from this dispersion of light to the stability of their church. They considered alike the spirit of innovation, and the spirit of inquiry, as their natural enemies. Besides this, the system still meets resistance from the penurious parsimony and stubborn love of darkness, prevailing in some parts of the province. Many villages neglect the support of their schools; many individuals, upon false pretexts, forbear sending their children to school, for the sake of saving the tax. The compulsory measures, and the penalties, prescribed by the ordinance, are used seldom, and with reluctance. The benevolent design has not been accomplished to the full extent of which it was susceptible; but, as far as it has been accomplished, its operation has been a blessing. That its effects have been very extensive, is not to be doubted, when we compare the number of schools throughout the province, in the year 1752, when they amounted only to one thousand five hundred and fifty-two, with that in the year 1798, when they were more than three thousand five hundred. The consequences of a more general diffusion of knowledge are attested by many other facts equally clear. Before the seven years war, there had scarcely ever been more than one periodical journal or gazette published in the province, at one time. There are now, no less than seventeen newspapers and magazines, which appear by the day, the week, the month, or the quarter, many of them upon subjects generally useful, and containing valuable information and instruction for the people. At the former period there were three booksellers, and all these at Breslau. There are, now, six in that capital, and seven dispersed about in the other cities. The number of printing-presses and of book-binders has increased in the same proportion.

Doctor Johnson, in his life of Watts, has bestowed a just and exalted encomium upon him, for not disdaining to descend from the pride of genius and the dignity of science, to write for the wants and the capacities of children. "Every man acquainted," says he, "with the common principles of human actions, will look with veneration on the writer, who is at one time combating Locke, and at another time making a catechism for children in their fourth year." But how much greater still is the tribute of admiration irresistibly drawn from us, when we behold an absolute monarch, the greatest general of his age, eminent as a writer in the highest departments of literature, descending, in a manner, to teach the alphabet to the children of his kingdom; bestowing his care, his persevering assiduity, his influence and his power, in diffusing plain and useful knowledge among his subjects; in opening to their minds the first and most important pages of the book of science, in filling the whole atmosphere they breathed, with that intellectual fragrance, which had before been imprisoned in the vials of learning, or enclosed within the gardens of wealth!—Immortal Frederick! when seated on the throne of Prussia, with kneeling millions at thy feet, thou wast only a king. On the fields of Leuthen, of Zorndorf, of Rosbach, of so many other scenes of human blood and anguish, thou wast only a hero. Even in thy rare and glorious converse with the Muses and with science, thou wast only a philosopher, an historian, a poet; but in this generous ardour, this active and enlightened zeal for the education of thy people, thou wast truly great—the father of thy country—the benefactor of mankind.

Benjamin Silliman 1805

English and Scottish Universities

Benjamin Silliman (1779–1864) was a distinguished professor of chemistry and natural history at Yale College. In 1804 the trustees of Yale appropriated funds for the enlargement of their library and the purchase of "chemical" and "philosophical" equipment from Europe. Silliman was commissioned to make the purchases and was encouraged to remain and study in Europe in order to enhance his knowledge of chemistry. He attended medical and scientific lectures at Edinburgh University and gained a first-hand knowledge of teaching at that institution. While visiting Oxford and Cambridge, he made observations which are typical of the ephemeral commentary indulged in by some Americans visiting English universities. Silliman

Benjamin Silliman, *A Journal of Travels in England, Holland, and Scotland and of Two Passages over the Atlantic in the Years 1805 and 1806* (Boston: Howe and Deforest, and Increase Cook and Company, 1812), second edition, I, 121–124; II, 215–218, 220–233, 310–315, 336–339, 343–344.

founded and for twenty years edited *The American Journal of Science and Arts*, and he was recognized for many years as the chief publisher of American scientific developments.

Oxford University

Oxford is sixty-three miles from Birmingham. We arrived in the former town a little after four o'clock in the morning, and I found a comfortable bed at the Angel inn.

The same causes which prevented me from remaining some time at Birmingham, will render my stay in Oxford so short, that I shall disappoint the reasonable expectations which you will form of receiving information concerning it. I however regret the circumstance the less, because I have it in view to visit Oxford again, when I am more at leisure.

The fatigue of travelling through the night prevented my rising in season for the morning service; but, in the afternoon, I went to the church of St. Mary, an ancient Gothic structure, belonging to Queen's College.

The officers and students of this college attended, and we had the best sermon which I have heard in England. I suppose the gentleman who delivered it was the Professor of Theology. His discourse was, in sentiment, correct, and in style manly, perspicuous, and elegant.

The officers and students all wear a loose black gown over their dress, which is like that of other gentlemen. They wear a black velvet cap, fitting the head exactly, like the crown of the hat before the modern high hats came into fashion. This cap is destitute of a rim or border, of any kind, either for ornament or use, and thus the face and eyes are completely exposed to the weather. On the very pinnacle of the cap is fixed a square board, covered also with black; it looks as a thin book would do, if laid on the crown of the head. From the middle of this, a tassel falls over on one side of the head. This is usually black, but, in the case of noblemen, it is of gold, and there are other variations in the singular costume which I have described, intended to designate academic as well as civil rank. The effect of the whole is somewhat ludicrous, at the same time that it is grave and even solemn. When the members of the university are out of Oxford, they throw off this garb, and appear like other men.

At the inn where I lodged, I accidentally met Mr. D——. We had been at Yale College together, some years ago, and neither of us, I believe, would have thought of our meeting at Oxford. We of course became associates; for it was an interesting discovery to find an old acquaintance where one supposed himself surrounded only by strangers, and we agreed to travel to London together.

Towards evening we made, in part, the circuit of Oxford and its environs, and viewed the exterior of most of the academic buildings, and the interior of some. The buildings are generally in the form of a hollow square; the included space forms a court which is commonly verdant and beautiful.

In one of the chapels we saw a curious production of art. It was a picture of a man, made by tracing the lines on a board with a hot poker. We were informed that one of the fellows, by amusing himself with burning a board with this instrument, gradually passed to attempting rude delineations, and ultimately acquired so much skill, as to leave this monument of his singular taste behind him; it is by no means deficient in elegance and effect.

Oxford is a place of great grandeur and beauty. It is situated in the midst of a country whose verdure is very rich and luxuriant. It stands at the intersection of the Thames and Cherwell, and these rivers and the canals are bordered by gravel walks, and rows of ancient, lofty, and venerable trees; these are so numerous in the town, that the buildings are often over-shadowed by them, and appear as if in a forest. The whole town has an unrivalled air of magnificence and dignity. No place ever impressed me with such feelings of admiration and awe, and I presume it is without a parallel in the world. Instead of the narrow and dirty lanes of trading towns, and the confused noise of commerce, there are spacious and quiet streets, with fine houses of stone, built in a very good taste. But what produces the principal effect is the great number of academic buildings, in a style of much grandeur, and rendered venerable by strong marks of antiquity. The effect is very much heightened by the frequent avenues of lofty forest-trees, and by the historical associations naturally connected with a university which claims *Alfred the Great* for its founder. The most considerable of the colleges here is that of Christ Church, founded by Cardinal Wolsey; and the most extensive and beautiful walk is in the rear of this.

Oxford contains nearly 12,000 inhabitants. It was distinguished for its strong partiality to Charles I. who held his court here during the whole of the civil wars. It is built principally on two streets, which cross each other at right angles, and the high street is considered as one of the finest in Europe. It is terminated by a beautiful bridge. The circumference of Oxford is said to be three miles, and its form circular. My travelling book says that there are thirteen parish churches, but I did not see them all. The number of colleges and other similar institutions is twenty-five. They informed me that the number of students in the university was about 1200, and that Christ Church college has more than any other. There is a fashion in these things, and the nobility and men of fortune are found principally at Christ Church. . . .

Cambridge University

It was nearly dark when we entered Cambridge, and as we passed rapidly by, I could merely distinguish the buildings of the university from those of the town.

After tea, I took a guide and went to Queens college, to the apartments of the master of the institution, Dr. M—, a man well known to the philosophical world. Unfortunately for me, he was engaged, and I spent only a few minutes in his society. We went next to the apartments of Mr. C— of Bennet college; his affable and polite deportment gave me a favourable opinion of the manners of the university.

An introduction to Mr. —, a fellow of Caius, or, as they here pronounce it Key's college, led me to that institution, where I was detained to supper. The establishment of the fellows, judging from these examples, are genteel; their apartments are large, handsome and well furnished, and apparently as comfortable as those in private houses. Our supper, according to the general habits of living in England, among people who are not dissipated, was frugal, but still ample and excellent in its kind, and it was rendered interesting to me, by the communications of the polished and enlightened man who was my host; although he had been bred in the university, his manners were those of a man of the world, in the best sense of that phrase, for he had travelled and visited other countries, and exhibited nothing of those prejudices, which have been so often charged to the English character. As a stranger I took the liberty of making numerous inquiries concerning the university, its courses of instruction, its police and discipline, and other interesting circumstances.

A certain number of the fellows perform duties very similar to those which the tutors discharge in our colleges, and on them I understand that the burden of instruction principally devolves; they meet their classes at appointed hours and places, and text-books of the different subjects are prescribed to the classes from which they are expected to obtain such information as is necessary to qualify them for a proper appearance before their instructers.

There is so much declamation in America, on the subject of the corrupt morals and dissipated lives of the youth at the English universities, in consequence of the alleged laxness of discipline, that I felt particularly solicitous to satisfy myself how this matter really was; but delicacy debarred me from pressing my inquiries on this subject as far as I could have wished. On the whole I concluded that this subject had been greatly misrepresented—that the majority of the youth are moral and studious, but, that the particular personal inspection into the habits of every individual member of the colleges, which is so rigorously practised in most of the American institutions of the kind, is here, in a great measure, unknown. The youth appear to be left more to their own discretion, and if no gross indecorum, offensive to good manners and sound morals, become public, I suppose the government will not interfere. There are, however, beyond a doubt, particular examples of a degree of dissipation and scandalous immorality, which, if they were taken as fair specimens of the whole society, would justify the highly-coloured pictures which have been so often drawn on this subject.

There can be no question that there is a difficulty in the English universities, which is almost unknown in the American colleges; I mean that which arises from the tacit but powerful sway produced over the minds of men by hereditary titles, honours, fortunes, and expectations of various kinds. In these universities there are sons of the first men in the empire, who are themselves, ere long, to fill the places of their fathers. That such men should not always be the most manageable subjects of academic discipline, and the fairest examples of sobriety and studious industry, is certainly not so extraordinary, as that there should be any youthful mind which is proof against allurements which have always drawn mankind with a syren influence. I believe that gross licentiousness is still obliged to make use of the veil of secrecy, and that some vices at least, here as well as elsewhere, shrink from observation.

It is said, that a short time since, some mischievous young men in the university, privately circulated a report among the amateurs of pugilistic combats, that there would be one, at a particular time, within 16 miles of Cambridge;—great secrecy was enjoined, that the officers of the university might not be alarmed, and the secret was so well kept, that every gig and saddlehorse in the town was engaged for the occasion, when the spectators, with a degree of punctuality, which, there is reason to believe, they had not often observed in their college exercises, assembled on the spot, but—no combatants appeared, and the whole turned out to be an imposition; they were ashamed and afraid to complain, but the thing transpired, and they were persecuted with such severe ridicule, that it was quite unnecessary to add any academic censure.

This love of sport, without much regard to the means by which it is excited, appears therefore to pervade the English universities as well as the American colleges. . . .

From King's Chapel, we went into the walks in the spacious grounds behind King's and Trinity Colleges, whence is a very fine prospect of these beautiful buildings.

Avenues of lofty trees, planted in fine verdant meadows, form academic retirements which must be peculiarly grateful, during the season of summer;—nor are they without interest and beauty, even now, when the falling leaves begin to cover the grass, and the chilly winds rather persuade one to seek the close room, and the fire-side.

The river Cam passes through these grounds, and although it is but a small and sluggish stream, yet, as it is water, and has a neat bridge, it affords a degree of variety, and augments the beauty of the scene, which is very little inferior to that behind Christ's College at Oxford.

But, if I may be allowed to give an opinion from so short an acquaintance with Cambridge, and a still more limited one with Oxford, the latter town is much superior in its general appearance, and particularly in the magnificence of its academic buildings;—but several of those at Cambridge are certainly elegant and some of them grand.

The town itself is not handsome; the University buildings stand about in it, here and there, without any general plan of arrangement; the streets are narrow and intricate, and the houses are far from being elegant; the town contains about 10,000 inhabitants.

The University buildings, both here and at Oxford, are constructed, generally, upon the old plan of the hollow square, that is, the building completely surrounds a portion of ground, which forms an interior court, to which is access through a handsome arched passage. Sometimes, these courts are very beautiful, especially when they have clean gravel walks and a share of verdure, but they are too frequently dismal enclosures, where damp air accumulates and becomes stagnant.

We visited the library of Trinity College. It contains about 30,000 volumes, arranged in recesses resembling alcoves, in a very long and beautiful room, of the age of Charles II. which produced many fine buildings in England.

In this apartment I saw the cobra de capello, the fatal snake of the East Indies; also a very beautiful chameleon and an Egyptian mummy. . . .

When one beholds these frightful remnants of mortality, he feels very little disposition to regret that the moderns are less perfectly acquainted, than the ancient Egyptians were, with the art of embalming. It is a miserable effort of man to evade the edict of heaven, *dust thou art, and unto dust shall thou return.*

Who can soberly wish that his body should escape the general law of decay and dissolution, that it may remain a hideous spectacle for posterity, the phantom of a form, attractive no longer when life has fled, and fit only to be committed to the dark and narrow house!

At the foot of the stairs, there were a number of Grecian antiques, with Grecian inscriptions.

In the chapel of Trinity College we saw a much admired statue of Sir Isaac Newton, who was educated in this institution.

By adverting to biographical memoirs of this, and of the sister University, any one will become convinced, that a very large proportion of the great men of England, for centuries past, have been derived from the two Universities, and by examining the records of the individual Colleges, it will also be evident that most of those who afterwards became distinguished in life, obtained the honours and distinctions of the University. It would be easy to establish both these positions by catalogues of names illustrious in science, in the professions, in politics, and even in war, and the present age affords a list not less extensive and renowned than any one that has preceded.

The popular position, that a regular public education is not more favourable to eminence than a private one, and that no conjecture concerning a young man's ultimate success, can be formed from his standing at college is, therefore, as unfounded as it is unreasonable. It is true that a youth, who has been distinguished in academic life, may, from indolence, vice, or misfortune, sink into obscurity, and a dull boy may, after he has left the classes, emerge, and discover talents that no one thought he possessed. A vigorous mind may also surmount the obstacles of a limited and imperfect education, and astonish mankind by displays of intellect and science far transcending the common standard of the schools; but, from such examples, no general consequences can be safely drawn, and we must admit that the thorough discipline of the mind is most successfully effected in the regular processes of an extensive academic education.

The dining-halls of a number of the colleges came in our way; the young men receive their dinners at these public tables, but take their breakfast and tea at their own apartments. The arrangements of the halls appear in general very similar to those in our colleges, but, there is more neatness and comfort, and even a considerable degree of elegance.

We saw the Senate-house, a magnificent building, in which the examinations and commencements are held.

The last public room which we visited, was the university library. It contains more than 90,000 volumes; but, I hardly know a more unsatisfactory spectacle to a transient visitor than a great library. It is rather distracting than gratifying merely to look at the backs of long rows of volumes, or just to inspect the titles. Examination of their contents is usually forbidden, or if indulged, is of little use, for, what can an hour, a day, a week, a month, a year, or even a life, effect towards reading 100,000 volumes. It is still highly important that such collections should be formed as great magazines of science and literature, whence the inquisitive and industrious may draw materials to be worked up in their various pursuits.

They showed us an Egyptian book, written on the papyrus. The papyrus was flattened, and, the characters, being traced in the cuticle by an instrument, a black powder was rubbed over, which stained the incisions permanently; the leaves were preserved by thrusting wires through them as they were laid face to face, and the whole was defended by two pieces of wood.

We now took a general walk about Cambridge and visited the various colleges. There are sixteen in the whole. Each institution is independent of the rest, as to its internal discipline and courses of instruction; it has separate offices, and is, in every respect, a distinct establishment, except, that the chancellor and other university officers have a general superintendance of the whole. The immediate instruction is performed principally by a certain number of the fellows who are appointed tutors. The gentleman with whom I was walking was both a fellow and a tutor, and, by making many and various inquiries, which were answered with politeness and intelligence, I was enabled to form something like a comparison between this university and our more circumscribed institutions in America. The latter are *comparatively*, more respectable than I had imagined, although in many things certainly inferior.

I am not disposed to pursue this comparison into details, both because I am deficient in the necessary information, and because it would be invidious with respect to the American institutions. For, we have in no instance a collection of independent literary societies, located in one place, and united under one head, to form a university, although most of the liberal arts and sciences are taught, more or less extensively, in our most respectable colleges. If the comparison were made at all, it would therefore be more proper to draw a parallel between some one of our colleges and some one or more of the individual colleges of the English universities. If this were done, our institutions would have less reason to shrink from the comparison.

In classical learning and philological literature, we are certainly far behind the English institutions, but, in mathematics, ethics, and the physical sciences, some of our institutions are probably equal to them. Indeed it is scarcely possible to say any thing on this subject in terms merely general, without involving material errors, for one American institution is distinguished for one species of knowledge, and another for another. Even the two great universities of England build their fame on foundations somewhat different. At Oxford, classical literature is cultivated to the comparative prejudice of mathematical learning, and preeminence in the former is the great criterion of distinction; while at Cambridge the greatest stress is laid on theoretical mathematics and natural philosophy. While every judicious American will, of course, discountenance that spirit of ostentation and vanity, which has sometimes infected our writings, and made us ridiculous in the eyes of Europe, he may still, with confidence, indulge this conviction, that, considering our youth, and various circumstances as a people, we have no occasion to be ashamed of our literary institutions, or to despair of their ultimately attaining every thing which can be useful to our country.

The degrees and honours of the university of Cambridge are not granted as a matter of course: take the following account of this subject from an English book.

"The system of education pursued is liberal, and the incentives to emulation and the rewards of merit very numerous. In this last respect, Cambridge is, perhaps, superior to Oxford, where, generally speaking, the opportunities of rewarding merit, by open foundations, are not so great as in the sister university.

"The grand examination of students is that which precedes the degree of bachelor of arts. It takes place in the Senate-house, on the first Monday in Lent term, and the three following days. The candidates from all the colleges, having gone through their respective courses of study, their examination in their own societies, and their exercises in the schools, are here examined impartially in public. The chief stress in these examinations, is laid upon mathematics and natural philosophy; and the greatest proficients in these are placed highest in the list of honours. When the examination is completed, the candidates are arranged in classes, according to their respective merits. The first class are called *wranglers*, and the senior wrangler is considered as the first man of his standing in the university. The two next classes are called *senior* and *junior optimes*, and these are all the degrees of honour. The rest of the candidates, if their ignorance is not too glaring, are suffered to have their degrees in a sort of multitude; and are sometimes jocosely denominated by their fellow students οἱ πολλοί [common herd]."

The number of persons in the different colleges varies extremely;—in some there are not more than from 40 to 60; in the greater number there are probably from 70 to 80 to 150; and in two of the colleges there are sometimes five or six hundred in each; the two to which I allude are St. John's and Trinity; the latter has usually a more numerous society than any other, for it is the college to which the nobility and young men of fortune resort more than to any other.

Both the officers and students of the universities wear academic gowns, and the ancient academic hood;—some minute variations in this dress, not easily distinguishable by a stranger, serve to mark the different descriptions of persons. I did not observe that the students paid their officers any external token of respect when they met them; both officers and students passed each other as if they had been entire strangers.

For the promotion of social and convivial enjoyment, there is a custom existing among the officers of several of the colleges, which gives a stranger an opportunity of seeing them under very pleasant circumstances. They dine, on particular days, at each others houses, in regular rotation, and the evening is devoted to relaxation. By the politeness of Mr. C ——, I was introduced at one of these dinners, and met a party consisting principally of masters or presidents, professors and fellows.

Our sitting lasted for hours; my seat was next to Mr. C ——, and, in the course of a very free conversation, he took occasion to observe, that it was impossible that any man born and educated 3000 miles from England, should speak the language so perfectly, that even an Englishman could not distinguish the difference between a stranger's speech and his own. This, he was pleased to say, was just the case between us; and he then, with much good nature and urbanity, insisted that I had been all the while amusing him with the story that I was an American, when it was so evident that I must be an Englishman, or must, at least, have been educated in England. I succeeded however, at length, in removing this gentleman's incredulity, although not his surprise. Probably every American traveller in England can relate similar occurrences with which he has been personally acquainted. We must not infer from them that the English do not know that their own language is spoken in the United States. Although we may pardon a Russian, or an unlettered Englishman for such a mistake, we must look for more correct information in a peer of the realm and a learned fellow of one of the universities. They, and all well-informed people in England, unquestionably know that the Anglo-Americans speak the English language; but they imagine that it is a colonial dialect, with a corrupt and barbarous pronunciation, and a vocabulary, interspersed with strange and unknown terms of transatlantic manufacture. That this is the result of prejudice or ignorance, is proved by the fact that a well-educated American may travel from London to John o'Groat's house, and thence to the Land's-end, and every where pass for a Londoner; this is the universal presumption concerning him, as will appear from the incidental remarks of the people of the country, and their questions concerning the news of the day.

I am well aware, that in the lapse of almost two centuries, since the first permanent English settlements were formed in America, the language must have undergone some changes. Words, then used in England, have since been dropped, and being in some instances still used in America, appear obsolete to an Englishman. In a new world, and under circumstances entirely novel, some new words and phrases have been invented; others, in common use in England, have been forgotten in America; old words have acquired additional significations, or have been stripped of their primitive, with the substitution of new meanings, and, in the mean time, similar changes have been taking place in England. But, after all, one is surprised that so great a similarity, I had almost said, such a perfect identity, of language, exists between the enlightened people of both countries. The best informed people of America speak the language (with a few unimportant exceptions) as the people of London do. It must be allowed, however, that the literary men of England speak and write the language with more purity and correctness than most people of the same description in America; and, in England, gross blunders at the bar and in Parliament are not so common as in the American congress and courts of law. But, if you compare England in the gross, comprehending all classes of people, with the mass of people of the United States, there cannot be a doubt that the latter have the advantage on this subject. The provincial dialects, which render the language of the common people of one county in England in a considerable degree unintelligible to those of another, and which, in many instances, incumber the style even of the country gentlemen with so much of the local *Shibboleth*, that they are instantly recognised in London, are almost wholly unknown in America, and the people from Maine to Georgia, and from the Atlantic to the Mississippi, speak a language perfectly intelligible to each other, and to every English traveller. Without therefore denying or entirely admitting, for the present, the charges of corrupting the style of fine writing, which is so often urged against us, I am clearly of the opinion that *the English language is more correctly spoken, at this time, by the mass of the American than by the mass of the English nation,* and that it has not undergone more rapid mutation in America, since the era of its settlement, than languages commonly suffer in the same period of time, in the natural course of things.

Our dinner presented no other incident worthy of notice;—conversation turned on various and common topics, and the manners of the gentlemen, although decorous and correct, were characterized by a degree of convivial ease and freedom.

In the evening we joined the ladies above stairs, and tea being over, I was invited to join several of the reverend masters and professors, in, what do you think?——A disquisition concerning the Hebrew points, the quadrature of the circle, or the possibility of perpetual motion?—— No—I was invited to join them in a rubber at whist!—not a gambling match, but a pastime.

It is somewhat remarkable that I should be invited to play at cards, for the first time in England, with academic gentlemen; they were so polite, however, as to excuse me, nor am I inclined to judge them with severity, only, it struck me as somewhat unfortunate that the usual instruments of gambling should be found in the hands of the guardians and instructers of youth, who are commonly prompt enough at finding out and applying to their own justification, the precedents derived from the conduct of their officers, while they will always have it in their power to plead amusement to repel the charge of gambling.

November 16.—Mr. C——, to whose unwearied attentions, all the while that I stayed in Cambridge, I am indebted for most of the pleasure and information I received, called on me, immediately after breakfast, and took me to the Botanical Garden, where I spent some time very agreeably. . . .

From the Botanical Garden, we went to the Castle-hill. I wished to survey Cambridge from an eminence, that I might gain a correct idea of its geographical situation. For this purpose I had before ascended to the top of the chapel of King's College, but the morning was hazy and the view was by no means so good as today from the Castle-hill. This hill derives its name from an ancient castle, one of whose gates is still remaining, and is said to have been erected by William the Conqueror. The remains of the castle are contiguous to the hill, and not upon it.

Cambridge is situated in the midst of a vast plain, bounded by remote hills of no great height. The city of Ely was in view, and a number of villages, but the University formed the most striking object in the prospect.

Returning into town, we called on Professor F——, to whom I had introductory letters, but whose absence had prevented me from seeing him before. I found him a very clever, intelligent man, with the most frank and friendly manners.

He took me to the laboratory, and displayed

every thing to my inspection. The laboratory is a good one, and the apparatus is extensive.

Besides Mr. F——, there is another professor of chemistry, Dr. W——, who delivers a course of elementary chemistry in the usual manner, but the course of Mr. F—— is somewhat peculiar. He demonstrates by experiment all the most important applications of chemistry and of mechanics to the arts of life, and particularly to the manufactures of Great Britain, many of the establishments of which he has, for this purpose, visited in person.

He is furnished with a complete collection of models and machines, adapted to this extensive plan, and the chemical apparatus of his colleague, Mr. W——, is used for the chemical demonstrations.

He has a small steam engine which serves, in the first place, to illustrate the theory and construction of this instrument; and, having put it in motion, he applies the moving power, thus produced, to work the rest of his machinery. He has a paper-mill and manufactures paper; a carding and spinning machine, with which he forms rolls and thread; he drives down piles, in the manner practised in the construction of bridges and wharves; he makes a hat, manufactures nitric acid, and, in short, exhibits to the young men all the leading applications of chemical and mechanical philosophy to real use. It is certainly a most happy plan, and, in the hands of so able a professor, must prove highly useful and interesting; and, it is said that Mr. F—— enjoys the honour of having invented and executed so important an improvement in education.

From this gentleman I received every attention of civility and kindness, as well as from the fellows to whom I had been introduced, and they all were so good as to endeavour to protract my stay, but I found it necessary to proceed, which I confess I did with reluctance, for I began to feel interested in a society where I found so much to interest my mind and gratify my feelings.

I left Cambridge with very pleasing impressions, and now regretted, more than ever, that circumstances had prevented my return to the sister University, and had limited my stay in Cambridge to two days.

But, it was already time for me to be in Scotland, and I therefore determined to go on that night. . . .

The University of Edinburgh

February 3.—"The University of Edinburgh was founded in the year 1582, by Queen Mary and James VI."

Although it is comparatively a modern institution, it has acquired a reputation, so extensive and well-deserved, that a stranger naturally looks for its buildings the moment that he walks out for the first time in Edinburgh. He will find them in the old town; the more ancient buildings are low and mean, and make no figure; but there is a magnificent front of hewn stone, facing a principal street of the old town, and forming a part of an extensive plan of university buildings, which they began to erect, a few years ago; this front, with a part of the wings, was completed, but their means failed, and this splendid monument of poverty and pride, rendered more impressive by an inscription commemorative of the royal origin of the University, remains a reproach to Scotland, and will soon, if neglected, become a ruin. It is said that they are waiting for the termination of the present arduous struggle with France, when they hope to complete the plan. I have heard it facetiously remarked, that the completion of these buildings would be a serious misfortune to the professors, for as they would live in them, it would take all their salaries to furnish the apartments with carpets.

The salaries of the professors are small, but the most valuable part of their compensations is derived from the fees paid for tickets of admission to their respective courses of lectures. This circumstance proves a great stimulus to exertion, and there is, as might be expected, a great disparity in the emoluments of the different professors. I believe there are no fellowships, and that the instruction of the University is performed by the professors alone. These are very numerous; —about twenty-four or twenty-six, if I am correctly informed. Almost every branch of science is taught; the medical courses occupy the most distinguished rank, but there is even a distinct professorship of agriculture.

Edinburgh presents a constellation of scientific and literary men, and, in proportion to its population holds, in this respect, a rank superior to that of any town in Britain, or perhaps in the world. The University embraces no small proportion of those who contribute to give Edinburgh this honourable distinction, and among these, Professor Dugald Stewart undoubtedly holds the most conspicuous place, as a man of general literature, and of impressive classical eloquence.

Dr. Gregory, professor of the practice of medicine, does honour to the memory of his father, the late Dr. Gregory, author of the Father's Legacy to his daughters.

Dr. Hope, successor of the late Dr. Black,

fills the chemical chair with much ability; he gives a complete and learned course, and exhibits an unrivalled example of neatness and beauty of experimental illustration.

The professorship of anatomy is still in the family of the Munroes; the present professor, who is now far advanced in life, has been a very distinguished man, but he has almost relinquished the active duties of the station, and transferred them to his son, who has been nominated his colleague and successor.

Professor Playfair is very able in the department of physics, and Mr. Leslie promises to fill with reputation the place of his illustrious predecessor Dr. Robison. I do not pretend to give a complete account of the ornaments of the University, or of those of the town of Edinburgh. I ought not to omit, however, to mention Dr. Barclay, an able private lecturer on anatomy, Dr. Thomson, the author of a celebrated system of chemistry, and Mr. Murray, a private lecturer on chemistry, a young man much distinguished for a clear philosophical mind, and a happy flow of luminous language.

Dr. Anderson has been rendered famous by his edition of the British Poets and by his various literature; the Bells are celebrated for their surgical works, and Dr. Brown and the two Dr. Duncans are well known to the medical and philosophical world.

Literature and science here receive the approbation and attention which constitute one of their most powerful supports, and most gratifying rewards, and Edinburgh appears to have less of the spirit of *mercantile selfishness* than such large town generally possess.

The buildings of the University do not contain chambers for the students; they afford merely lecture rooms, a library, and other public apartments. The professors generally have houses in town. One of them has a house at the college gate; it covers the spot of ground on which the building stood that contained Darnley, Queen Mary's husband, when he was blown into the air, by the explosion of gunpowder.

There are at present in the University of Edinburgh, about fourteen hundred students in all the classes, and, of these, about five hundred are medical students, who are collected from almost every civilized country. Most of them are from the British islands, but there are numbers from the continent of Europe, from the West Indies, and the United States. Of the latter description there are at present twenty-five in Edinburgh, and most of them are from States south of New England.

I was present this morning at Dr. Gregory's lecture, and sat next to a young Hindu who is here, as a student of medicine. He is a young man of a genteel appearance and an intelligent countenance; you would hardly think it possible that an olive complexion could afford so handsome a face.

The lecture happened to be upon the diseases of Europeans in the Asiatic countries, and I could perceive this young man's countenance change, every time that Hindustan was mentioned.

I do not know what degree of discipline is exercised among the younger classes of students in this University, but there appears to be none among those belonging to the medical school. They lodge in private houses in town, and spend their time as they please, nor does there appear to be any responsibility, except that created by the ultimate examination for the honours of the University, a distinction for which only a small proportion apply.

The examinations are conducted in Latin, and as it is not every candidate who is a sufficient adept either in this language, or in the several branches of medical science, to meet the ordeal with safety, recourse is had to the aid of a class of men, known here by the appellation of *grinders*. They teach young men to learn by rote, the series of Latin questions and answers which experience has shown, may be commonly expected, and by *grinding* them (as it is called) in this manner, from day to day, they at last enable ignorance and dullness to blunder along, through an examination. I received this account from an American, who was then himself undergoing the honourable operation of *grinding*. . . .

Opinions Concerning American Literature

April 19.—There is one acquisition which an American traveller in Britain will necessarily make, that will, in all probability, be very different from any thing he had anticipated; I mean a stock of humility, or at least of mortification, derived from the low opinion which he will find entertained on this side of the water, concerning many things in his own country.

I know there are individuals, and they are considerably numerous, whose admiration of America knows no bounds; whose language concerning us is always that of extravagant encomium, and who heap odium upon their own country, in proportion as they exaggerate the advantages of ours.

A few, (I am sorry to say, that as far as my observation extends they are very few) possess correct information and make that rational and candid estimate of the United States, which an unprejudiced American can hear without displeasure. People of this description are less numerous in England than in Scotland, where there is much more kindness towards us, and some share of real knowledge, concerning the American republics.

But, the general fact is otherwise. The greater number of people in both England and Scotland have but a very vague and incorrect notion of our geography, institutions, history, political divisions, and state of society and manners; and they listen, apparently with incredulity and impatience, to any accounts of the country which exhibit a favourable representation of it, especially if there be an express or implied comparison to the disadvantage of this. Nor, indeed, is it very extraordinary that this should be the case; we have ourselves been instrumental in bringing it about. We have exhibited so much of the *flatulency* of national vanity, and have made so many arrogant demands upon the admiration of the European world, that it is no wonder they have been disgusted. In our newspapers, in our anniversary orations, in many of our congressional speeches, and even in occasional sermons, we have praised ourselves with so little decency, and have monopolized with so little reserve every attribute of freedom, heroism, intelligence, and virtue, that we cannot be surprised if other countries should be somewhat reluctant to concede, what we so indecorously demand. They even doubt whether there can be much reality where there is so much vaunting, and in too many instances they do us the injustice to believe, that our manners have the coarseness and turbulence of the barbarous ages, and that our political liberty is little less than general licentiousness.

Our literary reputation is even at a still lower ebb. Of this no one needs any proof who reads the literary journals and reviews of Britain. I do not derive my impressions on this subject from the splenetic and captious spirit which too many of them exhibit towards every American production, but from the accidental droppings of conversation, and the general impression which is easily discovered by associating, with freedom, in British circles.

I called this morning upon a literary man in this city, and the conversation turned upon American literature. He was pleased to allow the Americans much genius, much keenness and energy of intellect, and a considerable share of information, but he thought we had

not yet *attained to taste*, and that most of our literary productions were turgid and bombastical. I admitted that the charge was, to a considerable degree, well founded, but, took the liberty to assure him that there was much sound literature and correct taste in the country, of which the European world had no evidence; because many of our writers are ardent young men, too often, little qualified for the tasks which they undertake, while most of those who are able to do us honour are too busy, too diffident, or too indolent to commence authors.

There is a serious impression existing in this country that we are in the childhood of literature; that we have no taste for the manly beauties of correct composition, and that the tinsel of epithet, and the sound of pompous declamation are alone acceptable to us. It must be confessed that the impression is not wholly unfounded; but the thing has been greatly exaggerated, and some of our best productions have been very little read on this side of the Atlantic.

It is, without doubt, an interesting thing to Americans, to know in what estimation they are held in the old countries of Europe. It is however difficult to find those who are well qualified to judge; and he who forms his opinion of us from the fastidious decisions of uncandid criticism; from the *petulant* volumes of European travellers in America; or from the popular bias of the majority in these islands, will be as far from the truth, as he who listens to our own inflated orators, or to the profuse and undistinguishing panegyric of our European admirers. . . .

Departure from Edinburgh

April 26.—It is impossible that any one should associate long among so warm hearted and friendly a people as the Scotch without permitting his feelings to become interested in their social circles. Mine have become so, in no small degree, and I could not remain unaffected by numerous instances of civility, kindness, and friendship. Accordingly, I have contemplated with pain the period of my final departure. Although happy to return to my country and friends, I cannot fail to realize with regret, that I shall never again behold those who have made my residence here so happy. But, such is the condition of human life. If we would avoid the pain of separating from our friends, we cannot have any, for, in proportion as they are more endeared, the anguish of losing them is increased, and he who would shun the suffering, so closely allied to the highest pleasures of the heart, must be a stranger to those pleasures also.

The influences of spring are now sensibly felt; verdure is fast returning to the trees, the hedge-rows, and the fields, and, at a period when the face of nature is about to assume its most beautiful livery, I am to commence my exile on the desolate ocean.

I had arranged all my affairs; my passport, after suffering some of the usual delays of office, had been granted by the Lord Provost; I had called on most of my friends, and exchanged with them those parting expressions of kindness, which, although depressing, are still grateful to the feelings; and I had seen, probably for the last time, but without taking formal leave, that family in which I have found so much cordiality and friendship, that I shall never cease to remember them with mixed emotions of pleasure and regret.

George Ticknor 1816

German Student Life at Göttingen

George Ticknor (1791–1871) studied both law and letters at Dartmouth College, and after graduating he spent some five years overseas studying and traveling. He was just twenty-three when he first left America for Europe, and a fellow traveler said of Ticknor that "few young men have ever left the United States better qualified by their previous education to profit by the tour of Europe." In addition to broadening his education during his two years at Göttingen University in Germany, Ticknor collected a private library and immersed himself in typical student activities and clubs.

When he was in Germany, Ticknor received an invitation to be professor of French and Spanish literature at Harvard. At the same time, his friend Edward Everett was also studying in Europe in preparation for the Harvard chair of Greek literature to which he had previously been appointed. The overseas postgraduate and professional studies undertaken by students at a university's behest were not uncommon at the time. It has subsequently become a time-honored practice which American universities continue to practice by encouraging their faculties to take sabbatical and study leaves abroad.

. . . You tell me you have been amused with the occasional hints I have given you of the life of a student at a German university. You shall then have more of them, and particularly an account of some events connected with this subject, which have lately occurred here under my immediate observation.

There are, at all the considerable literary establishments in Germany, secret associations among the students, consisting of all persons from the same country or province, which are not only connected with all similar associations at the same university, but with all similar associations throughout Germany. The bond of their union is a chivalrous, or, if you please, a captious rule of honor, and its basis is the sword. The object is not literary, but strictly municipal, and the whole advantage is the irresistible influence which the combination can give to its decisions, either against a student or a citizen.

At Göttingen, there have been, time out of mind, seven of these societies,—according to the seven principal States from which the students come,—as the Hanoverians, the Prussians, the Brunswickers, etc. They are in defiance of the laws of the university, and have often been broken up by the government, but have always reappeared under new names. Sometimes they have been called "Orders," sometimes "Bonds of Virtue," sometimes "Clubs of Honor," etc. The last were called "Landsmannschafts," or "Associations of Countrymen." Their object was twofold: to settle quarrels among their members, and to defend themselves against all impositions of the citizens. But the great power their combination gave them proved tyranny in injudicious hands, and the members were obliged to fight duels where no offense was really given, and the citizens were punished where no injustice or fraud had been practised. They

A letter from George Ticknor in Göttingen to Edward T. Channing in Boston, April 19, 1816; in George S. Hillard, editor, *Life, Letters and Journals of George Ticknor* (Boston: James R. Osgood and Company, 1876), pp. 89–94.

had but two modes of proceeding, and both were sufficiently summary. If one member was offended with another, his society compelled him to fight a duel, appointed the seconds and the witnesses, and saw that satisfaction was properly given. To be sure, these duels hardly deserve so imposing a name, for they were fought with such weapons and such armor that they were seldom bloody and could never be fatal; but still their number was so considerable that they were absolutely a nuisance, for every slight offence was settled by them.

This was the first mode; the second was when a member offended the club, or a citizen a member, and then the punishment was by "verschüss," or non-intercourse. If, for instance, a tradesman had cheated a student, if his landlord had treated him unkindly, or anybody with whom he had connection had offended him, he complained to his club. If they found the complaint supported and sufficient, the offender was put into "verschüss," —that is, no student was allowed to have anything to do with him. If he was a shopkeeper, his custom was gone; if he was a *restaurateur*, nobody would have his dinner from him, any more than if he sent out poison; and if he let rooms, nobody would take lodgings of him. In short, whatever might be the occupation of the offender, it was gone. Instances of this sort of punishment are not at all rare. Last year, a student, for having spoken disrespectfully of the "Landsmannschaft," was put under the ban of the Empire, and, after braving the whole University some weeks, and its marked contempt, went to Leipsic, but found himself received there with the same injuries, and was finally obliged to change his name and go to Jena. A baker, who had done nothing worse than sue a student for his regular bill, was put into "verschüss," and, after striving in vain to live independently of the students in a town supported entirely by them, found himself so much in debt, that in despair he shot himself. And the very man in whose house I live, having offended a student in his capacity of confectioner, was compelled, above a year since, to let his shop to another, and has been starving on its rent in the vain hope that the students will at last give up the persecution; but he has just sold it in despair.

These are the bad effects of this remarkable system. That it has its good effects also, you will easily believe; for, if it had not, it would not be tolerated a moment by the government, and indeed could not long exist among a large body of young men who are

really studious and regular to a remarkable degree, and whose notions of justice are, like those of all young men, essentially pure and unperverted.

The advantages of the system are, that it gives a character and *esprit de corps* to the whole motley mass of the students, which, in universities like these in Germany, could not otherwise be given to them; that it enables the pro-rector and professors, by governing a few of the heads of the clubs, to control the entire multitude under them more effectually than the laws will enable, or the spirit of the institution permit them to do directly; and that it introduces in their behavior to one another, and their conduct to the government, a degree of order and decorum, and a general gentlemanly spirit, which nothing can give to a thousand young men brought together where they have no responsibility, at an age when they have not yet learnt to behave well without a superior influence in some sort to compel to it. The evils, on the contrary, are the captious rules of honor which are maintained by it among the students, terminating in innumerable contemptible duels, and occasionally a flagrant injustice to a citizen,—though certainly to the citizens it does much more good than harm, for they are much more disposed and interested to cheat the students than the students can be to oppress them.

On the whole, therefore, the system seems to me to be bad, and one which ought to be exterminated, though at the same time I must confess to you that many of the professors think otherwise, and are persuaded that, while the laws of the University are so loose and weak, the students must have a municipal system of their own.

Much undoubtedly depends on the government for the time being. Under a vigilant pro-rector, who prevents these clubs from gaining too much strength or boldness, they may do good; but under such pro-rectors as professors may commonly be expected to be, who are interested to preserve their own popularity, and especially under a decidedly weak pro-rector, they must do much mischief. This has lately been the case here.

During the year ending in February, the pro-rectorship had fallen to two professors who did anything rather than execute the duties of first magistrates of the University, and, of course, during their government these secret "Landsmannschafts" had increased in boldness until their existence and acts were as notorious as those of the academical senate; and the duels multiplied till, contemptible as they are individually, they became an intolerable nuisance. Just at this time Prof. Mitscherlich, the editor of Horace, became in his turn pro-rector, and proved to be as much too severe as his predecessors had been too feeble and lax. He cited at once many students for inconsiderable and forgotten offenses, committed under the reign of the last pro-rectors, and was going on to purge the University of its follies more thoroughly than was prudent, or even desirable, when an event occurred which gave a higher direction to his inquiries and punishments. A student quarrelled with his club in the following manner. A house had been put into "verschüss," and a student being found still to frequent it, the sentence he had violated fell on himself. Exasperated at this, he threatened, if he were not reinstated, to expose the whole secret system to the pro-rector. You will easily imagine that this injudicious threat produced exactly the opposite effect from what he had intended. He was excommunicated with book and bell, and received with contempt and injuries where-ever he went. Still further enraged at what he ought to have expected, he actually sent a regular and ample memoir to the pro-rector, and fled the city. The moment the fact was known, or rather suspected, such a sensation was excited as no one can imagine who did not witness it.

There was no tumult or violence, but the whole appearance of the city was changed. The streets, always before filled only with young men hastening to their lectures, were now crowded with little "assemblages," as Gov. Gerry would call them, so that it was difficult to pass on the sidewalks; the benches in the lecture-rooms, where a vacant seat was a rarity, grew visibly thin and empty, and wherever you met a student he had the hurried and anxious air of a man of business. The whole character of things was altered. The first determination was to have personal vengeance on the traitor. Guards were posted on the roads to prevent his escape; for two nights a watch of three hundred patrolled the ramparts and the streets; and if he had been caught, he might have escaped with his life, but he would have boasted of nothing else. Fortunately his prudence, or that of the pro-rector, had secured his flight before his treason was suspected, and he has not since been seen or heard of. His infor-

mation, however, has enabled the pro-rector to arrest the heads of the clubs, and possess himself of their records, where he found a regular list of all the officers and members, amounting to between five or six hundred; and, among other curious documents, seized a protocol containing a detailed account of ninety-six of these harmless duels fought in five months.

So full a discovery precluded all subterfuge or defence. After a week of excitement and cabal, during which all study was suspended, and there was a kind of reign of terror in the University, the most prominent members of the clubs began to leave the city. This was immediately prevented by a public ordinance, laying them all under city arrest, and forbidding them to go out of the city gates under any pretence. This excited a new effervescence, for it indeed was a measure of needless severity, and fell upon the just as well as the unjust. New councils were held, and after much deliberation a deputation was sent to the government at Hanover, praying for its interference. This, however, produced no effect. The pro-rector still went on with his investigations, which were undoubtedly often vexatious and unwise, though certainly, in general, just; and at length, after three weeks of anxious and burning excitement, such as I should not have imagined the affair would have justified, five students were publicly exiled, *ab urbe et agro;* twenty-four received a *consilium abeundi,* or common expulsion; and the rest a general reprimand and warning.

Thus for the fifth or sixth time these secret clubs—which really grow out of the circumstances of the German Empire, and are perhaps formed by a kind of instinct in the German character—have been suppressed. About two hundred students have left the University in disgust; but they will not be missed three months hence, even if none of them return, as I suppose many will, on cooler reflection.

It is thought, however, that the want of these troublesome aids to the order of academic life will be occasionally felt during the next year in the rudeness, which, in such an interregnum, is always observed to creep into the manners of the students; and nobody doubts that under some other name or form they will reappear and be again crushed. . . .

Joseph Green Cogswell   1817

A Tutor's Educational Notes from Europe

Joseph Green Cogswell (1786–1871) attended Phillips Exeter Academy and graduated from Harvard College in 1806. He traveled to Europe in 1817 for additional studies and attended the University of Göttingen at the same time that his fellow countrymen Edward Everett, George Ticknor, and George Bancroft were there. He financed his three-year stay in Europe by serving as traveling tutor to a young graduate of Harvard, Oliver Thorndike. Thorndike's father paid Cogswell $1500 per annum plus expenses to educate and accompany his son abroad.

Upon his return to New England in 1821 Cogswell was appointed librarian and professor of mineralogy and geology at Harvard. He rearranged the Harvard library according to the "Göttingen plan," and in 1823 he and George Bancroft founded the Round Hill School in Northhampton, Massachusetts. The school was modeled after the German *gymnasium* and had a vigorous physical and intellectual curriculum, but it closed because of a lack of funds. After serving as editor of *The New York Review,* Cogswell persuaded John Jacob Astor to donate funds to establish the New York Public Library and became its first superintendent. He traveled to Europe in 1839 to purchase books for the library, and in 1842 he accompanied Washington Irving to Madrid as secretary of the American legation.

He kept extensive diaries and conducted a copious correspondence during his three voyages to Europe. The extracts below include notes on his stay at Göttingen University, his friendship with Goethe at Weimar, his trips to Fellenberg's school at Hofwyl in Switzerland, and his visit to Pestalozzi's at Yverdun.

Ipswich, *July* 14, 1816.. [To Mrs. C. S. Daveis, Portland.] When I parted from you, my dear sister, I promised myself the pleasure of soon meeting you again, and making another visit in the circle of my beloved friends in Portland, but herein my lot is disappointment, as in all my other hopes in life. On Friday last I agreed to devote myself anew to an exile from my native land, and expect, in the course of four weeks, again to bid adieu to all I love. . . . My destination is Göttingen, where I expect to remain, till a year from the coming October at least, and longer if George [Ticknor] and Edward [Everett] do not undertake their Grecian tour. If they do, I shall accompany them. I go out in company with a son of Mr. Thorndike's, who is to be graduated at Cambridge this Commencement, and continue with him while he remains abroad, for which his father gives me $1,500 per annum, and pays my expenses. This is connected with a plan which the Corporation of the College have in hand, to give me a permanent residence there on my return. . . .

Göttingen, *February* 16, 1817 [To C. S. Daveis, Portland.] . . . On the 1st day of October I landed in Holland. . . . The residue of October was spent on the banks of the Rhine, at Cologne, Coblentz, Mentz and

Frankfort, and in making the journey from the last named place to this, where we arrived Nov. 1. George and E. were then in Saxony, and did not return until the 5th. . . . I need not mention to you how my time was occupied after G. and E. returned; until the 11th, when we entered our regular lodgings and began the studies of the Semester, they were continually with me. . . .

On the 11th I turned all my forces to German, attending at the same time a course of lectures on the Modern Arts in Italian, and one on European Statistics in French. When I saw myself, fitted out in the style of a German student, with a large portfolio under my arm, trudging off to my lesson, with the regularity and punctuality of a school boy who fears the birch, it seemed that I must have gone back several years in life. At first I knew not how to reconcile myself to the situation of another period of pupilage, but habit effects anything. I soon made my tasks, construed my German and submitted to correction, with as much docility as if I had never known what it was to be myself a teacher and a governor. . . .

Thorndike behaves with perfect propriety, is very regular, studies well, and gives me no more trouble than any other companion would do.

Joseph Green Cogswell, *Life of Joseph Green Cogswell* (Cambridge, Mass.: Riverside Press, 1874), pp. 48, 50–52, 54–58, 60–63, 65–67, 79–81, 87–88, 114–115, 118–119, 125–126.

[To Mrs. E. Ticknor, Boston.] . . . The four belonging to our colony, or to use the technical word, our Landsmannschaft, assemble generally every evening, and I will venture to assert that there is no Landsmannschaft belonging to the University, not excepting the Dutch, composed of only two, in which greater harmony prevails. Now and then we get little Stephen[1] in from the country, which we consider an important addition in every respect, for he is a most delightful boy. . . .

Göttingen, *March* 16, 1817. [To C. S. Daveis, Portland.] Sunday Eve. . . . I have been out this evening to make what we should call at home, a sociable visit, where I staid till ten, and then brought G. to my room with me, and kept him till past eleven. . . . The social visit was made to Mad. Sartorius, who has been sick for three or four weeks, and still receives her company in her chamber. Herself, her husband a Prof. in the philosophical faculty, Prof. Welcker, also of the same faculty, George and myself were seated round a little tea table, and the evening was passed in a more rational, friendly and home like manner than any one I have spent in German society. . . . They amused us with some very pleasant anecdotes of their own literary men, particularly of Goethe, with whom they are intimate. One of these anecdotes shows so exactly the character of this great, but insufferably vain and affected man, that I give it to you. . . . Some fifteen or twenty years since, Constant, so well known in the literary world, went to Weimar, the Ferrara and the Florence of Germany, to see the brilliant geniuses which then gave such splendor to the court of the Grand Duchess. Being introduced to Goethe, he began in the style of a true Frenchman to load him with flattery, saying that the world was wondering at the stupendous productions of his genius, that he had secured to himself immortal fame, etc., etc. Goethe turned his large, fiery eyes upon Constant, and replied, ''I know it, I know all that, I know too that the world regards me as a carpenter, who has built a ship of war, of the first rate, upon a mountain, thousands of miles from the ocean—but the water will rise, my ship will float, and bear her builder in triumph where human genius never reached before.'' This is vanity which can have no parallel. Next week I shall be at Weimar and probably see this strange beast, and then per-

haps I may tell you something more of him.

On my way here from Frankfort I turned aside from the route to pass by Wezlar, and pluck a sprig or two from the lime trees, which shade the grave of the young Jerusalem, and, by a strange accident, I could have presented them to Charlotte[2] two days afterward, as I was introduced to her in the library, the first day of my arrival here. She is now arrived at that period when all the fire of youth and of love is faded from the eye, and still she has an eye that is not dumb, I can conceive that it must have been eloquent in other days. . . .

Berlin, *April* 17, 1817. [To Mrs. C. E. Daveis, Portland.] . . . I went to Weimar almost for the sole purpose of seeing Goethe, but he was absent on a visit to Jena, where I pursued him and obtained an audience. From all that I had heard of him, I was prepared to meet with the most repulsive reception, but, as I actually experienced the directly opposite, you will naturally infer that I felt not a little flattered, and therefore will not be surprised if I should give you a more favorable picture of him than you find in the ''Edinburgh Review.'' I sent him my letters of introduction, with a note, asking when he would allow me to wait upon him. In one of the letters it was observed that I had some fondness for mineralogy, and was desirous of seeing the great cabinet, belonging to the society of which he is President, at Jena. In a few moments he returned me an answer, that he would meet me in the rooms of the Society at noon, and there show me all that was to be seen. I liked this, as it evinced some degree of modesty in him, inasmuch as it implied that there was something, beside himself, worthy of my notice, and as it was very polite, too, in offering to take upon himself the trouble of going through the explanation of a collection, filling numerous and large apartments. At noon, then, I went to meet this great giant of German literature, the creator and sole governor of their taste. His exterior was in every respect different from the conceptions I had formed. A grand and graceful form, worthy of a knight of the days of chivalry, with a dignity of manners that marked the court rather than the closet, such as belong to Goethe, are not often the external

---

[1] Stephen Higginson Perkins (son of Mr. Samuel G. Perkins, of Boston), then at school near Göttingen.

[2] The young Jerusalem and Charlotte were real personages whose names had been publicly associated with Goethe's romance *Die Lieden des jungen Werther*, a book which created great enthusiasm at that time. . . .

characteristics of a man of letters. Soon after being introduced to him, with the politeness of a real gentleman, he turned the conversation to America, and spoke of its hopes and promises, in a manner that showed it had been the subject of his inquiries, and made juster and more rational observations, upon its literary pretensions and character, than I ever heard from any man in Europe. We talked, also , of English and German literature. I told him of the interest we were now taking in the latter, and found a very convenient opportunity to introduce a few words of compliment to himself, which was the least return I could make for his civility.

That you may not think I have made too great progress in German, I just observe that this conversation, which lasted an hour, was carried on in French. I suppose I might have managed the former; but I was afraid of going wrong, sometimes, with the titles of the Herr Minister von Goethe, and therefore proposed to him to adopt French, where I had only "Votre Excellence" to handle.

After we finished our literary discussions he carried me through the whole cabinet, and explained to me all its remarkables, with a facility that could not have been exceeded by a Professor of Mineralogy. When we parted he invited me to call on him, whenever I should be in Weimar, and so managed the whole interview I had with him, that I left him inclined to enter the lists in his defense, if I should ever have occasion. . . .

Göttingen, *Friday Morn.*, 23d *May* [1817, to G. Ticknor, Paris]. . . I go on very regularly, rising at four, study till six, then hear Hausmann on Geognosy, who is prime, as well in the understanding as the explaining of his subject. At 7 Schrader who teaches me very little; at 8 Welcker, who is exactly what you foretold he would be, abstract and obscure, always seeking to go where no one can follow him. . . . I really like him as a man and respect him as a scholar—indeed I almost love him, since a visit I made him one morning when he talked to me wholly of you, and talked as if he had a heart and had found out also in some degree the worth of yours. . . . From 9 to 11 I am at liberty to study—11 hear Hausmann privatissime in Mineralogy; this is accidental. A young man from Odessa whom I know, had begun the course and invited me to hear it with him. I could not refuse such an opportunity of prosecuting a favorite science. From 12 to 1 free,—1 to 2 in Botanic Garden or Library; 2 Heeren who lectures well; 3 with Reck; 4 Saalfeld in Northern His-

tory; 5 Blumenbach; 6 Benecke. . . . At 7 comes my drill sergeant and so ends the day as to the lectures I hear. At 8 I give Augustus one in Italian, and study as much afterwards, before 12, as accident and circumstances allow. With all this I do not want for exercise. I must needs walk 10,000 steps, at least 4 miles, every day. Saturday I make excursions with Schrader, and Sunday with Hausmann, who makes nothing of carrying us a round of 15 or 20 miles. . . .

Göttingen, *June* 27, 1817 [To G. Ticknor, Paris]. . . Hausmann has told me so much of the Harz, of its importance and wonders in a mineralogical and geological view, and Schrader of its botanical curiosities and beauties, that I could not rest while I thought I might leave Germany without seeing it. Accordingly as there is now a sort of half vacation, many of the professors being about to make the summer visit to Pyrmont, I resolved upon taking the next week for this tour and persuaded Everett to accompany me. We set out to-morrow morning and mean to return Sunday sennight. . . .

I never imagined that I should hear the story of the Windham frogs[3] in the auditorium of a German professor, but who can foretell the strange events which he may meet with in life.—Yesterday as Blumenbach was lecturing upon the Rana Ocellata, he amused the auditors with the Windham narrative and turned to me for confirmation; I shook my head—"Oh ja! oh ja!"—he repeated three or four times in his queer way. I kept on shaking my head, and then he came out with his authority, and who that must have been I need not tell you. He is infinitely amusing and probably as instructive as the nature of his college will admit. I find sometimes a little too much buffoonery; it seems strange that a man of such profound science as he is should treat his branch as if it afforded merely matter for amusement. . . .

---

[3]The anecdote referred to was this: The inhabitants of Windham, Connecticut, were alarmed one night in July, 1758, by strange sounds, which some thought to be the yelling of Indians, others to be warnings of the approach of the Day of Judgment. In the morning it was discovered that the bullfrogs who inhabited a pond a mile from the village, had carried on a deadly contest for the possession of a ditch, where after a severe drought, there remained a little water, the only moist spot in all the precincts where they lived. Many were found dead, and signs of battle were abundant. An old broadside giving a humorous account of this incident is reprinted in the *American Historical Record*, edited by B. J. Lossing, Vol. i. No. 5, May, 1872.

Göttingen, *July* 20, 1817 [To Prof. J. Farrar, Cambridge, U.S.]. . . . The article to which I referred above is an extract from a letter of Mr. Soldner at Munich to the Baron von Lindenau, giving an account of the new Observatory there, which appears to have qualities worthy of your attention, if similar ones have not already been considered by you. I translate such parts of the letter as I judge will be most important. . . But perhaps you have had all this a thousand times over. You must not laugh at me if you have. Building Observatories has not been my business, and I am not ashamed of my ignorance in regard to them. . . . I want to have you get into the way of forming correspondences in Europe, because it will do much for the *éclat* of the University. Your Observatory is not only to make you more nearly acquainted with the celestial luminaries, it will also show to the astronomers of Europe that there is at least one brilliant star in the American hemisphere. I shall not forget you whenever I go within a day's ride of an Observatory, particularly at Munich and at Ofen. . . . It is some satisfaction to me, always, to feel that no source of knowledge has been neglected, even if nothing is learnt by the investigation, and I have no doubt the same is the case with yourself. . . .

Everybody knows that from my youth upward, I have had a great lurch for exploring unknown regions, particularly the African deserts. The ill success of the late attempts, with better means than I could possibly command, compelled me to renounce this as impracticable, and hence my views turned to another quarter, but to a similar object, and after a great deal of conversation and advice with men of science in Europe, I have resolved upon gratifying this love of roaming by turning myself loose into the American wilds. This I do because I am convinced, from all that is now known of them, they must be very rich in respect to two of my chief subjects of inquiry, botany and mineralogy. Thus you see I have come to the very plan you marked out for me. I must confess, however, that I fairly exposed myself to your raillery. . . . You hit me also in another tender place, my dear sir, in the enumeration you make of the whole circle of the sciences, and the suggestion that I may find something among them to engage my attention. And here I must owe you one. I have nothing to retort upon you for instability, and not a word to say in my own justification. Having lived half of an ordinary life to no one purpose, it behooves me to make a better use of what may remain. The end of it must

decide if it will be as though I had not been. . . .

Göttingen, *Sunday*, 27th [*July*, 1817, to G. Ticknor, Paris.] 3 P.M. . . . I have made two experiments with Benecke in the library, and rejoice that I now get an hour of very valuable instruction, for one which was worth nothing at all. He takes the library first according to the arrangement on the shelves, and goes through the whole with me in that way, giving minute accounts of all the divisions and subdivisions, and of the practical application of the principles of classification and distribution. Afterwards he will do the same with the catalogues. If you think of any questions I shall not be likely to ask, tell me of them. This will be another acquisition which I shall owe to you, for I hardly think I should ever have thought of the study, had you not suggested it to me. As you put me in the way of acquiring this knowledge, I shall call upon you to tell me what use I can make of it, for I certainly see none myself. . . .

Geneva, *April* 26, 1818 [To G. Ticknor, Madrid.]. . . On my way here from the Simplon I walked from St. Gingoulph to Dovaine, a distance of thirty miles in eight hours; you see I am not wanting in the essential requisites for a Swiss traveller. . . . These are scenes which make me love life again. I forget myself and am happy as I gaze upon them. An elevation of a few thousand feet, above the level of the ocean, gives me a sense of independence. . . . produces as it were a new consciousness, and new sympathies, and new affections . . . . I do not remember to have heard you say much about Geneva. . . . Did it not occur to you that there was a great resemblance between them [the people here] and our good sober folks in Boston, the same gregarious disposition, the same love of talk and tea drinking, of political and religious conversation, in a word the same general habits and customs, except the villainous one of universal card playing, which is peculiar to the Genevans. I could not stand the siege much longer, it is quite as bad as at Rome. I have not had a single evening to myself since I have been here, any more than we did there, and the society is certainly not so interesting as it was there, or rather it is not so alluring.

Geneva, *June* 6, 1818 [To Mr. Elisha Ticknor, Boston.] Your kind letter of Dec. 15th has remained thus long unanswered that I might give you the information you wish about the Hofwyl institution, from my own personal knowledge and observation. Being at Berne, in the month of May, I went there and spent a day in examining this establishment. . . . Its object originally was agricultural, or rather, under the avowed object of improving the agriculture of his country, Mr. de Fellenberg had really in view the improvement of the system of general education. Like all philanthropists he was an enthusiast, and believed in the possible perfectibility of man. This he thought was to be effected through the medium of education. . . . Out of his school of theoretical agriculture grew a school for general and higher education, which has the character of being one of the best in Europe. Many of its characteristics are peculiar to itself, such as the dispensing altogether with rewards and punishments, the liberty allowed the pupil to defend himself when censured, and others which it would be interesting to examine as to their operation and influence; but the particular object of your enquiry is the establishment for the education of the children of the poor, and that is entirely distinct from the two already named.

His system embraced the two extremes of society; in his school the children of beggars and of sovereigns were to be taught to understand in what their duty and their happiness consists. . . . It was a noble effort and has already produced great good; when a little longer experiment shall have cleared it of some of its theoretic excellences, but practical defects, it will produce still greater, and very probably be one means of operating a real reformation in society . . . . I am sorry that I cannot give you some account of Pestalozzi's academy at Yverdun, which I have in like manner visited. . . .

Paris, *September* 1, 1818 [To Mr. E. Ticknor, Boston]. . . I have paid a second visit to Mr. de Fellenberg, at Hofwyl, with even greater satisfaction than I made my first. It was the day preceding a short vacation they have, once a year, of three weeks. Upon this occasion Mr. de F. gives the boys a little festival. It consisted in a concert, in which three fourths of the whole school joined, for music he considers a very important part of education,—after which a simple repast was given them in the grove adjoining the house, and more heartfelt joy I never witnessed in my life, not, as it seemed to me, because they were about to relax from their labors, but because they had the happiness to be placed for their education in a school, the head of which was rather a father than a master to them. I saw a thousand proofs of the

sentiments they entertain toward each other, and nothing could resemble more a tender and solicitous parent, surrounded by a family of obedient and affectionate children. There was the greatest equality and at the same time the greatest respect, a respect of the heart I mean, not of fear; instructors and pupils walked arm in arm together, played together, ate at the same table, and all without any danger to their reciprocal rights; how delightful it must be to govern, where love is the principle of obedience. . . .

Lausanne, *October* 28 [1819.] We have done wonders to-day to come from Concise to this place, beside making a long visit at Pestalozzi's at Yverdun. A painful visit it was to me, to see this good old man and real philanthropist going broken-hearted to his grave, for broken-hearted he must be, in contemplating the ruined state of the institution which he has been laboring his whole life to establish. . . . My regrets, however, are more for himself than for the public, for I do not believe his system carried to the extent he does, is the true method of storing the mind with knowledge. It would exclude memory altogether as a medium of instructing, and make use of reason alone, which is absurd. Reason must be furnished with ideas for the materials of its ratiocinations, and many of these must be laid up in and recalled by the memory. . . . This is the misery of all systems, that the makers of them are never satisfied with putting them in practice as far as they are true, merely, but have a foolish vanity of giving them universal applicability. . . .

Tours, *November* 21, 1819 [To G. Ticknor, Boston.]. . . You appear to entertain expectations that I shall finally consent to fix myself in Cambridge, and this can never be. Here, by the side of a good fire, with a nice carpet on the floor and my portion of coffee by my side, at six in the morning, in the placidest state of mind possible, in the good little city of Tours, where Thorndike studies and does everything else to my perfect satisfaction, and where, in a word, I am happier than I have been for more than six years before, I declare to you, with all due solemnity, that I cannot wear a professor's gown at Cambridge. I hope to see one institution in our country in which no person shall bear that title who is not truly a scholar, a classical one, I mean, and, as I am not that myself, I will not be such a recreant as to aid in keeping up the hungering, starving condition of the minds of our youth, for the sake of my daily bread. I am more sensible than ever upon this point. The character I gave last winter of the state of education among us, is commendation compared with that I should now give, and it is by the instrumentality of Cambridge alone, that I hope for a reformation.[4] In fact my scruples would be much less strong about accepting the same place in any other of our seminaries, . . . Now, the obstacles which oppose my being made professor do not apply with so much force to my being made librarian, and I do not say that I would not accept that office if I could have it. My deficiencies there would be somewhat counterbalanced, by the advantage of having one who knows so much, practically, of the book-selling trade in Europe, and who could so easily enter into correspondences abroad, and if I could see that I was useful I should be contented and happy. I cannot go to my grave in peace while I think I have lived in vain in the world, and when I get back to America I am resolved to embrace that course of life which promises me the fairest opportunity of doing good. And here I must beg you to let the subject rest, and say nothing more of Cambridge till we meet. . . .

Aberdeen, *August* 5, 1820 [To G. Ticknor, Boston.] Well, dearest G., my work in Europe is done, and I have no further *excuse*

---

[4]Ticknor had now entered on his duties as Professor of Modern Languages and Belles Lettres at Harvard College. . . .

for remaining here. My protégé, Oliver, was examined for his medical degree yesterday, and declared fully entitled to the honor; on Monday he receives his diploma and our first step, after that, will be a homeward one. . . . I will not say to what kindly influence it is owing, but sure it is, my heart is in every respect affectioned as you would wish it should be, toward home and the friends whom I am to meet there. I have had some strange revolutions of feeling since I came abroad, most of which I hope were produced wholly by external circumstances and consequently as fleeting as the causes in which they arose. Should you find any traces of them still remaining, when I return, depend on it they will soon be obliterated, by an intercourse with those friends who first gave my character whatever it has ever had of amiable and good. Till within the last two months I have always regretted that I came to Europe, because I felt that I had made but a poor exchange, by giving up my happiness for life for the acquisition of a little knowledge, and the gratification of a vain curiosity; but since I have found, that this sacrifice is not to be made, I have ceased to regret it, believing now that I have increased my means of being useful, without having lost the power of being happy. . . . I could not help telling you that, in expecting me home, you may expect to find me a better and a happier man than when you parted from me, worthy I trust, of your friendship and desirous above all things of preserving it. . . .

John Griscom   1819

Comparative Notes on Educational Innovation in Switzerland

John Griscom (1774-1852), a prominent Quaker educator, operated his own school in Pennsylvania from 1808 to 1818 and then traveled to Europe principally for reasons of health. The informal journal of his trip, *A Year in Europe*, describes his visits to schools, prisons, and hospitals in Great Britain, France, Switzerland, Italy, and the Netherlands; and its sales were sufficient to pay the expenses of his trip.

Greatly influenced by his visits to European correctional institutions, Griscom was instrumental in organizing the Society for the Prevention of Pauperism and Crime. In 1823 he helped establish the House of Refuge for Juvenile Delinquents in New York, which was the model for similar institutions in other states. Griscom is also remembered for his part in establishing a monitorial high school using Lancasterian principles, which existed from 1825 to 1831 in New York. His later career included service as a professor of chemistry and natural philosophy for four years at Rutgers Medical College, which he helped establish, and as prin-

John Griscom, *A Year in Europe Comprising a Journal of Observations in England, Scotland, Ireland, France, Switzerland, The North of Italy, and Holland in 1818 and 1819* (New York: Collins and Co. and E. Bliss and E. White, 1823), I, v-vii, 371-376, 381-389, 391-401, 415-424.

cipal of the Yearly Meeting Boarding School of Providence, Rhode Island.

His report on European schools was an unsponsored effort, unlike many of the other reports compiled by American educators who were sent to Europe specifically to study education. Henry Barnard, in evaluating Griscom's work a generation later, remarked that it had a "wider influence than any other similar report on the development of our educational, reformatory, and preventative measures directly and indirectly."

Preface

The relations between America and Europe are becoming every day more interesting and important. The unexampled rapidity with which the commerce, agriculture, and arts of the United States are extending and increasing; the extraordinary facilities now given to the social intercourse between the new and the old world; and the unabated spirit of enterprize and industry, which prevails in many parts of Europe; conspire to render these relations a concern of the greatest moment,—as tending, in no inconsiderable degree, to influence the tranquillity and happiness of a large portion of the civilized globe.

Under such circumstances, it must be considered, by persons conversant with human nature, as extremely desirable, that the people on each side of the Atlantic, should become more intimately and perfectly acquainted with each other; for it may, perhaps, be stated as a political, as well as social axiom, that the greater the intimacy, the greater probability of a cordial and pacific union;—that many of the rancorous jealousies and deep rooted prejudices, which are so apt to prevail between nations, as well as sects and neighbourhoods, would soften into kindness, were opportunities afforded of studying the bright as well as the dark sides of each other's character. And it requires but little ingenuity to perceive, that were there between nations a pervading sense of each other's merits, and a just feeling for each other's prosperity, it would be infinitely more difficult for the disaffected to bring about that condition of things, which is the most disastrous to human improvement, a state of open warfare,—and infinitely more easy to suppress the evil when it did prevail.

From these considerations it will be admitted, that books of travels, when written under the proper qualifications, are among the most useful kinds of literature;—that they furnish the principal means by which distant communities and nations become acquainted with each other's peculiarities, by which the useful arts are extended, and morals and manners are rendered more diffused and impressive.

It will be admitted also, that however beaten the track over which travellers may have passed, it is impossible to exhaust the stores of useful illustration, or to overcharge the picture of national and local representation, as long as truth and feeling guide the hand and qualify the pencil. It can never be said of the describer of nature, and more especially of human nature, as it may of the orator, who confines himself to some particular topic, that he has left nothing to be desired. So vast is the field of humanity, and so infinite are the shades which diversify the moral condition of the human race, that it is scarcely possible for two individuals to follow each other in the same, precise track of description. Not only do different observers see the same thing in different points of view, but each one has his particular sphere of observation, and will almost unavoidably throw some new light upon the subjects he attempts to elucidate. Hence every person who visits a foreign country will at once perceive, that, how diligent soever he may have been in studying that country through the medium of books, —there is a continual variety of untouched description, and that a small part only of the whole has been laid before him.

But notwithstanding these obvious truths, the Author cannot assure himself, that, even by the most reflecting and liberal-minded readers, he will be deemed to have acted wisely in exposing his sheets to the public eye. His journey was by no means undertaken with a fixed intention of exhibiting its occurrences beyond the circle of his family and friends. The motives to the voyage, were the renovation of impaired health, and the hope of spending a short time in Europe, both profitably and agreeably. The rapidity with which the journey was performed, and the multiplicity of objects which engaged his attention, prevented him from doing little more, while travelling, than to bestow a faithful attention to his note book; and since his return, other unavoidable avocations have delayed the filling up of the outline; but this delay, he trusts, has not been without its benefit, in the further development which time has given to some features of the narrative. . . .

Fribourg

Sept. 29, 1818. . . . At Fribourg, we obtained good accommodations and an excellent supper, at the Merchant's Inn.

Sept. 30th. Having a letter for Le Pere Girard, whose genius and philanthropy have qualified him to effect the most important improvements, in the education of the children of Fribourg, and to establish a school, which has become famous throughout Switzerland, I hastened this morning to the convent where he resides, and received the unwelcome intelligence, that it was the time of vacation, and that he had gone into the country, to stay some days. I inquired of one of his assistants, who there was, that could give me correct information, relative to the system pursued in the institution, over which the Pere Girard presides, and he referred me to the Chanoine Fontaine, as an enlightened man, and a friend of Pere Girard. Upon waiting for this ecclesiastic, at his house, he came in from the morning service, dressed in his priestly habiliments, and looked at me with some surprise. I apologised for coming to him without an introduction, and explained frankly the object of my visit. He then, very cordially, offered to give me all the information he could, and appointed 10 o'clock, to receive me and my friends. He regretted that Pere Girard was absent, as I should find him, he said, a very interesting man in conversation, and willing to communicate any information, relative to his system.

At the appointed hour, we went to the chanoine's, and were introduced into his picture room, which contained a very neat collection of paintings, one of which, he said, was by Rubens, (the descent from the cross,) and the original design of his great picture at Antwerp. He explained to us, loquaciously, the various pictures of the collection; and then, placing chairs in a circle, invited us to sit down, and commenced an eloquent statement, first of the etymology of the word *Education*, implying to draw out, or develope, and not to increase, or to superadd. He next adverted to the common error, as he called it, of supposing that mathematics can have much tendency to expand and mature the faculties of the mind; and urged the superiority of language, as an instrument or means of effecting this important end. He considered it of high importance, that plans of education should tend to open and perfect the qualities already existing in the mind, as the sun swells and opens the bud, and heightens the colours and fragrance of the rose. He informed us that the Pere Girard's views, and his own, corresponded on this subject; that the latter, being a man of penetration, and acquainted with human nature, and possessing a spirit of great philanthropy, had proceeded, step by step, trusting only to experience, in bringing the school to its present state of improvement. Prior to the commencement of his labours, the schools of Fribourg, were in a state of great depression, without system, and inefficacious, with respect to morals; that Pere Girard's greatest efforts had been, to make the scholars thoroughly acquainted with their religious duties, to render them sober and industrious; in short, to inspire them with a taste and a love for all that belongs to an honourable character, in the respective stations which they are to fill. His success, in this respect, the whole town was ready to attest. The Lancasterian plan of instruction, came opportunely to his aid; but he was rather a *"Belliste,"* than a *"Lancasterien."* The principle which he relies most upon, as an excitement to the energies of the boys, is emulation. This principle, properly directed, he is confident, does not produce envy, or any other injurious feeling. So anxious are the boys, in his school, to improve, they are known often to rise in the night to study; and so lively and interesting to them, has he rendered the exercises of the school, that very young children are fond of attending. A lady of distinction, (the ex-queen of Sweden,) visiting the school, observed a very young child in one of the classes. "Pourquoi viens tu ici, mon enfant?" said she, to the tiny scholar. "Pour m'amuser," was the answer. Still more surprised, she asked, "Comment? est-ce-que l'ecole t'amuse?" "Oh, Madame." said he, "nous nous amusons ici tous les jours." But, observed our learned informant, as there is always a struggle between light and darkness, so it was hardly to be expected, that Pere Girard's success, would not meet with opposition. His school has acquired so much celebrity, that not a day passes without visiters. In short, it was to have a little time to write, that he has left the town for a few days. A public examination is held every three months, with a great deal of form, accompanied with music, and a distribution of prizes, to the most meritorious scholars. It is a kind of public spectacle, which gratifies the town. But the religious principles of the Pere, are too liberal for the zealous friends of the Romish Church, and the bell of alarm has been sounded, with notes of danger to the true faith. A division has taken place, and, in the present government of the canton, there is a majority of the disaffected. They accordingly determined, by a decision obtained last month, to reinstate the Jesuits in their college, in Fribourg; doubtless with a view to counteract the influence of Pere Girard; and it is probable that they would soon proceed to place his school, "hors de combat," were it not for the very strong popular support, which it receives. The government of this canton is patrician; or, in other words, aristocratical. To retain their power, is a darling object with the patricians; and they are so well aware that the diffusion of learning and morals will work against them, that when the corner stone of a new and commodious house, now erecting for Pere Girard's school, was laid by a committee, the Avoyer, or chief magistrate, happening to pass, he said to one near him, "Voila le tombeau des patricians." The only excitement to emulation, which Girard uses, is an advancement in the classes, medals, and prize books at the examinations. But it is his constant effort to preserve such a tone of moral feeling, as to operate itself as a stimulus to honourable effort, and, at the same time, to prevent the evil consequences of emulation. That a most favourable change has been produced in the moral habits of the children of Fribourg, is generally admitted.

Our conversation with the Chanoine, was very interesting to us. He is a man of superior intelligence, of a comely figure, and pleasing address. We parted at one o'clock, and, on observing to him that we should be glad to see his cabinet, (for our printed guide informed us he had one,) he desired us to call again at two; an invitation we did not fail to comply with.

He introduced us into a room, completely filled with books, minerals, birds, fish, fossils, and other objects of natural history, arranged with great taste and effect. It was a very learned and neat little museum. His specimens of quartz crystals are uncommonly beautiful. He showed us a manuscript copy of the Bible, in illuminated letter, of very fine execution, and nearly four hundred years old. The whole collection does great credit to his industry, his learning, and his taste. His clerical dress, which he retained while we were with him, was neat and plain. We left him with sentiments of grateful respect, for the information he afforded us, and his cordial reception of strangers, without a formal introduction. . . .

Hofwyl

Oct. 2nd. . . . After getting our passports

examined, by the Austrian minister, at Berne, and taking our dinners at the table d'hote, we set off in a voiture provided by our landlord, for Hofwyl, two leagues from Berne, in order to visit the celebrated establishment, or "Institut d'education," of Emmanuel de Fellenberg. It was a rainy day. We passed through a pretty large wood, and arrived at Hofwyl, about 4 o'clock. I was introduced to Fellenberg, by three letters; two from Paris, and one from Geneva. The visiters that resort here are so numerous, and the attention of the principal so much taken up with them, I had been advised to anticipate some difficulty in getting access to him. On presenting myself at the door, I was received by a young man, who appeared to be his clerk, and who, introducing me into the office, requested me to write my name and residence in a book which he gave me. He then announced me to Fellenberg, who politely invited me into the parlour. I produced my letters, which appeared to give him much satisfaction. He is a man of middle age, of a mild and agreeable countenance, and of polite and genteel manners. He seated me on a sofa, and entered upon an explanation of the principles of his establishment, and the particular views of education, which had induced him to engage in it. He considers society as divisible into three distinct parts; the higher, (comprehending the noble and the wealthy,) the middling, and the poor. The greatest defects of education, he supposed to exist in the two extreme classes. That, these distinctions or classes among men, would always prevail, in every civilized country, he believed to be incontrovertible; and, of course, any attempt to break down the distinction, would be fruitless. It is, therefore, of consequence that they should be each educated in a manner conformable to their situations, but both in such a way, as to develope, to the highest extent, the best faculties of their nature; and, while it preserves the proper relation between them, it should, at the same time, encourage the feelings of kindliness and sympathy on the one part, and of respect and love on the other. This, he thought, could be effected upon no plan, so effectually, as by bringing them up side by side, so that they should have each other constantly in view, without any necessity whatever of mixing or associating. The rich, by observing the industry, the skill, and the importance of the labouring classes, would learn to entertain just sentiments respecting them, and the poor, by feeling and experiencing the kindly influence of the rich, would regard them as benefactors.

With respect to the best means of cultivating the faculties, which, in their due operation, are to promote the permanent happiness of men, he considers agriculture, as affording opportunities and advantages of the greatest importance, and next to this, the mechanic arts. Agreeably to these leading views, his establishment consists of two distinct parts; a boarding school of the sons of noblemen and gentlemen, in which no pains are spared, to provide them with teachers in every useful science; and of a house, in which boys, taken from the poorest class, are clothed and fed in a very plain, coarse, and farmer like style, and who work diligently in the fields, at employments adapted to their strength and skill. During two hours in the day, in summer, and more in winter, they are instructed in letters, and in music. They are likewise introduced into the workshops, and taught the business of a blacksmith, a carpenter, a wheelwright, a cabinet maker, a turner, a shoemaker, or a worker in brass, according as a particular talent for any of these, may manifest itself. The produce of the labour of these boys, bears no inconsiderable proportion of the expense of their maintenance and instruction.

After this brief explanation of his principles, Fellenberg introduced my companions and myself, to Count Louis de Villevielle, a gentleman from the south of France, who, reduced by the revolution, has attached himself to Fellenberg, and appears to live with him, as a sort of companion. He attends to strangers, and goes with them through the grounds, shops, &c. of the establishment. He proved to be a very sensible, well informed man, and altogether disposed to satisfy our inquiries. He conducted us to the workshops. In one of them, a new and handsome fire engine, of a large size, had just been completed in a style which would do credit to London or New York. In these shops, all the instruments of agriculture are made, and it is the constant aim of the principal, to improve upon the form and structure of them, and to invent others which experience may indicate the use of. As they make more than the farm requires, the surplus is sold to the neighbours.

In the evening the Count conducted us to the farmhouse, where the class of the poor boys are lodged, fed, and instructed. We found them at supper, on a kind of hasty-pudding, with whey and boiled potatoes. They breakfast on a piece of bread and an apple, or something as simple, and dine between eleven and twelve, on vegetable food alone. Once a week only, (on first day,) they have meat and wine. They are thus taught a lesson of simplicity, with respect

to their manner of living. The furniture of the house corresponds with the dress and clothing of the boys. After supper they went up stairs to the school-room, to take a lesson in music. Their teacher (Vehrly*) is a young man of very extraordinary qualifications. He received his early education from his father, who filled, in a distinguished manner, the office of schoolmaster for thirty years. He began at an early age to assist his parent in the discharge of his office. On coming to reside with Fellenberg, his views were further expanded, and he entered with enthusiasm into the concerns of the establishment, and willingly undertook the formation and direction of the class of the poor, in all their exercises, agricultural, literary, scientific, and moral. He lives with them, eats, sleeps, and works with them, dresses as they do, and makes himself their friend and companion, as well as their instructor. He is eminently fitted for such an occupation by his genius, his address, his temper and disposition, and above all by his religious principles. The school-room serves also for a shoemaker's shop, and probably accommodates, occasionally, the taylor and harness maker. The boys always take a lesson of one hour, between supper and bed. This lesson is frequently confined to music. They are taught it by principles, but they use no instrument but their vocal organs. Fellenberg lays great stress on music, as a means of bringing the mind and heart into harmony with truth, and of inspiring the mild and benevolent affections. He thinks it has been very beneficial in reclaiming many of these boys, from the vicious habits they had acquired from the low and exposed lives they had been subject to. By teaching them to sing religious songs, together with those that are simply patriotic, he says their attention is diverted from those vile ballads which are common among low bred people; and that they find, in this new entertainment, a happy substitute for the coarse and vulgar expressions to which they were addicted. The boys of this class appeared to be very healthy and contented. They are taught to pay the utmost attention to cleanliness. Their clothing in summer, is of coarse cotton, and in winter, of woollen cloth. They go barefooted, except when they work in the fields, or when the state of the weather requires them to wear shoes and stockings. They are always without any thing on their heads. Many of them, as might naturally be supposed, entered the school with the seeds of

---

*Johann Jakob Wehrli

scrophulous disorders; but by the effect of a simple and wholesome diet, cleanliness, and labour, they are restored to health with scarcely any medicine. Some of them, on their entrance, were feeble and debilitated, unable to endure cold, heat, or labour; but when once they have become accustomed to the regimen of the school, they willingly encounter rain, storms, and severe cold, whenever their work calls them abroad, without shrinking from, or regarding the exposure. They are taught to mend their own clothes. In summer they rise at five, and in winter at six; and after having dressed themselves and said their prayers, they receive instruction for an hour. They then breakfast, after which they go to work until half past eleven. They have then half an hour for dinner; after which Vehrly gives them a lesson of one hour. They work out till six, and after eating their supper, receive further instruction, which concludes with prayer, and they are generally in bed between eight and nine o'clock. But this distribution of time varies according to the seasons. In winter five or six hours a day are devoted to sedentary instruction. The morning of the first day of the week, is always devoted to exercises of piety, and after dinner some hours are given to instruction in sacred history. But their lessons are by no means confined to the school room. Vehrly takes pleasure in questioning them on subjects of natural history, geography, religion, morals, or any other useful topic, while they are at work in the fields or shops; and it may readily be conceived, that with this devotion to the improvement of his pupils, occasions will perpetually present themselves, of conveying instruction in every kind of knowledge, calculated to expand the minds of children, and to cultivate their best affections.

With regard to the most effective means of eliciting the powers of the mind, and of conducting the literary exercises of young people, great credit is due to Pestalozzi, whose veteran labours, as one of the most enlightened teachers of the age, were well known and acknowledged long before the commencement of the Hofwyl Institution. His plans of communicating knowledge, are in a great measure, practised by Vehrly. Much pains are taken to impress on the minds of the pupils, a deep sense of the importance of time, and of habits of industry; and from the reports that have been published by commissioners appointed to examine the establishments, it is evident that the most favourable results have attended these endeavours. The children are so effectually redeemed from their former vicious habits, that, in their most free and noisy sports, not an expression is heard, offensive to innocence or good manners. After working 10 hours in the day, they give themselves up, when their teacher permits, to the liveliest recreation; but a word from Vehrly, is sufficient to induce them to leave their sport and to engage in some other exercise. The progress which they make in knowledge, is truly surprising, when it is considered how adverse their former habits have been to all intellectual abstraction. In a few years, or even in less time, they learn to read, write and calculate, with and without the use of pencil or pen; the elements of drawing become familiar to them; and they acquire good notions of geometry, especially in its relation to field surveying, and its application to descriptive drawing. Botany and mineralogy constitute part of their amusements. They become well acquainted with all the plants of Hofwyl, and their different qualities, both the salutary and noxious. Of the minerals also, they acquire the names and principal uses, and they make collections of all that is valuable and curious in minerals and vegetables. Some of them are very attentive to the improvement of their little cabinets. The principal, when walking with them in the fields, is often called upon to decide disputes relative to the nature of stones or vegetables. But the most admirable trait in the character of this school, is the tone of religious feeling which, it is said, pervades it. This could not be accomplished were not Fellenberg and Vehrly, both strongly imbued with a sense of religious obligation, and unremittingly attentive to awaken those sentiments in the minds of the pupils. They have learned by heart more than 50 hymns, and many portions of sacred history. They are regularly attentive to one practice, which is a pleasing source of instruction, and at the same time serves to demonstrate the progress they have made in useful acquirements. At the close of every week, they write, in a book provided for the purpose, an account of whatever has impressed their minds with the greatest force. It may be either a moral reflection, a description of a plant, or an instrument, an account of a conversation, or an extract from some thing they have read. We saw some of these journals; they were mostly in the German language; and the greater number were written with remarkable neatness. Some of them contained drawings that evinced no inconsiderable skill, and an eye accustomed to accuracy of observation.

It will readily be conceived that a plan of instruction so admirable, and constantly directed to the best and purest affections of the mind and heart, can scarcely fail to redeem from indolence and vice, those whose habits have been the most degraded. And it has accordingly happened, that notwithstanding the boys under Vehrly's charge have been taken from the very lowest ranks, some of them the children of beggars, but one instance has occurred, of such inveterate vice, as to render it eventually necessary to abandon the culprit to his corrupt propensities, and expel him from the school.

In the religious exercises, which take place on the first day of the week, the boys of the poor school assemble with the superior class, but on no other occasion. . . .

Oct. 3rd. . . . Although the building, in which Fellenberg accommodates his superior class, is large, he is erecting two others. One of these is for the dwelling house and school-rooms of the students. It is about 100 feet long, and 60 wide, and will contain wine cellars, a chapel, ample dormitories, refectory, &c. for more pupils than his present number. The other building is for a riding-school below, and dancing and exercise rooms above. This building, which is also large, is constructed like many (if not most) of the country houses of Switzerland, by erecting an open and strong frame of wood, and filling the interstices with a mixture of clay and straw. This is moulded by the hand, into oblong portions, which are laid upon sticks, and are forced down in grooves made in the posts of the frame. The mortar is wrapped round the stick, so as to cover it; another is then forced down, &c. This wall is afterwards plaistered and white-washed.

The Hofwyl establishment, as I have before remarked, consists of two classes, the rich and the poor.

The class of the rich contains at present about 80. Twenty of these, consisting of children under ten years of age, are placed under the care of a respectable gentleman and his wife, in a house belonging to Fellenberg, situated about a mile from his own residence. A teacher or two have the charge of their instruction, both in and out of the house. From this house and ground we had a magnificent view of the eastern Alps. The elevation of some of the summits in this range, is but little less than that of Mount Blanc; and the extent of the chain covered with snow, was much greater than any I had seen. The air was very clear, exhibiting the rich white of this stupendous ridge of mountains, in the finest style imaginable.

The other sixty, constituting the most prominent part of the Hofwyl institution, are provided with more than twenty teachers, or professors. Among the pupils, are several princes, and the sons of ministers of state, &c. The price of board and tuition, varies from £100 to £300 sterling per annum. We were not admitted to the interior of the building occupied by these students. We saw none of their performances, of their schools, or their exercises, except a little riding on horseback, on saddles without stirrups; the horses trotting in a circle, guided by a rope held by a boy in the centre; the professor out: standing, likewise in the middle, and directing the rider how to sit. In this exclusion from the interior of his school, we were treated, by Fellenberg, like most, if not all, of his visiters. None are invited to the exercises, and none, of course, would go in without invitation. Either the trouble and distraction, which the general admission of his numerous visiters would occasion, oblige him to adopt this course; or, there is not, in the classification and operations of his school, enough of refinement, talent, and perfection, to support the name, and to correspond with the character of eminence he has succeeded in obtaining. My own impression is, that both these causes operate in producing his decision. The daily, and almost hourly, attendance and interference of company, would certainly be extremely troublesome. He does not profess, either, to have adopted any plan by which his pupils are rapidly brought forward. His system, as he explained it to me, is even opposed to a hasty progress. He wishes to allow his plants to arrive at full and vigorous growth, by a slow, cautious, and well directed training, and by carefully removing from the soil every obstruction; rather than to urge them by a hot-bed culture. He justly thinks, that all he can do, is to lay a solid foundation. That education is, or ought to be, the business of a whole life. Moral and religious principles, he regards as the basis of all that is excellent in man; and accordingly, great pains are taken to inculcate the doctrines of Christianity, agreeably to the profession of the parents and guardians of the pupils. The Catholic scholars have a clergyman or professor of their own sect, and the Emperor Alexander has provided for the instruction of the Russian pupils, in the principles of the Greek Church. Fellenberg's character, as a man of principle and piety, is, I believe, decidedly in his favour. He has the manners of a gentleman, and the whole exterior of his establishment, bears the marks of considerable taste and judgment. Beside the three schools already mentioned, he has another about half a mile from Hofwyl, where young men attend, during the winter, to courses of instruction in those subjects which relate to agriculture. He lectures himself, I believe, on the practical operations of farming. It is here too that the professor of chemistry has his laboratory and lecture room. We were introduced to him (Dr. Strobe,) and judged him to be a good chemist. He is also the physician of the establishment. His laboratory indicates an attachment to his profession and tolerable judgment in its practical details. The philosophical apparatus is, however, very unworthy of the institution, and ought not, I should hope, to be taken as a sample of the whole interior. In taking leave of Fellenberg, he expressed much regret at the shortness of our stay, and the consequent want of more opportunities of conversation. I cannot but regard him as a man of more than mediocrity of talent; a man of penetration and judgment; but rather prone, perhaps, like other German philosophers, to theorise on human nature, and to fancy that new and important discoveries are yet to be made in the principles of human action.

From the information we received from others, as well as from the statements of Fellenberg himself, it is evident that his plans have ever been regarded with jealousy by a great number of his most influential neighbours and fellow countrymen. He was at first condemned as a visionary: but when he had fairly demonstrated the practicability and utility of his schemes for the improvement of education, they accused him of sinister views; and alleged against him, that his motives were mercenary, having an eye chiefly to the profits of the establishment. This narrow-minded spirit has not been content with mere expressions of disapprobation and condemnation. The government of the canton has gone so far as to lay positive obstructions in his way, and to threaten him with the weight of their aristocratical authority. He had a few years ago devised a plan for diffusing some of the benefits of his experience in the government of youth, throughout the canton. He invited the teachers of schools to repair to Hofwyl during the period of their vacation, and there to avail themselves of such information, as the institution would afford, and their time would admit of. This offer was gladly accepted; but the next season the teachers of the canton were most arbitrarily interdicted by the government from resorting to Hofwyl. Fellenberg, thus very ungenerously thwarted in his wishes to do good, opened his establishment for the benefit of other cantons, and has thus had it in his power to extend still more widely the advantages of his system.[1] His great desire is to introduce a taste for agricultural pursuits, connected with an amelioration of the indigent classes.[2] He is himself of a patrician family; and his haughty compeers do not relish what they foolishly consider as a diminution of the dignity of their order, by his resorting to the task of an instructor. But though the Bernese government is thus actuated by ignoble sentiments towards the Hofwyl establishment, the most distinguished and enlightened characters in other parts of Switzerland, are decidedly in its favour. At Geneva it is considered as an honour to Switzerland; and if we may judge from the patronage that its founder has received from other countries; from England, Scotland, Germany, Russia, &c. it may be inferred that the Fellenberg system of instruction, is highly approved by the most competent judges of real merit in Europe.[3]

Without attempting to justify ALL the views which have influenced the founder of

---

[1] This part of the institution, which he called the *Normal School*, has been entirely prohibited by the cantonal government.

[2] His farm is intended to serve as a *model* of the best course of cultivation and management. About one twentieth of it is devoted to experimental inquiries, and the results are gradually adopted in his practice.

[3] By the latest information in my possession, the superior class consisted of nearly 100 pupils, taught by upwards of thirty professors! The course of instruction embraces the Greek, Latin, German and French languages and literature; History, civil and sacred; Geography; Mathematics, pure and mixed; natural and mental philosophy; chemistry; music; drawing; gymnastics, including riding, swimming, dancing, &c.; natural history in all its branches; and religious instruction.

The pupils rise at six in winter and five in summer; they breakfast at seven, eat a little at ten, dine at noon, take a luncheon at five, and sup at eight. Five hours are appropriated to study in the forenoon and four hours in the afternoon; the rest of the day being devoted to their gymnastic, agricultural, and mechanical exercises This arrangement however is not absolutely restrictive, but is made to conform to the varying circumstances of the establishment, the health and genius of the pupils, &c. The greatest pains are taken to cultivate the Hofwyl institution, either as it regards its general arrangement of distinct and independent classes, or its minute practical details, I have no hesitation in saying, that from all that I have read, and all that I have seen of this establishment, it does appear to me to be conducted upon principles which are calculated to afford the very best kind of education which it is possible to confer upon a young man, whatever may be the situation which he is to fill in active life. As it regards the poor, it is difficult to conceive how they could be brought up in a way which would better prepare them for filling the station of industrious, skillful and intelligent labourers. With respect to the rich, while they are cheerfully pursuing an excellent course of literary and scientific instruction, they are effectually preserved, by the principles of this institution, from those idle and vicious habits which so commonly result from the vacant time of colleges and universities. By turning their attention to agriculture and the mechanic arts; by inspiring them with a love of labour, or at least of a useful application of their strength and muscular activities; by exercising their ingenuity in the use of tools and instruments; by familiarizing them to an attentive observance of nature in her different kingdoms, and in the revolution of seasons,—a foundation is laid for those more expanded feelings and generous sympathies, which bind the upper to the lower classes of the community, and eventually tend to exalt the condition of humanity.

But the greatest recommendation of the Pestalozzian and Fellenberg plan of education, is the moral charm which is diffused throughout all its operations. It cannot but happen, (all other things being equal,) that pupils thus educated, will become not only more intelligent men and better philosophers, but also more moral and dignified members of society. I cannot but cherish the hope, that this scheme of education, of combining agricultural and mechanical, with literary and scientific instruction, will be speedily and extensively adopted in the United States. I am aware that it would have to contend with serious difficulties. The prejudices and habits of the people would be against it. The high notions of independence, so early imbibed and strongly cherished among us, would submit, in all probability, with an ill grace to the alternation of labour with the exercises of a school. The pulse of the nation has already been felt on this subject by a benevolent individual, (our friend M******,)* who, having visited the institutions of Pestalozzi and Fellenberg, was resolved, if possible, to establish one or more schools in the United States, on a similar plan. But after travelling from New York to lake Erie, he could find no one who would agree to second his views; none who did not consider the plan, as either unnecessary or impracticable. Thus discouraged he relinquished the project, though few persons in the world would have supported it by greater pecuniary sacrifices. Still I cannot but believe, that, if it were once intro-

---

their moral and religious sensibilities. The language chiefly spoken is the German. The internal or civil government, (if it may be so called,) of the school, is regulated by a constitution and bylaws, administered by the pupils themselves, and for which object they have their legislative and executive officers, under the supervision of the principal. The motives of emulation, as they are ordinarily excited by rewards, medals, honours, &c. or by a division into classes in the numerical order of first, second, third, &c. form no part of the Fellenberg system. His aim is to address his instructions to the more reasonable and noble principles of their nature, and by the number of his professors, (for he has had as many as thirty-five with less than 100 pupils,) to unite all the advantages of private, with those of public instruction.

It appears from a recent and very interesting exposition of the Hofwyl institution, by the Count de Villevielle, that the principal of that establishment began his enterprise with a fortune of 400,000 francs, (nearly $80,000,) and that by a prudent economy in his expenditures and management, he has, in the course of twenty-two years, more than doubled his original capital, notwithstanding the constant maintenance of 40 poor boys, and his liberal provision for those of the higher class.

Such is the attraction which Hofwyl now presents, to the enlightened curiosity of travellers in Switzerland, the number which daily visit the institution during the travelling season, cannot be estimated at less than 12 or 15. Of this number, it is scarcely possible that De Fellenberg, intensely occupied as he must be with his extensive concerns, can have time to see and converse with more than one. It is in consequence of the concourse of visiters, that so few are admitted to the interior of the school; for it would be an injustice to the parents, if, instead of devoting himself to the interests of their children, he should offer them as a daily and almost hourly spectacle to visiters.

*Believed to be Anthony Morris who later proposed the establishment of Fellenberg-type schools in America.

duced and brought fairly into operation, its superiority would be immediately manifest, and that the first successful example would be rapidly followed in different parts of the country. I have but little doubt, that on a good productive farm, of 250 or 300 acres, provided with suitable buildings, (which need not be very costly,) and well stocked, a school of twenty-five or thirty boys, conducted on the plan of Fellenberg's poor school, would maintain itself, and leave a gain in favour of the proprietor. A few such schools would soon impart, to a large and populous district of country, a moral tone, of incalculable importance to its highest interests and welfare. I know of no means by which a benevolent and wealthy individual could do so much good, at the same expense, as by erecting one or more such institutions, in any of our middle states. If white children could not at once be obtained to begin with, I would take the children of blacks. These could be procured of a suitable age, and taken on indentures to remain a certain number of years, or until they were of age, if it should be found requisite, as in some cases it might be. Such an experiment, with persons of this description, would be highly interesting. It would put to flight the ridiculous theory of those who contend for an organic inferiority on the part of the blacks. It would in time produce examples very beneficial to our black population; and in reference to the scheme of colonization, now becoming popular, it might prove extremely important, by furnishing individuals admirably qualified by education, habits, and morals to aid in the management of an infant colony. The great difficulty would be, either in America, or anywhere else, in finding persons qualified to conduct such schools. Such characters as Vehrly are rare. Without a deep sense of religion, united with the proper intellectual endowments, on the part of the teacher, the scheme could not prosper. Its basis is the mild, but fervent spirit of Christian love. It is, however, the happy nature of such a temper, to beget its own likeness in the hearts of others; and it might reasonably be presumed, that one successful example, would readily prepare the way for others.

We could not part with the Count de Villevielle, without feeling and acknowledging his indefatigable attentions. He is strongly impressed with the superiority of the Hofwyl system. In other places, he observes, *instruction* is the end, and *education* is only secondary. At Hofwyl, *education* is the end, and *instruction* is regarded only as the means of attaining it. . . .

Yverdun

Oct. 7th. . . . In our descent from Locle, we passed through or near Colombier, St. Aubin, Grandson, and other villages, and arrived at Yverdun about nine in the evening. We put up at the Hotel de la ville de Londres, where we found the accommodations rather of a superior kind.

Oct. 8th. Breakfast finished, our first and chief concern here was to visit the celebrated institute of Pestalozzi. This establishment occupies a large castle, the use of which was granted to Pestalozzi by the canton of Berne, when the town of Yverdun was included in that canton. The government of the Pays de Vaud, to which it now belongs, continues the grant. On entering the castle, we were invited into a private room. I gave my letters to the person in attendance, who took them immediately to the chief. The good old man soon came in, and seized me warmly by the hand, and seeing my hat on my head, he pointed to it in a sort of ecstasy, with his eyes almost filled with tears. I hardly knew how to interpret this emotion, and asked him if he wished me to take it off. He answered very earnestly, "no, no, no, keep it on, you are right." He seemed very glad to see us, and as he speaks French very imperfectly, and with an indistinct accent, he said he would call Monsieur G****** to talk with us. This gentleman soon came and entered immediately into a detail of the institution, its principles, its spirit, its arrangement, &c. He is an Englishman, and, as I found upon inquiry, brother to the lady whom I had seen at Lausanne. He has been some weeks with Pestalozzi, for the purpose of understanding his system thoroughly, in order to aid a sister in England in the education of her children. He enters warmly into its concerns, and will be useful in making it better known. He explained to us very clearly the leading ideas and views of human nature, which induced Pestalozzi to become an instructor of youth. The two great instruments with which he works are faith and love. He discards the motives of ambition and emulation, as unnecessary, and as tending to counteract the sentiment of good will toward others. He thinks there is enough in the intuitive understanding of every child to accomplish the complete growth and maturity of its faculties, if its reason be properly trained and nourished, and not warped by injudicious treatment. The common plans of education he regards as too artificial, too wide a departure from nature. Too much stress is laid upon the memory, while the imagination is too much neglected. If the native feelings of the heart, are allowed to operate, under the dominion of the native powers of the mind, drawn out and expanded by faith and love, the child is competent of itself to arrive gradually at the most correct and important conclusions in religion and science. There is a native and inherent life, which only requires to be cherished by genial treatment, to bring it into the full attainment of truth, and to the utmost perfection of its being. He therefore insists upon the greatest pains being taken to draw out this native life and to preserve it in full vigour. There is a constant danger of urging the child forward beyond its natural strength, of anticipating its conclusions and thus weakening its confidence in its own powers. In the plans he adopts nothing is to be got by heart. The understanding is to be thoroughly reached, and then the memory will take care of itself.

His school consists at present of about 90 boys, German, Prussian, French, Swiss, Italian, Spanish and English. It is divided into four principal classes, according to the attainments of the pupils. These classes are subdivided into others. There are seven school rooms in the castle, and twelve teachers or professors. His head professor, Joseph Schmidt, has been brought up in the institution, and is a very efficient and worthy man. He is a native of one of the German cantons, and speaks and writes perfectly the German and French. He is a man of modest demeanor, and entirely devoted to the institution. He has written treatises on several of the subjects taught in the school, and adapted to its methods.

We spent most of the day in the different school-rooms, witnessing the exercises of the scholars. Very few books are used, as it is expected the children can read well before they come there. But to describe the modes of teaching, so as to render them clearly intelligible, would require much more time and space than I can possibly allot to it, were I ever so competent to make it known. We saw the exercises of arithmetic, writing, drawing, mathematics, lessons in music and gymnastics, something of geography, French, Latin, and German. To teach a school, in the way practised here, without book, and almost entirely by verbal instruction, is extremely laborious. The teacher must be constantly with the child, always talking, questioning, explaining, and repeating. The pupils, however, by this process, are brought into very close intimacy with the instructer. Their capacities, all their faculties and propensities

become laid open to his observation. This gives him an advantage, which cannot possibly be gained, in the ordinary way in which schools are generally taught. The children look well, appear very contented, and apparently, live in great harmony one with another; which, considering the diversity of national character and temper here collected, can be attributed only to the spirit of love and affection which sways the breast of the principal of the institution, and extends its benign influence throughout all the departments. In the afternoon we went, with Pestalozzi, G******, and B******, a German clergyman, (who is here on a visit to the institution,) and one or two others, to visit a free school of twelve or fourteen children, which Pestalozzi has established in the village of Clendy, at a short distance from the castle. These are children taken from the families of poor people, selected on account of their character and talents, in order to be educated as teachers, with a view to extend and perpetuate the principles and operation of the system. One half of them are boys and the other half girls. Their principal instructer is a sister of Schmidt, the chief master, an exceedingly clever and interesting young woman. She has another sister also with her, younger than herself, who will soon become qualified to act as an instructer. These pupils were exercised before us, in drawing, in arithmetic, and in music. The girls, seated round a table, and busy with their needles, had questions in arithmetic given them by the mistress, which they were to solve by their heads. They are thus led on, from the most simple beginnings, to comprehend the principles of arithmetic, and to work questions with great expertness, solely by a mental process. A male teacher is provided for the boys, though the mistress often assists in their instruction. This little school promises to be well cared for, and of service to the Pestalozzian cause. We were much pleased with its appearance, and with the assurance it affords, that whatever there is of value and importance in this system, will not be lost.

The success of this mode of instruction, greatly depends on the personal qualifications of those who undertake to conduct it. There is nothing of mechanism in it, as in the Lancasterian plan; no laying down of precise rules for managing classes, &c. It is all mind and feeling. Its arrangements must always depend on the ages, talents, and tempers of the scholars, and requires, on the part of the teachers, the most diligent and faithful attention. Above all, it requires that the teacher should consider himself as the father and bosom friend of his pupils, and to be animated with the most affectionate desires for their good. Pestalozzi himself is all this. His heart glows with such a spirit, that the good old man can hardly refrain from bestowing kisses on all with whom he is concerned. He holds out his hand to his pupils on every occasion, and they love him as a child loves its mother. His plan of teaching is just fit for the domestic fireside, with a father or mother in the centre, and a circle of happy children around them. He is aware of this, and wishes to extend the knowledge of his plan to every parent. Pestalozzi is seventy-two years of age. It has been quite unfortunate for the progress of his system on the continent, that he pays so little attention to exteriors, regarding dress, furniture, &c. as of no moment whatever, provided the mind and heart be right.

Oct. 9th. The weather continuing wet, we resolved to wait till tomorrow, and take the diligence to Lausanne and Geneva. Much of the day was spent at the castle, in the school-rooms, and in conversation with G******. I omitted to mention, that we attended last evening, to the religious exercise which terminates the business of the day. The scholars assembled in a room called the chapel, but very simply furnished, with benches, and a table. When all were collected, Pestalozzi, directing his face chiefly to the boys, began to speak in German, moving about, from side to side, directing his attention, for some time, to the boys on his right, and then advancing towards those on his left. This motion, backwards and forwards, continued about twenty minutes; he was constantly speaking, and sometimes with considerable earnestness. It was altogether unintelligible to me, but I afterwards learned, that it consisted of a recapitulation of the occurrences of the day, noticing particularly everything of moment, and intermingling the whole with short prayers, adapted to the circumstances mentioned in the discourse. If, for example, any of the boys had quarrelled, or behaved unseemly to each other, or to their teacher, he would speak to the case, and accompany his remarks with a pious ejaculation. It is probable, that he sometimes engages more formally in this exercise. As it was, it appeared to gain the whole attention of his audience. It was concluded by reading, from a small book, what appeared to be a hymn or psalm.

A company of English visiters attended at the castle to-day, consisting of men and women. The boys performed some of their gymnastic exercises before them, consisting chiefly of simple, but simultaneous movements of the arms, legs, feet, head, &c., stepping, marching, turning, and jumping, all intended to exercise the various muscles, which give motion to the limbs and head, and to make the boys acquainted with the elements of all those movements. This exercise took place in one of the large bed-rooms. We attended, by invitation, last evening, a lecture given by Schmidt, the head teacher, to a number of young men, among whom were four Russians, sent by the Emperor to gain information, in England, and other countries, relative to the best modes of teaching. They had been in England, and spoke our language tolerably well. The lectures are to illustrate more fully, the principles and processes adopted in the Pestalozzian institution.

We had the company, this evening, at our lodgings, of Frederick Bucholz, who was late a chaplain to the king's German legion in England. He had been some time with Pestalozzi, and was able to inform us, more fully, with respect to some parts of the system, than we could obtain by a short visit to the school itself.

Oct. 10th. . . . We have had at our table d'hote, the last two days, ten or twelve boys, with their three preceptors, constituting a boarding school at Geneva. They are on an excursion, round the lake of Geneva, taking Yverdun in the way. They came to this place on foot, through the rain, and intended to perform the whole journey on foot; but the weather continuing very wet, they went off this morning in carriages. One of them is a young prince of Wirtemberg, about twelve years of age, of plain juvenile manners, exhibiting no extraordinary talent, but apparently of an amiable temper.

We left Yverdun in the diligence, after going again to the castle, and taking leave of some of the professors. Pestalozzi was not in; he had been to see us at the inn, but missed of us. Before we set off, however, the good old man came down again, and parted with us very affectionately. In the course of the two days which we have spent at the castle, he several times pressed my hand to his lips, and seemed to possess all the love and fervency of a true disciple in the cause in which he is engaged. If his personal talents, address, and management, were equal either to his genius, or his zeal, his influence would have been much greater even than it has been. Nevertheless, his life and labours will, I fully believe, be hereafter regarded as a most important epoch, in the history of education. When his

principles come to be more generally understood, they will be found to contain much that
is extremely valuable. It is to be feared, however, that many years will still elapse, before
the world is put in possession of a complete
explanatory view of his whole system. He does
not himself possess the faculty, (as Bucholz
informed me,) of explaining, in familiar and
intelligible terms, his own principles. He conceives with wonderful acuteness, and expresses himself in language of extraordinary
force and energy, but it requires a deep and
steady attention, to be able to embrace his
whole meaning. He has published largely in
explanation, and in support of his plans of
instruction; but there is so much of vernacular
pith—of idiomatic force and peculiarity, in his
style and manner, as to render it rather difficult to read him, and still more so, to translate his writings. He is now, however, anxious
to have all his works translated into English,
fully believing, that the merit of his plans will
be better understood, and his principles more
industriously supported by the English nation,
than by his own people. His career has been
marked with perplexities. He has had to
struggle intensely against poverty, neglect,
prejudice, and gross misrepresentation; but
his patience, his meekness, his perseverance,
his ardent love of his fellow creatures, have
borne him through all his trials; and notwithstanding his advanced age, the reputation of
his school, is now as high, if not higher, than
it ever has been. Towards those who have
generously contributed to aid him in his pecuniary difficulties, his heart glows with the
liveliest gratitude. Of two of my acquaintance,
one of London, and the other of Philadelphia,
who had thus befriended him, he could not
speak without evident emotion.

Henry Edwin Dwight

1825

Education in Prussia and the United States: Descriptions and Contrasts

Henry Edwin Dwight (1797–1832), one of the first American students registered at the University of Berlin, was the eighth son of Yale University President Timothy Dwight, Sr. After
his return to America in 1827, he and his brother, Sereno Edward Dwight, operated a German
type *gymnasium* at New Haven after the pattern of the Northampton, Massachusetts, Round Hill
School.

His account of German education is highly laudatory and analytical, and his detailed descriptions reveal a sophistication not easily discernible in other American travelers of his
time. But what is more important is his comparative analysis of European education on the
basis of religion. The table of contents in his *Travels in the North of Germany* contains the
inscription "Comparative Education of the People in Protestant and Catholic Countries,"
which is apparently the first recorded reference by an American to the analysis of education
specifically in both international and comparative terms. Therefore, Dwight can perhaps be
"formally" recognized as the first self-identified American "comparative" educator of the
nineteenth century.

Universities

The university of Berlin, until within a
few years, was merely a medical school.
In 1810, the three faculties of theology, law,
and philosophy, were added to it, and the
university was thus formed. It takes the lead,
this year, of all the German universities,
in the number of students, and also in the
number of lectures that are delivered. It
is now patronised more than any other in
Germany, not excepting that of Vienna; as
the Austrian government, of late years, has
been very unwilling to allow that freedom

Henry Edwin Dwight, *Travels in the North of Germany, in the Years 1825 and 1826* (New York: G. & C. &
H. Carvill, 1829), pp. 174–192, 243–254.

of literary discussion, which is indispensable to the prosperity of an university. That government, does not allow but one course of statistics, viz. of Austria, to be given in that institution, from the fear that even through this medium, some suspicions might enter the minds of the youth, that other countries, as they are more prosperous, may be also better governed. A law has recently been enacted, dated Vienna, January 26, 1826, (vide *Berlinische Nachrichten*, of February 2d, the same year,) that in the Austrian schools of instruction, no foreigner, who has passed the age of ten years, shall be received; and that cases of admission, under this age, shall not frequently occur. This law, illiberal as it is, is worthy of the source whence it proceeded, and must excite surprise even at Rome, where, as at all the other universities of Italy, foreigners are received on the same footing as the natives. It, doubtless, results from the fears which Metternich entertains, that political light will be introduced from abroad, to dazzle the youth so long accustomed only to Austrian darkness. It will, for ever, prevent the institution of Vienna, from rising numerically to the elevation it would otherwise attain, as from one-fourth to one-half of the students in every university of Germany, with this exception, are not natives of the kingdom, or grand duchy, in which it is situated.

The remarks made in my description of the university of Göttingen, are most of them applicable to that of Berlin. Like that, it is divided into four departments. In theology, there are seven professors and four teachers, who deliver twenty-eight courses of lectures. In the faculty of law, there are nine professors and five teachers, who deliver thirty-two courses of lectures. In the medical department, there are twenty-one professors and seven teachers, who deliver sixty-nine courses of lectures on every branch of surgery, anatomy, materia medic, physiology, medical practice, &c. In philosophy, there are thirty-five professors and fourteen teachers, who deliver ninety-three courses of lectures on almost every subject, included from the arts of singing and riding, to mathematics and Chaldaic. You will thus see that there are between two and three hundred courses of lectures delivered in this university. Each course here occupies four and a half months. In most of the courses, lectures are delivered four, five, and six times in a week; in a few of them, once and twice. You will perceive, by looking at the *Index Lectionum*, that

there are few subjects which hold a prominent place in moral, literary, or professional discussion, that are not here treated in an elaborate manner.

The great superiority of German universities to those of our country, and in truth, to all others, except that of Paris, results from the admirable subdivision of labour which exists there. This is as important in mental as in physical effort, and will always ensure equal success. One man, to use a hackneyed illustration, can not make more than five or six buttons daily, but ten men can make a thousand, by dividing and thus simplifying their labour. A professor who, like most of ours, is compelled to instruct in several languages, and write lectures upon the literature of as many nations, will never advance very far in either, and his opinions must be a mere compilation of those who have preceded him in the same departments. But, when an individual devotes most of his life to a single language, or, as the German professors often do, to two or three of the most distinguished works of its literature, he must, with moderate powers, arrive at a degree of excellence, which men of genius can not attain, where they waste their strength on the literature of three or four countries. It is an effect of this subdivision of mental effort, that we find such works as those of Heyne, Wolf, and Hermann, in classical learning; and to the want of it that, until within a few years, we have had no writer in oriental literature, or in that of Athens and Rome, who would sustain a moderate reputation in this country. When I left the United States, there were in Cambridge but four professors to instruct in the literature and languages of all nations, ancient and modern, and in Yale there was but one. Such a field is too wide for any one mind to grasp it. You may advance some distance on many beaten tracks, but you will never make any discoveries, unless you confine yourself to one or two.

You must not understand me as saying, that a professor of Hebrew should not be so familiar with Arabic, Syriac, Latin, and Greek, and with the modern languages, as to read them with facility. This is indispensable, if he will acquire an intimate knowledge of the Hebrew, or avail himself of the discoveries of others, and this the German professors do universally. It is rare to find one who cannot translate from six to seventeen languages, and they can often speak three or four; but they devote most of their strength to one, or even to a few works of a single language. By this division of labour, they have introduced in these institutions a more thorough course of exegetical instruction than has ever existed elsewhere. With us, if a student can give a grammatical translation of a few of the authors of classical literature, he is pronounced a fine Greek and Latin scholar, and he leaves the university in the blaze of a Salutatory or Valedictory.

Exegesis, so far as I am acquainted with our literary institutions, and I have friends connected with many of them, has scarcely become a part of classical instruction. Here they learn the construction of the ancient languages much more minutely than with us; so much so, that all the rules and exceptions of the syntax must be understood by the student. When he is familiar with these, he is supposed to have acquired such a knowledge of the language, as imperfectly to qualify him for commencing the study of its authors. Much more remains to be done before he can pursue an exegetical course to advantage. He must become thoroughly acquainted with the geography, the antiquities, the physical character of the country whose literature he is perusing, before he enters upon this mode of studying. In pursuing it as an exeget, he must study, most intimately, the character of the people, as moral, intellectual, and physical beings; be able to trace every custom and every image to its source; become acquainted with their mythology and philosophy; ascertain whether their opinions on these subjects were introduced by their intercourse with surrounding nations, or had their origin in their own peculiar character; make himself intimately acquainted with their history, laws, state of society, social intercourse, mode of life, their peculiar rites and ceremonies; examine the circumstances under which the author wrote his work, and of the nation at the time it was written; in one word, discover every thing connected with them as moral, intellectual, political, religious, social, and physical beings; so that he may, in the fullest manner, overcome all those difficulties which distance, time, and place, have thrown in the way of the reader. It is from the pursuit of this course, that so many of these professors appear, in their studies and lecture-rooms, to live more in past ages than in the present century, and to be more familiar with the manners and customs of antiquity than with those of Germany. It is thus that they learn to feel the true spirit of David, of Isaiah, Æschylus, Euripides, Dante, or Calderon, with almost the same force as

the contemporaries of those poets. Such a professor becomes, in fact, a lamp to guide the student in the darkness of antiquity.

It is not in ancient languages only, that they pursue this course of exegetical instruction. The remarks just made above, are as applicable to their lectures on modern literature, as to that of Greece and Rome. In fact, no other course of study is considered of any avail, and any other mode of lecturing would be the means of rendering every seat of the lecture-room vacant. This exegetical mode of study has been pursued with far more ardour, during the last seventy years, than before. Michaelis, in oriental literature; Heyne and Ernesti, in the ancient languages, created an interest in exegesis, previously unknown in this country. They have been succeeded by hundreds, perhaps it should be said by thousands, who have applied this mode of studying to the literature of almost every language, from China to the ultima Thule. The number of distinguished exegets, is much greater now than at any previous period. This remark is particularly applicable to the Orientalists and Grecians of this country; for these are the names which they receive when they arrive at eminence, being called no longer Germans.

The same subdivision of labour exists in almost every other department of instruction, as most of the universities possess cabinets and apparatus sufficiently extensive, to illustrate every branch of science. Though foreign languages and literature are pursued here with an interest unknown since the reformation, an equal ardour is manifested in the study of medicine, and in many of the branches of physical science. In consequence of this the German students acquire a thorough education in all the most important branches of knowledge. The distance between them and our own students is of course very great. The former, when they enter the universities are much better acquainted with the classical literature, than ours when they are graduated, and many of them are superior to many of our professors. This must continue to be the fact, so long as our literary professors are compelled to trace the immense field of classic or modern literature, and it may be added, so long as our universities continue on their present footing.

With us, as well as in Germany, the professors are chosen for life, but here the resemblance ceases. In the United States we give them a sufficient salary, to enable them to live pleasantly; and when once chosen, they realize that their fortune is made, that they have reached the ultimatum of ascent. Here they receive only half a subsistence for themselves and families; and whether they acquire the other half or not, depends entirely upon their own efforts. They perfectly understand, that nothing but a reputation for talents and attainments will fill their lecture rooms, and that to acquire this fame, the most indefatigable application and industry are necessary. Every department has its four or six professors and teachers, who deliver lectures on subjects so nearly similar, that a constant rivalry is produced. For example, to a student pursuing Greek literature, it is of very little importance whether he reads Sophocles or Euripedes, but it is very necessary that the professor whose lectures, he attends should be thoroughly acquainted with the author he attempts to explain. These gentlemen perfectly understand, as well as the stage and steamboat proprietors of our country, that if they are negligent, they will be deserted. This is not a little increased by the division into ordinary and extraordinary professors and teachers. The latter class who are paid nothing by the government, but are only permitted to deliver lectures, receive a Frederick d'or from each of the pupils, and are almost universally stimulated by necessity. Besides this they feel all the ardour of youth, and the consequent longing for reputation. To acquire subsistence and fame, they make unwearied exertions. Before them they see the extraordinary professors, whose title in the eyes of the students, gives them a prior claim; and to overtake them in the race they strain every nerve. The extraordinary professors see below them a number of young men, putting forth all their energy, while above them they behold the ordinary professors who have reached the highest point of ascent. This class are placed under the influence of two most powerful stimulants, the fear of being overtaken by the teachers, and the desire of surpassing the ordinary professors. The ordinary professors see below them two classes, at different distances, rapidly rising towards them, often almost treading upon their heels, and not unfrequently taking the lead in the number of their auditors, as well as in reputation. Under such a stimulus, they very rarely fall asleep, or relax their efforts, until age or debility arrives.

This continued strife has the happiest effect on the literature of this country, and in this respect, the German universities are better organised than any others in Europe. It is folly to suppose, that the mere influence of principle will induce most professors who do not feel great enthusiasm in their departments, to make the necessary efforts to arrive at excellence. They will often find bad weather in winter, and real or imaginary debility the rest of the year, an excuse for relaxation or indolence.

American professors are usually stationary from forty-five to fifty years of age, until their decease; or, to indulge the utmost charity, they advance very little after that period; here, they are continually acquiring fame by new attainments, and they are rarely unoccupied, even at seventy.

In the United States, the professors usually write but one course of lectures, which is delivered from year to year, until it loses with even themselves half its interest, from its monotony; here, there are very few who do not deliver two, three, and even four courses on different branches of their profession at the same time, which occupy them as many hours during three, four, and even five days of the week. With us, a professor is usually chosen at a very early period of life, and long before his attainments have qualified him for his station, with the hope that his talents and industry will justify the appointment. If, as is sometimes the case, they are chosen at a more advanced age, they are selected from one of the professions in which they have been so long occupied, that they have had but little time to devote to any thing but the practical part of it. This is particularly true of theology and medicine, and is almost equally so in the department of law. Though they make very good clergymen, lawyers, and physicians, very few of them, however distinguished are their talents, make able professors. A man designed for such a station, like an officer in the army, should be educated for his profession, and should go through all the gradations of ascent, until he arrives at the highest chair of instruction. It is almost as unsafe to choose a professor of theology, of law, or of medicine, because the person chosen was a good preacher, lawyer, or physician, as it would be to elevate a common soldier to the rank of general, because he performed his drill with great precision. The one requires as long a course of study and of diligent application as the other. Happily for Germany, a very different course is pursued here. Before an individual can reach the humble station of teacher, he must exhibit fine talents, and an amount of learning which few of our professors possess. In this station he remains a long time, and years must roll away, unless his attainments are very uncommon, before he is raised to the extraordinary chair. Previous to this elevation, he passes six, eight, ten, and sometimes fifteen years, in the most diligent research, relying entirely upon his own efforts for success.

When a professor at length takes the first ascending step, he is not considered qualified to receive the compensation or title of an ordinary professor. Here he remains many years dependant upon the three or four hundred dollars that he receives from government, and on the fees of his lectures for subsistence, until he shows the same decided superiority over his brethren of the same class, that he did when, as a teacher, he was called to the extraordinary chair. Even this is not enough. The German universities are all rival institutions, and the custom is universal, of appointing those who fill the prominent places in any one of them, to a similar place in another. To induce them to leave the chairs which they occupy, large pecuniary offers are made, and to these are not unfrequently added titles and decorations. The government of the university are thus under the necessity of retaining them by similar offers, or of seeing many of the students following the professor to a neighbouring institution. Learning and talent are thus thrown into the market, and become as much an article of commerce as any branch of manufactures. They are usually struck off to the highest bidder, unless the peculiar excellence of the library, as at Göttingen; or of the hospitals, as at Berlin, should induce the individual to make a pecuniary sacrifice for the sake of the greater facilities which his actual situation affords for arriving at eminence.

In consequence of this prevailing custom, an extraordinary professor is far from being certain of advancement to an ordinary chair, although he may have arrived at the first rank among his rivals in the university where he resides. If the fame of some other in a distant institution should surpass his own, he may have the mortification of seeing the vacancy filled by a stranger. The consciousness of this danger is a new motive to him to be ever active, and the thorough preparation which he makes, accordingly enables him, when he has at length arrived

at the *ne plus ultra* of ascent, to appear in every respect fitted for his station. Here he is still under the influence of the motives which have been already referred to, which tend to keep him constantly active. But with even these habits of application he might, at times, be persuaded to relax his efforts. Many of these gentlemen by the time they have reached the ordinary professorship, have acquired such fortunes or reputation as might induce them to cease from exertion and to live upon their past fame, like "a sword in its scabbard rusting ingloriously away," were not new motives still to be presented to their minds. These are the titles and ribbons which are conferred by the monarchs on those ordinary professors, who in that station acquire great distinction. As soon as a man here has acquired fortune he covets titles, for literary reputation is not sufficient to satisfy the boundless love of distinction. The desire of having a *Von* prefixed to his name, the hope of receiving the order of the black eagle of Prussia, of the white falcon of Weimar, of the great cross of the order of merit of Bavaria, &c., which from time to time are conferred on the literati of this country, induces him to continued exertions. The presentation of one of these increases his wish for more, until he becomes as desirous of them as an Italian vetturino is of his *buono mano*. With this system of advancement, bestowing its rewards exclusively according to the talents and industry of the individual, you will easily perceive that to be a professor in Germany requires an amount of learning and a course of preparation to which in the United States we are strangers.

Many of the preceding remarks are made with feelings of deep regret, and not in the spirit of censure. I am perfectly aware of the great difficulties that are thrown in the way of attainments in a country like our own: I am equally aware that the means of procuring an education in some branches of knowledge, particularly in exegetical theology, have not extensively existed till within a few years. Most of these difficulties can be henceforth overcome, with the aid of German ardour and German industry. This is the vinegar that will soften the intellectual mountains which the student is compelled to climb. With these no Alpine heights need discourage him, nor induce him to retire and leave the glorious country which lies beyond, unexplored and unconquered. With this he will surmount every eminence, and though Alps on Alps arise, he will continually advance, until standing on an intellectual Mount Blanc, the prospect of another clime and a distant age rises to his view, to reward him for his exertions.

The time I hope will soon arrive, when the faculties for acquiring knowledge will be within the reach of every individual. A theological professor who is not well versed in exegetical literature, does not exist this side of the Rhine, and few clergymen can be found in this part of Germany, who are not tolerably well acquainted with the Hebrew language and its literature. It would be unreasonable to demand, that our professors should be as profound scholars as those of this country: this at present is impossible. We have no libraries by means of which they can arrive at the same degree of excellence. With the exception of that of Cambridge, I have not seen one that contains, independently of its Greek, Latin, and English authors, one work in twenty which is indispensable to the eye of a German librarian, and which can easily be found in the large libraries of this country. With such a poverty of materials, how can it be expected that we should arrive even at moderate reputation in literature and science? But although the historian, the professors in modern literature, and especially the authors who write on subjects from the beaten track, can procure but few of the books to which they are referred in examining the subjects on which they write; those who fill the chairs of classical literature and of theology, will soon be able to procure such as are necessary to become thorough exegets in their departments. Even where these do not exist, it is delightful to reflect, that our commerce with Europe is now so extended, as to enable them at any time to procure them. Neither our literary men nor our clergymen, are in such indigent circumstances, as to prevent their availing themselves of the *chef-d'oeuvres* in foreign literature in their departments. A little of Hannibal's vinegar will enable them hereafter to surmount every obstacle.

No one can lament more than myself the poverty of our libraries. I should look upon the individual who would establish such a library in the United States, as that of Göttingen, as the greatest benefactor to my country, who has lived since the days of Washington. A residence near such a library as that just mentioned, near those of Berlin, of Dresden, or of *la Bibliothèque du Roi* at Paris, is almost enough, independently of family attachments, to reconcile a student to leave his country, and to reside in a foreign land. How long shall we wait before a small part of the literary treasures of the Continent are landed on our shores? When will our libraries become objects of interest to the eye of the foreigner? Our country is overflowing with wealth, and her physical and moral resources excite the astonishment of foreign nations. The time has gone by, for us to chaunt the old hackneyed song, "We must level our forests before we strike the lyre." The United States are at least twice as rich as Prussia, and are increasing in wealth with five times the rapidity. We have as yet very limited means of acquiring literary reputation, and not one university, in the German sense of the word. Prussia, with an equal population, has six national universities, each of which, Greifswald excepted, has from two to four times as many instructors as Cambridge; and that of Berlin, has greater literary resources than all the collegiate and university libraries and cabinets of the United States can afford.

When I speak of the universities of Germany, you must not understand me speaking of institutions which are the same with our own. They correspond only with the professional departments in our colleges. The students here, before they enter them, receive an education in the classics, at some one or two of the hundred gymnasia of the country, much superior to that acquired at our colleges; and in mathematics and physical science, one that is equal to that in most of the latter. To form a correct comparison, it is unnecessary to deduct all the academical students. I have now before me a list of all the students in the Prussian universities in 1825. More than three-fourths of these are pursuing theology, law, and medicine. The remainder are studying some one or more of the fifty or sixty branches of the philosophical department, many of them with the intention of devoting themselves to science or belles-lettres, while others hope to obtain places under government, or to lead a life of ease on their estates. In these six universities there were the last year, 4816 students.[1] In the medical schools of Philadelphia, Baltimore, New-York, Boston, New-Haven, Lexington, and Dartmouth, the only ones which deserve to be named, there were never more than 1300 students at a time, probably not more than 1100. The theological schools of Andover, Cambridge, New-Haven, Princeton, Auburn, New-York, and Virginia, they have never had

---

[1] In the winter of 1828, there were in the Prussian universities, *five thousand eight hundred and ninety* students. Vid. Foreign Review, No. 3d, page 266.

at any one time four hundred students. There are not one hundred young men studying law at all the colleges and universities of our country.[2] The number of graduates who are pursuing science and literature at these institutions, with the intention of devoting their lives to these pursuits, has never been fifty. Taking the largest of these estimates, we have in Prussia the number of students amounting to 4816; in the United States, to 1850. It should be recollected, however, that three-fourths of our students are the sons of our farmers, while not one in fifty is here the son of a peasant. From this you will be enabled to form a comparative estimate respecting the liberal education of the inhabitants of the towns in this country, and in the United States.

Happily for the literature of Prussia, as it must be admitted, this country is not a confederate republic, and it has but two prominent sects. There is, accordingly, no necessity for establishing a university in every department of the kingdom for as many different sects as there are departments. The money devoted to the support of these institutions, is not as with us, drawn off in forty or fifty channels, (for in the United States almost every state has one or two, and some of them three and four colleges,) each of which is soon dried up. Flowing as it does in a small number only, they make the wilderness to bud and blossom as the rose. The clamour of this or that province, this or that town, that the government is *spending the people's money*, that the university is not properly situated, and their consequent refusal to re-elect those who were instrumental in making such appropriations, are here unknown. The money thus appropriated is not, as with us, applied principally to buildings, to the mere outside of literature in the form of brick, stone, and mortar; but to the establishment and increase of libraries, cabinets and apparatus.

In the universities of this country, no buildings are erected, but those which are necessary to contain the *materiel* of literature. The lectures in most of the universities are delivered in the houses of the professors. In Berlin, it is true, they are held in the university edifice, but it is in the same building where the cabinets of natural history, anatomy, &c. are assembled. In Leipzig and Halle a few of the lectures are delivered in the public edifice; but most of them are at the houses of the professors. The amount of

money thus saved, to be appropriated to learning, is very great. To illustrate this, we may refer to two facts which have come under your observation. The new granite chapel at Cambridge cost, as I have always understood, sixty thousand dollars; and the two buildings at Andover, the chapel and college, eighty thousand. Two buildings at New-Haven, corresponding, in almost every respect, with those of Andover, and equally useful, though inferior in beauty, cost 24,000 dollars, or 12,000 each. Had similar edifices been erected at those places, there would have been left a surplus of 48,000 at Cambridge, and of 56,000 at Andover, for the increase of the libraries of those institutions. This sum, judiciously expended in Europe, would have procured for the former thirty thousand, and for the latter thirty-five or forty thousand volumes of standard works. What a different prospect would such an appropriation have presented to the eye of the scholar! What an influence would two such libraries, united to those which now exist in those institutions, have exerted on the public mind! They would soon have become the favourite residences of our students, the classic ground of our country; and graduates would have resorted to them from every college in the United States, to avail themselves of their literary treasures.

The prospects of our country, in a political point of view, are very brilliant; sufficiently so to satisfy the most ardent wishes of an American. My heart beats with pride and joy when I contrast its prosperity with that of the richest countries on the continent; and when I look forward to the future, I think I can see the United States rising with a grandeur and glory unequalled since the birth of time. In a religious point of view, it is equally flattering. The activity of our benevolent and religious institutions, leads one to hope, that the time is not far distant, when the silence of our immense forests, now only broken by the shout of the savage, and the howl of the wolf, will be exchanged for the sounds of many thousand "church going bells," and that from most of its hamlets, prayer will daily ascend from hearts overflowing with gratitude and love. The rapid increase of these institutions leads one to believe that, ere long, many of the ships which spread their canvass for a Pagan land, will bear missionaries, bibles and artists, to diffuse the blessings of Christianity and civilization to those buried in ignorance and sin. But with all this to excite our joy, there is, in our literary prospects, very little to gladden the eye. I fear that, in

[2]Reference is here made to the state of the medical, theological, and legal schools, previous to the year 1823, when I went to Europe.

this respect, we are to be the by-word of monarchists. Our cannon and our commerce will make us respected, perhaps feared, but will do little to excite the admiration of the literati of Europe. Who can look at Lorenzo de Medici, without feeling far more respect for him as the patron of genius, than as the richest man of Florence? Who can look at that republic, and distinguish its proud merchants, in the blaze of its literary fame? What intelligent American can look at England, and feel half the respect for her proud triumphs, from Crecy and Poictiers to Waterloo, that he does for her Shakspeare, her Milton, her Bacon, and Newton? The arches of triumph which commemorated those victories, have, and will, crumble into oblivion; but those proud names will shine with increasing effulgence, until time shall be no more.

Our universities, in some respects, resemble those of England; which, however well they may answer in a monarchy, are very ill adapted to a republic like ours. As a nation, we are the most intelligent on earth; as a literary nation, ours is the least respectable, the Catholic countries south of us, and those in South America excepted. Commerce, agriculture, manufactures, and politics, absorb most of our thoughts; and we feel perfectly satisfied if our sons receive an education similar to that of their fathers. In this respect, we have not advanced with the spirit of the age. American travellers are proverbial on the continent for their ignorance of foreign language and literature. Even few of our foreign ministers can talk fluently in other languages than their own when they leave our shores, while almost every *valet de place*, and servant of a large hotel in Germany, Russia, or Italy, can at least speak French, and many of them English. We appear to feel extensively as if the treasures of the mind were confined to the Latin, Greek, and English languages. For this reason not only the *chef d'oeuvres* of the continental nations, but the researches they have made in oriental and modern literature, are, to most of our countrymen, sealed books. How many hundreds of our lawyers are unacquainted with the celebrated code of Napoleon, because they have never learned the French language! How large a number of our physicians are equally ignorant of the actual state of their own science in Paris, for the same reason! How few of our clergymen are sufficiently acquainted with the German language, to avail themselves of the researches made in oriental literature, and of the great discoveries of the Germans in criticism.

The peculiar form of our government renders it excessively difficult to establish a university on a popular foundation, without irritating not only the feelings of every man who loves to harp upon national economy, but also of every sect throughout the state where the university is to be located. Our division into so many small republics, excites the very laudable desire in the minds of many of the inhabitants, to have a state university. The feeling with us almost universally exists, that a foundation must be laid for the religious instruction of the students. As the funds of the institution are not sufficient to endow a professorship, and build a chapel for every sect, one of them must, in this respect, be favoured; and in the eyes of the public, it is immediately transformed into an engine for promoting the views of Presbyterians, Episcopalians, or Baptists. Those belonging to other sects immediately become dissatisfied, and henceforward refuse, if they form a majority, to make the necessary appropriations to its support. If not sufficiently numerous to prevent this, they usually succeed by raising the hue and cry of wasting the public money, in which all young politicians unite, as this is the road to success at the ensuing election. Our literary institutions, like the hare, are thus hunted down; and if they escape destruction, they are compelled to pass an existence in silence, far removed from the notice of their pursuers. In this respect, a monarchical form of government possesses immense advantages over a republic. Most monarchs glory in being thought the patrons of learning, the Mæcenas of their countries. Fortunately for literature, they can dispose of the public funds to promote its prosperity, without being afraid of losing the votes of the lower classes in their vicinity. The cry of wasting the "people's money," raised by these and similar classes of society, who would rejoice to bring every one down to their own level of ignorance, as well as the poisonous breath of sectarianism, like the Simom and Sirocco, dry up all those fountains in our country which are necessary to the luxuriance of literature. Under their influence it often pines away; and if it survives, it flourishes like an exotic in a barren and frigid soil.

Were it not for our perfectly democratical form of government, we should be placed upon a footing somewhat similar to the small states of Germany. Like our individual states, they are too small in population and resources to exert much influence on the political world. Only one avenue to distinction remains, viz. that of literature. Accordingly we find in many of them, at least one university, which is patronised in the most liberal manner, and provided very abundantly with the *materiel* of instruction. A literary rivalry is thus excited, which is not only visible in the broad foundation on which they rest, but also in the strife which so generally exists among the monarchs, to obtain the most eminent literati of this country. No means within their power are left unemployed to attain the summit of excellence, and to increase the facilities for instruction. Accordingly you find that some of these states, whose territory and population are so small, as almost to escape your observation in a general survey of Europe, hold in the literary world a more distinguished rank than the country of the Czar, notwithstanding he can say with Philip, in Schiller's tragedy of Don Carlos,

"Die Sonne geht in meinem Staat nicht unter." [3]

Weimar, for example, with a territory not larger than many of the counties of New-York, and a population of two hundred and three thousand inhabitants, has a university of between four and five hundred students, [4] with two libraries, containing one hundred and forty thousand volumes, three learned societies, and several distinguished gymnasia, besides other schools of an elevated character. Baden, with a territory not so large as Massachusetts, and a population of but little over a million, has two universities, containing almost twelve hundred students, three public libraries, in which are assembled one hundred and forty thousand volumes, four lycea, and fourteen gymnasia, to say nothing of the numerous Latin schools which exist there. It is such institutions which give to these petty kingdoms and duchies their fame, without which they would be almost unnoticed, or if observed, soon forgotten by the traveller. More learned works have issued from the university of Göttingen in less than ninety-five years, than from the whole continent of America during the three centuries which have elapsed since its discovery. It is this literary reputation which has extended the fame of these countries to the most distant lands where students exist, and their patrons, in the eyes of every philanthropist, have much more reason to glory in their prosperity, than the autocrat in his million of bayonets. Why cannot most of our states, in proportion to their population, hold the same intellectual rank in the Republic of Letters? They might easily do it, were their government sufficiently enlightened to place our literary institutions on an equally broad foundation, provided the spirit of sectarianism would not violate the comparatively holy ground of literature, and by its proselyting breath cover it with ruin and desolation.

Before dismissing this subject, on which I have dwelt perhaps already too long, I must allude to a defect which exists in all our colleges and universities, one too, of which we seem to be totally unconscious. I allude to the appointment of tutors to instruct the three younger classes. The station itself is neither sufficiently lucrative, nor respectable, in the eyes of these young gentlemen, nor in those of the public, to induce any one of them to fix upon it as a *permanent employment*. The great majority of those who fill these places, are chosen from one to three years, after receiving their degrees. During this interval, many of them, it is true, have been employed in instruction in our grammar schools, in the hic, hæc, hoc, and the o, η, το of Latin and Greek literature, but others have been pursuing their classical studies, and are thus less qualified to become instructers then when they were graduated. Even the former have been most of the time occupied with the rudiments of these languages, and however well they may be qualified to give instruction in this respect, they do nothing towards explaining the author exegetically, or making their hearers feel his beauties. The recitations become mere dry translations, without any allusion to the antiquities, the state of society, or the circumstances under which the author wrote, his work often mere words, conveying ideas so faint, as to divest his poetry or prose of most of its beauty. The recitation is resorted to from necessity, consequently listened to with but little pleasure, and its termination diffuses joy over the faces of most of those who are present.

Independently of the youth and the want of preparation of this class of instructers, there is another evil quite as great, and which exists almost universally in our colleges. Most of the tutors at their appointment are pursuing their professional studies, or commence them soon after. The limited salary they receive, presents no inducement to them to continue any longer in this situation than

---

[3] The sun never sets on my dominions.

[4] Before the murder of Kotzebue there were almost eleven hundred students in that university. As Sand was a student of Jena, many of the German monarchs enacted a law, forbidding any of their subjects to join that university.

is necessary, as each of the professions hold out to them a much more flattering prospect. Instead of devoting all their time to preparing themselves for their recitations, not a small part of it is passed in studying law, medicine, or theology. They view these places as harbours, where they can safely lie during the storm which usually darkens the prospects of young men just preparing to enter on their course of life. Their future profession is the great object of interest, and one to which most of the energies of their minds are directed. Though in instruction they comply with their prescribed duties, they rarely do much to rouse the enthusiasm of their pupils, and quite as rarely find their own excited. Were their salaries increased two-fold, and they thus enabled to marry, there would be no difficulty in finding young men of talents who would gladly avail themselves of such stations, not for a few years only, but until they, by their attainments, were called upon to fill the vacancies in the professorial chairs of the colleges and universities of our country. Instead of finding themselves treated with so little respect as they often are by students, they would in their eyes be regarded as but little inferior to the professors, as many of them, from their age and attainments, would become their equals. The remarks I have made when speaking of the importance of thoroughly educating professors for their stations, are equally applicable to this class of instructers. Their labour might be greatly diminished, if each one, like the teachers in the German universities, would confine himself to one department, and instruct all the classes in that. They would then arrive at a thorough knowledge of their particular branches of learning or science, and be enabled to excite an ardent enthusiasm among their pupils. Their instruction, instead of being as it often is, not very interesting, would be prized by most of their pupils, and the recitation bell would be to them a summons to a literary banquet, no less agreeable than that which calls them to the refectory. . . .

Common Schools

I have made so many remarks respecting the universities of Germany, that you would not excuse me were I to omit giving you a sketch of the means of education provided for the great mass of the people, in the common schools. In this respect, as well as in her universities, Prussia is one of the most enlightened nations in Europe; indeed second only to Saxony, unless the southern part of Scotland is an exception. The Rhine provinces have been united to Prussia for so short a time, that their population has not yet begun to exhibit the same intellectual cultivation as the centre of the kingdom; still so broad is the foundation which has been laid for their improvement, that there is reason to hope, that they will, in the course of a few years, be little, if any inferior to their western brethren.

Prussian Poland, is in education, much inferior to the western part of Prussia. That "ignorance is the mother of devotion," has been as fully believed by her priests, as by those of Italy. With the exception of that part of Poland near the Baltic, little had been done to raise the character of the people, before the first division of that kingdom. Frederick the Great was too much occupied with war and belles-lettres to find time for the mental improvement of the great body of his subjects; while his successor, Frederick William the second, was too intent upon pleasure to do any thing for Prussian Poland. It remained for the present sovereign to provide the means of instruction for his Polish subjects, and to reorganise the schools of that part of his kingdom. Although they are much inferior to those of the old provinces, they are rapidly improving, and there is reason to anticipate a speedy mental renovation among a part at least of that unfortunate people.

The remarks that will now be made respecting the schools of this country, apply peculiarly to central Prussia, or to that part of the kingdom which excludes the provinces on the Rhine, and Prussian Poland. Perhaps Silesia also should be excluded, as when it was conquered by Frederick the Great, it was marked by that ignorance which is so characteristic of most parts of the Austrian dominions; and although it has long been united to Prussia, it has made much less progress in education than the rest of the kingdom.

It is an interesting subject to every traveller in Europe, to observe the difference which exists in the respective means of education in Protestant and Catholic countries. This is most clearly visible in Germany. In the Protestant states of the north, most of the peasantry can read and write, while in Austria and Bavaria the proportion is very small. Würtemberg which touches Bavaria, has a comparatively enlightened peasantry. When you travel through Switzerland, you can easily discover by the relative neatness of the villages and the prosperity of the people, as well as by their intelligence, whether you are in a Catholic or Protestant canton. Travel through Saxony, and you will not discover a child of ten years old, who has not acquired the rudiments of education; but cross the Bohemian boundary, and you will soon perceive that the peasantry are comparatively ignorant. In France after minute inquiries in every part of the kingdom which I visited, I learned that of the adults among the Catholic peasantry, a large proportion of them could neither read nor write; while among the Protestants, almost every child was instructed.

Far be it from me to imply that Catholic countries have not done much, very much, to promote the cause of literature. The efforts of Leo X. to revive the spirit of learning in Italy, exalt him, notwithstanding his anathemas against the Protestants, above the great mass of monarchs, who have embraced the religion of the Reformers. The patronage afforded by his father, Lorenzo de Medici, to letters and the fine arts, will be remembered with gratitude by students, when Florence shall be no more.

The great difference, however, between Protestant and Catholic countries, consists not in the number of scholars and artists who have been patronised, but in the foundation which has been laid for instructing the great mass of the people. Compare the Protestant countries of Europe, England, Denmark, Sweden, Saxony, and Prussia, for example, with Italy, Spain, and Portugal, or even with France. Look at Holland, and then at the Netherlands; at Protestant and Catholic Ireland. Look above all at the United States of America, and contrast it with Mexico and the republics of the South. Whence comes this mighty difference in European nations, which a few centuries since were all equally superstitious, and equally degraded? Why has Italy, for a long period the lamp of Europe, always had a peasantry but little superior in knowledge to the animals of her soil? Why are the common people of the Roman states, at this day, among the most ignorant and degraded of Europe? There the wealth and power of the Catholic Church has centered; nations for ages have brought thither their tribute; and still her peasantry have always been ignorant and debased. It does not result from the want of means on the part of the government. The money expended in the festivals of Rome for several centuries, would have provided all the people during that period with adequate means of instruction. The difference is found in the principles of Catholics and Protestants. The Reformers saw that an ignorant people were easily re-

duced to mere machines; that the only mode of securing to them their proper character, was by providing adequate means of instruction; and that without this instruction, the victory which they had gained would soon be lost. In every Protestant country, these means were accordingly provided by them, or by their successors, and the inhabitants of these countries have been the only nations, the great mass of which have been taught to read and write. It is on this elevated ground that the Protestant takes his stand; it is here that he feels an emotion of triumph swell his bosom, when he looks to what the Reformation has done to benefit the human race. He here beholds in a most striking manner, the difference between nations who receive their creed from compulsion or from conviction. It is after such a comparison, or rather contrast, that he places the Reformers among the illustrious benefactors of mankind.

The elementary schools of Prussia are entirely under the direction of the government. No one is allowed to act as an instructer in them, without a previous examination, and a written permission from the committee of examination. At the present time there are more than twenty thousand of these schools in the kingdom, of which seventeen thousand are in the villages, and the remainder in the towns. For the preparatory education of these instructers, one or more seminaries are established in every province, and are supported by the government. The object in forming these institutions, was to introduce a uniform system of instruction throughout the kingdom, as well as to prevent any person who was not qualified, from attempting to teach the peasantry. To these seminaries all those who wish to become instructers in the elementary schools are required to repair, where they are taught every thing necessary for their future station. Here they remain from two to three years, the time being regulated by their capacity, and their qualifications at the period when they commenced their course. They study, at these seminaries, geography, arithmetic, the German language, and the Bible. Here also they are taught the best modes of educating, and of governing children, as well as the subjects they are to teach. After they have finished their course at the seminaries, they are examined, and if found qualified, they receive a certificate to this effect. This paper, with a certificate of their baptism and moral character, which is signed by the pastor of the church they formerly attended, is presented to the government, or to its agents, who immediately enter their names on the list of instructers. By the establishment of these institutions, a uniform mode of instruction, has been introduced throughout Prussia.

The population of the United States is generally so intelligent, that many of the instructers of our elementary schools, are sufficiently well informed to teach the rudiments of education. There is, however, with us no systematic mode of instruction; and, in many instances, there is a great ignorance of the best mode of communicating knowledge to the minds of children. To understand a subject, will not of itself enable one to impart a clear view of it to others. This capacity can only be acquired by previous preparation, or by long experience. Few even of those who have been in the habit of instructing children for years, have that intimate and extensive knowledge of the subjects they teach, which is necessary for an instructer, whose object is to expand the mind of the child, and to excite his enthusiasm. Emulation doubtless exists to some extent in our schools, but it results principally from the desire of receiving marks of approbation, and from the little presents which are distributed to the youth. This, unquestionably, exerts somewhat of an auspicious influence, but it ceases as soon as the child leaves his school.

The great object of all instruction is *to excite a thirst for knowledge,* one which neither time nor distance can extinguish. It is not enough to impress certain facts on his mind, such, for instance, as are found in all our geographies, relative to the form, population, extent, &c. of the different countries of the world: there should be a constant endeavour to excite that curiosity which will prompt him to make subsequent inquiries for himself, to procure an amount of knowledge concerning the commerce, statistics, power, and comparative resources of nations, from which he will be always able to derive a fund of thoughts and arguments. He should be made a thinking, reflecting being; one who can discern the shadow, and not mistake it for the reality; one who can judge correctly on the great concerns of life, and who is not governed by others. The great difference between the southern peasantry of Europe and our farmers, is this, the one class are a mere machine, the other are a reflecting people. But, although the latter class are intelligent, they are below that point to which they might easily be elevated, were our common schools to assume the high character they would soon exhibit, if they were intrusted only to men of superior intelligence.

It is as necessary to educate an individual who designs to instruct others, as to educate a professor for his chair, or a general or commodore for military or naval command. Without such preparation, the instructer will be almost as unqualified to communicate knowledge, as a corporal would be to lead a division into action. In many of our states, we have large funds, the interest of which is appropriated to the maintenance of elementary schools. In Connecticut, this fund will soon be more than sufficient to provide the necessary means of instruction for all the youth of the state. Were the surplus to be applied to the support of a Seminary for the education of schoolmasters, the happiest results would soon be perceived. In such an institution, the young men would not only learn every thing connected with the usual subjects taught in our elementary schools, but might easily acquire that knowledge of theoretical agriculture, mineralogy, botany, statistics, and political economy, which would enable them greatly to enlarge the boundaries of knowledge in the villages where they reside. Persons thus instructed would easily become the prominent men of the villages where they resided. They would be enabled to direct the minds of not a small number of the villagers, as well as of their pupils, to subjects which would otherwise never have arrested their attention.

Were such schoolmasters provided for the education of the youth of Connecticut, the intellectual character of the mass of the inhabitants would, in one generation, not only become superior to that of every other people, but it would become the wonder and admiration of our country. To support such a Seminary,[5] and to provide it with the necessary *materiel* of literature, would not cost more than ten thousand dollars annually. Is it not desirable, at least, to try the experiment? How can we, for so limited a sum, accomplish an equal amount of good? Are not the minds and char-

---

[5] In the university of Leipzig, and perhaps in some others of Germany, lectures are delivered on education, in which the professor gives a historical view of the state of education in ancient and modern times, and examines all the important systems that have been formed upon this subject. In such a seminary as I have proposed, lectures of this kind, as well as those above referred to, should be given, and after a residence there of three or four years, young men would be qualified to instruct the great mass of the people, in such a manner, as to elevate the next generation far above the station filled by their fathers. Young men thus educated, would be certain of success, and by them every important vacancy would be filled.

acter of the rising generation, worth this trifling expenditure? Shall we always walk in the beaten track of our fathers, when prospects so bright and so glorious are opening to our view?

By the improvement of our common schools, those of a higher character would soon improve, and resemble at least, in some degree, the classical schools in Europe. This advancement would exert a most auspicious influence on the colleges of our state, and the inhabitants would acquire a character, superior to those of any province in the civilized world. Connecticut is too small in territory to exert much influence in our national councils. Many of the small states of Germany are almost invisible, when glancing your eye at the map of Europe, and like them, Connecticut is barely seen in a general survey of the map of the United States. Like them, however, Connecticut may rise to an intellectual elevation which shall excite the envy of those great states, which now surpass her so much in population and resources. There is no other way for her to exert an influence over the union. If she does not pursue this course, if she does not maintain her comparative literary eminence, she will soon cease to attract attention, and she will, ere long be unobserved, unless to contrast the spirit of her children, with that love of excelling, for which their fathers were so much distinguished. On the other hand, if she greatly enlarges the means of education for the mass of the people, and if her classical schools and colleges are placed on a broad and noble foundation, she will in less than a century, acquire that elevation of character, which will make her sons glory in their birth-place, and to be able to say, I am a citizen of Connecticut, will be to them a source of as much pride, as an Athenian ever felt in the age of Pericles, when looking at the city of Minerva.

Every clergyman in Prussia is required to visit the school or schools of his parish, and to ascertain whether the teacher fulfils his duties. He must confer with him often, must point out any defects which may exist in his mode of discipline or instruction, and see generally that he adopts the course which will best promote the interests of the school. Should the instructer not approve of the plans proposed, the question is referred to the superintendent of the district, who decides, and from whose decision there is no appeal. The clergyman of each parish makes an annual report to this officer, and the general report of the latter is sent to the Minister of Public Instruction once a year. A committee, consisting of one or more inspectors appointed by government, with the superintendent, or some person whom he may appoint, examine all the schools within their district, once or twice a year, to ascertain whether the reports made by the clergy are correct, as well as to form a general view of the state of education in their provinces. The existing defects and the necessary improvements are thus made known to the government, and such alterations are then made as are requisite.

The instructers are required to confine themselves almost exclusively to their professions, and not to pursue any one which will interfere with their business of instruction. Other pursuits are allowed in those cases only in which the receipts of the school do not furnish a subsistence. The duties of the teacher are numerous, as he is not only an instructer of youth, but is also a servant of the church. In the former capacity he must attend to the education of his pupils in the common branches of instruction, and also in biblical knowledge. Every morning and afternoon he is required to open the school with singing and prayer, and to close it with singing a hymn, in which such of his pupils as are capable unite. In the school, he is never to appear in dishabille, but as the ordinance of December 24, 1820, decrees, he must "never be without a cravat, nor wear slippers" before his pupils, as he would thus lose much of his influence. It is also enacted, that he shall never smoke in the school room; for so universal is this custom, that nothing but a royal ordinance could prevent it. In his capacity as a servant of the church, he officiates as chorister; for Germany is a nation of singers, and in those village churches where there is an organ it is his duty to play upon it. During the sickness or absence of the clergyman, he is required to officiate as his substitute; to read such a sermon as the preacher has previously selected, and afterwards to catechise the children. In the church, he must always appear in black, and when the pastor is present, must take charge of his scholars. In every situation he is required to yield the precedence to the clergyman. Without the permission of the latter he cannot be absent from the school; and with such permission no longer period than three days. Should he desire a longer absence, it is necessary to apply to the superintendent, without whose approbation no alterations in the prescribed mode of teaching are allowed.

Every parent is required to send his children to school as soon as they have reached a certain age, which, if I mistake not, is six years. It is the duty of the clergyman to visit his people annually, to ascertain if there are any parents who do not comply with this regulation. Should such parents, after having been notified by him, refuse to send their children, they are arraigned before a public tribunal, where they are punished by a fine. For the first week's absence of each child, the fine is one-thirtieth part of a rix dollar; for the second, one-fourth; for the third, two-thirds; and for the fourth, a rix dollar. Should he still continue to refuse to send his child, he is compelled to pay thirty fold. This penalty is imposed between the first of October and the first of April. From the first of April to the first of July, the child is not required to attend school but half of the time; and after the last mentioned period, until the first of October, parents are not required to send their children, as they need their assistance during the harvest months. The children must remain at school until they are confirmed, which usually takes place at fifteen years of age, though it is sometimes delayed by the parents until sixteen.

The school-house is erected at the expense of the parish, and must be sufficiently large to accommodate the scholars and the family of the instructer, who receives the use of it gratis. In the vicinity of this edifice is a small garden, and sometimes a few acres of land; of which he has the use so long as he remains the instructer of the parish. This building is not very elegant, as it usually contains but four or five chambers, but it is suitable for one whose income is so moderate as that of most of the instructers. Every parish has a treasury, from the funds of which the instructer is paid from seventy to eighty dollars per annum. Besides this amount, each parent pays to him six *pfennings* a week, or about six cents per month, for the instruction of each of his children. In some cases he receives also a small quantity of butter and flax from the parents. His whole income, exclusive of the rent of the school-house and the ground connected with it, rarely amounts to more than one hundred spanish dollars, if he teaches one of the village schools. Those who live in the towns receive about one hundred and fifty dollars.

All the books which are studied are selected by the consistory, and no new one can be introduced without its permission. The Bible is universally read by the children, and forms, as in our own country, the foundation of education for the youth of Prussia.

From this statement you will perceive how much this government has done for the people.

In no country in Europe, except Saxony and the south of Scotland, and possibly in one or two of the smaller states of Germany, is education so universally diffused as in the central part of this kingdom. These schools are established in every village. It may be said with truth of Prussia, that it is one of the most enlightened countries in the world; for among the younger of the population, it is rare to see an individual who cannot both read and write. I make use of the word younger, because many of the laws relating to education, were enacted during the reign of the present monarch, before whose accession the schools were in a much lower state than at present. No one can help respecting Frederick William for the wisdom he has exhibited, in thus improving the character of his subjects. This emotion will be stronger, when it is recollected that he is one of the most active members of the Holy Alliance, and that he is still not afraid of the general diffusion of intelligence among his subjects. He is here laying a broad foundation for the future prosperity of Prussia, and it is to be hoped also, for the future liberty of the nation. This event will not probably happen in many years, but it must come should these institutions continue for a century.

Although there are some defects in the plan which Frederick William has formed to diffuse intelligence throughout his dominions, the system is still so much superior to those of most Protestant countries, that you will perhaps feel no little surprise at this account of it; accustomed as we have been only a few years since, to class the Prussian peasantry below even those of England. Perhaps the greatest defect in the schools of Prussia, is the allowance of so limited a compensation to the instructers. In a country like ours, this evil need not exist; but in Prussia it is unavoidable, so long as it continues as poor a kingdom as it is at present. The price of produce is now so low, and the difficulties of finding a market are so great, that it is extremely inconvenient for many of the peasantry, to pay even the small sum which the law requires for the education of their children.

Allusion has been already made to the great benefit that might be derived from the establishment of seminaries, for the education of instructers. There is another advantage which would flow from such institutions. In the United States the business of instruction is, to a great extent, a secondary employment. It is one which occupies most teachers but a limited part of their lives. The young men who are thus employed, find in the almost immeasurable West a larger scope for their talents; while the young ladies and young widows, to whom the education of most children is committed, soon discover that matrimony is a much more desirable state, than the "delightful task of teaching the young idea how to shoot." Instructers in Prussia have no other employment. This is the great object of their existence; here is their permanent home. Were such seminaries established with us, by increasing the compensation of the instructers we might easily persuade them to make it the employment of their lives. It would then soon become a distinct profession, and many young men of respectable talents and acquirements would look to it as a future occupation. Instead of being compelled to exchange the instructers of our children so frequently, the schools would be re-organized, and the teachers would rarely think of pursuing any other profession.

From the remarks which have been made by me on the subject of education in Germany, as well as from my great approbation of the character of their universities, I hope you will not think that I am becoming too Germanic in my feelings, or that I have lost any of my attachment to my native land. I have, however, been too long absent from home, to use nothing but superlatives when speaking of every characteristic of our country, or to shut my eyes upon the improvements which exist on this side of the Atlantic. We have much in which we may glory; and when looking at the future prospects of our great nation, my heart often beats with pride, and I hope with gratitude, for our civil and religious liberty, as well as for our almost universal spirit of enterprise and religious philanthropy. But I trust that this admiration will not so dazzle my eyes, as to prevent me from seeing elsewhere the good which we do not possess, and from profiting by the view. Though we are able to teach the governments on the continent many political truths, we have yet much to learn from them in return; and peculiarly on the subject of education, before we shall attain that literary pre-eminence which is the blessing and the glory of Germany.

Anthony Morris   1827

A Proposal to Establish a Fellenberg School in Pennsylvania

Anthony Morris was in the regular stream of international visitors who went to Hofwyl, Switzerland, to observe Fellenberg's vocational and manual training school. He was greatly impressed with what he saw and suggested that a similar school would be suited to the educational needs of rural Pennsylvania. In the following letter of December 31, 1827, to Jonathan Roberts, president of the Pennsylvania Agricultural Society, Morris declaimed the role of an educational reformer saying, "I only claim the merit of endeavoring to introduce into our own country and into our own state, a system of education, which I have seen successfully established in Switzerland."

Morris clearly stated that he had diverse motives for wanting Pennsylvania to be blessed with the first Fellenberg Agricultural Institute in the United States. Wishing to see "such a system prepared for that portion of my family which remains to be educated," he and his son, James Pemberton Morris, were ready to make available a five-hundred-acre farm at Bolton, some twenty miles from Philadelphia. Morris proposed that William C. Woodbridge, who was one of the principal educators from the United States fully conversant with Fellenberg's school and its operation, be approached to fill the presidency of the new institute.

I am much gratified to find that your opinion of the Fellenberg system of education accords with those which I had expressed, as well as those I had received from other persons distinguished for their judgment, and devoted to the interests of agriculture and science, and to their extension throughout the Union.

To introduce into Pennsylvania, in the first instance, an Agricultural Institute, connected with a general system of scientific and liberal instruction, so extensive as to give, in the country, all the means of education now only attainable in colleges and cities, would be obviously an attempt beyond the resources of individual farmers, and must rely for its

A letter from Anthony Morris to Jonathan Roberts, president of the Pennsylvania Agricultural Society, in Washington, December 31, 1827; in *The American Journal of Education*, III (1828), 505–508, 568–571.

success on public opinion, that all powerful instrument in modern times, of effecting every end either of good or evil.

To ascertain, therefore, how far such a system would be sustained by public opinion in Pennsylvania, and generally in the United States, has been my first object. For this purpose my earliest references have been made to the agricultural societies of Pennsylvania, and to those individuals most known for their devotion to the extension of knowledge, and the improvement of our systems of education, especially in the country. Thus far my inquiries have resulted in the most satisfactory evidences of a general desire to improve the moral and intellectual character of our country population, and a conviction that this can only effectually be done by a system of education appropriate to this portion of our fellow citizens. Should further inquiry, by a more extended correspondence, confirm my impressions that public opinion is prepared for this system, a more detailed statement of its character, and the benefits expected from it, will be presented on the return of a gentleman to the United States, who went to Switzerland, and has resided some time at Hofwyl, with the express object of obtaining all the requisite information, and of whose character and talents we have the most satisfactory references here, as well as the opinion of Mr. Fellenberg himself, of his competency, and preparation for the part intended to be offered to him. I must defer, until his return, the statements and estimates to which you allude—he is expected in the spring.

No other fund has been contemplated as essential to the success of the establishment by its friends, than the subscription of responsible names for the requisite number of scholars; which, in the first instance, would be about one hundred, at perhaps two hundred dollars per annum for the school of general instruction. On the faith of these names, and presuming on the advance of one half year's tuition on its commencement, the requisite funds for preparation in buildings, &c., it is believed, might be easily raised in Philadelphia.

One hundred acres of land is supposed adequate to the agricultural department, and, for the exclusively labouring class, the experience of Mr. Fellenberg is, that the results of their labour paid for their education, subsistence, and clothing, leaving to each a moderate excess. To this class, and to that which would unite an agricultural to a liberal education, more or less extensive, according to the means and wishes of the scholars, the immediate benefits of the plan are most evident, in addition to the general benefit which the extension of the circles of science beyond our cities and colleges, would confer on the country.

On a farm prepared for a proper distribution of labour, having its buildings systematically arranged with every view to economy, provided with the due proportion of labourers, whom we will call apprentices, and possessing the requisite capital to conduct the whole system, (which Mr. Fellenberg has reduced to a science,) with the economy, regularity, and industry to which rural labours on such a farm may be subjected, you will readily see results in Pennsylvania, such as the Fellenberg system has realized in Switzerland, and school farms in which science would preside; and industry, intelligence, and happiness, would be the fruits, instead of indolence, idleness, and misery.

Such would be the happy change to the country population of Pennsylvania, should the system take root among us, and become the substitute of our roadside schools, which, in general, seem only intended to expose to travellers the rude state of science in our country, and the total want of an appropriate education for its population.

Our moderate farmers and mechanics would find at their doors a liberal and practical system of education prepared for their sons, and the labouring classes would be simultaneously employed and educated, as in the system referred to, the hours of relaxation from bodily labour, are devoted to intellectual improvement.

Thus, labour, is made to pay for education, and education to be the reward of labour, and both uniting in the same person to form a character as different from that of the uninstructed, undisciplined, and often intemperate clown, as the free, industrious, and intelligent farmer, mechanic and labourer of a republic ought to be, from the dependent, degraded, and ignorant slave.

We may in vain look for reforms from ignorance and intemperance in any other source than a good education, of which, perhaps, the best parts are, the early formation of good habits, the regular presence of good examples, the sure foundations of Christian doctrine, and the constant guards of a vigilant discipline; all these essential igredients seem more easily united in the country, than in colleges, and I have never seen them so efficiently united, as on the farm of the truly illustrious Fellenberg; hence my anxiety to have his system received and naturalized among us, and not only because it would be a public blessing, but because I wish to see such a system, prepared for that portion of my family which remains to be educated. You must not suppose that I aspire to the character of a reformer; I only claim the merit of endeavouring to introduce into our own country, and into our own state, a system of education, which I have seen successfully established in Switzerland, after an experience of near twenty years, during which time its operations and results have received the sanction of many of the most eminent scientific, literary and practically useful men in Europe; among these I will now only refer you to the late eminent Professor Pictet, and his brother Charles Pictet, of Geneva, the Count Capo d'Istrias, who visited the Institute at Hoffwyl, by order of the late Emperor Alexander, the late Hon. Mr. Horner, Brougham, and Mr. Jeffrey; the commissioners appointed by the Diet of the cantons of Switzerland, and to their report.

Such are the men who have visited, approved, and recommended the Hoffwyl Institution to their respective governments.

It would probably be a more arduous task to procure from the legislature of Pennsylvania the public patronage it so justly merits, than to establish an institution by individual efforts, and thus to anticipate legislation. We have seen extensive military schools rise up and flourish among us, by the efforts only of individuals, and attain celebrity in the objects of their institutions, without, perhaps, an adaptation to our national character and interests as universal as agriculture and civil education.

Individual effort seems, indeed, a safe and sure foundation for this system, and less liable to delay and defeat than legislation. The system had flourished in Switzerland, not only without the support of the government, but in opposition to the aristocratic features of the constitution of the Canton of Berne, because its principles are in accordance with the spirit of the age, and extend the blessings of education to the country population.

To this great class in Pennsylvania, the least attention has been paid. Human labour on our farms has been left almost to its own undisciplined operations. No science enlightens it; no system regulates it: it is not accompanied in the field by economy, nor by temperance, nor rewarded at the fireside of the peasant by content and competence. A day of undisciplined drudgery, stimulated in the field by whiskey, is often succeeded in the cabin of the cottager, by a night passed in the riot of intemperance, or the stupor of intoxication. A week of drunkenness may be purchased by a little more than a day of labour, and as long as ignorance shall be the inheritance of the labourer, intemperance will be his companion, and his consolation, against that listlessness and languor for which the resources of science are the only substitutes.

Should we conceal the prevalence of ignorance and intemperance among us, we should never succeed in removing them. It may be too late to hope for reformation or improvement in those farmers and labourers, who, having began their career in life without science or system, must expect to finish it without profit and without pleasure. But it can never be too early to lay a new foundation for the hopes and the prospects of the rising generation, enlightened by all the discoveries of the present day, and encouraged by the successful efforts and examples of such patriots as Fellenberg, who have never sought for a place beyond the farms cultivated by their fathers; nor for power, but over the passions and prejudices of their fellow creatures; and who, leaving to others the fields of political and party warfare (in which numbers will never be wanting) have devoted their lives to the moral and intellectual advancement of man.

An obvious defect in our national character is thought to originate from the inadequate portion of time which is generally devoted to the acquisition of knowledge, and particularly of elementary and classical knowledge, as the best foundation for every other; and from the miscellaneous and superficial education which a great number of the American youth receive, being neither adapted particularly to agriculture, professional, commercial, nor mechanical destinations in life, but leaving the unfortunate subject of such a system to be guided in his after pursuits, more by the false pride of parents and other incidental causes, than by any fixed and permanent principles. A change of system in this respect would probably do much to promote a change from an injurious and speculative versatility of character, to a systematic permanency in the pursuit of those objects to which an early system of education had been directed.

Our prejudices lead us to associate all ideas of schools and scholars, with houses, and desks, and benches; while the field itself, the great scene of the farmer and labourer's operations, is seldom suggested as the best school for his practical instruction.

The field lessons and labours in practical agriculture at Hoffwyl, are among the most animating and instructive lessons of man. It is, perhaps, there only that science and labour are seen, hand in hand, supporting and assisting each other, and that a system of education having its foundation in the pure principles of christianity, and separated from all sectarian controversy, is made subservient to the improvement, moral, intellectual, and practical, of man, in every grade of the human family. Is not systematic instruction in his occupation as essential to a farmer, a field labourer, and a gardener, as to a carpenter or a mason? Can system be obviously more necessary in any department of life than in our agricultural practices? And can any system be selected from the distant and diversified practices of our best farmers—a comparison between which and their results can never be fairly made. It is only where a variety of culture can be exhibited at one time in one place and on scientific principles, that comparisons can be made or just conclusions formed.

The principle of pattern farms, at the expense of the State, so long solicited in vain from our legislature by the politicians of former days, it would perhaps be useless at this moment to attempt to revive. You will see in this project a substitute for these, combining instruction with exhibition. To have some ground to go upon, I have selected Bolton farm, near Bristol, in Pennsylvania, as the locality for the first Agricultural Institute. It is an estate of my son James Pemberton Morris, who puts such parts of it as I may select any disposition, uniting in my wishes for the education of his children in such an institution. The farm consists of near five hundred acres, is situated in a healthy country, on the verge of the manor of Pennsborough, once the residence of the founder of Pennsylvania, and selected by him for its fertility and favorable position as to inter-

course by land and water; to which natural facilities will soon be added those of the Delaware canal, located near it, and communicating directly with Philadelphia at the distance of twenty miles from Bolton.

Next to the farm it is desirable to find the Fellenberg. This is the most difficult part, but will be surmounted, if Mr. Woodbridge, who has received practical instructions at Hoffwyl, will assume that character. Then are to be found the funds, which should come, I think, from the scholars, on the same system that has elevated to so merited an eminence among our scientific institutions, the Medical School of Philadelphia; no stated salary being annexed to each professor's chair, but the whole emolument arising out of the instruction from each, would be apportioned to its particular professor and assistant.

Such, sir, are the outlines of a plan for the introduction into the United States of a system of education believed to be adapted to the character of our country, and especially applicable to those interests and employments, in which the greatest numbers are engaged, and to which, heretofore, the least instruction has been extended.

My immediate object in this communication, is to obtain the expression of your opinion on the subject of it, which I have no other right to solicit, than that which is founded on a belief that it merits, and will receive, particular respect and attention from those classes, especially, whom it more immediately concerns. It is so far circular, as to be similar to those addressed to Mr. Fellenberg, of Hoffwyl; to Mr. Madison, to Judge Peters, the President of the Philadelphia Agricultural Society, from all of whom the most strongly expressed and favourable opinions have been received, and are in the hands of the chairman of the Committee on Agriculture in the House of Representatives.

William Channing Woodbridge   1832

Comparative State of Instruction in the United States and in Europe

William Channing Woodbridge (1794–1845) graduated from Yale College in 1811 and was principal of the Burlington Academy, New Jersey, from 1812 to 1814. He then returned to New Haven to study science and theology and in 1817 entered the Princeton Theological Seminary for

William Channing Woodbridge, "View of the Comparative State of Instruction in the United States and in Europe," *The American Annals of Education and Instruction*, II (July 1832), 329–336.

a short period. Returning to the teaching profession, he was an instructor at the Hartford, Connecticut, asylum for the deaf and dumb from 1817 to 1820. His first book on geography was published in 1821 and his second in 1824. Traveling to Europe for reasons of health, he remained abroad for five years and made a study of educational systems in Switzerland and Germany. Physically unable to teach again upon his return home in 1829, he purchased *The American Journal of Education*, changed its name to *The American Annals of Education and Instruction*, and published it until 1838.

In examining the state and prospects of a community, one of the most important elements is its condition in reference to Education.

In using this term, there is constant room for misunderstanding, in consequence of the various definitions given to it, to which we have formerly referred. For while some will regard it as comprising the mere elements of knowledge, and estimate the state of education by the number of individuals who can read and write, others consider it as embracing other branches of knowledge of direct practical value; others still do not permit the name of education to be applied to any but a course of classical and scientific instruction; and some would deem the accomplishments indispensable.

In a view of the comparative state of Europe and the United States, on this great subject, we must assume the distinction between Education and Instruction, which in our view is fundamental, and which is adopted by the most scientific writers on this great subject. We regard *Instruction*, then, as the mere communication of knowledge. We consider *Education* as the process by which character is formed, involving instruction, the discipline of the intellectual faculties, the discipline of the moral powers, and the training of the body as the instrument in all these operations. We consider it, in fact, as embracing *every influence by which man becomes what he is, or may be made what he should be.*

In considering, therefore, the respective state of the two continents, we feel ourselves called upon to consider the state of *Instruction* first, as entirely distinct from that of Education in its largest sense.

Instruction may be considered both in reference to its *extent* and to its *diffusion.*

As to the *extent* to which instruction is carried, there can be but one opinion. Occupied by the first wants of life, and the duties of a free government, our citizens have not found the opportunity, they have not felt the necessity, nor acquired the taste for profound study, in most branches of knowledge. They have been satisfied with that which prepared them for immediate action; and are called forward into life so early, that they have no opportunity to enter deeply into any subject. They have not been able to provide even *the means* by which others may attain the heights of learning, or the depths of science. These are *positive obstacles*. There are others of a *negative* character, which will be best illustrated by considering the positive advantages and facilities to the accurate and profound study of every branch of science and literature, in the most cultivated countries of Europe.

There are central points of wealth and influence in the governments of European countries, where measures can be taken for the promotion of these objects, which under our government, are impracticable. The prince, whose power or talents do not permit him to become conspicuous by his conquests, or his political influence, finds a wide field for distinguishing himself in becoming the patron of the arts and literature; a field in which he is almost sure of success, whatever his own qualifications may be, so long as he has the means of obtaining the libraries and cabinets of natural history, which shall be the object of general attention, and of collecting the men who shall be at once the heralds of knowledge, and the living testimonies to his munificence. On this ground, the princes of many of the smaller states of Europe, are more efficient patrons of learning than our own great republic, and vie with each other in these praiseworthy efforts. No small part of the magnificent libraries and apparatus, and of the invaluable results of literary labor, thus aided by the best means which can be collected from the four quarters of the world, must be ascribed to such efforts.

The contrast, in looking at our own country, is no less striking than painful. There are noble exceptions to the general rule; but how slow, how penurious, are our public bodies in bestowing *anything* upon literary institutions, or for scientific purposes. How anxiously does a large part of the community watch our General Government, lest they should *incidentally* do something to promote the cause of knowledge. An unhappy jealousy exists also against the attempt to elevate the standard of science and literature, lest they should be made the instruments of establishing a literary aristocracy. It is forgotten, that even in despotic governments, *the nation of literary men* has ever remained a *republic;* that the ablest and wisest, from whatever station they arise, have always attained the eminence and the rewards they merited; that nobility has been proud to receive them into its ranks, and despotism has felt itself honored in patronising them. It is forgotten that the common sailor owes his safety quite as much to the Principia of Newton, and the telescope of Herschel, and the profound researches and laborious calculations of Laplace and Bowditch, as to the art of the ship-builder; and that it is *science* and its votaries that have given the steamboat and the railroad-car to the traveller, and the gaslight to the citizen, and the safety-lamp to the miner, and the antidote to pestilence, to the trembling expectants of an invisible, deadly poison.

Unfounded, however, as this prejudice is, it exists to an unhappy extent in our country. Too many are ready to hold back others from any of the heights of science, which they cannot themselves attain, and few are ready to afford them the facilities for that profound study which only a small number of our race are willing to attempt in the minute and abstract, and yet essential branches of knowledge—a task which, it has been well observed, involves 'the most severe labor which is done under the sun.'

Another encouragement to the profound investigation of science and the laborious researches of literature in Europe, arises from the fact, that in most countries, it is the *safest* and *surest,* if not the *only road to distinction,* the only direction in which the mind can exert great powers; the only field in which the soul can expatiate, untrammeled by laws, unsuspected and unchained by the police.

The offices of state are assigned by inheritance or by patronage, in such a manner that most of the community are absolutely excluded from the hope of gaining influence or reputation as statesmen; and to attempt it, without a birthright or a patron, is a career almost as dangerous, as it is uncertain. On the other hand, there is a corresponding certainty that eminence in literature and science will gain them the respect and patronage of the government, and the applause of the nation; and when once the glitter of political glory is placed beyond our reach by an impassable barrier, it becomes comparatively an easy task for *philosophy* to perceive and feel the surpassing glory of literary honors, and to be conscious, that he who sways

the sceptre of the civilized world in an art or a science, or leads captive whole nations by the charms of his writings, holds a rank far higher than the despot who can only control the bodies of men and the soil on which they live, or the conqueror who imposes fetters upon their limbs, by the exertion of brute force.

It is the only safe direction, also, in which the man of talents, in these countries, can permit his powers to expand. If he allows them to enter upon the wide field of political or religious economy, he is in danger of being driven on by their impulse to opinions and expressions which will cost him his peace, or liberty, or life; while if he confines himself to mere intellectual pursuits, he is generally *secure* of all the rewards which royal munificence can lavish, upon success which it regards as a part of its own glory.

But to a noble mind, the strongest feeling connected with the subject probably is, that this is the *only field of action* in which it can go on without limit and without fear, *in the consciousness of absolute independence.* He who gains literary distinction which places him in the chair of a university, receives *the freedom of the world,* and is allowed and encouraged to go on without limitation, in every subject where he does not attack the safety of the state and the prisoner may thus enjoy an extent of range, which enables him to forget the walls which bar up his progress in other directions.

It should also be recollected, that on these very grounds, even policy dictates to the rulers to offer every stimulus, every facility for pursuits of this kind, in order that powerful and active minds may not be left at liberty to employ themselves in speculations or efforts on political subjects, a result of whose danger they have had so many examples. The king upon his throne, has learned to tremble before a single, powerful mind.

The contrast in the condition of the United States is obvious. Here, the road to distinction and wealth is through an active or political life. The mere votary of science and literature, cannot generally promise himself a high degree of either. Every citizen is called upon to take a part in the political, and social, and religious concerns of the community, and every one who possesses high intellectual power, is called upon to an extent which absorbs all the time and strength which is not demanded by the labors necessary for subsistence. He is stimulated by all the prospects of distinction which our country can offer, and urged by a sense of duty to make himself familiar with the great questions of politics and of social life, and to engage in active measures. In short, the motives and the demands for private, social, and public activity, and the little respect, the poor reward, which is bestowed upon *mere intellectual eminence,* serve as so many barriers to entrance upon a literary course, in place of the encouragements afforded in European countries.

The circumstances we have described, affect of course the character of the literary institutions of the respective continents. Those of the United States, originating as they do in the people, and maintained only by their suffrages and aid, can rise no higher than public opinion permits, and must limit themselves to the comparatively narrow field which that opinion prescribes. On the other hand, the public institutions of Europe derive their existence from the munificence and ostentation which we have described as a part of the policy of state, and the effort is continually made to elevate them to a higher point.

The result is, that the '*Lycées*' of France and the '*Gymnasia*' of Germany, give a course of literary instruction nearly equivalent to that of our colleges, surpassing them, in accuracy and extent, in most branches, and only falling short of them in not being combined with so much attention to science.

Such is an imperfect view of the comparative *extent* of literary and scientific instruction in Europe and the United States. In regard to its *diffusion,* the comparison is not easily made, in consequence of the difference in the character of the literary institutions of the two continents, to which we have just referred. If we compare the institutions which rank highest, under the name of universities and colleges, we may, however, approximate to correct results; and with this view, we present the following tabular statement of the number of students in the universities and colleges of the respective states and sections of the United States, and the principal countries of Europe. The materials for the former were derived from the American Quarterly Register of Education for 1831, a publication of uncommon accuracy and value. The European statistics are chiefly from the Weimar Statistical Almanac for 1831, the highest authority we know on this subject.

In reviewing this table, we shall perceive, that in accordance with an opinion often expressed, Scotland gives more of her youth a collegiate education than any other country in the world. Baden, Massachusetts, and Con-

necticut, fall little short of this standard; and these are the only countries in the world, according to these estimates, which have one collegiate pupil for less than 1,000 inhabitants. New Hampshire, according to the calculation of the American Quarterly Register, is the only American State besides, in which there is more than one for 1,500; while in Europe, Saxony, England, Hanover, Bavaria, Tuscany, Spain, and Russia, all have a proportion greater than this. It must not be forgotten, however, that the Universities and Colleges of Spain furnish nothing which deserves to be called, a truly liberal education. Vermont, Maine, New Jersey, South Carolina, Pennsylvania, New York, and Rhode Island, composing all the Eastern and three of the Middle States, and one of the Southern, have one student for less than 2,000 inhabitants, in which they are rivalled by Wurtemberg, Sweden, Portugal, and the Netherlands. Most of the Southern and Western States have from 2,000 to 4,000 inhabitants to a student. In this proportion, the highest compare with Switzerland, and the rest with Denmark, Naples, and Austria. The most recent Western States have only one to every 5,000 inhabitants; and still are placed on a level with France and Ireland. Russia, stands alone among the civilized countries of the world, and only gives a liberal education to one person in 15,000 of her population.

As a mass, it would appear that the Eastern States provide the advantages of a collegiate education, such as they are in the United States, for a greater proportion of their population than England, or any European countries except Scotland, Baden, and Saxony. The Middle States are as well provided as Wurtemberg, Sweden, and the Netherlands. The Southern States will compare with Switzerland in this respect; and the Western States, with all their destitution, are as well supplied with liberally educated men, so far as *numbers* are concerned, as Denmark and Austria.

One question deserves the attention of those who desire to supply the destitute portions of our country. In view of these calculations, can we believe that the North and East can over produce or educate a sufficient number of liberally educated young men to supply their own vacancies, and the pressing wants which this table presents at the South and West? It is evidently impossible; and the utmost which the more advanced states can hope to do, will be to furnish the men necessary to organise and direct the new institutions which must be formed or extended, in

Comparison of the Number of Students in the United States with That of the Countries of Europe

The number of *Academical* Students in the United States is here estimated at 3,475; Theological Students, 663; Legal, 88; Medical, not far from 2,000. They belong to the several States as here apportioned. For want of data, however, the Medical and Legal Students were divided among the various States according to their respective population.

American States	No. of Students	Proportion to Inhab.		European Countries	No. of Students	Proportion to Inhab.	
Massachusetts	770	1	792	Scotland	3,249	1	683
Connecticut	327	1	960	Baden	1,399	1	816
New Hampshire	241	1	1,118	Saxony	1,360	1	1,040
Vermont	186	1	1,509	England	10,549	1	1,132
Maine	238	1	1,611	Hanover	1,203	1	1,303
New Jersey	193	1	1,661	Bavaria	2,593	1	1,312
South Carolina	325	1	1,789	Tuscany	909	1	1,402
Pennsylvania	688	1	1,928	Spain	9,867	1	1,414
New York	986	1	1,940	Prussia	6,236	1	1,470
Rhode Island	50	1	1,944	Wurtemberg	887	1	1,731
Maryland	175	1	2,554	Sweden and Norway	2,687	1	1,732
Virginia	457	1	2,650	Portugal	1,604	1	1,879
Kentucky	249	1	2,766	Netherlands	2,998	1	1,979
Georgia	173	1	2,985	Sardinia	1,722	1	2,420
Mississippi	45	1	3,040	Switzerland	767	1	2,655
North Carolina	233	1	3,170	Denmark	578	1	3,342
Tennessee	211	1	3,245	Naples and Sicily	2,065	1	3,590
Ohio	285	1	3,290	Austria	8,584	1	3,786
Louisiana	46	1	3,335	France	6,196	1	5,140
Delaware	23	1	3,336	Ireland	1,254	1	5,707
Alabama	84	1	3,634	Russia	3,626	1	15,455
Missouri	28	1	5,003				
Indiana	65	1	5,101				
Illinois	28	1	5,624				

Sections of the United States				European Countries			
Eastern States	1,748	1	1,118	England	10,549	1	1,132
Middle States	1,995	1	1,844	Portugal	1,604	1	1,879
Southern States	1,485	1	2,612	Switzerland	767	1	2,655
Western States	957	1	3,516	Naples and Sicily	2,065	1	3,590
United States*	6,185	1	2,078	Western Europe	60,634	1	2,285

*In the American Quarterly Register for February, 1852, page 185—as said to be collected from the statistics of the institutions—we find the following estimates.

Number of Colleges in the United States, 59 (of which 12 are in New-England States, 13 in the Middle States, 15 in the Southern States, and 19 in the Western States and Territories); Theological Institutions, 22; Medical Schools, 18; Law Schools, 5;—Whole number of Instructors, 400.

Students in the Classical departments, 4,100; Medical departments, 1,863; Law departments, 88; Theological departments at 18 of the Institutions, 709; Total, 6,760.

Proportion to the Population: New England, 1 College Student to 1,331 inhabitants; Middle States, 1 College Student to 3,465 inhabitants; Southern States, 1 College Student to 7,232 inhabitants; Western States and Territories, 1 College Student to 7232 inhabitants; Western States and Territories, 1 College Student to 6,060 inhabitants.

Population of the Eastern States, 1,954,615—Middle, 3,658,698—Southern, 3,878,384—Western, 3,364-671.—Total, 12,856,004.

order to meet the demands of a population, now comparatively destitute, and every week becoming more destitute by its unparalleled increase. We would again remind the Patriots and the Philanthropists, and the Christians of the Atlantic States, that, *the West*, before the end of this century, *must govern the East—* must decide the fate of the Union. Does not their interest as well as their duty, call them to provide the best and most ample means for the education of their *future rulers?*

The comparative state of Common School Instruction is very different from that of Collegiate Instruction. In this, the United States have the pre-eminence, whether we compare them with the mass of European countries, or select individual examples. The Edinburgh Review admitted many years since, that 'The great body of the American people is better educated (instructed) than the mass of *any European community.*' The following table derived from the best sources, shews the proportion of children who receive Common School Instruction to the whole population, in several European countries, and in several of the United States, and furnishes statistical evidence of the truth of this remark.

Proportion of Pupils in Common Schools to the Whole Population

	Pupil	Inhab.
Wurtemberg	1 to	6
Canton Vaud, Switzerland	1 to	6.6
Bavaria	1 to	7
Prussia	1 to	7
Netherlands	1 to	9.7
Scotland	1 to	10
Austria	1 to	13
England	1 to	15.3
France	1 to	17.6
Ireland	1 to	18
Portugal	1 to	88
Russia	1 to	367
New York	1 to	3.9
Mass., Maine, Conn., estimated	1 to	4
All New England, at least	1 to	5
Pennsylvania, N. Jersey	1 to	8
Illinois	1 to	13
Kentucky	1 to	21

It will be seen in examining this table, that the proportion of children receiving Common School Instruction in New York and the Eastern States, is greater than in any country of the civilized world. So unusual is the proportion in New York, that Schwartz, the distinguished German historian of education, could

scarcely believe it correct. In Pennsylvania and New Jersey, whose destitution is the subject of so much well-founded regret and anxiety, the mass are still better taught than in most countries of Europe better than in Scotland itself; and even the Western States will soon have as much of common instruction as France. Still we should feel, that the neglect which may be for the time, safe in a despotism, is ruinous in a republic; for it undermines the basis of free institutions.

With regard to the *extent* of the instruction afforded in the common schools of the two continents, the comparison cannot be a general one. The common schools of the Eastern and Middle States, undoubtedly afford more extended instruction than those of most European countries. Geography and Grammar are extensively taught there. History is found in many of them; and in some, the attempt is made to give them a little knowledge of Natural History. All this would be deemed utterly superfluous in the instruction of the common people of most European countries; and as it is conducted in many of our schools, it certainly deserves the charge of superficiality, which is brought against it. But this is a defect in the modes of instruction, by no means essential to the plan, in a country where the comparatively easy circumstances of the whole community permit more time to be devoted to school instruction, and where republican institutions leave the door to office and influence open to all.

On the other hand, in the schools of Germany and Switzerland, a *practical* and *thorough* character is given to common school education which is not generally to be found in ours. The knowledge of the minerals, soils, plants and animals around them, and of the simple principles of agriculture, is deemed highly important. *Linear drawing* as the means of forming the eye, and as a supplement to writing, and *Music* as a means of cultivating the voice and the ear, are deemed essential to the education, even of a Swiss peasant, in the improved schools. In these respects, public opinion in this country, as in most European countries, is yet to be formed; but it is hoped that the efforts made in some of our schools, and the happy effects which have followed, will be the means of convincing those who confine their views and wishes to mere mechanical instruction, of the imperfection of the plan, and the importance of a more liberal course in the institutions of a free people.

In one respect perhaps, our schools differ from those of *every other Christian country—*

we mean in the great or entire neglect of *moral* and *religious instruction,* which is justly deemed as much more important than mere secular knowledge, as the character is more important than the talents. We should deeply regret any attempt to introduce *Theology* into our common schools; but we do hope the time will come, when it shall be felt, in accordance with the opinion so frequently expressed in public bodies of our enlightened men, that *the Bible* is a more essential book to the young than the Grammar or the Geography, and that a knowledge of JEHOVAH, is more important than any degree of familiarity with Jupiter and the gods of Greece and Rome.

Heman Humphrey   1835

Education in Scotland: Implications for the United States

Heman Humphrey (1779–1859) graduated from Yale College in 1805, was a minister in Pittsfield, Massachusetts, for some six years, and served as president of Amherst College from 1823 to 1845. In 1835 he traveled extensively through Scotland, England, and Ireland and visited France and Belgium. Humphrey's interests in both theology and higher education are discernible in the extract below on Scottish education, which gives a useful historical description coupled with a perceptive analysis of contemporary schooling. In much of his writing Humphrey took pains to contrast and compare educational conditions and needs in Europe with those prevailing in America. His account of primary education and school attendance in Scotland was not entirely complimentary, but it was based on reports and statistics furnished him by competent British informants.

The parochial schools of Scotland have been the admiration of enlightened men in all countries for two hundred and fifty years. Like civil and religious liberty, and all the noble institutions of that country, they are the offspring of the Reformation. Before John Knox rolled back the thunders of the Vatican upon the pope and his cardinals, and blew that mighty blast which shook down the walls of the spiritual Babylon in North Britain, the people were as deeply sunk in ignorance as they were in the superstition and idolatry of the great anti-christian apostacy. Very few, except the nobility, could read, and almost none could write. But as soon as Scotland had thrown off the Romish yoke, or rather, while she was struggling for life with "the man of sin," and the faggots were scarcely quenched in the Grass Market of Edinburgh, the reformers were busily employed in maturing a plan for the diffusion of letters throughout the country. They rightly judged, that to eradicate the errors of popery, and instil the faith of the Gospel into the hearts of the rising generation, the establishment of schools under pious teachers was essential. How anxious they were to see a school-house planted by the side of every kirk, and to make sound learning the handmaid of pure religion, is strikingly manifest in the following extracts from the "First Book of Discipline," drawn up by Knox and his immortal compeers, Winram, Spottiswood, Douglas, Willeck, and Row, and presented to the nobility in 1560, almost three centuries ago.

"Seeing that God has determined that his kirk here on earth shall be taught, not by angels, but by men; and seeing that men are born ignorant of God and godliness; and seeing, also, that he ceaseth to illuminate men miraculously, of necessity it is, that your honors be most careful for the virtuous education, and godly bringing up of the youth of this realm. For, as they must succeed us, so we ought to be careful that they have knowledge and erudition to profit and comfort that which ought to be most dear to us, to wit, the kirk and spouse of our Lord Jesus Christ. Of necessity, therefore, we judge it, that every several kirk have one school-master appointed; such an one at least, as is able to teach grammar and the Latin tongue, if the town be of any reputation. And further, we think it expedient, that in every notable town there should be erected a *college,* in which the arts, at least of rhetoric and logic, together with the tongues, be read, by sufficient masters, for whom honest stipends

Heman Humphrey, *Great Britain, France and Belgium: A Short Tour in 1835* (New York: Harper and Brothers, 1838), II, 131–144.

must be appointed; as also that provision be made for those that are poor, and not able, by themselves or their friends, to be sustained at letters.

"The rich and potent may not be permitted to suffer their children to spend their youth in a vain idleness, as heretofore they have done; but they must be exhorted, and by the censure of the kirk compelled to dedicate their sons by good exercises to the profit of the kirk and commonwealth; and this they must do, because they are able. The children of the poor must be supported and sustained on the charge of the kirk, trial being taken whether the spirit of docility be in them or not. If they be found apt to learning and letters, they may not be permitted to reject learning, but must be charged to continue their study, so that the commonwealth may have some comfort by them. And for this purpose must discreet, grave, and learned men be appointed to visit schools, for the trial of their exercise, profit, and continuance; to wit, the ministers and elders, with the best learned men in every town. A certain time must be appointed to reading and the catechism, and a certain time to grammar and the Latin tongue, and a certain time to the arts of philosophy and the other tongues, and a certain time to that study in which they intend chiefly to travel for the profit of the commonwealth, which time having expired, the children should either proceed to farther knowledge, or else they must be set to some handicraft or some other profitable exercise."

This is a very remarkable document. I very much question whether the whole history of human improvement can furnish the outline of an educational system at once so comprehensive, so simple, and so much in advance of the age in which it was drawn up; and certainly there is nothing which more strikingly shows what a wide difference there is between the genius of Protestantism and Popery. That the men who had themselves been taught to consider "ignorance as the mother of devotion," should all at once have such enlargement of views in regard to education, as soon as the light of the Reformation dawned upon their minds, and that they should find time to mature so wise a plan, while they were obliged to dispute every inch of ground with the enemy, and while, as yet, the conflict between darkness and light hung in such awful suspense, is truly wonderful. It would almost seem as if there must have been something supernatural in the illumination which guided them; for they could have derived but little assistance from the most enlightened nations whether ancient

or modern; and to this day, no material improvement has been made upon their system. If we did not know that our Puritan forefathers brought it along with them to New England, the similarity is so striking, that no one could doubt its Scottish origin, and the Prussian system of popular education, the most perfect and efficient probably, which the world ever saw, is manifestly indebted to the same source for all its essential elements.

It is not to be wondered at, perhaps, that a plan of religious and literary education so novel, and so much in advance of every thing else, gained its way slowly to that governmental patronage, which was thought essential to give it a fair trial. The views of Knox and his associates, thus promulgated in 1560, seem to have been for a long time regarded by the nobility, (to use their own phrase,) as "a devout imagination," and it was not till 1616, that James VI., hoping thereby to give popularity to Episcopacy, which he was striving to foist into the place of the Kirk in Scotland, sought to give effect to the system of the reformers by an act of Privy Council. Seventeen years after, in the reign of Charles I, it was still more formally recognized by act of Parliament.

But the church of Scotland did not wait these tardy and sinister movements of the government. Those good men, who saw so early and so clearly what was necessary to lay the foundations of Protestantism broad and deep throughout the country, determined to do what they could for the establishment of parochial schools, however neglectful the civil rulers might be of their duty. While they expostulated with the nobility for their supineness, they exerted themselves, as if all the hopes of Scotland depended on their efforts;— in so much, that in the Lowlands especially, popular education had made great progress, before the state came to their aid. It is stated in a document still extant, that only twenty years after the reformation, "so great had been the progress of religious instruction in the country where forty years before, the Bible was not suffered to be read, that almost every house possessed a copy, and that it was read in it."

In Dr. McCrie's Life of Melville, there is a Report of the visitation of parishes in the diocese of St. Andrews, in the year 1611 and 1613, to this effect, "That the parishes which had schools, were more than double in number to those that wanted them. Where they were wanting the visitors ordered them to be set up; and where the provision for the master was inadequate, they made arrangements for remedying the evil. This was the principle on which Scotland long acted; and by the moral machinery of pastors, school-masters, elders, deacons, and catechists, this country, which, in the fifteenth and sixteenth centuries, was the most barbarous and bigoted of European nations, and the devoted slave of the papacy, and whose priesthood held two-thirds of the landed property of the kingdom became, in the seventeenth and eighteenth centuries, the most thoroughly reformed and best educated nation in Europe.''

In 1646, when the Presbyterians had fully regained the ascendency, the Scottish Parliament passed an act requiring every parish to have a school-master, and ordaining, that if in any case, *heritors* or land holders neglected raising means for his support, the Presbytery should nominate twelve men to make the assessment upon their property. Indeed, strange as it may appear, the period between 1638 and 1660 seems almost entitled to be called the golden age of popular education in Scotland. In the universal diffusion of *religious* instruction it was decidedly so. "For," says *Kirkton*, a very respectable church historian of the times, "every parish had a minister, every village a school, every family almost had a Bible; yea, in most of the country, all the children of age could read, and were provided with Bible either by their parents or ministers. I have lived many years in a parish where I never heard an oath—and you would not, for a great part of the country, have lodged in a family where the Lord was not worshipped by reading, singing, and prayer. Nobody," he quaintly adds, "complained more of our church government than our taverners, whose ordinary lament was that their trade was hopeless; people were becoming so sober.''

It was thus by planting the school by the side of the kirk, that the reformed clergy raised the people of Scotland, both from feudal bondage and spiritual thraldom; and most grateful was the return which they every where received. During that period, school teaching was a *regular profession,* as much so as that of the ministry, and men were educated for it. Piety, no less than learning and aptness to teach, was regarded as an essential qualification in a school-master. The parish school was the nursery of the kirk, and the master was expected to co-operate with the minister in all his plans and efforts for the spiritual good of the rising generation. To command the best talents, and to place the teacher on the highest vantage ground in the discharge, of his duties, a house was pro-

vided for his family, and he received a liberal and permanent support. In the sacredness of his office the pastor was above him, but in talents and scholarship the school-master was expected to stand on nearly the same level.

It is this primitive and most desirable system of education which has secured for Scotland, and justly too, the highest meed of praise; and judging from my own impressions before I visited that country, it will scarcely be believed, by those who have not particularly inquired into the subject that during the greater part of the last two centuries, popular education has been on the decline, while her population has nearly trebled, and her wealth has increased a hundred fold. That this is actually the case however, no one I think can doubt, who will look at the statistics collected and prepared with great pains by the editor of the Scottish Guardian, and published three years ago under the superintendence of the Glasgow Education Association, and entitled, "*Scotland a half educated nation, both in quantity and quality!*" It is to this very able pamphlet that I am chiefly indebted for the facts upon which its startling title is based.

The first great shock which was given to the system of parochial schools in Scotland, was at the restoration of Charles II., when one-third of the clergy being driven into exile, the school-masters and catechists followed them, because they would not serve under the new Episcopal Establishment, and although the Revolution in 1688 restored both pastors and teachers to the great advantage of the country, the schools never recovered. The union with England, so auspicious in most respects, seems to have been an injury rather than an advantage to the cause of religion and learning in Scotland; for during more than a century, from 1696 to 1803, while her population and wealth were rapidly on the increase, no addition was made to the number of her schools and churches; and the value of the school-master's stipend had greatly diminished. In 1803, there was still but one school to a parish, however large or populous, and it may well be said that the profession of a teacher had become synonymous with poverty, when it is added; that the maximum salary was £11 2s. 6d. It was soon after raised, however, to £22 4s. 5d., and the minimum to £16 13s. with a house and garden containing about a quarter of an acre. As might have been expected, so pitiful an improvement did not answer the end. The school-master was poor and despised, receiving less for his services than the common artizans of the country, and eking out his miserable subsistence as he could.

As a natural consequence of this lamentable decline, it was found by a Parliamentary Board of Commissioners in 1816, that out of 416,000 inhabitants in the Scottish Highlands and islands, there were 100,000 adults who could neither read nor write. There were 171 parish schools containing only 8,550 scholars. *Two hundred and seventy-four* private schools were found however, which, with the former afforded the means of education to one *sixteenth* of the inhabitants. In all Scotland there were 942 parish schools, and 2,222 private schools; but the whole attendance did not exceed 176,000, that is, not more than a *twelfth* of the entire population was at school. Add to this, that from the smallness of the income in both classes of schools, the *style* of education was found to be very low, and the office of a school-master to be anything but inviting to men of competent education and talents. Some good probably resulted from the commission; for in 1828 the maximum salary was raised by act of Parliament to £35 and the minimum to £27. Still, nothing was done to extend the parochial system. After a hundred and twenty years, the schools remained at the same sacred number of one to each parish.

I should be glad to quote the eloquent requiem (shall I call it?) of the writer before me entire; but I must content myself with extracting a few sentences.

"Much and proudly, do we talk of our parish schools, and often do we eulogise the men who founded them in a barbarous age, and cherished them, amid difficulties and prejudices which we can now but little appreciate; —but what have we done to imitate their patriotism, or give effect to their benevolent designs? It is said that Romans never talked so much about Brutus and liberty as when they crouched most submissively to the will of the imperial tyrants; and surely, never did any age, talk more than the present, about education and the school-master; yet no civilized nation in Europe, is at present doing less to diffuse its blessings, and raise the standard of the qualifications of teachers of youth. We are vain of our past fame, as an educated nation, and talk of the prospective wisdom of men like Knox and Melville; but we are the degenerate descendants of a noble ancestry, who little imagine that the designs which they conceived, should be left well nigh to perish in an age boasting of its superior refinement, gathering wealth without measure —whose merchants live in luxury, unknown

to the ancient princes of Scotland, but who apply the accumulating *wealth and resources* of their country, to every possible purpose under heaven, save that of rendering the educational institutions which they founded adequate to the wants of their country."

In order to obtain a standard, by which to measure the actual condition of any country, in respect to education, it is necessary to ascertain what proportion of the population *ought* to be at school, so as "to ensure universal juvenile education." Now the Glasgow Association, say they find, that in Prussia, the educational age, being between *six* and *fourteen*, the proportion which ought to be at school, is one *sixth*; in the U. States of North America, the educational age, being between *five* and *fifteen*, one *fifth*; the actual school attendance in Prussia, in 1831, fell but a fraction below the estimate. In the State of New York, it was one *fourth*, that is 500,000 out of 2,000,000; and in Connecticut, not far from one *third*. The result to which they come, is, that at least, one *fifth* of the population of Scotland, too, ought to be at school.

"It may be assumed as a fact," says Mr. Dick, in his recent and very valuable work, on Mental Illumination, "that the number of children in any state from the age of *two*, to the age of fifteen years, is about *one-third* of the whole population. We find that in the States of Massachusetts, Maine and Connecticut, North America, there is one out of every *four*, of the population, attending a seminary of instruction. We may, therefore, fix on one *third*, including those, who should be in the infant schools, as the proper proportion. How many seminaries, then, would Scotland require, the population in 1831 being 2,400,000, and the one third, 800,000? Supposing 80 children, at an average, in every school, we must have no less than 10,000 schools, for the efficient instruction of all the youth, from two to fifteen years of age—but 2,500 of these, would be infant schools. According to Mr. Colquhoun's statement, the number of parishes in Scotland is 907, and the parochial schools are 1,005; so that it would be requisite to establish *ten times* the number of schools, that presently exist, in order to [attain] the efficient instruction of the whole population. If there are 1,000 private schools, or 2,000 in all, still we need 8,000 more, or *five times* the number, presently existing."

But let us take the more favorable estimates of the Glasgow Educational Association, already mentioned, and see in what aspect they present the actual state of education in Scotland. The basis, as above, is, that one *fifth* of its population, ought to be at school. The most recent and accurate inquiries, in regard to the educational state of the Highlands and Isles of Scotland, made by order of the General Assembly, show, that but one *tenth* of the population, are at school; that is, about 50,000 out of 500,000. And no less than 83,397 persons, between six and twenty years of age, are returned, as unable to read, either Gælic or English. Of the art of writing, a still greater number know nothing. In 132 parishes of the Lowlands, with a population of 215,000, only 20,000 are at day schools of all sorts—about one *eleventh* part, instead of one *fifth*. According to returns made in 1833, fourteen parishes in Perthshire, with a population of 24,025, had 2,811, or nearly one *seventh,* in school. In the parish of Annan, Dumfriesshire, a *tenth;* in Dundee, a *fifteenth;* in Stranvær, a *ninth;* in Cumbernauld, a *fourteenth,* and in New Monkland, a *twelfth.* The presumption, therefore, is, that even in the Lowland, and Midland counties, which may be regarded as the moral garden of Scotland, not much more than one *tenth,* are at school; that is, *one half* the number that ought to attend.

In the cities and large towns, the case is still more unfavorable. In the parish of Old Maschar, Aberdeen, containing 25,000 souls, at least, there are but a *thousand* children, in a course of primary education; that is, *one twenty-fifth;* in Dundee, one *thirteenth;* in Perth, one *fifteenth;* in one parish of Edinburgh, one *twelfth;* in three parishes of Greenoch, the same; in the large Abbey parish of Paisley, a *thirteenth* or *fourteenth,* and in Glasgow, about the same.

And it would seem that there is as great a deficiency in the *quality,* as in the *quantity* of popular education in Scotland. "The *style* of education," says the author of the able Glasgow report now before me, "may be judged from the remuneration of the teacher, his own education, his standing in the society where he exercises his profession, and the books employed, (used?) in the schools. The average income, from all sources of the parochial teachers in the Highlands, the General Assembly, estimated at £40 a year." In the Lowlands, it is somewhat higher, but still inadequate. The compensation of private teachers, is exceedingly penurious, as they are often obliged to put their fees still lower than are the very small fees of the parish schools, or have no scholars. The consequence is, that but few men of competent talents and education are willing to encounter

the toil and confinement of the school-room; and those of inferior qualifications, who do, are obliged to eke out their starved salaries by engaging in other employments.

The general tone of the Report to which I am so much indebted for the foregoing statistics, with reference to the decline and present alarming depression of popular education in Scotland, may possibly be somewhat too desponding. Nevertheless, it is unquestionably true, that looking at the past history, of the country, and its present condition, its first days after the Reformation were its best. The teachers, as a body, were better educated, better principled and better paid. The rudiments of learning were more universally diffused among the lower classes. A more careful inspection was exercised over the schools, by ministers and elders of the church, and by influential and pious laymen, who took a deep interest in their prosperity. And it is past all controversy, that for fifty years after the down-fall of Popery, thorough Bible instruction held a more prominent place, in the popular education of the country, than it does now, or ever has done since that golden period.

As several respectable Scottish writers have lately given us quite as much credit as we deserve, for the wisdom, liberality and efficiency of our common school systems in New England and New York, it may not be out of place for me just to glance at the subject. It is certainly a matter of high congratulation, that such liberal provision is made for the instruction of the poor; that our children of all classes are so generally sent to school, and that every body is taught to read and write. But it ought to be felt by all the friends of education, that our systems are susceptible of great improvements, and that they are loudly called for.

In the first place, we suffer exceedingly for want of a competent number of able and efficient teachers. And the reason is, our standard is altogether too low, and we keep it down by our penuriousness. Whatever we may demand and expect, and however loudly we may complain that good teachers are not to be had, we should not be willing to pay them if they were. In this case, as in every other, under our free institution, the supply will be in proportion to the urgency of the demand. If men of talents and enterprise were sure of being well paid, as teachers— of making their efforts and their literary acquisitions as productive in the school-house as any where else, the deficiency of which we complain would soon be supplied. But how can we expect it, so long as the wages of a school-master are kept below those of a common journey-man mechanic? Just so long as we compel our teachers to work *cheap*, we must expect to have CHEAP teachers.

In the next place, we suffer exceedingly for want of better systems of supervision. We have boards of education and visiting committees, to be sure. Parents take some interest in the schools, and the clergy, more; but, after all, much more must be done, be-fore we shall see them placed on that high ground which they ought to occupy.

In the last place, (for I cannot pursue the subject,) too little stress, by far, is laid upon the importance of *religious* instruction in our schools. The teachers, whether male or female, ought invariably to be persons of high moral qualifications, and as far as possible, of personal religion; and all our children ought every day to be taught to "fear God and keep his commandments."

Benjamin Smith   1836

Education in Prussia and the Training of Teachers

Benjamin Smith (1811–1893) graduated from Hampden-Sydney College in 1829, taught at the academy in Milton, North Carolina, until 1838, and then entered Union Theological Seminary. In 1836 he visited Europe and spent the major portion of his time in Germany conducting a special year-long study of the Prussian primary school system. Smith prepared a report of his trip for the Virginia House of Delegates in 1839, after similar reports by Victor Cousin and by Calvin Stowe had already been made public in 1831 and 1838 respectively. Although Smith's study had less influence on American education than did the two earlier reports, it did provide, specifically for Southern educators, an up-to-date account of both European education and a system of primary instruction which could be adapted for use in Virginia. His report closes with the admonition: "Let it not be supposed that a servile imitation of other countries is recommended. 'The true greatness of a people does not consist in borrowing nothing from others, but in borrowing from all whatever is good, and in perfecting whatever it appropriates.'"

Your favour of "September 4th, 1838," has been some time before me. You express your conviction, that the "facts" I have collected, and my "observations on the systems of education, pursued in some European countries, may be useful to the general assembly of our own state:" and you therefore, request me to communicate any information, I may possess, on the following topics:

"1. The mode of establishing schools; in Prussia particularly.
2. How the schools are organized.
3. What branches of education are taught.
4. How many months in the year the schools are continued.
5. Expense of tuition to each scholar.
6. What portion is required to be paid by the parent.
7. How teachers are obtained."

You add "with any other information you may consider valuable."

I now undertake, after the least possible delay, to comply with your request.

You are by no means singular, in supposing, that "facts and observations," on the systems of education, pursued in other countries, may be useful to our own; and in your selection of Prussia as the principal country, whose system deserves a detailed and accurate examination and consideration, you have but added your tribute of respect for her efforts in this cause, to those of other enlightened and patriotic statesmen, in this, as well as of the old world.

A few years since the French government deputed an eminent statesman of that kingdom, M. Victor Cousin, to visit Prussia, Wurtemberg, Saxony and the dukedom of Baden, in order to make a personal examination of their systems of education. His reports on the results of this examination, addressed to count Montalivet, minister of public instruction in France, were partially translated in

Benjamin M. Smith, "Report on the Primary School System of Prussia, January 15, 1839," *House Journal* of the Virginia House of Delegates, No. 26 (1839). For a copy of the complete document see also Edgar W. Knight, editor *A Documentary History of Education in the South Before 1860*, 5 vols. (Chapel Hill: The University of North Carolina Press, 1950), II, 410–460.

England, and have been republished in this country. The attention of many intelligent and distinguished men in England and America, was now much excited, to investigate more fully, the statements of these reports. The very fact, that the head of a military despotism had set on foot a system of instruction, designed to benefit every subject in his dominions, had expended large sums (one twenty-fifth part of the annual income of the kingdom being thus appropriated) in the endowment of literary institutions of every grade; in a word, that for forty years he had been engaged in promoting the moral and intellectual improvement of all his people, and that these efforts had been crowned with unexampled success. Such a statement as this, I say, was well calculated to excite the attention of a people who had been accustomed to regard an absolute monarch as a mere arbitrary despot, and to consider the security of his power as based in the ignorance of the people. The occasional reports of travellers through Germany, had already called attention to this new feature in the policy of despotism, but the information thus presented was not minute nor sufficiently extensive. To verify the statements of M. Cousin, several intelligent gentlemen from this country and England have repaired to Prussia, and given the subject a personal examination. Dr. Julius of Hamburg, known in the United States and England as the deputy of the Prussian government, to examine the penitentiary systems of this country, was invited to lay before a committee of the British parliament, such information as he possessed respecting the Prussian system of public instruction. In 1836, the legislature of Ohio deputed an eminent professor in a literary institution of that state, to make investigations on this topic, during a contemplated tour of Europe. The report which he presented on his return, was extensively circulated in Ohio, and an edition of 12,000 copies published and circulated in Pennsylvania, by order of the legislature.

The information thus laid before various legislative bodies, and the community at large, in many places, besides those referred to, has already served very important purposes; for although no one would suppose the institutions of one country can be exactly adapted to another, and much less those of a monarchy or military despotism, to a republic, yet many valuable hints can be derived, and much valuable aid obtained, from the experience of those who have been longer engaged in any special undertaking than we

have. And it is pleasant to the philanthropist to observe, that while Prussia was condescending, she might suppose, to learn from our infant republic the best methods of governing and reclaiming the refractory and abandoned, while the autocrat of Russia was disseminating among his people the publications of an American tract society, we, on the other hand, were willing to gather instruction on the establishment of schools from the military despot of Berlin. May the time soon come, when every species of national intercourse shall serve but to promote mutual benefit and the good of all!

But while, as we shall have occasion to notice, a very great zeal has been awakened on the subject of education, by these and other causes, in the United States, it may not be out of place to present some general views of the state of public instruction in some portions of continental Europe.

The smaller German states have already adopted a system, similar in its leading features to that of Prussia. In its practical operation, the system has advanced to a greater degree of perfection, perhaps, in the kingdom of Wurtemberg, and the duchy of Baden, than in Prussia itself. Bavaria is by no means behind it, and the kingdom of Saxony is in some features of her system superior. In the strong-hold of legitimacy and despotism, Austria, we find an edict by the emperor, with characteristic arbitrariness, stating, that "no person shall henceforth be permitted to marry, who cannot read, write and cypher." He is, however, benevolently providing means, by which all his subjects may comply with these requisitions.

Switzerland has, for some years, presented a most interesting field of observation to the friend of education. One man, the celebrated Fellenberg, has devoted his time, talents and wealth to this cause for thirty or forty years. His establishment at Hofwyl, near Berne, was commenced in the early part of this century, and has gradually increased, till it embraces institutions for every grade of academic study, from the high school down. His most useful labours have been those for improving the condition of schools by means of a teacher's seminary. With the high schools for the sons of the wealthy, he combined a gymnastic establishment and a manual labour department, for teaching the most useful mechanic arts and agriculture. This latter department is common to all the pupils, and many among the poor have materially aided themselves by their own labour. I cannot here give the details of this system. He has been extensively patronized by gentlemen in this country and England, and at one time numbered among his pupils several sons of the nobility in France and protégés of the emperor of Russia. The canton of Berne, and other parts of Switzerland, have reaped the most beneficial fruits of his exertions, in the improvement of the primary school teachers.

The new school law of France, the result of the combined talents and exertions of those celebrated men, Cousin, Montalivet and Guizot, has already produced decided changes in the policy of that kingdom. Up to 1828, the French government granted annually, the pitiful sum of $12,000 for primary schools, with a population of 30 millions.

In 1828, this sum was quintupled, and the government of "July 1830" has raised it, first to $140,000 and finally to $200,000 annually. This is but a beginning, and is only mentioned as an index of the interest already awakened. The vigorous and enlightened efforts of the present monarch, and those of his successor, should he be soon called to the throne, will doubtless effect more in the next ten years, than has been accomplished in the last, or any previous period; and we may hope to see this land of "political miracles," the subject of more beneficial and thorough revolutions, in the true basis of political prosperity, than she has ever yet undergone. It is with no common interest that we contemplate the efforts of the Russian emperor to expedite the adoption of a scheme of education, similar to the Prussian, in all parts of his vast dominions.

The empire over which he rules, mighty in resources, and commanding by position an influence on the three great branches of the white race, is, like our nation, one of yesterday, when compared with England and France. It is wearisome to imagination to predict its destiny and the future influence it will exert on the world. The present emperor, a son-in-law of the king of Prussia, has adopted his policy, and determined to reign in the hearts of his people. With despotism in any form, we republicans can have no sympathy, but if there can be a palliation, for such an institution, it must be afforded by such examples of the exercise of its power, as these afford. We may justly admire the benevolent effort, and its beneficial results, while we condemn the motive. The Russian system of education need not be delineated, since its most substantial parts, are but copies of the Prussian. A few facts, to evince the zealous co-operation of all classes, with the emperor and

minister, may be here stated, and thus also illustrating the interest in this subject, which pervades the northern and middle Europe.

Individuals in Siberia, and other portions of the empire, contribute from two to six thousand dollars, for the establishment of primary schools. One in Lialsk, has given as much as 10,000. In Novgorod the nobility contribute 12,000, and at Wologda, 9,000 annually to the gymnasia of those towns. In some places the citizens volunteer to support the schools, and one individual, besides procuring the erection of a schoolhouse, has contributed 2,000 dollars towards the support of the teacher. In Petersburg is a model school for teachers, from which 75 are annually sent out. Meanwhile, efforts are making, by awarding premiums to authors, to secure the best school books for children, and those of this country and Prussia are often translated, and adapted to Russia. Students from the Russian dominions are to be found in the German universities, preparing for usefulness at home, and those from the remote provinces, who devote themselves to teaching, are brought to Petersburg free of expense, to pursue their studies. There are already 6 universities, 67 gymnasia, 12,000 public, and 430 private primary schools in operation.

If any thing *can* compensate unhappy Poland for the oppressions of Russian despotism, the diffusion of the blessings of education may be expected to contribute greatly towards such a compensation; and she already enjoys a full share, in the exertions made in behalf of the whole empire.

But not only in Germany, France and Russia, do we discover developments of an unusual interest in this cause. Even the sultan of Turkey and pacha of Egypt, among other imitations of Christian civilization, are establishing schools and introducing the cultivation of the liberal sciences into their dominions. But recently, the latter, the most remarkable man of his age, perhaps, has instituted a female school of 100 pupils, in his seraglio, and procured an English lady to superintend it. In Paris and London, Turks and Egyptians, Greeks and Arabs, are to be found prosecuting studies preparatory for the business of instruction in their own countries.

Looking back to northern Europe, we discover Denmark, Sweden and Norway, with England and Scotland, either nationally or by individual efforts, evincing the most lively concern for the interests of popular education.

I may add to all this, respecting foreign countries, that an extraordinary interest on this subject has been exhibited in our own country. Already can several states proclaim that complete provision is made for the education of all their citizens. Ohio has introduced the Prussian school system so far as it respects seminaries for teachers. Similar institutions are recommended by Governor Ritner, in his recent message to the legislature of Pennsylvania; and their connexion with the academies of the state, has been proposed in New York. Kentucky and Tennessee have already entered on the adoption of systems contemplating provisions for the whole population of those states, and while penning these remarks, I learn that a bill has been reported to the Legislature of North Carolina, proposing a district free school system, for the whole state. In short, every portion of the civilized world, seems to be awake to the interests of general education.

Our national and sectional reviews, periodical pamphlets, and newspapers, have volunteered a very efficient aid in diffusing information on the subject of education, and every year we are flooded with addresses, speeches, reports of conventions and teachers' associations, all bearing on the same topic.

I rejoice too, that in Virginia, the flourishing state of some of our colleges and academies, not to mention the university, and the rapid increase of well conducted female schools, betoken a degree of interest in the general subject, far from lukewarm, while the determined effort, which you speak of making for primary schools, during the present winter, assures the public of your deep interest in this noble cause. I duly appreciate the honour you do me, in asking my aid, and while I feel unable to offer any "observations," or suggest any "plan," I readily undertake the humbler part of imparting such information as my opportunities have placed at my disposal. In the progress of my tour in Europe, I visited Saxony, Hanover, Baden and Wurtemberg, besides some other smaller states of Germany, Switzerland, France and England, remaining, however, but a short period, from four to ten weeks in each: and resided nearly a year in Prussia. By conversations with intelligent travellers from every part of Europe, and numerous reports and similar publications, I was enabled to procure the elements of such general statements as those already made. In Prussia, however, I enjoyed opportunities to verify by personal observation, the information derived from others, and add to it, the results of my own inquiries. I shall therefore be able to speak with more confidence of this country, and feel better prepared to answer your inquiries, which relate particularly to its institutions.

The present King of Prussia, doubtless deserves great credit for his exertions in the cause of education. But we are not to consider him solely responsible. The Germans have been generally distinguished for a literary spirit from the earliest periods of modern civilization. Their physical location, conspiring with the despotic nature of their governments, have driven them to seek distinction in literary pursuits. It was in Germany too, that the human mind was so violently agitated by the religious controversies of the 16th and 17th centuries. There the art of printing began to shed its lustre on the world. Many of its universities, now most celebrated, have been the offspring of modern zeal; but not a few of those still remain, whose foundations were laid in the remote darkness of the middle ages.

Frederick William, the elector, at the close of the 17th century, introduced many important improvements into his electorate for the benefit of his people, and among others, established and patronized many literary institutions of a minor grade than universities, very nearly resembling the present gymnasia of Germany. His immediate successor was too busy with the novel pomps of royalty, which his vanity had caused him to assume, and William Frederick I, too parsimonious to extend any liberal encouragement to education. Frederick the great, not only found time for personal attention to literary pursuits, but gave a rapid impulse to the study of the classics, and established and improved the high schools and universities. The short and inert course of Frederick William II, need not be noticed. The present king commenced his reign with a determined spirit of improving the condition of the lower classes. How much influence the French revolution exerted on his views of their importance, I stay not to enquire. In the very acme of national distress, in 1809, he began his preparations of extending the blessings of education to his people by introducing important changes in their political condition. The peasantry, till 1810 denied ownership in the soil, were permitted to become freeholders on liberal terms. The power of the nobles was broken, and the rare spectacle was presented, of but one step, from the throne of a hereditary and absolute monarchy, to the cottage. For a thorough reform of the body politic was commenced, based on these, among other principles: "That *equality before the law be secured*," *irrespective of rank* "*to every subject; justice be rigidly and punctually administered; and that, by the education of* THE PEOPLE, *and the spread of true religion, the general interests, and a national spirit be promoted, as the only sure basis of the national welfare.*"

Though furnished with a standing army of 50,000, with despotic irresponsible power, and obsequious servants, no effort was made to enforce any of the regulations for the promotion of education which followed these preliminary steps. Advancing from one position to another, introducing one plan after another, preparing the way for improvement before its annunciation, and interesting in his plans, some of the wisest and best men of his kingdom, he has in 30 years, brought into active operation, a system of public instruction, which neglects no child in his dominions, embracing a population of 12,000,000, with varieties of religion, national prejudice, language and habits.

The political divisions of the kingdom are, 1st, ten provinces, 2d, 26 regencies, 3d, three hundred and forty-five counties (or circles), 4, an indeterminate number of parishes (or communities) into which these counties are subdivided, and which vary in size, according to the density of population.

Formerly, whatever related to the cause of education, in the administration of the government, was assigned to the minister of the interior. By the present king, a separate department has been formed; "the ministry for public instruction, ecclesiastical and medicinal affairs." The minister in this department has for his assistance, a council composed of eminent ecclesiastics, physicians and professors, together forming a consistory. This is divided into three sections or boards, one for each interest: that for ecclesiastical affairs, composed chiefly of ecclesiastics, with a director at their head: that for public instruction, composed chiefly of laymen, with a director, and that for medicine, composed chiefly of medical men, with a director.

The number of each board is undetermined. A member of one may be a member of one or both the others, but with no increase of salary. Our attention is engaged only by the board for public instruction.

This consists at present of twelve members, whose salaries are $3500 to the director, and $22,000 for the other eleven. This board meets twice a week. By correspondence, official reports from lower authorities,

(to be mentioned below), individual knowledge, or proposition, or the agency of the minister, business is brought before them, and their decisions are in all cases final, with ministerial and royal approbation. Besides a general oversight of public instruction throughout the kingdom, this board has an immediate control over the universities. By means of a royal commissary, appointed by the minister, a correspondence is kept up between this officer and every university. They elect their senates or local governments, under the superintendence of this commissary.

On the other hand, the gymnasia, or institutions of secondary instruction, occupying a rank equal to that of our colleges, excepting the power to confer degrees, are placed under the immediate supervision of

Provincial Boards.—These correspond in the local governments of the provinces to the board of public instruction in the central administration. Here, however, the president of the province is at once director of the provincial consistory and of this board, which constitutes a part of it. This officer is merely the executive of the board, that possessing all the authority. Through him, a correspondence on all matters connected with education is carried on by the board on the one hand, and the minister on the other.

Attached to this board is an examining committee composed of professors in the university of the province, or that nearest to it, should there be none, whose duties are 1. To examine all pupils of the gymnasia, who design entering the university, or engaging in any literary pursuit controlled by the state. 2. To examine applicants for the offices of instructors in the gymnasia, whether rectors, professors or teachers.

Under the supervision of this board are also placed the teachers' seminaries, and all institutions of a grade above primary schools, and under universities, as private latin schools, polytechnic schools, and institutions for those who design becoming surgeons of the lower grade, or apothecaries. They have also a general control over the primary schools.

The immediate management of these, however, belongs to the regency, county and parish authorities, and this must now be explained.

In every parish there must be an elementary school, of which the pastor and some of the most considerable men of the place are appointed (partly by the state and partly by the people,) directors. When, however, as in Urban parishes, there exist several schools, and some higher than elementary, termed middle or citizens, schools, the magistracy constitute a *school committee,* presiding at once over the directors and schools, and reducing the whole to a harmonious management. These authorities, then, stand to primary schools in the same relation that the provincial boards do to the gymnasia.

But besides these, there are two other authorities to be noticed. There is for each county a school inspector, who overlooks the committees and directors, and to whom they must submit their whole system of management. He visits each school as often and unexpectedly as possible, besides making an annual formal inspection. He takes cognizance of all complaints, and forms the medium of intercourse between the several local authorities and the provincial boards. There is, however, another officer, a member of the regency council or government, who is placed above the inspectors, as well as schools of the various counties. This officer, styled school councillor, is in fact the true director of primary schools in the several regencies, and corresponds in his relation to them and their local authorities to the minister in his relation to the provincial boards and gymnasia. These two officers are paid.

Such may be termed the machinery of the system. It is seen that the subject of education thus occupies a station of importance equal to that of military or naval affairs, and its concerns are administered with all the promptness and energy which belong to any well conducted department of government. The details are left for local authorities, while general review and control are placed in the hands of the minister. Responsibility is devolved on all, and from the minister down, there are superiors to exact the fulfilment of every prescribed duty.

As your inquiries respect primary schools, particularly, I must omit any notice of the gymnasia and universities, although, in order to describe the governmental regulations for schools, it was necessary to advert to the authorities by whom they are controlled. From abundant data in my possession, it may be in my power at some other time to present a view of their internal organization, similar to that of the primary schools, to which I now call your attention.

It may be proper to observe here, that the government was engaged for ten years in modifying schools already existing and reducing to system the management of all the literary institutions of the country. The present system has not been the work of any

one plan or effort. No less than 226 different edicts on the subject have been issued in 40 years. The law of 1819, prescribing the principal regulations of primary schools, requires that wherever no school previously existed, it should be the duty of the inhabitants of towns and parishes to form school associations and appoint directors and committees under the authority of the officers of the province or county, who should take part in the name of the government in making these appointments. If any parish were unable to support a school, it might unite with one or more others, provided the children should never be obliged to walk more than $2\frac{1}{2}$ English miles. Provisions were also made for the union of different religious sects.

Every town of more than 1500 inhabitants was directed to establish a primary school of higher grade than the parish or elementary schools. If, however, unable to provide both, then the parish school should be merged into the lower classes of the town school. Also, wherever a gymnasium existed, its lower classes might be used as a substitute for the town school, if no separate institution of that grade could be found.

These schools, with others of similar character existing before the law was decreed, were placed under the immediate control of the directors and committees above mentioned. It was made their duty to levy the necessary contributions, with aid from the local magistracy; select and prepare plans of instruction, appoint the teachers, and secure the attendance of all children of a proper age to be at school. These local authorities are not paid. Their meetings must be held once in three months, to which they may invite the teacher. A more extended view of their duties is unnecessary, as it is enough to remark that they are the local executives of the government for carrying into operation every law connected with primary schools, of which they receive official advice by means of the authorities above them. They are immediately responsible to these, and in cases of difficulty with either teachers or people, the appeal may go up to the minister through the intermediate inspector, councillor and provincial board.

It was also provided by the law of 1819, that wherever schools existed before, under the management of persons appointed by their founders, or by them and the parish or church authorities with which they were connected, such might remain under their previous constitution. For all dependent on the royal bounty, the control was reserved to the state.

Every effort to raise the necessary funds for each parish and town school was directed to be made, and "their *claims must not be postponed to any other whatever;*" but if these efforts should not succeed, aid was guaranteed by either the provincial or national governments. Many schools were thus established, which have since exercised an influence on the community so salutary, that they no longer ask or need governmental assistance. This is an excellent commentary on the benefits of the system.

Having thus noticed the mode in which schools are established, let us now advert to those regulations which provide the necessary means for their complete organization. . . .

Teachers

From the law of 1819, which, with my personal observations, forms the principal source of my information on primary schools, I make the following extract: "A schoolmaster, to be worthy of his vocation, must be pious, discreet and deeply impressed with the dignity and sacredness of his calling. He should be thoroughly acquainted with the duties peculiar to the grade of primary instruction, in which he desires to be employed; he should possess the art of communicating knowledge, with that of moulding the minds of children; he should be unshaken in his loyalty to the state, conscientious in the duties of his office, friendly and judicious in his intercourse with the parents of his pupils, and with his fellow-citizens generally, and he should strive to inspire them with a lively interest in the school, and secure to it their favour and support."

To prepare teachers for answering such requisitions, is the object of the teachers' seminaries, of which you will find an account below.

Every applicant for a teachers' place is subjected to examination and probation on the following plan: A committee of examination, consisting of two lay and two clerical members is triennially appointed, whose duty it is to examine all candidates for the office of teacher in the common schools, in a certain district. Since the establishment of teachers' seminaries such a committee is connected with each of them. The notice of the meetings of this committee, are published in the provincial official gazettes. The clerical members conduct the examination on moral and religious character, and religious attainments. As these committees are appointed by the provincial government, the highest ecclesiastical authority of the province, if protestant, and the bishop of the diocese, if catholic, nominating the clerical members, they are directly responsible to the minister of public instruction. Such young men as sustain an examination, receive certificates signed by the committee, and if a graduate of a teacher's seminary, by the teachers of that institution. These certificates are of three grades, *excellent, good* and *sufficient;* and, moreover, define positively the bearer's fitness, whether for a town or village school. The name of the candidate is then entered on a list, copies of which are semi-annually published, for the information of the school directors and committees. Should the young man not be sustained, he may yet be permitted to occupy a lower station in a school as an assistant, be put off, or finally rejected on the spot, according to the degree and nature of his deficiency.

Any one whose name appears on these lists may be appointed. The appointing power rests with the school directors or committees, when the parish or towns support the schools by their unaided resources, with the founders or their trustees, when the school may have been established by private endowment and with the provincial government, when supported wholly by the royal treasury. In every case the brevet or testimonial of appointment, stating the duties of the station and its stipulated emolument, must be ratified by the provincial boards, and minute regulations are made, to secure regularity and an intelligent attention to the business. To dignify the station the teachers are publicly installed, by taking oath to perform their duties faithfully, and a presentation to the pupils, patrons and directors of the school, the municipal authorities, and often to more considerable bodies. They hold their places for life, unless promoted or disgraced and expelled. They are therefore placed under a most vigilant oversight, and subject to admonition, reproof or expulsion. Accusations may be brought against them, for derelictions in official duty, before the school authorities, who constitute a special court of justice in the case. Their decisions are subject to review and confirmation, or repeal, by the provincial authorities, lest local feuds or personal prejudices might procure injustice or oppression. Should the teacher be guilty of crimes for which he is amenable to the civil authority, his condemnation by that, is a virtual expulsion from office.

On the other hand, merit in the performance of his duties, however humble his station, rarely goes unrewarded. Complete lists of all appointments are annually transmitted to the minister, with statements of the income of each teacher, and the meritorious are designated, so that they may be promoted on the occurrence of vacancies, or, as is often the case, receive other marks of special notice and favour. Diligence and propriety of conduct are often rewarded by permission to travel at the expense of government, in order to derive improvement in their business, by inspecting the institutions of other countries. Others, whose opportunities have been slender, are sent to some teachers' seminary for one or two years, and others again are allowed additional salaries. Whatever might tend to lessen the dignity of the teacher in the eyes of the pupils or community, is strictly forbidden. He may not collect fees and gifts from door to door, as was formerly the case, nor engage in any employment of a dirty character, as the more laborious and servile occupations of a farmer's life. Nor can he follow any pursuit calculated to impede or impair his usefulness as a teacher, such as holding any office about a church, or other place which makes too great demands on his time and attention. For similar reasons, the teachers are exempted from serving in the army in time of peace, to that extent which is required of other citizens. In short, no measure is left unused to invest the office and character of the teacher with that dignity and importance, which are often denied them, but which they intrinsically merit everywhere. One additional item may be here inserted, that the government every where encourages the formation of teachers' associations for mutual consultation and improvement.

From a table now before me, I take the maximum and minimum, and averages of *salaries* allowed teachers of primary schools in towns and villages.

Those in the former or middle (citizens') schools, receive from thirty-five to eight hundred and forty dollars annually; those in the latter, from seven to three hundred and fifty. The average of the former, in the several regencies, ranges from seventy-one to four hundred and thirty-five dollars annually; of the latter, from twenty-one to one hundred and six. The averages for the whole kingdom are, for schoolmasters in towns, a hundred and fifty dollars annually, and in the village schools, sixty. These averages are based on the returns for 1821. But decided improvements have been since made, and the average for the latter, is now nearly eighty dollars, and for the former, a hundred and seventy. Indeed, but few masters of schools may be considered as penuriously supported; and the minimum salaries here noticed pertain generally to assistants and those females who, perhaps, as daughters or wives of the head teachers, are not entirely dependent. It must also be added, that in addition to these salaries, the head teachers are furnished with a house and two acres of land, and if bad, more for a garden and other purposes connected with a domestic establishment. They are moreover exempted from certain parochial taxes and charges, and from military service to a great extent in time of peace, and above all, at their death their widows and children are comfortably provided for; or should they outlive their ability to be useful, the feebleness and decrepitude of age are humanely remembered, and they are not permitted to want.

But after all, these salaries are not so small for Prussia, however they may appear to us. Provisions are absolutely cheaper than with us, and the advantages arising from a great advance in the arts and conveniences connected with domestic economy, reduce the price of living to a rate almost incredible. Wealth too, is a comparative term, and the poorest schoolmaster is often more independent than many of his patrons. The variations in the salaries of villages and towns need no explanation.

Tuition fees are included in these salaries, though in many cases they form a bare trifle, in others, are exceedingly moderate, and seldom exceed 25 cents monthly, even in towns. In particular cases they may be remitted entirely, though this is discouraged on the principle that "we value most, that for which we pay." Hence, in many cases, it is fixed at about $2\frac{1}{2}$ cents a month. . . .

Seminaries for Teachers

The last topic of enquiry presented in your letter will now be considered. You ask, "How are teachers obtained?"

Formerly, schoolmasters were appointed by the parish authorities, without any previous examination on their literary qualifications, excepting their knowledge of the catechism, and ability to read, write, sing and cypher. Numbers employed in keeping sheep in the summer, were transferred to the business of *keeping school* in the winter. The nobility who held some appointments, often conferred them on their valets and grooms, as rewards for services. Unsuccessful mechanics and merchants often supplied the place of teachers in the lowest schools, and disappointed candidates for the learned professions assumed the office of instructors in those of more elevated character. In short, the whole business was conducted very loosely, and often he who was good for nothing else, "would do" for an office of the most delicate and difficult nature.

In 1748, an institution for the instruction of teachers, was founded by a benevolent gentleman of Berlin, which in a few years received royal notice and patronage. The pupils were mostly young mechanics, who were scattered in various parts of the city, and much impeded in their studies by other avocations. Yet the institution did well in its time.

Frederick II. appropriated $2000 annually, (in 1771,) for the improvement of country schools, declaring that "primary education had been too much neglected: it is imperative to remove bad masters and replace them by competent men." As he had removed native custom house officers to make way for those imported from France, he ordered, with similar arbitrariness, that teachers should be brought from Saxony. But good teachers were not always to be had in Saxony. Frederick could theorize as a philosopher, and fight as a soldier, but he lacked patience and perseverance to contend with prejudice, and things went on very much as before till 1810, except in the province of Brandenburg, where partial success had attended the efforts of individuals and the local authorities, in establishing several of these institutions. At this period great improvements were made in the original school in Berlin; and after being adopted by the government, it was removed to Potsdam and reorganized under the uniform system which I shall now explain.

The government assumes the organization and support of these institutions. In some cases, private liberality had already endowed such schools to a partial extent, as seen above; in others, they have arisen on foundations designed for other purposes; and in others, they receive contributions from the regency governments in which they are established, or from benevolent individuals.

Their government is in the hands of the provincial school boards, under the inspection of the minister and central board. Every institution reports annually, the number, health, order, discipline, and morality of the pupils, together with the number and changes of instructors, the results of examinations, and any interesting occurrences connected with the school; also its wants, and suggestions as to its improvement. The frequent publication of these reports awakens and preserves a lively interest in their behalf, communicates a spirit of laudable emulation to the several schools, and diffuses through the community useful information on the science of instruction and the art of education.

Before proceeding to describe these schools, I will remark that clergymen or teachers of skilful character may train up masters for primary schools by permission of the provincial boards. This regulation is necessary, as there is yet a deficiency of these institutions. Every encouragement possible is held out to young men desirous of teaching to frequent some teachers' seminary; and one powerful inducement has recently been proposed, by making the graduates of such more eligible to places than others. Besides the great teachers' seminaries, as they are styled, of which I shall now speak, there are numerous establishments of similar character, though of lower grade and smaller size, designed to prepare teachers for the very poorest villages. These are greatly aided by government, as well as private liberality. In describing the larger, I shall of course describe these, so far as they rise in character to the standard of the former.

Every seminary for teachers must be furnished with *buildings* sufficient to accommodate the director and his family, the steward and his, and the teachers, whether married or single, if possible, together with all the pupils, so that the latter may constantly be under the eyes of their preceptors. Connected with these buildings must be a garden, bath houses, mechanic shops and grounds for gymnastic exercises.

They must, of course, be provided with the necessary apparatus for scientific instruction.

Instructors

A *director* and as many *assistants* as necessary constitute the faculty of each seminary. The number of the latter is of course varied —generally five or six—though sometimes not more than two, and sometimes as many as thirteen are needed. Five may be considered a fair average. The selection of directors has been made from the ranks of gymnasial teachers, or from those of the learned professions, where individuals may have distinguished themselves by their knowledge of the science of instruction, or otherwise manifested a peculiar aptitude for conducting such institutions. Hereafter these seminaries will supply their own teachers, while supplying those for the primary schools. The qualifications necessary for the regular instructors are of course those necessary for the highest grade of instruction in those institutions for which those seminaries design to prepare teachers. That is, they must be acquainted with the various branches of instruction in those schools; but they must, in order to give proper aid to those preparing to teach, possess a more thorough and accurate knowledge of each branch than if only required to teach children. A knowledge of the Latin and some modern languages is also required of the principal assistants.

Pupils and Course of Study

The *age* at which *pupils* may be received is seventeen or eighteen; though older persons may be admitted. None can enter younger. In order to [gain] admission, they must have received a good primary school education, must be sound of body, of good moral character, must possess musical talents and have improved them, so far as the acquisition of the art of singing, and the ability of performing on the piano forte and violin. The request for admission, must be presented the director, some time previous to that of entrance, and be accompanied by certificates to the possession of the above named qualifications, and also a promise of the father or guardian, or some responsible person, to guarantee the payment of the sum required for admission, in cases where any such requisition is made. Besides these provisions to prevent the admission of improper candidates, every applicant must sustain an examination on his knowledge of grammar, reading, religion, composition and arithmetic, together with his musical attainments and talents, both instrumental and vocal. Even with all the qualifications required, if a pupil is found to manifest no aptitude to teach, by his experiments in the schools for practice, attached to these seminaries, he may be dismissed. Every pupil receiving aid from the state, must obligate himself to teach for at least three years, after completing his course, or refund the money expended for his education.

The course of study prescribed, and the mode of instruction, must necessarily bear a strong resemblance to that already delineated for primary schools. On every branch, a greater degree of proficiency, is of course expected, and it is therefore taught more thoroughly and extensively. The scientific course of study, in our best colleges, may correctly represent it. The pupils are engaged during the first half of their course, whether of two or three years, (most generally, the course is completed in two years,) in the acquisition of knowledge from books. During the latter part of this first half of the course, the study of *paedagogies* is introduced by that of mental philosophy and psychology. The pupils are also instructed in the science of method, by which they are guided to the best possible means for acquiring or teaching any science or art. They are thus prepared for the duties of the latter half of the course which consist in experiments in teaching in the schools for practice already noticed, one or more of which are located conveniently to the seminary. These experiments are made in presence of the director, who corrects errors and gives hints, while they are thus engaged, and makes their exercises subjects of more special remark at a proper time.

Discipline

The discipline of these seminaries is strict, yet kind. As in the primary schools, the most diligent attention is given to secure regularity and system in every pursuit. This could not be otherwise, in institutions which prepare men for a business, requiring more than most others, the utmost order, punctuality and promptness. The punishments are, admonition, deprivation of privilege, suspension or expulsion.

Statistics

There are now thirty-three seminaries of this character in Prussia, besides the very small schools for similar purposes, already noticed. The government expends annually about $85,000 for their support. They contain about 1600 pupils, and thus afford nearly 800 teachers annually, which is only 50 less, than the annual need.

There could scarcely be devised a more efficient means of promoting the cause of common school education, with the same amount of money. These institutions are acquiring a great reputation. Most of what I have stated above, is the result of personal observation in a seminary, at Weisenfels, about 20 miles west of Leipsic, and of conversation with the highly accomplished and intelligent director of the institution. While there I met a gentleman from Scotland, the sole object of whose residence of three weeks, in the place, was the examination of the structure and operation of the school, in order to establish one similar to it, in his native country. I mention this fact, for the tribute is worth more, coming as it does, from a country, which has long been proverbial for the excellence of its primary schools. Similar visits have been made by gentlemen from Sweden, Denmark and England, and M. Cousin, in his reports, assigns these institutions, the most important place in the work of promoting the cause of primary instruction in Prussia.

Institutions of a similar character for the education of female teachers exist in Westphalia, according to Dr. Julius. As already intimated, however, there is great backwardness on this subject in Prussia, considering the general advancement made. It is probable that a better state of things will gradually succeed to proper efforts for the education of female teachers, and their abilities to instruct, may be more highly appreciated. . . .

I do earnestly desire that this report may aid you in your patriotic efforts. I fear, sir, that I have not succeeded in imparting just that kind of information you desired, in the best manner, yet whatever be the imperfections of the report itself, I flatter myself it presents the outlines of the Prussian system in such a manner as to render them intelligible. Should these afford you any useful hints, my object will have been accomplished, and I shall ever feel a most sincere pleasure, in reflecting on any effort of my feeble instrumentality, in such a cause.

Accept, sir, my assurances, &c., &c.,

BENJ. M. SMITH

Danville, Va., January 1st, 1839.

Suggestions on the Application of the System of Primary Schools to Virginia

On perusing the foregoing report, the question may naturally arise, "can this system be applied to our own state?" And as the answer is given, the importance of its consideration may be decided. But I take the liberty of remarking, that while no one can for a moment suppose the institutions suitable to a monarchy, *can* apply to a republic, still we may derive from them many important principles

of action, and obtain valuable hints, and discover plans worthy of imitation. In this view, I am disposed to consider the information contained in this report may be valuable.

It is with great diffidence I now propose to your consideration a few suggestions which have occurred to my mind on those plans and principles presented in this system, which appear to me worthy of entering into the composition of a system of primary schools for our own state.

1. The principle of state and parental obligation to educate all the children of the country, expressed by the phrase "school duty" among the Germans, must be recognized to some extent. Says a writer in the Foreign Quarterly Review. No. 24th: "If children provided their own education, and could be made sensible of its importance, it would be a *want*, and might be left to the natural demand and supply; but it is provided by the parents, and paid for by those who do not profit by its results, and is therefore a *duty* liable to be neglected." Numerous decisions of the English courts take a similar view of this subject; and I think some of our own laws are based on the correctness of this principle: thus, it is made the duty of every master to furnish his apprentice with a certain amount of instruction, and our state publicly proclaims its sense of obligation to the destitute by appropriating a large amount of money for their instruction. If, as Burke said, "education is the defence of nations," I see but little difference in the character of that obligation, which every state imposes on its citizens to perform military duty, and that which a state imposes, which obliges itself and parents to educate all the children. If, as we often hear, the prosperity and happiness, nay, even the existence of our republic, is based on the combined virtue and intelligence of the people, it becomes a question of practical importance and great moment, whether the state is not bound to see that this virtue and intelligence be promoted as far as education can promote them: and if the protection of life, liberty and property be that which every citizen may claim at the hands of the state, then may every one claim that every child be educated, and thus the safeguards of prevention of evil be added to those salutary restraints of law by which we are protected. To what extent this principle should be recognized in any plan of common schools, I am not able to say. I do not believe, in a popular government, any such principle, if recognized by law, could be enforced to its full extent, without much caution and previous efforts to

explain it fully and commend it to the approbation of the people.

2. The mode of supporting schools pursued in Prussia, recommends itself to our attention. The connexion of privilege with the performance of duty, or the suspension of sharing the benefits of schools, on sharing in their support, seems as necessary as the formation of a system.

We well know that the great obstacle to the operation of our present system has arisen from the very terms on which aid has been offered. You must confess the misfortune of poverty, ere you can receive the alms of charity, but poverty and pride are generally found together. I mean false pride, and no school commissioner need be told the numerous trials to which this feature of the system has exposed his patience.

Now, make the support of schools as the support of government, a matter of general taxation, based on some similar grounds as other systems of taxation; and though you may tax the childless to educate the offspring of parents, yet I believe the general benefits flowing to a community, from the universal diffusion of education, would more than repay such individuals, even in dollars and cents, for the apparently unjust expense to which they might be subjected. Is it no interest of the wealthy but childless man to have the value of property enhanced, the expenses of prisons and criminal prosecutions and poorhouses lessened? Does not education contribute directly to national wealth, by increasing the capacity of each individual in the community, and enabling him to turn his powers to the best account? by quickening ingenuity and promoting inventions and discoveries? by enabling men to push their researches farther into the powers and productions of the natural world? Let a comparison of Anglo-America with Spanish America, of England with Italy, of France with Spain, of Scotland with Ireland, and of Europe with China, or any part of civilized christendom with any part of Africa or Asia, answer such queries. "The muscular force of England and France are about equal," says Baron Dupin, "Yet the English by machinery have increased their force to a power equal to that of 25 millions, while France only rises to eleven." A single invention for supplying water to London saves to that city about 40 millions of dollars annually. But the position that education is wealth, is too obvious to need farther illustration.

I am well aware that many obstacles exist to the application of this principle. Our sparse population would render it impossible to furnish schools on this plan to some neighbourhoods, without great expense. But we are not to be deterred from the adoption of a principle, because its practical operation is liable to obstacles, in some cases. In neighbourhoods where a few wealthy persons reside, this principle would operate less injuriously on pecuniary interests, than the present system of private schools.

3. You have doubtless observed that the efficiency and success of the Prussian system, depend most materially on the qualification of teachers. How can the impregnable walls, in which ignorance is entrenched, be demolished, except by trained soldiers? This subject, as already observed, has attracted the serious attention of several legislatures. By the latest returns of the Massachusetts school board, the subject seems to awaken great interest in that state. Indeed, when we have devised the best theory of common schools, we are met at the threshold of all our calculations on its practicability by the question, "how can teachers be obtained?" For, in vain, may we speculate and plan systems, and declaim about popular ignorance, so long as we are unable to find men competent to teach. You may build school-houses in every district, 6 miles square, tax the people to the last point of endurance, pour out appropriations with princely munificence, and force children to school at the point of a sword, yet if you permit a man with "iron hands and wooden brains" to preside over your school, all will be vain and worse than in vain. Why should we educate a lawyer, or physician, or clergyman, why expect an apprenticeship of the mechanic, who shoes our horses, or paints our houses, and yet suppose that the most difficult and trying of all tasks can be performed by one who has had no experience and no instruction?

I am aware of obstacles here also. We are told that the business of teaching affords so little that we cannot secure the men. For our lowest schools, this is a serious obstacle. It does not apply to the academies and high schools. I am only permitted in this place, to throw out a few hints.

1. Educate teachers and you enhance their value. A good teacher can do more for a child in six months, than a bad one in two years. But farther, it is no difficult matter to perceive, that what is worth nothing, is dear at any price, and I apprehend one reason why good teachers are poorly paid, is because so many indifferent teachers have been too well paid.

2. Educate teachers and you elevate the dignity of the profession. Much of the aversion of young men to an engagement in this business, arises from the low station it has been permitted to occupy.

3. But supposing the work undertaken. It must be done by the state. This will cost a large sum, if separate institutions are established. I would venture to suggest the connexion of a teacher's department with each of our colleges, and also one for teachers of Latin schools, with the university. This would render the charge on the state lighter. By an appropriation to such institutions of a sum, sufficient to defray the tuition of every young man, who might be received as a candidate for the office of teacher, and another for supporting an additional professor in each, who should have the special charge of their instruction in the duties of their future office, I apprehend we might secure much of the benefits of teachers' seminaries, and avoid much of the expense, incidental to separate establishments. Some suitable arrangement might be made, requiring youth thus educated, to devote themselves to the business of instruction for a definite term. Provision could be introduced for defraying all, or nearly all the expenses of young men, of proper natural abilities, and the power of deciding on such cases, vested in the officers of the college, or better in certain persons in various parts of the state. Such a plan would cost much, it may be, but what then? Is it necessary to advert to the fact, that we are consulting to save the expenses incidental to an ignorant, uneducated community? England, with a population of six times that of Scotland, furnishes nearly 11 times as many criminals. Ireland, with a population about three times that of Scotland, and one half that of England, furnishes ten times the criminals of the former, and nearly as many as the latter. England sentences to death 480, Ireland 197, and Scotland 6, in one year. Judges and sheriffs will tell you, sir, that ignorance and crime are companions: and your own observation will confirm the statement. But I cannot dwell on this subject.

4. The systematic arrangement of the external organization of the Prussian school system, must be obvious to everyone. Can we not effect something of this kind? We have already something similar established. Our superintendent of the literary fund supplies the position of the minister. A board already exists. In every county men can be found to undertake the duties of school councillors and inspectors, and in every neighbourhood school directors may be had. We must, it is true, pay all, except the last, and these their expenses. Whenever the subject of cost comes up, I am irresistibly disposed to ask questions similar to those above. Let us here introduce another item on this point. How much does Virginia lose annually, in young enterprising citizens who emigrate to the west, for want of employment, above that of day labourers and mechanics? and how much money is annually carried to other portions of the country by birds of passage, who have stopped to teach long enough to pocket a few hundreds, aye, to sit in seats vacated by our own sons? I intend to foster no sectional spirit by these remarks. We should welcome teachers, if they come from China, so that they serve the state and *stay with us.* I am no politician, but have heard much of southern subjection to northern manufacturers. Will some politician inform us how much we pay to the northern manufacturers of school books and teachers? We complain that young men go northward for their academic education, and yet while they can acquire as good and cheaper educations, (in institutions better endowed than our own,) than can be had at home, they are not to blame.

5. The Prussian system provides for every grade of instruction, and holds out its assistance alike to the poor, the independent and the rich. We endow a university to which those can repair, who have 400 dollars a year to expend on their education; and we offer a common school education to the poor for nothing, while the middle classes, who mainly support the whole burdens of government, are left to provide for themselves. Ought this state of things to continue?

6. I presume we may derive some useful hints from the Prussian system, on the mode and subjects of instruction.

I cannot enlarge on this topic, without entering too much into details. The introduction of history, the study of our constitutions, of the first principles of natural science, and of drawing, and above all the elements of agricultural science, appears to me an object of great desire. I feel a peculiar delicacy in adverting to another topic,—I mean religion, not of a sect, but of the bible. I believe we might safely go this far,—to say in the proposed plan of elementary instruction,—"the bible shall be a class book, where the majority of the school patrons desire it." And lest I might be misunderstood, I will speak my sentiments in the language of a *French* philosopher, M. Cousin, "The less we desire our schools to be *ecclesiastical,* the more ought they to be *christian*. Religion is in my eyes the best, perhaps the only basis of popular education. I know something of Europe, and never have I seen good schools where the spirit of christian charity was wanting. Primary instruction flourishes in Holland, Scotland and Germany, and in all it is profoundly religious. I am not ignorant that this advice will grate on the ears of many persons, and that I shall be thought extremely *devot* at Paris. Yet it is not from Rome, but from Berlin, that I address you. The man who holds this language is a philosopher, formerly disliked, and even persecuted by the priesthood; but this philosopher has a mind too little affected by the recollection of his own insults, and is too well acquainted with human nature and history not to regard genuine christianity as a means of civilization for the people." Report on Public Instruction in Prussia, pp. 290–2. N. Y. edition, 1835.

And now, sir, I bring these suggestions to a close. Their worth is their only recommendation, and behind the sincerity of my desire to do good, I must shield myself from the imputation of presumption.

Let it not be supposed that a servile imitation of other countries is recommended. "The true greatness of a people does not consist in borrowing nothing from others, but in borrowing from all whatever is good and in perfecting whatever it appropriates."

I remain, with great respect, yours truly,

BENJ. M. SMITH
Danville, Va., January 15th, 1839.

Calvin E. Stowe   1836

Moral and Religious Lessons from European Schools

Calvin E. Stowe (1802–1886) graduated from Bowdoin College in 1824 and Andover Theological Seminary in 1828. During his long teaching career he was professor of Greek at Dartmouth College from 1831 to 1833 and professor of biblical literature at Lane Theological Seminary in Ohio from 1833 to 1850. For the next two years he served at Bowdoin College as professor of religion and later, from 1852 to 1864, at Andover Theological Seminary as professor of sacred literature. He also assisted in founding one of the earliest associations of professional teachers in America, the Western Literary Institute.

In 1835 Stowe published an influential paper on the need to provide special educational facilities for immigrants and to integrate foreign-born children into the public schools. Before he left for Europe in 1836 to purchase a library for the Lane Theological Seminary, Governor Lucas of Ohio requested him "to collect, during the progress of his contemplated tour in Europe, such facts and information as he may deem useful to the State, in relation to the various systems of public instruction and education, which have been adopted in the several countries through which he may pass, and make report thereof." Stowe's *Report on Elementary Public Instruction in Europe* made to the governor and the General Assembly of the State of Ohio on December 19, 1837, was distributed to all school districts in Ohio and was considered of such importance that the legislatures of Massachusetts, Michigan, North Carolina, Pennsylvania, and Virginia ordered reprints. No previous American report on European education had received such widespread distribution, which gave many Americans the opportunity to read such a thorough account of German education written by an intelligent observer and fellow countryman. American educators could compare Stowe's comments on Prussian education with the well-known and respected 1831 account of Victor Cousin entitled, *Report on the State of Public Instruction in Prussia,* which had become available in English in 1835.

The extracts below from Stowe's report include descriptions of Russian and Prussian education and answers to a comparative education questionnaire received from sources in Scotland, Prussia, and Baden. His interesting and prophetic notation of Russian education is included in spite of the fact that Stowe did not visit Russia and it is not first-hand. He said that Russian education "cannot but be deeply interesting to us since Russia has so many points of resemblance, and of striking contrast to our own country. Like the United States, her dominion

Calvin E. Stowe, *Report on Elementary Public Instruction in Europe Made to the Thirty-Sixth General Assembly of the State of Ohio,* as reprinted by the Massachusetts House of Representatives (Boston, 1838), pp. 3–19, 21–27, 51–59, 63–68.

extends over an immense territory, comprising almost every variety of soil, climate, production, and national character. Like ours her education institutions are comparatively new, and almost everything is to be begun in its elements.''

In March, 1836, just before I embarked for Europe, I received a communication from Governor Lucas, with the great seal of the State, enclosing the following resolves of the General Assembly, *to wit:*

"Resolved by the General Assembly of the State of Ohio, That C. E. Stowe, Professor in one of the Literary Institutions of this State, be requested to collect, during the progress of his contemplated tour in Europe, such facts and information as he may deem useful to the State, in relation to the various systems of public instruction and education, which have been adopted in the several countries through which he may pass, and make report thereof, with such practical observations as he may think proper, to the next General Assembly.

"Resolved, That His Excellency the Governor be requested to transmit a certified copy of the foregoing proceedings to Professor Stowe.''

In pursuance of the above resolutions, I communicated the intention of the General Assembly to Hon. A. Stevenson, the American Minister near the British Court, and he very readily furnished me with the credentials for the most satisfactory attainment of the object of my inquiries. I am also happy to remark, that the communication of Governor Lucas was a ready passport to my free admission to every institution in Europe to which I applied —and that my endeavors were seconded in the most encouraging manner by all the gentlemen connected with the educational establishments in the several countries through which I passed; and the warmest expressions of approbation were elicited of the zeal manifested by so young a state as Ohio, in the great cause of general education. Particularly in some of the old communities of central Europe, where it happened to be known that I was born in the same year in which Ohio became a sovereign State, it seemed to be matter of amusement as well as gratification, that a man who was *just as old as the State in which he lived,* had come with official authority to inquire respecting the best mode of education for the growing population of his native land; and they remarked, that our Governor and Legislators must be very enlightened and highly cultivated men. When in one instance I informed them that our Governor was a plain farmer, and that a majority of our Legislators were of the same occupa-

tion, the well known line which a Latin poet applies to husbandmen was applied to us:

O fortunatos nimium si sua bona norint.
Oh happy people, if they do but appreciate their own blessings.

In the progress of my tour I visited England, Scotland, France, Prussia, and the different States of Germany; and had opportunity to see the celebrated Universities of Cambridge, Oxford, Edinburg, Glasgow, Paris, Berlin, Halle, Leipsic, Heidleberg, and some others; and I was everywhere received with the greatest kindness, and every desirable facility was afforded me for the promotion of my inquiries. But knowing that a solid foundation must be laid before a durable superstructure can be reared, and being aware that, on this principle, the chief attention of our Legislature is, and for the present must be, directed to our common schools, my investigation of the Universities was comparatively brief—and the most of my time was spent in visiting the best district schools I could hear of, and also the high schools intended for the business education of young men, and the institutions for the education of teachers.

Before I proceed to the result of my inquiries on these topics, I would call the attention of the Legislature to some facts of a more general nature, which strongly impressed themselves upon my mind during the progress of my tour—and which, it seems to me, have a very important bearing upon the successful maintenance, if not the very existence, of free institutions in our country. I allude particularly to the wonderful change which has taken place in the policy of monarchial governments in respect to the education of the people. Formerly it was supposed that despotism could be maintained only by a sovereign with an army devoted to his interests, and dependent only upon himself for subsistence; an aristocracy which should monopolise the wealth and the intellectual culture of the entire nation; and a mass of people held in entire ignorance of their rights and privileges as men, and condemned to drudge for life for a bare and precarious subsistence—the mere dependents and slaves of the higher orders. But what is the aspect which the sovereignties of Europe now present?—and what is the change which is forcing itself along, even into the despotisms of

Asia and Africa? Ever since the revolution which separated this country from the British Empire, the idea of popular rights has been working its way irresistibly throughout the civilized world: and sovereigns who have had the sagacity to see the unavoidable results, have adapted their measures to the new aspect of the times. A new era in the history of civilization has evidently commenced. A despotic king of the Protestant faith, dreading the evils of an ignorant and unbridled democracy, such as was witnessed in the French revolution, has now for forty years been pursuing a course of instruction for his whole people, more complete, better adapted to develope every faculty of the soul, and to bring into action, every capability of every kind that may exist, even in the poorest cottage of the most obscure corner of his kingdom, than has ever before been imagined. Men of the highest order of intellect and most extensive attainments are encouraged to devote themselves to the business of teaching: the best plans for the furtherance of this object are immediately received and generously rewarded; talent and industry, wherever they exist, are sought out and promoted; and nothing is left undone that can help forward this great design.

The introduction of this system was preceded by political changes, which, considered as emanating from the government itself, have scarcely a parallel in the history of nations. When Frederick William III. ascended the throne of Prussia in 1797, the condition of the people was in many respects truly deplorable. But immediately upon his accession he set about reforming abuses, and introducing improvements. The odious religious edict was abolished—the administration of justice was thoroughly reformed, and rigid economy introduced into the royal household. The exclusive privileges of the nobles were taken away, and their power so completely broken, that there is now no hereditary aristocracy which can interfere with the sovereign, or oppress the people.

In 1810, the peasantry, who before had no ownership in the soil which they cultivated, and consequently no independence of character, by a royal decree, became freeholders on the following terms, namely: those who held their lands on perpetual lease, by giving up one-third, and those who held them on limited or life leases, by giving up one-half, to the landlord, became the owners in fee simple of the rest. The military is now so modelled that every citizen between the ages of 18 and 21 is in actual service in the standing army, where he is instructed in all that pertains to military life, and then returns to his peaceful occupations. Thus the army is made up entirely of citizens—and every citizen is a soldier; and there is no such thing as a standing army at the entire devotion of the sovereign, and independent of the people.

The prime minister, Hardenberg, in a circular published at the time when these reforms were in progress, declares, that "the new system is based upon the principle, that every subject, personally free, be able to raise himself, and develope his powers freely, without let or hindrance from any other; that the public burdens be borne in common and in just proportions; that equality before the law, be secured to every subject; that justice be rigidly and punctually administered; that merit in whatever rank it may be found, be enabled to rise without obstacle; that the government be carried on with unity, order, and power; that, by the education of the people, and the spread of true religion, the general interests, and a national spirit be promoted, as the only secure basis of the national welfare."

Another European king of the Roman Catholic faith, Louis of Bavaria, who is connected by marriage with the royal house of Prussia, moved by this example, and excited by emulation in behalf both of his church and kingdom, is now zealously pushing forward the same experiment among his own people, and already the Bavarian schools begin to rival the Prussian; and the University of Berlin finds its only equal in that of Munich. Louis has in one thing gone even beyond his brother of Prussia, in that he has granted to his people a real constitutional representation in the government, a privilege and a right which the Prussians have labored in vain to extort from Frederick William.

Even the Autocrat, Nicholas of Russia, (married to a daughter of the Prussian monarch, who inherits much of her father's spirit,) has been induced to commence a similar system throughout his vast dominions; and from the reports to the emperor of M. d'Ouvaroff, the Russian Minister of Public Instruction, it appears, that already from Poland to Siberia, and from the White Sea to the regions beyond the Caucasus, including the provinces so recently wrested from Persia, there are the beginnings of a complete system of common school instruction for the whole people, to be carried into full execution as fast as it is possible to provide the requisite number of qualified teachers.

Thus three sovereigns, representing the three great divisions of Christendom, the Protestant, the Romish, and the Greek, are now zealously engaged in doing what despotic sovereigns have seldom done before — enlightening and educating their people; and that too with better plans of instruction, and a more efficient accomplishment in practice than the world has ever before witnessed. Nor is the spirit of education confined to these nations. The kingdom of Wirtemberg, and the grand duchy of Baden, are not behind Prussia or Bavaria. The smaller states of Germany, and even old Austria, are pushing forward in the same career; France is all awake; Spain and Italy are beginning to open their eyes; the government of England—which has hitherto neglected the education of the common people more than any other Protestant country of Europe—is beginning to bestir itself; and even the Sultan of Turkey, and the Pacha of Egypt, are looking around for well qualified teachers to go among their people. In London and Paris I saw Turks, and Arabs, and Greeks, who had been sent by their respective governments to these cities, for the express purpose of being educated for teachers in their native countries, if not for the whole people, at least for the favored few. At Constantinople a society has been formed for the promotion of useful knowledge, which publishes a monthly journal edited by one of the Turks who studied in Paris; and the Sultan now employs a French teacher in his capital, whom he especially invited from France. And here too in our own country, in the movements of New England, New York, Pennsylvania, Ohio, Michigan, and several other of the states, we are strongly reminded of the educational zeal of the age.

In short the world seems to be awake and combining in one simultaneous effort for the spread of education; and sad indeed will be the condition of that community which lags behind in this universal march.

But I wish to direct your attention to the influence which these wide spread systems of education in the sovereignties of Europe, emanating from Prussia, must exert on our own institutions. The sovereigns to whom I have alluded, are not only educating the people, but they are laying aside the pomp, the trappings, and the lavish expenses of royalty, and by simplicity, by rigid economy, by an energetic and impartial administration of the government, are endeavoring to establish their thrones in the hearts of their people.

Frederick William, in his dress, appearance, and whole deportment, is as simple and unostentatious as an Ohio farmer; and few of our wealthy merchants ride in so plain a carriage, or sleep on so homely a bed as the monarch of Prussia. After witnessing the pageantry, the pomp and ostentation of the limited monarchy of England, one is astonished at the rigid simplicity of the great military despotism of central Europe.

In every stage of instruction it is made a prominent object, and one which is repeatedly and strenuously insisted on in all the laws pertaining to education, to awaken a *national spirit*—to create in the youthful mind a warm attachment to his native land, and its institutions, and to fix in his affections a decided preference for the peculiarities of his own country. Indeed the whole plan (which is well understood to have originated in Prussia, when the rapid spread of republican principles first began to threaten the thrones of Europe,) evidently is to unite with the military force which always attends a despotism, a strong moral power over the understanding and affections of the people. In view of this fact, an able English writer denominates the modern kingdom of Prussia, "that wonderful machine of state-craft—as a mere machine the most remarkable in existence—on the model of which most European governments are gradually proceeding to reform themselves." Already has this plan so far succeeded, that there is evidently in these countries a growing disregard for the *forms* of free government, provided the *substance* be enjoyed in the security and prosperity of the people.

Republicanism can be maintained only by universal intelligence and virtue among the people, and disinterestedness and fidelity in the rulers. Republics are considered the natural foes to monarchies; and where both start up side by side, it is taken for granted that the one must supplant the other. Hence their watchful jealousy of each other. Now when we see monarchies strengthening themselves in the manner described, are not republics exposed to double danger from vice, and neglect of education within themselves? And do not patriotism and the necessity of self-preservation, call upon us to do more and better for the education of our whole people, than any despotic sovereign can do for his? Did we stand alone—were there no rival governments on earth—or if we were surrounded by despotisms of degraded and ignorant slaves, like those of the ancient oriental world; *even then*, without intelligence and virtue in the great mass of the people, our liberties would pass from us. How emphatically must this be the case *now*, when the whole aspect of things is changed, and monarchies have actually stolen a march upon republics in the promotion of popular intelligence?

Efforts for Education in Russia

In a former report, which was printed by order of the Legislature in 1836, I gave a synopsis of the governmental regulations in Prussia respecting education, and I have not found by investigations on the spot, that the statements then made require any essential modification. I will here, however, take the liberty of stating some facts respecting the governmental efforts recently made in RUSSIA, to establish a system of popular education throughout that vast empire. These cannot but be deeply interesting to us, since Russia has so many points of resemblance, and of striking contrast to our own country. Like the United States, her dominion extends over an immense territory, comprising almost every variety of soil, climate, productions, and national character. Like ours, her educational institutions are comparatively new, and almost everything is to be begun in its elements; and, like us, she has received great accessions to her population by immigrants from almost every nation of Europe. Russia is unquestionably the largest and most powerful of despotisms; as the United States is the largest and most powerful of republics: and, while we enjoy the greatest political freedom that any government has ever permitted, she is held fast by the bonds of a severe autocracy. Add to this, Russia is the only European government, with the exception of Great Britain, whose territories border on our own. The fact, then, that a system of public instruction has been established in the Russian empire, is one of deep interest to us; and no less interesting will it be for us to know something of the nature of the system and of the means by which it is carried into operation.

The general system is that of Prussia, with such modifications as are necessary to adapt it to that widely extended, and, in some parts, semi-barbarous empire. For example, the whole empire is divided into provinces, each of which has a university—these provinces into academic districts, which are provided with their gymnasia for classical learning, and academies for the higher branches of a business education; and these

academic districts are again subdivided into school districts, each with its elementary school. As the heart of the whole system, there is at St. Petersburg a model school for the education of teachers of every grade, for all parts of the empire. Of the Universities, six had already gone into operation in 1835, namely: one at St. Petersburg, one at Moscow, one at Dorpat, in Livonia, one at Charkow, east of the river Dnieper, one at Kasan, on the Wolga, and one at Kiew. At other points Lyceums are established, with courses of study more limited than that of the Universities; and there is an institution at Moscow, especially for the education of the nobility. Of course, I shall not be understood as recommending for adoption by us whatever I speak of with approbation in reference to foreign lands; for the different circumstances of nations require entirely different systems. It is the part of a wise legislator to examine all the improvements within his reach, and from the whole, to select those parts only which are adapted to the peculiar circumstances of the people for whom he legislates.

The different institutions in Russia are established as fast as the circumstances of the people admit; and as teachers can be found to supply them. At the date of the last report of the Minister of Public Instruction, the number of elementary and parish schools was about 12,000—of private schools, 430—and of gymnasia, 57.

The governmental regulations for cherishing in the people a desire for education, and directing them in the attainment of it, are wisely adapted to the purpose. The Minister of Public Instruction publishes a regular periodical journal, in which he gathers up all the facts, information and arguments, to which this official station gives him access, and circulates them extensively through the nation. To illustrate the good faith, diligence and liberal-mindedness with which he executes his part of his office, I would refer to the number of his journal for August, 1835, in which he notices, with great approbation, the efforts of tract societies for the diffusion of moral and religious sentiments among the people, and mentions by name several publications of the American Tract Society, which have been translated into Russian, as having reached a third edition, and as being happily calculated to enlighten the intellect, and elevate the character of the people among whom they circulate. If the Minister of the Emperor Nicholas shows so much readiness to receive a good thing even from Democratic America, we surely will not be so narrow-minded as to spurn a good idea because it happened first to develope itself in Autocratic Russia. As a farther means of promoting education, every school director and examiner undergoes a rigid scrutiny as to his intellectual and moral fitness for those important trusts; and every candidate for civil office is strictly examined as to his attainments in those branches of learning requisite to the right performance of the official duties to which he aspires. As common schools are new in the Russian Empire, and as school-houses are to be built in every part of it, the government, knowing the importance of having these houses well planned and put up, has appointed an architect, with a salary of 1000 rubles a year, for every academic district, whose whole business it is to superintend the erecting and fitting up of the district school-houses in his particular province. When we recollect how many of the evils of our district schools result from the bad construction and wretched furniture of our school-houses, how completely, by these defects, the efforts of the best teachers may be nullified, and the minds and health of children, as well as their comfort, destroyed, we cannot but acknowledge this to be, for a country where every thing is to be begun from its foundation, a most judicious arrangement.

Canals, and other public improvements of this kind, are now in great demand, and, to further them, an institution has been established for the express purpose of teaching the arts requisite in their construction; and young men who intend to devote themselves to this business, are taken from the other schools and placed in this institution at the public expense. Special provision, also, is made for instruction in agriculture, and all the kindred arts, in order that the natural resources of the country may be fully developed. That religious instruction may be efficient, and, at the same time, the rights of conscience remain inviolate, clergymen of different christian denominations, where the circumstances of the people require it, are employed as religious teachers in the schools, their services compensated by government, and their families provided for, if necessary. The importance of female teachers is recognized, and every encouragement is held out to young ladies to engage in this work. Private teachers are subject to the same rules, and the same strict inspection, as the teachers of public schools; and, what is an improvement on the Prussian

plan, if the teacher of a private school becomes superannuated, or dies, in the service, his family are entitled to the same privileges as that of a public teacher, and receive pensions from the government adequate to their support and education. Thus all classes of faithful teachers are regarded and treated as public benefactors, and considered as entitled, not merely to a bare support while toiling and wearing themselves out in the public service, but to national remembrance and gratitude after their work is done.

Though the emperor of Russia is justly accused of unpardonable oppression in respect to Poland, yet he does not carry his oppression so far as to deprive the poor Polanders of the benefits of education, but is exerting the same laudable zeal to provide teachers for Poland as for any other part of his dominions. It has been found exceedingly difficult to obtain teachers who are willing to exercise their calling in the cold and inhospitable regions of Siberia. To facilitate this object, special privileges have been granted to Siberian teachers. Siberian young men are admitted to the university of Kasan free of expense, on condition that they devote a certain number of years to the business of school-keeping in Siberia. To forward the same object, a Siberian gentleman, by the name of Ponomarew, gives 6000 rubles a year for the support of the parish schools of Irkutzk, quite to the north-eastern extremity of Siberia, and has obligated himself, for ten years, to pay 500 rubles a year more, for the encouragement of the pupils of those schools.

Teachers from foreign countries are welcomed, and special provision is made that their religious sentiments be not interfered with, as well as that they do not impose their peculiar religious notions on their pupils. For the perfecting of teachers in certain branches, they are often sent abroad, at the public expense, to study in the institutions of other countries, where these branches are most successfully taught. Of these, there were in 1835, thirteen in Berlin—several in Vienna—and one in Oxford, England. School examiners and school committees, as well as school teachers, are required to hold frequent meetings for discussion, and for mutual instruction and encouragement.

It is the policy of the Minister of Public Instruction, not to crowd the schools with too many pupils — but to furnish as many teachers as possible, particularly in the higher institutions, that each individual scholar may receive a due share of attention.

As an illustration, I will refer to some of the universities. The university of St. Petersburg has two hundred and thirty pupils, and fifty-two officers and teachers, or one teacher to every four or five students. At Moscow, four hundred and fifty-six students, one hundred and sixty-eight teachers and officers, or one to every two or three students. That of Kasan, seventy officers and teachers, to two hundred and thirty-eight students, or one to every three or four students. That at Kiew, forty-three officers and teachers, to sixty-two students, or nearly as many of the one as the other. I would remark, however, that some of the teachers are merely lecturers on particular branches, and take no active part in the discipline or instruction of the institution, and a few attend only to its business concerns. Some of the universities, also, are not full, the institutions being new, and a full corps of teachers being appointed at the commencement. With all these allowances, however, we may set it down as a principle, that in the universities it is intended that there shall be one teacher at least to every eight or ten students. This may be going to excess, but it is certain that the ambition to multiply students beyond all the means of teaching, has been a great injury to education in American institutions. Education can never be what it is capable of being, unless the teacher can command time to become familiar with each individual mind under his care, and to adapt his mode of teaching to its peculiarities. To instruct only in masses, and to apply the same methods of instruction to all, is like throwing the drugs of an apothecary's shop into one great caldron —stirring them together, and giving every patient in the hospital a portion of the mixture.

It is peculiarly interesting in noticing the efforts of Russia, to observe, that the blessings of a good common school education are now extended to tribes which from time immemorial have been in a state of barbarism. In the wild regions, beyond mount Caucasus, comprising the provinces recently acquired from Persia, the system of district schools is efficiently carried out. As early as 1835, there were already established in those parts of the empire, fifteen schools, with sixty teachers, and about one thousand three hundred children under instruction; so that in the common schools of this new and uncultivated region, one teacher is provided for every twenty scholars. Besides this, there is a gymnasium at Tifflis, in which Asiatic lads are fitted to enter the European universities.

All teachers throughout the empire, according to an ordinance of February 26, 1835, receive their salaries monthly, that their attention may not be distracted by family cares. For the encouragement of entire devotedness on the part of teachers, and to prevent all solicitude for the maintenance of their families, the minister of public instruction is authorized to grant, to the widows and orphans of those teachers who have particularly distinguished themselves, not only the usual pension, but a gratuity equal in amount to an entire salary of two years.

The officers of government employed in the distant provinces of the empire, in the distant parts of Siberia, and on the borders of Persia, complained, that their remote location deprived their children of the advantages of the gymnasia and universities, which others enjoyed. To obviate this inconvenience, and to equalize as far as possible the advantages of education, the children of these officers are taken to the nearest gymnasium or university, and their travelling expenses defrayed by government. All the institutions of education are subject to the same rigorous examination as in Prussia, and the minister of public instruction is, *ex officio,* chairman of the board of examiners for the universities. As the duties of this office have become very laborious, the government, in addition to a liberal supply of other helps, in 1835 appointed General Count Protassow, who had for some time acted as a school director, assistant minister of public instruction.

I have already mentioned the model institution for teachers at St. Petersburg. In 1835, seventy-six teachers were graduated, and the number is every year increasing. Under the influence of this school, and other governmental arrangements, the methods of teaching are continually improving; and, in his report for 1835, the Minister observes, that the moral improvement of both teachers and pupils is such as to encourage the most pleasing hopes, that within the last two years, the national interest in the subject of education has very greatly increased, and that it has now become a matter of the deepest interest to the whole people; and that as to the methods of instruction, the old mechanical *memoriter* mode is continually giving way to the system of *developing the faculties.* Many facts are stated in the report, which confirm the Minister's remark, in respect to the growing interest in the minds of the Russian people, on the subject of education, illustrating the important fact, that among whatever people a good system of instruction is efficiently carried out, a deep and general interest will be excited. The nobles and the commons appear to emulate each other in the advancement of this cause. The nobility of Novgorod voluntarily contribute more than twelve thousand rubles a year for the Gymnasium in that place, and at Wologda the nobility contribute for a similar object nine thousand a year. At Cronstadt, the citizens volunteered to sustain a school at their own expense. At another place on the shores of the White Sea, the citizens have not only volunteered to maintain the school, but have also, of their own accord, entered into an obligation to erect a large and handsome stone building for the accommodation of the teachers and scholars. This was brought about by the zeal and activity of a single individual, whose name, though a barbarous one, ought here to be mentioned— Wassiligi Kologriew. This gentleman volunteered as an agent to promote the cause of education in the place of his residence, and besides giving his time and efforts, bore an equal share in all the expenses, and in addition, made a distinct donation of 2500 rubles for the advancement of the cause.

Another gentleman at Archangel, by the name of Kowalewsky, made a journey to a distant neighborhood inhabited by Samoiedes, Sirianes and other half barbarous tribes, to explain to them the advantages of education, and endeavor to establish a school among them. In this he was warmly seconded by the clergyman of the place, and, as the result of it, a single peasant or farmer, by the name of Anuphriew, engaged to support the school entirely for two years, and after that to contribute 300 rubles a year for five years longer, and in addition to this he contributed 1500 rubles for the erection of a school-house. The chief magistrate of the place also contributed, and allured by these examples the Sirianes put down nearly 15,000 rubles; and as soon as the requisite preparations could be made, the school was opened with great solemnity and appropriate ceremonies, in the midst of an immense concourse of intensely interested spectators. I shall be greatly disappointed if we cannot find in Ohio, enlightened men in our cities, and farmers in the country, willing to do as much for education as the gentleman of Archangel, and the hard-working peasant of the frozen regions of northern Russia.

A merchant by the name of Pluessin in Lialsk, made a donation of 10,000 rubles for the foundation of a district school in that place, and offered in addition, to have the school kept in his own house, and to furnish

it with firewood for three years. Tschistow, a citizen of Moscow, gave 2300 rubles for the purchase of school books, to be distributed among the poor children of the first school district in that city.

Numerous other instances might be mentioned of donations from persons in all ranks in society—in money, books, houses, fuel, or whatever they had it in their power to give for the support of schools; but the above may be sufficient to show the spirit of the people and excite us to emulation.

It must be observed that the government makes provision for the maintenance of all the district schools, gymnasia and Universities; and that this liberality of private citizens arises from pure zeal for the cause, and is applied to the extending and increasing the advantages derived from governmental patronage, to the purchase of books and clothing for the poorer children, the establishment of school libraries, and the providing of suitable rewards for meritorious teachers and pupils, and securing the means of access to the school-house, and proper furniture for it. Every effort is made to provide a plentiful supply of good school books, and to establish suitable libraries for the use of teachers. Quite recently, a Russian lady, a Miss Darzoff, received from the government a premium of 2500 rubles for compiling a little work, entitled "Useful Readings for Children."

In view of such facts as these, who is not ready to exclaim: "Well done, cold, semi-barbarous, despotic Russia!—may other nations more favored by nature and Providence emulate thy example!"

Internal Arrangements of the Prussian Schools

I will now ask your attention to a few facts respecting the internal management of the schools in Prussia and some other parts of Germany, which were impressed on my mind by a personal inspection of those establishments.

One of the circumstances that interested me most was the excellent order and rigid economy with which all the Prussian institutions are conducted. Particularly in large boarding schools, where hundreds, and sometimes thousands of youth are collected together, the benefits of the system are strikingly manifest. Every boy is taught to wait upon himself—to keep his person, clothing, furniture, and books, in perfect order and neatness; and no extravagance in dress, and no waste of fuel or food, or property of any kind is permitted. Each student has his own single bed, which is generally a light mattress, laid upon a frame of slender bars of iron, because such bedsteads are not likely to be infested by insects, and each one makes his own bed and keeps it in order. In the house, there is a place for every thing and every thing must be in its place. In one closet are the shoe-brushes and blacking, in another the lamps and oil, in another the fuel. At the doors are good mats and scrapers, and every thing of the kind necessary for neatness and comfort, and every student is taught, as carefully as he is taught any other lesson, to make a proper use of all these articles at the right time, and then to leave them in good order at their proper places. Every instance of neglect is sure to receive its appropriate reprimand, and if necessary, severe punishment. I know of nothing that can benefit us more than the introduction of such oft-repeated lessons on carefulness and frugality into all our educational establishments; for the contrary habits of carelessness and wastefulness, notwithstanding all the advantages which we enjoy, have already done us immense mischief. Very many of our families waste and throw away nearly as much as they use; and one third of the expenses of housekeeping might be saved by system and frugality. It is true, we have such an abundance of every thing that this enormous waste is not so sensibly felt as it would be in a more densely populated region; but it is not *always* to be so with us. The productions of our country for some years past have by no means kept pace with the increase of consumption, and many an American family during the last season has felt a hard pressure, where they never expected to feel one.

Especially should this be made a branch of female education, and studied faithfully and perseveringly by all who are to be wives and mothers, and have the care of families.

The universal success also and very beneficial results, with which the arts of drawing and designing, vocal and instrumental music, moral instruction and the Bible, have been introduced into schools, was another fact peculiarly interesting to me. I asked all the teachers with whom I conversed, whether they did not sometimes find children who were actually incapable of learning to draw and to sing. I have had but one reply, and that was, that they found the same diversity of natural talent in regard to these as in regard to reading, writing, and the other branches of educa-

tion; but they had never seen a child who was capable of learning to read and write, who could not be taught to sing well and draw neatly, and that too without taking any time which would at all interfere with, indeed which would not actually promote his progress in other studies. In regard to the necessity of moral instruction and the beneficial influence of the Bible in schools, the testimony was no less explicit and uniform. I inquired of all classes of teachers, and men of every grade of religious faith, instructors in common schools, high schools, and schools of art, of professors in colleges, universities and professional seminaries, in cities and in the country, in places where there was a uniformity and in places where there was a diversity of creeds, of believers and unbelievers, of rationalists and enthusiasts, of Catholics and Protestants; and I never found but one reply, and that was, that to leave the moral faculty uninstructed was to leave the most important part of the human mind undeveloped, and to strip education of almost every thing that can make it valuable; and that the Bible, independently of the interest attending it, as containing the most ancient and influential writings ever recorded by human hands, and comprising the religious system of almost the whole of the civilized world, is in itself the best book that can be put into the hands of children to interest, to exercise, and to unfold their intellectual and moral powers. Every teacher whom I consulted, repelled with indignation the idea that moral instruction is not proper for schools; and spurned with contempt the allegation, that the Bible cannot be introduced into common schools without encouraging a sectarian bias in the matter of teaching; an indignation and contempt which I believe will be fully participated in by every high-minded teacher in christendom. . . .

Institutions for Reformation

At Berlin, I visited an establishment for the reformation of youthful offenders. Here boys are placed, who have committed offences that bring them under the supervision of the police, to be instructed, and rescued from vice, instead of being hardened in iniquity, by living in the common prison with old offenders. It is under the care of Dr. Kopf, a most simple-hearted, excellent old gentleman; just such an one as reminds us of the ancient christians, who lived in the times of the persecution, simplicity and purity of the christian church. He has been very successful in reclaiming the young offender, and many an one, who would otherwise have been forever lost, has, by the influence of this institution, been saved to himself—to his country—and to God. It is a manual labor school; and to a judicious intermingling of study and labor, religious instruction, kind treatment and necessary severity, it has owed its success. When I was there, most of the boys were employed in cutting screws for the rail-road which the government was then constructing between Berlin and Leipsic; and there were but few who could not maintain themselves by their labor. As I was passing with Dr. K. from room to room, I heard some beautiful voices singing in an adjoining apartment, and on entering I found about twenty of the boys, sitting at a long table, making clothes for the establishment, and singing at their work. The Dr. enjoyed my surprise, and on going out, remarked—"I always keep these little rogues singing at their work, for while the children sing, the devil cannot come among them at all; he can only sit out doors there and growl; but if they stop singing, in the devil comes."—The Bible and the singing of religious hymns, are among the most efficient instruments which he employs for softening the hardened heart, and bringing the vicious and stubborn will to docility.

A similar establishment in the neighborhood of Hamburg, to which I was introduced by Dr. Julius, who is known to many of our citizens, afforded striking examples of the happy influence of moral and religious instruction, in reclaiming the vicious and saving the lost. Hamburg is the largest commercial city of Germany, and its population is extremely crowded. Though it is highly distinguished for its benevolent institutions, and for the hospitality and integrity of its citizens, yet the very circumstances in which it is placed, produce among the lowest class of its population, habits of degradation and beastliness, of which we have but few examples on this side the Atlantic. The children, therefore, received into this institution, are often of the very worst and most hopeless character. Not only are their *minds* most thoroughly depraved, but their very senses and bodily organization seem to partake in the viciousness and degradation of their hearts. Their appetites are so perverted, that sometimes the most loathsome and disgusting substances are preferred to wholesome food. The Superintendent, Mr. Wichern, states, that though plentifully supplied with provisions yet when first received, some of them will steal and eat soap, rancid grease that has been laid aside for the purpose of greasing shoes, and even catch May-bugs and devour them; and it is with the utmost difficulty that these disgusting habits are broken up. An ordinary man might suppose that the task of restoring such poor creatures to decency and good morals was entirely hopeless. Not so with Mr. Wichern. He took hold with the firm hope that the moral power of the word of God is competent even to such a task. His means are prayer, the Bible, singing, affectionate conversation, severe punishment when unavoidable, and constant steady employment, in useful labor. On one occasion, when every other means seemed to fail, he collected the children together, and read to them, in the words of the New Testament, the simple narrative of the sufferings and death of Christ, with some remarks on the design and object of his mission to this world. The effect was wonderful. They burst into tears of contrition, and during the whole of that term, from June till October, the influence of this scene was visible in all their conduct. The idea that takes so strong a hold when the character of Christ is exhibited to such poor creatures, is, that *they are objects of affection;* miserable, wicked, depised as they are, yet Christ, the son of God, loved them, and loved them enough to suffer and to die for them—and still loves them. The thought that *they can yet be loved,* melts the heart, and gives them hope, and is a strong incentive to reformation.

On another occasion, when considerable progress had been made in their moral education, the Superintendent discovered that some of them had taken nails from the premises, and applied them to their own use, without permission. He called them together, expressed his great disappointment and sorrow that they had profited so little by the instructions which had been given them, and told them that till he had evidence of their sincere repentance, he could not admit them to the morning and evening religious exercises of his family. With expressions of deep regret for their sin, and with promises, entreaties, and tears, they begged to have this privilege restored to them; but he was firm in his refusal. A few evenings afterward, while walking in the garden, he heard youthful voices among the shrubbery; and drawing near unperceived, he found that the boys had formed themselves into little companies of seven or eight each, and met morning and evening in different retired spots in the garden, to sing, read the Bible and pray among themselves; to ask God to forgive them the sins they had committed, and to give them strength to resist temptation in [the] future. With such evidence of repentance he soon restored to them the privilege of attending morning and evening prayers with his family.—One morning soon after, on entering his study, he found it all adorned with wreaths of the most beautiful flowers, which the boys had arranged there at early daybreak, in testimony of their joy and gratitude for his kindness. Thus rapidly had these poor creatures advanced in moral feeling, religious sensibility, and good taste.

In the spring, Mr. Wichern gives to each boy a patch of ground in the garden, which he is to call his own, and cultivate as he pleases. One of the boys began to erect a little hut of sticks and earth upon his plot, in which he might rest during the heat of the day, and to which he might retire when he wished to be alone. When it was all finished, it occurred to him to dedicate it to its use by religious ceremonies. Accordingly, he collected the boys together. The hut was adorned with wreaths of flowers, a little table was placed in the centre on which lay the open Bible, ornamented in the same manner. He then read with great seriousness the 14th, 15th, and 24th verses of the CXVIII. Psalm:

The Lord is my strength and my song, and is become my salvation.
The voice of rejoicing and salvation is heard in the tabernacles of the righteous.
This is the day which the Lord hath made. We will rejoice and be glad in it.

After this, the exercises were concluded by singing and prayer. Another boy afterwards built him a hut, which was to be dedicated in a similar way; but when the boys came together, they saw in it a piece of timber which belonged to the establishment, and ascertaining that it had been taken without permission, they at once demolished the whole edifice, and restored the timber to its place. At the time of harvest, when they first entered the field to gather the potatoes, before commencing the work, they formed into a circle, and much to the surprise of the Superintendent, broke out together into the harvest hymn: *Now let us all thank God.*

After singing this, they fell to their work with great cheerfulness and vigor.

I mention these instances, from numerous others which might be produced, to show how much may be done in reclaiming the most hopeless youthful offenders by a judicious application of the right means of moral in-fluence. How short-sighted and destructive, then, is the policy which would exclude such influence from our public institutions! The same effects have been produced by houses of reformation in our own country. I would mention, as one instance, the institution of Mr. Welles in Massachusetts.

Now, laying aside all considerations of benevolence and of religious obligation, is it not for the highest good of the State, that these minds should be withdrawn from vice and trained up to be enlightened and useful citizens, contributing a large share to the public wealth, virtue and happiness; rather than that they should come forward in life miserable criminals, of no use to themselves or the public, depredating on the property and violating the rights of the industrious citizens, increasing the public burdens by their crimes, endangering the well being of society, and undermining our liberties! They can be either the one or the other, according as we choose to educate them ourselves in the right way, or leave them to be educated by the thieves and drunkards in our streets, or the convicts in our prisons. The efforts made by some foreign nations to educate this part of their population, is a good lesson for us. All the schools and houses of reformation in Prussia, do not cost the government so much as old England is obliged to expend in prisons and constables for the regulation of that part of her population, for which the government provides no schools but the hulks and the jails; and I leave it to any one to say which arrangement produces the greatest amount of public happiness.

When I was in Berlin I went into the public prison, and visited every part of the establishment. At last I was introduced to a very large hall which was full of children, with their books and teachers, and having all the appearance of a common Prussian schoolroom. ''What,'' said I, ''is it possible that all these children are imprisoned here for crime?'' ''Oh no,'' said my conductor, smiling at my simplicity, ''but if a parent is imprisoned for crime, and on that account his children are left destitute of the means of education, and liable to grow up in ignorance and crime, the government has them taken here, and maintained and educated for useful employment.'' The thought brought tears to my eyes. This was a new idea to me. I know not that it has ever been suggested in the United States; but surely it is the duty of government, as well as its highest interest, when a man is paying the penalty of his crime in a public prison, to see that his unoffending children are not left to suffer, and to inherit their father's vices. Surely it would be better for the child, and *cheaper* as well as better, for the State. Let it not be supposed that a man would go to prison for the sake of having his children taken care of, for they who go to prison usually have little regard for their children; and if they had, discipline like that of the Berlin prison would soon sicken them of such a bargain.

Where education is estimated according to its real value, people are willing to expend money for the support of schools; and if necessary, to deny themselves some physical advantages for the sake of giving their children the blessings of moral and intellectual culture. In the government of Baden, four per cent of all the public expense is for education —they have a school with an average of two or three well qualified teachers to every three miles of territory, and every one hundred children; and that too, when the people are so poor that they can seldom afford any other food than dry barley bread, and a farmer considers it a luxury to be able to allow his family the use of butter-milk three or four times a year. In Prussia, palaces and convents are every where turned into houses of education; and accommodations originally provided for princes and bishops are not considered too good for the schoolmaster and his pupils. But, though occupying palaces, they have no opportunity to be idle or luxurious. Hard labor and frugal living are every where the indispensable conditions to a teacher's life, and I must say, that I have no particular wish that it should be otherwise; for it is only those who are willing to work hard and live frugally, that ever do much good in such a world as this.

I pass now to the consideration of a question of the deepest interest to us all, and that is, can the common schools in our State be made adequate to the wants of our population? I do not hesitate to answer this question decidedly in the affirmative; and to show that I give this answer on good grounds, I need only to state the proper object of education, and lay before you what is actually now done towards accomplishing this object in the common schools of Prussia and Wirtemberg.

What is the proper object of education? The proper object of education is a thorough developement of all the intellectual and moral powers—the awakening and calling forth of every talent that may exist, even in the remotest and obscurest corner of the State, and giving it a useful direction. A system that will

do this, and such a system only, do I consider adequate to the wants of our population; such a system, and such a system only, can avert all the evils and produce all the benefits which our common schools were designed to avert and produce. True, such a system must be far more extensive and complete than any now in operation among us—teachers must be more numerous, skilful, persevering, and self-denying—parents must take greater interest in the schools and do more for their support—and the children must attend punctually and regularly, till the whole prescribed course is completed. All this can be done, and I hope will be done; and to show that the thing is really practicable, I now ask your attention to the course of instruction in the common schools of Prussia and Wirtemberg, and other European States, which have done the most in the matter of public instruction. . . .

Character of the Common School System

The striking features of this system, even in the hasty and imperfect sketch which my limits allow me to give, are obvious even to superficial observation. No one can fail to observe its great completeness, both as to the number and kind of subjects embraced in it, and as to its adaptedness to develope every power of every kind, and give it a useful direction. What topic in all that is necessary for a sound business education is here omitted? I can think of nothing, unless it be one or two of the modern languages, and these are introduced wherever it is necessary. . . . In the Rhinish provinces of Prussia, in a considerable part of Bavaria, Baden, and Wirtemberg, French is taught as well as German; in the schools of Prussian Poland, German and Polish are taught; and even English, in the Russian schools of Cronstadt and Archangel, where so many English and American merchants resort for the purposes of trade. Two languages can be taught in a school quite as easily as one, provided the teacher be perfectly familar, as any one may see by visiting Mr. Solomon's school in Cincinnati, where all the instruction is given both in German and English.

What faculty of mind is there that is not developed in the scheme of instruction? I know of none. The perceptive and reflective faculties, the memory and the judgment, the imagination and the taste, the moral and religious faculty, and even the various kinds of physical and manual dexterity, all have opportunity for developement and exercise.

Indeed, I think the system in its great outlines, as nearly complete as human ingenuity and skill can make it; though undoubtedly some of its arrangements and details admit of improvement; and some changes will of course be necessary in adapting it to the circumstances of different countries.

The entirely practical character of the system is obvious throughout. It views every subject on the practical side, and in reference to its adaptedness to use. The dry technical abstract parts of science are not those first presented; but the system proceeds, in the only way which nature ever pointed out, from practice to theory, from parts to demonstrations. It has often been a complaint in respect to some systems of education, that the more a man studied, the less he knew of the actual business of life. Such a complaint cannot be made in reference to this system, for being intended to educate for the actual business of life, this object is never for a moment lost sight of.

Another striking feature of the system is its moral and religious character. Its morality is pure and elevated, its religion entirely removed from the narrowness of sectarian bigotry. What parent is there, loving his children and wishing to have them respected and happy, who would not desire that they should be educated under such a kind of moral and religious influence as has been described? Whether a believer in revelation or not, does he not know that without sound morals there can be no happiness, and that there is no morality like the morality of the New Testament? Does he not know that without religion, the human heart can never be at rest, and that there is no religion like the religion of the Bible? Every well informed man knows, that, as a general fact, it is impossible to impress the obligations of morality with any efficiency on the heart of a child, or even on that of an adult, without an appeal to some mode which is sustained by the authority of God; and for what code will it be possible to claim this authority if not for the code of the Bible?

But perhaps some will be ready to say, the scheme is indeed an excellent one, provided only it were practicable; but the idea of introducing so extensive and complete a course of study into our common schools is entirely visionary and can never be realized. I answer, that it is no theory which I have been exhibiting, but a matter of fact, a copy of actual practice. The above system is no visionary scheme emanating from the closet of a recluse, but a sketch of the course of

instruction now actually pursued by thousands of schoolmasters in the best district schools that have ever been organized. It can be done, for it has been done, it is now done, and it ought to be done. If it can be done in Europe, I believe it can be done in the United States: if it can be done in Prussia, I know it can be done in Ohio. The people have but to say the word and provide the means, and the thing is accomplished; for the word of the people here is even more powerful than the word of the King there; and the means of the people here are altogether more abundant for such an object than the means of the sovereign there. Shall this object, then, so desirable in itself, so entirely practicable, so easily within our reach, fail of accomplishment? For the honor and welfare of our State, for the safety of our whole nation, I trust it will not fail; but that we shall witness in this commonwealth the introduction of a system of common school instruction, fully adequate to all the wants of our population.

But the question occurs, *how* can this be done? I will give a few brief hints as to some things which I suppose to be essential to the attainment of so desirable an end.

Means of Sustaining the System

1. Teachers must be skilful, and trained to their business. It will at once be perceived, that the plan above sketched out proceeds on the supposition that the teacher has fully and distinctly in his mind the whole course of instruction, not only as it respects the matter to be taught, but also as to all the best modes of teaching, that he may be able readily and decidedly to vary his method according to the peculiarities of each individual mind which may come under his care. This is the only true secret of successful teaching. The old mechanical method, in which the teacher relies entirely on his textbook, and drags every mind along through the same dull routine of creeping recitation, is utterly insufficient to meet the wants of our people. It may do in Asiatic Turkey, where the whole object of the school is to learn to pronounce the words of the Koran, in one dull monotonous series of sounds; or it may do in China, where men must never speak or think out of the old beaten track of Chinese imbecility; but it will never do in the United States, where the object of education ought to be to make immediately available, for the highest and best purposes, every particle of real talent that exists in the nation. To effect such a purpose, the teacher

must possess a strong and independent mind, well disciplined, and well stored with every thing pertaining to his profession, and ready to adapt his instructions to every degree of intellectual capacity, and every kind of acquired habit. But how can we expect to find such teachers, unless they are trained to their business? A very few of extraordinary powers may occur, as we sometimes find able mechanics, and great mathematicians, who had no early training in their favorite pursuits; but these few exceptions to a general rule will never multiply fast enough to supply our schools with able teachers. The management of the human mind, particularly youthful mind, is the most delicate task ever committed to the hand of man; and shall it be left to mere instinct, or shall our schoolmasters have at least as careful a training as our lawyers and physicians?

2. Teachers, then, must have the means of acquiring the necessary qualifications; in other words, there must be institutions in which the business of teaching is made a systematic object of attention. I am not an advocate for multiplying our institutions. We already have more in number than we support, and it would be wise to give power and efficiency to those we now possess, before we project new ones. But the science and art of teaching ought to be a regular branch of study in some of our academies and high schools, that those who are looking forward to this profession may have an opportunity of studying its principles. In addition to this, in our populous towns where there is an opportunity for it, there should be large model schools, under the care of the most able and experienced teachers that can be obtained; and the candidates for the profession who have already completed the theoretic course of the academy, should be employed in this school as monitors or assistants, thus testing all their theories by practice, and acquiring skill and dexterity under the guidance of their head master. Thus, while learning, they would be teaching, and no time or effort would be lost. To give efficiency to the whole system, to present a general standard and a prominent point of union, there should be at least one model-teachers' seminary, at some central point,—as at Columbus,—which shall be amply provided with all the means of study and instruction, and have connected with it schools of every grade, for the practice of the students, under the immediate superintendence of their teachers.

3. The teachers must be competently supported, and devoted to their business. Few men attain any great degree of excellence in a profession, unless they love it, and place all their hopes in life upon it. A man cannot, consistently with his duty to himself, engage in a business which does not afford him a competent support, unless he has other means of living, which is not the case with many who engage in teaching. In this country especially, where there are such vast fields of profitable employment open to every enterprising man, it is not possible, that the best of teachers can be obtained, to any considerable extent, for our district schools, at the present rate of wages. We have already seen what encouragement is held out to teachers in Russia, Prussia, and other European nations, and what pledges are given of competent support to their families, not only while engaged in the work, but when, having been worn out in the public service, they are no longer able to labor. In those countries, where every profession and walk of life is crowded, and where one of the most common and oppressive evils is want of employment, men of high talents and qualifications are often glad to become teachers even of district schools; men who in this country would aspire to the highest places in our colleges, or even our halls of legislation and courts of justice. How much more necessary, then, here, that the profession of teaching should afford a competent support!

Indeed, such is the state of things in this country, that we cannot expect to find male teachers for all our schools. The business of educating, especially young children, must fall, to a great extent, on female teachers. There is not the same variety of tempting employment for females as for men, they can be supported cheaper, and the Creator has given them peculiar qualifications for the education of the young. Females, then, ought to be employed extensively in all our elementary schools, and they should be encouraged and aided in obtaining the qualifications necessary for this work. There is no country in the world where woman holds so high a rank, or exerts so great an influence, as here; wherefore, her responsibilities are the greater, and she is under obligations to render herself the more actively useful. I think our fair countrywomen, notwithstanding the exhortations of Harriet Martineau, Fanny Wright, and some other *ladies* and *gentlemen*, will never seek distinction in our public assemblies for public discussion, or in our halls of legislation; but in their appropriate work of educating the young, of forming the opening mind to all that is good and great, the more they distinguish themselves the better.

4. The children must be made comfortable in their school; they must be punctual, and attend the whole course. There can be no profitable study without personal comfort; and the inconvenience and miserable arrangements of some of our school-houses are enough to annihilate all that can be done by the best of teachers. No instructor can teach unless the pupils are present to be taught, and no plan of systematic instruction can be carried steadily through, unless the pupils attend punctually and through the whole course.

5. The children must be given up implicitly to the discipline of the school. Nothing can be done unless the teacher has the entire control of his pupils in school hours, and out of school too, so far as the rules of the school are concerned. If the parent in any way interferes with, or overrules the arrangements of the teacher, he may attribute it to himself if the school is not successful. No teacher ever ought to be employed to whom the entire management of the children cannot be safely entrusted; and better at any time dismiss the teacher than counteract his discipline. Let parents but take the pains and spend the money necessary to provide a comfortable school-house and a competent teacher for their children, and they never need apprehend that the discipline of the school will be unreasonably severe. No inconsiderable part of the corporeal punishment that has been inflicted in schools, has been made necessary by the discomfort of school-houses and the unskilfulness of teachers. A lively, sensitive boy is stuck upon a bench full of knot-holes and sharp ridges, without a support for his feet or his back, with a scorching fire on one side of him and a freezing wind on the other; and a stiff Orbilius of a master, with wooden brains and iron hands, orders him to sit perfectly still, with nothing to employ his mind or his body, till it is *his turn to read*. Thus confined for hours, what can the poor little fellow do but begin to wriggle like a fish out of water, or an eel in a frying-pan? For this irrepressible effort at relief he receives a box on the ear; this provokes and renders him still more uneasy, and next comes the merciless ferule; and the poor child is finally burnt and frozen, cuffed and beaten into hardened roguery or incurable stupidity, just because the avarice of his parents denied him a comfortable school-house and a competent teacher.

6. A beginning must be made at certain points, and the advance towards completeness must be gradual. Every thing cannot be done at once, and such a system as is needed cannot be generally introduced till its benefits are first demonstrated by actual experiment. Certain great points, then, where the people are ready to co-operate, and to make the most liberal advances in proportion to their means, to maintain the schools, should be selected, and no pains or expense spared, till the full benefits of the best system are realized; and as the good effects are seen, other places will very readily follow the example. All experience has shown, that governmental patronage is most profitably employed, not to do the entire work but simply as an incitement to the people to help themselves.

To follow up this great object, the legislature has wisely made choice of a Superintendent whose untiring labors and disinterested zeal are worthy of all praise. But no great plan can be carried through in a single year; and if the Superintendent is to have opportunity to do what is necessary, and to preserve that independence and energy of official character which is requisite to the successful discharge of his duties, he should hold his office for the same term and on the same conditions, as the Judges of the Supreme Court.

Every officer engaged in this, or in every other public work, should receive a suitable compensation for his services. This justice requires, and it is the only way to secure fidelity and efficiency.

There is one class of our population for whom some special provision seems necessary. The children of foreign immigrants are now very numerous among us, and it is essential that they receive a good ENGLISH EDUCATION. But they are not prepared to avail themselves of the advantages of our common English schools, their imperfect acquaintance with the language being an insuperable bar to their entering on the course of study. It is necessary, therefore, that there be some preparatory schools, in which instruction shall be communicated both in English and their native tongue. The English is, and must be, the language of this country, and the highest interests of our State demand it of the Legislature to require that the English language be thoroughly taught in every school which they patronise. Still, the exigencies of the case make it necessary that there should be some schools expressly fitted to the condition of our foreign immigrants, to introduce them to a knowledge of our language and institutions. A school of this kind has been established in Cincinnati by benevolent individuals. It has been in operation about a year, and already nearly three hundred children have received its advantages. Mr. Solomon, the head teacher, was educated for his profession in one of the best institutions of Prussia, and in this school he has demonstrated the excellencies of the system. The instructions are all given both in German and English, and this use of two languages does not at all interrupt the progress of the children in their respective studies. I cannot but recommend this philanthropic institution to the notice and patronage of the Legislature.

In neighborhoods where there is a mixed population, it is desirable, if possible, to employ teachers who understand both languages, and that the exercise of the school be conducted in both, with the rule, however, that all the reviews and examinations *be in English only.*

These suggestions I have made with unfeigned diffidence, and with a sincere desire that the work which has been so nobly begun by the Legislature of Ohio, may be carried forward to a glorious result. I should hardly have ventured to take such liberty had not my commission expressly authorized me to "make such practical observations as I might think proper," as well as to report facts. I know that I am addressing enlightened and patriotic men, who have discernment to perceive, and good feeling to appreciate, every sincere attempt, however humble it may be, for the country's good; and I have therefore spoken out plainly and directly the honest convictions of my heart; feeling assured that what is honestly meant, will, by highminded men, be kindly received. . . .

Queries on Education

The following inquiries, with some others not here included, were made out by a committee of the Association of Teachers in Hamilton county. I obtained the answers during my tour in Europe, from Mr. Wood of the Sessional School in Edinburg, Scotland, Rev. Mr. Kunze of the Frederick Orphan House, in Berlin, Prussia, and Professor Schwartz of the University of Heidelberg, in Baden. As I received the answers orally and in different languages, I cannot pretend to give them with verbal accuracy; but I have endeavored in every instance to make a faithful representation of the sentiment.

1. What is the best method of inculcating moral and religious duty in schools?

Mr. Wood. Every morning I have recitations in the Bible, accompanied with such brief and pertinent remarks as naturally occur in connection with the recitation.

Mr. Kunze. In Prussia the scholars are all taught Luther's Smaller Catechism; they have a daily recitation in the Bible, beginning with the historical portions; the schools are always opened and closed with prayer, and the singing of some religious hymns. The Bible and Psalm-book are the first books which are put into the hands of the child, and they are his constant companions through the whole course of his education, and required to be such through life.

Professor Schwartz. Every teacher should have a religious spirit, and by his personal influence, diffuse it among his pupils. The religious and moral instruction in the schools of Baden is similar to that in Prussia, as stated by Mr. Kunze.

2. What is the best mode for using the Bible in school?

Mr. W. Take the whole Bible just as it is in our translation; for the younger children, select the easier historical portions, and go through with it as the scholars advance.

Mr. K. In Prussia we have tried all sorts of ways, by extracts, by new translations, by commentaries, written expressly for schools; but after all those trials, there is now but one opinion among all acquainted with the subject, and that is, that the whole Bible, just as it stands in the translations in common use, should be a reading and recitation book in all the schools. In the Protestant schools, Luther's translation is used, and in the Catholic schools, the translation approved by that church. The children are required not merely to repeat the words of the translation by rote, but to give a good exhibition of the real sentiment in their own language.

Prof. S. Answer similar to Mr. Kunze's above.

3. Method of governing schools—moral influence—rewards of merit—emulation—corporeal punishment?

Mr. W. I use all the purely moral influence I can; but rewards for the meritorious are highly necessary; and as to the principle of emulation, I appeal to it more and more the longer I teach. The evils of emulation, such as producing discouragement or exciting envy in the less successful scholars, I avoid by equalizing the classes as much as possible, so that all the scholars of each class, may, as to their capabilities of improvement, be nearly on a level. I know no successful school for young scholars where corporeal punishment is disused. The teacher must retain it as a last resort.

Mr. K. The Bible, prayers, and singing, are most essential helps to the consistent teacher in governing his scholars; but premiums, emulation, and corporeal punishment, have hitherto been found indispensable auxiliaries. In our schools we have premiums of books, and in the orphan house there is a prize of fifty dollars annually awarded to each of the most meritorious scholars, which is allowed to accumulate in the savings bank till the pupil comes of age, when it is given to him to aid in establishing him in business. Each teacher keeps a journal, divided under different heads, of all the delinquencies of his scholars, and if any one has six in a month, he must suffer corporeal punishment. The instruction of punishment is a cow-skin; but no teacher is allowed to inflict more than four blows at any one time, or for any offence. This kind of punishment is not often needed. Of the 380 boys in the orphan house not more than two in a month render themselves liable to it. After the scholar enters the gymnasium, he is no longer liable to corporeal punishment; but in all the schools below this, it is held in reserve as the last resort.

Prof. S. I do not approve of rewards as a means of discipline. Emulation may be appealed to a little; but much of it is not good, it is so liable to call forth bitter and unholy feeling. The skilful teacher, who gains the confidence and affection of his scholars, can govern without emulation or rewards, and with very little of corporeal punishment. In a school in Heidelberg of 150 children under ten years of age, not two in a year suffer this kind of punishment. In Baden the teacher is not allowed to strike a scholar without obtaining permission of the school inspector, and in this way all hasty and vindictive punishments are prevented. The daily singing of religious hymns is one of the most efficient means of bringing a school under a perfect discipline by moral influence.

4. What is generally the best method of teaching?

Mr. W. As much as possible by conversation; as little as may be by mere book recitation. The pupil must always learn from the book.

Mr. K. Lively conversation. Very few teachers in Prussia ever use a book in recitation. The pupils study from books, and recite without them.

Prof. S. The living word in preference to the dead letter.

5. Employment of female teachers?

Mr. W. For young children they do well; and if good female teachers can be obtained, they might perhaps carry female education through without the help of male teachers.

Mr. K. Female teachers have not been much employed in Prussia, they are not generally successful. In a few instances they have done well.

Prof. S. Man is the divinely appointed teacher; but for small children female teachers do well; and in respect to all that pertains to the heart and the fingers they are even better than male teachers. It is not good that females should be educated entirely by teachers of their own sex; the female cannot be educated completely without the countenance of man to work upon the heart.

6. Is there any difference in the course of instruction for male and female schools?

Mr. K. None in the primary schools, but in the higher schools the course of instruction for males is more rigidly scientific than for females; and some branches of study are appropriate to the one class of schools which do not at all come into the other, and *vice versa.*

7. Public endowments for female schools of a high order?

Mr. W. There are no such endowments in Scotland.

Mr. K. There are very few in Prussia: only one in Berlin, but that a very good one. Female schools of a high order are mostly sustained by individual effort, under the supervision of the magistrates, but without aid from the Government.

Prof. S. We have none in Baden, nor are they needed for the female. The house is her school; and such are her susceptibilities, and her quickness of apprehension, that she is fitted by Providence to learn from real life; and she often learns thus, more successfully than boys can be taught in the school.

8. Number of studies to be pursued simultaneously in the different stages of instruction?

Mr. W. I begin with reading and writing (on slates) together, and as the scholars advance, increase the number of branches.

Mr. K. We begin all together, reading, writing, arithmetic, grammar, &c., and so continue throughout.

Prof. S. The younger the fewer, the older the more.

9. Infant Schools?

Mr. W. For children who are neglected by their parents, for poor orphans, and such like, they are excellent, but parents who are able to take care of their own children, ought to do it, and not send them to the infant school.

Mr. K. I regard them as highly useful for

all classes of children, the rich and the poor, the good and the bad; but the Prussian Government discourages them, except for the vicious and the neglected. The King admits them only where parental instruction cannot be had.

Prof. S. Highly useful, and very much increasing in Europe. In Italy, particularly in Lombardy, they are fast gaining ground under the care of truly Christian teachers.

10. The Pestalozzian system?

Mr. W. It has many good things, with some quackery. As a whole, it is too formal.

Mr. K. In Prussia, not approved as a whole and in arithmetic entirely disused.

Prof. S. One of the steps by which we arrived at our present stage of advancement; but we have got beyond it now.

11. Number of pupils to one teacher in the different stages of instruction?

Mr. W. In the elementary stages, if the teacher has good monitors,[1] he may safely take charge of from 100 to 600 pupils; as they advance, he must diminish the number, but only on account of the difficulty of obtaining good monitors in the higher branches.

Mr. K. In Prussia, generally about 40 in the elementary branches, and in the higher branches fewer.

Prof. S. In Baden the maximum is 80, on account of the difficulty, in that populous district, of maintaining a sufficient number of schoolmasters for the whole population. As the scholars advance, the number is diminished.

12. Systematic division of the different branches of instruction in schools?

Mr. W. ——

Mr. K. The schools in Prussia are all divided according to the different branches, and each branch has its own teacher.

Prof. S. Not good to attempt a systematic division in the elementary schools, but very useful for the higher schools. Young children need to be brought under the influence of one teacher, and not have their attention and affection divided among many.

13. Mode of instructing those who are preparing themselves to be teachers?

Mr. W. Employ them as monitors under a good teacher, with some theoretical instruction. This is matter of opinion, not of experience; for we have in Scotland no institutions for the preparation of teachers.

Mr. K. In the seminaries for teachers,

---

[1]Monitors, in Mr. Wood's school, occupy the place of assistant teachers, and each class has its monitor.

there are lectures on the theory of education, mode of teaching, &c.; but the pupils are taught principally by practical exercises in teaching the scholars of the model schools attached to these institutions, and they also labor to perfect themselves in the branches they are to teach.

Prof. S. The general principles of method may be communicated in lectures, but schools for actual practical exercise in teaching are indispensable. They must also become perfectly familiar with the branches they are to teach.

14. Estimation in which the teacher is held, and his income in proportion to that of the other professions?

Mr. W. With us, rising, in both respects, but as yet far below the other professions.

Mr. K. In Prussia, the elementary teachers are highly respected and competently maintained; they rank as the better sort of mechanics, and the head teachers rank next to clergymen. The salary low—that of the subordinate teachers, very low.

Prof. S. With us, the worthy teacher holds a respectable rank, and can sit at table with noblemen. The salary has recently been raised, but it is still below that of the clergyman.

15. Subordination among teachers?

Mr. W. Very desirable, but exceedingly difficult to carry it to any extent.

Mr. K. As strict subordination among the teachers of the school, as among the officers of the army.

Prof. S. Strict subordination must be maintained.

16. Mode of securing punctual and universal attendance of scholars till the full round of instruction is completed?

Mr. W. By acting on the parents.

Mr. K. By strict laws, rigorously executed.

Prof. S. By law.

17. Control of teachers over their scholars out of school hours?

Mr. W. The laws of the school are never to be violated, even out of school hours. Difficult to carry it any further.

Mr. K. The teacher has the control, so far as he can get it. Government sustains him in it.

Prof. S. In all that relates to the school, the teacher must have the control out of school hours.

18. How are schools affected by political changes in the administration of the government?

Mr. W. We have had fears, but as yet have suffered no actual evil.

Mr. K. We have no changes in Prussia.

Prof. S. The school must remain sacred and inviolate, untroubled by political changes.

19. School apparatus and library?

Mr. W. Very desirable, but little done that way, as yet, in Scotland.

Mr. K. Most of our schools are provided with them, and we consider them very important.

Prof. S. The teachers must have access to good books; and if they are industrious and skilful, the pupils will not suffer for want of a library.

20. How can accuracy of teaching be secured?

Mr. W. Every thing depends on the teacher.

Mr. K. Very accurate in Prussia; the Government will have it so.

Prof. S. The teacher must understand his profession, and devote himself to it.

21. Governmental supervision of schools, and mode of securing responsibility in the supervisors?

Mr. W. I cannot tell. In this country it is very inefficient, as it must be, unless the visitors receive pay for their services.

Mr. K. In this country the governmental supervision is very strict, and produces a very happy influence. The supervisors are paid for their work, and obliged to attend to it. Responsibility is secured by requiring minute and accurate periodical reports, and by a special visitation as often as once in three years.

Prof. S. The supervisors must be paid;

there must be strict subordination, accurate returns, and special visitations.

22. How are good teachers to be obtained in sufficient numbers?

Mr. W. I cannot tell. It is difficult here.

Mr. K. By means of our teachers' seminaries—we have them in abundance.

Prof. S. By teachers' seminaries, and private teaching, we have enough. In your country it must always be difficult while there is such an amount of business accessible which is so much more lucrative.

23. Extent of qualification demanded of elementary teachers?

Mr. W. In Scotland, there is no general rule.

Mr. K. & Prof. S. In Prussia and Baden, the demands are ample, and rigidly enforced.

24. Governmental supervision of private schools?

Mr. W. Of doubtful expediency.

Mr. K. Very strict in Prussia, and altogether beneficial in its influence.

Prof. S. Leave the private schools free, but regulate them, and see that the teachers do their duty.

25. Associations of teachers?

Mr. W. Not yet introduced in Scotland, but very desirable.

Mr. K. & Prof. S. Highly useful, and demanded and regulated by the Government. Written essays and discussions, and mutual communication of experience, the business of these Associations.

Alexander Dallas Bache   1836

European Primary School Notes and Educational Comparisons

Alexander Dallas Bache (1806–1867) graduated from the United States Military Academy in 1825 and was appointed professor of natural philosophy and chemistry at the University of Pennsylvania in 1827. He was chosen to be president of the newly established Girard College for orphans in 1836 and was immediately sent to Europe by the college trustees to study educational institutions and systems. He spent over two years in Europe, including some eight months in Britain where he visited many charitable institutions. In all, he visited over 270 schools and noted precise details of their curriculums, teaching methods, and administrative organizations. To illustrate his research, he constructed comparative education charts, including the one reprinted here on the number of hours spent at each activity in various European Institutions.

Bache's detailed report on European education remains as one of the most extensive accounts prepared by an American during the nineteenth century. It is divided into two parts; the first or minor part is devoted to institutions for orphans and destitute children similar to

Alexander Dallas Bache, *Report on Education in Europe to the Trustees of the Girard College for Orphans* (Philadelphia: Lydia R. Bailey, 1839), pp. iii–vii, 3–10, 157–159, 170–173, 199–208, 503–516, 655.

Girard College, and the second or major part describes primary, secondary, and tertiary-level schools in Ireland, Scotland, England, France, Holland, Prussia, Saxony, Bavaria, and Switzerland. The extracts below include the detailed instructions Bache received from the college trustees to investigate and compare European education and part of his report on infant, elementary, and secondary schools.

Instructions for the Tour

The origin and nature of the following Report, which has been ordered to be printed by the Trustees of the Girard College for Orphans, will be best explained by prefixing to it the instructions directing the tour, during which the information embodied in it was collected. These instructions were drawn up by the Committee on Scholastic Education, who were charged with this duty by the Board of Trustees.

Board of Trustees
Girard College for Orphans
September 19, 1836

A. D. Bache, Esq., President
Girard College for Orphans
Philadelphia

Dear Sir:—I enclose a copy of a resolution, passed by this Board on the 19th July last, authorizing you to visit Europe, under the instructions of the Committee on Scholastic Education. I also enclose, in quadruplicate, a commission from the Board, certified by the Mayor of Philadelphia, stating the objects of your mission, and asking the aid of all friends of science to facilitate your inquiries. The financial arrangements for your salary and expenses are, as you know, completed. It remains only for the Committee to add their instructions for your government.

Your familiarity with the subject of education, and your personal acquaintance with the views of the Board, of which you were a member, supersede the necessity of any detailed explanations in regard to the purposes of your voyage, or the best means of accomplishing them; and the Committee will, therefore, confine themselves to such general instructions as may regulate the course of your movements and inquiries.

The Board of Trustees are charged by the City of Philadelphia to prepare a system of instruction for the Girard College for Orphans. For this purpose they are anxious to have the most accurate information of the best means used for the same purpose elsewhere, and you have been selected to obtain it. Your object, then, is to visit all estab-lishments in Europe similar to the Girard College; and as these are found principally, if not exclusively, in England, Scotland, Ireland, France, Belgium, Holland, Switzerland, Italy, Austria, Prussia, and the rest of the states of Germany, these countries will form the natural limits of your tour. Accordingly, all institutions in each of those countries resembling the Girard College, or any others which promise to afford useful information in organizing it, you will see and examine. Your own reflection will readily suggest the points of information desired; and I will, therefore, merely enumerate a few, which may serve as a basis for your own extensive investigation. Of every establishment visited by you, we should wish to know—

1. Its history, general administration, and the nature and extent of its funds.

2. Its interior organization and government; the names, titles, and duties of all the persons employed in it.

3. Who are admitted to it, and the forms and terms of admission, and where it is professedly for the education of orphans who are considered as orphans.

4. The number and classification of the scholars, and their term of residence.

5. Their course of studies, in the minutest detail, from the commencement to the end of their residence in the institution, with the text-books and other works used.

6. As a part of that course, specially important to the Girard College, we should desire to know the regulations or the practice by which, among a large body of scholars, a portion, after continuing for some time in the institution, are permitted to begin their active career in life—while others, with greater aptitude or greater willingness to learn, are carried up to the higher branches of education. The nature and the mode of that discrimination would be highly interesting—as would also be—

7. The precise extent to which moral and religious instruction is proposed to be given, and is actually given, and also by whom and in what form that instruction is conveyed.

8. The mechanical arts taught—the mode of teaching them—the models, tools, and implements of all kinds employed—and the manner in which the practice of these arts is mingled with the routine of studies.

9. The system of rewards and punish-

ments in regard to studies or personal conduct.

10. The general police and discipline of the school.

11. The amusements—gymnastic exercises—games of all kinds, uniting instruction with agreeable relaxation—together with the number and extent of the vacations, pecuniary allowance, or personal indulgences to the scholars.

12. The diet and clothing of the scholars.

13. The regulations in regard to health, hours of study and of rest, arrangement as to sleeping and eating, and the whole routine of each day's employment.

14. The expenses of the school, including salaries and all incidents, with the average annual expense of each scholar.

15. The structure of the buildings, the arrangement of dormitories, refectories, play-grounds, and work-shops, illustrated by drawings, where they can be procured.

16. As a proper foundation for similar statistical inquiries in this country, you will collect all the information you can in respect to the proportion of orphans to the rest of the community.

These general heads of inquiry, which you can easily multiply, will indicate the wish of the Board that your examination should be thorough and practical. They already possess, or may easily obtain, all that books can teach on the subject. It is your especial duty to study the actual working of the machinery of education; to domesticate yourself, if practicable, in these institutions, and, by your own personal observation, to distinguish what is really useful from what is merely plausible in theory.

It is this anxiety that your investigation should be complete, which induces them not to fix at present any period for your return. How much time it may require cannot now be safely determined. They rely confidently on your diligence, and are sure that you will not prolong your absence without ample reason. While, therefore, they are very anxious to open the College with the least possible delay, they deem it so much more important to begin well than to begin soon, that they postpone naming any limit to your stay in Europe, until you are able to apprize them of your progress.

In respect to the purchase of books and apparatus, mentioned in the resolution of the Board, it is not their wish that you should, at this time, purchase a library, or an extensive philosophical apparatus. You will only inquire where they can be best procured hereafter, and, in the mean time, limit your actual purchases to text-books and other works used in schools, or which may assist your inquiries: to models, drawings, and such philosophical instruments as may be necessary or useful in opening the College, or which you may deem it expedient to procure in anticipation of the larger collection.

The materials and information thus acquired you will, on your return, present to the Board of Trustees, and at the same time, or as soon thereafter as practicable, you will prepare a final Report, with a plan for the government and instruction of the College—the result of all your examination and reflection.

In the mean time, you will keep the Board constantly advised of your movements.

With my best wishes that your mission may be as pleasant as I am sure it will be useful, I remain, yours truly,

N. BIDDLE
Chairman

Outline of Countries and Schools Visited

. . . While there can be no doubt that the general principles of education must be founded upon those of human action, and hence be common to all nations, it must be admitted that systems framed from such general laws would require considerable modification to render them applicable to different countries. Differences in political and social organization, in habits and manners, require corresponding changes to adapt a system of education to the nation; and, without such modifications, success in the institutions of one country is no guarantee for the same result in those of another. The difficulties, however, of working out a plan of education, from observation, appeared to me much greater at the outset of my undertaking than they do now, that I have seen how very many of the essentials are common to all well organized institutions having the same scope. A consideration of these difficulties induced me to make Great Britain the first point of my tour, since it was reasonable to infer that the successful methods of education there might be more easily transplanted, being more directly applicable at home than those of other countries. The examination of some of the more interesting institutions there occupied rather more than eight months; and, lest this portion of time should appear too great in comparison with that devoted to the Continent, it may be well to state the circumstances which absolutely required so considerable an allotment. Owing to the absence of any regular or central system of education, and of any general responsibility in the management of its institutions for public instruction, and to the entire freedom of individual effort, more time is required to obtain access to, and examine the establishments of Great Britain, than of any other country which I visited. A proper idea of the general arrangements can be obtained only by a study of particular cases, and each institution requires to be approached individually, and often in a different way, to secure a profitable entrance. As entirely different ideas frequently prevail in the organization of institutions of the same class, it is not sufficient, as it usually is elsewhere, to see merely a specimen to judge of the whole. For the special objects of my tour, the eleemosynary institutions were to be carefully inspected; and in the number of its Educational Charities, its Orphan Asylums, Bluecoat Schools, and Education Hospitals, Great Britain exceeds every other country in Europe. The city of Edinburgh and its vicinity alone contain five such institutions for boys, and no two of these are exactly alike in their regulations and administration, so that it was necessary to visit all to form precise ideas of their arrangements. If this be true of establishments having similar objects, in the same city, it may be inferred of those in different parts of the kingdom, and facts fully sustain the inference. It is true, to such an extent, that in preparing descriptions of these schools to present to the Board, I have found it difficult to classify them, so that by presenting, in detail, one institution as the type of a class, I might avoid the too great extension of this Report. The management of these institutions, the observation of which formed an important part of my duty, may serve in many points, especially in all that relates to the material comforts of life, as a model to those of other countries, in many of which I freely admit that more just ideas in regard to instruction prevail. Upon a review of the results of my visit to the institutions of Great Britain, it appears to me that the time was well bestowed, though more profitable experience in regard to instruction was acquired in less time in some of the countries of the Continent.

After completing a tour through some of the institutions of Ireland, Scotland, and England, I crossed to the Continent, and visited, in turn, the principal schools of France, Switzerland, Holland, Belgium, and the chief States of Germany, making also a rapid visit to Italy. The same subjects of inquiry did not, of course, interest me equally in these different countries, and I proceed to pass briefly in review their respective points of interest.

In Great Britain, the charitable institutions for education occupied most of my attention. There, as in other countries where similar establishments exist, and where no great or recent change has been made in public instruction, the instruction within them resembles more nearly that of the schools of the same grade in general, than in countries where such a change has been wrought. While engaged in visiting them, I did not neglect, however, institutions which afforded a less direct prospect of advantage. To illustrate by an example; although Heriot's, the Watsons', and other hospitals for education at Edinburgh and Glasgow occupied a large share of my attention while in Scotland, I visited, more or less in detail, at Edinburgh, the Model Infant School, the Circus-Place Preparatory School, the Sessional School, the High School, the Academy, the Western Academy, the Hill Street Institution, and the University; at Glasgow, the Infant and Juvenile Schools of the Education Society, the different departments of the High School, and the University. I also made an excursion to St. Andrew's, to visit the Madras College founded by Dr. Bell.

In France, the general system of education, especially as modified in its lower departments, and the schools for science and the arts, formed the special objects of examination. The orphans are, in general, associated with the foundlings, and distributed through the country at the expense of the state; the system presenting nothing, as far as my inquiries led, either for approval or imitation. The plan, of which I venture to speak thus freely, must not be confounded with the excellent system in the Grand Duchy of Weimar, which, though similar in appearance, differs essentially from it. In Weimar, orphan children, deprived of both parents, are distributed among families, as nearly as possible in the same station of life as the deceased parents, and a real superintendence, both moral and intellectual, is exercised over them by officers specially appointed for the purpose, and by the parochial clergy and schoolmasters.

In Switzerland, recent and great efforts, consequent upon the advance of true liberty, have been made among the republics, in behalf of general education. The school of Pestalozzi, at Yverdun, occupies a prominent place in the history of education; and the institutions of Fellenberg, at Hofwyl, have been frequently described. Others of great merit, but more recently established, are less generally known, and some of them will, as far as my limits allow, be noticed in this Report. I cannot, however, enter into the particulars requisite to present the striking results which the last seven years have produced in many of the cantons.

The common school system, as well as the eleemosynary institutions of Holland, deservedly attract much attention, and afforded interesting subjects for examination. There are peculiarities about both, and experiments have been made there which bear upon some of the most interesting questions in education. I need only refer, here, to those of the method of mutual instruction, and of the manner of supplying teachers; the latter of which experiments has led to a conclusion in favour of schools for teachers, which appears to me irresistible.

Among the institutions of the different states and free towns of Germany, I visited more or less in detail those of Prussia, Saxony, Austria, Bavaria, Wurtemberg, Nassau, Weimar, Frankfort, Bremen, and Hamburgh. The condition of public instruction, in general, in the different states, as well as of the different departments of it in the same state, is very unequal. Prussia is at present decidedly in advance of the other larger German States in the education of the people, especially in the manner and matter of the instruction. The ease with which every point connected with the schools is ascertained, is remarkable; and I look back to the time spent in them, and in intercourse with their teachers, as one of the most profitable portions of that occupied by my tour. As the various accounts which have been given of public instruction in Prussia have, in general, referred to the system more particularly than to the schools, I shall, in this Report, touch briefly upon the former, and go more into detail in regard to the latter. By reference to their spirit and minute arrangements, it is easy to see where they would apply as perfectly in a republic as in a monarchy. The instruction in many of the charitable institutions of that country has not kept pace with that in the schools in general, though there are others which have even led the way in improvement. Weimar has followed closely the Prussian model in its system of education, and the schools of Nassau may be said to be derived from the same source. The schools of Saxony were once famous throughout Europe, but the primary schools appear to have lost that rank; they are now, however, rapidly improving, by the same means which produced the present advanced state of instruc-

tion in Prussia—the education of teachers. In Bavaria, changes of system have been too recent to render general remarks of any value. I shall, however, give an account of the method of Graser, introduced into the schools of a section of the kingdom. In Austria, public instruction remains nearly on the footing upon which it was placed by the reforming emperor, Joseph the Second. There can be no doubt that it was once much in advance of the times, though the elementary department is at present behind that of most of the other German States. They still adhere to the incomplete plan of educating teachers in ordinary schools, and to antiquated methods of instruction. The Schools of Arts in Austria rank, however, with the best in Europe, and receive liberal encouragement from the government.

Of the many institutions which have claimed my attention, it would be entirely impossible to give even a meagre sketch within the limits appropriate to a Report,[1] and if it were practicable to go into details respecting all, many would be found not to repay the pains taken in reducing to paper a description of them. In making the selection, which is thus necessary, I shall endeavour to bring to the notice of the Board the countries in which the different departments of education are best carried on, and to give a sketch of the system of education, illustrated by the minutiæ of as many individual institutions as appear necessary to exemplify the system, and to render its results available for practice; endeavouring to render each account as complete in itself as the nature of the main object of my Report will permit.

The manner of collecting the information which I sought requires a passing notice. The introductions which usually flow in abundantly upon any one known to have a special object in visiting a country, opened to me the earliest and sometimes the best sources of information as to the existence, nature, and extent of institutions, and of the books necessary to give particulars in regard to them, and which are rarely known at a distance. By consulting these and other works and documents, and by comparison of various opinions, I was usually enabled to decide correctly as to the course which I ought to take, to see what was most deserving of attention. However, sometimes erroneous opinions deceived me, and I found that my course

---

[1]The whole number of schools visited was upwards of two hundred and seventy-eight; to some of these, however, I merely made a single short visit, others occupied me for several days.

had missed some interesting point, or had brought me to one of little interest. Occasionally the error was irremediable, but not often. Again, as it was necessary to employ all periods of the year, I found it impossible to arrange my visit so as to pass through a country at the period of greatest activity in the schools. Where the system of public instruction was central, like that of France, or Prussia, recourse to authority pointed out the proper institutions to visit, and gained admission to them. The personal acquaintance which the teachers of Germany have with each other, greatly facilitated my progress in its several states. Almost everywhere, indeed, I have reason to remember with gratitude the kind assistance rendered to me. Having ascertained the places which it would be, probably, profitable to visit and the institutions to be examined, I regulated the time and the attention devoted to them, by the interest which they appeared to present, returning to the same institution frequently or not at all, according to circumstances. As auxiliaries to my investigations during these visits, I procured the printed documents which existed relative to the institutions.

I also prepared beforehand a series of questions, to which, when modified to suit the particular establishment in regard to which detailed information was desired, I obtained answers from the head, or from one or more intelligent persons connected with the establishment.

The written and printed sources of information which are thus at the disposal of the Board, are 1st. A journal of my visits to different institutions, and of verbal information received in regard to them, with my remarks. 2d. Replies to a series of questions in regard to particular institutions, or systems of instruction. 3d. Statutes, by-laws, and regulations of different institutions. Laws and documents relating to public instruction, &c. 4th. Histories, descriptions, and text-books of different schools. 5th. Particular works on education.

These form a mass of documentary matter which, duly arranged and digested, will always throw the light of experiment upon doubtful points in the working of our system of organization. In many cases the documents, descriptive of the schools, give the actual results of suggestions contained in the works on education.

From this mass I propose to draw out some of the more prominent parts, and to call the attention of the Trustees specially to them. The personal experience gained by my tour will, however, as far as the Girard College is concerned, be its most important result. I could not expect the Trustees to follow me through descriptions or even notices of all the institutions which I have visited during my two years' absence, or listen to a record of the many failures and mistakes which I have seen, and which, though they have formed one considerable item in the experience gained, it would be truly an ungrateful task to record.

As best calculated to present the impressions, derived from this examination, of the actual results of education, I have adopted the descriptive form for my Report, and have purposely avoided summing up the conclusions, or presenting a review of them separately from the facts, that the force of the opinions may not be weakened by appearing out of this connexion. It is true that the remarks must be considered as general inductions from numerous facts, and not inferences from single instances, but these instances serve as their best illustration, if not sufficient, taken singly, to prove that they are just. These remarks suggested themselves at first as queries to be answered by further observation.

This Report will be divided into two parts, the first relating to the means provided for the education of orphans, the second to the systems of general education. Corresponding to these divisions there are two groups of institutions which present, in general, different objects for consideration; in the first, the government, discipline, and domestic economy, as well as the instruction are to be examined; while in the second, the instruction is the chief point of interest. Every individual institution in the first group should furnish moral, intellectual, and physical education; many in the second are necessarily more limited in their design. . . .

Infant Schools

As the pupils of the Girard College cannot be admitted before the age of six, they are past the infant period, and thus it may be supposed that I am departing from the rule which I have been obliged to lay down, in order to confine my Report within reasonable bounds. I am so fully impressed, however, with the importance of infant education, that I would not feel justified in passing over the period without a brief notice. The infant school system embraces so much of the philosophy of education, has been made so entirely an inductive branch, has been pondered over by so many minds of a superior order, that we cannot fail to derive advantage from a consideration of some of its principles and practical results. I am persuaded, that from the quarter of infant school instruction will one day come the reform of the English juvenile schools, and indeed this reform has already commenced, in the instance of the Juvenile Model School of Glasgow, and must extend widely, by the influence of its school for teachers.

The infant school system seems to have originated about the same time in Great Britain and Switzerland. In the former country, the first idea has been steadily improved upon, and there also it is now best carried out. Oberlin, the pastor of Steinthal (Ban de la Roche), collected the younger children of the poor of his parish into schools, where a female superintendent taught them spinning or knitting, and at intervals a little geography, from a Map of Steinthal and its Environs, or, by the help of pictures a portion of Bible or natural history. About the same time, the children of the workmen in Mr. Owen's extensive manufacturing establishments, at New Lanark, were collected in schools, for the purpose of healthful recreation, and of due care and of a certain degree of intellectual instruction; and, subsequently, a similar establishment was commenced by Lord Brougham, in Westminster. Mr. Wilderspin must, however, be considered as the author of the infant school as it now exists, having, in his connexion with a proposed asylum in another part of London, first proposed the name, defined the age, and established the true principles of infant education.

It is mainly by his instrumentality that the present system is now diffused so extensively over Great Britain. Of this system the infant schools of Liverpool, which he was engaged to reform, offered me an example for inspection, though not of the most favourable kind. The model infant schools of Glasgow, Edinburgh, and London, are improvements on the system, presenting marked varieties: that in London being derived, however, from the Glasgow model.

The necessity for the existence of such schools must vary much in different countries, and hence their not being adopted in all is no argument against the general principle of infant education. The want of such schools is most felt in a dense and manufacturing population, least in a scattered and agricultural one. Independently of essentially different degrees of usefulness, under different circumstances, various prejudices have concurred to prevent the introduction of these schools into some countries. Certain governments, as those of Germany in general, have not lent their influence to them, and the clergy have, in some parts of Europe, been as warmly opposed to them as in others they have been their friends. The deformed models which have been transplanted from England to other countries, have tended in many cases to foster these prejudices. In some of these the intellectual development of the pupils has been attempted to be carried on to their manifest injury, physically and mentally. In others, a mere mechanical and lifeless routine has been followed. The infant schools which I saw at Paris, called "écoles d'asile," seem to me to educate upon wrong principles, having adopted the mechanical arrangements of the English infant schools, without having seized their spirit. I believe, that depriving them of the female superintendence which they formerly enjoyed, to make them a part of the government system, will react further very injuriously upon them.

In some of the cities of Holland, as Rotterdam, Amsterdam, and Zwolle, I saw good infant schools. In the capital of Prussia they are beginning to take permanent root. In Austria. Proper, their condition is rather languishing, but in the Italian provinces they are deemed most important means of ultimately effecting a great change in the character of the people. At Venice the establishment is fostered by the government and liked by the people. At Milan is an admirable institution, growing out of that founded at Cremona, by the Abbé d'Aposti, who first introduced these schools into Italy. In Lombardy and Venice the schools are under the control of a society.

The best infant schools which I visited were decidedly those of Glasgow, Edinburgh, and London. The system of the infant schools of Lombardy, as I saw it at Milan, comes next to the English model, but is comparatively too verbal and precise, dealing too little with realities. . . .

Elementary or Primary Education

Elementary education may be considered in two points of view, both of great importance: as the sole education of the mass of the community, or as leading to higher instruction. In the former view, it requires to be complete, as a whole; in the latter, it is essentially preparatory. In reference to each, its character is materially different. In our country at large, we have been necessarily more occupied with creating common schools, than with elevating the standard of the instruction given in them. In the meantime, education has been advancing; and, unless we would be untrue to ourselves and to our political institutions, we must gather experience wherever it is to be found, and apply those practical results which are best adapted to our circumstances. In like manner, on the more limited field of the Girard College, we must raise our system upon the basis of the successful experiments of others, unless we would encounter the vexations incident to the acquisition of experience by our own failures.

The importance of primary instruction in both these references, has induced me to extend this notice of its present condition to a considerable number of countries, and to multiply the examples illustrative of the systems, where the schools are in a flourishing condition.

It happens, and I believe unfortunately for us, that the elementary schools of Great Britain are, in general, behind those of other countries of Europe with which we are less connected. Desultory, and sometimes conflicting, efforts at improvement have not made an impression proportioned to the wants of the people of that country, and have left them behind others, who have much less need of cultivated intelligence to enable them to fulfill the duties of citizens. Through the medium of schools for teachers, the importance of which is now recognised, the same rapid reforms may, however, be worked there, as have been effected in some countries on the continent. It will be found that, at present, I have been obliged to draw my examples of the schools for popular instruction in Great Britain from Scotland exclusively, but descriptions of departments for primary instruction will be found in some of the notices of secondary schools of other parts of the country.

Although the primary schools of France are not yet, in general, upon a level with those of Holland and Prussia, I have appended a brief notice of the system and progress of public instruction there. The view affords great encouragement, by showing how much may be realized by judicious laws, and in a well-arranged system of inspection. A rapid improvement in the schools in general will, no doubt, result from the operation of the normal schools.

The system of primary instruction in Holland is particularly interesting to an American, from its organization in an ascending series; beginning with the local school authorities, and terminating, after progressive degrees of representation, as it were, in the highest authority; instead of emanating, as in the centralized systems, from that authority. A fair trial has been given to a system of inspection which is almost entirely applicable to our country, and which has succeeded with them. They have tried an important experiment, in communicating religious without sectarian instruction; another, which has resulted in demonstrating the necessity of special schools for teachers; and another, entirely unfavourable to the system of mutual instruction. I have enlarged, therefore, upon the general account of their system of public instruction, and have given rather a general notice of the schools, than of any one in particular. I have, however, made one of the schools for the poor, which seemed to me superior even to those of the same class in Prussia, the subject of special description and remark.

. . . The Prussian system is the most perfect of the centralized systems, allowing considerable latitude in the arrangement of the individual schools, while all are subject to the influence of the central authority. It has not, as is commonly supposed, recently sprung into existence, but has been the work of time, has been altered and amended, and is still in progress. Its present condition is the result of experience, and thus it commends itself to enlightened imitation, by which I mean that which, laying aside what is inapplicable to the political or social institutions of the country adopting it, would employ the large amount of useful material which it contains. The schools contain much more that is applicable to our country than the system in general, and hence I have enlarged upon them, particularly upon the higher class of primary schools, which seem to me in better condition than those of any other of the larger European states. It is in what may be called the incidental parts of instruction, and which do not appear upon paper; in the spirit of the teacher, and sometimes in that of the books; that the peculiarities of national organization in these schools are chiefly to be found.

. . . The Austrian primary schools are chiefly characterized by a spirit of system, which exactly regulates the method and amount of what is to be taught, and when it shall be taught, throughout this vast empire. The mode of educating teachers tends to give them rather the routine than the spirit of their profession. My remarks apply to Austria Proper, and have no reference to the number, but to the general character of the schools. I was most favourably impressed with the earnest efforts making in the Italian provinces of Austria to spread primary instruction, an important measure where the schools have been so much neglected.

In the notices introductory to the description of schools in the different countries, I have endeavoured to give an outline of the organization of public instruction, of the regulations upon which it is founded, and of the mode of supplying teachers. The varieties in the schools are represented by some of the best which I visited, and of these I have given a more or less minute account, as the subject seemed to require, endeavouring, as in the former part of the Report, rather to notice peculiarities and differences than to repeat the same details in every case. In general, however, as before, the history and purpose of the school is first given, then its organization and government, then the admission and dismission of pupils, then the moral, intellectual, and physical education which it provides are discussed, and comparisons drawn between it and other similar institutions. These are interspersed with such remarks as reflection upon the subject may have suggested.

Besides the class of general primary schools, others which may be considered as of a special character have been planned, by which, while pursuing the studies of the elementary period, the individual is, at the same time, trained for his calling in after life. Such are the rural schools of Switzerland, which have also been transplanted to England and Ireland, and the manufacturing and industrial schools of France. . . .

Public Elementary Instruction in France

The present law regulating primary instruction in France, dates from the year 1833. Previous to framing it, M. Cousin was deputed by the Minister of Public Instruction to visit some of the states of Germany, the systems of which have the highest reputation, and especially Prussia. The information collected by him, and chiefly embodied in his Report, is supposed to have contributed in an important degree to the framing of the new law. By one of the provisions of this law, primary instruction is divided into two grades, elementary, and superior primary, and the least amount of instruction admissible in each grade is defined. In the first is enumerated moral and religious instruction, reading, writing, the elements of the French language,

and arithmetic, and the system of weights and measures prescribed by law. Linear drawing, is very generally added to these branches, and in many of the schools, vocal music is also taught.

To the subjects just enumerated, the law adds, as a minimum for superior primary instruction, the elements of geometry, with its common applications, particularly to geometrical drawing and surveying, the elementary principles of physical science, and natural history and geography, and particularly the history and geography of France. This superior primary instruction has spread but little, even in the metropolis of France, and the whole kingdom contained in 1838 but three hundred and thirty-two schools of the sort. In Lyons I found but one public school of this grade in 1838, and that but imperfectly developed.

While the law thus lays down the branches of instruction constituting the least admissible, it very properly says nothing about the methods of teaching. In the public schools there are, however, two leading methods, those of mutual and simultaneous instruction. The first is a modified Lancastrian system, originally introduced from England. The second is used chiefly in the schools of the "Christian Brothers," and its practices are derived from the founder of this religious body, the Abbé John La Salle. Specimens of both are to be found in the model schools attached to the Normal seminaries for educating primary teachers, of which there is one for every department of France, with one exception. Teachers educated in these establishments are expected to be able to use either method. In many of the schools fragments of the two are joined, constituting what has been termed a mixed system. It cannot, with propriety, however, be considered a special method, but is rather a modification, in various degrees, of one of the systems by the introduction of parts of the other. Of the schools upon the system of mutual instruction, I visited at Paris, with greater or less care, four, besides giving a glance at two others, in reference to musical instruction. Of those taught by the Christian Brothers I visited two. At Versailles, the two in connexion with the primary Normal schools, and the similar ones at Dijon. At Lyons, two of the first named kind and one of the second. The selection was made, of course, with reference to the merits of the schools in regard to which I had the best advice. Those on the plan of mutual instruction were inferior to the English model, and those upon the other system, to the similar schools in Holland, or in Germany, generally. Hence, I do not feel warranted in entering into details in regard to them in this Report. Primary instruction in France is in a state of transition, which, although it holds a fair promise for the future, presents, at present, but little for imitation in the individual schools.

I ought to notice that the mode of teaching music adopted in the mutual instruction schools of Paris, has proved highly successful, and that, in general, the results of the attempt to introduce vocal music into these schools have surpassed the expectation even of its advocates. The introduction of linear drawing has also been attended with success, but the mode of teaching from engravings is, I think, for the purposes in view, inferior to that used in the schools of Berlin.

It must not be supposed, from the foregoing remarks, that I undervalue the efforts lately made and now making in France, in behalf of primary instruction. The law itself was a great step. The system of inspection, which was begun in 1833, was carried out by the permanent appointment of one inspector to each department in 1835, and greatly extended by creating sub-inspectors in 1838, and is a most valuable auxiliary to the law. The regulation of the schools for girls in 1836; the increase of primary normal schools from forty-seven in 1833 to seventy-four in 1838; the increase of more than a million in the attendance on the boys' schools alone, between 1829 and 1838; the systematic encouragement to infant schools; all these are positive results, which have been already obtained, and on which France has great reason to congratulate herself. It was not to be expected that, with the previous deficiency in the number of schools for primary instruction in France, there would be great fastidiousness as to their character, which must, however, rapidly improve, if the introduction of well prepared teachers from the normal schools is allowed to have its full effect.

Primary Instruction in Holland

Among the primary schools of Holland are some of the best which I visited, and the whole condition of popular instruction is worthy of a nation which has ever been distinguished for its virtue and intelligence.

The primary instruction of Holland began to receive its present form at the close of the last century, and chiefly by the instrumentality of the "Society for Public Utility," the branches of which extended throughout the country. This society established model schools where they were required, published cheap text-books, excited discussions on methods of teaching, and stimulated the local authorities and others to the establishment of new schools. Always withdrawing its efforts when no longer needed in the cause, it avoided the effects of jealousy, by showing that it had no desire for control.

With a view to produce system throughout the then Batavian Republic, a law containing the general principles which should govern primary instruction was passed in 1806, and was accompanied by a series of regulations, to carry out its details. The most important provisions of the law are those for the inspection and management of the schools, and for the due qualification of schoolmasters, the establishment of individual schools being left to the local authorities. The system of inspection is eminently adapted to a country where centralization has never existed, and has proved highly successful in its operation. It begins with the appointment in each school district of an inspector, and, when the schools are numerous, gives him the assistance of a committee.

The inspectors of the different school districts of a province form the Provincial Board of Primary Instruction, who meet thrice every year, receive the reports of the inspectors, deliberate upon the concerns of primary instruction in the province, and make report annually to the minister of the interior. To carry out this system, the minister of the interior has authority to convene at the capital an assembly of delegates from the provincial Boards, to advise upon general matters. Only one such meeting has, however, taken place. In the general control of primary instruction, the minister of the interior is replaced by an officer called a referendary, and there is also an inspector general, who resides at the Hague.

To be admitted to the rank of teacher, certain preliminary examinations must be passed before the school-inspector, or local or provincial Board, according to the grade sought. There are four grades, requiring each a different examination. The lowest of these may be obtained at the age of sixteen, the third at eighteen, and the second at twenty-two. The second qualifies for the mastership of any primary school, and the first is, in fact, honorary. To pass the examination for the second grade, the candidate must be able to read and spell correctly, to write a good hand, must have a knowledge of the theory of the Dutch language, geography, history, arithmetic in all its branches, and a facility in imparting instruction. His moral and religious qualifications are also ascertained.

This general examination entitles an instructor to become a candidate for vacant schools, either public or private, but does not supersede the special examination or competition which may be required by their directors.

The law, besides, enjoins upon the local authorities, on the one hand, to furnish a sufficient number of schools for the population, and on the other, not to allow such a number as to render the income of the several masters inadequate to their support.

The definition of a primary school, as given in one of the regulations issued to complete the law, covers a wide field. According to it, a primary school is one in which youth is instructed in the first principles of knowledge, such as reading, writing, arithmetic, and the Dutch language, or the more advanced branches, such as the French, or other modern languages, or the ancient languages, geography, history, and other subjects of that description. There are several different kinds of schools, corresponding to different grades of instruction in these branches. Infant school instruction is included in the primary department, but it is not yet fully developed, being limited chiefly to Rotterdam and Zwolle.

The lowest schools are those for the poor (armen-scholen), and which are entirely gratuitous. The children enter at from six to seven, and remain until twelve or fourteen. As supplementary to them are evening schools, principally intended for revising former courses, and which should be attended until sixteen or eighteen years of age. As the attendance in these latter schools is not obligatory, the proportion of those who receive instruction in them varies much in different localities.

The next are called intermediate schools (tusschen-scholen), in which the pupils pay a trifling fee.[2] Both these are, in general, public. Some have been established by the school-committees, and after a few years have become self-supporting. The grade of instruction is rather higher than in the schools for the poor, but as the law does not prescribe any particular programme, it varies much in the different parts of Holland—a school which would be called intermediate in a small town ranking below one of the gratuitous establishments for the poor in one of the chief cities.

The amount taught depends, other circumstances being the same, upon the average age to which the children remain at school, and, therefore, varies also in the different parts of the kingdom.

The next grade, or burgher school (burger school), is, in general, a private establishment. It is distinguished from both the classes just enumerated by a larger fee,[3] and, in general, by a higher grade of instruction; but while in a single town or district it is easy to perceive this gradation, yet it is scarcely possible to observe it on a comparison of the country at large. In some places, the last mentioned school is called the Dutch school, to distinguish it from the following class.

The school denominated the "French School" is the highest of the primary division, and is, in general, a private establishment, though frequently of the kind classed by the law with private schools, but superintended, in reality, by the local school-committee itself. Besides the branches taught in the other schools, the courses of this embrace the French language, of which the pupils acquire a grammatical knowledge, and which they are enabled to speak with considerable facility. These schools prepare their pupils for entrance into active life, and serve, also, in some degree, as feeders to the grammar or Latin schools. The instruction in French is not, however, an exclusive mark of this grade of institution, as the descendants of the French emigrants, constituting the Walloon congregations, continue the teaching of this language in the gratuitous schools for the poor connected with their churches.

While, in point of fact, there is not the regular fourfold division of primary instruction which thus appears, it is difficult to draw a separating line.[4] The intermediate school connects the school for the poor and the burgher school, while in the burgher schools, the same branches are studied as in the French schools, except the French language. The less number of children under the charge of one master, the greater age to which the children in general remain at school, the generally greater capacity of the master, from the higher salary which his talents command, the greater family culture of the children before coming into and while in the school, render the average progress in the

---

[2]For example, in an intermediate school at Rotterdam which I visited, eight cents a week.

[3]The school fee at the burgher school at Haarlem is between six and seven dollars a year.

[4]M. Cousin, in his work, "De l'Instruction Publique en Holland," 1837, places the division between the burgher and the French schools.

burgher school of a given place superior to that in the intermediate school, and in this latter higher than in the school for the poor. I must say, however, that in more than one case, in the same place, I could detect no difference in the school itself, between the intermediate and the burgher school, except in the greater comfort of the accommodations of the latter; and I have already remarked that, in comparing the establishments of different places, the name is not an accurate guide to the grade of the school.

A sketch of the arrangement of the primary schools themselves would, I have thought, be rendered more compendious, without injury to its fidelity, by selecting for particular description one of the schools for the poor, which, as a class, rank higher in Holland than in any other of the European states, and engrafting upon the account of this, remarks on the methods of other schools; concluding by a brief statement of the particulars in which the intermediate, burgher, or French schools differ, in general, from the assumed type, or from each other.

Before doing so, however, there are some points fixed by the school regulations which require notice. The first is, that the system of instruction must be that called simultaneous, or in which all the pupils of a class take part at once. In practice, this requires to be varied by questions adapted to individuals, and the classes, therefore, must not be too large. In the intermediate schools I found, more commonly, classes of from thirty to fifty, the lesser number being well adapted to the method. With a well trained master, and a class of moderate numbers, this kind of instruction is the most lively that can be imagined, and when judiciously varied by questions put to all, but which only one is permitted to answer, it is also thorough. It is, in a great degree, the system already described of Mr. Wood's own class in the Edinburgh Sessional School.

The method of mutual instruction is not at all favoured in Holland. A very decided and general opinion against it appears early to have been brought about by the comparison of the English schools with their own. A prize was offered for the best dissertation on the subject by the society for public utility, and taken by M. Visser, inspector of primary schools in Freesland. This excellent dissertation which was published and widely distributed by the society, no doubt contributed to form or to strengthen the opinion which prevails at this day.

The only approach to the monitorial system in the schools of Holland is, that pupils who have an inclination to teach, and who will probably become teachers, are put in charge of the lower classes of a school. Thus, also, some of the best monitors of the Borough-road School in London are boys who are likely one day to follow the career of teaching. There is, however, a very wide difference between the use of a few apprentices to the profession, and that of a large number of monitors to give instruction. I had occasion to observe, however, that in many cases there was a want of life in the younger classes entrusted to these inexperienced teachers. If they are to be used, it would be better to employ them in classes which have some training, even though nearer the teacher's age and attainments.

The next point is in regard to religious instruction in the schools. There is unbounded toleration of religious creed in Holland, and while the necessity of religious instruction in the schools has been strongly felt, it has been made to stop short of the point at which, becoming doctrinal, the subjects taught could interfere with the views of any sect. Bible stories are made the means of moral and religious teaching in the school, and the doctrinal instruction is given by the pastors of the different churches on days appointed for the purpose, and usually not in the school-room.

The last point is in regard to the choice of school-books. The publication of them is not left to open competition. Every book, before it can be used in a public school, must be submitted to the examination of the minister of the interior, acting of course by deputy, and if approved, is admitted to the list of books which may be used in the schools. From this list the provincial board of primary schools select those which they consider best, to be used in their province, and from their list the teachers choose such as they approve. In private schools the teacher selects his own books, but he must report a list of them to the inspector.

There are two normal schools for the education of teachers for the primary schools, one at Groningen, established by the society for public utility, the other at Haarlem, by the government. Formerly all instructors were prepared in the different primary schools. They began to teach as early as twelve years of age, attending the evening school to make up their loss of time during the day. At sixteen they had served their apprenticeship, and were admissible to the fourth grade of teachers. This method prevails still to a considerable extent, but as it has been found to produce rather routine than intelligent teaching, the two normal schools have been established to supply the defect.

The *material* of elementary intellectual instruction consists in most countries of reading, writing, arithmetic, and a knowledge of the mother tongue, to which the geography of the country, and sometimes general geography, natural history, linear drawing and vocal music are added. Special exercises of the perceptive and reflective faculties are also included in the more improved intellectual systems. While the material is thus nearly the same, nothing can be more different than the results produced by the schools, according to the use which is made of it. In some the means are mistaken for the end, and if the pupil is enabled to read, write, and cypher mechanically, the school is supposed to have done its duty. In others these branches are employed as the means of developing the intellect as well as for the communication of useful knowledge; according as one or the other view is taken, the instruction is arranged in conformity with it. In Holland the intellectual methods of Pestalozzi have taken deep root, and the enlightened state of public opinion, in regard to elementary education, prevents in a great degree a mechanical system of teaching. . . .

General Remarks and Comparisons on Secondary Education

The variable nature of the circumstances bearing upon the secondary instruction of different countries, renders comparison, except in a general way, very difficult. A single example will serve to illustrate this position. The school into which the pupil is to be introduced, preparatory to professional life, though called by the same name, is essentially different in different countries. An English university, in its objects and aims, and consequently in its organization, is very unlike the faculties of France, or a university of Germany, and the secondary schools, which serve as feeders to these institutions, must be modified accordingly.

There are, however, high general purposes to be served in the mental training of youth, on the more or less successful modes of applying which, comparison will throw the light of experience. If a satisfactory intellectual education at Berlin requires the study of Latin, Greek, the vernacular, French, geography and history, mathematics, physics, natural history, and intellectual philosophy, it is not likely that the same can be accomplished elsewhere by the study of Latin, Greek, geography, a small portion of history, and less of arithmetic and geometry. If it is possible at Berlin to devote sufficient time to the branches enumerated in the Prussian programme, to make them really sources of mental culture and of positive knowledge, consistently with a thorough knowledge of the classics, it must be so in the same interval of time any where else. Hence there need be no apprehension even on the part of those who consider the attainment of classical knowledge for itself as the great end of instruction, in regard to the effects of an increased attention to other branches of knowledge, unless it can be shown that the German youth are inferior in these attainments, which has never, I believe, been even attempted, or unless it can be proved that they are naturally of higher intellectual powers than those of other countries.

To turn the details already given of secondary instruction to account, and to compare, in as brief a manner as possible, the Prussian gymnasia just described with the institutions for secondary instruction in the two other countries, some of the schools of which have been noticed, the Frederick William gymnasium may be assumed as representing an average of the Prussian gymnasia. There being nothing which can be considered as a *system* of secondary instruction in Great Britain, it is only by the comparison of single instances that an appreciation of the whole can be made. This comparison is rendered easy, and, in fact, reduced to ascertaining which of the schools of Great Britain most nearly resembles the Prussian gymnasium, by the detailed comparison already made of the several schools with each other. After completing the course just marked out, it will be my object to compare some of the features of the Prussian and French systems of secondary instruction, and a Prussian gymnasium with a French college. I would gladly have preceded this view by a comparison of the gymnasia of Prussia with those of some of the other German states, as Wurtemberg or Bavaria, and Austria, and that of the free town of Frankfort on the Maine, and even, subsequently, have extended the comparison to the Latin schools of Holland, and the colleges or gymnasia of Switzerland, but it would have been in vain to attempt this within the limits of the present Report. In the documents and notes which my tour has furnished, I have ample means for such a purpose, which I may at a future day accomplish, as it would throw the light of further experience on our operations.

Among the British institutions which I have described in more or less detail, no one approaches so closely to the Prussian gymnasia, in the outline of its course of studies, and in the time devoted to the different subjects, as the Hill-street Institution of Edinburgh. There are, it is true, strongly marked differences in the two courses, but not so great as between those of the Prussian institutions and of the more exclusively classical schools. It is certainly remarkable, that what is an established system in one country, should by many be considered as an innovation of doubtful expediency in the other. The pupils enter and leave the Scottish institution earlier than the Prussian, hence the courses must be forced, and the mature knowledge, the regular and progressive development which marks the pupils of the Prussian schools, cannot be acquired. The crowning courses of language are wanting, and the mathematics and physics are imperfectly learned, in general, from the too early youth of the pupil of the Scottish school. The two years between seventeen and nineteen spent in a Prussian gymnasium, are invaluable to both master and pupil. It must be observed, also, that one being a private school, and of recent establishment, labours under disadvantages in regard to procuring teachers which the public, long tried, and assured existence of the other, prevents their being subject to. With the advantages which the English grammar schools have in the age of their pupils, and the duration of their courses, over any private school, the introduction of the branches of knowledge considered essential in Germany, might be effected with comparative ease in them. I am convinced that, as soon as teachers were trained up for the change, and the pupils had become accustomed to it, the results would be most striking, and I do not consider the partial failure of the attempt, to which I have alluded, at Rugby, as at all conclusive. An experienced teacher in England made the remark to me, as a justification of the tendency to exclusively classical instruction in the secondary schools of Great Britain, that the nation having naturally a disposition to advance in material subjects, should be drawn away from them, and towards the ideal, by education; this was equivalent to saying that a nation should be educated against its nature and tendencies, which remark, it seems to me, need only be applied to the individuals forming the nation to show its fallacy.

In support of my inference as to the character of the classical instruction in the Prussian schools, it may not be amiss to observe,

that if the nearly exclusively classical example which I have given in Harrow school, be compared as to its course of studies in classics with a Prussian gymnasium, it will be found that, except in the article of Greek and Latin verse, which is in little or no repute in most of the gymnasia, the classical studies of these latter are fully equivalent to those of the former. I take it for granted that at Harrow the course is thoroughly acquired, and know that such is really the case in the gymnasia which I visited.

In regard to the methods of the British and Prussian schools in general, the recitation upon a lesson which has been studied from a text-book out of the school, used in the former, tends to foster habits of self-reliance, while that of mingling much oral instruction with the recitations used in the latter, renders the instruction more interesting to the pupils. When the latter method is employed, much less artificial stimulus from hope of reward or fear of punishment is necessary, and, if I may be permitted to judge from the examples which came under my notice in both countries, there is, on the average, more exertion on the part of a class in Prussia than in Great Britain. The prizes held out at the English grammar schools, in the way of scholarships at the universities, to those who distinguish themselves especially, insure a great amount of exertion on the part of young men of talent, whose subsequent success is appealed to as an evidence of the soundness of the system of instruction, with which it has little or nothing to do. The students find a similar stimulus at the university; a scholarship may, if the time be duly improved, lead to a fellowship, and thus to an honourable provision for life. With such strong motives to great individual exertion, a youth of talent might succeed in educating himself even without aid, or were the school system ever so bad.

In relation to the discipline in the similar secondary schools of Prussia and Great Britain, I would venture the remark, that in the former, it is generally much more advanced in its method, motives, and results, than in the latter. There are, of course, exceptions to this remark. The kind of relation existing habitually, especially in boarding-gymnasia, between the pupil and the teacher, in Prussia, is not unknown in Great Britain, but is an exception, and not the rule. In this respect, no doubt, a change is taking place, which will accelerate as it advances, and ultimately the principle will prevail, that the best interest of both pupil and teacher is to be found in the cultivation of mutual regard.

The organization of the systems of public instruction in Prussia and in France propagates a central influence through all parts of each, but by different means. Theoretically, the university of France is an empire within itself, with the grand master, actually the minister of public instruction, as the head, assisted by the university council. The academies, presided over by their rectors and councils, constitute the divisions of this empire. The execution of the university law, as regards the establishment of secondary instruction, is vested directly in the governments of the academies, who legislate merely in certain matters of detail. The minister of public instruction is also the central authority in Prussia, but the legislative, as well as the executive power, belong to the school-board emanating from the consistory of each province. It is true, that general laws made by the central authority cannot be contravened, but the very general nature of these laws leaves much for regulation by the local authorities, as has been seen in the diverse plans of the different gymnasia which have been presented in this Report.

The institutions introductory to the universities may, according to law, in either country, be public or private; but in Prussia, the private institutions have been obliterated by the public ones, and in France, are held in a miserable state of dependence upon them. Great efforts have been made, and are making, in the latter country, to free private secondary instruction from its trammels, and to enable it so far to compete with public instruction, as to keep this latter in a sound state. There are two grades of public institutions in France, namely, the royal and communal colleges, and only one in Prussia, the gymnasia; the former plan leading, according to the best authorities, to the recognition of establishments entirely incompetent to fulfil the objects of this kind of instruction.

The arrangement of academic degrees in Prussia and in France differs essentially, producing peculiarities in the introductory institutions. The academic grades in the faculty of letters and of sciences, after the lowest grade, or bachelor, are entirely distinct in the university of France. The bachelor of sciences must have a sufficient knowledge of letters to qualify him for the lowest degree in that department, but this degree once taken by a member of the highest class of a college, he need never enter the faculty of letters of the university. The qualifications of the literary man in science, and of the scientific man in letters, are not necessarily so high in the French arrangement as in the Prussian, where there is but one set of degrees for both. The plan of degrees in the university of France has the advantage which the variation allowed in the courses in the Prussian secondary schools supplies, in part, of allowing minds of different complexions to choose their career. As it is not incumbent on the man of science to pursue the course of letters in a faculty, the courses of rhetoric and philosophy would, in general, be lost to him, if they were not placed in the college course: the close study of these branches in the colleges, and their entire omission, or the little attention paid to them in the gymnasia, are striking differences in the two systems of instruction. The academic degrees of Prussia can only be taken by study in the faculties of the university, of which the secondary schools form no part: the corresponding ones in France are accessible to the youth leaving the colleges.

The examinations, which in Prussia must precede the matriculation at the university, are made in the gymnasia themselves, but under the direction of a special committee, while those for the degrees obtainable on leaving a French college are made in the university itself, and entirely by its authorities. The Prussian examinations are conducted in such a way as to render the system of manuals, by which pupils may be worked up to the precise minimum of attainment, almost impossible. The candidates are known to at least a part of the examiners, their former teachers, and their attainments have been accurately ascertained by them in the class-rooms, before coming to this test. The actual examining bodies having, in general, only the pupils of one gymnasium before them, are physically able to make the examination a thorough one. On the contrary, the examination for degrees in France, corresponding to those for the matriculation certificate in Prussia, are made in the university, by persons who are usually strangers to the pupils and their attainments, who have the arduous task of conducting the examination of all the candidates, and who are from these causes reduced to the necessity of rendering the examination less thorough, and more formal, and hence of allowing the opportunity for superficial preparation by manuals. The mode adopted in Prussia would undoubtedly give the public institutions a great advantage over private ones, did any such exist as independent establishments.

The use of written examinations in mathematics is adopted in the Prussian system, and not in the French, and with an originally strong prepossession in favour of the oral method. I now believe, from the facts which inquiry has brought before me, that the written form is a most valuable one, and that the two must be combined to give a thorough examination.

The subjects of secondary instruction in France and Prussia are essentially the same, but the manner of introducing them differs in most important particulars. The branches taught in a Prussian gymnasium are all obligatory; only the degree of study in some minor ones is left to the student, and the Hebrew language is reserved for those who intend to study theology; the Latin, Greek, German, French, religious instruction, geography, history, mathematics, physics, natural history, writing, drawing, and vocal music, are all studies to be regularly followed. While these branches are equally component parts of the course of the French colleges, with the exception of vocal music, and with the addition of chemistry, the modern foreign language, drawing, and writing, do not enter into the regular course, but are voluntary, being, however, furnished at the expense of the college. The branches which are not thus furnished can hardly be considered as parts of the instruction, being, as it were, merely tolerated.

The manner in which the same materials of instruction are combined in the programme of a French college and of a German gymnasium is so different, that it appears like attempting to compare things not homogeneous with each other, to bring them together for such a purpose. A glance at the arrangements of any one class in the two cases will show better what I mean than any description of this peculiarity. The German programme appears to have been carefully studied, the proportion of its parts to have been carefully elaborated, the arrangements as to order of study and time of study to have been carefully considered, and the whole presents a better matured and more finished system than that of the French college. It does not appear in the recent annals of this kind of instruction in Prussia, to have been doubtful whether letters and science shall be taught simultaneously or successively, or whether natural history shall be taught in the beginning, middle, or end of the course. The entire arrangement appears to me to be more compact and better ordered. It will not require a lengthened discussion to substantiate these views; attention need be called only to a few points in illustration of

them. The Prussian system lays down for the regular studies thirty to thirty-two hours per week for each class; the French includes but twenty-two hours. If from the thirty-two hours be taken the time allotted to studies considered voluntary in a French college, namely, six hours per week, the remainder, twenty-six hours, will still exceed by four hours the time occupied in the college recitations or lectures. The greater number of hours thus occupied is a real advantage in favour of the Prussian schools, since experience shows that thirty-two hours per week may be devoted to recitation, and the private study requisite for preparation be made by the student, without injury to his health. It cannot be doubted, from this comparison, that the branches composing the course of a gymnasium are more closely examined than those of a college. The details of the distribution of time in the separate classes confirm this deduction; for example, the time occupied per week by Latin, Greek, and German, in the upper third class of a Prussian gymnasium, is eighteen hours, and in the lower third and upper second class, each, seventeen hours, while in the parallel classes of a French college, in Latin, Greek, and French, but fourteen hours per week are employed. Further, the classical course is dropped entirely after the rhetoric class in the college, while in the gymnasium it extends to the close of the student's career. In regard to the scientific courses of the French colleges, the following points appear particularly worthy of notice. No instruction is given in mathematics higher than arithmetic, except two hours a week of geometry in the third class, until the pupil has reached the second class, in which, if he entered college at nine years of age, he arrives in his sixteenth year; and then all that he learns higher than this, if he follow the career of letters, is compressed into two years. Physics and chemistry for the student in this same career are taught in two lessons per week in the philosophy class. Natural history is thrown into the course of the sixth and fifth classes. A comparison of these defective arrangements with the regular instruction of the same branches, in their appropriate places in a Prussian gymnasium, fully justify the remarks, with which this paragraph commenced. Having attended the examination for the degree of bachelor of sciences at Paris, and heard recitations in the Prussian gymnasia, I am satisfied that the conclusions in regard to the superiority of the Prussian instruction in science are entirely just. The subject of religious instruction is one of such peculiar delicacy, that I am most happy to be able to submit the views of a high authority in public instruction in France, instead of my own, in regard to it, merely observing that I coincide, on this point, entirely in opinion with the authority to which I refer. M. Cousin says:—"There is no class in the Prussian gymnasium which has not a course of religious instruction, as it has of classical or of mathematical instruction. I have before said, and now repeat, that worship, with its ceremonies, can never be sufficient for young men who reflect, and who are imbued with the spirit of the times. A true religious instruction is indispensable, and no subject is better adapted to a regular, full, and varied instruction than Christianity, with a history which goes back to the beginning of the world, and is connected with all the great events in that of the human race, with its dogmas, which breathe a sublime metaphysics, its morality, which combines severity with indulgence, with its general literary monuments, from Genesis to the universal history."[5] Such an instruction M. Cousin demands for the colleges of his country, declaring that, though established by law, it does not now exist in them. The courses of rhetoric and philosophy, to which a considerable portion of time is given for the last two years of the student of letters, and an introduction to which begins even in the second class, are the chief ornaments of the course of the French colleges, and the sacrifices required by their introduction are amply compensated by their effect. The Prussian system postpones these courses to the university period, and requires every student who wishes to matriculate in other faculties, to go through them. The bachelor of letters, on leaving a French college, may begin at once the study of theology or of law, and the bachelor of sciences that of medicine. The German student must pass through the faculty of philosophy before he can begin the study of either of these professions. In regard to modern languages, the new recommendations for the Prussian gymnasia appear to me to place the French on a worse footing than before, but still a better one than that occupied by English and German in the French colleges. I cannot help hoping that this movement will not be followed up, and that the reasons for retaining the modern languages, as parts of a liberal education, will be found too strong to admit of their being so easily disposed of as

appears to be assumed in the circular from the Prussian ministry, which does not appear to have put forth its strength upon this question.

The methods of instruction in the French colleges, in the lower classes, resemble those of the English schools, with the advantage, that the pupils have the directors of studies to aid them when necessary. There are lectures, as well as recitations, in the higher classes, as in the gymnasia. In both the French and Prussian institutions there is a want of apparatus for illustration. In the courses of physics and natural history, it having once been determined that such instruction is essential, the implements necessary to teach to the best advantage should not be left wanting.

The government of the French colleges differs essentially from that of the boarding-gymnasia of Prussia. The question, whether it is advantageous to establish a boarding system in the midst of the residences of the parents of pupils, as in France, or to establish day-schools, as the Prussian gymnasia, is one that depends much upon national manners. My own convictions are, in the general, in favour of the Prussian system in this respect, and of encouraging the means of strengthening domestic ties, by leaving youth under parental control. The chief officer of the Prussian gymnasia, boarding as well as others, the director, or rector, is a teacher as well as a governor, while the provisor of the French college does not teach. The former arrangement has the advantage of bringing the director into contact with the pupils more closely; the latter allows a more thorough superintendence of instruction, discipline, and police. When the number of pupils is not very great, the former arrangement is, I believe, the more advantageous. It is, however, a matter almost of necessity, in institutions having such a numerous body of students as the Parisian colleges in general, that the presiding officer should have no other charge than that of superintendence, and it may further be desirable that he should be assisted by a censor, the second officer of the French college. There are no equivalent officers in the boarding-gymnasia of Prussia to the directors of studies, who have charge of the pupils during the study hours in the French colleges. One of the teachers, as at Schulpforta, takes a weekly turn to superintend the pupils, dwelling near them during the period of duty. This arrangement answers well, with the aid of the pupils selected to superintend sections, for a small number of students, but would be entirely inefficient in a Parisian college. The

_____

[5]Cousin, *Memoire sur l'instruction secondaire dans le royaume de Prusse*. Paris, 1837, p. 143.

directors of studies are most important officers in these institutions, especially as they are required to be competent to teach as well as to superintend, and the selection of them from among the adjuncts (agrégés), who are expectants of promotion, is an excellent arrangement. The professors and teachers in the French colleges, in Paris, are on the footing of the instructors in the Prussian day-gymnasia, living out of the institution, and having nothing to do with the discipline out of the recitation hours. This system has, no doubt, advantages, but the controlling disadvantage is the diminution of the moral influence of the teacher over the pupil. It is especially necessary, in establishments where young men are crowded together, and separated from the wholesome restraints of home and domestic discipline, to foster, by all means, the moral influence of the teacher, and to bring the pupil as near to him as possible. This is not done when the professor merely meets the student in the recitation or lecture-room for a few hours every day, and during the remainder of the time has no active care of, or interest in, his welfare. The existence of directors of studies is by no means incompatible with such a supervision by the professors. In both the French and Prussian institutions the highest officer, the provisor or director, administers the discipline, and the tone of it depends upon his character. The superintendence by pupils of sections of their fellows, is not allowed to degenerate into the "fagging system," the pupils being selected for the office, and constantly superintended by the teachers. From the location of the Parisian colleges, the details of their arrangements are not comparable with those of a Prussian country gymnasium.

The inducements to study are of a much more exciting kind in the French colleges than in the Prussian gymnasia. Both have a system of places in the class, differently arranged for the higher and lower classes, and both grade the pupils on leaving the institution. But in the French college there is a most powerful, I may say an excessive, stimulus from prizes, not only in the establishment, but from a comparison with others, and public attention is called to the successful youth, who is rewarded under the notice of the community of scholars, the university, and the public at large: his career depends upon successful competition from one step to another, until he has reached the higher places of society, and his selfish feelings are constantly and directly stimulated. It is more

easy to feel than to describe the influence of the minute particulars which constitute public scholastic sentiment, and which produce a very different atmosphere in the two classes of institutions. Emulation is not discouraged in the gymnasia, and intellectual and moral qualities are held in due esteem; but the development of mind is controlled by that of the moral sentiments, and there is in consequence less of strong personal rivalry than in the colleges. The reciprocal action of national character and education is so powerful, that it would be rash, without a much deeper examination than I can profess to have made, to say how far these differences are effects or causes. It is my duty to note them, and to comment freely upon them for our advantage, leaving the judgment to more competent minds.

With all the stimulus of the French colleges, there is one precaution neglected, which strikes at the root of the competency of the mass of students. The law in regard to stated half-yearly examinations is not executed. Incompetent students, unless grossly so, pass regularly forward with the competent into the higher classes. There is one period, in passing from the fourth to the third class, at which an examination has been applied, and with advantage; but there are three classes before the fourth, through which the students pass as a matter of course. It is obvious, that with so loose a system, the examinations for degrees must be relaxed, or the examiners take upon themselves a heavy responsibility. The regular examinations of the Prussian gymnasia afford the means of discovering the incompetent year by year, a result favourable both to the youths who are thus thrown into other careers, and to those who remain connected with these institutions.

The means for supplying teachers for secondary instruction must, I think, be admitted, so far as the normal school is concerned, to be superior in France to those of Prussia. The central normal school of Paris is certainly more advantageous than the detached philological and pedagogical seminaries of Prussia. This school is kept in vigour by competition from without, which, while it opens the career of instruction to those young men who may not be able from circumstances to avail themselves of the advantages of the normal school, reacts favourably upon the school itself. The candidate for the normal school must be at least a bachelor of letters, and must compete for his place. After going through its courses, he again passes through the severe ordeal of a com-

A Comparison of the Hours of Recreation, Rest, Exercise, Study, and School in Different European Institutions.

Place	Institution	Applies to	Number of Hours.										Years.
			Recreation	Gymnastics or other regular exercises	Meals & police. Prayers	Trades	Sleep	Study	Recitation in School	Bodily exercise and meals	Rest	Intellectual exercise	Age of Pupils
Edinburgh,	Heriot's Hospital,	Winter, Elder boys.	$2\frac{1}{2}$	1	$2\frac{1}{2}$	0	10	1	7	6	10	8	9 to 14
"	John Watson's Institution	" All,	$4\frac{1}{2}$	0	3	0	10	†	$6\frac{1}{2}$	$7\frac{1}{2}$	10	$6\frac{1}{2}$	$6\frac{1}{2}$ to 14
Liverpool,	Blue-Coat School,	Summer, "	4	$1\frac{1}{2}$*	$2\frac{3}{4}$	0	$8\frac{1}{2}$	$1\frac{3}{4}$	$5\frac{1}{2}$	$8\frac{1}{4}$	$8\frac{1}{2}$	$7\frac{1}{4}$	9 to 14
London,	Orphan Asylum,	" "	$4\frac{1}{2}$	$\frac{1}{2}$	$2\frac{3}{4}$	0	$9\frac{1}{2}$	†	$6\frac{3}{4}$	$7\frac{3}{4}$	$9\frac{1}{2}$	$6\frac{3}{4}$	9 to 14
Annaburg, (Prussia.)	Military Orphan-House,	" "	$3\frac{1}{2}$	1	$2\frac{1}{2}$	4	7	2	4	11	7	6	6 to $14\frac{1}{2}$
Frankfort, (on Maine.)	Orphan-House,	" Elder boys,	$2\frac{1}{2}$	1	$3\frac{1}{2}$	2	9	1	5	9	9	6	6 to $14\frac{1}{2}$
Halle,	Franke Foundation,	" "	5§	0	$1\frac{1}{2}$	0	$6\frac{1}{2}$	4	7	$6\frac{1}{2}$	$6\frac{1}{2}$	11	10 to 15
Hamburgh,	Orphan-House,	" All,	3	2	$3\frac{1}{2}$	0	$8\frac{1}{2}$	†	7	$8\frac{1}{2}$	$8\frac{1}{2}$	7	8 to 14
Prague,	St. John's Orphan-House,	" "	$3\frac{1}{2}$	1	3	0	$8\frac{1}{2}$	4	4	$7\frac{1}{2}$	$8\frac{1}{2}$	8	8 to $13\frac{1}{2}$
Struppen, (Saxony.)	School for soldiers' children,	Winter, "	$2\frac{1}{2}$	1	$2\frac{1}{2}$	3	9	2	4	9	9	6	6 to 14
"	"	Summer, "	4	1	$2\frac{1}{2}$	4	8	0	$4\frac{1}{2}$	$11\frac{1}{2}$	8	$4\frac{1}{2}$	8 to 17
	Secondary Schools.												
Liverpool,	Mr. Voelcker's School,	Winter, "	4§	0	$2\frac{1}{2}$	0	9	$2\frac{1}{2}$	6	$6\frac{1}{2}$	9	$9\frac{1}{2}$	8 to 18
Paris,	College of Louis XIV.,	Summer,	$2\frac{1}{4}$	0	$2\frac{3}{4}$	0	8	$4\frac{1}{2}$	$6\frac{1}{2}$ ‖	5	8	11	8 to 18
Prussia,	Schulpforta,	Winter,	$1\frac{1}{2}$ ‖	0	2	0	9	$6\frac{1}{2}$	5	$3\frac{1}{2}$	9‡	$11\frac{1}{2}$	14 to 19
Dresden,	Blochman's Gymnasium,	"	$2\frac{1}{2}$	1	$2\frac{1}{2}$	0	9	$3\frac{3}{4}$	$5\frac{1}{4}$	6	9‡	9	10 to 19
	Normal Schools.												
Prussia,	Weissenfels,	"	$1\frac{1}{2}$	1	$1\frac{1}{2}$	0	$7\frac{1}{2}$	$3\frac{1}{2}$	9	4	7	$12\frac{1}{2}$	16 to 20
"	"	Summer,	3	1	$1\frac{1}{2}$	0	7	$3\frac{1}{2}$	8	5	7	$11\frac{1}{2}$	"
France,	Dijon,	"	2	0	$1\frac{3}{4}$	0	8	5	$7\frac{1}{4}$	$3\frac{3}{4}$	8	$12\frac{1}{4}$	17 to 20

*Walking. † In school. ‡ Elder boys, eight hours. § Or regular exercise. ‖ In part voluntary.

In making this table, I have not aimed at rigid exactness in the fractional parts of the hour employed in certain occupations, but believe that they are sufficiently minute for the comparison intended.

petition for the place of adjunct (agrégé), in which he may be attached to some particular institution or not. In this place the powers of a young man are developed, and from it, if meritorious, he may rise in his career. The equivalent plan in Prussia secures competent instructors, but does not offer to them the advantages of the normal school.

In both France and Prussia, teachers are exempted from regular military service, and are entitled to retiring pensions in proportion to their services. . . .

Enoch Cobb Wines   1838

International Educational and Cultural Forces Relating to the United States

Enoch Cobb Wines (1806–1879) graduated from Middlebury College in 1827 and served as schoolmaster on the frigate *U. S. Constellation* from 1829 to 1831. He purchased Edenhill Seminary in Princeton, New Jersey, in 1832 and changed it to a boys school modeled after the German *gymnasium*. Wines was editor of *The American Journal of Education* from 1839 to 1849 and regularly included in it extensive accounts of foreign education. He held various educational positions, including teacher of languages at Central High School in Philadelphia in 1838, professor of ancient languages at Washington College from 1853 to 1859, and president of City University of St. Louis from 1859 to 1861. He accepted a position as secretary of the prison association of New York and visited Europe several times in the 1870's to study prison methods.

The extracts below suggest that Wines was interested in comparing educational systems on a theoretical and philosophical basis. He did, however, relate the practical results of education discernible through Britian's industrial revolution to the future awaiting the United States when educational systems became capable of fulfilling industrial needs.

Popular Education as a Public Duty

That education, based on Christianity, is adapted to elevate the character and promote the happiness of its possessors, is a position which it cannot require any laboured argument to prove, in the nineteenth century, to the citizens of the United States. It is a truth attested by universal experience, and capable of complete demonstration. Were I addressing a popular assembly on this subject, I would say to them,—Cast your eyes abroad on the world; consult time past and present; compare nations, families, and individuals respectively with each other;— your survey will lead you to this irresistible conclusion, that education, impregnated with the principles of true religion, is every where the great promoter of whatsoever things are true, whatsoever things are honest, whatsoever things are pure, lovely, and of good report; that it is the parent of virtue, industry, and order; that it is essential to the full benefits of gospel preaching; and that the want of it is the principal cause of the extreme profligacy, improvidence, and misery, which are so prevalent among the labouring classes in many countries.

A comparison between the Irish and Scottish peasantry would of itself be sufficient to establish this general fact. Among the former we behold little else than sloth, destitution, and crime; among the latter, even those who are in the worst comparative circumstances, a degree of comfort, the fruit of industry and order, is every where conspicuous. To what is this difference to be ascribed? The Irish possess as vigorous constitutions, and are as capable of enduring hard labour, as the Scotch. In the two great physical elements of prosperity, soil and climate, Ireland has a clear and decided advantage over Scotland. The difference then, making every allowance which truth and candour can require for the evils of misgovernment in the former country, is owing to the prevalence of intellectual and moral culture in the one case, and the want of it in the other. No other cause can be named, adequate to the production of the effect; and consequently to

E. C. Wines, *Hints on a System of Popular Education* (Philadelphia: Hogan and Thompson, 1838), pp. 30– 32, 48–50, 72–79, 88–93, 97–99, 110, 113–116, 157–165, 171, 173–175, 178–185.

assign any other would be, as you, gentlemen, well know, to violate one of the first principles of philosophy. In Ireland the education of the poor is deplorably neglected; few of them can either read or write; and almost all are ignorant of nearly every thing that it most befits a rational and accountable creature to understand. In Scotland an order of things exists essentially different. It is rare to meet with a person there who has not some education; schools exist in every parish; and the means of knowledge are brought within the reach of the lowest classes. The result, in each case, is such as has been already described; and such as must always take place under like circumstances. . . .

The Effect of Popular Education on Legislation

Universal education, then, is a pecuniary advantage to a nation, in the first place, by its effect on legislation. It would be easy to multiply proofs and illustrations of this most interesting truth. The argument is broad enough to fill a volume. The experience of all ages and nations might be made tributary in the gathering of materials for its construction. Who can calculate the riches often derived to a country from a judicious course of policy in relation to any one important interest, or even from the operation of a single wise law? In illustration of the former, take those extended systems of internal improvement, which have shed so much lustre on many of our states, and more than doubled their wealth. As an example of the latter, look at the law which secures to the author of any useful invention the pecuniary benefit resulting from the sale of the article invented. To what an amazing extent has it stimulated human ingenuity, and urged it on in the career of invention and discovery! And what arithmetic can calculate, what scale can measure, the activity and enterprize it has diffused through the community, the degree in which it has augmented the productive labour of the country, and the untold riches it has in this way poured into the lap of the nation?

This branch of the subject may be viewed in another aspect. We may select any period of the world—antiquity, the middle ages, or modern times—and compare the nations then existing with each other. We may compare, for example, in detail, England with France, France with Spain, Spain with Morocco, and Morocco itself with the kingdoms of interior Africa. We may institute a like process in reference to the same country at different periods of its history; as to Italy, for instance, before and after what is commonly termed the revival of learning. We may make our search into these matters as broad and as deep as we please; and what will be the result? We shall find, invariably, that those nations where the people have been best educated, have also been most distinguished for the wisdom of their laws, and have enjoyed a greater degree of prosperity, and reached a higher pitch of wealth than the others. It would be no labour for giants to pile Ossa upon Pelion, and to place them both on the top of Olympus, in the shape of proofs. But to do this would not harmonize with that character of generality to which the plan I have proposed to myself renders it necessary for me to adhere throughout these brief "Hints." I cannot, therefore, now stop to verify the assertion just made; but I make my appeal with confidence to history. Let my readers search it for themselves; and if they do not find that national prosperity and riches follow in the wake of education, as naturally as water seeks its level, or vapour ascends toward heaven, then have I read and studied in vain, and there is no one conclusion at which I have arrived, that I can rely upon with any confidence. But I am not—I cannot be mistaken. I would say, without hesitation, to any skeptic on this point—Carry your researches in reference to it in whatever direction, and push them to whatever extent you will, the result cannot but be a conviction, not to be shaken by the ingenuity of sophistry or the thunder of declamation, that the connection is not more inseparable between light and sun, between the shadow and its object, than that which exists, and ever must exist, between national prosperity and good laws, and between wise legislation and general intelligence. . . .

Education as an Aid to Ingenuity and Inventiveness

A system of universal and sound education would tend to quicken ingenuity, and thus to promote those inventions and discoveries, by the application of which to the arts of life the wealth of individuals and of nations is incalculably augmented. Men without education, or with comparatively little, may, by some fortunate accident—as the principle of making glass is said to have been discovered by some Syrian fishermen—or, by the mere force of original talent—as Paschal, while yet a youth, and before he had even heard of Euclid, actually rediscovered the science of geometry—

such persons, I say, may, by possibility, stumble upon some undiscovered principle, or strike out some new idea, which may be applied to purposes of great and general utility. But it is impossible that such cases should be of frequent occurrence. I hardly remember more than the two already cited as examples; and even as to these, the former is somewhat apocryphal, and it may well be questioned whether the latter is exactly a case in point.[1] Some previous knowledge and mental discipline, as well as genius, some acquaintance with the principles of science, are necessary to fit men for originating those curious combinations of thought, and pursuing those felicitous trains of experiment, which penetrate into the secrets of nature and the regions of invention, and bring back those bloodless trophies, which shed a real glory on our race, which exalt our conceptions of the power and dignity of the human mind, and which multiply, beyond expression, our comforts and our gains.

History, so far as its voice is heard at all on this subject, will fully bear me out in this position. Almost all the valuable discoveries and inventions on record have been made by educated men—self-educated, it may be, and struggling amid neglect or contumely, against obstacles insuperable by less resolute minds, till they have brought their labours to a happy termination;—and those nations where the general intellect has been most cultivated, and the light of science most widely diffused, have also been most distinguished for the number of their labour-saving machines, and for their improvements in the various branches of industry, by which wealth is accumulated. It is chiefly through the use of machinery that modern nations have been enabled so immeasurably to outstrip those of ancient times in riches; and it is by the same means that one nation now surpasses another in this respect.

In illustration of this point, President Young has made a comparison, founded upon the statistics of Baron Dupin, between the commercial and manufacturing condition of England and France. From this calculation it appears that the muscular force employed in commerce and manufactures in those two countries is about equal, being in each equivalent, in round numbers, to the power of six millions of men. Thus, if the productive enterprise of the two countries depended solely upon the animate power employed, France ought to be as great a commercial and manufacturing country as England. But the English, by means of machinery, have increased their force to a power equal to that of twenty-five millions of men, while the French have only raised theirs to that of eleven millions. England, then, owing to her superiority in discovering and inventing, has more than quadrupled her power of men and horses; France, on the other hand, has not quite doubled hers. "Is it," the learned President then pertinently inquires, "is it now any wonder that these islanders, with a narrower territory, smaller population, and less genial climate, should immensely outstrip their less intelligent and ingenious neighbour? And can we conceive a stronger proof of the actual pecuniary gain, that accrues to a nation from cultivating the intellect of her sons, than is furnished by such a fact?"

Let us look a little into this fact, to ascertain, if possible, how much England gains by her superiority in this matter over France. The actual commercial and manufacturing power of the latter country is only two-fifths of that of the former. The present annual value of the cotton manufacture in Great Britain, according to the Encyclopædia Britannica, is estimated to be about thirty-five millions of pounds sterling. Three-fifths of that sum, or more than twenty millions of pounds, is England's clear gain over her less skilful rival—an amount more than three times as great as the whole present annual revenue of the United States. And for this vast and ever increasing tide of prosperity, England is clearly indebted to popular education, which is the parent of intelligence, and the ultimate cause of all those improvements in the cotton manufacture, by which these amazing results have been secured.

There is a striking fact connected with the British East India cotton trade, which illustrates the wonderful superiority, in respect to their command over the elements of wealth, of those nations where the common mind is developed and stimulated by education. The manufacture of cotton goods was commenced in the East Indies, and for a long time, cotton fabrics were imported from that country into England. Now, however, in consequence of the introduction of machinery into England, and the perfection to which it has been brought, British manufacturers purchase the raw material in India, transport it seven thousand miles by water, pay a heavy duty to the state

---

[1] Paschal, though he knew nothing of geometry, was far from being uneducated. His father was one of the most eminent mathematicians in France, whose house was the constant resort of learned men.

upon it, convert it into cloth, and then send it back again, and actually undersell the natives in their own market.

The ingenuity of a single intellect, which might have slept for ever in ignorance and inactivity but for the influence of education, sometimes saves a nation more than it would cost to educate thoroughly all her sons. About a century ago, Hugh Middleton devised a plan for supplying London with pure water. It is estimated that a supply of wholesome water for that metropolis, if furnished by hauling, the method originally in use, would cost nine millions of pounds sterling. By Middleton's plan it costs considerably less than half a million. Thus London has, by one invention, been saved an annual expense, in the article of water alone, of more than eight and a half millions of pounds sterling, or about forty millions of dollars. This sum is more than enough to maintain good schools in the whole of England, Scotland, and Ireland.

Education, such as it exists at present among us, has already, by the inventions and discoveries of which it has been the source, increased the riches of this nation to an extent incalculably beyond all that the best system would have cost us. The application of steam to the propulsion of boats and railroad-cars, is alone more than sufficient to justify this remark. "It has already done more for every state in this union than all the power of industry, working by the old methods, could have effected for it in a hundred years. It has filled our houses with the productions of every country and climate, and has raised the price of every acre of our land, and almost every article of our produce." These are its direct consequences: but it has produced collateral effects, scarcely less auspicious to the prosperity and riches of the country, in the powerful impulse it has given to commerce, manufactures, agriculture, and all other branches of industry, by which men seek to create or to augment their fortunes.

But the advantages of the application of steam to these purposes, great as they are, scarcely bear a proportion to the aggregate of benefits derived from innumerable other inventions and discoveries. An instrument, called the cotton cultivator, has recently been invented, for thinning and weeding cotton, which, it is estimated, will perform the work of twenty men. I cannot, for want of the necessary data, which are not accessible to me where I write, enter into statements to show how much labour and expense are annually saved to the United States by Whittimore's card-making machine, and Whitney's cotton gin; but the amount must be immense. Who

can tell how much is saved to the husbandman, and the extent to which his gains are increased, by the use of the patent rake, and of the reaping and threshing machines, and by the invention and improvement of various other instruments for facilitating his labours?

We cannot, however, descend to particulars. The ingenuity of our countrymen has been directed, and often with the most gratifying results, to the invention of power-multiplying[2] machines, in every branch of human industry. A mere catalogue of the patents granted by the United States would fill several volumes. And to what are we indebted for this vast mass of labour-saving machinery, this multitude that can scarcely be numbered, of instruments for the accumulation of wealth? I reply unhesitatingly, — To the development of the popular mind by education. . . .

The connexion of sound popular education with the purity and perpetuity of its political institutions, was the third consideration suggested as showing that it is the duty of a free state to make adequate legal provision for the instruction of all her children. The discussion of this topic will now claim your attention; but only for a very brief space.

To the citizens of the United States is committed the solemn charge of perpetuating that liberty, and of maintaining those institutions, civil, social, literary, and religious, which it cost our fathers so much blood and treasure to establish;—institutions, which are at once the pride of our own country and the hope of the world. Yes—and I say it in no spirit of vain-glorious boasting, but with a deep impression of the responsibility which our position involves—we stand upon an eminence such as few nations have ever occupied. We are as a city set on a hill, whose light cannot be hid. The eyes of the world are upon us, —one portion regarding us with anxious but trembling hope, the other with a fiendish desire to see our fair prospects blasted, our honour prostrate in the dust, and our greatness and very existence among the things that were. Be assured, be assured, that our fall will be the triumph of despotism, and the knell of liberty throughout the world. The same pile

---

[2]I employ this word according to popular usage. I am well aware that it is not scientifically correct. There is really no such thing in art as an increased result, without a corresponding increase in the producing power. All that the most complex and ingenious machinery can do, is to concentrate power, to change its direction, or in some way to modify its action.

of ruins in which our constitution lies entombed, will cover the ardent hopes and cherished expectations of the friends of freedom every where. To maintain our free institutions, then, and to transmit them unimpaired to posterity, is no light trust, to be committed to rash hands and rasher heads. It is pregnant with the fate of empires. In its issue, are involved, for ages to come, the happiness or misery of a large portion of the civilized world. It is a trust most solemn in its nature, and the due execution of which demands, in every citizen, knowledge and judgment, as well as patriotism and vigilance.

It is not to be disguised that our political fabric is encompassed with dangers, and that there are elements of destruction at work among us, which, if left to operate without check or control, will ere long cause it to totter to its fall. I speak not this as a politician. The dangers to which I allude spring from our circumstances. They are inherent in our political organization as a nation, and our moral constitution as men. They would therefore exist, whatever party might chance to have the ascendancy for the time being. These dangers are numerous and multiform; but the two whose influence is most to be dreaded are, in my opinion, the facility with which foreigners are admitted to vote at our elections, and the loss of a proper independence of judgment and action in our own people, and a consequent susceptibility of being swayed to their own hurt by artful, selfish, and unprincipled party leaders.

Let me here guard against misapprehension and misconstruction. We have had, and still have, many naturalized citizens, whose talents and virtues are an ornament to our country; men of enlightened views and ardent patriotism; men sound to the core in their political and moral principles, and forward in every patriotic enterprise; men, in short, whose public services are a part of our national glory, and who are justly regarded as among the pillars of the state. It is not of such that I speak. I refer to that overflowing tide of immigration which disgorges upon our shores its annual thousands and tens of thousands of Europe's most degraded population; men without knowledge, without virtue, without patriotism, and with nothing to lose in the issue of any election. Are these persons fit depositories of political power? Have they any of that attachment to our institutions, and that knowledge of our form of government, which are essential to its safe exercise? Surely, either the honesty or the intelligence of the man who could maintain such a position, might well be questioned. There is danger, there

must be danger, impending over us from this source, as well as from the other.

Now what is the remedy for each? The proper remedy against the first mentioned of these dangers, would be a change in our naturalization laws; but such a change can scarcely be anticipated. The only practicable antidote to this, the only effectual safe-guard against the other, the only sure palladium of our liberties, is in so thorough an education of all our own citizens as shall nullify foreign influence, so far as it is dangerous, and secure real personal independence in the natives of the soil. Our very freedom will prove our bane, unless the people, the orginal source of all power, are so far enlightened as to be able to exercise the various functions of power aright. Universal suffrage, like many other things in this contradictory world, is either a blessing or a curse, according to circumstances. It is a blessing to a nation whose citizens use it with intelligence; it would be a curse to any people so far wanting in that attribute as to allow themselves to be made mere tools in the hands of ambitious demagogues. It is possible that a nation may be well governed, where the body of the people are ignorant; but it must be a government in which the people have no voice. Russia is governed with ability, but what imagination can paint the horrid scenes that would ensue upon the sudden introduction there of the right of universal suffrage? Freedom under such circumstances would be the most terrible of curses. It would become an instrument of destruction, to be dreaded in proportion to the degree in which it was possessed. No, the ability to reflect, examine, and judge, and the possession of elevated virtue, each attainable for the most part only through the instrumentality of education, are essential to the safe enjoyment and useful exercise of the privileges of freemen. It is a truth which we all acknowledge, but which we do not lay to heart as we ought, that intelligence and virtue are the bulwarks of a free government, that education is the parent of all true personal independence, and that in proportion to our intellectual and moral illumination will be our chances of surviving, in the vigour of perpetual manhood, the operation of those causes which have undermined all preceding republics, and which are already at work for our ruin. And let it not be forgotten that the importance of education is increasing every year in proportion to the vast influx of foreign voters, the increase of our native population, and the expansion of our people over a wider territory. . . .

How true is the celebrated aphorism of

Lord Bacon, that "knowledge is power"! It has been so in all ages and in every clime. It is a mighty instrument either for good or for evil. What a noble incentive this to labour for its acquisition! and how fearful the responsibility which the possession of it involves!

The Chinese government, the purest form of despotism on earth, the slow growth of uncounted ages, is upheld, and its vigour perpetuated, by EDUCATION. How forcible the argument thence derivable in favour of this exalted and exalting quality! And if it has force as applicable to such a country as China, it applies, as the logicians say, *a fortiori*, to civil institutions based, as ours are, on the principles of freedom and equality, and depending, confessedly, on the intelligence and virtue of the people for their security and vigour.

Now to sum up. It has been shown, I would fain trust conclusively, that the prevalence of good and thorough systems of popular education in the several members of our confederacy, would exalt the character of our citizens, and greatly augment their happiness in their civil, domestic, and individual relations; that every new degree of excellence in our primary schools, and every successive approach towards perfection in the system of education and universality in the enjoyment of its benefits, would add millions to the wealth of the nation where it abstracted only thousands; and that such education is inseparably connected with the right discharge of our duties as freemen, with the perpetuity of our glorious constitution, and with the progress of liberal principles and free institutions throughout the world.

These considerations must establish, if any thing can, the great, the paramount, the overshadowing importance, nay, the absolute necessity, of general education in a country like ours, and consequently the duty of the states to make adequate provision for it, and then to watch that the means adopted for that purpose be faithfully employed. For, it would be a position scarcely worthy of serious refutation, it would be in contradiction to all the lights of experience and observation, it would be little better than trifling, to contend that education can become universal and thorough, in a country where the government manifests no solicitude in its behalf, and puts forth no exertions to promote it. . . .

An Example from Germany

In Prussia, a country which exhibits the extraordinary spectacle of a despotic government and the most paternal anxiety, as well as the wisest plan, for the education of all the people, the popular schools are divided into two classes,—termed elementary schools, and burgher schools. . . .

. . . Observe, here is no theory—no programme of untried experiments: this is the actual education, actually given, and actually received. It is computed that thirteen out of fifteen children, from the age of seven to that of fourteen, are at the public schools; the remaining two are probably at the private schools, or educated at home; so that the *whole* are educated—and *thus* educated! Observe, this is no small and petty state, easily managed and controlled; it is a country that spreads over large tracts, various tribes, different languages, multiform religions: the energy of good government has conquered all these difficulties. But what you will admire in the Prussian system, is not the laws of education only, but the spirit that framed and pervades the laws—the full appreciation of the dignity and objects of men —of the duties of citizens—of the powers, and equality, and inheritance of the human soul. And yet in that country the people are said to be less *free* than in ours!—how immeasurably more the people are *regarded!*"

There is an article in the first number of a literary journal, recently established at the City of Washington, in which the Prussian system is attacked and decried as in no respect suited to this country, because, forsooth, Prussia is a monarchy! If the writer of said article means by this that it is not adapted to our use, because it teaches the laws and constitution of Prussia, so far I agree with him; but if he means that the great principle which is recognised as the basis of the system— viz. the necessity of a thorough education of all the people—and the wisdom and liberality with which that principle is carried out in its application, are at war either with our institutions, then, gentlemen, your own good sense shall be my only argument to refute him. I forbear to characterise his sophistry in the terms which it richly merits. Some good things *can* come out of Nazareth. Let us not be guilty of the flagrant illiberality of refusing to applaud and to imitate what is intrinsically excellent, because it happens to have originated with monarchists instead of republicans, and to exist on the southern coast of the Baltic instead of the western shores of the Atlantic ocean.

How poor and meager, in comparison with the education which Prussia and Saxe Weimar give to all their children, is that afforded by the generality of our common schools! Bulwer's description of the state of things in the elementary schools of England, is much more applicable to ours.—"Generally," says he, "throughout the primary schools, nothing is taught but a little spelling, a very little reading, still less writing, the catechism, the Lord's prayer, and an unexplained, unelucidated chapter or two in the Bible; add to these the nasal mastery of a hymn, and an undecided conquest over the rule of Addition, and you behold a very finished education of the poor."

I would not indulge in sarcasm, or be unjust, on such a subject as this. Even were I so disposed myself (which I am not), I am sure such a course would not meet with your approbation. I am free to admit, therefore, that this would not be a fair picture of our popular schools. Nevertheless, what do these institutions actually accomplish in the way of disciplining the powers of their pupils, and imparting knowledge? It would scarcely be unfair to say that, in a large proportion of them, the faculty of observation and comparison is not developed, nor the art of reflection taught, at all. And as to the knowledge they communicate, reading, spelling, writing, arithmetic, geography, and grammar, form generally the entire catalogue of studies in their courses of instruction. In reference to many of them even this list must be abridged, and in respect to still more, the branches enumerated are both imperfectly taught, and pursued to a very inconsiderable extent. The dignity of man, the powers of the human soul, the education of the senses, our rights and duties as men and citizens, and the works of the Creator by which we are surrounded, are subjects which, as you well know, are never dreamed of in the philosophy of most of our primary schoolmasters. The masters themselves are for the most part ignorant on these points, and multitudes of parents would oppose their introduction into school as branches of study. . . .

The Role of Teachers

But are we not, it may be asked, in the main, an intelligent, shrewd, well-informed people? I freely, nay, exultingly, admit that we are; but I deny that it is to our common schools that we are chiefly indebted for this character. As a nation, we are educated more by contact with each other, by business, by newspapers, magazines, and circulating libraries, by public meetings and conventions, by lyceums, by speeches in congress, in the state legislatures, and at political gatherings, and in various other ways, than by direct instructions imparted in the school room. And if so much general intelligence, as now unquestionably characterises us as a people, is the result of the present state of things, what might we not anticipate, if to all these influences were superadded the advantages of a well organised and comprehensive system of primary education? Results, glorious in themselves, and most auspicious to our prospects as a nation, might be looked for from such a union.

I say, A WELL ORGANIZED SYSTEM. But what are the conditions of such a system? Allow me to summon Mr. Cousin to my aid in answering this question. "The best plans of instruction," he says, "cannot be executed but by good teachers; and the state has done *nothing* for popular education, if it does not watch that those who devote themselves to teaching be well prepared; then suitably placed, encouraged, and guided in the duty of continued self-improvement; and lastly rewarded and promoted in proportion to their advancement, and punished according to their faults."

Here is the whole philosophy of good schools and sound education reduced within the compass of a nutshell. What are their elements? First, good plans of instruction; then, good teachers; next, provision by the state for preparing teachers for their work; fourthly, suitable encouragement and guidance in the duty of continued self-improvement; and finally, promotions and rewards for the meritorious, and punishments and disgraces for the unworthy. And these are all essential elements of a well organised system. Take away any one of them, and you destroy the proportions of the whole structure, and materially diminish both its strength and beauty;—take away the third—provision for the education of teachers—and you remove the corner stone of the whole system, and leave it comparatively powerless for any useful purpose. No general plan of popular education can be at all entitled to the epithet well-organised, which does not provide for the training of masters. This, in my opinion, is the first duty of a state with respect to schools; and without it, all other legislation in reference to this matter, whatever partial advantages it may result in, must stop short of the full benefits at which it ought to aim, and which it might accomplish.

There has been a radical error in the practice, if not in the opinions, of parents on this subject. They have acted as if they thought that he who was unfit for any thing else would make a very tolerable teacher for their children. No opinion could be more preposterous, no course of action more short-sighted. It is not thus that men think and act on other subjects. A mechanic must serve an apprenticeship of three, four, or five years, before he is allowed to undertake the formation of an elegant piece of furniture, or a complicated machine, when nothing can result from failure but the loss of the rude material and the workman's time. But we have been in the habit of committing the infant mind, that most delicate and complex piece of God's workmanship, to men who have never studied even the first principles of its structure; and that too at a time when its parts are most easily disarranged, and when such disarrangement produces the most fatal and lasting effects.

While such views thus practically prevail, it is in vain to look for the fruits of a wise system of elementary instruction. There is no conviction deeper or stronger in my mind than this,—that but little can be effected in this country towards elevating popular education, and establishing it on a firm basis, till we have a body of teachers regularly trained to their business, and the occupation of an instructer shall take its proper rank among the learned professions. When the title of school-master, now almost a reproach and a hissing, shall be a passport to respect, then, and not till then, will the general education become what it ought to be. And who, let me ask, is entitled to a higher degree of consideration and respect from the community than the devoted and laborious teacher of youth? Does the nature of a man's occupation confer any proportion of dignity, apart from the manner in which he performs its duties? We can scarcely deny that it does. What nobler work, then, can task the human energies than that of training immortal beings to act well their part in life, and to enjoy the rewards of virtue through interminable years: "It may be affirmed, without the least hesitation, that there is no office in general society more honourable or important than that of an instructer of the young, and none on which the present and future happiness of the human race so much depends. But in consequence of various circumstances, the office has been rendered inefficient for the great purposes of human improvement, and the teacher himself degraded from that rank which he ought to hold in the scale of society." He must now be raised to his proper elevation in that scale, or we must be content to forego the advantages of a higher moral and intellectual development of the popular mind. But the days of miracles are

over; and therefore it is that I conclude that this elevation is a result which can never take place, to the extent desired and needed, till SEMINARIES FOR THE EDUCATION OF TEACHERS shall have gone into general operation.

Institutions of this kind may be regarded as emphatically the intellectual want of the age, and especially of our own country. In Prussia this is no longer a want; it is already a realization. The number of such institutions in that kingdom is now fully equal to supply the entire demand for teachers throughout its territories. France has nobly followed the lead of Prussia in this matter, and her Normal schools will ere long furnish her with a corps of instructers every way qualified for their work. Many of the German principalities, and some of the cantons of Switzerland, have achieved the same thing. Similar establishments have been founded in Greece, and in some of the South American States; particularly that formerly under the presidentship of the accomplished and liberalminded Santander. And even in the heart of Africa, the monarch of Benin has invited a Mr. L'Espinat, a schoolmaster of Senegal, to establish in his capital a Normal school of mutual instruction.

Nor are these institutions so recent in their inception as many probably imagine. They owe their origin to the celebrated Francke who flourished nearly a century and a half ago. Beside his Orphan Asylum at Halle, stood a seminary for the education of teachers. From this time, education and the educator became objects of general interest throughout Germany; and since 1730, lectures on school keeping appear to have been universally delivered. Hecker, a pupil of the Franckean discipline, founded a school for teachers at Berlin in 1740; and one of these seminaries in Hanover was established as early as 1750. Normal schools were founded in Bohemia in 1770; and before the French revolution similar establishments existed in Usingen, Dessan, Cassel, Detmold, Gotha, Oeringen, and Kiel.

Thus you perceive how early the attention of other nations was directed to this great object of educating teachers, and how steadily and successfully some of them have pursued it. And who shall say that they have attached an undue importance to it? It is the very life-blood of an efficient system of popular instruction. In vain will you establish schools for the people, unless you place over them competent instructers. The wisest plan without this will be devoid of all vitality. But where will you get such teachers, unless you make them? Can you summon them from the "vasty deep" to do your bidding? You may call them, but they will not come; and for the best of reasons,—they are not in being. When will the states of this Union, the boasted land of common schools and general intelligence, awake to the importance of this subject, and put forth their energies to supply this deficiency? There is a torpor in the public mind in relation to it, for which it is not easy to account, and from the effects of which, if it be not shaken off, forebodings of the most gloomy character may well be entertained.

The institution of seminaries for the education of teachers, is no visionary scheme, no wild chimera of mine; their importance, their absolute necessity, is held by you, gentlemen, in common with all other intelligent men, who have examined enough into the matter to form a decisive opinion upon it. Are they not insisted on by some of the ablest writers and most enlightened friends of education on both sides of the Atlantic?—by Cousin in France, by Bulwer, Simpson, and Dick in England, by Bryce in Ireland, and by Woodbridge, Dwight, De Kay, and Dix in our own country? Mr. Burrowes, I understand, will urge the immediate necessity of establishing one or more in Pennsylvania, in his forthcoming Annual Report to the Legislature of that state. Their importance has been repeatedly affirmed in resolutions passed at popular meetings in various parts of the country, and especially by a highly respectable meeting held in the city of Philadelphia, about a twelve-month ago, when an elaborate argument was presented in favour of their establishment in a Report drawn up by the Rev. Gilbert Morgan, and unanimously adopted. Many of the first Literary Journals of the age have earnestly and ably maintained their indispensable necessity to a high order of popular education; and among them the Edinburgh Review, the Foreign Quarterly Review, and the London Quarterly Journal of Education, the American Annals of Education, and others too numerous to mention. . . .

Administration of Teachers Seminaries

It is a practical question of no small importance whether, if the proposed seminaries are established, they shall exist as independent institutions, or in connexion with and dependency on other institutions already in being,—either colleges or academies. Much may be said, with great plausibility and force, on both sides of the question; especially in favour of their connexion with colleges. Here we have buildings, libraries, lecture rooms, apparatus, cabinets, and learned professors, already provided, without any new outlay of money, and nothing seems wanting but pupils to be trained to become the future educators of our children. . . .

It is admitted, on all hands, that the profession of teaching ought to be as respectable as any other in society; and that it must become so, before it can be productive of all the benefits, which it is capable of achieving. It is also known, by all who know any thing about the delicate relations of cause and effect, how much men's feelings and opinions are influenced by names, appearances, and airy nothings, or that which seems little more substantial. Now the respectability of teaching will and must depend somewhat on the respectability of the institutions where instructers are trained. And will any man tell me that mere departmental appendages to colleges and academies can become as respectable in the eyes of the community, as original, independent institutions, with their own presidents, professors, buildings, libraries, apparatus, and all the other paraphernalia of educational establishments? It is impossible in the nature of things; and few, I imagine, will maintain that they can.

I shall content myself, and dismiss the argument, with one further consideration on this point. It is this: The young men who are preparing themselves to be teachers, will not be as well taught, either theoretically or practically, in the proposed college departments, as they would be in the teachers' seminary. You will not, I trust, misunderstand me here. Had I intended to cast any slur upon college instruction, I certainly would not address myself to a college Professor. All that I mean to say, and what I firmly believe, is, that Professors in colleges would not feel the same interest in their lectures and instructions to the pupils of a subordinate department in their respective institutions, that would be felt by the Professors in a Normal Seminary, where instructions of the kind in question would constitute their sole business. And besides this, the modes of teaching, adapted to common schools and to colleges, are so different, so almost opposite to each other, that it is no disparagement to an eminent and highly successful Professor in a college, to say that he is not the most fit person to instruct those who are to become the teachers of children. Teachers in colleges cannot properly be selected with much reference to their fitness for such a task; while the very reverse would be

true of the Normal school. There such qualification would be all in all. If it be said that
one Professor at least in each college would
be so chosen; my reply is, that in the teachers' seminaries *all* would be selected upon
this principle. From these premises the conclusion seems fairly deducible that the future
educators would themselves be better educated in seminaries with independent organizations, than in departments connected with
collegiate institutions. . . .

Teacher Recruitment

The question of securing the services of
these men, after they shall have completed
their course of studies, to the state in which
they were educated, is perhaps one of greater
practical difficulty. It is a question on which,
I confess, I have not bestowed much thought,
but the object contemplated I believe to be
entirely attainable. Permit me to suggest one
method, not as the only, or even the best
means of attaining it, but as one which has
occurred to my mind. It is somewhat similar to that employed by the General Government to secure a like object in reference to
the cadets educated at West Point. Let the
state not charge any of the seminarists more
than one half the actual cost of their education, and let her exact from each on entering
a written pledge, guarantied by friends, to
follow the profession of teaching for a specified number of years, say from three to five,
and to exercise it within her limits during
that period,—unless, on changing his purpose,
he first pay back to the state the whole sum
with interest, expended on his education.
Something like this, if I remember right, is
required of each pupil on entering the Normal
schools of Prussia. Let the state add to this a
judicious system of annual or triennial rewards, or honorary distinctions to be conferred on such as distinguish themselves by
the ability and faithfulness with which they
discharge their duties; and the end desired
would, I can scarcely doubt, be already well
nigh secured.

On the soundness of these organic principles for teachers' seminaries, I do not entertain the least doubt; but in forming such an
institution, an almost endless quantity of details would be requisite, in reference to which,
I frankly avow, I should be at great loss in
making up an opinion, and I doubt not many
others would find themselves in the same uncertainty. How can these doubts and the hesitation consequent upon them be removed? In

most matters of importance, where it is a
question how we shall proceed ourselves, it is
usual to consult the experience of others. But
whither shall we look for the lights of experience on this momentous question? There
is not, as far as I am informed, a single
institution of the kind proposed, established
by any state in this confederacy. The departments instituted for this purpose by the state
of New York, as mere appendages to a few of
the County Grammar Schools, cannot be considered as forming an exception to this remark. Mr. Dix, the able Superintendent of
Common Schools in that state, is not at all
satisfied with this plan. He says, "If the
foundations of the whole system of public instruction in New York were to be laid over,
it would be advisable to create separate seminaries for the education of teachers." There
is an institution for the training of teachers
in Andover, Mass., under the care of the Rev.
S. Hall, the author of several valuable works
on education, which is said to have been very
useful in its influence on common schools in
that state; but, if I am correctly informed,
it is not in any way connected with or dependent on the civil authorities of the commonwealth. And these establishments are,
as far as my knowledge goes, the extent to
which measures have been put in actual
operation for the specific object of educating
teachers in this country!

Whither, then, I ask again, shall we turn
our eyes for light to resolve our doubts, and
models that may help us in our hour of need?
To Prussia certainly, where institutions of
the kind in question are best organized, have
been longest in operation, and have produced
the most important results. I have said, and
it will not be denied, that it is customary, in
important matters, to consult the experience
of others. Is not this done in all the learned
professions, and in every pursuit of life?
Are not agents often employed for this purpose by individuals, by colleges, by incorporated companies, and even by sovereign
states? Suppose, for example, we were to hear
of the discovery of some new principle in
mechanics, more valuable than any hitherto
discovered, or of a new application of some
principle previously known, and to learn that
in some European country it had been applied
to machinery with complete success; suppose, further, that we were desirous of introducing this new principle, or application,
as the case might be, into our own manufactories, would we do it upon the mere representation of books, however well written
or scientific? No, surely; it is not in this

way that men act, where important pecuniary interests are involved. We would pursue a wiser course; we would send out some capable person, commissioned to make a thorough examination, and to bring back, not merely a written report, and plans on paper, but also his own personal knowledge, derived from personal observation. This is, in fact, often done. It is needless to enumerate cases; they are so common, that the memory of every man of the least information will supply them in abundance.

Let those states, then, that really desire to found systems of public instruction, fitted to bless the present generation, and worthy of being transmitted to posterity, act with the ordinary wisdom of intelligent individuals in undertaking an important enterprise. If they would set themselves intelligently about the first duty of a free state—to diffuse knowledge and virtue among its citizens—let them commission competent agents to visit the Prussian schools,[3] who shall be charged to take a general survey of the operation of the whole system, and to remain long enough at one of the best of the Normal seminaries to become perfectly familiar with all its organic principles, its details of arrangement, its modes of intercourse, discipline, and instruction, its examination, and, in short, with every thing appertaining to it in all its aspects and relations. After an adequate examination, let them return and spread the result of their inquiries severally before the states by whom they were employed. These will then be prepared to try the experiment of educating teachers under the most favourable circumstances, and if they fail, it will not be for the reason that, with a penny-wise pound-foolish policy, they groped their way in the dark, because they feared the expense of procuring those lights, which were within their reach. No objection, as it seems to me, could be made by any state to such a procedure, but its expense. Yet what would the expense be? A few thousand dollars at most—a mere nothing in comparison with the magnitude of the object to be secured.

It may, indeed, be urged as a plea to obviate the necessity of the course recommended, that we have the Report of Cousin on the state of Education in Prussia, and we may be called upon to say what need there is of further light. It is true that the eminent philosopher and educationist referred to, performed the duty assigned him with an ability honourable alike to himself and the French nation; and his Report is a mine of valuable information concerning Prussia, and of just principles in relation to education in general. But Cousin was not long enough in Prussia to become thoroughly conversant with her educational institutions.[4] His Report presents us with a variety of minute details in reference to the economy and regulations of the Normal schools, but he gives us no clear idea of the manner in which the various branches of knowledge are taught to those who are themselves to become the teachers of the primary schools. This, in fact, was hardly necessary under the circumstances; for he was to return, and to superintend in person the establishment of the national schools in France. Besides, it should be borne in mind that he wrote for a people differing widely from ours in their manners, customs, institutions, laws, form of government, and the whole structure of society. What the citizens of our several states need for their complete satisfaction is an examination by one of themselves,—a man familiar with their institutions and with their habitudes of thought, feeling, and action, who should pursue his investigations into the system with a constant reference to the question of its availability for their own republican purposes. They require for their guidance not only a Report from such a man, but that deep familiarity with the spirit of the system, and that intimate acquaintance with the minutiæ of its arrangements, and with its special modes of instruction, which can be gained only by personal inspection, and can never be fully shadowed forth in a written Report. Between a mere composition, however eloquent or able, and this full, fresh, breathing knowledge, there is the same difference that there is between a marble statue and a living man.

---

[3]This has actually been done by Ohio; a state which, though comparatively young, is already far in advance of many of her elder sisters, in her schools, her internal improvements, her eleemosinary institutions, and various other points of her public policy.

[4]He arrived there on the 5th of June, 1831, and left about the 1st of July of the same year.

Charles Astor Bristed   1840

Examinations and Student Life at Cambridge

Charles Astor Bristed (1820–1874) graduated from Yale in 1839 and went to England for five years to study at Cambridge University. His thorough and detailed account of English university life is written from a comparative viewpoint, and the immediacy of his previous studies at Yale is most discernible.

Comparing university goals and standards in America and Britain, Bristed analyzed the peculiarly medieval and classical examination system then in use at Cambridge. He examined the defects of American colleges and universities in scholarship and discussed some of their "supposed counterbalancing advantages." He felt that there were few people qualified to write an account of Cambridge student life and said that if he had "ever seen a decent review article on English university education, this book would not have been written." Of greater interest, however, is Bristed's proposition that there are "points in an English education which may be studied with profit and from which we may obtain valuable hints."

Preface

I write this book for three reasons:

First, very little is accurately known in this country about English Universities.

Secondly, most of what we hear respecting those institutions, comes through the medium of popular novels and other light literature, frequently written by non-University men, and almost always conveying an erroneous and unfavorable idea of the Universities.

Thirdly and principally, there are points in an English education which may be studied with profit, and from which we may draw valuable hints.

Few Americans have the opportunity of growing up into manhood among half a generation of the most highly educated class in England; nor is it indeed altogether desirable that many should have. I myself owed it to an accident. There are few persons among us qualified by their knowledge of the subject to do it justice. Had I ever seen even a decent review article on English University education, this book would not have been written.

It has been my object to give a picture of English University life just as it is; to do which correctly, I have been obliged to mingle gaieties and gravities. Should the reader not assent to my conclusions, he will at any rate have a tolerable idea of the facts. The same motive—a desire to depict accurately what I saw and experienced, and the impressions which such a life makes on an American—has obliged me to speak of myself more frequently than is altogether pleasant for either reader or author.

Of the bad arrangement and want of system displayed in the book, I am as conscious as the severest critic can be. These faults must be attributed to want of ability, not want of care. To deal with the minutiæ of a system so complicated as that of several independent Colleges combined in one University—rejecting what is unimportant, and lucidly setting forth what is worthy of remark—becomes an extremely difficult task where everything is so different from the corresponding arrangements among ourselves. My original intention was to present merely a series of sketches, without any attempt at filling up the connecting links throughout. I began the sketches, and two different Magazines at different times began to publish them, but were very soon afraid to go on, because I did not pretend to conceal our inferiority to the English in certain branches of liberal education. I then resolved to refrain, not merely from publishing, but from writing any more, until as many years as I passed in England had elapsed since my return thence. With the exception therefore of the first nine chapters, the whole of this work has been written during the past summer, and I can truly say that my opinions on all the matters discussed in it have undergone no important change for the last five years; all my observation has tended to confirm them.

Should this book fall into the hands of any Cambridge man, he may condemn it as abounding in petty and uninteresting details. If so, I would commend to his attention a brief apologue:—

An Arab traveller had occasion to visit London. On arriving there his attention was attracted by a great crowd in the street.

Charles Astor Bristed, *Five Years in An English University, 1840–1844* (New York: G. P. Putnam and Sons, 1851), pp. vii–viii, 44–57, 445–452, 455–475.

He drew near, and found to his surprise and disappointment that the object of Cockney curiosity was a camel, belonging to the caravan of some Barnum of the day. He wrote home to his friends, ''the frivolity and childishness of these English are intense. Yesterday I beheld a large concourse of people staring at an ordinary camel, that one of our boys would not have turned his head to look at.''. . .

An American Student's First Impression at Cambridge and on Cambridge

There are not a few persons in this community of ours, some of them not deficient in intelligence, nor entirely destitute of the spirit of benevolence, who think it a most desirable and praiseworthy thing to stir up all the mischief they can between England and America. These well-disposed individuals doubtless have their reward, which I never felt inclined to envy them; my own ideas always urging me to a directly opposite course, either from some mental blindness which kept me behind the progressive democracy of this advancing age, or because I never intended to put myself in a position which would oblige me to propitiate or toady Irishmen or slaveholders. Ever since my early boyhood it had been a leading idea with me that the great branches of the Anglo-Saxon family, distinguished by their language, by their ethical principles, by their judiciously liberal political institutions, from the rest of the world, ought to work harmoniously together; that a great deal of the bad feeling between them arose from ignorance, and was therefore removable by mere contact and information; and that a citizen of either country who had the opportunity, was doing his duty much better by endeavoring to promote a mutual knowledge of each other between the two peoples, and thus dispel antipathies having more a hypothetical than a real foundation, than by laboring to revive and foster old germs of animosity which time and the natural course of events were already doing so much to kill. In wishing, therefore, to stand well and make a good impression at Cambridge from my first entry, I was actuated not merely by a desire after the promotion of my own κῦδος [Kudos] (to speak Cantabrigically), but by an honest wish to represent my country well, and make the name of American respectable to many young Englishmen who had no personal experience of it. Indeed it was partly on this account that I had put myself in a position so disproportionate to my financial resources as that of a Trinity Fellow-Commoner.

I was well aware that in this endeavor there was considerable up-hill work to do, and sufficient discouragement to encounter; that as the American admirer of England is sure to get some hard knocks at home, so the American in England is apt to be looked at in a false light by the individuals of a nation to which he is well disposed.

Mere mistakes of ignorance I was always prepared for; and it is but justice to my English acquaintances to say that they were generally as glad to have such mistakes corrected as I was eager to correct them. This charge of ignorance is, as we all know, sometimes denied and sometimes slighted by Englishmen; but it is rather understating the case to say that the majority of English gentlemen know less than they should about the condition and institutions of a people so nearly related to them, and whose political and social movements they might study to so much advantage in reference to their own country. In our past history, short as it is, we would hardly expect them to be well up, coming into rivalry as it does with the more universally exciting events that took place in Europe contemporaneously; and other reasons may combine with national pride for making Waterloo a more familiar name to them than New Orleans; but surely an English gentleman who has attained his majority, might be expected to know that we have two Houses of Congress and that New York is not a slave State.

The old joke of presuming that a New Yorker or New Englander knows any man who may have gone out to Canada, St. Louis, or Texas, is really no joke at all, but a very common occurrence, which every American who has travelled or resided much in England must have verified for himself. Sometimes I have remarked instances where it might well be suspected that much of this ignorance was put on, and that—just as our public men assent to the romancings of Irish ''sympathizers,'' and wonder how England can be so blind and unjust as not to grant repeal, knowing better all the time—the Tory journalist when he asserted that bread was actually dearer at times in American than in English cities, *because* he had seen a New York shilling loaf which was not larger than a London tenpenny one, perfectly understood the relative value of the New York and English shillings. But in many cases no such explanation was admissible. The Liberals whom I met did not seem very much better acquainted with us than the Tories, but they were more anxious for information and better disposed towards us. The general bearing of such Tories, and that not merely young men or Dons at Cambridge, but Londoners, was very civil to me personally, but mingled with a sort of implied pity for my belonging to a country where a gentlemen was out of place, could not get his deserts, and must necessarily be κακόνουσ τῷ δῆμῷ [ignored by the mob]. For with the English Tory I found it a fixed idea that all our "Upper Ten" are bullied and plundered by the mob, just as it is with the American Radical, that all the mass of the English people are miserable serfs, and all the landed aristocracy bloated tyrants. With men of this sort I took a very summary course; neither more nor less than the ordinary American dodge of stoutly asserting and imperturbably maintaining our national superiority in morals and intelligence. Take the following as a specimen. *B.* at the Dean's table, enjoying the beneficial provender thereon. Enter (rather late) Strafford Pope, a young aristocrat with £30,000 a-year, and a large assortment of the most antediluvian politics. *P.* has heard that *B.* is an American, and takes a seat alongside him half intentionally; *B.* knows *P.* by reputation as one of the few reading Fellow-Commoners. They strike up a conversation in the pauses of the dinner; by and by the discourse takes a political turn.

P. A republic may be very well when we can make all men angels, but till then it can't answer.

B. Why, we make one answer very well, though our men don't pretend to be angels, and only some of our women.

P. Answer very well! You have no law—or, at least, no means of enforcing the law, you know. [An Englishmen always appends "you know" to the very thing you *don't* know, and won't admit.]

B. Oh, that's altogether a mistake on your part. I can see how it arises very naturally. You look around on your own lower orders and think how unfit they would be for political power; and so they are now, no doubt. But wait till virtue and intelligence are diffused among your people as generally as they are among ours, and then you will be ripe for a republic and will have it too.

Whether I believed in this magnificent formula of our superiority in virtue and intelligence to the rest of the world or not, it answered its purpose at the time completely, utterly putting down the Englishman, who was so upset with indignation at my quiet assumption, that he could not deliver himself of an articulate reply.

Some of the Fast men among the Fellow-Commoners and their toadies, whose love of deviltry was much greater than their wit, as soon as they heard of my nationality, determined to have some fun out of me; and accordingly invited me to various entertainments with the laudable intention of making me drunk and otherwise putting me through my paces. But these fellows gave me very little trouble; I may say it without vanity, for getting the better of them in any thing which required the smallest exertion of νους [brain] was like being first in a donkey-race. In all repartees and wordy warfare I gave them quite as much as they could manage. As to the fluids, I had the fortunate or unfortunate natural gift, not unimproved by practice, of a rather strong head, and could imbibe a pretty good share, even of the villanously doctored Cambridge wines, without disturbing my bodily or mental equilibrium; so that the men who had promised themselves the treat of seeing a drunken Yankee, only made themselves very comfortably tipsy in their attempts to intoxicate me, especially as I was too prudent to rely entirely on my natural capacities without having recourse to an occasional artifice. On one special occasion, I recollect there was a dead set made at me, almost every one present out of fourteen diners challenged me to drink repeatedly. I stuck to the Hock—or, more critically speaking, to something in a green bottle—the bottle and glass were colored, that was the main point; the colored glass enabled me to fill and empty, in appearance, many times, while in reality I only poured out and tasted a few drops; the result of which stratagem was that two or three of the party put themselves completely *hors de combat*, and were deeply impressed with a sense of my capacity.

Never but once did I come near getting into any difficulty on account of my country. One night after a dinner party, a Fellow-Commoner of older standing, who was leaving at the same time, carried me off to "show me another set." This other set consisted chiefly of the Beefsteak Club, some six or eight men who used to dine together once a week for the purpose of consuming incredible quantities of an extraordinary liquor called Cambridge Port, and having performed their usual duties, were then in what the Irish call a very high state of civilization. Among their guests was to my horror and disgust, a Fellow of the college, just about to take orders. Before I could find a decent pretext for evaporating, one of the most "civilized" undertook to banter me on my non-appearance in the classic regions of Barnwell. It is not very difficult to quiz a drunken man, and I showed this one up so completely before his friends, that he became quite furious, and proceeded to make some very personal remarks upon "Yankees," which provoked me to give him a rather dogmatic extempore lecture on the requisites of a gentlemen and the duties of hospitality and courtesy. He of the Beefsteak, comprehending dimly what I said, and being at a loss for words, made, by way of answer, a belligerent demonstration, to which, in self-defence, I was compelled to make signs of responding. But before hostilities were actually interchanged, several men seized hold of each of us, and the scene which ensued was sufficiently ludicrous. I had from the first been more amused at, than angry with, the obstreperous individual, and had not the slightest idea of fighting him unless he actually struck me; besides I was perfectly sober, which could not be said of any other person in the room except the old stager who brought me, so that I could observe quite coolly what was going on. One very well disposed and very tipsy man, who was great upon boats but very slow at books, endeavored to pacify me by relating the results of his own experience with moral deductions; but in four several attempts could get no farther than to inform me that he had been "f-five years in this u-university." Another, who evidently gave me credit for the most belligerent propensities, was expounding to me the laws of the University, which forbade duelling under penalty of expulsion for all concerned, and insisting that therefore it was impossible to call a man out, etc. Meanwhile the other party was surrounded by *his* group of friends, who at length succeeded in persuading him that he had been guilty of a great breach of decorum, so that in the end he began apologizing to me, and continued his excuses till they were almost as great a bore as the original offence. This incident did not fail to be repeated; and partly from the muddled condition of those who witnessed and assisted at it, partly from the inaccuracy of gossip, from which even Englishmen are not entirely exempt, it was repeated with various exaggerations, and finally settled into the form that I had drawn a knife on the asperser of my countrymen, and threatened him with instant annihilation.

Some trifling New York accomplishments, from which no one in my position could have expected much *a priori*, now came into play, and tended to give me consequence. It may seem ridiculous that a knowledge of particular meats and drinks, or the possession of a stock of well-cut trowsers, should have any

effect on a man's position in a community professedly literary; but it was these trifles more than any thing else that tended to raise the opinion which the younger portion of my new associates formed of me, and through me of the country.

One of the first things which surprises a young man from our Atlantic cities on visiting England, is the inferiority of the English in certain refinements of civilization, in which he was prepared to find them infinitely superior. It is with no small astonishment that the New Yorker, or Philadelphian, or Bostonian finds it almost impossible to get clothes made to fit in England; nor, while doing justice to the mutton and ale of the country, is he less disappointed to find that there is no variety—the eternal steak, chops and potatoes, and big joints everywhere; and that the national taste in wine is of the most barbarous description, most of the fluid consumed under that honorable appellation being half brandy. Moreover, having usually mixed more with Frenchmen, Spaniards, and Germans, and speaking what he knows of their languages more fluently than the Englishman of the same age, he has a decided advantage when any native of the Continent happens to be present, or when Continental matters are under discussion. After recovering from the first surprise of these facts, I cherished them *as* great facts, which enabled me to show my superiority to the "benighted British" when they least expected it; and more than one youth who thought to astonish the American savage by a display of the mysteries of civilization, was rather astonished in his turn at my summary condemnation of English tailors and cooks, and my ostentatious learning in French wines and dishes. It may be supposed that the Fellows were not moved by any vanities of habiliment, but their epicurean and convivial tendencies led them to respect any hints in the matter of edibles and potables. A more intellectual way of becoming known was in the University debating society. I had, more by practice than natural ability or inclination, acquired that knack of speech-making which about every third graduate of an American college possesses, and accordingly, at the first meeting of the *Union* after our admission, extemporized an argument on the Chinese war. In this way, however, it was not possible to gain much renown, the debating society being a very third-rate affair: mere oratory is about as much valued with the English as mere scholarship is with us. But in the legitimate business of the place I was not without resources. In accordance with the impulse first given by Newton, strengthened by other great scientific names, and only partially counteracted by such scholars as Bentley and Porson, Mathematics are made a necessary foundation for every thing at Cambridge; and the only road to Classical honors and their accompanying emoluments in the University, and virtually in all the Colleges, except Trinity, is through Mathematical, all candidates for the Classical Tripos being obliged as a preliminary to obtain a place in that Mathematical list which is headed by the Senior Wrangler and tailed by the Wooden Spoon. This preliminary passing in science being a terrible bore to the Classical men, and failure in it sometimes shipwrecking them for life, they consider themselves, and claim to be considered by others, victims and martyrs. Now I hated Mathematics as cordially as any Cantab of my contemporaries, and with more experience, if not more knowledge of the subject, while I really was fond of Classics; so as naturally to fall into the ranks of the aggrieved and complaining minority (there are about three Mathematical students for one Classical), and this helped to give me a position among those with whom I sympathized. In composition and cram I was yet untried, and the translations in lecture-room were not difficult to acquit one's self on respectably. Finally, whatever I did, derived an additional lustre from the blue and silver gown, the Fellow-Commoners generally being more disposed to *rowing* than reading, and not particularly distinguished in any way for their intellectual performances. Indeed they are popularly denominated "empty bottles," the first word of the appellation being an adjective, though were it taken as a verb there would be no untruth in it.

And now, what impression did my new associates make upon me? With those of my own standing, and nearly my own age, I was much disappointed and somewhat disgusted. These youths of eighteen or nineteen seemed precocious enough in vice, but the veriest schoolboys in every thing else—making a noise and throwing about pens and paper in the lecture-room, waxing uproarious at night over the worst liquors, working like schoolboys when they did work, translating with awkward literalness, and shifting most of the burden on the Lecturer when it came to Mathematics. In every thing but physical development and vicious tendency they seemed years behind American students considerably their juniors—except that some—and only some of them—executed beautiful Latin verses with great facility.

In some respects, my generalization was very imperfect and incorrect. It had been my mishap, partly from my position as Fellow-Commoner, partly from local accidents, to fall among a bad set of Undergraduates. Had I, in the situation of my rooms, or of my seat at lectures, lighted among some of the best Eton, or Rugby, or Shrewsbury men, my first impressions would have been considerably modified. But in one important point they were correct. The English student of eighteen is more a boy than the American of the same age, in manners, in self-possession, in world-knowledge, in general knowledge of literature even. How far this precocity on our part is an advantage, is a question of which we shall have more to say hereafter. At that time, deeming it an unmixed benefit, I was not a little proud of it, individually and nationally.

But while not particularly pleased with those of my own immediate standing, I took great delight in the society of another class —the Bachelor Scholars. These men, averaging about twenty-three years of age, the best Classics and Mathematicians of their years, were reading for Fellowships—that is, they were putting themselves through the best existing course of intellectual training and polish. Most of them well grounded in the grammar, and copiously learned in the vocabularies of the Ancient tongues, so that they read Latin and Greek more readily than one usually does French, were now working over their Classics to the utmost pitch of accuracy, branching them into philological discussions, enriching them with historic lore, and illustrating them from the literature of other languages. Some were carrying up the results of their mathematical drilling to the highest walks of pure science; and all were imbuing themselves with the sufficiently wide course of reading included within the limits of the metaphysical, or, as it is also and more correctly called, the *general* paper—a course which embraces Logic, Political Economy, Historical and Transcendental Metaphysics, and Ethics. Unsuccessful candidates, and others who wanted to laugh at the papers, used to call them *examinations on Whewell's books;* which, had it been strictly true, was saying a good deal for them, since the Professor of Casuistry has written no small quantity about various subjects.

The classical sympathies and mental symmetry of these men could be fully perceived only by a student like themselves, but any person not grossly illiterate must have been struck by their acquaintance with the literature of their own tongue—not the ephemeral and superficial part of it, but the classics of the language. For their relaxation, instead of cheap novels, political diatribes, or newspaper scandals, they read the old Dramatists, and the standard Essayists of bye-gone days. They formed Shakspeare clubs, to read and study *the* Dramatist—not exactly like those "Shakspearian Readings," in which the actor or actress is the chief attraction. The criticism displayed in their conversation was much superior to the majority of what is lauded when read in print; and when they talked, it was not declamation, or pamphleteering, or sophistical exhibition, aiming only to gain the victory and produce an effect on the listeners, but a candid communication of knowledge and opinion, and a search after truth. The regular and hearty exercise they took every day, maintaining their bodies in vigorous health, kept their minds elastic, and at the same time drove out all moroseness and peevishness, rendering them eminently genial. And, while generally in moderate circumstances, and living on (for England) a very moderate income, they had a taste for some of the enjoyments of art, which they gratified in their temperate, honest way. Without the means of luxury, they preserved a gentlemanly æstheticism. Their dress was simple, not to say economical, but its cleanliness and freedom from pretension dispelled any disposition to criticise it. They could not afford valuable paintings, but their rooms were hung with choice engravings, the accumulations of their undergraduate years, a few pounds' worth at a time. They lived habitually on plain and substantial provender; but on festive days, when an old friend turned up unexpectedly, or an examination resulted triumphantly, or on any other occasion that provoked revelry, they enjoyed a *recherché* dinner, and a bottle or two of good wine as much as the most scientific epicure. They had not the command of an opera, or indeed any place of public amusement, and for a great part of the year were confined to the somewhat monotonous country about Cambridge, but for a month or six weeks in the "Long" they rambled off to see the sights of Paris, or the galleries of Belgium, or the natural beauties of the Rhine and Switzerland, and came back far more delighted with their brief expedition than can be conceived by those who make it their business to worry from place to place in pursuit of diversion and excitement.

The great change and improvement effected by a few years of collegiate life was to me one of the first problems connected with the English Universities. Home experience had not led me to expect such a start between the ages of twenty-two and twenty-five. My own pursuit of classical study had been founded more on predilection for it than on a very strong conviction of its general utility; but now I began to consider whether there might not be in it more of this practical quality than I had ever yet given it credit for.

As to the Fellows, some of the younger men displayed much the same characteristics with the Bachelors; others of the older stock seemed to have grown somewhat rusty in their retirement; which led me to suspect, what indeed is a common opinion among the Fellows themselves, that the University is an excellent place for the regular seven years, or perhaps a few more, but after that time it is better for a man to leave it, unless he is strictly devoted to some purely scientific pursuit. And in this lies the value of the Trinity Fellowships, that being tenable (in the case of laymen) for seven years more (*not* involving residence) they afford a young man support until he can get fairly started in his profession, while the three years he has spent in reading for the Fellowship, themselves directly contribute to his getting the start by the regular and powerful mental training they put him through. But unfortunately many not otherwise so inclined are tempted into orders to keep their Fellowships. . . .

Inferiority of our Colleges and Universities in Scholarship

In comparing University education—that is to say, the highest and most liberal style of education—in England and in our own country, it is but natural, since Classical studies professedly lie at the foundation of it in both, that we should begin by contrasting the pupils' proficiency in such studies. What English scholarship is, the reader may have had some opportunity of judging from the preceding pages. What American is we shall now proceed to examine.

As I am about to say a great deal that is unusual, unpopular, and pretty sure to give offence, it may be as well, by way of preliminary, to anticipate a summary way of disposing of all my remarks, likely to be adopted in certain quarters. It is a stock argument against any man, possessing, or supposed to possess an independent property, and having ever travelled or resided abroad, when he makes any assertion not flattering to the popular vanity—an argument which may be briefly expressed thus: *This man cannot give any valuable information to American citizens, because from his position and associations he does not know what the duties of an American citizen are.* It is imputing voluntary or involuntary *incivism* to every well-educated and travelled gentleman, and thence deducing the conclusion that nothing which he may say on any question of practical importance is entitled to consideration.

People who reason thus, overlook one very important element of the question. The probability of a man's giving important information or valuable advice on any point, depends not merely on his opportunities to know and understand the truth concerning it, but *also* on his being free to tell so much truth as he does know. If he is under any strong bias of personal interest; if his pecuniary resources or his prospects of political advancement are likely to suffer by his telling unreservedly what he believes to be the truth, then his witness will be worth less than that of a man with less knowledge but more independence. An editor is certainly not in the position most favorable to the promulgation of unpopular truth, neither is a politician. The circulation of his paper or his availability as a candidate are considerations that will continually interfere with the convictions of his reason. No one who is directly dependent on the public for support dares to tell it the truth at all times. He who is indirectly dependent, like the man of business or the professional man without private means, is more at liberty, but not completely so. And when a man of either class has, by the exercise of his talents and industry, gained fortune and reputation, so that he may say what he thinks without danger and with a chance of effecting something, the probabilities are that, if a public man, he has so long habituated himself to the promulgation of the popular rather than the true, that his mind will continue to work in the same track; and that if a private citizen, he will be principally inclined to indemnify himself by the material comforts which wealth affords for the trouble he took to attain it, and will prefer a quiet life to the trouble of communicating his conviction to others.

In short, a man who has nothing to expect or fear from the public, who never intends to depend on their suffrages for anything, who does not practise politics or literature for a livelihood, who is not in danger of injuring his business by uttering unpopular opinions, who is not struggling for a place in fashionable society, and therefore not obliged to toady any individual or any set—such a man is almost the only one who can afford to speak the truth boldly, and is more likely than any other man to tell the truth, *supposing that he knows it.*

But why should he not know it? Is it on account of his wealth? Does that disqualify him from understanding republican institutions and what is good for republicans? I fancy there are too many men making or expecting to make fortunes for such a doctrine to be universally or very generally admitted. Moreover, if it be true, the Republic is not only certainly in danger, but must have contained the seeds of dissolution from its commencement, since the number of rich men among us has constantly increased and is increasing, in spite of laws, customs, and sentiments most favorable to the distribution of wealth. Is it because he has travelled and lived abroad? Let us take the extremest case. Suppose an American boy to have been left at a foreign school, to reside there during seven of the most important years in his life, to have partially forgotten his native language, so that he speaks a foreign tongue habitually and from preference, and has acquired the habits of his foreign schoolfellows and teachers. It may be urged with some plausibility that his education has not helped him to become the best kind of American citizen. But look a little further. A foreigner comes hither —one from the same country where this boy was educated; all these disqualifications exist in him to a much greater degree, yet after a few years' residence he is admitted to all the privileges of a citizen, and may hold any office except that of President. How thrice ridiculous to maintain that a portion of the American's previous life spent abroad incapacitates him more than the *whole* of *his* does the foreigner. It is worth noticing, too, that the persons most zealous in suggesting the *incivism* of wealthy and well-educated men among their own countrymen, are usually those most patronizing of emigrant foreigners, are Democrats first and Americans afterwards, and value their country chiefly as a refuge for the radicalism of the world. Suppose an American, from living or travelling abroad, has even acquired some foreign habits, that he drinks coffee when most of his countrymen take tea, or *vice versa*, or wears a hat of a slightly different shape from the ordinary, is he therefore unable to sympathize with his fellow-citizens, or to understand what is for their advantage? Have our adopted fellow-citizens no foreign habits? Do not some of them get drunk and riot, and abuse Englishmen and Protestants, and lie and cheat at elections here, exactly as they did at home? If we reject all reference to our naturalization laws, on the ground that they are a *fait accompli* and do not prove any principle, then we have the broad question—Does personal knowledge of another country disqualify a man for giving an opinion on the affairs of his own? Now I should be far from maintaining the opposite extreme to the opinion I have been combating, by admitting that foreign travel is necessarily a benefit to an American. There is a common-place of a certain class of men—two or three certain classes indeed—I heard it so often from countrymen whom I met abroad, and during the period immediately succeeding my return home, that I could calculate with almost mathematical certainty when it was coming. It usually runs in these words: *It is a good thing for a young man to spend some time abroad, and see something of foreign countries*, BECAUSE *he usually returns with a better appreciation of his own.* Now this I take to be quite as erroneous as the opposite conclusion. If the young man have some taste with not much principle, if he be only on the lookout for the pleasures of sense and wordly amusements, he will by no means return to his country better satisifed with it; on the contrary, he will have eaten of the lotus in Paris or some other continental city, and be always looking back to it with regret. But an earnest man (to borrow a phrase from my friends the Apostles) will be much more likely both to understand the deficiencies of his countrymen from living among people who have what they have not, and to appreciate their strong points from living among people who do not possess what they have.

Lastly, is a man less able to understand the duties of an American citizen, or to give his fellow-citizens any advice, because he has received an elaborate liberal education? Is he, for instance, less acquainted with political philosophy because he has studied the ancient writers of it as well as the modern, instead of the latter only, and those at second or third hand through the columns of a newspaper or a Congressional speech. Is he less able to judge of the tendencies of Popery in this country, because he has mastered its history and traced its workings in other countries, or the follies of Socialism because he has read the Fifth Book of Plato's Republic and Aristotle's answer to it? If so, the old Tory slander becomes a truth. Republicanism is *not* favorable to education except in a low and limited form.

I protest therefore against being read out of court by any of those persons who have given themselves a patent for looking specially after the public interest; and if any one of them, editor, lecturer, hack politician, or other sort of demagogue, who has just intelligence enough to be deceived by an American edition of the Cock Lane ghost, and just learning enough to tell his hearers that Plato proposed in his Republic the abolition of all family ties (which is just as correct as it would be to say that the Romish Church imposes celibacy on all its votaries) if any such man is prepared to attack me in the outset with the assertion that I do not know how American citizens are educated or how they ought to be, I tell him beforehand, in the plain language which it would do people of his stamp good if they heard oftener, that it is because I know too well both the evils existing and the probable results of a better system, because my advice tends to spoil his trade, that he would like to keep me from being heard. And now to the subject of this chapter.

Were I to be questioned by an educated foreigner, an Englishman or Frenchman, German, Hollander, or Dane, upon the standard of scholarship in our Colleges and Universities, I should be obliged to answer, not having the fear of King Public before my eyes, that it was exceedingly low, and that not merely according to *his* idea, but according to the idea of a boy fitted at a good school in New York. When I went up to Yale College in 1835, the very first thing that struck me was the classical deficiency of the greater part of the students and some of the instructors. A great many of the Freshmen had literally never heard of such a thing as prosody; they did not know that there were any rules for quantity: it may be imagined what work they made with reading poetry. Nor could their teachers, in many instances, do much to help them; one of our *classical* tutors did not know the quantity of the middle syllable in *profugus*, almost the first word in the Aeneid. The etymological part of Greek grammar (to say nothing of the syntax) was very imperfectly understood by the majority, and of those who made pretensions to scholarship there were not ten in a class who could write three consecutive sentences of decent Latin prose. The system of choosing the tutors to whose care the two lower classes were entirely committed, was enough to destroy any chance of rectifying the errors of bad and insufficient preparation. They were elected from the graduates who had taken a certain stand on the average of all their College course—say the first fifteen. Now a student might get among these fifteen—the "oration men"—by excelling in classics alone with very little ability in or taste for mathematics, or *vice versa*; but he was obliged to take such tutorial vacancy as came to him in his order of seniority; so the mathematical man might be set to hear classics or the classics to teach mathematics. The consequence of which was that not only the bad men did not improve, but the good ones were generally pretty well spoilt by the time they came to the Greek professor's hands in the third year. Not only was the course for all the students limited to the same books, and very small in quantity, so as to keep it at the level of the worst prepared (among whom were generally a large number of "beneficiaries" or charity students), but this small quantity was badly learned and taught; a student with classical taste had no encouragement for getting up his classics properly, for he had no chance of showing his scholarship or doing himself justice—his tutor could not appreciate him; consequently if ambitious, he was easily tempted to seek distinction in other things, the various associations for the cultivation of "speaking" and "writing" in which the College abounded. . . .

It may seem very unpatriotic to say all this, but when people are not generally awake to their own deficiencies their eyes ought to be opened, and their real friend is he who tries to do this, not he who, by claiming for the country what it does not possess, makes it and himself ridiculous in the eyes of foreigners, and tends to make them sceptical in regard to its real merits. Talk to a stranger of our chivalry towards women, our sympathy between classes, our benevolence for public objects, the diffusion of rudimentary education among the masses, etc., and he may be well disposed to believe you; but if you tell him at the same time that "So-and-So is a great scholar," when his works prove him to be a very inferior one, or that "Classics are on the whole as well taught at Yale and Harvard as at Oxford and Cambridge" (I have heard this roundly asserted, by a public man too), and your foreigner says to himself, "Here is my informant grossly astray on a subject of which I can judge at once; may he not be equally mistaken in some of the other excellences which he attributes to his countrymen?" The English have injured their character by a similar mistake of claiming too much. Insisting on a superiority in the arts of life—in dress,

cookery, and furniture, which they do not possess, and their claim to which is so easily disproved, they have caused foreigners to distrust their pretensions to higher excellences which are less obvious on the surface, and require longer and deeper experience and examination to appreciate.

Supposed Counterbalancing Advantages of American Colleges

Admitting that our colleges do not teach Latin and Greek so well as the European ones, the natural and ordinary defence is, that they teach other things, and those on the whole of more value, better. Let us examine the particulars of this defence. What are the other things taught?—are they better taught?—and are they more beneficial as means of liberal education?

And first, in relation to Mathematics. There used to be, and probably is still, a vague general impression at Yale, to the effect that the Mathematical course there is a very difficult and thorough one—that, in fact, Mathematics constitute one of the crack points of the institution. This fancy certainly derived some support from comparison with the Classical course, *as compared with which* the Mathematical was undoubtedly a good one. But that did not prevent it from being very bad, as tried either by an ideal standard, or by those existing in other countries. How *far* it reached is sufficiently shown by the fact that the Differential Calculus, the vestibule as it were to all high Mathematics, was among the *optional* studies at the end of the third year. The Valedictorian at the completion of the course, or the man who gained the first mathematical prize in the second year, need never have studied it. Nevertheless, a course of Mathematics stopping short of the Differential may be a very good one so far as it goes. But this was not the case with the course at Yale College. In many of its stages it was liable to the same reproach as the classical, of being a study of *books* rather than *subjects*. The learning and recitation of portions from day to day (for the annual examinations were little more than a form, and had no effect on the college honors) encouraged a habit of cramming from one day to another. A great deal of the work in the second or third year consisted of long calculations of examples worked with logarithms, which consumed a great deal of time without giving any insight into principles, and were equally distasteful to the good and the bad mathematicians. In fact, while the course was, from its daily recurrence through-out three years, and the amount of figuring it involved, more disagreeable to classics than a more difficult and rigorous investigation of principles requiring less dead mechanical work would have been, the best mathe-maticians of the class always grumbled at it quite as much as the best linguists did at the classical course. They complained, that with the exception of two prizes for problems dur-ing the Freshman and Sophomore years, and an occasional "original demonstration" in the recitation-room, they had no chance of show-ing their superior ability and acquirements, that much of their time was lost in long arithmetical and logarithmical computations, that classical men were continually tempted to "skin" (copy) the solutions of these examples, and thus put themselves unjustly on a level with them; and much more of the same sort. I am strongly inclined to think that a course of mathematics, covering as much real ground as the present one of three years, might be put into two without infringing more than at present on the special pursuits of the more classically disposed students, and with posi-tive benefit to the whole body. As it is, any student who enters upon his Senior year at Yale has *nominally* gone over a greater amount of mathematics than one of πολλοί[the people] at Cambridge—twice as much at least; but it does not follow that he really knows more or has enjoyed more of the peculiar benefits of mathematical training. I suspect that a man in the first class of the "Poll" has usually read mathematics to more profit than many of the "appointees," even of the "oration men" at Yale.

Secondly, as regards the sciences in gen-eral. The fact that during the last year various courses of lectures are delivered on the natu-ral and moral sciences, attendance on these courses not being optional as at an English University, but compulsory on all the students, will doubtless be considered by many persons a great point in favor of our Colleges. For my own part I look upon it as one of their greatest mistakes. The idea of being able to impart any adequate or permanent informa-tion to a large body of students in twenty-five lectures a-piece on a dozen different sciences, almost any *one* of which is work for a quarter of a man's lifetime, seems to me altogether visionary and chimerical. There are perhaps eight or ten of the hundred stu-dents present at each course who take an in-terest in the particular science, and derive some appreciable benefits from the lectures. It requires very little practical acquaintance

with the working of the system to ascertain that most of the auditors consider the lecture merely as part of a routine which they are obliged to go through.

Let it be admitted, however, that to have attended a certain number of lectures in scientific subjects is one of the desirable ac-complishments of a liberal education—nay, more, that it may sometimes evoke talent in the direction of some one science, which but for this accidental opportunity might never have been developed. Let us have the lectures then, by all means; but to make such lectures —for which no preparation is required and at which no notes are taken, which involve no reading before or after, and merely break in upon the student's day for two or three isolated hours—to make them a substitute for hard work and mental training, has surely a perilous tendency to effeminate the student's mind and give him desultory habits of thought. The youth who, under such a system of classi-cal and mathematical training as has been described, is ludicrously enough supposed to have acquired a sufficient knowledge of classics and mathematics, arrives at the end of his third year. Then the faculty virtually tell him, "You are a finished scholar and mathematician—all you have to do for the next year is to pack in all the sciences by means of lectures on each one three times a week during a term or two. All we ask of you is to attend a lecture of an hour's length three times a-day, and in the intervals you may read reviews and work them up into speeches and essays for your debating society." What should be an afternoon or evening amusement is made the work of the day.

I think a careful inquirer will find that the great *savans* of Europe have not been trained on such principles. Most of them have begun by being good mathematicians, and in many cases good scholars also; and at a maturer period of life they have brought well-disciplined minds to the particular study of their special pursuits.

Thirdly, there is a prevailing opinion among our students (how far it is accepted in other quarters of the community I will not pretend to say) that, in consequence of being left so much to themselves during the last year of their course, and of not overvaluing the College course at any time, they have much leisure for the perusal of literature and general improvement of their minds and ac-quisition of miscellaneous knowledge, in which respect they have the advantage over the English student.

Now as respects literature this is altogether a mistake. There certainly is a *kind* of literature in which our students are more at home than the English. They read more newspapers; they read more magazines; they read more political pamphlets; they read a great many more novels; they are well up in all that floating small literature of the day which an editor or periodical critic has to wade through as part of his business, and which any other man, especially any *young* man who wishes really to improve his mind, is much better without. But of the standard and classic literature of the language they do not read more or know more. They are not better acquainted with Shakspeare and Milton, with Wordsworth and Tennyson, with Bacon and Locke, with Gibbon and Robertson. They are not *by any means* so well acquainted with the old English Dramatists, the old English Divines, the essayists and political writers prior to Queen Anne, or the best ethical and logical writers of the present day. They take much of their knowledge at second hand from English reviews—reviews which the Cambridge man reads indeed with pleasure, but which from his previous acquaintance with the text and sources of them, he regards as subjects of his own criticism rather than authorities or oracles. They read rapidly, indiscriminately, and uncritically.

As to any superiority in miscellaneous information which the American student may have over the English one, much of this exterior knowledge is not owing to his collegiate training or want of training at all, but to his home and vacation life, the greater variety of people he encounters in his ordinary intercourse with the world. So much of it as is attainable from books, the English student picks up later in life, when he is better able to make use of it.

Fourthly, in all our Colleges English Composition and Public Speaking are encouraged in every possible way, both by the authorities and by associations of the students themselves, from the very beginning to the very end of the course. At an English University there is very little encouragement for either English Composition or Public Speaking. But to speak and write well, it is said, are the great aims and requisites of the minister, the lawyer, and the political man of any sort. They are the principal means of obtaining fame and power in a free country, and therefore are the highest intellectual ends of man; and that is the best education which best prepares the student for them.

Here we are arrived at the strong point of our Colleges and Universities. For it is the immediate object of an American College practically (whatever it may be with some of its Faculty theoretically) to make the students fluent speakers and ready writers, just as it is the immediate object of an English University to turn out good scholars and mathematicians. And the object is certainly accomplished: our Collegians learn to think on their legs and handle a pen with dexterity at a remarkably early age. The end proposed also, is a higher object to an ambitious young man. To aim at being a great author or orator, seems nobler and grander than to solve problems or read Aristotle in the original. As this is a very important matter, let us examine it in detail, beginning with a view of the effect which the admitted end of our collegiate education has upon our collegiate system as its workings are developed in one of the New England Universities.

Almost from the beginning of their course, certainly from the third term of their Freshman year, all students ambitious of distinction are, by common consent, divided into two classes, called in their own phraseology *scholars* and *writers*. The former class includes, by a singular extension of the term, Mathematicians as well as Classics—all, in short, who are prominent candidates for College honors; the latter, those who undertake to distinguish themselves in English Composition, either in the weekly readings of it before tutors and professors, the numerous debating societies among the students (into all of which orations and dissertations enter largely as part of the exercises), or the columns of the College Magazine. Sometimes a youth attempts to distinguish himself in both departments, and the attempt when made is frequently successful; but, as a general rule, the two classes of aspirants for fame are distinct. Closely connected with the "writers" are the speakers. Excellence as a debater, even when unaccompanied with a reputation for writing well, is much prized, and the happy possesor of both faculties is one of the College geniuses. The writers, including the speakers as subordinate to and in many cases coincident with them, are—and it is to this I wish to call particular attention —infinitely more honored and esteemed and envied and looked up to by the great bulk of the students than the "scholars" or College appointees. *The distinctions conferred by the students on one another are more prized than the distinctions conferred by the College authorities on the students.* So much so is this the case, that the prizes given by the Faculty for English Composition are not accepted among the students as tests of the best writers.

This state of things is induced by several different causes. The Faculty promote it indirectly by the inferiority of their Classical and Mathematical instruction, and by leaving the students so much to themselves during their last year. They promote it directly in more than one way: by giving "compositions" and "disputes" and "declamations" so large a place in the College exercises of the second and third years, by making the right to deliver a speech (at Junior Exhibition or Commencement) the highest reward for proficiency in College studies.

But whatever the causes, an outsider—one who had not the previous bias of being brought up under the system—looking at it from an external point of view, would be apt to say, "Here is a most anomalous and abnormal condition of things for an academical institution. The students have set up their judgment against that of their instructors. They declare that the means of education proposed for them by their teachers are the more ignoble, and those proposed for them by themselves the more worthy. They make themselves judges beforehand of that which it is the business of their tutors to qualify them for judging of. And their instructors receive these claims with assent—reluctant assent perhaps—but certainly not opposition, not even a negative one. What is this but self-condemnation on their part?"

It is not impossible, however, that the students, inadequately provided for by their teachers, may have provided for themselves a good means of education. Let us, therefore, examine the effect of practice in English Composition and Public Speaking, from an early age (say fifteen) as prominent elements of a liberal education.

First of all, it may reasonably be doubted whether the cultivation of two special talents which border closely on the domain of genius, and high excellence in which very few men can reasonably hope to attain, ought to be made the corner-stone of a general education. The very fact that it is a greater thing to be an orator than a scholar, is a positive reason for giving classics a preference over oratory in a *University* course. Not only does your end answer the proposed conditions better, but you have more likelihood of arriving at it. You cannot make every third man in a class a great orator or author, though you may give him a fluency and confidence in talking platitudes or a knack of stringing together common-places on paper; you can make every third man of a class a respectable scholar. Were it possible to send forth every College graduate throughout the country an orator, it would not be desirable. It would be an unfortunate example of mental alchemy.

"If all were gold then gold were no more wealth." Could we turn out every graduate a moderately good classic, we should give a taste and tone to the intellect of the country that would have a most favorable influence on oratory and authorship.

Let us look a little further. The *immediate* effects of the system we admit to be dazzling. The American student in his Senior year (when he may have attained the age of nineteen or thereabouts) has a readiness of tongue and pen, a confidence on his legs and a general dexterity of argument, unparalleled by his contemporaries in any part of the world. He will make speeches and write essays that are astonishing for one of his years when compared with the productions of older men about him. He seems to have shot up into full mental stature before he has reached the limit of his bodily growth. In all mixed society he will throw an English youth of the same age utterly into the shade. But let us examine how far this precocious splendor has any solid aliment or permanent source.

The Englishman's tardiness of development is in a great measure intentional. He is kept back to take a good start. He leaves school at the period of life when the American leaves College. Up to that time his studies have not been such as he can make an immediate display before the world with, but have rather been directed to strengthening and polishing his mind for future use. At the University his aim is to excel in the studies prescribed by the authorities of the place, not in something different from and partly antagonistic to these. However well-prepared, he finds numbers in advance of him, he can never complain that he does not know what to learn or can find no one to teach him. Whatever his school reputation, his vanity is sure to be speedily checked, and first of all by his private tutor, who "slangs" him for a mistake here or an inelegancy there. Then he makes mistakes in examination also, and "loses marks." If a thriving public-school classic and ready to carry all before him in that line, he is still obliged to read mathematics, to feel his inferiority at first and perhaps at last to occupy a subordinate place in them. If he has cleverness there is no lack of room to display it, but it is necessary that he should work hard also; there are great rewards of reputation as well as substantial emolument for the combination of intellect and industry, but none for disconnected and single exhibitions of brilliancy. The tendency of every influence about him is to make him cautious, self-critical and self-distrustful, careful and elaborate in his acquisitions, and consequently when he learns anything he takes hold of it as with a vice; when he says he knows it, you may be sure he does. And when he becomes a high Wrangler or First Class man, he does not infer that he is therefore bound to be a great statesman or orator at once, but only that he has good talents, a fair power and regular habits of work, by which, *if he continues to work*, he is likely, in course of time, to succeed in his profession. Or if he fails to take the stand he hoped, he can never charge his examiners with unfairness.

Our student, on the contrary, is from the first surrounded with influences calculated to excite and flatter his vanity. If he comes to College from a good school in New York or Boston, the chances are that he is set under a tutor who knows less of the rudiments of scholarship than himself. Hence the first lesson he learns is to despise his teachers. He hears it said all about him that the College appointees are for the most part poor dull fellows who never do anything to distinguish themselves in after life, that an Appointment is only worth taking as a mere extra if it can be got without taking much trouble for it, and that *writing* and *speaking* are the proper objects of his ambition. And the opinion respecting the appointees is partly true; a successful mediocrity has no great charm for a boy who is clever, and well enough prepared for something better. Thus he is led to depreciate the honors given by the authorities, and seek for distinction in another quarter. He aspires after those rewards which are in the gift of his fellow-students, and which he himself has a share in bestowing on others. He becomes habituated to making speeches and reading compositions before audiences of from thirty to a hundred, whose capacity to be critical is not equal to their disposition, and whose disposition is modified by their mutual interest; now and then he makes an unusually showy effort, and is applauded for it. His friends and acquaintances have not the same ability to find faults in his performance that a tutor has to correct the exercise of a pupil, nor does their position enable them to speak so freely without the risk of giving offence or incurring the suspicion of jealousy. If he succeeds in winning these popular honors, they are almost the exact counterpart of

similar ones in maturer life. He writes smart articles in the College magazine and is made editor of it; he gets a reputation for speaking in his debating society and is elected president, just as he might get sent to the state legislature when a man, for speaking well at public meetings. If he fails, his failure may be owing not to want of merit, but to want of popularity, or to intrigue and jealousy, of which there is always a great deal at work. Thus he brings the great world into the academic shades, and aims at being a public man while he should as yet be but a hard-working student.

And here his unguided and indiscriminate reading involves him in a double error. Not only is the object of his aim prematurely high, but the ideal of that object becomes continually lowered for him. He does not appreciate what he seeks to be. Though professedly working to form a style, he does not properly study the best models or confine himself to them. He swallows a great deal of second and third-rate matter. He acquires a childish fondness for metaphors more or less mixed, and generally for all sorts of figures, as if they were the sole test and standard of excellence in composition. In short he aims at *fine* writing, and sits down not to express his ideas on a subject, but to *write a piece*. So, in oratory, he knows little, except at second-hand, of Demosthenes and Cicero; rather more but not too much about Burke. He does not confine himself to the best models of his own country. He possesses well-thumbed copies of Webster's speeches and Everett's Orations, but he will turn from these at any time to the last imperfectly-reported stump speech—especially if he can utilize anything from it at the debating society. A secret conviction is generated in his mind that *he* could do nearly as well in their place as many of the men whose performances he reads—which may not be so very far from the truth —and here again his vanity is gratified. Moreover as his experience leads him to suspect that people are much in the habit of talking and writing about things of which they have but small knowledge, he comes to the conclusion that very small knowledge of a subject is necessary to qualify a man for talking and writing about it—he will consider himself prepared to discuss any point in metaphysics, for instance, after going through a course of *Stewart's Outlines*. The real acquisitions of a Senior Class in a New England College bear a lamentably small ratio to their conceit of knowledge.

One thing they certainly have mastered—

the art of electioneering. They have learned a great deal of human nature, as regards the way in which men can be "got round" and votes influenced. One of our large Colleges is an excellent school for a professed politician; whether this fact is particularly honorable to them, or whether that occupation is a particularly honorable and desirable one for all and many students, may admit of a doubt.

This brings us to another evil springing directly from the early and constant practice of writing and speaking. It encourages a *sophistic habit,* most dangerous for a very young man to acquire, since it puts him in an unfortunate frame of mind for the reception of knowledge and truth. I use the word *sophistic* not without direct reference to its origin, and to the intellectual training of the young Athenians by their itinerant professors—a training not far from having its counterpart among ourselves. What was this system as we deduce it from contemporary writers, especially Plato, who, indeed, often illustrates it himself unintentionally in his own course of argument? The Sophist was a professor of mental and moral philosophy; he taught his pupils to argue on all points of metaphysics and of ethics, including politics —to argue readily, dexterously, captiously, the discussion often declining into the merest hair-splitting and verbal quibbling. Victory, not truth—to effect a presumption rather than to secure the acquisition of knowledge, was the end of debate. The benefit proposed, sometimes without an attempt at disguise, to the pupil was, that he should be able to humbug the people and get on in the world (that is the plain Saxon of it), which he was to accomplish by being always ready to talk about anything, and never at a loss for a plausible argument.

Our young men leave college imbued with debating society formulæ. Their very slang is redolent of the society—its phrases are the phrases of their every-day life. If three or four of them are in a room together, one cannot say to another, "Smith, shut the door, please," without putting it into some such form as "I move Mr. Smith shut the door," or "I move Mr. Smith be a committee of one to shut that door." They are always ready for an argument, and will *tackle* a man of any age if there is a chance of a discussion. Recondite disquisitions are not to their purpose; but any popular question, such as a man can talk of from review and newspaper reading, they delight to raise a controversy about. They evince a great dexterity in taking exceptions, and are as quick to find instances against the generalizations of

others as to draw imperfect generalizations themselves.

Many years ago the father of a young Englishman who had distinguished himself at the University, and given other indications of uncommon talent, having destined his son for public life, wrote to a friend, an eminent Scotch advocate and politician, for advice how the young man should be trained to make him a successful orator. The answer, which was long preserved in the family, contained these suggestions among others,—"He must seek the conversation of older men, and talk at them without being afraid of them; he must talk a great deal merely for the sake of talking; he must talk too much in company."

The person who related this to me was most struck with the apparent paradox of the last clause—the ludicrous idea of the future orator *never talking enough* until he had *talked too much.* I was impressed by a different thought —the exactness with which our collegians anticipate this advice for themselves and carry it out. *They talk at older men without being afraid of them; they talk a great deal for mere practice in talking; they talk too much in company.*

Now the young man to whom this advice was given had the foundation of a thorough education whereon to build his rhetorical superstructure, varied knowledge to adorn, and a superior intellect to illuminate it. He started on a large capital in every point of view. If therefore he acquired a sometimes inconvenient habit of talking too much in company, there was still a probability that he would say much worth hearing; if his conversational sparrings with older men involved some violation of modesty, they were at any rate not likely to be disfigured by egregious errors. But when a youth acquires this talking facility and propensity without a proper training and knowledge to support it—when most of his authorities are at third or fourth-hand, hearsay, or the last newspaper article, or the confused recollection of what was at first imperfectly read, it follows inevitably that he must make many mistakes which his verbal dexterity will be continually brought into requisition to protect. And from this combination of inaccuracy of detail with facility of expression results one of our great national faults, *a tendency to defend rather than prevent mistakes; plausibility in explaining away or glossing over an error rather than caution in guarding against the probability of its occurrence.*

This feeling which, like the Spartan's conception of honesty, or the Parisian's of conjugal fidelity, places the evil of error, not in the original commission, but in the subsequent conviction of it, stands directly in the way of individual and national improvement. Its favorite mode of argument is the *ignoratio elenchi*, the ignoring of the main point in dispute, and joining issue on some irrelevant accident; of it and its favorite form of this mode is the *tu quoque*, a digression upon some personal demerit of the opponent. Thus both literature and politics are debased, and honest criticism or difference of opinion converted into matter of individual quarrel.

After all, the strongest objection to this literary precocity is that it defeats its own object. The ambitious student begins at the wrong end. He acquires manner before matter, and has a style in advance of his thoughts. His untimely blossoms do not fructify. His graces and ornaments of trope and metaphor, like the flowers which a child sticks into the ground to make a garden, grow faded and lose vitality for want of root and nutriment. He repeats his ideas, or those of others. He wrote fluently at eighteen, at twenty-six he writes a trifle perhaps more fluently but in no respect better. Some years ago, I heard an Italian say that his country produced many young artists of great promise, but none of them ever came to maturity. I thought at the time it was pretty much the same with our College geniuses. The class below me at Yale, out of a hundred members, had *thirty poets* —that is to say, men who had written *and published* verses. This is an extreme instance; but the number of "great writers" in my time (eleven years ago) at that College was very large. The number who have since attained any substantial literary distinction I could count on one hand and have some figures to spare.

The best education has its limits, and very marked ones. No physical training can develop an ordinary man into a giant or a Hercules. No intellectual training can *make* a genius. The error of our system is that it makes a great many ordinary men suppose themselves to be geniuses, while at the same time it does not develope their ordinary abilities in the best way.

I have often been surprised (until from the frequency of the phenomenon it ceased to surprise me) at the altered impressions made on me by these College geniuses in after life. I do not refer to their position or want of position in the world, so much as to the effect which their conversation had upon me. They seemed to have *come back to me*, if I may be allowed to use a sporting phrase.

Their remarks seemed trivial and commonplace, their ideas limited, till I was tempted to look down upon those whom I used to look up to. And more than one such man has confessed to me his regret at not having made better use of his College opportunities, and devoted himself more attentively to the legitimate studies of the place; and has owned his reluctant conviction that the time which he anticipated was borrowed at usurious interest, and the apparent gain had turned out a real loss.

The truth of what I have asserted, namely that our literary precocity overreaches itself, may be brought home very briefly to every unprejudiced and capable man. We accustom our youth to the practice of Composition much sooner than the English do theirs. *Do we on the whole write as well as the English?* Will any candid and well informed man say, from his heart, that the average of our books published every year is equal in quality to the average of theirs, or that the average quality of our newspaper and periodical literature is anywhere near theirs? I think every man *who can afford to have a conscience* will admit that there is a difference in their favor, and a greater difference than can be accounted for by the absence of an International Copyright Law. Yet, in order to justify our practice, we should expect as a result a *very decided superiority* to the English—*unless* we suppose an original inferiority of material. But the natural quickness and cleverness of the American mind are universally admitted. Our most bigoted enemies have never charged us with incapacity or stupidity. Our keenness of intelligence is all but proverbial among the nations. The inference seems unavoidable that there is something better in the English mode of training.

But our public speaking! *There* we have them! *There* we are unapproachable! Certainly this is our peculiar national excellence. Our few real and great orators will sustain a comparison with the few real and great orators of Europe; this much we may safely claim for them, and this is as much as will be conceded by the rest of the world. But it is in the general diffusion of a certain rhetorical facility, in the ability of every educated American to think and talk *on his legs*, that our superiority to Europeans consists. And doubtless it is a very convenient accomplishment for a gentleman to possess, one which an American is often proud of abroad, or before foreigners at home. But (leaving out of consideration so much of the price we pay for it as has been dilated on in the last few pages) it may be doubted whether the practical bene-fits accompanying its exercise are very great or altogether unmixed; whether our national speech-making talent does not, in some situations, cause an immense waste of time and ruinous delay of business, while in others it mocks both speakers and hearers with a delusive show of improvement. As to the combinations of writing and oratory, made to serve indifferently for either—the λόγοι ἐπιδεικτικοί [wise utterances], so much in vogue among us under the different names of "Addresses," "Discourses," "Orations" and "Lectures"—they are usually undertaken because the author received a flattering in-vitation and felt bound to put together an hour's worth of something—or because it was an easy and pleasant way of making pocket money—or because it was a cheap and convenient way of advertising something that he meant to bring out in book shape afterwards, and so make money of twice—or for any reason rather than an earnest desire and intent to teach the au-dience anything or make them think; an attend-ance at such Addresses, etc., is as much mental dissipation as the Frenchman's theatre or the German's concert.

Horace Mann   1843

A Preliminary and Critical Account of European Education

Horace Mann (1796–1859) graduated from Brown University in 1819, practiced law in Ded-ham, Massachusetts, from 1823 to 1827, and was a member of the Massachusetts state legis-lature for the next decade. In 1837 he became secretary of the Massachusetts Board of Educa-tion, and he is best remembered today for his annual reports to the Board from 1838 to 1849 and for his editing of *The Common School Journal* from 1838 to 1848.

Mann's widely publicized *Seventh Annual Report*, written in 1844 after a five-month trip visiting schools in Great Britain, Prussia, Saxony, Baden, Hesse, Holland, Belgium, and France, gives a critical account of the inadequacies of European education. The extracts below are taken from a preliminary report of his trip printed in *The Common School Journal* im-mediately upon his return. Mann reported that he had "seen many things to deplore, and many to admire." He had "visited countries where there is no national system of education at all, and countries where the minutest details of the schools are regulated by law." While he was critical of various aspects of European education, he did "not hesitate to say that there are many things abroad which we at home should do well to imitate."

For a considerable number of years past, the systems of Public Instruction, prevalent in some of the countries of Europe, have at-tracted much of American attention; and a highly laudable curiosity has been evinced, on the part of intelligent and liberal-minded men, to become acquainted with their nature and workings. Some persons, it is true, in the plenitude of a Chinese self-conceit, have asked, "Why seek among other nations for any improvements of our own? Are not we the freest and greatest and wisest people on the face of the earth? . . .

It is long since the great epic poet of the Romans uttered the wise sentiment, "*Fas est ab hoste doceri*,"—Learn even from your enemies. Sacred writ commands us to learn even from the brute creation: "Go to the ant, thou sluggard,"—the broad spirit of which in-junction is, learn from anybody, learn from anything, get wisdom, whether from friend or foe. "Wisdom is the principal thing, there-fore get wisdom."

As Editor of this Journal, and acting in an official capacity, as a kind of public coöperator or counsellor in whatever pertains to popular education, we have long yearned for this wisdom, and desired it above rubies. We have never exhorted others to acquire knowl-edge upon this great theme, but every word we have uttered has come, as with a violent rebound, upon our own heart, echoing deep and long, "Get knowledge thyself." We have never exposed what seemed to us short-sighted and untoward measures for advancing the cause, but a voice within has cried, "May there not be others to whose illuminated eye your more extended vision is the vision of the mole; may there not be other plans, conceived by genius or wrought out by experiment, compared with

Horace Mann, an editorial, *The Common School Journal,* VI (1844), 2–12.

which yours are toilsome and circuitous? Look, then, to the right hand and to the left. Explore every field that promises remuneration for the search. Ascend every eminence and survey the land. Nay, if you can obtain one new instrument of greater efficiency for the work, or discover one new idea, cross the ocean to make it your own.''

We have obeyed the monitions of this voice. We have visited every one of the countries of Europe, towards which any glimmering of new light, on this subject, has invited. And, on the whole, we have been gratified and instructed by the investigation. The instruction has been two-fold, that of warning as well as that of example. Europe exhibits beacons to terrify, as well as lights to guide. Over some of the fairest fields that God ever planted, out of the garden of Eden, the flood of ignorance has rested for thousands of years, deepening and corrupting from age to age, until now. No tongue of man can describe, nor mortal imagination conceive, the foul and hideous forms of poverty, and wretchedness, and crime, which have been engendered in the waters of this Dead Sea. Some men, indeed, possessed of talent and intelligence, and, in the world's opinion, accounted wise, after witnessing the attempts to reclaim these wastes, and seeing the dreadful shapes of misery and vice that have been revealed, have abandoned the enterprise in disgust. But what else could a reasonable man expect, if the waters of the Asphaltine Lake were to be drained off, but to find Sodom and Gomorrah at the bottom? And the labor of removing the ruins, occasioned by former transgressions, must be completed, before a new creation of health and loveliness can be begun. Shall we, then, suffer the same judgments to fall upon our own land; or, by foresight and timely exertion, shall we avert them? Have we not enough of righteous men, in all our cities, to save them?. . .

Nothing can be more clear than that the condition of education among the different nations of Europe, and among the great divisions of their religious sects, is the index and exponent of their condition, in all other respects. Learn, as to any nation, or denomination, what has been done to develop intelligence and improve the morality of its masses, and you already know, as a general fact, the relative amount of their happiness, and of their advancement in all the real constituents of a people's welfare. The thermometer does not indicate more truly the temperature of the atmosphere, nor the barometer its weight. There is no other criterion so general, so infallible. The indicia of a nation's welfare are not necessarily to be found in its locality or in its natural resources, in its wealth or in its power, in the number of victories which its heroes have won, or in the number of epics which its bards have written. A nation may be potent, like Russia, and still be a nation of miserable bond-men and bond-women. A nation may be magnificent in its exterior, like Great Britain, and still be tortured in all its vitals by the pangs of want and deadly wounds. Nor are the number of great men whose names adorn the annals of a people a test of the enviableness of their condition. Frederick the Great could fill his palaces with men of genius, while his subjects were perishing by famine and sword. If eligibleness of condition were enough, what spot on the two continents is better situated than Italy and other parts of the shores of the Mediterranean? and yet, on all these shores, there is not a government nor a city where a wise man or a father would wish to live himself, or to leave his children. But in some of the almost inaccessible mountains of Switzerland, in the marshes of Holland below the level of the sea, there are, or have been, communities, who, in the possession of intelligence, in the enjoyment of competency, and in the practice of the virtues, might well regard life as a blessing. And there are now some countries in Europe, which we have been taught to look upon with pity, almost with aversion, which are advancing more rapidly in all the constituents of human welfare, than the most favored nations of any part of the old world have heretofore advanced. All these differences of condition and of promise are referrable to one decisive, all-controlling standard,—the greater or less amount of mind-developing, character-forming education they have enjoyed. This is the criterion, the touch-stone. Decide by other tests, and you err; decide by this, and history will ratify the judgment.

In some other form we may, perhaps, hereafter, offer to the public the results of our inquiries into the condition of public schools, the modes of instruction, and the spirit manifested by that body of men who take upon themselves the formation of human character as it exists in the impressible periods of childhood and youth. But all that we can propose within the limits of an Introductory Article,—and by way of informing our readers that we have not been playing truant during a temporary absence from our post,—is to present a few general sketches, and a few statistical facts concerning the education condition of the leading countries of Europe, and perhaps dimly to shadow forth some of the more obvious consequences of its cultivation or neglect. Is it too much to expect that, from such a general survey, some lessons of practical wisdom may be derived?

So far as the number of children at school indicates the amount of education given, —at best a very fallible criterion, —that number, for several of the countries of Europe, is said, on pretty good authority, to be nearly as follows: In Switzerland, Germany, Holland, Denmark, the number at school may be set down as 1 to 6 or 7 of the inhabitants; in France and Belgium, about 1 to 10 or 12; in Ireland and Scotland, 1 to 11; in Spain, 1 to 346; and in Russia, 1 to 656.

England

Among those European countries which, with any propriety, can be called civilized, England is the only one which has no system for the general education of its people. In proportion to its population it expends more for education than any other country in Europe; but this expenditure is for classes, and not for the whole. The consequence, of course, is, an appalling degree of inequality in the condition of its subjects. The highest educational refinement exists side by side with the most brutish ignorance. The most elegant literary culture shines out among communities who cannot speak their native English tongue in a manner to be understood by Englishmen. Schools, colleges and universities, where the profoundest acquaintance with classical literature and with all its libraries of annotation and commentary is obtained, contrast with hovels within which a book was never seen, and whose occupants could not read one if they had it. A thirst for knowledge in a few, and a patronage of it by the government, which prompts them to invade the eternal solitudes of either pole, and to break through the phalanx of disease and death that guards the head-springs of the Niger, is applauded, and its objects pursued at immense expense, while there are tens of thousands around who do not know whether the land of their nativity is an island or a continent. There may be seen the loftiest orders of hierarchy, —bishops and archbishops, and the Defender of the Christian Faith, —with such miserable impostors and dupes as Courtenay and his followers. There is a church establishment twenty thousand strong, possessing an annual revenue of eight millions sterling, with thousands of native born subjects, arrived at manhood, who never heard the name of Christ. Such are the headings of only a few chapters in the terrific volume of English inequality. This is the condition of a country, in all whose multitudes of churches that Book is weekly read, which declares that God made of one blood all nations of men. The source, origin, cause, of all this is, the neglect of the masses by the possessors of wealth and of power;— mainly and primarily, the neglect of the education of the masses. That attended to, all else would have been changed. A few noble-souled individuals have attended to it, sought to foster and promote it, given money and time to accomplish it; but not the whole, not even any one *class*. The clergy have neglected it, forgetting that eternal truth, that God is a "God of *intelligence* as well as of love, and that exalted purity requires no less the cultivation of the intellect than the purity and warmth of the affections." The great landholders, the powerful lords of the soil, have neglected it. They advocate and defend the radical, fundamental, and, in the end, destructive error, that the masses of men are by nature incapable of self-government; and hence, by virtue of their theory, all necessity for inculcating the virtues of self-control, for imparting that interior light of intelligence which can guide and direct every man, is superseded. The great commercial classes of the nation have never been brought, like the clergy and the landholders, into immediate proximity and contact with the children of the realm, and so they, as a body, have paid no attention to the rising generation around them. In later times, a new department of labor has been opened, a new order in society has arisen, —the manufacturers, —who have not only lived among children, like the land-owners and the ecclesiastical body, but have prosecuted a kind of business in which the services of children could be made available. This was a new epoch. Enterprise, the love of gain of this nation, had before acted upon all the nations of the earth, and upon all the kingdoms of nature, and made them all tributary to its wealth. Here the spirit of cupidity was brought to act directly upon human beings, upon children. To gratify his passion, Herod sacrificed only children under two years of age, —helpless, unconscious, too young to suffer through the torments of fear, or the crushings of hope. But the English manufacturer suffers children to reach the age of hope, of fear, of conscious suffering; and then!—Moloch himself was a god of long-suffering, of tenderness, of boundless love, compared with them. They have tortured the body with years of pining, watching and hunger. They have pinched it with cold, and dwarfed and deformed it in all its proportions. The calm, restorative night,—that beautiful season which God has appointed and inwrought as an organic fact into the very structure of the universe, for the rest, refreshment and growth of his children,—they have stricken from the order of nature. Through its long watches they have bound children to their wheels. They have stived them in hot, suffocating rooms; when exhausted nature failed, they have plied the hellish lash. They have cut their pittance of compensation down, and down, and down, to the very minimum point of existence, because they could not work as long as water and steam. More than this, they have deprived them not only of the joys of childhood and the pleasures of knowledge, but of the consolations of religion and the hopes of immortality, so that they might coin their souls as well as their bodies into gold. Let any one read the reports of the English Factory Commissioners and Factory Inspectors, and he will say that the Fejee islanders, the Caribs, or the most ferocious tribes of cannibals that prowl in the interior of Africa, thousands of miles from the confines of civilization, ought to send missionaries to England, to raise, if possible, the English manufacturer to their own level of humanity. Under this manufacturing system, forms of privation, of suffering and crime, have grown up, such as have never before been known in any part of Christendom or heathendom. We have ourselves seen some of the abodes in which the victims of this system congregate,—houses, so called, erected on narrow courts,—courts opening at one end only upon a street,—framed back to back, with one story under ground, with no means of ingress or egress but through a front door, through which all the refuse and offal of the house must be daily cast into an unpaved court, to ferment and breed putrescence, and darken the heavens with its exhalations of disease and death. This mode of building is not confined to a solitary block or group, but in some places,—at Manchester, for instance, within and without the town,—squares and acres are covered with such dwellings, and such only. From their pallets of straw in these wretched sties, as we learn from the above-mentioned reports, children of the tenderest age are scourged up to travel three miles on foot to be at their tasks by daylight in the morning. At

noon, children still younger are sent to carry them an apology for a meal. We have seen the manner in which some of these victims of avarice and oppression live, less like human beings than like a knot of eels in their slime.

The horrible disclosures recently made in regard to the treatment of children in the mines, almost throughout the mining districts of England, are another record of the same turpitude and enormity. But it is painful to record these atrocities and sufferings. We wish only to draw attention to the consequences of such a systematic neglect of the moral and intellectual culture of children, and to deduce a moral in reference to our own duties. The victims of this neglect have now become so numerous that the paupers are one in twelve of the population of England. The frequency and the enormity of crime have materially reduced the value of life and property. This little island of Great Britain has already planted daughter colonies of convicts and malefactors in the islands of the three great oceans,—the Indian, the Pacific, and the Atlantic,—yet her selfish institutions breed them at home faster than she can convict and export them; and when we left England, in October last, portions of each of the three kingdoms were in commotion, and the government was marching large bodies of troops into Ireland, Scotland and Wales to put down insurrection by the sword.

The moral we derive from these facts, in reference to our own country, is, the duty of every class of men, and of every individual man, to do whatever in him lies for the welfare of the rising generation,—not to talk only, but to act; not to preach only, but to practise, lest those terrible retributions, which God, by his eternal laws, has denounced against such offences, come also upon us. Every farmer or mechanic who stints his child of knowledge, because he can *mint* his bones and sinews into money; every manufacturer who treats children as though they were merely *live* instead of *dead* machinery, who does not allow them a full measure of time for rest, a full measure of time for food, a full measure of time for sleep, and, above all, a full measure of time for the cultivation of mind and heart, is traitorous to the institutions of his country; or, what is worse, he is preparing a class of men who will, in the end, perpetrate more treason against the happiness of mankind, than it is possible for any one man, individually, to commit. The common criminal has but two hands; the man who cherishes ignorance lifts many hands against his country.

It would be as repugnant to our own feelings as it would be opposite to truth to include every English manufacturer in this sketch of the class. There are a few,—however painful to use words of limitation, we must say there are only a few,—who prove that they are humane and rational men. A few miles from Liverpool, for instance, there is the large establishment owned by the Messrs. Rollins, who have for years maintained a school for all the children, and kept open a reading-room for all the adults, upon their premises. They give, not money only, but time and personal encouragement; for one of the brothers meets with his operatives in the evening, instructing them, aiding their inquiries and giving countenance to their laudable efforts for self-improvement. Had England such an aristocracy as this, she would then, indeed, be "happy England." At what a bargain might she exchange her lords by the score for one real nobleman like these!

Scotland

Scotland has had what may with strict propriety be called a system of education, for nearly two centuries. By a clause introduced into an act of parliament, not longer than a man's thumb, it was declared "that a good and sufficient school shall be erected and maintained in every parish." How many of her Burnses and her Cunninghams, how much of the well-being of her inhabitants, and the celebrity of her literary name throughout all lands, does she owe to this brief provision. To her it was the fiat, "Let there be Light!" But her schools have not been what they should have been. In populous cities, and especially in great manufacturing districts, she is suffering many of the evils of the sister kingdom. It is estimated that only about one third part of the children of the country are educated in the parish schools. A portion of the rest are educated in private schools; a portion not at all.

As a specimen of the consequences even of partial neglect, when long continued, we give the following anecdote, on the authority of the Queen's Inspector of Schools for Scotland. He told us that, a few months ago, two benevolent gentlemen in one of their large towns, wishing to improve the condition of the laboring classes around them, brought together eighteen young men, from sixteen to twenty-five years of age, in order to give them some rudiments of moral and religious instruction. They put the question to the young men collectively: "Where was the birth-place of Jesus Christ?" Not one of them answered; all looked blank and stupid and said nothing. By-and-by the interrogators observed the countenance of one of them to be lighted up, and thinking that he was ready to reply, the question was put directly to him, "Where was Jesus Christ born?"—to which he answered, "Paisley [on the River Clyde]."

Holland

For many years past, Holland has maintained an efficient system of public schools. Their instruction seemed to us somewhat less thorough than that of Scotland, but, on the other hand, it is more general,—that is, the schools sustained by the government embrace a very much larger portion of the population than is done by the parochial schools in Scotland. Though there is no law in Holland prescribing the methods of instruction, yet, these methods are very uniform, being almost all copied from those of Mr. Prinsen, the head of the celebrated Normal school at Haarlem. Mr. Prinsen seems to have been the great lawgiver for Holland on the subject of schools, and is indeed almost a Napoleon among schoolmasters. There are two Normal schools in Holland, one at Groningen, the other that of Mr. Prinsen, at Haarlem. The fact that the methods of the latter have been so generally adopted, though the other is the older, seems to show that an intelligent community, and especially teachers, whose minds have been liberally trained, can decide between different systems; and one would think that this fact might serve also to show that we are in no danger at home of having all our methods of instruction stereotyped by our Normal schools, and all our teachers stamped by the same die, like coins struck in the same mint.

Belgium

Since Belgium separated from Holland, by the revolution of 1830, her schools have been neglected, and they have lately been described, by Mr. Ducpetiaux, as follows:

"Instruction in our schools is generally faulty and incomplete, and little merits the praise which has been bestowed upon it. The best thing that can be said in its favor is, that it is better than no instruction at all, and that it is more satisfactory to see children sitting on the benches of a school, even although they be doing nothing to the purpose, than to behold them working mischief in the streets. They are taught to read, write and figure a little; to teach them less is scarcely possible. We speak here of primary schools in general, and affirm that those who attribute a moralizing influence to the majority of these schools, deceive themselves in a manner the most strange and prejudicial to the interests of the class whose children are the pupils in these seminaries. A degree of instruction so limited, so meagre, is nearly equivalent to none whatever; and it is impossible that things should be in a better case, seeing that the education of the *teachers* themselves is of the most imperfect kind. Barely do these persons know the little which they undertake to impart; and they have, generally speaking, the most superficial notions of those methods of instilling knowledge, which they impudently attempt to apply in the case of those only a little more ignorant than themselves.''

Now, however, a law for Public Instruction has been enacted, (Sept. 23, 1842.) by virtue of which there is to be a complete organization of schools. At the head of the system are to be two Normal schools.

Prussia

But the most interesting portions of the world in regard to education are the Protestant states of Germany. It was Luther's reformation which gave being and birth to their systems of public schools. To emancipate mankind from Catholicism, he held it to be necessary that mankind should read the Scriptures. To enable them to read the Scriptures, universal education was necessary; and nothing could secure universal education but Common Schools.

One must study the history of Prussia to understand the magnitude and formidableness of the obstacles which the cause has had to encounter in that kingdom for two centuries and a half. Even now there are those who detract from the prerogatives of education as the means of conferring talent, power, wealth, the arts, prosperity, upon a people; and they cite Prussia as a proof that a nation may have as elaborate a system of Common Schools as talent can devise or unlimited power enforce, and yet be behind other nations having no such system, in invention, in skill, in all the arts of life, in everything that gives a nation historical eclat, in everything that

makes it feared for its power, and envied for its splendor. Why should Prussia, say they, with all its model systems of public instruction, be so much inferior to England in the useful arts, and to France in the exact sciences? As was said above, to understand these things, one must understand the history of Prussia. In the year 1797, when Frederic William III. ascended the throne, the condition of Prussia was most deplorable. The resources of the people had been exhausted to pay the hire of foreign mercenaries. All offices were conferred upon the families of the nobility. No incentive to honorable ambition was held out to the people at large. Civil despotism sucked the life-blood from the body of the people like a vampire, and religious despotism rode their spirits like an incubus. As to worldly enterprise and the desire of bettering one's condition, so strong in the heart of man, the community suffered under the most debasing and discouraging influences from the imperfect or corrupt administration of justice. Some of these evils were removed by that monarch, but the sorest of them all continued till many years later. In 1806, the disastrous battle of Jena was fought. Napoleon expended himself here, and left not an unbroken bone in the whole body of his antagonist. Up to this period a great portion of the population of Prussia were serfs,—absolute bond-men and bond-women,—of course weak, spiritless, without resilience. But it was the good fortune of Frederic to have one or two great men in his councils. Von Stein and Hardenburg are names that will live forever in Prussian history. Within the next three years, under their influences, these serfs were emancipated, elevated into owners of the soil they tilled, and made, comparatively, freemen. This was like a new creation of millions of men. It *was* a new creation of millions of men. To one who looks at the deep causes of things, it was as visible and palpable an act of creation as though the minister had stood forth, and, at the waving of his hand, millions of men had started from the earth, and rent the air with their shouts of joy. It was by the arm of these new-born men that Prussia was first enabled to cope with Napoleon. It was with these new-born men that she pursued him to Paris, in 1814. It was by these at last that the fate of Waterloo was decided.

It is easy to see that a nation, having had such wars to maintain, could not at once recover itself. After the body has been depleted almost to its last drop, it requires time even for a vigorous constitution to form new blood.

Besides, Prussia was not a commercial nation, and therefore could not gather into her coffers the wealth which other nations had earned. She was not a manufacturing nation, and so could not invite the world to come to her marts and leave their gold in exchange for her products. She was an agricultural nation, without a marine, and must, therefore, await the wants and the policy of others.

Here, then, are reasons enough for the comparative backwardness of Prussia. The spirit of the nation is not yet wholly awakened from the lethargy consequent upon so long a period of oppression. Its limbs were made torpid and stiff by the thongs that had bound them, and hence it is that its feet are not yet swift in the race of competition, nor its hands cunning in the works of art. If we stand at a prison door and see a captive brought forth from a long captivity, we ought not to expect to see him leap and dance for joy; we ought rather to expect that fainting and sinking will follow the debility of bondage.

But now we hesitate not to say that Prussia and some of her sister states, where the work of education, after the Prussian model, is going on, are rising more rapidly in the scale of civilization than any other of the nations in Christendom. Their growth is a surer growth. It is less liable to disaster or retrogression; and though Prussia herself is still nominally a despotism, yet we cannot hesitate a moment to predict that, on the very first crisis which arises, she will effectually assert her right to a free constitution, and will, at that time, have the intelligence that can safely administer and enjoy it. This improving condition of her people she owes to her schools;—nay, more, the schools have wrought out this great social revolution, in defiance of many adverse influences. The schools have lifted up the people, though weighed down by many burdens. The schools have been educating the childhood of the nation. The people cannot be said to have been born till they were emancipated. They are now rapidly maturing into the vigor and intelligence of manhood.

The only just mode of considering Prussia and some of the other German States, is, not to compare them with nations, a part of whose population has for centuries been acting under the stimuli of freedom, but with other nations whose systems of education, if systems they have, are as yet unanimated by the spirit of reform. Compare Prussia, Saxony, Wurtemburg, for instance, with Bohemia, Austria proper, Italy, and we shall see what education has done for the former.

Lancasterian Schools

The Lancasterian system, or that of monitorial instruction, prevails to a great extent in England, Scotland and Ireland. It is used in many of the private establishments in France, but it is considered that the French government, by its order of 25th April, 1834, "dividing all primary schools into three classes, according to the age and proficiency of the scholars," was meant as its death-blow in that country.

In Prussia, and in those parts of Germany where the subject of education is best understood, the Lancasterian method of instruction is most condemned. Substantially the same opinion prevails throughout Holland. Dr. Diesterweg, the head of the Teacher's Seminary at Berlin, and a great authority in Prussia, travelled, a few years since, to Denmark, for the express purpose of examining certain celebrated schools in that country, where the Lancasterian system was followed and highly approved. He has published an account of his journey. Although he went with a strong predilection in favor of the plan, yet he now entirely renounces his former opinion, and declares that, after having thoroughly examined the schools in Denmark, he utterly condemns the system as reducing the education of the people to mere mechanical repetitions, without any culture either of the heart or the understanding. From what we have seen of Lancasterian schools, we entirely concur in this opinion, and hope never to see that system adopted in this country.

S. G. H.   1844

A Critical Review of Schools in Rome, Italy

There are few American accounts of schools in the Italian states written during the early part of the nineteenth century. Most educational travelers from the United States found the Protestant schools of Britain and northern Germany and even the Catholic institutions of Switzerland, France, and southern Germany of greater interest. This amusingly critical description of schools in Rome reflects the national and religious background of the writer as much as it does the abysmally low standards of teaching in the schools he visited. Speaking of teachers from the religious orders, the author observed, "I have found among them many honest and zealous men, but who, never lifting their heads above the surface of the stream of life, do not perceive that, while the rest of the human race is sweeping outward towards improvement, they are not only stationary but even retrograding."

The author, S. G. H., is believed to be Samuel Gridley Howe (1801–1876), a graduate of Brown University in 1821 and Harvard Medical School in 1824. Howe served in the Greek War of Independence and traveled extensively in Europe. He later became interested in the education of the blind, and in 1832 he established and became the principal of the Perkins Institution and Massachusetts School for the Blind. Howe was intimately associated with Horace Mann in developing the common school system of Massachusetts.

There is not a school in Rome which must not be considered as a beacon to warn, rather than a light to guide, the inquirer. There are three schools in Rome commonly called the schools of the *Ignorantelli,* or the *Frères Ignorantins,* in French,—a term which seems to have been derived from the notion, once general, and not yet extinct, that the teachers must know nothing beyond the branches they teach, namely, reading, writing, and arithmetic. I say the notion is not yet extinct; for one of the masters, in a conversation with me, maintained the doctrine, and asserted that he would prefer that his sub-teachers should know nothing beyond the branches they taught,—should not read or study anything else, but spend their whole time in teaching, and in their devotions.

These three schools have thirteen hundred day scholars, who come at nine in the morning, and remain until noon,—return at two, and remain until six,—five days in the week, and who are taught gratuitously. The schoolhouses, like most of those in Rome, have an aisle in the middle of each room, with two or three rows of benches, rising a little above each other, on each hand. In front is a small stage, on which is the master's desk; and on each side of the door is a seat, much elevated above all the others, for the *dux,* or leader of the day,—the highest boy of the highest class. Projecting from the wall on both sides, there is a flag-staff, from which hangs over the heads of the boys a banner, one with the arms and devices of Rome, the

other with those of Carthage. Those ranged under the one are for the time Romans, those opposite them are Carthaginians. The contest is for superiority in the lessons, and the victors enjoy the triumph of a parade, with their banner flying, and sometimes with music.

In all the Roman schools you find this division of the seats, and with the avowed intent of pitting the boys against each other. I have seen scores of banners, but never observed any other than those of Rome and Carthage,—an extraordinary testimony which Romans still give to the superiority of the Carthaginians over all their other enemies. The high seat, each side of the door, is the post of the commander of each army,—the boy who stands and sits highest in the class.

Emulation is the main spring in the Roman, I may say in the Italian schools; it is excited in every possible form, by banners, by music, by badges, by prizes of various kinds. If the masters had a hundredth part of the emulation among themselves, and with those of other countries, which they inspire in their pupils, the schools would become tolerable, instead of being, as they are, among the most wretched in the world.

But to return to the *Scuolai degli Ignorantelli.* Each master has about fifty scholars in his room, and confines himself to a class for one year. The first teaches the elements of reading; the next, reading and writing; the higher one adds arithmetic. The boys go to school from three to seven years; they are, almost all of them, of active nervous

S. G. H., "Letter from Rome," *The Common School Journal,* VI (1844), 226–229, 329–337.

temperaments, and endowed with great natural vivacity and talent; nevertheless, they are prevented from becoming even tolerable readers and arithmeticians,—a fact which implies either great talent or great stupidity on the part of the masters. As for writing, I must confess I never saw any thing like it, even in the German schools; the system seems to me very slovenly, and the time consumed enormous; nevertheless the result is beautiful. A boy, in one of these schools, who can write small hand and capitals with ease and with the smoothness and grace of copperplate, would be called only a good writer; to be a *very* good one, he must, with a flourish of his pen, surround his page with spreadeagles, with dragons, and crocodiles; and if he aspire to any extraordinary distinction, he must bring in a human head and face, the features of which have a likeness to somebody or other. You would naturally suppose they must be taught to draw; but they are not; their power of execution comes probably from a greater natural endowment of those faculties by which we take cognisance of forms and outlines, and by which we imitate them. The reading is in the most whining, monotonous tone imaginable. I have heard hundreds of the best readers in the Roman schools; I have heard the masters read, and the priests read; and I have never heard one who did not whine or sing, except the boys in the Jews' school.

As for arithmetic, you will hardly credit the assertion, that living, active boys can be allowed the use of a slate and pencil for so many years, and yet be prevented from advancing beyond the very threshold of arithmetic; and yet such is the case in these schools. Questions which could be solved by a simple application of the Rule of Three, puzzled the best cipherers, if they were asked out of the common form.

The discipline of the schools seems paternal and good; the masters have the power of corporal punishment, but almost never use it; in fact, I think I may say *never* in these three schools. They use emulation, shame, exhortation and premiums of various kinds, but not the rod. Perhaps their character and dress of priests adds to their power; the boys regard them as spiritual teachers, as well as intellectual ones; and often when they come to the desk, they kneel and raise their hands. This, indeed, you see in most of the Roman schools. I have sometimes, on going into one of these schools, found a boy on his knees on the stone side of the door, others on their knees on the cold stone floor

of the passage ways, muttering over prayers with more rapidity than devotion; and, on my exit, after perhaps a half an hour, found them still on their marrow bones, the penance and the prescribed number of prayers not having been accomplished. This was for some offence which with us would have been punished by the ferula. You will easily calculate, without a slate and pencil, the increase of esteem with which this process will make a boy regard the great privilege of approaching his Maker in prayer. It reminds me of a pious old lady at home, who said to a boy, "There now! I meant to have let you stay at home from *meeting* this cold afternoon, but since you have been so naughty you *shall go;*—and, if you don't behave yourself, I'll send you to lecture this evening, too!" The little Yankee loved the meetinghouse as much more, as the young Roman does his prayers.

It is often said that the government and the teachers in Rome endeavor to manufacture popularity by keeping up the schools, while they take very good care not to let the pupils have any instruction which will really develop their minds, and give intelligence and strength to their character. This, I have no doubt, is true of the government, which, without going to any except the most trifling expense for public instruction, contrives to keep every instructer under surveillance and in perfect subjection; but I am sure it is not true of all the masters, or even of a majority of them. Many are earnest and honest teachers, but they are in a state of deplorable ignorance of the science of teaching. The slightest conversation with them betrays this. For instance, I have asked many what they thought would be the success of trying to teach a child to read in words, without spending so long a time upon the alphabet and the syllables; to which the first reply was that sort of stare of astonishment which would follow a grave question as to whether a child could learn to swallow food without first opening his mouth to eat; and when they are perfectly sure you are serious, they reply, "Why, how on earth can a child learn to read in any other way than by learning the alphabet and syllables?" One of the head masters, in reply to a question of mine whether he could not relieve the lassitude and weariness of his pupils by some gymnastic exercises in the open air, manifested great astonishment at the idea of gymnastic exercises; he had no conception of the thing; and another, after some reflection, asked if some of the institutions in Germany had not recently made some experiments in this way.

But what should they know about physiology, or even the laws of physics,—they, poor pallid priests, who from their tenderest years were forced to sit like automata, or to move like machines; whose boyhood was passed in seclusion, who never moved out of doors except to march in regular companies and in military order, under huge cocked hats, with their legs cramped in breeches and long stockings, and with a ponderous black cloak upon their backs, or long stripes of bombazine or flannel hanging like streamers from their collars and falling down to their heels? What should they know of the needs of childhood, who seem to think that fun and frolic are inventions of the Devil; that sinners alone are to shout and laugh; and that God made the green sward only for the children of the wicked to tumble upon,—the pure stream for the unjust alone to swim in,—the swift horse for the worldly alone to mount upon? What know they of the necessity of stimulating the brain by highly oxygenated blood forced bounding through the arteries by the alternate contraction and relaxation of hundreds of muscles,—they, whose flesh is as flabby as blown veal, whose whole growth runs to the adipose, who have not a hard muscle in their body except the flexors and extensors of their legs, and who, if ever in high health, have only the obesity of the stalled ox, or the stuffed capon?

These reflections may apply to the teachers of Italy generally who are of the priestly order, and I make them more in the spirit of sorrow than of reproach, for as individuals they are not to blame; they are moulded into their present shape by the institutions in which they are reared, and are not responsible for their mental organization, any more than for their physical peculiarities. I have found among them many honest and zealous men, but who, never lifting their heads above the surface of the stream of life, do not perceive, that, while the rest of the human race is sweeping onward towards improvement, they are not only stationary, but even retrograding.

An American who has not visited Italy can hardly conceive the nature of the obstacles which are purposely thrown in the way of the education of the people. Nay; even the travellers who visit this country seem rarely to inquire into the condition of the common people, or to penetrate deeper into society than can be done by an acquaintance with the consul, the banker, the landlord, and the *cicerone.* My visits to the schools always seem to excite great surprise. When it is

known I am a foreigner, the surprise increases; and when the master ascertains that I am an American, it amounts to amazement, which is sometimes expressed by the hesitating question of how it happened that I am not black! Hence you will hear from foreigners sweeping denunciations of this people as unfit for liberty, as cowardly, treacherous, wilfully ignorant and degraded. As if human nature ever, *by choice*, remained undeveloped or depraved! As if a rising generation, under a wise and paternal government, could grow up without making progress, and outstripping its predecessors in knowledge and goodness! No! for all the ignorance, the suffering, and the national vices of the Romans, the Roman government and the Roman institutions are responsible in the sight of God.

The entire control of public instruction is in the hands of the government, although it pays but a very paltry sum for its support. To have an idea of how perfect is the· *surveillance* of the people, you should remember that the whole city is divided into parishes, and each parish subdivided into sections, and assigned to priests, who are to make themselves acquainted with the doings, sayings, and thinkings, of every man, woman and child, in their parish or section. The whole is under the government of the Vicar General, or religious governor of the city. Every person is to go to confession at least once a year; if he fails to do so he receives an admonition from his priest; if this does not succeed in bringing him to his marrow bones, he is summoned before a higher authority, and the whole power of pomp, and office, and ceremonial, aided by appeal to his early superstitions and nursery terrors, is brought to bear upon him, and seldom in vain. A more summary and outrageous interference with his religious freedom is sometimes resorted to; a file of soldiers conducts him to the prison of the Sancto Officio or Holy Office, or, in plain English, the Inquisition; for it is the old Inquisition, and administered as of old, except that no *physical* torture is used, and that none but Catholics are amenable to it. In this prison, without any civil process, without being confronted with any accuser, without any chance of open trial, or of having a legal defender, he is kept until he promises to do better, to go to confession, and to be a Catholic. How often this latter process is resorted to, I cannot say, but I have knowledge of more than one case.

When a person is incorrigible he is doomed to excommunication, of which notice is given to the public, by putting up his name on the church doors, that they may avoid him like a mad dog. Now, though there are thousands who would not care a fig for this, (as far as it could affect their spiritual welfare,) who submit to the confessional with ill-concealed disgust, and who are obliged by the iron hand of power to play the hypocrite, yet there are very few who dare to brave excommunication.

You will see at once the hold which this machinery of the confessional gives to the priest over the instruction of children in schools taught by laymen. The master himself might not perhaps confess to his priest that he had been teaching his boys to exercise their own reason in adopting their faith, but the boys would tell their mothers, and they would tell the priest, should he ask them, which he would probably find unnecessary, for they would tell of their own accord. In a word, the whole of the public instruction here is under the entire control of priests interested in the preservation of the actual state of things, and opposed to any improvement, or any inquiry which may endanger it.

All the schools are kept three hours in the forenoon, and between two and three in the afternoon; but a considerable portion is occupied in the mummeries of their devotion, —nearly one hour and a half during each day, besides the whole of Saturday afternoon. Still more to diminish the time devoted to instruction, there are the numerous feast and fast days, which, with the recesses, amount to more than half the year; for, taking the fifty-two Sundays, the thirty-one days' vacation in October, the week of Christmas, and the ten days of Carnival, and fifty-two Thursdays on which there is no school, you have a total of 183 days in the year in which the poor children do not have even the scanty portion of instruction which the ignorant and hampered teacher could give them. From the Calendar of the Roman College now before me, it appears there are but 133 days in the year in which instruction is there given; and this college is surely the best school of Rome.

It is clear that a desire for display is the principal object of the Roman government, in what little it does for the public instruction. I say this deliberately, and am not alone in the opinion. A foreign diplomatic functionary here, who knows every man of consequence in the government, and who is much interested in popular instruction, told me that if I should ever publish a true account of the administration of public charitable institutions, or of the government, with regard to public instruction, I should never be allowed to visit the country again.

"Let BAD ENOUGH alone," seems the watchword of the powers that be; and with regard to popular instruction they desire only to preserve the *status in quo*. Some accuse them of wishing to bring back the darkness that brooded here of old; but I think they are satisfied with the fog that just allows one to grope his way along. It is wonderful to see how completely they shut out the light that is blazing all around them in Europe; for, notwithstanding there is no periodical press, notwithstanding the threefold censorship of the press, and the *cordon infernale* which surrounds the country, and keeps out newspapers, books, and even living men who would *talk* liberality, one would suppose that occasional sparks would fall upon the combustible materials within the crazy old structure, and set it in a blaze. But not at all; there is a quiet here equal to that of Balbec and Palmyra.

As for newspapers, not only do the officers of government effectually prevent the circulation of a single continental journal that has any pretensions to the name of one, but they carefully examine every one that comes through the post-office from abroad; and if it contains any liberal articles, or any news cheering to the friends of humanity, they stop the number. This is the case even with journals taken by the foreigners resident here. English journals too, which, probably, would be read only by the English, are stopped as well as the French and German. Greece, the old vassal of Rome, is up again; and Athens has a dozen newspapers, but not one of them is allowed to come through the post-office; the only news I can get from them is round about through France. By the by, did you learn how the Greeks resorted to the *lex talionis* in their enactments concerning the liberty of worship to be granted to Catholics? "Be it enacted &c.—that Catholics shall enjoy all the religious liberties, privileges, immunities, &c., that are granted to members of the Greek Church in the Roman States, &c." At present this amounts to entire prohibition of their worship. The enormous Index of forbidden books is getting every day larger; in fact, it is becoming so perfectly unmanageable that it will probably be thrown aside altogether, and the more convenient method adopted of publishing a list of books which people *may* read, as this will be a very small and convenient volume.

Literature in the Roman States is literally dead; copyright amounts to nothing, and there is no market for any books of value. Even the mechanical business of printing is done most wretchedly; and you see, in the government offices even, the old fashioned screw presses, pulled by a great strong man, inked by a big boy, and fed by another, all three of whom do not do more than one active journeyman Yankee printer.

The surveillance of the police over literature is so active, and so effectual in suppressing the least individuality of sentiment, that if an actor upon the stage ventures to introduce a joke of his own, or to vary from the text in the slightest degree, he is called to account at once, and told to confine himself to his copy. In short, the government seems to succeed completely in preventing any progress, though I hope it is only in appearance; for the few men of intelligence say that notwithstanding there is apparent indifference on the part of the people, they would nevertheless rise against their tyrants in a month, were it ascertained that the other powers would not interfere. Certain it is that no class except the priests has any attachment to the government. The nobles are entirely without any power under the present government; a marquis, a duke, or a prince, having not the slightest political influence, or any apparent advantage except precedence on certain ceremonials, and the *pas* in fashionable life. The middling classes have not the slightest political representation or power, but they pay heavy taxes without getting any benefit. The poorer and working classes know that not only can they not grow any richer as they grow older, but feel that it is very hard to get enough to live upon.

However, my intention is not to discourse to you upon political matters, but to give you such information as may interest you respecting the instruction of the people, and the condition of the schools. I shall speak first of the city of Rome itself; and as it may be said there is an immense deal of theology and a multitude of churches with very little religion, so it may be said there is a great deal of teaching, and a multitude of schoolhouses, with very little instruction. Schoolhouses, did I say? I have not seen a thing in Rome that would deserve the name, though I have sought very diligently, and visited scores of schools. I verily believe there is not a single one in the city built for that purpose, or I may say, at all well adapted for the accommodation of scholars. There are colleges and higher seminaries,—oh yes! the rich and the noble take very good care that there shall be provision for their precious offspring;—but the children of the poor can do

very well in the ground floor of damp houses, side by side with the stables, or in upper rooms or crazy garrets; and there you find many of the *Scuolae Regionarie,* or district schools, if I may so translate a word which implies merely local division. These Regionary schools of Rome are intended for the instruction of the children of the poor of Rome, and are, according to the best authority which I can find, 242 in number, and receive 4,922 children. These schools are of three kinds; the first, intended to receive children of both sexes under five years of age, are 179 in number, and have 3,726 children. They retain the girls, however, after five years of age. They are somewhat like the old dame schools of England, and are under the protection and surveillance of the government only so far as is necessary to see that no liberal or heretical doctrines are instilled into the tender minds of the young Romans.

They are kept by widows,—by broken down women,—by any one who cannot get a living in any other way. They receive a patent, or commission from the government, for which they pay a very small sum, and which is renewed every year.

According to the law, they ought to be examined, and to pass a severe ordeal as to moral and intellectual qualifications; but all that really is required of them is the certificate of their parish priest that they are good and pious Catholics. As for any examinations of their scholars, they seem to be more scarce than ever were those of our worst New England schools; indeed, as far as I could see, they had nothing to be examined in.

I will not trust myself at once to give any impressions of these schools,—for nothing in your experience will have prepared you for the disorder, dirt, idleness, and ignorance, which therein reign; but I will first give you an extract from the standard work on Roman Institutions, published in 1842, by Monsignore Morichini; a work which abounds from beginning to end, with fulsome panegyric of everything connected with the government. But the primary schools were too bad even for Morichini to praise by the wholesale; so that after lauding the principle of their establishment, and the Cardinal who *ought* to preside over their administration, he says: "Nevertheless, it must be confessed that the aspect of some of these schools is *rather comfortless.* Sometimes there are found in a single room on the ground floor, with but little light and little air, a great many dirty and disorderly children; some are crying, some are complaining, some are screaming;

one is swinging himself on a nail in the wall, one is lying on the floor in the dirt; others are sleeping, others are eating, and I do not know what all! In the repetition of their prayers there is a whining cant that certainly cannot form a pleasant association in their tender minds with so sacred a subject as communing with God. In these close quarters, often unhealthy too, the poor children are obliged to remain many hours without that exercise that is desirable and necessary even at their age. But not all the schools are of this sort; there were less bad; but I should not venture, nevertheless, to propose any of them for models, and I confess the need we have for better establishments of this kind."[1]

I think that this is the only instance in which the above author ventures to speak in anything like fitting terms of the establishments of which his work treats, though he might have said as much, and more, of prisons, hospitals, &c.; but, be that as it may, I can vouch for the fidelity of his description of the primary schools.

The schoolmasters, whom I saw, seemed very coarse, ignorant persons; the children were in every case disorderly, and there seemed no system at all except in the repetition of prayers. They pretend to teach reading in all cases; and in some they succeed in making the children conceive the difference between A and B,—but sometimes they fail to do even this. This matters little, perhaps, to the parents, whose object often is merely to get them out of the way at home. They pay as much as the mistress can make them, which is seldom more than two pauls, or about twenty cents per month, and generally less. The average number of scholars to a school being but a fraction over twenty, you may well conceive what grade of talents can be commanded by an income of eight dollars a month, out of which the rent is to be paid. Indeed, some of the schools had not more than twelve scholars; of course, the good women received less than five dollars per month; however, she must have some place to live in, and her only room served also for schoolroom.

So much for the 179 schools. Then there are 49, a grade higher, which receive girls over five years of age, though, as I observed before, in defiance of the law, girls some-

times remain in the first class of schools long after they are five years old; but not boys. In this matter, there is the greatest vigilance on the part of the parish priest, who would not be so much shocked at discovering that the schoolmistress could not read, as that she kept a boy,—even were it her own son,—in the school with girls, after he had passed his fifth birth-day. There is a degree of purism about this that is quite worthy those who hang up the images or pictures of naked saints and saintesses about the schoolroom, and at the corners of the streets.

In the school of the second order, there are girls over five years of age, to the number in the whole of eight hundred and seventy-six, and they are professedly taught to read, to write, and to sew. Most of them succeed in drawling out, in a singsong tone, one word after another of the Christian Doctrine, the standard school book, of which I shall give you some specimens hereafter. They come up, one at a time, to the chair of the mistress, kneel down on a stool at her feet, and after crossing themselves, make a desperate dart at the syllables, joining those that will join easily without any regard to their belonging to the same word or not;—pausing as much in the middle of words as between them, and manifesting a sovereign contempt for commas and periods, which they treat with great impartiality,—that is, neglect all alike.

A few, and only a few, learn to write; but then they are all taught to sew, and to knit, and some are taught embroidery.

The first class of regionary or district female schools are fourteen in number, and contain three hundred and twenty scholars. There is professedly taught in these schools, the elementary branches, grammar of the Italian and French languages, geography, history, and the finer kinds of needlework. The scholars pay in proportion to the means of the parents, and the schools have considerable reputation; but from the specimens I have seen, they would have reputation only in Rome. The girls cannot read with any ease or correctness; they write tolerably, and learn their own language pretty well, but as for French, geography, and history, they hardly know enough to know the difference between the subjects.

In none of the schools of the above kind, which I have seen, (and I have visited over twenty,) was there a map, a globe, or a blackboard to be seen. The attendance is very regular, owing to the fact of the parents paying for the schooling; and the discipline

[1]Degl' Instituti de Pubblica Carità, ed Istruzione Primaria, e delle Prigioni in Roma da D. Carlo Morichini, Prelato Romano. Roma, 1842. Vol. i., p. 305.

is mild. Emulation is the great incentive, the spring, indeed, which moves the machinery in most of the Roman schools; and, save in the lower ones, corporal punishment is very rarely resorted to. I have not found a single advocate for it, although all the masters say they have the power of resorting to it, in case of extreme necessity. They have this power indeed, always, but, to their credit be it spoken, they seldom use it. I always ask the question, both of schoolmasters and keepers of houses of correction for the young, do you flog? And the answer is, invariably, no!—and generally in a tone indicating surprise at the question.

Another, and perhaps a more important class of schools are those which go under the name of Sectional schools; and which are intended for boys over five years of age. They are fifty in number, and have about sixteen hundred scholars, generally from the indigent, but not the poorest class of society. These schools are under the control of the government, which, however, goes to no expense for their maintenance, and exercises only such control as will prevent any political or religious heresy being taught, and also obviate the possibility of any of the masters coming upon public charge in their sickness or old age. The first purpose is effected by means of the annual license and the espionage of the priest, and by occasional inquiries by a deputy of the Cardinal Vicar of Rome. The second is secured by making the masters pay three pauls, or thirty cents, a month, which goes to form a fund for pensioning them off, in old age or in long sickness. There are also two or three supernumerary schoolmasters, paid by the government, whose business it is to take charge of the school of any master who may be ill a few days. The retiring pension is about six dollars a month and cannot be enjoyed unless after a service of at least ten years. I have not heard a master speak of this arrangement with any satisfaction, and most of them seemed to look upon it with contempt.

Each master finds his own schoolroom, and collects as many scholars as he can; he keeps the school on his own account, and makes the parents pay according to their means, or rather according to their dispositions. The best school of the kind which I have seen had about sixty scholars, and the charge was invariably twelve pauls, or one dollar and twenty cents a month. Very few masters, however, have a reputation which will enable them to command a high price. In some schools I found less than a dozen boys about a forlorn

looking master, who seemed as though he were in need of the common comforts of life. Most of the masters are *foreigners*, as they are called, that is, Italians from other parts of the peninsula, generally the north, because the profession of schoolmaster is considered too low by the Romans for persons of their noble and elevated position!

There may be good teachers among this class of masters but I have not found them; on the contrary, I have conversed with many without meeting one who seemed to have the slightest conception of the true dignity of his calling, or any acquaintance with the modern improvements in the art of conducting schools.

They all pretend to teach reading, writing, and arithmetic; some of them add geography, history, and the Italian and French languages. I may safely say, however, that writing and the rudiments of the Latin language are the only branches that are thoroughly taught.

As for reading, the masters themselves do not know how to read well, and I doubt if many of them ever heard a good reader. Their aim seems to be to teach the scholar to emit the longest possible series of sounds with the least possible variation of tone, marking the words not by inflections of the voice but by a regular hiatus. They pay but little attention to the meaning of the words, and are content if the boy can give the proper sound to each group of letters.

They teach their scholars to write by dint of hard labor and continuous copying: and though their books, pens, ink, and desks are of the rudest kinds, and although they have no good method of instruction, nevertheless, so long continued is their perseverance, and such is the talent of the race for copying forms and outlines, that their success is great. You will find better chirographists in the Roman schools than in those of Massachusetts.

The rudiments of the Latin language are taught very thoroughly, as many of the boys are prepared in these schools for entering the Roman College. History is taught to a very limited extent, and geography on a still smaller scale. The sight of a globe would astonish the scholars, who very seldom see even a map. Natural philosophy is unheard of in the schools which I visited; and geology and astronomy would sound like cabalistic watchwords.

These schools are for the children of the better class of tradespeople; and those who do not go to the Roman College seldom receive any more instruction than they get in them; hence, you may judge what sort of men they make, and how little taste they acquire for reading or self-improvement of any kind.

There are not, as with us, the supplementary and all important practical schools which ripen elementary instruction into useful knowledge and train the boy up to the useful and active man; there are not the municipal offices, the jury boxes, the town meetings, the training fields, the caucuses. Alas! our brethren of Rome have none of those high privileges and manly duties; and without them, even were their schools better than ours,— were they the best that the world ever knew, —the people themselves would be only wise pedants; they would not be MEN.

Henry Philip Tappan 1851

Adaptation of European University Models

Henry Philip Tappan (1805–1881) graduated from Union College, Schenectady, New York, in 1825 and Auburn Theological Seminary in 1827 and later served as Congregational minister in Pittsfield, Massachusetts. He became professor of moral and intellectual philosophy at the University of the City of New York and was subsequently chancellor of the University of Michigan. He was forced to resign from both institutions—in 1837 and 1863 respectively—because of the academic controversy and hostility aroused by his rigorous and pioneering educational ideas. Tappan was greatly influenced by the carefully articulated Prussian system of education where only the most advanced courses were available at the university level, and he tried to realize the benefits of this system at Michigan.

He spent much of his later life in Germany and Switzerland where he died in Geneva. In the extract below, which illustrates his laudatory attitude toward German education, he noted that "the educational system of Germany, and particularly in Prussia, is certainly a very noble one. We cannot well be extravagant in its praise."

Leaving now the forms under which the University system was developed, let us return to the subjects of study. The reign of pure Scholasticism gradually yielded to branches more liberal—the ancient classics, mathematics, and physical science. The study of the ancient classics received a powerful impulse through the Italian schools, which produced many scholars of great eminence. The transition to the ancient classics was natural, from the common use of the Latin tongue. There was an affinity also between the logic of Aristotle and geometry. The study of the Peripatetic philosophy introduced the physics of Aristotle. The application of the Scholastic method to physical investigation made this branch of science indeed of little worth, and laid it justly open to the scornful denunciation of Bacon. Nevertheless there was progress, and the human mind was working up from the subtleties of the Scholastic philosophy to a region of greater freedom and light. The Universities were the centres of intellectual activity, where great men from time to time appeared, leading on the march of thought until the philosophy of Bacon changed the method of investigation, and Kepler and Newton revealed the true system of Nature.

It might have been expected, that with the advance of science, the Universities would have thrown off all the old scholasticism, and sprung forward in a new and glorious career. This, however, does not appear to have been the case so generally as the new era seemed to promise.

The changes in the French Universities were the effect of the convulsions of the Revolution, and the energy and patronage of Napoleon, rather than the result of a natural progress. The modern school of science and philosophy at Paris has been eminent; and the lectures of such men as Royer Collard, Cousin, Guizot, Jouffroy, Biot, and Arago, well nigh realize the ideal of a University.

In the English Universities the old tutorial and collegial system has continued to prevail. Oxford has been charged with the almost entire neglect of the mathematics, and Cambridge with a corresponding neglect of the classics. The Edinburgh Review of April, 1810, remarks: "We believe ourselves warranted to say, that the examinations at Oxford, till within a very few years, so far as

Henry Philip Tappan, *University Education* (New York: George P. Putnam, 1851), pp. 35-51.

they were scientific at all, and not confined to the learned languages, turned entirely on the Aristotelian and Scholastic logic. The college lectures, according to the best of our information, were guilty of this same neglect; they gave no account of the great modern discoveries, or of the method that had led to them. Some few individuals might pursue natural philosophy to a certain length; but it entered not at all into the general plan of education. To judge, so far as we have been able to learn, from the subjects of public examination, or from the general course of study, one would have thought that the fame of the great discoveries which had been made during the last hundred and fifty years, had never reached the University of Oxford.''

Improvements have since been introduced, and greater improvements are in progress, particularly in the University of Cambridge; but it appears an indisputable fact, that the system of the English Universities has been lamentably deficient, and has by no means yet attained a completeness demanded alike by their long standing, and the character of the age to which they have come down. The Edinburgh Review of April, 1849, asks: "But, even as a preparatory training, is the actual benefit ever found to justify their high pretensions? Is there any man alive who can say, not with truth, but even with conviction, that the best or most laborious scholars and mathematicians of the University are the best lawyers, physicians, philosophers, or statesmen of England? The very reverse is the plain, if not the acknowledged fact. It would be difficult to find at present, among the most eminent leaders in Westminster Hall, any whose academical course was distinguished by studies, or crowned with honors, either mathematical or classical. The extent to which academical distinctions have lately been thrown into the background in the professional and public life of England, has gone lengths which really surprise us.''

As a general system, the English Universities present us only courses of Collegial study of a very limited extent, pursued under tutors, and followed by examinations for a degree. The attainment of the degree appears to be the great end of study. Neither a principle of utility, nor of philosophical education, governs. There are indeed higher honors, the reward of higher studies. And unquestionably profound and elegant scholars are made on the foundations of the fellowships. We are speaking of the tendency of the system, and not of the opportunities afforded in these venerable seats of learning, to those who are disposed

to study and learned retirement. But the men who should be permanent professors, like Whately and Arnold, can find at the Universities no amply-endowed professorships, or thronging classes yielding adequate fees; and hence are compelled, with few exceptions, to take the head masterships of schools, or to retire into the church; and leave the instruction to the fellows of the colleges. The truth is, that the English Universities still feel the incubus of the old Scholasticism, and reap the effects of the changes introduced under the Chancellorship of Laud. They are antiquated institutions, which do not meet the requirements of a new age.

As the Universities grew out of the Church, are in their origin Church institutions, their condition will be found to keep pace with that of the Church. Hence, in Spain, where the Schoolmen were longest cherished, and where the power of the Priesthood extended over everything, the Universities, instead of advancing with enlightened Europe, have remained fixed in scholastic and ecclesiastical solidity. In Italy they have retrograded.

On the other hand, in Protestant Germany, what an advance has been made! In no part of the world has University education been so enlarged, and made so liberal and thorough. The Universities of Protestant Germany stand forth as model institutions, if there be such to be found; and the whole system of education, from the Common School upward, exhibits an intellectual progress which commands our admiration. In Germany, the emancipation of the Church was the emancipation of the Universities. The rationalism which now prevails, whatever may be its errors, is a symptom and a consequent of the intense reaction which there took place against the prescriptions of ecclesiastical and academical authority; and which must ultimately correct itself by the same force by which it came into being. The Universities of Scotland have exhibited a similar freedom and independence, without running into a similar excess. With a high tone of general scholarship, they have had also a distinct philosophical school of distinguished merit; and no country has contended more nobly and steadfastly for civil and religious freedom.

Now the English Universities exhibit the same correspondence to the church out of which they have sprung, and to which they belong. Two strong elements in the English Church have ever been, a zeal for the prerogative, and a stiff adherence to the apostolical succession. Many of us Protestants who have no great regard for either, think that the forced reformation of the English Church by Henry VIII., and the modifications which he gave it, never separated it sufficiently from Rome. It indeed received a new head, but retained many of the old errors. The Universities have in like manner been the strongholds of Toryism and high-churchism. The part which Oxford in particular has acted in our own times by her publications of a Romish tendency, and by the defection of some of her members, shows the direction and strength of her ecclesiastical bias. Oxford is governed by church influences, and these hold her in scholastic bondage, and bind her under a reverence for the past, instead of leading her onward with the awakening spirit of philosophy, and the enlargement of the sciences.

Neither Oxford nor Cambridge have ever had a school of philosophy. In this they have been left behind by France, Germany, and Scotland. England has had philosophers, but they gave no lectures, and formed no schools at the Universities. What had Bacon, Locke, and Coleridge to do with the Universities? What had the Universities to do with them? Ecclesiastical prescription can never allow a free philosophical movement. We can understand at this point of view the fact affirmed by the writer in the Edinburgh Review, that the examinations at Oxford, "so far as they were scientific at all, and not confined to the learned languages, turned entirely on the Aristotelian and Scholastic logic; and that the new logic, such as is explained in the Novum Organum of Bacon, was never mentioned." Professor Whewell, of Cambridge, the learned author of the Philosophy of the Inductive Sciences, and of the History of the Inductive Sciences, has done much to awaken a philosophical spirit in that University, and has contributed essentially to the bringing about of manifest improvements in the course of education. His work On Liberal Education in general, is one of great value and interest. The distinction which he makes between *permanent* and *progressive* studies, is important and suggestive; the view which he takes of the discipline of the human faculties is philosophical and lofty; the proportions in which he distributes classical and mathematical studies, strike us as judicious; and his recommendation of the geometrical method in preference to the analytical as a discipline for the reasoning faculty, is wise and worthy of all attention.

That the English Universities are improvable, and improving, we fully believe. But never, while paralyzed by high-church influence, can they fully develop their great capacities, and collect within their precincts, and under their government, schools of philosophy and science formed of the great wits and profound thinkers of England. It is easy to get up scholasticism under prescription, but investigation and productive thought must be free as birds upon the wing—they must bear themselves along by their own native vigor, in their own native element. And we must run the risk of flying in the wrong direction sometimes, or we can have no flying at all, unless it be the wretched flying of a decoy-pigeon—fluttering within the limits of the string held by the hand of its master. Universities may, indeed, make learned men; but their best commendation is given when it can be said of them, that furnishing the material and appliances of learning, setting the examples in their professors and graduates, breathing the spirit of scholarship in all that pertains to them, they inspire men, by the self-creative force of study and thought, to make themselves both learned and wise, and thus ready to put their hand to every great and good work, whether of science, of religion, or of the state.

We have spoken of the German Universities as model institutions. Their excellence consists in two things: first, they are purely Universities, without any admixture of collegial tuition. Secondly, they are complete as Universities, providing libraries and all other material of learning, and having professors of eminence to lecture on theology, law, and medicine, the philosophical, mathematical, natural, philological, and political Sciences, on history and geography, on the history and principles of Art, in fine, upon every branch of human knowledge. The professors are so numerous that a proper division of labor takes place, and every subject is thoroughly discussed. At the University every student selects the courses he is to attend. He is thrown upon his own responsibility and diligence. He is left free to pursue his studies; but, if he wishes to become a clergyman, a physician, a lawyer, a statesman, a professor, or a teacher in any superior school, he must go through the most rigid examinations, both oral and written.

Collegial tuition in the German Universities does not exist, because wholly unnecessary, the student being fully prepared at the Gymnasium before he is permitted to enter the University. Without the Gymnasium, the University would be little worth. The course at the Gymnasium embraces a very thorough study of the Latin and Greek languages, a knowledge of the mathematics below the Differential and Integral Calculus, general history, and one or two modern languages besides the German, and Hebrew if the student design to study theology. The examinations are full and severe, the gradations of merit are accurately marked, and no one below the second grade is permitted to enter the University.

The Gymnasia thus guard the entrance of the Universities. Besides, the University course would not be available to him who had not prepared himself for it. It presumes certain attainments, and passes by the elements of the sciences. It is true, indeed, that a student may neglect his opportunities in the University, but then he throws away all hopes of professional life, and of employment in the State.

The Educational System of Germany, and particularly in Prussia, is certainly a very noble one. We cannot well be extravagant in its praise. Thorough in all its parts, consistent with itself, and vigorously sustained, it furnishes every department of life with educated men, and keeps up at the Universities themselves, in every branch of knowledge, a supply of erudite and elegant scholars and authors, for the benefit and glory of their country, and the good of mankind.

In comparing the University system of Germany with that of England, it is worthy of remark that Germany has also admirable common-school systems for popular education, while England is strikingly deficient in this respect. In the one case a properly-developed University system has reached its natural result of invigorating general education; in the other the priestly privilege of a cloistered learning is still maintained.

The Colleges of America are plainly copied from the Colleges of the English Universities. The course of studies, the President and Tutors, the number of years occupied by the course, are all copied from the English model. We have seen that in the English Institutions, the name of University alone remained, while the collegial or tutorial system absorbed all the educational functions. In America, while Colleges were professedly established, they soon assumed a mixed character. Professors were appointed, but they discharged only the duty of tutors in the higher grades of study; so that the tutors were really assistant professors, or the professors only tutors of the first rank. Our Colleges also have from the beginning conferred degrees in all the faculties, which in England belongs only to the University. By establishing

the faculties of Theology, Law, and Medicine, some of our colleges have approached still more nearly to the forms and functions of a University. By assuming the title of University and College indifferently, as we are prone to do, we seem to intimate that we have some characteristics belonging to both, and that we deem it in our power to become Universities whenever we please. Sometimes the only advance made to the higher position, is by establishing a medical school; which, however, has little other connection with the college than its dependence upon it for conferring the degree of Doctor of Medicine.

If we understand aright the distinction between a College and a University, the latter is not necessarily constituted by collecting together schools under the different faculties. These may be merely collegial schools. A University course presumes a preparatory tutorial course, by which the students have acquired elementary knowledge, and formed habits of study and investigation, to an extent sufficient to enable them to hear the lectures of professors with advantage, to consult libraries with facility and profit, and to carry on for themselves researches in the different departments of literature and science. A University course may be indefinitely extended at the pleasure of the student. He may here undertake the fullest philosophical education possible—passing from one branch of study to another, and selecting courses of lectures according to the state of his knowledge, and the intellectual discipline which he requires; or, having accomplished a satisfactory general education of his powers, he may next, either enter upon professional studies, or devote himself to some particular branch of science as the occupation of his life. In the German Universities any one, whether he designs to give himself wholly to a student's life, or to fit himself for a professor's chair, may, after undergoing the requisite examination, obtain from the faculty to which he belongs, permission to teach, without receiving any compensation, and only as a form of education. The professors extraordinary are selected from these licentiates, and receive a small salary. From these again the professors of the different faculties are usually selected. Every person of these three classes may lecture upon any subject he pleases: but professors are obliged, besides, to lecture on the branches particularly contemplated in their appointment. In this way at a University alone can the intellectual life be varied and enlarged. A University is literally a *Cyclopaedia* where are collected books on every subject of human knowledge, cabinets and apparatus of every description that can aid learned investigation and philosophical experiment, and amply qualified professors and teachers to assist the student in his studies, by rules and directions gathered from long experience, and by lectures which treat of every subject with the freshness of thought not yet taking its final repose in authorship, and which often present discoveries and views in advance of what has yet been given to the world. In fine, a University is designed to give to him who would study every help that he needs or desires.

A College in distinction from a University is an elementary and a preparatory school. A College may be directly connected with the University, or it may not. Its original connection with the University was partly accidental, and partly necessary. It was necessary to provide convenient habitations for students who flocked to hear the lectures of the doctor or professor. Many of these students might require private tuition, in relation both to preparatory and additional studies, and thus the Colleges would become places of separate study, under masters appointed for that purpose. This must especially have been demanded in the early period of the Universities, when preparatory schools were not common.

In Germany the Gymnasia are really the Colleges. The education which they furnish is more thorough, we believe, than what is obtained at the Colleges of either England or of our own country. In England, schools like that of Rugby, under the late Dr. Arnold, and those of Eton and Westminster; and in America, those schools commonly called *Academies*, and indeed other classical schools, are of the nature of a college, only of a still lower grade, and more elementary. In passing from the classical school to the college the studies are not essentially changed, nor is the kind of discipline. Hence, a student in our country can prepare at the second, third, and even fourth year of collegial study. In college there may be less of juvenile discipline, and there are generally greater advantages. What gives the college, however, its chief distinction, is the power of conferring academical degrees. We may say, therefore, the academy prepares for the college, and the college prepares for a degree. In England the colleges are directly connected with the University. But, it appears the University has fallen into desuetude, and colleges alone remain.

In our country we have no Universities. Whatever may be the names by which we choose to call our institutions of learning, still they are not Universities. They have neither the libraries and material of learning, generally, nor the number of professors and courses of lectures, nor the large and free organization which go to make up Universities. Nor does the connection of Divinity, Law, and Medical Schools with them give them this character. For law and medicine a thorough preparatory classical discipline is not required. In this respect the last is the most deficient of the two, and great numbers receive the academical degree of Doctor of Medicine who have never received an academical education. The degree of Doctor of Laws is more sparingly bestowed than any other; and this, as well as Doctor of Divinity, is never bestowed introductory to the entrance upon professional life. The schools of Theology approach more nearly to the University character than any other, since a collegial discipline is generally required preparatory to an entrance therein.

The course of study in our colleges, copying from the English, was, at their first institution, fixed at four years. The number of studies then was far more limited than at present, and the scholarship was consequently more thorough and exact. There was less attempted, but what was attempted was more perfectly mastered, and hence afforded a better intellectual discipline. With the vast extension of science, it came to pass that the course of study was vastly enlarged. Instead of erecting Universities, we have only pressed into our four years' course a greater number of studies. The effect has been disastrous. We have destroyed the charm of study by hurry and unnatural pressure, and we have rendered our scholarship vague and superficial. We have not fed thought by natural supplies of knowledge. We have not disciplined mind by guiding it to a calm and profound activity; but, we have stimulated acquisition to preternatural exertions, and have learned, as it were, from an encyclopaedia the mere names of sciences, without gaining the sciences themselves.

John Wesley Hoyt   1867

An Official United States Survey of Foreign Education

John Wesley Hoyt (1831–1912) graduated from Ohio Wesleyan University in 1849, attended Cincinnati Law School, and later graduated from the Eclectic Medical Institute in 1853. He then taught chemistry and medical jurisprudence until 1857. In 1870 he founded the Academy of Sciences, Arts, and Letters of Wisconsin, and he served as its president until 1874. He was governor of the Wyoming Territory from 1878 to 1882 and the first president of the University of Wyoming from 1887 to 1890. Hoyt represented the United States as an educator at various international conferences—as Wisconsin state commissioner at the 1862 London International Exhibition and as a national commissioner at the 1867 Paris Universal Exposition and the 1873 Vienna International Exhibition.

The extracts below, from Hoyt's report on education made at the Paris Exposition in 1867, include descriptive accounts of the educational systems of France, Holland, Belgium, Prussia, Austria, Switzerland, Spain, Portugal, Greece, Denmark, Sweden, Russia, and Italy. Hoyt mixed value judgments inconsequently with statistical details, and although the following extracts exclude many of these statistics, they illustrate the type of official descriptive accounts on foreign education made for the United States government. They are neither imaginative nor truly comparative, but they reflect an official viewpoint on contemporary educational developments in Europe.

In order to make more intelligible the subsequent references to the different classes of educational institutions to be treated of in this report, as well as all discussions of them and the relations they sustain to each other, it seems proper, first of all, to present in concise form a general outline of the present condition of education in the various countries which, by virtue of their educational representation at the Exposition, have demanded my attention.

In pursuance of this plan, it is my purpose to present, first, the educational spirit and policy of each of the nations represented, with their general statistical results; and, secondly, the results as manifested in the condition of the several great classes of institutions everywhere recognized.

In the collection of statistics, I have necessarily depended upon the authority of others. No pains have been spared, however, in seeking the best sources of information, personal application having been made in many instances to the heads of departments themselves, and it is believed that, in general, they present a very correct showing of the state and progress of education in the countries to which they refer.

In considering the different nations, the order observed will be that of their local occurrence in the Palace of the Exposition, except as to the United States, which, for convenience, will be presented last.

France

Since the year 1831, when the enlightened Guizot sent the no less able and distinguished Victor Cousin to Prussia to study and report upon the system of education in that country, much progress has been made by the cause of popular education in France.

Before that period, the imperial government and the subsequent royal dynasty had established and liberally supported many institutions for secondary, superior, and the highest culture; but the wants of the millions had been almost entirely ignored. The present, however, is full of activity and hope.

The French system of public instruction is all-comprehensive, embracing, alike, the highest and the lowest schools in the empire; the spirit which animates, and the power which controls and directs them, having their center at the throne, and diffusing themselves through the medium of officers of the departments, arrondissements, cantons, and communes, into which the empire is divided, thus reaching, or aiming to reach, the whole people.

The official classification of the schools for public instruction is usually: 1. primary, including all elementary and the lowest grade of normal schools; 2. secondary, comprising the royal and communal colleges, lyceums, and the second grade of normal schools; 3. superior, embracing the "academies" having

John W. Hoyt, *Report on Education: Paris Universal Exposition, 1867 Reports of the United States Commissioners* (Washington, D.C.: U.S. Government Printing Office, 1870), pp. 15–17, 19–25, 29–41, 44–45.

"faculties" of science, letters, law, medicine, and theology, together with a single superior normal school.

The control of these several classes of institutions is vested in the imperial council of public instruction, formerly known as, and even yet constituting that theoretical body, the University of France; and consisting of the minister of public instruction, three senators, five bishops or archbishops, three councilors of state, three members of the court of appeals, eight inspectors-general, three clergymen belonging to the Lutheran, Reformed, and Jewish churches, five members of the Institute, and two heads of private educational establishments; the intention of the government being to give the various religious orders and institutions of the empire a fair representation in the school system, which is intended to fit all classes of persons for respectable citizenship. It is also worthy of note that this liberality of purpose observed in the constitution of boards, councils, and committees is traceable through all subordinate ramifications of the system.

All the members of this grand council are annually named by the Emperor; its meetings being semi-annual for the consideration of existing and amendatory regulations. There is also a council of thirty, with the minister at its head, entitled the superior council of improvement for special secondary instruction; a health commission of ten for all classes of schools; and a committee of patronage for infant schools, consisting of the archbishop of Paris, a senator, two chiefs from the staff of the minister of education, and twenty of the distinguished ladies of France.

Subordinate to the imperial council are regulations and officials not unusual in any important particular, yet usually ample and well-devised as by an authority intending to have itself felt and its results beneficial to the furtherance of the great end in view.

To insure efficient working and a faithful performance of duty by teachers in the various grades of schools, numerous inspectors are provided—eight inspectors-general for superior instruction, three for the faculty of letters, three for the faculty of science, and one for each of the faculties of law and medicine; eight inspectors-general for secondary instruction, four for letters, and four for science; four inspectors-general for elementary instruction, and four honorary members of inspection, co-operating with each several class. There are also academy inspectors, numbering as many for all the academic districts as there are included departments. These inspectors are assisted

by a rector, who is in charge of the normal and primary instruction for that district. More recently the infant schools are supposed to be under the supervision of the Empress, assisted by a number of ladies, salaried by the state, and numbering one for each academic district, which is the largest school division of the empire; and finally, there are a large number of departmental inspectors for the primary schools, amounting to one for each arrondissement, the civil division between a department and a commune, being no less than 363.

Private schools are allowed and encouraged, but instructors in these must pass the examinations required of those serving in the public schools; and the proficiency of their pupils and general school management are subject to a like oversight.

While it is obligatory upon the people to establish and maintain the required primary instruction in each commune, aid being given only when school fees and local taxes fail of sufficiency, attendance upon the schools is not obligatory. The age at which those who do attend pass out of any public instruction of this grade is determined quite as often by the ages at which they receive their first communion in the church to which they belong as by their attainments in school knowledge. For the Catholic church, this age is twelve; and for the Lutheran, sixteen. Thirteen-fifteenths of the French population is of the communion of the church of Rome.

Religiously considered, in the administration of its school system, the government is most judicious and liberal, recognizing the equal rights, before the law, of Catholicism, Protestantism, and Judaism, the three great generic and irreconcilable religions of Western Europe. Instructions in religion are given in all public schools; but no child is obliged to receive instruction in any creed denied by the parents; and in all cases where it is practicable and desired, separate schools for the children of differing denominations are provided. There is nothing in the law either requiring or disallowing this practice, it being, as in the question of mixed or separate schools for boys and girls, left to the circumstances of the communities and the discretion of the local authorities in charge of the schools. As a rule, there seems to be a preference for separate schools for the sexes and the religious orders. . . .

Holland

Public instruction in Holland is divided into the usual grades, with primary schools, ordinary and superior, in one of which all private ones of this class must rank.

The scheme of organization is simple. The minister of the home department is the supreme officer in charge of this interest. The eleven provinces of the kingdom are divided into eighty-nine school districts, and these into communes, in each of which there must be a primary school in the care of a local board; and each commune of 3,000 persons has a school commission. For each district there is an overseer, who is chairman of all the commissions within his jurisdiction. At the head of the districts embraced in a given province is a provincial inspector, salaried by the state, whose duty is to superintend all the schools in his province, receive the reports of district overseers, and once a year to sit in the council of provincial inspectors, under the presidency of the minister, upon the general interests of primary schools throughout the kingdom.

Secondary instruction is provided for and looked after with an equally Dutch straightforwardness of action.

Children are admitted to these schools without distinction of creed; and while it is the avowed purpose to have primary instruction "tend to develop the reason of the young and to train them to the exercise of all the Christian and social virtues, the teacher is to abstain from teaching, doing, or permitting anything contrary to the respect due to the convictions of dissenters." In short, the teacher is expected and enjoined to cultivate the Christian virtues, but is prohibited from teaching any form of theological doctrine. Religious instruction, outside of the family, is left to the different communions, the school law favoring no one of them, though it expressly provides that "school-rooms may be used at the convenience of any of them, for the religious instruction of children attending the schools, out of school hours."

Primary schools must be in operation throughout the entire year, except during the time of recognized holidays.

The support of the primary schools, as in most countries, is required of the communes, which must also furnish them in sufficient number, the state deputies and the government being judge of that sufficiency. In the event of a commune proving unable to support the needed schools, the province in which it is found and the state share equally in meeting the expense.

The law further provides for a liberal minimum compensation to teachers, and that the communes furnish them a residence and garden. It also fixes the maximum number of children to be placed under the care of an unaided teacher.

Attendance upon school is not obligatory; but is made practically somewhat so, by prohibiting parents from receiving relief from charitable institutions whose children have not been duly instructed in the elements of a popular education. . . .

Belgium

The school system of Belgium is very imperfect, yielding but inferior results.

As in France, the kingdom is divided into provinces, corresponding to the French departments, arrondissements, cantons, and communes. The minister of the interior performs the functions of minister of public instruction.

The law recognizes the following classes of schools:

1. Primary, including communal schools, founded, supported, and administered by the communes; private adopted schools, often a substitute for the communal, and receiving a consideration for instruction given; and private free schools, usually those of denominational orders, and which admit poor children gratuitously.

2. Superior elementary, or high schools.

3. Secondary, or intermediate schools, preparatory to the university, and known as Atheneums.

4. Normal schools, primary and secondary.

5. Superior schools—universities with faculties of philosophy, medicine, law, and theology.

The public communal schools are established and managed by the communal authorities, which are practically quite independent as to their establishment at all; though, if done, the schools are subject to the supervision of the government through cantonal inspectors appointed by the minister. It is the duty of the inspector, whose term is three years and who receives a per diem for service rendered, to visit each school within his canton twice in each year, and report to his next official superior, the provincial inspector. Of provincial inspectors there are nine; one for each province. They are appointed in like manner, with corresponding duties for their province, besides that of presiding at the cantonal conferences of teachers and making a report of the proceedings, as well as of all inferior inspectors, to the minister of education.

Once a year these provincial inspectors meet in council at Brussels, under the presidency of the minister, to consider all educational interests that may arise.

Teachers can only be appointed, upon favorable examination by a clergyman and a layman, from among candidates who have had at least two years' training in an approved normal school; and when appointed, are removable by the inspector, upon consultation with the communal council.

In the superior elementary schools, it is provided that one of the best in each province may incorporate into its scheme a course of normal instruction for persons fitting themselves to teach in the lower schools. Provision is made in the organization of the Atheneums for instruction in various industrial branches.

In addition to these courses, normal and industrial, separate schools are founded for higher advantages in acquiring proficiency in the art of teaching and in the application of science to the pursuits of life.

Superior education is furnished in two universities of the state, at Ghent and Liege, and two outside of government patronage, that of Louvain being Catholic, and that of Brussels liberal.

In special culture, there are schools of arts, manufactures, mines, and civil engineering, in connection with the state universities, and a superior commercial institute at Antwerp.

The policy of the government is, like some of its European neighbors, to give as little assistance as is possible to elementary instruction, and keep good the right to superintend its character and operations—that of the Belgian authorities limiting it almost within the encouragement given to communal school-house building, by loans of money to that object, returnable within a given number of years. From 1842, when the present school regulations were adopted, to 1851, there was such a decline in the public interest growing out, as it seemed, of the voluntary policy permitted in the communes, that few of them either owned or provided school buildings. At that date the government opened a credit of 1,000,000 francs with the communes in aid of school-houses, so that at this time they own some 2,500, capable of accommodating over 256,000 pupils. Still, looking at the condition of the education of the common people as favorably as possible, Belgium presents the spectacle of a militia of which scarcely over thirty per cent. can read and write, and a school population, two-thirds of which commence the labor of life in self-support without the rudiments of anything that can be called education.

Secondary and all intermediate education fares better, but is yet unsustained, in any just sense, by the public treasury. When superior and special institutions are considered in reference to the ways and means of their existence, the state shows to better advantage in the two universities of its care and those independent, giving instruction to nearly 2,000 students, while meeting more than half of the annual expenses of such schools as prepare for the higher professional positions of life.

It supports schools for the blind and deaf-mutes, for orphans, and for juvenile criminals. It liberally sustains a national observatory, about 20 public libraries, three conservatories of music, with more than 1,000 pupils incited to excellence by liberal rewards, and more than 50 schools and halls for drawing, painting, sculpture, and architecture, which together instruct scarcely less than 10,000 students, all of which institutions are aided or supported by public funds.

Prussia

First among the nations to adopt systematic regulations for the instruction of the people, and faithful to this policy through the strifes and upheavals of more than three hundred years, Prussia is fully entitled to its present rank as first in the educational world.

Owing to the war of 1866, and the absorption, as a consequence, into the kingdom of a number of the smaller states of North Germany, the school system of Prussia is undergoing modifications. At the date of this writing, however, none of these have been promulgated, even if determined upon, and this account must be understood, therefore, as referring to the period immediately preceding that great event.

The principal divisions are provinces, of which, in 1866, there were ten, and these are subdivided into regencies, circles, and parishes.

Its system of public instruction wears the features of a strong government. At its head stands the minister of education and of ecclesiastical and medical affairs, and a central council, of which he is president. This council is divided into sections corresponding to the three general interests of the department; the one devoted to the establishment and care of schools being the educational cabinet of the minister, and occupied in devising plans and executing such measures as meet with his approval and have the sanction of the law.

Next below is the provincial council, having general control of secondary education, and primary normal schools. A subdivision of this consistory (*Schulcollegium*) has charge of the primary schools of its province, being empowered to execute the statutes made and provided, and to decide upon the use of textbooks, subject to the approval of the minister, to whom all its transactions are reported.

Immediately below this is the church and school section of the supreme council of the regency, charged with the examination and appointment of teachers in the primary schools, with keeping the schools in good condition, and with collecting and disbursing school funds. It is presided over by the school councilor, (*Schulrath,*) who is a member of the regency council, and entitled to a seat in the consistory of a provincial council, to which, on behalf of the church and school committee, he makes report.

The educational officials of a circle are the councilor of the circle (*Landrath*) and the inspector, a clergyman, whose duty to watch over the schools of the several parishes of his circle is an essential part of his ecclesiastical functions. Finally, each parish must have its school, and each school its committee of supervision, (*Schulvorstand,*) consisting of the curate, two magistrates, from two to four notable persons of the parish, and its inspector, usually the parish clergyman.

In the larger towns and cities the general management of all the schools is intrusted to a board called the school deputation. This board consists of the burgomaster, (mayor,) members of the municipal council, pastors, and directors of the higher schools, while there is also a committee of management for each school.

Each of the heads of council, from the highest to the lowest civil division of the country, is appointed by the government, and each has the power of veto over the acts of the council, board, or committee over which he presides, and, in certain cases, over the appointing or elective school privileges of the people. Thus the entire school system is in the hands of the central power at Berlin.

The schools rise in gradation in the following order: Elementary, lower burgher, higher burgher, real, pro-gymnasia, gymnasia, and universities. There are, besides these, normal schools of the three grades, and a great variety of special schools devoted to instruction in the practical arts, in the application of science to industry, in liberal professions, and in the fine arts.

Religious instruction is an invariable rule, though the state expressly provides that "children whom the law allows to be brought up in any other religion than that which is being taught in the public schools, cannot be compelled to attend the religious instruction given in the same." The latest regulations upon this subject (1851) are to the effect that, "in the people's school all possible regard shall be had to denominational relations, and religious instruction left to the conduct of the respective religious bodies." As a rule, where Protestants and Catholics are each in sufficient number to render it practicable, separate schools are established. Any parish, however, may have a mixed school, if there is general agreement to do so, and the authorities concur. Most of the public schools are open to all children of proper age and qualifications, without respect to sex.

In regard to support of schools, each parish must maintain its own, if able, and being unequal to the charge, the circle, the province, and the state join equally in meeting the expense.

Provision is made for teachers in exemption from military duty during their studies, preparatory for and when engaged in instructional service, if, in the opinion of the authorities, they cannot be spared from their work; also, for compensation while thus employed, and for support when no longer able to serve. The number of pupils that may be placed under the care of one instructor is always regulated by law.

While attendance is strictly obligatory upon the schools provided during school age, from seven to fourteen—unless by special permission—parents furnishing instruction in other ways are not released from support of the public institutions. To increase the necessity for the education of children whom poverty or the avarice of parents might tempt to place at work, to the neglect of school opportunities, the law prohibits, by severe penalties, the employment of any person under sixteen years of age, unless satisfied by certificate from the school authorities that he has a knowledge of the required rudimentary branches of education. Exceptions are made in cases where an employer of large numbers of young persons maintains a good school, at his own expense, for the instruction of his employés during a certain number of hours each day; and a default to furnish any child in such employ this opportunity, three times in five years, forfeits to the employer the right to forever after engage in his service any under that age.

The Prussian government, while dispensing from its general funds only so much as is needed to make good the deficit in local taxes and school fees for primary instruction, does yet, by its school enactments and liberality, so keep equal to their demand the great body of its people, that all ranks and denominations seem to have a common pride in the maintenance of their position as leaders of popular education. And since the people are the basis of all financial possibilities within the dispensation of public authorities, their readiness to contribute to all classes of secondary, special, and superior schools must be equally great, since, besides its nearly 25,000 common schools, with an attendance of about 3,000,000 children, Prussia presents an array of institutions of the higher and highest rank no less honorable to its liberality and wisdom. No enumeration of these will be made here, as in the body of this report there will be frequent occasion to refer to them in illustration of the grades under discussion. In no country in the world, however, is the public outlay of means for schools of all classes more liberally responded to by the popular, voluntary purse—a standing argument against the few who undertake to make it appear that the people who are compelled to have elementary education do not value it, or make haste to add to it; and a perpetual memorial to other nations in favor of popular school instruction. . . .

Austria

A statement of the number and classes of schools found within the Austrian empire would give evidence of a satisfactory condition of education in that country. Besides the eight universities of its superior instruction, there are 65 lyceums of philosophy; 2,138 gymnasiums; a number of professional and technical schools, and of lower, secondary, and primary almost enough to make a school, of some sort, for each parish. But where there is a spirit of national interest, and a really efficient working in the public school system of a country, there will not be found any difficulty in procuring its records and statistical reports. Such reports, with the freshness and accuracy of a people awake to so great an interest, could not be found. Again, it must not be forgotten that the schools

now established suffice for a population of 36,000,000.

Justice to the liberal spirit, both in and outside of the government, demands, however, that there be taken into the account of its present condition the difficulties with which it has to contend in establishing anything like a national system of public instruction. Principal among these are the great diversity of its populations, with no homogeneous principle of unity among them, and the powers of a church and an aristocracy, both averse to the liberal diffusion of knowledge among the masses of the people. These, like an incubus of great darkness, have rested for generations upon the vast possibilities of its intellectual development.

In view of all the circumstances, the actual number and grades of such schools as do exist are creditable to the government.

The general system of organization embraces a council, superior and subordinate, of superintendence and inspection, in which the civil and church authorities are of equal numbers and powers, the whole under the control of the minister of education.

The classification of schools is similar to that of Prussia, though the inferior primary schools are quite below, and the superior ones much less numerous, and all less efficiently managed than those of its enterprising neighbor.

The qualification of teachers and school attendance are so loosely provided for, and so little looked after, that the average actually in school, from seven to twelve years—the Austrian school age—is but little over fifty per cent. for the whole empire. In the German provinces, where the people come more directly under the influence of a liberal culture of other people, the statistics show, in a population of 12,000,000, a superior grade of higher schools, and of primary 11,158, with a board of instruction numbering 17,853, and an attendance of 1,645,816 children, making a per cent. of the school population of, for different portions and years, eighty-six and ninety-four.

In 1864 the municipal council of Vienna made a step in advance of any portion of the kingdom by establishing in each of the eight parishes of the city a superior *Bürgerschule,* (citizens' school;) and later, by memorializing the council of public instruction, to the end of securing to their national system the efficiency of that of Prussia.

While considering the ways and means of providing for such changes as were involved, the Austria-Prussian war of 1866 seemed to

delay so desirable an accomplishment; but
the more immediate contact of the less cultivated Austrian soldiery with the better educated and victorious Prussians, and the fact
that not only their own government, but the
intelligence of all civilized peoples, attribute the advantage of the latter to the more
thorough mental discipline acquired in their
schools over that of the comparatively uneducated enemy, are telling with more certainty than human prescience could have pre-
dicted upon the Austrian demand for a better
popular education.

Switzerland

The Swiss system of popular education
possesses peculiar interest to the people of
the United States, owing to the general resemblance it bears to our own. There is,
in fact, no national system, each cantonal
division of the republic, of which there are
twenty-five, having its own system complete.

An account of these, in detail, would be
neither profitable nor practicable, and a mere
outline will be given of what, for the want of a
more fitting term, may be called the school
system of Switzerland.

The spirit of this system is at once
Christian and democratic. Its administration
rests primarily in the cantonal minister of
public instructions, with shared or delegated
aid from a board made up of three or more
members elected from the communes, or
sections, which are the only school divisions
known to the cantons. These communal
directors are, one for each, elected by the
people to look after the school of its locality,
and furnish, at discretion of the minister, a
board, of such as he may select therefrom,
to co-operate with him for the general good
of the entire canton, which answers substantially, for the purposes under consideration,
to the State of our federal Union.

The gradation of the schools is essentially
German; and for the inspection there is a
plan adopted similar to that noticed in several
other countries—the communal inspectors
reporting to the cantonal, and these to the
minister, in regard to whatever relates to the
fulfillment or evasion of the law and the
general condition of the schools.

The provisions for securing good teachers
are admirable, and in evidence that it is far
enough from either the theory or practice of
the Swiss citizen to consider a poor teacher
as better than none, or a better teacher,
at advanced pay, more expensive than one less
qualified at a cheaper rate.

Attendance is obligatory in most of the
cantons unless it can be shown that children
not in the public schools are receiving equally
good instruction in private schools or at
home; and even then, so jealous is the state
in its guardianship of this great interest,
children having instruction outside of the
public schools must undergo examinations to
ascertain whether their proficiency equals
that demanded by the system publicly administered. In some of the cantons the prescribed
school age is from seven to fourteen, and in
others from six to sixteen.

Notwithstanding this generally enforced
acceptance of the instruction provided, there
is a large margin in the construction of the
law as to the length of the school year, and
provision made for allowed discontinuance,
after the twelfth year, of such children as
are very inconveniently situated, or who are
a necessity to poor and infirm parents.

The policy in regard to the support of the
schools is much the same as that in Germany,
and a general interest is maintained in them
as vital to both individual and national prosperity. Whether their children attend these
schools or not, all persons liable to taxation
contribute to their maintenance; and eight
days before each annual commencement, a
copy of the school law is sent to every person
interested in its observance.

The gymnastic and military exercises connected with the public schools form a very
interesting feature, and help to keep good the
popular enthusiasm in regard to them. So
much importance does the government attach
to this branch of the public instruction that
it sends each year, at its own expense, suitable young men to the great gymnastic establishment at Dresden, to qualify themselves
to teach the best practices of the world in
their own institutions. The skill of improvement and adaptation to their home needs,
with which these "best practices" of other
countries are adopted, has often been noticed
by foreigners, and from a distinguished
French school commissioner brought the
statement, "that Germany might well send, in
its turn, some of its best subjects to study
gymnastics in the cantonal schools of Switzerland.". . .

One cause of the efficiency of public action
in the cantons of confederate Switzerland
ought not to be overlooked. While the population of the country is of diverse nationalities
and represents extremes of devotion in the
great classes of religionists—Catholic, Protestant, and liberal—it has been the policy
of the several governments to tolerate all

religious beliefs; nay, to treat all alike generously, but, at the same time, to enforce the duty of public instruction, notwithstanding the opposition of any sect. In this work Switzerland has had a fair amount of hinderance, but in evidence of the independence of the state in this regard may be cited a resolution, passed in 1867 by the grand council of Bern, the substance of which sets forth, "that the absolute obedience which members of religious orders owe to their superiors being found incompatible with legal requirements concerning instruction, no persons belonging to such orders shall henceforth be employed upon the public educational staff, and that all such persons now employed are to be considered as having resigned."

Spain

One of the first European states to establish great universities in the Middle Ages, and for subsequent centuries the nurse of science as well as the "cradle of great captains," for the past hundred of years Spain has so lagged in the great march of the nations that the world has well-nigh lost all hope of seeing her ever awake and put on new energy for the fulfillment of a mission more in harmony with the spirit of modern times; but the past few years have shown that she has not yet gone into hopeless decay—that she too has shared in the educational impulse destined to reach every portion of the earth, and is now determined to advance to an honorable position among the more progressive and enlightened nations.

Public education in Spain is under the general direction of the minister of public works, commerce, and instruction, and a royal council—embracing six sections, to wit, primary instruction, philosophy, ecclesiastical science, jurisprudence, medical science, and administration of public instruction.

The general division of instruction is into primary, which is gratuitous and obligatory by law; secondary, which includes the colleges and all institutions of like character and grade; superior, or faculty education, which embraces the university courses; and professional, which is given in the special schools for music, painting, sculpture, and architecture, bridges and highways, forests, arts and trades, &c. The clergy, which has its courses and theological faculties in the universities, has, besides these, over sixty episcopal seminaries, in which there is a wide range of studies, leading from the Latin grammar up to the doctorate. In 1864 these ecclesiastical colleges numbered 23,614 pupils.

In presenting the extensive and highly interesting collections destined to have place in Classes 89 and 90 of the Exposition, the Royal Commissioners for Spain made the following very encouraging statements:

"Within the past few years primary instruction in Spain has had considerable development, in consequence of the many encouragements that have been given to this interest by the government and of the sacrifices imposed upon themselves by the municipalities. In fact, the expenses incurred for the *personnel* and *matériel* of the schools amount to a third of their budgets. Since the publication of the law of the 9th of September, 1857, which regulated the pay of teachers, and fixed the proportion that each center of population should pay, according to the number of inhabitants, in aid of primary education, the number of schools has increased prodigiously, and has even doubled within the last ten years. We can certify that now there is not a single hamlet that has not its teacher and the necessary resources for the maintenance of one school for each of the two sexes. If we add, moreover, that this same law has rendered primary instruction obligatory, in granting to judges the power to condemn to a penalty, the extent of which varies according to the offense, all parents who do not send their children, between the ages of six and nine years, to the schools, we shall have the explanation of why the schools have multiplied in so short a time and the number of pupils reached a very considerable figure; also the ground of our hope that in a few years Spain will, in this respect, have nothing to envy the most civilized nations of Europe.

"This result, so satisfactory, has been obtained also through the creation of normal schools, which have been improved by successive special regulations, and which each year furnish the necessary number of teachers of every grade. These schools have also facilitated among all classes of society the means of acquiring those primary ideas which are the basis of more extensive information in every department of knowledge. On the other hand, the provincial inspectors have rendered important service since the date of the creation of that office, whether in stimulating the zeal of municipalities for the establishment of new schools or in inciting teachers to give instruction as extended as the faculties of their pupils and the circumstances of the locality will permit.''

The objects exposed in the educational classes of Group X [of the Exposition] embrace every department of primary instruction, together with a great number of popular scientific and other works designed for a wider diffusion of knowledge among all classes of the people, and, in the aggregate, were a most welcome indorsement of these words of the Royal Commission, as well as additional warrant for the reference I have myself made to the future of education in Spain.

Portugal

Public education is even more backward in Portugal than it was in Spain twenty years ago.

The schools are primary, secondary, (chiefly lyceums,) and superior, (including all above secondary.) These interests are under the direction of the minister of the home department and a royal council.

The regulations in regard to teachers and the obligatory education of children are fair in letter, but none of them are enforced with spirit and energy, so that the number of schools, and of children in attendance upon such inferior ones as do exist, is lamentably small.

Greece

It is not possible to think of the past glory and present wretchedness of Greece without sad reflections upon the transitory nature of even national eminence.

Greece, once the intellectual mistress of the world, adorning its civilization with the triumphs of her genius in every department of art, science, literature, and philosophy, to-day a feeble community, ranking but as a petty kingdom, and that only by the grace of nations having no existence in the days of her ancient glory!

But there are still sparks of living in the embers of her departed greatness, and we find her, through representative lovers of learning, demanding a place for educational contributions in the Universal Exposition of 1867.

Under the system of instruction inaugurated within the past quarter of a century, no little progress has been made in diffusing the blessings of education among all classes of the people. Over 50,000 children are now in the primary schools, over 5,000 in the Hellenic, (a secondary school based upon the study of Greek,) some 2,000 in the gymnasiums, over 600 in the University of Athens, and a considerable and yearly increasing number in the normal, industrial, scientific, and professional institutions.

Denmark

The Scandinavian states have long been noted for the excellence of their common schools and the universality of rudimentary education among the people.

In Denmark popular education has been provided for and fostered by the government for more than three hundred years. Under the law, operative since 1814, the general control of this interest is in the hands of a minister of public instruction and subordinate superintendents for the several departments of the kingdom.

Each parish is obliged to furnish good primary-school buildings, with teachers for the instruction of children in reading, writing, arithmetic, the Lutheran Catechism, grammar, history, and geography. There are normal schools for the training of teachers, which add to these more primary branches studies in mathematics, the natural sciences, pedagogy, gymnastics, drawing, and music.

The secondary schools are high or grammar schools, and furnish instruction in the Danish language and literature, in Latin, Greek, French, and German, and advanced courses in mathematics, the natural sciences, &c., and are found only in larger towns and cities—about thirty in number for the entire country.

The schools are well managed, and bring corresponding results, the profession of schoolmaster being honored and education valued.

Schools of superior rank are liberally sustained and patronized, the income of the University of Copenhagen reaching to nearly $75,000, with an attendance of students there and at the University of Kiel, which has an income of about half as much, and libraries embracing 175,000 volumes.

In special education, there are schools polytechnic, military, naval, of forestry, and medicine, an academy of the fine arts, and those usual for the unfortunate.

From the first movements of the state in the direction of popular education, it was compulsory, to the extent that the church refused confirmation—without which no person could be employed, apprenticed, or married—to such as could not read and write; and under the present law it is unconditionally imposed upon all parents that their children shall receive instruction in some approved school from seven to fourteen years of age, and the law is respected and effective.

Sweden

The government of Sweden nobly began the work of popular education almost two hundred years ago, demanding of every youth who would be confirmed by the church—without which the royal road to marriage and all the avenues of success in life were closed to him—that he should show that he was able to read and write. The result of this intelligent and thorough educational policy, well followed up by the adoption of improved systems, is that at the present time, while occupying an inhospitable and half barren country reaching north to the Polar Sea, Sweden probably has as small a per cent. of persons within its borders who cannot read and write as any country in the world.

The Swedish system embraces the usual classes of schools, the primary being mainly under the control of the clergy, who are of the Lutheran faith. To each diocesan consistory, having care of all the schools within its ecclesiastical jurisdiction, inspectors appointed by the state have, more recently, been added, the improved condition of which testifies to the advantage secured.

The law of 1864 required the establishment of a school in each parish; but the sparseness of the population in portions of the country rendered the law, of necessity, inoperative, and the authorities fell back upon the perambulatory system that had been so successful in Norway. There are at this time more than 16,000 of these itinerant schools held for a few weeks, or for a few days in each week, in given localities, and furnishing instruction to about 125,000 pupils.

In the more thickly settled portions of the kingdom the parishes are divided into districts, each having its permanent school, the whole number of which is over 2,000, with 150,000 in attendance; in the higher public schools are 6,000; in private schools, 20,000; 150,000 educated at home—making a total of nearly 500,000 receiving public primary instruction, or some education of equal value.

The quality of the culture secured at these schools may be judged from the studies pursued in the most elementary of them, and everywhere advanced and improved upon in the permanent schools of towns. These studies are religion, the Swedish language, geography, mathematics, Swedish and general history, natural history, writing, music, drawing, and gymnastics.

The legal minimum compensation of a teacher is not so much money, but an amount of the necessaries of life, such as corn, firewood, pasture, a garden, a house, &c. If a faithful teacher and well liked, he may expect to, and usually does, receive more from the school patrons; but this much he is guaranteed, and in case of failure in the school district to meet his needs, the government comes to his aid.

Attendance upon the schools is obligatory between the ages of nine and fifteen.

Secondary education is given in schools of learning—corresponding to the pro-gymnasia of Germany and grammar schools of England —gymnasia, and apologist schools. The first two afford instruction in the higher mathematics, Greek, Latin, German, and French, and are preparatory to the university. The apologist schools teach the same, with less of the classics, and answer more nearly to the real schools of Germany.

Normal and special instruction can be had, to a considerable extent, in its 8 normal schools, 1 school of agriculture, 2 horticultural schools, 7 schools of forestry, 9 schools for the arts and trades, 1 for naval construction, 9 for navigation, and an extensive polytechnic school.

Superior education still flourishes in its two ancient universities of Lund and Upsala, with their 77 professors and 1,500 students. . . .

Russia

This grand empire is making no less rapid strides in educational matters, under the enlightened policy of the present Emperor, than in the development of its vast resources and the general amelioration of the political and social condition of its population.

Since the foundation laid for intellectual culture by Peter the Great, universities and other institutions of a high order have had an existence in several of the larger cities. So long, however, as a large majority of the people were slaves, and it was the policy of the government to keep them so, scarcely anything was done for the establishment of a grade of schools lower than professional and gymnasia—such as were essential to the education of the nobility, and to qualify the few for different branches of the civil service. But the shackles of serfdom were no sooner knocked off than the people began to call for schools. Even the late serfs undertook, of themselves, in many instances, the work of establishing them; so that, while in 1861 there was scarcely a public school for the peasantry in the empire, at the close of the second year of their emancipation 8,000 schools had sprung up, all of them for and supported by this class of persons.

The government, also, recognizing the necessity of education for the people, has adopted measures for the multiplication of schools of every grade. Nor has the educational movement stopped here. The church has awakened to this great interest, and is more actively enlisted in the cause of education than ever before, so that the schools supported by the church alone furnish instruction to nearly or quite 350,000 children, and the total number of pupils under instruction in the whole empire has advanced since the date of emancipation from less than half to more than a million, increasing the proportion of children in school from one in one hundred and fifty to one in sixty for the entire population.

Just previous to 1864 the budget of the minister of public instruction had grown to 950,000 rubles, of about seventy-five cents each. In 1864 the Emperor had determined to establish many new parish or village schools, and, accordingly, 450,000 rubles more were added, making the total of that year for his department (the military, naval, engineering, and other like schools being under the universities) of 1,300,000 rubles. In 1865 the public aid to education had increased to 6,467,452 rubles. It should be borne in mind, however, that a large proportion of these sums was for secondary and superior schools—the parish schools for elementary instruction being carried on, as in other European countries, with but little help from the state.

The school division of the empire is into great circles, (ten,) provinces, districts, and villages or parishes. It was the original intention to have at least one university at the chief city of each circle, a gymnasium at the capital of each province, a lower secondary school in each district, and a primary school for every parish, the officers of the university circle to have general supervision of the schools of the three subordinate grades.

In the departments of secondary, superior, and special education so much of this plan

has been realized that Russia now possesses seven well established universities, with a total of 600 professors and 6,000 students; one superior normal school at the capital and several of lesser rank; three lyceums; over 90 gymnasia; about 500 district schools, (equal to American high schools;) some 70 theological seminaries; law schools apart from the universities; independent schools of medicine, surgery, and pharmacy; two or three schools of high order for instruction in the oriental languages, with over 1,000 pupils; two academies of the fine arts, with schools of art, instructing more than 1,000 students; a normal agricultural institute, and nearly 100 agricultural schools of various grades; an imperial school of mines, with 10 district and 70 primary mining schools scattered over the empire; one central and several subordinate polytechnic schools; 15 schools relating to naval and marine affairs; two schools of engineering; numerous technological institutes and industrial schools; together with general and special libraries, and a rapidly increasing number of scientific, literary, and industrial societies of almost every class known in the world.

At the present rate of its educational development, it cannot be many years before Russia will be entitled to rank among the most enlightened as well as the most powerful of nations.

Italy

In common school education, Italy finds herself in the same category with Spain, though far ahead of that country in the condition of science, letters, and art, as well as in the number of her institutions of higher learning, and in the multitude of her learned men. With all the glory that belongs to her as the nursing mother, for more than twenty centuries, of letters, of jurisprudence, of medical science, and of physics, as well as of art, the masses of the people are still in darkness. But Italy, too, has once more felt the electric touch of liberty, and to-day her educational Cavours, Victor Emanuels, and Garibaldis, with "Free and Universal Education" as their watchword, are now waging a war against ignorance and intolerance that must drive them, ere many years, from that beautiful and classic land.

The first efforts for the improvement of the instruction of the people began in Tuscany and Lombardy, under the stimulation and direction of Lambruschini, Thonar, and other distinguished educationists, through the medium of the journal of education known as the "Guida dell' Educatore," and quickly followed by the publication of valuable text-books for the schools, were not only successful in the provinces where they originated but extended themselves into other portions of northern Italy. But this was about the time of the enthusiasm awakened in many parts of Europe by the introduction of the Lancasterian method of teaching; and after a most extraordinary multiplication of blocks, charts, and other appliances for the schools that were exceedingly faulty, the work of progress lapsed, leaving the whole field of education in a fog of uncertainty as to means and methods; so that the present work of sifting methods and wisely directing the new movement, to be done by the educational leaders of Italy, is even more difficult than the pioneer work of their predecessors.

On this head, the author of "L'Italie Économique," in 1867, published by authority of the royal commission representing that kingdom at the Exposition, makes the following remarks: "At this moment, schools, books, methods, and instruments multiply themselves; but, it is necessary to say, without order, without preconceived direction. There are in the schools a few good books, in the midst of a multitude of bad ones, and such of these books and instruments as are esteemed and used in one province are unknown in another. The misfortune is, that no one knows for himself, and no competent person has taken it in hand to examine all these things and determine which to exclude and which to adopt for the use of the schools. If the Exposition should teach this alone, it would confer an immense advantage. A discernment, grave and assured of the best books, best instruments, best geographic charts, and best methods in use, even now, in all Italy, would contribute much to their diffusion and aid a revolution the most salutary that one could desire at this moment. Then would there work out for itself a career of progress, after the example of the most civilized nations, and perhaps make apparent what distinguished and impartial men have already affirmed, viz., that in the matter of public instruction Italy possesses a richness of which she has not yet become sufficiently conscious.". . .

Great Britain and Ireland

In the revision of the educational code of Great Britain, adopted in 1867, will be found some noticeable improvements bearing upon the condition and prospects of its elementary schools.

An annual sum of money is granted for public instruction administered by the department of education, of which the lord president is head. The object is to promote the education of the children of manual laborers. The means used are to aid local effort to establish and maintain elementary and normal schools for the instruction of children and training of teachers for this department. All schools receiving aid from this grant must be in the interest of some recognized religious sect, or have daily readings from the authorized Scriptures. They must also be open to the inspection of persons appointed by her Majesty in council, the committee on education having consulted with the religious bodies interested before nominating inspectors, who may not in the least interfere with the religious instruction given, or with the management of the schools, their duty being simply to ascertain whether the conditions of the aid given are fulfilled, and to report to the department.

Aid to establish schools in building, improving, and fitting up school-rooms and dwellings for teachers, is limited to the amount contributed by proprietors, residents, or employers of labor in the parish, or within four miles radius of the school. No aid is given to establish normal schools, buildings and fittings being obtained by voluntary contributions from those interested.

Aid is given to maintain both elementary and normal schools, upon the conditions hereinbefore named, to which are added the attendance and proficiency of pupils, and the qualifications and faithfulness of teachers.

Endowed schools, to receive aid, must meet the conditions required of those of lower grade, the annual grant to a school of this class being reduced by the amount of endowment income, the reduction being omitted when both grant and income do not exceed 15s. per scholar by average for the year.

Normal colleges, to which the normal schools are inferior departments, have aid to the amount of £20 per annum for each master, and £14 for each mistress—until the sums have reached, respectively, £100 and £76—who, having been trained there for two years, have completed the prescribed probation and obtained certificates for teaching in the same school until, with an intervening year, they have had two favorable reports from inspectors of the same, or been reported by the proper authorities as having completed a like period of service as elementary teacher in the army or royal navy, the poor, law, industrial or reformatory schools.

Masters and mistresses who have been trained for but one year may obtain certificates upon the same ground as those for two, in which case five annual grants of one-half the above-named sums are made to the institutions where they have been instructed.

The early history of education in Scotland compares more than favorably with that of England. Almost four hundred years ago it was enacted that children of the barons and freeholders should be sent to the parochial schools from the ages of six to nine years, and after that to seminaries of higher grade. Neglect of this duty met with a penalty very severe for the fortunes of the times. Later, and almost two hundred years since, legal steps were taken for the establishment of a school in every parish, with provision to assess the lands for that purpose.

Compulsory attendance has been the policy of the Scottish government; and the support and position accorded to instructors of youth from that early time, with the advance since made, not only in salary for service, but in the quality of that rendered, show that it has been the intention to magnify the office of the teacher, and to make the school-room tell upon the national prosperity both at home and abroad.

But as the old plan of leaving the education of the people pretty much alone has been found, in England, incompatible with the growth of liberal sentiment in the world and the growing importance of *the people*, so the old systems of schools in Scotland have proved unequal to the advancing needs of the times, and both countries are now experimenting as to the ways and means of a more efficient national scheme of public instruction.

William B. Hazen   1872

Comparative Education: A Military Viewpoint

William B. Hazen (1830–1887) graduated from West Point Military Academy in 1855, reached the rank of major general during the Civil War in 1864, and was appointed chief signal officer in 1880. In 1870 and 1871 Hazen made two six-month visits overseas as a military observer to report on European armies and tactical developments for the United States Army. He was with the German armies during the Franco-Prussian War and was later military attaché to the United States legation at Vienna during the Turco-Russian War. The following extracts, taken from Hazen's account of the Franco-Prussian War, suggest that the French defeat can be blamed on a poor system of public education and on a generally illiterate and apathetic population. Hazen praised the Prussian systems of education and military training but finds little to commend in the French systems.

Comparison of American, French, and Prussian Military Schools

It will be seen that in France the military schools do not, as in Prussia, form a distinct department, but are under the Minister of War, and also that only about one-third of the officers of the army are, of necessity, educated men, while in Prussia all must be so. It will be also noticed, that at the French schools there is almost a total absence of moral control, while in Prussia the opposite is true.

The great lack of a good preparatory education is loudly complained of in France,

and most of the first year in all the military schools is required to make up for this deficiency. The almost total neglect of mathematical subjects at all the special schools is very noticeable. The course at the Polytechnic is general, and the exact sciences enter into it largely. The great attention given everywhere to drawing, and all practical subjects of a military character, is very striking. The idea seems to be to take the French mind as it is, and adorn it, rather than, by a careful course of exact study, to improve it. There is, in fact, a disposition to diminish the already moderate mathematical element in the military education, and to increase the

William B. Hazen, *The Schools and the Army in Germany and France, with a Diary of Siege Life at Versailles* (New York: Harper and Brothers, 1872), pp. 289–291, 378–382.

literary studies. In the French system, the entire school course is given before service is seen, while in Prussia a certain amount of actual service must precede any theoretical course at the schools; nor is there in France, as in Prussia, any provision for recognizing, utilizing, and educating the talent of young men who have, by a few years' service, developed mental superiority.

It may not be amiss to compare these schools, in a few particulars, with our own at West Point. The Prussian system, which makes service universal, and in the highest degree respectable—even aristocratic—is enabled to secure the best possible officers without entire dependence upon exact school instruction; but in France we find, as with us, a partially voluntary military system, an attempt to make officers without previous training, and schools where the state endeavors to keep up the science of the profession by educating a portion of its officers.

The distinctive differences between the French and American systems are, that in France study and instruction are forced, under constant surveillance, and carried on in the lecture-room with very little use of text-books, while ours is almost entirely a course of voluntary private study of text-books, the recitation and blackboard being merely to test the students' actual progress in knowledge. Theirs is largely a practical course, including some literature, and very little mathematics; ours is largely mathematical, with about the same amount of literary study, and much less attention to drawing, with a practical course less extended in some respects, but vastly more general and thorough in others. While French students are but slightly educated in tactics and drill, except in their own arm, and the infantry and cavalry receive but a two years' course, and the standard of proficiency is so low that ninety-five per cent. graduate, our own school gives a thorough four years' course of civil education, embracing the whole range of exact sciences, makes each cadet proficient in every branch of service, and sets the standard of study so high that but thirty-three per cent. of the cadets can reach it. Theirs is little else than barrack life, and it is doubtful if this system can develop personal character of that high order sought at West Point, where each cadet is made to work out by himself, in his own way, his various tasks, while living like a gentleman in his separate room, paying great attention to neatness, the toilet, and the bath, controlled through his own sense of uprightness and integrity, rather than by surveillance.

The school buildings nowhere approach the excellence, neatness, and appropriateness of our own, nor did the cadets, wherever I met them, show the trimness and manliness of those at West Point. These comparisons will apply pretty generally to the English military schools, so far as I have been able to understand them. They are all institutions of special courses, and do not undertake to give a complete education in all the arms.

After seeing much of the best of the European armies, I believe that at the breaking out of our war our little regular army was officered by better technical soldiers than any army in the world, and this I believe to be due to West Point. . . .

Education and the Common People of France

Of the condition of the mass of the French people I have hardly spoken. Tourists, writers, and humorists are silent upon the subject. Mr. Kay, who has written so much and so well upon elementary schools in Germany, and small proprietorships in France, says nothing upon the former subject. Mr. Arnold reached them once at Toulouse. Mrs. Blunt has given us light in her magazine articles, but the actual condition of the great mass of French peasantry is to the world a sealed book. We have seen that the state has provided a primary school for about every six hundred of her people, corresponding to about one to each of our townships. At some time, about two-thirds of the children of France attend these schools, and a portion, perhaps half of them, perhaps more, pass through the primary course. The rolls of the army and other statistics and sources of information, show that somewhere between twenty-five and thirty-five per centum of the population can not read or write. Of the half who attend the primary schools irregularly, the amount of instruction is exceedingly limited, and the primary course itself is very elementary. Mr. Arnold says that the people of France are "not in the least bookish," and are "almost incredibly ignorant;" and, as regards the peasantry: "The merits of the French school system are undoubtedly more in the probable future than in the present or past, but the schools are there; and in the rise of the people in wealth and comfort is probably the only obligation that can draw these people to them."

After the third of the nation who can not read or write, there comes another third whose acquirements scarcely amount to any thing. One boy in about three hundred of the inhabitants passes through the higher institutions, corresponding to our high schools and colleges, and one in about fifteen hundred receives an education of the first order.

This ought to give some notion of the condition of the French people in respect to education. In viewing the great struggle with Prussia, this subject, I fear, has not received due weight. The common people of France seldom read books. They have no magazines, and newspapers are scarcely known among them. A city like Rheims, Rouen, or Asnières of fifty or sixty thousand inhabitants, usually publishes two or three little sheets, about such as we always find in every village of four or five hundred inhabitants in Kansas or Nebraska, and not more than a hundredth part of the population read them. The peasantry of France comprise upward of twenty-five million of the population, and, in villages of four or five hundred up to two or three thousand, one would look in vain for that leaven of respectable society which we find everywhere in our own country. The exceeding ignorance of these people is, of course, accompanied by superstitious and groundless suspicion. They are little controlled by reason, but seem, like the people of the South in our war, to possess the faculty of believing whatever is favorable to themselves. This peculiarity M. Gambetta availed himself of in forcing public feeling in France by the grandest series of falsehoods ever told from a chair of state. It was this that led them to condemn and execute as a spy every man who could not account for himself to their liking, and that caused their non-combatants to fall upon the wounded and isolated German soldiers and slay them, always believing that their own people would at once recover the ground.

We have no population that at all corresponds to the poorer peasantry of France. Even the mountain inhabitants of East Tennessee and Kentucky are vastly superior in intelligence and character, though not in morality, to the French peasantry. The old men are vicious, and wear a fierce and dismal expression of countenance; while the old women, usually with a white cloth about their heads, have faces as totally blank and destitute of any human expression as many of the lower animals. The children usually have round, fat, unintelligent faces. The young men, during my stay in France, were mostly with the army, and the young women were attractive only from the universal charm of youthful maidenhood.

These people live by agriculture and the common trades, in villages of a few hundred inhabitants. Their houses are usually of stone, one and a half stories high. Near the front door, which always opens directly on the street, is kept the compost heap for enriching the little farm. In Paris I have seen thousands of men, who labored upon the roads with a horse and cart, living in the streets, and sleeping under their carts upon an old sheepskin, from one year's end to the other —their poor old faces showing no more animation, hope, or happiness, than the horse which was their only companion. I fear that our people who visit France keep their eyes generally toward Paris, the Tuileries, the Bois du Boulogne, and the Grand Opera, and see little of real French life. . . .

It is to be hoped that we shall no longer look on France as an example of civilization worthy of admiration and imitation.

I claim little originality for the foregoing pages. I was compelled, by my limited time in Europe, to avail myself largely of the labor of others, and have written the book at a remote frontier post, without libraries, and compelled to rely upon the courtesy of our ministers at Berlin, Paris, and London for the necessary volumes of reference. I thank these gentlemen for their kind assistance.

I found much to admire in the simple, earnest life of the German people, who have accomplished so much by rational and persistent labor, and I have tried to be just in my criticisms upon French character and methods.

Our own service should derive important lessons from the Franco-Prussian war, and I submit this work to the public, and especially to my brother officers, as my contribution toward that result.

Birdsey Grant Northrop   1873

Should American Youth Be Educated Abroad?

Birdsey Grant Northrop (1817–1895) graduated from Yale College in 1841 and Yale Theological School in 1845. He was minister of the Congregational church at Saxonville, Massachusetts, until 1857 when he resigned from the ministry to become the agent of the Massachusetts State Board of Education. In 1867 he was appointed secretary of the Connecticut State Board of Education, a position he occupied until he retired in 1883.

In *Education Abroad,* a collection of essays, Northrop wrote a devastating polemic against "a foreign education for American youth," and he was remarkably successful in gaining the approval and strong endorsement of his views by the foremost American educators of the day. Among those who were persuaded to have their endorsements of Northrop's views published in his work were Charles W. Eliot of Harvard University, Mark Hopkins of Williams College, and James B. Angell of the University of Michigan.

The practice of educating American youth abroad has been steadily growing for a long period. But the present year has witnessed an unprecedented exodus of our youth to Europe. The extraordinary attractions of the Vienna Exposition are not the only explanation of this great migration. The fancied superiority of European Schools, the supposed economy of living on the continent, and a vague ambition for "foreign culture" have alike contributed to this result. More than all, fashion has given its sanction and created a furor in favor of European education. Example is contagious. The multitude now departing are likely to draw thousands more. Principals of foreign schools, soon to arrive, are already advertised to leave New York in August or September to escort the pupils committed to their care. Their circulars, some of them offensively pretentious, are sent widely over this country. Resident agents are employed to push their schemes.

The discussion of this subject is therefore timely. Connecticut cannot render a better service to her own schools or to the country, than by helping to check a fashion which practically disparages our own institutions, and withdraws the sympathies of those who would otherwise liberally support them.

American and European schools have their distinctive excellences, and can each learn much from the other. Of late the schools of Prussia have been over-praised. Though justly lauded by Horace Mann, Professor Stowe and others, thirty years ago, they do not retain the same preëminence. Relatively there has been greater progress in some other lands.

The Prussian system, though of acknowledged excellence, is in some measure stereotyped. A just pride in the laurels won, now tends towards satisfaction with past achievements. Such complacency does not foster that spirit of progress and improvement so conspicuous in Austria and America. The commendations well deserved in the days of Dinter no longer belong exclusively or specially to the Prussians. Stimulated, indeed, by their illustrious example at the outset, others have overtaken them in the race. These remarks apply to their public school system rather than to their magnificent universities and other higher institutions, which open opportunities for the broadest culture to the graduates of our colleges, especially to those in training for professorships, with fixed principles, studious habits, and disciplined minds. For the want of these requisites many American students fail to receive substantial benefit, even from the German universities. Inadequate preparation and application make those grand lecture courses comparatively worthless to them. Such passive absorption is not the true process of education. But aside from the universities, the so-called golden opportunities of continental culture have been greatly exaggerated.

For our youth, American schools are better than European. To send our boys or girls away to foreign boarding schools is a great mistake, or rather, one of the fashionable follies which is just now having its day. With fashion one cannot reason. I do not object that this fashion is costly in money, for that is one of its attractions, but costly in what is worth vastly more than gold, namely, character and practical culture. This fash-

Birdsey Grant Northrop, *Education Abroad and Other Papers* (New York: A. S. Barnes and Co., 1873), pp. 5–13; and in Stewart E. Fraser, editor, *The Evils of a Foreign Education or Birdsey Northrop on Education Abroad* (Nashville, Tenn.: Peabody International Center, 1967), pp. 1–9.

ion of to-day, experience and a wiser self-respect will surely rectify when the comparative results of the two systems come to be better understood. The fond hopes so often wrecked in foreign lands will at least serve as beacons in the future. It is not in France alone that a moral malaria pervades the atmosphere. The example of other cities besides Paris and Naples refutes the plausible but pernicious aphorism of Burke, that "vice loses half its evil by parting with all its grossness." In these luxurious centres a voluptuous refinement veils the grossest immorality under simulations of delicacy, if not under the sanctions of law, and *licenses* vice herself, if only robed in the semblance of propriety. A thin veneering covers the foulest corruption. To offend against *taste* is worse than to break the ten commandments, and vice has less to fear than vulgarity.

If parents accompany their children and still surround them with the restraints and inspirations of home, these objections are mainly obviated. The great advantage of foreign travel I freely admit. Personal observations abroad may happily supplement the school, remove narrowness, and stimulate the desire for knowledge. There is some sense in the old saying, "Drill a child thoroughly in the elements, and then set him on a horse and trot him round the world."

In the German schools the course of study is so unlike ours, the subjects and methods so peculiar, and the processes so *slow,* as to weary, if not disgust, the American boy. To him the school rules seem odd, if not arbitrary. Many American boys I found there ill at ease, if not discontented, grumbling and homesick, because, they said, these strange methods are not so well fitted to serve the practical ends of life, and meet the conditions of success in America.

In philological studies and researches, in the refinements of art, in music and in manners, European schools excel. But this linguistic and aesthetic culture, admirable as it is, poorly compensates for the loss of a more practical training, and for the neglect of our own vernacular and literature, too common with our boys educated abroad. These exiles return too often un-Americanized, if not un-Christianized. After carefully observing both processes and results, with large numbers educated abroad and at home, the conviction is forced upon me that the thousands of our youth schooled abroad return with an education less substantial than that afforded here, and what is far worse, with character less matured, even if not impaired.

The breadth and art, the elegance and re-finement, with perhaps the assumption of foreign airs, or aping of European customs, are by no means the surest conditions of success, in the practical duties and stern realities of American life. It should be remembered, too, that laws, customs, manners and institutions educate as well as the school. Like an atmosphere, this influence surrounds the child and unconsciously moulds his character. This element, healthful and invigorating in republics, is repressive in monarchies, where you witness on every hand an obsequiousness to rank, a deference to usage, an unquestioning submission to mere authority, unfriendly to the elasticity, the independence, and still more to the aspirations of the juvenile mind. The *gendarme* standing at every corner is only one of many reminders that there is always near you, or rather *over* you, the outstretched arm of resistless power. The incentives and methods employed in school government in America are more healthful and stimulating than those found abroad, where school discipline conforms to the prevailing political ideas and is essentially despotic. The military spirit is now dominant and all-pervasive in Germany. The school is one of the appointed agencies for diffusing aristocratic ideas and fortifying monarchical institutions. Education naturally conforms to the prevailing political sentiments. Our system aims at the development, protection, and prosperity of the individual. There the State is always the central figure. With us the Government is for the people as well as of the people. There the people are for the Government, and the children are taught that they belong to the State, somewhat as they do to their parents.

The juvenile mind, pliant and docile, yields to surrounding associations. Political freedom favors individual independence and manliness. Our youth should therefore be educated as Americans, and be well grounded in American ideas and principles. In the knowledge of men and things, in courage and aspiration, in push and energy, in solid utility, in the adaptation of means to ends, Americanism means more than German-ism or any other national*ism*.

To profit by the superior scholarship of the German gymnasium, the full course should be mastered, which occupies eight years. A partial course will be but a beginning in many branches, with the completion of none. The American boy needs about two years of preparation, especially in mastering the German language, for he cannot catch the spirit of the school while the recitations are in an unknown tongue.

Among the valuable results of such a ten-years' course may be named, 1. A thorough mastery of the German language, one of the most difficult as well as one of the most important of modern languages. 2. The most thorough training in the ancient classics, including both writing and speaking Latin, if not Greek. 3. Familiarity with German history and literature, with something of general history. 4. Besides the usual mathematical studies, prominence is given to drawing, music and "manners." The aesthetic element is carefully developed. Admitting then, the excellence of this instruction, does it compensate for the want of home influences at this formative period—from eight to eighteen years—when character is largely moulded and fixed? Then, more than ever, a youth needs the impulses, the instructions and aspirations that cluster around home, kindred and friends.

American society and associations, giving a practical knowledge of our modes of thought, intercourse and influence, are the very educational forces needed by the American student who aspires to lead or control public sentiment. The best training for public life in Germany is not, of course, the surest promise of success here. For American boys, German history is disproportionably prominent. As in the study of geography they wisely begin with the school-house, and then the village or city where they live, and build up all the world around that centre, so all the historical world revolves around Germany as the center. In connection with the thorough study of their own annals, love of country is most thoroughly and ably taught in German schools.

These manifold agencies, to a remarkable degree, develop the noble sentiment of devotion to Fatherland. But the patriotism there taught is so intimately associated with loyalty to the king, that it is inoperative on American boys. Discarding Caesarism, these inculcations of the duty of homage to the emperor, and of the doctrine of the divine right of kings, are foreign to them. The real truth, so much better than regal assumptions and royal prerogatives, they do not learn, and so the ties are not formed that should bind them to their native land. Constantly hearing laudations of monarchical governments, and disparagements of free institutions, the youth exiled at ten years of age do not learn to prize and love their native land. The magnificent architecture, the grand libraries, art galleries, churches, cathedrals and palaces, the museums, monuments and triumphal arches, the zoölogical and botanical gardens, impress their tender minds with such a glamour that they come into unconscious, if not avowed sympathy with this depreciation of their own country, and are virtually denationalized.

The experience of American colleges is believed to be nearly uniform as to the superiority in the qualification of candidates trained at home over our youth prepared for college abroad. The number of the latter class is relatively small. But the instances of eminent success, either in college studies or practical life on the part of American boys, chiefly educated abroad, are rare and exceptional.

It is plausibly said that our girls and boys are usually educated abroad in private boarding schools specially adapted to foreign youth. While there are some excellent schools of this kind, there are many others superficial and pretentious. The public schools of Germany are greatly superior to their private institutions. An eminent American author, with the best opportunities of observation, says, "There is no end to the swindling and pretence on the part of boarding schools in France and Germany." Says another, "My boy was swindled out of ten years' progress in a boarding school abroad." A prominent gentleman in Washington now acknowledges "results prove that sending my boy three years to Germany was unwise." An artist whose tastes and business favored his continuing abroad, where he had spent six years, and became thoroughly acquainted with European methods of education, says, "I have returned to America for the sake of my children." Similar experiences might be multiplied.

On such a question as this, opinions may be more influential than arguments. Certainly the mature judgment of our most experienced educators, those who have had wide opportunities for observing both methods and results at home and abroad, is entitled to special consideration. I therefore presented this question to the presidents of our leading colleges, and other eminent educators of our country, requesting their views, with liberty to print them. All but one thus addressed have replied, substantially endorsing my own convictions. Their position, culture and experience give weight to the opinions expressed, especially as some of them were once advocates of foreign education. The opinions of such men must command attention. Indeed they comprise the most authoritative verdict ever rendered on this subject.

The letters appended are given in the order of date, omitting only personal allusions. Though differing in their points of observation and in the objections named, they all concur in the same general conclusions. The following summary embraces the more prominent points urged:

1. All agree that the elementary and preparatory studies should be pursued at home.

2. Nearly all concur in the view that the collegiate course also should be completed in our own country.

3. There is a general agreement in favor of first completing the ordinary professional course in our own institutions.

4. Many favor a post-graduate course for the fuller pursuit of certain specialties in some of the great universities of Europe.

5. For the elementary and undergraduate studies, the experiments of *mixing* American and foreign systems of education fail oftener than they succeed. The gain is but a fraction compared with the loss. "It is surely to save at the spigot and let out at the bunghole."

6. Many cases are cited of persons who now deplore the mistake of their juvenile exile abroad, and their want of early training in incipient citizenship and the practical lessons of American life. "Such facts are attested by the sad experience of hundreds of American families."

7. One correspondent characterizes the class of persons described as cosmopolitan as ''an unhappy, useless and sterile breed''; and another speaks of them as a "hybrid class, neither Europeans nor Americans, ill adapted to practical duties in either hemisphere, out of adjustment with our society, and out of sympathy with our simple American life."

8. Superintendent Fallows cites the testimony of the leading German educators among us. While they complain of certain defects in our system, they are emphatic in saying, "American schools in processes and results are the best for American children."

9. Some affirm that competent Americans succeed better in teaching modern languages than foreign professors. Though knowing less of the language taught, they understand better the difficulties to be overcome, and the way to meet them.

10. American teachers show more tact and skill in stimulating and controlling American boys. Some speak of the want of adaptation and of success on the part of foreign teachers in American schools and colleges in the control of their classes.

11. Those who have been abroad from five to eight years in their preparatory course are usually found far behind their old school associates in their studies.

12. The "code of honor" prevalent in German universities is deprecated. The marks of the duel, which some American students have brought from Heidelberg and other German universities, are not here held as badges of honor.

13. The lecture-room system "is ill adapted to *ordinary* students, however profitable to advanced scholars."

14. The constant advocacy of monarchical government, and disparagement of republican institutions, together with the displays and pomp of royalty, tend to denationalize and un-Americanize the susceptible youth resident abroad from the age of ten to twenty years. The statesmen of Europe are experts in the use of pageants, displays and amusements. These specious proofs of princely munificence, and of regal sympathy with popular wants, are really effective forces to develop the loyalty of the masses, if not to repress thought and paralyze efforts for liberty.

15. National sentiments, traditions and histories, as well as social sympathies, strongly mould the plastic mind of childhood. Our exiled youth not only lose these needed lessons, but also those healthful local attachments which should bind them to the homestead, the neighborhood, the town or city, and the State.

16. The special facilities for studying modern languages abroad are generally conceded. Some, however, contend that the mastery of the principles and philosophy of a language by the study of its grammar and lexicon gives a higher discipline than the art of speaking acquired merely by conversation. Such fluency of speech comes by imitation—is easily gotten and soon forgotten, unless retained by practice. The power to read German authors is a higher attainment than the ability to use glibly the fewer phrases and smaller vocabulary recurring in ordinary conversation.

17. The methods and motives of school government are more healthful and inspiring at home than abroad. The "tunding," caning and flogging, so common in England, are barbarous. The discipline in European schools is essentially arbitrary and despotic. The military spirit is pervasive, and ill suited to American youth. The schools, instead of holding their graduates with pleasant memories, are often referred to with regret, if not disgust.

18. The cheapness of living was once an attraction to German schools, but the late Prussian war and the lavish expenditures of

some Americans have combined to advance prices, so that economy no longer invites to European schools. To some their greater cost has only made them seem the more aristocratic and attractive.

19. The moral risks incurred by our youth in foreign boarding schools are great.

20. Conceit is too often fostered with boys inclined to accept the semblance for the substance. "It sounds large to say, 'I was educated at Berlin.' " Modesty is the characteristic of true scholarship. While the genuine student is unharmed, the very young or superficial may become unduly inflated, and "get a foolish and hurtful taint of foreign airs."

21. The advantages of foreign travel after the requisite preparatory studies are fully conceded by all and urged by many.

22. Last and least, though by no means an unimportant objection, is the cost of foreign education. The average number of Americans visiting or resident in Europe is over fifty thousand, and the present season still larger, by reason of the International Exposition. The number at school is now greater than ever. The export and appreciation of gold and corresponding depreciation of our currency are sensibly affected by this mania for European education.

Joseph Parrish Thompson   1873

German and American Education: A Critical Comparison

Joseph Parrish Thompson (1819–1879), pastor of the Broadway Tabernacle Congregational Church from 1845 to 1871, was well known as an Egyptologist and theological writer. He helped to found *The New Englander* and *The Independent* and was a regular contributor to *The North American Review*. He was long a resident of Germany and died in Berlin a few years after the following article was published in *The New York Observer*.

Thompson corresponded with Birdsey Grant Northrop, secretary of the Connecticut State Board of Education, providing him with critical material on European education. Thompson's account comparing German and American education is based on a careful, lengthy, first-hand analysis of the topic, and he believed that "the superiority of European education is pretty much a tradition, which many cling to through ignorance of what has been gained in America in the past generation." Perhaps of greater importance is Thompson's suggestion that after graduation the "well-balanced" American student should go for a year or two of "eclectic study" at a German University. Likewise, he suggested that a German student who was looking forward to public life, would greatly benefit from a year or two at an American university studying political philosophy and the constitutional history and law of the United States.

The question of sending American youth abroad to be educated is of high public importance, since it concerns, in no small degree, the future of American scholarship, literature, patriotism, manners and religion. As a contribution towards these principles, I propose to give an analysis of the German and American methods and courses of instruction, with reflections suggested by a somewhat close observation of German training and its results upon mind and character.

1. For the easy acquisition of the French and German languages by their children, parents who can arrange to live in Europe might do well to reside for a term of years in France or Germany, with children between five and twelve years of age. In such cases it is assumed that the children, while mingling in school and at play with children of another tongue, will be kept under the social and moral influences of an American home; will learn lessons of patriotism and of religion with the English speech; and will be trained in the table manners, the personal habits, and the social courtesies, in which the well-bred Englishman or American is so superior to the average German, and even to the Frenchman. If you do not wish your child to eat with his knife, to suck down his soup like a maelstrom, to help

Joseph Parrish Thompson, correspondence, in Birdsey Grant Northrop, *Education Abroad and Other Papers* (New York: A. S. Barnes and Co., 1873), pp. 68–74; and in Stewart E. Fraser, editor, *The Evils of a Foreign Education or Birdsey Northrop on Education Abroad* (Nashville, Tenn.: Peabody International Center, 1967), pp. 64–70.

himself to butter or salt with his own knife
—because there is neither butter-knife nor
salt-spoon upon the table—to comb his hair
and blow his nose vociferously where others
are eating, to talk at the top of his voice, to
mix all sorts of vegetables in greasy gravies
steaming with onions, and to content himself
with a teacupful of water for his daily
ablutions, and with the alternate ends of the
same towel for a week, and to carry huge
chunks of black bread and raw sausage in a
bit of dirty newspaper to school for his
lunch; if you do not wish him to puff cigars
with his infant breath, and to utter a "Gott!"
a "Bewahre!" or a "Herr Jesus!" at every
incident of school or play; if you would not
have him learn to sit stolidly staring at a
lady in church without offering her his seat,
or to shove her off the sidewalk by always
keeping to the right; in a word, if you would
not have your child grow up in all things the
reverse of the quietness, the cleanliness, the
decorum, the courtesy, that mark the true
English and American gentleman, then do not
place him in his growing and plastic years
in any average "pension" in Germany. If
circumstances should necessitate his entering such a home, wait till he is old enough
to stand it or stomach it, without sacrificing
those properties of life which are inculcated
in good American families. To sum up all on
this head, if you can arrange to live abroad,
and thus to surround young children in their
earliest years with the healthy influences of
home and the invigorating atmosphere of
patriotism, in that case you may contrive,
without detriment to other interests, to give
them the facility of acquiring modern languages, and also the taste for nature and art,
which may be cultivated to such advantage at
any well-selected point in Europe. But, on returning to America, you will need to take
special pains lest the knowledge of foreign
tongues should be lost through want of
practice in speaking. Experience shows that
a language picked up so easily in childhood
may be dropped almost as easily through
disuse in riper years.

2. Young men and young women, between
twenty and twenty-five, who have passed
through the customary training of American
schools and colleges, and who have sufficient
stability of mind and character to be entrusted
with the care of their own principles, habits
and opinions, may be sent abroad to good
advantage for the pursuit of some specialty
in literature, science and art, under celebrated teachers, and for that enlargement of
mind, that generosity of judgment, that

amenity of feeling, that cosmopolitan appreciation of men, peoples and institutions, which a
sagacious and susceptible spirit will gain
from travel and residence in foreign lands.
A thorough college course at home, supplemented by an eclectic course at a German
university, and this again capped with the
professional course in America—or the latter
two inverted—would give a young man the
best possible preparation for his calling in
life. The sending of American youth abroad
with such a preparation, and for such accomplishments, is by all means to be encouraged; and the college officers at home will
be found the best advisers as to time, place,
and lines of study.

3. But for the interval between twelve
and twenty, Germany can offer to American
youth no better means of training than they
have at home, *nor so good a preparation for
American life as American schools and colleges provide.* A youth at this period might,
indeed, be well-enough educated abroad, so
far as mental culture is concerned, though
this is questionable; and if attended throughout his course with parental guidance and control, he might be kept true to the tone of
American manners, ideas and principles—yet
even then he must suffer a lack of discipline
in the English language, in American history,
and above all, in the practical, common-sense
American logic, and a loss of the *esprit de
corps* of the American Fraternity of Letters,
and of the inspirations of American patriotism and progress, for which no facility in
foreign tongues could ever compensate.
There will be exceptional cases, *but no wise
American parent who can avoid it will subject a child to the risks and privations of a
European education during the critical period
from twelve to twenty—certainly not alone!*
The private schools of Germany are so far
inferior to the best private schools in the
United States that these can be left out of
the estimate, and the comparison will be made
most fairly between the *Gymnasium* of Germany and the Classical Academy and College
of America, which cover the same period of
life, and between the *Polytechnic Schools* or
the *Gewerbe-Akademie* and the corresponding Scientific School—say, for instance, the
"Sheffield" department at Yale University.

The course of study in the Gymnasium
covers a period of nine years; in the first
five years the student is exercised in the following studies;

1. *Religion:* History of the Old Testament,
the Gospels, the Catechism, and the Songs
of the Church.

2. *The German Language:* Readings and declamations, studies in the Sagas, the poets and the historians, with lectures and grammatical practice.

3. *Latin:* Grammar, with oral and written translation, prosody, selections from Ovid, Cæsar de bello Gallico.

4. *Geography:* Physical and political.

5. *Mathematics:* Arithmetic to decimals; Algebraic signs and formulas; Elements of Geometry.

6. *Natural Science:* Preliminary lessons in the Animal Kingdom, in Botany, Mineralogy, and Anthropology.

7. *Greek:* Grammar, translation and composition, selections from Xenophon's Anabasis.

8. *French:* Grammar, Chrestomathy and composition.

9. *History:* Greek, Roman, and German.

To these are to be added lessons in drawing, in writing, and in singing.

Compare this with the studies at Phillips Academy or at Williston Academy, and you will see that in classical and mathematical studies the first five years in a Berlin Gymnasium do not carry a student so far as is required for admission to the Freshman class at Yale. In geography and history no greater advance is made; and the study of German and French would be at the expense of English to an American boy at a time when he most needs to be exercised in his native tongue. Is it wise, then, to send him abroad for no greater advantages than these?

The remaining four years of the Gymnasium run nearly parallel with the collegiate course in America.

Compared with the course at Yale College, neither in extent nor variety of instruction, in text-books nor in topics, is there a shadow of advantage in the German Gymnasium over the American College.

Why then send a boy of sixteen to Germany? The comparison given above of the course of study in a Berlin gymnasium with that pursued in the parallel years at Phillips' Academy and Yale College demonstrates to the eye that, in respect of discipline in the classics and the mathematics, and of general attainments in literature, history, and science, the American youth from 12 to 20 would gain nothing by forsaking his home-schools for the schools of Germany. The Gymnasium is the gate-way to the University; in the University, Faculties corresponding to the schools of Law, of Medicine, and of Theology in the United States, and to the post-graduate Faculty of Philosophy and the Arts

lately established at Yale, Harvard, Princeton, and other colleges, are grouped about a common center; instruction is given wholly by lectures, and the student selects his own course, and in that course his favorite professors. The Gymnasium and the University are sought by the sons of the wealthy, the titled, and the cultivated classes, with whom education is a passport to good society, and also by young men who are looking forward to one of the liberal professions, to the civil service, to a professorship, or to the pursuit of literature, philosophy, or science, in some specialty of the higher learning. This course is denominated "the *spiritual* culture."

But Germany has been awake also to the demands of recent times for an education directed to more practical ends, and based more largely upon the physical sciences and the knowledge of things than upon letters and the classics. For such an education provision is made in the *Gewerbe*-schools, crowned with the *Gewerbe*-Academy or Polytechnic. The course in the latter as to topics and aims is parallel to that of the Scientific schools in America, and since the German Polytechnic is supposed to offer special advantages to American youth, I propose to test this claim by an analytical comparison of the best specimens of each—say the Polytechnic at Carlsruhe or Berlin with the "Sheffield" at New Haven. In the *Gewerbe*-school, which is preparatory to the Polytechnic, the division and subdivision of classes, correspond with that of the Gymnasium; but the four upper classes will answer for a comparison with—say the "Hopkins Grammar School" at New Haven, as a preparation for the Sheffield. These classes study as follows.

1. *Religion:* Biblical History; Heathenism and Judaism; the first century of the Church; the Reformation; the Augsburg Confession, and the Canon of the Scriptures.

2. *German:* the poets, lyric, epic, and dramatic; history of German literature in the Middle Ages and in modern times.

3. *French:* Thierry, Rollin, Voltaire, Souvestre, Montesquieu, Barran, Molière, Guizot, with grammatical exercises, translations, and criticisms.

4. *English:* Survey of English literature; study of selected authors, in which Dickens' Child's History of England, and Irving's Sketch Book are combined with Bancroft, Macaulay and Shakespeare!

5. *History and Geography:* Greece, the Orient, Rome, the Middle Ages and Modern Times.

6. *Mathematics:* Algebra, Logarithms, Geometry (both analytic and synthetic), Trigonometry, Stereometry, elements of Differential and Integral Computation, with special reference to Analytical Mechanics.

7. *Physics:* Heat, Electricity, Magnetism, Motion, Steam, Electrodynamics, Cosmical Physics, Optics and Acoustics.

8. *Chemistry and Natural History:* Botany, Zoology, elements of the Anatomy and Physiology of plants and animals, Crystallography, Inorganic Chemistry, Organic Chemistry, Geognosy, Chemical Technology with laboratory work, elements of Comparative Anatomy. Neither Latin nor Greek is taught at all in this school.

In comparison with the Academic preparation for a Scientific School in the United States, the *Gewerbe*-school shows a superiority in the study of French (and naturally of German), and in the departments of Physics and Natural History, where the studies of the Freshman year in the Sheffield are, to some extent, anticipated in the *Prima* of the Gewerbe. But in Mathematics, Geography, History and English, the Academy boy in America is carried quite as far as the Gewerbe boy in Germany; and besides, the Academy boy has a training in Latin and Greek, in Cæsar, Cicero, Virgil and Xenophon, of which the Gewerbe boy has nothing at all, though one would think that a scientific education should embrace at least the rudiments of the languages from which the whole terminology of science is constructed! Thus far then the account between the Academy and the Gewerbe is fairly balanced, and the apparent superiority of the Gewerbe in preliminary scientific studies disappears when we pursue the comparison between the "Scientific" and the "Polytechnic"; for it is then seen to be not at all a difference of quantity or degree in the matter of a scientific course, but simply of the distribution or classification of studies through a given term of years.

Commonly the boys in the Gewerbe-school are of a lower grade socially than the boys in the Gymnasium, especially in large cities; —as a friend expressed it, "Gentlemen send their sons to the Gymnasium and the University, only the common people send to the Gewerbe-schools." From ocular and nasal inspection of some of these schools, I must say that an American boy of nice family ought not to be subjected to such companionship, for if "cleanliness is akin to godliness," the average Germans have sadly fallen from grace! And for that matter, even in the Berlin

University, an American student informs me that his German seatmates disgust him daily, in the brief intervals of the lectures, by taking from their pockets bread, cheese and sausage, done up in a smutty newspaper, eating with a jack-knife, and then combing their hair with unwashed hands. Such habits are largely national, but one sees less of them in the Gymnasium and the University than in the Gewerbe-school. Many boys use the latter as boys once used the Free Academy in New York, as a recommendation for business. The catalogue of one of the best of these schools in Berlin shows that the lower classes average about 100, the middle classes only from 40 to 50, and the upper classes dwindle to 10 or 12!

Coming now to the Polytechnic, to which the Gewerbe-school is preparatory, how does this compare with the corresponding Scientific School in America—say the "Sheffield" at New Haven? [I beg to be understood that I take Yale University as a standard with no invidious reference to other American colleges, but because I am familiar with Yale, and have its latest catalogue at hand.] To draw out in detail the comparison of studies, text-books, exercises, etc., between Sheffield and a German Polytechnic, would require too much space; so the reader will be so good as to accept the writer's testimony, from a minute analysis, that each and every study, in each and every subdivision, is as specifically and as thoroughly provided for at the Sheffield Scientific as at the Carlsruhe Polytechnic, not excepting the German and French languages, with only this proper difference, that the prominence given in the Polytechnic to German history and literature, in the Sheffield is assigned to English literature, history and composition. If a boy does not master his own language, as to style and expression, between 12 and 20, he never will; and no matter how many foreign languages he may know, his knowledge will be of no avail, unless he can use it readily, clearly and effectively in his own tongue.

The superiority of European education is pretty much a tradition, which many cling to through ignorance of what has been gained in America in the past generation. What would I not give to-day to have had in my youth the classical and literary training of a German Gymnasium and University as compared with what Yale College could offer forty years ago! But for the youth of to-day the difference is not worth the voyage across the sea. Unless private reasons should otherwise direct, the *undergraduate* period, whether in the College or in the Scientific School, can be spent to better advantage at home than abroad, even for the general object of intellectual training, apart from the specific adaptation of that training to American life.

After graduation, the well-balanced student should come to Germany, if possible, for a year or two of eclectic study at a University. For the same reason the young German who is looking forward to public life, and who would fit himself for the responsibilities of these times, should go to Yale or Harvard for a year or two of study in political philosophy, and in the Constitutional history and law of the United States. And what a world of good it would do these young German licentiates to spend a year or two at New Haven, Andover or Union in learning to put *thought* into their sermons. The immense superiority of the American pulpit over every other excepting that of Scotland lies in its thinking power; and it will be a sorry day for the American churches if, in a blind quest of popular effect or of the baser element of commercial success, they shall part with one iota of what has made their strength, their glory, and their increase. Said a leading English minister to me, "Your American preachers *think* where we Englishmen *talk!*" Said the greatest Professor of Theology in Germany, "We have no such preaching as the American in Germany. Ah! if we could only .have your union of thought with heart, of strength with feeling, of science with scripture, we might get hold upon the mind of Germany with the Gospel."

This thing lies partly in the mental habit of the American, but much also in the method of training—the breadth, the comprehensiveness and the logical vigor of the American education, compared with the minuteness, the particularity, the exhaustive traditionalism, and the speculative fantasy of the German.

James Morgan Hart   1874

German and English Universities: Models for America

James Morgan Hart (1839–1916) graduated from the College of New Jersey in 1860 and from the University of Göttingen in 1864. He also studied philology at Berlin, Geneva, Leipzig, and Marburg. Hart was professor of modern languages and English literature at the University of Cincinnati from 1876 to 1890 and taught at Cornell University from 1890 to 1907.

Hart's comparative account of German, English, and American universities is based on several years' residence and study in Europe. He did not visit either Oxford or Cambridge, so some of his comparisons were not based on first-hand experience. He was on surer ground when he contrasted the character and atmosphere of a German university with an American institution, specifically, Marburg with Princeton. His highly readable work concludes with useful suggestions for Americans considering studying abroad and became standard reading for those undertaking graduate studies at a German university.

Comparison of German and English Universities

I approach this part of the subject with reluctance. Not having visited either Oxford or Cambridge, my knowledge of the English university system is at best only second-hand, and confessedly imperfect. English scholarship ranks high in America. We are apt to regard the best men of Oxford and Cambridge as prodigies in their respective departments. Without intending to speak in disparagement of the English universities, I venture to put in a word of dissent from the indiscriminate praise that is heaped upon them in Mr. Bristed's work. One has only to study attentively Matthew Arnold's report on the educational system of Germany, above all to read between the lines and detect what the author thinks but dares not express, to gain the conviction that higher education in England labors under many and grave evils.

The chief objections that may be urged against the English system, so far as I can formulate them, are as follows. The education afforded by Oxford and Cambridge is

James Morgan Hart, *German Universities: A Narrative of Personal Experience Together with Recent Statistical Information, Practical Suggestions, and a Comparison of the German, English, and American Systems of Higher Education* (New York: G. P. Putnam's Sons, 1874), pp. 321-325, 327-355.

illiberal, is expensive, and is comparatively unproductive of results.

It is illiberal both in its quantity and its quality. All told, the number of students at Oxford and Cambridge is between 3,000 and 4,000. Leipsic alone has almost as many. In the German Empire, the matriculated students (according to the University Calendar for the present summer) are in round numbers 16,000. This includes twenty universities, but not the Catholic Academy of Münster. It does not include non-matriculating attendants at lectures, of whom there are 1,816 at Berlin alone, nor does it include the Austrian universities. In other words, there are five men pursuing a higher education in Germany for one in the United Kingdom. To this it may be objected that the comparison takes no note of institutions like the universities of Edinburgh and Glasgow, Trinity College (Dublin), and others of a more limited nature in the city of London. But do Edinburgh, Glasgow, or Trinity rank with Oxford and Cambridge? I put the question as a foreigner, one who is free from petty local prejudices or jealousies. Are not the students who set the tone better prepared at Oxford and Cambridge than elsewhere? Is not the instruction, as a whole, of a higher order? Do not Oxford and Cambridge claim to be the seats of learning by eminence? When an English writer speaks of "university men," does he not mean, as a matter of course, Oxons and Cantabs? Regarding the amount of study accomplished, the scope of the curriculum, prestige, wealth of endowment, social and political influence, we shall be constrained to place Oxford and Cambridge by themselves, as the best that the English system can exhibit. This will not hinder us from admitting the personal superiority of many Edinburgh and Glasgow graduates.

As the best, then, that the United Kingdom can exhibit, I must pronounce Oxford and Cambridge illiberal in comparison with the stately list of universities that begins with Berlin and ends with Würzburg. Oxford and Cambridge do not represent the entire Kingdom, do not train the men from all classes of society and for all the professions. The German university is national property, the English is not. It is a private corporation, pursuing objects of its own selection and heeding public clamor only when that clamor becomes too loud, too unmistakable to be longer neglected. It is sectarian in its character and in its tendency, aristocratic in its atmosphere, and—severe as the expression may sound—bigoted in its mode of instruction. It is sectarian because it is a Church of England institution. Now the Church of England is as liberal as any church well can be. The very circumstance that it is broken up into so many factions or cliques only proves as much. Yet broad and generous as it may be, it is still narrow in mind and heart as compared with mankind at large. Is it not strange, then, well nigh intolerable, that a country like England, claiming to have shaken off all the fetters of spiritual and political bondage, should tolerate such exclusivism in letters? Dissenters, Catholics, and Jews, it is true, can now pursue their studies at Oxford and Cambridge, and are admitted to competition for university prizes. But since how long? And even now, can the Dissenter, the Catholic, or the Jew look upon Oxford or Cambridge as his university, are any of the professors his professors, is any part of the curriculum shaped with reference to his tenets? In Germany, the Catholics have their own universities, or, in Protestant countries, their paritetic faculties. Among the professors are not a few Jews, men of the widest reputation. Every German, irrespective of creed, of sectional jealousy, feels that any German university can be his, that wherever conflict of religious opinion comes in, allowances are made for his peculiarities. The consequence is that all the German universities are knit together by the strongest of spiritual bonds. Students pass freely from one to the other, without so much as dreaming of jealousy or of drawing invidious comparisons. The 16,000 young men now attending the twenty German universities are put on a footing of the most absolute equality as to rights and obligations. Nor is this all. These universities meet the intellectual wants of the entire nation. Not only is no man excluded from them, either theoretically or practically, but every man of literary, scientific, or political aspirations must attend them. They are the only avenues through which one can hope to enter the professions. They are shaped so as to furnish instruction of the highest order in every branch. One can scarcely mention a subject of investigation that is not taught at every German university by one, or ten, or perhaps twenty men of ability. The universities are State institutions, open to all citizens as a matter of right. They are under the control of the Ministry of Public Instruction, they are the Corinthian capital of the national system of education. They are just as much national property as the public schools, the courts, the post-office.

What is the contrast presented by Oxford

and Cambridge? Young men are compelled to wear an absurd mediæval garb, one that might afford a good question for our debating societies, namely, whether it was intended by nature for ornament or for use. Young men are compelled to attend the religious services of a church which does not represent the entire nation, are compelled to live by routine, to keep hours. And finally, they are compelled to follow prescribed courses of study. Everywhere compulsion, nowhere the freedom that the German is taught to regard as the prime element in study. The instruction at Oxford and Cambridge is excellent in its way, but it runs in too narrow grooves, it has too much the character of training for a boat-race, and too little the character of "science." Those who compete for fellowships and prizes are hampered in many ways, being forced to acquire a certain amount of superficial familiarity with branches outside of their chosen department. The classical men are bored with mathematics, the mathematical men are bored with the classics. It is only within twenty or thirty years that the "natural-science" men have had any chance whatever. . . .

. . . The reader must bear in mind the distinction between the college and the university. Trinity College is the seat of classic learning, yet the University of Cambridge, as a whole, is mathematical in its proclivities. The college favors a certain set of studies, the university another. A new Master is appointed for the college, who threatens to change its character. Those students who had entered Trinity College in good faith, supposing that no more than a limited amount of work in mathematics would be exacted from them, find their prospects of college preferment suddenly overcast. With them it was not merely a point of honor, but a question of pecuniary loss. They were cut off from the chances of a Fellowship. Can anything be imagined more arbitrary, more spasmodic? One man is to have the right of setting and upsetting. Education, which should be planned in accordance with definite principles, is to be made a matter of individual caprice.

Neither Oxford nor Cambridge is a university in the true sense of the term. It is a congeries of colleges. Each college has its own organization, its own administration, its own body of students and instructors. The university has but a nominal share in the instruction and the discipline. The most that it does is to set the requirements for the Tripos. In Germany there are no colleges.

The faculties of the university are co-ordinated. The rectorship passes year by year from one faculty to another. The student is responsible to his faculty for the quality of his work, but the discipline is administered by the university at large. The theologian, the jurist, the classical philologist, the mathematician, the student of medicine, the historian, the geologist, are co-equal. No one can claim precedence over the other. Merit is not gauged according to preconceived opinions as to the respective superiority of classics over mathematics, or vice versa, or of the two over the sciences of nature. Each student has his own branch of study, and ranks as good or bad according to his performances in that branch alone.

To make this perfectly clear, I should place side by side, in tabular array, the list of hours and studies of Oxford, for instance, and of some German university, say Leipsic. But the space is wanting. I give in a subsequent place the list for Leipsic alone. The reader who wishes to inform himself more fully, need only contrast it with the Oxford calendar. After making the comparison, he will scarcely be tempted to rank the two institutions as equals.

The secret of the German university instruction is this. It rests upon a broad basis of well graded public schools. How England stands in this respect, has been abundantly shown by Matthew Arnold. The English have no schools that correspond to the German gymnasiums. Both Oxford and Cambridge, with all their pretensions, have to make good the defects of even such schools as Eton, Rugby, Harrow and Winchester. I have cited in another place the courses, in whole or in part, of two gymnasiums selected at random as representatives of their class. They show that the public schools of Germany teach all that a man need master in the way of general discipline. The classics are well taught, but so are mathematics, the modern languages, the natural sciences, history, and belles lettres. The *Primaner* who gets his *Maturitätszeugniss* (certificate of ripeness) is fully the peer of the best sixth-form boy of Rugby in classics—even Mr. Arnold admits that—and, what Mr. Arnold passes over in silence without expressly admitting, he is superior in everything else. He knows all that can be expected of a well educated man in the way of general information on general topics. For his special training, and for this alone, there remains the university.

An additional defect of the English universities is their practice of testing schol-

arship by close competitive examinations.
The Honor-men of Oxford and Cambridge,
the Scholars and Fellows, are undoubtedly
men of superior attainments. They have done
a prodigious amount of work in a very short
time. The question is, whether the work is
of the right kind, and whether it is done in
the right way. After reading attentively Mr.
Bristed's work, and others, I am forced to
the conclusion—shared moreover by the leading scholars of Germany—that competitive
examinations are not the proper test of scientific study. Speed, knack, what the English
call "pace," is unduly exalted at the expense
of thoroughness and originality. The candidate
for honors reads certain works and authors
because he has every reason for believing
that they will be "set," he neglects others
because he knows that they are not "set." In
other words, he subjects his individual preferences to the conventionalisms of the examiners. Term after term, year after year, he
is kept on the stretch. He asks himself repeatedly the question: Can I afford to do this?
Will it not be safer to do that? He has not the
opportunity of branching off into some unexplored field of study and producing novel,
independent results. Questions which the
English Honor-man passes over, on the plea
that they will probably "not pay," are
precisely the ones which the German student
takes up with patience and energy, in the
hope of achieving reputation as an original
thinker. Besides, the strain involved in preparing for a competitive examination is too
severe. It exhausts the mind and the body.
Success is too dearly bought, failure is dis-
heartening. The soundest thinkers of England,
I believe, are slowly awaking to the consciousness that the prize-examinations of
Oxford and Cambridge do not answer their
purpose satisfactorily.

In the next place, the instruction at Oxford
and Cambridge costs too much. Compared
with Germany, England is an expensive country. Yet the cost of living at an English
university is largely in excess of what it
should be, even for England. The reason is that
prices are arbitrary, and the style of living is
conventional. The tone is set by the many
wealthy young men, noblemen and parvenus,
who have more money than they know how to
spend properly, and who launch accordingly
into all sorts of extravagance. What with
"tigers," horses, dogs, boating-clubs, elaborate dinners and suppers, they make an
ostentation of wealth that either throws the
poorer students completely into the shade, or
forces them into ruinous competition. This

can scarcely be said of the German universities. The wealthy students of Berlin or
Bonn or Leipsic do not exercise a like influence over their fellows, for the reason
that they do not come in such close personal
contact with them. In England, a student
has the same associates for three or four
years, lives with them in the same quad-
rangle, recites in the same classes, attends
the same chapel and church, sits at the same
Commons. In Germany, each man lives by
himself, selects his rooms and his dining-
place according as his means may permit,
and associates only with men who are personally congenial. If he has had the ill luck to
make the acquaintance of a "fast" set in
his first semester, it is an easy matter to
reform by cutting them in the second. If
the worst comes to the worst, he has only
to try a change of air by removing to another
university. It was a common saying in my
day, that the Heidelberg idlers came to
Göttingen, after a semester or two, to do
their studying.

Not only are the expenses of living at
Oxford and Cambridge out of all proportion
to the benefit received, but the atmosphere
of both places, particularly of Oxford, is
thoroughly aristocratic. I do not condemn this
unqualifiedly as a fault. If England sees fit
to maintain her aristocratic institutions, it is
not for the foreigner to take her to task
therefor. Yet this concession should not
prevent us from looking the facts full in the
face and estimating their bearing and probable
results. The higher education of England is
in the exclusive possession of the higher,
say rather the highest classes. Not that all
the students come from the nobility and the
bourgeoisie parvenue. The real study at both
Oxford and Cambridge is done by the sons
of toiling barristers, country clergymen of
the Church of England, and other persons of
limited means. Yet even these students are
under the influence of the aristocratic element. They themselves are aristocrats in
disguise, they represent the side lines of the
nobility. Most certainly they are not
democratic. The popular element in England
is excluded *de facto* from participation in
the real or supposed benefits of Oxford and
Cambridge. If we examine, on the other hand,
the mass of students in any German university, we shall find that it is composed
of representatives of every class, from the
highest nobility, perhaps the royal family
itself, to the lowliest shop-keeper and district tax-collector. From this results the
happy equality that characterizes the Ger-

man seats of learning. They are neither aristocratic nor democratic in the political or the social sense, but they are what they should be,—national. They exist for the entire nation, they are supported by contributions from the national purse, and they supply the nation in turn with all its clergymen, physicians, lawyers, teachers, men of science. Hence the respect, I may say the enthusiastic affection, the unbounded pride that the nation as a whole takes in its universities. It is not pride in any one university, in Berlin or Leipsic, nor in any one professor or set of professors, but in the system as a system, that affords to all an equal chance of first-rate education at the lowest possible price. Now much as we respect Oxford and Cambridge, great as may be our veneration for the names and associations that cluster around them, we cannot in fairness regard them as in this sense national. They are English, intensely English; they could not exist outside the factitious atmosphere that envelops English "society." Yet they do not represent the entire nation, only its governing classes. We do well to think with admiration of the great scholars that have lived and died on the banks of the Isis and the Cam. But we shall do better to judge them also by what they have failed to accomplish. What have they done for the *diffusion* of science and of culture in England? Have they not, by their exclusiveness, their prejudice, helped, unconsciously perhaps yet not the less directly, to make the English folk what it is, the most benighted, the most illiterate, the most helpless, the most brutal among all the nations that call themselves civilized? Oxford and Cambridge are at this day not seats of learning pure and simple, they are the trysting places of the nobility and the *bourgeoisie parvenue*. The noblemen are in need of money to preserve and round off ancestral acres, the wealthy seek after titles. At the university, then, are laid the foundations of future alliances political and matrimonial. Probably half the students who go to Oxford and Cambridge, do so not to study but to "form connections." And the possible results? It is not for me to predict coming events. Yet should the fourth estate succeed in sending a certain number of representatives to parliament, enough to form a majority with the Dissenters and the Catholics,—such a conjuncture is anything but impossible,—what position would the English universities occupy? Could they make any reply to the searching demand: What have you done for us? Of what good to us are your scholarships, your fellowships, your Regius professors? Why should we refrain from reconstructing you from top to bottom?

Finally, the English university system is comparatively unproductive of results. It may seem presumptuous in any one man to break thus the rod of judgment over the backs of so many hundreds older, wiser, more renowned than himself. Yet surely any one claiming to be a scholar has the right to judge other men's scholarship by what it accomplishes. Personally acquainted with not one of the many professors and fellows of Oxford and Cambridge, I can estimate them only by what they do and by what they fail to do. Regarding science and scholarship in the aggregate, then, I venture to assert that there are only two departments in which the English are at the present time prominent, viz., pure mathematics and natural history. In all the others, they play a subordinate part. And in these two departments themselves, the universities have but a small share. Such men as Tyndall, Huxley, and Darwin, move outside the university sphere. It may be doubted even whether they meet with as hearty support and encouragement in their own country as they do in Germany and in France. In the departments of law, history, speculative philosophy, philology, orientalia, theology, the English universities produce scarcely anything that can be called first-rate. Let us take up some of them in order. As for law, neither Oxford nor Cambridge pretends to give a legal education. Oxford looks upon its honorary degree of D.C.L. as the choicest gift in its power to confer. Yet Oxford is incapable of teaching the Pandects. Were an Oxford fellow, I do not say an undergraduate, to undertake the study of the Civil Law, what help could he obtain from the university? The very first thing that he would have to do would be to learn German and French, because in those languages alone would he find available text-books. Even in the English Common Law, Oxford and Cambridge do nothing. The lawyer pursues his studies at the Temple, and at the Westminster Courts. Should he be foolhardy enough to venture upon the history of the Common Law, where will he find aid and encouragement, any professors who can guide him in his researches, can tell him what to read and how to read it? He must work by himself, must spend years of toil in forming mere preliminary judgements, such as the German student picks up in his first semester. In other words, there is not in all England a school of legal history or legal philosophy. Nor are the English better off in the matter of political history. The leading historians of the present generation are Freeman, Froude, Trollope and Lingard. As to Froude's merits, the reader may consult the stinging reviews of him in the *Historische Zeitschrift*. With regard to the others, can any one compare them for a single sober moment with men like Ranke, Waitz, Wattenbach, Droysen, Jaffé, and von Sybel? Is there any spot in England, inside or outside the universities, where history is taught as an independent branch of science? The English do something for the history of their own country, but not much more than the Germans are doing for them. Whereas they do nothing for the history of Germany, next to nothing for the history of France, Italy and Spain. The most that they do is to appropriate the hard-won researches of continental scholars and serve them up to the public in the shape of palatable magazine articles. Still worse is the case with philology. One might suppose that the shades of Bentley and Porson would rise from the dust and castigate their degenerate successors. The only philologist of general reputation connected with the English Universities is Max Müller, a German! It would be superfluous to call off in this place the long array of names of men who have made Germany famous in this department, all the Grimms and Bopps, and Schleichers. What have the English to set up against them? When the student of philology begins his investigations into the origin of language, into the relations of the Indo-Germanic, the Semitic, the Ugric families of languages, what English authorities and text-books does he consult? Even in the field where, above all others, we have reason to expect much of English scholarship, namely, the very limited department of *English* philology, the state of things is, to speak mildly, humiliating. The only scientific, rational grammars of the English language are the works of two Germans, Koch and Mätzner. The only critical edition of the body of Anglo-Saxon poetry is by a German, Grein. And that same German is obliged to suspend his edition of the body of Anglo-Saxon prose because he discovers that the English text-editions upon which he relied are untrustworthy! No Englishman thinks it worth the while to go out of his way to study the *Hildebrandslied* or the *Nibelungenlied* or *Parzival*, yet he suffers the German to invade him in his home and instruct him upon Beovulf, Cynevulf, and Aelfric.

It is needless to push the comparison farther. While the Germans, restless, enterprising, thoroughly trained, have ransacked the libraries of all Europe, making themselves at home in the political and literary history of every country, editing rare works in old French, old Spanish, Italian, Slavonic, Norse, inventing new theories and processes and bringing them within the reach of every student, the English have rested on their labors, in insular exclusiveness. They have trod their round of Tripos and Little-Go, they have written clever verses in Latin and made smooth translations and "floored" papers, but they have not produced their share of scholars. They are laggards in the great international handicap, because they are overweighted with routine and with narrow-minded devotion to certain studies. Is it because the English spirit has lost its quondam energy of initiative? For one, I am loth to believe it. I have not lost faith in the brain-power of the Anglo-Saxon race. What that race needs is emancipation from the thraldom of caste in education. Should the fourth estate do nothing worse than reconstruct Oxford and Cambridge, Eton, Harrow, Rugby, and the entire system from top to bottom, its advent to power might be hailed as a blessing.

Comparison of German Universities and American Colleges

To enter into an elaborate comparison of the German and the American systems of higher education, feature by feature, would not only swell the present work beyond reasonable limits, but would expose the one making it to the charge of being unpractical, unpatriotic, radical, aggressive, *doctrinaire*. The time has not yet arrived when the real friends of educational reform can look for a fair, rational discussion. Passion and prejudice run too high, there is too much dogmatism on the part of both conservative and innovator. The argument of the advocates of the existing regime might be framed somewhat in this wise. The American system is American, it has grown out of the needs of the country, it is adapted to the formation of national character, it gives our young men what they require for playing their part in public life. Moreover, we are here, strongly entrenched. Beside us there is none else, we cannot be dispossessed of our vantage ground, what are you going to do about it?

Now there is not one of the above propositions that is not susceptible of being overhauled and corrected, or at least modified. But the time for doing it is not yet at hand. The American public is still indifferent, as a public. It is not aroused to the vital connection between the State and education in all its stages, highest as well as lowest. The explanation of the signal failure of the movement in behalf of Civil Service Reform is to be found in the circumstance that the public is apathetic. The nation at large does not care whether it has better office-holders or not. It secretly approves, rather than disapproves, of the principle of succession in office. After a man has been post-master or revenue-collector for four years, it is only fair—argues the American mind—that he give some one else "a chance." Such is public opinion, and it is idle to quarrel with it. A similar view is taken of education. We do not need highly educated men. So long as our graduates can spell with tolerable accuracy, have a modicum of the classics and mathematics, can write and declaim with fluency, what more do you expect of them? They must become "practical," must learn the theory through the practice, and rough it with the others. Right or wrong, this is the average estimate set upon the value of college education. The public does not perceive the importance of any thing higher and more systematic. Indeed, I am tempted at times to believe that the colleges have exceeded, on some points, the demands of their friends. They give more than is expected of them. There are symptoms of a desire to react from the progress made during the past fifteen years. In making this assertion, I have in view, not so much Yale and Harvard as the colleges in the Middle and Western States. Urged on by a spirit of rivalry which is in itself deserving only of praise, these latter have made their curriculum more extensive and have also enforced its requirements more strictly. In doing this, they have gone a step too far, they have outrun the capacities of the preparatory schools. Up to the outbreak of the Civil War, the American college was an easy-going institution, where one was not forced beyond his natural gait, but had leisure to follow his inclinations, and especially to read. This has been changed. New professorships in the natural sciences have been created, and the chairs have been filled with energetic young men, enthusiastic in their vocation, and—I trust they will pardon the bluntness of the expression—rather intolerant towards those who do not keep pace with them. Many of the professors in the older departments are also young men who have studied abroad,

are equally enthusiastic, and equally intolerant. The result is that we are called upon to witness a curious phenomenon, one that must act as a disturbing element in every system of education, to wit, a *direct conflict of studies*. Our undergraduates have at the present day too many studies, and are hurried through difficult and disconnected subjects at too rapid a rate. The new professors in the classics and the new professors in the natural sciences threaten to tear the child asunder between them, and there is no Solomon at hand to decide upon the true alma mater. Viewed in this light, the assertion now going the rounds of the press and attributed variously to Mr. Beecher and Mr. Fields, namely, that our colleges have not succeeded in producing one first-rate man in any department since 1855, will perhaps receive its explanation. Whatever the college of by-gone days may have failed to do, it certainly gave its pupil a better opportunity than his successor now enjoys, of maturing in conformity to the laws of individual being.

The present remarks will be confined to three points: the want of connection between College and State, the question of economy, and the question of discipline.

The College, unlike the German University, rests upon nothing and ends in nothing. We shall not obtain a just conception of the University unless we view it in its twofold bearing. It is, on the one hand, the keystone of the arch of public-school education in Germany. Everything in that system leads up to the university by a series of carefully graduated steps. The gymnasium rests upon the *Volksschule*, the university rests upon the gymnasium. The whole cannot subsist without each one of the parts. On the other hand, the University is the door of approach to all the professions and also to public office. Whoever is not content with trade and commerce must submit to its liberalizing discipline. Without the public schools as a basis, and state-service or the professions as a goal, the University would speedily lose its right of being.

It will be needless to dwell upon the contrast presented by the college. I have said that it rests upon nothing and ends in nothing. By this is meant that the college is wholly dissevered from the state. It does not rest upon the system of public schools, neither is it the place where candidates prepare themselves for state-service. Massachusetts excepted, there is not a state where public schools attempt to fit young men for college. The needful preparation can be obtained only at academies and private schools which are exempt from state control and which pursue each the plan that seems to it best. However excellent these schools may be, they do not constitute a well organized, uniform system. The college ends in nothing, because its curriculum is not enforced as the condition precedent to civil and professional appointment.

Dropping abstract terms, I put the case of real "national education" before the reader in the shape of an imaginary example. Let us suppose the state of New York to enact a statute to the following effect: "As soon as may be practicable, the academies of this state shall be reconstituted as public schools of the first grade. The teachers now in office shall be required to pass an examination equivalent to that for B.A. or B.S. in some one of the acknowledged colleges of the state. Future applicants for the position of teacher in the academies and grammar schools must have passed through the full public school course, beginning with the grammar school and finishing with the college, and received the degree of B.A. or B.S. The colleges shall be placed under the supervision of the State Board of Education. The trustees of a college shall have the right to propose nominations for professorships, but the governor of the state shall exercise his discretion in rejecting unsuitable nominees. No college shall be considered as a state institution or entitled to recognition as an institution of learning, that does not submit to the regulations of the state authorities. As soon as the provisions of this act shall have been carried out, no one shall be admitted to the bar or bench of this state, or be permitted to practice medicine in the state, or be employed as teacher in the public schools, who shall not have received the degree of B.A., M.D. or B.S. from some state college acknowledged as such. Furthermore, no one shall be eligible for appointment or election to state-office without such degree. Finally, all private schools wishing to be placed on an equality with the state academies or grammar schools must conform in all respects to the curriculum of the academy or the grammar school, and must submit to the state requirements in the matter of holding examinations and appointing teachers."

Such an ideal enactment, imperfectly sketched as it is, will nevertheless, I trust, bring the case home to the reader. It is of course impracticable. Yet I venture to say that until we are prepared to introduce and maintain something of the sort, it will be useless to talk of Civil Service Reform and University Education. Our office-holders may be improved somewhat in quality, our colleges may give a higher grade of instruction, but we shall not have a body of trained officials, neither shall we have a system of universities. Our colleges teach already all that can be demanded of institutions that receive no official recognition from the state, and that are viewed with indifference, not to say skepticism, by the leaders in mercantile and political life. Let the reader extol our college system to the best of his ability, I still maintain that so long as three fourths of our national and state representatives, nine tenths of our office-holders, and the majority of the teachers in our public schools are non-graduates, it is the most extravagant optimism to regard the colleges as playing any acknowledged part in *national* life. The famous Simmons case proves this beyond controversy. If there be any city in America that has just reason to be proud of its public-school education, it is Boston. If there be any college in America that has done more than another for the promotion of learning and culture, and that is merely waiting for the word to constitute itself into a bona fide university, it is Harvard. Yet Boston and Cambridge combined were unable to prevent the appointment of a man notoriously incompetent, a man whose mere nomination, under a system like that of Germany, would have been an impossibility.

It would not be difficult to show that in point of economy also our colleges have much to learn from Germany. The reader's most careful attention is invited to the tabular statement of income and expenditure for the university of Leipsic, presented elsewhere. Two of our colleges, Harvard and Yale, have each—if I mistake not—as large an income as that of Leipsic. If smaller, the difference is certainly inconsiderable. Yet both Harvard and Yale would be slow in provoking a comparison between themselves and Leipsic. To what, then, must we look for the explanation of this disproportion in America between the outlay and the results effected? In part, but only in a small part, to the relatively higher figures of professors' salaries in America. Each one of the full professors at Harvard receives $4,000 a year, I believe. At Yale, the salaries are very nearly as high. No one will have the shabbiness to assert that the pay is too high. As a class, American professors are insufficiently recompensed. After years of toil and annoyance, they can be thankful if they are able to keep themselves and their families out of debt. Were the salary of every professor doubled, the increase would be nothing more than justice. It is difficult to understand why professors, who are men of ability and culture, who devote themselves unselfishly to the best interests of the nation, should not be paid as liberally as our best lawyers and physicians, why the guardians of the spiritual interests of men should fare worse than those who look merely after their bodies and estates. It is not more than six years ago that the president of Harvard was forced to admit in public that his senior professor received less than the chief cook of the Parker House! Things have been bettered since then, but they have not been radically cured.

Now for this state of affairs the party chief in responsibility is the college itself. Not Harvard, nor Yale, nor Princeton, nor Cornell alone, but the spirit of our college system. We have been misled by rivalry into copying after England in the feature that is least worthy of imitation. I mean—buildings! Had the money which has been sunk in brick and stone and mortar during the past twenty years been judiciously invested, the salary of every professor in America might be doubled at this moment. If this assertion sounds extravagant, the reader has only to scrutinize carefully the condition of any one of our colleges, to note the amount of money expended upon costly edifices, and then to judge for himself whether that amount, if placed at interest, would not add at least fifty per cent to the annual income. What are the buildings necessary for keeping up a college? Those which contain the libraries and apparatus, and the rooms suitable for lectures and recitations. Whatever goes beyond this, is superfluous. We may derive some wholesome lessons on the point from examining into the conduct of the German government in re-establishing the university of Strassburg. Although barely three years have elapsed since the annexation of Alsace, the university has a full staff of eighty professors, and a body of six hundred students. Yet the university of Strassburg has not at this day *a single building that it can properly call its own.* To estimate such a policy of organization with due regard to its extraordinary singleness of view, we must bear in mind that it was not induced by stint of funds. Prince Bismarck, as Chancellor of the Empire and Administrator of the Imperial Provinces, had *carte blanche.* Probably no man since the days of Cardinal Wolsey enjoyed a like opportunity of immortalizing himself in stained glass and stone. The French indemnity money was pouring into the German coffers in a steady stream, Germany was wild over its sudden accession to wealth. It would have cost but a word from the Prince to divert a paltry fraction, say twenty of the thousand millions, to the glory of German architects and the greater glory of the unificator of his country. But the Prince knew too well what he was undertaking. He knew that the strength of a university does not consist in its array of dead buildings, but in its force of live men, that the ultimate test of the capacity of a university is its ability to pay professors. So the Prince quietly let the twenty millions take their natural course into the imperial treasury, and contented himself with organizing the Strassburg university after the model of all the others, to wit, as an unobtrusive congregation of eminent men in the receipt of good salaries. For the mere appliances and paraphernalia of learning, for permanent laboratories, library buildings, botanical gardens and the like, he trusted to the future, and to the general principle that, given the skilled artisan, the workshop will follow of itself.

Will it be necessary to descant upon the painful contrast afforded by our colleges, to show, instance by instance, how we have spent our money upon the workshop, until we have none left wherewith to pay the workman? The city of Philadelphia expended two millions of dollars upon Girard College. It succeeded in erecting a Grecian temple that is the wonder of the tourist and the terror of the teacher. After years of tinkering and patching, the rooms are even now scarcely suited to the purposes of instruction, and the instructors themselves are scantily paid.

Instead of scattering my remarks over a number of colleges, permit me to concentrate them upon that one with which I am most familiar, namely, Cornell. Much has been bruited about of late as to Mr. Cornell's dishonesty. It is needless to say that the charges were completely disproved by the Committee of Investigation in their report, but it may not be superfluous to add that nobody connected with the university put the slightest faith in the charges. On the contrary, it was a matter of almost public notoriety in Ithaca that Mr. Cornell was at one time rather embarrassed in his finances, in consequence of the obligations into which he had entered gratuitously for the benefit of the university. There is not the shadow of a doubt but that the intentions of Mr. Cornell have always been strictly honorable. Yet it is not the less evident that the affairs of the university have been badly managed from the outset. Instead of beginning on a modest scale, and developing the field of operation gradually, keeping pace with the growth of resources, the managers of the university started it in extravagance and then conducted it with the most humiliating parsimony. There was but one object for which money seemed to be forthcoming, and that object was ostentatious architecture. The Cascadilla was completed and the North and South Universities were erected at an expense of not less than $250,000. Ample accommodation for lectures and recitations—which was all that was needed—could have been had for $75,000. Furthermore, instead of locating the university in the town of Ithaca, where it would have been comparatively accessible, it was pitched upon the crest of a hill four hundred feet high and exposed to the inclemency of the weather. By dint of lavish expenditure in planting trees, it is possible that the buildings may be sheltered, in the course of a generation, from the searching east winds. But nothing can ever screen them from the furious northerly and westerly gales that sweep across the lake every winter and spring. Only one who has himself struggled for half a mile through the snow against a cutting north-wester, and reached his lecture-room half blinded and benumbed, scarcely able to collect his thoughts or to keep his teeth from chattering in the presence of the class, will appreciate the trials of our model American university furnished with "all the modern improvements." The casual visitor, who views the grounds on a pleasant day in June or October, knows nothing of all this. He perceives only the beauty of the landscape, and congratulates the university on its admirable location! The expression, as I have heard it again and again, always sounded like the cruelest of friendly mockeries. A fine view on a fine day is but a sorry atonement for months of wearing toil and exposure. How shall we explain this mania, peculiar to America, of locating public institutions on hill-tops? Is it that the whole world may see what feats of architecture we are capable of, crude conglomerations of bald, unrelieved lines, distorted chimneys, unsymmetrical windows, or do we desire the votaries of knowledge to look upon her temple as an Alpine "station?"

Had Mr. McGraw, Mr. Sage, and the other donors given, not buildings, but the money expended on buildings, had the university husbanded its resources and lived year by year within its income, had it refrained from luxuries, such as high-priced lectures from outsiders, and the purchase of questionable libraries; in short, had the university patterned in only this one respect of economy after the German universities that it professes to regard as its beau ideal, its available capital would be greater than it now is by the round sum of one million dollars.

Cornell University is not the only institution that has made the mistake. Every college in the land can tell the same story with variations. Harvard, Yale, Amherst, Dartmouth, Princeton and the others have received during the past ten years many handsome donations, but these donations have come usually in the shape of buildings. Few of the donors appear to have stumbled upon the patent fact that what a college needs in the first place is money, in the second place money, in the last place money, or upon the equally patent fact that every building entails upon the college additional expenses. A chapel costing $70,000 forces the college to an annual outlay of $1,000 to $2,000 for repairs, heating and attendance. Let us consider the most common form of donation. A friend of — college, we may say, wishes to bestow the handsome sum of $200,000. Instead of endowing four or five professorships, thereby directly relieving the college from so much pressure on its general income, he erects a handsome dormitory, capable of holding fifty students. Each student pays for his suite of rooms $250 per annum, an excessive amount for the forty academic weeks. The aggregate rental would be $12,500. From this are to be deducted the expenses for insurance, repairs, heating, and servants' wages, say $3,000. The net yield to the college, then, is only $9,500. Whereas the original fund, if judiciously invested, would have yielded $14,000. There is a waste, accordingly, of $4,500, to say nothing of the extra burden of worry and responsibility imposed upon the college authorities.

Is it surprising that the expense of collegiate life should have increased so rapidly within five years? Our colleges have grown rich in appearance, but in reality they are little better off than they were fifteen years ago. They have added one stately building after another, they have surrounded their students with objects that incite to extravagance, they have encouraged, directly or indirectly, an almost luxurious style of living, yet they are not a whit more independent of student support.[1] In fact, they have been forced to raise their tuition-charges. The Senatus Academicus of Leipsic could dismiss five hundred students at a blow, without curtailing the regular official salary of any one of its professors by so much as a penny. I doubt whether the American college can be found that would venture to send away twenty of its students, and *keep them away*. The truth is that the salaries of the professors depend too much upon the tuition-fees paid by the students. This the students themselves have found out, and they are prepared to act upon it. They know that dormitories, chapels, libraries, laboratories, by whomsoever erected in the first place, are supported by the tuition-fees that come from them. They hold the purse-strings, and they have already begun to assert their so called rights.

Intimately connected with this matter of economy is the further one of discipline. The German university court, whenever it does interfere, is inflexible; it can afford to be. Conscious that the university is a state institution, and that the government is pledged directly to its support, it is not diverted from the strictest administration of justice by the dread of diminishing the income derived from students. The vacillating policy, the alternate spasms of laxity and strictness that mark the course of discipline in an American college, on the other hand, are too well known to require more than a mention. Those of us who have passed or are passing through college know that such a thing as strict, even-handed justice does not exist for students. Private failings are punished with too much severity, public disorder with too little, and in general there is a want of fixity of purpose. The quality of the discipline varies from term to term, even from week to week. I remember the instance where two students, room-mates, arraigned for precisely the same offense, were punished, one by suspension for three months, the other by suspension for six. The secret of the difference was that they were not tried at the same faculty meeting. Not one of those professors who voted for the respective sentences perceived the gross injustice of the discrimination until attention was directed to it by myself, as registering clerk of the faculty. It is not my object to discuss the grave question of public disorder and the proper way of meeting it, for I believe that there is only one way, not attainable at present, and that way lies in the absolute monetary independence of the college itself. Until professors' salaries can be secured by better means than precarious student-support, we have no right to expect a thorough reform. Professors are after all only men. Situated as they are, they cannot afford to be stricter, they must temporize, must yield here and there to student clamor and to inveterate traditions and prejudices. At the same time, I cherish the belief that it is possible to effect at least a partial reform, by changing the mode of administering discipline. The change would consist in abolishing the present cumbersome faculty-meetings and in lodging the entire control in the hands of the president and say two advisers. A college faculty, to speak the plain, unvarnished truth, is a body without a soul, without a sense of responsibility, for the simple reason that the individual is lost in the multitude. It is impossible to obtain from an aggregation of twenty or thirty men anything like uniformity of action. The whole is broken up into groups, or cliques, which do not act in concert, and according as one or the other of such cliques may be present on a given occasion, the voting will be decided one way or the other. Furthermore, college professors, as a class, have loose notions as to what is really evidence, and what is not. Although sitting as judges, they have not received a legal training. They are determined in their opinions only too often by hearsay, vague rumors, and general reputation. Finally, their functions are too heterogeneous. They are in direct conflict with the cardinal principle of Anglo-Saxon justice, to wit, the separation of legislative powers and judicial.

The college faculty enacts laws and regulations, and then proceeds to carry them out, not infrequently legislating *ex post facto*. It seems to me that this evil might be remedied by diminishing the number of faculty-meetings to one a month, and by restricting the action of the faculty to the discussion and adoption of general measures. The carrying out of those measures could be intrusted to a select Executive Committee, consisting of the president and two professors (chosen with regard to their legal attainments) and responsible directly to the trustees. Without claiming for such a tribunal infallibility, I am confident that it would have at least the following merits. It would expedite matters wonderfully. None

---

[1] The average yearly expenditure of the class of 1874 at Yale is stated at over $1,000.

but the members of a college faculty can estimate the amount of time wasted in mere parley. Three men will accomplish as much in an hour as twenty men in an entire afternoon. In the next place, the rulings of a tribunal of three would be uniform. Each member would be bound inflexibly by his previous action. And in the third place, there would be personal responsibility; students, parents, trustees, and outsiders would know whom to hold accountable. Under the present system, the burden of responsibility is shifted from man to man, and the student who may feel himself aggrieved is never at a loss for pretexts for raising the cry of injustice. There is no risk run in impugning the decisions of a faculty of twenty, but to attack a committee of three is a step from which the ordinary student would shrink. The establishment of an Executive Committee, as indicated above, would introduce a healthier tone of feeling between faculty and students, and would rid the professional vocation of many trials and annoyances.

Joshua L. Chamberlain   1878

Lessons and Results for America from the Paris Exposition

Joshua Lawrence Chamberlain (1828–1914), a graduate of Bowdoin College, Brunswick, Main, in 1852 and of Bangor Theological Seminary in 1855, was a professor of rhetoric and modern languages prior to the Civil War.   During the war he distinguished himself as a general with the Army of the Potomac and was decorated with the Congressional Medal of Honor for his conduct at the Battle of Gettysburg. He served as governor of Maine from 1866 to 1870 and as president of Bowdoin College from 1871 to 1883. He was one of the United States Commissioners at the Paris Universal Exposition of 1878, and the following extracts on European education are from his report on this exposition.

In seeking to draw from the Paris Exposition such lessons as we might profitably give or receive in exchange with the most advanced nations of Europe, it would be difficult and perhaps of little advantage to undertake to say what particular country is behind or before others in certain respects in which they differ and certain directions in which they tend. A movement may possibly be a backward one, or a forward movement may be carried too far.

But it may perhaps be safely concluded that a movement which is directed by the efforts of the most enlightened minds, after deliberation and free discussion and exchange of ideas, and which is the accepted result of the best experience and observation, may properly be regarded as a true advance. If one country has made better attainments than others in directions so determined, it may be said that it is "ahead" of them.

1. One of the tendencies which seems to be in accordance with the general voice of reason and experience is that represented by the watchwords of the progressive party in education throughout Europe—"Education ob-ligatory, gratuitous, and neutral in religion." It would not be correct to say these ends have been better attained in the United States than in some other countries. With respect to the absence of tuition fees for public school instruction we are clearly in advance. As to the obligatory requirement of a certain degree of education, but few of our States, if any, have reached the point attained in several other countries.

Where instruction is provided at the public expense there is certainly a strong reason to require children to profit by the privilege; and there can be no doubt the tendency of society is toward that end. With regard to the third point, the religious neutrality of public education, it already exists in the modified form of unsectarianism in the United States. Whether we can ever be induced to enforce an absolute neutrality in which the general principles of Christianity on which our codes of morals and tests of virtuous character are based, shall have no favorable presumption, but all religions and no religion shall have equal regard, is a question we may have to face. But probably unsectarianism will be a

Joshua L. Chamberlain, *Report on Education: Paris Universal Exposition, 1878 Reports of the United States Commissioners* (Washington, D.C.: U.S. Government Printing Office, 1880), pp. 341–347.

satisfactory resting point for our people. Most European nations which have declared for neutrality of religion in the schools have insisted that they shall still inculcate the "Christian virtues." It would appear that the Christian nations of the earth are not yet ready to reform the calendar.

2. Another subject of comparative study is coëducation. The feeling in Europe is very decided for separate schools for the sexes. There are indeed some mixed schools for the lowest grades, and in cases where the circumstances of a people of certain localities render this necessary (as has been shown in the course of this report), but in general it may be said there is not a country in Europe in which young men and young women are taught together.

If we grant that some of the feeling here referred to results from false teachings, and low views of the true significance and office of sex, and the correspondingly low state of sexual morality in such countries, there are still natural and permanent reasons why coëducation of the sexes is not likely to become the settled policy of advanced educational systems. Even in this country the tendency is toward separate schools for older pupils, as it must be observed that the first-class institutions for the separate education of girls are better patronized than those which, being principally designed for young men, are thrown open also to young women.

3. In the employment of female teachers for primary schools the practice in Europe has until lately been widely different from that of the United States. They have been very largely employed in the United States and scarcely at all in Europe. The present tendency seems to be from both extremes. There is an energetic movement in the progressive countries of the Old World to open the way for what seems to be the natural vocation of woman, while it is apparently felt in America that we have given up the schools too much to the charge of women, and a reaction in this respect has begun. There is a just mean somewhere. But it will probably remain true that the reserved force and the power to command and to deal with masses, which is a characteristic of manhood, will be deemed an essential factor in the proper discipline of youthful character, and the successful administration of schools on any considerable scale.

4. In respect to school books, Europe is too far one way, and we are too far the other. Most of the school books of Europe are poorly printed and poorly bound. This may be said especially of Germany, north and south. But then these books are cheap. On the contrary, our school books are too fine and too costly. The printer's and the engraver's art have reached such a point here, and publishers have so vied with each other to make a "splendid book," that we have run into a bad extreme. Our text books have too often become picture books; that is to say, the pictures are not for illustration but for ornament and luxury. The educating influence of such artistic work may possibly count for something, but the added expense is a serious item for the mass of children. A school book ought to be attractive, but should not be burdensome with beauty. Our attention has recently been called to the hard finish and glaring whiteness of much of the paper used in our fine books, and in some of our fine school books, which is very trying to the eye and likely to be injurious to the eyes of the young. In this respect, certainly, most countries of Europe have the advantage of us, the paper being soft and tinted so as not to throw a violent reflection of light. We might exchange some ideas with our friends abroad, with advantage to both parties.

5. Great attention is given in the schools of Europe to penmanship. Three hands are usually taught—the gothic, the round, and the current. The first is used for headings. The fault of the current hand is a tendency to stiffness and angularity. But there is a cheering absence of superfluity of hair-lines, and this goes to promote legibility, which is supposed to be one aim of penmanship. The excellence of the writing, of which there was a vast amount presented at the Exposition, was its clearness, strength, and legibility. To this might justly be added the excellence of beauty, meaning by this the symmetry and truth of the curves and angles. In this country we have lost something by giving up almost entirely the round full-faced hand we may be fortunate enough to see in the writings of our fathers.

6. We are behind Europe in the education of the senses, of the power of observation, and manipulation. The sharp competitions of the different countries of Europe demand the cultivation of the eye and hand, and long practice has given an aptitude and ability transmitted perhaps as an inheritance and so become a second nature. But we certainly need to do a great deal more in this direction, and we cannot begin too soon. If the brain of man conceives the strategy by which we master nature, it is by the eye and the hand that the real victory is to be achieved. A

large amount of the educational effort of this country is directed to sharpen the wits and quicken the inventive genius of our people, but our lack in bodily training will before long make itself painfully evident.

7. In respect to the education of girls, Europe is in some respects far behind us. In the lower grades we succeed in giving equal facilities to girls and boys; but in higher, and especially in the highest grades, it would seem that we are hardly keeping pace with the newly awakened Old World.

8. All countries are now striving to improve their school buildings. The marked feature of the school houses in the towns and cities of Western Europe is the "covered court," a free covered space, sometimes lighted from the side and sometimes canopied with glass, where the children may not only take their exercise in all weathers alike, but where they may also take their noon meal. The buildings are not generally above two stories high, and the best of them are now so constructed that the light shall come only on one side of the room, and so as to fall over the pupil's left shoulder. It is claimed also that this has a good educating effect upon the eye and upon the judgment of form and of the truth of light and shade.

9. It must be conceded that there is an economy of force in the system of graded schools. But observation at home and abroad has raised a serious doubt whether the advantage of the economical result may not have been at the expense of the best educational effect. It seems as if the classification of children has become too sharp and scientific, the grading too fine. This is especially observable in the case of the younger children. In the order of nature, children learn largely by example; and even in the presence and atmosphere of older ones, the younger seem to grow unconsciously and by imbibition. But shut up to themselves, the little ones, who have not yet learned to study books with real interest, when their appointed routine task is over have only to sit blank and inane; whereas, by merely looking on while others are doing work even wholly above what the younger can comprehend, they might gain more of real knowledge than by the methods which the teacher so painstakingly and painfully employs. It is a serious question whether it would not be better to make fewer grades, even if it spoils our theory of "progress by differentiation."

10. The relation of the government, or rather the body politic, to the schools of a country, and the extent of its powers and duties with regard to them, is a question which enters into that of the theory of the State, and will probably be differently regarded according to the theory of government which may be dominant in any mind or in any country. But the tendency is unmistakable in Europe, and in America also, to extend practically the care of the State over the schools to any and every degree which the best interests of education may demand. This is seen in things small as well as great. It is coming to be the practice in Europe to provide scholars with everything needed for their school work; and even so distinguished a philosopher and savan and so conservative a mind as M. Gréard, Inspector General of Public Instruction in France, recommends that the city of Paris should pay for the dinners of all the scholars in its schools. But the question chiefly at issue in this country is scarcely raised at all in Europe, namely, whether the State has any duty or right to provide a higher grade of education than the primary at the public expense. All that is proper to be said on this matter in a paper like this, is that, however conservative our theories may be as to the sphere of government or the proper objects of taxation, the movement of the age is in sympathy with the public provision for instruction of the higher and even highest grades, and it is likely to be irresistible.

11. Another and equally interesting question of education in the State is its relation to the forms of government. We claim in this country that the common schools are the foundation of our liberties—this is, of the guarantees of our liberties. Popular education is doubtless essential to republican institutions, but the converse would hardly hold true —that republican institutions are essential to popular education. A strong central government, if it is well disposed, can be a much more efficient educator than a democracy or a republic. A democracy, left to itself, is by no means sure to aspire to rise beyond its present condition, and certainly could not be always trusted to carry education to its highest point. It would require a rare enlightenment and ennoblement of spirit for a pure democracy to foster an education which naturally produces an aristocracy. Saxony, Wurtemburg, and many other states of Germany, abundantly illustrate what a strong government can enforce in the way of general education. But when benevolent monarchies thus foster the common school they well know that the tendency of popular education is adverse to all absolutism, and that they are

preparing the way for republics. By such tides of action and reaction the world moves. But the representative element in all governments, even the strongest monarchies, is one of the striking characteristics of the present times. In all of them the wisest and best are devising methods of a more complete enfranchisement of the people. Whatever the form of government, the movement of all the civilized nations of the earth is towards freedom,—by which word we mean a condition where the will of the people, and not the will of a monarch or of any master, makes the laws and rules the land. An extreme conservative influence, like that of the Roman Catholic Church, may in some countries make education a question of politics. Thus we see the progressive and liberal parties in France and Italy and Spain—parties whose principles we should call democratic and republican—enthusiastic in the cause of popular education. In order for men to comprehend their duties they must know their rights, and they can only know these by discovering their destinies through learning their capabilities.

12. Connected with this is the deep interest now felt in the enlightened countries of Europe in the study of social and political science. Our schools and colleges in America are far behind in this matter. Nor can there be any branch of the "humanities" more important or more urgently demanded by the times than the knowledge of the facts, the forces, and the laws by which civilization advances, and man emerges from the brute. Nowhere is this study more demanded than in our own country, and never more than at the present time.

13. Among the observations from which valuable suggestions can be drawn is that in regard to the present tendencies of the great schools of Europe to diffuse their light as widely as possible among the people. Not content with educating those within their walls, and with conducting original investigations in science, they are throwing open their lecture-rooms, and even going out into the neighboring towns, for the purpose of giving popular courses of instruction and making the people sharers in the advancement of knowledge. These aristocratic institutions taking pleasure in such work afford a striking example, creditable to them and to our times. More of this sort could be done in our higher schools of learning. The college should not only be a place where a student can get an education; it should be a light set on a hill, to shine into the dark places below it.

14. Our final thought naturally turns to the educating influence of these international exhibitions. As children learn by example and observation, so do men, and so do nations. A principle of natural selection on a grand scale works here. Each people shows its best, and every other admires and learns; and where, in any point, one surpasses all, the most able may make this excellence their point of departure, and the very least may take it as their goal. Thus each one learns its best hold and line of work; the sharpness of competition is softened by the interchange of human sympathies and quickening ideas, and the excellences of each become the common wealth of all.

James Russell Soley   1880

A Contrast in Naval Education: Britain and France

James Russell Soley (1850–1911), a teacher and writer, became assistant professor of English at the United States Naval Academy in 1871 and was head of the department of English studies, history, and law from 1872 to 1882. From 1883 until his death Soley supervised the publication of the Civil War naval records, serving as Assistant Secretary of the Navy from 1890 to 1893. His descriptive account of European naval education is possibly the only one of its kind written by an American educator during the nineteenth century. Juxtaposing concise and extensive accounts of naval training in Britain, France, and Germany, he left it up to the reader to make comparisons and suitable deductions.

James Russell Soley, *Report on Foreign Systems of Naval Education* (Washington, D.C.: U.S. Government Printing Office, 1880), pp. 26–28, 89–90, 109–115, 117, 152–153.

History of Naval Education in Great Britain

The way in which the present complicated system has grown up can only be fully understood by reference to former regulations.

The Naval Academy was first established at Portsmouth dockyard in 1729, for the education of 40 students. The age at admission was between 13 and 16. In 1806 the name of the school was changed to the "Royal Naval College," and in 1816 the age was fixed at from $12\frac{1}{2}$ to 14 years. The course lasted two years, and comprised various branches of elementary mathematics and English studies, somewhat similar to the present Britannia course. After leaving the college, the students served for a year as "volunteers of the first class," on board cruisers, and were then rated as midshipmen. After six years' service as midshipmen, and after passing an examination in seamanship and navigation, they became mates (the present sub-lieutenants), and were eligible for promotion to lieutenants. During the term of service at sea, some little instruction in navigation was given by the chaplains, or naval instructors, if there happened to be any on board.

Only a part of the young officers of the Navy went through the course at the Naval College, and those who did had no incentive to continue their studies after they left it. Accordingly, in 1837, the college was abolished, and the efforts of the Admiralty were directed towards the improvement of the corps of naval instructors.

In 1839 the Royal Naval College was again opened, but on an entirely different basis; in fact, it was practically another establishment. It was to provide "further means of scientific education" for a certain number of officers and mates, the latter of whom studied at the college for a year. At the same time the instruction given on shipboard was improved and broadened. By subsequent orders the college was extended so as to take in, in a certain measure, students in the higher ranks of the Navy and marines, officers qualifying for the marine artillery, masters, naval instructors, and engineers. Its intention was to teach advanced pupils, and it corresponded to the present college at Greenwich, as its predecessor had corresponded to the Britannia.

But the Admiralty, which, in 1837, discovered the want of higher education in the Navy, and to that end abolished the old college, in 1857 discovered the want of elementary training, and again opened a junior school, this time, however, without abolishing the other.

The new school was the beginning of the present Britannia system, though much has since been changed in details. It comprised a stationary training ship, an easy entrance examination, and a course of fifteen months, afterward lengthened to two years. The limits of age at admission were fixed at 13 and 15 years, which were changed in 1859 to 12 and 14, then to 12 and 13, and lastly to 12 and $13\frac{1}{2}$. In 1868 a special sea-going training ship was attached to the school, but this has since been discontinued, and cadets are now sent to sea in every variety of large cruiser. The course in the sea-going ship lasted a year. The examination for admission to the school was competitive, only half the number of candidates examined receiving appointments. The number nominated varied from 40 to 80, and the number appointed was always one-half; but competition was entirely done away with in 1875.

After leaving the special training ship, cadets were rated midshipmen and began their regular duties in ships of the fleet. Here they had still some limited instruction from naval instructors, or navigating officers, or officers specially detailed for the duty. A half-yearly examination of a somewhat crude character was held by the captain, and at the end of two years and a half (later eighteen months) midshipmen passed the thorough intermediate examination in navigation, chart-drawing, surveying, steam, French, and seamanship. In 1873 both the half-yearly and the intermediate examinations were discontinued, and in their stead full examinations were held in January of each year. These new annual examinations differed from the intermediate examinations in several points, but chiefly in the addition to the required subjects, of arithmetic, algebra, geometry, trigonometry, mechanics, and hydrostatics. The change was made on account of the general complaint that junior officers forgot or neglected the elementary mathematics they had already learned. In 1875 the annual examinations were placed in July, and the half-yearly examinations were revived in December, a regulation still in force. Meanwhile a more important change had been accomplished in the final abolition of the Naval College at Portsmouth, which had been in existence since 1839, and the opening of the new college at Greenwich, with a vastly improved organization, on the 1st of February, 1873.

It will be well to notice in this connection the School of Naval Architecture, first opened in 1811 at Portsmouth, and closed, for no particular reason, in 1832. It was reorganized, with considerable changes, as the Central School of Mathematics and Naval Construction, and closed, with as little reason as before, about 1853. In 1864 a third school was opened at South Kensington, which, in 1873, was united with the Naval College at Greenwich; and this last organization bids fair to be permanent.

It will be seen from the above sketch of the history of naval education in England that, while there has been undoubted progress, it has been after a long series of changes, experiments, renewed experiments, and expedients of all kinds, from which even now it cannot be said that a harmonious or satisfactory system has been evolved. In fact, it is rather a combination of makeshifts, resulting from a series of tentative and spasmodic efforts in almost every form which naval education is capable of taking. The naval administration never seems to have looked at the subject as a whole, from the beginning in the entering examination of cadets to the final stage at the promotion to sub-lieutenants, and to have worked out a systematic plan which should have both consistency and coherence. It appears rather to have adopted from time to time such partial views as were presented to it by advocates of a particular theory, by officers who leaned one way or another, a process which has sometimes resulted in its going back upon its own tracks, and making experiments which had been already proved failures. This is partly due to the want of attention hitherto given to the subject, a want which is now in a fair way to be met. Every year more is to be heard in the way of discussion of naval education, and every year more comprehensive and reasonable views seem to gain ground. That the government is likely to stop at its present stage in reforming the education of officers is very improbable; and as the Naval College at Greenwich is now firmly established, it will hardly be many years before further, and perhaps more radical, changes take place in the English system. . . .

General Character of British Naval Education

Made up as the English system is of diverse elements, it has a certain unity throughout, which is due solely to the fact that the whole is practically under one head. Except for the gunnery training, for which the Excellent is responsible, and the seamanship, which is instilled by some process on board ship, the whole training of officers is under the direction of the Director of Studies at Greenwich. His control does not go so far as the devising of a general plan; that is a matter for the Admiralty. But the specific application of the plan in all its details rests with him; and it is safe to say that whatever may be the faults of the English system, they do not lie in the application of it. From the time the young lad of twelve or thirteen passes his examination for a cadetship down to his last voluntary course as a captain, through the Britannia, the course afloat, the sub-lieutenants' collegiate course, and the subsequent voluntary studies, his education is in the hands of Dr. Hirst, under the Admiralty rules, and it is managed with all the wisdom and judgment that the rules will permit. The importance of this single head for the whole system cannot be overestimated.

In the English service there seems to be a theory that a naval officer be a creature of a delicate and sensitive organization, whose regard for his profession and whose zeal for a high standard of professional attainment must be stimulated by surrounding him eternally with all its minor details, to an extent unknown in any other walk of life. To make a sailor, he must begin at twelve or thirteen, even though he does not go to sea for two years, to accustom him early to his duties. During these two years he must live on board a ship, and be able to climb the rigging, to familiarize himself with details; though the ship lies at anchor in a river, a few yards from the shore, and carries no spars but her foremast and head booms. He must sleep in a hammock to inure himself to hardship. In the opinion of the majority of officers, he must have his college for higher instruction in a naval port, or he will forget his duties; and he must pursue his scientific researches in a dockyard, because he will be surrounded by officers engaged in the work of the profession, with whom he can discuss articles in the professional magazines.

If the naval profession has become what many enlightened officers of the present day would have us believe, an occupation involving accurate scientific knowledge, the system of training in England has a tendency to grasp the shadow while losing the substance. The expedients adopted with reference to the higher education of voluntary students, and the admirable courses of instruction for officers who have taken up one branch of the service, notably in the Excellent and Vernon, do much to remedy the inherent defects of the system; and the promotion in two grades by selection excludes the most incompetent officers from

positions of great responsibility. But it seems
impossible that the injurious effects of the
method of training pursued with young
officers, during the first eight years of their
professional life, should not be felt by the
vast majority throughout their whole career.
The peculiar features of this training have
been already pointed out: the discouraging
efforts in the Britannia to attain a point hopelessly beyond the young student's reach; the
five years of desultory training on board the
great cruising ships, passed in a struggle to
retain and comprehend a mass of undigested
facts and principles, crammed for the immediate purpose of passing an examination;
and, finally, the review course, where the student first finds himself fairly on his feet, in
his relations with his instructors. The fatal
defect of the system has been aptly set forth
in a remark of one of the Greenwich professors, in his evidence before the commission, where he says that the standard for
sub-lieutenants is the same as that for cadets
in the Britannia; but the essential difference
lies in the fact that at Greenwich the students
actually reach the standard, while at Dartmouth they do not. No one who has had much
experience in educational methods will deny
that such a system must be productive of
harmful results when applied rigorously to
the training of a body of young men; and one
is therefore led to the conclusion that the high
scientific and professional attainments of
many English naval officers are not in consequence, but in spite, of their early education. . . .

The French Naval School

The school at which nearly all the cadets
of the line of the French Navy receive their
education is on board the old wooden line-of-
battle ship Borda. The Borda is anchored in
the roads of Brest, about a mile and a half
or two miles from the town. The interior
of the ship is cut up and rearranged to suit
the needs of the school, as in the case of the
Britannia, though the details of arrangement
in the Borda are quite different. The poop
extends to the main-mast, and contains the
cabins of the commanding officer, although the
latter does not live on board. The spar-deck
forward of the poop is used as a gymnasium.
The combings of the main hatchway are
removed, and the deck flushed over; and
there is the usual supply of rings, parallel
and horizontal bars, &c., that form the outfit of a small gymnasium. On the upper gun-

deck is the mess-hall, with pantries and
offices forward. The students sleep on the
lower gun-deck. On this deck are also the
two study-rooms (*salles d'étude*), one for each
division. All these rooms are forward of the
main-mast. In the after part of the ship, on
the two gun-decks, are the officers' quarters
and wardroom, and also the lecture-rooms.
These are two in number, and are built in
the shape of amphitheaters, the floor being
laid in steps rising towards the back, and
extending from the lower to the upper deck.
The furniture in all these rooms is of the
simplest character, consisting of small stationary tables, desks, and benches. The
library is small, inconveniently placed, and
contains few recent books. The space between decks in the room devoted to this purpose is too small to admit of standing up-
right. The library seems to be little used. The
battery of the Borda consists of B.L.R.
guns of the most recent type, of 12, 14,
and 16 c. m. Two corvettes are attached to
the establishment, one a sailing-vessel, the
other a screw-steamer.

Personnel. The Naval School, like all other
adjuncts of the station at Brest, is under
the general authority and supervision of the
Préfet Maritime of the II arrondissement. At
its head is a captain; next in rank to the captain is a commander (*capitaine de frégate*),
who has the same general duties as com-
manders on board sea-going vessels.

The authority of the Préfet Maritime is
not confined to mere formalities. He makes
all the administrative arrangements necessary for carrying on the working of the school,
especially those in regard to police and interior service. He makes inspections at discretion, but he is required by regulation to
inspect regularly three times a year—in
January, April, and August. The two first
inspections are preceded by the inspections
of the material administration of the school,
made by the commissary-general, and by the
commissary in charge of equipments. Reports
are made to the Ministry of Marine of the
result of each of these inspections. In regard
to various details of government the captain
frequently advises with the Préfet; and, finally, the latter is the presiding member of
the board of improvement (*conseil de perfectionnement*).

The captain of the Borda is the director
of the studies of the school as well as of the
discipline. The commander, or executive officer, has charge of the interior police and
service, of the conduct of students, and of
practical and professional instruction. He

keeps a conduct book and a punishment book, and gives the students a mark for conduct every quarter. With instruction in the scientific and miscellaneous branches he has nothing to do, the instructors in these branches being wholly under the direction of the captain.

The instructors consist of eight lieutenants, twelve professors, and one principal mechanician. The lieutenants have charge of the courses in seamanship, naval architecture, gunnery, and practical navigation, there being two for each branch, one taking the upper and one the lower class. Four of the lieutenants act as chiefs of sections (*chefs d'escouades*) and keep a constant and careful oversight of the members of their sections. They transmit orders to their respective sections, and receive complaints or requests from them. It is their duty to regulate all those minor matters of detail, pertaining to the daily life of the pupils, that are not covered by general instructions. A close personal relation is thus established between the members of each section and their chief. He sees that all articles in their possession, such as clothing and books, are properly kept and cared for, and that they have no unauthorized objects. He keeps their weekly allowance books, and, in case of permission to incur extra expenses, for special instruction or what not, he is required to certify that the lessons have been properly given, or that the articles purchased have been duly received. Of course these duties involve frequent inspection and constant personal intercourse; and the chief of section is the person to whom the student naturally looks for advice and assistance, and who is to aid and stimulate his efforts to perfect himself as a naval officer. The other lieutenants perform the ordinary duties of officer of the day; but all of them, including the chiefs of sections, have a share in the regular detail of the ship's duties; and all have to note delinquencies on the part of the students and to enforce the discipline of the ship. They can only inflict reprimands; cases requiring severer punishment must be referred to the captain or commander. The senior lieutenant is in charge of two auxiliary vessels; the instructor in practical navigation has the direction of the observatory on shore; while a third lieutenant is charged with the small-arm practice.

The twelve professors at the Naval School are divided as follows:

Professors of analysis and mechanics 2
Professors of astronomy and navigation 2
Professor of physics and chemistry 1
Professors of literature, history, and geography 2
Professors of English 3
Professors of drawing 2

The professors do not reside on board the ship, but are brought off from shore every morning in a small steamer attached to the school, in time for the morning lecture.

The other officers of the school are, a principal mechanician, instructor in steam-engineering; a chaplain; an assistant commissary, who has charge of all administrative matters other than military or academic; three surgeons; and an accounting officer and storekeeper (*agent comptable économe*). The latter officer has the direction of a variety of matters, such as the care of public property, the preparation of estimates for stores and materials, receipts, disbursements, and purchases, and the correspondence of the captain of the school with the parents of pupils.

To the list of officers should perhaps be added the members of the two boards of examination, whose functions are subsidiary to the main purpose of the school, though the members are not attached to the Borda. One of these boards conducts the examination for admission, the other the annual and final examinations. The latter board is composed of naval officers of high rank, together with a member of the corps of hydrographic examiners. The pharmacist-in-chief at Brest usually examines in chemistry.

The crew of the Borda numbers about 150 men. The warrant and petty officers are carefully selected by the captain of the Borda, and six or eight of them, in addition to their regular duties, assist in the instruction of the students in practical exercises connected with the specialties to which they belong. These special branches include seamanship and gunnery, and the specialties of helmsmen, topmen, machinists, and captain of arms. A similar number of non-commissioned officers of the marine artillery (*adjudants*) perform the details of disciplinary service. At their head is the captain of arms, and the whole force comes directly under the executive officer. Their duties include the hourly oversight of the pupils, the frequent inspection of their desks, chests, and lockers, and of all their belongings, and duty as watchmen by day and by night. They are directed to enforce the regulations of discipline, and to report all infractions. In fact, in all matters of detail they perform the police of the ship.

There are four boards or committees that occupy an important place in the organization of the school. The first of these is the committee on improvements (*conseil de perfectionnement*). It is composed of the Préfet Maritime, as president; the captains of the Borda and of the Flore, the sea-going practice-ship of cadets; and the members of the two examining boards, of admission and graduation. It meets annually, revises the programme of study, and considers and proposes other changes in the organization and methods of the school. These changes are submitted for approval to the Board of Admiralty (*conseil d'amirauté*) at the Ministry of Marine.

The council of instruction or academic board (*conseil d'instruction*) is composed of the captain and commander of the Borda, the two examining boards, three professors or instructors, appointed for one year by the Préfet, of whom one is in the professional, one in the scientific, and one in the literary or "general" department, and the commissary.[1] The duties of the board are to consider and report upon measures proposed by the secondary council, or referred to it by the Minister. The latter include the distribution of scholarships (*bourses*), and of indemnities for outfit.

The secondary council of instruction (*conseil secondaire d'instruction*) is composed of the same members as the council of instruction, except the examining boards. It acts as an advisory board to the Préfet Maritime and the captain of the school, by whom various questions relating to academic organization are submitted to it. It has also the initiative in all propositions relating to the instruction and course of study, and it conducts the re-examination of deficient pupils, making recommendations as to the final disposition of doubtful cases. It considers proposals for the purchase of scientific works, periodicals, and apparatus. Its other duties include the preparation of the term and yearly class-lists, and, in general, it attends to those matters of detail which concern the academic interests of the school. The captain of the school is president of the council, and any of the instructors or professors who are not members may be required to attend its discussions, but only with a consulting voice.

The fourth of the governing boards is the council of administration (*conseil d'administration*). It is composed of the captain and commander, the commissary, and the two senior lieutenants, chiefs of sections. It keeps the running account with the Ministry of Finance, and with the pupils, and it has general charge of receipts, disbursements, and purchases. The "accounting officer and storekeeper" (*économe*) acts as its agent.

Examination for Admission. The examination for admission to the Naval School is one of the most important parts of the French system of naval education, on account of its scope, its method, and its close relation to the system of public instruction in the country. It is competitive in character. Its requirements are high and extend over a considerable range of subjects. Finally, it is based directly on the programmes of study in the *lycées*, the principal schools for secondary instruction in France. It has several other noticeable features, but it is to these three that its important effects are chiefly due.

The method of organization is simple. The examining board consists of four examiners, chosen each year by the Minister of Marine, two in scientific, and two in literary or general subjects. A captain in the Navy is president of the board, but his duties are confined to administrative matters. Junior officers are assigned to take charge of the examination-room. A special examiner is appointed to mark the drawings handed in by candidates.

The examination is in two parts, written and oral. The written examination is held first, and candidates are required to obtain a certain mark—35 per cent. in mathematics, 25 per cent. in literary subjects, and 15 per cent. in drawing. Those who fail to reach this standard are excluded from further competition. To save candidates the expense of a long journey, the simple and excellent method is adopted of having different centers of examination, at any one of which candidates may present themselves. The centers are ten in number—Paris, Brest, Cherbourg, Lorient, Rochefort, Toulouse, Toulon, Bastia (Corsica), Algiers, and Lyons. At these places written examinations are held simultaneously on the 11th, 12th, and 13th of June in each year. As most of the places designated are naval stations, or stations where a number of naval officers are constantly on duty (all, in fact, except Lyons and Toulouse), the service of conducting the written examination is attended with no special expense to the government.

---

[1] It must constantly be borne in mind that the word commissary denotes a member of the administrative corps of the Navy, and has no connection with what in English is understood as the commissariat.

Useful as this system is found in France, its advantages would be even greater in the United States, on account of the immense distances to be passed over by candidates from all the Congressional districts, in reaching any given point. At present it happens, and under the existing system it must continue to happen, not infrequently, that young men whose means do not warrant the expense are obliged to take a journey of 1,500 or 3,000 miles to present themselves at an examination which they are totally unprepared to pass. The only way to avoid this is by holding examinations simultaneously at different centers. The principal navy-yards furnish convenient points, with all the materials ready at hand. In this way Boston and Portsmouth would be centers for New England; New York and Philadelphia for the Middle States; Annapolis, Norfolk, Port Royal, and Pensacola for the Southeast, and San Francisco for the extreme West. To these might be added Cincinnati, Chicago, Saint Louis, and New Orleans for the center. Such a system would present great advantages, and at the same time be easy of application and attended with little or no expense.

Persons desiring to compete in the examination for admission to the Naval School are obliged to enter their names as candidates at the prefecture of the department in which they reside, between the 1st and 25th of April, preceding the examination at which they intend to present themselves. They must be at least fourteen, and not more than seventeen, years of age on the 1st of January preceding their application. This condition is rigorously applied, and no dispensations are ever granted to candidates above or below the limits. The average age of candidates admitted has been found to be about 16 years. At the time of entering their names, candidates are required to present the following papers:

1. Certificate of birth.
2. Certificate of French nationality.
3. Physician's certificate of vaccination.
4. Choice of center of examination.
5. Bond of parent or guardian for payment of fee for board and tuition, amounting to 700 francs a year.
6. Bond of parent or guardian for payment of outfit, amounting to about 1,000 francs.

The regulations for conducting the written examinations are prescribed with considerable minuteness, particularly with a view to prevent irregularity or unfairness in marking. The questions are the same at all the centers of examination. They are sent in sealed envelopes from the Ministry of Marine to the prefects and subprefects in whose jurisdiction the examination is to be held, and by whom they are transmitted to the naval officers in charge of the examination.

The examinations are held with closed doors, at the day and hour prescribed. Not more than twenty candidates can be placed in one room, and warrant officers are detailed for the surveillance of these rooms; at least one to every ten candidates. At the beginning of each day's session the officer in charge opens the envelope in the presence of the candidates, and reads aloud the questions. At the close of the session he collects the papers and transmits them to the ministry of marine. Here the duties of this officer cease. The papers are sent to the president of the board of examiners, who detaches the headings containing the name of the writer, after having placed on both headings and papers a corresponding series of numbers. In this condition, numbered, but not named, the papers are turned over to the proper examiners to be marked. When the marking is finished, the board meets and draws up a list, still without the names of candidates, of the marks given to each numbered paper. The president then opens, in the presence of the board, the sealed envelope in which he had previously placed the headings, and the final report of the written examination is drawn up. This is published in the *Journal Officiel*, and is the only notification received by the candidates of their success or failure at the preliminary examination.

The oral examinations follow immediately upon the written. Like the first, they are held at various cities, the board of examiners making a tour for this purpose. The places of the examination are the same as before, except in the case of Bastia and Algiers, candidates from Corsica and Algeria presenting themselves at Toulon. The first examination is held at Paris, July 1, and at the other cities in succession. Each candidate must pass a medical examination before a board composed of the president of the examining board, a commander, and a naval surgeon. This always precedes the oral examination. Candidates who have failed at the written examination, or who have absented themselves from any of the tests, or who have made use of any improper means of assistance, are ruled out before the oral examination begins.

The final classification is prepared under the direction of the jury of examination, composed of the examining board, together with two naval officers of high rank, sitting at Paris. The marks, ranging, according to the usual scale in France, from 0 to 20, are multiplied by the prescribed coefficients, and the sum of the products gives the final mark. In case two candidates have the same mark, the oral examination decides their final position; and if the result is still the same, greater weight is given to the scientific branches. Thirty additional marks are given to candidates who have taken the degree of bachelor of letters. From the final list the minister appoints the members of the entering class at the naval school in the order of classification, and in accordance with the number required. A letter is accordingly sent to each successful candidate, which he is to present to the major-general (chief of naval staff) on his arrival at Brest, before the beginning of the session. After a second medical examination, and after making the necessary deposit, he is regularly entered at the school.

The scope of the examination for admission is defined in the programmes of certain classes in the *lycées*. . . .

. . . As far as instruction goes, both lycées and colleges may be classed together, though the latter are usually less completely organized and provided with a less numerous staff of instructors; but in general they follow the programme of the lycées as far as they can. This includes nine regular classes, with a division (*bifurcation*) in the programme, above the second class, for students who desire to confine their attention more particularly either to science or to literature and philosophy. The higher classes are known as the classes of elementary mathematics and the higher mathematics, on the one hand, and of rhetoric and philosophy, on the other. The highest classes reach a standard as high as that of the sophomore class at our highest universities, or of the senior class at many of our colleges. Leaving out the last two years, the French schools correspond nearly to our best Latin and high schools. They are admirably organized and carefully inspected; their methods of instruction and programmes of study are based on sound principles, and they produce the best results. Of course it is a great advantage to a professional school to be able to draw its pupils from such a source, and thus to be assured that they have a preliminary training at once broad, thorough, and complete. There is no greater drag to the efficiency of an institution for higher education than the want of good fitting schools —a want such as is felt at the present moment

at our Military and Naval Academies, and nowhere felt more severely. This want in France is supplied to the fullest extent and in the most satisfactory way. The great national schools, including the Polytechnic, Saint-Cyr, the normal school, and the naval school at Brest, receive the great majority of their pupils from the best schools that exist in the country. They are thus enabled to make the qualifications for admission high, to do away with all those elementary branches of instruction that form no proper part of the work of a professional school, and to concentrate the energies of their pupils upon studies of a high character, connected more or less directly with the profession in view. The high standard of admission and the competitive examinations are not productive of cramming; on the contrary, they are far less so than a lower standard would be, even in a test examination, where the preparation is given in inferior schools, with a month or a fortnight of private tuition just before the examination. At the examination for admission at Annapolis, limited as it is in scope and trifling as are the subjects that compose it, a large number of the weaker candidates are prepared by this latter process. In France where the programme of the examination is based directly on that of the schools—in fact, is identical with it in most subjects—there is no such difficulty. . . .

General Character of French Naval Education

It was remarked by Captain Hore, the naval attaché of the English embassy in Paris, in his testimony before the Committee on the Higher Education of Officers, in 1870, that the English had no system of naval education. and that the French had too much system. That there is much truth in the first part of the observation will be acknowledged by every one who has examined the matter at all, and Captain Hore, being himself an English officer, was in a position to know. But his judgment upon the French system must be taken with some allowance, and certainly his testimony before the committee does not indicate such an acquaintance with the subject as would entitle his opinion to great weight.

The fault of "too much system," if it means anything, means a sacrifice of results to methods, an effort which looks rather to the perfection of the machinery than to the work done by the machine. It is a fault very commonly charged to French methods of administration, and one to which, perhaps, they are largely open. It is a necessary consequence of extreme centralization, and it affects to some extent the system of public education, including both the secondary and the professional schools. Its injurious effects are felt, however, rather in minor details and in exceptional instances than in the general result. In most respects the public-school system, although highly organized, is sufficiently elastic to meet the wants of individual cases. As to the training-schools for this or that professional service, and especially for a military service, it is doubtful whether a flexible system is as productive of good results as a more rigid one; and in the French naval schools there is certainly in matters of theoretical and practical instruction much greater flexibility than is to be found in those of almost any other nation. The system of oral teaching, without the restrictions of a text-book and supplemented by individual explanation and interrogation, cannot be other than an elastic one. With regard to discipline, however, it must be confessed that if French boys are at all like other boys, a great many rules might be relaxed with direct and positive benefit.

The broad features of the French system of naval education may be readily recognized from the detailed description that has been given. They consist in a unity of purpose underlying the whole plan; a rational organization, with a distinct perception of the ends in view, and an adaptation of means to reach the ends proposed; the exaction of a high standard of preparatory training; and great originality, freedom, and thoroughness of instruction. Looking at the details, we find, in the case of line officers, a system of local examination for admission, competitive in character, with requirements based on the programmes of the best schools in the country. These are followed by a three years' course of theoretical and practical training. The first two years are passed in a stationary ship, with all the disadvantages that such a school-house entails—disadvantages in this case even greater than in that of the Britannia. The only compensating advantage is that of making possible an excessively rigorous discipline, an advantage of more than doubtful character. The course of theoretical instruction is the fullest and most advanced *required* course pursued by the cadets of any navy in the world except that of Germany, and the practical and professional branches receive an ample share of time and attention, although the course in these subjects is rightly considered as only preparatory to the work of the practice-ship. It is, nevertheless, extensive and thorough, including frequent exercise in the details of seamanship, gunnery, navigation, and the manipulation of engines. Following the two years' course comes the third and final year in a sea-going practice-ship, with review and completion of the course, in the theory and practice of subjects purely professional.

The other corps of the service are as well taught as the line in the particular duties of their several professions; for it may be taken as a cardinal maxim of professional education in France that a man cannot be expected to know how to do a thing by a process of inspiration or intuition, or even by "picking up," but that he must be *taught* to do it. Hence, they have a thorough course of instruction for the men who are to build their ships, to fight their ships, to govern the employment of the motive power of their ships, to conduct the details of internal administration on board their ships. The constructors have a four years' course: two years at the Polytechnic, the first school of mathematics in the world, and two years at their special school of application, with practice in the great ship-building and engine-building establishments. The engineers or mechanicians have a series of courses and examinations preceding each promotion, whose extent and character leave little to be desired for this branch of the profession. Finally, the administrative officers or commissaries are taught effectually the principles, the laws, and regulations which are to govern them in the future exercise of their duties.

It will be seen that the education given to officers in general is of a high and extensive character. This supplies the want of special subsequent training to some extent, but not wholly. There is a decided need at present of facilities for higher education in the branches which particular inclinations may lead individual line officers to take up. It is not unlikely that such a higher college, similar in purpose to the half-pay courses at Greenwich, may in time be established; though there is by no means the same necessity for it that exists in England.

Charles William Eliot   1888

A Comparison of American and French School Programs

Charles William Eliot (1834–1926) graduated from Harvard College in 1853. He was assistant professor of mathematics and chemistry at Harvard from 1858 to 1863, professor of chemistry at the Massachusetts Institute of Technology in 1865, and president of Harvard from 1869 to 1909. Eliot is considered one of the leading innovators in American higher education during the nineteenth century and introduced many progressive changes in Harvard's curriculum and administration. He traveled abroad to study education in France, Germany, and England from 1863 to 1865 and in 1867.

Eliot's comparative study of French and American public school curriculums is a classic descriptive analysis of educational systems. His speech below, prepared for school superintendents, suggested methods whereby the whole primary and secondary school program in the United States could be shortened and yet enriched. Eliot felt that American educators should emulate the French program in order to allow students to enter college at eighteen instead of nineteen without lowering the standards for a bachelor's degree. He made the perennial complaint, still prevalent among American educators, that there was too great a preponderance of women teachers and said that "herein lies one of the great causes of the inferiority of the American teaching to the French and German teaching."

In the process of improving the secondary schools, colleges, and professional schools of the United States,—a process which has been carried on with remarkable energy since the Civil War,—certain new difficulties have been created for the higher education in general, and particularly for colleges. These difficulties have to do with the age at which young men can get prepared for college, and therefore with the ages at which boys pass the successive stages of their earlier education. The average age of admission to Harvard College has been rising for sixty years past, and has now reached the extravagant limit of eighteen years and ten months. Harvard College is not at all peculiar in this respect; indeed, many of the country colleges find their young men older still at entrance. The average college graduate is undoubtedly nearly twenty-three years old at graduation; and when he has obtained his A.B. he must nowadays allow at least three years for his professional education.

In respect to the length of time required for a satisfactory professional training, there has been a great change since the War. Twenty years ago the period of residence at Harvard University for the degree of Bachelor of Laws was eighteen months; now it is three years. Many of the States of the American Union have passed laws which practically make three years the normal period of study before admission to the bar. Ambitious medical students are giving four years to their medical training. Twenty years ago the leading colleges were satisfied to take men just graduated in arts as tutors in Latin, Greek, and mathematics. Now they expect a candidate for a tutorship or instructorship to have devoted two or three years to study after taking his bachelor's degree. School boards and trustees have become correspondingly exacting. In short, professional education in the United States is becoming constantly more thorough and elaborate, and is therefore demanding of aspirants to the professions more and more time. The average college graduate who fits himself well for any one of the learned professions, including teaching, can hardly begin to support himself before he is twenty-seven years old.

This condition of things is so unreasonable in a new country like the United States—being hardly matched in the oldest and most densely peopled countries of Europe—that some remedy is urgently demanded; and the first partial remedy that suggests itself is to reduce the average age of admission to college to eighteen. This reduction would

Charles William Eliot, "Can School Programmes Be Shortened and Enriched?" *Educational Reform: Essays and Addresses* (New York: The Century Co., 1905), pp. 151–176; and in United States Bureau of Education, *Circulars of Information, 1888,* Vol. II, No. 6, Proceedings of the Department of Superintendence of the National Educational Association, at its Meeting in Washington, February 14–16, 1888 (Washington, D.C.: U.S. Government Printing Office, 1888), pp. 101–115.

save about a year. In effecting this saving of time, it is greatly to be wished that no reduction should be made in the attainments which the average candidates for admission now brings to the American colleges; for it is probable that the saving thus effected will not be sufficient in itself, and that the public interests will require in addition some shortening of the ordinary college course of four years. College men, therefore, are anxiously looking to see if the American school courses can be both shortened and enriched,—shortened, so that our boys may come to college at eighteen instead of nineteen, and enriched, in order that they may bring to college at eighteen more than they now bring at nineteen, so that the standard of the A.B. may not be lowered.

The anxiety with which men charged with the conduct of college education look at this question is increased by the relative decline of American colleges and universities as a whole. This relative decline, which was pointed out nearly twenty years ago by President Barnard of Columbia College, is very visible of late years. The population of the United States is supposed by the best authorities to increase about one third in every period of ten years. In the ten-year period from 1875 to 1884 inclusive, the universities and colleges included in the tables published by the Commissioner of Education show an increase in their number of students of only 11 per cent., instead of $33\frac{1}{3}$ per cent. If we select from the same tables the ten-year period from 1876 to 1885, the increase is 16 per cent.; but the explanation of this higher percentage of increase is that the total number of students in the year 1876 was abnormally low, being 2400 below the number of 1875. If we add to the institutions enumerated as universities and colleges all the schools of science and all the higher institutions for the education of women, we still find that this enlarged list of institutions has not gained students at the same rate at which the population has increased, although the schools of science have made very large gains in the decade referred to. Thus the increase in the number of students in universities and colleges, schools of science, and women's colleges, all taken together, was only 23 per cent. in the ten years from 1875 to 1884 inclusive. Obviously there are serious hindrances affecting all the institutions which receive young men and women at the age of eighteen or nineteen to keep them under liberal training for three or four years. One of these hindrances undoubtedly is that the

colleges as a whole held too long to a medieval curriculum; but a greater hindrance, in all probability, is the burden imposed upon parents when their elaborately educated sons cannot support themselves in their professions until they are twenty-seven or twenty-eight years old. Hence the importance of the inquiry, Can school programmes be shortened and enriched?

In studying this problem it is natural to turn first to the schools sometimes called preparatory—that is, to the best high schools and academies; but if we examine the courses of study in these schools we find that the four years during which they keep their pupils are generally crowded with work. Thus the Phillips Academy, at Exeter, New Hampshire, one of the best academies in the United States, has a four years' course which is so full that hardly any suggestion can be made for compacting or abbreviating it. But what are the requirements for admission to Exeter? "Some knowledge of common-school arithmetic, writing, and spelling, and of the elements of English grammar." These requirements might reasonably be made of a boy leaving the primary school at eight years of age; yet the average age of admission to Exeter is sixteen and one half. Now, Exeter is an academy which does not content itself with such low terms of admission unless under compulsion. It would require more if it could get more from the average candidate; but it draws its pupils from a wide area, and its experience is against making greater demands. The Exeter course is itself encumbered with some studies suitable for a boy of ten. Thus it devotes much time to arithmetic, and teaches the very elements of English and English literature. A secondary school which is obliged to take its pupils in the average condition of the boys who enter Exeter can hardly do more for them in the four years between sixteen and twenty than is now accomplished at that academy. What is true of Exeter is true of the whole body of upper schools. They have to make good the deficiencies of the lower schools. It is necessary, therefore, to examine the American school programmes from the beginning, to start with the primary school and go on through the grammar school and the high school, searching for the places where time and labor can be saved.

The subject seems to be one chiefly interesting to colleges, but really it has a much broader scope. In the first place, whatever improves the school programmes for those children whose education is to be prolonged, perhaps, until they are twenty-five years old, will improve the programmes also for the less fortunate children whose education is to be briefer. The public schools will never send to higher institutions any very large proportion of the children who are trained in them; but their programmes may best be made substantial and systematic by fitting them to the needs of their most intelligent and fortunate pupils. Moreover, we may reasonably strive to make every grade of the public-school programme,—primary, grammar, and high,—and, indeed, every year in any programme, a thing good in itself, as well as a good introduction to the course of study which lies beyond it. The better the programme is in itself, the better it will be as a preparation for further study. To the primary and grammar schools this principle applies in all its fullness. In the high school and academy the principle needs qualification for the foreign languages only, and for that portion of the programme options should be allowed. The question, Can American school programmes be at once condensed and enriched? has, then, a wide scope, and touches the interests of the whole population.

As evidence conducing to the formation of a just opinion upon the practicability of shortening and enriching our school programmes, an actual comparison of two public-school programmes,—one French and one American,—covering the ages of eight to seventeen inclusive, is printed at the end of this document. One programme is that of the French secondary schools, which is followed all over France in the institutions called *lycées;* the other is the programme made by uniting the first three years of the Boston grammar schools with the complete course of the Boston Latin School. It is assumed that the Boston schools are a fair type for the country Indeed, the Boston Latin School is supposed to be the best, as it is the oldest, American classical school which is supported by local taxation. In the tables referred to the programmes are placed side by side, so that the courses for the same years of age can be conveniently compared. It is in each case the classical course which is tabulated; but a similar comparison could be instituted between the corresponding programmes in which Latin and Greek are replaced by other subjects. In the French schools Latin and Greek can be in large part replaced by mathematical and scientific studies, and in Boston the English High School offers a programme like that of the Latin School, but with similar substitution of mathematical and scientific studies for all the Greek and

some or all of the Latin. The present purpose can be fully accomplished by limiting the comparison to the classical programmes. The French programme was chosen rather than the programme of a German gymnasium, because it is a lower term of comparison, the German programme being more comprehensive, elaborate, and difficult. The French programme is a recent reduction of a programme in force from 1880 to 1885, the reduction amounting to about twenty per cent., and the number of recitations per week in the two programmes (French and American) is nearly the same. It is the best of foreign programmes as a term of comparison, because France is socially a democratic country, politically a republic, and industrially a country whose chief reliance, in the strenuous competition to which its population is exposed within and without, is the intelligence and skill of its producing classes. In all these respects France and the United States closely resemble each other. Moreover, the French boy has no possible advantage over the American boy in strength of constitution, intelligence, or endurance; on the contrary, he is not so large a boy as the American on an average, and he is not so well fed.

A very brief examination of these two programmes side by side reveals several important facts. The French programme is decidedly the more substantial; that is to say, it calls for greater exertion on the part of the pupil than the American, introduces the children earlier to serious subjects, and is generally more interesting and more stimulating to the intelligence. For example, at eight years of age the French boy begins to study a foreign language, either English or German; the American boy begins to study a modern language five years later, at thirteen, when the best period for learning a foreign tongue is already past. The French boy of eight begins the study of history in a very interesting and stimulating way through the study of biography; the American boy gets no history until he is thirteen, when he begins Greek history. The French boy of eight gives just one third of the time to arithmetic that the American boy gives, and in the whole course does not give to that subject more than one third the time the American boy gives; yet, for practical purposes, the French are quite as skillful with numbers as the Americans. The French boy gets at natural history earlier than the American boy, and in better subjects. Again, the French programme represents an actual fact, the large majority of French boys passing regularly through it at the ages indicated in the programme; whereas the programme of the Boston Latin School, prepared for the years from eleven to sixteen inclusive, actually covers the years from thirteen to eighteen inclusive. In comparing the attainments of the Boston boy with those of the French boy we must therefore add two full years to the ages set down in the American programme. The inferiority of the Boston programme then becomes very conspicuous. There is no single subject touched in the American programme in which the French boy does not accomplish more than the American. This appears very clearly in comparing the amounts of Latin and Greek set down in the two programmes, but equally plainly in geometry and physics. Moreover, the French course extends a year beyond the American course, and in the class called philosophy gives a comprehensive survey of philosophy and ethics, a thing never attempted in the United States with boys of seventeen, yet found practicable and in the highest degree useful in the French republic. The preponderance of the French language, the mother-tongue, in the French programme is most noticeable. Until Latin and Greek are introduced, French occupies half of the whole course. When the study of Latin and Greek is at its height, French still claims a substantial portion of the programme; and in the final year, the year called philosophy, French resumes almost exclusive possession of the programme. Great improvements have been made during the last ten years in the study of English and English literature in the best American schools; but the mother-tongue does not yet hold anything like the place in American schools that French holds in the French schools. In the French lycées geometry comes before algebra, and with the help of drawing is treated thoroughly before algebra is seriously attacked, plane geometry being finished by the time the boy is fourteen years of age. At the Boston Latin School, on the other hand, plane geometry is not completed until the boy is seventeen according to the programme, and nineteen in reality. This brief discussion of the two programmes may reasonably convince any one that the French boy makes a much greater total attainment by the time he is eighteen than the American boy has a chance to make at the best American schools by the time he is nineteen. Thorough study of them will only strengthen this conviction.

The comparison thus instituted gives no warrant for impatient, revolutionary action. The transformation it suggests is not to be wrought in a year, but should be the aim of patient labor during many years. Everybody knows that foreign institutions of education cannot be imported; that a nation's educational institutions are strongly influenced by its political, ethical, and industrial conditions, and that the improvement of schools and colleges must necessarily be slow. It may, however, be justly inferred from this comparison of programmes that the condition of secondary schools in the United States is at present one of inferiority; that the country ought not to be satisfied with that condition, and indeed should strenuously exert itself to improve it, there being opportunity in American programmes for both condensation and enrichment. If it be said that the American boy turns out pretty well after all, and that the American community, as a whole, is as intelligent as the French or the German community, the ready answer is that free institutions are in themselves a considerable education for the population; but that the advantage which the nation has over Europe in possessing free institutions ought not to reconcile it to a position of inferiority as regards schools; it ought to aim to have the best schools, too. If it be practicable to make American primary and secondary schools better, the work of improvement should be set on foot.

The fair inference from the [below] tables being that improvement is practicable, it will not be unprofitable to consider some of the means of improving the American public school, from the primary grade through the high school.

1. In the first place, better programmes need better teachers. The great difference between the French and German secondary schools and the American is in the quality of the teachers. Two modes of improving the general body of teachers in the public schools demand special attention. In the first place, school committees, superintendents, teachers themselves, and all friends of public education should constantly strive to procure a better tenure of office for American teachers. The American schools will never equal the schools of Germany and France until well-proved teachers can secure a tenure during good behavior and efficiency, like teachers in those countries. Consideration, dignity, and quietness of mind go with a permanent tenure, and the public-school service will never compete successfully with the service of private educational corporations in this country until the public employ is as good as the private employ in this regard. Secondly, the average skill of the teachers in the public schools may be in-

creased by raising the present low proportion of male teachers in the schools. Herein lies one of the great causes of the inferiority of the American teaching to the French and German teaching. The proportion of women teachers in American schools is vastly greater than it is in Europe. The larger the proportion of women in any system of public schools, the larger will be the percentage of new appointments every year, and the larger the amount of work done by temporary substitutes. New appointments and substitutes generally mean inexperienced teachers, or, at the best, teachers suddenly put to work in unaccustomed places. This superiority of men as teachers has, of course, nothing whatever to do with the relative intelligence or faithfulness of men and women. It is a well-known fact that many women enter the public schools as teachers without any intention of long following the business; and also that women are absent from duty from two to three times as much as men. Young men who take up teaching as a temporary expedient are also unsatisfactory material. The schools need the life-work of highly trained and experienced teachers. After these two most important means of raising the average quality of public-school teachers come lesser means which ought not to be neglected; thus, superintendents and committees can do something to improve teachers by invariably advocating the expenditure of money for teaching, rather than for mechanical appliances or buildings. Cheap teachers and expensive apparatus and buildings are precisely the reverse of wise practice, particularly if the fine buildings are not fire-proof after all. Again, the teaching of the public schools can, of course, be improved by the establishment of teachers' examinations, which secure a better preparation in the average teacher, and by methods of supervision which make known the relative merits of teachers who are on probation. Good progress has been made in this direction during the past ten years (1878–88).

2. The second direction of untiring effort should be to the improvement of programmes; for the programmes are all-important to the steady development of the whole system of schools from top to bottom. A good programme will, of course, not execute itself; it must be vivified by the good teacher; but an injudicious programme is an almost insuperable obstacle to the improvement of a city's schools. As a rule, the American programmes do not seem to be substantial enough, from the first year in the primary school onward. There is not enough meat in the diet. They do not bring the child forward fast enough to maintain his interest, and induce him to put forth his strength. Frequent complaint is made of overpressure in the public schools, but Friedrich Paulsen is probably right in saying that it is not work which causes overfatigue so much as lack of interest and lack of conscious progress. The sense that, work as he may, he is not accomplishing anything will wear upon the stoutest adult, much more upon a child. One problem in arithmetic which he cannot solve will try a child more than ten he can solve. One hour of work in which he can take no intelligent interest will wear him out more than two hours of work in which he cannot help being interested. Now, the trouble with much of the work in the public schools is that it is profoundly and inevitably uninteresting to the childish mind. To enrich the school programme, therefore, and to make serious subjects follow each other in it more rapidly than now, is not necessarily to increase the strain upon the child; it is, however, necessarily to increase the skill demanded of the teacher, and hence the improvement of teachers must go hand in hand with the improvement of programmes. The best way to diminish strain is to increase interest, attractiveness, and the sense of achievement and growth. American teaching in school and college has been chiefly driving and judging; it ought to be leading and inspiring. Here are these beautiful fields—I will show you the way through them. Here are these rewarding exercises—I will show you how to practise them. Here are these heights—I will lead you up them.

3. Much time can be saved in primary and secondary schools by diminishing the number of reviews, and by never aiming at that kind of accuracy of attainment which reviews, followed by examinations, are intended to enforce. Why should an accuracy of knowledge and of statement be habitually demanded of children which adults seldom possess? How many well-educated adults can add long columns of figures correctly, or find the least common multiple or the greatest common divisor of six or eight numbers? Nothing but practice can keep one skilful in these exercises, and we may reasonably be grateful that few people are compelled to keep in the necessary practice. Few adult minds retain accurately considerable masses of isolated facts; and it is commonly observed that minds which are good at that are seldom the best minds. Why do we try to make children do what we do not try to do ourselves? Instead

of mastering one subject before going to another, it is almost invariably wise to go on to a superior subject before the inferior has been mastered—mastery being a very rare thing. On the mastery theory, how much new reading or thinking should we adults do? Instead of reviewing arithmetic, study algebra; for algebra will illustrate arithmetic and supply many examples of arithmetical processes. Instead of re-reading a familiar story, read a new one; it will be vastly more interesting, and the common words will all recur—the common words being by far the most valuable ones. Instead of reviewing the physical geography of North America, study South America. There, too, the pupil will find mountain-chains, watersheds, high plateaus, broad plains, great streams, and isothermal lines. The really profitable time to review a subject is not when we have just finished it, but when we have used it in studying other subjects, and have seen its relations to other subjects and what it is good for. For example, the French programme puts a review of arithmetic, algebra, and geometry into the last year. With all his mathematical powers strengthened by the study of algebra and geometry, and with all the practice of arithmetic which his study of mensuration and algebra has involved, the boy returns at seventeen to arithmetic and finds it infinitely easier than he did at fourteen. Further, the French boy has escaped those most exasperating of arithmetical puzzles which a little easy algebra enables one to solve with facility. Many an educated New-Englander remembers to this day the exasperation he felt when he discovered that problems in Colburn's Sequel, over which he had struggled for hours, could be solved in as many minutes after he had got half-way through Sherwin's Algebra. Is it not an abominable waste of the time and strength of children to put them to doing in a difficult way, never used in real life, something they will be able to do in an easy way a year or two later? To introduce any artificial hardness into the course of training that any human being has to follow is an unpardonable educational sin. There is hardness enough in this world without manufacturing any, particularly for children. On careful search through all the years of the public-school programmes now in use, many places will be found where time can be saved and strain lessened by abandoning the effort to obtain an exaggerated and wholly unnatural accuracy of work. It is one of the worst defects of examinations that they set an artificial value upon accuracy of attain-

ment. Good examination results do not always prove that the training of the children examined has been of the best kind.

4. In almost all the numerous collections of school statistics now published in this country, it appears that the various grades contain children much too old for them, who have apparently been held back. This phenomenon seems to be due partly to the ambition of teachers and partly to the caution of parents. To illustrate with a specific case: in the Boston primary schools, which are intended for children of five to seven years of age inclusive, 44 per cent. of all the children for three years past were over seven; and in the grammar schools of the same city, which are intended for children of from eight to thirteen years inclusive, from 20 to 24 per cent. were over thirteen. It has already been mentioned that the average age of admission to the Latin School is not eleven years, as indicated in the programme, but thirteen years. It is really thirteen years and three months. For three years past, from one third to one half of the graduating classes of the Boston grammar schools have been more than six years in the schools, the programme calling for but six years. In the Boston primary and grammar schools the tendency is in the wrong direction; that is, in 1887 there was a larger proportion of pupils over age than in 1877. The ambition of teachers tends to keep children too long in the several grades, because they desire to have their pupils appear well at the periodical examinations, and also because they like to keep in their classes the bright children as aids to the dull ones. The caution of parents tends to produce the same difficulty because they fear over-pressure; not comprehending that with children, as with adults, it is not work so much as worry that injures, or finding that the existing system adds worry to work. The exaggerated notion that it is necessary to master one thing before a child goes to another is also responsible for the retardation of children on their way through the regular course. The result of this retardation is that the boy comes too late to the high school or to the Latin School, and so fails to complete that higher course if he is going into business, or comes too late to college if his education is to be more prolonged. The great body of children ought to pass regularly from one grade to another, without delay, at the ages set down on the programme; and any method of examination which interferes with this regular progress does more harm than good. Of late years many experiments have been

made on semiannual promotions and other means of hurrying forward the brighter children. The aim of these experiments is laudable; but the statistics suggest a doubt whether semiannual promotions really promote, and whether they do not disturb to an inexpedient degree the orderly progress of the school work. In general the work of any school must be laid out by years, and on this account irregular promotions will hardly provide a remedy against the common evil of retardation.[1]

5. If we look back a generation, or two generations, in the history of American schools, we shall find that the time spent in school by children during a year has been decidedly reduced; although great improvements have been made during the same period in the ventilation of school buildings, and various bodily exercises, such as singing, gymnastics, and military drill, have been introduced. This reduction of school hours has gone quite far enough, and some steps need to be taken in the other direction. The ideal school should be so conducted that the child's physique is not impaired by attending it, or his enjoyment of his daily life lessened.

---

[1]Irregular and rapid promotion has been greatly facilitated since 1888.

Then longer school hours would not be unsafe or unwelcome. It should be the teachers that need rest and vacation, and not the children. In cities vacation schools seem to be a desirable addition to our present organization. A long vacation may be a very good thing for children who have at home some intellectual resources, or who can go to the country or to the sea in vacation, and there learn some things not found in books; but for children of ignorant or heedless parents, who have nothing of intellectual life to offer them at home, a long vacation is likely to be a serious injury, particularly in cities and large towns. Vacation schools tend to bring forward, or keep up, the least favored children, thus accelerating the general rate of progress during the year.

The chief objects of this address are, first, to point out a serious difficulty which is embarrassing the whole course of American education; and, secondly, to indicate briefly a few of the directions in which labor may be wisely spent in improving our school system, to the general end that the pupils may receive a better training in a shorter time. The professional experience and zeal of superintendents and teachers will know how to devise and execute appropriate measures of relief and improvement.

French and American Public-School Programmes Compared

PROGRAMME OF STUDIES (1885) IN THE SECONDARY SCHOOLS OF FRANCE.

CLASSICAL COURSE.

[In the preparatory class and in the eighth and seventh classes the number of hours of teaching per week is 20, including 1 hour a week for drawing.]

PREPARATORY CLASS. Age 8 yrs.

FRENCH. 9 1/2 hours a week. Reading, spelling, writing, and the most elementary rules of grammar.
GERMAN OR ENGLISH. 4 h. a wk. Exercises in reading and writing. Pronunciation. Accent. Indispensable paradigms.
HISTORY. 1 1/2 h. a wk. Biographies of illustrious men—travelers, patriots, inventors. Talks on great personages in French history down to 1789.
GEOGRAPHY. 1 1/2 h. a wk. Meaning of the principal terms in physical geography, illustrated from the town or county. Outlines of the physical geography of France. Geographical drawing, illustrated with the globe, chart, and blackboard. The continents.
ARITHMETIC. 1 1/2 h. a wk. Mental arithmetic—whole numbers.
OBJECT-LESSONS. 1 h. a wk. Coal, metals, coins, clouds, rain, snow, ice, springs, brooks, lakes, wells, canals, sea-water, salt, wind, storms, familiar animals and plants. [This set of subjects lasts 2 yrs.]
DRAWING. 1 h. a wk. Straight lines, angles, circles, polygons, stars, ellipses, spirals, the curves of plants, first notions of perspective. [This set of subjects lasts 3 yrs.]

PROGRAMME OF STUDIES (1887) IN THE BOSTON GRAMMAR SCHOOLS (FIRST THREE YEARS) AND THE PUBLIC LATIN SCHOOL.

[In the Grammar Schools the number of hours of teaching per week is 22, including the drawing and music.]

SIXTH CLASS. Grammar School (1st year of course). Age 8 yrs.

ENGLISH. 11 hours a week. Oral and written exercises. Reading. Science lessons, pictures illustrating trades, etc., stories reproduced. Recitation. Writing from blackboard and from dictation. Letter-writing. An authorized reader.
GEOGRAPHY. 2 h. a wk. The earth a ball. Maps. Hemispheres, continents, oceans, climates, most important countries, peoples, cities.
ARITHMETIC. 4 1/2 h. a wk. Whole numbers to 100,000. Decimals. U. S. money. Liquid and dry measures. Oral exercises.
ELEMENTARY SCIENCE. 2 h. a wk. Human body with reference to hygiene. Plants (May to July), seedlings, sponge, coral, oyster, clam, snail. Shells, air, wind, rain, frost, snow, hail, ice.
DRAWING. 1 1/2 h. a wk. Circle, ellipse, oval. Curves. Polygons. Drawing from dictation and from memory.
MUSIC. 1 h. a wk. Exercises and songs. Writing exercises.

FRENCH PROGRAMME

EIGHTH CLASS. Age 9 yrs.

FRENCH. 9 h. a wk. Reading, spelling, writing, grammar, and little compositions. Descriptions reproduced.
GERMAN OR ENGLISH. 4 h. a wk. First notions of grammar, reading, writing, spelling, common phrases. English text-book—Miss Edgeworth's Tales.
HISTORY. 1 1/2 h. a wk. Outline of French history to Louis XI.
GEOGRAPHY. 1 1/2 h. a wk. Elementary geography of Europe, Asia, Africa, America, and Oceanica. Voyages of discovery.
ARITHMETIC. 2 h. a wk. Whole numbers. Exercises in mental arithmetic. Easy problems.
OBJECT-LESSONS. 1 h. a wk. Exercises on some of the objects mentioned in the programme for the preparatory class.
DRAWING. 1 h. a wk. Same as for the preparatory class.

SEVENTH CLASS. Age 10 yrs.

FRENCH. 9 h. a wk. As in previous years. Syntax.
GERMAN OR ENGLISH. 4 h. a wk. Grammar. Auxiliary and irregular verbs. Easy prose. Exercises in reading and conversation. English texts—Sanford and Merton, and Old Poz.
HISTORY. 1 1/2 h. a wk. History of France from Louis XI to 1815.
GEOGRAPHY. 1 1/2 h. a wk. Elementary geography of France.
ARITHMETIC AND GEOMETRY. 2 h. a wk. Whole numbers and decimals. Metric system. Geometrical figures.
STONES AND SOILS. 1 h. a wk. Limestones, lime-kilns, mortars, plaster, clay, bricks, pottery, quartz, flint, grindstones, granite, sands, drift, mold, soils, fossils, quarries, volcanoes.
DRAWING. 1 h. a wk. Same as for the preparatory class.

[In the sixth and higher classes the number of hours of instruction per week is 20, with 2 hours of drawing in addition.]

SIXTH CLASS. Age 11 yrs.

FRENCH. 3 h. a wk. Grammar. Extracts in prose and verse from French classics. La Fontaine's fables. Simple compositions.
LATIN. 10 h. a wk. Elements of grammar. Viri Romæ. Translation of French phrases into Latin.
GERMAN OR ENGLISH. 2 h. a wk. Grammar, reading, conversation, written exercises. English texts—Edgeworth's Tales, Aikin and Barbauld's Evenings at Home, Primer of English history.
HISTORY. 2 h. a wk. Ancient history of the Orient—Egypt, Assyria, Palestine, Phœnicia, Persia.
GEOGRAPHY. 1 h. a wk. Europe and the Mediterranean basin.
ARITHMETIC AND GEOMETRY. 1 h. a wk. Common fractions. Decimals. Sphere, poles, meridians, parallels. Latitude and longitude.
ZOÖLOGY. 1 h. a wk. Man. Vertebrates. Articulates. Worms. Mollusks. Fauna of the principal regions of the globe.
DRAWING. 2 h. a wk. Perspective with shadows. Drawing from ornaments in relief, from architectural fragments, from the human head. [These subjects serve for 2 yrs.]

FIFTH CLASS. Age 12 yrs.

FRENCH. 3 h. a wk. As in preceding year. Extracts from La Fontaine, Boileau, Racine, Fénelon, Buffon.
LATIN. 10 h. a wk. to Jan. 1, 8 h. thereafter. Grammar, syntax, elements of prosody. Extracts from Phædrus, Ovid, and Nepos. Latin theme, written and oral.
GREEK. 2 h. a wk. from Jan. 1. Grammar, accent, paradigms.
GERMAN OR ENGLISH. 2 h. a wk. Reading, writing, conversation, translation. English texts—Scott's Tales of a Grandfather, Franklin's Autobiography, Primer of the History of Greece.

BOSTON PROGRAMME

FIFTH CLASS (Grammar School). Age 9 yrs.

ENGLISH. 11 h. a wk. Same methods as in preceding year.
ELEMENTARY SCIENCE. 2 h. a wk. Hygiene. Plants (Sept. to Nov., and May to July). Animals—lobster and insects. Sun, moon, and stars. Drainage of vicinity. Rocks and soils.
GEOGRAPHY. 2 h. a wk. Important countries—our own first. Natural features, climate, productions, people, government, customs, and cities.
ARITHMETIC. 4 1/2 h. a wk. Whole numbers and decimals continued. Avoirdupois weight, and units of time. Oral problems in common fractions.
DRAWING. 1 1/2 h. a wk. Objects in two dimensions. Octagon, spiral, simple ornament.
MUSIC. 1 h. a wk. Chromatic scale. Breathing. Songs.

FOURTH CLASS (Grammar School). Age 10 yrs.

ENGLISH. 10 h. a wk. Oral and written expression, including writing 5 h. Reading 5 h. More advanced books and methods.
HYGIENE. 1 h. a wk. Continued.
ARITHMETIC. 4 1/2 h. a wk. Common fractions. Long, square, and solid measures. Decimals continued.
GEOGRAPHY. 3 h. a wk. Meridians and parallels, zones, winds, and ocean currents, climate as affecting man. Physical geography of North America, South America, and Europe. Map-drawing. Apparent motions of sun, moon, and stars. Seasons.
OBSERVATION LESSONS. 1 h. a wk. Common metals, minerals, and rocks.
DRAWING. 1 1/2 h. a wk. Ornament. Geometric forms. Elementary design from plant forms. Objects based on the oval. Cylinder, cone, and vase. Drawing from memory.
MUSIC. 1 h. a wk. Scale and staff intervals. Different keys to three sharps and four flats.

[In the Latin School the number of hours of instruction per week is 20, including 2 hours of military drill.]

SIXTH CLASS (Latin School). Age 11 yrs.

ENGLISH. Not less than 3 h. a wk. Reading aloud and recitation of selections from prose and poetry. Reading the history of the United States. Grammar. Oral and written abstracts. Writing. Spelling.
LATIN. Regular forms. Latin into English, and English into Latin. Writing Latin from dictation. Vocabulary.
GEOGRAPHY. Physical and political geography, with map-drawing of the United States, the countries of Europe, and the other countries of North America.
ARITHMETIC. Review. Metric system. Percentage, with applications.
GEOMETRY. Oral. Forms and simple propositions.
PHYSIOLOGY. Oral instruction, to begin March 1.
MILITARY DRILL. 2 h. a wk.

FIFTH CLASS (Latin School). Age 12 yrs.

ENGLISH. Not less than 3 h. a wk. Prose—Tanglewood Tales, Autobiography of Franklin, History of England; poetry—selections from Holmes, Bryant, and Scott. Methods those of previous years.
LATIN. Translation of easy prose and of Cæsar's Gallic War, Bks. I and II. Unprepared translation. Writing from dictation. Committing passages to memory. English into Latin—sentences like Cæsar's.
GEOGRAPHY. Physical and political geography of South America, West Indies, Asia, Africa, and Oceanica, with map-drawing.

FRENCH PROGRAMME

HISTORY. 2 h. a wk. History of Greece.

GEOGRAPHY. 1 h. a wk. The oceans. Physical geography of Africa, Asia, Oceanica, and America. Principal states, capitals, and commercial ports. European possessions.

ARITHMETIC AND GEOMETRY. 1 h. a wk. Rule of three. Interest, discount, measurement of areas and volumes.

BOTANY. 1 h. a wk. Organs of a plant—root, stem, leaf, flower, fruit, seed. Divisions of the vegetable kingdom, illustrated. Outlines of the flora of the principal regions of the globe.

DRAWING. See the preceding year.

FOURTH CLASS. Age 13 yrs.

FRENCH. 2 h. a wk. Grammar finished. Extracts from Racine, Madame de Sévigné, and Montesquieu. Differences between French and Latin construction.

LATIN. 5 h. a wk. first 1/2 yr.; 6 h. a wk. second 1/2 yr. Extracts from Vergil and Ovid. Cæsar's Gallic War. Quintius Curtius. Latin composition, oral and written.

GREEK. 6 h. a wk. Grammar, elements of syntax, simple compositions. Extracts from Xenophon and Lucian.

GERMAN OR ENGLISH. 2 h. a wk. Reading, writing, conversation, translation. English texts—De Foe's Robinson Crusoe, Irving's Voyages of Columbus, Miss Corner's History of Rome.

HISTORY. 2 h. a wk. History of Rome.

GEOGRAPHY. 1 h. a wk. Geography of France. French colonies.

GEOMETRY. 1 h. a wk. Straight line, angles, triangles, parallelogram, circle, secant, tangent, measure of angles.

GEOLOGY. 1 h. a wk. first 1/2 yr. The principal rocks. Continuous changes of the earth's crust. Principal geologic periods, primary, secondary, tertiary, and glacial.

DRAWING. 2 h. a wk. From architectural fragments. The human figure, from prints, and bas-reliefs. Some mechanical drawing of architectural designs.

THIRD CLASS. Age 14 yrs.

FRENCH. 2 h. a wk. Authors—Corneille, Racine, Boileau, Bossuet, Fénelon. Compositions. Outlines of literary history. Free library of French authors.

LATIN. 5 h. a wk. Grammar reviewed. Prosody. Considerable portions of Livy, Cicero, Pliny, Sallust, Vergil.

GREEK. 5 h. a wk. Grammar continued. Extracts from Homer, Herodotus, Xenophon, Lucian.

GERMAN OR ENGLISH. 2 h. a wk. All varieties of instruction. English texts—Vicar of Wakefield, Tales from Shakspere, Macaulay's History of England, Vol. I.

HISTORY. 2 h. a wk. History of Europe, and particularly of France, from 395 to 1270.

GEOGRAPHY. 1 h. a wk. Geography of Europe, physical, political, and economic. Geography of each state.

ARITHMETIC, ALGEBRA, AND GEOMETRY. 2 h. a wk. Arithmetic finished, including square root and proportions. First principles of algebra. Plane geometry finished through area of the circle.

PHYSICS. 2 h. a wk. 1/2 the yr. Gravity, properties of liquids and gases. Specific gravity. Barometer. Heat.

DRAWING. 2 h. a wk. Decorative figures. Caryatids. Friezes. Doric, Ionic, and Corinthian orders. The human figure, and figures of animals.

SECOND CLASS. Age 15 yrs.

FRENCH. 3 h. a wk. Selections from ten authors covering the sixteenth to the nineteenth centuries inclusive.

LATIN. 4 h. a wk. Prosody. The meters of Horace. Authors—Vergil, Horace, Cicero, Livy, and Tacitus.

GREEK. 5 h. a wk. Grammar reviewed. Considerable portions of Homer, Euripides, Plato, Xenophon, and Plutarch.

LITERARY HISTORY. 1 h. a wk. is devoted to the history of Greek (10 lectures), Latin (10 lectures), and French (15 lectures) literatures. This hour is taken from the hours appropriated to the three languages.

GERMAN OR ENGLISH. 2 h. a wk. Grammar reviewed. Reading, conversation, translation, composition. English texts—Julius Cæsar, The Deserted Village, The Traveler—a romance of Scott, A Christmas Carol, David Copperfield, extracts from English historians.

BOSTON PROGRAMME

ARITHMETIC. Oral and written. Percentage, including simple and compound interest, discount, and partial payments. Compound numbers. Ratio and proportion. Powers and roots.

GEOMETRY. Mensuration, with oral geometry.

ZOÖLOGY. Oral instruction, to begin March 1.

MILITARY DRILL. 2 h. a wk.

FOURTH CLASS (Latin School). Age 13 yrs.

ENGLISH. Not less than 3 h. a wk. Prose—Church's Stories from Homer, Two Years before the Mast, Plutarch (Greek Lives); poetry—selections from Lowell, Gray, and Goldsmith. Abstracts, descriptions, oral exercises.

LATIN. Cæsar's Gallic War, Bks. III and IV; Ovid, 1000 lines; Æneid, Bk. I. Some prosody. Same methods as before.

FRENCH OR GERMAN. Pronunciation. Regular verbs. Translation of easy prose. Writing from dictation. Vocabulary. English into French or German.

GEOGRAPHY. General reviews. Astronomical and physical phenomena. Political and commercial relations of different countries.

HISTORY. History of Greece, with historical geography.

ZOÖLOGY. Oral instruction, to begin March 1.

ALGEBRA. Including the generalizations of arithmetic.

MILITARY DRILL. 2 h. a wk.

THIRD CLASS (Latin School). Age 14 yrs.

ENGLISH. Not less than 3 h. a wk. Prose—Plutarch (Roman Lives), Addison's papers in the Spectator, one of Scott's novels; poetry—Macaulay's Lays, some of Tennyson's, Emerson's, and Wordsworth's poems. Abstracts, compositions, and translations from a foreign language.

LATIN. Æneid, Bks. II-IV. Sallust's Catiline. Easy passages from Cicero. Unprepared translation. Committing passages to memory. English into Latin.

GREEK. Forms. Translation of 25 pp. of the Anabasis. Unprepared translation. Greek from dictation. Vocabulary. English into Greek.

FRENCH OR GERMAN. Reading. Oral and written translation of modern prose. Dictation. Committing passages to memory. Vocabulary. English into French or German.

HISTORY. History of Rome, with historical geography.

BOTANY OR PHYSICS. To begin March 1.

ALGEBRA. Including the generalizations of, and applications to, arithmetic.

MILITARY DRILL. 2 h. a wk.

SECOND CLASS (Latin School). Age 15 yrs.

ENGLISH. One play of Shakspere. Part of the English required for admission to college. Recitation of prose and verse. Translations. Compositions.

LATIN. Cicero, four orations. Vergil's Bucolics, and review of Æneid, Bks. I-IV. Translation at sight. Committing to memory. Vocabulary. English into Latin.

GREEK. Anabasis, I-IV. Sight translations from Xenophon. Greek from dictation. Vocabulary. English into Greek.

FRENCH OR GERMAN. As in previous year.

HISTORY AND GEOGRAPHY. History and geography of Greece and Rome completed.

ALGEBRA. Through quadratic equations. Algebra and arithmetic reviewed.

GEOMETRY. Plane geometry begun.

BOTANY OR PHYSICS. To begin March 1.

MILITARY DRILL. 2 h. a wk.

FRENCH PROGRAMME

HISTORY. 2 h. a wk. History of Europe, and particularly of France, from 1270 to 1610.

GEOGRAPHY. 1 h. a wk. Geography of Africa, Asia, Oceanica, and America. Meteorology. Climatology. Productions. Commercial relations. Steam and telegraph lines.

ALGEBRA AND GEOMETRY. 2 h. a wk. Algebra completed through equations of the second degree. Solid geometry to the cone.

PHYSICS. 2 h. a wk. 1/2 the yr. Electricity and magnetism. Acoustics.

DRAWING. 2 h. a wk. Same as in the preceding year.

CLASS OF RHETORIC. Age 16 yrs.

FRENCH. 4 h. a wk. Eleven authors of seventeen, eighteen, and nineteen centuries. Fifteen lessons on the history of French literature from the time of Louis XIII.

LATIN. 4 h. a wk. Portions of Terence, Lucretius, Vergil, Horace, Cicero, Livy, and Tacitus.

GREEK. 4 h. a wk. Portions of Homer, Sophocles, Aristophanes, Plato, and Demosthenes.

GERMAN OR ENGLISH. 2 h. a wk. Authors in English—Shakspere, Washington Irving, Byron, Tennyson, Dickens, and George Eliot.

HISTORY. 2 h. a wk. History of Europe, and particularly of France, from 1610 to 1789.

GEOGRAPHY. 1 h. a wk. Physical, political, administrative, and economic geography of France and its colonies.

GEOMETRY AND COSMOGRAPHY. 2 h. a wk. Solid geometry finished—through the sphere. The celestial sphere. Earth, sun, time, moon, eclipses, planets, stars, universal gravitation, tides.

CHEMISTRY. 2 h. a wk. first 1/2 yr. Hydrogen, oxygen, nitrogen, chlorine, sulphur, phosphorus, carbon, silicon, and their most important combinations. General notions of the metals, oxides, and salts. Principal organic compounds. Nomenclature and notation.

DRAWING. The human head from nature. Landscape from prints and nature.

CLASS OF PHILOSOPHY. Age 17 years.

PSYCHOLOGY, LOGIC, ETHICS, AND METAPHYSICS. 9 h. a wk., of which 8 h. are for the general course and two French authors, and 1 h. for one Latin and one Greek author. The two French authors are chosen each year from a list containing works of Descartes, Malebranche, Pascal, Leibnitz, Condillac, and Cousin. The course includes an account of sensibility, intelligence, and volition, of formal and applied logic, of conscience and duty, of family and country, of political duties, of labor, capital, and property, of immortality and natural religion.

HISTORY. 2 h. a wk. Contemporary history, 1789 to 1875.

ARITHMETIC, ALGEBRA, AND GEOMETRY. 4 h. a wk. Review of the whole course in these subjects.

PHYSICS. 2 h. a wk. Optics. Applications of physics—steam-engines, magneto-electric machines, electroplating, telephone.

PHYSIOLOGY, ANIMAL AND VEGETABLE. 2 h. a wk. Nutrition, organs of sense, voice, apparatus for movement, nerves. Vegetable nutrition and reproduction.

DRAWING. 2 h. a wk. Same as in the preceding year.

BOSTON PROGRAMME

FIRST CLASS (Latin School). Age 16 yrs.

ENGLISH. The English required for admission to college. Recitation of prose and poetry. Translations and compositions.

LATIN. Æneid, Bks. V-IX. Cicero, three orations. Translation at sight. Methods as in previous year.

GREEK. Selections from Herodotus. Translation at sight. Iliad, Bks. I-III, with prosody. Greek composition.

FRENCH OR GERMAN. Prepared and sight translation from one or more French or German classics. Reading a history of France or Germany. Other methods as in previous years.

GEOMETRY. Plane geometry completed.

MILITARY DRILL. 2 h. a wk.

[There is no equivalent in the Boston programme for the Class of Philosophy in the French programme.]

Louis R. Klemm

1888

Subjective Descriptions of European Education

Louis R. Klemm (1845–1925) held positions as principal of the Cincinnati Technical School, supervisor of the German department of the Cleveland public schools, and superintendent of public schools in Hamilton, Ohio. His intensive study of European schools was based on a ten-

Louis R. Klemm, *European Schools: Or What I Saw in the Schools of Germany, France, Austria, and Switzerland* (New York: D. Appleton and Company, 1889), pp. x–xii, 1–3, 102–104, 409–413

month tour of France, Prussia, Saxony, Bavaria, Austria, and Switzerland in 1887. Klemm intended his book to be a comparative study which would disprove the fallacious "opinion that European methods of teaching can not be adapted to American schools" and thus contribute "toward improving the schools of a country which deserves to have the best schools on the face of the earth!" His writing is subjective and generally interesting, with few pretensions to comparisons except in the most pungent terms. Speaking of Swiss schools as "simplicity misplaced," Klemm revealed that he had never been more disappointed than when he visited the schools in Switzerland. He said, "the poverty, or let me say the simplicity, of these schools in aims, in methods, and in equipment fairly disgusted me."

An Introductory Preface

This book is not, like many official reports, weighed down with statistical data and ponderous descriptions of school systems. It says very little of school houses and sites. The course of study is mentioned only when it is absolutely necessary, and even then in outlines only. The book contains observations in European schools, or "Chips from Educational Workshops." The author has endeavored to offer the reader truthful delineations of the present status of didactics and methodology in the public schools of Germany, France, Austria, and Switzerland. Lessons which he heard are sketched as faithfully as a quick pencil could gather and the memory retain them. Numerous devices in use in Europe are offered in sketch illustrations, and copies of pupils' work where they could conveniently be used. The manual training-schools of Europe are shown in their results; the different systems of drawing and industrial training of girls are compared. Each branch of study of the elementary schools is represented by sketch-lessons, and successful methods of teaching are illustrated by *verbatim* reproduction of model lessons.

The book is written for the purpose of offering a "standard of measurement" for our own schools; a statement of what is done in the schools of Europe, and how it is done. If it should succeed in disproving the opinion that "European methods of teaching can not be adapted to American schools," the author will be most happy. This fallacious opinion is upheld very obstinately. It is heard from the rostrum, found in the educational press, urged in season and out of season; but, since it is merely an opinion, it can be disproved by facts alone, and they are already furnished by hundreds of excellent teachers in this country who adopt and adapt what is good in the theories and practices of their European brethren.

Though the author had frequently advocated methods used in Germany, he had never called them "German methods" nor felt called upon to refute the fallacy of their non-adaptability, knowing that some day he would have an opportunity of answering it more successfully than by entering into controversies. The facts offered in this book, it is hoped, may not seem strange, for they are not decorated with fancies. They can be verified by stacks of pupils' work collected by the author himself on his visits in hundreds of schools of various types. Speculations are rare in this book, though the writer states his opinion freely, and indulges in comparisons perhaps too freely.

He went to Europe with the intention of seeing what was worth reporting. Schools inferior to the average American school he avoided. He strove, during a journey of ten months, to see the best that Europe could offer him, and in this volume he thinks he has pictured the best results, described the most advanced methods, and given a great number of valuable hints that will be serviceable to teachers who have not sunk back into that detestable state of self-sufficiency and satisfaction which is the arch-foe of progress.

The most warm-hearted thanks are due to all who aided the author with valuable advice in selecting "points of observation"; thanks also to the Government officials in France, Prussia, Saxony, Bavaria, Austria, and Switzerland, but particularly to the Minister of Public Instruction in Berlin, Dr. von Gossler, and to the director of "écoles primaires" in Paris, Monsieur J. Buisson. By their generous kindness the writer was enabled to see what few American visitors have had occasion to see.

May this book infuse a little enthusiasm into teachers who consider their professional duties distasteful; may it strengthen others who are earnestly striving to reach a higher level of perfection; and may it contribute its share toward improving the schools of a country which deserves to have the best schools on the face of the earth! . . .

The reader may permit me to introduce the book with an argument. I wish to state emphatically that what is urged in our country, and advocated under the caption "German methods," does not deserve that name. German methods have nothing specifically German about them, so long as they aim at assisting intellectual growth. The faculties of the mind are essentially the same in different craniums. It matters not whether I have to teach the children of a Zulu-Kaffir, or an Indian tribe, or children of English, German, French, or American birth—the leading features of my procedure in teaching them would be the same. It is only matters specifically German, as, for instance, the peculiar form of government and other things, such as customs and habits, that bear upon the government of schools, which can not, and should not, be urged for adoption in our country. But it has never occurred to any one to urge institutions foreign to the spirit of our free institutions as specifically German methods. What is applicable to the education of the human being, not of the German as such, is urged, and that, as was said, is not specifically German.

There can be no objection to such methods, if their object is to facilitate the growth of the mind, the strengthening and steeling of the will, and the skill of the hands, though they be erroneously called German methods, because in Germany they were first applied. To think that there must be special avenues to the mind of the German child, that can not be used for the American, is either the height of presumption, which disdains to use anything not indigenous to the American soil,[1] or a total disregard of the true definition of the term "method," to wit: *"Method is a way of reaching a given end by a series of acts which tend to secure it."*

The end in view being the same, why should not the method be the same? I take it for granted that the reader's innate sense of truth permits him to see that the end in view in German and American schools is the same, as far as intellectual culture is concerned. For proofs, he may read Comenius's, Pestalozzi's, Froebel's, and Diesterweg's principles and maxims, and compare them with expressions of our home authorities. I will not burden this chapter with them. The lessons I describe in the following pages may convince him that there is nothing specifically German in "German methods." What I find

in them is specifically human, and can be applied in any school.

"But," wrote a learned doctor, with whom I had exchanged arguments on this point, "your argument, that the faculties of the mind are the same in different nations and individuals, might lead us to adopt Chinese methods, because the Chinese children's senses are the same as all other children's."

Why should it? We do not wish to adopt and adapt inferior but better methods. If, perchance, the Chinese should hit upon a more direct and profitable method of teaching, I should not hesitate a moment in adopting it. But the Chinese have not developed the art of teaching to any high degree, and have not invented or discovered methods worth recommending. Why, therefore, should we adopt their methods?

Any one who travels through Europe as I did for nearly a year, seeing, observing, testing, inquiring, examining in all domains of activity, in society, in schools, in factories, in government offices, etc., would see that in Europe American methods are adopted and applied with an alacrity worthy of a good purpose. I saw applied numerous American inventions, American methods of carrying on trade, of industrial pursuits, of managing public and private affairs, etc., *ad infinitum.* American machines and devices, all that we are justly proud of, are there copied, sold, used, and applied. Why, might I ask, do not the Europeans adopt the Hottentot's methods? It is the same argument, and deserves the same answer: It is the better, not the inferior methods that they want.

Our almost insular seclusion from the other civilized parts of the world should not make us exclusive in thought and action. National pride is a grand virtue; but, when it becomes derogatory to our own interests and shuts our eyes to the progress of other nations, that pride becomes a vice. Not having a standard measure of length, how can we measure a distance! If this book, in a modest way, succeeds in furnishing a standard of excellence by which true-hearted American teachers may measure their own performances, it is all I desire and hope for. . . .

French Pupils in German Schools

Despite the bitter hatred Frenchmen entertain against Germany, they are alive to the superiority of the German schools and try to profit by them. It is now nearly ten years since the French national school

---

[1]Colonel Parker and other typical American teachers unhesitatingly adapt (nay, adopt) "German" methods, and give due credit to the sources from which they draw. . . .

authorities resolved upon a direct acknowledgment of that superiority by sending annually several graduates of French high-schools to attend the last two years of the course in German high-schools. No indifferent material is sent, to be sure, but only boys who have won the first prizes. As I have stated elsewhere (in the article, ''A Distinction with a Big Difference''), the German secondary schools are well adapted to talented pupils, while weaker ones are weeded out. These French boys, then, coming as they do like ''picked nines,'' are not objected to by German school authorities. They say there is no reason whatever to refuse them admittance, inasmuch as they conduct themselves properly, and usually are a credit to the schools they attend.

These boys are directed to stay a half-year or a year at one school and then go to another. They are not allowed to stay two full years in one town, lest they might enter into ties too close to suit the French Government. They are directed to take board and lodging in private families, and to live exactly as the pupils of German gymnasiums do. The Government pays all expenses during their stay in Germany. At the close of each year the students are required to send in a report of what they experienced and of the manner in which they utilized their time. Of course, the frequent changes of schools and place of habitation are inconvenient, but they enable the young men to see a good deal of that country which ignorant Frenchmen before 1870 thought lay near the north pole!

I had opportunities to learn something of the contents of the reports sent home to the Minister of Instruction, and must confess that they are mostly true to life and tally with my own observations. Most of the young men are very much pleased with the reception they find among the people, the teachers, and fellow-pupils. They praise the delicacy and tact of their German hosts, a fact which the wounded spirit of Frenchmen is apt to appreciate. Some admit that the senseless agitation in France concerning ''revenge for 1870'' makes their stay in certain places unendurable. All, however, are loud in praising the instruction they get in school.

They are unanimous in saying that the German high-schools are far superior to the French lycées. Especially in mathematics, they think, the German schools prove superior. The way the students are made to work out problems in geometry, trigonometry, oral arithmetic, etc., the self-activity

to which the pupils are led, and the independence and self-dependence in thinking, are commended. Instruction in the sciences also is thought superior to that in France. Particularly enthusiastic are the reports about gymnastic drill. This is not astonishing if we consider that the indulgent French youth is not drilled much at home in bodily exercises. An equal share of praise is given to the teaching of music. In referring to this the young Frenchmen speak with animation of the German songs, which they consider very melodious.

As far as instruction is concerned they have but one opinion; but they do not like the rigid discipline exercised in German high-schools. Why, they are not even permitted to smoke, not even in the sanctum sanctorum of their own bedrooms! The slightest deviation from the straight road of virtue is punished severely. They are ''not treated as gentlemen,'' but ''as boys,'' are obliged to doff their hats when they pass a teacher, and are generally treated as unripe youths. Though I can not myself like the rough treatment I noticed here and there, I must admit that the German teachers are consistent in regarding no school-boy a gentleman. However pretentious he may be, he is a minor, and as such can not lay claim to the dignities of a full-grown man. Of course, I full well understand that in a republic this is considered heresy; but we may admit the consistency practiced in German schools where the treatment of pupils is a reflection of the mode of government, monarchical government, in which respect for authority is ''learned by doing.''

In one particular the German high-schools find condemnation on the part of these French students. They say Germans pay less attention to show—that is, to legitimate show. For instance, they care naught for rhetorical polish, and their recitations are considered good when the essential facts are brought out correctly. The garment of thought is neglected. Their teaching of drawing also is less refined than that in France. This may be true in the high-schools, but I can testify to a wonderful improvement in drawing in the lower schools which has not reached the upper grades as yet. I trust, though, that in ten years that branch of the curriculum will be fully up to the French standard. . . .

Switzerland and Alsace: Simplicity in the Wrong Place

Simplicity in manners and customs is a

proverbial virtue in the citizen of a republic ever since the time of Lycurgus; and Cincinnatus and Curius, Fabricius and Fabius are noted examples of ancient Rome of that simplicity and civil virtue which seem to vanish before the conquering progress of culture. Without being conscious of it, we connect in our mind simplicity with honesty, and, though luxuriously inclined ourselves, we can not but do homage to a true example of simplicity when we meet it. I went to Switzerland, and there found what I never expected to see—a sample of simplicity in the wrong place, a misdirected simplicity, coupled with a miserly economy and a brutal honesty—mark the words!

The Germans, and in these latter days the French also, consider the best barely good enough for their children. They are therefore always on the alert to catch what improvements are offered in common-school education. I will not speak of material things, such as books, etc., but will confine myself to the world of ideas. There is no new idea in the realm of education that they do not instantly welcome; no device whose usefulness they will not test without delay; no method that they will not at once apply in some experimental station; no principle which they will not quickly seize to serve them as a subject for discussion; no branch of study which they will not give a place in the curriculum of some school.

It is an undeniable fact that the German school lives in the most unrivaled luxury with regard to ideas, branches of study, text-books, and other material things. Whether the fact that it is equally well supplied with teaching forces is the natural consequence of the undying aspiration and remarkable activity of the German school, or whether the latter is the result of the fact that the schools are manned with professional teachers, is a question of no importance here; for Switzerland, where I found a deplorable absence of that luxury referred to, has also a profession of teaching.

Having spent nearly nine months in France, Germany, Austria, and other countries of Europe, I came to Switzerland fully prepared to witness in the land of Pestalozzi a progress in the schools of the people such as would take my breath away; but never was I more disappointed than when I did see schools in Switzerland. The poverty, or let me say the simplicity, of these schools in aims, in methods, and in equipment fairly disgusted me. I confined my observations to "peo-

ple's schools"—that is, the primary schools, which in many places have a four years' course. Spending some time in many classes of various schools, and comparing the courses of study and the methods applied, I gathered a fair picture of the *status quo* of the Swiss public school for the lower strata of society, which does not satisfy me.

In order to be able to defend this sweeping assertion in case it should be attacked, I provided myself with the printed courses of instruction, the manuals used by the teachers, and some samples of pupils' work which were offered me by the teachers as excellent specimens. Judging from these proofs in black and white and from ocular evidence, I concluded that the proverbial republican simplicity is here found in the wrong place. Since education in Switzerland is, as with us, not a matter of legislation of the Confederation, but of each separate canton, it is reasonable to suppose that my experiences are exceptional ones, and I am perfectly willing to offer the benefit of the doubt to any one who feels unjustly treated by my criticism.

Let me proceed to state in what way I met with the "simplicity" referred to. I purposely avoid mentioning the names of the cities I visited. The results in drawing are very poor. There is a manual for instruction in drawing, in use in one of the larger cities, showing the work to be done in four years. This course is primitive to a fault. It can not be alleged to be an antiquated document, for it bears the date January, 1887. . . .

I awaited a lesson in geography anxiously, to see whether in that branch also the same "conservatism" was exhibited. To be sure it was! The geographical horizon of the pupils in the fourth year did not extend beyond the little landscape surrounding the city, and the maps by the pupils of this home geography were the rudest possible. I was requested to look them over. The pride of the teacher over this work was so evident that I asked him to let me have a few to show my friends in America. The request flattered him, and he selected a few of the best, which I am ready to exhibit as proofs of my statement. From these best ones one may judge of the worst.

In language the results seemed anything but satisfactory, the teachers having to contend with an abominable dialect. How narrow the teachers of these Swiss schools are may be seen from the fact that they actually make a difference in pronunciation of ei and ai, two diphthongs for which the

German language has but one sound: Rhein
and Rain, mein and Main, are indistinguish-
able by the ear. Exercises in orthography
are painfully monotonous, and the school-
tone in reading and reciting found here is
so abominable that it resembled a sing-song
such as can be surpassed only by the old-
fashioned oral spelling of the American
school of times gone by: "C-o-n, Con,
s-t-a-n, stan, Constan, t-i, ti, Constanti,
n-o, no, p-l-e, ple, Constantinople."

In singing, too, the results were unsatisfactory. No two-part music in the fourth
school year, nothing but the simple melodies
of popular and sacred airs, did I hear.
Since it is reasonable to suppose that teachers
and pupils put their best foot foremost when
a visitor is present, I take it for granted
that they regaled me with the best they could
set before me. My visit occurred during the
last month of the school year, and it can
therefore not be urged as an excuse that the
course of each school year had only just begun. The school year in Europe generally
closes at Easter.

A hand-book for teachers, entitled "Principles of Instruction in the Primary Schools,"
which I procured, is full of narrow views
and antiquated methods. No wonder the teachers looked like sleepy horses in a treadmill!

Nowhere here did I find that fire of enthusiasm, that personal magnetism, so often
observed in other European and in American
schools. Oh, what a disappointment that was
for me, who had come to Switzerland with
eager expectation to find ideas and practices
worthy of being transplanted to the fertile
soil of the New World! Three cities I visited
in Switzerland, and much money I spent in
traveling and in costly hotels, and found
nothing worthy of note. I left the country
sorry that I was poorer by a cherished
illusion.

Still, I must not close this chapter without doing justice in some manner to the
fact that reports of others are not in harmony
with mine. Whether these people applied a
different standard of measurement, or I
happened to strike the wrong places, I can
not say. I read glowing accounts of some
special Swiss schools, regular mines of
information regarding theory and practice, and the professional journals published
in that country also are, as a rule, not so
conservative and backward as one would
think, judging from what I saw in the schools
I visited; but my sense of justice will not
permit me to gloss over what seemed to me
faulty *in toto*.

James Russell Parsons, Jr.   1891

Prussian Schools Through American Eyes

James Russell Parsons, Jr., (1861–1905) graduated from Trinity College in 1881. He served
as school commissioner in Rensselaer County, New York, from 1885 to 1888 and United States
consul at Aachen, Germany, from 1888 to 1891. Parsons was appointed inspector of teachers'
training classes in New York in 1891. His account of German education below and the following
account on French education were based on an extensive series of visits to educational institutions in both these countries. Andrew Draper, superintendent of public instruction for
New York State, commissioned Parsons to undertake these studies of the major aspects of
elementary and secondary education in Prussia and France, so that American educators
could "see more clearly the strong points and discern the weak points of our own system."
Draper described Parsons' work as "surprising in the clearness and perspicuity of its
statements as well as in its completeness and comprehensiveness."

Scope of Report

The aim of the following report is to give,
in a condensed form, from the standpoint of
a New Yorker, the organization, classification
and work accomplished in Prussian elementary schools properly so called. Other

schools in which elementary work is done,
such as the middle schools (*Mittelschulen*),
are not touched upon except generally and
as it becomes necessary in stating the qualifications of teachers and school commissioners.

James Russell Parsons, Jr., *Prussian Schools Through American Eyes*: *A Report to the New York State
Department of Public Instruction* (Syracuse, New York: C. W. Bardeen, 1891), pp. 1–11, 15–16, 19–21,
75–77, 81–82.

The reader follows the would-be elementary school teacher through the elementary school, the school preparatory to the normal, the normal school and the final examinations.

An attempt is made to state clearly and concisely the minimum of work required of each Prussian child and the provisions by which the accomplishment of this work is secured.

Maintenance of Elementary Schools the State's First Duty

In Prussia the support of the elementary schools is considered the first and most important duty of the State. Even in time of war these schools must not be closed. The teachers who have passed the final examination and received definite appointments are sure of their pay, even though the schools to which they are appointed cease to exist. Teachers in elementary schools are on the same footing with clergymen as regards freedom from the payment of taxes; they have but six weeks' instead of three years' military service, and for this time their wages as teachers and those of their substitutes as well must be paid. They are also freed from the duty of quartering soldiers in time of war. Finally, at the close of their active service, they draw pensions from the government.

Inferiorities of the New York Elementary School System

When Prussia was defeated by the armies of the great Napoleon, she turned her attention toward the perfection of her system of education. At the close of the Franco-Prussian war, France followed the same course, which resulted in the adoption of the essential features of the elementary school system of Prussia.

The New Yorker, anxious for a high degree of perfection in the elementary schools of his State, must be struck forcibly by the following merits of the Elementary School System of Prussia. Furthermore, if sufficiently interested to push his investigations farther, he can test in France, under a re-

publican form of government, the operations of laws assuring similar advantages:

1. Compulsory education laws, necessitating a full and regular attendance of the children of school age.

2. Official courses of study fixing the work to be accomplished in each of the different grades of schools. Uniformity is thus secured in the work done in all schools of the same class.

3. Definite qualifications and experience in teaching for eligibility to the office of school commissioner.

4. Provisions elevating teaching to the dignity of a profession and making the tenure of office secure.

5. Trained teachers in rural as well as city districts and a school year of at least forty weeks.

6. General supervision of instruction for children of school age in private schools and families, including the qualifications of instructors.

New York elementary schools will never compare favorably with those of Prussia without similar provisions. Until these provisions are secured, advanced schools are of secondary importance. The first duty of the State is to provide suitably for a good elementary school education.

As stated by M. Victor Cousin in 1833, primary instruction is too far advanced in Prussia to render it necessary to make very frequent reports on the subject.

Cousin reviewed carefully the state of primary instruction in Prussia in the year 1831, under the firm conviction that the experience of Germany, and particularly of Prussia, ought not to be lost upon the French people.

"National rivalries or antipathies," said he, "would here be completely out of place. The true greatness of a people does not consist in borrowing nothing from others, but in borrowing from all whatever is good, and in perfecting whatever it appropriates. I am as great an enemy as any one to artificial imitations; but it is mere pusillanimity to reject a thing for no other reason than that it has been thought good by others. With the promptitude and justness of the French understanding, and the indestructible unity of our national character, we may assimilate all that is good in other countries without fear of ceasing to be ourselves. * * * There are branches of the public service which must be secured against all casualties by the State, and in the first rank of these is primary instruction."

---

[1]The only exceptions, excluding those unfit for any intellectual training, are children mentally, morally or physically incompetent. The education of these children is cared for in special schools for dullards, reform schools and institutions for the deaf, dumb and blind. The stupid are brought as far as possible in the elementary school course, generally in regular schools, sometimes in special schools for dullards.

The suggestions of M. Cousin were followed in the main, though, it must be granted, after a long delay. In New York, once convinced of the necessity of reforms, we move with incredible celerity. It is interesting to note that the report of Cousin, published in 1833, emphasizes what are today the main defects of our system of primary instruction.

Superiorities of the Prussian Elementary School System

A careful observer of the work done in Prussian elementary schools will detect, naturally enough, many imperfections, and yet he will return to this country with the feeling that Prussia is far in the lead of us. Take as an example a wealthy school district in New York State where parents are alive to the advantages of a good education. Suppose, as is often the case with us, that teachers and supervising officers are thoroughly competent, that the length of the school year approximates that of the Prussian school year, and that the attendance of the children is regular. The work done in these schools is fully equal to that done in the best Prussian elementary schools. Unfortunately, however, up to the present time, such schools have been exceptions here and not the rule as in Prussia. Our children learn as easily as the Prussian children, but under existing laws the pupils of the average New York school district, between the ages of 6 and 14, can not compete with the children of the average school district in Prussia. It is in vain that New York State goes on spending more and more each year for educational purposes. Without legislation insuring a full and regular attendance of the children of school age; without definite uniform qualifications for supervising officers as well as teachers; without an approximate equalization of local taxation for school purposes; without State supervision of instruction given in private schools and families, we shall never attain anything approaching uniformity in the work done in our elementary schools.

It is very unjust to make the sweeping assertion that no good elementary school work is done in New York State. I have visited many schools in countries of the old world as well as in New York, and have never seen better elementary schools anywhere in the world than the best schools here at home. Every Prussian child between the ages of 6 and 14 must, except in cases of severe illness or other extraordinary

cause, be present at every session of the school he attends. The lists of the children of school age, in charge of the local police (in rural districts the Burgermeister), are kept so carefully that it is impossible to escape the provisions of the compulsory education laws, as much so as it is to evade the military service. Dispensations amounting to more than four weeks in the school year are never given to children under 12 years of age, and to them only when sickness in the family or other unusal cause make it advisable.[2] Even then such children must prove the attainment of a sufficient degree of proficiency in the work laid down by law for elementary schools. Examinations are held regularly to determine the pupils' ripeness in such work, and they may be forced to attend school beyond the close of the fourteenth year of age, when, through previous irregular attendance or lack of diligence, the results of the examination are not satisfactory. Pupils leaving elementary schools, before the close of the fourteenth year of age, to attend a higher school, must submit to the school commissioner a certificate from the director of such higher school. Again, should the pupil leave such higher school before having attained the age of 14, the director must notify the school commissioner a second time. In every province there are houses of correction for children of school age who can not be otherwise controlled. The school commissioner and *Landrath* decide as to the sending of children to these institutions. Unless the parents are very poor, they are forced to pay the costs. In 1885 there were 180 of these houses of correction (*Rettungshäuser*) in Prussia, 141 of which were established since 1848.[3]

Would it not be very difficult to find many children of New York State who, between the ages of 6 and 14, had not absented themselves for long periods from school? With us most trivial excuses are accepted, and the time lost in these eight years is considerable. It is no wonder, then, that the Prussian children of 13 and 14 are, in general, far in advance of our children of the same age. In our cities and villages, however, where the school year approximates in length that which the Prus-

---

[2]Children under 12 years of age are forbidden to work in factories or mines. Those between 12 and 14 are restricted by law to six hours a day.

[3]Between October 1, 1878 and March 31, 1886, 11,101 children were sent to these houses of correction (*"Statistisches Handbuch für den Preussischen Staat,"* Berlin, 1888).

sian decrees fix definitely for their elementary schools, I contend that the children are not as far behind as we should expect them to be, when we consider their irregularity in attendance.

Qualifications of School Commissioners

Within the past few years, much has been done to call the attention of the people to the essential defects in our school system. There has been a great improvement all along the line and yet, with one exception, that of uniform qualifications and examinations for teachers' certificates, the most important defects are still to be remedied.

The teachers in our public schools must now attain a certain standard, and yet, contrary to the precedents established by other countries and contrary to reason, the officers who supervise the work of these teachers, the school commissioners, have but one qualification, as the *sine qua non*, that is, ability to secure a plurality of the votes cast at a popular election. There are many thoroughly efficient school commissioners in the State. Under existing laws, however, these cases may be considered as accidents. The inefficient officers worry the teachers whose educational qualifications are far superior to their own; add an immense amount of unnecessary work to the Department of Public Instruction; and make our school system a laughing-stock to other countries where such inconsistencies are unknown.

In order to understand the qualifications required of school commissioners (*Kreisschulinspektoren*) in Prussia, let us review briefly the requirements of male teachers. 1. *Elementary schools*. It may be stated at the outset that almost all the male elementary school teachers are normal school graduates. To insure similarity in training and a thorough knowledge of character, few foreigners and few beside normal school (*Schullehrer-Seminar*) graduates are admitted to the male teaching force. From 6 to 14 the would-be teacher has attended, let us suppose, an elementary school. He must then absolve the three years' course laid down for the preparatory schools (*Präparanden - Anstalten*). These preparatory schools (*Präparaden-Anstalten*) are special institutions which fit for the normal (*Schullehrer-Seminar*). He is now ready for the normal school. At the close of a three years' course at the normal school he is admitted to the first teachers' examination. If successful, he must next

practice as candidate or assistant teacher not less than two years and not more than five years before his admission to the final test (*Zweite Prüfung*). It is a most excellent idea to defer this final test until the applicant has been tried in the school-room. In this way only can decision be reached as to teaching capacity, discipline, etc. If teacher fails to pass the examination within five years, he is dropped. 2. *Middle schools*. For teachers of lower classes the same requirements with the addition of ability to teach a foreign tongue, or natural history in its broadest sense, and the attainment of the mark "good" in all subjects at the final examination (*Zweite Prüfung*). For higher classes, a special examination provided for middle school teachers (*Prüfung der Lehrer an Mittelschulen*). There is really no gradation between elementary and middle schools. The latter merely go on somewhat further with elementary school work, introducing French, Latin and English. 3. *High schools* (*Realschulen, Realgymnasien, Progymnasien and Gymnasien*). All high school teachers, except those engaged in technical departments, must first absolve the nine years' gymnasial course, which commences at the close of the third school year. Next comes the university course of three or four years. The candidate is now ready for the State examination. The subjects for this State examination (*Staatsprüfung*) are divided into four classes: 1. The ancient languages and German; 2. Mathematics and natural sciences; 3. History and geography; 4. Religion and Hebrew. At the close of one year's practice to test teaching capacity, he receives a second certificate and is thereupon engaged provisionally. On account of strength of competition he is often forced to wait as many as six years before receiving a permanent position. The advancement to the position of head master (*Oberlehrer*) follows generally in Prussia, after the twelfth year of service, always providing that the teacher has done well in the State examination and has also been successful in teaching. 4. *Normal school teachers and directors;* directors of schools preparatory for the normal; directors of middle schools and higher schools for girls (*Töchterschulen*) must pass a special examination provided for those who are to hold such positions (*Prüfung der Rectoren*).

The school commissioners (*Kreisschulinspektoren*) are either former regular high school teachers, generally doctors of philosophy, or more rarely theologians, or former normal school teachers. All must have had practical experience in teaching. It is not regulated by law how long they must have taught, but to insure efficiency, before permanent appointment as school commissioner, they are engaged provisionally for six months or longer. As with us, school commissioner districts vary greatly in size and in number of schools.

Other Supervising Officers

In addition to the school commissioners (*Kreisschulinspektoren*), there are (2) local school inspectors, generally the clergyman or mayor; (3) boards of education, consisting of the local school inspector, local officials and from two to four citizens; there is no salary attached to these offices; and (4) the government school councilors (*Regierungsräthe und Schulräthe*); and (5) *Landräthe*. The *Kreisschulinspektor* corresponds to our school commissioner. The other officers may be compared with our (2) and (3) school trustees and boards of education, (4) State department members (5) supervisors.[4]

Recommendation for New York

The uniform examinations for teachers' certificates are now definitely established in New York. No person should be eligible to the office of school commissioner who does not hold a teacher's license of the first grade or its equivalent, and who has not, in addition, practical experience as a teacher. In this way, we should establish at least a minimum of qualifications for this important office.

Compulsory Education Laws

The necessity for effective compulsory education laws has been thoroughly canvassed in this State. We understand fully the legal provisions made by other countries in this respect. New York is most generous towards

[4]Prussian schools excepting *Fortbildungsschulen* (for young workmen and apprentices), which are under the jurisdiction of the minister of commerce, are controlled by the minister of education at Berlin through the provincial school consistories (*Provinzialschulcollegien*), provincial and district governments.

her public schools. Every year the expenses of these schools are increasing. From $5,735,460.24 in 1865, the grand total for 1889 was $16,691,178.24, a sum nearly equal to one-sixth the total annual cost of the maintenance of the immense standing army of the German Empire or to one-third the annual cost of public education in Prussia. We are, as a people, most generous, and yet we are always anxious to get the worth of our money. Our public schools are for the people. Here, if anywhere, under a government by the people and for the people, an elementary school education is a matter of necessity. All the children between fixed ages should be forced to improve the educational advantages the state offers. In this way only can we make good and intelligent citizens of the rising generation.

Compulsory education laws are most effective in Prussia, as will be seen from the fact that for some years, the average number of recruits to the army, without elementary school training, has not exceeded two per cent, and in many parts of the kingdom has been less than two-tenths of one per cent. The most favorable statistics come from Hohenzollern, Schleswig-Holstein, Hanover, Berlin, Westphalia and Saxony; the most unfavorable from the eastern borders. . . .

State Supervision of Private Schools

As regards State supervision of private schools in the matter of qualifications of teachers and courses of study in the common school branches for pupils of school age, comparatively little has been said or written in this State. This discussion, however, will surely follow the enforcement of compulsory education laws. Before going abroad, I had often thought of this question in reflecting upon some of our inefficient private schools. High tuition bills are far from indicating a high grade of instruction. Fortunately, most of our private schools are very good. The patrons of all these schools and all interested therein should be willing to advocate that the teachers in private schools throughout the State possess at least the qualifications of teachers in public schools. This is the provision made abroad, and I have learned to appreciate its value.

Under compulsory education laws, the State fixes a *minimum* of work to be accomplished and a given time in which it is to be done. It then becomes the duty of the State to overlook all institutions where this elementary instruction is imparted. Private schools should be tested by the State to see if this *minimum* be attained. In all matters of opinion or in all work which is not laid down by the State, these schools should enjoy perfect freedom. If, however, New York is opposed to State supervision of private schools, uniformity in elementary school work may be secured by fixing the qualifications of private school teachers and compelling pupils to pass annual examinations in the work laid down by the State. Instruction given in families could be regulated in the same way. Compulsory education, to be efficient, necessitates a high degree of carefulness. There should be no loop-holes and nothing should be left to chance, if we desire uniformity in our elementary school work.

Courses of Study

The work to be accomplished in each Prussian elementary school is definitely laid down by law. Each school is not a law unto itself as to what shall be done and when and how this is to be done. I have learned by practical experience that the work in ungraded schools compares most favorably with that of graded schools. The courses of study vary little except as regards division of time and classes. The reader will note this by a comparison of the courses of study for ungraded schools and schools with two departments. Indeed, inasmuch, as the courses of study of schools with more classes would have involved a repetition of the same work, I have given only the division of time and general regulations for these schools.

Upon first visiting Prussian elementary schools, I heard the statement from school commissioners that the most thorough and systematic work is often done in ungraded schools. Whatever the standard of literary qualifications may be, some teachers will lack teaching capacity, and though Prussia is very careful in practical tests of teaching capacity, nevertheless even there some incompetency will creep in. A good teacher in an ungraded school, after having had the same children eight years, will often do better work than that done in graded schools where children change teachers upon promotion to another department. In this State, however, it would be very difficult to find many ungraded schools taught by the same teacher for the period of eight years.

Teachers are often promoted with their classes, so that they instruct the same class three or four years. In exceptional cases, where teachers are incompetent, this plan works great injustice. Generally speaking, it is advantageous both for pupils and teachers.

Length of School Terms and Vacations

An examination of the decrees regulating the length of vacations in different government districts shows a difference of from one to three weeks in the time elementary schools remain in session annually. Forty-two weeks is the *minimum*, forty-five weeks the *maximum*. The hours of instruction per week vary in primary and advanced divisions from twenty to thirty-two, as will be seen by reference to courses of study.[5] In the government districts of Magdeburg and Hanover, the elementary schools are open at least forty-three weeks annually. Patriotic festivals, viz., the Emperor's birthday and the anniversary of Sedan, and general religious festivals not occurring in regular vacations are included. Patriotic festivals are celebrated by appropriate exercises in the schools. In Jewish schools, the vacations are arranged to include the Jewish festivals.[6] The length of the school year for Romanists, Protestants and Jews is substantially the same. Instead of taking Saturday, as with us, Prussian elementary schools are closed Wednesday and Saturday afternoons. Upon these half-days there is no instruction except as it may be necessary to fill out the time required for gymnastics and manual training.

The rural elementary schools in the government district of Potsdam are in session forty-two and fifty-seven hundredths weeks annually, the city and suburban schools forty-two and twenty-nine hundredths. . . .

In 1889, the average length of time the schools of New York were in session was thirty-five and five-tenths weeks. The Prussian children gain from six to ten weeks a year.

The township system, by equalizing local taxation, would enable us to increase the legal school year to at least forty weeks.

---

[5]Half-day schools and schools with three classes and two teachers give only twelve hours instruction weekly in the lowest division.

[6]In Dusseldorf, sixteen holidays are allowed for the Jewish festivals. Those not falling in regular vacations must be made up, when exceeding the number of holidays in other schools.

Prussian Elementary Schools Are Free

In this respect Prussia has passed through three stages. Under the first elementary schools were entirely self-supporting; under the second they received State aid, but were still largely self-supporting; under the third, Laws of 1888 and 1889, elementary schools were made free and the State pays a larger proportion of the cost of maintenance. Districts must pay for repairs, new buildings and cost of heating. If unwilling to provide proper school accommodations for the children of school age, they can be forced by the government to do so. Poor districts may receive special government aid to meet such expenses.[7]

In France the elementary schools are not only gratuitous, but books, paper, ink and school supplies generally are provided free of charge. More than this, the children of indigent parents are furnished with warm food in winter, with shoes and with clothing. In Prussia books and school supplies are free only for the poor, who are also provided with food and clothing, that they may be enabled to attend school. Each district has its *caisse*, the revenues of which depend upon government and district grants or assessments made upon large landholders.

Teachers' Wages

The direct aim of the laws of June 14, 1888, and March 31, 1889, was to lighten the burden of local taxation for schools for children of school age. These laws have had a beneficial effect in increasing slightly the wages of teachers.

Teachers' salaries are still quite small in Prussia, particularly in the case of females. Allowances are generally made for house-rent and fuel. Teachers in rural districts are provided with a house and garden. Their salaries are often not much more than half those paid city teachers of the same grade, and yet, as regards professional training and character of work, they are fully equal to city teachers. It must be borne in mind, however, that city life is, as a rule, far more expensive than country life.

In comparing with salaries paid in New York, several things are to be considered.

1. The great difference in the purchasing power of money.

2. The absolute security of the teacher in his position.

3. The fact that he draws a pension of from one-fourth to three-fourths of his salary upon his retirement, the amount depending upon the number of years of official service.[8]

The average annual salary received by teachers in Prussia in 1886 was $267.50. The average for the same year in New York was $409.27. The Prussian teacher, however, received fuel and dwelling free, in addition to his regular salary. . . .

Language Used in Teaching

Since 1889, except in the case of religious instruction in districts with a large foreign population, the German language has been used universally in teaching all subjects in Prussian elementary schools. Up to 1887, the Polish language was in use in schools made up of Poles, and up to April 1, 1889, pupils in North Schleswig were taught in the Danish language.

Statistics of 1886 show that ten and thirty-five-one-hundredths per cent of the total number of children in attendance upon public elementary schools spoke only the Polish language at home. The percentage of children in whose families German was the only language spoken, was eighty-six and fifty-eight-one-hundredths. In the families of the other thirteen and forty-two-one-hundredths per cent, either another language was spoken in addition to German, or only a foreign tongue.

Number of children in whose families only Polish was spoken	500,315
Number of children in whose families only Sclavonic dialects were spoken	31,473
Number of children in whose families only Danish was spoken	24,088
Number of children in whose families only some language other than German was spoken	4,049
Total	449,925
Number of children in whose families only German was spoken	4,188,857
Number of children in whose families German and another language were spoken	89,465
Total	4,838,247

---

[7]In some districts the State pays the entire cost of maintaining the elementary schools. In other districts, excepting a small portion of teachers' salaries, the State pays nothing.

[8]In 1886, there were 4,211 pensioned elementary teachers in Prussia. The average pension was $170.25 (681 marks); 49.89 per cent of all pensions was paid by the State.

From this we see that the difficulty of teaching more or less in a foreign tongue existed in 1886 in the case of quite a considerable percentage of the school children.

With children entirely ignorant of German, the difficulty will not be overcome before the third or fourth school year.

Special text and reference-books have been issued for schools with a large foreign population. Courses of study are modified to meet the needs of such schools, and teachers receive special training therefor.

The Prussian government moved very carefully in this matter. Experiments seemed to prove the advisability of adopting the German language generally, and reports show that the results are very satisfactory.

The experiments made before adopting exclusively the German language in schools made up of foreigners were most interesting. The Minister of Public Instruction conducted these experiments in person. It was everywhere found that children who had not spoken a single German word before entering school, not only made great progress in the elementary school *curriculum* when the instruction was given in German, but also expressed themselves best in their native tongue. The ministry was at last satisfied that it was advisable to adopt the German language exclusive of all others. . . .

Training of Children in the Love of the Fatherland

In Prussian schools the utmost pains are taken to foster the spirit of patriotism. The law requires that a likeness of the Emperor be placed in each school-room. Courses of study improve every opportunity to call attention to the importance of cultivating a national spirit. From the cradle, the Prussian child learns the national songs. At every step one is reminded that Prussia is a land of patriots.

In New York the appointment of Arbor Day was the first movement toward the recognition of the importance of this subject in connection with our schools. This attempt to cultivate a national spirit is most praiseworthy. Teachers and all school officers should spare no pains in developing a proper spirit of patriotism and love of our free institutions. If this were done as in Prussia, the history and geography of our own country would no longer be looked upon by pupils as dry and uninteresting.

Text-books

A complete list is made by the government of all text-books which may be used in the schools. This list must be followed. The director of a high school and the school commissioner in the case of an elementary school, are forced, if they desire to introduce a new book, to state the defects of the old one and the advantages of the proposed substitute and submit this statement, with a copy of the new book, to the government. There is but one time of the year in which new books may be introduced.

Prussian elementary schools use fewer text-books for pupils and more reference books for teachers than New York elementary schools.

The paper, binding and printing of our school-books is much better than that of the German books. Our books present a much more attractive appearance, but are more expensive in consequence. German text-books are often mere outlines. The first book in geography covers only the government district. Each government district uses a special book for this purpose. This peculiarity is worthy of note. Another peculiarity is the text-book in the *Realien*, embracing geography, history and natural history. The readers offer at times an illustration of the danger of pushing too far a principle good *per se*. This principle is to take up only the work of standard authors. Statistics and descriptions of America and rapidly growing cities and countries in other parts of the world, written years ago, do not give as a rule a very correct idea of the state of things to-day. Readers in present use in Prussian elementary schools contain examples establishing the justice of this criticism.

All pupils must be supplied with books. In the school lists of pupils, the occupation of the father is always given, and it is the duty of the teacher to know what children must be supplied with books. Except in the case of poverty, when books and stationery are furnished free of charge, parents and guardians can be forced by law to provide them. This happens, indeed, very seldom.

As is the case where teachers are properly trained, Prussian instructors use text-books very little in recitations. I have often been present for hours at recitations in elementary schools when the teacher did not refer a single time to a text or reference book.

Text-books are free only to the children of indigent parents. They are not printed by the government. In drawing up the official lists of text-books which may be used, care is taken to avoid an unnecessary variety. The State aims to insure uniformity in each province in the text-books used in all schools of the same class. . . .

Interest of the General Public in School Work

This is in striking contrast with the indifference of the people of New York. Parks and skating-rinks, botanical and zoölogical gardens, gymnasia and swimming schools, libraries and museums are opened to the school children. Teachers attend with their classes special theatrical performances of German and foreign classics.

Religious Instruction

Religious instruction is the foundation-stone of elementary school work in Prussia. This instruction, both in the public and in the private schools, is compulsory. It is regulated by law, is entirely impartial, and is considered an essential part of the education of each pupil. Roman Catholics, Protestants and Jews have masters of their own faith, but no one can give religious instruction who is not authorized by the general government. Except in the country, all elementary schools are confessional. In the case of these rural mixed schools, the religious belief of the teacher depends on that of a plurality of the pupils. To entitle children to special religious instruction other than that of a plurality of the pupils, there must be at least twelve pupils who demand it. When possible, it is desirable that schools unite for this purpose.

In the maintenance of local schools, Jews and Christians have the same legal rights. In Jewish secondary schools, Christian teachers are sometimes employed, but not *vice versa.* Indeed, with the exception of schools of art, of industry and of navigation, the Jews can teach only in Jewish schools. Every synagogue community is forced by law to give the necessary instruction in Judaism to children between the ages of 6 and 14. It may be said briefly that pupils must receive instruction in accordance with the religious belief of their parents. Unbaptized children of Roman Catholics or Protestants receive naturally religious instruction in accordance with the faith of their parents. A teacher can not force a pupil

to receive other religious instruction than that in the faith of his parents, except at the request of these parents.

It must not be overlooked that Prussian parents can choose for their children a public school, a private school or instruction in the family. All private schools, however, are under the immediate supervision of the government, and teachers in these private schools must have the same qualifications as the teachers in the public schools. Furthermore, if instruction be given in the family, the government has the duty, through her supervising officers, to see that said instruction be an equivalent for that given in the public schools. Inasmuch as religious instruction is an essential part of the elementary school *curriculum*, the teachers must be qualified. The time-tables under Courses of Study, given in the sixth chapter, show how regular this religious instruction is, both for Roman Catholics and for Protestants.

In connection with religious instruction, it should be stated that clergymen in Prussia, are to a certain extent officers of the State. A majority receive a part of their salary, sometimes half, directly from the State treasury. They must all have absolved the gymnasial course of nine years and the university course of three or four years or a theological course in a divinity school of recognized standing. . . .

School Discipline and Miscellaneous Regulations

The teacher in Prussia has much more authority over his pupils than the teacher in New York. He exercises this authority both in and out of school, and it covers, also, children of other classes than his own in the same school, but not pupils of other schools.

Corporal punishment is allowed, but same must not be carried out to such an extent that the health of the pupil suffer in consequence. If the pupil be too severely dealt with, the teacher is disciplined by the *Provinzial-Schulcollegium.* Very severe cases subject teachers to fines of 300 thalers [9] or imprisonment for three years. If the injury be permanent, the teacher is imprisoned for five years in a penitentiary or for one year in a State prison. The former confinement brings with it generally the loss of citizen-

---

[9]A thaler is equal to 71.4 cents.

ship. Ordinary imprisonment does not necessarily involve these consequences. Imprisonment from two to ten years follows in cases where injuries were given intentionally.

If death result from injuries received, the person inflicting these injuries is imprisoned not less than three years in a house of correction (*Zuchthaus*) or three months in a State prison (*Gefängniss*). Circumstances under which the injury was given receive careful attention.

Fines, up to 2,000 thalers for the benefit of the person injured, may be inflicted.

An official teacher or other employe of the government, who, in the exercise of his office, inflicts or permits the infliction of serious injuries, is imprisoned for not less than three months. If there are extenuating circumstances, the imprisonment may be shortened to one day or a fine of 300 thalers. If the injury be exceptionally severe, imprisonment for two years follows. Extenuating circumstances may limit this imprisonment to three months.

The following decrees regulate the infliction of corporal punishment by school teachers:

1. Corporal punishment should be resorted to only when other disciplinary means have failed, and then only in cases of obstinate persistence in lying, great stubbornness and disobedience, gross immorality and persistent lack of industry.

Teachers are not permitted to form the habit of resorting to corporal punishment daily and hourly. When possible, little children and girls of all ages should not be punished in this way.

2. In the case of little children less than 9 years of age, the teacher must use a light switch; in other cases, a pliant stick not thicker than the little finger may be employed.

3. Girls are to be hit upon the back alone, boys upon the back or the *Gesäss*. The force of blows must be moderated. In inflicting corporal punishment the clothing must not be removed.

4. The use of a thicker stick or rule, hitting with hand, fist or book in the face and head, hair-pulling, ear-twisting or that of other parts of the body, punching in the breast, back and head, or other like punishments, are forbidden.

5. Pupils are not to receive corporal punishment while at their desks, but in an open space of school room. It should be administered at the close of the recitation

hour, never in the hour devoted to religious studies.

6. Switch and stick should be in teacher's closet during the hours for instruction, not directly at hand.

7. The grounds and extent of the punishment inflicted must be recorded in the teacher's register.

8. In cases requiring very severe measures, whether faults were committed on or off the school premises, the teacher should notify the local school inspector and inflict the punishment in his presence. In large schools such matters are brought before a conference of the teachers, and the punishment is inflicted in presence of the director (*Rector*).

9. When teacher has been too severe in inflicting corporal punishment, he is disciplined by the *Provinzial-Schulcollegium*. Serious cases subject him to penalties fixed by the penal code. School inspectors must forward well grounded complaints, even though injuries inflicted be not serious, to the *Provinzial-Schulcollegium*.

10. Teachers often found guilty of excess in inflicting corporal punishment, in addition to the other penalties, forfeit, for long or short periods, the authority to inflict corporal punishment.

11. To lessen complaints brought against teachers, disciplinary measures should be often discussed, and all teachers, especially the younger, should study thoroughly the decrees relating thereto.

It is to be noted that no actions against teachers can be brought, either in civil or criminal courts, except in cases where a child has received some real bodily injury, wound or bruise. This is also the case when local school inspectors and school commissioners have inflicted corporal punishment.

A glance at the regulations for pupils in higher schools shows that they are closely watched at all times:

1. If the school director ascertains that pupils are living in a *pension* which he deems unsuitable, it is his duty to notify the parents or guardians of such pupils. If no attention be paid to this notification, the pupils are expelled.

2. Pupils from other districts can not select nor change their boarding-place without the authority of the school-director.

3. Pupils from other districts are under the special oversight of the *Ordinarius*.

4. Pupils who absent themselves from the

city or village over night, even though they lose no study or instruction-hour, must have the permission of the *Ordinarius* or school-director. This applies to pupils from other districts not dwelling with parents.

5. Pupils must have permission of *Ordinarius* or school-director to attend theaters and balls. Pupils residing with their parents at home must procure the permission of parents to attend theaters, and can only attend public balls in the company of parents or guardians.

6. Pupils who give private lessons must procure the permission of *Ordinarius* or school-director.

No outsider is permitted to enter or disturb a public school under five thalers fine or imprisonment.

Teachers must be on hand fifteen minutes before school opens. Tardiness should be closely watched.

Children may not be kept at school so as to lose midday meal, nor should they be kept after school until dark.

Children are not permitted to give presents to teachers, nor are they allowed to take up collections.

Children under school age are not allowed to be present in the school-room during school sessions. The teacher is not permitted to wear slippers during school-hours.

The pupils are forbidden to frequent taverns, confectioneries, saloons. They are not allowed to attend dramatical, musical and acrobatic performances, except in the company of parents or guardians. They are encouraged to protect useful animals and government property, such as railways and telegraph lines. They are warned against the careless use of fire-arms.

Teachers should watch over the private reading of pupils. They should be protected from obscene literature. . . .

Conclusion

The superiority of the Prussian system of elementary education, as compared with that of New York, may be summed up in one sentence. *Prussia sends all her children between fixed ages to school, and protects them while there from the imposition of bad work.* Frederick the Great aimed to accomplish this in 1763. From his day the system has been perfected gradually, and stands to-day without a rival.

Since 1871, France has followed in the footsteps of her rival, and the standard of work done in elementary schools has advanced with a rapidity which seems almost incredible.

In 1888, the cost of public education in Prussia, including the secondary, trade schools, technical schools and universities, was reckoned at $1.7717 *per caput* of total population. Allowances for rent and fuel slightly increased these figures. Army and navy schools were not included.

The cost of public education in New York in 1888 (census of 1880) was figured at three dollars and eight cents *per caput* of total population.

Every impartial person must admit that Prussia secures in good results the full value of the money expended, and that New York does not.

The methods in use in Prussia can not be adopted as a whole in New York. This is clear. Nevertheless, wise legislation would secure for us similar advantages, as the example of France, a sister republic, demonstrates.

Our model elementary schools would then become the rule, and not the exception, as at present.

James Russell Parsons, Jr.   1892

French Schools Through American Eyes

The belief that everything American is perfect constitutes a form of false patriotism which seems to be growing in this country, particularly in the field of journalism. There is a large and increasing class of men who can not bear an adverse opinion touching anything American "without falling into these hysterics of holy horror, which are the usual refuge of ignorance and stupidity." If we are to realize, however, the promise

James Russell Parsons, Jr., *French Schools Through American Eyes: A Report to the New York State Department of Public Instruction* (Syracuse, New York: C. W. Bardeen, 1892), pp. 7–11, 135–136.

of becoming the greatest nation in the world, we must cultivate the power of discrimination. We must learn to reject that which is bad; to adopt and perfect that which is good wherever it may be found. "The true greatness of a people," said M. Victor Cousin in 1833, "does not consist in borrowing nothing from others, but in borrowing from all whatever is good, and in perfecting whatever it appropriates."

There is no branch of the public service in which this power of discrimination is more needed than in primary instruction. France has succeeded in assimilating all that is good in the systems of elementary education of other countries without destroying the unity of her national character. What France has done, New York can and should do.

The problem of the French and Prussian teacher is to accomplish a fixed amount of work in a set time with a given number of children between fixed ages, who must attend school regularly. What is the problem confronting the New York teacher? To accomplish an indefinite amount of work in an indefinite time with an indefinite number of pupils between five and twenty-one years of age, who attend school when they feel disposed to do so. Compared with this, the secrets of perpetual motion and of the squaring of the circle are as nothing.

Whatever may be the opinions as regards secondary and higher education, the extent to which they should be gratuitous, the fields into which they should be carried by the State, almost all civilized people are unanimous in recognizing the universal necessity of an elementary education in those schools which represent the body of the nation. In order to make good and intelligent citizens, a minimum of school work is essential, and the most enlightened have now settled on the period of seven or eight years for its accomplishment.

As stated last year in my report on Prussian elementary schools, it would be most unjust to make an assertion that no good elementary school work is done in New York State. I have visited many schools in countries of the old world as well as in New York, and have never seen better elementary schools than the best schools here at home. More than this, I am aware that there are many schools to-day in obscure corners of my own country, or hidden among the hills of the school commissioner districts, which no thoughtful person can visit without being most favorably impressed by the faithful, conscientious and efficient work of the teachers. Working for very small salaries, struggling against the disadvantages of irregular attendance and a short school year, it is marvelous what these teachers accomplish.

But it is in vain that New York State goes on expending more and more each year for educational purposes. Without legislation insuring a full and regular attendance of the children from six to thirteen or fourteen years of age; without a minimum of qualifications for supervising officers as well as teachers; without an approximate equalization of local taxation for school purposes; without State supervision of instruction given in private schools and in families, we shall never attain anything approaching the uniform excellence of the work done in Prussian and French elementary schools. . . .

Throughout France there is at the present time a fermentation of thought in matters pertaining to public education. This is particularly true in cities and large centers of population. In speaking of the expense of public education in Paris, Albert Shaw says:

"Probably no other city in the world secures equally advantageous results from the outlay upon schools. Under the compulsory education act the attendance of children in elementary schools has actually been made almost universal. But Paris does not stop with elementary education in reading, writing and numbers. It maintains a marvelous system of industrial and trade schools for both sexes, in which almost everything that pertains to the production and traffic of Paris is taught and encouraged. American and English visitors at the exposition of 1889, will remember the remarkable display of the Paris industrial schools, especially in lines of decorative manufacture and art. It is in these schools that Parisian dressmakers, milliners, artificial-flower makers, furniture designers, house decorators, skilled workers in metals, and handicraftsmen in scores of lines of industry are educated to do the things that keep Paris prosperous and rich. It is public money wisely spent that maintains such an educational system. I need not refer to the higher schools of science, of classics and literature, of engineering and of fine art. All the flowers of civilization are encouraged by the Paris municipality. The yearly expenditure of a moderate but regular sum for the promotion of fine arts, by means of the purchase, under a competitive system, of designs for public statues, of pictures and mural designs for schools and various public buildings, and of other artistic works, not only educates the popular taste and adds to the adornment and beauty of the city, but

helps to keep Paris the art center of the world, and thus to maintain what, from the economic point of view, is one of the chief and most profitable industries of Paris. The mercantile schools that train so many thousands of women as well as men in bookkeeping and penmanship are also an admirable investment."

We turn now to the special consideration of what has been called the most complete national system ever devised, of compulsory, gratuitous and secular public education.

History teaches us that after great wars, and especially disastrous wars, public attention turns toward education. August 10, 1807, William III, King of Prussia, said: "The State must regain in intellectual force what it has lost in physical force." Men like Humboldt, Fichte and Stein were not wanting, and the result was the reorganization of national education, substantially completed in 1813.

The story of France from the close of the Franco-Prussian war is another striking illustration of this fact. For more than half a century the attention of the French people had been directed to the defects in their system of education. Strong men had devoted their lives to remedy these defects, and yet comparatively little was accomplished until France had been conquered by Prussia and her very existence was threatened.

The study of public education in France is particularly interesting to Americans. The laws, measures and methods, adopted by a sister republic to insure the requisite training for good and intelligent citizens, are not looked upon so suspiciously as those enforced under more despotic forms of government.

The documents setting forth the condition of public education in France are remarkable for precision, clearness and brevity. A study of the new code of primary instruction (*Nouveau Code de l'Instruction Primaire par A. E. Pichard*, 1890), will convince the New Yorker that our code should be thoroughly revised. It is a brave man, indeed, who has courage enough to venture an opinion on school matters in New York. Statutes are often contradictory and we are in almost as bad a condition as the Prussians who have no code of public instruction at all, but are forced to depend on a few general laws and many local decrees. The French system of primary instruction, however, is so clearly set forth in the code that it is very easy to understand. As a consequence there is much

less contention than in New York, and a great saving of time and money.

The object of this report is to state as clearly and as concisely as possible just what the French system of primary instruction is, and the results which are accomplished under this system.

As in my report on Prussian elementary schools, an attempt is made to state clearly and concisely the minimum of work required of each healthy French child, and the provisions by which the accomplishment of this work is secured. The reader follows the would-be teacher through the Kindergarten (*école maternelle*), the lower and upper primary schools, the normal school, and the final examinations.

In France as in Prussia primary instruction is secured by the State against all casualties. It is uniform and invariable, because the primary schools represent the body of the nation and are destined to nourish and to strengthen the national unity. Compulsory education laws necessitate a full and regular attendance of the children of school age. Official courses of study fix the work to be accomplished in each of the different grades of schools. Teaching is elevated to the dignity of a profession and the tenure of office is secure. The State is most generous in supporting schools in poor and thinly populated districts. Trained teachers are found in rural as well as in city districts and the school year is at least forty weeks in length. The State supervises the instruction of children of school age in private schools and families, insisting on definite qualifications for private instructors. A minimum of qualifications is established for all teachers and inspectors of schools. Special teachers must hold the certificate of capacity for their particular lines of work.

These in brief are the principal advantages of the French elementary school system. New York elementary schools will never compare favorably with those of France without similar provisions. Since 1871 the standard of work done in French elementary schools has advanced with a rapidity which is without a parallel in the history of education, and which would seem entirely incredible to those not familiar with the tremendous sacrifices the Republic has made since the war. . . .

Several authorities have asserted that the French admit the superiority of Prussian schools, because French parents have sent their children in many cases to Prussian secondary schools. This argument had force as far as secondary schools were concerned, but it should have been restricted to these schools.

If France continues to make as much progress in her secondary schools as she has made during the past few years, the comparison with those of her rival will be as favorable as in the case of elementary schools. At present she is endeavoring to avoid the objections which have been urged by Germans against their own system of secondary instruction, and seems to be working along better and more practical lines, though it must not be overlooked that this work in France is yet in its infancy.

Schools, like prophets, are often not without honor save in their own country. We have many examples of the truth of this statement. Parents in New York often send their children away to be educated, when they would receive better instruction in the public schools at home. In the same way German parents send their children to France and French children are sent to Germany, though in these cases the acquisition of a modern language is often the principal reason.

We must also bear in mind the fact that the reputation of Prussian schools has been established for more than half a century, while the French system of public instruction dates almost entirely from the Franco-Prussian war, and in a large measure from 1882. The schools of Prussia have been perfected gradually from 1813, the date of the completion of the reorganization of the system of education.

With this fact in mind we do not expect to find such a high degree of perfection in the French as in the Prussian schools, and are indeed surprised that comparisons, based on results attained in so short a time are so favorable.

There is no system of public instruction which is not weakened by poor schools. I have heard lessons in technical grammar in Kindergärten in Paris, and I have visited second and third rate schools in Germany. When pupils have expressed surprise that as an American I was neither red nor black, and asked what language was generally spoken in the United States, I have not drawn general conclusions as to faulty methods of instruction because my other visits had convinced me that Prussian and French elementary schools have attained uniform degrees of excellence while our model elementary schools are exceptions to the rule.

It has been stated by prominent authorities that the French or Prussian child of 12 is about two years in advance of the American of the same age. It is most unjust to make such comparisons unless they are accompanied by explanations. It is not because the French or Prussian pupils have greater natural capacity than the American, but simply because from their sixth or seventh year of age they have been forced to attend school regularly for at least 40 weeks annually, and have been protected in school as far as possible from the imposition of bad work.

In France and in Prussia the laws fix a minimum of instruction for elementary schools, and surround the schools with all safeguards. The result is that the general standard of the work accomplished approaches that maintained in our best elementary schools.

In New York the laws do not prescribe the work for elementary schools. Each school is practically a law unto itself as to what shall be pursued and how. Furthermore, the legal school year is about ten weeks shorter than in Prussia and France, and attendance is irregular. The result is that our model elementary schools are exceptions to the rule.

Isaac Sharpless 1893

Comparative Education and Administration: England and America

Isaac Sharpless (1848–1920) graduated from Harvard College in 1873 and served at Hartford College as instructor in mathematics from 1875 to 1879, as professor of mathematics and astronomy from 1879 to 1884, and as president from 1887 to 1917. He was the first president of the Friends Historical Association at Philadelphia. The article below is based on his travel experiences in England during the winter of 1890 and 1891, when he visited schools

Isaac Sharpless, *The Relation of the State to Education in England and America*, Publication No. 87 (Philadelphia: American Academy of Political and Social Science, 1893), pp. 1–22.

and interviewed educators. Although he was generally critical of English education, he favored the English provisions for careful accounting procedures and regulations for enforcing compulsory school attendance.

Historians may differ as to whether our American institutions sprang from England or Holland. They may agree to divide the honors and may possibly be willing ultimately to accord to America some originating power of her own. The question of the cause of the divergence in the institutions of the two great Anglo-Saxon nations is an interesting one, and probably no phase of it is more interesting than that which deals with educational systems.

A great factor in the divergence has undoubtedly been the fact that English systems have been built up by the slow accretions of ages, every proposed addition being required to show proof, not only of its inherent usefulness, but also of adaptability to the other parts of the edifice already erected; while here to a much greater extent the ground has been cleared and we have been able to consult utility in determining our structure. Then again, we have been willing to learn from foreigners. The cosmopolitan character of our population is but an index of a cosmopolitan character in our institutions. Holland, Germany, Scandinavia, as well as England, have been probed by minds open to receive and adopt any suggestions, and these have been woven often unconsciously into our systems. England, with a more homogeneous population and great belief in her own ability to solve all her own problems without assistance, has made a slower but perhaps more characteristically national growth.

Furthermore, over all *our* development has continually hovered the great democratic idea, directing the way to institutions in which it may find a fitting permanent abode. The people ultimately will secure a system giving equal chances, for the people are supreme. The mother country boasts of her equal and in some cases greater political liberty, but it is useless it seems to me to deny that in essential democracy, a democracy which gives a chance for every talent to be fully developed, she is still behind us, though in the past twenty years she has probably gained on us in the race. She still says of democratic ideas what the student in theology gave as an answer to the question as to the church's doctrine on the subject of good works: "A few of them will do no harm;" while we have embraced these ideas readily and fully and are continually modifying all our institutions, social, political and religious, in their direction.

It is not, however, the purpose of this paper to trace the causes, but some of the facts of divergences in the systems of State education in the two countries, and the subjects of contrast which will be treated of are four.

1. The guarantees which the State receives that its money is properly expended by the schools.

2. The provision which it makes for education from the age of fourteen to the age of nineteen.

3. The enforcement of education on unwilling parents and children.

4. The attitude towards religious and Biblical teaching.

1. The English follow up their appropriation with most detailed care. It is not given into local hands to make what they can of it. The system is popularly called "payment by results," and this expresses the general idea supposed to govern the method. Every shilling given is supposed to be given for a result already obtained. "Have you taught a boy to read and write and cipher?" the government says to a school. "We will not take your word for it, we will ascertain for ourselves, and if so, we will pay you for it." "Is your school in a fair state of discipline and organization? If our inspection satisfies us on this point we will give you a shilling per child. If it is very good we will give you 1*s.* 6*d.*" "Will your children fairly pass our examination in geography? we will give you a shilling a piece; will they do it very well indeed? we will give you two shillings a piece; will they not pass? we will not give you anything," and so on through the list. The epigram of Robert Lowe is supposed to sum up its merits. "If the system is costly it shall be efficient; if inefficient it shall be cheap."

If inspectors were omniscient and infallible, accurately gauging all the good results a school produces, hampered by no instructions and swayed by no prejudices, there could probably be no better system devised than this. It would secure the very greatest good from every penny appropriated.

About $7,000,000 are paid out by the general government on the basis of this arrangement in aid of education, and this covers about twenty-seven per cent of the total cost of maintaining the schools.

Any denominational or private school, if it fulfills certain general conditions as to religious instruction, quality of teaching, and charges to parents, can be a recipient of this grant.

With regard to the whole system of inspection and "payment by results," a strong controversy has been, and still is raging in England. For it, it is urged that it is necessary for the government to have assurance that the purposes, for which so much public money is voted, are secured; and the fact that so many of the schools are in private hands makes this all the more important. It is also said to be a guarantee against the tendency, which seems to be especially strong in English schools, particularly those most closely connected with the universities, to give too much attention to a few bright scholars, at the expense of the duller ones; for evidently such a course would not satisfy inspectors and win grants. Its friends also claim that it is the cause, to a large extent, of the increase in salaries of teachers, and affords a certain means of informing managers as to the relative value of the different teachers, and thus enables them to graduate salaries in proportion to pedagogic or grant-winning abilities. It is certain that salaries have steadily risen under the operation of the system, that teachers hold a higher place in the estimation of the community and that the best of them have a very handsome remuneration for their services. There is not the level of uniform compensation for teachers of a certain grade, which prevails in most other countries, but the system often makes it economical to secure and retain good teachers, even at an advance over others who are doing, in an inferior manner, the same work. The average salary of men teachers in the public Elementary Schools in England is about $600, and of women, $375, while in Pennsylvania it is about $325 for men, and $250 for women, and the expenses of living are greater.

On the other hand, the "cramming" which the system produces is violently protested against. To meet the demands, real or supposed, of the inspector, education is sacrificed to the process of forcing into the scholars, available and grant compelling knowledge. Facts in geography, for instance, count for more than real brain power in a test by an external examiner. The teacher is hampered in the adoption of methods which seem to him best, by the fear that they will not produce the kind of results which the government inquires for, and the scholars are filled with a sort of knowledge which disappears as rapidly as it was gained. One hears many complaints that the children

who leave school at twelve or fourteen often lose almost all their school acquisitions in a few years. This danger is fully recognized by the department, and inspectors are strongly urged not to lay too much stress on mere knowledge. . . .

These questions of the development of high ambitions, of character, of good habits, and of physique cannot be too strongly urged on the attention of elementary schools. Together they are more important than any intellectual attainments. They stand the wear and tear of life better, and do more to assist their possessor to prominence and success. If the system does not allow their encouragement, it is a severe indictment against it. It is undoubtedly true that they do not count for very much in obtaining grants. It is also true that success in them is often very difficult to estimate. Probably the department is doing all that it can to secure them. A grant for "discipline and organization" of 1s. or 1s. 6d. may be made, and inspectors are instructed that they "will have special regard to the moral training and conduct of the children, to the neatness and order of the school premises and furniture, and to the proper classification of the scholars." They are also to be satisfied "that all reasonable care is taken in the ordinary management of the school, to bring up the children in habits of punctuality, of good manners and language, of cleanliness and neatness, and also to impress on the children the importance of cheerful obedience to duty, of consideration and respect for others, and of honor and truthfulness in word and act."

This is excellent; and if under the system good teachers are allowed to get these results, even if to do it certain studies are neglected, there would be but little left to desire.

These arguments do not seem to have undermined the belief of most Englishmen connected with education that "payment by results" is advantageous, or at least necessary for the present.

They have probably produced serious modifications, which have tended towards the idea that it is the work of inspectors to see that school officers do their duty, rather than test very minutely the advancement of the individual scholar in special subjects. These modifications satisfy many of the objectors; and though the clamor does not lack energy and volume, it is more likely to produce further modification than to cause the abolishment of a system which is unquestionably effective in toning up many schools that would otherwise be bad, and which satisfies the Englishman's idea of fairness, and of the propriety of equivalence for public money expended.

Such is the carefully guarded English system—without loop-hole for waste, and with a continual stimulation to goodness of a certain sort.

In Pennsylvania our State Legislature appropriates $5,000,000 annually towards the schools, about one-third the total revenue, and nearly as much as the English Government. What security does it have against squandering? None, except what it imposes on the school districts in connection with the money they raise for themselves.

There are general laws governing the sort of schools the State will recognize. The teacher must be examined and certificated by the County Superintendent. The schools must be kept open at least 120 days in the year; every person between the ages of six and twenty-one must have the privilege of attending them; and orthography, reading, writing, English grammar, geography, arithmetic, physiology and hygiene, must be taught by a teacher whom the Superintendent pronounces efficient and the local directors appoint.

All of this has to be certified to by the County Commissioners for each district as a condition of receiving any money from the State. This report being received by the State Superintendent he must pay the money in proportion to the number of *resident taxables* in the district. The State cannot go back on the local returns. There is no question of quality of instruction. "Results" have nothing to do with it. The grant creates comparatively little stimulation. It is largely a device to relieve local taxation. The Constitution directs that at least $1,000,000 shall be given, and undoubtedly this was originally for the purpose of imposing conditions on backward communities as to quality of teachers, length of school year and subjects to be taught. But the State is rich and the districts are poor, and public opinion demanded an increase of State aid, so the appropriation rose finally to $5,000,000 with but little change in legislation. Of course the increase gives still greater power to enforce State provisions. No district can well afford to throw away lightly so large an increment of revenue, coming to it as a gift and adding no additional responsibility. But it is doubtful whether, despite the well-meant efforts of County Superintendent and school officers, sufficient betterment of the schools has

resulted from the increase. It was done to relieve local taxation, and it has done this. The other effect, to add to gross revenues and consequent efficiency of the schools, is a matter of doubt, except in a few districts already alert.

The county which fulfills the minimum requirements of the law, keeps its schools open for six months of twenty days each, employs the cheapest talent the County Superintendent will pass, and teaches however lamely the prescribed studies, knows it will receive its share of the funds just as if it paid double salaries, had ten months of school year and made its schools first rate, and hence feels no great pressure to improve.

In the English system a State officer, absolutely independent of the locality, follows up the appropriation and on the basis of his report it is granted. In America, for while the local idea is very strong in Pennsylvania, it may in this respect be taken as a typical State, all is left to the locality. The easily fulfilled general conditions are compatible with very poor schools. County superintendents elected by the directors, and seeking election every three years, are not always very rigid in examining teachers. They cannot be, for the directors fix the salary and these will not draw in all parts the best material, and yet in a sense the law is complied with, and the commissioners elected by the same constituency certify this to the State officer, who has no option but to pay the money.

The English system applied to Pennsylvania would first destroy an immense number of weakly schools, and then it would build up in their places schools of better sort and would work up the tone of unwilling and lethargic communities.

And yet I would not wish its adoption. The strength derived from local independence is a factor we cannot ignore.

The continual burden of working up to the requirements of an external examiner is such a fetter on a good teacher that one would not want it. If our worst schools are worse than the English, I believe our best schools are better, for in many places a teacher is asked for no results except her general tone and impression on the school, and this is as it should be.

But we are throwing away a chance to build up the school systems in weak districts, and it seems to me that some constructive legislation is needed to secure the benefits of payments by results without its evils.

I am not competent, nor is this the place to enter into details, but as a basis of this system I think we should have, appointed and paid by the State, a number of officers whose business should be, each in a well-defined district, to report in a perfectly general way as to the efficiency of the schools and their fitness to receive aid. They should be paid by the State, so as to make them independent of local influence, and they should have power, not in the least to interfere with local effort, but solely to report on its success; not on each study, not on each school, but on the district. They should take into account possible and not ideal results. They should say to directors, you must make better schools, or you shall not have State money, or not as much State money. They would in time, if properly selected and disciplined, become influential in shaping policy and methods, but this would only be an indirect effect of their employment. Their main duty would be to secure the necessary guarantees that the large sum of $5,000,000 annually given by the State is properly expended. By some such device as this you might secure all the advantages of English "payment by results," with no derogation to local enterprise and a continual uplift of the average standard of the schools.

Instead of saying, we will give you a quarter for every child taught geography, and then taking possession of the school to ascertain the facts and deducing the appropriation by this arithmetical process, our inspector would report: "In such a district the school is not giving as good intellectual and moral results as one has a right to expect. I would recommend a reduction of its appropriation, until it shows itself competent to use it better." The district might find it actually cheaper to keep up a good school than a poor one. If a good teacher, costing a few dollars a month more, could receive from the State treble the increase of her salary, American shrewdness would dictate her employment, and after all the great secret of a good school is to place a good teacher in contact with children and fetter her by no restraints. The appropriation is now large enough to make its reception worth an effort.

2. Another point of contrast in the two countries is their attitude to secondary education. There are no State-aided secondary schools in England. A large number of schools, many of them since the reorganization of 1868 excellent schools, most of them dating their origin to the time of the Re-

formation, give the English boys of means a good education preparatory to business, technical schools or the universities. They have a noble history, excellent traditions, an efficient teaching staff, and are the most interesting features, because the most distinctively English, of the whole English set of educational institutions. But being old foundations, they are not distributed in accordance with the population. Many populous new towns have none, while in other quarters there is a redundancy. It was the noble dream of the reformers to place a grammar school for rich and poor in every parish, and have every one point to the universities, so that the poor boy, by scholarships in the universities which they often provided, should find his way clear to the Bachelor's Degree. Had their successors possessed their spirit the dream would have been a reality. But the rich have monopolized the schools, and even the university scholarships, and a poor boy, except in rare instances, cannot rise above the elementary schools. Even the middle classes, which profit most by a secondary education, are excluded, except they happen to reside near one of these old endowed schools. For these schools the State does nothing. They do not wish anything from the State, and will not willingly accept any favors coupled with conditions. They have their endowments and their constituency. They do a good work in limited lines, and they are not anxious to give up their independence and become a part of any system involving government examiners, conscience clauses and certificated teachers. Hence they do nearly nothing, except in a few localities, to supply secondary education to the great middle classes of English boys. They are for the rich. But England is on the eve of a great reorganization of its secondary system. A recent private letter from a gentleman who will have a hand in shaping the movement says: "We are just starting on a very difficult voyage over here—the organization of secondary education, and there will be fierce fighting over it. I believe in the State supplying what has been left unsupplied, and requiring some very general conditions to be satisfied by what is in existence. Others would have everything under the direction of the State —them I shall fight to the death. The storm will break in about four months—a new government may delay it for a year—but storm there will be." And the Vice-President of the Council on Education, the practical head of the department, has said within a few weeks: "I find throughout the country a rising flood of public opinion in favor of some further development of secondary education, and a growing conviction of the need for lessening the chaos which lies between the now completely organized system of elementary education and the universities." The gaps of the system will be filled up by State-established schools. Those already existing will be co-ordinated without too much curtailment of their liberties, and we will see a system arise, wrought out in the, if tardy, yet thorough and effective, English manner. England is no longer ruled by the rich, and the sentiment that they alone should be educated is passing away before the growth of a great Democratic wave, which, now represented in Parliament and Councils, is granting to all classes the chances to the best the country can afford.

There are but a score or two of men in both the historic universities who have ever been in a State-aided school. Ninety-nine per cent of all their students come from the fifteen per cent of the people who are called the upper classes. The prospects before an ambitious poor boy, except in rare instances, are cheerless in the extreme. The life of labor of the father is to be reproduced in the son, with only the advantage given by an improved elementary education of which the father probably has none at all.

America has been wiser or more fortunate. Our public school system has embraced the high school—an institution often with grave faults, but supplying a good opportunity, more often of the modern sort, to almost all boys and girls who ought to have it, and who will value it. It is the stepping stone between the elementary school and the university, in many States practically the only one which exists. Any one who can be supported to the age of seventeen or eighteen can go to college and any one can satisfy those aspirations which often are aroused later in life by a book, a lecture, a newspaper article, or a conversation. Every American college knows the young man of perhaps twenty-three or twenty-four, with a hiatus of years in his educational life, of a very slender patrimony, and shallow financial resources, but somehow suddenly aroused to a burning desire for a college degree and the learning which it implies. Such a late awakening would in England be absolutely futile. If it ever occurred it would be dismissed as an impossible dream. Such a person might almost as well aspire to be ruler of the United Kingdom. But here it is very possible of realization. He finds a free

high school in the nearest town. From there he readily passes to a college or university, in many States, practically free and supported by State funds; in others, with a number of scholarships reserved for the poor and deserving, so arranged that they can be readily applied for without loss of independence, while the vacation affords the chances to replenish his resources for personal expenditure.

It is the free secondary school which makes this possible, which gives to every boy and girl a chance for the best in the way of education that the country can offer. How weak then is the cry of demagogues, and of some who are not demagogues, that the public purse should supply only the education of the masses, the three "R's," and that all beyond this savors of aristocracy. It would be unfortunate indeed, if, just as England is emerging from its blindness and traditionary ideas into the light of which Matthew Arnold was the apostle, and though he knew it not, the prophet, we should allow any one to convince us that the people's money should go to elementary schools alone, thus hopelessly condemning to ignorance and inferiority many lives which were meant for something better.

Where a whole community patronizes the public school system and representatives from all sorts of people sit side by side in primary, grammar and high school, which is the case in New England and the Northwest, there is not much danger of any attack on State-aided public education in any of its parts being successful. It is to be hoped there is not anywhere, but the great strength of endowed, denominational and private schools in Philadelphia is creating a large class who have no direct interest in the free high school. Such schools in sufficient numbers are an excellent and useful stimulus to a public school system, competing with it for its brightest children, but if they become too popular they tend to make class distinctions and lessen that concern of all for the educational advancement of all which is the life of a democracy. An improvement and extension of our facilities for free secondary education in our large cities seem to me to be a great need. So far from this being open to the charge of taking public money for the support of the few, it seems to be the very essence of the democratic idea. Every child does not need a secondary education, but every child needs to have the opportunity, if his intellectual and moral resources render it desirable for him.

3. Another point of contrast is in the matter of compulsory attendance. It was not till 1880 that this was made binding on all school boards of England. The requirements are now about as follows:

All English children are compelled to attend school after the age of five years, until they have passed the standard fixed by the local laws. This varies in different parts, but is usually the fifth or sixth standard; when the child is on an average twelve or thirteen years old. If, however, the child is a bright one and can pass his standard at the age of eleven, he may be withdrawn from the school and placed at remunerative work on half time and at school the other half, for two years. At thirteen all compulsion ceases, unless by that time the child has not passed the standard for children of ten, in which case he must attend a year longer. This regulation is enforced with considerable strictness. A parent whose child does not attend regularly, and who has no good reason for absence, is liable to a fine not exceeding five shillings. If the parents are drunken and neglect their children habitually, or if the children have fallen into criminal habits, they may be committed to an industrial school, where they are kept for a greater or less time, educated, fed and in some cases housed at night. These schools are not popular. The parents are expected to pay two shillings a week, but this from such parents is very difficult to collect, and parent and child are often willing to promise regular attendance at an ordinary school as a condition of release. Often the poor look on industrial schools as prisons, which indeed they are.

It is pretty difficult to evade these laws. The first attempt is to keep the children off the school lists, and the nomadic character of the lower classes of London, renders this sometimes difficult to detect. Children are hidden away upon the approach of officers and their existence resolutely denied. Once on the lists the only escape is feigned illness. Many and ingenious are the artifices employed. A child found wading in a pond gave bronchitis as a reason for non-attendance at school, while head and other aches, violent under observation, but suddenly disappearing, are not infrequent. The laws are said to be very unpopular with a limited class, who cannot understand why they should be forced to educate their children against their will, and in addition (until 1891), to pay the school pence. The existence of this class is the excuse for the compulsory law, which will probably, as has been the case in

Prussia, in time extinguish it.

More respectable are the objections of those who, while admitting the necessity of compulsion, complain of the sweeping character of the laws, and the strictness of their enforcement in many places. From the age of five, every child must attend twice a day, five days in the week, for forty weeks in the year. Irregular attendance, as well as truancy, renders a parent liable to fine, and school boards are invested with great powers, which they must exercise, to detect evasions of the law on the part of children or parents or employers.

This is in strong contrast with the methods in the United States. Though all our schools are free, only part of the States have any compulsory laws, and of these only a very few rigorously enforce them.

They seem to be the only safeguards we have against falling to a secondary place in educational standing. Practically, all the European States, north of the Mediterranean peninsulas and west of Russia, are satisfied as to their efficacy; and we cannot depend any longer with safety on *drawing* to our schools, even though we make instruction, books and stationery free, the whole of the child population which ought to be at school. Without the immigration of the past twenty-five years we might have done this, but that has wholly changed the conditions.

Compulsory education usually makes itself unnecessary after a few decades. If a whole generation of men and women can be educated, they do not need much pressure to induce them to send their children to school. Ignorance tends to perpetuate itself, and so does education. In a permanent population the necessity for compulsory laws ought gradually to disappear. The first step is the difficult and important one. England has taken this step, and taken it with an emphasis which admits of no doubt that she means never to go back again. We have not. We have tried the other expedient of encouragement, but evidently this is not sufficient; and, before illiteracy further gains on us, we should seriously consider whether the welfare of the State does not demand that we should follow the course which France took so tardily, and England more tardily still, but which, once taken, no country has ever repented of. Notwithstanding various sources of weakness, the Royal Commission of 1886–88, which made an exhaustive inquiry into the subject, reported that compulsion had unquestionably increased the attendance in three ways: by its direct influence on parents;

by the disgrace a parent feels at being brought before a magistrate; and by the fact that the completion of a certain standard would allow the child to be placed at remunerative work.

Taking England over, the average attendance is about seventy-eight per cent of the number on the school register; but as this number includes many children under five, to whom the compulsory laws do not apply, it is probable that eighty-two per cent would more correctly represent the average attendance of children above this age. In the United States the attendance is about sixty-seven per cent of the enrollment; in Pennsylvania, seventy-three per cent, and all are not enrolled.

In 1891 there were twenty-seven States and Territories which had enacted compulsory laws, sixteen of which had passed them in the preceding five years; but most of them appear to be in favor of the law, but against its enforcement. Thus New York reports, "We have a compulsory law on our statute books, but it is a compulsory law which does not compel." Illinois says, "It is doubtful if this law has caused an increase in the attendance upon our schools of 100 pupils," and she has since repealed it. From Maine, "I am not aware that the provisions of the act were ever anywhere enforced;" and so on through the list. Indeed, except in two or three New England States, it is doubtful if compulsory laws have produced any serious effect in the United States. In some cases this is through defects in laws, more often as the result of a failure of public opinion to support the enforcement. There is no reason in the political history of Pennsylvania to show that the experiment would result more favorably here than elsewhere, and yet we are losing ground yearly for want of such a provision. While the population has increased twenty-two per cent in the past ten years, the school attendance has only increased one and one-half per cent. New York gives similar figures.

This is not reassuring. Europe has tried the experiment and it has succeeded, becoming each year more popular and easy of enforcement. We know the remedy, we can probably in time secure the law, but we care so little for laws which no one is personally interested in administering that whether passed or not we have no great hopes that it will cure the evil. That we need compulsory education is a matter about which there ought to be little doubt in the minds of those who have studied the history of the move-

ment. Whether any law would give it to us and turn the tide of illiteracy is a doubtful question. It is a condition of affairs demanding the earnest thought of all citizens. It will hardly do to acknowledge ourselves beaten by the problem. There are facts enough attainable to show what is necessary in the way of a law, and we ought ultimately to make it efficient.

4. It is difficult to say anything new on the religious question. And yet one cannot well omit it, for on no point is the divergence of the two nations more apparent.

England approached the subject of popular education with societies representing religious bodies, or formed with reference to religious questions already partly in possession of the field. They could not be ignored, and the completed system had to be dove-tailed around their creations which occupied, but did not cover the ground. Hence, they were left in possession, taken into the system, received State grants and were allowed to propagate their religious views undisturbed. They were more than embraced, they were protected from competition whenever they offered sufficient educational privileges to equip a district. Otherwise they were supplemented. But in return for this financial aid and protection they were to arrange their time of religious instruction so as to place it at the beginning or end of the school day, and every dissenting parent was to be at liberty to remove his child without prejudice to his other work, during those minutes. Moreover, the State was not to examine or give any grant for the religious instruction. In this way Catholic schools, Methodist schools, Church of England schools, and schools managed by the British and Foreign School Society, whose motto was religious, but undenominational education, all came within the public school system, and all pursued unmolested their peculiar methods of religious instruction.

To fill up the gaps of the system a set of schools called Board Schools, managed by boards elected by the district and partially sustained by local taxes, was created. To one of these two classes of schools English boys or girls, between five and eleven (in some cases fourteen), are required to go.

Even in the Board Schools religious instruction may have a prominent place. It depends entirely on the locality. Of the 2255 school boards in England and Wales in 1886, about three-fourths had adopted more or less elaborate schemes of what they called religious but undenominational instruction. In all cases the Bible was the basis of this work. Three hundred and ninety-four others read the Bible without comment, and only ninety-one omitted the subject altogether.

The scheme of the London Board is a seven years' course of Bible history and religious teaching, occupying a half hour per day. To illustrate this, one year's requirements taken at random will be given:

"Memory work: John xiv. 15–31; Ephesians vi. 1–18; lessons from Samuel and Kings, with special reference to the lives of Samuel, Saul, David and Solomon; the life of Christ from third Passover to end of Gospels; Acts of the Apostles, first two chapters."

Such a course as this continued all the years of a child's education will undoubtedly give a Christian bias to his mind. It is undenominational only in so far as it fails to draw any distinction between Christian sects, but it pays no regard to any unchristian beliefs. The holders of such are, however, protected by the liberty, a liberty in fact not frequently exercised, to withhold their children from this course while securing all the other benefits of the school.

England seems to be wedded to religious instruction, requires it in her public elementary schools by the wishes of the great majority of her people, and by perhaps an equal majority desires or is willing that this should be on a Christian basis.

In Pennsylvania, in seven-eighths of the public schools, the Bible is read by the teacher without comment, and this usually constitutes the sum of the religious instruction given. In many States this is omitted and the tendencies are more and more to bring our schools to the condition of the French, where every form of religious instruction is jealously excluded. The logic of our position, which implies the absolute separation of church and State, is rapidly driving us to this place. We must apply the same principles to Catholics, Jews, and unbelievers we do to Protestant sects, if in any locality they demand it. We cannot consistently with our general theory, levy taxes to force teaching down children's throats against which their consciences protest and while I believe it is a good thing to give even the weak ideas of religion usually gained by an unexplained reading of the New Testment and would hold on to it as long as I could, I should give it up in the face of any serious and respectable protest if we are to maintain our present theory of public schools.

And yet this is to my mind not a satisfactory result to come to. The American nation needs more rather than less religious instruction. The formal reading of the Bible is often a lifeless form. The children do not know the subject read about. One word of explanation is often worth the whole chapter read. The home, the church, and the Sunday School combined do not give nearly sufficient to many children, none at all to many others, and if we are to rule it out of the schools absolutely, we will also largely rule it out of the life of the nation. Also while natural ethics may be taught and be effective, it is not so pointedly taught as when reinforced by the religious sanction. Hence I do not believe that the absolute secularization of the schools can be permanently satisfactory except in so far as the nation lowers its standards, and I would be glad to find some compromise, if you will call it so, by which the great majority of the people, of any school district, could have a definite positive teaching of such a general sort as they might approve, not sectarian, with such an arrangement of hours as not to force the attendance of the minority of conscientious opposers. Even unbelievers are often glad or at least willing to have definite religious and moral ideas taught their children, and it hardly seems to me worth while for the great mass of the people, especially those of Anglo-Saxon descent inheriting the religious tendencies of the race, to witness their own growth in religious indifference, for the sake of a theory, if an equally satisfactory result for the rest of the nation can be secured by another arrangement.

If in a district of 100 families, ninety-five desire and would be greatly profited by the infusion of general religious truth, and cannot get it except through the schools, why not excuse the five from attendance and give it.

That the English educational system, in general, has certain advantages over ours, it would, it seems to me, be useless to deny, and we would not be true Americans if we did not recognize and copy good wherever we can find it, and yet, on the whole, we have a decided superiority, which the contrast we have been over, not at all complete, would not reveal.

Our system has a tremendous and overflowing vitality, which promises more for the future than the well-fitted machinery of England. Did you ever live in a country town during the week of a teachers' institute? It is a greater attraction than the new railroad or the circus. The air is saturated with educational questions. The teachers, often of the same social grades as the best of the residents, are received into the homes and made the central features of the excitement. The American free school is discussed, extravagantly, perhaps, in certain features, but on the whole, intelligently. Better still, have you ever been to a State or National Educational Convention? The discussions do not impress one as being in the least shallow or vaguely general. They seem to be the deliverances of men of thought and training and experience, who talk of questions of which they know, anxious for results, willing to face every problem as it arises, and absorbingly interested in the subject. They are stirred up themselves and they manage to communicate to others. They go to their localities, each one an enthusiastic agent of the cause of education.

Thus our country is permeated with educational life. England does not know so much of it. Her teachers do not read professional literature as ours do. They do not meet in conventions as ours do. They do not communicate popular enthusiasm for education as ours do. They are often more highly trained, but frequently inferior in social grade and fineness of instincts. It is this pervasive and contagious individual ambition for education and intense belief in it among all classes of native Americans, inducing a jealous guard over the interests of our schools as fundamental to our whole national structure, which is to me the most striking contrast with the educational condition of our brethren across the Atlantic.

John Tilden Prince   1897

Comparisons of American and German Schools

John Tilden Prince (1844–1916) studied at the Bridgewater Normal School and Harvard University and received his Ph.D. at the University of Leipzig in 1889. He later taught and was superintendent of schools in Waltham and Watertown, Massachusetts. Prince's writings were clearly intended for comparative purposes, and he showed this purpose at the outset of the extract below by stating that he would attempt to answer the question "How does our system of schools compare with that of Germany?" In the conclusion to his article he summed up his negative answer by stating that "our schools are poor in comparison with the schools of Germany."

I shall attempt to answer the question which is frequently asked: How does our system of schools compare with that of Germany, and what useful lessons, if any, relating to public school education may we learn from that country?

First, however, there is to be met the question whether a knowledge of the educational practices of other nations will help us to improve our system and methods of education? Upon this question there seems to be a wide difference of opinion. On the one hand it is asserted that no two nations have the same conditions of life,—either social or civil,—that the schools of a nation are a growth peculiar to itself, as are its laws and customs, and therefore that they can be perfected only by trial and experience under the peculiar conditions of their origin and existence. On the other hand it is urged that the universality of the needs of men as human beings should be recognized; and as the highest end of education is to make good and wise men rather than citizens of any particular state, or workers at any given calling, there should be some common means pursued by which this highest and common end is reached. A knowledge of the common means thus employed serves a double purpose: first, in proving the efficacy of true theories of education; and secondly, in guarding against false ones. Thus the success and mistakes of one people may be used for the benefit of all others.

The history of education shows that this principle of co-operation or the transmission of theories through their embodied practices has been a potent factor in the development of true methods of education. It was recognized in the times of Ratich, Comenius,

John Tilden Prince, *Methods of Instruction and Organization of the Schools of Germany for the Use of American Teachers and Normal Schools* (Boston: Lee and Shepard, 1897), pp. 216–237.

and Pestalozzi, when hundreds of teachers from various countries flocked to see the practical working of theories which were not fully understood or believed. And when we reflect upon the influence of the imperfect and crude attempts of these men to embody in practice theories which, without such practice, might have fallen upon dull ears,— an influence which has extended throughout the civilized world,—we cannot resist the conclusion, not only that it is useful for one nation to study the practices of other nations, but that it is the surest and best way of extending and perfecting the science as well as the art of education.

In seeking to find where we may learn most of that which will be useful in improving our schools, we naturally turn to the countries where lived the great reformers whose names I have just given, and where the fiercest pedagogical conflicts have been waged. In these countries—Germany, Austria, and Switzerland—we find a system of education scientific and thorough in its character, broad in its scope, and uniform in its practices. So good, indeed, are the schools of these countries that they are constantly visited by foreigners who are either drawn thither by professional interest, or sent officially to study their system and to observe their methods.

Nor are the interest and zeal in behalf of the schools new to the German people. Ever since the Reformation, the government has encouraged the establishment of institutions of learning of every kind to such an extent as to call to the service of elementary education the best thought of the country. True, that thought has been erratic and at times abnormal in its application, yet it has always been vigorous and powerful, whether exercised in the severe, classical formalism of Trotzendorf and Sturm, or in the free naturalism of Comenius and Basedow. The experience, therefore, of Germany in the management of her schools has been a thoughtful one; and as such it commands our respect, and invites our attention to some features of their system of schools in contrast with some of our own.

Organization

Whatever may be said of the superiority of natural over acquired qualifications for the teachers' calling, no one, I suppose, will doubt the general statement that the efficiency of teachers is enhanced by special preparation

for their work. That being conceded, we turn to inquire how much so-called professional preparation is demanded of teachers in the United States. From a recent report of the Commissioner of Education it will be seen that in California, Illinois, Kansas, New Hampshire, New York, Massachusetts, Pennsylvania, Vermont, and Wisconsin—the only States making full reports—only one teacher out of every seventeen was in 1886 a graduate of a normal school. A larger proportion, or about twelve per cent, of all teachers employed are reported as having attended a normal school. These States, doubtless, have other training-schools in which some of the teachers have received more or less professional training. Making a liberal allowance for the number attending such schools, and for the probable advance that has been made, it is safe to say that not more than one-fourth of the present teachers of the above-named States have had any professional preparation for their work. The character of elementary education in these States is certainly as high as it is in the rest of the Union. It may be said, therefore, that as many as three-fourths of all the teachers of this country at the present time entered upon their work without the slightest theoretical knowledge of the science or art of teaching. In other words, a majority of the people of the country regard teaching as less of an art than carpentry or horseshoeing, for which some preparation at least is thought to be necessary. When it is considered that a large proportion of these untrained teachers are new to their work every year, the seriousness of the matter becomes apparent. The enormous waste of money which is occasioned by the misdirected energies of this army of novices is of little consequence beside the irreparable injury which their experiments and mistakes cause to the children.

To raise this low standard of requirements for teaching to the standard which Germany has set will be no easy matter; but that it must be done before we can seriously make a comparison of the schools of the two countries, or even before we can claim that there is a profession of teaching in this country, is beyond question.

Our normal schools should demand a higher degree of scholarship for admission than they now demand, or else their courses of study should be broader and more extended than they are in most States of the Union. There should also be given in the normal course a greater opportunity for professional practice than is now given. Graduation from such a course, or its equivalent, should be required for the position of teacher in all elementary schools. Of the secondary school teachers there should be demanded, in addition to graduation from college, at least one year of professional training.

To establish this high, or an equally high, standard of requirements for teaching is the duty of the state. Wherever in the state there is inability to reach it, assistance should be given; and wherever in the state there is unwillingness to reach it, force should be used. If such a policy should be opposed on account of a fear of centralization, let it be remembered that centralization is dangerous only as the central power usurps or takes away individual and local rights. It is plain to see that the delegation of this power to the state protects in the best possible way the rights of both individuals and separate localities.

Efficient service depends not only upon intelligent effort, but also upon a continuance of that effort. A frequently changing personality in any department of industry means a loss in unity of purpose and effort, and consequent weakness. This is especially true in teaching, which requires united and harmonious efforts toward a common purpose. If we step to-day into any one of the one hundred thousand schoolrooms in Germany, we shall find a teacher who feels that he is engaged in his lifework, and in a large proportion of those schoolrooms we shall find teachers who have the practical assurance of their government, that their continuance in office depends only upon good behavior and faithful service. Very rarely are the permanently elected teachers changed from the position to which they are appointed, and more rarely still are they dismissed from service.

Aside from the efficiency of these professional workers, their permanence of place makes their efforts felt in a way not known in a system of constant changes like ours. From recent statistics we learn that an average of twenty-six changes occurs in the United States yearly in every one hundred teachers' positions; that is, the average length of the teacher's service is less than four years. In some quarters the rule is to "make a change" every term, the term consisting of ten or twelve weeks. So accustomed are we to a want of permanency in the teacher's position, that we regard it not out of place for a young woman to make it a convenient waiting-place for matrimony, or for a young man to use

it as a stepping-stone to one of the so-called learned professions. What other business would permit such a large "tramp" element to impair its efficiency, or lower its standard of effective usefulness?

In this matter, as in that of the qualifications of teachers, the state should take a decided stand. Having demanded of teachers the best possible preparation for their work, the state should give them, or oblige the municipalities to give them, a permanent tenure of office during good behavior, good health, and professional faithfulness. In this act of justice to teachers there is found the only safeguard against the evils of frequent changes of teachers on the one hand, and of political wire-pulling on the other.

A good plan of studies is to the teacher what the chart and compass are to the navigator. By its aid progress in the right direction may be measured; without it there is likely to be much work done which is aimless and useless, if, indeed, it is not absolutely injurious. The making of a good plan of studies implies not only a knowledge of the subjects to be studied, but also such acquaintance with the powers and capacities of the growing mind as to know the proper sequence of subjects, and the relative amount of work to be done in successive periods. Such knowledge, it must be admitted, is scientific, and can be acquired only by long and varied experience.

In many parts of the United States the arrangement of a plan of studies is left to the local board,—a board which is made up of men who can, it may be, run a farm or factory, but who have no special fitness to direct teachers in respect to subjects of study. As a consequence there are many towns which have no plan of studies for their schools, absolutely no guide to what is expected to be done, beyond the wishes of parents who are ambitious for their children to go through or over many books. This may not be less harmful than a faithful adherence to the requirements of some plans which are made by persons wholly unfit to make them. And all these hindrances to good and systematic work are but little worse than the constantly changing courses of studies which ambitious school committees, superintendents, and principals are fond of putting out as essential improvements over what has preceded, or as proofs of their ability as reformers.

Instead of these doubtful guides, which are as likely to be incorrect as correct, and which are subject to frequent changes, there should be a general plan for each grade of schools, made and sanctioned by high professional authority, and authorized as a guide for every school in the state. These plans should be subject to such enlargement and explanations as local superintendents or principals may think necessary. Thus we should follow in the main the policy of Germany, whose plans of study may be said to be the result of the best educational thought of the state: on the one hand so well defined as to make the teacher's duty clear, and on the other hand so unrestricted as to leave much freedom and independence of action.

In estimating the value of an educational system, the attendance of children upon the schools should not be left out of the account. No school system can be said to be good which is not supported by laws requiring a certain standard of education for all.

How far the practice of many parts of our country is from this standard appears from statistics which show that in twenty-one States there are no compulsory laws of school attendance, and that in other States, according to the Commissioner of Education,[1] "in many instances the compulsory attendance law, if not actually a dead letter, is practically so." In many of the Northern States where the percentage of attendance is the highest there is gross neglect, not only in enforcing the laws of compulsory attendance upon the schools, but also in providing proper truant schools. This neglect is due largely to the fact that the execution of the laws is left to local authorities, who for political and social reasons fail to do their duty. Members of the school board do not stand a good chance for re-election who by an enforcement of the law entail extra expense upon the town; and they are few, especially in country towns, who are willing to proceed against a neighbor, or a neighbor's children, in case of a violation of the law.

To prevent the evil of illiteracy, as well as the enormous waste of money, which our records of school attendance imply, is a matter of no small concern, and should receive the immediate attention of both state and nation. It may not be possible for us to adopt the same rigorous policy of coercion which Germany enforces with her strong military spirit, and with her complete state police system. But that we should follow her example of protecting the rights of children, so far, at least, as to make school attendance compulsory up to a certain age, must be

admitted, especially when we consider the dangers of ignorant citizenship in a government like ours. Having made these compulsory laws we should see to it that the means of executing them are as effective as are the means of executing other laws upon the statute book.

Experience has proved the necessity of wise supervision in most departments of labor; and nowhere is the necessity more apparent than in a complex system of schools, involving various interests and requiring great technical skill. Germany has for many years observed this principle in the management of her schools, and the results clearly demonstrate its importance. In that country organization of the schools, the examination of teachers, the criticism and direction in methods of teaching, in short, all duties involving wisdom and skill, are given mainly into the hands of professional men.

No uniform method of school supervision is practised in this country; each state, and in some states each town, determining the methods to be employed. The schools of most of the cities, and of some of the large towns, are well supervised by skilled superintendents, who are appointed on account of their superior qualifications. The weak points in the supervision elsewhere, which means, of course, in the larger part of the country, are quite apparent to all who know the worth of intelligent direction in school affairs. In some sections there is absolutely no supervision of the schools other than what is done by members of school boards, who, as a rule, have little time to attend to the duties of their office, and who are likely to have neither natural nor acquired fitness to criticise and direct the teachers' special work. In other sections county superintendents are either appointed by a board, or elected by popular vote. Some of these persons are, doubtless, efficient supervisors; but their field of labor is frequently so large as to prevent their service from being felt to any appreciable degree in the schools. In general it may be said, therefore, that a greater part of the school supervision of this country is ineffectual because of the largeness of the supervisor's field of labor, or of his dependence in election to and retention in office upon the will of the people, or of his want of proper qualifications to perform the duties of his office.

Important as is a recognition of the value of skilled or professional supervision, the perception of its province and limitations is

[1]Report, 1886–87, p. 56.

no less so. Germany's policy of having the work of teachers guided wisely, without having it cramped and narrowed, is a policy which America might adopt with profit to her schools. Skilled supervision, which should be provided by law, implies wisdom,—the wisdom which can be possessed only by *professional* superintendents.

Teachers and Teaching

Having considered the conditions under which the schools are maintained, and some possible reforms of those conditions suggested by Germany's experience we have next to inquire what lessons intimately connected with the work of the schoolroom may be learned from Germany's practice.

The central object of interest and of profitable study is the teacher, whose influence in educational affairs is deservedly strong. This influence is not newly acquired. It is an inheritance from the past, a transmission of powers won by the courage, zeal, and intellectual strength of the teachers of three centuries. Beginning with the Reformation,— the time from which the present school system of Germany dates,—the teacher has filled a prominent place in all educational reforms; not only in promulgating new philosophies and methods of teaching, but in putting into practice new courses of study, in calling forth for education the active interest of princes and people, and, whenever it was necessary, in shaping legislation relating to education both high and low. It is this inheritance of influence in educational affairs into which the German teacher of to-day has come; and most worthily, as I believe, does he use and keep it.

He does not wait for writers of occasional and sensational articles to shape public opinion,—writers whose criticisms of the schools rest on no knowledge of their condition, and whose conception of their needs has not the basis of philosophy or experience. Neither does he allow newly fledged members of school boards to initiate schemes of reform which may not have merit enough to last through a single administration. The German teacher does not take his cue from such men, nor does he wait to take his cue from anybody. He prefers to have the first as well as last word in all questions of reform, whether it be in methods, programmes, or organization. To him belongs, almost exclusively, the privilege of educating the public in school affairs through the public press.

He uses professional association meetings, of which there are many, in discussing questions of reform, and he exercises the right of petition to the government all the more readily because he knows that his petition will receive consideration.

The present notable measures of reform of higher education had their rise in associations of teachers who formulated their opinions two years ago in a monster petition of over twenty thousand signers to the Prussian Diet. Whether it was this petition which caused the appointment of the recent commission in Prussia, it is hard to say; yet there can be no doubt that the schoolmasters themselves began the discussion of questions considered in the conference last December, and the goverment's confidence in their ability to pass judgment upon the subjects presented was shown in the large number of schoolmen appointed to serve on the commission.

The influence of the teachers in inaugurating reforms and in guiding legislation is due partly to the fact that they are, upon main issues of administration, clear and united, partly because they insist upon being heard, and partly because their action is pointed and systematic. I well remember the earnestness and point of a discussion carried on by a village association in Southern Germany. The association consisted of eight men, —all the teachers of the town. The subject was manual training. Two or three meetings had been held previously, and the conclusions of the association were carefully noted in a series of statements, after being discussed and voted upon. These conclusions were to be sent to a higher body which was to formulate all conclusions received, and print them in what is called a Year Book. Who can doubt that conclusions thus reached would and should have great weight in the counsels of the Nation?

It is influence of this kind which our American schools most need. Not only do teachers fail to make themselves felt, as they should be felt, in certain features of school legislation, but they are obliged frequently to give way to the politician in matters purely professional. In some places promotions are made, examinations are conducted, and even courses of studies are arranged, by persons who can lay no claim to professional knowledge.

Whatever the cause of the teacher's want of influence in directing educational affairs in this country, certain it is, that so long as the schools are controlled by politicians, independent of professional advice, there will be poor schools and a waste of money. It is to be hoped that the practice of Germany in heeding the advice of teachers in all matters relating to education will in good time become the settled policy of all parts of this country. That time may come when the high requirements for teaching already spoken of have been fully met.

I have spoken of the teacher's influence in Germany in what may be called outside affairs. In the schoolroom his personality is even more marked. Here we learn the secret of his power, which is that he is in earnest in carrying out a purpose. That is what most impresses visitors from abroad. They may not always think the purpose a good one; but the value of a well-defined purpose is clearly seen, especially when behind that purpose—as is generally the case in Germany—there are both intelligence and professional training. Ask any teacher of the elementary or secondary schools in Germany the reason for any particular method or practice, and you will find him ready with an answer, given in a way which leaves no doubt as to his sincerity, even though he does not convince you of the wisdom of his course.

One general purpose quite manifest in schools of all grades is that of leading the children to think for themselves by the use of objects and pictures, and by questioning. The latter feature of the recitation is particularly noticeable. The questions asked are not strictly Socratic, but they are of such a character as to impress or to develop ideas. When they are of the latter kind they are called "development questions," leading the pupils to pass from the known to the unknown, or to discover an effect from a known cause.

Another characteristic of the work of German teachers is the frequency of giving reviews. The salient points of previous lessons are frequently reviewed, especially those points which have some relation to the subject in hand. The reason for some of the reviews seems to be twofold—first, to refresh the pupils' memory, and secondly, to present all parts of a given subject in their logical relation.

In all information studies—history, geography, reading, and natural history—the teachers show that they have a large fund of information which is always ready for use in the recitation. The necessity of the teacher's proficiency in this regard is, perhaps, not so great in America where the text-book is supposed to give much needed information; yet the great interest which is awakened in the recitation whenever such information is given by the teacher, and the increased confidence and power which such communication gives, are advantages which our American teachers would do well to consider.

Perhaps the most noticeable difference between recitations here and in Germany, is in the manner of the teacher. In Germany the teacher always stands and manifests a vigorous, watchful interest, both in the subject matter and in the pupils. I would not have our teachers adopt the same vigorous means of securing interest and exactness as are sometimes employed by German teachers, but I wish they could have some of their enthusiasm in the schoolroom.

There should be provided by the state or municipality far more apparatus than is now generally provided for the schools. In large graded schools the apparatus should be conveniently located for use in a room provided for the purpose.

There should be in convenient places for the benefit of teachers, museums containing all kinds of apparatus, text-books, and reference books. It is to our shame that we have not long ere this established institutions of this kind, which have been found in other countries of such great practical value to teachers.

It may not be advisable to include in our courses of studies all the branches of instruction which are taught in Germany; but, even in this respect, we may get some assistance from German courses. Nature and elementary science lessons, for example, have as prominent a place in the elementary school programmes of Germany, as arithmetic or geography have, and no good reason can be given why they should not have equal prominence in our programmes. With the possible exception of reading and writing they are, when properly taught, the most valuable subjects in the elementary school course. Two or three hours a week, therefore, should be given to lessons upon plants, animals, and minerals in the lower and middle grades, supplemented by elementary physics or chemistry in the higher grades.

The interest which the German boys of the people's schools manifest in the study of geometry, is an indication of the place which that study may have in our grammar school course, first in supplementing the study of form in the lower grades, and secondly, in accompanying the study of arithmetic in the higher.

The introduction of these subjects of instruction would necessitate lessening the amount required in other subjects, and that can best be done, perhaps, in arithmetic and geography, which are at present overloaded with useless details.

When we consider the time that is frequently taken to complete the grammar school course, and the apparent advantage which German children possess in having a short preparatory course for the high school, it seems advisable to rearrange our classification or courses of studies, so as to permit pupils to begin earlier than they now do the direct preparation for a special classical or scientific course.

Following the lead of Germany in placing great emphasis upon the study of the mother-tongue, we should do far more in English in all grades than is generally done in respect to both language and literature.

Again, more time than is now generally allowed should be given in our high schools to a single science. Instead of a one year course in chemistry, for example, there should be a course of three or four years, so as to give time to develop a scientific spirit and to make the study of practical worth.

And finally, Germany's example of giving all the children of the schools a regular, methodical, and continuous course in physical training may well be followed by us.

In what I have said of the German schools I have felt called upon to emphasize their good features only. With such elements of strength, we should expect to find some elements of weakness. These faults have their origin in the ends or purposes of a people who are intellectually strong, and whose political safety lies in keeping up a military spirit.

Few text-books are used in the elementary schools of Germany,—fewer, I believe, than is good for the pupils,—*first*, because a knowledge of the use of books and a good habit of using them are most valuable to people of any walk in life, and *secondly*, because a proper use of them prevents too great dependence upon the teacher. The programmes

of graded schools are so arranged as to prevent pupils from studying independently and without interruption in school; and the constant talking of teachers, however stimulating it may be to pupils, is not without its bad effects. Moreover, the demands upon pupils, especially in the high schools, are frequently so great as to make school work a grinding burden, and so intensive as to preclude opportunities for general culture.

Again, so far as I could learn, the cultivation of the will is sadly neglected in many of the schools of Germany. The higher forms of self-control and self-respect are lost sight of in discipline, and obedience is often exacted by the severest means. In these particulars, at least, the teachers of Germany can learn wisdom from us. Perhaps they will be willing to do so when the menacing armies upon either side of their country are disbanded, and when circumstances no longer compel them to train their children for the stern conflicts of war.

One word, in closing, upon our own prospects for the future: I have said that our schools are poor in comparison with the schools of Germany. And yet, I believe I am not inconsistent in saying that the best we have are better for us than the best that exist in Germany would be. The trouble is, our very good schools are far too few. Instead of finding good schools everywhere, as we do in Germany, in the country as well as in the city, and in all parts of each, we are obliged in this country to make a hunt for them, even in the most favored places. When they shall be found not the exception, but the rule, not depending upon exceptional conditions, but resulting from a wisely planned organization, then we shall not have to sit at the feet of Germany as learners, but we can bid the teachers of that country come to us, and learn how to train boys and girls into intelligent, self-respecting, self-ruling, and God-fearing men and women. It is for American teachers to work steadily toward the accomplishment of this much-desired end.

On American Education

Introduction

The American school is a microcosm of American life. There reigns in it the same spirit of freedom and equality; the same rapidity of movement, scarce leaving time for work to be thoroughly well done; the same desire for progress, eagerly catching at every new idea, ever on the lookout for improvements; the same appeals to ambition, the same sensitiveness to praise and blame, the same subordination of the individual to the mass, of the scholar to the class, as of the citizen to the nation; the same prominence given to pursuits of a utilitarian, over pursuits of a refining aim; the same excessive and exhausting strain on the mental and physical powers; the same feverishness and absence of repose;—elements of strength and weakness, of success and failure, mingled together in proportions which make it almost impossible to find any one discriminating epithet by which to characterize the resultant whole.[1]

American education, the schools and universities, and the whole development of an indigenous culture have long been the favorite topic of comment for countless foreign visitors. Some of these visitors came to stay and contributed significantly to the young republic as it established itself during the nineteenth century. Others were equally appalled and fascinated by the development of a roisterous and independent American culture that was so different from the Old World and yet was still linked to it through language, literature, political institutions, and even in some ways through education. These links, particularly with Britain in the early part of the nineteenth century but later also with Germany and France, were strengthened by both the American traveling to Europe and the foreigner visiting the United States during the entire century.

This section of the documentary collection emphasizes the attitudes of foreigners as they traveled throughout the United States visiting schools and commenting on the "American way of life." As in the previous section, the concentration is almost entirely, and perhaps arbitrarily, on the nineteenth century. The documents—written primarily by British, German, and French commentators with a leavening of Australian, Chinese, Hungarian, New Zealand, and Swedish contributors—include writings by political scientists, clergymen, merchants, military officers, novelists, as well as by teachers and educational officials. There is a modest balance between the entertaining writing of men such as Thomas Hamilton and Frederick Marryat, retired British service officers, and the intellectual brilliance of men such as Paul Bourget and Michael Sadler. Some of the commentators were professional pedagogues, and others were merely interested travelers. However, in spite of the wide variety of the authors' nationalities, professions, styles of writing, and interests, the documents show that:

Never was there a populous land whose inhabitants were so uniformly judged en masse, *or one about which the truth has been more generalized and less discriminated.*[2]

The American author of the quotation above, Henry T. Tuckerman, in his century-old pioneering work *America and Her Commentators* wrote about the self-evident value of foreigners discussing all aspects of American life under the widest range of conditions and suggested that:

---

[1] James Fraser, *Report on the Common School Systems of the United States and the Provinces of Upper and Lower Canada,* of the School Inquiry Commission on Middle-Class Schools, Vol. II (London, 1866); in *The American Journal of Education,* III (1870), 578.

[2] Henry T. Tuckerman, *America and Her Commentators with a Critical Sketch of Travel in the United States* (New York: Charles Scribner, 1864), p. 444.

Numerous as are the books of travelers and commentaries on America—ranging from the most shallow to the most profound, from the crude to the artistic, from the instructive to the impertinent—so far is the subject from being exhausted, that we seem but now to have a clear view of the materials for judgment, description, and analysis. It required the genius of modern communication, the scientific progress, the human enterprise, the historical development and the social inspiration of our own day, to appreciate the problems which events will solve on this continent; to understand the tendencies, record the phenomena, define the influences and traits, and realize the natural moral and political character and destiny of America.[3]

The nineteenth century saw literally thousands of well-educated, literate men and women come to the United States to explore its natural resources and cultural needs. The literature of the time abounds with the tales of travelers including Alexis de Tocqueville, Frances Trollope, and Charles Dickens. In addition to the works of these well-known writers, there is a wealth of commentary on American cultural patterns and the resultant schools that has not yet been exhaustively explored. What was and still is so fascinating about the United States educational system to observers from Europe, Asia, and even Africa and Latin America? The apparent insatiability of curious travelers in the nineteenth century has certainly not abated in the twentieth century. Is this because these travelers are automatically exposed to the American system of education which occupies a focal point in most American communities? Or is it because American education represents an attractive, widespread, and popular system?

One great paradox of the commentaries on the American educational and cultural scene is that one of the leading English comparative educators, Matthew Arnold, chose not to discuss the schools and formal educational processes in either a detailed or scholarly manner. In his *Civilization in the United States*, Arnold discussed his visit to America in 1883 and said candidly that he found Americans dull and uninteresting. Charles Dickens made a visit to America forty years earlier, in 1842, and he, like Arnold, was not overly impressed with much of what he saw. His strictures on the American press were devastating and perhaps justly uttered. Dickens, however, had a warm personal regard for American education and, speaking of American intellectuals, he said:

Cultivation and refinement seem but to enhance their warmth of heart and ardent enthusiasms; and it is the possession of these latter qualities in a most remarkable degree, which renders an educated American one of the most endeavoring and most generous of friends. I never was so won upon, as by this class; never yielded up my full confidence and esteem so readily and pleasurably as to them.[4]

Other visitors from England, Harriet Martineau and J. S. Buckingham, who traveled in the United States from 1834 to 1836 and from 1837 to 1844 respectively, had a more liberal and optimistic outlook than Dickens and Arnold. Miss Martineau, in *Society in America*, observed that all children, even the poorest, in all parts of the country, received the advantages of education. She believed that the only children seen on the streets during school hours were truants because the general provisions for schools in America were certainly more than adequate for its population. Buckingham included his liberal views and laudatory opinions in encyclopedic works on his American journeys. In 1837 he noted that New York teachers were better trained and more efficient than the teachers at the national and Lancasterian schools of England. He also believed that the "average proficiency" of New York pupils was superior to that of English pupils.

It was perhaps inevitable that the British travelers, many of whom were very well educated, should take a special interest in American colleges and universities. In the middle of the nineteenth century J. M. Phillippo, an English missionary to Jamaica, estimated that the United States contained some 123 colleges with 435 instructors and over 10,000 students. W. E. Baxter, a Scottish graduate of Edinburgh University, gave a most laudatory evaluation of American institutions of higher learning in 1846. He believed that Edinburgh and Göttingen had found their equals in Andover, Auburn, Princeton, and Yale and suggested that these American institutions surpassed such hallowed British institutions as Oxford and Cambridge

---

[3] *Ibid.*, p. vi.

[4] Charles Dickens, *The Works of Charles Dickens, Vol. XXVII: American Notes* (New York: Peter Fenelon Collier, n. d.), p. 284.

in theological training and eminence. Harvard, of course, drew many visitors, and it was the favorite place for academic tourists traveling in the North, while the University of Virginia was often the mecca for visitors to the South. St. Louis University, a Jesuit school chartered in 1832, drew the most visitors in the West, although many went to the University of Nashville, where President Philip Lindsley was a regular host to foreign educators. These were all small universities. In the late 1840's Harvard could only boast three hundred undergraduates and twenty professors, and St. Louis University had barely two hundred students, many of whom were drawn from countries in Latin America. The University of Virginia was the largest with nearly one thousand students. Again, it remained for one of the sharpest British critics, Charles Dickens, to make the most laudatory comments on American colleges. In spite of their various defects, Dickens noted:

they disseminate no prejudices; rear no bigots; dig up the buried ashes of no old superstitions; never interpose between the people and their improvement; exclude no man because of his religious opinions; and above all, in their whole course of study and instruction, recognize a world . . . beyond the college walls.[5]

The avowed primary goal of American education, and certainly of the common school, was the inculcation of civic responsibility and democratic attitudes. It was to be expected, therefore, that many of the travelers and "honorary educational inspectors" would comment on this aspect of American education. For the most part, these men acknowledged that the standards of instruction were at least efficient, if not satisfactory. Joseph Sturge, in his *A Visit to the United States*, noted that in 1841 the mere acquiring of knowledge was secondary to the forming of intelligent opinions on the important social and political questions of the day. This view of American "education for democracy" was shared by Hugo Reid; and in his *Sketches in North America*, based on his sojourn in the United States during 1859 and 1860, he hailed the common school as a bulwark against despotism and as a guarantee against the emergence of class barriers.

There were visitors, however, who were opposed to what they saw and deplored the developments they witnessed in the common schools. The most vigorous attacks on American public education generally came from conservative authors who reacted sharply against the entire concept of compulsory public and secular education. Some of these men felt that a school without religion was "irreligious" rather than merely "non-religious." This view was expressed by J. P. Lewis in *Across the Atlantic*, based on his journey of 1848, and by S. M. Maury in her 1846 account, *An Englishwoman in America*. J. R. Godley believed in the religious control of the public schools and insisted that regular religious exercises of a spiritual nature were an important diversion from such material studies as the physical sciences. His *Letters From America*, based on a visit in 1842, reflected his zealous High Anglican and Tory views. He was critical of all American religious and political institutions and revealed his antagonism toward the nascent development of the common school in America.

Alexis de Tocqueville, a Frenchman who wrote at the beginning of the nineteenth century, noted what he believed was an easily identifiable tendency in America to favor the mediocre. Thus, American education could produce great inventors, aggressive businessmen, and hardy farmers, but few really great scholars, scientists, authors, poets, and artists. Mediocrity was tolerated in American schools because of the virtually boundless economic opportunities in the world beyond, which could more than compensate for the lack of intellectual brilliance and academic dash so necessary in a "truly cultured society." While American schools could promote a mind that could discover principles of instant practical importance, they were unable to promote a mind that could enjoy meditation and leisure or encourage children and young scholars to pursue truth for its own sake. This view was partially shared by another Frenchman, Paul Bourget, who firmly believed that "the indispensable corollary of the study of the life of a people is the study of the educational processes of that people."[6] He held the view, which many foreigners had and still have, that facts, not abstract ideas, are the whetstone of the American public schools. Bourget amply expressed this view when he spoke of the American mind:

---

[5]*Ibid.*, p. 210.
[6]Paul Bourget, *Outre-mer Impressions of America* (London: T. Fisher Unwin, 1895), p. 276.

its almost total lack of abstract ideas, and its amazing power of recognizing reality, of ma-nipulating it in the domains of mechanics as well as in that of business. The aim is, to the most remarkable degree, to confront these awakening minds constantly, indefatigably with the fact.[7]

Another Frenchman, Christopher Langlois, who wrote at the end of the century, succinctly summed up the American concern for education. He closely inspected the schools and suggested four principal causes which made Americans compulsively support their schools and defend them vociferously against foreign criticisms:

1. A general realization that a people who govern themselves must be educated.
2. The necessity of education in the assimilation of foreign people.
3. The idea that each person has the right to make the most of himself.
4. The effort to prevent the rise of a caste system.[8]

This summation suggests that those who desire to understand American education should have a knowledge of American political and social ideals. Accordingly, when analyzing and interpreting foreign comments on American education, it is necessary to consider the author's ideals and background. While the author has probably made it his concern to view the educational system critically, his impressions may still be tinged with a nationalistic viewpoint.

On the whole, the foreigners who visited the United States during the nineteenth century were favorably impressed with the American system of education. Many of the commentators were not professional educators and may be called "intellectual tourists." Others came for a close inspection of the schools. All of these men found a system of education that was not perfect, yet they found that the fundamentals of education were being taught throughout the country. The schools seemed satisfactory for a dynamic and expanding country which required what was practical rather than what was aesthetic, contemplative, and erudite. Americans sometimes appeared indifferent to some of their intellectual, social, and political inadequacies, but they were proud of their educational institutions. The foreigners found that Americans had unlimited faith that time, energy, and enormous economic resources would obviate or make up for those deficiencies which were sometimes so irritating to visitors. Americans had made their own educational system for the masses, and no amount of educational borrowing, intellectual plagiarism, or dependence on the broad-based English inheritance from the eighteenth century could have produced it.

The storehouse of writings on all aspects of life in the United States by foreign authors is enormous. Many of these writings have been the subject of other compilations and anthologies. However, this section of materials on the American educational efforts of the nineteenth century includes many works which have never before been part of a documentary collection and contains a judicious selection of well-known works. There is a temptation in compiling an anthology to overuse the well-known authors, such as—on the subject of nineteenth-century American education—Frances Trollope, Charles Dickens, Frederick Marryat, James Bryce, Harriet Martineau, and Alexis de Tocqueville, whose popularity has exceeded their expectations. However, nearly half of the following documents were written by men who were not directly in the field of formal education and were not specifically concerned with teaching, with the schools, or with the educational process. These include, for example, Pierre Samuel Du Pont de Nemours, Isaac Fidler, Israel Benjamin, and Paul Bourget. The rest of the authors in this section were engaged in teaching or education and were professionals in their field rather than casual observers. These include Michael Sadler, Emil Hausknecht, and W. Gatton Grasby, from England, Germany, and Australia, respectively.

Included in this section are three documents written by Americans—David Murray, Louis R. Klemm, and John W. Hoyt. These are included because the authors made attempts to set American education in its proper world perspective and to contrast the American educational system to other systems. Hoyt related nineteenth-century university trends in Europe and

---

[7]*Ibid.*, p. 288.

[8]Christopher V. Langlois, "Notes sur l'éducation aux Etat-Unis," *Revue internationale de l'enseignement*, No. 49 (1905), pp. 289−309; in W. J. Osburn, *Foreign Criticism of American Education*, Bureau of Education Bulletin, No. 8 (Washington, D.C.: U.S. Government Printing Office, 1922).

discussed their implications for higher education in the United States. Klemm's statistical and tabular presentation of educational information contains useful comparisons, and Murray's essay, written for the Japanese government, includes an analysis of the value of a national system of education. Another American contribution is a description of the first large-scale teacher-training program for foreign students in the United States. This unique program was not duplicated for half a century and brought a group of Cuban teachers to Harvard University for summer school in 1900.

The documents in this section include descriptions of elementary, secondary, and higher education, of rural and urban schools, and of public and private institutions. Suggestions for improved teacher training and pedagogic techniques are found throughout. The authors were almost universally disposed to comment, contrast, compare, and criticize as they surveyed the panorama of American education. They were sometimes influenced by personal likes and dislikes, but their comments should be evaluated in terms of accuracy, information, and constructiveness.

R. E. Hughes, an Englishman, saw his country's school system as a "half-way house" in education between the German and American systems. Laishley, a New Zealander, viewed American education in an international perspective and set out in tabular form the main characteristics of the leading systems of education so that his countrymen and colleagues could benefit from his extensive researches. His work represents perhaps the best nineteenth-century presentation of education dissected carefully into its many component parts. Huang tsun-Hsien and David Murray had Asia, China and Japan respectively, in mind when they wrote. These two countries loom large in the early history of American international education, and Japanese and Chinese students were the first and largest contingent of government-sponsored foreign students in the United States. The impressions of many of these students have been recorded and are available in published compilations.

Some of the extracts included in this section were written by men who came to America as immigrants, tourists, or businessmen. These men often combined business and travel together by using their notes as a basis for publications which became lucrative sources of income. Some of them came to America purposely to write books on their journeys or to prepare handbooks for immigrants; others came to see a unique country with entertaining but peculiar political and social customs, and, in spite of their prejudices and preconceived notions, they found America fascinating. Many of these mere travelers or "literati" were able to capture the spice and excitement of American education as reflected, for example, in a frontier school or in the magnificence of an educational exhibit at an international exposition, but some of the visitors who came specifically to study American education and culture wrote pompous, boring, overlaudatory, or overcritical accounts of what they had seen.

Americans have always tried to follow the practice of seeing "ourselves as others see us." The beginning of the nineteenth century often saw tourists and scholars scorning American education and culture. These men sometimes suggested that Americans should use European schools as models, and the comparisons they made usually showed the American schools unfavorably. The American pockets of culture at the time—Boston, New York, and Philadelphia—were considered no match intellectually or by any standard of higher education to any principal city of Europe. By the end of the nineteenth century, however, a radical change in the attitudes of foreign visitors had taken place. The comparisons were still being made, but the American common school, the emerging high school, and even the universities were no longer subjects of scorn, amusement, or mere indifference. Americans had forged new educational models which captured the imagination of even the most critical European observers. The observers from Asia, the Middle East, and Australasia were even more appreciative. They were intrigued and impressed with much that they saw, and they believed that America had developed many political, economic, and social benefits which they could use as models.

Thus, the nineteenth century saw a steady transition from mere commentary, advice, and casual criticism to a more scientific, methodological, and professional study of American educational accomplishment. It also saw the attention of foreign visitors, which during the early part of the century had been occupied by the schools of New York, Boston, and Philadelphia, become broader to include all kinds of education in all areas of the United States. By the turn of the century, American education and its concomitant cultural patterns were well established and were recognized as equal to the best in the world.

Pierre Samuel Du Pont de Nemours   1800

A French Plan for the National University of America

Pierre Samuel Du Pont de Nemours (1739–1817) was a student of natural science and medicine before he became interested in political economy, particularly the French school which he named "physiocracy." He served various French governments and from 1772 to 1774 was secretary of the Council of Public Instruction in Poland. In 1783 he aided in the negotiations with Britain which led to the treaty of independence for the United States. Du Pont participated actively in the political upheaval preceding the French Revolution and was a member of the States-General in 1789. However, his conservative views ultimately led to his imprisonment in 1792 and forced his emigration to the United States in 1799. The following year Thomas Jefferson asked him to prepare a plan for national education, and although it was never adopted in the United States, it became part of the French educational code.

Du Pont returned to France in 1802 and promoted the sale of Louisiana to the United States. He became vice-president of the Paris Chamber of Commerce and in 1814 assisted Talleyrand in restoring the Bourbons to the French throne. He was appointed secretary general of the provisional government and made counselor of state by Louis XVIII. Du Pont was forced to flee when Napoleon returned to power in 1815, and he again settled in the United States. The plan for American education which Du Pont prepared in 1800 included the excerpt below on higher education. This plan was the first major proposal for a national system of education in the United States prepared by a foreign educational consultant.

We have until now used the word University to describe as a whole the schools founded by the Government in which the study of sciences, begun in our colleges, is carried to a higher development, and other branches of knowledge are taught for which there has been less preparation.

And we have thus used the term, because it was for the establishment of a University that we were asked to write this treatise.

But the noble and scholarly man who so graciously asked for it, did not mean by the word University only a place for instruction in the highest sciences. He positively excluded from his project any classes for such accomplishments as could be studied without the help of a public institution.

The name *University* comes from Europe and implies the claim of our great institutions of learning, that they introduce their students to the universality of human knowledge.

These *Universities* of the old world were or are divided into four departments.

1st. The Department of Theology, which was never the universal theology, or morality founded on the knowledge of God, on the proofs of his wisdom and goodness, on the duties which he imposes on men by the physical constitution that he has given them and by their relations to each other and to other animals; but only the theology of the dominant religion of the country.

The Universities of Salamanca, of Paris, of Oxford, are very different in their Departments of theology.

2d. The Department of Law. There are taught in France the canon law or papal law, and the civil law of the Romans under their last emperor, but little or no French law.

I do not know whether law is better taught in England, but from the amount of trickery that can be accomplished by the civil law of England, and which reaches even to the United States, I think it would be wiser to use all the powers of philosophy, morality and justice to simplify the law itself, rather than to waste the powers of youth in its study. Unfortunately the complications and obscurities of laws and their application often create what is called *a good business*, and men who have learned this *business* and live by it, and because of it are frequently elected to the Legislatures, become, almost in spite of themselves, decided enemies of reform.

3d. The Department of Medicine. That includes a great number of interesting sciences, which, when they are absorbed by minds formed for the study of nature and disposed to respect its laws, are a wonderful training for the intellect, and are pro-

Pierre, Samuel Du Pont de Nemours, *National Education in the United States of America*, translated from the second French edition of 1812 and introduced by B. G. Du Pont (Newark, Delaware: University of Delaware Press, 1923), pp. 121–147.

foundly useful to humanity by the knowledge they give of illness and the opportunities to relieve, console, encourage and help those who suffer. The knowledge of how to heal is still in the hands of God. English physicians, masters and models of the American doctors, while otherwise able scholars and very learned, seem to be ignorant of that important fact. They too often operate, and their patients die more frequently.

4th. And last, the Department of Arts, where mechanics are not taught, nor hydraulics, nor drawing, nor painting, nor sculpture, nor architecture, nor music:

But *Latin*, as thoroughly as a dead language can be taught;

Greek, rather poorly, except in the universities of Scotland and some of Germany;

Latin poetry, or rather, the rules of versification; poetry is not taught, *nascuntur poetae*;

Rhetoric, so aptly defined by Montaigne as *the art of making large shoes for little feet*, is, of all arts, the one most certain to spoil one's style.

They add to rhetoric, to distort the mind, *debating*, under the name of logic, with the stupid and barbarous principle that any proposition may be both attacked and defended: *quidquid dixeris argumentabor*.

However, all our great men have overcome the misfortune of having gone through these studies, as some vigorous constitutions survive the abuse of bleeding, of opium, of kermes, of emetics, and of calomel.

Above these two extinguishers of intelligence there is a third, an unintelligible theological gibberish called *metaphysics*.

And at the end of the course, in the last months of the last year, they talk a little of *geometry*, casually of *physics*, and of *astronomy*, but in such fashion that the students know much less of them than our pupils of the primary schools.

After having taken what are called degrees in these four Departments, one is supposed to possess universal knowledge; and there was a time when one held proudly to the proposition *de omne scibili*.

Our *University* will be different.

It will include our *primary schools*, our *colleges*, and our *special schools*. For all these institutions will be branches of our public education. And the special schools will be only the summit or the completion.

I would not therefore give the name *University* to the special schools, though it may have a useful side; namely, that of adopting accepted standards, and of convincing Euro-

peans as well as Americans that youth can be as well taught in America as in Europe.

It should be provided by the law concerning education, that the *General Council* and the *Committees of Public Instruction;* the *special schools* for the most advanced studies; the *colleges*, of which the object is chiefly to develop literary and scientific men; and the *primary schools* which will give the most important knowledge to all citizens—shall together constitute the University of North America.

A young man who had gone through a primary school, college and the special schools would be a *scholar of our University*.

This should be defined clearly and precisely, as must always be done in matters of legislation, and as nearly as possible in everything. Nothing is more unfortunate, particularly when it has to deal with matters of education where it is so necessary to be exact in the choice of expressions, than a meaningless word or an ill-chosen one.

Let us consider now the special schools that should be established at Washington City.

There should be, it seems to me, four schools:

One of medicine;

One of mines;

One of social science and legislation;

One of higher geometry and the sciences that it explains.

I do not see any reason for their being dependant on each other, nor of their having any connection except that they will be in the same building, where there will also be the public library, the museum, the botanical garden, the quarters of the General Council of Education, and the philosophic society.

This palace of science seems to me to be one of the monuments with which the eighteen States would wish to embellish their capital.

We have seen that the State's pupils, chosen to be sent to the special schools, have decided on their professions and have prepared themselves to study for them by a longer or shorter period of post-graduate work in the college.

Those who wish to study medicine will repeat the work in chemistry, physics, natural history, and ancient languages. That will require three years.

Those who wish to study mining must do their preparatory work in the class of geometry and in those of natural history and chemistry. Two years will be sufficient.

Geometry and algebra will occupy those who are interested in astronomy, navigation, shipbuilding, or higher mathematics; and it is possible that they may be prepared in one year, though two may be necessary.

Finally those who would be members of the bar, or study the science of government, should apply themselves to the classes in natural law, national law, history, political economy, and languages ancient and modern. They will need three years.

When they arrive at the special schools, they will be worthy of receiving lessons and capable of understanding them.

The four schools being directly administered by the Council of Education, they do not need a general *Principal;* but each of them should have its own, who will select his colleagues, and will explain to the students in what classes they are to begin, in what order and with what purpose they are to go to other classes; also which subjects they should review, and when.

Let us examine the necessary number of classes.

School of Medicine

It will have five classes:

The first of anatomy;

The second, of animal economy and pathology. The professor of this class will have the title, rank and authority of *Principal;*

The third, of surgery and child-birth;

The fourth, of materia medica and pharmaceutical chemistry;

The fifth, of botany.

Young men who do not intend to study medicine but wish to know more of natural sciences may join the classes of anatomy and botany. But no one shall be accepted as a Doctor of Medicine without having passed successful public examinations in all five classes.

The Professor of Botany will direct all work in the garden and will take his pupils for walks in the country.

The Professor of Anatomy will give several lessons on comparative anatomy, which will impress on the students the anatomy of man. Beside the work in his own amphitheatre, he will direct and supervise the experiments of each of his pupils out of the class-room; and as they improve he will have each of them in turn demonstrate in the amphitheatre, in his presence, for the instruction of their fellow-students.

The *Principal* and the Professor of Surgery under him will have charge of the hospitals and will take their pupils to them, warning them of the dangers of having patients near together in a hospital; and that care must be taken to make complications of diseases less frequent and less severe by filling the rooms with fresh air and by placing the beds far apart. When one builds in a locality where it is possible to have all the land that is necessary, a hospital begins with a very great advantage. It should be possible at Washington City and the sea board cities of America to require hospitals only for sailors without friends or acquaintances, and to care for others in their own homes.

The medical professors shall be authorized to take one of their pupils when they visit patients who have sent for them; but never two pupils at once, and always the same one to the same patient. For a sick man does not object to seeing a consultant with his doctor, but a new face might distress and harm him. For this same reason, if the physician has found his pupil useless during the first visit, he should not take him again.

All of our pupils will have had at *college* at least two good courses of theoretical and practical chemistry. With the help of a class in pharmaceutical chemistry it will be easy for them to apply those principles to materia medica and to pharmaceutics.

These students of medicine will be educated men who, as post-graduates, reviewed in college their courses in Greek, Latin, chemistry and natural history. They will not be held back in the medical school by constant reviews, which are necessary at college for inattentive pupils, whose memories are quick but not retentive; but we have already advised that of their own accord, after consulting the Principal and the professors, they review any courses in which they are most interested. Anatomy, pathology, surgery—each demands more than one year of study for those who wish to do more than talk about it; and our students must be able to use their knowledge and help suffering humanity. They will have time enough. A man who wishes to be a physician should give his whole youth to preparation; for until he is thirty years old he will not inspire much confidence. In the meantime he should learn to deserve it; a patient's faith in his physician is one of the most powerful remedies.

We have placed the class in botany at the end of our medical course, as a recreation and relief; we feared that if it were studied earlier it would be a dangerous distraction and amusement.

The study of botany is very healthful and very entertaining; while that of anatomy, although most interesting, is depressing and unhealthful—it means overcoming much that is abhorrent. Surgery, which demands that one forget the sympathy inspired by the cries of pain and the repugnance of dipping one's hand in blood, requires a courage not easily attained. The lovers of Flora find it hard to leave her laughing valleys and delicious woodlands to return to the altars of pain and the temples of death.

Moreover, it has been observed that few botanists wish to become physicians, unless they were so before. But society does not need a large number of professional botanists. They are like great mathematicians: two or three of the highest rank, five or six of the second, are sufficient. It is not so with physicians, if they have philosophic minds, if they do not pretend to cure everything, if they do not insist on giving drugs, if they know natural history, if, like Hippocrates, they can use and purify air and water, they can accomplish much for the state and are the best instructors of practical philosophy, of enlightened benevolence. We must not let them sacrifice the utility of the fruit to the charm and beauty of the blossoms. We must not train our youth for his own amusement—*non sibi, sed patriae*.

School of Mines

I have no desire that the United States should give much thought to gold mines, which are very rare and happily are unknown in that country. But coal mines, indicated, not far from the coast, by immense beds of micaceous schist, and by a multitude of valleys which were formerly bays situated in the beds of ancient lakes and now dried up; copper mines, lead mines, above all iron mines, seem to be numerous there and of excellent quality. They require, therefore, serious attention.

And in a country where the population is not great compared to its immense territory, where the price of labor will probably be high for two or three centuries, these mines can only be worked when science and intelligence overcome the difficulties of labor and expense. The temptation to work them exists and will increase. It must be so managed that it will not be ruinous.

Under these circumstances a school of mines seems to me to be necessary.

This school should have three classes:

One of mineralogy, of which the professor shall be the *Principal* of the school, and shall nominate the other two to the Council of Education.

The other two professors will teach:

The first, docimastic [the science of assaying minerals] chemistry;

The other, subterranean geometry and the machinery that may be necessary for mining.

These three studies will be grasped easily by pupils who in our colleges have learned some idea of natural history, and have had a good training in chemistry and thorough preparation in elementary geometry and mechanics.

However, we shall require of them a year for each course in the school of mines.

We believe that they will then be ready to understand a mine and to direct its exploitation with economy and intelligence.

School of Social Science

The school of *social science* shall be limited to two classes:

The first will be under the *Principal* of this school, who will select his colleague. The Principal will teach the general theory of government; that of internal administration and political relations; the law of nations, statistics, colonization. This will be the *school of statesmen*.

The first principles of it will have been studied in childhood in the books of the primary schools and continued in college in the class of ethics, as well as in the courses on history and political economy.

But in the special school the students will not be limited to general maxims, nor to outlines of history; they will examine in detail the strength and the interests of different nations, their sagacity, their errors, and the consequences that follow. By using political arithmetic, explained with thoughtful criticism, they will learn not to accept figures on the population, culture and commerce of a country from directories, almanacs, worthless books on geography, the haphazard or prejudiced accounts of travellers; nor even to depend on statements that seem more authentic and are quite as misleading, such as official financial reports, which never allow for waste and suppress secret transactions; nor the statements of the records of the custom-house of which the clerks cannot and will not report fraud, collusion, contraband, and who have no knowledge whatever of the shipments of silver, gold, precious stones, jewels, and compact merchandise like lace.

The pupils will be taught to connect every fact with others that relate to the same subject; to balance them, to judge one by the other; to determine the truth between two exaggerations, one of excess and one of diminution; and to put facts together with sagacity so that gradually the mind will arrive at something that is very near the truth. It is surprising to find how very accurately one can obtain definite information by this method on matters that were absolutely hidden under a chaos of statements and contradictions.

Political truths demonstrated by facts are no more convincing to the trained mind than they were without demonstration; but they are much more imposing to the multitude. It is important that the members of a government shall add the weight of erudition which impresses the public to that of reason which only affects philosophers; and that by the force, the depth, the fluency of their discussions, they can, in legislative bodies or executive councils, repulse or suppress thoughtless assertions that might lead to dangerous situations. It is not enough in political combats to be courageous and to be right; it is necessary to be well-armed and able to fence.

Another branch of this great science, a branch that is most important to a country like the United States, which has behind it three million square leagues of wild and uncultivated land, is that which concerns colonization; the art of persuading, explaining, conquering by kindness; to establish by means of honesty and by carefully planned labor increasing happiness, uprightness and success for the new nation; the art of enriching others and one's self by advances made with apparent but well-considered lavishness.

I do not say that this last branch of social science is as yet fully grasped and perfected; but the rudiments are known and the *Western Territory* gives unlimited opportunity to test its principles by experience. Organized groups are beginning to appear there, like grass in a forest. It would not be difficult to learn to sow and cultivate them like plants in a garden.

I think that the work of this class should continue for two years; and as the pupils can do much of it by themselves—reading, extracting, criticising the works which the Principal-Professor suggests—I think they need a lesson only once in two days. They are to exercise their discrimination more than their memory.

This Principal-Professor will hold the class on Monday, Wednesday and Friday for the pupils of the current year, and on Tuesday, Thursday and Saturday for those who are in their second year. The intermediate days will be for the work of the pupils themselves; in this science above all it is necessary not to *think* but to *know*, and to develop by one's own intellectual effort and talents and by the finest perceptions of one's own mind.

The other class of *social science* will be devoted to the *civil and criminal* law of the country.

But I most urgently advise that law shall not be considered permanent law until every effort has been made to find the source of the reasons and methods for prolonging litigation, which multiplies feuds, which chills friendliness, which checks reciprocal advances of great value in a country still very bare of population, and which forces on the nation a burden that is detrimental even to its treasury. I implore that before everything else the source of these evils shall be stopped or at least diminished by definite laws, by simple rules of procedure which can always hasten the end of a law suit.

If all trials were decided by chance—by throws of dice, justice would be done half the time.

But in a nation that is generous, thoughtful and honest and where judges are elected, judging is never done by chance. Therefore any plan that will bring about greater promptness in the process of law will be a good one.

When the complication of formalities, the facility of quibbling, and the piling up of *illegalities*, often by collusion, which involve a review of the whole affair, have affected three hundred law-suits, it may be that one of them has been somewhat better judged; but the delays occasioned to the other two hundred and ninety-nine have done more harm than can be offset by the perfect decision in the three hundredth.

But it is not true that complication of formalities, facility in quibbling and discovering illegalities, can ever lead to a wiser decision.

Any honest and intelligent man can judge a short trial; when a suit becomes complicated, it needs eagles and angels.

Why is America so obstinate in imitating

everything English?—and particularly the things that England herself rightly considers mistakes in her government, and which she would have reformed long ago if they had not been bound up with the interests of a numerous and powerful corporation?

Why does not this daughter of thirty years pride herself on improving on her mother?

My dear Americans, revise your *civil law* and do not let it be taught with the *authority of the State* until you have made the laws and the processes as good as you know how.

As for your law concerning impeachments for crime, you can scarcely alter that.

School of Transcendental Geometry

This school will be devoted to the highest geometry and to those ordinary sciences that depend on it.

There will be five classes:

One of *transcendent geometry* [all mathematics beyond Euclidian geometry]; the professor of this class will have the duties and rights of Principal of this school.

One of *astronomy;*

One of *hydrography* and *navigation;*

One of the *construction* and *rigging* of ships;

One of *engineering,* both civil and military, and for artillery.

The names of these classes is sufficient indication of the knowledge that the third will have gained from the second, and that the three lower ones will gain from the first.

As it will be the professor of the first class who will find his colleagues, and nominate them for the approval of the General Council of Education, he will require their cooperation. He can give the course such an administration that its pupils will have a valuable training and will not deteriorate to the methods of the ordinary worker.

We have now in France the most wonderful construction for the hulls of battle-ships and we owe it to one of our greatest geometricians, *Borda,* who was chief of staff to d'Estaing, in the war for the independence of the United States.

It is said that the best battle-ship in Europe is the *Conception* which *Gauthier* built for Spain on Borda's principles.

And the two best frigates are the *Pomone* and the *Méduse,* of which Borda himself directed the construction at Brest; they have both, unfortunately, been taken by the English. He built us other excellent vessels.

It is a great misfortune that he died without having applied to the rigging those calculations and improvements which he so successfully applied to the ship itself. But one of his successors will do it.

As to *engineering* for civil and military construction, no nation is in such need of canals as the United States, and most of their ports have no means of exterior defense.

The Cost of Four Special Schools

I shall not include in this expense the price of the buildings, for I consider them a public monument for the embellishment of the capital, and I suppose they will be built by the Government for the special schools and all other establishments relating to science.

The public library should not belong to the schools, but it should be at their service and chosen principally on the advice of the professors.

We need, therefore, in estimating the expense account, only consider the salaries of the professors and some other slight costs.

There will be fifteen professors, of whom four will be Principals.

I do not think the Principals should be offered less than *one thousand dollars* salary, or the other professors less than *six hundred* dollars.

Their salaries should place them in a rank above the professors and even the Principals of the colleges; for the public, which judges very superficially, always believes that a man is paid in proportion to his value.

So the four Principals
will receive . . . .   4,000 dollars
The other eleven professors   6,600
A porter to clean the rooms   200
Other expenses   300
        Total . . . . 11,100 dollars

At this price alone we would not have Principals and professors worthy of the positions.

We will give them here, as in the colleges, contingent fees.

And in order to be able to give the professors and Principals whom we wish to engage for our schools, an idea of the income they may expect, we must make an approximate estimate as we did for the Principals and professors of the colleges.

These calculations are suggestive and cannot be absolutely exact.

The students in the special schools are, like those in the colleges, of two kinds—the ones chosen for their abilities, to be educated at the cost of their States; the others, at the expense of their parents or themselves.

We have supposed that the State of Virginia will send each year ten students at the expense of the state to the special schools; that would be one from each college.

If the other states send students in the same proportion we shall have, allowing for the varying populations of the states, *seventy-five* pupils each year whose expenses at the schools of the Republic will be defrayed by their own States. So that in ten or twelve years and thereafter, there will be about *three hundred*, the enrollment depending upon whether they have selected courses requiring five years, or four, or three.

The students supported by their parents or themselves may amount to twice or three times as many; for there will be two or three times as many young men anxious to enter lucrative professions which require the higher education, as there are State pupils who deserve that education at the public expense; and as students of any age will be received at these schools, many grown men will follow the courses for pure love of study.

The students will receive from the State that sends them a pension of *two hundred dollars*, of which *one hundred and fifty* will be given to them for their food and other personal expenses, *fifty* will be given to the professors—*forty* to the one in whose class the student is working and *ten* to the *Principal* of the school.

Those who are in the Principal's class will give him the whole of the contribution.

Each student will choose the profession that he wishes to adopt and, in consequence, the school that he wishes to enter, but while he is in that school he will follow the advice of the Principal as to the order in which he will enter the prescribed classes.

The students whose expenses are paid by themselves or their families, will pay *one hundred dollars* a year, of which eighty will be for the professor whose course they are following and twenty for the Principal of the school.

When they are in the Principal's class, the hundred dollars will not be divided.

We will not repeat the statements we have already made in explaining the salaries for the colleges; it is enough to say that this arrangement will assure to the professors and above all to the Principals of our special schools much larger incomes than the most distinguished scholars can hope to earn in other countries.

This excellent position will be reached by degrees, but even at the beginning the terms will be generous.

At first there will be no State-aided students and it would be unwise to expect more than a hundred and forty or a hundred and fifty each year for the first years, divided according to their choice among the different schools.

For the first year it will be necessary to open only the four principal classes and two dependent classes—they will be the classes of *anatomy*, Animal Economy and Pathology, Mineralogy; *docimastic chemistry*, Social Science and Transcendent Geometry. The other classes will not be opened till the second, third, or fourth year as they may be needed.

This precaution—which may be demanded by the requirements of instruction, though it may not be for the interests of the treasury of the institution—must be observed: no professor shall begin with less than *fourteen hundred dollars* and no Principal less than *two thousand*, and their incomes shall increase each year for ten or twelve years. At the end of that time, the least important chair in our special schools will be worth *four thousand dollars or twenty-one thousand francs* to the professor; some will offer half as much more and the four Principals from *forty to fifty thousand francs* each.

Such incomes will make it possible to choose from the foremost scholars of all countries in selecting professors and Principals for our special schools. The ambition of every learned man in the world will be that he may one day attain to one of the chairs. Washington City will become the Bokhara, the Benares, the Byblas, the Cariath-Sepher, the city of knowledge. Men of the highest reputation will be assembled there as professors; perhaps Europeans will not be considered properly educated unless they have studied in its schools.

Such is the advantage that Athens once enjoyed; today it belongs to Edinburgh and Gottingen. To obtain it we would only need to secure the most illustrious scholars of Gottingen, Edinburgh, and other scholastic cities, promising them a brilliant future that can be attained only by the perfection of their knowledge and that can be secured only by sustained preeminence.

Our professors will form the nucleus of

an admirable Philosophic Society. Engineering will do wonderful things in a country where it will be so tremendously rewarded. It will make therefore its most powerful efforts and will urge forward all other sciences. We shall have increased knowledge by giving it a worthy home. We shall have done well for America and for the world.

John Davis 1802

Educational Tutoring in the South

John Davis (1774–1854) was born in Salisbury, England, and went to sea at the early age of eleven, making two voyages to the East. In spite of his lack of education, Davis acquired the reputation of a poet and author. Many of his works eventually sold well in the United States, but during his travels in America from 1798 to 1802, he was forced to take what work he could find as a tutor and writer.

Traveling extensively in the South, Davis visited South Carolina, Georgia, and Virginia. In 1798 he served for six weeks as a teacher in a college in Charleston, was dismissed, and then obtained a position as tutor to the children of Thomas Drayton in his homes at Coosawatchie and Sullivan's Island. During the summer of 1801, he held a brief appointment in a Quaker family in Virginia and for three months in 1802 was a master in a "field" school in Prince William County. While looking for work as a tutor in South Carolina, Davis had the interview which he described in the following extract.

I landed at *Charleston* with Doctor *De Bow,* who had clad himself in his black suit, and though a young man, wore a monstrous pair of spectacles on his nose. Adieu jollity! adieu laughter! the Doctor was without an acquaintance on a strange shore, and he had no other friend but his Solemnity to recommend him. It was to no purpose that I endeavoured to provoke him to laughter by my remarks; the Physician would not even relax his risible muscles into a smile.

The Doctor was right. In a few days he contrived to hire part of a house in Union-street; obtained credit for a considerable quantity of drugs; and only wanted a chariot to equal the best Physician in *Charleston.*

The Doctor was in possession of a voluble tongue; and I furnished him with a few *Latin* phrases, which he dealt out to his hearers with an air of profound learning. He generally concluded his speeches with *Nullius addictus jurare in verba magistri!*

Wishing for some daily pursuit, I advertised in one of the papers for the place of Tutor in a respectable family; not omitting to observe that the advertiser was the translator of *Buonaparte's* Campaign in *Italy.* The editor of the Gazette assured me of an hundred applications; and that early the next morning I should not be without some. His predictions were verified; for the following day, on calling at the office, I found a note left from a Planter who lived a mile from the town, desiring me to visit him that afternoon at his house. I went thither accordingly. Every thing indicated opulence and ease. Mr. H—— received me with the insolence of prosperity. You are, said he, the person who advertised for the place of Tutor in a respectable family? I answered with a bow.

Planter. What, Sir, are your qualifications?

Tutor. I am competently skilled, Sir, in the *Latin* and *French* languages, not unacquainted with *Greek,* conversant with Geography, and accustomed to composition in my vernacular idiom.

Planter. But if you possess all *that there* learning, how comes it you could not get into some College, or School.

Tutor. Why, Sir, it is found even in Colleges that dunces triumph, and men of letters are disregarded by a general combination in favour of dulness.

Planter. Can you *drive* well, Sir?

Tutor. Drive, Sir, did you say? I really do not comprehend you.

Planter. I mean, Sir, can you keep your scholars in order?

Tutor. Yes, Sir, if they are left entirely to my direction.

John Davis, *Travels of Four Years and a Half in the United States of America; during 1798, 1799, 1800, 1801, and 1802* (Bristol: R. Edwards, 1803); the extract is taken from the edition by A. J. Morrison (New York: Henry Holt and Co., Inc., 1909), pp. 51-58.

Planter. Ah! that would not be. Mrs. H——, who is a woman of extensive learning, (she lost a fine opportunity once of learning *French,* and only a few years ago could write the best hand of any lady in *Charleston,*) Mrs. H—— would superintend your management of the school.

Tutor. Mrs. ——, Sir, would do me honour.

Planter. Mrs. H——, Sir, is in the real sense of the word, a woman of literature; and her eldest daughter is a prodigy for her age. She could tell at nine years old whether a pudding was boiled enough; and, now, though only eleven, can repeat *Pope's* Ode on Solitude by heart. Ah! *Pope* was a *pretty* poet; my wife is very fond of *Pope.* You have read him, I make no doubt, Sir. What is your opinion of his works?

Tutor. In his Rape of the Lock, Sir, he exhibits most of the *vis imaginandi* that constitutes the poet; his Essay on Criticism is scarcely inferior to *Horace's* Epistle to the Pisoes; his Satires——

Planter. But I am surprised, Sir, you bestow no praise on his Ode on Solitude. Mrs. H——, who is quite a critic in those matters, allows the Ode on Solitude to be his best, his noblest, his sublimest production.

Tutor. Persuaded, Sir, of the critical acuteness of Mrs. H——, it is not safe to depart from her in opinion;—and if Mrs. H—— affirms the Ode on Solitude to be the sublimest of Mr. *Pope's* productions, it would be rather painful than pleasant to undeceive her in opinion.

Planter. That is right, Sir, I like to see young men modest. What spelling-book do you use?

Tutor. What spelling-book, Sir? Indeed—really—upon my word Sir,—any—oh! *Noah Webster's,* Sir.

Planter. Ah! I perceive you are a New England man, by giving the preference to *Noah Webster.*

Tutor. Sir, I beg your pardon; I am from Old England.

Planter. Well, no matter for that,—but Mrs. H——, who is an excellent speller, never makes use of any other but *Matthew Carey's* spelling-book. It is a valuable work, the copyright is secured. But here comes Mrs. H—— herself.

Mrs. H—— now entered, followed by a negro girl, who held a peacock's feather in her hand. Mrs. H—— received my bow with a mutilated curtsy, and throwing herself on a sopha, called peremptorily to *Prudence* to brush the flies from her face. There was a striking contrast between the dress of the lady and her maid; the one was tricked out in all the finery of fashion; while the black skin of the other peeped through her garments.

Well, my dear, said Mr. H——, this young man is the person who advertised for the place of tutor in a respectable family. A little conversation with him will enable you to judge, whether he is qualified to instruct our children in the branches of a liberal education.

Mrs. H——. Why independent of his literary attainments, it will be necessary for him to produce certificates of his conduct. I am not easily satisfied in my choice of a tutor; *a body* should be very cautious in admitting a stranger to her family. This gentleman is young, and young men are very frequently addicted to bad habits. Some are prone to late hours; some to hard drinking; and some to Negur girls: the last propensity I could never forgive.

Mr. H. Yes, my dear, you discharged Mr. *Spondee,* our last tutor, for his intimacy with the Negur girls:—*Prudence* had a little one by him. *Prudence* looked reproachfully at her master; the child was in reality the offspring of Mr. H——, who fearing the inquiries of the world on the subject, fathered it upon the last tutor. But they must have been blind who could not discover that the child was sprung from Mr. H——; for it had the same vulgar forehead, the same vacant eye, and the same idiot laugh.

Mr. H. Do, my dear, examine the young man a little on literary matters. He seems to have read *Pope.*

Mrs. H. What, Sir, is your opinion of Mr. *Pope's* Ode on Solitude?

Tutor. It is a tolerable production, madam, for a child.

Mrs. H. A tolerable production for a child! Mercy on us! It is the *most sublimest* of his productions. But tastes differ. Have you read the works of *Dr. Johnson?* Which do you approve the most.

Tutor. Why, Madam, if you allude to his poems, I should, in conformity with your judgment, give a decided preference to his Epitaph on a Duck, written, if I mistake not, when he was four years old. It need scarcely fear competition with *Pope's* Ode on Solitude. At this moment the eldest daughter of this learned lady, of this unsexed female, tripped into the room on light, fantastic toe. Come, my daughter, said the lady, let this gentleman hear you repeat the Ode on Solitude. Excuse me, Madam, cried I, taking up my hat and bowing.

Do you hear the child, Bawled Mr. H——. I pray you, sir, to excuse me, rejoined I.

Mrs. H. It will not take the child ten minutes.

---

[1]It has been my object in this scene to soften the conditions of private tutors in America, by putting up Mr. H — *in signum terroris et Memoriae* to other purse-proud planters. I write not from personal pique, but a desire to benefit society. Happy shall I think myself should this page hold the mirror up to the inflation of pride, and the insolence of prosperity.

Tutor. Ten minutes, Madam, are the sixth part of an hour that will never return!

Mr. H. Politeness dictates it.

Tutor. Excuse me, I entreat you, Sir.

Mr. H. I cannot excuse you, I shall hire you as tutor, and I have a right to expect from you submission. I may perhaps give you the sum of fifty pounds a year.

Don't mention it, Sir, said I. There again you will have the goodness to excuse me. Madam, your most obedient. Miss, your very obsequious. Sir, your humble servant.[1]

My walk back to *Charleston* was along the shore of the *Atlantic,* whose waves naturally associated the idea of a home I despaired ever again to behold. . . .

Thomas Hamilton

1831

Education and National Characteristics

Thomas Hamilton (1789–1842) was educated at the University of Glasgow and was later in the British Army for some eight years. He served in the Peninsula Wars, in Nova Scotia and New Brunswick, and in the army of occupation in France in 1815. Retiring from the army in 1818, he joined the editorial staff of *Blackwood's* magazine. His novel *Cyril Thornton* which appeared in 1827 was popular in its day. In another work, *Men and Manners in America,* he revealed himself as a shrewd and kindly critic.

During his tour of American schools and institutions, Hamilton met and was entertained by John Griscom and George Ticknor. He recounted the especially generous reception he received from educators and intellectuals and the admiration he felt for the educational provisions of the United States which, he said, reminded him of the Scottish devotion to public education.

Introduction

It was not till more than a year after my return, that I finally determined on publishing the result of my observations in the United States. Of books of travels in America, there seemed no deficiency; and I was naturally unwilling to incur, by the public expression of my opinions, the certainty of giving offence to a people, of whose hospitality I shall always entertain a grateful recollection. I should, therefore, gladly have remained silent, and devoted those hours which occasionally hang heavy on the hands of an idle gentleman, to the productions of lighter literature, which, if not more attractive to the reader, would certainly have been more agreeable to the taste and habits of the writer.

But when I found the institutions and experience of the United States deliberately quoted in the reformed Parliament, as affording safe precedent for British legislation, and learned that the drivellers who uttered such nonsense, instead of encountering merited derision, were listened to with patience and approbation, by men as ignorant as themselves, I certainly did feel that another work on America was yet wanted, and at once determined to undertake a task which inferior considerations would probably have induced me to decline.

How far, in writing of the institutions of a foreign country, I may have been influenced by the prejudices natural to an Englishman, I presume not to determine. To the impartiality of a cosmopolite I make no pretension. No man can wholly cast off the

Thomas Hamilton, *Men and Manners in America* (Philadelphia: Carey, Lea and Blanchard, 1833), pp. iv-vi, 52–57, 59–60, 75–77, 95–96, 121–125, 190–196, 198–199, 257, 409–410.

trammels of habit and education, nor escape from the bias of that multitude of minute and latent predilections, which insensibly affect the judgment of the wisest.

But, apart from such necessary and acknowledged influences, I am aware of no prejudice which could lead me to form a perverted estimate of the condition, moral or social, of the Americans. I visited their country with no antipathies to be overcome; and I doubt not you can bear testimony that my political sentiments were not such, as to make it probable that I would regard with an unfavourable eye the popular character of their government. In the United States I was received with kindness, and enjoyed an intercourse at once gratifying and instructive, with many individuals for whom I can never cease to cherish the warmest sentiments of esteem. I neither left England a visionary and discontented enthusiast, nor did I return to it a man of blighted prospects and disappointed hopes. In the business or ambitions of the world I had long ceased to have any share. I was bound to no party, and pledged to no opinions. I had visited many countries, and may therefore be permitted to claim the possession of such advantages as foreign travel can bestow.

Under these circumstances, I leave it to the ingenuity of others to discover by what probable—what possible temptation, I could be induced to write in a spirit of unjust depreciation of the manners, morals, or institutions of a people so intimately connected with England, by the ties of interest, and the affinities of common ancestry.

It has been said, by some one, that the narrative of a traveller is necessarily a book of inaccuracies. I admit the truth of the apophthegm, and only claim the most favourable construction for his mistakes. The range of a traveller's observations must generally be limited to those peculiarities which float, as it were, on the surface of society. Of the ''sunken treasuries'' beneath, he cannot speak. His sources of information are always fallible, and, at best, he can appeal only to the results of an imperfect experience. A great deal which necessarily enters into his narrative, must be derived from the testimony of others. In the common intercourse of society, men do not select their words with that scrupulous precision which they use in a witness-box. Details are loosely given, and inaccurately remembered. Events are coloured or distorted by the partialities of the narrator; minute circumstances are omitted or brought into undue prominence, and the vast and varied machinery by which fact is manufactured into fallacy is continually at work.

From the errors which, I fear, must still constitute the badge of all our tribe, I pretend to no exemption. But, whatever be the amount of its imperfections, the present work is offered to the world without excuse of any sort; for I confess my observations have led to the conclusion, that a book requiring apology is rarely worth it. . . .

New York

Professor Griscomb, a member of the Society of Friends, was obliging enough to conduct me over a large seminary placed under his immediate superintendence. The general plan of education is one with which, in Scotland at least, we are familiar, and I did not remark that any material improvement had followed its adoption in the United States. To divide boys into large classes of fifty or a hundred, in which, of course, the rate of advancement of the slowest boy must regulate that of the cleverest and most assiduous, does not, I confess, appear a system founded on very sound or rational principles. On this plan of retardation, it is, of course, necessary to discover some employment for the boys, whose talents enable them to outstrip their fellows; and this is done by appointing them to the office of monitor, or teacher, of a subdivision of the class. This mode of communicating knowledge has its advantages and its faults. It is no doubt beneficial to the great body of the class, who are instructed with greater facility, and less labour to the master. But the monitors are little better than scapegoats, who, with some injustice, are made to pay the whole penalty of the comparative dulness of their companions. The system, however, I have been assured, both in this country and in England, is found to work well, and I have no doubt it does so in respect to the *average* amount of instruction imparted to the pupils. But the principle of sacrificing the clever few, for the advancement of the stupid many, is one, I still humbly conceive, to be liable to strong objections. Of establishments on this principle, I have seen none more successful than that of Professor Griscomb. Every thing which zeal and talent on the part of the master could effect, had obviously been done: and on the part of the scholars, there was assuredly no want of proficiency in any branch of knowledge adapted to their age and capacity.

School Discipline

A striking difference exists between the system of rewards and punishments adopted in the schools of the United States, and in those of England. In the former, neither personal infliction, nor forcible coercion of any kind, is permitted. How far such a system is likely to prove successful, I cannot yet form an opinion, but judging solely from the seminary under Dr. Griscomb, I should be inclined to augur favourably of its results. It has always, however, appeared strange to me, that the American should betray so strong an antipathy to the system of the public schools of England. There are no other establishments, perhaps, in our country, so entirely republican both in principle and practice. Rank is there allowed no privileges, and the only recognised aristocracy is that of personal qualities. Yet these schools are far from finding favour in American eyes. The system of fagging, in particular, is regarded with abhorrence; and since my arrival, I have never met any one who could even speak of it with patience. The state of feeling on this matter in the two countries presents this curious anomaly: A young English nobleman is sent to Westminster or Winchester to brush coats and wash tea-cups, while the meanest American storekeeper would redden with virtuous indignation at the very thought of the issue of his loins contaminating his plebeian blood by the discharge of such functions.

The difference of feeling, however, seems to admit of easy explanation. In England, the menial offices in question form the duties of *freemen;* in America, even in those States where slavery has been abolished, domestic service being discharged by Negroes, is connected with a thousand degrading associations. So powerful are these, that I have never yet conversed with an American who could understand that there is nothing intrinsically disgraceful in such duties; and their being at all considered so, proceeds entirely from a certain confusion of thought, which connects the office with the manners and character of those by whom it is discharged. In a country where household services are generally performed by persons of respectable character, on a level, in point of morals and acquirement, with other handicraftsmen, it is evident that such prej-

udice could exist in no material degree. But it certainly could not exist *at all* in a country, where for a certain period such services were performed by *all*, including every rank below royalty. Let the idea of personal degradation, therefore, be wholly abstracted, and then the question will rest on its true basis, namely, whether such discipline as that adopted in our public schools, be favourable to the improvement of the moral character or not?

In England, the system is believed from long experience to work practically well. No man will say, that British gentlemen, formed under the discipline of these institutions, are deficient in high bearing, or in generous spirit; nor will it readily be considered a disadvantage, that those who are afterwards to wield the united influence of rank and wealth, should, in their early years, be placed in a situation, where their personal and moral qualities alone can place them even on an equality with their companions.

It is very probable, indeed, that a system suited to a country, in which gradation of ranks forms an integral part of the constitution, may not be adapted to another, which differs so widely in these respects, as the United States. Here, there is no pride of birth or station to be overcome; and whether, under circumstances so different, the kind of discipline in question might operate beneficially or otherwise, is a point on which I certainly do not presume to decide. I only assert my conviction, that in this country it has never yet been made the subject of liberal and enlightened discussion, and therefore that the value of Transatlantic opinion with regard to it is absolutely null. The conclusion adopted may be right, but the grounds on which it is founded are evidently wrong.

Having resolved to devote the day to the inspection of schools, I went from that under the superintendence of Professor Griscomb, to another for the education of children of colour. I here found about a hundred boys, in whose countenances might be traced every possible gradation of complexion between those of the swarthy Ethiop and florid European. Indeed, several of the children were so fair, that I certainly never should have discovered the lurking taint of African descent. In person they were clean and neat, and though of course the offspring of the very lowest class of the people, there was nothing in their dress or appearance indicative of abject poverty. The master struck me as an intelligent and benevolent man. He frankly answered all my questions, and evidently took pride in the proficiency of his pupils.

School for Children of Colour

It has often happened to me, since my arrival in this country, to hear it gravely maintained by men of education and intelligence, that the Negroes were an inferior race, a link as it were between man and the brutes. Having enjoyed few opportunities of observation on people of colour in my own country, I was now glad to be enabled to enlarge my knowledge on a subject so interesting. I therefore requested the master to inform me whether the results of his experience had led to the inference, that the aptitude of the Negro children for acquiring knowledge was inferior to that of the whites. In reply, he assured me they had not done so; and, on the contrary, declared, that in sagacity, perseverance, and capacity for the acquisition and retention of knowledge, his poor despised scholars were equal to any boys he had ever known. "But, alas, sir!" said he, "to what end are these poor creatures taught acquirement, from the exercise of which they are destined to be debarred, by the prejudices of society? It is surely but a cruel mockery to cultivate talents, when in the present state of public feeling, there is no field open for their useful employment. Be his acquirements what they may, a Negro is still a Negro, or, in other words, a creature marked out for degradation, and exclusion from those objects which stimulate the hopes and powers of other men."

I observed, in reply, that I was not aware that, in those States in which slavery had been abolished, any such barrier existed as that to which he alluded. "In the State of New York, for instance," I asked, "are not all offices and professions open to the man of colour as well as to the white?"

"I see, sir," replied he, "that you are not a native of this country, or you would not have asked such a question." He then went on to inform me, that the exclusion in question did not arise from any legislative enactment, but from the tyranny of that prejudice, which, regarding the poor black as a being of inferior order, works its own fulfilment in making him so. There was no answering this, for it accorded too well with my own observations in society, not to carry my implicit belief.

The master then proceeded to explain the system of education adopted in the school, and subsequently afforded many gratifying proofs of the proficiency of his scholars. One class was employed in navigation, and worked several complicated problems with great accuracy and rapidity. A large proportion were perfectly conversant with arithmetic, and not a few with the lower mathematics. A long and rigid examination took place in geography, in the course of which questions were answered with facility, which I confess would have puzzled me exceedingly, had they been addressed to myself.

I had become so much interested in the little party-coloured crowd before me, that I recurred to our former discourse, and inquired of the master, what would probably become of his scholars on their being sent out into the world? Some trades, some description of labour of course were open to them, and I expressed my desire to know what these were. He told me they were few. The class studying navigation, were destined to be sailors; but let their talents be what they might, it was impossible they could rise to be officers of the paltriest merchantman that entered the waters of the United States. The office of cook or steward was indeed within the scope of their ambition; but it was just as feasible for the poor creatures to expect to become Chancellor of the State, as mate of a ship. In other pursuits, it was the same. Some would become stone-masons, or bricklayers, and to the extent of carrying a hod, or handling a trowel, the course was clear before them; but the office of master-bricklayer was open to them in precisely the same sense as the Professorship of Natural Philosophy. No white artificer would serve under a coloured master. The most degraded Irish emigrant would scout the idea with indignation. As carpenters, shoemakers, or tailors, they were still arrested by the same barrier. In either of the latter capacities, indeed, they might work for people of their own complexion, but no *gentleman* would ever think of ordering garments of any sort from a *schneider* of cuticle less white than his own. Grocers they might be, but then who could perceive the possibility of a respectable household matron purchasing tea or spiceries from a vile "Nigger?" As barbers, they were more fortunate, and in that capacity might even enjoy the privilege of taking the President of the United States by the nose. Throughout the Union, the department of domestic service particularly belongs to them, though recently they are beginning to find rivals in the Irish emigrants, who come annually in swarms like locusts. . . .

Tribulations of a Foreign Student in New York

I am tempted here to relate an anecdote, though somewhat out of place, as it did not occur till my return to New York the following spring. Chancing one day at the Ordinary at Bunker's to sit next an English merchant from St. Domingo, in the course of conversation, he mentioned the following circumstances. The son of a Haytian general, high in the favour of Boyer, recently accompanied him to New York, which he came to visit for pleasure and instruction. This young man, though a mulatto, was pleasing in manner, and with more intelligence than is usually to be met with in a country in which education is so defective. At home, he had been accustomed to receive all the deference due to his rank, and when he arrived in New York, it was with high anticipations of the pleasure that awaited him in a city so opulent and enlightened.

On landing, he inquired for the best hotel, and directed his baggage to be conveyed there. He was rudely refused admittance, and tried several others with similar result. At length he was forced to take up his abode in a miserable lodging-house kept by a Negro woman. The pride of the young Haytian (who, sooth to say, was something of a dandy, and made imposing display of gold chains and brooches,) was sadly galled by this, and the experience of every hour tended farther to confirm the conviction, that, in this country, he was regarded as a degraded being, with whom the meanest white man would hold it disgraceful to associate. In the evening, he went to the theatre, and tendered his money to the box-keeper. It was tossed back to him, with a disdainful intimation, that the place for persons of his colour was the upper gallery.

On the following morning, my countryman, who had frequently been a guest at the table of his father, paid him a visit. He found the young Haytian in despair. All his dreams of pleasure were gone, and he returned to his native island by the first conveyance, to visit the United States no more.

This young man should have gone to Europe.—Should he visit England, he may feel quite secure, that, if he have money in his pocket, he will offer himself at no hotel, from Land's End to John O'Groat's house, where he will not meet with a very cordial reception. Churches, theatres, operas, concerts, coaches, chariots, cabs, vans, wagons, steam-boats, railway-carriages and air-balloons, will all be open to him as the daylight. He may repose on cushions of down or of air, he may charm his ear with music, and his palate with luxuries of all sorts. He may travel *en prince,* or *en roturier,* precisely as his fancy dictates, and may enjoy even the honours of a crowned head, if he will only pay like one. In short, so long as he carries certain golden ballast about with him, all will go well. But when that is done, his case is pitiable. He will then become familiar with the provisions of the vagrant act, and Mr. Roe or Mr. Ballantine will recommend exercise on the treadmill, for the benefit of his constitution. Let him but show his nose abroad, and a whole host of parish overseers will take alarm. The new police will bait him like a bull; and should he dare approach even the lowest eating-house, the master will shut the door in his face. If he ask charity, he will be told to work. If he beg work, he will be told to get about his business. If he steal, he will be found a free passage to Botany Bay, and be dressed gratis on his arrival, in an elegant suit of yellow. If he rob, he will be found a free passage to another world, in which, as there is no paying or receiving in payment, we may hope that his troubles will be at an end for ever. . . .

Intelligence of Businessmen

Though I have unquestionably met in New York with many most intelligent and accomplished gentlemen, still, I think the fact cannot be denied, that the average of acquirement resulting from education is a good deal lower in this country than in the better circles of England. In all the knowledge which must be taught, and which requires laborious study for its attainment, I should say the Americans are considerably inferior to my countrymen. In that knowledge, on the other hand, which the individual acquires for himself by actual observation, which bears an immediate marketable value, and is directly available in the ordinary avocations of life, I do not imagine the Americans are excelled by any people in the world. They are, consequently, better fitted for analytic than synthetic reasoning. In the former process they are frequently successful. In the latter, their failure sometimes approaches to the ludicrous.

Another result of this condition of intelligence is, that the tone even of the best conversation is pitched in a lower key than in England. The speakers evidently presume on an inferior degree of acquirement in their audience, and, frequently, deem it necessary to advance deliberate proof of matters, which, in the old country, would be taken for granted. There is certainly less of what may be called floating intellect in conversation. First principles are laboriously established and long trains of reasoning terminate, not in paradox, but in commonplace. In short, whatever it is the obvious and immediate interest of Americans to know, is fully understood. Whatever is available, rather in the general elevation of the intellect, than in the promotion of individual ambition, engrosses but a small share of the public attention.

In the United States one is struck with the fact, that there exist certain doctrines and opinions which have descended like heirlooms from generation to generation, and seem to form the subject of a sort of national entail, most felicitously contrived to check the natural tendency to intellectual advancement in the inheritors. The sons succeed to these opinions of their father, precisely as they do to his silver salvers, or gold-headed cane; and thus do certain dogmas, political and religious, gradually acquire a sort of prescriptive authority, and continue to be handed down, unsubjected to the test of philosophical examination. It is at least partially attributable to this cause, that the Americans are given to deal somewhat too extensively in broad and sweeping aphorisms. The most difficult problems of legislation are here treated as matters on which it were an insult on the understanding of a school-boy, to suppose that he could entertain a doubt. Inquire their reasons for the inbred faith, of which they are the dark, though vehement apostles, and you get nothing but a few shallow truisms, which absolutely afford no footing for the conclusions they are brought forward to establish. The Americans seem to imagine themselves imbued with the power of *feeling* truth, or, rather, of getting at it by intuition, for by no other process can I yet discover that they attempt its attainment. With the commoner and more vulgar truths, indeed, I should almost pronounce them too plentifully stocked, since in these, they seem to imagine, is contained the whole valuable essence of human knowledge. It is unquestionable,

that this character of mind is most unfavourable to national advancement; yet it is too prominent not to find a place among the features which distinguish the American intellect from that of any other people with whom it has been my fortune to become acquainted....

Harvard University

One of my first morning's occupations was to visit Cambridge University, about three miles distant. In this excursion I had the advantage of being accompanied by Professor Ticknor, who obligingly conducted me over every part of the establishment. The buildings, though not extensive, are commodious; and the library—the largest in the United States—contains about 30,000 volumes; no very imposing aggregate. The academical course is completed in four years, at the termination of which the candidates for the degree of Bachelor of Arts are admitted to that honour, after passing the ordeal of examination. In three years more, the degree of Master may—as in the English Universities—be taken as matter of course. There are three terms in the year, the intervals between which amount to about three months. The number of students is somewhat under two hundred and fifty. These have the option of either living *more academico* in the college, or of boarding in houses in the neighbourhood. No religious tenets are taught; but the regnant spirit is unquestionably Unitarian. In extent, in opulence, and in number of students, the establishment is not equal even to the smallest of our Scottish Universities....

Education in New England

In these States, the education of the people is likewise the subject of legislative enactment. In Massachusetts, public schools are established in every district, and supported by a tax levied on the public. In Connecticut they are maintained in another manner. By the charter of Charles the Second, this colony extended across the Continent to the Pacific, within the same parallels of latitude which bound it on the East. It, therefore, included a large portion of the present States of Pennsylvania and Ohio, which being sold, produced a sum amounting to £270,000 sterling, the interest of which is exclusively devoted to the purposes of education through-out the State. This fund is now largely in-creased, and its annual produce, I believe, is greater than the whole income of the State arising from taxation.

In these public schools every citizen has not only a right to have his children edu-cated, but, as in some parts of Germany, he is compelled by law to exercise it. It is here considered essential to the public interest that every man should receive so much in-struction as will qualify him for a useful member of the State. No member of society can be considered as an isolated and ab-stract being, living for his own pleasure, and labouring for his own advantage. In free States, especially, every man has important political functions, which affect materially not only his own well-being, but that of his fellow-citizens; and it is surely reasonable to demand that he shall at least possess such knowledge as shall render it possible for him to discharge his duties with advan-tage to the community. The policy which attempts to check crime by the diffusion of knowledge, is the offspring of true political wisdom. It gives a security to person and property, beyond that afforded by the law, and looks for the improvement of the people, not to the gibbet and the prison, but to in-creased intelligence, and a consequently keener sense of moral responsibility.

Speaking generally, it may be said that every New Englander receives the elements of education. Reading and writing, even among the poorest class, are universally diffused: arithmetic, I presume, comes by instinct among this guessing, reckoning, ex-pecting, and calculating people. The school-master has long been abroad in these States, deprived, it is true, of his rod and ferule, but still most usefully employed. Up to a certain point he has done wonders; he has made his scholars as wise as himself, and it would be somewhat unreasonable to expect more. If it be considered desirable, how-ever, that the present range of popular knowledge should be enlarged, the question then arises, who shall teach the school-master? Who shall impress a pedagogue (on the best terms with himself, and whose only wonder is, "that one small head should carry all he knows,") with a due sense of his deficiencies, and lead him to admit that there are more things between heaven and earth than are dreamed of in his philosophy? A New Englander passes through the statu-tory process of education, and enters life

with the intimate conviction that he has mastered, if not the *omnescibile,* at least every thing valuable within the domain of intellect. It never occurs to him as possible, that he may have formed a wrong conclusion on any question, however intricate, of poli-tics or religion. He despises all knowledge abstracted from the business of the world, and prides himself on his stock of practical truths. In mind, body, and estate, he believes himself the first and noblest of God's crea-tures. The sound of triumph is ever on his lips, and, like a man who has mounted the first step of a ladder, it is his pride to look down on his neighbours, whom he over-tops by an inch, instead of directing his attention to the great height yet to be sur-mounted.

This folly, indeed, is not peculiar to the New Englander, though in him it is more strongly marked than in the inhabitants of the other States. It enters into the very essence of his character; it is part and par-cel of him, and its eradication would in-volve an entire change of being. "A blessing be on him who first invented sleep," says Sancho Panza, "for it covers a man all over like a cloak." And even so Jonathan may bless his vanity. He is encased in it from top to toe; it is a panoply of proof, which renders him invulnerable equally to ridicule and argument.

If to form a just estimate of ourselves and others be the test of knowledge, the New Englander is the most ignorant of man-kind. There is a great deal that is really good and estimable in his character, but, after all, he is not absolutely the ninth wonder of the world. I know of no benefit that could be conferred on him equal to convincing him of this truth. He may be assured that the man who knows nothing, and is aware of his ignorance, is a wiser and more enviable being than he who knows a little, and imagines that he knows all. The extent of our ignorance is a far more profit-able object of contemplation than that of our knowledge. Discontent with our actual amount of acquirement is the indispensable condition of possible improvement. It is to be wished that Jonathan would remember this. He may rely on it, he will occupy a higher place in the estimation of the world, whenever he has acquired the wisdom to think more humbly of himself.

The New England free-schools are estab-lishments happily adapted to the wants and character of the people. They have been found to work admirably, and too much praise cannot be bestowed on the enlightened policy which, from the very foundation of the colony, has never once lost sight of the great object of diffusing education through every cottage within its boundaries. It will detract nothing from the honour thus justly due, to mention that the establishment of district schools was not an original achievement of New England intelligence. The parish-schools of Scotland (to say nothing of Germany) had existed long before the pilgrim fathers ever knelt in worship beneath the shadows of the hoary forest trees. The principle of the establishments in both countries is the same, the only difference is in the details. In Scotland the land-owners of each parish contribute the means of education for the body of the people. The schoolhouse and dwelling-house of the master are provided and kept in repair by an assessment on the land, which is likewise burdened with the amount of his salary.

It has been an object, however, wisely kept in view, that instruction at these seminaries shall not be wholly gratuitous. There are few even of the poorest order in Scotland who would not consider it a degradation to send their children to a charity school, and the feeling of independence, is perhaps the very last which a wise legislator will venture to counteract. It is to be expected, too, that when the master depends on the emolument to be derived from his scholars, he will exert himself more zealously than when his remuneration arises from a source altogether independent of his own efforts. The sum demanded from the scholars, however, is so low, that instruction is placed within the reach of the poorest cottager; and instances are few, indeed, in which a child born in Scotland is suffered to grow up without sufficient instruction to enable him to discharge respectably the duties of the situation he is destined to fill.

When Mr. Brougham, however, brought forward in the British Parliament his plan of national education, which consisted mainly in the establishment throughout the kingdom of parish-schools, similar to those in Scotland, one of the most eminent individuals of the Union[1] did not hesitate to arrogate the whole merit of the precedent for New England. I have more than once since my arrival heard Mr. Brougham accused of un-

worthy motives, in not publicly confessing that his whole project was founded on the example set forth for imitation in this favoured region. It was in vain that I pleaded the circumstances above stated, the company were evidently determined to believe their own schools without parallel in the world, and the Lord Chancellor will assuredly go down to his grave unabsolved from this weighty imputation.

In character there are many points of resemblance between the Scotch and New Englanders. There is the same sobriety, love of order, and perseverance in both; the same attachment to religion, mingled with more caution in Sanders, and more enterprise in Jonathan. Both are the inhabitants of a poor country, and both have become rich by habits of steady industry and frugality. Both send forth a large portion of their population to participate in the wealth of more favoured regions. The Scot, however, never loses his attachment to his native land. It has probably been to him a rugged nurse, yet, wander where he will, its heathy mountains are ever present to his imagination, and he thinks of the bleak muirland cottage in which he grew from infancy to manhood, as a spot encircled by a halo of light and beauty. Whenever Fortune smiles on him, he returns to his native village, and the drama of his life closes where it commenced. . . .

University of Pennsylvania

Of all the American colleges beyond the limits of New England, that of Pennsylvania is perhaps the most distinguished. Its medical school is decidedly so, and an Esculapian armed with a Philadelphia diploma, is held to commit slaughter on his fellow-creatures according to the most approved principles of modern science. Till within a few years, however, the scientific and literary departments of this institution had fallen into comparative neglect. But a revolution in an American college is an easier affair than the introduction of the most trifling change in such establishments as Oxford or Cambridge. The statutes were revised by a board of trustees appointed for the purpose. The system of education was corrected and enlarged, and men of competent talent and acquirements were invited to preside over the various departments of instruction. A new edifice was erected, and an extensive addition made to the former beggarly account

[1]Mr. Webster, in his speech delivered at Plymouth in commemoration of the first settlement of New England.

of philosophical apparatus. The natural consequences followed. The number of students was considerably increased, and the benefits of the institution were augmented, not only in magnitude, but in extent of diffusion.

In this establishment, there is no discretion permitted in regard to the course of study to be followed by the student. Every one is compelled to travel in the same track, and to reach the same point, whatever may be his future destination in life. It is, perhaps, quite right that such portions of a university course should be considered imperative, as relate to the preparatory development of the intellectual powers; but it does appear somewhat absurd to insist on cramming every boy with mathematics, chemistry, and natural philosophy. In America, the period devoted to education is so short, that there can be no folly greater than that of frittering it away in a variety of pursuits, which contribute little to the general elevation of the intellect. It is the certain result of attempting too much, that nothing will be accomplished. With such a system of education, the standard of acquirement must of necessity be greatly lower than in other countries, where excellence in some one department constitutes the great object of individual ambition. The truth of this position is in perfect accordance with the state of knowledge in America. In illustration of it, I shall direct the attention of the reader to an extract from the report of the Board of Trustees of this very University of Pennsylvania. Alluding to the prescribed course of education, these gentlemen assure the public, that "Its object is to communicate a *profound* and *critical knowledge* of the *classics;* an *extensive acquaintance* with the *different branches* of *mathematical science, natural philosophy,* and *chemistry,* combined with *all the varieties of knowledge* comprehended within the sphere of *moral philosophy, logic, rhetoric, metaphysics,* and the *evidences of Christianity. This course of instruction will occupy* FOUR YEARS!"

Had the number of years to be devoted to the acquisition of this vast mass of knowledge been *forty* instead of *four,* the promise of the Board of Trustees might still have been objectionable on the score of hyperbole. In Europe no body of gentlemen connected with any public seminary, durst have ventured on such a statement. Respect for their own character, and the certainty of ridicule, would have prevented it. But in America it is different. The standard of knowledge being there infinitely lower, the Trustees promised nothing more than they might reasonably hope to accomplish. On the Western shores of the Atlantic, a young man is believed to have "a profound and critical knowledge of the classics," when he can manage to construe a passage of Cæsar or Virgil, and—by the help of the lexicon—haply of Xenophon or Anacreon. And so with the other branches of acquirement. In mathematics, it is scarcely meant to be implied that the student shall have mastered the works of La Grange or La Place; nor in metaphysics, that he shall even understand the philosophy of Kant or Cousin, but simply that he shall have acquired enough to constitute, in the eyes of the American public, "an extensive acquaintance with the different branches of mathematical science, combined with all the varieties of knowledge comprehended within the sphere of moral philosophy, logic, rhetoric, and metaphysics."

It thus appears that what in one country would be nothing better than impudent quackery, becomes the language of sober truth in another. The same terms carry different meanings on different sides of the water, and the cause of the discrepancy is too obvious to be mistaken. Having alluded to this subject, I would willingly be permitted to offer a few observations on the interesting question,—How far the condition of society in the United States, and the influence of its institutions are favourable, or otherwise, to the cultivation of philosophy and the higher literature?

State of Literature

The termination of the Revolutionary war left the United States with a population graduating in civilization from slaves to planters. The scale went low enough, but unfortunately not very high. The great mass of the white population, especially in the Northern States, were by no means deficient in such education as was suited to their circumstances. In a country to which abject poverty was happily a stranger, there existed few obstacles to the general diffusion of elementary instruction. But between the amount of acquirement of the richer and the poorer orders, little disparity existed. Where the necessity of labour was imposed on all, it was not probable that any demand should exist for learning not immediately-connected with the business of life. To the grower of indigo or tobacco; to the feller of timber, or the retailer of cutlery and dry goods, the refinements of literature were necessarily unknown. In her whole population, America did not number a single scholar, in the higher acceptation of the term, and had every book in her whole territory been contributed to form a national library, it would not have afforded the materials from which a scholar could be framed.

It is true, that in several of the States there existed colleges, but these were little better than schools without the necessary discipline; and had their pretensions been greater, it is very certain that such poor and distant establishments could offer no inducement to foreigners of high acquirement, to exchange "the ampler ether, the diviner air," of their native universities, for the atmosphere of Yale or Harvard. At all events, the Americans had no desire to draw our men of letters from their learned retreats. In the condition of society I have described, it was impossible that learning should engross any portion of the public favour. Even to the present day, the value of education in the United States is estimated, not by its result on the mind of the student, in strengthening his faculties, purifying his taste, and enlarging and elevating the sphere of thought and consciousness, *but by the amount of available knowledge which it enables him to bring to the common business of life.*

The consequences of this error, when participated in by a whole nation, have been most pernicious. It has unquestionably contributed to perpetuate the very ignorance in which it originated. It has done its part, in connexion with other causes, in depriving the United States of the most enduring source of national greatness. Nor can we hope that the evil will be removed, until the vulgar and unworthy sophistry which has imposed on the judgment, even of the most intelligent Americans, shall cease to influence some wiser and unborn generation....

Thomas Jefferson

Whatever were the defects of Jefferson, he seems to have been impressed with a deep consciousness of the deficiencies of his countrymen. He saw that the elements of knowledge were diffused every where, but that all its higher fruits were wanting. He endeavoured, not only to rouse his countrymen to a sense of their intellectual condition, but to provide the means by which it might be improved. With this view he founded a university in his native State, and his last worldly anxieties were devoted to its advancement. Jefferson felt strongly, that while philosophy and literature were excluded from the fair objects of professional ambition, and the United States continued to be dependent for all advances in knowledge, on importations from Europe, she was wanting in the noblest element of national greatness. Though the commerce of mind be regulated by loftier principles than more vulgar traffic, it should consist, unquestionably, of exchange of some kind. To receive, and not to give, is to subsist on charity; to be a mute and changeling in the great family of nations.

The obstacles to success, however, were too great for the powers of Jefferson to overcome. In a community where the gradations of opulence constitute the great distinction between man and man, the pursuits which lead most readily to its attainment will certainly engross the whole volume of national talent. In England there are various coexistent aristocracies, which act as mutual correctives, and, by multiplying the objects of ambition, give amplitude and diffusion to its efforts. In America there exists but one, and the impulse it awakens is, of course, violent in proportion to its concentration. Jefferson, therefore, failed in this great object, towards the accomplishment of which his anxious thoughts were directed. As a politician, he exercised a far greater influence over the national mind than any other statesman his country has produced. But in his endeavours to direct the intellectual impulses of his countrymen towards loftier objects, the very structure of society presented an insuperable barrier to success.

America Unfavourable to Literature

I am aware, it will be urged, that the state of things I have described is merely transient, and that when population shall become more dense, and increased competition shall render commerce and agriculture less lucrative, the pursuits of science and literature will engross their due portion of the national talent. I hope it may be so, but yet it cannot be disguised, that there hitherto has been no visible approximation towards such a condition of society. In the present generation of Americans, I can detect no symptom of improving taste, or increasing elevation of intellect. On the contrary, the fact has been irresistibly forced on my conviction, that they are altogether inferior to those, whose place, in the course of nature, they are soon destined to occupy. Compared with their fathers, I have no hesitation in pronouncing the younger portion of the richer classes to be less literal, less enlightened, less observant of the proprieties of life, and certainly far less pleasing in manner and deportment.

In England every new generation starts forward into life with advantages far superior to its predecessor. Each successive crop—if I may so write—of legislators, is marked by increase of knowledge and enlargement of thought. The standard of acquirement necessary to attain distinction in public life, is now confessedly higher than it was thirty years ago. The intellectual currency of the country, instead of being depreciated, has advanced in value, while the issue has been prodigiously enlarged. True, there are no giants in our days, but this may be in part at least accounted for, by a general increase of stature in the people. We have gained at least an inch upon our fathers, and have the gratifying prospect of appearing diminutive when compared with our children.

But if this be so in America, I confess my observation is at fault. I can discern no prospect of her soon becoming a mental benefactor to the world. Elementary instruction, it is true, has generally kept pace with the rapid progress of population; but while the steps of youth are studiously directed to the base of the mountain of knowledge, no facilities have been provided for scaling its summit. There is at this moment nothing in the United States worthy of the name of a library. Not only is there an entire absence of learning, in the higher sense of the term, but an absolute want of the material from which alone learning can be extracted. At present an American might

study every book within the limits of the Union, and still be regarded in many parts of Europe—especially in Germany—as a man comparatively ignorant. And why does a great nation thus voluntarily continue in a state of intellectual destitution so anomalous and humiliating? There are libraries to be sold in Europe. Books might be imported in millions. Is it poverty, or is it ignorance of their value, that withholds America from the purchase?[2]...

Effect of Democratic Institutions on the Mind of the Country

. . .Acquirements of any sort, therefore, which the great mass of the people do not value, or are incapable of appreciating, are of no practical advantage; for they bring with them neither fame, nor more substantial reward. But this is understating the case. Such knowledge, if displayed at all, would not merely be a dead letter in the qualifications of a candidate for political power, it would oppose a decided obstacle to his success. The sovereign people in America are given to be somewhat intolerant of acquirement, the immediate utility of which they cannot appreciate, but which they do feel has imparted something of mental superiority to its possessor. This is particularly the case with regard to literary accomplishment. The cry of the people is for *"equal and universal education;"* and attainments which circumstances have placed beyond their own reach; they would willingly discountenance in others.

It is true, indeed, that with regard to mere professional acquirements a different feeling prevails. The people have no objection to a clever surgeon or a learned physician, because they profit by their skill. An ingenious mechanic they respect. There is a fair field for a chemist or engineer. But, in regard to literature, they can discover no practical benefits of which it is productive. In their eyes, it is a mere appanage of aristocracy, and whatever mental superiority it is felt to confer, is at the expense of the self-esteem of less educated men. I have myself heard in Congress the imputation of scholarship bandied about as a reproach; and if the epithet of "literary gentleman" may be considered as malignant, as it did sometimes appear to be gratuitous, there assuredly existed ample apology for the indignant feeling it appeared to excite. The truth, I believe, is, that in their

---

[2]The value of books imported from Europe during the year 1829−30 for public institutions, amounted only to 10,829 dollars! Even of this wretched sum, I am assured the greater part was expended in works strictly new. Of the old treasures of learning, America seems content to remain destitute.

In regard to science, it is a fact scarcely credible, that the second maritime power in the world does not at the present moment possess a single astronomical observatory, and is dependent on France and England for the calculations of an ephemeris by which her ships may be enabled in tolerable safety to navigate the ocean!

political representatives, the people demand just so much knowledge and accomplishment as they conceive to be practically available for the promotion of their own interests. This, in their opinion, is enough. More were but to gild refined gold, and paint the lily; operations which could add nothing to the value of the metal, or the fragrance of the flower.

The consequence of all this has been, that the standard of judgment, in regard to public men, is decidedly lower in the United States than in most countries of Europe. It is, perhaps, natural that the demand for political accomplishment should not precede its necessity; and I am far from wishing to assert, that American statesmen have not been hitherto found adequate to all the wants of the commonwealth. But if it be the great object of enlightened institutions to encourage the development of the highest faculties; and, generally, to raise man in the scale of intellectual being: if knowledge be confessedly power, and freedom from prejudice a nobler enfranchisement than mere physical liberty, then I fear that, in reference to this great and ultimate function, those of the United States will be found wanting. I am far from arguing, that science and literature should be indebted for their promotion to a system of direct encouragement. Such policy is always dubious, and has rarely proved successful. But I certainly regard, as one most important standard of excellence in a government, the degree in which, *by its very constitution,* it tends to call into action the higher powers and qualities of the human mind. It is a poor policy, which, in matters of intellect, looks not beyond the necessities of the present hour. There is no economy so short-sighted, as that which would limit the expenditure of mind; and assuredly the condition of society cannot be desirable, in which great qualities of every sort do not find efficient excitement and ample field for display.

How far the influences which have hitherto prevented the intellectual advancement of the Americans, may hereafter be counteracted by others more favourable to the cultivation of learning, I presume not to predict. There is certainly no deficiency of talent in the United States; no deficiency of men, stored even to abundance with knowledge, practically applicable to the palpable and grosser wants of their countrymen....

Eloquence of Congress

In Congress, the number of men who have received—what even in the United States is called—a classical education, is extremely small, and of these the proportion who still retain sufficient scholarship to find pleasure in allusion to the words of the great writers of antiquity, is yet smaller. The great majority are utterly and recklessly ignorant of the learned languages, and the whole literature imbodied in them; and it is evident that, with such an audience, any appeal to classical authority is mere waste of breath in the one party, and of patience in the other. It may appear strange, under such circumstances, but I have no doubt of the fact, that in the course of a session, more Latin—such as it is—is quoted in the House of Representatives, than in both Houses of the British Parliament. Indeed, it is ludicrous enough to observe the solicitude of men, evidently illiterate, to trick out their speeches with such hackneyed extracts from classical authors, as they may have picked up in the course of a superficial reading. Thus, if a member be attacked, he will probably assure the House, not in plain English, that the charge of his opponent is weak, and without foundation, but in Latin that it is *"telum imbelle et sine ictu."* Should he find occasion to profess philanthropy, the chances are that the words of Terence, *"Homo sum, humani nihil,"* &c. will be mispronounced in a pathetic accent, with the right hand pressed gracefully on the breast. In short, members were always ready with some petty scrap of threadbare trumpery, which, like the Cosmogonist in the Vicar of Wakefield, they kept cut and dry for the frequent occasions of oratorical emergency....

Conclusion

I have now done. I fear it will be collected from these volumes, that my impressions of the moral and political condition of the Americans are on the whole unfavourable. I regret this, but cannot help it. If opinion depended on will, mine would be different. I returned to England with a strong feeling of gratitude for the hospitality I experienced in all parts of the Union; and I can truly declare, that no pride or pertinacity of judgment will prevent my cherishing the sincere wish, that all the evils which appear to me to impend over the future destinies of this rising country may be averted, and that the United States may afford a great and lasting example of freedom and prosperity.

Let enlightened Americans who visit

England write of her institutions in the same spirit of freedom which I have used in discussing the advantages of theirs. It is for the benefit of both nations that their errors and inconsistencies should be rigorously and unsparingly detected. A blunder exposed ceases to be injurious, and instead of a dangerous precedent, becomes a useful beacon. When a writer has to deal with fallacies affecting the welfare of a community, he should express himself boldly. There should be no mincing of word or argument—no equivocation of dissent—no dalliance with falsehood—no vailing the dignity of a good cause. Truth should never strike her topsails in compliment to ignorance or sophistry, and if the battle be fought yard-arm to yard-arm, however her cause may occasionally suffer from the weakness of its champions, it is sure to prove ultimately victorious.

Alexis de Tocqueville   1831

On Women's Education and on the Study of Greek and Latin Literature

Alexis de Tocqueville (1805–1859), a French author and political commentator, was born in Paris where he later studied and practiced law. In 1831 he petitioned the French government for permission to travel to the United States to study the penal system of that country. In addition to this official mission, he pursued his own special interests, namely an analysis of American society, government, and democracy in action. He traveled widely in the United States and made copious notes of all that he observed.

The excerpts below on education are from DeTocqueville's *Democracy in America*, written upon his return to France in 1833. The first American edition of his work was available in 1838, and it has long been regarded as one of the finest writings on American life as seen through the eyes of a foreigner during the nineteenth century.

No free communities ever existed without morals, and as I observed in the former part of this work, morals are the work of woman. Consequently, whatever affects the condition of women, their habits and their opinions, has great political importance in my eyes.

Among almost all Protestant nations young women are far more the mistresses of their own actions than they are in Catholic countries. This independence is still greater in Protestant countries like England, which have retained or acquired the right of self-government; freedom is then infused into the domestic circle by political habits and by religious opinions. In the United States the doctrines of Protestantism are combined with great political liberty and a most democratic state of society, and nowhere are young women surrendered so early or so completely to their own guidance.

Long before an American girl arrives at the marriageable age, her emancipation from maternal control begins: she has scarcely ceased to be a child when she already thinks for herself, speaks with freedom, and acts on her own impulse. The great scene of the world is constantly open to her view; far from seeking to conceal it from her, it is every day disclosed more completely and she is taught to survey it with a firm and calm gaze. Thus the vices and dangers of society are early revealed to her; as she sees them clearly, she views them without illusion and braves them without fear, for she is full of reliance on her own strength, and her confidence seems to be shared by all around her.

An American girl scarcely ever displays that virginal softness in the midst of young desires or that innocent and ingenuous grace which usually attend the European woman in the transition from girlhood to youth. It is rare that an American woman, at any age, displays childish timidity or ignorance. Like the young women of Europe she seeks to please, but she knows precisely the cost of pleasing. If she does not abandon herself to evil, at least she knows that it exists; and she is remarkable rather for purity of manners than for chastity of mind.

I have been frequently surprised and almost frightened at the singular address and happy boldness with which young women in America contrive to manage their thoughts and their language amid all the difficulties of free conversation; a philosopher would have stumbled at every step along the narrow path which they trod without accident and without effort. It is easy, indeed, to perceive that even amid the independence of early youth an American woman is always mistress of herself; she indulges in all permitted pleasures without yielding herself up to any of them, and her reason never allows the reins of self-guidance to drop, though it often seems to hold them loosely.

In France, where traditions of every age are still so strangely mingled in the opinions and tastes of the people, women commonly receive a reserved, retired, and almost conventual education, as they did in aristocratic times; and then they are suddenly abandoned without a guide and without assistance in the midst of all the irregularities inseparable from democratic society.

The Americans are more consistent. They have found out that in a democracy the independence of individuals cannot fail to be very great, youth premature, tastes ill-restrained, customs fleeting, public opinion often unsettled and powerless, paternal authority weak, and marital authority contested. Under these circumstances, believing that they had little chance of repressing in woman the most vehement passions of the human heart, they held that the surer way was to teach her the art of combating those passions for herself. As they could not prevent her virtue from being exposed to frequent danger, they determined that she should know how best to defend it, and more reliance was placed on the free vigor of her will than on safeguards which have been shaken or overthrown. Instead, then, of inculcating mistrust of herself, they constantly seek to enhance her confidence in her own strength of character. As it is neither possible nor desirable to keep a young woman in perpetual and complete ignorance, they hasten to give her a precocious knowledge on all subjects. Far from hiding the corruptions of the world from her, they prefer that she should see them at once and train herself to shun them, and they hold it of more importance to protect her conduct than to be overscrupulous of the innocence of her thoughts.

Although the Americans are a very religious people, they do not rely on religion alone to defend the virtue of woman; they seek to arm her reason also. In this respect

they have followed the same method as in several others: they first make vigorous efforts to cause individual independence to control itself, and they do not call in the aid of religion until they have reached the utmost limits of human strength.

I am aware that an education of this kind is not without danger; I am sensible that it tends to invigorate the judgment at the expense of the imagination and to make cold and virtuous women instead of affectionate wives and agreeable companions to man. Society may be more tranquil and better regulated, but domestic life has often fewer charms. These, however, are secondary evils, which may be braved for the sake of higher interests. At the stage at which we are now arrived, the choice is no longer left to us; a democratic education is indispensable to protect women from 'the dangers with which democratic institutions and manners surround them.

What was called the People in the most democratic republics of antiquity was very unlike what we designate by that term. In Athens all the citizens took part in public affairs; but there were only twenty thousand citizens to more than three hundred and fifty thousand inhabitants. All the rest were slaves, and discharged the greater part of those duties which belong at the present day to the lower or even to the middle classes. Athens, then, with her universal suffrage, was, after all, merely an aristocratic republic, in which all the nobles had an equal right to the government.

The struggle between the patricians and plebeians of Rome must be considered in the same light: it was simply an internal feud between the elder and younger branches of the same family. All belonged to the aristocracy and all had the aristocratic spirit.

It is to be remarked, moreover, that, among the ancients books were always scarce and dear, and that very great difficulties impeded their publication and circulation. These circumstances concentrated literary tastes and habits among a small number of men, who formed a small literary aristocracy out of the choicer spirits of the great political aristocracy. Accordingly, nothing goes to prove that literature was ever treated as a trade among the Greeks and Romans.

These communities, which were not only aristocracies, but very polished and free nations, of course imparted to their literary productions the special defects and merits that characterize the literature of aristocratic times. And indeed a very superficial survey of the works of ancient authors will suffice to convince us that if those writers were sometimes deficient in variety and fertility in their subjects, or in boldness, vivacity, and power of generalization in their thoughts, they always displayed exquisite care and skill in their details. Nothing in their works seems to be done hastily or at random; every line is written for the eye of the connoisseur and is shaped after some conception of ideal beauty. No literature places those fine qualities in which the writers of democracies are naturally deficient in bolder relief than that of the ancients; no literature, therefore, ought to be more studied in democratic times. This study is better suited than any other to combat the literary defects inherent in those times; as for their natural literary qualities, these will spring up of their own accord without its being necessary to learn to acquire them.

It is important that this point should be clearly understood. A particular study may be useful to the literature of a people without being appropriate to its social and political wants. If men were to persist in teaching nothing but the literature of the dead languages in a community where everyone is habitually led to make vehement exertions to augment or to maintain his fortune, the result would be a very polished, but a very dangerous set of citizens. For as their social and political condition would give them every day a sense of wants, which their education would never teach them to supply, they would perturb the state, in the name of the Greeks and Romans, instead of enriching it by their productive industry.

It is evident that in democratic communities the interest of individuals as well as the security of the commonwealth demands that the education of the greater number should be scientific, commercial, and industrial rather than literary. Greek and Latin should not be taught in all the schools; but it is important that those who, by their natural disposition or their fortune, are destined to cultivate letters or prepared to relish them should find schools where a complete knowledge of ancient literature may be acquired and where the true scholar may be formed. A few excellent universities would do more towards the attainment of this object than a multitude of bad grammar-schools, where superfluous matters, badly learned, stand in the way of sound instruction in necessary studies.

All who aspire to literary excellence in democratic nations ought frequently to refresh themselves at the springs of ancient literature; there is no more wholesome medicine for the mind. Not that I hold the literary productions of the ancients to be irreproachable, but I think that they have some special merits, admirably calculated to counterbalance our peculiar defects. They are a prop on the side on which we are in most danger of falling.

Isaac Fidler

1832

An Immigrant's Anecdotal View of the State of Learning in America

Isaac Fidler was an English clergyman, classical scholar, and linguist. His lack of success during ten years of temporary church appointments in London led to dissatisfaction with British society and aristocracy, and he emigrated to America in 1831 with his family and servant.

Fidler was bitterly disappointed with his reception in America and was unable to secure help from the Episcopal authorities nor from the publishers of classical manuscripts for whom he had wished to write. He could not find a congenial teaching appointment and discovered that even Harvard College had no appointment for a "Sanscrit or Persian scholar." Prospective employers suggested that he forget his previous training and take up a new profession. Fidler quarreled with many of those who had befriended him and with most of the intellectuals with whom he came in contact. The excerpt below shows that his views on American education and learning were bitterly prejudiced because of his inability to secure a suitable teaching post.

Isaac Fidler, *Observations on Professions, Literature, Manners and Emigration in the United States and Canada Made During a Residence There in 1832* (London: Whittaker, Treacher, and Company, 1833), pp. 46–62.

Fidler was finally forced to accept a position as clergyman at a nonconformist church in Thornhill, near York, Upper Canada. But the wilderness and primitiveness of the region made him return to New York by the autumn of 1832. He believed that it was futile to consider settling in America and ultimately returned to England.

When I had held two or three conversations with a gentleman, to whom I had a letter of introduction from London, with reference to my plan of teaching, particularly the languages of the East; he told me that, in his opinion, my best measure would be to go back to England. "The Americans do not yet want any thing with the East Indies. They are not colonizing other countries, but peopling their own; and have more need of being taught how to handle the axe or the spade, than how to read Hindoostanee. Had you been a strong active hardy ploughman, you might have been worth encouragement, but as it is, I can give you none." What this gentleman and his family told me, I found to be perfectly correct. The attempt would be useless and absurd to persuade a people, in love with money, and with themselves; doating upon their own perfections, and their superiority over all the nations of the earth in learning, arts, and arms; and despising, or pretending to despise, the English most heartily, that an individual from Great Britain had arrived in their country to teach them languages they do not know. It would be equally useless, to attempt inducing them to pay for information, which they could not at once convert to purposes of gain. A little further inquiry among those, with whom my letters and introductions brought me in contact, soon induced me to abandon the intention of opening a school for instruction in Eastern languages. Dr. Milnor himself thought the attempt could be only futile and followed by disappointment. He imagined, however, that another kind of school might be opened, which would be more likely to succeed. A day-school, with liberal terms, he said, *might* answer my expectations.

As the same thing had been suggested by other gentlemen of some consideration, it became worthy the attention of one, circumstanced like myself, to investigate more closely the character of day-schools in general, and the mode of conducting them. I soon found, that a common schoolmaster, in that country, is not regarded with much respect; and that education, in such schools, is on a contracted scale. It is true, that high claims to skill are advanced by teachers, and parents are flattered with reports that their sons are in such and such classes, and have studied such and such books.

School Insubordination

The hours of attendance in day-schools are about five and a half each day, for four days, and four for the remaining two days of the week. In some seminaries, there are sixty or eighty pupils taught by one, or at the most, by two masters. Such schools, generally close at three in the afternoon. Here insubordination prevails to a degree subversive of all improvement. The pupils are entirely independent of their teacher. No correction, no coercion, no manner of restraint is permitted to be used. It must be seen, from this picture, that general education is at a low ebb, even in New York. Indeed, all who know any thing of teaching, will see at once the impossibility of conveying extensive knowledge, in so few hours per day, and upon such a system. Parents also have as little control over their offspring at home, as the master has at school; and the leisure hours of idle boys are, in all countries perhaps, alike unproductive of improvement.

Two or three anecdotes were related, to convey to me an idea of American schools. The best teacher whom the United States could ever boast of was a blind athletic old man, who was so well acquainted with the books he taught, as to detect immediately the slightest incorrectness of his scholars. He was also a great disciplinarian; and, though blind, could, from constant practice, inflict the most painful and effective chastisements. From the energetic mental and bodily powers of this teacher, his pupils became distinguished in the colleges and universities of America. They were generally, at their admission into public seminaries, so far in advance of other students, that, from the absence of inducements to steady application, they there, for the first time, contracted habits of idleness. They also became less obedient and subordinate to collegiate regulations than the other scholars, when the hand of correction, of which they formerly had tasted, was no longer extended over them. Thus, a two-fold evil was produced by the discipline and skill of this blind teacher. Since that time, corporal punishment has almost disappeared from American day-schools; and a teacher, who should now have recourse to such means of enforcing instruction, would meet with reprehension from the parents, and perhaps retaliation from his scholars.

My inquiries, when this statement was made to me, were naturally directed to the real means of which a teacher might be allowed to avail himself, in order to inculcate his instructions on the more inattentive of his pupils.

"He must," replied a gentleman, "put up with their behaviour, but by no means punish them; and should his patience be exhausted, he must then acquaint the parents with their conduct. Allow me," continued he, "to mention to you a circumstance which occurred under my immediate observation:—A schoolmaster was appointed to a parish or district school, over which I had some influence. A rumour was circulated that he made use of chastisement, and an investigation took place. The report was confirmed by a public examination; and a notice was, in consequence, conveyed to him, that he must relinquish either his rod or his school. His answer imported that the latter, if either, would be abandoned. I entered one day whilst he was employed in attending to some lessons with which his scholars were engaged. He was, himself, rather an odd-looking person, and his visage frequently assumed involuntary contortions and grimaces, when his mind was ruffled or agitated. I observed a little boy, who was very deaf, amusing himself with laughing at the grotesque figure and odd contortions of his master. The teacher observed this act of impropriety, and after reprimanding the little fellow for neglect of his books, threatened to punish him in case of repetition of the offence. The master, on observing that what he had said produced no effect, forgetting the deafness of his pupil, inflicted on him immediate punishment. I felt indignant at this conduct, and, after sharply rebuking him before his boys, convened a meeting of the trustees, of whom I was one, and had him summarily dismissed."

I inquired what course a schoolmaster must pursue if any of his scholars should turn out obstinate and refractory, or if he have one more intractable than the rest. Is the master still obliged to tolerate patiently the most insubordinate conduct?

"He should expel the offender," was the reply. "In a college of ours, there was a student notoriously offensive and ungovernable. On one occasion, his instructor having observed something improper in his conduct, deemed him worthy of reprehension, and summoned him to his desk. The young man, suddenly extending his hand to the watch-chain of his teacher, jerked his gold timepiece out of the pocket, and dashed it instantly on the desk. A meeting of the trustees and members was convened, and the young man was *dismissed*."

College Education

In a country like America, where there is nothing in the patronage of colleges, and where expulsion from a public institution entails no disgrace, nor disqualifies for any kind of business or pursuit, it appeared to me improbable that much attention to instruction could be secured. I therefore asked if such a system of education could lead to eminent acquirements?

"In our country," he replied, "education is generally completed at the age of sixteen or seventeen, even in colleges and universities. Young men enter at that age and sometimes earlier, into business or professions. The clerical profession must be excepted. Learning, to a great extent, is not required for store-keepers and merchants' clerks. Yet the students in our colleges are generally acquainted with the rudiments of Greek and Latin; also with common arithmetic, and the usual course of mathematics. This is sufficient to enable them to comprehend any allusions which occur in reading or conversation. And a foundation being once laid, it is in their power, if choice induce, or opportunity allow them, to prosecute any branch as far as they please."

"But yet," said I, resuming the subject of common schools, "if schoolmasters are allowed no coercive influence over their scholars, is it not a difficult matter to meet with respectable persons willing and able to undertake a task so laborious and ungrateful?"

"There are always found," he replied, "some respectable young men, who, intended for other professions, are willing to devote two or three years to a parish or district school, in order to improve themselves, and save a little money to help them forward. And even others, on leaving the university, frequently begin their career by conducting an inferior school. These, becoming noted, by degrees, for their good conduct and steady application, rise from one station to another, till at last they fill a professor's chair in some college or university."

"It appears then," said I, "that common schools in the States are regarded as very subordinate situations; and are not of sufficient importance, to secure the continued residence of a really respectable person. There must either be teachers of doubtful character and qualifications, or a continual fluctuation, in your district schools."

Anecdote of a Teacher

He assented to the correctness of these remarks; and then proceeded in the following narration:—"There are always found persons both qualified and willing to conduct such schools, notwithstanding their subordinate situation, and also the smallness of salaries annexed to them. The following anecdote will convince you," he continued, "that we are at no loss for teachers. Sometime ago, a gentleman came over from Ireland, with high and satisfactory testimonials, desirous of obtaining a professorship in some of our schools or colleges. He applied to several gentlemen in the States; and to me, among others. I was very desirous of promoting his object, and recommended him to the trustees of several colleges and schools, one after another, yet he could never succeed. His failure did not arise, in the least degree, from deficiency of talents or of character; but merely because he was a stranger, and was opposed by many candidates, who had greater personal interest than himself. Disheartened, at last, by frequent disappointments, and reduced in his circumstances, he supplicated me to use my utmost exertions in his behalf. There happened soon after to be a school on Long Island vacant, and I had sufficient influence with the electors to procure his nomination. The stipend, indeed, was rather small, but was enough to furnish a subsistence. This Irish gentleman, after filling the situation for some time, fell sick, and grew desirous of returning to his native country, and to his relatives, from whom, during his American sojourn, he had heard no account. He had been unable to save any thing, or, to speak more correctly, was in debt. How to return, he did not know; and in this forlorn condition, he again applied to my benevo-

lence. I made his condition known to some friends of mine, who subscribed a few dollars, and procured him a passage to Ireland. He promised to write to me, on reaching his native country; but his gratitude evaporated, and I heard of him no more."

Second Anecdote

The foregoing anecdote was related to me by a person of conspicuous standing in New York, and the truth of it is unquestionable. A story, in some respects similar, but with a tragical and melancholy ending, was told, to dissuade me from emigrating far back, or accepting any office in America out of the Atlantic States. The person who related it, was possessed of elegant manners, and from England.

A person from England, with every characteristic of a gentleman, who had moved in better circles, solicited the place of schoolmaster in a country village, and was successful. The emoluments arising from his teaching were barely adequate to the supply of indispensable necessaries, and left him without any of those little comforts which sweeten civilized life. The boors and storekeepers of the village, unaccustomed to such a schoolmaster, observed, indeed, the propriety of his conduct, and his sad and silent mien; but took no interest in him, beyond the education of their children, and the exercise of a prying curiosity, which he was unwilling, and all others were unable to gratify, by any information or disclosure. He entered into none of their parties, partook of nothing cheerful, nor joined in any pastimes. He found, in the contracted souls around him, no kindred spirit with his own; none, with whom to interchange ideas, or communicate his griefs. His mind had, consequently, no intervals of social relaxation; and his bodily wants were but scantily supplied. His nights were spent in a wretched apartment, and on a bed of straw; and his days, in educating those, who were strangers to the feelings of civilized life, and whose earthly existence would be bounded by rustic toils, or sordid calculations. This situation he filled for some time, with increasing sadness, but without a murmur or complaint. At last, his strength became completely exhausted; and, unable longer to attend his school, he was confined to a solitary room. Too poor to hire attendance, he prepared his own food, and lived by himself. Some of the neighbours, not having seen or heard of him for a longer time than usual, entered his lonely abode, and found his lifeless body stretched upon the straw, where, bereft of every earthly comfort, he had sickened, without a hand to aid him, and died in absolute solitude. His pockets and apartments were ransacked, to discover his real name, and the place of his nativity; but every inquiry was useless. An impenetrable secrecy rested upon his birth and misfortunes; and his remains were deposited by strangers in unconsecrated ground, without a sigh of sympathy, or even common Christian burial.

American Rudeness

"The Americans," continued my informant, "are, in general, strangers to the finer feelings; and take pleasure in humbling those whose manners differ from their own. If you retire back from the larger cities, which have received a tincture from European residents, you will have ample opportunities of realising this tale, in almost every particular. Your family, indeed, will keep you from utter solitude; but if your children mix at all with those around them, their conduct towards yourself will be so contaminated with republican principles, as will become a source of hourly vexation. Such places are fitted only for the rudest people, and offer no correspondence with minds in the least refined by good society, or humanized by literature."

In conversation with an American clergyman, I once expressed myself thus:—"It appears strange to me, that so many should be found willing to engage in school-teaching, which, even here, must require expensive qualifications, and which, notwithstanding, is so little respected, and so badly paid." "The expensive preparation, of which you speak," he replied, "is generally defrayed by the public; and the respect is perhaps greater than you have been led to imagine, although not equal to what a clergyman or a lawyer receives. A schoolmaster's character is less obtrusive or conspicuous, than that of other professions: but he is not, on that account, less respected. His standing in society is equal to respectable traders, and persons in the minor professions. But perhaps it may afford you some insight into this subject, when I tell you, that in the New England States alone, there are between one and two millions of dollars, of public funds,

annually expended, in affording education to the children of those, who could not otherwise obtain it. The sons of these people, after having obtained a grammatical, and, in many instances, a collegiate education, go abroad into the world without a dollar, to fight their way. No school or college affords an opening, which cannot instantly be supplied. And a small salary is perhaps as much as they could obtain by labour, or in business. Besides, in point of respectability, a school possesses some advantages; and may lead to higher degrees of advancement, if filled by merit." To this I merely observed, "that I never before felt so strongly the force of Alexander's reply, when asked if he could contend at the Olympic games." "I could readily contend," he answered, "if kings were my competitors." "If clergymen of eminence in learning were frequently so engaged, I could open a day-school in your country. But at present, I will content myself with pushing my inquiries," "You had better," said he, "consult other teachers."

State of Teachers

In one of my interviews with Dr. Wainwright, he advised me to open a school in New York, and to charge the following terms; ten dollars per quarter for boys under ten years, fifteen for those above that age, and twenty for such as might read the higher classics. These, although not the highest terms, are considered respectable. He supposed I might soon have a school of fifty or sixty scholars. The terms above mentioned are two, three, and four pounds sterling, per quarter, respectively. It would be difficult to raise a day-school in England with higher terms and greater numbers; especially when we take this into consideration, that the higher classics in America would be lower classics in this country. Perhaps a person would imagine that a considerable saving might be made from such a school. Yet I believe most people, engaged in schools, in New York, relate a different tale. They deduct house rent, which is nearly double of what it is with us; and clothes, which are fifty per cent. higher; and fuel, which is also higher. They then remember, that sickness is more prevalent, and that medicines are more expensive. After years of experience, they learn the fact, that a few hundred dollars go but a little way in housekeeping.

Frederick Marryat   1837

A Young Ladies' Academy

Frederick Marryat (1792–1848) entered the British Royal Navy in 1806 and resigned in 1830 to devote himself to writing, using his naval background as the basis for a series of popular adventure novels. Marryat, a well-known and experienced traveler, arrived in the United States when he was forty-five years old. Popular and well-received, he reciprocated by writing of the country in generally favorable terms.

While traveling by steamboat up the Hudson River to Albany, he stopped to visit the Albany Female Academy founded in 1814. Marryat's visit coincided with the examination and graduation exercises described in the extract below. His behavior at these examinations was later criticized by George Combe, the Scottish phrenologist who visited the seminary three years later in 1840. Combe recounts that:

In this institution Captain Marryat has forfeited some reputation. He mentions that at the public examinations he secretly assisted the young ladies with their French exercises and received their acknowledgements confidentially for the favor; the young ladies maintain that all the rules of gallantry prescribed to the Captain an invoiable eternal secrecy on the subject; instead of observing which he has published an account of the whole transaction in his work on America; betraying their confidence, and as they say, at the same time, indulging his own vanity.

. . . I set off for Albany, where I had an engagement, having been invited to attend at the examination of the young ladies at the seminary.

Here again is a rivalry between Albany and Troy, each of them glorying in possessing the largest seminary for the education of young ladies, who are sent from every State of the Union, to be finished off at one or the other of them. Here, and indeed in many other establishments, the young ladies upon quitting it have diplomas given to them, if they pass their examinations satisfactorily. They are educated upon a system which would satisfy even Miss Martineau, and prepared to exercise the rights of which she complains that women have been so unjustly deprived. Conceive three hundred modern Portias, who regularly take their degrees, and emerge from the portico of the seminary full of algebra, equality, and the theory of the constitution! The quantity and variety crammed into them is beyond all calculation. The examination takes place yearly, to prove to the parents that the preceptors have done their duty, and is in itself very innocent, as it only causes the young ladies to blush a little.

This afternoon they were examined in algebra, and their performance was very creditable. Under a certain age girls are certainly much quicker than boys, and I presume would retain what they learnt if it were not for their subsequent duties in making puddings, and nursing babies. Yet there are affairs which must be performed by one sex or the other, and of what use can algebra and other abstruse matters be to a woman in her present state of domestic thraldom.

The theory of the American constitution was the next subject on which they were examined; by their replies, this appeared to be to them more abstruse than algebra: but the fact is, women are born tories, and admit no other than petticoat government as legitimate.

The next day we again repaired to the hall, and French was the language in which they were to be examined, and the examination afforded us much amusement.

The young ladies sat down in rows on one side of the room. In the centre, towards the end, was an easel, on which was placed a large black board on which they worked with chalk the questions in algebra, &c.—a towel hanging to it, that they might wipe out and correct. The French preceptor, an old Emigré count, sat down with the examiners

Frederick Marryat, *A Diary in America, with Remarks on Its Institutions* (London: Longmans, Orme, Brown, Green, and Longmans, 1839); the extract is taken from the edition by Jules Zanger (Bloomington, Ind.: Indiana University Press, 1960), pp. 94–97.

before the board, the visitors (chiefly composed of anxious papas and mammas) being seated on benches behind them. As it happened, I had taken my seat close to the examining board, and at some little distance from the other persons who were deputed or invited to attend. I don't know how I came there. I believe I had come in too late; but there I was, within three feet of every young lady who came up to the board.

"Now, messieurs, have the kindness to ask any question you please," said the old Count. "Mademoiselle, you will have the goodness to step forward." A question was proposed in English, which the young lady had to write down in French. The very first went wrong: I perceived it, and without looking at her, pronounced the right word, so that she could hear it. She caught it, rubbed out the wrong word with the towel, and rectified it. This was carried on through the whole sentence, and then she retreated from the board that her work might be examined. "Very well, very well, indeed, Miss, c'est parfaitement bien;" and the young lady sat down blushing. Thus were they all called up, and one after another prompted by me; and

the old Count was delighted at the success of his pupils.

Now, what amused me in this was the little bit of human nature; the *tact* displayed by the sex, which appears to be innate, and which never deserts them. Had I prompted a boy, he would most likely have turned his head round towards me, and thus would have revealed what I was about; but not one of the whole class was guilty of such indiscretion. They heard me, rubbed out, corrected, waited for the word when they did not know it, but never by any look or sign made it appear that there was any understanding between us. Their eyes were constantly fixed on the board, and they appeared not to know that I was in the room. It was really beautiful. When the examination was over, I received a look from them all, half comic, half serious, which amply repaid me for my assistance.

As young ladies are assembled here from every State of the Union, it was a *fair* criterion of American beauty, and it must be acknowledged that the American women are the *prettiest* in the whole world.

George Combe

1840

A Phrenological View of American Education

George Combe (1788-1858) was a Scottish phrenologist and educator. After attending Edinburgh University (1802–1804), he entered the law profession. In 1815 he met Johann Spurzheim in Edinburgh, and two years later they renewed their acquaintance in Paris. Combe soon became the leading advocate of phrenology in Britain. He founded the British Phrenological Society in 1820 and the *Phrenological Journal* in 1823. He traveled and lectured throughout Germany and the United States as well as Great Britain. His ideas on popular education were put into practice in a school which he founded in Edinburgh in 1848.

During his visit to America, Combe became acquainted with many prominent educators including Horace Mann. He was not overly optimistic about the future of the United States, stating that "the educational institutions ... appear generally to be defective." He believed, however, that the study of phrenology would greatly improve American education, and that it was "calculated to benefit the people of the United States, by enabling both teachers and pupils to act with intelligence and cooperation in instructing and training." His account of education below was written principally from a psychological and sociological viewpoint.

American Civilization

Mons. Guizot, in his "History of Civilisation in Europe," has well observed that the degree of civilisation which any age or country has attained is indicated by the

"development of social activity, and that of individual activity; the progress of society, and the progress of humanity. Wherever the *external* condition of man is quickened and ameliorated—wherever the *internal* nature of man is exhibited with lustre and grandeur—

George Combe, *Notes on the United States of North America During a Phrenological Visit in 1838–40* (Philadelphia: Carey & Hart, 1841), I, 241–248, 261, 264, 272, 326–329, 336–340.

upon these two signs the human race ap-
plauds and proclaims civilisation, often in
spite of fundamental imperfections in the
social state." Let us apply these principles
to the United States.

In no country, probably, in the world is
the external condition of man so high as in
the American Union. The enterprise, intelligence, activity, and economical habits of
the people have multiplied to an astonishing
extent all the physical elements of human
enjoyment. It was observed to me by a gentleman who is minutely and extensively
acquainted with the United States, that in
this country no man who is able and willing
to work need to go supperless to bed. In this
he far understated the fact. Laborers here
are rich compared with the individuals in
the same class in Europe. Their food is
wholesome and abundant; their dwelling-
houses comfortable and well furnished; they
possess *property*, and enjoy many of the
luxuries which property, in a state of civilisation, is capable of purchasing. The American cities contain great wealth; and
reckoning the whole property, and the whole
population of the Union, and dividing the
value of the one by the sum of the other, my
impression is that the product would show a
larger amount of wealth for each individual
in the United States, than exists in any other
country in the world, Great Britain alone
probably excepted. In the United States this
property is so equally diffused, that it is
really national.

The formation of railroads and canals,
the multiplication of steamboats, ships,
machinery, manufactories, and houses, the
extension of the productive soil; in short,
the advance of all that ministers to the well-
being of "the external condition of man"
proceeds in the United States on a gigantic
scale, and with extraordinary rapidity. We
must grant, therefore, that whatever other
"imperfection" may exist "in the social
state," this fundamental element of civilisation abounds in a high degree. . . .

The Anglo-Saxon race, which chiefly has
peopled the United States, has been richly
endowed by nature with mental qualities. It
possesses, in a high degree, all the faculties
classed under the three grand divisions
before mentioned; but, to attain their complete development, they need cultivation. In
the United States the development of the
mind of the mass of the people is accomplished by the following influences:—1*st*, By
domestic education. 2*dly*, By district schools.
3*dly*, By religious instruction. 4*thly*, By pro-

fessional instruction; and, *lastly*, By political
action.

By Domestic Education

The object of education in the family
circle is to develope and regulate the affections, as well as to instruct the understanding. So far as a stranger can discover by
observation, or learn by inquiries, the family
education in the United States is exceedingly
various, and depends for its character much
more on the natural dispositions of the
parents, than on any system of instruction.
In general the parents are in easy circumstances, are happily matched, are good-
natured, active, and frugal; and these
qualities insensibly cultivate similar dispositions in the young; but there are of course
numerous exceptions; and education has not
advanced so far among the masses as to
render domestic training systematic. Every
family has its own manners, maxims, and
modes of treatment. Speaking generally, the
faculties of the child are allowed free scope
in the family circle, without sufficient enforcement of self-denial, or of the subordination of the lower to the higher powers.
The first useful lesson to a child is that of
self-restraint, or of foregoing a present
enjoyment at the call of duty, or for the
sake of a higher, although more distant,
good. Many American children appear to be
indulged in their appetites and desires, and
to be too little restrained in the manifestation of their propensities. Egotism, or the
idea that the world is made for them, and
that other persons must stand aside to allow
them scope, is a feature not infrequently
recognised. The consideration of the manner
in which their sentiments and modes of
action, will affect other individuals of well
regulated and well cultivated minds, is not
adequately brought home to them. In short,
the active manifestation of the moral sentiments in refined habits, in pure and elevated
desires, and in disinterested goodness, is
not aimed at systematically as an object in
domestic training. I speak of the masses
composing the nation, and not of the children
of well educated and refined individuals.

In intellectual cultivation, domestic education is still more defective, because in the
masses the parents themselves are very imperfectly instructed.

On the whole, therefore, the domestic
training and instruction appear to me to be
imperfect, viewed in relation to the objects

of enlarging the mind's sphere of action, of conferring on it the power of self-restraint, and also the ability to discover and successfully to pursue its own permanent welfare.

Of Common School Education

From the various remarks which have already been presented in these volumes, the reader will be prepared to draw the inference that, viewed in relation to the three objects before mentioned, the common school education in the United States is also imperfect; I should say very imperfect. The things taught (chiefly reading, writing, and arithmetic) are not in themselves education. If sedulously and wisely applied, they may enable the individual to obtain knowledge; but the common schools stop short of supplying it. They even communicate very imperfectly the art of acquiring it; for some of the teachers are themselves ill qualified; their modes of teaching are defective, and the attendance of the children at school is brief and irregular. The addition of a library to each school-district was dictated by a perception of the magnitude and importance of the deficiency in this department. It appears to me that besides great improvements in existing schools, still higher seminaries are wanted, in which the elements of natural, moral, and political science, with their applications to the purposes of individual and social enjoyment, may be taught to the whole people.

One, and probably the most important, element in an education calculated to fit an individual for becoming an accomplished member of the American democracy, is *training* the faculties to their proper modes of action. This can be accomplished only by calling them all into activity, and by communicating to the higher powers the knowledge and habit of governing the lower. Mere intellectual instruction is not sufficient for this purpose; the propensities and sentiments must be trained in the field of life. . . .This end will be best accomplished by communicating to children the knowledge of their own faculties, and of their spheres of use and abuse, by placing them in circumstances in which these may be called into action, and superintending that action in such a manner as to cultivate the powers of rapid judgment and steady self-control. The play-ground is an important field for conducting this branch of education. The principles and practice of it are explained in the works of Wilderspin and Stow already referred to. This depart-

ment of education is in a very humble condition in the United States; and yet to them it is all-important. Every one of their citizens wields political and judicial power; he is at once the subject of the law and its pillar; he elects his own judges, magistrates, and rulers, and it is his duty to obey them. If ever knowledge of what is right, self-control to pursue it, and high moral resolve to sacrifice every motive of self-interest and individual ambition, to the dictates of benevolence and justice, were needed in any people, they are wanted in the citizens of the United States. A well *instructed* citizen will consider the influence of any law on the general welfare before he consents to its enactment, and a well *trained* citizen will not only obey that law when enacted, but lend his whole moral and physical energies, if necessary, to enforce its observance by all, until repealed by constitutional authority. An *ill-instructed* citizen will clamor for the enactment of any law which promises to relieve *him* from an individual inconvenience, or to confer on him an individual advantage, without much consideration concerning its general effects; and an *ill-trained* citizen will seek to subject the magistrates, judges, and the law to his own control, that he may bend them in subserviency to his interest, his ambition, or his inclinations, from day to day, as these arise and take different directions. The *ill-trained* citizen takes counsel of his self-will; and self-will, uninstructed and untrained to the guidance of moral principle, leads to destruction.

Phrenology is calculated to benefit the people of the United States, by enabling both teachers and pupils to act with intelligence and co-operation in instructing and training. It presents views of each mental power, and of its spheres of use and abuse, so simple and intelligible that children can understand them, and teachers can act upon them.

Lecturing to the people in lyceums is extensively practised in the United States, and as a mode of public instruction it is well calculated to advance their intelligence; but hitherto, owing to the defects of their education in the primary schools, it has not yielded half its advantages. As formerly mentioned, the lectures delivered in lyceums are generally of a miscellaneous character, developing no subject systematically, and sacrificing profound interest to variety and temporary excitement; yet no other lectures would attract persons of mature age, whose minds had not been opened up, in their elementary education, to the value of scientific knowledge. If the simpler elements of the natural sciences were taught in childhood, the mind, when it expanded into vigor, would long for fuller developments of their principles, and the lectures in the lyceums might then assume a high character of usefulness.

Viewing the object of education, then, to be to communicate knowledge by which the sphere of the mind's action may be enlarged—to train each individual to self-control and the love of good—and to enable him, by these means combined, to pursue successfully his own welfare, the educational institutions of the United States appear generally to be defective.

Of Religious Instruction

The objects of religious instruction are twofold; first, To obtain Salvation in a future life; and, secondly, To conduce to practical virtue in this world. I regard the first as belonging to the sphere of theology, and as beyond the jurisdiction, equally of the philosopher and the civil magistrate. By the principles consecrated at the Reformation each individual has the exclusive right of judging on this subject for himself, and for those whose souls Providence has intrusted to his care. I merely remark, that I perceive great differences existing in the opinions of American sects regarding, first, the extent of the danger to which the human soul is exposed in a future life; and secondly, the means by which this danger may be avoided; but that each sect exhibits a means of salvation which it considers commensurate with its own ideas of the danger.... The grand motive of the clergy of all sects is, no doubt, the love of souls; but there is a secondary circumstance which is, probably, not without some effect in securing their exertions, namely, the knowledge that the acceptance of their peculiar doctrines regarding salvation is the bond which binds the people to their ministrations, and that the more successfully they impress a firm conviction of their views on their flocks, the more secure do they feel in obtaining the means of their own subsistence, and the greater also are their power and influence over their people. This branch of religious instruction, therefore, appears to be in a salutary and satisfactory condition in the United States....

Professional Callings

The great majority of the people of the United States are engaged in arts, manufactures, commerce, navigation, agriculture, divinity, law, and medicine; and their pursuits are therefore useful, and productive of enjoyment. As the paths of industry are rarely obstructed by bad laws or artificial obstacles, American civilisation, in this department, will bear a favorable comparison with that of the most advanced nations. These avocations, however do not fully develope the highest faculties of the mind. They cultivate Acquisitiveness, Self-Love, and the love of Distinction, more than Benevolence, Veneration, Conscientiousness, and Ideality. They call the intellect into activity, but many of them do not necessarily direct it to moral objects. They are deserving of all praise as important elements of civilisation, indeed as necessary to the very foundations of it: but in order to exhibit the *"internal* nature of man with *lustre* and *grandeur,"* higher pursuits must be added to and mingled with them. The schools, colleges, and the pulpit, must supply the lustre and grandeur in which the avocations of common life are necessarily defective. Great improvements in professional attainments remain to be made in the United States. American divines are not in general so learned as those of England, but they appear to be more practical; while the professions of law and medicine in the rural districts, comprising nineteen-twentieths of the whole United States, stand in need of large accessions of knowledge to bring them to a par with the same professions in the enlightened countries of Europe.[1] The improved education which I have suggested would render the practice of the professions in some degree scientific or philosophical pursuits, in which

[1] If professional knowledge be measured by its ready adaptation to the exigencies of the case, the disparity between the professions in Europe and in the United States is far from being so great or so evident as is implied in the text. The European physicians, for example, may be better lexicographers or linguists, but they are not, proportionately to this kind of learning, better read in medicine nor better practitioners than the Americans. On the score of composition and style, the communications in the American Medical Journals, are in the average superior to those in the British periodicals of a similar character. This statement is not made hastily nor without due consideration.

each individual would endeavor, in his vocation, to appropriate the laws which the Creator has established as essential to success, and the calm calculations of reason would, to some extent, regulate the impulsive and empirical movements which have hitherto been fraught with so much suffering to the people.

Political Institutions

The American Declaration of Independence announces that "all men are created equal," a proposition which, however liable to be disputed in some respects, has (leaving out of view the African race) been practically adopted as the fundamental principle of all the institutions and legislation of the United States. It is the most powerful maxim for developing the *individual*, in all his faculties and functions, that has ever been promulgated, and it has certainly produced great results. It is probably the first abstract proposition that is cloathed with an intelligible meaning in the mind of the American child, and it influences his conduct through life. It sends forth the young citizen full of confidence in himself, untrammelled by authority, unawed by recognised superiority in others, and assured of a fair field for every exertion....

Obstacles to Reform

. . . Again,—in conversing with the friends of education on the imperfection of their schools in the department of *training*, and suggesting the advantages of inviting Mr. Wilderspin to come to the eastern cities and show them infant training in practice,— they acknowledged the defect, expressed themselves convinced of the benefit of a visit from Wilderspin—and said that there would be no difficulty in raising by subscription, the sum of money requisite to try the experiment; but one and all added that public opinion would not sanction such a step, and that if they ventured on it, they would do more harm than good to the cause of education. Again, when a scheme was hatching in Massachusetts to overthrow the Board of Education, there were not a few influential persons in different parts of the state, who, in private, acknowledged themselves to be the friends of the board, and who justly estimated its value, yet who had not suffi-

cient moral courage publicly to declare their convictions, and to support it. I was informed of this fact by a gentleman deeply interested in education, resident in another state, who travelled through a large portion of Massachusetts at the time in question, and who made it an object to ascertain the state of opinion on the subject. Once more, when agitation for the abolition of slavery commenced in the New England states, public opinion gave up the individuals who favored it almost to martyrdom.

... The common schools are placed under the management of directors and inspectors chosen by the people, and the reformers must obtain these offices before they can give effect to their benevolent designs. But the people, being ignorant of the nature and utility of the proposed changes, are easily operated upon by the insinuations, misrepresentations, and declamations of the hostile parties, who are scattered every where among them, and who by these means experience little difficulty in rendering the reformers unpopular, and thus preventing their election. The gentlemen who told me that the proposal to invite Wilderspin to the United States, would retard, instead of forwarding, the desired improvements in training, were sound in their judgment; because the prejudices of the people against foreigners, and their dislikes to innovation in their school systems, would, while they were ignorant of the nature of the proposed improvement, have ensured the exclusion of its projectors from office, and placed its opponents in power over the schools. The remedy for this evil is gradually to open up the subject to the public mind in lectures and through the press: or to carry the scheme into execution in some private seminary, and then show it to the people in action. After they comprehend its advantages, they will adopt it. And accordingly, the project of improvement by training is not abandoned by those who perceive its value; but they are proceeding prudently to prepare the people to receive and sanction it. So far from this condition of things being an unmitigated evil, it is attended with many benefits. It leads moral reformers to consider their measures thoroughly, and by anticipating opposition, to detect the weak points of their schemes. It also imposes on them the necessity of addressing the reason and moral sentiments of the people, and of *thus aiding in cultivating their rational nature;* and, in my opinion, the ultimate test of the merits of all institutions, is the degree in which they promote the accomplishment of this end. ...

Whatever estimate may be formed of the adaptation of the new philosophy to the wants of the American people as a guide to opinion, there can be little doubt that some general moral influence which should command respect and pervade the Union, would be highly useful. The division of the country into states, and these into counties and townships, each of which becomes an absorbing focus of interest to its own inhabitants, retards the diffusion of much valuable knowledge, and to some extent paralyses moral effort. I met with highly intelligent persons in Connecticut, interested in education, who knew nearly nothing of the organisation and action of the board of education in Massachusetts, although this state is divided from Connecticut only by a line. Not only so, but before I left the United States, the Common School Journal of Connecticut had ceased to be published, owing to the want of subscribers. It was a very ably conducted, useful, and cheap periodical, but it did not discuss politics, nor theological controversy, nor news; it was full only of high moral and practical information relative to the improvement of education; and this object interested so few persons that it could not find subscribers sufficient to support its existence! In Pennsylvania still less is known by the public of what is doing in Massachusetts or the other states in mere moral pursuits; and so with other portions of the Union. Large numbers of religious papers are published in the states, but the circulation of nearly the whole of them is local. ...

Austria and Prussia

... "Why should you send your son abroad to spend your money and imbibe false notions? Our [Austrian] schools and colleges are sufficient to teach all that a good subject needs to know."

The general effect of this form of government, then, is, that it is fitted to render happy all the humbler class of minds, those individuals who have neither desire nor talents to extend their efforts beyond the private sphere; but that it chains up, and thereby obstructs the enjoyment of the men of powerful intellect and high moral endowments, whose sphere of action is public life. The nobler the mind, the more heavily does the leaden load of despotism weigh upon its powers. Farther, it imposes fetters on the general mind of the nation, and retards progression. The government must move before the people are allowed to stir; and where all rational motives for progression are withdrawn from it, its advance must be slow, or if its pace be accidentally quickened by the genius of an individual sovereign, the effects of his liberality and energy are lost, because the people are not prepared to follow in the path which he opens to them.

The government of Prussia was in much the same state as that of Austria, until it was overthrown by Napoleon in the war of 1807. After its restoration, however, it saw its error. Under the old regime, its subjects had been kept in such profound ignorance, and so thoroughly oppressed, that they possessed neither mental energy nor national feeling, and so fell an easy prey to the invading French. It became the interest of the government to rouse its people from this lethargy, and to excite sentiments of patriotism. This was accomplished by making the serfs free, and instituting a system of universal and comparatively high education. The effects of the change were marvellous: In one generation Prussia stood forth a regenerated nation—full of energy, activity, intelligence, and profound national feeling. But the form of the government was little changed. It continues to be a despotism, but a more liberal and a much more enlightened despotism than that of Austria. The education which it provides for its people is superior to that of any other country in Europe, and I believe superior to any which even you can boast of. The government is well administered. It regulates every thing, but it does it well. Its police and custom-house officers are civil gentlemanly men; its post-office department is regular and safe, but it opens letters without scruple when it wants political information; it keeps the stagecoaches, post-horses, and roads of the state in excellent condition, but it monopolises them all. If, however, a single passenger more than the stage will carry presents himself at the hour appointed for its starting, another vehicle is instantly provided for him. The laws are just, and impartially administered. Life and property are as safe as in any country in the world; industry is fostered; and learning and philosophy are patronised. In what, then, is the Prussian government inferior to yours?

I have said that happiness is the result of the activity of all the faculties. The Prussian government, while it does every thing *for* the people, and does it well, allows the people to do exceedingly little for themselves. It educates them, and elicits talent, but it allows that talent little scope in the social circle, except in its own service. It permits the towns to choose some of their municipal officers, but their number and powers are small.... In short, under this monarchy, as under the empire of Austria, self-action in regulating social interests is denied to the people, and the object of the government is to draw into its own service all the energy, talent, and attainments of the nation, and to leave the mass the passive recipients of its impressions. It desires intelligence in the masses, because it needs mind and energy for its own defence against hostile nations; but it refuses to allow free scope to the mind and energy which it has evoked, lest they should subvert its own authority, and introduce self-government. Here, therefore, as in Austria, commonplace persons are happy; but the higher minds are cribbed and limited in their natural and best spheres of action, except when enlisted by the government in its own service. As civilisation must be measured chiefly by the intelligence, power of self-action and self-control of the masses, the Prussian government, by denying the right of political action to the people, limits their advance in mental improvement. It, however, allows religious freedom; for men of all forms of faith are equally eligible to fill public offices.

The United Kingdom

Let us now advert to the government of Great Britain and Ireland. That country has enjoyed political liberty for centuries, and claims to be the parent of your freedom. In Britain we enjoy the right to say and print what we please, in what form we see proper, and also to go where, and to do what, our own inclinations dictate, on the simple condition that, in pursuing our own gratifications, we shall not unjustly interfere with the rights of our neighbors. We may worship God, also, in any manner that appears to our own consciences to be most acceptable to the Divine Majesty. Life and property are secure, and the paths to wealth and honor are open to all. In Britain, then, it may be supposed that every faculty has as ample a scope for action as in the United States; but there are two bulwarks which arrest, or misdirect, the activity of the intellectual

powers and higher sentiments of the people. The first of these is the hereditary peerage, invested with political power and special privileges. It maintains in possession of great legislative, moral, and political influence, a body of men who owe their superiority, not to personal attainments, but to birth alone. If man be a rational being, the objects of his reverence, and the standards by which he forms his manners and opinions, should possess the highest natural gifts, most assiduously and successfully cultivated. A hereditary peerage presents to the public mind of Great Britain and Ireland, standards which do not possess these attributes of natural and acquired superiority. It, therefore, obscures the moral perceptions of the middle and lower ranks, by training them to pay that profound homage to high birth which is due alone to intelligence and virtue. By its influence it also misdirects the ambition of the aspiring minds in all the lower grades, and renders them more desirous to be admitted into its ranks, by any means, than to merit distinction for superior wisdom and morality. It is not open, as a matter of right, to all, but is to be attained by favor, with or without merit. It maintains a class so far removed from contact with, interest in, or dependence upon, the mass of the people, that it is little moved by their sufferings, and little disposed to elevate their moral and intellectual condition, or to do them justice in the exercise of its legislative powers.

The hereditary peerage operates injuriously also on the lower and middle classes of society, by leading their active and ambitious members to turn away from their fellows whom they should protect and advance, and to adopt the interests and prejudices of the aristocracy, into whose ranks they aspire to gain admission.

The second obstacle to the free action of the mind in Britain is the existence of established churches. These have consecrated opinions formed, in the dawn of modern civilisation, by theologians who partook much more of the character of monks and schoolmen than of that of philosophers or practical men of the world, and these opinions stand immovably enacted and ordained by Parliament as the legal guides to salvation, against which advancing reason and science employ their demonstrations in vain. A vast priesthood, amply endowed to maintain these opinions, resist improvement as innovation, and denounce free inquiry as profanity and infidelity. The consequence is the reign of hypocrisy, and the prostration of the religious sentiments by many individuals at the shrines of interest and ambition. . . .

Practical Education in America

Most of you will probably acknowledge the advantages of education, point to your common schools, to the large sums appropriated by the states for public instruction, and ask what more can any reasonable man desire? With every feeling of deference towards your learned men and divines, I would answer that you stand in need of a philosophy of mind capable of guiding your steps in your efforts to bestow education on your people. Many will say—Is not common sense sufficient to enable us to manage with success both our political and educational institutions? I repeat the observation of Archbishop Whately, that men never acknowledge the sufficiency of mere common sense to the accomplishment of any important undertaking when they fully understand its nature and the difficulties that must be surmounted to ensure success. A blacksmith will probably assure you, that common sense is sufficient to enable you to farm, if he knows nothing about farming; but if you ask him whether common sense will enable you to shoe a horse, he will unhesitatingly answer, that if you try the experiment, you will probably get your brains kicked out for your rashness and presumption. Do you imagine, then, that the successful direction of the affairs of a great nation, and the training of the human mind, demand less of scientific skill and experience than shoeing horses?

But allow me to ask, what do you understand by common sense, which is supposed to be such an all-sufficient guide in the United States? What is called common sense means the notions which have entered the mind of any individual, from such occurrences and sources of information as he happens to have enjoyed. Men's capacities differ, their opportunities of observation differ, and hence their common sense differs. The individual who professes to have no theory, no hypothesis, no system, but to follow plain common sense, has a theory: it is that formed by his innate capacity, aided by his own individual experience.

In some of your academies, the talent for English composition is supposed to be the most valuable attainment that can be communicated to the young; in others arithmetic and mathematics are regarded as the best studies for developing all the faculties; while one female teacher assured me, in all seriousness, that the human mind is a blank; that all minds are alike in their native capacities, and that she can evoke whatever talents and dispositions she pleases. This is her theory, and she has practised on it for many years! You must have observed how the practices of teachers differ; you cannot suppose that each adopts his own method without some reasons for preferring it;— these reasons, however limited and lame, constitute his theory. In point of fact, they all have theories, and the vast differences in their notions prove that nature is not the author of them; because she is always consistent with herself, and gives one response to all. When we have studied nature we agree. Hence, the great principles of astronomy, chemistry, physiology, and of other branches of natural science, are no longer in dispute. But on the subjects of morals, religion, and education, the diversity and conflict of opinion are boundless. Does not this indicate that our notions on these subjects do not yet rest on a scientific basis? in short, that we enjoy no sound and practical philosophy of mind?

To you this state of mental science is an evil of the greatest magnitude. In this country you need not only education, but an education that shall communicate to youth the knowledge, maxims, and experience of age. Here you commit political power to the hands of nearly every man who has attained majority. Your population doubles every twenty-three or twenty-five years. The actual majority of your voters is probably under thirty-five or thirty-six years of age. There is no other country in the world which is ruled by men so young and so inexperienced. I was told before I came here, that the Americans are the most excitable nation on the globe; that you take fire in a moment, and instantly rush to action, whether it be in speculation, in legitimate enterprise, in war, or in political change; and since my stay among you, I have heard the deep-toned war-cry uttered with a force and unanimity which is full of fearful omen. And the cause of this may be discerned. The mind, till thirty-five, acts more under the impulse of the feelings than under the guidance of intellect. By the very laws of our nature, Combativeness, Destructiveness, Self-Esteem, Love of Approbation, and Acquisitiveness, are then more energetic than they are at fifty or sixty; and at that period also experience is more deficient. Life has not been long enough to enable us to accumulate wisdom, to detect the illusions of passion or of vain glory—to supply the deficiencies and correct the errors of an imperfect education.

In your country, then, above all others, your school education should teach your youth the specific knowledge of the constitution and powers of physical nature, and the means by which they may be applied to the promotion of human happiness—of the constitution of the body, and the laws of health—of the constitution of the mind, and the means by which we may be best trained to the discharge of our duties in the private, domestic, and social circles—of the laws by which wealth is created and distributed; and of the influence of morals and legislation on the welfare of the individual and society. As you do not wait until your voters, who wield the destinies of your country—who make peace and war—who make and unmake banks—who make and unmake tariffs affecting industry to the core—and who make and unmake even your schools, colleges, and churches—I say, as you do not wait until age has given them wisdom and experience, but place the helm, at once, in their hands, and allow them to act, while they are still full of young blood, and all the energy, confidence, and rashness that attend it—you are called on by every consideration to perfect your schools, so as to communicate to them the dictates of a wisdom which cannot be dispensed with, and which will not otherwise be attained. . . .

The Future of American Education

Yours is a noble destiny. Providence has assigned to you the duty of proving by experiment, whether man be, or be not, a rational and moral being, capable of working out his own way to virtue and enjoyment, under the guidance of Reason and Scripture, unfettered by despotic power, and unchained by law-enacted creeds. Your institutions and physical condition call all your faculties into vivid action. Among these, the animal propensities, as I have remarked, are not dormant; but those observers err, who allow their attention to be arrested only, or chiefly, by the abuses of the propensities which appear in your people. Virtue consists in meeting and overcoming temptation. As you, then, by possessing freedom are tempted above other nations, you will show a virtue above them all, if you nobly resist every seducing influence, and march boldly onward in the paths of rectitude and wisdom.

The subjects of a despot, whose every thought and action are ruled by other minds, have little merit in exhibiting order and decorum in their public conduct. You will prove the true strength of your moral principles, when you restrain your passions by your own virtuous resolves, and obey just laws enacted by yourselves. It is to aid you in this admirable course of action, in so far as the feeble abilities of one individual will go, that I now address to you these observations. And I again ask, Do your schools teach all that your young voters should know? all that the best of your citizens would wish them to know, when they act as electors and arbitrators of the public welfare?—I believe not. If you ask how they can be improved you will be answered by as many projects and proposals for education, as if you had inquired for the philosopher's stone.

So far from education supplying this knowledge, it appears to me, that a vast proportion of your people have not yet obtained a glimpse of what, I hope, is destined to constitute the real greatness and glory of your country. I find here, the ambition of many individuals directed towards raising the United States to the rank of the richest and the most powerful nation in the world. They bend their whole minds to the increase of her commercial, agricultural, naval, and military grandeur. This is not wrong; but it is not *all*. Thousands of your young men pant for war, in order to wreath the laurels of victory round the brow of their native country; and they call this patriotism. I desire to see higher and better views entertained of the glories and destiny of the United States. History presents only the records of wars, devastations, and selfish aggrandisement pursued by all governments that have ever existed;—republics, oligarchies, monarchies —all have run one wild career of immorality and ambition. If your nation consider herself to have no higher vocation than these, she ceases to be an object of moral interest to the philanthropist and philosopher. If her annals be destined to record the contests only of faction against faction, of party against party, or of the nation against foreign nations—the friend of human improvement must turn from her in despair. The grand duty assigned to Americans is to raise up and exhibit to the world, a nation great in virtue; to show, for the first time, since history began, a people universally educated; a people prosperous, refined, happy, and gigantically great, by the realization in their institutions, in their private lives, and in their public actions, of the principles of Christianity.

Per Adam Siljeström   1851

The Relationships of Institutions of Higher Learning to Scientific Life

Per Adam Siljeström (1815–1892) was born at Calmar, Sweden, and educated in Swedish primary and secondary schools. He was active in elementary education curriculum reform, visiting England in 1848 and the United States two years later to study the elementary school problems of these two countries. Siljeström's researches were embodied in one of the first comprehensive accounts of American education written by a European during the century. It was intended originally for Swedish readers and includes a comparison of English and American schools. He established a "New Elementary School" in Stockholm, patterned in part on the educational developments he noted in the United States.

In 1864 Henry Tuckerman said in his *America and Her Commentators* that Siljeström "gave to his countrymen an able description and exposition of the American system of popular education, which is justly esteemed for its fullness and accuracy." The widespread development of an effective system of public education in the United States impressed Siljeström, and for the English edition of his book, he wrote the following preface.

The United States are the only communities in the world which from their very commencement were prepared to establish popular education as one of the fundamental pillars of the social and political fabric; they are the only communities in which the highest possible degree of enlightenment in the people has been practically and universally recognized, not only as a very desirable object from the philanthropic point of view, but also as constituting the principal cog-wheel in the machinery of State.

The question as to the influence of the higher educational institutions on learned and scientific life in America suggests some very important reflections. The first point that arrests the attention in connection with this subject, is the very inferior position which lectures hold in the American universities as compared to those of Europe. Here we are accustomed to attach much importance to academical lectures; and one of the chief distinctions between our universities and our schools of a lower grade consists in this, that instruction in the former is given exclusively according to the acroamatic method. In America, the common school method, with its lessons and "recitations," is continued up to the degree of bachelor of arts, although, particularly as regards certain subjects, lectures are also partially employed; and the same may be said of the theological and legal schools, and particularly of the former. In the medical schools, however, lectures are employed exclusively, no doubt to the great detriment of the students; for as long as there is a question of teaching in the strict sense of the word, and of studying for an examination—whether this be of a higher or a lower degree—lectures are, in my opinion, a very defective means of instruction. There is no method like the common school method of questionings and repetitions for enforcing serious and profound study, but of course applied with such modifications as the more advanced age and knowledge of the pupils may render advisable. Every other mode of proceeding is liable to induce superficiality and what is called cramming. It is, however, undeniable that much good may be effected by lectures, and they are of course quite indispensable as regards all subjects which require to be illustrated by experiments or by collections of natural objects, which cannot be conveniently exhibited to the pupils elsewhere than in the lecture room. Indeed, I am so persuaded of the usefulness of lectures, that I would wish to see them introduced even into the lowest grade of schools; but they must be used with moderation and only occasionally, and not so much on account of the actual amount of instruction which they are calculated to convey, as with a view to awaken and keep alive the interest of the pupils, to introduce new ideas and opinions, or to suggest higher and more general views, &c. In the present times, when it is so easy to obtain good elementary works on all subjects, it seems to me quite ludicrous, that the chief occupation of a professor should be to lecture year after year upon

Per Adam Siljeström, *The Educational Institutions of the United States, Their Character and Organization,* translated from Swedish by Frederica Rowan (London: John Chapman, 1853), pp. 373–397.

the *elements* of a certain science, particularly if this science be not a branch of experimental philosophy. Is it possible to imagine anything more wearisome to the lecturer, or more useless to the auditors? Yet is not this the general character of the lectures in our universities?

There is one particular reason, which renders it very unadvisable to attach so generally, as is now the case, the obligation of lecturing to the office of the teachers in our universities. The chief aim of a lecture is to awaken interest in the auditors for the subject treated, and this object cannot be attained unless the lectures possess the special qualifications required to command the attention of a numerous auditory. But a man may be an excellent scholar and an excellent teacher, without possessing that richness of imagination, and that wealth of ideas, which, together with some minor qualifications, are necessary to constitute a good lecturer, and through which he can alone produce an effect on his auditors; and if he do not produce an effect, of what avail is it that he lectures? And how is it possible even for the best-qualified lecturer to go on, week after week, without being exhausted, and becoming indifferent in consequence? In a word, it seems to me, that the nature of lecturing is such, that it ought by all means to be left to the professors themselves, to judge whether or not this mode of instruction should be adopted.

The reader will perceive that it is not my desire to depreciate the value of lectures as a means of conveying instruction, but merely that the usual academic lectures should be superseded by others of a higher character and having a higher aim. Lectures of the kind I am alluding to are of the greatest importance for the development of a higher intellectual life within the domains of science, literature, and art; but in this case the lectures must not be considered merely as a method of instruction, nor be used merely as appendages to higher or lower educational institutions. They must, on the contrary, be *free* and *public*—free, as regards the lecturer, so that no man be bound to lecture, who does not feel himself called so to do, and that every man who feels the calling be not impeded in so doing—and public, so that the mighty impetus, which lectures are calculated to give, may, if possible, strike every chord in the nation likely to vibrate at the touch. Let us never forget, what history and daily experience teaches, that science, poetry, and art are not the exclusive privileges of universities, academies, and schools, but may and do flourish beyond the precincts of such institutions, and that therefore the means of awakening and keeping alive a taste for their culture, ought to have as wide-spread a sphere of action as possible. Lectures, the most important of these means, cannot therefore be considered as having attained their proper standing, until, instead of being an obligatory part of the official functions of certain teachers, they have become the free utterances of men feeling themselves called to the vocation—until they cease to be merely a part of a school method, and become what I would term, in the higher sense of the word, *popular* lectures.

In this respect America, in which country popular lectures on all subjects are very common, possesses a great advantage over Europe, although as regards academical lectures, she is far behind Europe. I must not, however, be misunderstood when speaking of "popular" lectures, as being of much importance with regard to the development of a higher intellectual life. By popular lectures I do not understand, any more than the Americans understand, lectures in which the public are merely treated to a *réchauffé* of the sumptuous fare enjoyed in the learned and scientific coteries; or, in other words, in which old and well-known facts are put forward in a popular form. Such ought not to be the case. Why should not the thinker and the investigator himself present to the public, through the medium of public lectures, the result of his researches, or his new ideas and views[1]? Why should not popular lectures enjoy the privilege of being original? This privilege they do enjoy in America—at least in a great many cases—and the consequence is, that a few "popular" lectures exercise a much greater and more beneficial influence on scientific and literary life, than a whole year's course of dull *ex-officio* lectures at a university on the oft-repeated elements of one or another science. The popular lectures in America, to which I am alluding, may no doubt in some cases prove inferior, and in others they may be the utterances of charlatanism, for, as regards these lectures, as well as in all other matters, good and bad are mixed together; but gradually, as the general culture of the nation has risen, and scientific life has been developed, the popular lectures also have assumed a higher character.

[1]Of course I do not mean that this could be done in every case.

But although, for the reasons here stated, I see no ground to deplore the great dearth of lectures in the universities of the United States, as compared with those of Europe— and although I think that the former may, in spite of this dearth, maintain their position as nurseries of science and literature— there are, in my opinion, other grounds for doubting whether those institutions really answer their object. It is well known how dependent the Americans have hitherto been on Europe in all matters relating to science and literature, and that in a great many cases, they have contented themselves with borrowing and imitating. This imitation is also evinced in the constitution of their learned institutions, particularly of their colleges, which have been organized after English models. As in England, so in America, these institutions are little more than seminaries for teaching the classical languages and mathematics; all other subjects are considered as subordinate, and are treated with more or less negligence. Now, with all respect for the classical languages, and particularly for mathematics, as educational means, it must still be allowed, that these two branches of science alone are not sufficient to satisfy the youthful mind's craving for intellectual food; and whatever be the opinion on this subject, it cannot at least be maintained that scientific culture, as it is understood in modern times, is at all promoted by college education in America. Idolatry of the classical languages is as common in the new world as in the old; and the only difference is, that the antiquated pedantry, which generally goes hand in hand with this idolatry, appears even more preposterous in America, in the midst of the fresh life of a new community. In Europe it is in unison with the many other antiquated forms and institutions which are still upheld; but that which in consequence may seem quite natural here, appears almost ridiculous in America. It is not, however, difficult to explain how this state of things could be maintained in the United States, when we remember, as I have said above, that, as regards learning and science, but little self-dependence has been evinced in that country, and that the learned education has hitherto been, as it were, isolated and almost exclusively in the hands of some small private corporations, which, possessing the right to fill all vacancies occurring in the number of their own members, must have been peculiarly fitted to perpetuate old prejudices. With few exceptions, the learned educational establishments of America, although they receive public support, and are in a measure under public control, cannot be looked upon as popular institutions; and the consequence of their not being so, is at once rendered strikingly evident, when they are compared with the admirable activity and energy which reigns throughout the strictly popular division of the educational system. I entertain the conviction, that as long as the classical pedantry which now prevails in the higher educational institutions be not got rid of, and a more popular system of government be introduced, these institutions will never exercise that influence on the scientific culture of the nation, as, under other circumstances, they might and would exercise. If the same defects, which have here been indicated, be found likewise to prevail in the higher public schools, this is, I think, entirely owing to that want of self-dependence, which, as I have said, still characterizes the higher scientific and literary life of America. I have no doubt, however, that gradually, as the public school system extends its action to higher spheres, the system of instruction will adopt a new and more effective form.

Those who have had opportunities of becoming acquainted with the literature of the United States, cannot but be struck with the extraordinary improvement that has taken place within the last few decenniums, and cannot fail to observe that the present is fraught with rich promises as to the development of a more general taste for literature and science in the country. That the Americans are not as yet further advanced in this respect ought not to cause surprise; indeed there is more reason to be astonished that, in spite of all the obstacles with which they have had to contend, they should have advanced so far. Among the obstacles to which I allude, I may point to the dearth of scientific museums, &c., and more particularly of extensive libraries, such as have been accumulated in Europe in the course of centuries, and which cannot be the growth of a day. According to returns made in the year 1850, the libraries in America were as follow:—38 State libraries, with a total of 283,037 volumes; 98 libraries belonging to private associations (including Athenæums, Lyceums, Mechanics' Institutes, &c.), with a total of 562,229 volumes[2]; 119 college libraries, with 580,901 volumes; 134 libraries belonging to associations among the students, and containing 259,089 volumes; 222 libraries belonging to special and incorporated

[2]This return, I think, can hardly be correct.

academies, containing 315,287 volumes; 33 libraries belonging to learned societies, with a total of 143,576 volumes (in addition to the common school and Sunday school libraries). Very few among these libraries, however, are of any importance. Only four among the number—viz. the library of Congress[3], one in Philadelphia, one in Boston, and the college library in Cambridge, which is the largest—contain more than 50,000 volumes. How very imperfect they must all be, when considered from the scientific point of view, I need hardly mention, nor either how great a drawback this imperfection must prove as regards scientific investigation and researches in America. There are, however, circumstances that give rise to hopes of a better state of things in the future, and first and foremost among these is the foundation of the *Smithsonian Institution* in Washington, and of the *Astor Library* in New York. The latter has lately been founded by the will of John Jacob Astor, who died in 1848; bequeathing a sum of 400,000 dollars for the foundation of a public library in the city of New York. According to the will of the testator 120,000 dollars were to be immediately applied to the purchase of books, and 75,000 dollars to the erection of the building, and the interest of the remaining sum to the maintenance and gradual extension of the library. Of the Smithsonian Institution I shall speak hereafter.

Of collections coming under the head of natural history, such as geological, mineralogical, and zoological, there are several very valuable ones, although none that can be compared with the best in Europe; and these collections have of late years greatly increased both in number and in riches, particularly as regards the natural products of America, partly owing to an increased interest in scientific investigations, and partly owing to the geological and topographical surveys which have been undertaken in several States at the public expense. There are also a great number of collections of scientific instruments and apparatus, but chiefly such as are used for lectures, and certainly they cannot be compared with the better scientific cabinets of Europe. In point of observatories and astronomical instruments, however, America is singularly well supplied; in several of her observatories are found some of the best and most expensive instruments in the world. The observatories in Washington and Cambridge

can bear comparison with the best in Europe, and besides these there are several others, which, though of inferior grade, hold a very respectable position. Altogether it may be said, that in point of *number*, America is rich in scientific collections, but comparatively few have any high scientific value.

All the better scientific instruments are imported from Europe; and up to the present day the higher branches of instrument manufacture cannot be said to exist in America. The instruments made there are chiefly intended to meet the demand of lecturers. It will readily be conceived, that it is not because the Americans, who excel in all kinds of handicrafts, are incapable of manufacturing such instruments as are required for the highest scientific purposes, that these are not produced in the country itself. Indeed, proofs of their skill as mechanicians are not wanting in many other directions; but the importation from Europe of the class of instruments in question is only a further evidence of the absence of all artificial fostering of particular trades, every branch of industry being left free to develope itself according to the natural course of circumstances. When, therefore, scientific investigation and general scientific culture in America shall have attained the height and extension which there is every reason to hope they will attain in the proximate future, then the higher branches of scientific instrument manufacture will also flourish in the country, and rival those of Europe.

Among the causes which have retarded the development of scientific life in America, must also be reckoned the want of men possessing the will and the power to devote themselves exclusively to science and literature. Such men have hitherto been few in number, and, with some brilliant exceptions, not of very distinguished abilities. That it should be so is quite natural. In Europe, where a numerous class of scholars have been reared by the fostering care of the Government in the midst of a surrounding mass of ignorance, this class may be looked upon as an artificial flower used to conceal the barren and sterile soil; and as such it is connected by no natural ties with the general culture of the people and very often does not even feel an interest in the latter. In America, however, where, as I have before said, things are generally allowed to take their natural course, popular culture has been the first step in the series of developments, and constitutes the soil in which all higher intellectual culture is rooted; and I have no doubt

---

[3]This has since been partially destroyed by fire.

that the plant that has thus developed itself will one day bear striking testimony to the richness of the soil from which it has sprung. All signs seem, indeed, to indicate that its budding time is at hand, and I have little doubt that another generation will see it put forth a richness of bloom, such as Europe does not even dream of at this moment.

I am quite alive to the drawbacks under which those who enter the literary career still suffer in America. The reader has had occasion to learn in the course of these pages, that a simple teacher in a popular school is often better paid than many of the professors of the universities, and this fact affords a good standard by which to measure the relative degree of patronage which is bestowed on popular education and on a learned education in that country. However, it is not the vocation of common school teacher, but the higher rewards of the industrial and political career, which in the most cases draw men of talent and knowledge from the path of literature and science. But this does not at all seem to me an insuperable difficulty. When the taste and interest for science has become more general and more deeply rooted, and, by the foundation of museums, libraries, &c., the means of scientific investigation have become more accessible, the scientific talent in the country will be developed independently of all pecuniary rewards. Indeed many circumstances have of late years contributed to awaken this spirit of progress in America. Among these are the frequent visits paid to Europe, whence the young Americans bring back with them to their homes a more extended knowledge of the nature and scope of scientific labours[4], and a greater interest in them; while also the occasional removal of some scientific European to America is not without an influence.[5]

Among the strongest inducements to scientific studies which have occurred within the country itself, I reckon the geographical and topographical surveys alluded to above, undertaken on a grand scale by the separate States, as also the scientific works which

Congress caused to be carried on in connection with the surveys of the new territories extending along the shores of the Atlantic and the Pacific. The numerous staff required for these undertakings, although the scientific attainments of many of its members may not be of the highest character, will nevertheless in all probability form a nucleus around which all those who are interested in natural science will gradually group themselves. Not less important are the inducements to historic and philologic researches which have of late sprung up, and which have already borne good fruit. It is undeniable that, although the number of those who devote themselves to serious scientific investigations is as yet but small, it is nevertheless increasing in a remarkable degree; and although an exclusive devotion to literature and science has hitherto, by the great majority, been considered incompatible with the duties which a citizen owes to the State, persons may now be met with who have placed themselves in this category.

There is one institution in America which promises to exercise a considerable influence on the development of science and of scientific life. This is the Smithsonian Institution in Washington, which has only been in activity during the last few years, and regarding which I subjoin some notices.

An Englishman, John Smithson by name, having bequeathed by will upwards of half-a-million dollars to the United States for the foundation in Washington of an institution, bearing his name, "for the increase and diffusion of knowledge among men,"[6] and the trust having been accepted by the Government of the United States, the learned institution in question was finally organized in 1846. The fund by that time amounted to 750,000 dollars. In virtue of the Act of Congress granting a Charter to the Institution, it is placed under the direction of a "Board of Regents," consisting of the President of the United States, who acts as chairman; of the Vice-President; the Chief Justice of the Supreme Court of the United States; the Mayor of Washington (those are members *ex officio);* three Members of the Senate, and three Members of the House of Representatives, elected in and by their respective houses, and of six other Members elected by the two houses concurrently. In

---

[4] I could, for instance, name several young American chemists who have studied in the laboratories of Europe.

[5] The political disturbances in Europe, which force so many men of talent and information to emigrate, will, no doubt, exercise a great influence on the intellectual and artistic development of America.

---

[6] Smithson had never been in America; and, as far as I have been able to learn, he could have had no personal reasons for selecting the United States as the executors of his will.

addition to this supreme ruling body, the officials of the Institution are, one secretary, one assistant secretary (who is at the same time librarian), and an executive committee, consisting of three members. The Act alluded to above further enacts that a library, a museum of natural history, and a museum of mineralogy and geology, shall be attached to the Institution, and further, that it shall be provided with the instruments necessary for carrying on physical investigations, as also that the delivery of popular lectures shall be included in its objects. The regular plan of organization having been left to the Regents, it fell happily into the hands of persons fully competent to undertake the responsible task, and able to dispose, in the most judicious manner, of the immense sums confided to them for the advancement of science. In connection herewith, Professor Bache, who was one of the Members of the Executive Committee, and Professor Henry, the Secretary, are particularly deserving of mention. The detailed plan of the Institution, drawn up by the latter, is a masterly document, in point of science, as also an excellent interpretation of the concise provisions of Smithson's will, and would alone suffice to show the high scientific position attained by the writer. According to this plan, the chief functions of the Institution will be to encourage original scientific investigations, to publish the results of these, and to issue annual reports on the progress of science. The transactions of the Institution have already been introduced to the learned world under the name of the "Smithsonian Contributions to Knowledge;" and researches into the natural history, meteorology, &c., of the United States, have been commenced under its auspices. No branch of knowledge is excluded from the sphere of the Institution. By judicious economy, it has been possible, after erecting a stately palace for the purposes of the Institution, and having made several purchases for the library, as well as for the collection of scientific instruments, to invest a sum of 650,000 dollars, the annual interest on which, amounting to about 40,000 dollars, is to be applied to the maintenance of the Institution; the half being appropriated to the extension of the collections, the other half to the support of scientific investigations and observations, the publication of learned dissertations, &c.

There are several other learned and scientific institutions in America with similar objects, but none of them command as extensive resources as the Smithsonian Institution. As regards their organization, these institutions come under two heads, some being organized somewhat on the pattern of the old European academies of science and literature, others on more democratic and popular principles, such as obtain in the various modern literary and scientific associations. There can be no doubt as to which of these systems will ultimately prevail in America, and will be the most effective as regards the advancement of literature and science. I must indeed be greatly mistaken, if the civilization of the future do not everywhere pronounce in favour of the more popular organization. To render this more clear, I will cast a glance at the learned and scientific societies of Europe, and at the influence which they exercise at present on the development of science and literature in our hemisphere.

It is impossible to approach without a feeling of reverence institutions whose history is so intimately connected with the history of modern science and literature, and with the names of so many individuals of high merit. Yet if, without allowing ourselves to be blinded by the halo which surrounds them, we examine them more closely, we cannot but detect that "there is something rotten" in these institutions, which prevents their exercising the quickening influence which might be expected from them in the present day; and I have no hesitation in saying, that this is the *spirit of caste* which prevails in them, and is a necessary consequence of the manner in which they are organized.

In the first place, I think there is not a single thing effected by the institutions in question, which might not as well be effected without them. They publish Transactions; but are there not many instances to show that this can be done by others, as well as by academies? They sometimes supply the Governments with information and advice on scientific subjects; but might not such information be obtained from other and equally reliable sources? Might it not, for instance, be obtained as well from the very same persons, who sit in the judgment seat in the academies, after they have doffed their academical uniform? Further, as regards the scientific collections, the maintenance and extension of which are entrusted to the academies, it may be said that for this purpose funds are required, but not academies. Finally, as regards the encouragements given to science and learning in the form of prizes or pecuniary assistance for carrying out independent researches and investigations, &c., these are no doubt very valuable and very necessary; but has it not been proved in our day, that scientific and literary associations can hold forth the same encouragements without being subjected to an academic organization? Has not, for instance, the British Association for the Advancement of Science put forth a degree of activity and exercised an influence which has never been equalled by any academy? If such be the beginning, (for in fact only a *beginning* has been made as regards the attempts to exercise, by these means, an influence on the development of higher intellectual life,) may we not with good reason look forward to a new era in literature and science? And may it not be said that the time of the academies has gone by, and that we ought to be on the look-out for other means by which to attain the object in view?

While fully acknowledging the good that academies of science and literature have effected, we ought not to overlook the disadvantages accruing from the mode of their organization. These disadvantages are such as could not but arise when learning and genius were forced into the narrow bounds of a corporation, dressed in uniform, and even sometimes invested with political rights. Under such circumstances, it is almost impossible that intrigue, narrow-mindedness, and the spirit of caste should not be developed; and we ought not to be surprised at seeing tractableness and decorum more valued in academies than true merit, and mediocrity and academical gravity more highly appreciated than true learning and genius; nay, even mental incapacity and scientific and literary nullity making their way, if they be but accompanied by a sufficient amount of subtle party spirit. We ought not to be surprised at seeing in these institutions a cringing respect for rank, power, and riches, nor at beholding the means intended for scientific and literary purposes used as instruments for promoting the ends of private favour or disfavour, or of political intrigues. We ought not to be astonished at seeing dawning talent neglected, nay, even opposed, by institutions whose duty and vocation it ought to be to seek for such talent, and to rear it with fostering care, but which jesuitically make it their business to "honour" talent when it has already obtained celebrity, in order that they may clad themselves in the borrowed lustre. Whoever is at all acquainted with the internal history of the class of institu-

tions to which I am here alluding, cannot deny that all that I have said is more than hypothetically true. Unfortunately, such things exist in reality in a much higher degree than most persons have any conception of.

But if such be the case, we must not flatter ourselves that the consequences will not be felt beyond the halls of the academy. Moral disease is always contagious; and the corruption, the existence of which is revealed by the symptoms to which I have alluded, must exercise as baneful and retarding an influence on the development of science and literature as the trade guilds exercised on the development of the manual and mechanical arts.

The sciences are no longer secrets known to a certain brotherhood only, and the time will come when they will no longer thrive within the musty chapter-houses in which the antiquated guild-spirit loves to keep them imprisoned. The time will come when scientific and literary development will be placed on a *popular* basis, by which I mean not only that they will exercise a more powerful influence on all classes and individuals, but also that they will be cultivated and advanced by all. America, in particular, must look forward to such a development on a democratic foundation; and, for my part, I cannot doubt that the results, should they even not be felt for some decenniums, or even for some generations, will ultimately incalculably exceed all the results we have ever experienced of the activity of our present learned and scientific institutions. In America, in particular, it will be proved, and, indeed, it has, in a measure, already been proved, that the more exclusive a learned or scientific body be, and the more it departs from the democratic form as regards its organization, the less influence it will exercise on the advancement of literature and science. The mean and corrupting spirit of coterie cannot exist in America as long as the present political and social institutions prevail.

Another question connected with the above subject, and which is of much importance, is, whether circumstances in America are more favourable for the development of some branches of science than of others, and, if so, which are the branches that are most favoured? Those who hold the Americans to be pre-eminently a practical people—and the number of these is very large—are generally inclined to think that the natural sciences not only are exclusively cultivated in America, but also that they form the most essential ingredient in the national culture. I confess such was my own impression before I visited the country, but I found the reality very different from my expectations. Although I had constant opportunities of admiring the fresh and active mental life that prevails throughout the country, and which reveals itself in all directions, I was much surprised to find how comparatively low a rank the natural sciences held as regards this mental life. I have already shown that, although the natural sciences are not entirely excluded from the learned schools, the latter must nevertheless be considered chiefly as institutions for teaching the classical languages; and it is easy to see what a bias this must give to the thoughts and interests of the scholars. Further, if we observe what is taking place independently of this class, within the sphere of popular education;—if, for instance, we observe what are the subjects most generally treated by the public lecturers, we are surprised to find that history, philosophy, æsthetics, in a word, the subjects which are included under the name of polite learning, occupy an incomparably greater amount of attention than the natural sciences; and if we look into the periodical literature, as well as other branches of original literature, we find ourselves plunged into an ocean of poetry, elocution, philosophy, &c., while only here and there we see the natural sciences rearing their heads above the surrounding waters. Indeed, it is surprising to meet in "practical" America so many persons who are quite at home in all the theoretical-philosophical systems of Germany, &c. I do not, of course, mean to deny that America possesses many very eminent scientific men, and that the natural sciences also are very generally cultivated among the people; but, as compared to other subjects, they certainly hold the subordinate position which I have indicated, and it is easy to discern to what side American civilization particularly tends.

If we inquire into the causes of this state of things, we shall find that they chiefly reside in the political institutions. Independently of the inducements to the study of rhetoric, history, and philosophy, which are held out by public life, there is another, and a deeper reason, why the "humanities" must always maintain a superior position in a democracy. In the ancient republics it was the same, and, when we contemplate the height to which the polite sciences attained

in those republics, we cannot help feeling surprised that the natural sciences should have made so little progress among the people of antiquity. But the cause is this: in a democratic community *man* is the chief object of interest, and therefore the studies which relate to man must have the most attractions. In an aristocratic or despotic State only comparatively few individuals are considered of any weight or value, all others are merely important in as far as they serve as means for the attainment of some object, never because of their humanity, and to encourage inquiries into the capacities and possible developments of the human mind, would be in direct opposition to the interests of such forms of government. The Emperor of Russia will certainly not be found to favour independent historical and philosophical research—a research which tends to show what *man* has been, and what he may be on earth; but he will not object to grace his country with rich and excellent observatories, and to see the lustre of his reign increased by the discoveries of many a renowned astronomer, who possesses the quality, invaluable in his eyes, of centring his whole attention on the heavens. There is no reason why he should not overwhelm with honours the chemist who analyses the minerals from his Siberian mines, in the miserable depths of which, however, languishes many an individual whom he has sent there to expiate the offence of having endeavoured to analyze the deepest and most sacred feelings of the human heart. He listens with pleased attention to descriptions of all the animals and plants in his vast realm, and encourages every attempt to improve the breeds of domestic animals, but let no one attempt to speak of or endeavour to ameliorate the condition of his 60,000,000 Russian serfs. How different is it not in a republic, where the people as a whole, and every citizen in particular, is of infinite greater value than all the kingdoms of nature together! It seems to me self-evident, that in such a State the sciences that relate to man must predominate; and in America this is so much the case, that the interest felt in man seems even to be extended to his physical being, for although human physiology is not the science which is *most* cultivated, yet it enters much more into popular education than in Europe.

But, however correct this reasoning may be, and however much some circumstances seem to bear witness to its truth, it would nevertheless be precipitate to conclude that the natural sciences will not thrive or attain any high degree of development in the United States. If we hold in view the height to which these sciences have at present attained, and the rapid progress which they are every day making, it is impossible to believe otherwise, than that, in spite of less favourable conjunctures, they will take root and flourish in all countries where liberty of investigation produces taste for investigation. Besides this, we must not forget the extraordinary improvements in all branches of industry in the United States, and the intimate connection which exists between modern industry and the natural sciences, a circumstance which is quite sufficient to secure to these sciences every support and encouragement which they may require.

All that has been said in this chapter about literature and science may be equally applied to the fine arts. These also suffer, and will long have to suffer, from the absence of galleries, &c.; yet there are many evidences which show that the fine arts also are in course of development. When I mention—what will probably be known to the reader—that America already possesses artists who have won a European reputation, that it is becoming more and more common to decorate even private houses with works of art, and that annual exhibitions of paintings take place in the United States, I have at least stated some points which will serve to give an idea of the present state of the fine arts in America and of their future prospects.

One of the two or three art unions in New York, and the largest in the Union, had in 1849 about 18,000 members. This union pays as much as 1000 or 1500 dollars for the best pictures that it purchases. From this it appears that, although the fine arts in America are still in their infancy, they do not entirely lack encouragement. On the contrary it may be expected that, in a country where the power of association is so well known, this power will be brought to bear upon the fine arts also, and will do more to raise them, than could be effected by the capricious support of a few scattered Mecænases.

Israel Joseph Benjamin   1859

The Consequences of a Lack of Education

Israel Joseph Benjamin (1818–1864) was born in Falticeni, Rumania. A timber merchant for much of his early life, he later traveled widely to visit Jewish congregations in various parts of the world. Modeling his travels after the earlier journeys of Benjamin of Tudela, a medieval Spanish traveler, he visited North Africa and Asia in 1845 and North America in 1859. Benjamin's travels in North America are described in a two-volume work which was published shortly before he died in London.

Benjamin noted the problems that Jewish girls and women in the United States were having in obtaining an adequate education. This disturbed him because he felt that "not half the American Jewesses of the future are ready to take worthily and to fill properly the places in life appointed to them." He stated that "like electricity, enlightenment must have conductors to spread broadly through the community; the best conductors are the schools and the press." He was concerned that these "conductors" were not strong enough in America, and contemptuously dismissed higher education for its "shallowness," stating that tailors "become physicians in thirty-two weeks" and watchmen suddenly become "attorneys."

While Benjamin was critical of some aspects of American education, he had high praise for many American political institutions. His comments are informative, especially since they came from a self-made and virtually self-educated, though widely read, man.

The first and highest of the peremptory demands that religion and duty make upon every man of Israel is to give his children a good education, to prepare them for life, and to put into their hands the means for making their own way. The American schools furnish a guarantee of one aspect of this duty. But there is cause for concern that the

Israel Joseph Benjamin, *Drei Jahre in Amerika, 1859—1862* (Hanover: Selbstverlag des Verfassers, 1862); translated and edited by Oscar Handlin, in *This Was America* (Cambridge, Mass.: Harvard University Press, 1949), pp. 270–282. Copyright 1949 by the President and Fellows of Harvard College. Reprinted by permission.

provision, wisely made, to exclude there-from all religion and the study of the Holy Scriptures, leaves the daughters of Israel much neglected.

Jewish boys are, in the course of events, taken care of in religion, as are the sons and daughters of the Christians; they either attend a Jewish school or receive private instruction. But the case of the girls is quite different. In what a sad condition is the religious preparation of the future Jewish wives and mothers! How little they learn of their duties toward God and men! What do they know of the commandments which bind them as daughters of Israel? Should not those who are bound by the holiest religious duties be soundly prepared to fulfill them? These duties are numerous and heavy and one is astonished that not half the American Jewesses of the future are ready to take worthily and to fill properly the places in life appointed to them. Yet that is far too true.

The causes lie in neglect of their education. To illustrate this contention and to corroborate its truth it will be worth while to sketch the kind of schooling that American Jewish ladies now receive.

The mother of a daughter, any good-hearted, passably wealthy woman, seeks to impress upon the immature minds of her children as much good as she can. This private influence lasts until about the age of five. Then the child, it is clear, must go to a public school, or what seems more respectable, to a so-called "Institute." In the latter establishment the child begins a normal course of study, makes the acquaintance of friends of other religious persuasions, and may without shock and without meaning kneel down in the mornings at the opening of the school during the prayers offered by scholars of other religions.

After school, she prepares her lessons for the next day or plays as all children do. On going to bed or on getting up she may say a Hebrew or English prayer with her mother, but she learns little and knows nothing of what Judaism means. So the education of the girl continues until she is fifteen, except for the slight difference that in time she leaves the institute and goes to a high school or "college." At fifteen begins a new period in her life. At her birthday her mother and father have promised she will be free, she leaves school, graduates to her great joy.

What useful knowledge has she acquired in all this time? All in all, very little! She has passed ten precious years of her life in contact with all sorts of books, but has made little progress; the time is wasted, and generally forever. What she has acquired is of no use to her. She does not understand the use of the needle, has no knowledge of housework, and even less of higher things. Ask who created her, who clothes her, who gives her daily bread; she may give the proper answer, but more likely will say, "I did not learn that in my books."

During the ten years her good parents have increased their wealth and form the praiseworthy resolution that their daughter should not forget everything she learned. To complete her education they engage a music teacher, a singing teacher, a drawing teacher, a governess who will provide instruction in French, and also in sewing and weaving. To cap it all, they add a teacher who will furnish a Hebrew education and who will introduce her to the alphabet of a language in which she should, even as a child, have been lisping the name of God. The maiden, as might be expected, finds this last in the line of instructors irksome. The language seems silly, and also too difficult. She cries at her lessons, so that her indulgent parents, who suffer at her tears, give notice to the teacher who should have been the first engaged and the last dismissed. They have, however, out of a deficiency of true religious feeling, blundered onto the opposite path; they hire him last and let him go first.

Having in this manner completed her religious education, the young woman goes on much as before, saying the few prayers she learned as a child from her mother in English. If she occasionally visits the synagogue, she uses a prayer book in the same language. The remaining teachers soon earn the same dismissal as the Hebrew teacher. The maiden becomes capricious through the parties, balls, and soirees which now absorb her attention; her mind is distracted, she is hungry for the praise of the young men, and has no thoughts for learning. The young lady—she no longer lets herself be called a girl—believes that her education is complete in all branches and considers herself prepared to take her place in the world, prepared to make a man happy and to become a Jewish mother. I must also note that this is but one instance among a thousand that occur in this country with only slight variations.

Who is to blame for this altogether neglected education, the heedless girl or the overindulgent parents? I believe neither the maiden nor the parents are responsible. The former is like any other child; the latter do everything in their power to give their daughter the best possible education. They spend their wealth, their energy, their time, even their lives to make possible the highest attainable training, and they convince themselves without a doubt that they are successful. To their great distress they soon, but too late, become aware of their errors.

I blame neither the young woman, nor her parents. Rather the responsibility rests upon all the members of the whole Jewish community which as a body should, as is the case in England, France, and Germany, meet a general need and establish a Jewish school for boys and girls.

Having spoken about the education of Jewish women I would like to make a few comments on the training of Jewish young men, which is, alas, scarcely any better. The Jewish boy is sent to school from the age of six to sixteen, and learns to read, to write, and to reckon. No father has, however, spirit enough to indulge in a measure of scientific education or to allow his son to attain a higher education. As soon as the boy has a minimum of learning he is taken into the business, naturally without having attended a commercial school, since that is not necessary; the techniques of trade consist entirely of practical, mechanical exercises for making money. With facility in that line he soon earns the title of an educated man.

Only in the larger places has there recently been any concern with religious education and with knowledge of the Hebrew language. From all this it is sufficiently clear that no great learned men will spring up from among the American Jews. It is particularly notable that Jewish children very quickly find themselves at home in the American element. It is significant that they speak with their parents neither in German nor in Hebrew, but only in English and will answer only in that tongue, no matter in what language they are addressed. And so they adhere entirely to the American ways.

America worships two idols. First is that deaf, dumb, blind Mammon before whom the masses humbly bow in this land. They kneel before him, setting their honor aside, day and night thinking only of amassing wealth, of building palaces. The second idol, on the contrary, sees, hears, walks, and talks, and is above all full of life; it is the female sex. Both idols live together in constant warfare. What one builds, the other tears down; what

one accumulates, the other scatters; what one makes good, the other spoils.

The reign of the women is here complete. Unbelievable as it may sound, even in the courts the word of a woman of the lowest classes is given more credence than that of the most respectable man. I was told in New York that this legal situation was a few years ago carried so far that girls who took a fancy to a man they saw in the street would learn his name, address, and condition and go to court with the complaint that he had made a promise of marriage and failed to keep it. The men were then compelled to be married, against their wills, without the slightest consideration of the consequences of such a forced union. When married women no longer enjoy their passions, their love of dress, their idleness, and the other conditions under which they live, they leave their husbands and take no notice even of their children. Such incidents are almost a matter of course. They make daily reading matter in the American newspapers.

Let us examine more closely these women who are capable of perpetrating such evils. The American women have fine and gentle features, are very delicately built, and know better than any others in the world the art of adorning themselves. They are very bright in conversation, always vivacious, and passionately love music, singing, and dancing. Their education is poor and they have little understanding of how to raise children. Many, in fact, do not wish to have any children at all, out of fear of losing their beauty, and not infrequently resort to any remedy. A New York physician asked me whether the wicked custom still existed in the Orient by which women take a certain medicine to prevent pregnancy. There is also a reference in the Talmud to women who take a preparation in order to remain childless. An American doctor could surely earn a million dollars in a single year dispensing this concoction. I informed my questioner that I had made no observations on this subject but would not fail to note it on my next trip.

The women have a characteristic, innate, and ineradicable aversion to any work and to household affairs. They love sweets and delicacies to a degree that there are nowhere in the world so many dentists as here, and all make a good living. They are indispensable because the unbounded taste for sweets rots the teeth, so that artificial ones must take the place of the natural. What is more, many ladies allow whole rows of teeth to be extracted, as I myself saw, in order to replace them with prettier ones. And though this is known and should frighten the other sex away, yet their beauty and enticements still allure men with irresistible force.

Of love, the salt of the earth, these females know nothing. Let the man only have money enough to indulge them in luxuries, then he is good enough for a husband, be he old or young, handsome or plain, religious or atheist. Let the money vanish, and with it will go faith and love. I might mention here an interpretation of a passage in the Talmud. We know that Eve, who ate and got her husband to eat the apple that brought mortality with it, was created from Adam's rib while he was asleep. Now the Talmud tells us that "when God decided to create man, he took a bit of earth from every part of the world and thereof fashioned man." Surely the rib, from which woman was created, must have originated in American soil and therefore had sensuality inherent in it. While Adam was poor and unable to satisfy her taste for luxuries, life was a burden to her and she sought to do away with herself, and with him; or, alternatively, she gave him the apple out of jealousy so that he should not take up with another woman. Such instances are not rare, in America at least.

I sought the source of woman's position here, and believe that it lies in the circumstance that, at the first peopling of America, there were so few females that a man counted it a great fortune to find a woman. He had little choice and was compelled to overlook her weaknesses and deficiencies, married her more often than not like an idol. Though there is now by no means a shortage of women, this attitude is well established.

Before us lies a little pamphlet, a speech made in New York by a lady on America and the destiny which, she says, "the Spirits" have prepared for it. The idea finds credence, and people stream from all quarters to listen to the inspirations of the Spirits commanded by the lady. This single incident characterizes the American spirit; it is deplorable that such a gross swindle should find admirers and adherents amongst a people whom Morse and Mitchell in their geography call most enlightened. How can one be angry with the witchcraft, the manias, and the other superstitious incidents pursued by humanity from time immemorial when the most enlightened people raises up in its midst Mormons, Millerites, and similar abnormalities! Why speak of the delusions of the Middle Ages when we saw with our own eyes the most enlightened nation flock to the prophetess of this superstition. And one may be sure that a fraud will find more believers, supporters, and participants, the bigger, the sillier, and the more absurd it is.

The calm and dispassionate observer might, in the face of such manifestations, have doubts as to the soundness of human understanding and come close to thinking that the world will easily be inherited by villains and swindlers. It is hard to say this, but it must be said. He is no true friend who only smiles at his neighbor and gilds the flaws in his character. And he is no true friend of the American people who enhances and supports the self-complacency and the self-deception from which the Americans suffer. The author of these lines loves this land and its people as his own and chooses it by a free choice. He may be allowed to speak freely, for what he says comes not from a passion for finding fault.

First of all, the claim to be the most enlightened of peoples is a kind of self-deception. In this land there is not a single seat of learning that could be compared with such minor universities as those of Padua, Jena, Göttingen, or Halle, to say nothing of the great institutions in England, France, in Berlin, St. Petersburg, and Vienna. This is one of the most certain criteria of learning. Enlightenment is not a plant that grows of itself, that springs spontaneously from the soil without care and attention; it is rather a blossom that never unfolds without the supporting hands of man.

From what sources could exceptionally enlightened principles, practices, or doctrines have been fashioned here? Like electricity, enlightenment must have conductors to spread broadly through the community; the best conductors are the schools and the press. The American public schools are scarcely two decades old and still suffer from the deficiencies which normally retard new institutions. The shallowness of the colleges, academies, and seminaries is commonly known. Young ladies study astronomy before they know how to spell properly; young men attain the doctorate after they rush through a mixed-up mass of Greek, Latin, mathematics, French, German, natural philosophy, chemistry, history, geography, logic, mental and moral philosophy, and still other subjects, in two or three years without ever having mastered one of them. Tailors, shoemakers, farmers, shop assistants become physicians in thirty-two weeks; policemen, watchmen, constables all of a sudden become attorneys. Any man who feels in himself the capacity for becoming a preacher, teacher, politician, statesman, or diplomat soon finds himself a sphere of activity. The whole ridiculous superficiality is yet not by far so clumsy and disgusting as the pedantry of the half-educated teachers and pedagogues who kill the spirit with words and formulae. Can we then see here a soil to nurture the most enlightened of people? The schools are still too young and the colleges too immature.

The press is likewise not strong enough. This field is dominated by the absence of principles, by the concern with making money only, and by a superficiality that makes pictures and other devices conceal its shortcomings. Here, too, other nations have a great advantage. There is no journal in the United States that is worthy of being placed beside the press of London, or the French and German periodicals. Here every kind of trash finds in the press some defender and patron, if only it will pay well enough. The result is that the newspaper is not always a beacon of light for the community, not always the honest and true chronicler of daily history, not the torch of progress and learning, but often simply a speculative enterprise in the hands of profit-seeking parties who only publish that which will do them the most good. One will seek in vain for earnestness or love of the truth, and more easily come upon articles that simply excite sensations, upon bombastic words and immoral announcements. The press is not here the mistress but too often only the pitiful servant of the people, gathering up the crumbs of news that fall from the richly laden table of humanity. Such a press could not and can not lift a people to the highest levels of enlightenment.

Nor will contemporary literature do so. With the exception of a few old names there are no sparkling intellects or radiating geniuses in the arts. But we will be countered in defense of the country with the assertion, "It is the freedom for which our fathers bled and died, it is the constitution and the laws which our wise ancestors left us which make us the most enlightened people." More properly they should say, "which should have made us." Truly, such examples should have inspired a quite different spirit. The constitution and institutions only show that the fathers of the republic were very enlightened. But what is the status now of the constitution, in theory and practice? We must remain silent. Where is the constitution? Where is our liberty? We ask often but get no answers.

The firmest and most imposing structure of state that yet was erected by human hands on the solid basis of political and religious liberty, personal and civic freedom, is now threatened by a crash brought about by its own sons.

Its present shortcomings arise from no organic defects in the government of the United States, but rather from a rotting element of demagoguery which is found in many lands. The current position of the United States and the misfortunes that befell it, blow by blow, at the beginning of this war, encouraged its enemies to slander its constitution and derogate its institutions.

This war began through the abuse of freedom and wealth, just as a man may kill himself through overindulgence and immoderation. This abuse of the unlimited wealth of the land and of freedom took two forms, materialism and the neglect of learning. As quickly as our steamboats cut through the sea and as quickly as our locomotives fly across the western plains, even more quickly do we rush into materialism and ignorance. To make money now has a magnetic, a magic attraction. Public officials accept offices, and others long for them, simply to enrich themselves. They set themselves no more honorable objective; no purer motive moves them. The good of the commonwealth concerns them not at all. There are, of course, exceptions; honor and the public good are the stars that guide a few, but for the overwhelming mass it is money that serves that function. Have ever so many traitors among officials been discovered as here in the past few months of political squabbling? The reason is clear. Treachery is more profitable than loyalty; and he who is faithful only for the sake of gold is easily drawn into a betrayal when the tempter has a longer purse. Wealth is the key to respect, honor, and esteem.

Almost every man is therefore constrained to become a merchant, a banker, a speculator, or a manufacturer, to secure a position that will bring a sizable income. The child learns from his father, the pupil from his teacher, the scholar from his professor, that gold commands a mighty power in every circle of society. Cupidity enters the bloodstream at the expense of every gentler, better, and higher feeling, and is nourished with sacrifices of spiritual capacities and happiness. Thousands give up their health and their lives in the service of Mammon.

In consequence of this general overwhelming passion, the human spirit is altogether repressed; the determination, from childhood on, to make money, deforms the beauty of nature, the pleasantness of humane education, the truth of science, the loftiness of art, the holiness of religion, of morality, of truth, of honor, of duty. Everything is pushed to the background, takes a subordinate role. This is the center from which our demoralization proceeds. Why should the number of dishonest officials and of traitors seem remarkable? They travel the same road as all the others; they also make gold like the others and do not differentiate themselves from the crowd.

Here lies the source of the disease; this is truly the cancerous growth. The spirit of the American people is troubled by an illness that must arouse the liveliest apprehensions, an illness that ought not to be found in a constitutional state. The result is that now, after fifty years as a going concern, often brilliantly, the United States stands at the brink of the precipice and runs the risk of a fall unless a man appears who will help with advice and deeds.

We come now to the second point mentioned above, the place of learning. This too, like all else, is only the slavish handmaid of passions which are only worked up by the pursuit of wealth. Learning is not loved for its own sake; it is not resorted to as a sun to light up the way; it is rather another article of commerce. There are shops where professional politicians make up politics, and priest factories which deal in religion. The position of a professor, of a scholar, a thinker, a rabbi, or a preacher is thought of as his business. We have no time to do anything for ourselves and demand that our fellow men should earn money just as we do. We rejoice, when for our comfort they manufacture in advance shoes, boots, clothing, hats, also medicine, magnetic pills, galvanic circuits, health, morals, religion, truth, or any other commodity. For that reason, produce any absurdity whatsoever, if it is ridiculous enough to create a stir in this country it will be believed. Delusions, quackery, shams, ridiculous and childish superstitions each makes a profit and, as a matter of course, lasts a certain time, until it must make room for some other, from Barnum on down to the fortune-tellers, from Dr. Townsend's Sarsaparilla to the various stomach bitters, from John Smith and Miller down to Mr. Lederer of New York. We are so often deceived because we wish to be deceived.

Under such conditions science cannot thrive. Where these are the prevailing conditions, they lead to the following conclusion: Everyman knows everything and is capable of doing anything. Circumstances teach here any man knows everything and can set himself to any job without studying it and without previous experience. In this country we come across a professor who allowed himself to become a bookbinder and bookdealer, that is to say a good husband. His life's task was unsuccessful. Instead of applying himself to science to develop and further to educate himself, he was compelled, like all those around him, to make money after his fashion. We meet a professional astronomer, distinguished in his subject, but who must occupy himself with civil engineering. Most fortunate are many doctors who never learned very much but give themselves over to boasting and swaggering and who do not miscalculate in doing so. Quacks and frauds have the greatest influence and are almost every place the arbiters of the spirit. Everyone must concede that learning still stands here at a very low point. The students have no time to concern themselves for long with serious studies, they must hurry right through. But in the rush there can be no thorough mastery of any subject.

There is no trick to being a captain, so long as the sea is quiet, but when a storm blows up the experienced seaman begins to take precautions. As long as freedom and unity reigned undisturbed over the American ship of state, every man was good enough and competent to hold office; but now, at the first serious storm, the consequences emerge of the simple-minded system by which every man knows and is capable of everything. Yet the trial through which we must now pass will show us how small we are in our overblown pride, will teach us that there are higher and more important interests than gold and luxury. So long as it is the highest aim of each individual to amass goods and possessions, so long will that also be the highest aim of a nation which, after all, is made up of individuals.

Some of the general causes having been sketched above, it is now time to say something of the more particular elements. The weaknesses of a community must in large measure be reflected in the school, the church, and the state, the institutions with the greatest influence upon the members of the community.

The press has more than once revealed the fact that the public schools are only hothouses for memory, calculation, craftiness, and indifferent minds, and leave untouched and altogether uncultivated the higher capacities of youth, the noble impulses and lofty ideals of young hearts.

After a child's love of learning, his aptitude for reflection, and his independent thinking have been thoroughly stifled by several years of eternally deadening spelling, he is crammed full of a mass of names, from geography, history, and grammar. These remain only words, are never understood, never take on flesh and blood meanings. The child absorbs nothing but words. For assistance he has the textbook, which the poor student must learn without comprehending. The mind is in this manner exercised and overtaxed for six or eight years at the expense of the higher intellectual capacities, and nine times out of ten the scholar forgets, since it is all absorbed without reflection, in one year what he has learned in six.

Arithmetic also belongs in the class of studies of dead words. Here, too, in most cases there is only an exercise of the capacity to remember. Even in the most fortunate cases when it is properly learned with a plan and system to develop ideas, it then develops simply the capacity for cold, earnest, and sly calculation that is by no means natural or educational for the young spirit.

What is left now for the moral aptitudes of youth which also should be fostered, and what is done for that? Nothing. They earn not even a glance in education. In this case, externals reflect the internal conditions; and the site and structure of the schoolhouse characterize the spirit of the school. We see schoolhouses on a plot of land on which no blade of grass, no tree sprouts, while in Europe on most of the land around the building luxuriant flowers and plants flourish, and in the larger cities exceptional sums are spent on gardens, to aid in learning botany, more particularly pomiculture and gardening, and to awaken a feeling for nature. In American schools there is not the least idea taught about living nature; everything presented to the student is dead and deadening. He is offered only words and more words,

and gloomy calculations which are alien to nature, which do not suit the moral feelings, and which have no regard for the thousand beauties of God's creation, or for the honorable impulses which rest in the breasts of men and live in the figures of history. Under such conditions does the student leave the public schools and enter into the general stream of life.

Let us now glance at the few exceptional cases—very few, in comparison with the number who attend the elementary schools—who go on to the academies, the seminaries, high schools, colleges, or however else the facilities for higher education may be entitled.

We begin with the young ladies who are expected to learn Latin, Greek, and mathematics, subjects which are not included in our first part. No greater perversion of nature is conceivable! The young woman whose every nerve is sensitive, whose heart is full of gentle emotions, in whom the admiration of the good and the beautiful is innate, must fix in her memory mathematical formulae and the paradigms of Latin and Greek which she will forget within a year after having graduated with honors. Similarly with history; here there is no effort by the instructor to demonstrate the connections of cause and effect, to demonstrate the wisdom of Providence or cautiously to use it as a model for life. The teacher simply says, "You must learn ten pages for the next assignment," and so the poor creatures overload their minds without deriving the least profit from their torments.

A few mechanically learn music (piano), drawing, and painting, but the principles of aesthetics with their very intimate consequences for feminine feelings are altogether neglected. Others get to the study of natural philosophy and chemistry, but without instruments or laboratory. They investigate astronomy without observatories, learn botany in the winter in their rooms, and study the crystallization of snow and ice in the summer; the conception of uniting studies with nature itself and with its manifestations seems to occur to no one.

Let us now turn to the institutions for young men, in which we discover precisely the same deficiencies, joined to a superficiality that comes from the neglect of the older and newer classics. Of all the branches of knowledge, only mathematics is truly studied.

No one learns in the schools how to study

by himself; the great goal toward which all the reading is aimed is to pass examinations. The human is thus alienated both from art and nature; all is judged by its immediate utility.

The consequence is that we meet among educated men so much egotism, so little interest in the public welfare and concern for private good. A gentleman, to whom I once expressed my astonishment at the number of perjuries and public frauds, remarked to me, "Not all are infected, not all are corrupt, only those, unbelievable as it may sound, who are well educated; we get fresh men from the common mass." There is a creeping disease here which must be healed from the roots unless this republic be brought ever nearer decay.

James Fraser

1865

An Official English Report on American Education

James Fraser (1818-1885), an Anglican prelate, was educated at Lincoln College, Oxford. He was appointed fellow of Oriel College as a tutor in 1842 and served as a clergyman in Wiltshire and Berkshire from 1847 to 1870. Fraser was then consecrated Bishop of Manchester. He was appointed assistant commissioner of the Royal Commission on Education in 1856, and during the year 1865 he visited the United States and Canada in an official capacity.

Fraser's observations of American schools are both professional and philosophical. He was an amusing and fair commentator noting that "an American teacher may be immoral, ignorant . . . but he, and particularly she, could hardly be dull." He reported that he saw inefficient schools in America but the "drowsy dullness . . . and the inattentive habits . . . which characterize so many an English school, I never saw."

In endeavoring to comprehend and appreciate this system of common or public schools—for the two epithets are used indifferently—it is absolutely necessary that the European observer should throw his mind, if possible, into the conditions of American life, should take his point of departure from a few leading social principles, and keep constantly before his eyes certain salient social phenomena, which have (so to speak) necessitated its form, give to it its significance, underlie its action, maintain its motive power, determine its methods, and fix its aims. The *principles* have been already referred to; they are the principles of perfect social equality and absolute religious freedom. The *phenomena* are the restlessness and activity of the American character, —without, perhaps, the culture and refinement of the old Athenian, but with all his versatility,—the absorbing interest of political life; the constantly rising aims of each individual; the ebb and flow of commercial enterprise, and the immense development of the spirit of speculation; the intense energy of the national temperament, its rapidity of movement, its precipitancy, its impatience of standing still. Many an American in the course of an active life will have turned his hand to half a dozen different professions or ways of getting a livelihood. "The one lesson we are taught all through life," a person one day humorously but truly said to me, "is to be *dis*contented with our station."

And it is this temper more than any other, intensified by the opportunities that the country affords and the prizes that it holds out to enterprise and ability, which is the motive power that sustains the schools. Corresponding, therefore, with these ideas, and reflecting these phenomena, must be the proper system of education. And the correspondence is marvellously exact, the reflection wonderfully true. The American school is a microcosm of American life. There reigns in it the same spirit of freedom and equality; the same rapidity of movement, scarce leaving time for work to be thoroughly well done; the same desire of progress, eagerly catching at every new idea, ever on the look out for improvements; the same appeals to ambition, the same sensi-

James Fraser, *Report on the Common School Systems of the United States and the Provinces of Upper and Lower Canada*, of the School Inquiry Commission on Middle-Class Schools, Vol. II (London, 1886); the extract is taken from *The American Journal of Education*, III (1870), 577-580.

tiveness to praise and blame, the same subordination of the individual to the mass, of the scholar to the class, as of the citizen to the nation; the same prominence given to pursuits of a utilitarian, over pursuits of a refining, aim; the same excessive and exhausting strain on the mental and physical powers; the same feverishness and absence of repose;—elements of strength and weakness, of success and failure, mingled together in proportions which make it almost impossible to find any one discriminating epithet by which to characterize the resultant whole.

I. First, then, the system is in perfect harmony with the other institutions of the country. It is democratic, equal, free. But democratic institutions do not work with their full freedom and equality where the rapid growth of material prosperity is introducing social distinctions, and where, if not an aristocracy of birth or nobility, yet an aristocracy of wealth is being insensibly, but surely, formed. And so the American schools, particularly in the large cities and in the higher grades, are practically in the possession of the middle class. The sons and daughters of the wealthiest (with a few exceptions, which only prove the rule) are not in them; nor, in many places, the sons and daughters of the poorest either. The efficiency of the system—in the sense of its actually supplying the wants of every class of society, and really furnishing *common* schools—is nearly in an inverse ratio to the prosperity of the district in which it operates.

And further, the school, from its very harmony with other institutions, is exposed to the same corrupting influences; and as in some places the posts of municipal authority have fallen into the hands of unscrupulous politicians, who use their vantage ground to promote, not the public weal, but the interests of their party, so, we have seen, in the same places it is distinctly alleged that the politicians are doing their best to taint and spoil the schools.

II. Again. The system exactly answers the wants of the people; their wants, I mean, as they understand them themselves. The principle of local self-government being supreme in the constitution of the schools, what people require, that they can have; at least, all is in their own hands.

What ought to be the school's greatest source of strength—the fact that its destinies are in the hands of those who are to profit directly by its advantages—proves,

under the influence of selfish or sordid motives, in too many cases to be its principal element of weakness.

III. The system is a cheap system. In places where sordid views prevail it is made cheap at the cost of efficiency; by reducing the time during which the school is kept open to the narrowest limit; by cutting down the salaries of the teachers to the lowest sum; by neglecting to furnish it with the needful supplies of apparatus and books. But in cities where the support is most liberal, and indeed any sum that is asked for is given, still the system is cheap; 25s. to 30s. a year per child in the lower grades, 6l. to 10l. per year in the high school. The economy results from the principle of grading, and from the number of children of equal attainments in the same class who can be taught by the same teacher as though they were but one. Schools in England might be made as cheap if they could be organized on the same system. Throw all the schools of Edinburgh or London under one board of management, grade them, entrust each teacher with the oversight of 50 pupils, and the cost per child would probably be as low with us as it is in the United States. But in a graded school the class is the unit to the teacher's eye, and not the individual girl or boy, and what is gained in cheapness is almost lost again in thoroughness; and it is too much the tendency of all teachers, without the direct encouragement of the system under which they are working, to act upon the maxim, "Occupet extremum scabies.". If discrimination is a high gift in a teacher, there is very little scope or necessity for its exercise in a graded school.

IV. The spirit of work produced under the system both in teachers and pupils, and the discipline of the schools, are both high. The teachers are constantly under the eye of the public, are placed in keen competition one with another, and anxiously look forward to the figures which will show in the Superintendent's next report how their school compares with other schools of the same grade. They are kept up to the full tension of their strength; sometimes, indeed, the tension is too great for their strength, and I frequently heard teachers say they wanted rest—a want which their worn, hectic looks abundantly showed.

Continued idleness, again, in a pupil, such as is allowed without any very strong effort to correct it, at Eton and elsewhere, would not be tolerated in an American school. The influence of idleness is felt to be contagious.

If a boy won't work he must not by a bad example corrupt his schoolfellows—he must be withdrawn. Discipline, too, is nearly perfect in the best schools, but it is of a kind to which it would be hopeless to attempt to get 500 English boys of the upper or middle class to submit, and which even by many Americans is considered too repressive and mechanical.

I do not know that the aggregate results of the system can be better summed up than by saying that there exists in America a general diffusion of intelligence rather than any high culture or profound erudition. If I were to compare them with the results of the best education at home, I should say that an American pupil probably leaves school with more special knowledge, but with less general development. He would have more acquaintance (not very profound, though) with certain branches of physical science; perhaps more, certainly as much, acquaintance with mathematics, but not more acquaintance with modern languages, and much less acquaintance with ancient languages and classical literature. I think our best teachers are better (perhaps because more regularly educated) than their best; but our worst teachers are incomparably worse, duller, more immethodical, more indolent, more uninteresting, than anything I saw or can conceive of being tolerated among them. An American teacher may be immoral, ignorant, and in many ways incompetent, but he, and particularly she, could hardly be dull. Liveliness and energy, hiding sometimes perhaps a multitude of other sins, seem to be their inherent qualities. I saw in America many inefficient schools, but the drowsy dullness of the teacher and the inattentive habits of the children, which characterize so many an English school, I never saw.

The mistake that is commonly made in America is one, I fear, that is taking some root in England—a confusion of thought between the processes that convey knowledge and the processes that develop mental power, and a tendency to confine the work of the school too exclusively to the former. It is perhaps the inevitable tendency of an age of material prosperity and utilitarian ideas. Of course, the processes of education are carried on through media that convey information too, and a well-educated man, if not necessarily, *is*, at any rate almost necessarily *becomes*, a well-informed man. But, in my sense of things, the work of education has been successfully accomplished when a scholar has learnt just three things—what he really *does* know, what he does *not* know, and *how* knowledge is in each case acquired; in other words, education is the development and training of *faculties*, rather than, to use a favorite American word, the "presentation" to the mind of *facts*. What was Aristotle's conception of the man whom he calls "thoroughly educated?" Not, I take it, a man of encyclopædic information, but a man of perfectly trained and well-balanced mind, able to apply to any subject that may occupy his attentions its proper methods, and to draw from it its legitimate conclusions. Hence, the proper functions of a sound system of education are to quicken the observation, strengthen the memory, discipline the reason, cultivate the taste; and that is the best system which gives to each faculty of our complex nature its just and proportionate development. The American schools devote themselves far too exclusively to the two former aims; the latter two receive much less attention than they deserve. The results are such as might be expected to flow from any one-sided and partial treatment of the human mind. Subjects are constantly "memorized" without being understood, and hence their stay in the memory is precarious and transitory, while, though facts are observed, they are not sufficiently classified, and the reasoning powers and the taste, the latter especially, are left to form themselves pretty much at will. The programme of the schools, particularly in the higher grades, is too wide and multifarious. Subjects are taken up for a while and then dropped (and presently forgotten) to make room for others that have been long waiting their turn. When occasionally expressing my surprise that an important subject like a language, French or German for instance, after being studied for three or four terms, then disappeared from the programme, and did not seem afterwards to be resumed, I was met by the invariable explanation that it got "crowded out." I doubt whether American school managers accept the maxim, "Ne multa sed multum," as true of the process of education. In nothing did the managers of the Boston schools seem to me to give greater evidence of good sense and wisdom than in the manifest desire they showed to contract their programme into narrower limits, and to attach more importance to sound methods than to showy but superficial results.

I have spoken of the cultivation of taste as an element of education. The great defect, in my judgment, in American taste, literary as well as other, is, speaking generally, its apparent incompetency to appreciate the beauty of simplicity, which really constitutes the charm of the merely graceful and the grandeur of the sublime. De Tocqueville has noticed, with his usual perspicacity, the preference of American orators and writers for a bombastic and inflated style.

In touching upon this point of national taste some allowance must be made for the rareness, inevitable in a new country where the conquest of the soil and the development of material wealth is the primary concern of the people, of art-museums, picture galleries, and those other instrumentalities which have been found so efficacious in older civilizations in teaching the public mind to recognize and appreciate the grand, the beautiful, the pure. There are said to be fine works of art in the possession of private collectors in America; but there is hardly such a thing as a public gallery of paintings or of sculpture worthy the name.... With so few standards, therefore, of artistic beauty and proportion to exhibit to the eye, there exists all the greater need that the best models of accurate thought and chastened feeling, as expressed in language, should be presented to the mind; and as the printing press has made the whole range of classic literature common ground, it is to be regretted that influences which are out of reach are not compensated by others which are at hand, and that Homer and Virgil, Plato and Cicero, Sophocles and Terence, are not made to do for America what they, in conjunction with Phidias and Raffaelle, and the other potent magicians in the world of art, have done for Europe.

The tone of an American school—that "nescio quid" so hard to be described, but so easily recognized by the experienced eye, so soon felt by the quick perceptions of the heart—if not unsatisfactory, is yet incomplete. It is true that the work of the day commences with the reading of the Word of God, generally followed by prayer. It is true that decorous if not reverent attention is paid during both those exercises; but the decorum struck me as rather a result or a part of discipline than as a result of spiritual impressions; there was no "face as it had been the face of 'an angel;'" no appearance of kindled hearts. The intellectual tone of the schools is high; the moral tone, though perhaps a little too self-conscious, is not unhealthy; but another tone, which can only be vaguely described in words, but of which one feels oneself in the presence when it is

really there, and which, for want of a better name, I must call the "religious" tone, one misses, and misses with regret....

It ought not to be hard to conjecture, after what has been said, which type of child abounds most in American schools. I doubt if the latter temper, however charming to the sentimentalist, would be either appreciated or fostered by those who watch the development of youthful faculties there. To "seem for aid parental to sue all wistfully" would be deemed at best an amiable weakness, likely to interfere seriously with ultimate success in life. The sooner an American boy learns to stand alone and depend solely on himself, the better all who are concerned about his well-doing seem to be pleased. The quick "thrill at touch of praise," the desire to excel, the ambition to be foremost, are found to be the most powerful motives to study, the most efficient instruments of discipline. Indeed, it may be doubted whether they are not employed to excess for this purpose. It is the custom to request visitors to the schools to make little speeches to the assembled pupils. The staple of most that I heard was the well-worn theme of the infinite career that lay before them, and the possibility of every boy who listened to the speaker becoming President of the United States, or occupying a position equally honorable and equally to be coveted. To my judgment, and in the judgment of not a few Americans themselves, there is far too much of this. Such addresses, no doubt, are stimulating; but it must be recollected that there are unhealthy stimulants; and I was told stories enough by sober people, who disapproved of the practice, of many a boy, conscious of talents and urged on by such motives, who, attempting one of these grand careers and failing, sank at last into nothing better than a discontented and mischievous politician.

It might be thought also that amid the wildness of religious fancy and the strangeness of theological opinions, which prevail in America to an extent far beyond anything within an Englishman's experience, the blessings of a fixed creed would be more easily recognized and more strongly felt than where traditional beliefs still largely influence public thought, and men are less tossed about by winds of doctrine. It is unnecessary to say, however, that no attempt to lay the foundations of such a creed, or in any way to presume that such a creed even exists, is made in the common schools.

I do not like to call the American system

of education, or to hear it called, *irreligious*. It is perhaps even going too far to say that it is *non-religious*, or purely secular. If the cultivation of some of the choicest intellectual gifts bestowed by God on man— the perceptions, memory, taste, judgment, reason; if the exaction of habits of punctuality, attention, industry, and "good behavior;" if the respect which is required and which is paid during the reading of a daily portion of God's holy Word, and the daily saying of Christ's universal prayer, are all to be set down as only so many contrivances for producing "clever devils," it would be vain to argue against such a prejudice. But if, as I believe, the cultivation of any one of

God's good gifts and the attempt to develop any one right principle or worthy habit are, so far as they go, steps in the direction, not only of morality but of piety, materials with which both the moralist and the divine, the parent and the Sunday-school teacher, may hope to build the structure of a "perfect man" which they desire, then it is manifestly ungenerous to turn round upon the system which does this, which supplies these materials of the building, and is prohibited by circumstances over which it has no control and to which it is forced to adapt itself from doing more, and stigmatize it with the brand of godlessness.

Sophia Jex Blake   1866

A Coeducational College: Oberlin

Sophia Jex Blake (1840–1912), an English author, studied medicine in London at a time when medical careers were not open to women. She was not permitted to receive a degree and went to the United States in 1866 to travel and to continue her medical studies. During her stay in America she visited Antioch and Oberlin Colleges which particularly interested her because of their experiments in coeducation. Some of the students were Civil War veterans and their manners and speech upset Sophia Blake greatly; she thought that "the roughness of manners at Oberlin seemed greater than elsewhere." As an Englishwoman she was particularly disturbed by the "barbarous English" of the students; however, she gave full credit to Oberlin for opening a college career to women, something which she had been denied.

As we did not find the President at home when we first called on him, he very kindly paid us a return visit in the course of the afternoon, and gave us the most unqualified welcome to Oberlin, together with offers of personal aid and hospitality, which were, we found, the forerunners of similar kindness, almost without exception, throughout our whole tour of visits in the West, and, indeed, in all parts of the States into which we went. All the professors, teachers, and students with whom we came in contact showed us equal cordiality; and, our object being once understood, we were invited to attend any or all the "recitations" and classes at pleasure, and gladly took large advantage of this permission.

Every English traveller with such an object as ours in view, must, I think, be struck with the cordial welcome offered, and the facilities liberally given, by almost all in authority at the different centres of education in America, and, while acknowledging

it with the utmost gratitude, will probably be inclined to wonder regretfully whether an American teacher coming over to England would be likely to attain his or her object with equal ease. Of course, a great deal must be allowed for differences of temperament and habit, and the natural distinctions between an old country, with time-honoured usages both for good and evil, and a new one, where things are hardly enough systematized for comfort; but the fact is, I am afraid, undeniable, that it is a great deal easier to see, mark, and learn, in one country than in the other.

Who has not wished that such a thing as mental photography were possible? While I write I am conscious of the strongest wish to convey to those who care to know about Oberlin, and cannot see it for themselves, just the impression which my own mind received during a stay of ten days; comprising a series of constant visits to the different class-rooms, and frequent conversations with

Sophia Jex Blake, *A Visit to Some American Schools and Colleges* (London: Macmillan and Company, 1867), pp. 8–47.

the professors and teachers. But I find myself met at the outset by the extreme difficulty presented by the total unlikeness of all
I saw to anything English with which I can
compare it, the widely different conditions
of society in which the writer and the reader
find themselves, and the unfamiliar tones of
thought and life, of which it is so hard for
the one to convey an idea to the other.

Perhaps the present life of Oberlin will
be best understood by a reference to the
history of its origin and progress.

I take the following account of "Oberlin,
its Origin, Progress, and Results," from a
pamphlet by Professor Fairchild, originally
produced as an Address to the "Alumni of
Oberlin, 1860," and simply condense the information therein contained.

The plan of Oberlin originated with Rev.
J. Shipherd, the pastor of a Presbyterian
Church, and combined the expression of very
strong religious feeling with the desire for
an extensive and cheap system of education
for both sexes. It "involved a school, open
to both sexes, with various departments,
Preparatory, Teachers', Collegiate, and
Theological, furnishing a substantial education at the lowest possible rates," with
facilities for self-support by manual labour.
This school was to be surrounded by a
"Christian community, united in the faith of
the Gospel," and a convenant of "consecra-
tion to the work" was framed, binding its
subscribers to a "common purpose of glori-
fying God in doing good to men," to a
"community of interests as perfect as if a
community of property;" to an appropriation
of any surplus obtained by industry and self-
denial to the spread of the Gospel; to a
renunciation of "strong and unnecessary
drinks, even tea and coffee," and of "all
bad habits" (in which their successors, at
least, seem not to include incessant spitting),
as well as "tight dressing and ornamental
attire;" and to an endeavour to "extend the
influence of Oberlin to our fallen race."

These descendants of the Puritan fathers
succeeded, in 1833, in obtaining a site for
their purpose, in the centre of dense forests
still uncleared in the northern part of Ohio;
log cabins were erected in the same year;
and though the "Indian's hunting-path still
traversed the forest, and the howl of the
wolf was heard at night," a school was
opened at Christmas, and by the end of the
first year the pupils numbered one hundred.
In 1834 the first "*College* class" was organized, and in the course of that and the
following year students flocked in numerously, though for more than two years "the

devious tracks through the forests were
often impassable to carriages."

The distinctive spirit of Oberlin soon
found expression in a flourishing theological
school, the members of which spread through
the country during vacations, teaching and
preaching with great energy, as well as encouraging "temperance" and "anti-slavery"
meetings on all occasions, to the admiration,
as may be supposed, of some, and the great
disgust of others.

In the winter of 1834–5, the Trustees
took up their definite position with regard
to one of the questions then even more bitterly agitated than now, and decided it by the
free admission of all coloured students on
equal terms with the whites. This step marks
an epoch in the educational history of America; for though solitary coloured students
had been admitted at Dartmouth College,
New Hampshire, and possibly elsewhere, no
such proclamation of welcome had hitherto
gone forth from any educational body, and
the extreme opposition which the measure
called forth is the best testimony to the
merit of its supporters.

The original founders of Oberlin were
anxious to combine manual labour with
mental study, and made it obligatory on all
students to work with their hands for four
hours daily, thus defraying chief part of their
expenses. This feature has been now materially modified, and labour is no longer compulsory, though it is still very common to
find pupils of both sexes who support themselves wholly or in part by the labour of
their hands, as a large proportion of the
students have very small independent means,
and there is, I suppose, hardly one person
of any wealth among the whole number.

While sitting in the matron's office, I
heard more than one of the female students
request exemptions from the study of geometry, or natural philosophy, or chemistry,
because she "could not get through all her
housework, and she had to work for her
board."

The amount of earnestness and industry
which such pupils would be likely to bring to
their studies can be best appreciated by
those who have had the great pleasure of
teaching night classes in London, or elsewhere, the students at which worked with
their hands all day, and looked up at their
teacher in the evening, with that eager thirst
for knowledge you so seldom see in the eyes
of any other class.

As the College itself sprung from small
beginnings to rapidly increasing dimensions,
the buildings connected with it have been

successively erected at different times, and in various styles of workmanship. The oldest building of all, which was erected in 1833, and contained the germs of all the future departments, has passed from the hands of the College, and is probably now hardly recognisable. The next in age is the Ladies' Hall, built in 1834, a plain wooden building, in questionable repair, which is about to be superseded by another, already finished, in brick, of much larger dimensions. Other buildings have grown up around, placed at irregular intervals, some without, and some within, the square of ground more especially belonging to the College, and containing the Young Men's Hall, the Chapel, &c. &c.

The appearance that Oberlin now presents is that of a loosely-built village, or, in local parlance, "city," with numbers of ill-defined streets, more or less thickly sprinkled with unpretending wooden houses, and converging into a somewhat closer group in the immediate vicinity of the College. The population is now estimated at about three thousand, besides the students, whose numbers average another thousand.

The life of the whole community is in more or less close connexion with that of the College, almost every person in Oberlin being there either to receive or impart instruction, or to minister to the material wants of those who do one or the other.

The roads are still somewhat rude, and the pathways or "sidewalks" are made (Western fashion) entirely of planks, cut in short transverse lengths,—the crossings being also of planks, laid longitudinally. These planks make a sufficiently pleasant and even footway when first laid, but are apt soon to warp in the sun and rot in the rain, needing frequent repair or renewal.

The whole place has an appearance peculiar to itself, and very hard to render by description.

There is an utter absence of all the appearances and pretensions of wealth, and though the universal frugality had its painful side, (in the case, for instance, of the professors, whose meagre salaries must be terribly apt to cumber them with the cares from which they so much need to be free,) there was, at the same time, something very refreshing in the sight of a community where money did *not* rule,—where it was the normal state to have very little of it, and where nobody thought it necessary to strain after any particular appearances.

In the morning, when the students first meet, and at the times of changing the classes throughout the day, the streets present a very bright and busy look. The students of both sexes come hurrying along from their various "halls," or from the private houses where they board, for none of the buildings are together, and every one has to pass, often many times a day, along the different roads and pathways, in going to the different classrooms. Each professor has his own domain, and to this each class comes at its appointed hour, passing away, when its time has expired, to some other building, to attend another recitation.

The two sexes are about equally represented among the students, though the full College course is taken by a smaller number of women than of men. "Coloured" students—varying widely as to hue—form about a third of the whole number, and I suppose there is hardly any community in America where the coloured and white races meet on so real and genuine a footing of equality as at Oberlin.

Oberlin College, as now existing, comprises several distinct departments, each of which has its plan of study laid out separately, and to any of which all qualified students are admitted, without distinction of age, sex, or colour. The College course proper is designed to "afford as extensive and thorough a course of instruction as other Colleges" in America; and, on the completion of the prescribed course of study, male and female students alike receive the Academical degree. I heard with great interest, that in the year of my visit (1865), it so happened that the only woman who graduated was a coloured girl, originally a slave, who had not even then paid her full ransom to her former owners. . . .

The number of students in the "College proper" in 1864–5 was 112, of whom 95 were male and 17 female.

The Theological Department, though usually comprising but a small number of students, holds a very prominent place in Oberlin College. It is designed to prepare students for the University, and its undergraduates are usually somewhat more advanced in age than the others, and are wont to take a leading part in the meetings for prayer, and similar purposes, which form so large a feature in Oberlin life. The number of students last year was 13.

The Scientific Course comprises a somewhat exceptional course of study, and is, I suppose, chiefly resorted to by students whose education has been further advanced in other directions, or who desire to cultivate, for some special purpose, the subjects which it embraces. In 1865, it numbered 28 students.

The Ladies' Course is designed for girls who desire a thorough education, and yet do not aspire to graduate in the College proper. In some studies, however, the students recite with the College Classes, where the stage of progress is similar in each. The number of students in this department was 175.

The Preparatory Department is placed under the management of one of the Professors, and the classes in it are mainly taught by graduates or undergraduates of the College, of either sex. The attendance in this department is very numerous, comprising both students who desire to fit themselves for entering of the College course, and those who wish for a thorough groundwork of education, without expecting to pursue their studies further. In the latter class especially one may expect to find those "working students" who have had small opportunities of early instruction, and now seize eagerly on mental study while supporting themselves by manual labour. At the time of my visit, Oberlin, as well as the other Western colleges, showed visible signs of the recent Peace, in the number of military or semi-military jackets scattered throughout the class-rooms, the wearers having left their homes, or their half-completed studies, at the national summons, and now returned to resume their books with an ardour and simplicity in no wise lessened by their warlike experience.

It was a very curious sight to go into the recitation-rooms, and see some benches filled with young men "bearded like pards," and others with young women of corresponding age, many of them of different shades of "colour," labouring painfully at the elements of grammar or geography, under the auspices of some young undergraduate (more often a woman than a man), often much their junior; while side by side with them would sit, perhaps, children of twelve or fourteen, their equals in book-learning, if in nothing else.

Besides the General Preparatory Department, there is another division specially adapted for girls preparing for the "Ladies' Course," but the classes of the two sections are not, I think, kept distinct, except where studies pursued are different. The whole number of students in the Preparatory Departments was 570.

The general system of instruction at Oberlin (and, indeed, with some modifica-

tions, throughout most of the Schools and Colleges I saw in America) differs considerably from that most generally approved in England.

Certain text-books, none of which were familiar to me, are appointed for study, and the students are generally given a certain portion to be mastered before their next meeting.

The class-hour is little more than a daily examination by the Professors, whose share of actual teaching (with few exceptions) seems to be infinitesimal.

The Professor of Physiology, indeed, gave something more resembling a lecture, and illustrated his teaching by reference to a skeleton at his side, and the Professors of Geology and Chemistry were also provided with cabinets of specimens.

It is part of the plan pursued here to attack a subject very vigorously by means of *daily* recitations, and an amount of study which, if thorough, must be very stiff, and so to "be through with it" in two or three terms, when its place would be taken by another study, to be in its turn completed in short space; there being thus only three or four subjects pursued simultaneously. We were told, for instance, that students were "expected to have studied Algebra one term before entering College, and then to *complete* the subject in their first term." This statement greatly amazed and bewildered me, till I saw the text-book in use, the author of which (Professor Loomis, of Yale,) professed only to have summed up therein so much of the more practical parts of the science as might be mastered "*in the time usually allotted* to the study in American Colleges."

It is only right to say that we had previously heard some accusations against Oberlin of want of thoroughness in study, and the recitations at which we were present hardly convinced us of the injustice of the charge.

Be these charges more or less well founded, I do not doubt, however, that the results produced by this College are such as are invaluable to the class of students seeking instruction, and are very likely adequate to the demand in the West, where, even less than in the New England States, the full requirements of elegant scholarship would be likely to find appreciation.

The total number of students at Oberlin in 1864–5 was 901, of whom 409 were males, and 492 females.

Of these students, a considerable number

board in the College "Halls," the "Ladies' Hall" being wholly occupied by female students, some of whom repay their expenses by doing the housework, and "Tappan Hall" being similarly appropriated to young men, all the students of both sexes who "room" in either place meeting for meals in the refectory attached to the Ladies' Hall. A larger number still board in those neighbouring families "whose piety is satisfactory to the College authorities," and the rules of the College apply equally to all.

Recitation hours begin after breakfast, at 8 A.M. and continue till noon, when dinner is served, and after this few classes meet, except for the study of French and the Natural Sciences.

The female students are under the general direction of a Matron, who issues a small book of rules for their observance, and who is to be found either personally, or by deputy, at her office in the Ladies' Hall for the adjustment of all small matters. The Professor who is at the head of the Preparatory Department has also an office surrounded by a kind of bar and railing, to which the young men can come for similar purposes of inquiry, and a second book of regulations is issued for their benefit.

In each set of rules occurs a prohibition of all games of chance or skill, including even chess and draughts, and *"all use* of intoxicating liquors."

A library of moderate dimensions is provided for the use of students, on payment of a small fee, and contributions to this library are greatly valued.

The daily routine of recitations was the same on four days in the week, Saturday being mainly appropriated to Bible classes, and Monday to what they called Rhetorical Exercises.

It is perhaps as another remnant of the old Puritan feeling that one finds pretty generally in North America a disregard of the idea of sanctity of place,—manifesting itself in the use of the churches and chapels of most denominations for various purposes not strictly religious. The speeches and recitations on "Class-day" at Harvard University are made in the chapel. I have been present at a meeting in a chapel on behalf of hospital funds; and therefore it was by no means exceptional that the Oberlin Rhetorical Exercises were held in the College chapel.

The students whose turn it was to take part in the performance on the day of our visit mounted in turn the platform ordinarily used as a pulpit, and recited more or less perfectly speeches and essays, previously prepared and committed to memory; the girls, however, being allowed the privilege of *reading* their compositions. Some of the essays had considerable merit, and afforded scope for a variety of styles both grave and gay. I have jotted down in my note-book the titles or mottoes of a few: "All men are free and equal" (which was, very curiously, the first essay we heard in America); "Rome was not built in a day;" "On Short Cuts" (the moral thereof being, "The short cut home is the furthest about"). Then came a political essay, of which I failed to catch the name, but the general refrain seemed to be "the determination of the North, and the ferocity of the South." Then one "On General Education," in which we were informed that "education was the abomination of monarchs, because they knew its results would hurl them from their thrones." After the two last rather childish productions it was refreshing to have a really able essay "On Windows," in which a senior undergraduate spoke strongly and cleverly about the prejudices through which we see things, and of how much "lies in the eye of the beholder." Only the undergraduates of the College proper take part in these exercises, the rest of the students attending as audience, with also many of the Professors.

It is hard to give an English public any just idea of the state of society here, because nothing parallel could exist in England.

The general average of Oberlin students may, perhaps, be most fairly compared to that of Government students in our training colleges, and yet the comparison is very inadequate, for they represent here the *whole* of society, and not a single class; and this, of course, essentially affects their habits, manners, and tone of mind. They are all supposed to be "gentlemen and ladies" (and indeed the readiness with which democratic America claims these titles is truly edifying), and acknowledge no social superiors. Thus, they have on the one hand no higher standard of manners by which to profit, and very little consciousness that such is needed; while on the other they have no temptation to strain after the pretensions of a class above their own, and thus escape much essential vulgarity. Many of them displayed a great degree of kindness and real courtesy, though with an almost absolute deficiency of polish of manner, which characteristic may, indeed, perhaps be called rather national than local.

In two respects the roughness of manners at Oberlin seemed greater than elsewhere: firstly, in the queer attitudes indulged in by the students during class hours, and secondly, in the incessant spitting that went on then as well as at all other times. It certainly did strike one with amazement when watching one of the recitations to see young men with their heels poised on the back of the next seat about on a level with their heads, or their legs stretched out on the seat beside them, while an examination was going on in perhaps quite abstruse branches of study, which are usually in our minds associated with a very considerable degree of culture.

A lesser degree of the same thing has often struck me throughout those States which I visited,—everywhere the external accessories of cultivation seem to lag far behind the degree of actual study and learning; and this, joined to the barbarous English which is so very general, makes it hard for a European to recognise and allow for real scholarship beneath an exterior of person, of speech, and of manner, which in England hardly ever co-exist with it.

As a rule the girls seemed considerably more civilized than the young men,—partly, perhaps, because the feminine instinct, to a great degree, forbade just those special actions and habits which were peculiarly disagreeable in the latter.

The teachers and professors seemed generally to belong to exactly the same order as the majority of the pupils, but some of them have had the advantage of travel, and have availed themselves of it very intelligently.

I think, perhaps, that those familiar with a Moravian community or a German University could enter more readily into the nature of these Colleges than any others.

In Oberlin the original Puritan spirit is still strong, and shows itself in the modern form of desire for revivals, rumours of one hoped for being afloat at the time of our visit. The religious "exercises" are very frequent— morning prayer in the families, and evening prayer in the chapel, forming but a small part of them. There were innumerable "Sabbath-schools" and prayer-meetings announced from the pulpit on Sunday, and during the week prayer-meetings and lectures seemed of daily occurrence. A custom, moreover, obtains here which it is hard for a stranger to admire, viz. the opening of *every* recitation with either a hymn or a prayer; the names of the students being first called over, then the prayer offered or hymn sung, and then the subject of study proceeded with. The first time I was present on such an occasion was at the lecture on physiology. The names were called; instantly on the conclusion of the list some one struck up, "All hail the power of Jesu's Name," and, as the last word of the verse died out, the lecturer began briskly, "What did I say were the physical functions?" I confess that to me at least the effect was rather striking than edifying.

The morning sermon on Sunday was decidedly of the sensational order, with one or two accounts (apparently for imitation) of people, mentioned by name, who received such vivid spiritual impressions as to fall into swoons in church, and remain so (one of them at least) for sixteen hours. The sermon concluded with an invitation to the congregation to come and hear the sequel thereof in the afternoon, and an interjected remark that "those who needed it most wouldn't"—the personal application of which remark we still could not help risking.

Several prayer-meetings were held during the week, at one of which, specially "conducted by the students themselves," we were present. A theological student presided, and the proceedings having been opened by prayer and a hymn, he invited every one to speak as he or she felt able, requesting each to be "as brief as possible, as he felt that God was among them, and that many ought to speak that evening." One after another the students rose, some with quiet composure, but more with evident hesitation and excitement. One young man prayed very earnestly, and asked the people's prayers for "a young man under conviction, whose tears God had seen;" another testified of the "good done to his own soul;" a third "said a word for Jesus, and how He answered prayer;" two or three with tears in their eyes feared that they "were not Christians, but desired the prayers of the rest that they might become so;" another declared that he "had felt great comfort in religion, but now had nothing comforting to say;" and one very young man asked the prayers of all for himself, and asked them too "for his father, who" (and his voice broke) "was sixty years of age, and—a sinner." Some of the girls spoke too, but on the whole there seemed to me among them less of the painful intensity of feeling which characterised so many of the young men, and this struck me the more as opposed to the ordinary estimate of the religious susceptibility of the two sexes.

There seemed a general feeling abroad that the excitement of the evening might be indicative of the "first drops of a great shower of revival." The whole scene was to me very impressive (as must be any exhibition of deep feeling in whatever direction), very novel, and, I am afraid I must add, very sad. It seemed almost impossible that a state of feeling such as was here indicated, could pervade a society in which general healthiness of tone prevailed. In so far as revivals depend on a morbid state of spiritual excitement, and that again on imperfectly developed bodily health, there seemed at Oberlin every facility for their advent. A less robust set of students I have seldom seen, with manners gentle and kind, but more subdued than seemed suited to their age had they been in full mental and physical health. The place impressed me as flat, and not very healthy (though the contrary is asserted) and the water had to be filtered for drinking. From what I saw I imagine that no adequate system of cleansing or drainage prevails; and, though violent epidemics may be rare, I think the effects may be seen in the general under-baked look of the whole number of students and Professors.

No suitable provision was made for physical exercise or relaxation, and no gymnasium existed for either sex. During our ten days' stay we saw no sign whatever of athletic sports or exercises, unless indeed some of the students belonged to a company of firemen recently established, who exercised in front of our windows. The utmost physical recreation seemed to consist in a country walk, and I doubt if even this was common, though a large number of the students had just returned from the disbanded army. This absence of desire for physical sports seems more or less common throughout America, and is very strange in the eyes of those accustomed to the exhibition of animal spirits in the English youth of both sexes.

There seems an absolute deficiency of vitality in Americans in this respect; they seem for the most part born without the love of physical exertion which so distinguishes their English cousins. And co-existent with this there seems to be on the other hand a greater readiness for study, a greater willingness to apply steadily to learning and find pleasure in it for its own sake, than we often find among students of the same age in England. Certainly the amount of actual mental work exacted and obtained from the youth of both sexes in America seems to me greater than could usually be got in England, and, as far as my observation goes, the students themselves do not rebel against it, as I think is more or less the instinct of healthy English boys and girls.

I do not pretend to account for these differences, nor indeed to do more than record my own impressions on the point, but it is one that has struck me repeatedly.

Another feature in Oberlin College which impressed me unfavourably was the very low scale of prices, and consequently inadequate payment of the Professors. Of course the missionary character assumed by the College from the first must be taken into account, and it is in some sense consistent with this that the Professors should consent to labour for a rate of remuneration barely sufficient to provide them with the necessaries of life, and, in cases where they have large families, often inadequate to furnish them with domestic service. But, as far as I could learn, there exists no real necessity for so very low a scale of charges as are made for instruction, many at least of the pupils being able to pay at a somewhat higher rate. I do not, however, know how far it would now be in the power of the Faculty to raise more money by fees, as the only existing endowment (consisting of about $7,000 per annum) was raised by the sale of one thousand perpetual scholarships, the holders or lessees of which are entitled to a free education, and it is on this basis that nearly all the students are entered.

In the Theological Department, even without these scholarships, instruction is free. In the other departments, the above-mentioned scholarships may be "rented" for about $3 a term,—the whole charge for the year amounting therefore (according to the rate of exchange) to about thirty shillings, to which is added another ten shillings charged for "incidental expenses." Board can be obtained in the Halls and of the neighbouring families for sums varying from eight to fifteen shillings a week; and in the College Halls, where the charge is lowest, it may be still further diminished by manual labour for the good of the community. No one, at least, can complain that education is here an expensive luxury!

I have now to speak of the point which first interested me in the idea and existence of Oberlin, and which first made me desire when on the other side of the Atlantic to see this and other similar Colleges with my own eyes, and from them draw my own conclusions: I mean the joint education of the sexes, as here existing.

The subject is one sure to be bitterly contested; for on the one side are ranged all the old habits of thought of the many, who see in the new system the downfall of all propriety; and on the other the unmeasured enthusiasm of the few, who believe it to contain the germs of all future progress. Between the two it is sufficiently hard to decide; and it is only as a contribution to the data from which to form a conclusion that I have endeavoured carefully to collect, and now honestly to state, such evidence as I could find to bear on the subject.

At Oberlin the regulations are such that it is the education alone which is common to both sexes, the social life being completely separate, with the exception that the meals in the Ladies' Hall are shared by the occupants of Tappan Hall. At prayer-meetings, indeed, all the students may meet, and at the different lectures in the chapel, as well as at all recitations in the class-rooms; but they are strictly forbidden to walk to and from such meetings with those of the opposite sex, or to have any intercourse with them out of hours; and, as far as I could learn, the regulations seemed to be well obeyed.

In the class-rooms the girls generally occupy the front benches, and the young men those behind, or sometimes one side of the room is appropriated to each, as in the chapel a general division runs down the middle.

I conversed with many of the Professors on the subject of this joint education, and also inquired the individual opinion of each as to the relative mental powers of the male and female students.

On the general issue, I found almost complete agreement in favour of the joint education. With regard to the latter inquiry, some diversity of opinion existed.

Besides the oral testimony which I was at pains to collect, I was referred to a small pamphlet on the subject, prepared by the same Professor whose record of Oberlin's early history I have already quoted.

The first advantage of the system, as there set forth, is its economy, the provision requisite for educating the youth of one sex being, as is urged, usually sufficient for both, or at least capable of being made so with small addition, and thus a double gain secured at little more than a single outlay. It is, I suppose, undeniable, that where provision for educating both sexes is not made,

it is the girls that will go to the wall, as is seen almost everywhere in England when once we pass beyond the limit of national schools, where both sexes are more or less commonly taught together, or at least provided with similar facilities for instruction. Professor Fairchild argues that, in the Western and more thinly populated states, where no large endowments are available, the women will be especially sure to suffer, "unless the same school can meet the wants of both."

The next argument brought forward is the mutually beneficial effect which is likely to be exercised by male and female students when brought together for the purposes of study. "That society is most happy," says the pamphlet, "which conforms most strictly to the order of nature as indicated in the family relation, where brother and sister mutually elevate and restrain each other." "A school for young men becomes a community in itself, with its own standard of morality and its laws of honour;" but in a college for both sexes the student will find a "public sentiment not so lenient as that of a community of associates needing the same indulgence." "There is no healthful discipline where the order of the school is not maintained by public sentiment; and, if those may be trusted who have had experience, there is no more successful method of securing such than by uniting the sexes in pursuit of study." The influence of this union in the matter of discipline is allowed to be "doubtless more important for young men than for young women;" and, similarly, the balance of benefit is said to incline to their side in the tendency of joint education to produce a "purer moral atmosphere" than that common in a society of their own.

"A more correct idea of the character of the female sex" is another advantage to be expected by young men under such a system, says Professor Fairchild, adding, modestly, that he is unable to affirm whether a false estimate of the other sex, similar to that so often to be regretted among young men, exists in ladies' boarding-schools; "but, if so, they need a similar remedy." Allied to this last gain is "a more thorough common sense, as opposed to morbid sentimentalism," which may, it is hoped, result from a well-regulated association of the sexes; and also "a higher degree of social cultivation." "A wholesome incitement to effort in study is another advantage naturally resulting." "The general elevating influence of a proper association of the sexes in society at large is universally admitted, though social philosophers may fail to explain it. Who shall deny that the same power operates with at least equal effect upon the young when associated as pupils in the same school?''

The pamphlet next goes on to consider the old objection of the ''different spheres of action,'' and contends that the aim of every school and college ''should be to furnish a general cultivation as a basis of preparation for any or every sphere.'' As to the inquiry whether ''young ladies will be able to maintain their standing with young men,'' Professor Fairchild speaks from personal experience, and assures us that ''ladies ask no indulgence, and receive none. If an experience of twelve years in a school of five hundred of both sexes affords ground for judgment, the difficulty may be regarded as wholly ideal.'' Some studies should, he thinks, be properly pursued in separate classes, as is the case at Oberlin with anatomy and physiology. With regard to the classics, he argues that ''proper discrimination'' will evade all difficulty; that ''such authors as Plato and Xenophon, Cicero and Tacitus—as noble and chaste as the entire range of literature affords—may be read in mixed classes without causing a blush;'' and adds, ''It might be well even in schools for young men to keep within such limits.''

The argument that a public school or college is not the place for young women because of the coarseness of manners that prevails, leads Mr. Fairchild to ask whether the school which is dangerous for one sex will be safe for the other, and whether (unless young men need much *less* safeguard against impurity than young women) it would not be better to resolve that such influences should prevail as could but be healthful for each, rather than to exclude girls from the corruption tolerated for boys. ''Our judgment in regard to the propriety of the matter,'' he adds, ''must be determined not by what schools are now without the influence of female society, but what they will be when that influence is secured.''

By isolating women from men, moreover, he argues that they may be made into prudes, on the one hand; or, ''snatching the boon of education which should have been freely bestowed,'' they may, on the other, become really and offensively masculine from the very position of antagonism into which they find themselves forced.

The pamphlet concludes with a few words on the supposed danger of hasty attachments and marriages which may arise, on which

point the author remarks, that ''there is something in the association of every-day life which appeals to the judgment rather than to the fancy,'' and that weeks and months of steady labour over the same problems or at the same sciences will not be more likely to create romances than casual meetings at fêtes and balls.

In talking with the other Professors on the same subject, I found the above opinions confirmed, and was assured that hardly an instance had arisen where harm came from the system of joint education, and that many good results undoubtedly did follow.

In speaking of the relative abilities of the male and female students, I found more difference of opinion. The Professor of Chemistry and Physiology thought that the girls played their part in the recitations about as well as the young men, but did not consider them so well qualified for the lengthened consideration of a scientific subject.

The Professor of Greek told me that he was unable to see much difference between the students of the two sexes: ''But for the difference in sound of voice, I should find it hard, or impossible, with my eyes shut, to tell one from the other. If I am to find a distinction, I may perhaps say that, speaking generally, the ladies have more intuitive quickness in construing, and earlier acquire elegance in composition; while the gentlemen seem more able to seize on points touching the philosophy of the language. As regards power of attention and application, I have never remarked any difference, and the work done is usually about equal.''

The Professor of Biblical Literature, who had the chief management of the Theological School, had had much less to do with female than with male students. He said that he had had, however, quite as good work done by young women as by young men, and that in rhetorical exercises and composition he often found them to excel the young men in delicacy and elegance of expression. On the whole, however, he inclined to the belief that the balance of mental strength lay on the side of the young men. In answer to a question of mine, this Professor said that they had never received applications from women for systematic training for the ministry, though one or two female graduates had afterwards become preachers; but that, if such applications were made, the Faculty would certainly not refuse to admit them, but would, in each case, as at present, leave the responsibility of electing such a calling to the individual conscience.

The Professor of Mathematics spoke, perhaps, more strongly than any in favour of the equality of the male and female intellect. He had been a Professor at Hillsdale College before coming to Oberlin, and gave us letters of introduction to that place, where the same system of education is pursued, though with certain differences. On the point in question he said, "I have found the work done by ladies to be fully equal to that of the gentlemen—*fully;* and it has more than once occurred that the best scholar in my class was a lady. Ladies are generally the quickest at recitation, and will repeat long problems more accurately than most of the young men. I do not know that they have any counterbalancing defect. As to strength and power of application, I know that the advantage is said to lie with the men, but I have not found it so."

These were the chief conversations with Oberlin Professors on this subject, though I talked about it more or less to others, and found that, substantially, the same opinions prevailed.

In giving the foregoing account of Oberlin, I have felt bound to report, as fairly as I could, both sides of the picture; and, if I have been obliged to dwell on some points not altogether to be commended, I hope that I have not failed also to show how much there is that is truly good, genuine, and valuable in this simple community, in the midst of which one cannot live for even a few days without a feeling of attachment to those who are so ready with their kindly welcome. Whatever shortcomings or errors may be recorded against Oberlin, it should ever be remembered in her favour that she took the initiative before all the world in opening a college career to women, and in welcoming, on equal terms, all students, of whatever race or hue. This double glory shall surely be hers in the memories of men when much on which she now prides herself more may be forgotten.

John Wesley Hoyt   1867

Application to America of European Developments in University Education

The extract below is taken from John Wesley Hoyt's report on education given at the Paris Universal Exposition in 1867. For further information, the reader should refer to the extract by Hoyt in the previous section of this book entitled "On European Education."

We have seen that the German idea of a university—which is the nearest perfect yet realized—is that of an institution affording the highest and most thorough general culture, in connection with the best instruction and training for the more intellectual professions. The careful reader of the preceding chapter has also noticed a recent disposition to bring other departments than those of theology, law, and medicine within the pale of the learned professions, and thus to extend the area of university education by the incorporation therewith of more or less perfectly developed schools and faculties not formerly included. Political economy and statesmanship are thus making advances toward an ultimate, and indeed an early, recognition as a complete and independent faculty. The universities of Munich and of Tübingen already afford examples of this sort. The fine arts are likewise advancing their claims to a place in the university beside the recognized professions; and the day is probably not very remote when the great schools of art in both the Old and the New World will constitute university faculties. On this side of the Atlantic, Yale College, Michigan University, Washington University at St. Louis, and perhaps several others, have already inaugurated this important change in the constitution of the American university. Moreover, in connection with several of the great German universities, as heretofore stated, and with some of the Italian, various schools of the scientific and more material professions, such as schools of agriculture and of engineering, as well as of veterinary science and of pharmacy, have been established; while the Swiss Federal University at Zurich, the

John W. Hoyt, *Report on Education: Paris Universal Exposition, 1867 Reports of the United States Commissioners* (Washington, D.C.: U.S. Government Printing Office, 1870), pp. 389–398.

Danish University at Copenhagen, and the Finnish University at Helsingfors, have, of late, each been materially transformed and enlarged by the development therein, or the consolidation therewith, of more or less comprehensive polytechnic schools. Our American universities—those of them, I mean, in which there have been established colleges of agriculture and the mechanic arts—are not without precedent, therefore, as to this mode of enlargement, this innovation upon the constitution and scope of the ancient university.

This same spirit is also manifest, though in a less marked degree, in the English universities, in whose behalf an effort is now making, first, for the restoration of the old faculties of law, medicine, and theology; and, secondly, for the creation of new departments of study, such as history, political economy, and the fine arts—destined, in course of time, to become full faculties, equal in rank and honor with the others.

It may be assumed, therefore, that a present leading tendency of the university is to an enlargement of its scope by bringing within the range of its educational work the whole circle of superior and special studies, regardless of the relative rank they have heretofore held in the world's estimation. And while it hardly requires a word of argument to show how truly such enlargement is in harmony with the spirit of the age and with the educational wants of the industrial classes, there are certain questions connected with the organization of the new schools thus incorporated, the importance of which is so vital as to require the most careful consideration; for if, by enlarging its scope, we are to degrade the university from its ideal rank as an association of professional schools, bound together by the strong attractive force of a central school or schools of general culture, in which the *wissenschaftliche Geist,* the scientific spirit, of the German university is the animating and controlling principle, and make it a mere aggregation of inferior schools established in the interest of the *Brodwissenschaften,* or bread-and-butter sciences, and loosely held together by a community of sordid aims—if such were the inevitable result of an extension of the boundary lines of the university, then it were a thousand times better that the present narrow limits should remain unchanged, and that the schools of the practical sciences be grouped together on a separate foundation of their own, after the manner of the great separate polytechnicums of Europe or the Industrial University of Illinois. I mean to say, in other words, that the university, as the fountain-head of true learning of every sort, must be maintained at a high level and kept pure at all hazards. It is thus, and thus only, that the intellectual supremacy of a people is either attainable or maintainable; and, accordingly, it is a matter of the greatest moment to determine whether the expansion now in progress must of necessity lead to a degradation of the university standards. Touching this question, there will doubtless be a difference of opinion as to its susceptibility of *a priori* settlement. But, to my mind, no proposition not already placed beyond dispute by actual demonstration is clearer than that it is possible to open the door of the university to every one of the higher branches of study and every one of the numerous professions that engage the intellectual efforts of man, without the least sacrifice of its high character. How should it be otherwise? It is not the sciences alone that are correlative; there is a correlation of all the knowledges, to what domain soever they severally belong; and in their higher range the relation is one of equality of rank, not of diversity. If the votaries of one set up for it a higher claim because, forsooth, in its sublime elevation, it is altogether above the range of the practical, it is because of the narrowness of their limitations—because they have not yet learned that all knowledge and every kind of learning that is worth anything is both theoretical and practical, and either the one or the other according as it is studied in its essence or in its extension into the sphere of human activities—because they have not yet learned that great yet simple lesson, the essential unity and harmony of all truths, so that it is impossible for any man to know the whole of any one thing until he has gained the mastery of all things. And if, on the other hand, the industrial classes are so generally condemners of the abstract and theoretical, and worshipers of the practical, it is because they have been so long cramped, fettered, and blinded by narrow and foolish notions of an essential antagonism between the different classes of society, and between the different departments in the world of letters, science, and the arts—because they have not yet stood upon a plane of intelligence high enough to see that the real interests of any class are so wisely and beautifully interwoven with the interests of every other, that, practically, the good of one is the good of all; that even the most practical of all the practical sciences has, of necessity, its source in the abstract and theoretical; and that as, in truth, all branches of knowledge are essential parts of one complete system, so the growth and completeness of each is promoted by the utmost intimacy and equality of association.

It seems to me that this very nature of the relation that exists between all the departments of learning, confirmed, as it is, by the known liberalizing power of such association upon the minds of all who are brought within the circle of its influence, is, of itself, convincing proof, not only of the desirableness, but also of the practicability and wisdom, of so enlarging the scope of the university as that it shall become, not in title merely but in reality, a central source of universal knowledge.

May we not consider it settled, then, that this the leading tendency of university education at the present day is philosophical, and therefore entitled to encouragement? Undoubtedly. But encouragement is not all that is wanted; the movement is eminently in need of the guidance of practical wisdom. The uncultured world, seeing, not the secret sources of knowledge and the tedious processes by means of which it has been reached, but only the results, lacks appreciation of profound culture, and is impatient of thorough and protracted courses of study. Leave the university in such hands, and everything would be contemptuously thrown out, with the brand of "useless," that could not yield immediate practical, and for the most part material, results; the branches and departments allowed to remain would be reduced to the narrowest possible limits; all subordinate institutions, from the college down to the primary school, would be correspondingly degraded in their standards; learning and science would quickly degenerate into a pitiful charlatanism; and the most rapidly advancing civilization lapse into a hopeless barbarism.

Here, then, we have the means of security. The university must be made not only a central source of proved and accepted knowledge, but also a central place of universal culture—an institution a recognized and important office of which shall be to search for and discover the yet concealed truths that wait for new explorers in the universe of mind and matter. It must have for its object the extension as well as the diffusion of knowledge. And its ideal results must be, not simply the learned theologian, lawyer, philologist, and physician; nor yet these supplemented by the successful agriculturist, the skillful architect, the practical engineer, and that entire host of well-trained professional workers who constitute the visible vanguard of the great army of material progress; nor yet a great people, provided with the best conditions of material development, luxuriating in the wealth of its own production and rejoicing in the superiority of its physical power; its ideal results must also, and above all else, include the highest type of individual manhood and a nation preeminently distinguished for the high quality of its intellectual culture and the grandeur of its moral influence on the rest of the world. Again, I say, degradation of the university is liable, nay almost certain, to follow in all cases where the idea of a profound and exalted culture is subordinated to the idea of direct practical availability. But insure to the former its legitimate central place in the comprehensive scheme, make the high faculties of general science and philosophy the heart and soul of the whole institution, and it will surely become a vitalizing and elevating influence, holding its "practical" no less than its professional faculties to a higher standard than, as isolated schools, they could possibly attain.

It is needless to say that in America, where, as yet, we have no high faculty of philosophy, and where there is so little of the *wissenschaftliche Geist* in any quarter, and hence so little elevating and sustaining power, there is little danger of a degradation of university standards, for the reason that they are already, and always have been, about as low as they could be got. But does not this very fact, so discreditable to our country, constitute a powerful argument in favor of at once creating such faculties in all our would-be universities, both on their own account and because of their needed influence on the professional faculties, new and old? One thing is certain, namely, that unless measures are promptly taken for the creation of such faculties, that same superficialness which now marks the professional schools of the country will continue to characterize them. Nor will this be the worst of the case; for if our American universities are to continue in their present course of expansion by multiplication of professional schools, without the required improvement in their standards, instead of fulfilling the important office of stimulating and lifting up the colleges and the public schools of the country—an office of the utmost importance, and one for the thorough fulfillment of which they should be held responsible—they are almost certain to degrade them, as a class, even below their present inferior level.

At Yale and Harvard there are signs of an earnest desire to supply this great want of American education; but unless I have misapprehended the present character and objects of the few brief and disconnected courses of lectures thus far offered to their students and to the public generally, they constitute but a single first step of the many that require to be taken, before we shall be able to point to even one faculty of philosophy corresponding in rank to the *philosophische Facultät* of the German university.

But expansion of the university is not likely to stop with the incorporation of new faculties. There is also discoverable a tendency to expansion by the division of existing faculties. In some instances the new faculties amount almost to the creation of a new department, great in its importance and extensive in its scope, around the nucleus of a single branch of study formerly included in one of the ancient faculties. In other cases the new faculties are formed by a natural and equal division of the studies previously embraced in the faculty of philosophy or its equivalent, and the subsequent expansion of these divisions into full faculties, each covering a wider field and demanding of the student the same term of study as a condition of admission to the laureate, as was required previous to the division.

Examples of the first kind are presented by the *staatswirthschaftliche Facultät* of the Bavarian and Wurtemberg Universities, which is an offshoot of the *juristische* or *Juristen Facultät*, as may be seen by reference to the University of Vienna, in which political philosophy, though not yet advanced to the rank of an independent faculty, nevertheless has an important place in the law faculty, there known as the *rechts- und staatswissenchaftliche Facultät*. The schools of engineering, of agriculture, of veterinary science, of pharmacy, &c., already noticed as having, within late years, sprung up in many of the universities of the Old World, also properly belong to this general class.

Examples of the second class—of new faculties formed by the equal division of the original faculty of philosophy, so long the foundation school of the European university, into schools of philosophy and letters, and schools of the mathematical, physical, and natural sciences—are still more common, being found in many countries. Thus in Italy, instead of the ancient faculty of philosophy, we now have, as the basis of the professional faculties, the *facotà di filosofia e lettere*, and the *facoltà di scienze, fisiche, matematiche e naturali;* in France, the *faculté des sciences* and the *faculté des lettres;* in Belgium, the *faculté des sciences* and the *faculté de philosophie et lettres;* in Denmark, the *philosophiske Facultet* and the *mathematisk-naturvidenskabelige Facultet;* in Holland, the *facultas disciplinarum mathematicarum et physicarum* and the *facultas philosophiae theoreticae et literarum humaniorum;* in Russia, the historico-philological faculty and the physico-mathematical faculty. So likewise in this country the same tendency, though on a lower plane and without the same necessity, is observable in the division of the university department of general culture into the "regular" or classical and the scientific courses that exist in so many of the universities; while in at least one—the University of Wisconsin—there are found distinct and co-ordinate colleges or faculties of letters and of science and the arts.

Now, if this multiplication by division were nothing more than a partition of studies, with an assignment of the ordinary academic, mathematical, and scientific studies to one division, and the academic courses in language, literature, and philosophy to the other, it is clear that there would be not only no expansion whatever in such cases, but, on the other hand, an actual and very prejudicial contraction of the already too narrow range of studies the completion of which has been essential to the baccalaureate; and yet, practically, it is, with few exceptions, this very partitioning of studies that is now going on in this country. In the European countries, however, the division is either a real expansion, by taking in new studies and extending the upward range of the old ones, or at least a systematic and philosophical arrangement of the numberless studies embraced by the full faculty of philosophy, according to the somewhat different needs—at this advanced stage in the student's life quite beyond the *academic* range—of those who are preparing for the "learned" or for the scientific and "practical" pursuits.

That the faculty of philosophy in the German university has not yet undergone a division similar to those found in the other European countries is doubtless due to the limitless range of this faculty, to the singular freedom of choice allowed to all who attend the courses of instruction embraced, and to the more liberal, though by no means more easy, terms on which the doctorate in this faculty is conferred. Still another reason may be found in the fact that, in Germany, the university is still almost exclusively a door to the "learned" pursuits; admission to the scientific and industrial pursuits being gained chiefly through the technical, industrial, and polytechnic schools, in all of which the German States so far excel. And yet, notwithstanding these peculiarities of the case in Germany, it is by no means clear to my own mind that the university there is not susceptible of improvement by the proper organization of two separate faculties, similar in general cast to those found in the other countries named. Nor is there much doubt that such a change will come, in course of time, with the organization therein of the new faculties of the scientific professions. That freedom of the German university, which, opening the vast domain of letters, science, and philosophy to all who choose to enter upon and occupy it, bids them choose for themselves such range of study as seems most in harmony with their individual tastes and aspirations, and allows them to continue therein even to the end of their days, is most admirable, surely, and should be fostered and protected with the most jealous care. But for such students as have fixed and definite aims sharply outlined, both by their bent of character and the uncompromising necessities of life, there is doubtless an advantage in finding, already formed, such groupings of studies as have been determined by the wisest educators, and proved by the experience of years to be best calculated to perfect their preparation for their respective callings in life—that is, if we may assume that the student, still feeling his way and only advancing by the aid of others, is less wise than the master, already familiar with the great highway, and even the by-ways, his feet have need to tread.

Intimately connected with this organization of faculties we have the question of discipline; concerning which, however, I deem it important to say only this much, namely: that the manifest and true tendency is a fair compromise between the rigid rule of the French and English universities on the one hand and the extreme license of the German university on the other; neither of which secures the best results. These contrasting policies have naturally grown out of the different governing ideas that characterize the universities of those countries respectively, and which, indeed, are essential to their differences in grade and real character. For the English university, as already shown, is only a *haut lycée*, and in no proper sense a university at all. It proceeds, therefore, upon the hypothesis that the students who resort to it are still boys, whose object is elementary culture and discipline, and whose need is the stimulation of examinations and high prizes and the severe restraints and penalties imposed by arbitrary authority. Whereas the German university is based on the theory that they who resort to its halls are young men already disciplined in mind and fashioned as to habits of intellectual and moral life, and hence duly prepared to enter upon their career of superior study in that true scientific and philosophic spirit whose glory is that it lifts the student by its own inherent power of inspiration high above all need of arbitrary rule and artificial stimulation.

That neither of these theories is perfectly adapted to the end proposed is apparent after a careful investigation; for, in England the proportion of students who attain to anything more than a *pass* degree, or even entitle themselves to that, is very small, while at the best of the German universities it is rare that more than a third of the whole number manifest their possession of the true *wissenschaftliche Geist* by continuous laborious effort during their period of study. Even at Berlin the scientific spirit which animates the whole institution and gives vitality and power to its teaching in every department, fails with the majority to supply the place of official and professional supervision. To the authorities of this, the foremost of the world's universities, it may with propriety be said, "This ought ye to have done and not left the other undone." The scientific spirit is above all price; but even the University of Berlin would accomplish yet more if, to its magnificent material and intellectual provisions for the education of the thousands who throng its famous lecture rooms, there were added such requirements as to attendance, and such frequent tests of progress and proficiency as have ever been found essential to hold the less ambitious and as yet uninspired majority of students to their work.

The English methods being simply a perpetuation of past errors, the French a system begotten of the too military spirit of the nation, and the German policy a natural reaction upon the too rigid systems that had been long in vogue when it was adopted, it is not strange that the leading educators of these and of other countries are at present earnestly striving to determine the golden mean.

Touching the organization of the professoriate, one risks nothing in conceding that the German universities, including the Swiss and Austrian, present the best models; and the wonder is that these have not been already universally adopted by other countries. Extraordinary professors, performing the office of assistants, with moderate salaries or half salaries, and thus supplementing the instruction given by the ordinary professors, at a considerable saving to the funds of the institution, are found, indeed, in all the European universities; but the *Privatdocenten*, giving private lectures on subjects of their own choice, dependent entirely upon their own powers of attraction for auditors and compensation, and powerfully stimulating both extraordinary and ordinary professors, for whose private pupils and fees they are authorized competitors, and for whose very places even they may be aspirants—these are a class of teachers peculiarly German, and a class of whom, in view of the great saving they make to the university, and the quickening and vitalizing influence they exert upon every department and member thereof, it is not too much to say that they are the most important class at present belonging to the university corps of instructors. That so important a feature of the professoriate as this is destined to be adopted at an early day, wherever practicable, seems to me almost certain. But with all the economy that may be used, in their organization and management, it is coming to be understood that it is not possible in any country to establish and maintain a real university without vast sums of money. And accordingly there is observed a corresponding tendency in those countries where the true idea of a university is best comprehended to a concentration of means and intellectual forces in a few great institutions, rather than practically squander them upon a great number of half-endowed, sickly institutions, which are not only not worthy of their high title, but whose meagerness and necessary imperfections constitute them a positive hindrance and curse to the cause of university education. It was the want of a due appreciation of this that led to the establishment in early times of so many universities in Italy and Germany. It will be remembered that as early as the year 1500 Germany alone had fourteen, and that the number continued to increase for a long time after that; every town of the second or third rank insisting on having its university, until at last, yielding to the contempt in which the majority of them had long been held by the learned men of the times, happily sustained by the necessary territorial changes that came of the political commotions of the eighteenth century, those of them whose life was most sickly, such as those of Erfurt, Mainz, Helmstadt, Frankfort-on-the-Oder, Rinteln, Duisburg, Bamberg, Cologne, Munster, Paderborn, Dillingen, and Salzburg, were suppressed.

Italy, whose mania for numerous universities had run *pari passu* with that of Germany, has not even yet effected the requisite work of suppression. The need of such work has long been felt by leading minds, however, and has at length been fairly undertaken by the government, whose purpose it is, by reducing the number of state universities from fifteen to about half the number, and by the adoption of more thorough regulations for their management, to raise them to the high level of the foremost universities of Germany.

So, also, there is, of late, a growing appreciation in Great Britain of the importance of a more judicious concentration of means upon a less number of institutions, in order to the upbuilding of such as shall be more worthy of the high demands alike made by the country and the times. In pursuance of this felt necessity, the Scotch universities are to be consolidated; Queen's University, Dublin, is empowered to grant the degrees heretofore conferred by the colleges at Cork, Galway, and Belfast; and the University of London is gradually absorbing the degree-conferring powers of a large number of similar institutions in England.

In this country alone, where the ambition of new cities and new States, as well as of numberless religious sects, strongly wars against this true policy of the higher education, the opposite tendency still prevails. But even here more rational ideas of what constitutes a true university, and of the large amount of money and professional talent requisite to maintain such an institution, are rapidly gaining ground; so that we may reasonably hope to see a check, ere long, put upon the present insane policy of multiplication without regard to the necessities of education.

It thus appears that university education, notwithstanding its present low condition in most countries, and its serious imperfections in all, is characterized by tendencies that promise great things for the time to come. So much is already beyond question, namely, that the university of the future is to be not the mere *college* of America, nor even the college supplemented by one or more poorly organized and more poorly equipped professional schools; not that loose aggregation of grammar schools, supplemented by a few poorly attended courses of university lectures, that wear the title, by courtesy, in England; not the French grouping of academical faculties, limited—especially in the departments of letters and science—to a quite too narrow field of study; not the university of Spain, or Portugal, or Italy, from whose faculties for the higher general culture the powers of attraction and inspiration have long since departed; not the Scandinavian or Slavonian university, cast in the mold of mediæval times, or at the best a mixture of the old and more modern types; nor yet the Germanic university, found, with but minor modifications, in all the States of Germany, in Austria, Switzerland, Holland, and Denmark, and which, though wherever found it presents the highest existing type, is nevertheless everywhere too limited in scope and generally too lax in its regulations—not any of these, but rather an institution more ample in its endowment, broader in its scope, more complete in its organization, more philosophical and practical in its internal regulations, and certainly not less high than the highest in all its educational standards; an institution above and beyond the best of the gymnasia, Latin schools, high schools, academies, and colleges, and, on its own higher plane, existing for the extension and diffusion of all branches of knowledge; a broad and noble institution, where the love of all knowledge, and of knowledge as knowledge, shall be fostered and developed; where all departments of learning shall be equally honored, and the relations of each to every other shall be understood and taught; where the students devoted to each and all branches of learning, whether science, language, literature, or philosophy, or to any combinations of these constituting the numerous professional courses of instruction, shall intermingle and enjoy friendly intercourse as peers of the same realm; where the professors, chosen, as in France and Germany, after trial, from among the ablest and best scholars of the world, possessed of absolute freedom of conscience and of speech, and honored and rewarded more nearly in proportion to merit, shall be, not teachers of the known merely, but also earnest searchers after the unknown, and capable, by their own genius, enthusiasm, and moral power, of infusing their own lofty ambition into the minds of all who may wait upon their instruction; a university not barely complying with the demands of the age, but one that shall create, develop, and satisfy new and unheard-of demands and aspirations; that shall have power to fashion the nation and mold the age unto its own grander ideal; and which, through every change and every real advance of the world, shall still be at the front, driving back from their fastnesses the powers of darkness, opening up new continents of truth to the grand army of progress, and so leading the nation forward, and helping to elevate the whole human race. Such an institution would be to the world its first realization of the true idea of a university.

Adolf Douai and John Straubenmueller   1868

German Schools in the United States

The letter below was sent to Henry Barnard, United States Commissioner of Education from the German Teachers' Society of New York, by their president and reporter, John Straubenmueller and Adolf Douai, respectively. They asked that the circumstances and plight of the German schools in the United States be publicized and that the letter be incorporated in Barnard's annual report to the United States Congress. The authors traced the origins of the German schools and distinguished the various types found in the United States. The excellence of German methodology, the articulation between school grades, and the carefully planned curriculums were emphasized. The authors stressed the fact that these schools were exponents of the best of European pedagogical experimentation, and they deplored the appar-

Adolf Douai and John Straubenmueller, "German Schools in the United States," *The American Journal of Education*, III (1870), 581–586.

ent indifference of the general public or common school devotees. In an eloquent discussion of religious, cultural, and pedagogic factors, they argued the case for the encouragement, support, and continuation of the German private school in the United States.

...There are several hundreds of German schools in this country. Permit us to explain briefly the causes and reasons that have led to the foundation of these schools, since it may to many seem superfluous for Germans to support schools of their own in a country where, in the public schools, a general and gratuitous instruction is guaranteed to the children of parents of all nationalities.

The first of these reasons and causes is that our German-born population find that their children rapidly unlearn the German tongue, English being not only the common idiom of all nationalities in this country, but also a language easier than almost any other to acquire, to wield, and to pronounce. This fact sadly disturbs the family relations, the efforts of parents toward the education of their children, and the respect due to the parents from the latter. For when their children speak among themselves, even at home, nothing but English, they form, as it were, a foreign element within the family. The great mass of the immigrated Germans learn, during the first generation, hardly English enough to understand all their children talk among themselves, and thus they are unable to discover their secrets, to warn, to guide, to correct them. The children deeming English, the common language of the country, a better one than any other, begin to slight their parents, who have not a perfect command of the same, to enjoy the fun of having their own secrets, inaccessible to their parents, and end in refusing obedience to them, and in no longer keeping company, when half-grown, with their nearest relations not perfectly Anglicized. That these facts are productive of a great many evils, and even engender juvenile crime and profligacy, can be easily understood.

But this, sad as it must be called by every unprejudiced observer, is not all. The better class of Germans—and the immigration of now-a-days increases from year to year in the degree of education and respectability represented by them—sorely regret that their children and children's children should lose the privilege of commanding the two master languages of the world, English and German, at the same time. The treasures of the German literature being in no respect inferior to any other, and the usefulness in practical life of speaking and writing a plurality of languages being obvious to every intelligent mind, why should German-born children, who may so easily reap the advantages of a plurality of tongues, lose them by sheer negligence of the parents? It is certain that all the citizens of this great country should have a common language as a means of mutual intelligence and a characteristic feature of their nationality; but it is not adverse to the American idea, that the citizens of this country should derive untold advantages from their ability to freely converse and communicate with the natives of other countries, and to enjoy their national literatures. And of all languages, the German—the language of the greatest poets of modern times, of the most profound science and philosophy, and of a nation, destined to become, in no distant future, the foremost in Europe—seems to be entitled to appreciation by American citizens generally; so much the more so, as it is the mother of Anglo-Saxon and modern English, and is spoken in this country by about five millions of men—a number rapidly increasing.

But a third reason and cause leading to the foundation of German schools in this country has, in the eyes of some, even been paramount to those beforementioned, important as they are. Germany is the cradle of the reformation of schools, and the German schools, as a whole, might, from the latter part of the eighteenth century down to the middle of the present, be justly considered as by far the best in the world. It is, then, but natural that immigrated Germans, coming from a great many excellent schools in their old country; and being conscious of and thankful for the great advantages derived from them, should desire that their children may grow up under the same benefits, and that the United States, this dear country of their choice, may profit to some degree from the existence of schools instituted after the German model, even though the latter be modified according to the peculiar circumstances and requirements of the American nationality and idea.

Of the three causes just mentioned, each, according as it was prevailing over the other two in the minds of the founders of German schools, gave rise to a different kind of school. Where the idea of preserving the family relations, and together with them the parental religious denomination, prevailed, there *denominational* German schools were founded, of which there are in this country nearly as many as there are German church buildings and societies. Where, however, the second reason obtained preference to the other two, *private* schools were undertaken and patronized. Where, lastly, the third reason was paramount to the two others, without necessarily excluding them, *society* schools on shares sprang into existence. A few, however, of the private establishments must be classed with this third class.

1. We need not dwell long on the denominational class of German schools. Their existence dates as far back as the German immigration into this country. As soon as the new-comers felt able to support a church and a minister of their creed, there was also a beginning made of instructing their children in the mother tongue, so that they might be enabled to understand German preaching, and to sustain the family relations intelligibly. It was, of course, clearly the interest of the ministers to become either themselves the teachers of German, or at least the founders of schools in this tongue, if they wished to continue their denomination beyond the first generation. But a great majority of the early German clergymen, down to almost our own times, being very illiterate, their teaching did not amount to much, and does not even now. During the last two or three decades, it is true, a sufficient number of able German teachers came over from the mother country, so that the character of these denominational schools might have been extensively improved. But there being little intelligence among these congregations and their clergy, they could not understand the requirements of a good school, and that able teachers cannot be expected to thrive on so low salaries as from two to four hundred dollars a year, and to perform, into the bargain, the menial work of sextons and attendants to their ministers. Thus it is that hardly half a dozen of the several hundred schools of this kind ever have been worthy of the name of schools (among which, two deserve honorable mention, the St. Matthæus Church school in Walker street, New York, as it was under Director Hardter's leadership, and the "Zion's Schule" in Baltimore, since it came under Dr. Herzog's care,) and that from two to three millions of descendants of Germans now in the country have wholly, or almost wholly, lost the understanding and use of their native language.

2. The *private* German schools are of a modern origin. When, after the unsuccessful revolutionary fermentation of 1830, a more intelligent class of Germans began to emigrate and to spread the love of the German language and literature even among Anglo-Americans, the first of these private institutions were founded in the great commercial centres, New York, Philadelphia, Baltimore, Cincinnati, and St. Louis, whence they spread to some other places, especially since, after the unfortunate end of the revolution of 1848, the number of intelligent German immigrants considerably increased. It was chiefly the commercial class of citizens who patronized these schools. With them it was less the motive of sustaining the family relations which prompted them to so doing. Being themselves conversant enough with English, they, for the most part, also talked English at home; but they valued the great advantages connected with understanding several tongues, and wished to secure these for their children. No doubt this second class of German schools was and is of a far higher order than the denominational; but being made subservient to the private interests of their founders and proprietors, and being based solely on their commercial utility, not on an ideal conception of the compass, duties, and importance of the school, as it ought to be, all these schools, with the exception of a few to be mentioned under the third head, remained one-sided concerns, with underpaid teachers, a more or less aristocratic tendency, a bad discipline, and much outward show, without a corresponding interior value.

3. The third class of German schools, those founded by societies on shares, and a few by private enterprise, owe their origin to the ideas which succumbed in the mother country in the revolution of 1848, and stamped so different a character on the emigrants of that period. The generation of men of that time came from the most excellent German schools; educated there at a time when these schools had reached their highest degree of excellence. For it must be noted here that meanwhile the German governments, having found out what an enemy to monarchical institutions and established (state) churches they had thus far fostered in these excellent schools, have since 1850, intentionally lowered the standard of popular education, so far as depended on them. The generation of men just mentioned regarded the German model school as the "palladium" of their ideas, their liberalism, their philo-

sophical conception of state, religion, and society; they almost revered it religiously. Every intelligent man among them had an exalted notion of what the school is to be, and even the great mass of the then immigrants seconded their efforts to transplant the German model school to the hospitable soil of their adopted country. But having, most of them, lost their property through the revolution and emigration, and being obliged to struggle for many years with the hardships of a new existence to be founded, their new schools were doomed to be, till in part now, embarrassed by the insufficiency of means allotted to them. A majority of these schools were established or, at least, fostered into existence by the "Turner" (gymnastic) societies, spread all over the country; but most of these societies consist of men of very moderate means, and their schools, therefore, consist rarely of more than two classes. They charge very moderate tuition fees, allow their teachers better salaries than the denominational and most private schools, but yet rather scantily, and make both ends meet by pic-nics and charitable collections. Of a still higher character are those society schools which were independent of any organization, the founders being chartered by the legislatures of the several States as school (academical) societies, and the necessary capital, with which buildings were built and furnished, being gathered by small shares. The current expenses are defrayed by the tuition fees, new shares, or subscriptions. The tuition fees are moderate, and the chief, if not the only, source of income; still the teachers' salaries are the highest of all paid in German schools, although, with the exception of those of one or two principals, not exceeding $1,000 per annum....

The characteristic features of the schools of the third class are the following: They aim at the German ideal or model school, improved by the addition of a perfect knowledge of English, of more freedom from theoretical pedantry and impractical schematism, and by a tendency to inculcate liberal views and independent thinking. All exclude religious instruction to this extent that no prayers are offered, and the Bible is not read in school. They all require in their teachers a superior skill and talent, and have thus far succeeded in obtaining a supply of such at moderate salaries; but now the supply seems to diminish, as the intellectual standard of teachers coming over from the old country is, with some excep-

tions, inferior to that of the preceding generation. It is evident, then, that they all will, in future, have to pay higher salaries corresponding to the high order of talent demanded for their classes; and in consequence of this they will have to enhance their tuition charges, now averaging from $30 to $120 per child, to higher figures; and they may be successful therein, the liberality of our Germans toward their schools increasing with their opulence.

They are divided into as many classes as their means will allow, numbering each, if possible, no more than 40 pupils, some of them far less, only a few considerably more. This is an indispensable condition of success for this system. Our course of studies is so extensive that to gain time is with us to gain everything, so much the more so as the pupils will leave the school at the age of fourteen or sooner, unless they have already acquired a considerable proficiency in their studies, and in their mental growth the very stimulus toward absolving the whole course of their school. But practical life, or a course of higher studies, lures them away to the very last, before the sixteenth year of age is fulfilled. From sanitary reasons it is not deemed prudent to receive pupils into the elementary classes before the sixth or seventh year of age is over. Within that short, intervening space, then, of eight years at best, and without overtaxing the physical powers of youth by home work, the wonderful task is to be achieved of imparting to all the children (a very small percentage excepted) a correct and fluent use and understanding of English, German and French to about equal proficiency in each; of mathematics, all except the "calculus" and the most difficult problems of geometry and trigonometry; of natural philosophy, in all its more important bearings, not neglecting a general, and in a few branches, even a more special survey of natural history; of geography and history, treating more thoroughly those of America and Europe, but excluding no other part entirely; of bookkeeping and practical arithmetic; finally, of penmanship, drawing, singing and gymnastics, (and, with the female department, of needle—work.) This great task can be achieved only by a rapid advancement of the pupils from class to class; and this would be impossible with a large number of pupils in the same class or with pupils of different degrees of development. The work is, however, facilitated by the institution of *Kindergartens,* according to

Fr. Froebel's system, of which there is one connected with Dr. Gercke's, and one with the subscriber's, Dr. Douai's school, while those once connected with the Boston and the Hoboken institutions no longer exist. These Kindergartens, receiving children of from four to seven years of age, are now somewhat more generally appreciated, wherefore we may forego describing them here. In the system of the German model school they, beside their general importance for developing harmoniously all the mental and physical powers of tender youth, subserve the useful purpose of imparting to the pupils an equal proficiency and correctness in the understanding and oral use of English and German, as far as can be expected from children of this age, so that on entering the lowest elementary class they can easily understand both the English and German teachers and can make themselves easily understood by either. It may be feared that the use of two languages at the same time in so tender an age might stunt the development of one or either. But experience shows that the Kindergarten system is up to the task of preventing jumbles of that kind; nay, it is a fact that French-born children, having to contend with three languages at the same time, when having gone through the Kindergarten, will, as a class, turn out our most brilliant pupils up to the highest classes. Another fact here deserves mention, namely, that our system of instruction and education, although beginning with children of four or five years of age and carrying them through such an amount of mental work as no other schools in the world, presents the most satisfactory hygienic statistics. The mortality in most of our better schools—certainly of all that have fallen under the observation of the subscribers— does not exceed the very low figure of two or less in a thousand per annum, and diseases of all kinds are comparatively very rare, the attendance at school very regular, as far as depends on sanitary causes, and accidents seem to be still rarer. We can boldly challenge the closest medical examination of our schools in this respect.

Still, with the advantages just mentioned of classes not crowded, well graded and well officered, with a Kindergarten to prepare suitably the elementary beginners, and with the health and bodily vigor of the pupils well cared for, the said task could not be performed but for the admirable system and methods as devised by more than half a century of educational experience in the best German schools. The general characteristics of this system, condensed into the fewest possible words, consist in doing thoroughly and durably whatever is done, in attempting little at a time, but completing by a wise use of the material of instruction, so that the intellect, the imagination, the memory, the will, and the sense of beauty and order, may each profit so far as may be therefrom; and in arranging the succession of lessons so as to lead very gradually from the easier and perceptible to the more difficult and abstract, from real objects to notions and ideas, and from the simple to the complicated. Our teachers are well trained in understanding and carrying out philosophically the system, and to render the various methods invented and adapted to every branch of instruction serviceable to the fundamental idea. They are, as a rule, left free to follow their own method, provided the same do not conflict with the system and general idea. Thus there is a variety of methods of instruction in elementary reading, but the tedious spelling of Anglo-Saxon schools is, as a rule, done away with. In the best of our schools English and German reading is gone through to the end of the first reading book in three months with the quickest of the pupils; in half a year with a great majority; in one year, at latest, with the rest; and all they can read they must be likewise able to write legibly and correctly on their slates. These reading methods are more or less phonetic, and the intellect is called into activity in analyzing the sounds of the words and the pictures, of their written or printed representatives into their constituted elements, and in recomposing them into spoken and written or printed words. In elementary arithmetic the value of numbers must first be objectively demonstrated, and fluently understood before ciphering begins. Addition and subtraction within the space of the numbers from 1 to 20 are followed by multiplication and division within the same numerical space; then follow the four "rules" to within 100, later to higher figures, always combining mental arithmetic with practice in ciphering. Numeration and pronunciation of larger numbers follow when the pupils can form a notion of what a million, &c., is. The first acquaintance with fractions can, with great advantage, be introduced even before numeration. Great stress is laid on the ability of the pupils to attack arithmetical tasks intelligently and to solve them correctly and expeditiously, both with and without the use of figures. A thorough training in arithmetic, like the one mentioned, renders it possible to begin geometry and algebra profitably with children of ten years of age. In these branches also the foundation is laid with great care in the manner of object lessons. The pupils must first, from examples given, find out the new notions introduced and express them properly in their own words, discover the rules, laws and demonstrations themselves, and apply examples of their own to the rules already mastered. A definition is never merely learned by heart, much less a theorem or its demonstration. The pupils must find them as much as possible for themselves, and frequent oral repetition or written exercises impress the matter in all its bearings—not merely the words for it—upon the memory. In the same way grammar is treated, which must be begun after the ninth year, if three languages are to be mastered in a high degree before the end of the sixteenth. Example and object precede rule and definition; the understanding of the thing itself, its name; the laws and rules of language must, as much as possible, be discovered by the learners themselves; and the correct use of the language must be based, not on usage alone, but on a conscious and intelligent practice of the laws and rules; finally a fluent and beautiful command of language, orally and in writing, must result from a frequent exercise in translation from each of the three languages into the other; and artistic ability, from logical clearness of mind and a perfect understanding of the subject to be treated. The pupils therefore are prevented from expatiating stylistically on matters beyond their horizon of experience. So with us natural philosophy is taught in the manner of object lessons. We present before all the experiment, call on the pupils to tell what they see, or otherwise perceive with their senses, and to tell it in appropriate language, to derive the laws proven by the experiment, and to draw all necessary conclusions from them. In the study of natural history the real objects of nature are, whenever it is possible, brought forward to draw information, full and conclusive, directly from them, and to endear this study to all the pupils. History and geography are, as much as possible, combined, to shed mutually light one on the other, and the former is treated in a conversational manner, so as to interest the class in the objects presented; the latter drawn directly from the globe and the map, starting from

home and spreading step by step to the rest of the world, while the pupils are exercised in sketching maps understandingly. The former, leaning thus on the latter, becomes in the hands of a skilful and well-posted teacher a picture of the gradual development of the human race into what it is. Drawing is taught according to different methods; but in most of our better schools the elementary faculty of drawing lines of all kinds is thoroughly practiced, while some include the laws of perspective, drawing from nature, and painting in water colors. In singing some of our schools can favorably compare with any schools in the country, teaching the use of the elements of the system, and performing in two and three parts. In gymnastics, what is called calisthenics and light gymnastics, is practiced carefully, so as to invigorate the system to bear the required mental strain, and to give every pupil the full and beautiful use of all his limbs. We forbear going any further into details, our aim being merely to direct the attention of all sincere lovers of education to the undeniable results of our system and methods; and to open channels of communication between the Anglo-Saxon and German reformers of schools on the larger scale. The two nationalities, and the representatives of their best interests do not yet sufficiently understand each other, though much good for our common country might result from their intercourse and inter-dependence.

In short, the German system of education is *organic*, an organism of a complicated yet simple and beautiful kind; and no single part of it can be borrowed and embodied into a different system without discarding its principal advantages. It aims at educating the whole man together and harmoniously, at developing in the future generations, above all, *man* himself in the full sway and enjoyment of all his faculties and inclinations, by means of a universal training in all the chief branches of science and art, as far as the extant degree of preparation allows; and developing at the same time the *professional man* and *citizen* by means of helping his peculiar talents and inclinations along on the right track. It discards and spurns every kind of one-sided instruction and training, as impairing the harmony of development and the future destiny of our descendants. And if it achieves a great deal it is because it opens in its pupils all the fountains of talent and character, knows how to address and interest the whole man in the youth, and to make

him, from infancy up, self-active and independent, so that he enjoys continually the
greatest of all pleasures, the consciousness
of mental and physical growth, and feels
unbounded and well founded confidence in all
his powers because he has learned how to
use, to apply, and to enhance them.

The very universality of this kind of education is the secret of its success in every
single branch of instruction; its very thoroughness insures its rapidity of progress,
especially in later years. It is comparatively
easier to acquire two or three languages
than one, provided it is done with the aid of
comparative philology and very thoroughly
in the beginning. It is easier to learn arithmetic, geometry and algebra at the same
time than either one, because they illustrate
and explain each other. It is easier to study
and understand history and geography than
either singly, because their contents are
inseparably interlaced and interwoven. It is
easier to become an adept in penmanship
and in drawing simultaneously, than in one
separately, provided always that a thorough
proficiency is attempted. Just so it is easier
to render all instruction morally educating,
and all moral education instructive, than not,
because the one helps the other practice
by enriching its means and powers. Finally
it is easier to combine, with great results,
the *material* purpose of instruction (acquisition of knowledge and skill) with its *formal*
purpose (development of all the powers of
the organism) than to carry out each independently of the other, for in proportion as
the powers and abilities grow, the amassing
of skill and knowledge are furthered and
made pleasant, and in proportion as knowledge and skill grow, the mental powers are
increased, always provided it is done with
system and thoroughness.

The foregoing remarks will suffice to
defend and explain what otherwise, in our
system, might seem to become an over-
taxation of the youthful mind, or else an
inducement to superficiality. The better class
of our German schools will, it is hoped,
on careful scrutiny be found exempt from
such reproaches. It is only with pupils received at too late a period of life, or else
previously neglected in education, that they
cannot exhibit sufficient results of their
labors. Their own pupils will, after having
finished the entire course, stand comparison
with any other pupils of the same age in
almost every single branch of learning and
skill. This much seems to be proven by the
experience of a dozen years.

So—it will be asked—your system withholds your pupils entirely from the public
school? They must, in order to reap the
benefits of your system, absolutely go without the advantages of the common school
system? Do you then not fear that, by separating them during all their schooling time
from the intimate acquaintance and competition with all their future fellow-citizens, you
convert them into aristocrats, unfit them for
the life and duties of a republic, and estrange
them to their country? Our answer, long
and well pondered, is: We do not, at least
not to a dangerous degree. Our schools are
patronized by all classes of citizens, and
admit each, to our knowledge, a number of
poor children gratuitously, or at reduced
rates of charges. They do so from motives
prompted by the above considerations and
apprehensions, and do so to the extremity
of their means. Besides, even the common
public schools are as yet liable to reproaches of the same kind. The different
classes of population live, at least in our
larger cities, in separate districts and
localities; rich parents have, therefore,
always a chance to send their children to
such public schools where they are associated with none but their equals in social
condition, while poor children meet, as a
rule, with none but poor children in the
common schools of poor districts.   And
wherever the school superintendents do not
favor such exclusive movements, wealthy
parents can afford to send their darlings to
private establishments—especially boarding-
schools. As long as the keeping and patron-
ization of private schools are not by law
forbidden, our schools, as not subject to
greater, or even the same exceptions and
reproaches, than other private schools,
ought to be looked upon with equal favor.
Besides our wants are peculiar, and cannot
otherwise be remedied, unless the public
schools are assimilated in character to our
own, and our language is well cared for
therein, of which, indeed, a slight beginning
has been made in some eastern and western
cities.

No class of citizens would more exult-
antly greet the day when they could give
up their own private schools, because the
common schools were assimilated in character to theirs, their language well taught,
and the children of all classes of citizens
freely meeting in them, than the Germans.
Their whole turn of mind is democratic
and republican in the best sense of these
terms. But that this day is yet distant, we

have reasons to fear. One of them is that we so rarely find for our schools American-born teachers of English who are competent to enter into the spirit of our system, and pliable enough to adapt themselves to our methods of instruction and education. The same holds good of French-born teachers of French. We therefore apprehend that it will take many years before the superior advantages of our system will be generally appreciated, as well as before the great number of teachers required for carrying it out all over the common schools of the country are prepared for such a task. On the other hand, if we do not find teachers enough of Anglo-Saxon lineage fit for our schools, there is no lack of pupils of the same nationality who enter our schools and into their spirit, and their number seems to be on the increase.

There is quite a literature of German-American school-books printed and published in this country, comprising chiefly reading books—German, and a few English, according to our system—arithmetics, grammars, vocabularies, editions of classical poetry, and the like—not enough, however, to cover all our wants, so that a number of books remain to be imported from Germany for the benefit of our schools. Those published in the Old World are not in all respects what our system and the peculiarities of our country demand, and by degrees they will all be replaced by books here published. Text-books of science and art are discarded in our system as degrading the teacher into more or less of a machine for re-hearsing recitations, stunting the use of the intellect on the part of the pupil, and con-

verting the school—which should be an organism—into a labor-saving mechanism, a kind of manufactory. We hold that the teacher, if he is worthy of that dignified name, is the best imaginable text-book; our instruction and repetition in all sciences proper are oral, with just as much of written exercises on the part of the pupil, and dictated paragraphs on the part of the teacher, as are indispensable for cultivating the memory, and exercising self-activity in home-work.

The prospects of our German-American schools are not very bright. While, on the one hand, their field of activity is enlarging from year to year, and their self-supporting power increasing, the number of teachers up to the task does not increase in the same ratio, simply because teaching is, even in this country, the worst-paying investment of talent and time, capital and energy. A great many of our best teachers have been driven away from their life-long calling to better paying pursuits; and many more will yet be estranged to their vocation by the endless sacrifices of health and means, connected with instituting model schools and conducting them. It is for these reasons, and because the future immigration of able German teachers will hardly supply the future demand, that the subscribers wish that the Anglo-Saxon schools should henceforth more and more embody the model school; that Anglo-American teachers should more and more adopt the Pestalozzian system, instead of the Anglo-Saxon; and that the teachers and friends of education of Anglo-Saxon and German nationality should more and more communicate and rival with each other to further this great end.

Anthony John Mundella   1870

The Views of a British Member of Parliament

Anthony John Mundella (1825-1897) was born in Leicester, England, and became prominent as a member of parliament. He was interested in education, particularly technical and trade school education and was influential in the parliamentary debates leading to the passage of the 1870 Forster Education Act concerning elementary education in England. While traveling on business trips to the Continent, he studied the educational systems of several of the German states, including Prussia and Saxony. As a result, he was in a position to compare education in Britain, Germany, and the United States.

The letter below to General John Eaton, United States Commissioner of Education, was Mundella's answer to a request for the comments of foreign politicians regarding American

A letter from Anthony John Mundella to John Eaton, United States Commissioner of Education, November 2, 1870, in *Report of the Commissioner of Education, 1870* (Washington, D.C.: U.S. Government Printing Office, 1870), pp. 30-31.

schools. Mundella compared the schools he had visited in the United States favorably to those of England. He noted, however, that American schools provided inadequate technical, industrial, and art education. American educators had already become aware of this deficiency, and a "supervisor of drawing" had just been brought over from England; within a few years after Mundella's visit numerous art schools, such as the Boston Normal Art Schools, were established.

I have much pleasure in answering your inquiry as to my opinion of the American school system. I may congratulate you without reserve on possessing, in all the States through which I have passed, the best and most commodious school-houses in the world. Nothing which I have seen in any European country will compare with them; the State of Massachusetts, I think, and more especially the City of Boston, standing pre-eminent. The normal schools which I have seen are excellent, and the attainments of the teachers, especially of the female teachers, beyond anything I could have expected, and far beyond anything I have witnessed elsewhere.

The munificence of the American people in the sections I have visited, in providing schools, is, in my opinion, entirely without a parallel; a good education being offered free to every American child. If I have any regret it is to notice that where such ample, almost lavish, provision has been made, there are still many who partake very sparingly only, while others absent themselves altogether from the feast. If you could introduce a plan for enforcing regular attendance for a course of years, as is done in Germany, your educational system would leave little or nothing to be desired. I may state, from long experience, that where the education of children is wholly dependent upon the parents, selfishness, or the indifference, or intemperate habits of many, will cause a considerable number to be entirely neglected, or only partially educated; and, in a country like yours, where the only guarantee for your free institutions is the intelligent assent and support of the citizens, the State and the nation have a right to demand that those who share in the government of the country and enjoy its privileges shall have had the advantage of education and a virtuous training.

In my opinion the successful working of the schools in Boston is mainly attributable to the fact that large compulsory powers are exercised by the school board of that city. I can quite understand that American citizens generally need no compulsory powers to enforce the education of their children, but with the immense influx of emigrants from all quarters of the world, too many of them, also, entirely illiterate, it is not safe to commit to the discretion of such persons the question whether the future citizens of this country shall or shall not be educated. It appears to me that a great impulse could be given to the work of education in every State by the exercise of some central inspection and supervision from your own Department. Great emulation, I think, would follow from a fair annual estimate of the quality and result of the instruction afforded in every State, emanating from some central authority. I think the District of Columbia might, and ought to be, made a model for every other section of the Union.

My observations have been entirely confined to the elementary, grammar, high, and normal schools, and institutions for technical instruction; but I have not seen any of your universities or professional colleges, and am unable, even if I were qualified, to give an opinion as to their extent and value.

While there is so much room for congratulation, there is an immense field remaining unoccupied which cannot be neglected without grievous loss to the nation. I refer to technical, industrial, and art education, which, so far as national and State effort is concerned, seem to have been much neglected. The Cooper Institute of New York, and the Institute of Technology at Boston and Worcester, are bright exceptions. The first I regard as one of the most noble and useful instances of private benevolence I have ever encountered.

David Murray

National Education: An American Plan for Japan

David Murray (1830–1905), an American educator, graduated from Union College in 1852. He then served at the Albany Academy until 1863, first as an instructor and for six years as principal. For the next ten years he was a professor at Rutgers College, and in 1872 he received a request from Arinori Mori, Japanese Chargé d'Affaires in Washington, to prepare a memorandum for the Japanese government on "the necessity for a national system of education." Requests were also sent to Theodore Woolsey, William Stearns, Mark Hopkins, James McCosh, Charles Eliot, and Birdsey Northrop. However, Murray's memorandum below was deemed by the Japanese as the most thoughtful presentation, and it led to his appointment from 1873 to 1879 as adviser to the Japanese Ministry of Public Education. Inazo Nitobe, a prominent contemporary educator from Japan, noted that Murray "rendered valuable service in helping to carry out the elementary school system, an outline of which had been formed before his arrival."

The problem of education is justly regarded by statesmen as the most important in all the circle of their duties.

All other functions of government, such as the repression and punishment of crime, the encouragement of national industries, the development of commerce, the defence against enemies, all are inferior in importance to that training of the young which determines the character of the nation. Education, by its benign influence on men, when in their formative and plastic period, renders the severer interferences of government unnecessary.

Good and intelligent populations need but little government. Repressive enactments, and the expensive machinery of armies and police, would, under such circumstances, become superfluous. And just so far as education can render a nation intelligent and virtuous, so far is it relieving the rulers from the more painful exercises of power. The nations which have in modern times exerted the greatest influence on the world's history, those which have made the most rapid progress in wealth and power, are those which have made education their special care, and have furnished the most general and the most thorough culture to their citizens. The two nations which in the past century have advanced most in wealth, population, fame, and influence, are the United States and Germany. In these nations, if there is any one feature in which their systems of government excel, it is in the liberality and profusion with which the means of education have been provided. Differing widely in other circumstances, they have still shown this common aim in their efforts to render education universal, and to leave no human soul within their territory without the opportunity for development.

It is worth while to consider how education does so materially and actively influence the life and well-being of a nation. And following essentially the divisions of this subject suggested in the letter of the Japanese chargé d'affaires, we may consider—

1. *The Effect of Education upon the Material Prosperity of a Country.*

National prosperity is held to consist in the accumulation of wealth in the hands of the inhabitants, in the general activity of trade and exchange, in the increase of the productions of a country, and in its general growth in population. These circumstances, which constitute material growth, are sure evidences also of the existence of happiness and contentment among the people, and have no small share in producing them. Education does three things which bear upon the material prosperity of a country:

1. It stimulates in the mind of the individual a desire to improve his present condition, and aids him in devising ways and means.

2. It teaches what has been done in other lands, and by other men in like pursuits.

3. It opens up to him the principles which underlie his vocation, and gives him a sure scientific basis for his future efforts. For example, in agriculture, which must, in all countries, be regarded as a leading industry,

David Murray, "National Education: Its Necessity, Advantages, and Institutions," *Education in Japan: A Series of Letters Addressed by Prominent Americans to Arinori Mori* (New York: D. Appleton and Company, 1873), pp. 88–108.

the ignorant tiller of the soil plods on year after year without ever dreaming that improvement in his traditional methods is possible, or imagining that any change would improve or increase the products of his ground. On the other hand, place the educated man in the same circumstances; he is not satisfied with present achievements; he must secure larger and better crops for the same expenditure of labor, and he must improve the implements and methods with which his work is done. He has learned from books and from teachers what others have accomplished, and he finds much that applies to his own peculiar circumstances. And, lastly, his knowledge of principles enables him to judge of the applicability of these methods, and to devise means for himself of rendering his art more perfect. Improvements of this kind in agriculture always begin among the intelligent, and, like leaven in bread, extend to the whole mass. One wise and judicious man is a centre of influence to a whole neighborhood. The good examples are followed, sooner or later, by the unthinking imitators, and so the educated classes become themselves in turn educators of others.

What is true of agriculture is true of every great national industry. In many of these, education is even more directly influential, because a greater degree of technical skill is necessary for their successful prosecution.

The development of the mineral resources of a country must depend largely upon the employment of skilled engineers, who have been trained up for such pursuits.

Science has taught the geologist to detect the hiding-places of all precious and useful metals, and to trace their extent and predict their value. Science has taught the methods of converting the raw materials of a country into finished and valuable productions. It has devised machinery to supplement the labor of the human hands. It takes the cotton, the flax, the wool, and the silk, and turns them into cloths. It takes the metallic ores from their native beds, and by subtle transformations converts them into the thousands of articles required for human use.

To originate and carry on these extensive industries which constitute the wealth and material prosperity of a nation, requires a large body of educated men. It requires operatives of skill and intelligence. It requires superintendents and engineers and chemists, especially and highly educated. And, over all, it requires that the capitalists

who possess the means to enter upon these great industrial schemes shall also possess the knowledge which will give them the confidence to enter upon them.

The nation which proposes, therefore, to develop its resources, must begin by providing for its young men the necessary education to enable them to appreciate and conduct these enterprises. From its promising youth it must be able to train up a future army of engineers, navigators, ship-builders, architects, iron-masters, and manufacturers, who shall do for their country what the Watts, the Stephensons, the Brunels, the Bessemers, have done for England, and what the Fultons, the Franklins, the Morses, the Henrys, have done for the United States. Besides the general education which the nation ought to supply to all, it must, to aid these industrial enterprises, provide the special technical education which they demand.

For Japan this branch of the subject has most profound interest. Rich in all agricultural and mineral resources, it presents a boundless field for the applications of modern technological science.

Standing as the conspicuous advance-guard of the Eastern world, it has unrivalled facilities for founding and developing a great system of industries, which will render it as eminent in national wealth as it is already eminent in a spirit of political progress.

2. *The Effect of Education on the Commerce of a Nation.*

Commerce brings nations into relations with each other. The seclusion of an empire from the rest of the world not only narrows and represses the national character, but, by its effect upon commercial relations, cuts it off from one of the chief sources of national wealth. In order that these relations should be mutually satisfactory and mutually advantageous, a common ground of intelligence and culture must exist between them. Those engaged in commerce must possess such a knowledge of each other's wants, productions, laws, and institutions, that this intercourse may not be a system of over-reaching, but an equitable and honorable interchange of products. Commerce is conducted on certain great laws, which must be understood by those who would successfully conduct its transactions. It involves a knowledge of finance and exchange. It necessitates ship-building and marine engineering and navigation and practical astronomy. It calls into exercise the best powers of the best minds of a kingdom. It requires, in short, on the part of its promoters, not only that technological training which its various employments call into play, but a liberal education fitted to develop the highest faculties.

Japan is so singularly well situated for cultivating commercial relations with other nations, that with judicious management it cannot fail to become the great commercial nation of the East.

It has a rich and fertile country; it can supply an abundance of staple articles of trade; it has fine harbors; and it has a commanding location in the great lines of traffic. The great geographer, Ritter, of Germany, long ago pointed out the commercial value to a country of a great extent of coast-line. The access by water on all sides, the indentations of bays and rivers into the interior, afford a facility for carrying on trade that cannot fail to enrich it. The insular location of England, and the opportunities for commerce to reach her on all sides, have produced their effect in rendering her the greatest commercial nation on the globe.

Japan, in respect to the Asiatic Continent and the western coast of America, holds a position almost identical to that of England in respect to the European Continent and the eastern coast of America. It requires but the introduction of the modern appliances of commerce and the judicious encouragement of the Government, to create out of Japan an equally colossal commercial power.

It is, however, the work of time, and in that work education must be a principal instrument. It is that which must stimulate the national mind to strive after the advantages of commerce; and it is that alone which can train up a body of men fitted by knowledge, skill, and enterprise, to carry on its vast and far-reaching schemes.

3. *Effect of Education on the Social, Moral, and Physical Condition of the People.*

Education in its best sense is the training of the whole man, physically, intellectually, and morally. To satisfy perfectly the great ends of his being, he must be vigorous and healthy in body; he must have a mind well stored with knowledge, and ready for any emergency, and he must be so established in honorable principles that he will use his powers for the best interests of his fellow-men. Education, then, if it attains even in a feeble degree these ends, must tend to the improvement of the human race. Whenever education has been extended, and as fast as it has been extended, society has been elevated in comfort and happiness.

Most of the physical evils under which

men suffer are the results of ignorance. The ignorant laborer will starve where the intelligent will find profitable employment. The opportunities for profitable industry may be all around, but the ignorant have no eyes to see them. The earth opens her treasures to those who know how to touch the hidden springs by which they are guarded. Men eat unwholesome food and drink unwholesome drinks, and generate diseases in their bodies, because they have not learned the laws of health. They live in filthy and unhealthy dwellings, and suffer fever-pests to collect around them, because they are ignorant of the poison they are thus drinking into their veins. Education, by imparting a knowledge of sanitary laws, would save men from a vast number of these ills to which they are exposed. And even many of those diseases which cannot be prevented in human society, are capable of being cured by the educated skill of the physician and surgeon. Consider what medical science has done for the human race. How many disorders which were once fatal are now under its control! How much pain and suffering are now spared to us! How many physical injuries and infirmities which were once deemed incurable has surgery been able to relieve! Even battle-fields are invaded by the white tent of the hospital, and the surgeon follows the soldier and tries to save what war has left of wounded and disfigured humanity. Sanitary and medical science has added a perceptible amount to the average human life. Men, on an average, in countries where these sciences are cultivated, live longer now than two centuries ago.

Consider, too, the amount which has been added to human life by the more expeditious modes of travelling and transmitting intelligence. Weeks and months of time which were once spent in the exhaustive labor of travelling are now saved for more profitable employment. By improvements in machinery the hard and heavy labor of the human race has been lightened, and the time thus rescued can be used in the cultivation of the higher powers.

Education has not only originated these vast ameliorations in the condition of the human race, but enables them to avail themselves of these superior advantages for the purpose of higher culture.

But the happiness of man does not depend upon his physical condition solely or even mainly. The social well-being of a community, therefore, will not be complete where every man has enough to eat and is comfortably housed. Our sacred Book says,

"Man cannot live by bread alone." He must have intellectual and spiritual food as well as physical. Even at the hardest, but a small part of the twenty-four hours is consumed by men in business. It is vastly important for their happiness, therefore, that they should be provided with intellectual resources. The educated man possesses these in abundance. Science and literature, the history of his own and other lands, the problems of law and government, the study of man in his history and his destiny, are subjects which may occupy the leisure of the highest minds. Education directs the man to these high themes; and thus, by withdrawing him from lower pursuits and baser gratifications, raises the standard of human character, and increases the happiness and dignity of the race.

4. *The Effect of Education on Laws and Government.*

In all good governments the administration of affairs naturally falls into the hands of the more intelligent and better-educated classes. Education, therefore, affects laws and government more immediately than any other interest. The educated men of a country are mainly the leaders of opinion, and both make and execute the laws. Woe to that country where the ignorant bear rule, and where men of culture are compelled to make way for those who rise by corrupt practices or brute force!

That nation is badly governed which is governed by power alone. A sense of justice and equity, a confidence in the impartiality and integrity of rulers, is more potent in maintaining order than standing armies.

Laws are the highest embodiment of human wisdom. They are founded on the principles of human nature, and upon the experiences of history. Little by little they have been accumulated through past ages. To gather out from the rubbish of the past, and from the experience of other lands, that which will best serve the wants of a country, requires the wisdom of the most cultivated minds. A class of men to whom these tasks are to be intrusted must be trained up with special care, and their efforts must be rewarded with encouragement and honor. It must not be supposed that men fitted for such duties will grow out of the ground. A system of training must be adopted to fit men for the public service, and by judicious dismissions and promotions the good and the intelligent must be retained, and the corrupt and incompetent must be set aside.

While education is especially necessary in those engaged in the cares of government,

a general system of education will render the task of government more easy. Laws intended for the ignorant and vicious may be greatly modified when applied to a nation elevated by education. The history of laws in progressive nations exhibits a continual change from the more severe penalties to the milder, and from a more restrictive policy to a more liberal.

When once the intelligent public opinion of a nation has been educated up to self-restraint and individual responsibility, much that would otherwise require the paternal care of the government may safely be left to the suggestions of self-interest.

Such are some of the considerations which bear upon the subject of national education, and which indicate, with no uncertain emphasis, the importance to every country of making the most liberal provision for its promotion. Liberality here will be economy elsewhere. What is spent on education will be saved a hundredfold in armies, and police, and courts of justice.

Education in a nation means standing and influence among the powers of the earth; it means well-trained officers and soldiers to defend it in times of war; it means ships, and steamboats, and railroads, and commerce; it means the cultivation of science, and philosophy, and art; it means the development of a national literature in which the best thought, the inner life, and outward achievements of the nation, shall be embodied.

To attain these great results requires time. Nations cannot be built up, nor torn down, nor changed, in a day. England has been experimenting since the days of Alfred the Great, and her testimony is that, as she has advanced in culture and education, she has increased in wealth and power, and that her mistake has been in not making education sufficiently free and extended. Germany, since the days of Frederick the Great, has been patiently perfecting her system of education, so that every German child, whether peasant or noble, may receive a thorough education; and it was Germany's education, Germany's universal culture, which triumphed over France in their recent struggle. If there is any one circumstance in the government and the policy of the United States of which she may be proud, it is her free and almost universal education. Every child may find within its reach a school in which the essentials of an education may be obtained. States vie with each other in the liberality with which education is sustained, and statesmen take their most commendable pride in devising the most perfect systems of schools.

It will be advisable after this general summary of the advantages of education, to consider how these advantages may be best secured:

1. Every nation must create a system of education suited to its own wants.

There are national characteristics which ought properly to modify the scheme of education which would be deemed the most suitable. The culture required in one nation is not precisely what is required in another. There are traditional customs which it would be unwise to undertake to subvert. There are institutions already founded which are revered for their local and national associations, which without material change may be made the best elements of a new system. Every successful school system must be a natural outgrowth from the wants of the nation. If, therefore, changes are to be made in the educational system of any country, wisdom would suggest the retention, so far as admissible, of those institutions already in existence. This is but a proper concession to national self-respect, and will go far to make any new features acceptable.

In this respect, Japan has no reason to wish for radical and sweeping changes. Her schools are already an integral part of the national life. Her young men trained in these schools bear a favorable comparison to those of other lands. Her public men in their intercourse with other nations have shown by their sagacity and energy that education is not neglected in her ancient empire.

2. A nation ought to aim at universal education.

It is not meant by this that all children should have the advantages of the highest education. The circumstances and the capacities of many would not admit this. But the effort ought at least to be made to give to every child the elements of an education. This the government owes to itself. It is economy to do this. It is cheaper to educate the people than to govern them uneducated. After this, higher education ought to be liberally provided for all those whose circumstances and capacities would justify it.

3. Female education is equally important with male education.

The employments of woman do not carry her into the same places of public trust or into active business, but in her proper sphere she is equally important as a member of human society. Her education, therefore, is to be as carefully provided for. She must receive that culture which will make her the acceptable and equal companion of man. The comfort and happiness of home depend largely upon her, and it is the part of wisdom to give her the means of making it refined and cultivated. The care and supervision of children naturally fall into her hands during their most impressible years, and the guardians of the future men and women of a nation ought, in common prudence, to be well educated.

4. Education should be both practical and disciplinary.

There are two ends which the education of a man secures. The *first* of them is the development of his intellectual powers. All studies accomplish this in a greater or less degree. The mind is like the body—exercise tends to strengthen and develop it. The man who masters the difficulties of his studies in youth acquires the intellectual vigor to overcome the difficulties of actual life. While, therefore, it is desirable, as far as possible, to educate him in those subjects which he will use afterward, still sciences are not to be rejected because their immediate utility may not be apparent. The culture received from the study of poetry, languages, mental and moral science, and art, is equally or even more valuable than that imparted by practical sciences.

The *second* end of education is to furnish the student with a knowledge of those things which his future occupations will require. This knowledge is as various as the occupations to which men devote themselves. Judges, lawyers, statesmen, teachers, engineers, astronomers, miners, merchants, all will require a different preparation for their duties. Still all learned occupations are alike in this, that they demand a certain culture of mind, which will enable them to master the difficulties of their professions as they arise. Those learned professions, therefore, may thus far be classed together, and the preliminary general culture may properly be imparted in the same institutions. Furthermore, all scientific occupations agree in requiring certain general principles of science which lie at the base of all their pursuits. Beyond this, each profession requires a special preparation peculiar to itself, which may in part be imparted in professional schools, and in part can only be learned by a system of apprenticeship in which each candidate is required to study his profession for a certain time under another before he is permitted to enter into its full privileges.

5. What educational institutions are required.

We are now prepared to point out the different classes of institutions which the contemplated general education of a people will make necessary:

(1.) A class of schools denominated in the United States common schools. They should be fitted to educate children from the earliest school age up to the age of fourteen or fifteen years. They should furnish them instruction in all elementary branches of learning, such as reading, writing, and spelling their native language correctly; the Arabic system of notation and arithmetic, as being the key to all future improvements in science and exchange; the history of their own and other lands. Such subjects should be taught to all children, rich and poor, peasant and noble. Such schools Japan already has in liberal measure, and therefore Japan has the best of all foundations for a complete system of education. Such schools should be brought under government control and inspection, and increased in number and efficiency as fast as the circumstances of the empire will warrant.

(2.) A higher grade of schools is necessary for those who desire and are fitted for a higher education. In the United States those schools frequently have elementary departments connected with them, so that children here may be trained from their earliest years; but the distinctive features of these schools must be the more advanced departments, in which the student may be carried forward into the higher branches of learning, such as the elements of science and mathematics, the study of foreign languages, history, geography, and literature. The studies in these schools may occupy the youths until in most cases they are prepared to enter upon the active duties of their chosen life-occupations. Institutions of this grade would be required in the important centres, and should be multiplied as fast as the supply of suitable candidates will justify.

(3.) For those who propose to enter some learned career, as the higher branches of the government service, or some learned profession, institutions will be required of a still more advanced character, corresponding with the colleges of the United States and England. In them the very highest general culture should be given.

Science in its general principles and many of its applications should be taught, illustrated with the most approved apparatus, by competent teachers. The principles of philosophy, of law, and government, of political economy, and finance, should be studied.

On the success of these institutions much will depend. They will be centres of influence radiating in all directions. They will attract to themselves young men of talent from all the walks of life, and inspire them with an ambition to do something good and great. From them will come the young men full of fire and ardor, who will be the pride and glory of their country. Not many such institutions will be required, but they need to be well equipped with all the best apparatus of modern learning, and manned by enthusiastic and competent instructors.

(4.) Technical schools will be required to give special instruction in various professions and arts. Thus in a maritime country navigation must be taught, and the use of the essential instruments and methods of the profession. Engineers trained in the building of roads, railroads, bridges, steam-engines, and machinery, need a special education. Every country must establish so many and such technical schools as its circumstances call for.

(5.) Last, but not least important, are schools for training teachers. There is a science in teaching, and the men who are to have the training of the precious youth of the land must themselves be prepared for their duties. When new methods and new subjects of instruction are to be introduced, this becomes especially necessary. For this purpose, normal schools are established in various countries and the teachers drilled for their duties. Science-teachers are received into laboratories and instructed in the use of apparatus and in the methods of illustrating the subjects by appropriate experiments.

(6.) In addition to the different classes of schools above enumerated, the best results in education will call for the establishment of *museums*, generally in connection with the highest institutions of learning. In these are to be gathered the various collections which illustrate science and the arts. Specimens of minerals, rocks, timbers, useful products, and manufacturing skill of the country, should be here brought together for instruction and comparison.

And, to close this enumeration of institutions, the government will find it necessary, in connection with the instruction of navigation, to establish an *astronomical observatory*.

To it are to be intrusted the preparation and publication of sailing-charts and the books and tables for determining the latitude and longitude and time on board of the vessels. Every maritime nation has found it necessary to provide for this. England has her national observatory at Greenwich, France at Paris, Russia at Pulkova, Germany at Berlin, and the United States at Washington. For a nation whose language and methods of computation and reckoning of time are so different from all other nations, as Japan, it will be necessary to establish an institution to have charge of and give instruction in these important subjects.

Ferdinand Eduard Buisson 1876

French Views of American Schools

Ferdinand Eduard Buisson (1841–1932), a French educator and politician, was co-winner (with Ludwig Quidde) of the Nobel Peace Prize in 1927. He served variously as a professor of pedagogy at the Sorbonne and later as Director of Elementary Education in France. From 1902 to 1924 he was a Radical Socialist member of the Chamber of Deputies. Buisson's recognition as an educator stems principally from his efforts in securing a system of free, public, compulsory, secular education in France. He is also well known as the editor from 1882 to 1893 of the *Dictionnaire de pédagogie et d'instruction primaire*.

In 1876 Buisson and six assistants were appointed by the French government to examine and report on the American school system. This team of educational experts from the Ministry of Public Instruction made a detailed inspection of the school exhibits at the Centennial Exposition held in Philadelphia during 1876 and also visited schools in various states from Massachusetts to Missouri. The results of their studies are presented in an extensive publication which took some two years to prepare. The critical but thorough efforts of Buisson and his colleagues were regarded highly by American educators. Birdsey Northrop, Secretary of the Connecticut Board of Education, included a translation of the highlights of Buisson's study in his annual report of 1879. In an introduction to this translation Northrop said:

If this Report has not the monumental character of De Tocqueville's Democracy, *it is by far the most comprehensive and the most valuable analysis thus far made of public instruction in the United States. It is our whole free school system, its organization, working, methods and results, set forth in its glories and in its faults, in its strength and in its weakness, by a critic as sympathetic as he is acute.*

A republican government needs the whole power of education, said Montesquieu. This sentiment never found a fitter illustration than in the United States. If any people ever used this "power of education," or united its destinies to the development of its schools, or made public instruction the supreme guarantee of its liberties, the condition of its prosperity, the safeguard of its institutions, that is most assuredly the people of the United States. This role assigned to the school in social life has long been the most characteristic feature which foreigners have observed in American customs. This solicitude for the education of youth grows with the growth of the country, enters more and more into public opinion, and is incorporated in more decisive acts. What in the beginning might seem a burst of enthusiasm has gradually assumed the force of a profound conviction. No longer the work of philanthropists, or of religious societies, it has become a public service for which states, cities and towns include in their ordinary taxes sums which no country in the world had hitherto thought of consecrating to education. So far from restricting itself to elementary education, this generosity extends so as to provide free institutions of superior secondary instruction. Public opinion approves, nay, enacts these sacrifices, so clear has it become to all eyes that the future of the American people will be what its schools make it.

Many causes conspire to give the American school this unique importance. At first it was the influence of the Protestant element. The early settlers of New England knew of no grander duty, or more precious privilege than reading the Bible. Holding ignorance to be barbarism, they early enacted that each town shall have a school and

Ferdinand Eduard Buisson, "French Views of American Schools," in Birdsey Grant Northrop, *Annual Report of the Board of Education of the State of Connecticut presented to the General Assembly, January Session, 1879, Together with the Annual Report of the Secretary of the Board* (New Haven, Conn., 1879), pp. 55–75.

that each family shall instruct its children. In proportion as their government became democratic, that which at first was only a religious duty became also a political necessity. Where everything depends on the will of the people, that will must be enlightened, at the risk of utter ruin. Education, useful elsewhere, is here essential. Universal suffrage means universal education or demagogy.

This country is peopled by the constant immigration of men of every race, class, and religion, who have little in common but the desire to better their condition. The mixed and ignorant crowds who form the bulk of this immigration tend to group themselves according to their nationality. Hence they need to be Americanized as soon as possible. The Irish, German, French, Scandinavians and Spaniards must not desire to constitute themselves a nation in the nation, but these immigrants must themselves be the American nation and make their boast of it. What is the instrument of this marvellous transformation? What institution has so infused the American blood into these thousands of colonists, who have hardly had time to forget Europe? It is the public school, and its usefulness in this direction alone justifies its cost. Suppose that instead of these public institutions, the new immigrants could find only private schools, all would be changed. Each would follow his own ideas and customs, each group would constitute itself apart, perpetuating its language, traditions, creed, its ancient national spirit and also its own prejudices. Instead of accustoming the child to a healthful contact with conflicting opinions, the school would be a confessional, the distinction of rich and poor, of the child that pays and the charity pupil would perpetuate and pronounce itself. It is a capital fact for America, thanks to daily contact in the public schools, that the antipathy of the white to the colored child has begun to yield. And the United States without this fusion of races, without unity of language, without the equality of social classes, without the mutual tolerance of all the sects, above all, without the ardent love of their new country and its institutions, would that be the United States at all? All that this country has become and is now, is literally due to the public school.

In proportion as a nation advances, the dangers which the school is to avert go on increasing. For this reason they redouble their efforts and liberality for schools. As the native population does not increase as fast as the foreign or mixed population, the time may come when the American element, the native *Yankee*, will be in the minority. Hence the United States omit no measure fitted to imbue the new population with the American spirit and so assimilate them that they shall seize and make the national traditions their own.

The Profession of Teaching in the United States.—In France a person enters the career of teaching with the view of creating for himself a stable and permanent position. Those who abandon it before obtaining their retiring pension form the exception. The young beginner expects to live and die a teacher, and as each year adds to his previous experience, the time comes when, possessed of adequate theoretical and practical knowledge, he is able to discipline his class methodically and successfully.

Not at all thus is it in the United States. The profession of teacher seems to be a sort of intermediate stage in one's career— a stage at which the young woman awaits an establishment suited to her tastes, and the young man a more lucrative position. For many young people, this transitory profession simply furnishes the means of continuing their studies. Few male teachers remain more than five years in the service; and, if the lady teachers show a longer term, it is not to be forgotten that marriage is usually the end of their desires, and that, once married, they almost always resign their positions. It has thus come to pass, by the mere force of circumstances, that the school authorities have been led not only to establish various regulations for the application of school laws, but also to lay down detailed courses of study containing the subjects to be taught in each kind of school, in each class, often in each division, and this for each term, if not for each month in the year. The time-tables in schools that are at all regularly attended are fixed in advance, the text-books are chosen by the school board; and finally, school manuals, often of great value, are furnished as a *vade mecum*, from which teachers may derive information as to methods and the various details of daily work.

Time-Tables.—A class in an American public school, even in the cities, comprises at least three divisions or sections, and in some classes with not more than forty-five pupils, five sections are found. But while in France it is a principle not to go beyond three divisions, and to bring these together as frequently as possible in collective lessons, such as reading, writing, history, geography, object lessons, and dictation— whereby these exercises receive the amount of time required for some degree of fullness in the development of the subject,—the American system rarely admits a combination of this kind. Each division has its own separate lessons in the different branches, with an *occasional* exception in the case of oral spelling and object lessons. Thus in a session of two and one-half hours of actual work, we have counted in the primary schools and in the country schools as many as fourteen distinct exercises—a number reduced to seven in the grammar schools; but there is always one-half at least of the pupils that remain unemployed, while the others receive their lessons or go through their "recitation," as it is called in the United States. This everlasting coming and going of *study* and of *recitation* gives rise to a perpetual movement in the class-room.

Moreover, as monitors are never employed, it comes to pass that a very limited period of time can be given to the lessons, and even this time is diminished by the frequent changes of place, for generally, in recitation, the pupils leave their seats and arrange themselves standing, along the class-room wall, and then return to their seats during the fifteen minutes or half hour of "study," their place in the meantime being taken by others. In many a time-table we have seen lessons in reading, arithmetic and history reduced to ten and even to five minutes, and, in like manner, general lessons in botany and physiology cut down to five minutes in the first grade of a grammar school.

What is to be expected from such a procedure? It is in vain that the best arranged programmes are put into the hands of teachers, or that the most valuable pedagogic directions are laid down for their guidance—their intelligence and their devotion must both be foiled by the vices of such a system.

The time-tables—rarer, by the way, than any other documents—appear to us the weak part in the organization of American schools. There is nothing to indicate that most important matter, to wit, the work of those divisions which the teacher has not immediately in hand. The pupils are "studying," they told us, but what are they studying? Undirected and unwatched, we have our fears as to this "studying." Of course, there must be a great abuse of copying work, that mechanical task so justly proscribed in

France; and worse still, it cannot be possible, owing to the lack of time, to develop the reasoning and observing powers of the children. Instruction, reduced as it is, per force, to dry recitations or mechanical exercises, is barren in the lower grades, where this evil is the worst, while in the higher grades it cannot but be fettered, and must produce results below what might be expected from so choice a body of teachers, and so excellent an organization.

School Manuals.—Every one of the various courses of study that we examined has joined to it, by way of complement, pedagogic directions for the use of teachers. Prepared, as these are, by competent persons, they bring the attention of teachers to the carrying out of the courses of study, the mode of conducting recitations and the nature and aim of practical exercises; in a word, they give the school system a unity that secures the regular progress of instruction, while it renders inspection more effective.

Country Schools.—Owing to the representations of certain enthusiastic travelers, a most lovely idea of the American rural school-house is common in France: it is pictured as a nest among flowers. Thither resort, each morning, on prancing ponies, red-cheeked lassies and lads, grave and proud and respectful to their young mates as our cavaliers of the good old times. The mistress—herself young—smilingly receives them at the entrance, o'ershadowed by great trees. How remote is the reality from this picture, this charming exception to a state of things still in its rude beginnings! We traversed the vast plains where the husbandman struggles against an unconquerable vegetation, and the still half-wild valleys in the regions of iron, coal and oil,—and it was not our lot to find any such school idyl.

In the country, stone or brick schoolhouses form the exception; frame buildings, so cold in winter and so scorching in summer, are much more numerous, and the loghouse has not yet disappeared. In the most flourishing States, what complaints are made against defective school accommodations! Let it not be said that, in describing the rural schools of the United States, we have sought out exceptional cases; we have tried our best to do justice to that great country, but we cannot conceal the fact that in the rural districts the school-houses are poor affairs and poorly equipped. Thus in Pennsylvania and New Hampshire, out of twenty-two teachers' reports, fourteen stated that the class-rooms were absolutely destitute of everything in the way of means for visual instruction, that is, there were neither maps nor blackboards; two schools had one map each; one school possessed an old globe; other schools no blackboards and no reading books; a single school was furnished with suitable apparatus.

The Courses of Study in Ungraded Schools are still in the tentative period, not to say in a state of chaos. Some are too succinct and barely outlined; others reflect the personal predilections of the teacher and show that ingenuous pedantry so often found associated with total inexperience. Sometimes a good deal less than the required course is done; sometimes it is greatly exceeded; such studies as history, music, composition, drawing and book-keeping being taken up, and in some cases algebra, physiology, geology, natural philosophy, and rhetoric even.

The worst evil from which rural schools suffer is irregularity of attendance. Teachers and superintendents bitterly complain of this. As a partial remedy, and as a means of allowing children to attend school without wholly depriving parents of their help, some States have lately established a number of "half-time" classes, in which attendance is reduced to a single session per day. This measure has everywhere been followed by good results, and it would perhaps be advantageous to introduce it into our French system, for the summer term at least, and in the case of the older pupils.

The Country School-houses are still in many instances built of wood, as are many of the finest dwellings, but they are frame buildings well put together, painted, and conveniently lighted. More frequently the constructions are of pressed brick with stone trimmings and slate roofs. You have only to see these coquettish school-houses, in the midst of vast lawns, shaded with fine trees and surrounded by palings, to judge of the place which the school holds in public opinion. It is indeed a national institution, devoted to the education of "boys whose votes will decide the fate of the Republic, and of girls, one of whom may be the mother of the president of the United States."

What specially distinguishes the country school-house of the United States from that of Europe is the absence of lodgings for master or mistress. Nowhere in the United States is this arrangement found. It is an evidence of a state of things not without its unfortunate side: the teacher is engaged for a year simply; he is paid by the month, and most frequently his certificate has but a limited duration. Under these circumstances he but comes and goes; when he is not a resident of the locality, he takes board for the school term and has nothing but a study or office in the school-house.

School-houses of New York City.—In the school buildings in New York City everything is sacrificed to the reception hall with its vast platform, fitted to hold a desk, several arm-chairs and a piano. In the hall it is that the stranger visiting the school is received. The movement of five or six hundred children entering in good order, to the sound of the piano, from six or eight adjoining rooms, while the folding doors opening below, show the smallest scholars ranked on steps—all this makes a fine show; but it is purchased too dearly, if the studies and the health of the children are to suffer thereby, as we cannot but think that they must.

The Kindergarten.—Infant Schools, which in France precede the primary school, form no part of the public school system of the United States. The few infant schools which exist are private establishments, or else free institutions, without legal recognition. Nevertheless, since 1871, Kindergartens on the Froebel plan have been attached to some of the public schools of Boston and St. Louis, and these establishments are every year gaining ground in a quite marked manner in all the States. The obstacles still encountered by the Kindergarten arise partly from American domestic manners, and partly from the prejudice which this German importation arouses in the minds of certain superintendents.

Woman in America is much less employed than she is in France, Belgium, and England, in industrial employments that take her from her household. "Home, Sweet Home" is for the Anglo-Saxon a species of worship, and in this sphere the wife is to maintain order, peace and happiness, by attending to her husband and children. It is not to be thought of that she should go to a place of employment in the morning and stay there till evening. The hearth must not be cold nor the house forsaken. And this is the motive that withdraws married women from public school-teaching. For what would become of her "home," and who would take care of her husband and children, when she was at school—generally considerably removed from her abode? In America the mother is the first instructor of her children, and generally she teaches them to read before sending them to public school.

In the Kindergarten exhibits at Philadelphia we noticed everywhere the application of Froebel's ideas, designed to interest children while amusing them, to excite and direct their attention, to accustom them to represent or put together objects of their own devising.

But with Americans the practical spirit is too strong for them readily to accept what does not offer an immediate result. One of the objections they urge against the Kindergarten is that it does not teach reading, writing and arithmetic (the three R's). Indeed, these institutions are not likely to meet full acceptance in the United States until it shall be shown that the general training they give to very young children will induce rapid school-progress, until it shall be shown that children bring from the Kindergarten a certain stock of practical notions. Besides, there is the question of expense, and how can $16 be gotten for the education of a child of from 3 to 7 years of age, when this costs only $10 or $12 for a pupil of from 7 to 10 years of age? If the Kindergarten has made its way at but a few points in the United States, it is the object of an active advocacy and has the sympathy of eminent educators. The application it has already received tends to free the Froebel system of any too exclusive form, and to adapt it to the wants and the genius of the country. This same result we should seek to attain in France, with the view of infusing life into our infant schools, and awakening the faculties of the child, instead of putting them to sleep by merely mechanical modes of procedure.

Reading.—The reading of the French language certainly presents sufficient difficulty; but the extreme complication and the numerous anomalies of English pronunciation render the teaching of reading in that tongue a still more delicate problem. Hence, in the United States, great ingenuity has been expended in the discovery of practical and speedy methods. Germany has furnished many plans which have been ingeniously modified and applied.

The ancient alphabetic method is now scarcely used at all in good schools. It is the longest and most monotonous method—and it is the method best known in France. This method was not represented at the Exposition. Even in the country schools in the United States, there are not on the average twenty in a hundred that use the old spelling plan, and in many States it is not employed at all. Manifestly public opinion has pronounced for the new methods.

In the phonic method, imported from Germany, the teacher drills the child first in the pronunciation of the sounds of the language, then in distinguishing the signs by which these are represented. He thus proceeds from the sound to the symbol, from the letter uttered to the letter figured, in place of passing from the name of the letter to its phonic value, which is often very difficult. However, this method, applied strictly and in its whole scope, assumes that, as is the case of German, a given letter always corresponds with a given sound, and this is not the case with the English language. Hence many objections have been raised to the purely phonic method, which indeed had to be modified into the word method or the phonetic method.

The phonic method, even when aided by all the American improvements of the word method, will always meet with grave objections. Excellent for German and Spanish, in which a letter has rarely more than a single power, it encounters in French, and still more so in English, anomalies resulting from the constant use of the same sign for different sounds, or of two different signs for the same sound, not to speak of useless double consonants, silent letters, etc. This consideration has led to the invention, by Dr. Edwin Leigh, of a method based on the same principle, but which in its application has recourse to typographical innovations. In many schools the teachers make use of the Leigh method in connection with the word method, and this is called the *eclectic* method, for in America every new device assumes a pretentious name.

In most of the schools visited by us, special importance is attached to class exercises in pronunciation. The lady teachers throw a certain ardor into the work of articulation, and, if need be, they show the play of the vocal organs in the production of a given sound or element, as for instance *th* hard, or guttural *r*, etc. It is to be desired that this were done in France, and that our teachers appreciated the utility of this vocal gymnastic, as bearing on reading or even on spelling. No pains are spared to give the pupils a correct pronunciation, not only in the primary but also in the most advanced classes. The master reads in a loud intelligible voice a passage from the Reader suited to the grade. The pupils repeat it in the same tone and with the same inflections. This is one of the liveliest and most curious exercises in an American school, and one which we have often witnessed with the keenest interest. The preceding account proves what importance is attached to reading in the United States. The method employed, very generally a rational one, secures the speedy acquisition of reading, and inspires pupils with the love of reading; this is, doubtless, one of the reasons why there is no other country where people read better or read more.

The Mother Tongue.—The courses of study and the directions for teaching the English language reveal everywhere a truly practical spirit, and are full of judicious considerations. It is with entire justice that distinction is made between language training and grammatical study. It is readily understood that the English language, in which the laws of concord amount to scarcely anything, may content itself with this practical study. French, which deals more in rules and orthographic details, requires more attention to grammar.

Two abuses strike us in the numerous papers on grammar and analysis that came under our eye. 1. The complication of parsing and analysis. In France also we carry written parsing too far, for everywhere routine acts in the same way and transforms into a mechanical exercise what, within proper limits, ought to be a valuable intellectual discipline. 2. Subtlety of distinction and complicated terminology. In grammatical instruction it seems to the Americans that the simplicity of English syntax ought to be made up for by a lavish use of scholastic distinctions, which, unfortunately, correspond to nothing in the construction of language. Dictation exercises which occupy so prominent a place in our French schools, are rare in the United States.

A feature that deserves unreserved praise, and which we found in the better schools in the United States, is the development of the inventive faculty of the pupil by means of composition-exercises outlined in the most general manner. Even in the primary schools the teachers are beginning to require the pupils to write out an account of what is represented in a picture in the text-book or in a chromo placed before them. This is a capital exercise, and one that we cannot too strongly recommend for adoption in our French schools. The task consists simply in practicing the scholar in observing attentively, in telling what he sees, and in telling this in an orderly manner.

Geography has long been a favorite study in American schools. It could not be otherwise in a country that has so many reasons for devoting itself to this science,—the im-

mense extent of its territory, the great diversity in its physical conditions, resources and population, the importance of its commercial relations with the whole world, not to mention the circumstances of its origin, whence it results that no land is absolutely foreign to it.

In response to a well understood want, geographical instruction early assumed a methodical form: this form, without being original, has still an American character, something national and *sui generis*. The old mode of instruction, bristling with repulsive nomenclatures which in nowise spoke to the mind or the imagination, and which merely loaded the memory, is still doubtless found in a multitude of rural schools; for in speaking of the United States in general, it must never be forgotten that there is a distance of nearly half a century between the country school, properly so-called, and the town or city school.

One of the happiest symptoms that strike the attention at the slightest examination is that geographical study now almost always begins where it ought to begin—*by making the child acquainted with the neighborhood, by a plan of the class room, the schoolhouse, the street, the village;* in a word, a knowledge of the points of the compass, not merely on the map and as a matter of definition, but in nature, in a given locality. This very fact is an indication justifying the belief that geographical reform has penetrated deeply into educational practice, for it is generally by such beginnings that this reform ends. It is more difficult to bring about a rectification in the manner of teaching these rudiments than it is to perfect subsequent instruction. And that this progress has been made in the United States is manifest in every way,—by the text-books, the courses of study, and the numberless specimens of work done by the scholars. The strong point in all this new geographical training is that it is really a series of object lessons, that it begins with the child's own stock of knowledge instead of overwhelming him with abstractions and definitions.

Without overlooking the progress already made, we received the general impression that the new methods have not yet penetrated into the heart of primary teaching; they are known and applied sometimes in an admirable manner in the larger cities and in *élite* schools, but they are still unknown in most country schools, and between these two extremes are thousands of schools which as yet have hardly begun to feel the influence of the new ideas, and thousands that have the letter without the spirit thereof. The following features of American geographical teaching are recommended as worthy of imitation:—

I. *To begin with the synthetic method, which, starting with local geography; progressively enlarges the horizon of study, but not to dwell too long on local geography; to give pupils notions of general geography and cosmography as soon as they are able to receive them.*

II. *To practice pupils early in map drawing from memory and in reproducing on the blackboards the proximate forms of countries.*

III. *To insist on the descriptive part, without going out of the way to seek the picturesque, and paying particular attention to imparting correct ideas on the relief of countries, their general features, the nature of the soil, climate, production, etc., above all, great attention to what the English call "physiography."*

Arithmetic.—In American schools nothing is equal to the care with which the child is trained in the intelligent application of the four ground rules. No sooner does the pupil know the simplest numbers, 1, 2, 3, that is the *a b c* of calculation, than means are found for setting him to work in combining them by addition, subtraction, multiplication and division, in such a way as to bring into play all the faculties of attention, reflection and judgment. Beyond this first stage, the teaching of arithmetic generally quits the good way we have indicated, and ceases to be the supreme agency of intellectual culture. It seems as though the sole aim now were to impart hastily the practical means of resolving this or that kind of operation.

The principles that might light up the progress of the pupil and exercise his wits are almost voluntarily left aside. He commits to memory how, in a given case, he should state a proposition, what rule he should follow—whether or not he has learnt the *why*—and he applies the rule, with confidence and in a routine manner to exercises similar to that which served as an example. Practice before theory—such is the idea that generally prevails. And the method of proceeding is generally as follows: The teacher, or one of the most advanced pupils, sets forth on the blackboard each point in an operation to be learned, while the pupils follow, verifying in their book the course indicated; then the latter reproduce on their slates the same work, retain the rule by heart and apply it, point by point, to new

examples. The rationale of the procedure is given only in case the curiosity or good sense of the scholar calls it out.

Great efforts are now making to bring back arithmetical teaching to a more rational way, to ally in just measure theory and practice, by a recurrence to the principles of analysis as well as of synthesis. By the solution of a good many problems of the same kind, dealing with quite small numbers the pupil is led to formulate for himself the method to be pursued in the exercises assigned to him. His memory is then not the only faculty brought into play; he reasons and draws conclusions; his good sense develops, he acquires correct language, acquires a taste for what he does, and gains strength for greater difficulties. Arithmetic has its principles and its axioms, just as geometry has, and it is by setting them forth, by developing them logically that the pupil's intellect is sharpened and his judgment exercised and himself fitted for the intelligent practice of calculation.

Drawing in the Public Schools.—Six years ago drawing was taught only in certain special schools, and that in a very imperfect manner: there were no models, no methods, no materials, no masters. A committee was formed, and in a few years a whole system of instruction was devised. In some states, Drawing has been made obligatory; four methods, strictly graded and completing one another, bring the arts of designing within the reach of pupils of all ages; public expositions are increasing; all regular teachers are put in the way of teaching this branch of education; a normal school of art, to which flock pupils from all parts, has been founded and a fruitful emulation has arisen among various cities. If we take into account that these are the fruits of a few years of trial, it must be acknowledged that such remarkable results were never before obtained in so short a time. The following are the recommendations made on the subject of drawing:

I. *To commence drawing as soon as the child enters school, by slate or blackboard exercises, using the aid of squares or better style of points regularly placed in such a way as to leave to the pupil the drawing of the lines.*

II. *To advance gradually from the straight line to elementary geometrical figures, then to more complex combinations, and so to industrial and ornamental drawing.*

III. *Especially to practice the eye by ele-*

*mentary studies in perspective, by the rec-
ognition of distances by sight, and by the
observation and comparison of forms.*

IV. *To proscribe drawing by mere fancy
or chance, which falsifies the taste.*

V. *To organize for pupil-teachers methodical courses of drawing suited to their
future wants.*

High Schools.—Everywhere High Schools
are the special object of attention on the part
of School Boards and towns having over 500
families—say from 2,000 to 2,500 inhabitants,
do not shrink from taxing themselves for
their suitable accommodation. In most cases,
these schools are for both sexes. No part of
the American school system is more essentially national than are the High Schools, no
part of the system presents features that
are more original, or, in some respects,
further removed from European ideas, no
part of the system is worthy of more profound study. Peruse the course of study in
these High Schools; think of those children
of workmen and work-women passing four
or five years in adorning, strengthening and
cultivating their minds by studies that
everywhere else are reserved for the well-
to-do classes, and tell us if these institutions do not bear the very seal and impress
of American civilization. Need one be astonished, then, at the frank pride with which the
American citizen speaks of these schools?
Has he not a right to be proud when, by sure
documentary evidence, he shows us the son
and the daughter of the humblest artisan so
mentally elevated that between them and the
privileged of fortune no difference of culture,
no trace of intellectual inferiority, is to be
discovered? If it is glorious to see society
freely giving to the poor the benefit of a
public school education, is it not a still
more extraordinary spectacle to behold a
nation that deems it would wrong its humblest citizens were their children denied *any*
opportunity for the full and free expansion of
their minds? Here is a country where there
are hundreds of free High Schools, on the
same footing as the most primary establishments. They are of one body with the common schools, are administered by the same
authorities, supported by the same funds,
and intended for the same population; and
yet, instead of being limited to the strictly
essential studies, to the minimum of knowledge required to take children out of the
official category of the illiterate, these
upper schools are established on the basis of
what may be called the higher instruction.

They are not professional schools, nor are
they bastard imitations of the classical college, nor yet low grade universities—they
are in the fullest sense popular schools,
intended to give the people the best, purest
and loftiest results of liberal education.
They open up no special pursuit—they lead
to all pursuits, without exception and without
distinction. They do not make an engineer,
an architect, or a physician, any more than
they make an artisan or a merchant, but they
form bright, intelligent youths trained to
studies of every kind, qualified to select for
themselves among the various professions,
and skilled to succeed therein. One graduate
will enter the university, another will go
into business; there will be differences of
occupation among them, but there will be no
inequality of education.

*So far as social equality can possibly be
reached on this earth, it is attained by the
American High School.* In other countries it
is to be feared that the children of different
classes of society, though brought together
for a while in the public school, must soon
find themselves separated by the whole distance between their respective families;
indeed, it must be so, since one child enters
on his apprenticeship and thus stops short
in his intellectual development at the very
time when the other is just beginning his. In
the United States every effort is made to
delay and to diminish this separation, to
carry as far as possible, and as high as
possible, that common instruction which
effaces the distinction of rich and poor.

If it be true that the prosperity of a republic is in the direct ratio of the replenish-
ment of its middle classes, of the abundance
and facility in the indefinite recruiting of
these classes, then the High School of the
United States, whatever it may cost, is the
best investment of capital that can possibly
be made.

Summary of Conclusions.—1. The common schools of the United States are essentially a national institution; they are dear to
the people, respected by all, created,
sustained and enriched by a unanimous spirit
of patriotism which for a century has shown
no falling off; in a word, they are deemed
the very source of public prosperity, as,
par excellence, the conservative and pro-
tective institution in their democratic
government and republican manners.

2. The school organization is rigorously
municipal. The law simply establishes as a
principle the necessity of public instruction,

leaving to each community to provide for its own needs in its own way.

3. The higher direction and the inspection of the public schools are confided to elective boards. From this peculiarity arise various results, as, for instance, the frequent renewing of the Boards and Superintendents, the unfortunate influence of political prejudices and local interests, the liability to sudden changes in the school organization, and, finally, *the necessity imposed on the people to keep themselves informed on the school questions, as matters on which they have constantly to vote.*

4. The public schools are in all grades absolutely FREE: the abolition of fees was in every State the signal of the new birth of the public schools; it brought into these establishments the children of all classes of the population, and constantly tends to bring them nearer and nearer together.

5. The public schools are absolutely unsectarian.

6. Compulsory education, made matter of law in some States, has doubtless aided the development of common school instruction. The results thus far ascertained are not very striking; and besides it is impossible either to pass or to carry out the measure in the very region where its urgency is most pressing, that is, in the South. In general, the most practical form that compulsion has assumed is the hunting up of vagabond children or the adoption of various measures to force them into school, to begin with, and then, if need be, to transfer them to reform schools or other special establishments.

7. Public school instruction in the United States does not form a course of study apart, strictly limited to a minimum or completely distinct from classical instruction; it comprises three degrees—the primary, the grammar school, and the high school course—sometimes combined in a single school, and again subdivided among three different schools, but in all cases *connecting with the higher education,* whether literary or professional, so that a child of the working class has the opportunity of gratuitously continuing his education as far as his tastes and aptitudes permit.

8. The training of teachers is now almost universally regarded as the essential condition of sound, popular education, and the number of State Normal Schools is rapidly increasing.

9. As the career of teaching is often taken up merely provisionally by young men or women who do not intend to continue in the field, there results a very grievous instability in the teaching force—though it should be observed that there is some compensation for this evil in the fact that it draws into the work a large number of young schoolmasters full of ardor, equipped beyond the needs of the common school course, and untrammelled by the spirit of routine.

10. The coëducation of the sexes is the rule in the American public school system, and except in some of the great cities is becoming more and more the rule. The results of this usage are generally represented as excellent in both the moral and the intellectual aspect. The only or at least the chief objections heard, are based on the excess of labor which the system imposes on young girls.

11. From these causes and from the marked taste of Americans for innovation and new departures, it has come to pass that the schools of the United States show a diversity of organization, and a multiplicity of forms, courses of study, textbooks, and methods, which result in much experimentation and a lamentable loss of time; but which, by leaving a great deal to the free choice and responsibility of teachers and local authorities, interests them directly and personally in the success of the school.

12. Thence result, also, extraordinary efforts and boundless liberality directed to giving the schools, both in the construction of the buildings and in the establishment and maintenance of the institutions, an air of comfort, of amplitude, and almost luxury, which is not merely a satisfaction to municipal pride, but is mainly the means of giving the public schools the prestige necessary to bring within their fold all classes of the population without distinction.

13. The great publicity given to the Reports of Committees and Superintendents, the interest taken by the people in school statistics, and the beautiful and simple organization of the National Bureau of Education do more for the growth and improvement of educational institutions than could possibly be accomplished by the *orders of any administrative authority,* even though clothed with the most extensive power.

14. If, with all these educational facilities, the United States still show a considerable proportion of illiterate population, the explanation is found, first, in the fact that the whole South is yet a region to be conquered for public school instruction, and secondly, because immigration is incessantly

bringing in a fresh contingent of illiterate adults.

15. The educational methods of the United States are in general distinguished from our own by two characteristics, which may by turns be either advantages or defects. On the one hand they tend to become essentially objective, synthetic, analogical, active. On the other hand, they are eminently practical, being planned and practiced with reference to the wants of life and to direct utility.

16. And so in the choice of subjects to be taught, the American system is marked by the selection of the most indispensable matters, of the most rapid methods, of the most positive successes, of those advantages which if not the most important for mental improvement, have the most direct bearing on the present or future interest of the pupil,—an aim which is very well in principle, but which, when too exclusively sought, stamps study with an empirical and utilitarian impress, gives a narrowness to education, and to a certain extent cramps the mind itself.

17. As regards methods of teaching, the American system recommends itself by a frequent appeal to the pupil's own powers, to his intellectual and moral spontaneity. It cares less for the logical order of ideas than it does for the natural order of impressions; it leaves a large independence to the teacher and a still larger to the scholar,—whence an extreme diversity in the modes of procedure and a not less striking inequality in the results. Many and many a time one is struck with the hasty, rapid, almost improvised character of a plan of education which trusts implicitly to good instincts, good sense, and good will, which aims ever to address the eye, the memory, the imagination, which would thus gain time over the old strictly didactic methods, but which by so doing, runs the risk of becoming somewhat superficial, and is in danger sometimes of dispensing too much with the severe but fruitful labors of abstraction and reasoning.

We are not of those who, ignorant of the marvellous proofs of moral and material vitality which the United States have shown, think that we have discovered in this grand body the germ of decomposition and prophesy its near ruin. This is perhaps *the* people, of all the earth, which has in its immense domains the grandest deposits of natural riches; in its temperament and character the most powerful motive to action; in its historical traditions the noblest example of energy, efficiency, courage and civic honor, and in its institutions the system best fitted to favor the rise of liberty, and these are some of the forces which ought to resist the toughest trials. But while we do not overlook these most promising signs, we do not conceal the formidable problems which the country has still to solve. The antagonism of races, traditions and interests which brought on the bloody conflict between the North and the South, the irruption of the blacks into public life, a just but terrible punishment of a civic wrong, the difficulty of long maintaining the bonds which unite people so diverse, spread over a territory so immense; all these are grave questions. These however are thrown in the shade by a danger more immediate, and that is the alteration, say rather the corruption of political morals, the question of elections, and especially the election of President, whether this shall be made by the intelligence and virtue of the people, or whether it will veer about and become the prey of intrigue and corruption.

Henryk Sienkiewicz   1876

Rural Schools

Henryk Sienkiewicz (1846-1916), a Polish novelist, studied philology at Warsaw University and graduated in 1870. He traveled extensively in the United States between 1876 and 1878. Sienkiewicz's best-known literary work was *Quo Vadis*, written in 1895; he was awarded the Nobel Prize for literature in 1905.

During his travels in the United States, Sienkiewicz noted that "the accepted system of teaching is by demonstration." Visiting a one-room country school he found that "the starting point in a lesson in geography is the schoolhouse itself," and "the teacher constantly

Henryk Sienkiewicz, *Portrait of America*, edited and translated by Charles Morley (New York: Columbia University Press, 1959), pp. 23-25.

extends the horizon of [the children's] knowledge until it includes the whole earth." Sienkiewicz enjoyed these visits and felt that the United States could expect "remarkable results" from the investment being made to build schools among the "Indians, buffaloes, grizzlies, jaguars, and rattlers."

Roaming with a gun on my shoulder along the banks of the Cosumnes and in the neighboring hills, lured by curiosity and—shall I confess?—by the charms of the teacher, I frequently stopped at the solitary little school. It is a small building, consisting only of one room. The benches are arranged according to the latest scientific methods. On the walls are maps of the United States, Europe, and other parts of the world. Between two maps hangs a motto made out of dried flowers by the children: "Knowledge is power." Facing the benches is the teacher's elevated desk, which, however, she seldom occupies; instead, walking among the pupils, she conducts the lessons in a peripatetic manner, so to speak. Moreover, since the children vary in the degree of their mental development, almost every one requires individual instruction. Reading, writing, and arithmetic are, of course, the main subjects, but the lessons also include zoology, botany, geography, and the like.

The accepted system of teaching is by demonstration, an exceedingly practical method which is now in common use. The teacher's starting point in a lesson in geography is the schoolhouse itself. The children learn how houses are built and for what purposes the rooms are used. After learning about the school, they become acquainted with the countryside in which the school is located, the towns, the rivers, then the entire state, next the United States. The teacher constantly extends the horizon of their knowledge until it includes the whole earth. In the study of zoology and botany the children learn first of all about the fauna and flora of their own vicinity. They study a large number of plants which they see daily on their way to and from school, and the teacher describes the harmful and useful properties of these plants. In the same manner she acquaints her charges with animals and minerals.

Thanks to this excellent system there is in the entire United States scarcely a person among the younger generation who cannot read, write, or calculate, who does not understand politics, and who, in short, is not more or less prepared for his duties as a citizen. The hope is well-founded that such schools and teachers will awaken civic honesty and public conscience, which at present are apparently being bandied about by playful young kittens.

There are many schools like the one described above. Wherever several farms are established on the prairie, there among the Indians, buffaloes, grizzlies, jaguars, and rattlers a small school is immediately erected which the children attend daily, even from a distance of several miles. The United States spends more money than any other country on education, and remarkable results may be expected from this investment in the not-so-distant future.

The education of youth, especially on the elementary level, is almost exclusively in the hands of women. I have already discussed the good features of this system; I shall now speak of the bad, for every medal has two sides. Each teacher is generally an "interesting young lady" in whom loneliness nurtures a very romantic disposition. Youth and blood cry out for fullfillment even on the prairie. As a result it frequently happens that some young knight of the prairie, some trapper or farmer, adorned by the maiden's imagery with rainbow colors of heroism, sinks into this imagery as torrents of rain into the ground, and then occur trysts under the sycamore tree, then a hushed "I am yours—you are mine" and other possessive pronouns, declined through all the cases. Then a whispered, "Eternally, ah, eternally!" And finally, as Slowacki says:

. . . things evil and sinful
Concerning which the Bible speaks.[1]

The result is that the morals and the duties of the teacher suffer in so far as the devil gains. As a result of the laws of this country, however, such relations are a ladder from which one either breaks one's neck or, more generally, goes to the altar. It is well to write this, if only for the benefit of my compatriots who, when abroad, are astonishingly enterprising in this respect.

[1]Juliusz Slowacki (1809-1849) is one of Poland's greatest poets. The lines cited are taken from the stanza on "first love" in Song II of the poem *Beniowski*.

Huang Tsun-Hsien   1881

The Closure of the Chinese Educational Mission in America

Huang Tsun-Hsien (1845–1905) wrote the poem below in the autumn of 1881, while serving on the staff of the Chinese Legation in Tokyo. In the introduction to his translation of Huang's work, William Hung noted:

The Chinese Educational Mission in Hartford, Connecticut, represented one of the most fascinating episodes in the history of relations between China and the United States. During its short life of nine years, 1872–1881, the Mission brought to America one hundred twenty Chinese boys in their early teens. They were placed first in selected American homes for general and tutorial guidance and then in a number of schools and colleges, for preparatory and professional training in the sciences and technologies then mostly unavailable in China.

It was mainly the lack of cooperation among the Chinese officials in charge that led to the sudden termination of the Mission and the summary recall of the boys. Yet despite their incomplete training, despite the atmosphere of distrust awaiting them at their return, most of these boys were able to justify amply the inspiration and encouragement they had received from their American teachers and friends by subsequent decades of service to China's modernization. Some of them rose high in the government and professions. Thus, though there were heartbreaking experiences, the story as a whole is heartwarming.

When our Dynasty came to have relations
    with the Western regions
We were at the height of power and
    prosperity:
From the south, the Kingdom of Loochoo,
From the east, the Kingdom of Korea,
From the north, a treaty-bound state,
An empire known as Russia,
They all sent hither their young men
To study under the professors of the
    Imperial Academy.
When the Emperor visited the Hall of
    Classics
Amidst the magnificent display of Court
    etiquette
Epigraphic copies of canonical texts were
    taken out of boxes,
Treasured canopies were stretched over the
    temple yard,
Where students read standing with books
While numerous barbarians stood around in
    the outer court.
Oh! what a manifestation of grandeur!
Alas! it has become only a memory of the
    remote past.

For since the Court had to take refuge in
    Jehol,
The country has weakened miserably.

Six or seven Powers around the globe
Are as vultures waiting with covetous
    glances.
Neither the literary style fit for stately
    occasions
Nor the rhymes demanded by examinations
Can, in the opinion of two or three elder
    statesmen,
Help the country out of its predicament.
To plant talents for the future,
It is necessary to have foreign education.
These statesmen memorialized the Throne
    to send students abroad;
An Imperial decree ordered officers to take
    charge:
Let preference be given to ability,
Then consideration to the status of the
    home.
But aristocracy thought success through
    literary examinations
As easy as plucking a hair from one's own
    beard;
The bound volumes of antithetic essays
    contain precious models;
Should youths be ordered to stop reading
    them?
Far, far off, the Western Hemisphere,
Farther than the world's edge.
A boy from a well-to-do home should not
    be exposed to the least danger;

Huang Tsun-Hsien, "The Closure of the Educational Mission in America," translated and annotated by William Hung, in *Harvard Journal of Asiatic Studies*, XVIII (1955), 51–56.

Should he dare to meet sea monsters by
 taking the voyage?

Only the sons of humble homes
Will prefer profit and think lightly of
 separation.
The sparrows on a frozen hilltop,
Wearing short their beaks and crying daily
 of hunger,
Will think of the joy of flying off
To somewhere,--anywhere.
Thus farm boys in rags,
Mere babes with tousled hair,
Were granted liberal scholarships
And provided with wardrobes for a glorious
 trip.
The sailors were experienced travelers;
Even they were surprised by what they saw:
"These are poor children;
How could they have come to enjoy such
 privilege?"
Nonetheless, a Minister brought them to the
 ship;
Disembarking, they rode away with him in
 brilliant carriages;
At last they were turned over to the
 Principals
Who were to direct them in everything.

In the large building with more than a
 hundred rooms,
With the yellow dragon-flag raised aloft on
 the outside,
You enter a classroom to find it empty;
You see the professorial chair never
 occupied.
The learned teachers are having their sound
 naps,
Comfortable and undisturbed.
Where are students?
They are nowhere to be found
They have gone with their lady tutors,
Like hens and chicks.
They twitter all day long in the avian
 language
In the hope the little ones might learn it
 perfectly.

Among them the highly talented students
Are often extraordinarily good.
The rest just hit or miss;
Many have lost themselves in the
 environment.
They step on a thousand flowers in the red
 carpet;

They look out of four windows framed with
 green glass;
They ride on golden-reined horses to
 marble-pillared palaces;
They feast off silver platters and drink
 from ever-brimming cups.
The ignorant country lads, having seen
 little before,
Are easily swayed by such strange
 luxuries.
When a letter comes from home, telling of
 poverty
And asking "How are you now doing?"
The answer is "I eat two chickens a day;
I recall not how you burnt the door to cook
 the hen for a parting feast.
You say you have no more cereal;
Well, why not just eat meat?"
A caller wants to discuss conditions in the
 old country;
The boys blush and know not what to say.
Though they can use the foreign tongue to
 call one another to play,
To summon the waiters to the dinner
 tables,
To chat on varying subjects among
 themselves,
Or to sing high-pitched solos,
Yet, as for the Shanghai or the Canton
 dialect,
They have forgotten and ceased to
 understand.
Some even practice the Christian religion,
Follow people into churches
To partake of the eucharist
And to turn the leaves of the Scriptures.
They live in a mirage, a paradise,
And are showered with fragrant blossoms
 by the fair ones.
They have found the country of superb
 happiness;
They are too happy to think of their
 fatherland.

Then came the new Principal, Mr. Wu,
And his associate, who was fond of showing
 bureaucratic powers
And who said, "These are runaway horses;
We have to bridle them before we can ride
 them."
The students were called together
And ordered to make obeisance at the threat
 of the whip.
The weaker ones only screamed in pain;
The stronger boys turned around to
 remonstrate.
"You are wild whelps,

Not so polite as timid mice."
"Who wants to be scolded like a beast
Or to suffer violence in public?"
Angered, the Principal memorialized the
    Government
And pressed exaggerated charges:
"These pupils are completely incorrigible
And have learned nothing save truancy.
With such schooling they will either become
    barbarian slaves
Or remain simply stupid Chinese.
The nation has wasted much money
On them—and for what good?"
The Government instructed the Ministers:
"Make a careful selection of those to be
    retained."
One of the Ministers was partial to the
    students
And made up his mind to give them every
    support.

Mollified, the Principal regretted
His own words—too difficult to retract
The other Minister had just got off the train,
And he vented his displeasure with abusive
    words:
"I'll hear none of this business;
Let me enjoy my clams."
The Principal rose up in a rage
And painted like an air pump made of bamboo.
Thus, one word of disagreement
Set them as far apart as heaven and earth.
One hundred wretchedly unhappy boys,
Each and every one had to be sent home.
It was as if a melon field had been raked up
    by the vines and roots;
Oh! so many were crushed!
Before their recall was finally decided upon,
Americans wrote letters back and forth.
Former President Grant
and college presidents So-and-So
All spoke good words for the Chinese
    students,
And wished to have them become stars of
    the two nations.
"Since they have not studied long,
It is too early to tell whether they will
    succeed.
But the bright ones among them
Are certainly not dumbbells.
This is like breaking up a banquet
Or tearing off decorations.

You have expected us to love and help these
    boys,
Why do you now leave us out of all
    consideration?"
His Lordship, the State Minister, replied:
"Merely the dismissal of the faulty ones."
Yet, suddenly all were recalled to be
    disbanded;
There is loud protest about our deception.
The resentment may find expression in
    inhospitality;
Soon there will be the exclusion of Chinese
    laborers.

We recall the popularity of Western science,
Reaching its zenith in the K'ang-hsi period.
Mathematics then included geometry,
And medicine many foreign prescriptions.
Missionaries served either as official
    astronomers
Or as attendants in the Southern Study of the
    Imperial Palace.
In the translated treatises on mechanics
How numerous and impressive the
    contrivances are!
Unfortunately, in the Imperial Academy
The curriculum has not included Western
    learning.
Withal, on the promotion of science
Now depends the future of the nation.
A decade's effort in training youths
Will lay the foundation for a century's
    wealth and strength.
Why treat this matter as child's play
And send only the sons of the humble and
    obscure?
You cannot expect tall pines to grow on a
    little mole,
Nor can you beautify a disfigured face by
    painting eyebrows.
So we have let a magnificent, far-sighted
    policy
Be ruined by mere private quarrels.
The offense calls not for such severe
    punishment,
And it is perhaps too late to repair the
    injustice.
Alas, the stumbling of one misstep!
I fear there will never be another chance.
As I watch the ocean liner sailing homeward
Ten thousand thoughts fill my bosom with
    sadness.

R. Laishley   1886

Comparative Educational Charts and Notes on Education in the United States

R. Laishley, a New Zealand educator and author, served as a member of the Auckland Board of Education and the Auckland University Council. As an official of the New Zealand Department of Public Instruction, he was sent to Europe and the United States to study and report comprehensively on educational developments. Laishley's extensive report is one of the first comparative studies of its kind prepared by a New Zealander. In addition, the charts on comparative education that he prepared are among the most detailed and concise made during the entire century.

In compliance with the request contained in the letters to me, dated the 1st October, 1883, from the Hons. the then Premier of the colony, and the then Minister of Education, I now submit the results of my investigations respecting State education in Europe and America.

The countries written of are Great Britain, France, Switzerland, Italy, Germany, Belgium, and The United States; as it was to those countries, as special centres of educational life and progress, that I directed my attention.

It is conceived that the aim of national education is in each country the same; although the methods adopted may, necessarily, differ, as being, more or less, dependent on climatic, religious, financial, political, or, indeed, geographical conditions.

In studying, therefore, the subject, I have endeavoured to keep in view that three questions should be the tests of any existing system, or proposed innovation, viz.:—

(1.) What is the true aim of national education?
(2.) In what respects, if any, do the means employed in any other country differ from those in the Colony? and
(3.) Whether there are such conditions as account for, or justify, any difference?

It has been also borne in mind that it does not necessarily follow because a particular *régime*, or feature, is the best suited for one place that it is so for another. Thus where a people is all, or virtually all, of the same creed, it is presumed that no serious difference on the religious aspect of national education can arise.

Similarly, financial discussion could not, it is conceived, become important where no State assistance is needed; so that it is impossible to indiscriminately cull all the excellences—excellences they may be so far as any particular habitat is concerned—of a national system, and by patchworking, irrespective of climatic, religious, monetary, political, or geographical conditions, to produce a model system. "But the objector who tells us that the educational experience and opinions of foreign countries are valueless to us because of the divergence between their civilization and ours, betrays his ignorance, and reveals his incompetence for educational direction. Modern civilization is rapidly tending to uniformity and unity. Each nation is hastening more and more to adopt the innovations and improvements of all the others. The educational element of civilization forms no exception to the general drift of things. Methods of teaching have nothing to do with national boundaries. The best is the best everywhere. The essential elements of a good school system are the same in every country."[1]

In aiming, however, at perfection, it is inferred that the special conditions must be considered. Even then, the result of an innovation either by the omission or addition of a feature may not, of course, necessarily be satisfactory; however well tried such an

---

R. Laishley, *Report upon State Education in Great Britain, France, Switzerland, Italy, Germany, Belgium, and the United States of America; Including a Special Report upon Deaf-Mute Instruction*, printed for the New Zealand General Assembly (Auckland, New Zealand, 1886), pp. 1-6, 69-70, 83.

[1]John D. Philbrick, "City School Systems in the United States," Circulars of Information for the Bureau of Education, No. 1 (Washington, D.C., 1885), p. 8.

much as we can only weigh the probabilities for or against success in deciding on any proposition, if hitherto untried where a innovation may have been elsewhere: inas-trial is proposed. We know the defects, if any, of the *status quo*, but the possible effects in practice of a proposition as yet untested in a new field can, of course, only be esti-mated by probabilities.

The religious and financial aspects of national education have especially engaged my attention; because they must, it would seem, always involve the most serious issues in any State system: and, certainly, in the case of the Colony—which is my immediate con-cern—they are the features which admit of the greatest discussion.

It is most seriously questioned whether the British—a *de facto* religious—system tends to diminish crime, and whether a secular one is not distinctly dangerous.

It is not for me to enter here, however, into the questions as to—

(1.) Whether religion is the foundation of morality, or conducive to it, or whether morality can be taught without it? or

(2.) Whether by teaching no religion a creed is not as arbitrarily taught as if Calvinism, or any other form of ism, were inculcated? or

(3.) Whether, even if a majority of the public be against an alteration of the law, it be not the duty of a Government not to obey public opinion, but to mould it? and

It suffices for my purpose to believe—

(1.) That there should be on the part of a State great care that the utmost consideration be shown towards the religious feelings of all;

(2.) "That no form whatever of merely secular instruction will satisfy the great majority who believe that education without religion is impossible;"

(3.) That there will be, if there be not already, "a strong reaction against allowing sectarian jealousy to cause numbers of the population to grow up without the simplest elementary knowledge;" and

(4.) That friction, as between the State and religionists, retards, if it does not prevent, the perfect working of any State educational system.

And, if any proof were needed, surely the anti-clerical agitations in Belgium in 1884 show the seriousness of the questions involved in the arbitrary exclusion of re-ligious teaching from public schools.

I have therefore endeavoured to devise such a system as will satisfy, virtually, all; being, however, well aware of the risk—in the phrase of the Eastern poet—of finding a tiger while beating the jungle for a deer.

As regards the gravity of the financial question I need only point to the very startling amount of taxation for educational purposes; which we should indeed recognize as star-tling were it in the form of a separate direct education rate. The large cost of—

(a) Elementary day schools (including scholarships), and normal schools;

(b) Secondary and university tuition (including the annual value of the endowments);

(c) Native schools;

(d) Summer deaf-mute institution;

(e) Industrial and orphan schools; and of

(f) Public libraries—

would, then, indeed, be keenly *felt*.

Immense reductions in expenditure should, in my opinion, be made, and direct local tax-ation adopted.

There are four other subjects to which also special attention is invited—

(1.) TEACHERS—because—

(a) "The teacher is the key to the whole situation—he is the heart as well as the brain of the ele-mentary school system;"[2]

(b) The backbone of a good system is thorough training of *all* teach-ers—and

(c) The pupil-teacher system is fraught with injury to the taught and the teacher.

(2.) INFANT SCHOOLS — because, to quote an opinion given to me by Pro-fessor Huxley, "the value of these cannot be overrated."

(3.) PHYSICAL TRAINING — because circumstances clearly tend to con-vince—in accordance with what Mr. Matthew Arnold has expressed to me—that it should be a main feature in school training, and not a sub-sidiary one, and should be looked

---

[2]*Report of the Committee of Council on Educa-tion, 1882-83*, on England and Wales, pp. 257, 278.

upon as the necessary basis to be attended to above all other things—by reason of its being an essential preliminary to a sound and retentive mind; and

(4.) TECHNICAL INSTRUCTION — especially in view of—

(a) The complaint, so often urged in the Colony, that agriculture is not profitable; and

(b) Whether greater prominence ought not to be given in national study to what would tend to be useful in the development of the resources of the Colony, in preference to the greater attention paid to purely literary attainments?

The stress laid upon drawing by the Royal Commissioners for Technical Instruction in their report, and by other authorities, is especially noticeable. Indeed, at the International Education Conference in 1884 the President said: "The monopoly of the three Rs is doomed, and the enthronement beside them of three Ds — drawing, drill, and adroitness—approaching."[3]

The remarks upon education in Great Britain are more elaborate than those relating to any foreign country: because we naturally, at least in the first instance, look there for example. In all cases, however, the main difficulty has been to write upon various systems so tersely as to fairly represent all features, and yet not to weary with minutiae. Numerous references are therefore made to publications, which are forwarded herewith where practicable and necessary. When no more detailed information than the text affords is required, the footnotes need not, of course, be noticed; but it is hoped that they may, whenever additional knowledge is needed, prove useful by facilitating investigation.

Of the report as a whole, I cannot refrain from recording how greatly my European and American experiences have tended to confirm me in the view that "of education information itself is really the least part" —that knowledge is not necessarily power— and that in order to render it power, there must exist the ability to rightly utilise it. Until, therefore, physical training, and mental

and moral discipline, are pre-eminent in State training, it is a serious question whether national education must not fail of its true goal.

In the countries visited every facility has been granted to study their institutions. Moreover, through the courtesy of the Secretary to the Education Department in England I was enabled to attend the Education Conference of European and American delegates, held in London in August, 1884; and thereby enjoyed the great advantage of learning the views of an international assembly of high educational authorities.

Further, as whatever value may attach to this report must greatly depend upon its accuracy, I have submitted the several sections to the perusal of experienced authorities in the respective countries: and, although nothing appears except from my pen, and no one other than myself is responsible for comments or conclusions, yet, I trust, the precaution taken may be considered to minimise the risks of error in statement. . . .

When this report was originally forwarded in May, 1885, I wrote as follows:—

"I had, until recently, hoped that it would have been practicable to include herein information obtained by me in the United States of America. But, in consequence of the continuous labour that I have found it to be requisite to bestow on the subject of education in Europe—which subject has necessitated close attention from the time I landed in England in January, 1884, up to the present date—it has been impossible as yet for me to visit America. It is still, however, my intention to do so soon; and, if thereupon my views upon national education there materially alter, I will communicate with the Government by sending a supplementary report. It may, however, be stated that the opportunities I have had of personal intercourse with Americans and others intimately acquainted with the subject; the advantages afforded by attendance at the conference last year; and the study of publications, including the latest official ones received by me from the Bureau, Washington, recently, enable me, with some degree of confidence, to arrive at conclusions."

Since thus writing, I, in January last (1886), visited the United States; and, in consequence of personal inquiry and observation, now add more data, and confirm what was previously stated.

There are several very interesting questions which may with especial advantage be

---

[3] Canon McColl, paper at the International Education Conference, *Health Exhibit Literature* (London, 1884), Vol. XIII, p. 3.

State Education in Great Britain, France, Switzerland, Italy, Germany, Belgium, and the
United States of America

	GREAT BRITAIN	FRANCE
Religious Instruction— (a) Consideration shown (b) Basis of education	(a) By means of local option, with conscience clause, and provision against sectarian teaching in Board schools, and by means of denominational aid. (b) System nominally secular, but practically religious. Regulated by Boards (subject to approval of Department), and managers of voluntary schools respectively.	(a) and (b) System strictly secular; although the system purports to be absolutely neutral in, and not hostile to, religion. But religious instruction optional in private schools. Instruction in all public schools can only be given by laymen. Monks and nuns precluded from teaching in municipal schools. Even the name of God excluded from the municipal schools of Paris.
Gratuitous primary education	(a) Graduated scale of fees, with remissions in cases of poverty. Class books free. (b) Some free schools. Fees and remissions regulated by Boards (subject to approval of Department) and by managers of voluntary schools respectively.	Instruction in— (a) Infant, (b) Elementary primary schools, and (c) Superior primary schools, entirely gratuitous. School necessaries also gratuitous; and in Paris penny dinners provided by municipality—free for really poor. No separate free schools. In communal schools of Paris annual treats given to the most deserving children. In 1885 law passed providing wholly gratuitous education after examination for one child in every family of more than six.
Compulsory attendance	Regulated by Boards. Age, 5–13, virtually everywhere in England; Scotland 5–14. School life there does not usually begin before 6. In certain cases, attendance compulsory till 14 in England. Permanent exemption obtainable by means of certificate of proficiency, or attendance at other approved schools. Temporary exemptions granted for husbandry purposes, or for reasons somewhat similar to those available in colony.	From the age of 6 complete to 13 complete. Enacted by State. Remarkably high percentage of average attendance at primary schools, especially in cities. Exempt if receiving instruction at home or at private school, or if certificat d'études obtained; which certificate is considered evidence of better training than if child had passed all English standards. Other exemptions available for half-timers, and temporarily.
Protection of children against injurious employment	In England employment forbidden under 10 or afterwards during compulsory period until certificate of proficiency (4th Standard) is obtained. But in Scotland law prohibits full time employment under 14 till 5th Standard passed.	Children can only be employed as "half-timers," in trades or agriculture, under age of 13, by consent of public authorities, unless a certificat d'études is obtained at or after 11 years of age."

	GREAT BRITAIN	FRANCE
School age	No limit; but apparently attendance under 3 and over 14 not contemplated for day school, or under 14 and over 21 for evening school.	No definition or limit, except law relating to compulsory attendance. Infant schools admit from 2 years of age, and programmes are framed accordingly.
Local government, by locally-elected authorities	Elected Boards, with large powers, including powers (subject to approval of Department) to (a) Borrow money to erect, &c., schoolhouses; (b) Make by-laws regulating compulsory attendances, religious instruction, fees, and remissions; (c) Found free schools and (without such approval) to claim or levy rates to cover deficiencies in income. One of the chief defects in the administration is that local Boards have little real power, and therefore feel little responsibility.	A certain amount of local government, including powers of local taxation, although less than, for instance, in Great Britain, Germany, Switzerland, Belgium, or the United States. It is the State which supremely controls all classes of educational institutions.
Sources of support	(a) Board schools mainly by grants, fees, and rates, claimed or levied by Boards. (b) Voluntary State-aided schools (about 76 per cent of whole number of schools), mainly by grants, fees, and private contributions.	Primary schools— (a) Communes (mainly), (b) Departments, and (c) State. State now spends annually eighty millions of francs on primary instruction.
Teachers	(a) Pupil-teachers. (b) The normal schools are voluntary, which State inspects and aids, but does not manage or support. Two years' term. In Scotland practically affiliated to universities. Tuition not gratuitous. (c) For Board schools appointments made and salaries adjusted nominally by Boards, but virtually by Department. Incomes dependent largely upon results. (d) Pensions and gratuities granted, although only to a very inadequate extent. Not available for teachers engaged since 9 May, 1862.	(a) Pupil-teaching virtually defunct. (b) Proper qualifications indispensable—brevet de capacité. (c) There are not only normal schools for training masters in all the Departments, but in many schools for training mistresses, and also two superior normal schools for training normal-school teachers. Examinations for admission: Pupils enter about 18. No religious teaching. All residential; three years' course gratuitous. Visiting specialists. (d) Appointments of teachers in primary schools made by Prefects on proposition of departmental Inspectors. (e) Salaries low, but fixed. (f) Pensions and gratuities granted. Women much more freely employed as teachers than in Germany or Switzerland.
Infant schools	When average attendance of infants 20 or more in a school, a distinct department or class of ordinary primary school is formed; children from 3 years, separate teachers, mainly females. Object teaching the specialty. No individual examination under 6 years of age. For scholars not sufficiently advanced for 1st Stand. Special normal school instruction in infant school teaching; but teacher not less than 18, approved by Inspector, may have charge of class of 60 or less. No home lessons. Grants computed only on av. attendance. Number over 7 years of age comparatively small.	The arrangements are deemed excellent. Froebel method adopted in great part. Taught and inspected exclusively by females, who must be of certain age, and qualified. Attendance not compulsory under compulsory age. Limitation of numbers for each teacher. Gymnastic exercises taught. Infant classes added to primary school when separate schools impracticable. The infant schools are probably more thoroughly and systematically provided for than in any other country.

State Education in Great Britain, France, Switzerland, Italy, Germany, Belgium, and the United States of America

	SWITZERLAND	ITALY	GERMANY
Religious Instruction— (a) Consideration shown (b) Basis of education	(a) Not only is religious liberty carefully protected by Federal law, but great consideration is shown. For instance, although Berne is a Protestant canton, Roman Catholic schools have been established there by the school authorities. (b) Religion, as a rule, the basis of education in primary and secondary schools; occupying, as a rule, the first place on school programmes. Religious instruction regulated by cantons.	(a) Religious feelings protected by a conscience clause. (b) Religious instruction by lay headmasters imparted in nearly all primary schools on Saturdays. But it forms no part of school examination, nor does proficiency in it aid class promotion. In secondary schools and universities, no religious instruction. Roman Catholic dignitaries dissatisfied because religious instruction is not in State schools the basis of education, and when given is not conducted as they approve.	(a) Not only is religious liberty protected, but great consideration is shown towards (virtually) all. (b) Religion universally the basis of education, occupying the first place on elementary school programmes. Religious instruction also included in normal school course.
Gratuitous primary education	Universal, but only during the compulsory-age periods. Infant-school instruction not gratuitous except for those unable to pay. In most of the cantons school necessaries are not given gratuitously. Main reason given why instruction has been made gratuitous—that free schooling gives powers of compulsion that can then be enforced with greater stringency.	Primary education in day schools (including infant schools) gratuitous.	Primary education not, as a rule, gratuitous. For instance, gratuitous in Berlin, although not, as a rule, in Saxony or Bavaria, or indeed even throughout Prussia. Where primary schools not free, free schools usually provided for poor children. But available for all unable to pay. Instruction in infant schools is not, as a rule, free. In supplementary schools the law varies according to the State. Books not generally free, except in cases of poverty.
Compulsory attendance	Average period, say from the age of 6¼ to nearly 14½. Compulsory-attendance laws in all cantons; but period not universally the same. It even differs in a canton according to localities. Large attendance percentage. On leaving primary school further attendance obligatory at continuation school for those who do not then attend a secondary school.	Period 6–11, including one year at infant school. But owing to lack of schools in some sparsely-settled districts, education is in some places only nominally compulsory. Moreover, even where there are schools compulsory provisions are frequently not strictly enforced; and attendances therefore are small. For five-sixths of the pupils in some places the holidays virtually extend from middle of June to middle of November.	Period 6–14 at primary school. In some places further attendance is obligatory. For instance, in Saxony those children who at the expiration of the 8 years have not satisfactorily progressed must attend one year longer. And, in some places, boys after the 8-course, if they are not being elsewhere educated, must attend a continuation school for three years longer. Attendance good—"a habit of the country."
Protection of children against injurious employment	Children carefully protected by Federal laws, (a) Against employment when under 14, or (b) Under 16, for more than 11 hours a day altogether in school and at work; (c) Instruction at school and in religion must not be intruded upon by work; (d) Under 18 forbidden to work on Sundays, or at night; (e) Certain industries forbidden.	No law against employment of uneducated children, or of children at too young an age.	Children are protected. Terms vary in different States. In Prussia, for instance, industrial work for wages prohibited under the age of 9; in Baden 11, and so forth.

	SWITZERLAND	ITALY	GERMANY
School age	No time-limit defined. Children frequent infant schools from about the age of 3. Pupils generally leave secondary school about the age of 15.	The ordinary public primary instruction consists of five courses of one year each, commencing at the age of 6. The usual age of entering into secondary schools is 10 or 11.	No limit; but there are certain ages, as elsewhere, when it is considered that pupils should attend certain grades of schools, and learn certain subjects. Gradation of tuition considered excellent.
Local government, by locally-elected authorities	Each canton absolute control (except over Zürich Polytechnic School) over education, subject only to (a) General principles laid down by Confederation, and (b) Ultimate rights reserved to Confederation. Control includes power to regulate religious instruction, to levy direct local taxation, to fix compulsory-attendance period, to manage expenditure and administration details. Cantonal education managed by Boards. Exceptional division of nation into independent sovereignties a cause of excellence.	Whole system supremely controlled by Minister and Council; but in each province there is a School Board, under the presidency of the Prefect. There are also communal and municipal authorities.	State supremely controls; but there are large powers of local government, including powers to (a) Regulate religious instruction (subject to protection of minorities); (b) Levy direct local taxes; (c) Control expenditure, and (d) Manage administrative details. Under Minister in each State is State Board. There are also Boards for provinces and districts and school committees in each parish. Exceptional division of nation into sovereignties a cause of excellence.
Sources of support	Communes and municipalities mainly support the primary schools by direct local taxation. But cantons aid by taxes levied for the purpose, and support entirely the normal schools.	(a) Mainly the Communes and municipalities, by means of direct local taxation, and (b) The State.	Primary and (generally) secondary schools, mainly supported by local taxation, levied by communes and municipalities, and by fees, with aid from States in case of need. But universities and polytechnics are maintained by the States, and by fees.
Teachers	(a) No pupil teachers. (b) Teachers must be qualified. (c) Normal schools—terms, 3 or 4 years; gratuitous tuition. (d) Salaries small, but fixed. (e) Pensions, at least in some cantons. (f) Co-operation of teachers in inspection. "Instruction is better in foreign popular schools than in ours, because the teachers are better trained. The methods of teaching ... are more gradual, more natural, more rational than in ours."—M. Arnold. "Switzerland the most efficient country as to school staff."—M. Arnold. Female teaching not favoured, especially for higher classes.	(a) Teachers must possess certificate of morality and diploma. Those for primary schools are nominated by local authorities, for 3 years. (b) Normal schools—course 3 years gratuitous, non-residential, although annexed, there is often a pension for receiving a certain number of bursary or paying pupils. Elementary school annexed to normal school. (c) Pension granted by State. There are also private associations which grant pensions.	(a) No pupil teachers. (b) Must possess diploma. (c) Normal schools—Admission only after passing examination; not gratuitous; except for those not able to pay; course 3 to 6 years—some for training masters and some for training mistresses; although latter not so numerous. (d) Salaries small, but fixed. (e) Pensions granted. Proportion of pension to salary varies in different States. Usually, however, the amount depends upon duration of service. Female teaching not favoured, especially for higher classes. Co-operation of teachers in inspection. Thorough training of teachers. Better trained than in England.
Infant schools	Do not necessarily form a link in State education. Attendance only voluntary. They are, however, encouraged by cantonal governments, and children largely frequent them from the age of 3 up to 6. Instruction not gratuitous, except for the poor. Time mainly occupied with Kindergarten exercises.	An infant-school course of one year is the first stage of compulsory-attendance period. In Naples are considered the first step in State education. It is said "if salles d'asile could be opened where little folks could have proper care, there would be an increase of school attendance at the ordinary primary schools."	Attendance not compulsory, but children usually frequent them from 2 to 6. They are to be found in most places; but they are not universally public institutions; nor are they favoured in Germany, medical opinion being against school training before 6. All, however, are subject to State inspection. Kindergärten exercises are not formally recognized as a necessary step in State education.

State Education in Great Britain, France, Switzerland, Italy, Germany, Belgium, and the United States of America

	BELGIUM	THE UNITED STATES
Religious Instruction— (a) Consideration shown (b) Basis of education	(a) Recent law confers a certain amount of power to localities to subsidise denominational schools, but does not show consideration towards all minorities. (b) State system is secular, subject to important reservations. For instance, communes may place religious and moral teaching at the head of the programmes of all or some of their primary schools. Such teaching must, however, be given at the beginning or end of the other instruction. Children whose parents request it are to be excused from assisting. Inspection, however, does not extend to religious and moral instruction.	(a) and (b) There is no universal rule; but in most places a certain amount of religious instruction is given. The system, however, must be deemed secular. The influence of the school, however, is wholly on the side of morality and religion; although religious training is virtually entrusted to church and family agencies, which maintain, it is claimed, very full provision for the work. There is dissatisfaction, however, and therefore friction.
Gratuitous primary education	Infant schools—gratuitous instruction for poor; in other cases a small fee. Primary—50 cents to 2 francs per month, but gratuitous for poor if parent goes to Burgomaster and says he cannot pay. In some communes, free schools. Secondary, higher elementary—25 to 60 francs per annum. Royal Athenæum, 60 to 100 francs per annum.	Primary education is gratuitous. Books, &c., are also, in some places, given. There is also gratuitous instruction in high schools. Infant schools do not form a part of public school organization, but where there are voluntary infant (Kindergarten) schools, instruction is gratuitous. Sometimes in cities special schools for wastrels, but generally not.
Compulsory attendance	No laws compelling attendance at school, or tuition for any period.	In the majority of the States and Territories there are no compulsory attendance laws; and where they do exist, in twenty-two instances, the obligatory term is generally very limited, and the laws not uniform. Agents of truancy employed in some States. Want of sufficient accommodation also potent cause of poor attendances.
Protection of children against injurious employment	There is no restriction against the employment of uneducated or young children.	There are only ten of the States and Territories which have enacted laws for regulating the employment of uneducated or young children.

School age	Defined to be 6–14. The usual period for frequenting primary schools is between the ages of 6–7 to 14, unless child goes to secondary school in first instance.	Defined in all the States and Territories—18 different legal school ages. Longest extending from 4 years of age to 21, covering a period of 17 years. Shortest from 8 years of age to 16. Average from 5½ to 19½ years. Pupil generally begins at 6 and ends at 15 or 16.
Local government, by locally-elected authorities	Primary communal schools are managed by the communes. Two or more communes may, when necessary, be allowed by the King to unite in founding or supporting a school. The Communal Councils determine the number of school teachers.	The Confederation has no control over public education. Each State has sole control; but the powers of the States are not usually exercised by the States, but by subordinate organizations, or corporations, into which the States are divided for judicial and municipal purposes, such as counties, townships, and cities. These corporations are generally allowed large legislative and administrative powers, and general supervision only is exercised by the States.
Sources of support	Infant schools: Communes (primarily but not mainly), State (mainly), provinces, and fees. Primary: Communes (primarily but not mainly), provinces, State (mainly), and fees. Secondary: Towns usually give building, and State makes up difference between fees and cost of tuition. State contributes far the greater proportion of cost of all educational institutions. Universities under immediate care of Government.	"Common schools" are supported— (a) In part by State school funds, accumulated from national grants of land, (b) From appropriations made from State revenue, and (c) In part by local taxation (mainly). Special aid granted to sparsely-settled sections of the country.
Teachers	(a) No pupil teachers. (b) For primary schools, teachers must be Belgian or naturalized, and possess diploma as primary teachers on graduating from a public normal school, or one subject to State inspection, after attending course at least 2 years; or have diploma of secondary teaching (2nd deg.); or passed exam. for teachers before Board organized by Govt. (c) The State, the provinces, and the communes can establish normal schools. There are several—some for training masters, and some for training mistresses. All training free, and when necessary food supplied; course 3 years; gymnastics part of training. Besides the State schools there are 34 normal schools adopted by Govt. (d) Appointments in prim. schools by Communal Councils, who may suspend, but dismissal to receive approval of permanent committee; and teachers and Council right to appeal to King. In secondly, schools, appointed by King to superior positions, by Ministers to others. (e) Salaries fixed; small. Minim. limit. Pensions given.	(a) Female teachers very largely predominate. (b) Normal school arrangements defective. Tuition not always gratuitous, but free tuition very general. (c) Examinations, certifications, qualifications, and appointments not, as a rule, satisfactory. (d) Salaries, as a rule, small. Teachers must, in New York, Michigan, and Connecticut, have knowledge of effects of alcohol upon the human body. There are some teachers' libraries.
Infant schools	These schools are maintained by the communes primarily, State, and fees. Instruction is gratuitous, except for the not poor. Teachers are specially trained for infant-school teaching. Programme generally based on the method of Froebel. Usual age of frequenting, 3–6.7. They are joined to ordinary day schools in the communes where authorities deem them necessary. The Communal Council regulate everything relating to their establishment and organization.	Do not enter into theory of American school organization, but in some places there are voluntary infant schools, conducted upon Kindergarten method. These schools are gratuitous and rapidly increasing, and are encouraged, and in some cases assisted, by Boards. Kindergarten exercises have been introduced, to a certain extent, into public primary schools for children not over 7. There are some State infant asylums.

State Education in Great Britain, France, Switzerland, Italy, Germany, Belgium, and the United States of America

	GREAT BRITAIN	FRANCE	SWITZERLAND
Classes of state schools	(a) Infant. (b) Primary day. (c) Evening, But in Scotland universities and secondary education are recognized. In Wales three colleges are aided by the State. (d) Technical schools.	(a) Infant schools and classes. (b) Elementary primary day schools. (c) Superior primary schools. (d) Evening and Sunday schools. (e) Secondary—i.e., Lyceums and communal colleges. (f) Higher educational institutions. (g) Technical schools. French elementary schools considered in advance of the English; not only generally as preparatory for technical schools, whilst German and Swiss schools excel the French.	(a) Infant schools are not necessarily the 1st grade. (b) Primary day schools. (c) Supplementary schools (compulsory for those not attending secondary school). (d) Secondary (higher elementary). (e) Colleges (Gymnasien and Industrieschulen) (f) Polytechnic school, and (g) Universities (5) There are also apprenticeship schools.
Subjects of study in primary schools	Religious instruction as directed by Boards and voluntary school managers. (a) Obligatory subjects— Reading, Needlework (for girls in day schools). Writing, Arithmetic, (b) Optional subjects (Class)— Singing, Geography, English, Elementary science, Drawing, History. (c) Optional subjects (Specific)— Algebra, Animal physiology, Euclid and Botany, mensuration, Principles of agricul. Mechanics, Latin, Chemistry, French, Physics, Domestic economy. (d) And any other secular subject under certain conditions. Over-pressure complained of.	(a) Physical education, and preparation for industrial education— Hygiene, Gymnastics, Military exercises (for boys), Manual work (for boys). (b) Intellectual education— Reading, Geometry, Writing, Drawing, French Elements of the phys- language, ical and natural History, sciences, Geography, Agriculture and hor- Civil rights, ticulture, notions of Singing. political economy, Arithmetic, (c) Morale. No standards; home lessons. Over-pressure not generally complained of, but opinions expressed that too much was done.	In Berne, as fairly representative of the cantons— Religious instruction, Natural history, Language (maternal), Singing, Arithmetic and calcu- Writing, lation of dimensions, Drawing, History, Gymnastics (boys), Geography, Needlework (girls). In addition, in the superior schools, French or German, and geometry. No standards. In certain places black slates abolished to prevent myopia. Over-pressure not complained of.
Physical training	Not obligatory, or specifically recognized as a code subject. Perhaps, in view of art, 12 in code, it is contemplated as coming within terms of art 16 or 17.	Physical education is placed before intellectual or moral: and gymnastics occupies the first place on the programme, after hygiene. Even children from 2 to 5 commence with exercises manuels, and from 5 to 7 have gymnastic exercises. Number of hours calculated to be about the same as in England or Germany. The systematic stress laid upon, and the attention paid to, the subject, however, is very marked.	Deemed to be so important that Confederation has legislated for its promotion; and cantons must attend to it. It is specially intended as a preparation for military service. Teachers have to be specially trained.
Inspection and examination	(a) All State-aided schools are inspected. (b) Inspectors appointed by, and under sole control of, department. (c) Special Inspectors for normal schools. (d) Inspectors' functions very important. (e) Arrangements for examining evening scholars. Regulations relative to examinations, home lessons and punishments noteworthy. Individual examinations dispensed with	(a) All Inspectors are nominated by the Minister. (b) There are lady Inspectors for infant schools. System of inspection excellent; less mechanical than in England. Some Inspectors selected from same class as in England; many more from schoolmaster class. Inspectors, relatively to teachers, well paid. Regular medical inspection ad-	(a) Headmasters take part in cantonal inspection. (b) Inspectors are appointed for a limited term. (c) Jurisdiction of Inspectors over private as well as public schools.

Continuation schools and half-time scholars	Evening schools not recognized by statute, but in discretion of Boards subject to approval of Department. Fees low, and prizes given; but attendance declining. Grants earnable subject to inspection. No limit as to age. Continuation schools otherwise do not exist. Half-time scholars recognized by code; but numbers decreasing. They are said to learn much quicker than other scholars.	Evening and Sunday schools, as "continuation" schools, for adults as well as children of both sexes, are considered to be a feature in France; and arrangements are made for "half-time" scholars. Most of the adult schools are Sunday schools.	Continuation schools numerous and important. Supplement teaching of primary school and prepare for industrial pursuits, or a technical school. Attendance compulsory for a term after leaving primary school unless child joins secondary school. Small charge made unless pupil too poor to pay.
Secondary and higher schools	No support or aid granted by State, except to (a) Scotch universities, and indirectly to secondary education in Scotland, (b) Three colleges in Wales, and (c) Science and art department. The few graded schools established by Boards receive no special grants. But look at syllabus relating to "specific subjects;" and note that higher-class schools in Scotland are inspected at State expense.	Public instruction liberally aided by grants and scholarships contributed by (a) State, (b) Departments, and (c) Communes. Instruction not gratuitous; but fees low. Young children admitted into lower divisions of colleges and lyceums by special elementary preparation. Modern languages and science largely substituted in secondary schools for Latin and Greek.	These are mainly supported with public moneys; but education is not universally gratuitous, although frequently so. Thus, in Lucerne, tuition universally free, in Zürich secondary schools free, but higher schools charge fees. In all cases, however, the fees are small, and in case of need the charge is remitted. Attendance optional. The Industrieschulen are trade schools, the Gymnasien classical.
Technical instruction	Promoted in two ways— (a) In primary schools by means of drawing (class subject), and grants payable in respect of "specific subjects;" and (b) Votes to Science and Art Department.	Most liberally promoted by (a) Blending theory and practice in primary schools, (b) Evening, Sunday, apprentice, and continuation schools and classes, (c) Science and art schools, and (d) Lectures of all kinds. Instruction gratuitous: except nominal fee in some cases for lectures. Evening schools considered especially excellent.	Not only are there supplementary schools, but also (a) Apprenticeship schools, (b) Industrieschulen, (c) Other technical institutions, and (d) Zürich Polytechnic School.
Scholarships	No public-money scholarships except those granted by Science and Art Department. But there are scholarships available for primary-school scholars, supplied by private benevolence.	State freely grants scholarships (bourses) for scholars in primary and higher schools. But the comparative smallness of the amounts, especially of those available for superior primary schools is noticeable.	Small public-money scholarships granted, but only to those who (a) Pass requisite examination, and (b) Require them in order to pursue their studies.
State supervision respecting private schools	There is no State control or supervision in Great Britain over private schools or private tuition. The only provision is that a Board must be satisfied that a "child is under efficient instruction."	Private schools are not under general State control, but are subject to State supervision in respect of (a) Morality, (b) Sanitary arrangements, (c) Keeping a register of, and reporting absences, (d) Books used not being such as are contrary to actual Constitution or principles of Government. Teachers must possess the brevet de capacité, except in certain very exceptional cases of age and experience.	Each canton has power to make regulations in respect of private schools as well as public, and they are inspected by the same inspectors as the public schools. Only perhaps 2 or 3 per cent of children attend them during compulsory period.

State Education in Great Britain, France, Switzerland, Italy, Germany, Belgium, and the United States of America

	ITALY	GERMANY
Classes of state schools	(a) Infant. (b) Primary. (c) Secondary: technical, gymnasia, colleges. (d) Universities. (e) Other technical (including evening and Sunday schools for workmen). The work proper to each institution must be performed in it before pupil allowed to proceed to higher institutions.	Generally— (a) Infant (not everywhere public schools) (b) Primary; (c) Supplementary (attendance in some places compulsory, when education not pursued at secondary school); (d) Preparatory secondary (this frequently 6–9 1st stage); (e) Modern; (f) Upper modern; (g) Classical; (h) Polytechnic; (i) Universities.
Subjects of study in primary schools	Inferior degree— Religion, Reading, Writing, Arithmetic (elementary), Italian language, Metrical system. Superior degree— Subjects as above (increased knowledge), Composition (more rules), Penmanship, Geography (elementary), History (the most remarkable events in national), Elementary physical and natural science, and their principal applications to the usages of life. In boys' schools there is added geometry and drawing (lineal). In girls' schools, also work proper to their sex. Over-pressure not complained of, but one of the highest (Roman Catholic) authorities on education at Rome is of opinion that there are far too many subjects taught in the State schools.	Taking Saxony as an instance— Religion and morals. The German language, including reading and writing. Arithmetic. Geometry. History—geography and geology—natural history—physics. Singing. Drawing. Needlework (for girls). No standards. Horticulture in Baden compulsory. Class numbers regulated by law. Home lessons usual. Over-pressure, as evidenced by defective eyesight, &c.
Physical training	Gymnastic exercises receive attention; although they do not form such a prominent part of State education as in some other countries.	Marked recognition of importance of drill and gymnastic exercises. Liberal expenditure upon it. Recognized that without such physical training the severe examinations could not be undertaken. Widely admitted that even more than at present is desirable.
Inspection and examination	The importance of yearly examinations, whereby (amongst other things) fitness for promotion to or attendance at a higher school may be judged, is insisted upon. But inspection frequently brings "no visible results, and is looked forward to without anxiety and without hope."	In addition to ordinary inspection, each primary school every third or fourth year is carefully inspected by an expert member of a Board of Education. The Inspectors confer and co-operate with the teachers.

Continuation schools and half-time scholars	There are no continuation schools for children after leaving the primary schools notwithstanding the early termination of the compulsory period. But there are evening and Sunday schools for adults; and "pupils graduating from the 3rd grade are expected to attend an evening school for a year."	Continuation schools important feature in Germany. Attendance compulsory in some places, where pupils on leaving primary do not join secondary school. Some preparation for industrial pursuits. Instruction is not universally gratuitous, although when fees are charged they are small. Half-time system exists, but to no great extent.
Secondary and higher schools	Organization of secondary schools has higher reputation than that of primary schools. Technical schools prepare for trade or technical institutes. Lyceums or colleges for universities. Entry at secondary schools is at 10 or 11. But preliminary examination required on entry, and on promotion from one class to another. There are higher schools for girls. Admission only gained to lyceums or colleges on presenting satisfactory certificate of license from gymnasium. Applicants for admission to university must produce certificate from lyceum, and undergo preliminary examination.	Instruction not, as a rule, gratuitous, except when scholars have distinguished themselves and are not able to pay; then free tuition generally available. In certain schools certain number of free places, and sometimes dinners or suppers and dinners, available for poor scholars. Generally day schools. No state secondary schools, as a rule, for girls. But there are some excellent ones.
Technical instruction	Generously fostered with State and other public moneys: (a) Tech. schools (including evening and Sunday schools for workmen), (b) Technical institutes, (c) Professional schools (including women's work schools), (d) Higher tech. institutes. Art schools plentiful, and reputedly superior. "A permanent commission has been established in connection with the Ministry of Agriculture. It is to have a general oversight of industrial museums, schools of art, as applied to industries, schools of design for working men, in fact of all institutions which have to do with industries as taught to the working classes."	In addition to supplementary schools, science and art everywhere fostered, especially science. Thus: (a) Apprenticeship schools, (b) Trade schools and women's work schools, (c) Real schools, (d) Higher technical schools, and (e) Polytechnics. There are also art schools. Workshops in primary schools not yet introduced; but drawing well taught. Special teaching of horticulture in Baden; and there are some domestic-economy schools for girls. Most adult schools in Germany, France, and Belgium are Sunday schools; and the technical schools on the Continent are said to be mainly founded by manufacturers.
Scholarships	For those rich in talent but poor in fortune, the State annually votes a sum. There are also scholarships available out of private gifts.	No State scholarships; but there are some scholarships in universities available from Royal or private legacies. They are, however, only awarded to scholars, (a) Who have distinguished themselves, and (b) Are too poor to otherwise continue studies. They are generally small.
State supervision respecting private schools	The provincial Boards of Education have supervision, under the Minister, over private as well as public schools in respect of sanitary and moral matters.	Private schools are under Government inspection and supervision. Teachers must be thoroughly qualified and possess diploma. Comparatively few private schools, and little private tuition.

State Education in Great Britain, France, Switzerland, Italy, Germany, Belgium, and the United States of America

	BELGIUM	THE UNITED STATES
Classes of state schools	(a) Infant. (b) Primary (at least in each commune). (c) Supplementary. (d) Secondary (higher elementary and Royal Athenaeum). (e) Universities. (f) Special (including scientific and art schools, and women's work schools). Roman Catholics have good primary, secondary, and normal schools; and university at Louvain.	(a) Primary, 6–9–10. (b) Grammar, 10–14-15. (c) High (for boys, and also for girls), 14–15—17-18. (d) Colleges. (e) Universities (also night and technical schools).
Subjects of study in primary schools	Religious and moral teaching optional with communes. Reading. Writing. Elements of arithmetic. Legal system of weights and measures. Elements of the French, Flemish, or German language, according to wants of locality. Geography. History of Belgium. Elementary drawing. Notions of agriculture. Needlework (for girls). Additional teaching under certain circumstances. There are also Crèches institutions. Cookery is an obligatory subject in all the girls' schools of Brussels. Over-pressure not complained of; but there seems to be too many subjects and too much work for proper digestion.	Reading and writing. Grammar. Arithmetic. Geography. Drawing and vocal music quite general. Rudiments of natural science, taught orally, in most city schools. Declamation a favourite exercise. In some places special masters to teach music and penmanship. School libraries encouraged in some States. Over-pressure complained of.
Physical training	There is great attention paid to physical training in the State schools.	Neglected; free and vocal gymnastics being the only muscular exercises in primary schools, and they are not practised in even all the city schools. Military drill, however, in addition to other gymnastic exercises, is given in many of the high schools.
Inspection and examination	Supervision of primary schools confided to communal authorities, and Government Inspectors. Each province has one or two Inspectors appointed and dismissable by King. Such Inspector must visit schools in his province at least once in two years. Under Government Inspectors; cantonal ones nominated by Government. They must visit schools in their cantons at least once a year. State pays salaries. For secondary schools Inspectors appointed by Govt. Inspection does not extend to religious and moral instruction; and is regulated by Govt. Once at least every 3 mo's cantonal Inspector calls together teachers of his district, and report sent to principal Inspector. Each principal Inspector presides annually at a conference of teachers, and sends an annual report to the Minister.	Superintendents answer in great part to our Inspectors: but they are political officers, and ill paid: and in majority of cases do not give the whole of their time to the work. System of inspection not satisfactory.

Continuation schools and half-time scholars	Continuation schools are numerous and important. Instruction is free, and they are carried on by the State mainly to promote industrial knowledge. Drawing is the basis of instruction in them. Carried on in evenings and on Sunday mornings. Other evening schools exist, but attendance decreasing. Half-time factory schools established in some places.	Free evening schools in cities for adults and children are common. But they are not a success, the chief cause being inefficiency of teachers. Special attention in them to reading, writing, arithmetic, and to certain industrial studies.
Secondary and higher schools	Higher elementary—81 for boys and 36 for girls—entered at 6–7 if child sent to preparatory school annexed, otherwise 9–15 when not intended for higher schools. Latin and Greek are not taught. Under immediate care of State. Royal Athenaeums—20, all day schools, although in some places boarding-houses in connection. Entrance examination. Usual ages 11–18. Instruction divided into (a) Literary, and (b) Scientific or professional. In each seven classes. No Latin taught on professional side. Under immediate care of State. Answer to English public schools such as Eton or Harrow.	High schools form portion of gratuitous public school system. Academies and seminaries, generally founded and supported by private enterprise, are numerous. Not controlled by State, but free from taxation.
Technical instruction	Earnestly promoted by Government. Instruction largely gratuitous. (a) Apprenticeship and artisan schools held in evenings and on Sunday mornings. (b) Professional schools (including women's work schools). (c) No polytechnics, but higher technical instruction carried on in Brussels University. And very numerous technical and art schools. Most of the adult schools are Sunday schools; and the Communal Councils regulate everything relating to the establishment and organization of adult schools.	(a) Great attention to colleges of agriculture and mechanics, where sexes are educated together. (b) Commencem't of blending mental and manual instruction in primary schools. (c) Certain gratuitous evening industrial schools, where books and supplies are free. (d) Art schools not numerous. "Our systems of instruction have come down to us strong on the intellectual side, but weak on the practical." In Massachusetts every city or town over 10,000 must maintain an evening school.
Scholarships	Both State and municipal scholarships, and several private bequest ones. But only granted when (a) Student is deserving, and (b) Needs it as a means towards pursuing higher studies. For primary-school scholars, 100 to 200 for three or four years, provided satisfactory examination passed each year. Royal Athenaeums, 200 to 400, according to necessities of pupil; six years. Also some established in connection with normal schools, not exceeding three years.	There are scholarships available in consequence of private gifts.
State supervision respecting private schools	The Government do not exercise any control or supervision over private schools or scholars. But denominational schools receiving State aid are subject to three conditions— (a) Instruction must come up to a certain standard, (b) Children of poor must be received gratuitously, and (c) Government inspection. There are private normal schools, as well as other classes of private schools.	There is no State control or supervision over private schools or private tuition.

studied in connection with the United States; and as they are of grave importance, and especially deserving of attention in new communities—such as the Colony—where as yet institutions have not been permanently developed, some of the most prominent are here referred to:—

(1.) Whether a system of complete gratuitous State primary education has a demoralizing tendency, as inclining to weaken a sense of parental responsibility and influence?

(2.) Whether the present scope of the popular educational teaching in force—for instance, in Great Britain and the Colony—does not tend to discourage manual pursuits, and thereby retard the general development of the material resources of a country?

(3.) If so, whether the giving of a greater prominence, in a national course of study, to all that which would tend to be useful in the practical development of such resources, would not be distinctly preferable to the larger attention now paid to purely literary attainments? and—

(4.) Whether that inventive skill, for which the United States is so renowned, may not be attributed—

(a) To the ambition engendered by such democratic institutions as enable even the highest post to be attainable by industry and ability, coupled with

(b) That instruction in many schools and systems of schools which provides that stress is laid upon the practical method of conducting investigations for the purpose of verification and of original discovery.

It is not within the province of this Report to discuss these questions, but I venture to commend their consideration to those interested in educational progress, and to suggest that no country presents such materials for their solution as the United States, with over 50,000,000 of inhabitants, and with a school population of at least 16,794,402. . . .

In the American system there is much that induces commendation; especially—

(a) Large powers of local government, including powers of direct local taxation;

(b) Compulsory-attendance laws so far as they exist, although they exist only to a limited extent;

(c) The promotion of technical instruction, including prominence given to drawing;

(d) The requirement in certain States respecting the knowledge of the influence of alcohol on the human body; and

(e) The provisions, so far as they extend, against the improper employment of children.

But public education in the United States has not arrived at that condition which justifies its imitation as a complete system.

For instance, respecting the States generally, there exists the want of adequate provisions affecting (a) school accommodation, (b) compulsory education, (c) length of school terms, (d) training, standard of qualification, and appointment of teachers; (e) religious instruction, (f) physical training, (g) inspection, (h) infant-school arrangements, and (i) injurious employment of children; involving an unjustifiable amount of illiteracy, incompetent teaching in too many cases, religious friction, and a very general absence of that thoroughness, without which veneer is apt to take the place of substance—causes which, as it seems to me, must, if unamended, not only retard the progress, but sap the core of any nation.

There must, however, be much to learn, even if there be not everything to imitate; for, apart from the large questions which may with especial advantage be studied in connection with the States, and in addition to much that may be commended, to arrive at a clear perception of error must be distinct gain. Moreover, the immense mass of data on educational subjects not only relating to the States, but to all parts of the world, annually collected and gratuitously distributed by the Bureau, is indeed a most valuable contribution and aid to educational progress, and deserves to be extensively and gratefully availed of. . . .

Joshua Girling Fitch   1888

The American High School

Joshua Girling Fitch (1824–1903), an English educational reformer, graduated from the University of London. He served as principal of the Borough Road Training College of the British and Foreign School Society. His work at the Training College was highly praised by Matthew Arnold and led to his appointment as an inspector for the Education Department (from 1863 to 1894). He was knighted for his services to education in 1896.

Fitch was responsible for preparing two major reports on foreign education and for recommending innovations in English education. The first report, compiled in 1888, concerned American schools, and the second, written in 1891, discussed the workings of the "free school system in America, France and Belgium." Michael Sadler, a distinguished English comparative educator, says that Fitch's "interest in the study of American education was always strong and his admiration of American educational effort profound."

It should be observed that the American high school is unlike any institution in England. It is essentially a continuation school, and is in close organic connection with the primary or grammar schools. It does not receive pupils till the age of 14, and all its arrangements pre-suppose that, before entering it, the pupil has gone successfully through the "grammar" grades. An English "grammar school" or middle school exists side by side with a public elementary school, but has no relation to it. The latter takes scholars from 6 to 7 to 14, and the former from 7 or 8 to 17 or 18. The two are attended by scholars of very different social ranks, and each has its own course of instruction fashioned from the first on the theory that the course will extend to a certain age, and that this course must, in view of that fact, have a completeness of its own. The broader and more liberal aims of the English grammar school affect the character of the daily lessons from the first. Subjects are begun in it by the age of 10 or 11 which do not come into the curriculum of the elementary school at all. Hence if by means of scholarships or otherwise a boy of promise is to be taken from the lower school to the higher, it is necessary to choose him early, say at 11 or 12, and to transfer him to the one from the other at once. He would not derive the full advantage of the higher school course if he stayed to complete the seven standards of the elementary school. But in America the "ladder" is differently constructed. The end of the grammar school curriculum coincides with the beginning of that of the high school. Both schools are generally under the same management. And, except for the fact that it is the poorer parent who is compelled to withdraw his child earliest for labor, both are attended by the same class of pupils. Hence a good deal of the waste of power in England, owing to the separation of children of different social ranks into distinct schools during the period of purely elementary education is avoided. Our "higher" schools are higher, not because they are occupied in doing advanced work, nor because relatively to the needs of a scholar in the early stage of his education they are giving better elementary instruction, but partly because they contemplate the extension of the studies to a later age, and mainly because they are attended by pupils whose parents are rich enough to pay for their education, and therefore do not need the help of a Government grant.

The supply of high schools is not uniform throughout the country. They are to be found in most though not all of the great cities. The public school law of Massachusetts requires a high school whenever the place contains 500 children of school age; and that State contains no less than 229 high schools. The public school system of the city of New York includes no high school. The place of such an institution is partly supplied by the College of the City of New York, which gives a scientific and literary training to young men, and partly by the Normal school for young women—which is not, as its name seems to imply, an institution wholly for the training of teachers, since its lower classes give a good general education, and since many scholars enter it without any intention of proceeding to the higher departments in which special professional training is given to future schoolmistresses. When it is considered that instruction in all the schools

Joshua Girling Fitch, *Notes on American Schools and Training Colleges* (London: Macmillan and Company, 1890), pp. 27–70.

which are once incorporated into the public school system is gratuitous, it is not a little remarkable that the proportion of scholars availing themselves of this provision is so small. In Chicago, for example, a prosperous city of 875,000 inhabitants, amply supplied with excellent schools, there are only 2,000 scholars in the high schools, of whom less than 500 are boys; and of these it is computed that less than half remain long enough to complete the course. In Boston, a city in which the appreciation of knowledge and culture has long been exceptionally high, the elementary schools are attended in all by 55,451 scholars, of whom 2,211 are in the highest class and 3,429 are in the second class, corresponding to our 7th and 6th Standards respectively. The grammar school diploma was in 1887 awarded to 1,992 "graduates." This gives a proportion of scholars successfully completing the elementary school course in a given year of about one twenty-eighth of the whole number of pupils, and, assuming an average stay in the schools of seven years, this points roughly to the conclusion that one-fourth of the scholars will probably proceed to the end of the course. In the same year the schools of the London School Board are reported to have presented 264,791 scholars for examination in standards, of whom 6,379 were in and above the 7th Standard, a number not amounting to one-fortieth of the whole, and suggesting that if seven years be the ordinary length of the school life, not many more than one-sixth of the scholars now in board schools will remain long enough to complete their course by passing in Standard VII. Considering, however, that the scholars in the London board schools belong almost all to the wage-earning class, and that those of the Boston public schools include the children of persons of all social grades, the comparison is nowise unfavorable. If we had, as in Boston, statistics showing the total number of scholars of all ranks who remained under instruction till 13, 14, and 15 respectively, it may be doubted whether London would appear at any disadvantage. Yet the statistics of Boston give a higher average of scholars in advanced schools and classes than those of any other city in the States, whose figures I have had an opportunity of examining. Of the 1,992 who "graduated" in the Boston grammar schools, 1,081, or 54 per cent., subsequently entered either the English or the Latin high schools. This fact represents a very satisfactory proportion. But applying the same test, and by taking into account the numbers who reach the advanced class in the high schools, it appears that little more than one-fifth complete the four years' course and become "graduates" of the high school.

Comparison of English and American School Attendance

Indeed, a comparison of the general statistics of school attendance in America with those of our own country cannot fairly be made without keeping in view the fact that here the public elementary schools are designed for the children of the laboring class, and are not used except to a very small extent by parents above that class. But the educational returns of America extend to the children of all the classes who attend public schools at all. It should also be borne in mind that according to the latest returns the population of the United States (57,929,609) is, roughly speaking, about double that of England and Wales. In the light of these facts the following figures are significant: The report of 1887 of the Commissioner of Education shows the number of scholars on the rolls in all the public schools to be 11,805,660, and the average number in daily attendance to be 7,571,416, or 64 per cent. In the report of the English Education Department for last year 4,635,184 were enrolled on the registers of the elementary schools of England and Wales; of whom 3,527,381, or 76 per cent, were in average daily attendance. This average, it must be observed, is computed in England on a minimum of 400 school attendances, or 200 days, in the year. But in many parts of America the schools are open less than half this number of times. For example: In the State of Connecticut, which is said to take the lead in regard to the enforcement of attendance, the law is satisfied with 120 days' attendance in the year; and in many districts of that State schools are open only for six months in the year. The average term of the school in the State of Mississippi was 84 days in the year 1887. In the State of New York the Act requires 14 weeks of school attendance in the year. The new compulsory law of 1887 for the State of Maine, which is designed to supersede the less stringent regulations hitherto in force, requires attendance for 16 weeks in the year.

One obvious conclusion from these returns is that the system of free schools does not necessarily secure a high average of regularity in attendance. There are compulsory laws in several of the great cities, and truant officers whose business it is to enforce them; but they are in most cases very leniently administered, and in many towns, and over large tracts of country, they do not exist at all. It is the experience of all school authorities that wherever wages are high, and there are many openings for juvenile labor, the children drop off in great numbers at 11 and 12 years of age; and that there are no public measures which are effective enough to prevent it. The rule which so often prevails in the states of Germany, requiring attendance at a continuation school or *Fortbildungs Schule* in the case of all scholars who fail to reach a certain standard in the ordinary day schools at 13 or 14, has no force in the American States. Statistics of actual illiteracy have not been compiled in such a way as to furnish data for any comprehensive induction; but those of several States may be usefully compared. In the State of Massachusetts the last report computed that there were, in 1885, 122,263 "illiterates," forming 7.73 per cent. of the population. Of these, 6.79 per cent. were born in Massachusetts, 4.58 in other States, and 88.63 per cent. were foreign born. These figures include illiterates of all ages, many of whom have come into the State after reaching maturity. If only the minors from 10 to 20 are considered, they will be found to be only 9.92 of the total number as against 11.99 in 1875. This is one of the most favorable statements, and shows how very large a part of the ignorance and poverty of the New England States is imported. But other figures offer a striking contrast. In Alabama, out of a population of 1,262,505, no less than 433,447 over the age of 10 were unable to write. Michigan, with a much more generous school system, had, out of a population of 1,648,690, only 63,672 illiterates; and Arkansas, out of a population of 1,542,359, had 410,722.

The School Buildings and Furniture

In regard to the material fabric of the schools generally, only two or three facts need to be mentioned. The teaching is conducted in separate class-rooms, but provision is nearly always made for one hall large enough to contain the whole of the pupils, and available for collective exercises, and for the annual prize giving and other ceremonials. In some instances both of these objects are fulfilled in the same apartment. At a large school in New York I saw several hundred scholars assembled for the opening exercise and singing, and immediately afterwards a number of partitions, which had been ingeniously attached to the roof, descended at a signal, and the whole of the large hall was at once transformed into a number of separate class-rooms. The schools generally are less amply furnished with playgrounds than schools of corresponding grades in England; and it seemed to me that much less use was made of them during the mid-day recess. Some of the elementary schools, especially in New York, were too crowded for health or comfort. The official regulations issued by the City Superintendent prescribe the following as the minimum of floor-space and air-space per pupil: "In the three lower classes of the primary schools, five square feet and seventy cubic feet; in the three higher grades, six square and eighty cubic feet; in the four lower grades of grammar schools, seven square feet and ninety cubic feet, and in the four higher grades, nine square feet and one hundred cubic feet per scholar." Space, however, is exceptionally valuable in the city of New York, and these minima are generally exceeded in other places. The plan of seating pupils at single separate desks is common and has many advantages; but it does not economize space well. It fills a room with desks, so that there is no space for collective movement or for causing the class to vary its position by occasional standing; and if the numbers are large the scholars are spread over so wide an area that the teacher's voice is needlessly tried.

One very useful mechanical device, which is not without an important incidental effect on the whole character of the teaching, is to be found in nearly all the best American schools. It is the continuous blackboard, or blackened surface extending all round the room, after the fashion of what house painters here call a "dado." I am frequently struck in England with the waste of power caused by the smallness of the blackboard surface accessible to the teacher. More than half of what is written or drawn in illustration of the lessons I hear at home is rubbed out directly, and before it has served its purpose, simply because room is wanted to write or draw something else. English teachers have yet to learn the proper use of a blackboard. There is much waste of time whenever anything is sketched or written upon it, and not afterwards read or referred to, and made an effective instrument of recapitulation. Unless the questions, "What have I written here?" "Why did I write it?" "What is the meaning of this diagram?" "Can you explain it to the class?'' occur later in the lesson, the board should not be used at all. Nor unless the series of demonstrations, examples, or pictures remain within sight of the learner during the whole of the lesson, and for a time afterwards, is it possible for him to go back and get a clear notion of the right order of its development, or to see any continuity or wholeness in it. An American teacher generally understands this. He begins at one end of the wall behind his *estrade* and goes on to the other end; erasing nothing, but letting all the parts of his subject be illustrated in order, and referring back to them from time to time. And at the end of his lesson he sends some of the scholars to the side walls to work out in the presence of the class other problems, to reproduce a diagram, or to write an illustrative sentence. There is plenty of room on the walls for failures as well as for successes. Both are retained within sight of the pupils for a time; and in the hands of a skilful teacher the good and the bad exercises are equally instructive. The wall surface is also available for many other purposes—setting out the work to be done for home lessons; writing out the sums which have to be worked, the lists of words which have to be wrought into sentences; or giving a specimen map or diagram for imitation.

The power of rapid and effective freehand drawing is cultivated more generally, and with more success, among the best American teachers than among our own, and it gives them a great advantage. A diagram sketched out then and there to illustrate a science lesson, a map which grows under the teacher's hand as one fact after another is elicited and explained, have a far greater effect in kindling the interest of children and fixing their attention than any number of engraved or painted pictures, however good. Whatever forms part of the permanent decoration of a schoolroom is apt to be taken for granted, and practically disregarded by children. But a new drawing made *ad hoc* and associated with something which at the time is being enforced or made interesting by the teacher has a value of a far higher kind. The new regulations of our own Science and Art Department respecting the conditions of the drawing certificate for teachers emphasize strongly the importance of uncopied and free blackboard drawing. But the best of the American training colleges have for several years given special attention to this part of the teacher's qualification. I have seen the students of a normal school busily engaged during the midday recess of the juvenile practising school in dashing off with a few simple strokes outline pictures of birds and flowers, of ships or of houses, or copies of the little illustrations to be found in story books; so that when the children returned they should find something new all round the room to look at and to talk about.

Drawings and Manual Instruction

It will be seen from the tabulated statement of the requirements in the various grades how large an importance is attached to drawing in the American schools. It is, in fact, the one form of manual training on the value of which all the best educational authorities are agreed. Many misgivings are expressed even by some of the ablest of those authorities about the educational value of other kinds of *Hand-arbeit*, but none as to the importance of drawing and design. In America, as in England, discussions about ''technical'' and manual instruction excite great public interest. But there are two classes of persons who advocate the introduction of such training into schools; and there is a little confusion between the objects severally aimed at by these two classes. One section of educational authorities desires to train skilled handicraftsmen, and sees with alarm the increasing distaste of the American boy for manual labor. It is said with truth that by far the larger proportion of mechanical trades is in the hands of foreigners. This is not altogether surprising. The air of America is full of commercial speculation and enterprise, and of restless ambition. New royal roads to success, new ways of making rapid fortunes, are opening every day. A lad of any promise is attracted to the ''store,'' to the railroad, or the office, and thinks that mechanical labor, if not just a little servile and undignified, is at any rate a very slow process for ''getting on'' in life. It is believed by many of the advocates of manual training that the best corrective for this growing evil will be the introduction of organized hand-work into the ordinary curriculum of a school; and it is hoped in this way not only to increase the tactual skill of the pupil, but also to awaken an intelligent interest in such work, and to invest it with more dignified associations. Other persons view the whole problem in a different aspect. They believe that, apart from all considerations of industry or utility, the right training of the fingers and the senses is a valuable part of general education, and has an important reflex action on the intelligence of the pupil and on his fitness to perform any of the duties of life. Some very valuable and costly experiments have been tried in many places to meet one or other of these two views. The Technological Institute at Boston, the Pratt Institute at Brooklyn, and the Manual Training School at Chicago have mainly for their purpose to increase the scientific knowledge, the skill and the producing power of those who may look forward to becoming the captains of industry and directors of manufacture. The institutions established by Dr. Felix Adler and Dr. N. Murray Butler in New York, and the Manual Training School at Philadelphia, are types of schools having a more distinctly educational aim. All of these institutions are the product of private munificence, and none of them except the last is incorporated into the public-school system of the city in which it is situated. It is to the energetic initiative of the school superintendent of Philadelphia that the introduction of this new experiment into that city is mainly due. He defends it, not on grounds of any industrial or economic needs, but solely on educational considerations. He says:

Manual training is founded on the claim that it gives a more complete education than is afforded by the course of instruction now followed in the schools. It undertakes so to modify the existing methods of training as to yield an education that shall make the graduate of the public school a more harmoniously developed and efficient member of society. The instruction given in our schools is too one-sided. . . . To a very large extent the schools neglect the training of those powers which bring the mind into true relations with its physical environment. A very large portion of the time of pupils in schools of every grade is devoted to the study of words. Educational reformers for nearly 300 years have been seeking to remedy this defect. The introduction of object lessons and of science instruction were well-meant efforts in this direction, and manual work is nothing more than a further extension of the same principle. It seeks to train the hand and the eye, not for the purpose of superseding the action of the mind, but as the efficient agents of the mind in gaining a truer and fuller knowledge of the world. Emerson says in his terse way that "manual labor is the study of the external world." It is in the spirit of this maxim that

the new education seeks to widen the training of children in the direction of the harmonious development of mind and body through such agencies as the best experience may dictate.

It cannot be said that these principles, though accepted by many of the most thoughtful educators in the States, have so far prevailed as to affect the recognized curriculum of school studies in any of the great educational centres. I learned with interest that the School Committee in New York had determined to introduce manual training by way of experiment into nine of their (lower) primary schools and six of the grammar (or upper primary) schools. But on inquiry I found that this meant little more than the adoption for the first time of the little mechanical occupations of the Kindergarten and drawing into the younger classes, and of needlework as a new employment for girls. The *Slojd* or Swedish system of training by woodwork and the use of carpenter's tools is not, so far as I can learn, adopted by any school authority. Drawing, as I have said, is the one manual art about the value of which all are agreed. And, after all, it is the one manual art which is least likely to degenerate into mechanism or to lose its educational character. It is quite conceivable that the arts of carpentering, modelling, sewing, and fashioning paper and metal may, when once acquired, become mere routine, and cease to have any effect on the general development of the learner's capacity and intelligence. But drawing and design are arts capable of infinite developments and applications, and, when once acquired, can never lose their power to stimulate thought, to purify taste, and to call forth new efforts.

Teaching Drawing by Correspondence

An interesting and novel experiment has recently been tried with a view to make the study of drawing more general throughout the States. The "Prang Institute" at Boston has devised a plan for home study and for instruction by correspondence, with a view to meet the needs of teachers in remote places who feel the need of further guidance as to the best mode of teaching. They are furnished with materials, copies, and definite instructions, and their performances in drawing, modelling, and design are sent regularly to headquarters for criticism. Large numbers of teachers have availed themselves of this arrangement, though at a distance from oral instructors, and are pursuing regular courses of exercise under guidance. I have seen many of the exercises produced under these conditions, and am assured that many of them show unusual excellence. . . .

Infant Schools

Infant schools, in the English sense of the word, are almost unknown in America, chiefly because the course of primary instruction is not generally supposed to begin till the seventh year. In Boston, however, "kindergarten" schools were established, in the first instance, by the private efforts of a benevolent lady, and have since been taken over and incorporated into the public school system. In St. Louis also the system of Fröbel was introduced as a voluntary experiment and afterward adopted by the board. In both cases, however, the "kindergarten" was regarded at first as a thing apart from the ordinary primary school. The system and methods were wholly unlike, and the games and manual employments of Fröbel constituted almost the whole occupation of the children. Some disappointment was experienced at the result by many teachers. It was found that this playful discipline did not afford the best preparation for the serious work of the ordinary primary school. The English ideal of an infant school—one in which elementary instruction in reading, writing, and counting is interspersed with simple lessons on the phenomena of nature and of common life, and with interesting and varied manual employments, has not prevailed in America. I confess I greatly prefer it. It seems to me to put what is commonly called "kindergarten" methods and discipline into their proper place, rather as organic parts of a good and rounded system of juvenile training, as helps to the general development of the observant faculty and to the acquisition of knowledge, than as constituting even in the earliest years a separate organization, having aims and principles different from those which should prevail during the rest of the school life. Whatever is good and true in the principles of Fröbel and Rousseau, is applicable not to infants only, but also to the discipline of children of all ages. Separate Fröbelian institutions, for "kindergarten" training and manual employments alone, are in my opinion foredoomed to failure.

Reading and Writing

I did not think either the reading or the writing of the scholars whose performances I witnessed were better, age for age, than those which one meets with every day in good elementary schools at home. Less use is made in the lower classes of large hand as a means of showing the true forms and proportions of letters, and as a general rule the style of writing appropriate to small-hand is adopted from the first. The use of the type-writer is now so much more common in American houses of business than in England that I had few opportunities of seeing the handwriting of the youths who had gone from school into such houses; but what I saw has not been clearer or more readable than that of lads of the same age in London. The reading books as a rule are bright, well illustrated, and attractive; but rather more fragmentary than our own, and are generally designed rather to form a taste for reading than to convey much information. I was very glad to find that the absurd practice so common in English schools of constantly interrupting the reading lesson for exercises in oral spelling was everywhere discouraged in America. Spelling is a matter for the visual memory and for transcription, not for oral recitation. *Pictures* of words need to be seen and recognized, and time is terribly wasted by the mere utterance of the letters that compose them. The following passage from the "manual" issued by one of the city school superintendents deserves the attention of English as well as American teachers:

"Do not use concert drill. The impression made upon the mind by writing the same word often and by frequent reviews in the form of dictation will be found much better aids to the memory than any amount of oral repetition. It is next to impossible to prevent concert exercises in spelling from degenerating into a mere unconscious utterance of words, a species of action destructive of every purpose for which a well-ordered school is maintained."

One exercise in reading I found in the grammar schools of America which might be usefully adopted here. Scholars are set down for a quarter of an hour to read a page or two in silence, and are told that at the end of the time there will be questions and conversation upon it. We often act as if the only reading to be performed in school was reading aloud in class. Thus the habit of using a book in the one way in which its use will be of most value to a scholar in after life— reading to himself and feeling himself responsible for getting at and appropriating its meaning—is not properly acquired.

Oral Composition

Much more attention is paid than in our schools to what I may call "oral composition," to exercises in which the scholar is called upon to stand up and reproduce a story, or to say what he knows or what he thinks about the subject. *E.g.*, a list of words which have occurred during a reading lesson is written on the board, and the scholars are called on individually to rise and make sentences, containing one or more of the words. A rough outline picture is drawn, and the scholar is asked to make a little story about it. Answers to questions are expected to be given in whole sentences, not in single words. Time is reserved at the end of the lesson for recapitulating parts of it by the scholars themselves, with less of prompting and questioning than is common in our schools. Often a boy or girl is called on to come forward and catechise the class on what has been learned. No doubt this causes delay, and makes a lesson seem to move slowly and to cover but little ground; but the principle underlying the practice is entirely right. There is no true teaching unless the learner is made to speak his own words, as well as to listen to those of an instructor.

> *Minds that have nothing to confer*
> *Find little to perceive.*

This is not unfrequently overlooked. The opposite practice, which I have often to complain of at home, has the disadvantage of giving the learners too little to do for themselves. The teacher often hurries on, asking questions which admit of being answered in single words; satisfied if he secures interest and attention and if the scholars seem to acquiesce in what he states. But he needs to be reminded that acquiescence is not knowledge; that it is very possible to assent to many propositions without understanding them; and that Charles Kingsley's playful description of a school in which "the master learned all the lessons and the scholars heard them" is not wholly a figment of a novelist's imagination.

Elocution

The great facility possessed by the average American in the art of public speaking is not only fostered by the numerous conventions and ceremonials which form so conspicuous a feature of transatlantic life, it is largely encouraged by the discipline of the schools. Children are practised from the first in looking large numbers of other children in the face and reciting with courage and self-possession. English readers of American books, must, however, be on their guard against misunderstanding the word "recitation," which so frequently occurs in them. It does not mean, as with us, an elocutionary effort of any kind; but it simply denotes any oral lesson or catechetical exercise. Nevertheless, recitation in our sense of the word is practised in various forms. If the scholars have prepared a written exercise they are asked to read it aloud to the class. Solos are to be heard as well as choruses in the music lessons. The teacher will often write or select from a book a little dialogue, which is learned by three or four picked scholars, and recited in the hearing of the class with much dramatic action and emphasis. Connected with every school and college, from the primary school up to Harvard University, there is an annual ceremonial day, on which, in the hearing of parents and the public, the pupils who have written the best essays or who can do anything particularly well, are called on to declaim or otherwise display their powers. It is needless to say that these exhibitions are very popular, that they keep up a sense of pride and local interest in the public schools, and that they powerfully stimulate the more ambitious scholars. That they also encourage self-consciousness and the love of display, that the show compositions are often not original productions, and that there was a slight air of unreality and pretentiousness about some of the "commencement" exercises which I witnessed, must, I fear, be admitted. This drawback is fully recognized by many of the best teachers with whom I conversed on the subject, but when due precautions are taken I cannot doubt that there is a genuine advantage in these displays, both as means of enlisting popular and parental sympathy in the work of education and as an incentive to scholars to do their best.

Memory Exercise

It seemed to me that an undue proportion of what was learned was learned by heart, and that even the oral exercises which were supposed to be spontaneous were too much alike, and conformed too often to certain conventional patterns which were in constant use in the schools. What is oddly called "memorizing" is a very favorite exercise; but it is often confined to the reproduction of scraps of information or short passages from textbooks. Many more rules, definitions, and aphorisms are committed to memory in American than in English schools. I heard in one class the boys get up one after another and give by rote in succession a few sentences recording the names, dates, and chief performances of the eighteen presidents of the United States. In another school, the girls recited in order the names of principal inventors and discoverers, with a description of the exploits of each. Of course, all these facts are worth knowing, but the particular words in which the compiler of the text-book has embodied them have no value in themselves; and as far as they have any effect at all, learning them by rote tends to discourage any effort of thought about the subject itself. I am glad to know that in England the only purely *memoriter* exercise prescribed in the Code is the learning of good poetry, in which not only the substance is interesting, but the form is itself valuable, and has a grace and charm and therefore an educative value of its own. The practice so common in our best schools at home of learning by heart in the highest classes one hundred of the noblest lines of a play like *Julius Caesar*, and reading in connection with the whole drama some of the history of the period, is very little followed in the American schools. In many of them a great deal of what is learned by heart has no literary merit, and can therefore do little to improve the vocabulary or to refine the taste of the learner.

Arithmetic

The teaching of arithmetic is greatly helped in America by the fortunate circumstances that all the money is decimal, and that a good many of the antiquated terms found in English tables of weights and measures are not in use. Hence all compound arithmetic is easier, and time is saved which can be well devoted to the explanation of principles and to examination of the properties of numbers, and the reasons for arithmetical processes. In most of the schemes of instruction the arithmetical course is laid out in a careful and logical order; the method of Grube being very generally adopted. The characteristic feature of this method is that it does not regard addition, subtraction, multiplication, and division as four processes graduated in difficulty, and to be learned in succession; but it assumes that the true progression is from small numbers to large. Hence the beginner takes, for example, the number twelve. He is made to see and to count cubes, balls, or other objects. He adds, subtracts, multiplies, and divides all the numbers up to twelve. He is shown or helped to find out in how many ways that number is made up of parts. He learns all its fractions and aliquot parts; he applies the number to hours, to money, and to inches, and whatever arithmetical process is possible within that narrow limit he learns to perform. After that he proceeds in the next class, say, as far as the number 50, and will take up the arithmetic of one dollar, not going beyond the limit, but performing every operation within it. Big numbers and elaborate notation are reserved till later. It is believed that by knowing all the properties of small and manageable numbers, and by varying the exercises upon them, the scholar obtains a far better mastery over figures, and a truer preparation for dealing with more complex magnitudes, than if he works in succession a number of sums in groups, each group illustrating a single rule. The method seems to me a good and rational one, and I was much pleased with the results. It is certainly more interesting to the children. The helpless way in which scholars at home sometimes ask, when a question is given, "What rule is it in?" is a sure proof that they have been unintelligently taught. . . .

One excellent practice is in general use in the best American schools which I have seen. A scholar is frequently asked to make sums, to set a question in a rule, and to come forward and work it out in the presence of the class. Sometimes, when a process has been explained, the home lesson does not take the form of set exercises to be wrought out; but the scholars are told to invent for themselves, and work by next day any sums they like in illustration of the rule. On the whole, it does not seem to me that the boys and girls are working questions quite so difficult as those of the same age in England, or that their answers are more generally correct. Ability to manipulate numbers is understood to come earlier than power to comprehend mathematical demonstration, and such demonstration is often deferred. But, speaking generally, the rationale of the rules is often better explained than at home. It should be observed that in the exercises for solution much care is taken to give practical problems such as would occur in ordinary business—writing out bills, commercial letters, calculations of bank interest, and fictitious ledgers and cash-books.

Object or "Observation Lessons," etc.

All the schemes of instruction insist in some form on object lessons, or "observation lessons," as they are often called. In some cases hygiene is the favorite subject, in others botany, in some natural history, in others the ordinary scenes and incidents of town or country life. Grammar and analysis are included in all cases; but in the earlier classes the English exercises consist mainly of simple composition and punctuation, and the use of capitals; formal grammar being deferred a little later than in English schools. The logical analysis and synthesis of sentences receive a good deal of attention. But verbal analysis, the structure and decomposition of words, the meaning of significant prefixes and final syllables, and the grouping together of words having a common root, or a common element in meaning—an exercise which in judicious hands is found so stimulating in many English schools—is not always prescribed or practised. I could observe little practical difference between American schools and our own in regard to the teaching of geography and history. The maps were often excellent and well finished, but not better than are to be seen any day in London Board schools; and our own method of beginning with the geography of the immediate neighborhood, and connecting from the first physical geography with commercial and political facts, is generally adopted. If the scholars showed, as a rule, a fuller acquaintance with the history of their own country than English children of the same age, it may be accounted for by the fact that there is much less of it to learn. Few of the prescribed lessons go back even to the colonial days. It is to the glorious annals of American progress during the century succeeding the Revolution that the attention of the scholars is chiefly directed.

Lessons in Patriotism

Closely connected with this subject, another feature of American schools deserves particular mention. Special lessons are everywhere given on the American Constitution, on the rights and duties of American citizens, of the President, of Congress, of the Senate, and of the States. National anniversaries are very religiously observed. "On the school days immediately preceding the 4th of July and the 22d of February (Washington's birthday) in each year," say the regulations of the New York School Board, "the principals of all the grammar schools in the city shall assemble the pupils of their respective schools and read, or cause to be read, to them either the 'Declaration of Independence' or 'Washington's farewell address to the people of the United States,' combining therewith such other patriotic exercises as may be advisable." There can be no doubt that in this and other ways, the schools try successfully, not only to inform the children about the government under which they live, but to inspire them with a pride in their country and its institutions. An American boy thinks that in no other country would it be possible for him to enjoy real freedom, or so many civic privileges. I was talking to a class once about the meanings of some words which were written on the board as a verbal exercise, and "equality" being one of the words, I asked the boys to put it into a sentence. One after another made up a sentence about the equality of all American citizens, and when the question was further put, "Equality in what?—in height, in size, in fortune, in good looks, in wisdom, in goodness?" the negative answers were followed unanimously by the phrase, "in political rights." It was evidently the feeling of the class that such equality in political rights existed nowhere else in the world. One may be amused at this, but it is nevertheless true, on both sides of the Atlantic, that a boy is more likely hereafter to do something to make his country proud of him, if he is early taught to be proud of his country, and to have some good reason for being proud of it.

In the country places, throughout the States of the Union and the provinces of the Canadian Dominion, it is a common practice to set apart one day in April, May, or June for planting trees, shrubs, and flowers in the school precincts, and for the general ornamentation of the school premises. The authorities permit this to count as a lawful school day. During the forenoon the grounds are levelled, stones and refuse removed, holes made for the trees, a flower-bed is laid out or a part of the ground is sodded or seeded with lawn grass. While the boys are thus engaged, the girls are employed in putting in order and ornamenting the schoolroom, arranging flowers, and displaying specimens of maps, writing, and other manual work. Trees planted are associated with the name of a class or a teacher, or of some public event.

Discipline

One could not help being impressed everywhere by the excellence of the discipline, and the more so as it is said to be maintained almost uniformly without resorting to corporal punishment. Indeed, in most of the State and city regulations teachers are absolutely forbidden to inflict such punishment at all. There was no lack of evidence of high animal spirits outside the schools; but within there seemed to be little difficulty in maintaining discipline. Even at the universities, at Columbia and at Harvard, where I witnessed both the out-door sports and the academic ceremonial, I was struck by the dignity and seriousness of the students in the college itself, the absence, not merely of rowdyism, but of all unseemly shouting or unruliness.

General Character of the Schemes of Instruction

The chief feature in the schemes of instruction is the minuteness with which all the details are specified and the little room that is left for the discretion or special preferences of the teacher. In the high schools and universities the practice of prescribing "elective" subjects is very common; but here the choice is open to the parent or scholar, not to the teacher. In the schemes for primary and grammar schools, corresponding to our public elementary schools at home, there are hardly ever any alternative or optional subjects. There is a fixed *menu*, and not, as in the English schedules, provision for a *diner à la carte* in the form of a list of class-subjects, or specific subject from which the teacher may choose that which he can teach best, and which is most useful or most appreciated in his own district. Every subject is obligatory. The books to be used, the limits of work to be done in each grade or standard, are, in most cases, rigidly prescribed. I was looking at the copy-books in one school and observed that the series of exercises was graduated on a novel and rather elaborate theory, beginning with an analysis of the parts of letters. I asked the teacher whether she found the plan worked well. She replied that it worked

ill and that she greatly disliked it; but, she added, "these copy-books are prescribed by the school superintendent and we must not use any other." Repeatedly I have been told, when asking some simple question closely connected with the subject in hand, that it was "beyond the grade." A class of boys of 13 was working fractions, and when I was questioning them on a fraction and suggesting that other figures similarly related would express the same fraction, I happened to use the word "proportion." The teacher stopped me at once· with the remark that proportion did not come until the next grade. There is certainly less room for spontaneity or originality of plan on the part of the teacher than in our own country. It seemed to me, too, that many of the authorized time-tables cut up the day's work into too many short lessons on different subjects, and that the teaching was often scrappy and superficial, affording less room for the thorough examination of a subject than might be desired. Text-books and certain accepted formulas appeared to dominate the work of the classes too much, and, in spite of the undoubted merits of some features of the educational system, I have not the least reason to believe that American boys and girls are more soundly taught or are provided with a better intellectual outfit for the business and duties of life than English children of the same age, who are brought up in a good elementary school.

The School Superintendent

The chief executive officer and the adviser of the local educational authority is the School Superintendent. He occupies a position wholly unlike that of any scholastic officer in any country in Europe. Within his own domain, whether a State, a county, or a city, he combines in himself the characters of a minister of public instruction, an inspector of schools, a licenser of teachers, and a professor of pedagogy. Under the sanction of his board or committee he draws up the detailed regulations for the work of all classes in the schools, and often appends to them a manual, or at least an explanatory memorandum prescribing the method in which each subject shall be taught. He conducts, with the assistance of his staff of inspectors, the periodical examinations for determining the list of promotions among scholars from grade to grade. He sets the questions. He examines all candidates for the office of teacher in his district, and awards to them diplomas authorizing their employment in schools, and stating the grades of teaching for which they are severally qualified. It is part of his duty to hold "institutes" or assemblies of teachers, and to instruct those of them who have not been previously trained in the work of their special classes. He often conducts voluntary periodical conferences with the older teachers, and gives lectures to them on the history and philosophy of education. He is assisted by a staff of inspectors or supervisors who visit schools under his direction and share with him the duty of examining children for promotion. Sometimes he has an ingenious plan for availing himself of the services of the teachers in the annual examinations. He arranges that each question shall be answered on a separate sheet of paper, and then confides the marking of all the answers to one given question to one person. In this way he secures uniformity of judgment and avoids all suspicion of partiality. At his central bureau are often to be found a good professional library, for lending and reference, for the use of teachers; specimen juvenile libraries suited to different classes of schools, and a museum of objects and appliances illustrative of the best methods of teaching. One of the ablest of the school superintendents showed me some large portfolios and bound volumes in which he has carefully collected and dated during some years past the best specimens of work done at the annual examinations, drawings, written answers to questions, themes, compositions, and the like. He was thus able, he said, to compare the work of one year with another, and to form an exact estimate of general progress or of the working of any new experiment.

The person charged with these multifarious and important duties has almost invariably—I never met with one exception to the rule—been himself a teacher. Not, indeed, an *elementary* teacher, for if he were it is urged with some truth he would not be so likely to secure the confidence and respect of those whom he superintended, and would not be qualified either to examine high schools or to advise the board in reference to the due co-ordination of the work of primary and secondary instruction. But he has nearly always before his appointment served with distinction as master in a high school, or as professor in a normal or other college. He is, therefore, familiar with all the details of school work, and able to give valuable counsel in regard to methods. To this fact

he owes much of his influence among teachers and much of his public usefulness. If to the same fact he also owes certain prepossessions, and a certain lack of intellectual detachment, which render it difficult for him to recognize impartially the merit of good work of very different types, it must be admitted that these are possible disadvantages. But, in the opinion of the best authorities, they are enormously outweighed by the advantages which he has derived from his previous educational experience.

The main drawback to the usefulness of the school superintendent is the precarious tenure of his office. He is appointed by a local school committee, which is itself directly or indirectly the product of popular election, and which is liable to frequent changes. He is himself subject to triennial, or even to annual, re-election, and cannot count on that re-election unless he is *persona grata* to the local authority of the day. He is entitled to no pension and to no compensation for loss of office. He is, it is true, not one of that large army of functionaries whose offices become vacant on the accession of a new president, for he is not an officer of the Federal Government, but of the State or the city. Local politics, however, are subject to fluctuations certainly not less frequent and decisive than those of the Union itself. Every school superintendent has, therefore, a personal interest in local elections, which sometimes necessarily identifies him with party controversies, and which must, in any case, tend to withdraw his attention from his proper duties. Moreover, he has a strong motive to ingratiate himself with those who will have the power to re-elect him. The exercise of patronage is the pleasantest and often the most coveted part of the prerogative of a local alderman or committeeman. He wishes, it may be, to procure for a niece or other *protégée* an appointment as teacher. Her qualifications may not be high, but the fiat of the school superintendent will entitle her to a diploma, and that officer is under the strongest temptation to grant it on lenient terms. This is not the place in which to dwell upon the large question of Civil Service Reform, which is so anxiously discussed by American statesmen, but within the sphere of educational work the need for it is no less felt than in the Customs or in the Post Office. A body of public officers like the members of the permanent Civil Service in England, bound by the traditional etiquette of their profession to hold themselves aloof from all party politics, and to place their best services at the disposal of chiefs of different administrations, yet, at the same time, secure in their position *quamdiu se bene gesserint*, does not exist in America. Till it exists the nation will not induce the ablest men to take up departmental duty as a life's profession, nor will it obtain even from those who now undertake it the fullest and highest service which they are capable of rendering.

Practically inseparable from the American system, there is another danger, on which definite statements could not be properly made without great caution, even were the data for accurate generalization less obscure and more accessible than they are. The school authorities in their official programmes prescribe not only subjects of instruction, but also, in most cases, the books and the apparatus which should be employed. Occasionally, but not frequently, there is an authorized list of books from which the teachers are under certain conditions free to choose. More often the list of school-books is definitely enforced. Large pecuniary interests—those of publishers and producers of school appliances—are therefore involved. The smartness and energy of American traders are well known, and since the introduction of a new series of copybooks or of a manual may bring a large profit to a business house it is not surprising that the way is open to a good deal of subterranean influence if not to actual bribery. It is known that some great publishing firms spend considerable sums in manipulating the elections for school committees, with a special view to the adoption of particular reading-books or text-books. A great temptation is therefore presented to those officers who are charged with the duty of framing the lists of school requisites, and experience shows that this temptation is not always resisted.

This difficulty is partly, though not wholly, avoided by the practice which is adopted in the Province of Ontario. Here, when the Minister of Public Instruction approves a reading-book or text-book, the Education Department buys up the copyright, and thus becomes a distributor, without any intermediary agent, of its own books. This plan makes it next to impossible that any officer of the department should have a private commercial understanding with a publisher. But it does not overcome the graver difficulty. The selected book, however good, will certainly not be in the judgment of *all* the best teachers the fittest book for their own purpose, nor that which they can use the most effectively. And even though it may be, on the whole, the best

book which could be chosen, the fact that its use has been enforced by authority tends to discourage the most valuable forms of educational enterprise, and to make the production of a still better book difficult.

Inspection and Examination

The subject of school superintendence connects itself closely with the whole question of inspection and examination, and with the means adopted in order to secure the continued efficiency of the schools. A comparison of these means with those employed in our own country might prove misleading, inasmuch as the conditions are wholly dissimilar. There is nothing in America analogous to the Education Department in England, distributing from a central office a vast sum annually voted by Parliament in aid of local effort, and at the same time leaving all initiative—the choice of teachers, of books, and of methods, and the whole of the organization and daily discipline—to independent local bodies. The boards and committees of an American county or city are themselves the school managers; they appoint, pay, and dismiss teachers and prescribe plans and machinery, and their income is derived from one source only—the public fund, placed at their disposal by the taxpayers. They have in their hands many means of keeping up the standard of the schools, while the central government in England has but one—the power to grant or withhold subsidies, and to proportion the amount of those subsidies to the proved efficiency of the teaching. The method generally adopted by the various school authorities in America is to issue a very definite programme, to prescribe minutely the work to be done in each "grade" or class, to put forth also a manual or explanatory memorandum indicating the methods which are to be adopted in teaching each subject; and then, by means of frequent inspection, to find out whether these directions are habitually carried into effect. There are examinations, of course, especially when once a year the scholars are individually tested in order to determine whether they are qualified for promotion; but the main purpose of inspection is to ascertain whether the teachers are using the approved methods and conforming to the official programme. This plan of inspection has some obvious merits; but it is open to many objections, and is deeply disliked by many of the best teachers. In England, if the universities examine the public schools, if external examining authorities make an annual report upon a grammar school or a girls' high school, or if H. M. inspectors examine an elementary school, it is with the *results* of the work that they are concerned. The methods, the books, and the organization are left to the discretion of the teachers, who, whether engaged in higher or lower schools, would regard as an intolerable restraint the authority of any external body which laid down for the daily work of each class regulations as minute as those contained in some of the American manuals. Such regulations, though they are often drawn with great ability, and though they are of undoubted value to inexperienced or unskilful teachers, have a tendency to discourage originality, to destroy all sense of freedom and elbow-room on the part of the best teachers, and to make school work run in too mechanical a routine. While I was in New York an indignation meeting was held, and attended by many teachers and friends of education, to protest against the existing system, to set up a society for the reform of the city schools, and to denounce the "hated manuals" put forth by the board. Very strong language was used at the meeting and in the press. "Our system," it was said, "does not properly educate, and is conducted too much on the principle that the teacher's work is to cram the pupil with hard facts. The school system of this city is nothing more or less than a magnificent piece of machinery, crushing out, whether designedly or not, all individuality. Uniformity is the thing aimed at, and the uniformity achieved is that of mediocrity." I thought I had heard language of this kind somewhat nearer home, but I had never before heard it used against public authorities because they did not measure the teaching in schools by its results, but would insist on minute and mechanical rules controlling the processes by which the results were produced. And over and over again I have been asked by teachers what sort of test was applied to educational work in England; and when I have replied that it was the business of officials here to ascertain what work had been done, but not to criticise methods, except in so far as those methods were shown to have failed to achieve their purpose, teachers have invariably told me that they would greatly prefer being judged under such a system, and that it would be far more tolerable and effective than their own. The truth is that till the end of time any conceivable system which subjects either teaching work or any other work to external criticism is sure to be unsatisfactory to some of those who are criticised. But once admit that public authority is to be brought to bear on school work at all, there are, it would seem, only two possible ways of doing it. Whether the immediate object be to award credit to the teachers, or to assess the share of a public fund to which the school should be entitled, or to make a report for the information of the public, is immaterial. The work of a school must be estimated either by its methods and machinery or by its results; and of the two the former plan hampers teachers and restricts their freedom far more than the latter. It presupposes that the method approved by authority is the best in all circumstances and in the hands of all teachers; and it greatly discourages all independent effort and all invention of new and better methods.

Louis R. Klemm   1890

Systematic Comparisons of American and European Education

The following extract is from a study prepared by Louis R. Klemm (1845–1916) for the U.S. Commissioner of Education. Klemm was officially recognized as a "specialist in foreign school systems," and his compilation illustrates the government's interest in making statistical information available as a basis for educational comparisons. Although only two tables are reproduced below, the original study included six tables and four diagrams on education in Europe and America between kindergarten and university levels during 1890. For further information, the reader should refer to the extract by Klemm in the previous section of this book entitled "On European Education."

Louis R. Klemm, "Education in Europe and America," in *Report of the Commissioner of Education, 1889-90* (Washington, D.C.: U.S. Government Printing Office, 1893), I, 549-550, 553, 558.

The accompanying charts and diagrams are a continuation of a systematic comparison, commenced in the Annual Report of 1888–89, Part I, pages 75–78, showing the sum total of educational efforts in Europe and Pan America between kindergarten and university.

Various lines of inquiry were pointed out last year as standards of comparison, but for reasons then stated only one was applied, *i.e.*, "What portion of the population of each nation in Europe and America is under school influence?" This year the inquiry is extended to two other questions, *i.e.*, "What is the cost of elementary instruction per capita of the population?" and "Is elementary instruction gratuitous, or is a tuition fee charged?" It will be seen that while most of the blanks which appeared in last year's tables are filled this year, new blanks occur in the new columns. It is to be hoped that they will disappear as quickly as those of last year. . . .

In the result of this inquiry we have systematically excluded from the count all institutions such as "infant schools" and "kindergartens," because they represent the prescholastic age. Also excluded are all professional schools, such as universities, polytechnical, medical, pharmaceutical, and art schools, conservatories of music, in fact, all special schools except normal schools, not because the latter are not special and professional schools, for they are, and

needs must be, but because they are not sufficiently designated as special schools in the statistical material at hand.

This then brings the age, commonly called "school age," within the years 6 and 18 (or 20). These limits are not in all cases and in all nations the same, which may account for a small percentage of difference in the number of enrolled children. Again, the sum total stated for Great Britain and Ireland does not contain the number of secondary students, while they are included in nearly all other countries. Secondary instruction being entirely left to private enterprise in England, it is not possible to obatin reliable statistics concerning it. It would be but just to add from $1\frac{1}{2}$ to 2 per cent to the ratio given in order to place Great Britain and Ireland on a similar basis with European continental countries. But aside from little unavoidable discrepancies and possible errors, these tables and diagrams reveal facts which invite the most earnest attention.

With regard to the new colums: (a) Cost per capita, and (b) Tuition fee paid or not? it is regretted that the officials of some countries do not report the amount of expenditures by provincial and local authorities, and only state the amount paid by the central governments. These items were inserted rather than leave blanks. But they are marked thus (*), which means from state only. . . .

Education in Europe Between Kindergarten and University, 1890

Arranged According to Ratio of Children in School

Countries.	Date of census or estimate.	Population.	Date of report.	Children enrolled in school.	Ratio to population.	Cost of elementary instruction per capita of population.	Pay tuition or not.
Bavaria	1890	5,589,382	1890	1,187,792	21.2	. . . . .	Pay and free schools.
Baden	1890	1,656,817	1889	342,764	20.6	. . . . .	Do.
Saxony	1890	3,500,513	1889	706,946	20.2	$2.28	Free.
Prussia	1890	29,959,388	a1890	5,874,390	19.6	1.86	Pay and free schools.
Switzerland	1888	2,917,740	1890	570,935	19.5	2.03	Free.
Württemberg	1890	2,035,443	1889	388,262	19.0	1.67	Pay and free schools.
Germany (Empire)	1890	49,421,064	a1890	9,300,000	18.8	. . . . .	
Lübeck	1890	76,485	1890	14,403	18.7	2.17	Free
Bremen	1890	180,443	1890	32,191	18.0	1.94	Do.
Finland	1889	2,305,916	1890	406,966	17.6	*.50	Pay and free schools.
England and Wales	1891	29,001,018	1890	4,825,560	16.6	1.30	Pay and free.
Scotland	1891	4,033,103	1890	664,466	16.4	1.40	Free.
Great Britain and Ireland	1891	37,888,153	1890	6,184,858	16.3	. . . . .	Pay and free.
Hamburg	1890	622,530	1889	96,356	15.6	. . . . .	Free
Norway	1891	1,199,176	1888	308,507	15.4	.80	Pay and free schools.
Sweden	1890	4,784,675	1890	736,790	15.4	.70	Do.
France	1891	38,343,192	1889	5,807,157	15.1	1.34	Free
Ireland	1891	4,706,162	1890	694,832	14.7	1.05	Do.
Netherlands, the	1890	4,564,565	1890	657,611	14.2	1.42	Pay and free schools.
Belgium	1890	6,147,041	1890	827,958	13.5	1.60	Do.
Austria	1890	23,895,413	1889	3,132,088	13.1	*.22	Do.
Austria-Hungary	1890	41,231,342	1889	5,312,656	12.9	. . . .	
Hungary	1890	17,335,929	1889	2,180,568	12.6	.42	Do.
Denmark	1890	2,185,159	1885	239,940	11.0	1.54	Do.
Spain	1887	17,550,246	1885	1,859,183	10.6	*.21	Do.
Italy	1890	30,158,408	1889	2,733,859	9.6	.79	Do.
Greece	1889	2,187,208	1884	140,155	6.4	. . . . .	
Portugal	1881	4,708,178	1887	276,688	5.9	*.25	Pay and free schools.
Bulgaria	1890	3,154,375	1890	171,983	5.5	*.12	Free.
Russia	1889	95,870,810	1890	a3,000,000	3.1	*.13	Pay and free schools.
Servia	1891	2,162,759	1889	58,575	2.7	*.23	Free.
Turkey	a1885	4,786,545	1882	126,471	2.6	. . . . .	Small fee.
Roumania	a1887	5,500,000	1890	138,800	2.5	*.20	Free
Montenegro	a1890	236,000	1889	3,300	1.4	. . . . .	Do.

         * From State only.   *a* Estimated.

Education in America Between Kindergarten and University, 1890

Arranged According to Ratio of Children in School

Countries.	Date of census or estimate.	Population.	Date of report.	Children enrolled in school.	Ratio to population.	Cost of elementary instruction per capita of population.	Pay tuition or not.
North Central States (United States)	1890	22,362,279	1890	5,647,308	25.0	$2.81	Free
United States (entire)	1890	62,622,250	1890	14,377,536	23.3	2.24	Do.
South Central States (United States)	1890	10,972,893	1890	2,558,378	23.3	.98	Do.
South Atlantic States (United States)	1890	8,857,920	1890	1,903,468	21.5	.96	Do.
North Atlantic States (United States)	1890	17,410,545	1890	3,694,067	21.2	2.76	Do.
Canada	1891	4,829,411	1889	998,823	20.8	1.85	Do.
Western States (United States)	1890	3,027,613	1890	574,315	19.0	3.34	Do.
Jamaica	b1891	639,491	1890	75,680	11.8	*.21	Do.
Surinam	1889	55,968	1889	5,684	10.0	. . . .	Pay and free schools.
Guiana (British)	1891	284,887	1890	27,884	9.6	.44	Do.
Trinidad	1890	208,030	1890	19,685	9.4	.70	Do.
Uruguay	1889	683,943	1888	54,513	8.0	.75	Do.
Paraguay	1887	329,645	1891	25,594	8.0	.99	Free.
Honduras (British)	1891	31,471	1890	2,450	8.0	*.32	Pay and free schools.
Costa Rica	1891	238,782	1890	17,500	7.3	1.55	Free.
Argentine Republic	1887	4,086,492	1890	276,983	6.8	a2.55	Do.
Guiana (French)	b1890	25,796	1888	1,658	6.4	. . . .	
Martinique and Guadeloupe.	1888	324,462	1888	18,073	5.5	. . . .	
Honduras	1889	431,917	1890	b23,000	5.3	*.32	Pay and free schools.
Venezuela	1890	2,285,054	1891	104,840	5.0	*.16	Free.
Mexico	1889	11,632,924	1888	543,977	4.7	.32	Do.
Ecuador	b1889	1,271,861	1890	58,308	4.6	. . . .	Do.
Chile	1891	2,766,747	1888	122,664	4.4	. . . .	Do.
Guatemala.	b1890	1,452,003	1890	57,380	4.0	.37	Do.
Salvador.	1891	777,895	1889	28,473	3.7	. . . .	
Cuba	1890	1,521,684	1887	50,000	3.3	. . . .	
Nicaragua	b1890	400,000	1887	11,914	3.0	. . . .	
Peru	1886	2,700,945	1890	71,435	2.6	.11	Pay and free schools.
Colombia	1881	3,878,600	1889	93,187	2.4	. . . .	Free.
Bolivia	1888	1,192,162	1890	27,764	2.3	*.63	Do.
Brazil	1888	14,002,335	1889	305,193	2.2	.51	Do.
Santo Domingo	1888	610,000	1890	b10,000	1.6	. . . .	Do.
Haiti	1887	960,000	1890	b10,000	1.0	. . . .	Do.
Puerto Rico.	1890	806,708	. . . .	. . . .	. . . . . .	. . . .	

*From State only   a Depreciated paper money.   b Estimated.

W. Catton Grasby 1891

An Australian's View of Education in America and England

W. Catton Grasby (1859–1930), an Australian educator, traveled on behalf of the Education Department of South Australia to study education in Europe and North America. Some of the results of his study are included in the extracts below. He compared the educational system of England with that of the United States and made a series of recommendations for Australian educators to follow. It has become customary for generations of Australian educators to visualize their culture and system of education somewhere between that of Great Britain and the United States. Catton Grasby was no exception, and in discussing the status of teachers, he noted that "Australia occupies an intermediate position between her two older relations in this matter."

Status of Teachers

A difference is noticeable in the position which the teacher takes, and the respect in which the work is held, in England, Australia, and America. I place the names in this order, because Australia occupies an intermediate position between her two older relations in this matter. So many of the public and professional men of the United States have used the school as a step in Ambition's ladder, and so many of the wives of her prominent citizens have either been actively engaged in the work of teaching, or have graduated in the high or normal schools or colleges with those who have become teachers, that the pedagogical profession is held in higher repute than in the mother country, where the public elementary school is for "common people," and where to make son or daughter a teacher is more often considered an ambitious aim in itself. The fact that male teachers in the United States so frequently merely look upon the work of teaching as a temporary expedient to earn money to place themselves in an occupation more remunerative and less irksome, is the cause of much of the weakness of the male in comparison with the female American teacher.

In the past men have, to a large extent, taken to teaching to earn money to go to college; or, having graduated at college, teach until they have saved sufficient to commence the practice of the law. Such men will not, as a rule, be first-class teachers. It is only when a man's heart is in his work, that he will do best work. Some taking to the profession with this object, find that they have such a liking for it they can never leave it. Such are the most successful. As a rule, the door leading to success opens to those having the key of talent and energy. Others, and these seem to be the more numerous, take to teaching as the most available occupation until "something turns up," and continue for the same reason. These men form the drag which hinders the progress of educational reform. The worst teaching I saw in America was by men who were graduates of some of the best universities. They taught as they had been taught when they were boys at school. They are the conservative party at the Association meetings and teachers' Institutes. Their standing as university men gives their words weight, which they should not possess.

This custom, I believe rapidly passing away, of thus looking at the work of a teacher, has been productive of much harm. Except in individual cases, men will always aim at those positions in which it is possible to win the widest reputations, the highest honours, the largest incomes, and the best social position. While the relics of savagery linger to such an extent that the drones of the national hive, the fomenters of quarrels, thrive best—nay, exist at all—in consequence of the barbarism of our natures; while the profession of suppressing crime and fomenting national quarrels and wholesale butchery is more highly honoured than training boys for useful lives; while it is considered an "advance" to leave the education of a child, in order to publicly lie in defence of a criminal who has been allowed to reach his condition of degradation by neglect in early life, it is not to be wondered that the world's progress, though sure, should be slow.

Proportion of Male and Female

In the United States there are upwards of four hundred thousand teachers, of whom

Catton Grasby, *Teaching in Three Continents: Personal Notes on the Educational Systems of the World* (London: Cassell and Company Ltd., 1891), pp. 231-241, 295-298.

thirty-seven per cent. are men. This statement will astonish the average American, nearly as greatly as the visitor who goes from city to city and finds women reigning almost supreme throughout the public schools. When I further state that of the ninety-six thousand *public elementary teachers* under the English Education Department, only thirty-one per cent. are males, that is to say, according to statistics, the proportion of male teachers is less in England than in the United States, it will be thought necessary to find some explanation for the unexpected result.

In the first place, the number given for the United States includes *all grades* of teachers. If it were possible to find the number of teachers in the primary and grammar schools of the States, the comparison would be very different.

I was fully aware that there has been for some time a decided tendency in England to increase the proportion of female teachers, but I was not aware that it had developed to the extent which it has. Only forty-one per cent. of all certificated teachers, twenty-six per cent. of the assistants, twenty-seven per cent. of the pupil-teachers, and twenty-five per cent. of the candidates for engagement as pupil-teachers, are males.

In London the experiment of employing women teachers for standards I. and II. in the Boys' Departments of a limited number of selected schools was tried a few years since, with such success that the Board decided to continue and extend the principle. There are now nearly twice as many lady as gentlemen adult teachers, while only twenty-one per cent. of the pupil-teachers are males. At the same time women are not found in charge of boys' schools, as in America. There is always a man at the head.

Returning to the consideration of the proportion of male teachers in the United States, some curious results are obtained. Where education is worst, the proportion of male teachers is highest; while in the centres where it has made the greatest progress, and where the schools are most efficient, it is becoming a curiosity to find a male teacher in the primary and grammar schools.

In New Mexico seventy-eight per cent. of the teachers are men, in Utah fifty per cent., in Arkansas seventy-three per cent., Carolina sixty-two; while for the whole of the South Central States it is sixty-one, and for the South Atlantic group of States it is fifty-three. I have no practical experience of any of these States except Utah; but the census shows that illiteracy is increasing at a greater ratio than the population, and it is chiefly for them that the advocates of the Blair Bill wish to devote eighty millions of dollars from the national treasury.

If we examine the figures for the groups of States where education has received most attention, we find that in the Atlantic Division only twenty-two per cent. are men, and in the North Central group of States thirty-four per cent. Taking individual States, the difference becomes still more marked; New Hampshire has ten per cent. of men in her schools, Massachusetts ten per cent., Rhode Island twelve per cent., New York State seventeen per cent., California twenty-one per cent. Taking a few of the cities and towns, it will be found that in Chicago only four out of each hundred of the primary and grammar-school teachers are men. In Boston there are twelve, Springfield seven, Providence six, Washington nine, San Francisco six, New York City thirteen, Long Island city not three, while there are fourteen smaller cities which employ only female teachers. Philadelphia has three per cent. of men, St. Louis nine per cent., Minneapolis three, St. Paul five per cent.

In Toronto, Canada, there are only thirty male teachers in the schools, having an attendance of sixteen thousand children, or just ten per cent.

In South Australia forty-five per cent. of all the regular teachers are males. Of the head-teachers eighty-one per cent. are men; of the assistants and pupil-teachers twenty-nine per cent. are males.

I collected a number of opinions as to the cause and effect of the great and growing disproportion of ladies in the schools; some of which I will summarise.

The consensus of opinion in England appears to be, that the increase of proportion of lady teachers has been brought about in the first place principally through motives of economy; but now it is considered that for some departments of the work they are better than men. If this tendency continues, co-education will follow as a natural sequence.

The Clerk of the Liverpool School Board, after watching the result of the gradual increase of the number of lady teachers, is of opinion that except for the higher classes of boys they are preferable to the majority of available men.

The same opinion was given by other School Board and Voluntary school authorities.

The head-master of one of the finest,

though not the largest, Board-schools I saw, whose staff of assistants consisted of five female and two male teachers, said he liked female teachers best except for the two upper classes. Said he, "Female assistants are more easily managed, and *I can get a deal more work out of them.*" That reply is characteristic of many I received: "Female teachers carry out instructions better," "Lady teachers are more careful of details," and so forth. On the other hand, there are not wanting a large number of men who predict dreadful consequences if the present tendency is allowed to continue. The work is too hard for women, say some; and in England there is some truth in the statement, but that is no argument against ability. "Boys need strong management;" "They lose self-respect when they have to remain under women," are remarks often heard.

The principal of the Normal School, Boston, considers that the paucity of male teachers, and the lack of means for training them, is one of the weak spots in the school system of the towns. He greatly regrets that there are not more men in the schools, though under present conditions he considers it a good thing. They have to be obtained where they can, and often are not of the first order: they have had no training, teach as they were taught, and have no grasp of the higher part of the teacher's profession. The consequence is that they are seldom on the progressive side of the education movement, and retard its progress. One of the most difficult tasks of a progressive teacher or superintendent is to fight against the ignorance and prejudice of these men. That they are often college graduates makes matters worse, for they hold up their diplomas as guarantees of capacity, and the people grant their claims.

The same gentleman says that the usual reason assigned for the employment of female teachers is that they are more sympathetic; but after seeing male teachers in Germany teaching junior classes, he is of opinion that men properly trained are more sympathetic than women. "The real reason is economy. We do not pay women more than about 1,750 dollars, and we cannot get first-class men for that."

Among other opinions I sought were those of the managers of the education departments of several large publishing houses. One gentleman who had formerly been a teacher, and afterwards a State superintendent of schools, said: "It is chiefly a question of money. First-class men are, however, looking more to the profession of late since they

see that in consequence of the development of the System of Superintendence there will be better opportunities. At present, it is no doubt true that the men do not show to advantage, and the progressive movements are largely carried on by women."

Another business man, but also having experience of the schools, in reply to my inquiry, said:—

"It is chiefly a question of money. A 1,500 dollars woman is superior to a 1,500 dollars man, and so on down or up the scale. A first-class woman can be secured for a salary which would not secure a second-class man. The women are anxious to take up the work, while the men are equally wishful of finding other occupations."

Questioning Superintendent MacAlister of Philadelphia who is looked upon as one of the most progressive men in the United States, and who has worked marvels in the improvement of the Public Schools of Philadelphia, he said: "There are fewer men in proportion in Philadelphia than in any other large city in the Union. I think women make better teachers than men; they are brighter, quicker, more sympathetic, and less conservative than men. We have some splendid women in our schools." There is a magnificent Normal School for the training of women, but no means whereby a man may receive special training as a teacher. I therefore suggested that the comparison between men and women teachers was hardly fair. A man is taken without any preparation, and placed to do the same work as a woman who has had a special training; and because he does not do it as well or better, it is argued that he is not as well adapted for teaching as a woman. They may be educated, cultured gentlemen, but unless the arguments in favour of teaching being a profession are devoid of weight, it is not to be wondered that they are opposed to "New Systems" which, in the nature of things, they do not understand.

He admitted that there was much to be said in the way I had indicated; but when a man became a teacher, he should read and understand the signification of his work.

A plan was being considered for giving the necessary training to men, who, at present, were often the greatest hindrances to the progress of true education.

I made a number of inquiries in Toronto. One principal said: "Plenty of men could be engaged, but women are cheaper, and the short-sighted authorities will make that the chief consideration. Our boys leave school early because they have to be under female teachers; boys over ten require a man's force of character. The upper classes of both boys and girls should be taught by men. There are only half a dozen male assistants in the whole of the city, at a salary of not more than seven hundred and fifty dollars, while the maximum salary of a female assistant is six hundred and fifty dollars, and only two or three receive that.''

The same statements were repeated over and over again, in a multitude of forms; but I have no hesitation in saying that the prevalent opinion is that, while women cost less, they are just as effective as men.

How Teachers Act Towards Strangers

In one characteristic, all countries are alike. It seems to be the rule everywhere that as soon as a visitor enters a school the teachers change their work. There appears to be a great reluctance to allow him to see the school in its normal condition. When this desire simply leads to a general brightening-up of both pupils and teachers, while the regular work is carried on in the ordinary way, I am glad that it should be so. I go to a school wishing to see it in its real condition, under the most favourable circumstances. All fine days are not equally bright; a humorous man is not at all times equally witty; a poet has not always the divine gift of song. A school may be excellent, but there are times when it is out of harmony, just as there are times when work proceeds with more than ordinary vigour and smoothness. If I am to make but one visit, I do not wish to see it under either of the unusual circumstances, but would choose that which is too good rather than the unfavourable. Even a cipher does not present exactly the same appearance from every point of view. Many objects, having been seen from only one position, are unrecognisable from others; comparatively few people would recognise a side-view of their own faces.

Many teachers find it absolutely impossible to conduct their work in the ordinary way in the presence of visitors. I can, I think, generally detect when this is the case. Some men and women, however, while lacking the power to be natural, have developed to an astonishing degree the power to hide, under a formal bearing and appearance of stolid indifference, their intense excitement and the acute suffering they feel. This is a great misfortune. The children see their teacher is not the same as usual when a stranger is present, and become different too. Both are alike uncomfortable, and both deserve strongest sympathy, and neither get it.

Very different is the lazy teacher, who gathers himself together on such occasions, and adds to the opinion of laziness with which his pupils regard him the further despicable one of dishonesty and hypocrisy. All ''show off,'' and the casual visitor thinks what a fine teacher and well-disciplined class he has seen. The behaviour of children, like that of teachers, varies greatly in different places when a visitor enters a school.

In San Francisco, immediately a visitor enters the room, all rise, step out of the desks with perfect order and quietness, and stand, respectful and silent, until the visitor is formally introduced, when they gracefully bow, and in many schools say, with winning grace, ''We are pleased to see you, sir.''

Nothwithstanding the opinion I shall presently express, I must candidly own that the custom has much to recommend it. Had I seen it burlesqued in even a few of the scores of rooms I visited, I should condemn it; but I did not. It was performed with greater grace in some than in other schools, but it was only a difference in degree where the worst was good. While it is evidently a result of drill, nothing could be more free from the stiffness one generally associates with drill. The attention, due to the Delsarte System of Calisthenics, must be the secret of the grace of movement. It is essentially pleasing to the visitor; and while I would much rather have entered without form, I cannot but recognise that the training must have a great influence in producing that courteous, self-contained bearing so noticeable among the Californian people. As anyone who wishes to gain an insight into the schools will not confine his observations to a mere formal visit, the chief objection is thereby removed; for, after this formal introduction to teachers and pupils, he can pass from room to room while the work is proceeding in the ordinary way. As I proceeded East, I observed, with the increasing conservative tendencies of the people, a gradual lessening of this formality; but, at the same time, a growing tendency to put the pupils through sets of exercises to show their proficiency. I did not go to hear what the children knew, but to see how they were taught. This weakness was most marked in New York City, whose schools seem to have had great influence in forming the English opinion which I have read and heard of American teaching.

There seemed to be so great a desire for me to see what they thought good, with a corresponding apparent disinclination to allow me to see what I wished, that I found it profitable to spend less time in the Empire City than I had intended. I came to the conclusion that there is more system and less education in New York than in any other city of the Union I had visited. In contrast to this, I was pleased to find in many places that, unless I was accompanied by a superintendent or other official, the pupils did not change their positions nor cease work at all, apparently not noticing me; while the teachers politely but silently acknowledged my presence and continued their work.

At one large convention of teachers, the Superintendent particularly impressed upon his hearers the importance of this, emphasising the point that visitors should not be allowed to interfere with the regular work of the school. "Anyone," said he, "who is really interested in the school would much prefer to see it in its normal condition; and anyone not so interested should not be considered." The majority of Australian and English, as well as American, teachers, would do well to adopt this advice. . . .

English Estimate of American Education

I believe that the average Englishman forms far too low an estimate of American education. Particularly is this true with regard to the Universities. For this he, or rather his insular character, is not more to blame than the American's love for high-sounding phrases and titles, which have caused the misconception. This love of effect has prompted him to use, in trivial matters, expressions which, to English minds, convey a much higher meaning. For example, the term "graduate" conveys to an English mind the idea of one who has taken a college course, and received the hall mark of a university degree. When, therefore, he hears an American boy or girl of fourteen talking about having "graduated," his notions of propriety receive a shock. It is an innovation, and he does not like innovations except when brought in with proper decorum and powerful patronage. As a matter of fact, the American boy thinks no more of "graduating" than the Leeds lad does of passing his seventh standard; but his appropriation of a term used only in the higher exclusive sense seems to give him an air of presumption.

Again, one hears of the teacher in charge of an ordinary public school spoken of as the "principal," a term which, in England, designates the head of a more pretentious seat of learning: "head master" being used in elementary and middle class schools. Then, the terms "faculty" and "alumni" are used with great deference in the older land. To the conservative Britisher, with his decorous respect amounting almost to reverence for the old associations of expressions connected with profound learning, it seems undignified and little short of ridiculous, to hear the teachers of a high school spoken of as "professors," the staff as the "faculty," and the pupils, boys and girls of from fourteen to eighteen, "alumni." These are but small matters, and with American associations are perfectly natural, but afford a field for the satirist. On the other hand, they are quite as important as many of the points which give the American equally false ideas of England.

The official statistics show that an immense number of untrained teachers are taken into even the city schools of the States each year; and the reader unacquainted with the country draws a reasonable inference that the teaching must be very poor. But what would happen if the English Board schools were practically staffed each year with raw untrained material of the same character as the present teachers, but without their special experience, throws little light on the American condition of things. A group of Arabs looks picturesque in an oasis of the desert; but place it in Ludgate Circus, with lamp-posts substituted for palms, and London fog for sunshine, and a scarecrow has charms as great. Things can only be judged in their environment.

Another source of misconception is the supposed character—I am not in a position to state what foundation now exists for the opinion—which many of the institutions called colleges or universities have for rapidly transforming working men of ambition into graduates with LL.D., Ph.D., D.D., etc., tacked on to their names, leading to the statement that it is a greater distinction to have no degree than to be an American doctor of laws. When talking of this, a gentleman of exceptional ability said: "Fools enough in all conscience manage to obtain degrees in England, with all the exclusiveness of our Universities; what must it be where the strictures are absent?" I will not answer the question; but may it not be that the fool is in the same position on both sides of the Atlantic?—he does not differ greatly the world over—but that after the degree has been won the man has still to prove his worth for practical purposes of life, or there will be no use for him any way, whether he be in one or the other country. I have not found it to be a cardinal doctrine of belief among the University men of England that undergraduates always make study their *chief purpose* at college. In some way, and with various aids, they "get through." Many of these afterwards settle down to work, and carve out names for themselves. They are not the "fools" my friend spoke of, and yet they did not deserve the degree at the time they received it. Now if this can be, it is possible that a man —although he has been but a carpenter and lacks that indescribable bearing, nowhere acquired as at the great Universities, which marks the English gentleman—by his natural ability, wide reading, and much seclusive study, in the course of three years' hard work such as a physically strong man, urged by ambitious motives, can endure, may actually earn a far higher degree than those who have done the compulsory work of Cambridge, and who, by being well coached up, at the end of the term "got through," may be, fairly well. Were I to judge the English University-man by the young men, not a few, with whom I have travelled; and the American by the Doctors, Masters, or Bachelors who commenced life as tradesmen or farmers, first earning the money with which they paid their expenses at college, I should not hesitate long in deciding that the latter were the better men. But I would be doing equal injustice in each case. Yet the ideas held of each other by the average subject or citizen of the two great divisions of the English race is not any more correct than the absurd example I have given. Did each understand the other, much ridicule on each side would be turned to admiration.

George Birkbeck Hill   1893

Oxford and Harvard Comparisons

George Birkbeck Hill (1835–1903), an English author and editor, was educated at Pembroke College, Oxford. He taught at Bruce Castle School for ten years and was headmaster there from 1868 to 1877. Returning to Oxford in 1887, he devoted the remainder of his life to writing.

Hill's contribution to comparative education lies entirely in his work comparing Oxford and Harvard. He spent barely a semester at Harvard in Cambridge, Massachusetts, but he read widely and used reports published by the university as well as faculty interviews to substantiate his findings. He intended his book to be a criticism of both Oxford and Harvard and skillfully interwove into it a series of suggestions for academic reform at his own institution.

The Harvard system of academic organization and administration particularly impressed Hill, who viewed the system prevailing at Oxford as chaotic. The finance and support of higher education in America also impressed him, and he prophetically noted that "the millionaire who shall endow research [at Harvard] has not yet appeared on the stage of the New England Cambridge. Perhaps he is within the prompter's call."

Academic Standards

In America, it is clear, a better classification is needed both in the schools and in the Universities. Democratic equality has been allowed, it seems, to invade even the province of the mind. All the realm of learning is in common. It is felony, not to drink small beer, but to ask for stronger ale than most heads can stand. In the school there should be that sixth form which the dull and backward are never suffered to encumber; and even in this sixth form there should be no absolute equality of study. The ablest scholars, while they did all that was done by the others, should have a wider range of subjects. In the University there should be established that division between "passmen" and "classmen" which is for the benefit of the slow and ignorant almost as much as of the well-trained scholar. He must no longer be made to work on the same lines as the dunce and the idler, merely doing well what they do ill. It is on a

George Birkbeck Hill, *Harvard College by an Oxonian* (New York: Macmillan and Company, 1894), pp. 241–252, 312–316.

higher level he should study, and at a greater pace that he should advance. At Harvard, as I am informed by one of the most eminent of the Professors, "it is perfectly possible for the best scholars (in rank) to earn their rank and their scholarships too in courses of study in which the lowest in rank can pass without censure. This is intolerable; and yet it would require a severe wrench to break us off from it. Our higher courses, it is true, give students an opportunity to study on a higher level; but we still give our rank and our scholarship to those who stand highest in the general competition; and it is much easier to *stand high* in a lower course than in a higher." To attain the highest success the student has to reach the top in each one of the sixteen courses through which he has passed in his four years at College. Whether he has stood on the summit of sixteen mole-hills or sixteen mountains matters not a whit.

These evils, great as they undoubtedly are, have happily been lessened by the elective system. Real scholars would not sacrifice rank to knowledge, but would choose the higher courses. Thus by a natural process they would classify themselves. It is in the Graduate School, however, free as it is from all artificial rewards, that the Professor who has the cause of learning deeply at heart finds his greatest comfort and hope. In it, I am told, there are students as good as the best in Oxford and Cambridge—not perhaps so ready and versatile, for they have not passed through a long and often harmful course of systematic training, but nevertheless nowise inferior to them in knowledge and in a love of learning.

In our ancient Universities, though of late years far greater freedom has been given than of old, nevertheless, the battle of "elective studies"—to use the American term—is still going on. At Oxford and at Cambridge no one can take his degree who has not some knowledge of Greek and Latin. At Oxford he can bid farewell to the classics when he has passed his first examination;[1] but without some Greek and Latin, enough to be a worry, but scarcely enough to be an advantage, the University is barred even to the most ardent learner. It is but a short while since, at Cambridge, the attempt to make Greek an optional study was defeated by an overwhelming majority. In neither University does the widest knowledge in one department make up for total ignorance in an-

other. A student might write as good Latin as Erasmus ever wrote, and might in Mathematics give the promise of a second Newton, or in Natural Science of a second Darwin,—unless he knows his Greek irregular verbs, Oxford and Cambridge will have none of him. . . . It is much to be wished that our universities, if they cannot make up their minds to altogether abandoning compulsory Greek, should get over the difficulty by some ingenious fiction. They might, for instance, decree, that in the case of a student who shows unusual proficiency in any great branch of learning, it shall be taken for granted that he does know Greek, and that the examiners shall no more presume to test his knowledge of that language than Don Quixote presumed to test the strength of his patched-up helmet. . . .

. . . In Harvard the degree is not won, as in the English Universities, by success in three or four public examinations, conducted by Boards of Examiners, but by the student satisfying his instructor in each one of the eighteen courses through which he passes in his four years. The instructor, I was told, does not altogether go by the answers in the examinations which he himself commonly holds, but he takes into consideration the difficulties which may have arisen through such circumstances as illness or the death of a near relative. He considers, moreover, a student's habits—whether of idleness or industry. One of the Professors whom I consulted thought the standard too low; another said that the system works well if each Professor examines his own class. He alone, who had taught them, was competent to test the students' knowledge of what they had been taught. At the end of each course "the standing of each student is expressed, according to his proficiency, by one of five grades." He who, at the close of his career, is found to have attained the highest grade in fifteen courses, takes his degree *summa cum laude*. The highest grade in nine courses, or the highest or second in fifteen, confers a *magna cum laude;* and the highest or second in nine courses confers a *cum laude.* The *summa cum laude,* moreover, is conferred on any one who, in a special examination, conducted by a committee of the Faculty, near the close of the Senior year, has shown great proficiency in any department.

Such a system of examinations as I have described does not put the students through that severe course through which the highest students of Oxford and Cambridge pass—

---

[1] Responsions, once vulgarly known as *the little go*, but now as *smalls*.

a course which, so long as it has not strained the mind or weakened the body, admirably fits a man for the severest toil of professional life. He who, with health unimpaired, is placed at Oxford in the First Class in the School of Literæ Humaniores, or at Cambridge high among the Wranglers, is not very likely in after life to be daunted or baffled by any kind of work, however hard or dry it may be. It does to perfection that which it was meant to do. It fits men for the great world—for success at the Bar and in public life. It turns out great lawyers and great statesmen. It keeps up a constant supply of leading-article writers—men who can rapidly make themselves masters of facts and as rapidly set them forth in a clear and able form. It confers infinite dexerity and readiness. On the other hand, it breaks down a certain number—perhaps not many—by the excessive strain it puts upon them, and it unfits still more for the scholar's life. It is for success, not for knowledge, that the struggle has been, and it is success and not knowledge that far too often is its great reward. "Do not spoil your careers," the late Master of Balliol used to say to his undergraduates. He was the last man to have agreed with Mr. Lowell's notion of a University, that it is "a place where nothing useful is taught."[2] I have heard of a humorous saying of the Master's that "Diogenes Laertius was a learned man in the worst sense of the word." There are learned men even worse than Diogenes Laertius—men gifted with great powers, who, having by their learning won a high reputation, then turn traders, and instead of increasing knowledge, traffic in it. The Oxford and Cambridge scholars are far less likely than the scholars of a German University to spoil their careers by giving themselves up to the noble, but ill-requited life of a man of learning. It is not in the Schools of either of our great Universities that is awakened that ardent spirit of research, that love of knowledge for its own sake, which is the glory of Germany. *Finis coronat opus.* The First Class, or the Wranglership, is achieved, and the goal is won. In a way as strange as it is absurd, these high distinctions sometimes chill aspirations. I have heard a great Greek scholar at Oxford pleasantly describe how a First Class man often becomes afraid of his own reputation— the reputation which he gained before his moustache was fully grown. Throughout life he will not give to the world any piece of

[2]*Harvard College, 250th Anniversary*, p. 216.

learned work, lest it should not be found up to the high-water mark of his two and twentieth year. In Harvard there is none of this blaze of glory that comes at the end of a strain prolonged through many years. It is no training place for mental athletes. But while something thereby is lost, much is gained. There are no false suns to dazzle the scholar's eyes. It is not the goal of a four years' course, with its shining pillars, that lies before him, but the boundless horizon of the great ocean of truth all undiscovered.

The Fellowships which the University offers to graduates are not prizes for what they have already learnt, but means of support while they learn more. No young Bachelor of Arts is splendidly rewarded for his success in examinations by an annual allowance of two hundred pounds for the next seven years. There is no Derby Scholarship that adds one hundred and fifty-seven pounds to the youth who, in all probability, has already won more money prizes than any man of his standing. There is no Tom Tiddler's ground where the "brilliant" men[3] pick up gold and silver. All the money that is given, is given not to reward students, but to support them in further studies. They either go to work in some foreign university, or far more commonly, they stay on to work in the Graduate School—that School in which Ticknor's vision of the real university is fast taking a substantial and a noble form. It was founded in 1872; but "for many years its development was retarded by illiberal and artificial rules of admission. . . . In the meanwhile other universities, unhampered by inconvenient traditions, working on freer lines, and amply provided with fellowships of considerable value, with free tuition added, in many cases, to their stipend, outstripped us in the path we were entering."[4] "The enthusiasm," writes Professor Goodwin, "with which our best Universities are now organizing studies for Bachelors of Arts, and the increasing resort of graduates to these centres of learning, show the power of this movement towards true university education, a power which is just beginning to be felt. We owe special gratitude to the Johns Hopkins University

[3]At Oxford, and perhaps also at Cambridge, a "brilliant" man is an undergraduate who does "brilliant" work and writes "brilliant" essays. It not unfrequently seems the *brilliant* must have much the same derivation as *lucus—a non lucendo.*

[4]From a *Circula of Ten of the Members of the Administrative Board of the Graduate School*, dated November 20, 1893.

at Baltimore, which called public attention to the importance of this movement by its bold experiment of establishing its Graduate School before any other department was organized, and by devoting its chief energies to this from the beginning. In these new Graduate Schools we see the brightest hope for the future American University."[5]

It is in this school that the best of the students not only gather knowledge but help to increase it. Here it is that is done "that work which is the highest duty of every university, without which no institution has ever been called a university by men who weigh their words with full intelligence,—the work of advancing the boundaries of knowledge by the original researches and the joint labours of its professors and its students."[6] Graduates of other Universities are flocking to it from all sides; nay, even Professors, who, having obtained a year's leave of absence, descend from their chairs to take their seats once more on the scholars' bench. Among these ardent students I had the pleasure of meeting the President of one of the smaller Western Universities. Such a body of men as this gives a higher tone and a more vigorous life to the whole University. It inspirits the work of the Professors, who no longer have to travel year after year the same round. It sets a higher standard before the undergraduates, who have in their midst "men full of the spirit of independent work, and of a sense of the value and meaning of learning." It opens up to them other and nobler fields of fame than the baseball and football grounds, and a greatness immeasurably above the greatness of the mightiest of athletes. The rapid growth of this school shows how much it was needed and how excellent are its methods. In 1886 it numbered but sixty-four resident students, and in 1889 ninety-six. It can now boast of two hundred and forty-five. Besides these it has eleven non-resident Fellows, of whom eight are studying in Germany and two in France. "It is already larger than Harvard College was fifty years ago."[7] One thing is wanting. It has none of that social life which not only throws a charm over the years spent in a great University, but which teaches a lesson which cannot be got out of books. "The majority of the students in the Graduate School," writes

an Instructor in Philosophy, "are forlorn atoms, and their concourse is too fortuitous ever to make a world. A man who has been only at the Graduate School is not a Harvard man."[8] This statement, I am told, is somewhat overdrawn. Groups are formed of the men of each district of the country. The Californians, for instance, would hang together, and so would the students from the maritime provinces. The day, it is to be hoped, will come before long when, in some noble building, they will all share in a common life.

It was not till 1886 that admission to the school was put on a sound footing. It was in that year that the governing bodies at last shook themselves free from the conviction that none must come to study at a University but those who are candidates for a degree—a conviction which still constrains Oxford. They rose to the thought that at a University it is knowledge which should be sold and not distinctions, and that for all who thirst for it the gates of the fountains of learning should be opened wide. Every one is freely admitted who can show that he has already learnt enough to be able to follow the higher studies. In this school he finds "perfect freedom both in teaching and in learning. It has no degree in courses for which all students are candidates, and consequently no paternal supervision of each student's daily work."[9] Many indeed aim at the higher degrees of Master of Arts or of Doctor of Philosophy or Science, for no longer are the higher degrees conferred without examination. Up to 1872, as is still the case in Oxford and Cambridge, the Master's degree had been given after a certain lapse of time as a matter of course. Now it is only awarded after a further study of one year at the College —a study which may be confined to a single department. The Doctor's degree is given "on the ground of long study and high attainment in a special branch of learning, manifested not only by examinations, but by a thesis, which must be presented and accepted before the candidate is admitted to examination, and must show an original treatment of a fitting subject, or give evidence of independent research."[10]

In America it has hitherto been more difficult even than in England to give men the love of the scholar's life—the life of

[5] *The Present and Future of Harvard College,* p. 16.

[6] *A Circular,* etc.

[7] *Annual reports,* 1892-93, pp. 28, 110; *Catalogue,* p. 287.

[8] *Educational Review,* April, 1894, p. 320.

[9] *The Present and Future of Harvard College,* p. 23.

[10] *Catalogue,* p. 299.

"plain living and high thinking." On that
vast continent the great and rapid conquests
of man over wild nature, with the splendid
rewards that followed in their train, tempt
almost all the ablest men away from the
world of thought to the world of action. Even
some of the lately-founded universities seem
not unlikely, by the aid of their noble endowments, to bear their part in corrupting pure
learning. In their eagerness to secure, perhaps not so much the ablest Professors as the
fame of having them, they offer needlessly
high salaries. During the academical year
1891–92, "seven universities and colleges
made ineffectual efforts to draw teachers of
Harvard into their service. Four Professors,
four Assistant-Professors and six Instructors declined offers of higher pay and higher
titles at other institutions." Among the causes
"which bind its teachers to the University,"
President Eliot reckons "the dignity and
stability of the institution; the perfect liberty
of opinion; the freedom in teaching—every
teacher teaching as he thinks best, except as
the more experienced teachers may persuade
and inform the less experienced; the great
resources of the University in books and
collections, and the fact that any teacher can
at any time cause books desirable in his
department to be bought by the Library;
the separation of Cambridge from the luxurious society of great cities, etc., . . .
and lastly, the consideration which learning
and high character traditionally enjoy in Eastern Massachusetts, independent of pecuniary
condition."[11] . . .

Teachers

In nothing does Harvard differ more thoroughly from Oxford than in the perfect
organization which exists in her army of
teachers. In Oxford the teachers are divided
into two main bodies, entirely independent
of each other and under no central government—the University Professors and the College Tutors. Over the Professors scarcely
any control exists; they rival the Cyclopes in
their independence. The tutors are governed
each by the Corporation of his own College.
Of this Corporation he is commonly a member. The Colleges are twenty in number.[12]

To the Professors and Tutors must be added
the University Readers,[13] who are under a
special Board; the Assistants and the Demonstrators in the Museum who are under the
control of their Professors; and the teachers
of the Unattached Students—the students, that
is to say, who are undergraduates of the University, but are not members of any College. In all the confusion of such a system
as this, if system it can be called, there is
a great waste of labour and of money, and
an unfair inequality of payment. There are,
or there have been till lately, Professors
of great learning who have lectured to empty
benches—I might say to empty chairs; for,
unable to face the forlorn look of the lecture-rooms, they have given their instruction
in their own studies. Even there there has
been an appearance of vacancy. On the other
hand, there are Tutors who, never failing
to draw together a large number of students,
are nevertheless miserably paid for their
work, and see no sure opening before them
of advancement. In our army of learning there
is no Field-Marshal's baton in every soldier's
knapsack. There is no clear and well-marked
path of promotion, on which a young man can
with confidence set his foot, sure that high
merit will in time bring him to a high position.
However able he may be, he has chance
fighting heavily against him. The learned
author who is at present throwing a stream
of light on the reign of the first two Stuarts
and of the Commonwealth, skilled though he is
as a teacher, has never been made a Tutor
in the College, or a Professor in the University, which he so greatly adorns. From
the College at the beginning of his career
he was shut out by religious intolerance,
just as from the same College another
distinguished student and teacher, many years
later, was thrust forth. From a University
Chair he has been excluded mainly through
the absence of organization in the staff
of teachers. He is by no means a solitary
example. Mr. Freeman was not made Professor of History until he was too old to
learn the teacher's art; Mr. Froude, when
he succeeded him, had passed the
Psalmist's limit of three-score years and ten.
The two distinguished scholars who have
recently been raised to the Chairs of Greek
and Latin, in a wealthy and properly organized
University would have been made Professors

---

[11]*Annual Reports*, 1891–92, p. 8.

[12]I exclude Keble, for it is not a College in the
sense in which the word has always been used at
Oxford. It is governed by a Board of outsiders.
Neither do I reckon the two Halls.

[13]They, roughly speaking, answer to the Assistant-Professors, but they are independent of the
Professors. In some departments indeed there is
only a Reader and no Professor.

twenty years earlier. So often does it happen in Oxford that men are not promoted till they are past their prime, that not uncommonly a Professor's salary is looked upon, not as wages, but a reward. Little surprise is caused by the nomination of a man from whom fresh work can hardly be expected. That he has done good work is, with many, a full justification of his appointment. It is his claims, and not the claims of the students, that are examined. His well-earned pension as a hard and successful worker in the field of learning is to be provided at their expense. Through the whole of the University far too much is spent in rewards and far too little in wages. Were the wealth of the foundations more wisely used, teachers would be more fairly remunerated, and learned men and students of nature, who may have no gift for teaching, would be able to count on a decent maintenance whilst they laboriously advanced the boundaries of knowledge. In Harvard, provision for such men as these is as yet but very imperfectly made. The millionaire who shall endow research has not as yet appeared on the stage of the New England Cambridge. Perhaps he is within the prompter's call.

It is in the organization of the great body of teachers that Harvard excels. An undergraduate who greatly distinguishes himself, after taking his degree, with the help of a scholarship, if he is a poor man, will continue his studies in the Graduate School or in some foreign university. In due time he joins the staff of teachers as a Lecturer, Demonstrator, or Assistant. His appointment is but for one year. In all likelihood it will be continued if he shows his fitness for the post. If he does not, he is weeded out while he is still young enough to seek his living elsewhere. The University is not saddled with an incompetent teacher, who, as sometimes happens in our Oxford Colleges, is kept on through pity, to the great injury of the students. He, however, who successfully passes through this period of probation may hope before long to become an Instructor or a Tutor with a longer engagement; and, later on, an Assistant-Professor with much higher pay and an engagement for five years. At last he arrives at the full Professorship. He can rise no higher, unless he is made President; but with length of service and with merit his salary increases up to a certain limit. The average age at which a man becomes full Professor is thirty-five years. If in any of these grades of advancement there is no vacancy in Harvard, an able

teacher may count on receiving a "call" from some other University. Should he there greatly distinguish himself, he is scarcely less sure, when a vacancy does occur, to be recalled to his old College. The chance of promotion has greatly increased of late years, not only by the foundation of other seats of learning, for each of which a whole staff of Professors is needed, but moreover by the rapid growth in all the chief departments of the University. This has indeed gone on by leaps and by bounds. In the last twenty-five years the number of students, as I have said, has increased by more than two thousand. Instead of forty-eight Professors and Assistant-Professors there are now one hundred and eighteen, and instead of thirty-three Tutors, Instructors, Demonstrators, and Assistants there are now two hundred and four. Twenty-five years ago there were in all eighty-one teachers; they now number three hundred and twenty-two. This augmentation is still going on. This year there are eighteen more Professors and Assistant-Professors than there were two years ago, while the lower ranks of teachers have in the same short time been increased by fifty-one.

In the method which is followed when a vacant Chair has to be filled up or a new Chair is created, Harvard, in common, I believe, with American universities in general, sets us an excellent example. No application is made for the post by a crowd of eager candidates; no testimonials are sent in—testimonials in which one side of the shield only is shown, in which truth so often is divided from falsehood by the thinnest of partitions. The members of each Faculty have made themselves acquainted with the merits of the most eminent teachers in other seats of learning; should Harvard herself not furnish the right man, they know where he is to be found. He is offered the post; he is not exposed to the loss of dignity which invests a suitor. One man is honoured by the selection which is made of him; none are wounded in their feelings by being passed over. The selection is not confined to citizens of the United States. Two years ago two new Chairs were founded at Harvard, one of Economic History, the other of Experimental Psychology. To fill them an invitation was sent across the Canadian border to an Oxford Master of Arts, a Professor in the University of Toronto, and across the Atlantic to a German Doctor of Philosophy, a teacher in the University of Freiburg.

How happy would a University be where,

with a perfect system of subordination by which merit is sure of recognition, should be combined the social life and the friendly intercourse and all the opportunities for the interchange of thought and knowledge which are found in every one of our Oxford Colleges. Each one of them is the gathering-place, the home, of a small knot of learned men. Each of the Common-Rooms is a centre of kindly feeling and hospitality. Of these we have twenty; Harvard has not one.

It will be easier for Oxford to take to herself all the good that there is in the Harvard system, than for Harvard to add to her vigorous and admirable organization all that charm and pleasantness of life which make an Oxford man's College scarcely less dear to him than Oxford herself. By an Act of Parliament the one reform can be in great part effected; the other could only come about by the slow changes of long years.

Emil Hausknecht   1893

German Criticism of American Education

Emil Hausknecht (born in 1853), a German educator, was professor at the National University of Japan in Tokyo and then became director of the second Realschule in Berlin. The International Education Congress held in connection with the Columbian Exposition of 1893 brought a number of prominent European educators to the United States. Among these were many Germans, including Ernst Schlee, Stephan Waetzoldt, Constantine Norrenberg, and Emil Hausknecht. The reports of these men were described by Americans as not "in every case absolutely correct, on the contrary they exhibit palpable errors." On the other hand, the Germans received considerable publicity in Germany and were praised for "working scientifically, thinking philosophically and acting honestly." Hausknecht in particular, was praised for the impartial and objective manner in which he wrote his account of American education.

He who has had the pleasure of crossing the United States, leisurely observing what he saw, and who has had the privilege of finding in his various places of sojourn the kindest reception and enlightening expression of ideas on the part of leading persons in science and promoters of popular education; he who has seen with his own eyes, especially in the West, the innumerable palace-like institutions for public education, churches, libraries, and Christian association buildings for young people, and gymnasia for schools, and in a measure has learned the piety and liberality of their promoters and founders, will know that in that country, though it is partly still in primitive development, yet everywhere progressing with gigantic strides, and disregarding Old World prejudices, something higher rules than "filthy lucre," which, under the present circumstances of civilization, can scarcely be called "filthy" any longer.

A prominent preacher expressed himself during the Sunday services in Trinity Church, previous to the beginning of the winter semester of Yale University in the old and venerable Elm City of New Haven, as follows:

"It is a passion for education, a noble eagerness for knowledge and culture that has become a perfect craze, that has seized the whole American people at present." Dr. W. T. Harris, the United States Commissioner of Education, said to me in one of our pleasant and instructive interviews: "It is a heart hunger for education, a ravenous appetite for culture that is felt in all strata of society, in the middle and lower classes of the people, as well as in the upper classes; it works like an elementary force, and urges onward and upward." We need not wonder that things sometimes are placed topsy-turvy in a country the people of which create everything through their own power and out of themselves, and it must be borne in mind that in the peculiar development of its conditions it lacks a centralized government, one that thinks for all, and guides the people even in questions of detail; a government in which the traditions of experienced and well-qualified experts is embodied; of men who are conscious of the object to be attained. Neither have the States of the Old World, moving in regulated conditions, always avoided mistakes in the domain of education, and it is

Emil Hausknecht, "The American System of Education," in *Report of the Commissioner of Education, 1892-93* (Washington, D. C.: U.S. Government Printing Office, 1859), I, 522–529.

these very States which have to overcome a system firmly established in order to do justice to new principles arising from special conditions.

The cause of this universal desire for education in America is partly found in the fact that the common school education is quite inefficient and inadequate. A general law for compulsory school attendance is not in existence, and an astonishingly large ratio of the population has grown up without any instruction in school. All the more intense becomes the consciousness of the want of an education in after years, particularly in a country where there are no rules and regulations for the preparation for professions or occupations. If with us anyone "changes saddles" (that is, his profession), his action is in most cases subject to the disapproval of public opinion, or to that of his circle of acquaintances. In America—at least as yet —everyone, even a common laborer, may become anything and everything, even President, if he understands how and has learned enough to make wise use of circumstances. It is quite immaterial how he acquired his knowledge, or whether he can by written testimonials prove to be in possession of such knowledge. It is not at all a rare case to meet men who, as boys, peddled matches, newspapers, and other things in order to support mother and sisters, and who at times, when they had saved enough, "did a little toward getting an education," until finally they had worked their way up to be social leaders of the people. Every inhabitant of that country has an exalted opinion (mostly exaggerated) of his own capacity, hence it is not to be wondered at that the intense aspiration toward an "education" for practical reasons permeates all the laboring classes. Every sensible workman, who likes to speak of the equality of all citizens, and yet instinctively feels the inequality caused by difference in social position, aspires to be, or at least wishes to be, considered a gentleman in his appearance, manners, and actions. As a gentleman he does not drink liquor, and smokes little or not at all.[1]

The motives that urge the cultured and wealthy classes to a liberal and incessant participation in raising the level of education of the lower classes are quite different. They have long recognized that a constitution resting upon the principle of democracy, like the American, finds its greatest enemy in the ignorance and want of judgment of the masses, and believe that this danger may be met by popular education as high and extended as possible. To these political motives may be traced back (partly at least) the efforts made in behalf of advanced instruction for girls. The men are almost exclusively occupied from an early age in obtaining a livelihood; though, by life's experiences and the reading of journals, magazines, and books written in popular style, they endeavor to educate themselves, the average "schooling" the boys get is of a comparatively brief period; hence it is deemed advisable to secure for the girls— the mothers and teachers of the future generation—the benefits of a most thorough education.

It is of course plain that, aside from these political considerations, often exclusively philanthropic motives come into play which lead to liberal bequests for purposes of education.

After these general remarks a few features of the American system of education may be discussed. I have neither leisure nor available space to enter into the minute details of the entire system. It seems to me advisable, however, to touch upon a few points necessary for a general comprehension of the entire system before entering into a discussion of any separate branch. It shall be done briefly and without claim upon systematic arrangement.

There is no national organization of the school system, embracing uniformly the entire school system of the country; in fact, it would be impossible, owing to the unequal development of the separate States, which, taken together, have an area fifteen times the area of the German Empire. The Bureau of Education in Washington, a part of the Department of the Interior, is merely a statistical bureau of public instruction, without any authoritative or directive power. The establishment, maintenance, and organization of the school system are concerns of the separate States, and they devote themselves to this task with great zeal. Public opinion, conscious of the fact that the healthy development of the State depends upon a well-organized school system, tries to attract a large immigration from other States by establishing excellent institutions of learning. Furthermore there is a noble rivalry kept up among the States, which is the cause of there being few States that do not think their institutions the best in the Union, the "best

---

[1]However, chewing and spitting seem to be allowed to a gentleman. Children, even young girls (but scarcely of the better classes), chew gum or nibble popcorn.

in the world," or at least nurse a conviction that they soon will be.

The supreme authority in school matters is, in most States, vested in a State board of education, which endeavors to elevate the whole system of public education of the State according to a uniform plan, and whose especial anxiety is to promote the general and professional education of the teachers, both men and women. In some States the number of women teachers reaches the high proportion of 90 per cent of the total number. To the large cities, which consider it an honor to do as much as possible for education, the law grants almost complete liberty in levying school taxes; this liberty increases the "joy in giving" and the possibility for new, progressive measures. The highest degree of perfection of any of the numerous school systems may be found in Boston, or, generally speaking, in the State of Massachusetts. Comparatively well developed are the schools also in Minneapolis, St. Paul, Indianapolis, and Washington. A similar opinion may be held concerning entire States like Massachusetts, Connecticut, New Jersey, Minnesota, Iowa, Michigan, and others.

Immense sums are expended for the maintenance and elevation of the system of instruction, not only by the States and communities, but likewise through grand and liberal bequests and donations. Aside from colleges and a few other institutions instruction is gratuitous; some States, like California, Wisconsin, Virginia, Texas, Michigan, and others, have even free "universities," which however, with the partial exception of Ann Arbor, actually rank as colleges. Appliances also are furnished free, and not only textbooks, but everything needed in manual training and cookery, and in physics and chemistry, for which every pupil has his own experimenting and work table. With regard to the advantages of free text-books and the uniformity caused thereby, the opinions differ. Free schoolbooks for entire States seem to have essentially influenced the quality of the books by paralyzing the productive energy of authors. New and more methodically arranged schoolbooks are rare of late years. Gratuity of the entire instruction and free text-books and appliances belong to the many devices which have been resorted to in order to allure as many pupils as possible into school, and to keep them there, since compulsory attendance can not be enforced.

In theory America possesses the common school (Einheitsschule). After the primary school, intended for children from 6 to 10, follows the grammar school for children from 10 to 14; the continuation of this institution is the high school of three or four yearly courses, which is partly an institution for the preparation for practical life, and partly a preparatory school for the college. The grammar school corresponds more or less with the upper grades of our people's school of six, seven, or eight grades. It is fundamentally different from the English grammar school, which may be compared to our gymnasium, and like our gymnasium ("Real-Gymnasium" and "Real-Schule") stands entirely outside of the system of the common school. An American boy who has passed through the grammar school is said to have graduated, while an English boy who goes through the course with credit up to 14, is said to have passed the seventh standard. While thus, in theory, the course through the American common primary, grammar, and high school leads to the college, the facts do not correspond to this everywhere. The colleges distrust the education of the high school and, indeed, the transfer from a high school to a college is possible only when the former has observed the conditions of admission required by the college, and when it stands in more or less intimate relations to the respective college. Comparatively few high schools maintain such relations. Those high schools on the other hand, which are considered primarily preparatory schools for colleges, distrust the education offered in the grammar schools; so that some parents who intend their children to enter the high school, withdraw them from the grammar school before the completion of the course, and have them privately prepared for an entrance examination to the high school.

The colleges are a kind of intermediate institution between our gymnasium and university, representing the work of the upper grades of a gymnasium and that of one or two years at a university, as we understand those terms. They are mostly institutions with dormitories, lying remote from the noisy din of cities, surrounded by park-like grounds. In the colleges physical exercises are very popular. While, with few exceptions, no beer drinking or smoking is found, yet the student's life here is very gay, full of fun and pranks. To be sure, work is done here, and a great deal of it, for at the end of each of the three or four terms of the year an examination has to be passed. Unlike our universities, most American colleges have the purpose of transmitting knowledge. The chief object of our universities, which is to guide the students to independent scientific production, lies entirely outside of the scope of the college. But some colleges attempt this by retaining their own graduates, i.e., those who have passed the finishing examination after a three-years' successful attendance at college, and offering them in so-called post-graduate courses (in contradistinction to undergraduate courses) opportunities for scientific work. A few colleges admit only post-graduate students. Such institutions are called, at times, universities. The term university is frequently given to other institutions that do not deserve it, and are not recognized as such in the learned world. Altogether there are nearly 400 colleges in the United States. . . .

The foregoing paragraph made us acquainted with another characteristic of the American system of education, the so-called coeducation, simultaneous instruction of boys and girls in the same class rooms, and in the same subjects,[2] in the primary, grammar, and high school, as well as in colleges and universities. Formerly coeducation was resorted to much more frequently in Germany than now. In the Western States of America it was first used as a makeshift, but it has in the course of the last ten years spread farther and farther East, and is now found in all the New England States, which are remarkable for their firmly-fixed institutions and high degree of culture. The most important of the higher institutions of learning in New England reject coeducation in high schools and colleges, I think, with good reason. In quite a number of States coeducation is practiced in all schools. Concerning the advantages and disadvantages of this mode of education lengthy and heated controversies have been filling the columns of the press.

As a makeshift coeducation is better than nothing. As a principle, it entirely ignores the needs of the separate sexes arising from the differences in the development of boys and girls. Boys and girls in the ages from 14 to 18 must be differently treated, both in regard to the intellectual and the emotional nature. Coeducation is possible, however, in America more than in Germany or elsewhere, because custom and education have given to the girl and the woman greater freedom and

determination in their manners and appearance, and have also given them strong protection against encroachment and improprieties. Coeducation is possible in America for two other reasons: The week has only five school days, Saturday being a holiday, and the school day has only five lessons, of which one is usually a study hour. Besides, grammar and high schools require much less severe intellectual effort and a much more concentrated and simple exertion of the mind than is required in our secondary schools for boys. In the grammar schools foreign languages are not taught at all; in the high schools only two foreign languages are taught, of which the second scarcely proceeds beyond mere rudiments.

In modern languages I have found everywhere (with the exception of Boston, which certainly has the best schools) a method of instruction which beggars description, for it is a waste of time and calls for no intellectual labor on the part of pupils and teacher. The consequences of beginning the study of foreign languages so late are very serious. They are manifested in the very small amount of knowledge in the languages with which the student enters college, so that there he is frequently subjected to mere elementary exercises. The consequences are seen also in the defective linguistic-logical discipline of the mind, which perhaps more than the discipline in mathematical forms of thought is a requisite of all profound intellectual progress, be that in linguistic or in mathematical and scientific branches. This discipline is especially necessary, in fact an essential requisite of independent intellectual work, and the present American method of beginning the study of languages is entirely inadequate. The other disadvantage of a defective linguistic discipline, namely, the want of thorough comprehension of the mother tongue in America, is compensated in most colleges by excellent exercises in the written and oral use of English.

Another peculiarity of the American system of schools is the extensive employment of women in teaching, not only in primary and grammar schools, where they are employed almost exclusively, but also in high schools, and at times in colleges. It is unquestionable that some women are gifted with special physical and intellectual powers, able to successfully cope in scientific equipment, methodical skill, and pedagogical tact with many of the best male teachers in (let us say, in order to remain on the firm ground of actual observation) Latin, Greek,

---

[2]Except in gymnastics and manual training; instead of this branch the girls have instruction in female handiwork, and, in the grammar schools, lessons in cooking.

physics, chemistry, and mathematics.[3] Generally speaking, the lower degree of physical power of resistance in woman causes a lower degree of executive ability. A more extensive employment of thoroughly prepared men in high schools would very perceptibly raise the level of these schools. But men are not numerous as teachers in America, not even in the high schools. Public life offers positions with much higher emoluments than those of the schoolmaster and professor. The one circumstance that comparatively few men devote themselves to teaching in grammar and high schools, reacts naturally upon the quality of the teachers engaged; but of course I do not mean to say that there are no thorough teachers in these institutions.

Generally speaking, it may be asserted that one kind of high schools, called English high schools, in which modern languages and natural science predominate over the classical languages, is, according to our conception, scarcely more than an advanced elementary or citizen's school. In these schools, if they happen to have one or two thoroughly equipped male teachers for one or two scientific branches, acceptable results are found. The Latin high schools seem to be better in every respect. Of course there are a few exceptionally good English high schools.

A peculiar feature of the American school system is the development which manual training has had. It is an acquisition made since the World's Exposition at Philadelphia, and an imitation of the Russian system, which was suggested by Dr. Woodward, of St. Louis, and has since spread over the whole Union. Manual training is now either given in special, technical, or manual training high schools, which are admirable, or has been made an integral part of the course in primary, grammar, and high schools, as, for instance, in the city of Washington. In the so-called manual training high schools, which are a third kind of high school beside the English and classical, ten hours a week are devoted to work

in the shops, five to drawing, and ten to scientific instruction.

I must deny myself the pleasure of entering into the historical development of this interesting and important branch of instruction, nor can I state here the psychological arguments upon which it is based; but I will state that the growth of manual instruction as an organic branch of the public school system and the great popularity and progress of Froebel's educational ideas (surprising to us as Germans, but very significant for America) has led to a complete revolution of didactics, to the so-called "new education," the education "by doing," in contradistinction to the old memoriter method. A further result of this instruction "by doing" are the independent exercises of the pupil in experimenting, mentioned before. These experiments are made, of course, under direction of the teachers in physics and chemistry.

For the preparation of teachers the States have their normal schools; for that of the three learned professions (theology, law, and medicine), divinity, law, and medical schools. Very few of these institutions require a college education for admission. Many of the medical schools shut one eye, if the candidate for admission has scarcely reached a degree of education required for admission to a high school. The Massachusetts Institute of Technology in Boston is a polytechnicum of the first rank. Its president is the renowned political economist, Gen. Francis Walker. Besides, there are trade and industrial schools. The Drexel Institute in Philadelphia is a very grand institution for art, science, and industry, and is richly equipped and well organized. It admits students of both sexes. Drawing and modeling—subjects which, though extensively taught in America, are but little developed—seem to be very well represented here. The main object of this institution for popular culture (this epithet is used in the true sense of the word) is the training of teachers; it prepares—(1) Teachers and supervisors of drawing in public and private schools; (2) teachers of science in high schools and academies; (3) directors and teachers in physical culture; (4) instructors in manual training; (5) instructors in cookery; (6) instructresses in dressmaking and millinery; (7) assistants in library work, i.e., mostly girls; the employment of women in the lower positions in libraries is a very extensive one in America, the land of public libraries. The American public libraries are distinguished more than the generous English

---

[3]One observation seems to me worthy of mention. It was made in Wellesley College. In a class consisting of some 20 young ladies studying mathematics, the students showed themselves so well acquainted with differential calculus that there could be no question as to their ability to use and comprehend it. This visit was made in company of the school superintendent of Berlin, Privy Councilor Prof. Dr. Bertram, whose quick observation and expert judgment aided me during a part of my journey in the fall of 1893.

libraries by facilitating and simplifying the use of books for the reading public by making the books accessible, by advising and guiding the readers in the selection of reading matter, and by making the use of reading rooms as comfortable and pleasant as possible.

For Indians and negroes an excellent institution exists at Hampton, Va., the normal and agricultural institute for negroes and Indians. I visited it in the fall of 1890. The young Indians of both sexes received here, besides instruction in the common school branches and religion, a training in trades, agriculture, female handiwork, cooking, tailoring, washing, ironing, etc. The negro children in the Northern States are taught together with the white children; in the Southern States, including even Maryland and the District of Columbia, they have their special schools. It was interesting to hear in a colored high school in Washington a 15-year-old negress translate Cicero's Pro Milone. The colored teacher of Latin, a graduate of Harvard, also spoke German fluently. The teacher of physics and chemistry, like the principal, a colored man, was a Ph. D., who had first studied at Harvard, afterwards at Heidelberg and Berlin.

Aside from some institutions established by the Catholic Church and other religious communities, no religious instruction is given in American schools. However, it can not be said that therefore an atheistic atmosphere prevails in school and society. Nowhere is religious life as active and intense as in America. I do not think, as is alleged, that this remarkably strong participation in religious life is a consequence of the separation of church and state and the exclusion of religious instruction from the schools. It is said that because the schools do not indulge in overfeeding their pupils with Bible verses and hymns (as is alleged to be the case with us), attendance at church is better and more voluntary, dictated by the desires of the heart. The conditions are altogether different in America. As everywhere in the Anglo-Saxon world, so it is, especially in America, that the mind (or should we say an aberration of the mind?) which ripened the reformation has again awakened and hastens, as Carlyle says, to a search for new forms in which the essential contents of Christianity are to be molded. Hence the numerous bequests for pious purposes; hence, also, the numerous churches and pulpits well supported by devout and charitably inclined adherents of different sects; hence, also, the fact that a book like

Robert Elsmere, by Mrs. Humphrey Ward, is found everywhere, and has eager readers and commentators wherever the English language reaches—and English is the universal language which spans the globe. This same spirit pervades a good part of the laboring people. I myself have heard on the commons of Boston and other cities on Sunday afternoons, in religious socialistic speeches addressed to all who were willing to listen, the ever-recurring idea of a socialistic Utopia that the world could not be improved unless the kingdom of Jesus were restored in its original form, and its social plans carried out. . . .

A characteristic feature of the American high schools is the fact that the pupils are being made acquainted in every branch of study with the accessible literature relating to it and receive suggestions for the use of popular scientific works touching upon the subject. Works of reference of various kinds are found in great number in every high school. The cause of this procedure, especially important in the writing of essays on literature and historical subjects, is partly explained by the necessity of resorting to these books because of the often very inadequate knowledge of the teachers, which requires that the pupils be offered reliable material in reference books. It is partly explained, also, by the strong desire to educate for self-activity and independence; this is a tendency very prominent in English and American schools.

A thing worthy of imitation is the continuous blackboard in American schools, a blackboard, either of natural slate or made of slating fluid, attached to the four walls, except where the wall is broken by doors and windows. This gives ample room to teachers and pupils for blackboard work. Sketches, figures, etc., sometimes in artistic perfection, illustrating mathematics, geography, and natural history, can be retained on the blackboard for many a day; there is still room left for quotations from noted authors, for golden rules of life and proverbs, which may be renewed weekly.

The fact that in the courses of study in colleges such ample opportunity for the study of the Spanish language is given appears curious to us Germans. Though the well-established relations between the Union and the Latin-American States might explain it, it is reasonable to suppose that the recent popularity of Spanish as a study stands in close connection with Pan-American desires and aspirations to crowd out European nations, especially Germany, from commerce in South America. Looked at from a purely commercial standpoint, the study of Spanish has for the Germans, at present, a prominent importance. Thorough acquaintance with Spanish is fully as important to us as a knowledge of French. Far more important, however, is a thorough knowledge of English, the universal language that spreads over the whole world.

E. F. M. MacCarthy   1895

The United States and English Systems Compared

E. F. M. MacCarthy (1838–1917), an English educator and Episcopal clergyman, served as headmaster of King Edward's Grammar School, Birmingham, and vice-chairman of the Birmingham School Board. He was a close observer and ardent supporter of many aspects of the "American Common School system." He enthusiastically believed that there was "much that may be prudently imitated in the methods and workings of the American schools."

MacCarthy was impressed with the availability of secondary education for so many children in America, which he noted was not the case in England. On the other hand, he decried the laxity in establishing a nation-wide system of compulsory education in America. His account covers with clarity many aspects of elementary and secondary education and teacher training in the United States.

Primary and Grammar Schools

It is not an easy matter to grasp the philosophy of a foreign educational system. Education is not an art, like the art of swimming for instance, where, though the methods of teaching and practice may vary considerably, yet the purpose which the art seeks to achieve, viz., how to propel the body along the surface of water without getting the head underneath, is, all the world over, the same. On the contrary, the purpose of a national system of education will differ very materially in different countries. Education is the organized and scientific initiation of the young into the duties of civilised life. Each different ideal of civilisation will, therefore, produce its own peculiar ideal of education.

Now there are undoubtedly strong differences between American and English ideals. Let us cite one conspicuous instance of such difference. The American people (by which here and elsewhere is meant the people of the United States) have always been their own law-makers, and so, from the earliest period of their national history, they have placed in the forefront, as their object in founding a public system of education, that of training up law-making, as well as law-abiding, citizens. But this object was certainly not the guiding principle of those who initiated and developed popular education in England. The voluntary and denominational movement of the early part of this century had confessedly no other than religious and philanthropic aims on behalf of the poorer classes; and as time went on it received recognition and support from the State almost entirely on these grounds. And, although our first national movement on behalf of education, in the year 1870, received a great impulse from the middle and upper-class consciousness of the danger of leaving "our masters" in ignorance of their letters, yet the arrest of that movement at its present incomplete stage shows that we still realise only imperfectly that other ideal of education as a course of training for the law-makers of England. The English ideal in the past has not been that of an American State which sets up as a fundamental axiom:—"Since the efficient government of the State requires the harmonious cooperation of the masses, it is a condition for the welfare of the State to provide schools in which the children of the people grow up together without class or sect distinction, so that a more homogeneous population may make the action

E. F. M. MacCarthy, "Western State Education; The United States and English Systems Compared," in W. Wilson Hunter, ed. *State Education for the People in America, Europe, India, and Australia with Papers on the Education of Women, Technical Instruction and Payment by Results* (Syracuse, New York: C. W. Bardeen, 1895), pp. 82–104.

of the Government harmonious and energetic."[1]

Again, neither is it an easy matter to master the details of a foreign educational system. This is especially true of the "American Common School system." And the reason is not far to seek—in one sense, there *is no* American Common School system. So difficult is it for an Englishman, with his Education Department administering the Education Acts, issuing its annual code of regulations, and thus virtually determining for all public elementary schools the duties of managers, the qualifications of teachers, and the course of instruction, to realise "local option" as the fundamental principle of a public school system, that it becomes necessary to emphasise this fact at starting. There is *no* American Education Department, *no* American Minister of Education. The Commissioner of Education at the head of the United States Bureau of Education at Washington is rather a Registrar-General for education than a Minister of State—a sort of statistical head centre who has no more control over educational bodies than the Registrar-General in England has over the births, deaths, and marriages of human bodies which he records and tabulates. In fact the functions of the United States Government in the matter of educational legislation are of the narrowest kind. Apart from the scientific military training of the Army and Navy, which is entirely in its hands, it limits itself to making endowments in the shape of land-grants to the several States for the purposes of common school education or for the promotion of scientific agriculture and the mechanical arts. It has also furnished endowments for the support of Universities in all new States formed since 1787. The duty and responsibility of making provision for the education of its population rests with the several States individually; and each State has, of its own proper motion, though some in the South only tardily, come to recognise this duty by establishing a common school system in its midst. And this system differs, or may differ, from the corresponding system of other States.

First, this individuality is shown in the different modes of election, the widely varied composition and functions of the several State Boards of Education. In some States the Boards are composed mostly of professional teachers, in others, chiefly of State officers. Then, in some States, the State Superintendent

(*i.e.,* Inspector, though not with analogous functions to Her Majesty's Inspectors of Schools) is elected directly by the people, in others by the Governor, in others, again, by the Legislature, in others by the State Board of Education itself; and his duties, powers, and prerogatives are equally diverse.

Again, some States enforce compulsory school attendance, others do not; and where compulsion is carried out, the "bye-laws" (as we should call them) regulating the ages between which they are enforced, the minimum number of attendances required, the penalties for their breach, and the conditions of exemption, vary with each State.

The principle of local self-government which underlies the social and political constitution of the United States asserts itself still further by each State assigning to the municipalities of cities and townships within its borders the power to elect their own School Committees or School Boards, only retaining the right of prescribing their organization, officers, and general powers. These City Boards have also been organized on every variety of plan. The New York Board is elected by the Mayor. In Philadelphia the Board is elected by the Judges, who are themselves elected by popular vote, and the Board is associated in its task of school management with certain "school directors," who are elected by the people, three for each ward in the city. In Cincinnati the Board is elected partly by the people in wards and partly on a "general ticket;" and so on. These City School Boards have power (subject to the State educational laws) to constitute school districts, elect school officers, collect taxes for school purposes, and arrange for the examination, appointment and rate of pay of teachers, to build schools, arrange courses of study, prescribe the regulations for the government of the schools, and to administer these schools. Hence there are further opportunities for diversity in educational machinery and policy owing to the individual local circumstances, the ever-varying political and social temper of each city and town. And it should further be borne in mind that America is far less homogeneous in itself than England. Over that wide area, varieties of race and tradition, of climate and environment, have impressed even upon individual cities, marked divergencies from a uniform ethical, social and political standard. Boston is not as New Orleans, nor Richmond as San Francisco.

But, amidst all this diversity of ideal and theory, of detail and practice, there is

---

[1]National Council of Education, Proceedings, 1887.

an underlying unity, an undercurrent of common sentiment in educational matters which is strong enough to set the course of the stream very much in the same direction all over the United States, in obedience to the "genius" of their national institutions. The Common School is universal; it is open to all classes; it is free; and it is either unsectarian or secular, *i.e.,* neutral, in religious matters. Let us glance at these points in order.

First, *the Common School is to be found everywhere,* in the remotest farming town where scarcely 20 children of school age can be counted within a radius of two or three miles, no less than in the large cities.[2] And every Common School is under the control and management of a local board, variously designated in different parts of the United States, but everywhere practically what, from the point of view of local *representative* control, we in England would call a School Board. The School Board is, therefore, universal. Its foundation rests on the idea that every locality is competent to manage its own educational affairs. But this only within limits. Each State has its own State Law, which is administered by the State Board of Education. The State lays down by law that Common Schools of a certain grade and range of study shall exist within a given area, that the schools shall be open for a minimum number of days, and (where it has adopted the principle of compulsion) fixes the requirements as to school attendance, and the penalties for truancy. The function of the State Board of Education is to obtain and publish the returns required by law from the School Boards, and to apportion the State Fund (where such exists) arising from grants of land, bequests or endowments. But the State Board has no *legal* control over the *management* of the schools, and can exercise no authority with reference to local taxation, the erection of school buildings, the appointment of teachers, or the organization, discipline and course of study in the schools. These matters are entirely in the hands of the local School Boards. The State Board does, however, exercise considerable influence in the form of "moral suasion" beyond the limits of its legal powers, by the acquiescence and good-will of the School Boards. It exercises this function more especially among the rural School Boards. Practically it leaves the city School Boards alone in the management of their schools; for experience has shown that the public spirit of a city community is an ample guarantee, in spite of occasional abuse of the position by struggling politicians, for the presence of a sufficient number of competent administrators upon the School Board, and for the efficiency, energy, and enterprise of its working.

In the rural parts of the States, however, it is frequently far otherwise. The only available members of the Board are farmers; they live two or three miles from each other, and from the school; they do not profess to be qualified for the work, and only serve on the School Board because "somebody must." A School Board so composed will not only frankly recognise its inefficiency, but will court the assistance and guidance which the State Board of Education is prepared most freely to render. For the discharge of these functions towards the rural Board the State Board employs Superintendents or Agents whose duty it is to collect and diffuse information as to the condition of the schools, to inspect and examine when invited, to point out weaknesses, and to make suggestions for improvement. But beyond this they are careful not to go.

Now contrast this with the English system; and, for this purpose, for "State Law" read "Education Acts of Parliament," for "State Board of Education" read "Education Department," and for "State Fund" read "Parliamentary Grant." Further, for "School Board," we must read "Managers of a Public Elementary School," for the English law recognizes equally as "Managers" either School Boards, or a body (of three persons at least), representing a voluntary or denominational agency. The analogy thus suggested between the English and American systems holds good very fairly, but the following points of differentiation will at once strike the observer. In both countries, the education of the people is regulated by a central law. But the strength of a law depends upon the degree to which it can be enforced, and with regard to education, the leverage which in both countries makes for the enforcement of the law is mainly the money grant which the administrators have at their disposal. That money is the "State Fund" in one case, and the "Parliamentary Grant" in the other. Now, in America, the State Fund even at its largest (as, probably, in Massachusetts) bears a very much smaller proportion to the sum raised by local taxa-

---

[2]In America, a *town* (old English *township*) corresponds to the English village or group of villages forming a *rural* area; and a *city,* to the English municipal town, forming an *urban* area.

tion, than the Parliamentary Grant in England does to the sum raised locally either by rates and fees, or by subscriptions and fees. Consequently on this ground the power of the Education Department over Public Elementary Schools in England is much greater than the power of the State Boards of Education over the Common Schools in America. But, further, the Education Law in England is wider and more far-reaching. By "the Code," which is strictly an annual appendix to the Education Acts, the Education Department has a very direct control over the buildings, the teachers employed, and over the organization and internal management of a public elementary school; it appoints inspectors, who can claim admittance at any time into a school for a close examination and inspection of the school in all these particulars, and the amount of Parliamentary Grant, even to the extent of total withdrawal, is subject to a minute assessment of the merits of the school as to its condition, teaching-staff, and educational results.

It is admitted, by thoughtful Americans, that their policy (as regards the rural Boards) has its elements of weakness as well as of strength:—"It may allow to be left for a long time untouched many errors and defects in the management of the schools which might at once be removed if the State were to lay its hand directly upon them; and it may seem thus to fail, and may perhaps really fail, in bringing the schools with sufficient promptness to the best attainable results. But, on the other side, in its reliance upon the intelligence and carefulness of the people themselves in their several localities, and through the necessity of working only through such agencies, it may secure, in a more permanent form, the gains that are made."[3]

May not Englishmen admit that our policy also has its elements of weakness as well as of strength; that too much centralization and too little trust in local interest in education is a characteristic note of our system, just as too little of the former and too much of the latter is of theirs?

Secondly, *the Common School is open to all classes*, rich and poor, of every station or social rank. The "legal school age" (*i.e.*, the range of ages between which a child or young person can legally claim to be educated at a Common School) is determined in each State by its State Law, and is accepted, with only a slight modification here and there, by

the Cities or Towns which are entitled to have their own School system. The usual range of school age is from five or six to twenty or twenty-one. It is the function, then, of the Common School system to supply any demand for education which can reasonably be made on behalf of young persons between these ages. Obviously, therefore, there can be no such limitation in the American system to merely elementary education as pertains in England, where Parliament has limited State recognition to Elementary schools which are provided for the child-population between three and thirteen years of age, and practically turn the scholars out of school when they have passed the highest "standard" of an elementary course of instruction set forth by the "Code."

In America, then, every State requires by law that there shall be, first, a sufficient number of schools for the instruction of every child who may legally attend school in orthography, reading, writing, English grammar, geography, arithmetic, drawing, the history of the United States, the constitution of its own State, and of its own city or town, and in good morals. Higher subjects are required to be taught where expedient. These schools are, in working, universally divided into *two* departments, called Primary and Grammar schools; but this division has no foundation in the nature of things, but is made purely as a matter of convenience. The Primary School receives children from the youngest school-age up to about ten or eleven; and they then pass on to the Grammar School, there to complete what practically is the elementary course. The arrangement has the advantage of enabling small Primary Schools to be placed nearer the homes of the younger children, who are then transferred, when able to walk longer distances, to a large and well-grounded Grammar School, which is thus fed by a group of Primary Schools. But, secondly, the State law requires that there shall be maintained in every town of so many hundred (500 in Massachusetts) families, in addition, a *high* school, and, sometimes, makes further provision, as in Massachusetts, that every town of 4000 inhabitants must widen its high school curriculum by the introduction of such additional subjects as Greek, French, Astronomy, Moral Science and Political Economy.

There are, or were until very recently, no schools, in the Common School system, corresponding to our English Infants Schools, receiving children at three (or even under three) years of age up to about seven. With-

[3] Report of Massachusetts Board of Education, 1880-1.

in the last few years, however, as a result of a number of experiments by private persons to adapt the Kindergarten or Froebellian system to American conditions—notably at St. Louis—Schools on the Kindergarten model (called Sub-Primary) have been established as part of the Public School system. Following the lead of St. Louis, Milwaukie and Philadelphia have Sub-Primary Schools firmly established. Boston has lately joined this goodly company, and has taken over the fourteen Kindergarten schools in that City, previously supported by private benevolence; and other cities are rapidly taking steps in the same direction.

Before passing on to the work of the High Schools, a few criticisms on the work of the American Primary and Grammar Schools, based on the writer's own observation and examination, may serve as an estimate of the comparative efficiency of American and English public Elementary Schools, to be taken for what it is worth. The average age of children in the lowest grade (or class) on admission in American city schools is nearer seven than six, and, as a consequence of the child's first introduction to mental training at an age nearly two years greater than the corresponding age in England, where Infant Schools are universal, it follows that the average age of children doing work corresponding to any given English Code Standard is greater in America than in England. This disparity seems to hold good all through school life, though in diminishing degree, that is, American children never entirely make up for the time lost through the lack of Infant Schools, so as to be as young in any "Standard" as English children. As no payments to the teachers, either from the State Fund or the local taxes depend upon the "results" of examinations, the scholars are not driven at so great a pace. The pace might be somewhat increased, without physical strain. There seems to be a little too much "marking time." Promotion from stage to stage takes place at long intervals (sometimes as much as a year, as in England), and follows rigid rules. Consequently, as in England, promotion is not rapid enough for the more intelligent scholars. Those who complete the course, going right through to the highest class of the Grammar School, at fourteen or fifteen years of age, are comparatively few, more girls than boys, in the proportion sometimes as high as two to one; and these go through a "review" of the work of past years, and may be said to leave school with a thoroughly sound practical edu-

cation. Large numbers, however, especially in those States which have no compulsory law (*i.e.*, in about half of the States), have left school by eleven, indifferently equipped, and these must soon lose most of what they have acquired. Those who leave between eleven and thirteen do not seem to have had the opportunity of being so well equipped with an Elementary Education as corresponding English children. Doubtless, this defect in their school training is largely made up for, afterwards, by greater adroitness and adaptability—the result partly of inherited faculty, and partly also of the wider education in the ways of the world, acquired during those early years up to seven, which are spent by English children in the narrower community of the Infant School.

High Schools

In passing from the Grammar School to the High School, which is equally open to him under every State Common School System, the scholar is being lifted, by the enlightened provision of the community, out of the region of elementary, into that of secondary, education. Herein America is in marked contrast with England. In England the provision for Secondary Education follows the track of the old endowments of the Tudors and Stuarts, and is almost wholly wanting outside of that track. But the distribution of these endowments is in no way based on the needs of modern England, so that a village like Ewelme in Oxfordshire has far more than it can profitably use; a populous town like Sheffield, far less. In many small country towns, endowed Secondary Schools are to be found which neither Acts of Parliament, Royal Commissions, nor new Schemes of government have been able to galvanize into life. Vested interests have been too powerful for the masterly Recommendations of the Schools Inquiry Commissioners of 1868, which proposed to divide the country into educational districts, and to co-ordinate the endowments within each area by such redistribution as would meet the latter-day wants of the community. Though the composition and constitution of governing bodies have been largely, and, in many cases, beneficially re-modelled, it has not always been possible, even for Parliamentary Commissioners, to eliminate elements antagonistic to reform. Hence, even the funds derivable from endowments, scanty as they are for the needs of the England of to-day, are far from being appropriated to the best advantage; and the late Mr. Matthew Arnold, preaching the doctrine of "organize your Secondary Education" incessantly for five-and-twenty years, felt himself to be only a *vox clamantis in deserto*, and the disregard of his voice to be a terrible "blow for the declining age of a sincere but ineffectual Liberal."[4]

But America knows nothing of these characteristic English difficulties. There, whatever Secondary Education exists (except that given by a few private schools and academies in the wealthier cities) is provided as part of the Public School System by the local School Board, and is supported out of the taxes annually raised from the whole community for the purposes of Education. This is, indeed, the most distinctive feature of each State Common School system. The facilities for higher education are not capriciously distributed, by the chances of ancient or modern bounty, but are to be found in the midst of all fairly populous cities and towns in the State.

But though the cause of higher education escapes our difficulties, it must not be supposed that it has no difficulties of its own. It is obviously essential to the proper management of any kind of higher education that the managers should be socially in sympathy with those for whom they are providing the education, that they should have an adequate conception of the value to the many of the higher mental training for the few, and be conscious of aims based on broad views of the fruitfulness of intellectual life in a nation. Now, unhappily, there comes across the usually healthy political life of an American city a sick season—a time when the unscrupulous, the mercenary, the self-seeking, to whom "everything human and divine has its price," has full sway; it is then that the better elements either retire from public life in disgust at the treatment to which they are subjected, and in despair at their powerlessness to stem the tide of deterioration that has set in, or are elbowed out of the honourable posts they occupied by the mean devices of those who use these posts for their own dishonourable ends. Sad times these for higher education: for the selfishness of the demagogue immediately suggests to the burdened taxpayer, "Why

should you be called upon in your poverty to pay for the Latin and Greek and other accomplishments which are of no use to your children, and which ought to be provided for the rich man's children at his own expense?" Most cities have had their days of re-action, when it has been a severe struggle to maintain a proper standard of secondary instruction in face of an outcry like this. But the struggle generally ends in the triumph of the better elements; and many of the State legislatures have checked the recurrence of such untoward times for higher education by changes in the mode of election and constitution of School Boards, which have made them less directly dependent on popular whim and less capable of manipulation by political machinists. "In this direction, however, much remains to be desired."[5]

The English Endowed or Public School and the American High School being thus the outcome of such different circumstances as have been described, present numerous and marked points of contrast. An English Endowed School would admit scholars of *all* ages, from eight or nine years old and upwards; its standard of attainment qualifying for admission would vary with the age of the candidate; and each pupil, on being admitted, would be placed in that class in the school where the attainments were as nearly as possible similar to his own. The batch of admissions at a particular entrance examination, though the greater proportion would be entered in the lowest class of the school, would be distributed over a wide range of classes. But in America the almost universal rule is to make the condition of admission to a High School either that the candidate shall have passed at least the previous year in some upper elementary school (*i.e.*, Grammar School, so called), and have *graduated*, *i.e.*, satisfactorily completed the course of instruction there, or shall show in an examination attainments equivalent to such graduation. Consequently, all the pupils entering a High School at a given time are as nearly as possible of the *same* age and attainments. Having previously reached the first grade (or class) of an American Grammar School, they will average fourteen or fifteen years of age, and will have all reached a certain standard in the subjects named above as forming the course of instruction in Grammar Schools. Consequently, though of such

---

[4]See Mathew Arnold's article "Porro unum est necessarium," *Fortnightly Review*, November, 1878.

[5]City School Systems, by Dr. John D. Philbrick, Circular of the Bureau of Education, 1885.

an advanced age, they will, as a rule, have studied no *foreign* language whatever, ancient or modern.[6]

The High School course (in a city) extends over four years, but sometimes, as in the newer cities of the West, only three years. But the average length of stay in the school is only a little over two years, and in the case of boys, even less than that;[7] while the number of those who complete the course only ranges from one-third to as low as one-sixth of the number admitted to the school. It follows that a High School accommodating 300 scholars will admit nearly 150 from the various Grammar Schools at one annual or two semi-annual admissions. The scholars enter the same class and travel more or less *pari passu* through the school. This class will be divided into sections, and a large amount of choice will be allowed to each pupil, according to the parental views as to his (or her) future career in life. In some cities, the popular demand (to which the High School must bow) has compelled the introduction of three or even more "*elective*" *courses* of study (not subjects merely) in the same school—a classical or commercial or a general English course.[8] The pupils in the several sections belonging to the same year are taken together in those general subjects which are common to one or more of these courses, such as History or Algebra, and where any branch of a subject is pursued to a greater extent by one set of pupils more than another, further subdivisions may be formed. As a consequence of this great liberty of "election" on the part of scholars as to the course of study they will pursue, the High Schools of America are almost all

taught upon the "departmental" system, *i.e.*, each member of the teaching-staff is a specialist, having his own special department of school-work—one, or, it may be, two subjects which he teaches throughout the school—one teacher taking all the Latin, another Algebra and French, another Geometry and History, another English, and so on. This system is not the usual one in English Endowed and Public Schools (though it is largely practised in the High Schools for Girls which have lately been established), where each master has his own class for a given half-year, which he takes in a wide range of subjects, only passing his boys on to "departmental" masters for modern languages, mathematics or science. But such a plan would be impossible where electiveness of studies is carried to such an extent as in America.

As may well be imagined from this description, the difficulties of elaborating an effective school programme, which shall ensure the full employment of every teacher and scholar during the school hours are considerable. But the Departmental system in America has its drawbacks as well as its difficulties. In the Grammar Schools from which the pupils have been drafted into the High School, they have been accustomed to the class-teacher system, where scholar and teacher are thrown together for the greater part of the day's programme for a half-year or even a year at a time, and the relations between them become intimate, and even parental, in character. But all this is changed when they come to the High School. There each teacher gives instruction to perhaps 200 different scholars every day, and consequently teacher and scholar do not get, even at the end of the year, much beyond an attitude of amiable neutrality. It is admitted that the pupils feel this reduction of personal interest in themselves keenly, and that this is one reason of their abandoning the High School course so frequently soon after admission.

Coming now to the special studies of the American High Schools many circumstances will occur to the mind as militating against the attainment to the same high standard of work which is reached by a thoroughly efficient Endowed or Public School in England. It is obvious that, where the study of a foreign language is only commenced at the advanced age of fourteen or thereabouts, no such proficiency in Latin and Greek is attainable as compared with that which an English boy can show who was introduced to one

---

[6]Except, possibly, German, if they should happen either to be of German parentage, or of American parentage living in cities with a large German population, when, as is the case with Welsh children in a public elementary school in Wales, they will have received a *bilingual* training (English and Welsh) in the elementary school itself.

[7]In many of the High Schools, especially in the centre and west of the United States, boys and girls are taught in the same school, and the proportion of girls to boys in the highest class of the High School is 3, 4, or even 5 to 1. This, of course, means that the women of America are better educated than the men.

[8]Sometimes there are *two* English courses, one for children of English-speaking, and the other for children of German-speaking, parents, and called respectively the English-English, and the German-English courses.

of these languages at eight or nine years of age.

Again, a very general age for admission to an American University, even to the older institutions of Harvard and Yale, is seventeen; consequently a boy who showed marked capacity or taste for classical studies would be passed out of the High School and on to the University at a much earlier age than in England, and the High Schools would not be called upon to carry the classical course beyond his requirements at seventeen years of age. In a word, the head scholars of an American High School are just three, or at most four, years removed from their Latin declensions; in an English High School they would be more nearly eight to ten years from that initiation into the Latin tongue. The fundamental difference between these schools in the two countries cannot be more concisely put. Latin or Greek Verse Composition is unknown; the Professor of Classical Literature at John Hopkins University (Baltimore) told the writer that he thought he was the only man in America who could write Greek Iambics, and he was an Oxford man. Latin Prose Composition is not taught to any great extent. Most of the classical work that would be shown up by the scholars of the first class of an American High School, aged seventeen or thereabouts, would only pass muster in an English Public School for boys of fifteen. Great attention is, however, paid to Mathematics. Pupils do not, as a rule, study more than *two* foreign languages, so that those who are following the complete classical course, and taking up both Latin and Greek, are not taught any modern language. It is not usual, even among those who have elected for the English or Commercial courses, to find more than one modern language studied, which would be either French or German. German is the most popular of these two "Electives," and naturally, because of the large German-speaking element to be found in most of the great cities. Several branches of Science: — Physics, Physiology, Botany are included in the possible curriculum. Much more attention than in corresponding Schools in England is paid to English Language and Literature, Constitutional History (of the United States), and General Geography. The complaint is still frequent in the Reports of Superintendents that in these and the science subjects the tendency is to require of the pupils mere memorizing of the paragraphs of their text-books, "dull as a bill of lading and scrappy as an invoice." The slavery to text-books

has never been so conspicuous in English High Schools, though it cannot be said that the schools of this country are altogether free from it. Teaching here, as there, is frequently an artificial, not a natural, process. And it must be so in any part of the world where more people profess the art than those who have a natural aptitude for it, or have taken the pains to study its principles. The moral of all which is—train your teachers.

But there are two institutions which must be excepted from most of the foregoing criticisms on American High Schools—the Latin High School, and the English High School, at Boston. That city is, as everybody is aware, the nursing-mother of American National Education. *Noblesse oblige,* and whatever Boston does in the matter of Education is always worthy of its traditions and its enlightened educational faith. It has recently (1881) erected for the Boys' Latin and English High Schools, under one roof or series of roofs, what may be indeed called a . school-palace, vieing in the completeness of its equipment and architectural fitness with anything of which Vienna—that city of school-palaces—can boast. The late Bishop Fraser visited (in 1865) the English High School when it was in its old premises, and said of it even then, in his Report to the Schools Inquiry Commission, that "it ought to be put in a glass-case and carried over to England," as a specimen of what a school for the training of the English Middle Class for professional and business avocations should be. Would not his heart sink within him in despair at England ever rising to the same lofty conception of what is true wisdom in regard to the education of the middle classes, if he saw this school as it is now, in all the magnificent surroundings of its new home, with the most perfect class-room arrangements, with science lecture theatres, laboratories and gymnasium, and with every newest device for securing the orderliness, health, and efficient instruction of its pupils! The English High School for boys was originally founded in 1827, but the Latin High School is by far the oldest American Public School, dating from 1635, five years after the original settlement of that city and a year before the founding of Harvard University. This latter school, alone of American High Schools supported by public funds, bears a close resemblance to our Public Schools or First Grade Endowed Schools in England. The object of the school is distinctly to prepare boys for the University, and parents are required to signify their intention of giving their sons a University education. It is not a Finishing School, preparing boys for business life, as the American High Schools of the ordinary type profess to be, and as the other—the Boston English High School—is, but it is a Preparatory School for the University. Instead of admitting boys only on condition of their having completed the Grammar School course, they are encouraged to enter much earlier, and the admission Examination only requires a standard to be reached equivalent to the third class of the Grammar School, instead of the first. Thus boys of twelve, or even eleven, find their way into the Latin High School, and as they stay till seventeen, and sometimes till eighteen years of age, and devote their time mainly to the classics —with some mathematics and science in addition—it follows that the majority of them go to College with six or seven years of thorough classical training as a foundation for further study.

Recently also, the Board School for Boston has erected Girls' Latin, and Girls' English High Schools in another part of the city, and with courses of instruction precisely the same as those in the corresponding schools for boys. These schools are the result of an agitation carried on over many years to obtain for girls the privilege of being trained to an intelligent womanhood on the same grounds, and by the same means, as boys had long been trained to an intelligent manhood. The maxim of *co-education*, which is that boys and girls should be educated together, up to any age, in the same school and in the same class-rooms is not accepted in Boston. This principle has been very generally adopted in High Schools in the cities of the newer Western States of America, and in towns of small population in the Eastern States, for obvious reasons of economy; but it does not meet with favour in the larger of the old communities in the East, and has led to considerable abstentions from the use of the Public High School on the part of the wealthier classes in the West, who prefer to send their daughters at all events, and even their sons, to private Academies. Though co-education finds many able and honest advocates among prominent educationists on *à priori* grounds, parents of families find that it bristles with practical difficulties. The question is a wide one, and cannot be satisfactorily dealt with in this essay. But with regard to *High* Schools—and we are now speaking exclusively of such schools— where the scholars are of ages from four-

teen to eighteen and are drawn from homes of widely-different surroundings and social ideas, it may be assumed—to quote Dr. Philbrick's words—"that separate education of the sexes and not co-education in the High School grade of the city schools is the normal finality to which all civilisation tends." With this verdict, most English people will, doubtless, agree.

In closing these remarks upon American Secondary Education as part of the Common School System, we conclude, as we began, by emphasizing the one great and glaring point of contrast between America and England:— Whatever the shortcomings of the American High School, its glory is that it exists everywhere; maintained at the public cost of the tax-payer, within reasonable reach of every family of the middle classes, and accessible to the brighter intelligences among the poorest; while, whatever the excellences of the English Endowed School, where it is found in good working order, the crying grievance is that it exists only in a few favoured but isolated spots, and the bulk of the middle classes of England as well as the exceptionally gifted of the working classes,

look up, and are not fed,
But, swoln with wind and the rank mist they
draw,
Rot inwardly.

In lifting up his lamentation over this glaring defect in our English educational system, Matthew Arnold, though dead, yet speaks words of wisdom and of justice when he says:[9]—"The existing resources for secondary instruction, if judiciously co-ordered and utilised, would prove to be immense; but undoubtedly gaps would have to be filled, an annual State grant and municipal grants would be necessary. That is to say, the nation would perform, as a corporate and co-operative work, a work which is now never conceived and laid out as a whole, but is done sporadically, precariously, and insufficiently. We have had experience how elementary instruction gains by being thus conceived and laid out, instead of being left to individual adventure or individual benevolence. The middle class, who contribute so immense a share of the cost incurred for the public institution of elementary schools, while their own school supply is so miserable, would be repaid twenty times over for their share in the addi-

---

[9] See his article in the *Fortnightly Review* quoted above, p. 89.

tional cost of publicly instituting secondary instruction by the direct benefit which they and theirs would get from its system of schools. The upper class, which has bought out the middle class at so many of the great foundation schools designed for its benefit, and which has monopolised what good secondary instruction we have, owes to the middle class the reparation of contributing to a public system of secondary schools."

Free, Compulsory, and Secular Education

. . . throughout the American Common School System—alike in Primary, Grammar, and High Schools—and in all the States without exception, instruction is gratuitous, or, in ordinary parlance, *free*.

The adoption of the principle of Free Schools has only become general in the United States within the last quarter of a century. In Massachusetts, and in those of the New England States where the original settlements were made. and the State svstem set up, in the 17th century, by Presbyterian exiles from England, the "Free" School was adopted from the very first. The explanation of this is, that the *Presbyterian* exodus from these shores (which is not to be confounded, as is often the case, with the *Puritan* exodus to Plymouth in the "Mayflower") was largely composed of men of means and of fair social position among the middle classes—country squires, clergymen, lawyers and merchants, such as the Winthrops, Vanes, Eatons and Bellinghams; and these men had been educated in English Endowed Grammar Schools, in all (or almost all) of which instruction was entirely (or almost entirely) gratuitous. These men, therefore, carried the principle of *free* education with them from England; and it is their *special* glory that they enlarged the conception of this "free" principle so as to cover the educational needs of every, even the poorest, citizen of the new communities across the Atlantic, all the while that "the poor," *i.e.*, the labouring classes in the mother country, remained without any education till the present century, and even now do not receive it at the public cost, without school fees. But the difficulty of raising sufficient funds for educational purposes, as the population of the community increased faster than its wealth, led even the New England States to fall back upon the expedient of school fees, except Massachusetts, which has under all financial stress remained true to the spirit

and letter of its earliest Education Law. And so, school fees were exacted in the form familiarly known as "rate-bills," from all parents (except in cases of poverty, which had to declare and prove itself) in all but this State until about the middle of the present century. Then an agitation commenced against them, largely on the ground that "attendance was repelled by directly taxing it"; and this, gaining force and volume as it progressed, slowly and steadily prevailed, first in one State and then in another, until, by the year 1871, the rate-bill had entirely disappeared, and instruction in the Common Schools of every State became entirely gratuitous. The effect of the removal of direct taxation from school attendance has been just what was anticipated: greater enrolment and more regular attendance have been characteristic of the school returns uninterruptedly since the abolition of fees.

A further movement is gaining ground for the gratuitous supply of text-books and stationery. The arguments for this extension of the principle of gratuitous instruction are partly economic and partly moral: (1) Expense would be saved, because the books would be purchased on more advantageous terms by the School Board, and, when they had served their purpose with one batch of scholars, would be available for use by the next batch coming up to that grade; and (2) The invidious distinction between the well-to-do who can afford to buy books and the poor who, under present regulations, can only obtain their books gratis on a personal plea of poverty, would be obliterated. The policy of supplying free books has been adopted for seventy years in Philadelphia and for fifty years in New York, and its success has led to its adoption in many other cities. The State Law of Massachusetts, which made the provision of text-books by a city or town optional by an enactment in 1873, has since 1884, made it compulsory upon all cities and towns to furnish all pupils in the public schools with free books and stationery.

This is the place to say something about *compulsion*, or the enforcement of attendance at school by legal enactment. The American States have shown very great reluctance thus to interfere with the legal rights of parents over their children, and to assert the legal rights of children as against their parents. But they are rapidly recognising the stern logic of facts which, presented in the form of annual statistics of child-vagrancy and adult-illiteracy, are convincing them that parental indulgence, negligence and greed, are greater sources of danger to the community than any encroachment could be on parental liberty to deprive his offspring of education. "The State, though it has provided a free gift to its children, yet finds it necessary to compel its acceptance"—this is the painful conclusion to which the American mind is coming, but only very slowly and unwillingly. Barely one-half of the States (only 16 or 17 out of 38) have as yet adopted any compulsory laws, and these, where they are in force, are generally very mild in character, and are still more mildly administered. The most stringent compulsory law does not require attendance for more than half the number of weeks in the school year, and then only from children above eight years of age; the offence of truancy rarely touches more than exceptional and flagrant cases; the penalties for the breach of the law on the part of parents and guardians are (except in Massachusetts) slight and ineffectual, and only in Massachusetts, and perhaps in one or two cities, are truant officers appointed to search out cases of illegal employment, or are penalties attached to such illegal employment of children of school age. In many States where the law (as in New York State Law, 1875) looks strong, it is practically a dead letter.

The contrast with England in this respect is most striking. Though England has *not* provided education as a *free* gift to her children, she has yet determined to enforce its acceptance. And, having determined this, she has set to work in spite of the retention of the school fees to carry out compulsion with a rigour which is in marked contrast to the mildness of American compulsion. In England, the Law, first introduced in 1870, and strengthened by further enactments in 1876 and 1880, is now universal; it applies to all children over *five* years of age; it requires regular attendance morning and afternoon for five days in the week all through the school year; it imposes penalties upon parents for the irregular attendance of their children as well as for their truancy and vagrancy, and upon employers for illegal employment of children who should be at school; and it has armed School Boards, and School Attendance Committees in non-School Board areas, with very large powers, which they are obliged to exercise, for following up and detecting offenders, whether children, or parents, or employers of labour.

The question that is now arousing considerable public interest in England, and pressing upon practical statesmen for solution, is whether the community can fairly and reasonably enforce such a stringent compulsory Law without making the education to which it applies a free gift for the compelled, at the public cost.

. . . and lastly, instruction in the Common Schools is confined to secular subjects entirely in three-fourths of the States;[10] and in the remaining States, religious instruction of an unsectarian character is either required to be given (in New Hampshire alone), permitted to be given, or not forbidden to be given, by the teachers, with the right of children to absent themselves; and this permission is very variously made use of, the amount of religious instruction in most cases being limited to reciting the Lord's Prayer and reading the Bible without comment.

The Common School is only one of the agencies recognised as operating for the development of the perfect manhood of an American citizen, and, as the School does not usurp, so neither does it ignore, the functions of the Church and the Family as co-partners with it in this development. This is the explanation of the attitude of America towards religious instruction. Moreover, there are practical considerations which have influenced this division of labour. The existence of a Roman Catholic population in a city—if these children are to have the same educational rights as those of all other American citizens to the schools to which all alike contribute by taxation—has of itself the effect of confining the teaching exclusively to purely secular subjects. The Roman Catholics will not accept unsectarian religious teaching at any price; they will not allow the children to be present at the reading from a version of the Bible (the Authorized Version) which, though accepted by Protestant Churches, is repudiated by their own Church. Protests are raised, from time to time, against what is considered so disastrous for morality and religion as a school system which, though it enjoins the teaching and inculcation of moral principles, largely precludes reference to the highest moral sanction. American State and City Reports are very reticent on this subject from fear, possibly, of stirring up a

_____

[10] Twenty-seven out of the thirty-six States who furnished Returns to the Royal Commission on the Elementary Education Acts, see Blue Book, Foreign Returns, 1888. The remaining nine States are Florida, Maine, Michigan, New Hampshire, New Jersey, Oregon, Pennsylvania, Vermont and Virginia. Ohio made no Return.

heated discussion which would hinder the progress of the school system; but on the whole it seems as if the secular platform is maintaining its ground in spite of an occasional charge of "godlessness" which can be so readily met, as it has been met by the following words of Secretary John W. Dickenson of the Massachusetts State Board of Education:[11] "The public schools are condemned by some because they are godless institutions. The charge should be carefully examined for its meaning. If it means that theology is not one of the branches of study required or permitted to be taught, the charge is true, and the public Common School could not live a day if it were not true. If it means that the schools are anti-religious in any sense, the charge has already been shown to be unqualifiedly false. It must be false, unless the cultivation of good intellectual and moral habits is opposed to a faithful consideration of the highest truths that refer to our future, as well as to our present, well-being. What harm can come to a true religion from the ability to read, or to perform arithmetical problems; from a knowledge of the constitution and uses of things in the natural world; from an understanding of the principles and forms of our civil Government; from the power to reason correctly; from a training in the practice of good manners; or from the cultivation of the virtues, which are the ornament of society and the basis of a republican constitution? It seems hardly possible that in this age of the world, and in this civilised State, religion should stand in fear of general intelligence, or of personal freedom."

The Training of Teachers, and "Teachers' Institutes"

No survey of American Common School Education would be complete which did not include some account of the provision made in the several States *for the supply of teachers and for their efficient training.* The right to select the teacher is possessed, and tenaciously clung to, by each local School Board, and the only control, which each State can and does exercise over the qualifications of the teachers employed within its area, lies in fixing the conditions under which it is prepared to grant licenses to teach (after examination by the State Superintendent), and in refusing all "appropriations" from the

State Education Fund to any City or Town Board which employs unlicensed or uncertificated teachers. Most of the States issue such licenses or certificates, and exercise the power of the purse—with greater or less effect upon the Boards according to the length of that purse—to exclude uncertificated teachers from the Public Schools. The qualifications required are very various, and for teachers in the rural districts, often deplorably low; but, as a rule, no one is allowed to undertake any subjects except those for which his certificate shows him to be qualified. The School Boards of the great cities, in like manner make the possession of a certificate from the City Superintendent a condition of employment as a teacher.

The source of supply of Teachers is found in the "Graduates" of the Grammar or High Schools, or from those who have spent one year or more in Normal Schools or at the Universities. The age at which young persons commence teaching may be as young as 16 or 17, but is rarely less than 18 in cities and populous towns. The English "pupil-teacher" system is not found anywhere in the States. By far the larger proportion of teachers engaged in the common schools are women. The teachers in the primary schools, all but the principals (and sometimes even the principals) of Grammar Schools for both sexes, and some of those in High Schools for boys are women. They stay in the profession longer than the men, intending, unless they marry, to make a livelihood by it. The men, on the other hand, largely use teaching as a stepping-stone to other literary professions, or to the many avenues of commerce which are continually opening up in such a country of new enterprises and new conquests over primitive nature as America. The scale of pay for men (except in Massachusetts) is not at all calculated to counteract this influence, being decidedly low, considering the high rents and great cost of living; and is often (in the Western States) very slightly higher than that of women. Then most of the Boards, especially those outside the cities, make the appointments of their teachers terminate at the end of each school year; and the shortness of the engagement, and the insecurity of re-engagement, greatly favour and encourage this tendency to treat "school-keeping" as a temporary occupation.

By way of comparison and contrast, it may first be noted that, in England also, the appointment of the teacher rests solely with the School Boards or Bodies of Managers, while Parliament (through the Education De-

---

[11]See Report, Mass. Board of Education, 1888, p. 78.

partment) lays down as a condition of sharing in the Government grant, that the Head Teacher, at least, shall hold a Government Certificate, and that the rest of the staff shall possess certain qualifications; and here, also, small schools in rural districts are allowed to be in charge of head teachers with qualifications of a comparatively low standard (known as the "provisional certificate"). The Teachers in English Elementary Schools are mostly recruited from the Elementary schools themselves—a state of things rendered possible, and indeed purposely created, by the "pupil-teacher system," whereby young persons of both sexes may, and do, enter the profession at the early age of 14. The numerical preponderance of women over men engaged in teaching is not so great as in America, in spite of the existence of Infant Schools staffed wholly by women, because here, as a rule, boys are taught, after the infants' stage is passed, entirely by men. Again, in marked contrast to the American phenomenon, the vast majority of the men who enter the profession (certainly if they get beyond the pupil-teacher stage and become assistants, or go to a Training College), take it up as a means of livelihood and adopt it permanently. This great advantage to education which the English schools possess over the American is largely secured to them by comparative fixity of tenure, and by the higher rate of salaries for men (taking into account the smaller cost of living) which generally obtains in England, no less than by the tendency characteristic of this country to choose a career and stick to it.

But the American States have not remained satisfied with simply requiring, where they could, that the teachers employed should possess some kind of certificate attesting to a certain amount of knowledge of the subjects to be taught, but they have, most of them, realised the paramount necessity of some training for them in the art and science of education. Accordingly, second to none of the means by which each State—as a State—influences the Common School instruction within its borders, its great concern has been to secure this professional instruction. The last half-century, commencing with the year 1839, when the first State Normal Schools were established by Massachusetts at Lexington (transferred to Framingham) and at Westfield, has witnessed the founding of nearly one hundred of these Normal Schools (or Training Colleges, as they would be called in England); and, if we add to these the Normal Schools and Teachers' Training Classes set up by counties and cities, a grand total of 134 Public Normal Schools is reached, maintained by public funds, and, in most cases, free of charge to those students who declare their intention of following their profession in the Common Schools. Of these Normal Schools, Wisconsin alone supplies five, Massachusetts six, New York State nine, and Pennsylvania no fewer than eleven. The demand for professionally trained teachers is still largely in excess of the supply, and the States are every year founding additional Normal Schools. In the Southern States, where the need is most felt and the State resources are subject to most strain, the Peabody Trust has stimulated and assisted local effort (as in Virginia, South Carolina, and Tennessee) with liberal appropriations.

In the Cities which have taken professional training in hand, the machinery for this training assumes various forms, adapted to local circumstances. The High School for Girls at Philadelphia, which has been presided over for the last twenty-five years, by the veteran Principal, George W. Fetter, is the Normal School for that city. Out of a total of nearly 2000 Pupils (Rep. Bureau of Educn., 1887–8), 228 Pupils were enrolled for the Teachers' Training Course, and 575 Students were in the Practising Schools attached, which embrace boys, girls, and Kindergarten departments. This Normal School has a three years' course, commencing at about fourteen years of age, and a fourth year of studentship in the Practising Schools, before teaching certificates are awarded. New York City has a corresponding institution on an equally large scale, and it is estimated that nearly one-half of the students who have graduated at this School (here called a College) are teaching in the Common Schools of the city. In other cities, we find a Training Class formed as an extra year's course in the High School, or a Normal Department attached to the State or local University which may happen to be situated in its vicinity. The State Normal Schools, which are mostly for women only, though some are for both sexes, usually arrange for day or non-boarding students only, each student making private arrangements for residence in the neighbourhood of the School; but some of them receive Boarders, while there are three or four State Schools (in Massachusetts and New Jersey), which are restricted to boarding students. Each State makes its terms of admission, which are dependent upon examinations equivalent to the higher Grammar, or middle High School, grades. The usual age of admission is sixteen for women, and seventeen for men. The "graduating" course varies considerably in length, from one year in some States, to three or four in others. No religious instruction is given in Normal Schools.

In treating of the professional training of teachers in America, mention, and very conspicuous mention, is merited by a piece of machinery entirely of American origin, and quite peculiar to that country. This is "The Teachers' Institute." This kind of organization, the first experiment in which was made by the voluntary efforts of Dr. Henry Barnard, at Hartford, Conn., in 1839, has since been universally recognised as a most valuable supplement to, or substitute for, professional training in the Normal School proper, so that all the States with few exceptions, have now incorporated into their School laws regulations for the holding of Teachers' Institutes, and have set apart appropriations for their support, even making attendance compulsory in some cases upon all teachers engaged in public schools.

A Teachers' Institute may be defined concisely as an "itinerant normal school" for the professional education of teachers actually engaged in teaching. The Institute is organised under direction of the State Superintendent, who associates with himself one or two principals of Normal Schools, and some of the ablest City or Town Superintendents in the district in which the Institute is to be held, and thus a Normal School is extemporized at a given centre, which holds a session for some days or weeks there, and then migrates to another centre, passing from place to place during the autumn months. By this means an Institute normal training is brought within easy reach of every teacher in the State once every year. The instruction is generally given gratuitously at the expense of the State, and, wherever the Institute is held, all sections of the residents combine to reduce the cost which would fall upon the teachers for board and lodging by hospitably housing or entertaining them during the session of the Institute. The duration of each session varies inversely with the other provision which the States, Counties and Cities have made for normal training. Where, as in Massachusetts, a large proportion of the teachers actually employed in the schools have already received normal training in a Normal School proper, the Institute session lasts for only one clear day. But where, as in the more Western and Southern States, the large majority of the teachers are not normally trained, the Institute Session is made to extend to two, or even three weeks. Other supplementary aids to the professional training and general culture of teachers are to be found in Township Institutes, Teachers' Conventions and Associations, which exist in nearly every town having a graded system of public schools; also in Teachers' Reading Circles for the study of works on Pedagogy and Moral Science; and in Holiday or Summer Normal Schools, where recreation, social intercourse, and professional study and discussion combine to promote healthiness, good fellowship, homogeneity and a high standard of educational ideals among American Teachers.

Conclusion

In bringing this survey of the American Common School system to a close, the writer is again impressed with the inefficacy of facts and figures, reports and statistics, however deftly handled, to strike the characteristic note of the American system, so as to convey to an English mind all that it conveys to an American. The system is the creation of the all-pervading democratic idea, which, Minerva-like, leapt into full being in the seventeenth century: in England, the feudalism of the middle ages still survives, and is only slowly being transmuted by the infusion of the democratic idea of the nineteenth. When our English Royal Commission on the Education Acts sent its paper of inquiries the other day to the several American State Boards of Education asking, among others, the question, "From what class of society are the teachers drawn?" that State,[12] which gave back the laconic reply, "We are democrats," put the fundamental *differentia* between the English and American mind into the clear view which a flash of lightning momentarily produces on a landscape in darkness. "Among the important virtues," says Mr. Secretary Dickenson,[13] "which the public school is adapted to cultivate, is patriotism or love of country. The love of benefactors is a natural affection. It springs up in the mind on the perception of favours received. The public school is the free gift of the State. It is the best gift of a government to its people. As the scholar

----

[12] The State of Mississippi, see Blue Book, Royal Commission on Education Acts, Foreign Returns, 1888, p. 273.

[13] Report of Secretary of the Massachusetts State Board of Education, 1888, p. 77.

comes to understand its value to him as an individual and a citizen; as he becomes aware that his intelligence and the free government which protects him are, in an important sense, the results of its developing influences, his love of country grows stronger, and his desire to promote its welfare increases. In the same way it may be shown that the public school, by its organization and exercises, is adapted to cultivate all the social virtues, and at the same time to train the children to that self-control and independence in thinking which are the necessary characteristics of the people of a self-governed State."

No doubt there is much to be avoided by England in the methods and working of the American Common Schools. But is there not also much that may be prudently imitated? After all, we English may well take a lesson from the American people of enthusiasm for, and a genuine belief in, education *as a civilizing and ennobling force.* No one in America fears (secular) education, or looks with dread upon any of its possible consequences to society. There it is reverenced, deeply reverenced, as a *saviour* of society. And the teachers, as Education's priesthood, share in that reverence, and receive accordingly that respect and deference which goes so far to compensate priesthoods all the world over for meagre material prospects and emoluments. We cannot be said to have yet learnt that lesson in England.

Paul Bourget   1895

Impressions of American Education

Paul Bourget (1852–1935), a French critic, poet, and novelist, was educated at the Sorbonne. The author of several books on poetry as well as psychological novels, he was elected to the Académie Française in 1894. Bourget visited a sampling of schools in the United States: "Boston as sufficiently representative of primary instruction; Harvard as representing universities for men and Wellesley those for women; of technical schools, West Point, the military academy, the St. Cyr of the United States." In spite of the limited number of schools he visited, he succinctly noted many of their characteristics. Bourget wrote in an entertaining and penetrating manner about many aspects of American education. His work is descriptive rather than comparative; nonetheless, he ably related his knowledge of both French and British education to the American scene.

When one has seen a certain civilization in some of its fully developed representatives, and has formed an idea, correct or incorrect, of its good qualities and its defects, its value and its insufficiency, it remains to test these notions by a counter experiment, if I may so speak. One must try to see in the formative state these individual men or women, whom one has already seen exercising their matured powers. To put it more simply, the indispensable corollary of the study of the life of a people is the study of the educational processes of that people. The nature of the instruction given by a country to its youth is doubly instructive; for on the one hand it reveals the educator's conception of men,—hence of the citizen, hence of the entire nation,—and on the other hand it permits you if not to foresee, at least to have a presentiment of what the future of the nation will be, when once the children and youth thus brought up shall become the nation in their turn.

For example, is it possible perfectly to understand England without having understood Oxford, and the sort of seminary of "gentlemen" established there many centuries ago? You seat yourself on the turf of New College, at the foot of the ancient ramparts of the city; in the close of Wadham, near the apse of the chapel built by Dame Dorothea, whose statue may still be seen, stiff and severe under the folds of her robe of stone; on the edge of the pool of Worcester, where De Quincey dreamed; in the grandly quiet park of St. John's. Only to see the young barbarians, as Matthew Arnold called them, playing tennis in the beautiful setting which owes everything to the dead, only to follow them, as in their flannel suits they seat themselves in a canoe and glide along the venerable walls of these ancient cloisters; or on horseback,

Paul Bourget, *Outre-Mer Impressions of America* (London: T. Fisher Unwin, 1895), pp. 276–280, 287–291.

trotting beside the grassy graveyards scattered everywhere in this city,—all the future of this youth is unveiled to you. The boy who has been in such surroundings during his impressionable years must be, he cannot but be, just what in fact nine out of ten Englishmen are: healthy and traditional, capable of all endurance, of all physical daring, and deeply, thoroughly conservative, even when he believes himself to be a radical; respectful of the past in his most intense ardor for individual action, because he has felt it too deeply, too much realized its benefits, to be anything else.

On the other hand, you visit a French *Lycée* with its barrack-like buildings, its narrow, hemmed-in playgrounds, the promiscuity of its dormitories, the bare ugliness of its studios and class-rooms. What more is needed to show you that the young men there brought up must be physically impoverished, nervously overstrained, robbed of joy and spontaneity. Discipline, too little individualized to be intelligent, must inevitably either cow or irritate him. He comes forth from it either a functionary or a refractory, crushed or revolted, nearly resembling the man careful only of his own interests and the anarchist, two equally baleful types of the civilized man, wasting himself either in feeble platitudes or in destructive insanity. Such is the fatal end of a system of culture apprehended as the reverse of nature and tradition, first by the men of the Convention and then by the Emperor, the most ill-omened of all their ill-starred works, most calculated to dry up, at its source, the energy and virtue of our middle class. Here, as everywhere, education explains history, because it explains customs.

It is not always easy to grasp the influence of a whole social system upon the schools, and again of the schools upon the social system. In the United States, in particular, the very character of the nation makes it almost impossible to define its system of education, spread as it is over an immense extent of country and absolutely without central direction. The power of states, of cities, especially of individuals, to initiate action conspires incessantly to modify the innumerable centres of instruction which have spontaneously blossomed out upon this soil where social forces seem to have a plasticity very like the plasticity of natural forces in the youth of the planet. The chances are great that each educational building will be constructed on a different plan, for each educator is apparently a man with his own ideas, and each pupil even is an elementary personality.

I remember when I was in Newport being entirely nonplussed by the question of a negro who waited upon me in the hotel, a sort of black giant whom up to that time I had admired solely for his dexerity in carrying in the flat of his hand a tray loaded with six or seven entire dinners.

"Is it true, sir," he asked me, "that you are going to write a book about America?"

"Perhaps," I replied. "But why do you ask?"

"Because I should much like to have a copy to read this winter in college."

"The negroes are so vain," said a New Yorker, to whom I laughingly related this dialogue. "He wanted to make you think he knew how to read." And he added, "Since you are collecting anecdotes about the 'colored gentlemen' don't forget this one. The other week Lord B——, one of the first nobles of England, was travelling beyond Chicago. At a certain station one of the Pullman car porters approached him with the words, 'They tell me that you are Lord B——.' 'Yes,' replied the other. 'Would you give me your hand?' asked the negro. The nobleman thought this request showed a touching humility. He extended his hand to the unhappy son of slavery, who perhaps had formerly been himself a slave. What did the darkey do but shake the nobleman's hand with the proud remark, 'You know, Lord B——, I am an American citizen and I propose to tell all my fellow-citizens that the British aristocracy is all right!'"

My witty interlocutor was mistaken. It was not in braggadocio that the waiter in the Newport hotel had spoken of his college. I had the proof of this when, in the course of the winter, being in a little Southern city in which the newspapers had made known my presence, I received a letter which I cannot refrain from setting down here in all its artlessness, so significant does it appear to me.

"I write you a few lines to let you know that I have succeeded in entering college as I hoped to do. I entered January 1, and am getting along very nicely with my studies. My wish was to take the full, regular course, but I am not able to do so as I must support myself while in school. I must therefore content myself with the normal and scientific course. I do not precisely know what I shall do next summer. I have thought of going back to the hotel in Newport, but nothing is decided. I am looking for a copy of your book when it is finished.''

What can be the spirit of a college on whose benches a servant, twenty years old and more, may take his place for six months in the year, between two terms of service, and the fact not appear in the least exceptional? What must be our opinion of the man himself, his demands of life, the thoughts he exchanges with his fellow-students; what of an entire society in which such features are of daily occurrence? Once more measure the abyss that separates the Old World from the New. And yet the very exclamation that falls from a foreigner's lips on meeting such incidents—"How American that is!" is a proof that he recognizes a certain character common to all the manifestations of this singular country, however unlike they may be. . . .

Admitting that the school is an entirely local creation based upon the good will of individuals, the methods of instruction ought to be all alike conformed, not indeed to abstract and conventional theories but to the peculiar needs of the city, its individual and encompassing life. A short tour of investigation suffices to show the traveller that in fact education is minutely and systematically organized here with a view to the adaptation of the individual to his surroundings. The teachers are both men and women, but especially women. These zealous creatures earn nearly nine hundred dollars a year. Most of them are unmarried, and though in constant contact with male teachers "cases of scandal," as they say here, are extremely rare. These women teachers are, above all, moral persons. Their sense of responsibility enables them to exert an all-pervading influence over the children and youth whom they instruct. Perhaps we may find here one of the reasons for the peculiar respect in which women are held in America. They are a part of the strongest and most tender impressions of youth.

It is worth while to see these school-mistresses, most of them pretty, teaching their classes, especially in the primary schools, where girls and boys of ten to twelve years sit side by side. They proceed mainly by questions put to the school at large, the pupils asking permission to reply by raising the hand. The mistress chooses one, then asks another question, looking up this or that one who is backward. It is very simple, very animated, very pleasant. The great variety in the exercises, none of which lasts more than half an hour, forbids fatigue. In the beginners' classes, as also in the grammar grades, the feature which most strikes a middle-class Frenchman, of grammar school education, is the constant use of the concrete and positive method. Modelling in clay plays an important part in this method of instruction. In almost every schoolroom that you may visit you will see a whole collection of figures modelled by the children of both sexes, who follow you with curious eyes,—simple objects made in the likeness of the humble realities that surround them, a carrot, a loaf of bread, a biscuit, a butterfly, a flower. Here are some busy with a lesson in which they must draw and describe a potato that lies before them. Others are busy copying some leaves. They must identify the tree and give some positive facts about it. Others have just finished some rather complicated woodwork, made after patterns drawn with chalk upon the blackboard; pigeonholes, boxes, pieces of carved wood that might be adjusted to some machine. In all these details you recognize the same principle; to make the eye, the mind, and the hand work together; to train the child to observe, and to regulate his thought and actions in accordance with his observation.

After seeing these methods of education, you understand better certain peculiarities of the American mind,—its almost total lack of abstract ideas, and its amazing power of recognizing reality, of manipulating it in the domain of mechanics as well as in that of business. The aim is, to the most remarkable degree, to confront these awakening minds constantly, indefatigably with the *fact*. The exercises which they choose are the evident proof of this. Thus I have seen the pupils in a somewhat advanced class occupied by way of written exercise, in replying to a newspaper advertisement for employees. When they are grown up, they will have such advertisements to draw up. These things are facts, and this education bows to facts. They will need to write letters relative to travelling, and here is a class of little girls of twelve who have just been dealing with the subject: "A trip to Europe.''

I read two of the copies that the teacher is correcting. The first is the work of a child who has never been abroad. It is a very dry and meagre production, which, however, reveals a minute effort after accuracy. The child names the ship on which she is supposed to have made the voyage. She mentions the day of setting out, the length of the voyage, the number of miles made each day, the name of a hotel in Liverpool and one in London. All these details are accurate and real. She has heard relatives or friends mention them, and she has retained them. The little girl of the second paper has actually made the journey. She had observed and remembered each daily event, the incidents, the meals, the conversation of her mother and the stewardess. She had observed the small size of the London houses and the air of "refined gayety" of Paris. It is all told without effort and sometimes with a good deal of naturalness. It seemed as if I were tracing to its source that talent for conscientious and truthful writing which in America even more than in England has produced an enormous amount of feminine literature. The attention here is carefully directed to the daily current of events. Fifteen or twenty years hence this little girl will go to the poles or to Egypt and her notes of travel will appear in some magazine, if indeed she does not undertake some monograph on art or history, science or literature, or if again she does not try her hand at a "short story," that brief and sensational study of life, in narrative form, which is really the summit of excellence in American literature.

Returning from these visits, you must take up the report of the school committee, to read it with the picture before you of these boys and girls with their spirited, resolute faces, these masters and mistresses with their lively, familiar ways, these light and well-ordered schoolrooms, these well-stocked laboratories—all this little world of study in which nothing calls up the thought of discipline or constraint. You will receive the fullest light on the whole system of instruction by reading the part of the report entitled "Examination Papers." This is a list covering pages and pages of questions put to the pupils in written or oral examinations. There is not one, from the simplest to the most difficult, which was not designed to put the child's mind in an atmosphere of positive action, to connect it with facts by a firm and sufficient tie. In the matter of spelling, for instance, the easiest dictation exercises contain facts of domestic life or counsels of practical utility.

"While I remain in the country this summer my time will be occupied in active recreation." "John, come here. Did you hear me quoting the old saying, 'A stitch in time saves nine'?"

If the examination is in composition, subjects like these are given:—

"Wanted: a young woman in a photographic gallery. Must have practical and artistic experience and good references. Address, Room 15, 154 Tremont Street, Boston, Mass. Write the letter that you would write if you desired this place."

"Write a letter to some one you know who has never been in this school. Describe the playground, the building, your room."

"Write to a friend, giving advice as to her health, telling her the things you have learned about the care of the body."

If it is geography, this is how they prepare children for their future travels:—

"Sail from Cape Ann to Cork, with a cargo. What goods would you take and what would you bring back?"

"Make an excursion from San Francisco to Paris. Describe the route. What articles would you bring back?"

Then follow an infinite number of questions upon climates and products, both vegetable and mineral, and the division of industries.

If the study is mathematics, mental arithmetic will occupy the first place, of course, and all the problems will refer to processes of buying and selling.

If it is history, all the questions turn upon the annals of the great Republic, and especially on New England.

"When and by whom was Boston founded? Describe the Tree of Liberty, the Boston Massacre, the Boston Tea-party. Describe a New England village, a Sunday morning in colonial times. Give an account of the landing in Massachusetts Bay and a short description of the leaders of the first colony."

Evidently the pupil who is prepared to reply on all these points has been educated with a view to becoming a business man in a democracy and if possible, in a special city of the democracy. The citizens who manage this vast organization for civic instruction are finding, nevertheless, that in these programmes there is too little room for the workingman. The report sketches a project for a new school of mechanical arts, more complete than any other. It will be called— no doubt by this time it is already called— "The Mechanical High School." The prospectus is summed up in these words, which I transcribe textually:—

"For the first time in Boston the child who is to enter industrial life will have, at the public expense, the same opportunities for preparation which have long been given to those who are preparing for business or professional life."

Having reached this point, it seems to me that these people must have attained their ideal, which can be expressed in one word: *the complete identification of education and life.*

Ernst Schlee   1895

The Latest Educational Reform Movements in the United States

Ernst Schlee (1834–1905), a German educator, was director of the Realgymnasium in Altona. He was a member of the Berlin Conference of December 1890, called by Emperor William "for the purpose of simplifying the courses of study" in German secondary schools. Schlee visited the United States during the Columbian Exposition and based his criticisms of American education on the reports of the Committee of Ten and the Committee of Fifteen appointed by the National Education Association. The work of these committees concerned secondary and elementary education respectively, and was closely followed by thoughtful educators from Germany. Schlee noted that the recommendations of the NEA committees provoked considerable discussion in American educational circles and remarked that "the United States resembles a hotbed of pedagogical discussion over which the gods must rejoice."

The fundamental points which the committee of ten recognizes as fixed are (1) that the number of lessons per week be not increased, (2) that the conditions of admission to college be not increased, and (3) that the principle of unity upon which the common school rests be not disturbed. This last-mentioned point meets all demands for a differentiation or bifurcation previous to the eighth year of the course. In other words, that the pupils intending to enter college and those intending to devote themselves to business pursuits should have precisely the same elementary instruction. Yet the committee declares it impossible to prepare a suitable programme for the secondary school having a course of four years if it be built on the present course of the common school. Either instruction in foreign languages, mathematics, and natural sciences should begin in the elementary school or the secondary school should begin two years earlier, and leave only six years for the elementary school. It is claimed that elementary instruction, both with regard to matter and method, is continued too long. In all the sub or special committees the complaint was heard that the high school did not find sufficient preparatory knowledge in the pupils, and that it had to begin with all secondary branches at the same time.

Of all claims for an earlier beginning of secondary branches none was more emphatic than that for foreign languages. The valuation of modern foreign languages is naturally different in America from the European, for the American does not recognize the need of them as languages of communication. Still, knowledge of foreign languages is considered by him of great value for the training of the mind, especially for a more thorough comprehension of the mother tongue, although this is not attributed to the power of a special formative and logical training as it was formerly in relation to Latin grammar. On the other hand, the comprehension of the German language is acknowledged as a means to a recognition of German science. While the committee in its general discussion emphasized more the pedagogical gain arising from the study of foreign tongues, in the details of its plan of study it points to this more practical aim. The report does not arrive at a complete equalization of these different aims.

The committee goes farthest in its recommendations concerning modern languages, the chairman designating this as most novel and striking. They are, that German or French be introduced as a regular study in the fifth school year, tenth year of age. The report adds that Latin would offer the same advantages, but living languages seemed more suitable for grammar schools, as the upper grades of the common schools are called.

The subcommittee on Latin considers it desirable to increase the demands in that study and regrets the fact that the study of Latin is commenced at a much earlier date in England, France, and Germany as compared with America. Still the committee thinks it undesirable to make a radical change, and is satisfied with the suggestion of beginning Latin one year earlier, devoting to it five hours per week. The committee on mathematics likewise advocates earlier occupation with geometry, and so, too, the committee on natural sciences claims several years for instruction in simple natural phenomena, in botany, zoology; and again, the committee on history calls for two years of study in history, American and universal history.

Ernst Schlee, "The Latest Movements in Education in the United States," in *Report of the Commissioner of Education, 1896–97*, (Washington, D.C.: U.S. Government Printing Office, 1898), I, 178–185.

The question arises whether all these proposals can be united within the limits of the common school system. Doubtless some changes might be introduced in the grammar school easily without doing violence to its character as a common school. For instance, concrete geometry may be added to mathematics; that is, the introduction to the study of geometry by means of the senses and with the aid of drawing, measuring, without formal proof. Instruction in natural sciences may also be limited to a discussion of important phenomena, animals, and plants. But the unity of the system becomes questionable when instruction in modern tongues as an optional branch is introduced; still more by the introduction of Latin, ancient history, and algebra as optional branches. These subjects should become compulsory branches during the last year's course of the elementary school. It is true ancient history does not seem as necessary for the Americans as it is for the Germans, because they have no history of the Middle Ages of their own, although their language and literature have borrowed much more from antiquity than we have. Consider the many antique proper names in America, as for instance, Athens, Sparta, Ithaca, Cincinnati, Capitol, etc. A connected history of classic antiquity is not related to the general culture of the people, and receives its value only in connection with higher education. And yet there is a proposition to teach Latin one or possibly two years in the elementary school. The subcommittee for instruction in Latin and the entire committee of ten leave this point somewhat unexplained and merely propose an earlier beginning, while at the same time offering suggestions tending to make the former non-active.

In contradistinction, the committee of fifteen takes up Latin, with five lessons per week during the last school year of the course of the elementary school, and at the same time definitely adheres to the principle that the instruction for boys and girls should be precisely the same to the fourteenth year of age. This committee expects much from these weak beginnings in Latin, which are not continued, as it also does of algebra. Quite contrary to the sometimes excessive demand, heard in Germany also, for a definite conclusion and finish of the elementary education, the committee is of the opinion that a brief instruction in secondary subjects, like Latin and algebra, has a higher value than any elementary branch that might be substituted for them. Especially a year's instruction in Latin would place a pupil far above those who only studied English grammar, without Latin, for the beginning of any branch (discipline) lays special weight upon its fundamental ideas. During the first week of Latin lessons, the pupil is made acquainted with the remarkable phenomenon that a language can express by declensions and conjugations what his mother tongue does by means of prepositions and auxiliaries (English: to him, Latin: ei). He learns with astonishment that quite a different order of the words in syntax is to be followed, and that root words have still a concrete meaning, while the same words or their derivations in the mother tongue are abstract. These observations are mental germs, which grow and result in a better mastering of the mother tongue. Similarly the result of studying the elements of algebra are judged. For a young philosopher this might be found true, but for the majority of elementary pupils they are imaginings devoid of substance.

In this question we may see the pivotal point of the whole present educational movement in America. The weakness of secondary education is correctly recognized. The attempt ought to be made to begin earlier with foreign languages and mathematics, but any attempt to fit this plan for the entire common school, which naturally finds much opposition in America, must miscarry. Moreover, since the grammar school in the South and everywhere in rural districts closes with the sixth school year, America will have to follow the example of all other civilized countries and allow the high school and the elementary school to go side by side for a number of years. The propositions of the committee of fifteen, compared with those of the committee of ten, appear to us as a step backward. . . .

With reference to the organic connection between the high school, college, and university, the committe of ten entertains the opinion, based upon actual conditions, that the course of study should be arranged essentially for those boys and girls who do not intend to continue their studies in a higher seat of learning; that is to say, those who do not intend to enter the college, and that a preparation for higher education could only be a secondary object of the high school. But starting from the theoretic presupposition that the chief branches, if treated thoroughly, are, as regards their formative power, of equal value for admission to college, the committee considers it right that the colleges make special conditions regarding the extent and duration of school studies and require proofs as the committee on English, for instance, does by demanding that no pupil be admitted to college who can not write good English. But on the whole the committee seems to favor the suggestion that a satisfactory graduation from a four years' course be considered a suitable preparation for college or any other scientific institution. In other words, that the examination for graduation in the high school do away with an examination for admission to college; and the committee considers this profitable for the schools, colleges, and the entire country.

The subcommittees of the committee of ten express themselves in detail concerning the method of instruction. Their reports show that pedagogical theory in the United States is everywhere abreast with the present status of science, and that it is very familiar with German pedagogy and psychology from Pestalozzi to Wundt. Although the statements do not bear the character of borrowed thought, but appear to have been thought out independently, still special portions bear a very familiar face; thus, for instance, when the committee on history speaks of political economy (Volkswirtschaftslehre). There is not another question in which the persons consulted show a greater variety of opinion. Some distinguished superintendents and principals wish to have this branch taught during the last year of the high school course; some even demand daily instruction for twelve weeks, other teachers declare that there is no place for that branch in the secondary school. Under the circumstances the committee thought it wise not to recommend formal instruction in political economy, but that the most important principles be presented in connection with the history of the United States and commercial geography. The subject would therefore appear first in its most elementary features during the third year of the grammar school, and then again during the last two years of the high school. It would appear not as a special science, but as an explanation of conditions of the commonwealth and of political questions.

Observe this passage concerning the mother tongue: "Both with reference to the high school and the lower schools, the committees declare that every teacher, in whatever branch he may instruct, must consider himself responsible for the use of good English on the part of his pupils." Similar to the committee on natural science, the committee on history emphasizes the necessity of written accounts, narrations, and other compositions; and if the propositions of the nine committees

become realities there would be at least one written composition daily for every pupil, which, in the interest of good English, is important.

In the face of the method of instruction in vogue in America it is particularly remarkable that all these committees consider the acquisition of mere knowledge not the aim of education, but the development of the mental powers and comprehension, exercises in observing, developing thought and expression. For this reason the various committees intend to limit the use of the text-book method and recommend its exclusion from grammar schools in studies like grammar, mathematics, and natural sciences. This method may be explained as follows: The text-book or guide is first studied, i.e., memorized by the pupil, mostly in school in so-called study lessons, and then the teacher asks for the contents of the lesson during recitations. While this reciting is going on he explains, corrects, and enlarges the matter as occasion demands. The committee of fifteen (whose report on method of instruction, written by Dr. Harris, takes its stand more on the solid ground of existing circumstances, not merely from necessity, but also from appreciation of these circumstances) gives special instruction for the treatment of this method, and recommends, for instance, the dividing each class into two divisions, so that the one study (memorize) while the other recite. The committee of ten, however, and especially its subcommittees, make oral lessons—that is, free instruction by the teacher—everywhere the principal thing. They wish that the teacher lead the child to observe and to start from observation and experience. In the interest of geography and natural sciences they recommend that one afternoon per week be utilized for excursions into the open air, and they suggest the utilization of the free Saturdays for exercise in natural-science laboratories. They further recommend more extensive equipment of the schools with means of instruction, more drawing wherever possible, and not merely means of demonstration for the teacher, but also means for the exercise of the pupils. Special subcommittees present a methodical order of experiments, 57 for the instruction in physics and 100 for chemistry.

However, for all this teachers are necessary, and these are found in few schools. The committee of ten, and almost all its subcommittees, point to this great want and make recommendations for the preparation of suitable teachers. The committee on geography, which furnished the most extensive report, recommends a course very much in harmony with the new Herbartians (for instance, Frick), namely, to make geography a central branch and not to restrict it to a mere description of the surface of the earth, but include in it the elements of botany, zoology, astronomy, and meteorology, with all sorts of discussions concerning commerce, politics, ethnology, etc., and this commission submits a course like the one treated with us only in its first beginnings. The committee of ten designates these propositions as revolutionary, although as an ideal course which it is impossible to carry out everywhere and immediately.

We give about the same criticism to the reports concerning instruction in the sciences, including history. Some of the propositions betray that they are put forward by academic professors whose judgment is not guided by pedagogical experience; for instance, when we see that for botanical instruction in the elementary school it is proposed to furnish every pupil with at least a microscope, alcohol, glycerin, and iodine to aid his investigations of plants; or when we see the pupils of the senior high school class instructed to judge the authority of sources, especially the difference between real sources and representations at second hand; or when it is seriously recommended to allow the pupils of the same class in history to use two, three, or four parallel textbooks for the purpose of accustoming them to comparison and criticism.

However, these little things do not detract from the value of the whole. The report of the committee of ten has for America the importance of an official pedagogy, scientifically progressive and professional, which will exercise an important influence upon the American school for a number of years.

And now to the committee of fifteen. For the purpose of continuing its reform propositions, the National Education Association in 1894 appointed another commission, this time of fifteen men, who should solve the same problem for the elementary school, and sketch the principles of municipal school management, and make suggestions for professional preparation of teachers.* To facilitate the work, this commission was divided into three sections, each of five members. Following the example of the committee of ten, they put themselves in communication with all parts of the country by submitting

a number of questions to many learned men and educators, and calling for expressions of opinion.

It is not necessary to enter into the reports on the two subjects mentioned last, however important they may be for America, since they are closely connected with public institutions differing from ours. It may be remarked though that the proposals for school management intend to serve reform by making the municipal school commissions independent of political influence by means of appointment instead of election. This will increase the independence and responsibility of the school superintendent. The last question, the one concerning preparation of teachers, is perhaps the most urgent one in the United States, but its solution finds the greatest difficulties in the prevailing social conditions, which will wreck the suggestions, however logical they may be. They are, that the general education of teachers, male and female, should be four years in advance of the course of the school in which they instruct; hence that elementary teachers should have graduated from the high school, and teachers of secondary schools have passed through college; besides, that both should have pursued a partly theoretical and partly practical course of pedagogy in a normal school.

More important by far is the first of the three problems, and the report concerning it has all the more interest to us, inasmuch as it is composed by Dr. Harris, the present Commissioner of Education. We have touched upon the report in previous pages.

Its peculiar importance may be found in the fact that it has caused a commotion in the educational world of America such as has never been witnessed before. The department of school superintendence had proposed the subject, "Correlation of studies in elementary schools." This term is of doubtful meaning—at any rate, its meaning is disputed in America—more so than with us the term "concentration in instruction," a term that is used with more different interpretations by our new Herbartians (Ziller, Stoy, Kern, Dillmann, Frick) than by Herbart himself, who meant it to be a connection of the entire instruction for systematic training of the soul of the pupil. In the department of superintendence, however (as is seen from the meeting of the department at Cleveland, February 19 to 21, 1895), it seemed to have been the intention to call for a report upon the different kinds of concentration and a general application of Herbartian principles to courses of study and methods of instruction. One is all

---

*Their report was presented in 1895.

the more induced to think so since not only the committee of ten, but also the subcommittees on history, geography, and natural sciences had expressed themselves quite in the sense of the new Herbartian school, and had especially suggested a combination of related branches in instruction. They had not only used the expression "association," which was plain enough, but had also used the word "correlation." We quote from page 16: "While these nine conferences desire each their own subject to be brought into the course of elementary schools, they all agree that these different subjects should be correlated and associated one with another by the programme and by actual teaching; that every subject recommended for introduction into elementary and secondary schools should help every other, and that the teacher of each single subject should feel responsible for the advancement of the pupils in all subjects, and should distinctly contribute to this advancement." The report was expected to solve the same problem which Frick had attempted to solve in the meeting of principals of the Province of Saxony in the year 1883.

But Dr. Harris, on the whole, belongs to a conservative class of men. His scientific learning is not so much toward the natural-scientific as it is toward the historic-philologic direction. The analysis of definitions forms with him the starting point of investigation, and in the development of his course for the elementary school he does not hesitate to go back to Charlemagne's trivium and quadrivium. He can not be counted among the representatives of the grammatical specialists, since he knows how to value a correct realistic instruction and does not try to make grammar a favorite factor in the so-called formal training. Yet he stands on the philologic side of the question, and regards language as the center of instruction in elementary schools. He may have been induced to emphasize this more particularly, since in public education in America the interest in natural sciences predominates, which may be seen from the fact that the pedagogical influence of Preyer finds much applause. We may also add that Dr. Harris is a Hegelian and, particularly in psychology, an opponent of Herbart. Finally, a misunderstanding added to the agitation, for he did not use the term "correlation of studies" in the sense in which it was used in the questions submitted. In short, he did not, as was expected by a number of educators, furnish an essay concerning the proper relation of branches in the course of study. In his fine and well-weighed manner he enters upon the order in which the branches should enter the course in harmony with the development of the pupil. He then explains more particularly what Stoy designates as "statics of instruction;" that is to say, the selection and amount which would promote an all-sided harmonious development of the mental powers and interests, and how a course of study should be framed to introduce the pupil into the totality of human knowledge of the present day, and prepare him for the practical demands of the world in which he is to live.

However well this may have been thought out, there is much abstract deduction without actuality in it. The kind of correlation of studies which many had thought of he merely touches by characterizing and rejecting the artificial combination of instruction in "Gesinnungs- und Kulturstufenstoff," rejected by the American Herbartians, as is done by our modern Herbartians in Germany, and he did it in referring to Ziller's example of Robinson Crusoe. To combat the perversity of artificial concentration was wise and proper, especially the mixing up of the branches of study, which is found in Germany here and there trumped up in model lessons in which essentials are torn apart and thrown aside in order to make excursions into other fields. But Dr. Harris not only neglected to point out the correct method of association and concentration, but also failed to show the establishment of centers and unities within each branch of study by means of selection and grouping; nor did he touch upon the assistance of the various branches to one another by means of suitable reading matter and drawing; nor did he suggest a method of comprehensive relation of knowledge, but he provoked his opponents by placing his views, which are correct enough, to be sure, in direct contradistinction to the endeavors of the Herbartians. In place of concentration he advocated, especially for the beginning of instruction, the principle of analysis and isolation, so that everything individual and characteristic found in any branch of study should be clearly comprehended and become effective. While on the other side, in exaggeration of a correct idea, the study of the child's soul is made the basis of the whole science of pedagogy, Harris emphasizes sharply that it is not the psychology and the physiology of brain cells which determine the kind and extent of the branches taught, but the demands of the civilization in which the child is born, so that it be enabled to perform its duties in the family, in civil society, in state, and church. The method of instruction is to him a secondary consideration, and for external matters each science will suggest its own directions.

The consequence was that after the report was read in Cleveland February 19 to 21, 1895, the debate disclosed an almost universal and violent opposition. However, the study of educational questions, especially the Herbartian pedagogy in America, has received a stronger impetus than it would have received if the report had represented Herbart's views. According to information received from an American educator, there have never been such animated discussions in the educational world in America as at present. The United States, it is said, resembles a hotbed of pedagogical discussion, over which the gods must rejoice.

Harvard College Annual Report   1900
Expedition of Cuban Teachers to Harvard

Two Harvard graduates, Ernest Lee Conant (1884) and Alexis E. Frye (1890), were residing in Havana, Cuba, after the end of the Spanish-American War in 1898. Frye was the military-appointed superintendent of schools for Cuba, and Conant was practicing law in Havana. Together they conceived the notion of sending Cuban teachers to a summer school at Harvard University and wrote to Harvard President Charles W. Eliot requesting that the teachers be permitted to attend the Harvard summer school for six weeks. The university authorities agreed to the plan, and the Harvard summer school in 1900 became the first and certainly the largest summer school for foreign students ever seen in the United States. The program catered to over 1200 Cuban teachers and represented a unique American experiment in international education unparalleled for half a century.

Requesting Permission for the Expedition

> *Headquarters Division of Cuba*
> *Habana*
> *February 6, 1900*

President Charles W. Eliot
Cambridge, Mass.

Dear President Eliot: We are planning to carry as many Cuban teachers as possible (perhaps 1,000 or more) to the United States next summer, and as alumni of old Harvard and with the firm belief that our alma mater offers the best facilities, we naturally turn to her for help.

These teachers will have for their object hard study as well as a tour of observation through our country. The general plan will be as follows: The party will leave Cuba on Government transports or on chartered steamers about the last of June. It is our wish that the steamers may land us directly in Boston, and that the teachers may attend the Harvard summer school for six weeks.

The next four weeks will then be given to travel and visits to the great cities, perhaps crossing the continent to San Francisco. We are sure that this brief outline will tell you the whole story. You can readily see what tremendous results would follow with 1,000 intelligent men and women (after such a broadening experience) scattered over the island . . .

Of course the one great item is expense. Can it not be arranged so that the instruction for six weeks at Harvard shall be free? With this as a starting point, we shall organize a committee in Cambridge and Boston with a view to securing free accommodation in homes during the six weeks. We shall ask various cities to plan temporary entertainment. If we cannot secure government transports, it may be possible to secure some appropriation in the island to pay the cost of steamer travel. The teachers are poor; they need this summer's outing and work. They need it for themselves and they need it for the sake of our own country.

The school laws of Cuba (see article 23 of decree sent you) require courses of summer

---

"Expedition of Cuban Teachers to Cambridge, Massachusetts," from the annual reports of the president and treasurer of Harvard College, 1899-1900, pp. 36-49; the extract is taken from *Report of the Commissioner of Education, 1899-1900* (Washington, D.C.: U.S. Government Printing Office, 1901), II, 1378-1385.

*study from the teachers. This will be one of
the great means of educating teachers now in
the schoolroom and who cannot attend normal
schools. Many of these teachers lack even the
elements of education; many of them have
hardly been beyond the limits of their own
towns. We can not carry normal schools to
every town and city; but we can carry the
teachers to educational institutions, and we
want the best, namely, Harvard. We want the
teachers to breathe the atmosphere of the
greatest school in America. We want them to
feel the history and associations, to enjoy the
facilities of libraries and laboratories. We
want them to come in contact, not only with
the strong minds of the professors, but also
with hundreds of the brightest and best teachers in America who will this summer be in
Cambridge. We want these teachers to have
the culture that comes from travel; we want
them to carry this culture back into the Cuban
homes and the Cuban schools. We want these
teachers to know our country, to know our
people. We want the ties between the two
countries drawn closer, so that all feeling of
antagonism may melt away, in order that our
country may do a higher and better work for
Cuba . . . .*

*Of course we know that the work ordinarily
done in the Harvard summer school would
need to be adapted to the teachers of Cuba.
The work is of too high a grade in general,
and the subjects as a whole are such as are
not taught in the public schools of Cuba. Without interfering in the slightest degree with
the summer school, could you not plan a
parallel school with a course specially fitted
to the needs of the Cuban teachers? More
than nine-tenths of these teachers can neither speak nor understand English. There are
enough, however, with a knowledge of English
to form a medium for transmitting the work
of the summer school to the others. . . .*

*As soon as we know whether Harvard Uni-
versity will extend this invitation and will do
this grand work we will bend every energy to
complete the plans, and we shall succeed. We
have submitted the proposition to General
Wood, and it goes almost without saying that
he will give his powerful support to the movement.*

Sincerely yours,

               ERNEST L. CONANT
               ALEXIS E. FRYE

Approval of the Plan

This letter, which was received in Cambridge on the 12th of February, was considered on the 13th at a special meeting of
the president and fellows; and the president
was then authorized to reply in the affirmative, if General Wood favored the plan. A
few days afterwards a telegram was received from General Wood strongly indorsing
the project, whereupon the following telegram
was sent to Superintendent Frye: "Frye,
Habana. Yes. Eliot." Notices of the project
and of the affirmative answer of Harvard were
thereupon published in the Cuban newspapers,
and an active discussion immediately arose
as to the feasibility of the plan. It was
contended that it would be impossible for
young women to go on such an expedition,
in violation of the social habits of the Cuban
people; the Catholic Church in some places
manifested opposition to the project; and at
first the general sentiment of the people
seemed to be adverse. Superintendent Frye
was at some disadvantage, because he had not
traveled over the island, and was personally
known in Habana and the immediate neighborhood only. Nevertheless, in the course of a
month it became evident that there was so
much interest in the project that it was expedient to devise the arrangements for the
expedition in detail, and to announce them as
soon as possible. Thereupon, Mr. Frye
visited Washington and Cambridge about the
1st of April. In Washington he secured the
cordial cooperation of Secretary Root, who
subsequently expressed his approval in a
cordial letter to President Eliot, dated May 8.

Subscriptions for the Cuban Summer School

When Mr. Frye began to discuss the details of the expedition with the Harvard
authorities, it soon appeared that the university would really become responsible for
the health and safety of the members of the
expedition while in Cambridge, and that it
would, therefore, be expedient for the university to supervise the lodging, feeding,
and protecting of the members of the expedition during the six weeks of their stay there.
It also appeared that the regular summer
school would not be suitable for the Cuban
teachers, and that special courses of instruction would be needed. Thereupon, a public
meeting was held in Boston to describe the
objects of the proposed expedition and call
attention to them; and a circular was issued
by the president and fellows of Harvard
College asking the community for the means
of paying all the expenses of the expedition
too far from the yard. It was necessary to

during its six weeks in Cambridge, including board, lodging, instruction, excursions, and entertainments. Subscriptions began to come in before the end of April, and continued to flow in until the middle of August. The sum asked for was $70,000; and that sum was ultimately provided, and a little more, the total subscribed being $71,145.33.

The subscription list is an interesting one because of the large number and the variety of persons who took part in it. It was emphatically a popular subscription, and represented all classes of the community. Very little personal solicitation was necessary. The circular was distributed widely, and the newspapers from time to time called attention to the state of the subscription. One large contribution came by order of the court from the unused balance of the fund raised near the outbreak of the war with Spain to provide means of caring for the sick and wounded among the troops in Cuba (the volunteer aid fund). When this fund was distributed in accordance with the order of the court $20,000 of it came to the subscription for the Cuban teachers.

Plan of Instruction

The plan for the instruction comprehended (1) two lessons a day in English; (2) a course of eighteen lectures in Spanish on physiography, illustrated by as many excursions to different points of geographical interest in the neighborhood of Boston; (3) two courses of lectures in Spanish on historical subjects— one on the history of the United States, the other on the history of the Spanish colonies in North and South America; and (4) lectures on free libraries, on the organization of the American schools, and on imitation and allied faculties in children. Through special gifts received from Mrs. Quincy A. Shaw, a course of illustrated lectures on the kindergarten was provided for the Cuban women teachers, and a workshop course on American sloid for a selected number of Cuban men. Laboratory instruction in physiography being out of the question for so large a number of persons, field study was adopted as the best substitute. The instruction in English was to be given in 40 sections—20 for men, and 20 for women. The teachers selected for these sections were in general young graduates and undergraduates of Harvard College and Radcliffe College. Each teacher of English was to give two lessons a day to his or her section—one from 8 o'clock till a quarter before 9, and

the other from half past 11 till 12. The lectures were all to come between these two English lessons, and no lesson or lecture was to be more than three-quarters of an hour long. Sanders Theater was to be used for all the lectures; and the English lessons were to be given in 40 rooms, all of which were in the college yard. The afternoons were to be devoted to excursions, each Cuban teacher being provided with at least three excursions each week. Sundays and evenings were to be left free.

Arrangements in Cuba and in Cambridge

On the 16th of May a circular was issued by Superintendent Frye in Habana, setting forth the project as fully as was then possible, giving all details concerning the transportation of the teachers to Boston on Government steamers, describing the arrangements made in Cambridge for the accommodation of the visiting teachers and the probable advantages of the trip. The circular also gave instructions concerning clothing, baggage, medical attendance, health certificates, vaccination, and other details. The university had limited the number of Cuban teachers to 1,450, which is the capacity of its largest lecture room, Sanders Theater. Moreover, the two dining halls would not accommodate well more than 1,450 persons in addition to the regular summer school. Superintendent Frye was therefore obliged to provide means of selecting these 1,450 persons from the 3,500 teachers who were already at work in the public schools of Cuba. The selections were made by Cuban authorities exclusively—in general by the school boards already established all over the island. As soon as Superintendent Frye's circular had been distributed through the Cuban towns and villages, the work of selection began.

In the meantime, the following arrangements had been made in Cambridge: Students occupying rooms in college dormitories offered their rooms in sufficient number to accommodate all the Cuban men teachers. Rooms enough were then engaged in houses within half a mile of University Hall to accommodate all the women teachers in groups of from 8 to 16 in a house. Each householder undertook, for a price agreed upon, to receive a certain number of teachers, provide them with furnished rooms, and give them a simple breakfast. The use of three houses was given without rent; and several others were offered but not accepted because they were engage a business agent who should have charge of all the arrangements for the accommodation of the visitors in Cambridge; and his first task was to provide rooms for the women teachers. Since many of the students who offered their rooms in college dormitories were unwilling that their beds, linen, and blankets should be used, it was necessary to hire these articles in large quantity for six weeks' use. It was decided that the Cuban women should eat their luncheons and dinners in Memorial Hall, the capacity of which is 756 seats; and that the men teachers should eat all their meals in Randall Hall, a portion of that hall, however, being reserved for the regular summer school, which consists of both men and women, the women being in the majority. In both halls the Cuban teachers were to be provided with a bill of fare for each meal arranged by the steward, and every teacher was to take whatever he or she wanted from that bill of fare. In Randall Hall, the members of the regular summer school followed the ordinary rule of that hall, which is to order by the plate and pay for exactly what is ordered. Two methods were in use, therefore, at every meal in Randall Hall—one for the Cubans, the other for the American summer school.

By the end of June the business manager, Mr. Clarence C. Mann (A. B., Harv., 1899) had completed his arrangements, and had opened an office in Holden Chapel as headquarters for information—in fact, for all the business of the expedition. He had also engaged about twenty chaperons to live in or near the houses in which the women were lodged, and a large number of clerks and guides, most of whom were Harvard students in the law school, the college, and the scientific school. All the chaperons, and most of the guides, spoke some Spanish. In addition, a few interpreters were employed. Subsequently it became necessary to engage an additional number of chaperons. These ladies lived in the houses with the Cuban women teachers, ate with them at Memorial Hall, helped them with their English lessons, went shopping with them, adjusted their difficulties, attended to their ailments, tried to prevent overwork and overexcitement, directed them gently, and befriended them heartily. The success of the expedition, so far as the women teachers were concerned, was largely due to these ladies.

The Embarkation and Voyage

The embarkation of the Cuban teachers took place at 14 different ports on the north and south sides of the island, and began on the 22d of June. Some of the teachers from inland towns were as much as a week in getting from their homes to their ports of embarkation, such are the difficulties of travel in inland Cuba. Some of the transports touched at four ports, others at but two. On one transport only women embarked; on another only men; on the other three came both men and women. The vessels, being intended for the transportation of troops and supplies, had to be especially fitted up to their new function, and even then they were far from providing the ordinary comforts of ocean liners. Fortunately, the sea was smooth, and the weather fine, though hot. Up to the last moment there was grave doubt how many teachers would actually sail on the five transports. A printed list prepared in Secretary Frye's office in Habana about the middle of June contained the names of 1,397 persons; but nobody felt sure that all these persons would actually embark. The first positive statement of the number of persons to be entertained at the university came by telegram from General Wood as follows:

H Habana, June 29, 1900—2.19 p.m.

President Eliot, Harvard, Boston:
    Transports left Cuba as follows. . . .June 25, McPherson from Gibara, 110 males, 96 females; total 206. . . .June 26, Crook from Matanzas, 295 males. . . .June 26, Buford from Cienfuegos, 51 males, 67 females; total 118. . . .June 28, Sedwick from Sagua la Grande, 428 females. Total 1,047 so far. McClellan leaves from Nuevitas. As soon as her departure is reported will wire you.

                    WOOD

Habana, June 30, 1900—11.56 a.m.

President Eliot, Harvard, Boston:
    In addition to my telegram of yesterday, McClellan left from Nuevitas 29th with 156 males, 70 females; total 226. . . .Total teachers sailed to date, 612 males, 661 females; total 1,273.

                    WOOD

The expedition was, then, 177 persons short of the maximum number named by the university; but in a country where the means of communication are few and difficult it was a remarkable feat to get 1,273 teachers on board the transports within six weeks of the issuing of the first circular letter of instructions from Superintendent Frye's office.

The Arrival at Cambridge

The first transport reached Boston rather earlier than was expected, on the afternoon of June 30, and the last arrived on Wednesday, July 4. The transports landed their passengers at the navy-yard where excellent arrangements were made to prevent the intrusion of any inconvenient public. With the aid of two Spanish-speaking guides in each car, the transportation of the teachers to Memorial Hall in Cambridge was managed rapidly and safely. Other guides had charge of the transportation of the baggage and its distribution in Cambridge. At Memorial Hall each teacher received a pin bearing a number, by which number the teacher was thereafter to be recognized as a member of the expedition. At the same time each teacher received a map on which were marked all the college buildings and all the houses in which any Cuban teachers were to live. An excellent map of the vicinity of Boston, furnished by the Appalachian Mountain Club, was also placed in each teacher's hands, and, finally, a table in Spanish of all the lessons, lectures, and excursions of the first half week, arranged by days and hours. By the employment of thirty or forty messengers and guides, most of whom could speak some Spanish, the distribution of the teachers to their several quarters was accomplished with reasonable dispatch. At first it was necessary to conduct the teachers—especially the women—from their rooms to the dining halls and to Sanders Theater, but in a day or two they learned the way.

Hospitalities and Excursions

The first lesson was given on the morning of Thursday, July 5, when the division of the whole body into 40 sections was made at Memorial Hall, and each section was guided from the hall to the recitation room which that section was to occupy throughout the six weeks. The first excursion, which started on Thursday afternoon, labored of course under some difficulties, because the meeting places were unfamiliar and most of the teachers knew nothing about electric cars, but in two days the whole machinery of the Cuban school was in operation, and thereafter it ran with remarkable smoothness. The excursions were of three kinds: The geographical excursions, which formed a portion of the instruction in geography; the excursions to several characteristic manufacturing establishments, and the excursions of a social nature. Only one of these last was provided by the university,

but there were many others that were arranged by private persons.

The Catholic societies of Boston and Cambridge had made arrangements, with the cooperation of the university, to offer to the Cuban teachers facilities for reading and writing in rooms provided by the university within the college yard. For the men, Harvard 1 was devoted to this purpose; for the women, rooms in Phillips Brooks House. In both places the Catholic societies kept their representatives throughout the day and evening, and were enabled to show the Cubans very acceptable hospitality. The Catholic societies also gave two concert dances each week for the Cuban teachers in the Hemenway Gymnasium and took all the responsibility for the management of these entertainments. Three concerts, which were very largely attended and were much enjoyed, were given in Sanders Theater—one by the Baptist societies of Cambridge, one by the Catholic societies, and one by the Cubans themselves. Each week a programme in Spanish was issued, in which all the lessons or lectures and all the excursions were carefully described, and the numbers assigned to each excursion were given.

At the Catholic church on Holyoke street, St. Paul's, special services were held for the benefit of the Cuban visitors throughout their stay, and these services were well attended. Through the good offices of Archbishop Williams, Father Fidelis, a graduate of Harvard College in 1861, who had become familiar with the Spanish language through long residence in South America, was brought to Cambridge for the express purpose of attending to the religious wants of the visiting Catholics.

The attendance at the English lessons was excellent, hundreds of the teachers being very regular in their attendance. At the lectures in Spanish in Sanders Theater the attendance was not so good, and yet it was creditable, particularly at the lectures on physiography, which were handsomely illustrated by means of lantern slides. The lessons in sloyd were followed eagerly; and the kindergarten lessons were well attended, considering that hours could not be found for all of them which were altogether free from other appointments. The attendance at the excursions was about 60 per cent of the whole number of teachers. The weather was hot much of the time, and the Cubans were not accustomed to walking any distance. Those excursions which demanded much walking were not pleasurable for them, and were attended as a matter of duty.

Physique of the Visitors

The physique of the visitors necessarily attracted the immediate attention of those who were responsible for their welfare. The ages of the Cuban teachers ranged from 16 to 60, but the extremes were not numerously represented. The selecting bodies in Cuba had selected too many elderly people, who were, of course, incapable of learning English, or indeed of absorbing readily new ideas. About 10 per cent of the men were over 44 years of age, and about 10 per cent of the women were over 38. To the Cuban authorities, however, it may have seemed expedient to select for the excursion some persons of influence or high standing in their several communities, whose presence would be a safeguard for the younger members, and who would be able to impress their views on their own people after the return of the expedition. There at first seemed to be too large a proportion of delicate and feeble persons, but the very favorable physical experience of the expedition shows that this feebleness was more apparent than real. . . . Physically the Cuban women seemed decidedly superior as women to the Cuban men as men; and this appearance was borne out by the measurements taken by Dr. Sargent, the Cuban women comparing more favorably with the American women than the Cuban men with the American men. Most of the Cuban teachers gained steadily in weight while they were in Cambridge, and many returned to Cuba in a better condition of health than when they came thence. This gain of weight may have been due to the fact that they were much more active while in Cambridge than they are habitually in Cuba. The men had to walk to and from all their meals and to their language lessons and their lectures, and there was some walking on the excursions. The women walked from their rooms to luncheon and dinner and to their daily lessons and lectures, and many of them went on from two to three excursions per week. Going up and down stairs was also an unwonted exercise for most of the visiting teachers, rural Cuban houses being in general only one story in height.

Health and Conduct

Of the 1,273 members of the expedition, not one died during the entire absence of the expedition from Cuba; and when the transports landed their passengers at the 14 ports from which they had taken them every person was able to walk ashore. There was no serious accident to any member of the expedition. The health and safety record is certainly remarkable, considering the strong climatic change which the whole expedition had undergone, and the unwonted fatigues and exposures of their life in Cambridge and during the fortnight of travel which succeeded their stay in Cambridge.

With the rarest exceptions the Cuban teachers were habitually gentle and polite to each other and to all the Americans who were brought in contact with them. The men gave no trouble whatever in the College dormitories, and both men and women were neat in their persons and tidy in the dining halls. The men smoked incessantly. Only very few of the women smoked at all, and those in private.

What the Cubans Learned

The chief result of the expedition was the opening of the minds of these 1,300 intelligent people to a flood of new observations and new ideas. There was a great diversity among them as regards education and capacity. As General Wood said in a letter written from Habana on the 24th of February to Maj. Henry L. Higginson, "You will find all classes among them, from the highly educated to those of very limited education, but they are all enthusiastically interested in educational matters, and to these people and to the children they are teaching we must look for the Cuba we hope to build up. These men and women will come back to Cuba with very many new ideas and very much better fitted to teach." A fair proportion of them learned much English and got a new conception of science and history teaching, but many of them were too old to learn a new language, or, indeed, to acquire much intellectual training of any sort, yet all saw with their eyes the American ways of living and the outside, at least, of many American institutions, such as schools, hospitals, asylums, libraries, churches, and theaters. They made two voyages on the ocean; they had a hasty view of New York, Philadelphia, and Washington; they caught a glimpse of the country on their rides through New Jersey, Pennsylvania, and Maryland, and they became well acquainted with Cambridge and the neighborhood of Boston, from Marblehead on the one side to Point Allerton and Nantasket on the other. They came in contact with a considerable number of American educated young people and found them serviceable, cordial, and friendly. When the expedition was about to leave Cambridge for the fortnight's journey, the Cubans wished to have the young men who had worked for them and with them in Cambridge accompany them on their journey, and Superintendent Frye so arranged it; and it was with real regret that the guides and the guided parted at Philadelphia, whence the transports sailed for Cuba.

It is to be observed that the men and women who did the real work for the Cubans in Cambridge were for the most part decidedly young in years—most of them were from 19 to 24 years of age. These young people worked with zeal and energy in a long-sustained, alert care taking. On some occasions the clerks and guides worked all night without relaxing the labors of the day, and this in unusually hot weather.

The Expense Account

The expedition spent six weeks and a half in Cambridge; and the total cost, including instruction, entertainment, board and lodging, transportation on excursions, medical care, and the cost of clerks, guides, chaperons, and interpreters, was $68,105. A balance of about $3,000 still remains of the money raised by subscription. If, however, the full number of 1,450 had reached Cambridge, the money raised would hardly have sufficed. The details of the expense account include some curious particulars. Thus, the women in Memorial Hall, with their chaperons, cost fully 25 per cent more than the men in Randall Hall, although they took but two meals in Memorial Hall while the men took three in Randall. The numbers in the two halls were about 700 in Memorial and 600 in Randall. The medical care cost over a thousand dollars, although there was no case of very serious illness, and in spite of the fact that three Cuban physicians accompanied the expedition, whose services were always at the disposition of the sick. For the better treatment of slight indispositions it was found desirable, before half the stay of the expedition in Cambridge was over, to hire a house as an infirmary, and to provide the patients with a resident woman physician and a trained nurse. The lodging of the women in private houses cost more than twice as much as the lodging of the men in the college dormitories, because the students gave the use of their rooms, whereas the Cuban women's rooms had all to be paid for. One month's salary was paid to the Cuban

public school-teachers while they were in Cambridge. There were 1,181 of them, the remaining 92 being teachers in the University of Habana and the institutes, private school-teachers, and Cuban chaperons and interpreters, together with three physicians and two priests. The bursar paid with perfect precision these 1,181 persons $60,257.70 in a little over two hours. In order to offer safe-keeping for the moneys which might be in the possession of the Cuban teachers, the university proposed to receive temporary deposits of money, to be returned to the depositor on demand. This offer was an expedient one; but the Cuban teachers did not avail themselves of it, only $485.50 being deposited by them during their stay in Cambridge. The Cuban teachers paid for the two books which were used in the English courses, and for their own laundry work; they rode to and from Boston on their own errands at their own cost; but all their other expenses were paid from the subscription so long as they were in Cambridge.

The visitors expressed very warmly, both in public and in private, their sense of obligation for the hospitality they enjoyed at the university, and for the educational and social privileges which had been provided for them. In general, they seemed interested and light hearted. The dining halls resounded with their rapid and lively talk during all the meals, and every evening after dinner the women lingered long in the vestibule of Memorial Hall, to which men were admitted. Nevertheless, there was a very pathetic side to the whole experience. Many of the members of the expedition had gone through severe sufferings and anxieties; they had lost friends and members of their own families in the long-continued fighting; they had been sick and half starved, and in all sorts of peril; and they were wholly uncertain concerning their means of livelihood, their appointments as teachers being but temporary, and expiring soon. The contrast between these experiences and their situation at Cambridge was sharp and profound; and then they were to return to their impoverished island, where both the industrial and the political situation are full of grave anxiety. None of them were sure of reappointment to their places as teachers; all were to be examined anew not later than December. In short, though the present was enjoyable, the future was anxious. It was natural that they should bid good-bye to prosperous and friendly Cambridge with mingled sentiments of gratitude, pleasure, and sadness.

R. E. Hughes

Halfway Education: Britain Between Germany and America

R. E. Hughes (1866–1924) was educated at Oxford and London Universities and was one of the earliest modern English educators to develop a comparative methodology in education. He attempted to apply this methodology scientifically to the study of various "systems of national education" and to "bring to bear upon educational statistics and reports, those principles of scientific evaluation which would be applied in such a study as comparative anatomy." His first book, *Schools at Home and Abroad,* published in 1902, provides the extract below on comparative education. His second book, published a year later, was directly couched in comparative terms and was aptly titled *The Making of Citizens: A Study in Comparative Education.*

That the amount of trained intellect, of skilled brain-power which a nation possesses is the only true measure of its power is beginning to be accepted.

Natural resources and hereditary aptitude will for a time compensate for a lack of this, but the danger is the more insidious flattering as it does national vanity and deluding into a false security. The commercial greatness of Germany to-day differs in this respect from that of America that it has been attained in a great measure despite natural obstacles. Our own commercial power like that of America is mainly due to natural resources and national aptitude. It is fortunate for us that a national characteristic, namely self-depreciation is crying aloud in pessimistic tones, and warning us of the dangerously false position we are in. It is not technical nor commercial education that we need as much as a better and more comprehensive scheme of national training. More skilled intellects prepared to take up this problem and that problem, not so much because a training in the solution of similar problems has been received but because the intellect has been trained to attack scientifically all problems.

The foundation stone of every system of national training is the school of the people, the primary school. Two nations by their commercial competition have been forcing the above truths home to us, and it is with the hope of learning other lessons from our rivals that this paper is written. It is not in any sense a comprehensive comparison, but rather a series of impressions gathered from many sources and placed in juxtaposition here.

In Germany to-day the "caste" feeling is acute, in England it is less so, in America it has, as a political force, disappeared. In Germany the Volksschule is, generally speaking, for one class only, the labouring class; in England the elementary school though originally designed for the poor is open to all, but utilised mainly by the labouring and lower middle classes; in America the common school is in theory for all classes, and in practice is largely attended by all classes.

In Germany primary education is partially free, in England entirely free, whilst in America not only is primary education free, but to a considerable extent secondary and academic are also free.

Lastly, private schools have almost entirely disappeared in Germany: as a matter of fact there are 404 private elementary schools in Prussia; in England as competitors of the elementary school they are moribund; in America they are flourishing.

German education though not so minutely organised as, say French education, is intensely bureaucratic. The State, through its officers trains, appoints, and pensions teachers, compels effectively every parent to send his child to school, prescribes the books to be used, sometimes proscribes methods, leaves to the locality but little of initiative or control, but to its servant the teacher secures a sound status and considerable freedom of method in carrying out a prescribed curriculum.

In the United States on the other hand the doctrine of individualism has been carried to its logical conclusion. The Federal Government has practically no control over the education of its future citizens. The sole function of the Federal Government is the annual publication of valuable reports, and the collection and publication of statistics which, owing to their voluntary nature, are incomplete.

Each state is a law unto itself in matters

R. E. Hughes, "The Halfway House: A Study in Comparative Education," *Schools at Home and Abroad* (New York: E. P. Dalton & Co., 1902), pp. 9-18, 20 – 23, 25 – 51.

educational, and within each state every variety of educational efficiency may be found. Here teachers are licensed to teach for one, there for three years; this town employs only "trained" teachers, that one employs the cheapest it can get (for example more than half the teachers in the State of Utah have received only an elementary school education). This city has at the head of its educational administration a pedagogue of international reputation, that one boasts of a gentleman who fills up the interstices of a busy life by "bossing" the schools. Beside some of the finest schools in the world are some of the poorest. There is an extraordinary variation in efficiency of American schools, less perhaps of English, and certainly still less of German schools. Public interest in education is much keener in Germany and America than in England. In America all classes are interested in education, in Germany the learned classes, in England—well, no class. It is no uncommon thing for audiences of a thousand or more to attend a course of lectures or a conference on educational topics in America.

People of wealth and social position often attend university lectures in Pedagogy. It is a significant fact that America and Germany have each over 250 educational periodicals, whereas I doubt if we support *one tenth* of that number at home. Again, some of the most interesting and pregnant work of the day is being worked out in American schools and colleges. Child study, the rational basis of any system of training, is gradually being monopolised by Americans, and in other directions American thought is leading the educational world.

That she means business is shown by the royal bounty of her wealthy sons, who, as a free-will offering to the good cause gave in one year, 1899, fourteen million pounds sterling for the better education of Columbia's children and young people. Even the gravest defects of American education, such as irregular attendance, etc., may have their compensation. In time, doubtless, the parent will voluntarily see the folly and extravagance of thwarting the training of his child, and such a time it may be said is worth waiting for. Germany with her magnificent system of school attendance has still to deplore the rapid rate at which so many of her children degenerate after leaving school into all the indifference of an uneducated class, whereas America can boast that despite their meagre equipment her children leave school with a keen desire for more education, which by means of newspapers, lectures, and courses, they are generally able to gratify.

In America every career is open to the enterprising youth, in Germany it is generally fixed for him when he is nine years old. The educational ladder is practically complete in America, in Germany it is almost unknown and until recently, undesired.

The German Kindergarten for children under six years of age is not encouraged by the state and receives no public assistance whatsoever. The German government evidently considers that a child should not attend school until he is six years old. Indeed, the vast majority of German children never do. It is only in a few of the larger cities that the Kindergarten is found. The State does not permit the Kindergarten to teach any of the subjects of the elementary school curriculum, and looks upon them merely as places where children are looked after. The fact that no certificate is required by the State to teach in a German Kindergarten, although required of family tutors and governesses, is significant of the attitude of the State. It would seem as if it had never recovered from its first suspicion of the Kindergarten as a godless institution.

Some of the finest Kindergartens in the world are to be found in America. The *principles* of Froebel and Herbart found a congenial soil in America. American ideas on education have been largely taken from Germany, but American ideals are of home manufacture, and the pedagogic world is the richer for it. Moreover, there is an admirable independence in the world of American pedagogy, so that though Froebel and Herbart are the sources, they are by no means the autocrats of the best American teaching. It is interesting to observe that the average German teacher, primary and secondary, has no superfluity of respect for the apostle of self-activity. The German secondary school teacher has sympathies more akin to those of the English public schoolmaster than to those of the American pedagogue.

The beginning of the American Kindergarten was due to the efforts of private individuals such as Miss Blow and Mrs. Quincy Shaw, and it was only after many years' successful work that these schools were taken over and extended by the local school boards. Many of these American Kindergartens are well built and nicely furnished. As in the German Kindergarten everything is done to make the place homelike and pleasant. The pictures on the walls are constantly changed

according to the season. A piano is always
provided. Each child has a small wicker chair
for himself, and the children are gathered,
about ten in number, around a table just as
they are in the German Kindergarten. In
St. Louis only two children sit at each table.
Each group of ten is a class, and there may
be two of these in a room. The American
Kindergartens are generally open for three
hours daily, in the morning only. The training of these city Kindergartens is admirable,
but the pity of it is there are so few of them.
There are practically none outside the larger
towns. Indeed there are only 4,363 Kindergartens in the States; these employ 8,937
teachers, and have 189,604 pupils out of a
total school population of fifteen million.
England with a school population of five and
a half million has two million children attending the infants' schools. The Kindergarten
as understood by Froebel and found in America
and Germany is rare in England. There are
signs of a considerable revolution taking
place in the curriculum and methods of the
English infants' schools, but whether these
will, or can, ever develop into real Kindergartens is a moot point. The English infant
school hitherto both in its methods and its
architecture has been modelled closely upon
the pattern of the elementary school.

Play-rooms are rarely provided. It would
seem no greater expense to build an alternat-
ing set of class-rooms and play-rooms as
is done in Antwerp, so that whilst one half
the children occupies the class-rooms the
other half occupies the play-rooms.

The English class is invariably too large,
and the training of the teacher in the principles
of the Kindergarten too fragmentary for the
real Kindergarten to flourish here, *at present.*
The fact is the Kindergarten is a most expensive system of training which only wealthy
bodies can undertake. Dr. Harris was able
at St. Louis to reduce the cost of the Kindergarten to a reasonable sum[1] by utilising the
gratuitous services of people anxious to make
themselves practically acquainted with the
details of the Kindergarten system.

Although English infant schools based on
the principles of the Kindergarten are few,
yet everything points to an increase. There is
a divine unrest apparent; the spirit is moving
on the waters. We have as a people recognised that these most impressionable and ac-
quisitive years of childhood should be utilised

for training. We alone of the three nations
have provided a system of training which, if
not pedagogically perfect, is at least comprehensive.

But it is in the primary schools—the people's schools that nations are made and
unmade. It was to the Volksschule that Bismarck credited Königgrätz, and it is in our
elementary schools, if anywhere, that imperial England will learn her trust and her
burden.

The German rural school is generally a
plain substantial building. It has one play-
ground for both sexes, which is often planted
with trees.

The building is of two storeys, the upper
one being the master's house. A school pump
in the playground is the only lavatory accommodation provided, and the cloakroom is represented by a series of hat pegs in the corridor and class-room.

These small one-class schools are worked
in three sections by the teacher, and the time-
table is so arranged that the oral lessons
are taken consecutively in each section.

The teacher is a civil servant; he has
absolute security of tenure and a relatively
good social position. His upbringing has generally been rural; one third of all German
primary teachers spring from the farming
class, so that his sympathies and tastes are
in harmony with his environment. Further, on
the whole he is relatively as well off as the
town teacher so that he feels quite content
with his position. But he *has* grievances,
and one of them is the serious under-staffing
of many German rural schools. A school of
90 to 100 children is not rare, and the
half-time school is a fairly regular feature
of many parts of rural Germany. The older
children come in the morning and the younger
in the afternoon, so that one teacher may have
from 100 to 150 pupils to deal with in one
day. The same institution flourishes in some
parts of America, and even the cities of New
York, Washington, and Minneapolis have had
to resort to it, owing to inadequate school
accommodation.

In 1896 there were in Prussia 92,001 full-
sized elementary classes but only 78,431
class-rooms for them. The remaining 13,570
had either to share a class-room or attend
half-day. For every 150 rural classes there
are only 100 class-rooms. Further 12,578
classes had no teacher of their own. Over six
hundred thousand Prussian children are
taught in half-day schools and nearly one
million in ungraded schools.

Nearly one and a half million Prussian

---

[1]Namely to about six dollars per child which is
much less than the cost per child of the city primary
school.

children are taught in overcrowded classes, though a class is not technically overcrowded until there are over 80 children in the rural and 70 children in the urban class to one teacher. In some cases as many as 170 children to one teacher are recorded. To give each class a teacher and to reduce each to its normal size of 70 or 80 children would necessitate the appointment of 20,000 more teachers.

Then one hears of the local managers in Germany fixing the hours of school meeting early in the morning or late in the evening, so that the daily labour of the children may not be unduly interfered with. In the States the same end is achieved by not opening the school at all during the period that child labour is serviceable. Another grievance of the German rural teacher is the question of extraneous duties which one fifth of all the teachers are called upon to perform.

The rural school is no more popular in Germany than in England. It is said that one of the sons of Prince Bismarck will not hear of the school teacher on his estate having a better house than an agricultural labourer. Herr von Below-Saleske declared that, "people don't need much school learning in order to grub potatoes." Herr von Helldorf thus summarised his educational programme: "I am not for teaching arithmetic to the agricultural labourer. It will only spoil him. He has got to lead horses and handle the plough, not figures."

So powerful is the Agrarian Party that the state has been compelled to allow boys of school age in East Prussia to leave school and serve as shepherds. The poet has expressed the American farmer's thought in words which appear to voice rural opinion all the world over:—

. . .There ain't no great good to be reached By tip-toein' children up higher than ever their fathers was teached.

The English rural school is perhaps as well housed as the average rural school in Germany. The German school is kept in a better state of repair, but in hygienic and sanitary conditions the English school is on the whole superior. The English teacher however lacks security of tenure, his upbringing is probably urban, and many inducements are held out to him to leave the country for the town school.

In America, about half the total number of school children are taught in rural schools. "It happens that ungraded rural schools with

a very small attendance are to be found even in the most thickly peopled States and often in proximity to cities. Rhode Island (in 1895) reports 158 out of its 263 schools as ungraded, and 64 of them containing fewer than 10 pupils each; three towns have in the aggregate thirty-nine schools averaging fewer than ten pupils. Vermont in 1893 reported 153 schools with six pupils or less each. Massachusetts in 1893–4 reported sixteen towns with an aggregate of nearly 100 schools with an average of eleven pupils. New York in 1894–5 reported 2,983 schools with fewer than ten pupils each, and 7,529 with less than twenty." Indeed we hear of an official visit to a school in New York State where the teacher had no pupils at present but was expecting two later on. Meanwhile embroidery kept her employed. American rural schools are open for probably not more than half the number of days per annum that the English or German rural schools are.

The teacher of one year will probably not be the teacher of the next. To many young people keeping school in this way is but an opportunity for making a little money towards some higher aim. . . .

America, like England and other parts of the world, is finding out the defects of small administrative areas in education, and the cry for bigger areas is raised by all educators who have given a thought to the problem of the rural school.

The rural school problem has received considerable attention from American educators, and the report of the Committee of Twelve on Rural Schools is one of the most valuable reports ever written. American educators have attacked the problem in quite a new way. Instead of taking the school to the children they take the children to the school. By this means these small ungraded schools of ten or twenty children become a fully graded school of 300 children. The advantages are obvious. It is economical and the further education of the children beyond the common school can be provided for. The motor-car has infinite possibilities of educational reform wrapped within its throbbing breast. Another interesting experiment is the introduction of the faculty system into rural schools by which a number of small rural schools are placed under one head or principal, who, besides being teacher of one of the schools, also acts as a kind of superintendent over the other schools and by advice and help trains the other teachers in the best methods.

The newer urban schools of Germany have

an accommodation for about 1,600 children and are built on the class-room and corridor system. The class-rooms, all facing the north, accommodate each about 60 children, but as only 6 sq. feet is allowed each child the rooms often appear crowded.

In England the minimum space allowed for each child is 10 sq. feet and in America in the newer schools 20 sq. feet is said to be taken as a minimum.

No lavatory accommodation is provided in these German schools other than a pump in the playground and drinking fountains in the corridor. In the basement, however, shower baths are some times fitted for washing the children weekly and on the south side of the building we get a teacher's room, conference room, and a room for periodically weighing and measuring the children. A very fine gymnasium is attached to the school. The school rarely, if ever, possesses a library for the pupils.

The newer English primary and higher primary schools are built with a Central Hall from which class-rooms open out. It is not as finely furnished a building perhaps as the German school but fulfils its function in life equally well. It sometimes has a gymnasium, one or two Science Laboratories, and occasionally swimming baths in the basement. Special rooms for cookery, and laundry work, and woodwork, may also be attached. The newer American schools differ in no essential respect; more use is made of iron in the construction, perhaps, and the staircases are beautifully wide. All the Chicago schools are supplied with bath tubs. The offices are in the basement where there is sometimes also a bicycle stand. The windows in all the class-rooms are carried to within 6 inches of the ceiling. The frame of the window is very lightly made. On the second storey is a fine assembly hall with seating accommodation for all the children attending the school. The school is heated and ventilated by the Plenum system, as indeed are both the English and German school.

It is impossible to distinguish between the relative excellences of these three schools; even experts differ. One tells us that the death rate of American school children is higher than of European children, because of the poorer hygienic condition of the American school, whilst another asserts that the American school building is externally and internally superior to French, German, or English schools. . . .

The fact that so much of the teaching is entrusted to women may lead to a lack of virility and strength in the training. There is a very outspoken criticism in the report of the school superintendent for Detroit. "Is it not possible that the increasing number of incorrigibles may bear some relation to this sentimentality? I know that I am terribly heterodox in suggesting that a good sound thrashing occasionally would be of more benefit to a capricious spunky youngster than all the goody-goody talks so correctly advocated. We are getting too many Mamma's pets and Lord Fauntleroys, and I fear our system has a tendency to perpetuate it. Give us more good hearty moral discipline, more Sanfords, and Mertons, and Tom Browns."

In many American schools the boys daily salute the national flag in the central hall of the school, and recite a vow of fealty to it. This custom has recently been transferred to Manilla where its efficacy will have a severe test.

It must not however be forgotten in comparing systems of discipline, that school discipline is largely a matter of school architecture, and that the class-room system has been much longer the vogue in Germany and America than in England.

Let us listen to the teaching in these three class-rooms.

The German teacher is highly trained and well informed. We notice how carefully he recapitulates and secures the ground, how little he relies upon any text book. Indeed the German child has no text book, except for arithmetic. The teacher speaks in a low natural voice, but he insists upon his pupils speaking out. In arithmetic we notice that he allows a pupil to come out and state and work a problem on the blackboard in front of the class. But this is the exception; as a rule the German teacher makes himself the source of all his pupil's knowledge. The instruction is almost entirely oral. There is very little written work in books and what there is is largely a "fair" copy of what had been previously done on the slate.

The weakness of German teaching is, I think, the lack of cultivation of the child's self activity. No sufficient appeal is made to experience, the child is rarely taught to dig out knowledge for himself and, when he leaves school and teacher behind him, he is helpless. However, he has fulfilled his obligations to the State and may now with equanimity relapse into a blissful state of indifference to education. School has but rarely engendered in him a love of education, and though he may be compelled to attend a Continuation School for a year or two longer it is but a postponement of the joyful day when he will be released from this further obligation to the State. No portion of the curriculum specially appeals to him. As a rule his manual dexterity has not been trained nor a permanent love of knowledge kindled by his school life. He takes with him from school a respect for constituted authority (which indeed he probably took with him to school) a desire to do his duty in that state of life unto which it has pleased God to call him, no more; and perhaps a few gems of national poetry or song which he may be able to carry about with him a few years longer. Public opinion on educational matters amongst the labouring class in Germany is much the same as in other lands, and I do not think that there is any higher educational enthusiasm amongst German labourers than there is to be found amongst the same class in England; but the German is more law-abiding and perhaps his sense of parental obligation is keener, or to put it another way, has not been blunted by too much being taken off his hands by the State.

The pupils, boys and girls, in the American class room, have each a text book of the matter of the lesson, and generally the lesson consists of the teacher testing the children's knowledge of the book. "The American text book is a peculiar institution, self-contained and complete in itself. It is plentifully illustrated with pictures and maps; it is divided into lessons or portions; it supplies questions for the teacher, names all other books that throw light on each particular lesson, in fact, does the teacher's work for her." (Zimmern). Often indeed the questions she asks are taken from the book itself, even the answers she should receive are sometimes given therein. Some of the brighter children appear to monopolise the lesson, as the system lends itself to that. Although the lesson is mainly oral, there is very little oral teaching. There is much testing and appeal to memory. In a Chicago school, Dr. Rice tells us that a teacher said to her class, "Don't stop to think but tell me what you know." Then again one misses the ordered development of the German lesson, the imparting of wisdom out of a full mind, the studied care of the limits. So powerful is the tyranny of the text book in some parts of America that we have heard of a candidate being asked "According to what text book do you teach?" "One trouble with many people is that they began text books so early in life, and followed them so closely that they

have never learned to distinguish their own thoughts and opinions from those of the books; in fact, they are scarcely aware that they have opinions of their own" (McMurry). Besides this the very exhaustive criticism of Dr. Rice would appear to show that unscientific mechanical teaching as well as absurd fads flourish to an extraordinary extent in some American cities[2]. . . . In South Dakota the superintendent reports that the teaching of the evil effects of alcohol and tobacco is so effective "that nearly every pupil is ready to give a temperance lecture at a moment's warning." It may, however, be pointed out, that such teaching is not altogether a monopoly of America, and in spite of these occasional peculiarities, much admirable work is done in American schools. Language is carefully taught. The children speak out loudly and clearly like German children do, and not like our children too often do. This is probably why most Americans are much better conversationalists than English people. The children's self-activity is cultivated in the American school, they are taught to dig out knowledge for themselves. In every school the children are taught to use Webster's Unabridged. Practically all urban American schools have a fine library besides which the public library of every American town provides suitable books and special accommodation for all children who can write their names. American pupils are expected to find out knowledge for themselves, and so the school library is an indispensable portion of the equipment of every efficient American school.

Some of these school libraries, especially those of the high schools, are the acme of comfort and utility, and in them much of the total school time is often spent.

---

[2] Detroit (Michigan)—The Board of Education of this place has got into trouble with the female teachers in its schools. It has lately been studying hygiene and high art together with theories as to the kind of figures calisthenics ought to produce if persisted in by ladies. The consequence is that the board came to the conclusion that its women teachers would look more Grecian and graceful if they abstained from wearing corsets, and orders were accordingly issued to the ladies to discontinue using those articles of attire. The board explained that in its opinion corsets interfered with the teacher's efficiency in taking graceful poses, that the ladies would look more "elegant" without the proscribed garment, and that the result would be the teachers would be able the more effectively to impress their scholars and educate them in an appreciation of the beautiful. The teachers are revolting.—*Dalziel.*

The helplessness of the American pupil in his teacher's hands is not evident to him or to us. His self-respect is preserved and his self-resource cultivated. He leaves school ready to begin the real education of life, *i.e.*, self-training, and naturally alert, ambitious, and confident, he develops into the pushful, resourceful, American citizen of to-day. Although this method of teaching may have been originally adopted because the teacher was untrained, yet there can be no doubt that the system has great advantages and admirably suits American characteristics.

The foreign observer in criticising the English teacher is apt to lay stress upon what he considers the poor discipline of an English class. This inborn restlessness is a national characteristic of which we as a people may reasonably be proud, and most chary in curbing. It is this restlessness that has carried our folk round the globe. Often this busy hum, this continual restlessness of the British class-room is the surest evidence of the children's self-activity. Is it not preferable to the deadly stillness of a "well-disciplined" school? In any case it is not the difficulty to the English teacher that his critic imagines.

English training-college teachers and professors have long since known that the first lesson the future teacher has to learn is to maintain discipline, consequently this training receives very careful treatment from the first. Hence what to another teacher would be a task absorbing a large proportion of his energy has become to the trained English teacher a mere matter of habit, largely automatic. Little of his total energy is absorbed in this essential matter. A German or American teacher would, I grant you, find practically all his energy required in merely securing discipline in an English class-room, but that would prove nothing more than that he did not understand the boys. The trained English teacher would seem to be, on the whole, a fair mean between the German and American teacher. His training has especially fitted him for the practical work of teaching. He is a master of the technique of the class-room and the practical details of instruction.

He may lack the deeper pedagogic training, the philosophical grasp, the ripeness, so to speak, of the German, and also the vivacity and enthusiasm of the good American teacher, but, on the other hand, there is a thoroughness and conscientiousness in his work, combined with resource, which enable him to triumph over difficulties that would prove insuperable to a less practically trained teacher.

His initiative and resource are, I venture to think, higher than his German colleague's and his technical outfit as a teacher more thorough than that of the American teacher. The incubus of educational tradition does not press as heavily on the American as on the English, nor on the English as much as on the German teacher.

His teaching is more oral than the American but less than the German; he uses text books much more than the German, but much less than the American. Finally, whatever may be the faults of English teaching they must not in common fairness be laid at the door of the English teacher, but at that of Mr. Robert Lowe who invented the system of payment by results

Fortunately that has passed away, and there is appearing in our teachers a finer spirit, a keener interest in the purely pedagogic side of their calling, a higher sense of the dignity, privileges, and obligations of their profession, which are full of the happiest auguries for the future. Finally let it be said that the good teacher is a cosmopolitan; he is not confined to the Old or New World.

The written work of our English pupil is considered to be superior to that of the American both in neatness and style. Accuracy and other virtues engendered by a systematic and careful training are characteristic of the English pupil, whilst vivacity and originality are characteristic of the American pupil. Civic duty and patriotism are carefully cultivated both in the American and German urban school; in England both are studiously neglected.

Arithmetic absorbs more time in the English and American than in the German school; indeed an American Superintendent tells me that it is the fetish of the American school, and another American says, "In our country schools arithmetic is a fetish; no subdivision of the book and no problem in the book may be omitted; 'to go through the arithmetic' is the ambition of the child, and the ambition of the parent for the child." [Report U.S. Bureau of Education, 1893–4.]

The needlework of the English girls is superior to that of either the American or German girl, and cookery, laundry work, and cottage gardening are more generally taught in the English school than in the other two schools. Physical training receives more attention in England and America than in the German School, but this is supposed to be compensated for by the subsequent two years' military service, but no such training ever engenders the valuable virtues of the play-ground.

The degree of illiteracy of these countries is as follows:—

			Date
England and Wales . 6.4% men	7.3% women		1891
Scotland . . . . 3.4% men	5.3% women		1891
Ireland . . . . 19.4% men	19.4% women		1891
Germany . . . . . . 0.24% men	. . . .		1894
United States . . . . 13.3% men	and women		1894
France . . . . 7.4% men	. . . .		1890

Americans, however, reasonably enough point out that the incoming population, composed as it is largely of the scourings of Europe, accounts for this high figure for the States. In some of the Southern States, however, *illiteracy is actually increasing faster than the increase of population.*

The amount annually devoted to the education of each child in the States is £3 15s. 0d., in England, £2 9s. 11d., and in Prussia £1 14s. 0d.

Although America is spending nobly upon education, yet in but few civilised countries is the educational outlook, in some respects, so full of serious import to the community.

The most serious matter, perhaps, is the fact that in some of the largest American cities thousands, and even, in some cases, tens of thousands of children are said to be growing up destitute of a school education. In New York, Chicago, St. Louis, and Philadelphia the numbers are appalling. This is due to lack of school places, and the excuse urged is that it is impossible to keep up with the growth of these cities. But in reply it may be urged that some German cities have grown equally rapidly yet no such state of things is allowed to occur there. In the whole of the kingdom of Prussia there are less children kept from school for this reason than in New York city alone. The Empire city in its despair has organised half-day schools to minimise the danger. The fact that the annual vote for education in this city is not only insufficient to provide these needed premises, but sometimes even to pay its teachers, is perhaps the better guide to the true cause, though the substitution of huge tenements for ordinary dwelling houses has, in recent years, had something to do with bringing this state of things about.

I have tabulated the figures for some of the larger American cities for the year 1897–8.

City	Number Enrolled	Places Provided	Deficiency
New York	471,251	385,091	86,160
Chicago	236,219	220,575	15,644
San Francisco	50,101	39,495	10,606
Boston	85,320	77,835	7,485
Detroit	37,131	32,599	4,532
New Orleans	29,522	23,383	6,139
Philadelphia	173,363	146,475	26,888
Milwaukee	40,210	38,424	1,786
Buffalo	56,718	53,071	3,647
St. Louis	75,922	66,722	9,200
Grand Rapids	21,434	15,928	5,506
Washington	44,698	42,437	2,261
Indianapolis	33,853	18,830	15,023
Mobile	8,092	7,000	1,092
Atlanta	14,338	10,555	3,783
Minneapolis	33,673	32,000	1,673
St. Paul	23,790	22,356	1,434
Cincinnati	44,635	44,700	. . . . .

The only localities in England and Wales which show a deficiency of school places at present are these towns:—

Town	Number Enrolled	Places Provided	Deficiency
Bootle	9,321	8,696	625
Coventry	10,521	10,449	72
Gateshead	21,156	20,252	904
Gloucester	7,894	7,539	355
Ipswich	11,348	10,999	349
Lincoln	8,243	7,877	366
Middlesboro	16,392	16,214	178
Newport, Mon.	12,890	12,716	174
Northampton	11,953	11,839	114
Southampton	16,990	16,252	738
South Shields	18,203	17,877	326
Sunderland	26,908	25,166	1,742
Walsall	15,136	14,030	1,106
Yarmouth	9,563	9,108	455
Cardiff	30,661	29,055'	1,606

For the Kingdom of Prussia in 1890 the figures were:—Children of school age, 5,299,310; of these

Attending public schools, ...	93 per cent.
Attending private schools, ...	5½ per cent.
Had no room, ...	3,239

Did not attend owing to physical or
   mental incapacity,. 10,041
Failed to attend without sufficient
   excuse,. . . . . 945 or $\frac{2}{100}$ of
                             1 per cent.

In England and Wales there are more than sufficient places for all children of school age. In 1899 there were in the Counties 4,757,687 places for 4,112,501 scholars enrolled, and in the County Boroughs there were 1,683,458 places for 1,559,902 scholars.

American official statistics show that the number of children enrolled on the school registers is larger in proportion to the population than in any other country. Unfortunately the laws of compulsory attendance, where they do exist, are rarely enforced.

In 1897–8 only 68 per cent. of the numbers enrolled attended school regularly. Further, the American school is not opened, as is the English school, for *at least* 200 days.

In 1897–8 the average school year for the whole of the States was 144.3 days.

Rhode Is.,	191 days.	Mass.,	186 days
Michigan,	160 days.	N. Carolina,	68.8 days
Arkansas,	69 days.		

In other words, the average American child will receive from three to five years of school instruction of 200 days; the average English and German child will get quite seven years.[3]

Children leave school early in the States as well as in England, particularly the boys, who, it has been said, as they grow older rather resent being taught by female teachers.

"In the classes composed of children from ten years and upwards there was an increasing preponderance of girls. It is stated that over 50 per cent. of the children who ever enter school leave before the age of ten. If this be so, a much larger proportion of boys do not attend school after that age."—*Grasby*.

In spite of such facts an American writes, "That the public system of education has been carried in our country during the last half century to a degree of perfection heretofore unknown to any country of the world none will deny; and that to-day the United States is far in advance of all other nations in this respect will also be admitted."

---

[3]Number of years schooling (of 200 days) each individual receives in both public primary and secondary School in 1899:–N. Atlantic Div., 5.67 years; S. Atlantic Div., 2.78 years; S. Central Div., 2.88 years; N. Central Div., 5.14 years; Western Div., 5.28 years.

Wiser Americans, however, bitterly bewail this state of things. Truant officers have been appointed in New York State, as well as three State inspectors whose duty it is to assist or compel the local authorities to enforce the law. We at home know how futile such efforts are, unless backed by a rigorous administration of the law. Elsewhere we hear of citizens banding themselves together for using *moral suasion* to get the children to school!

The attendance in Germany is, I consider, perfect—that is to say, there is practically no avoidable leakage. In France, too, a fairly high figure is reached. These results are not altogether due to a keener love of education, but it is, I imagine, to both being military States, where parents obey the law as a matter of course. The law of compulsory attendance is so clear and so automatic that it never occurs to a German parent to attempt to evade it.

"Make your educational laws strict and your criminal laws may be gentle, but leave youth its liberty and you will have to dig dungeons for old age," says Ruskin.

Every birth in Germany is recorded, and twice a year a census of the school population of the district is taken by the police and the list given to the school master. Every absence is reported to the police by the teacher, and they make enquiries and, if necessary, fine the parents. That is all.

In England and Wales the average attendance of all children is 81.6 per cent., but of older children—that is of comparable age to German children—the figures are 87.5 per cent. One of the main causes for the better attendance in Germany is that there are more schools in proportion to the population than in England. In Prussia there are 36,138 public elementary schools, in England only 15,199 (excluding infants' schools). Children rarely walk any considerable distance to school—in fact, only one child out of every 25 walks one and a half miles or more to school in the Fatherland. In the whole of Prussia there is one school to every 874 inhabitants; in England, one to every 1,550 inhabitants, and in America, one to every 300 people.

The Prussian elementary schools are practically all denominational. There are 24,487 Protestant, 10,725 Catholic, 246 Jewish, and 680 *"Mixed"* schools. The city schools average 418 pupils each, and those of the villages and country 109 pupils each.

The German teacher is pedagogically the finest trained teacher in the world. For practical skill in the handling of large classes the English teacher is unequalled. For spontaneity, vivacity, and enthusiasm it would be difficult to find a peer of the American teacher. But these are generalities.

The German teacher is trained for six years—three years in a preparatory normal school where his elementary training is deepened but not widened much, and three years in the normal school where a similar training is given, together with the special technical training required for his professional duties.

During the last year he teaches in the model school for from six to ten hours weekly. Every German Training College must have attached to it not only a graded but also an ungraded model school.

A foreign language may be, but only occasionally is, taken up by the student. Students in Training Colleges are not allowed to take notes during a lecture. The Germans hold that taking notes distracts the listener and diminishes seriously the value of the lecture. Germans are invariably good listeners. German educational reformers, like English reformers, are asking for a widening and enrichment of the normal school curriculum, and for utilising the secondary school (Realschule) for the training of teachers.

The graduate of a German Training College does not receive his full diploma until he has passed a further examination in pedagogy at the end of at least two years. During these two years he is carefully watched and helped by his training college teachers. He is then appointed to a school where, in some provinces, he is expected to stay at least three years. He possesses absolute security of tenure, and is entitled to a sick pension after ten years' service, and a full service pension at sixty-five. He is fairly well paid, and enjoys a good social status. That the profession is popular is shown by the fact that about one-fifth of all German teachers are sons of teachers.

Women teachers have not hitherto received fair treatment in Germany. They come generally from a higher social class than the men, being largely the daughters of military or professional men, too poor to provide the dowry so indispensable for a German girl's marriage.

These women have generally been through a middle or secondary school course and have sat for the examination of secondary teachers, but have failed in some one or other subject, and so get only the lower diploma—that licenses them to teach in the primary school.

The Training College accommodation for women is also very inadequate, and even the men teachers in girls' schools are rather looked down upon by the male teachers of other schools. Altogether the position of women teachers, or even a teacher of girls, is not altogether a desirable one in Germany, but this feeling will doubtless disappear in time. The head teacher of all girls' schools and at least one other teacher must be males. These men teachers have a very pleasant sympathetic way with the girls.

The English teacher, under favourable circumstances, begins to teach, or rather assist, when about fifteen to sixteen years of age, and for three years spends half a day in the school. The remainder of the day is spent at a special school for pupil teachers, where the instruction is given generally by University graduates who are also trained teachers, and under favourable conditions as regards equipment and accommodation. There are probably few institutions in the kingdom of the work of which less is popularly known than these central schools. To compare the condition of the pupil teacher of to-day with that of say ten years ago is foolish, and many observers and critics of the English teacher have failed to recognize or fully appreciate the revolution these institutions have silently effected.

The English teacher is said to have two years' training; it would be more correct to say that under favourable circumstances he will receive five years' thoroughly sound training. The number of University graduates too in our primary schools, though small, is increasing, and a rapidly increasing proportion of English teachers are receiving what is practically a University training in our Day Training Colleges.

No, the real defect of our English trained teacher is that we haven't got enough of him. Seventy-two per cent. of English male teachers, and forty-nine per cent. of female teachers are trained. If both are combined there are only fifty-eight per cent. of our certificated teachers who are college trained; the others *are* "trained," it is true, and have passed precisely the same examination, but have not received the advantages of a normal school training. Behind this insufficiency of the college trained teacher is the inadequate training college accommodation in England. The present training college accommodation suffices for a teaching force of 42,000 instead of 62,000. Prussia and Germany generally are able to turn out annually just the number of trained teachers required for the schools of the country. This they are able to do with great exactitude, owing to the preparatory lists drawn out by the inspectors and provincial councils of the probable requirements of the district for each year. German Training Colleges are smaller and more numerous than ours, and are generally located in small provincial towns.

No unqualified teachers, such as our Article 68, are employed in the German school excepting for the teaching of needlework. This, in rural districts, is taught by the master's wife, or a woman from the village. I wonder how many American teachers in out of the way places would find that that was the only article in the English Code which just about covered their qualifications! Neither America nor Germany has anything quite similar to our pupil teacher, but in the schools of Chicago there are what are called "school cadets," who are young people who intend becoming teachers. They assist in teaching all day, and are paid seventy-five cents for the toil. In Germany too, a boy of fourteen or fifteen is often found helping the master to teach his school of from eighty to a hundred children. These boys usually develop into fully fledged teachers. That there is something to be said for our system is the opinion of America's greatest authority, Dr. W. T. Harris: "In my opinion we have something to learn from this monitorial system (i.e., the P. T. system of England). The kindergarten and ungraded school in rural districts can, it seems to me, adopt a form of the Lancasterian system which would serve a good purpose. The cost of the Kindergarten may be reduced to one-fifth of what it is under the present plan, and the ungraded school may train its higher pupils more effectively as pupil teachers than by the present stereotyped system." And one of the leaders of German pedagogy, who is himself a rural teacher, has strongly advocated the introduction of the pupil teacher system into the German country school.

Indeed it would seem that the rural school anywhere in the world cannot, under present circumstances and with reasonable economy, be worked without employing persons of the nature of pupil teacher and Article 68. It is largely the reluctance to employ such that causes the fearful understaffing of many German rural schools. There is a wonderful similarity in the difficulties of the rural school all the world over. A man crosses a ditch in much the same way whether in Timbuctoo or California.

Of the English qualified teacher 34 per cent. of him is male, and practically the same proportions (i.e. 31 per cent.) hold for the American teacher, whereas of the German teacher there is only about 13 per cent. female. Of the whole teaching staff of the English school however, 75 per cent. is female. In England as in America the rapidly growing preponderance of the female teacher is mainly due to economic reasons, but in Germany this is not so much so.

Curiously enough, or perhaps obviously enough, where education is most advanced in the States, there the female teacher thrives best:—e.g., In Chicago only 6.6 per cent. of total teachers are male. In New York State City teachers 8.0 per cent. are male, and of the State teachers 21.0 per cent. are male. And of normal school pupils the females form:—93 per cent. in Massachusetts, 99 per cent. in Connecticut, 100 per cent. in New Hampshire.

The American male teacher will soon be as extinct as the bison. At present his habitat is mainly the backwoods and morasses of the Southern States.

Of the American teacher the most diverse views may reasonably be held, for she is as diverse as she is numerous. No general statement of her capacity can be made not even for the teachers of each State.

Towns vary, States vary, Massachusetts for example, has nearly 40 per cent. of its teachers graduates of normal colleges, and the New England States generally have a considerable proportion of teachers who have received some training.[4] But this training is often rather meagre.

"According to the judgment of a very competent American school teacher, the work done in normal schools does not compare with that of a German seminary."

Indeed an American writer asserts that "A preparation in pedagogics for the profession is almost entirely wanting; in fact, the principle has been enunciated that a teacher in the public schools need not know more than he must teach, and that a knowledge of his text book is sufficient." Even the principals of primary schools will deny the need of professional training for the teacher. The fact that some of the finest Training Colleges perhaps in the world are American in no way affects the above statements.

---

[4] "No state makes a better showing than Massachusetts, but in 1897-98 only 38.5 per cent. of her teachers in public schools had received normal instruction, and only 33.5 per cent. were normal graduates."—Hinsdale.

Of all American primary teachers it has been said, that one third have passed through a normal school of some kind or other. Where the remaining two-thirds obtain their qualification is somewhat difficult to say. "It may be presumed that less than one-sixth of the supply of new teachers come from the training schools especially designed to educate teachers" (Dr. Harris).

"But the true professional competency of our teachers taken all in all, does not become fully apparent until we consider that not more than a small percentage of persons engaged in teaching in the public schools of this country are normal school graduates. Of those teaching, besides the normal school graduates, others have simply attended a normal school, high school or academy, for one or more terms, while a very large number of licences to teach are granted to those whose education does not extend beyond that received at a grammar school, with or without a little extra coaching." (Dr. Rice). It may be pointed out that the American grammar school is simply our "senior mixed" *i.e.* a primary school for children between ten and fourteen years old.

The system of certification by which the local school authority licenses its teachers for a varying number of years, has a double effect. On the one hand it unsettles the teachers, and gives them no security of tenure, not even that of the English teacher with his life certificate; on the other hand, it prevents stagnation, and encourages the introduction of new ideas and experiments. In the State of New York, of all the teachers employed—

1,115	received a diploma from the State Superintendent.
3,927	held normal school certificates.
28,536	were licensed by local officers.

This renewal of the certificate is, in the majority of cases, a mere formality, but whereas the German teacher has an official life of twenty-five years, that of the American is five years. In spite of this, "The office of teaching in the average American school is perhaps the only one in the world that can be retained indefinitely in spite of the poorest incompetence." (Dr. Rice).

Just as, in considering the strength of the English teaching staff, it was necessary if we would form a true estimate of its comparative power, to consider not only the college trained, but also the school trained teacher, as well as the preliminary train-

ing now so largely given in the special school for pupil teachers, so, in considering and estimating the technical outfit of the American teacher, we should obtain a very inadequate estimate of the real strength, if we neglected to consider the many subsidiary agencies for training which have been so highly and largely developed in America.

In the first place comes the School Superintendent, who is as a rule the executive officer of the State, County, or Township educational Board. This Board be it remembered, has no Whitehall to stimulate or moderate its educational zeal as may seem necessary. Of its own sweet will it may make of its land an educational Paradise or desert.

Hence in a pushing, go-ahead town, anxious to attract a good class of residents, one of the chief attractions offered may be a magnificent set of schools. A few leagues away parsimony may take ample revenge. Let us return to the School Superintendent, who, in the best circumstances, is a highly trained expert, but in other cases too often an astute politician. The State Superintendent for Maine in his report for 1896 writes—"Of the School Superintendents (in this State) 35 per cent. are farmers, the rest are teachers, physicians, housekeepers, merchants, lawyers, clergymen, carpenters, lumbermen, labourers, druggists, journalists, fishermen, postmasters, engineers, painters, stonecutters, blacksmiths, and one each of express agents, book-keepers, guides, saw-filers, surveyors, ferrymen, barbers, painters, manufacturers, haberdashers, railroad postal clerks, dairymen, and spinsters. Four per cent devote all their time to this business. The rest devote such time as they are willing to take from their personal affairs."

One of the chief duties of the Superintendent is to train the teachers up to his methods and ideals. His tenure of office will probably not be long; meanwhile he will probably make things hum. So much power is concentrated in the Superintendent's hands that, for the time being, he is the educational autocrat of the district. He sometimes selects the text books, invariably prescribes in detail the methods, defines the curriculum and fixes the ideals. Indeed there is no room left for the teacher's initiative. This is all very well for a poor, untrained teacher, but for a well trained teacher it must be painfully galling. "The truth is, that as a rule our teachers are too weak to stand alone, and therefore need constantly to be propped up

by the supervisory staff." (Dr. Rice). I
have by me an admirable scheme based
upon the soundest principles of modern
pedagogy, drawn out by the Superintendent
of Schools in a Californian town. It is
really excellent, and affords evidence of how
the light is encircling the globe. It is a far
cry to California, yet the land of the setting
sun would seem to be coming the land of
the rising sun. But, however admirable, such
a detailed scheme in method would never
be tolerated in England nor even in Germany.

The American teacher is treated like a
child. She is told what to eat and how to
eat, what to teach and how to teach. Perhaps
one may summarise the whole matter thus:—

Germany gets a highly trained teacher and
leaves him largely alone. The Government
inspector sees him once in about four or
five years. (The constant visits of the
parochial inspector are of course neglected in
making this statement.)

England gets a less highly trained teacher,
gives him free play as to method but
sends her official to see him twice a year.

America gets a teacher and teaches him,
and sends her official to see him many
times a year.

Let us hark back to other subsidiary
methods of training the teacher in America.
It is said that American teachers are always endeavouring to improve their professional knowledge, whereas the average
English teacher only rarely follows up the
pedagogical training received in the Training College. It is certain from the number
of American periodicals and books on educational topics that there is a much larger
circle of educational readers in America
than in England.

Even English writers on education obtain
a wider circulation in America than at home.
Teacher's meetings again are much more
highly organised in America and in Germany,
and are less concerned with the politics
than with the pedagogics of education than they
are in England. Meetings of this kind are held
monthly in Germany, which the teachers are
compelled to attend, their expenses being
defrayed by the State. The district inspector
presides, and the papers read are on pedagogic questions of interest to the teachers,
and such conferences are concluded by a
convivial concert and supper which serves
to cement the pleasant feeling of *camaraderie*
so essential to the success of the profession.

In America too the School Boards pay
their teachers' expenses and compel them to
attend these meetings. These may extend over

three or four days, and the public attend
largely and take a keen interest in the discussions. Railway companies and hotel proprietors offer special facilities for such
gatherings.

However, after all is said and done, it is
the opinion of Americans themselves that
matters educational will never be on a sound
footing in America until a real profession of
teaching has been established. At present
such a profession can hardly be said to
exist. An American official report states:
"In the United States the profession of teaching seems to be a kind of waiting room in
which the young girl awaits a congenial
ulterior support, and the young man a more
advantageous position." But here again one
must be wary of drawing conclusions thus.
In America a man and woman too plays many
parts; no profession is closed, no career
barred to the enterprising American.

He may indeed be everything by turn and
nothing long: a lawyer to-day, a superintendent to-morrow, a divine on Sunday.
Teaching is in this respect like other professions in America, and the philosopher
may perhaps wisely pause to consider whether
such a state of affairs is not in accordance
with the eternal fitness of things where you
have a big people settling down in a new
home. America is crystallising out, and as
yet it is difficult to say what shape the
crystal will take on.

Finally a word as to payment of teachers.
For the year 1897–8 the average annual pay
of American teachers was for males £109,
females £93, calculated on the monthly pay
sheet. For the same year, 1897–8, the
average pay of English teachers was for
males £124, females £83. The salaries of
English headmasters has increased 35 per
cent., and of headmistresses 48 per cent.,
during the last twenty-five years.

In the kingdom of Prussia the average
pay of male teachers, according to statistics
collected in 1896, was for city teachers £96,
and for country teachers £64, or a general
average for male teachers of £77 per annum.
For female teachers the average pay in city
schools was £66, and in country schools
£54, or a general average of £61. The female teacher in America gets 85 per cent.,
in Prussia 80 per cent., and in England only
67 per cent. of the salary awarded to the
male teacher. The smaller difference in
America is probably due to the relatively
higher efficiency of the bulk of the American female teachers as compared to the bulk
of male teachers. A pedagogically trained

male American teacher is somewhat of a *rara avis.*

It must be remembered, however, in comparing these figures that the length of the school year, like the buying capacity of money, varies considerably in these three States, and also that in Prussia all schools have a dwelling house attached, and that firing is allowed for the school house, and further that in Germany and England teachers are entitled to pensions. Moreover all German country schools are provided with a garden for the use of the master. These items, namely, house, garden, and firing, were duly considered in the above figures for Prussia, but not in those of England and America. Of English schoolmasters 25 per cent., and of mistresses 12 $\frac{1}{2}$ per cent., are provided with school residences.

It is a significant little fact that teachers are not paid during absences from school or during holidays in the States.

Let me say something as to the attitude of the school to the people. In America it is customary for any visitor to a city of any claims to progress to be shown around the schools. As a rule the American school is the finest architectural structure in the town. So customary is this visiting that chairs are placed in each class-room for the convenience of callers. One of two results probably follows, either the class work is disturbed or a certain priggishness is liable to be engendered. American teachers admit this, and some of them would gladly see this custom abolished.

In Germany a parent visiting a school without a special permission from the authorities (which is rarely granted), is fined. No encouragement is given to a parent to take any active part in the training of his child. It is true that once a year parents are invited to the school "examination," which is the only examination that the school holds, but every item of the programme is carefully rehearsed beforehand by pupil and teacher before being submitted to so critical an audience. Many of the teachers would like to see even this little pleasantry abolished.

The picture of an irate mother exhausting her vocabulary on the school doorstep occasionally seen in England makes one inclined to feel that there is something in the German view of the matter.

But these facts are significant of the school and State attitude towards the people.

The working classes in Germany take no active interest in the school. In England they vote at Board elections; in America they take a pride in them and show you round. After all, the differences are those of a bureaucratic and a democratic State. England is the half-way house.

Postscript

As I lay my pen down, strains of music reach me. There across the way is a group of German lads of from thirteen to twenty years of age. They seem weary after many days' travel through this pleasant land of England. Sad, stern faces with set jaws they seem to pull forth the music automatically from their strings. What brings these lads so far from home? Why have they left their beautiful Fatherland behind, and why do they hurry thus to the West? See how their faces brighten as the evening sun pours his light into their faces. What are they thinking of? What means this picture? It is the children crying for the light, for freedom, for self-development. Behind them are restraint, bureaucracy and conscription;[5] in front they see life and liberty. Small wonder is it that these German children become American citizens so readily. Of what advantage is it that a man gains the whole world of knowledge and loses his own soul. Better the intellectual levity of America than the cultured servitude of Europe. And as I muse, the lads break into fresh music, not indeed "Die Wacht am Rhein," but—"The New Jerusalem."

---

[5] I have heard it stated that conscription is popular in Germany, but I have also read that there are 20,000 desertions annually from the German army. I wonder which is true?

Michael E. Sadler   1902

Impressions of American Education

Michael E. Sadler (1861–1943), an English educator, was educated at Winchester, Rugby, Trinity College, and Oxford. He became secretary of the University Extension Lectures Sub-Committee in 1885 and was a member of the Bryce Commission on Secondary Education from 1894 to 1895. He then served as director of the Office of Special Inquiries and Reports until 1903, when he was appointed to a professorship at the University of Manchester. In 1911 he became vice-chancellor at the University of Leeds, and from 1923 until he retired in 1934, he was master at University College, Oxford.

Sadler gave the speech reproduced below at the annual congress of the Educational Institute, Glasgow, Scotland, on December 30, 1902. The key to his views on American education lies in his dictum that "the comparative study of national systems of education is a delicate enterprise. . . . But the first requisite for the intelligent study of a foreign system of education is sympathy." He lived up to this principle and his views on American education were as sympathetic as they were generous. His criticisms were balanced but stimulating and focused on the more obvious defects in American education without being hackneyed. Prophetically, in calling for better relations between Britain and the United States, Sadler stated that "too much depends for the future of the world on the outcome of the great educational movement in America."

At rare intervals in the history of a nation there comes a great outburst of physical and intellectual energy which, with over-mastering power, carries forward the masses of the people, together with its leaders, in an exhilarating rush of common effort. In the United States of America such a movement is in progress to-day. It reveals its force at three points—the American workshop, the American office, and the American school. Of the tremendous power of the movement no one who has witnessed it can doubt. But whither it will lead he would be a rash man who would dare to prophesy. These great national movements often turn in new and unlooked-for directions with an accumulated force which breaks old bounds and tears entrance into new channels. Those who seem to lead the movement believe that they can guide it toward some chosen goal. But they often find themselves swept along in the flood toward some unexpected issue, thru gaps in ancient barriers which looked immovable, but prove to have been sapped and weakened by slow and hidden changes in national character and in national belief.

The great movement now going forward in American education is but one aspect of the national movement which is stirring to its depth the whole of American life. Hence its profound significance, not only to Americans, but to the Old World, and not least to us who, geographically, politically, and spiritually, are, as it were, the link between the Old World and the New.

It is appropriate for us, here in Glasgow, to consider the meaning of these things. The fame of Glasgow is significant of sea power and of trading enterprise, and in regard to both of these the United States seem destined to play a great part in the world's history.

And it is fitting in a congress of Scottish teachers to consider what American schools and universities are seeking to accomplish for American life, because in the great movement now going forward for the deepening and strengthening of American education, men of Scottish or Scotch-Irish ancestry are bearing a prominent and influential part. These men are proud to trace back their descent to the Covenanters or to those Scottish Presbyterians who, settled in Ulster in the earlier part of the seventeenth century, found themselves driven to emigrate two generations afterward by the hostility of the English Parliament toward the flourishing growth of Irish manufactures.

Before I plunge into the details of my subject, I will venture to say one word as to the point of view from which to approach it. A great and famous Scotch philosopher, once, I believe an unsuccessful candidate for a chair in this University, used to say that the power of seeing the favorable rather than the unfavorable side of things is a turn of mind which is worth as much as being born to an estate of ten thousand a year. The Americans have this turn of mind. They prefer to talk about the bright side. They

Michael E. Sadler, "Impressions of American Education," *Educational Review*, XXV (March 1903), 217–231.

leave the dark side to one's natural powers of observation and of inference. No one can form a shrewd judgment on American education who merely sees what he is bid to see, and who refrains from employing his critical faculty as well as his organ of admiration. The comparative study of national systems of education is a delicate enterprise. The path to truth lies between Scylla and Charybdis; between harsh, censorious judgments of other people's failings and too ready belief in the superior merits of other people's achievements. But the first requisite for the intelligent study of a foreign system of education is sympathy. We must do as we would be done by. We must endeavor to enter, to the best of our power, into the spirit of patriotism and self-sacrifice which always animates any living and progressive system of national education. Imitate it in any mechanical or literal way we cannot: profit by it we can, but in order to profit we first must sympathize. Look at the favorable side first; then the defects will reveal themselves in due course and in due proportion. Then, and not till then, the way is open to a measured judgment. But it is both good sense and good manners to think first and chiefly of the favorable side of a foreign system to which we are admitted with graceful hospitality and in the spirit of professional comradeship. And I am inclined to think that if we, as a nation, take to heart the favorable side of American education, we shall find it worth a good deal more to us than ten thousand a year.

1. The first thing to which I would draw your attention is the fact that America—progressive America—heartily believes in education. That is the heart of the whole matter. America believes in education. The American school is radiant with a belief in its mission, and it works among people who believe in the reality of its influence, in the necessity for its labors, and in the grandeur of its task. It is the old story. The essential thing is faith. Faith can move mountains of inertia, and ignorance, and class selfishness. This glowing faith in the power of education is the saving grace of modern American life. All witnesses agree on the one point that in education all intelligent Americans heartily and unfeignedly believe. I have even heard it said that they don't really believe in anything else.

The words of Washington in his Farewell Address fell on fruitful ground. "Promote, as an object of primary importance, institutions for the general diffusion of knowledge.

In proportion as the structure of a Government gives force to public opinion, it is essential that public opinion should be enlightened." That is one of the first principles of American policy. The Monroe doctrine is the second. Round the frieze of the Public Library of Boston, Mass., there are carved in plain letters fifteen words which sum up this central doctrine of American democracy: "The Commonwealth requires the education of the people as the safeguard of order and liberty."

Thus regarded, education becomes at once a national thing. Its chief power in America is to make Americans. Stand at the Battery in New York and watch the great liners coming up the Narrows from the Old World. That is the gate of America, and thru it pass the poor immigrants of varied nationality, bringing with them a strange medley of discordant ideals, and in some cases not a little anti-social distrust of law and government. These are the raw materials of American democracy. The school is the mill which grinds up these diverse materials into one consistence. Once let that machinery stand idle or fall into disrepair, and the civic unity of America is imperiled.

But national unity is a moral thing. The means of conserving it must therefore make use of moral, as well as of purely intellectual, influences. Patriotism, tho protected by identity of economic interest, has its deepest roots in other than self-regarding instincts. And to those hidden sources of national strength any education, worthy to be called national, makes confident appeal. This is the note of all that is best in the new educational movement in America. It seeks to touch the springs of character. Its ideal is not a selfish and exclusive culture, but scholarship engaged in social service. "It is not scholarship alone," if I may recall those stirring words of Dr. Chalmers, "it is not scholarship alone that tells on the great masses of society, but scholarship impregnated with religion."

2. Thus America believes in education because education is making America. But the essence of a democratic commonwealth lies in the individuality of its citizenship. This eager belief in individuality is the second characteristic of American education to which I would invite your attention to-day. American firms advertise for "a live man." The American primary school is determined to produce a live child. For some tastes it succeeds only too well, but that is another story. For the work of the earliest grades of

American education, the harshest critic would give little else than praise. In the first four years of school life the American child is stimulated to self-expression and self-realization by teachers skillful in their art, and unwearied in their practice of it. The brushwork, the modeling, the simple compositions, the beginnings of scientific education, which distinguish this stage of American education are often excellent. Much is done to produce alertness of mind and body and to cultivate the faculty and habit of self-expression. What is too often lacking, as a background to all this stimulation, is wise restraint and discipline at home. Many American parents, in their desire to give their children a good time, seem to shrink from exercising parental authority in matters in which home and school should work together, and in which the school may fairly claim the help of the home. That, however, is an evil not wholly confined to the western hemisphere.

The atmosphere of the American school and college is an atmosphere of equality and of independence. Energy and self-confidence thrive in it. Whatever else is sacrificed, the individual is encouraged to express himself and to realize his native capacity as best he may. This readiness to encourage individuality is a characteristic of American life. It has profoundly changed the organization of their universities thru the development of what was called "elective studies." The same lesson is working in their secondary schools. And we can see the same principle at work in American industry, where great pains are taken to encourage the individual workmen to make suggestions for the improvement of processes of manufacture or distribution, and where there is almost a passion for hearing new ideas and for experimenting with new appliances.

But thoughtful Americans perceive that to stimulate individuality and self-expression is only half the work of a good school. The other half is discipline. Is there not high authority for the belief that the true beginning of wisdom is desire of discipline? But just as the yearning for individuality implies a philosophical ideal in which the individual plays a determining part, so does the belief in discipline postulate a social ideal—a striving after some ordered organization of society —in which the stress is laid on duties rather than on rights. And here it is that American thinking has been weak, and American life is at present somewhat thin and poor. In old days the strength of American charac-

ter lay in the discipline of Puritan society. But the bonds of that society burst under the pressure of modern life, and then there rushed out a wonderful energy, which had been long confined within the restraints of the older discipline. This energy, this powerful individuality, carried the descendants of the old Puritan stock thru the chief part of their new task of subduing to settlement and to the needs of agriculture and industry the northern part of the United States as far as the Pacific by means of the adventurous courage of pioneers and the resources of applied science. But this stage is nearly accomplished. What is needed next is a new social discipline, a new social ideal, dominating the lives and inspiring the devotion of the common people. But this is the very point at which chaos reigns. The problem of problems in American education is to foresee the social organization for which the children must be prepared. No American writer discusses this question with a clearer sense of its urgency than Dr. John Dewey, of the University of Chicago. "We must make," he says, in his *School and Society,* "each one of our schools an embryonic community life, active in the types of occupations that reflect the life of the larger society, and permeated thruout with the spirit of art, history, and science. When the school introduces and trains each child of society into membership with such a little community, saturating him with the spirit of service, and providing him with the instruments of effective self-direction, we shall have the deepest and best guarantee of a larger society which is worthy, lovely, and harmonious." Yes; but how shall we set to work to get some clearer notion of what the duties, the relationships, and the extent of these future adult communities are going to be? And what, in preparation for such adult duties, is to be the task of the home as compared with that of the school? Dr. Dewey indicates the drift of the need —a need not confined to America—but he throws little light on the future evolution of American society.

3. Thus the American believes in education, because education equips individuals for the tasks of American citizenship. But those tasks are changing, because applied science has changed some of the fundamental conditions on which rested the old order of society and the balance of power between the great nations of the earth. Applied science, too, has drawn into inevitably closer political relationship the nations of the Old World and

the New. The American flag in the Philippines is the symbol of the change. Education therefore must change together with the change in the world conditions, because it is with the new conditions that education must train the rising generation to cope. This conviction that great changes are impending in the subject-matter of education is the third great characteristic of American educational thought to which I would call your attention to-day. In every type of school strenuous American teachers are endeavoring to tear out the non essentials. "Don't be cumbered up with a lot of unnecessary luggage in education," the American teacher pleads, "cut down your transport; don't make your pupils carry an ounce of unnecessary weight; confine yourself to the essentials; revise all your old traditions; lop away all superfluities. There is so much that a man ought to know that we must reduce the cost of the production of knowlege to the lowest possible figure by employing labor-saving appliances in education, and by avoiding to the utmost the waste of precious time."

This is the mood of the vigorous American teacher. It is also the mood of the vigorous American manufacturer. "If I were asked," says Mr. Young in his recent *Review of the American cotton industry*, "if I were asked to attempt in a single sentence a definition of the improved management [which characterizes the American manufacturer], I should say it is this: unceasing study and close analysis of the costs of production, and unresting endeavor to diminish any and every element in them by any departure from existing routine, or by any outlay of additional capital which close calculation may show to be probably advantageous. To follow this policy is no American monopoly. But to follow it successfully these are necessary—a trained intelligence, an untiring energy, a complete freedom from the trammels of tradition, and a certain bold tho calculating adventurousness."

May I, however, in passing suggest the doubt whether we are able at present to decide with any sort of certainty what are non-essentials in our system of education. The enthusiasts of the French Revolution thought that intellectual enlightenment would suffice to bring about the social millennium. We know how far their confidence was misplaced. Nor has the modern world, which owed so much to the humanitarian enthusiasm of the French Revolution, yet beaten its swords into plowshares. In 1791 the famous Dr. Anderson, of Glasgow, sent to the National Convention in Paris a prophetic gift—a model of a newly invented cannon. They hung it up with the inscription. "The gift of science to liberty." Liberty must sometimes wish that science had thought of giving her something else. Anyway, can we not imagine debate arising on the subject whether or not military drill is an essential or non-essential of the modern elementary and secondary school? And unless appearances are very deceptive, military excitement is not wholly distasteful to the young American.

4. Some people are fond of informing us that, in the future, the extension of national trade will depend a good deal on the magnitude and efficiency of national armaments. Be that the case or not, we may at least hazard the prediction that industrial and commercial success will require the fulfillment of four primary conditions: (1) hard work and imaginative power on the part of the directors of industry and their organizing subordinates; (2) the harnessing of applied science in the service of business; (3) intelligence and skill among the rank and file of the industrial army; and (4), not least important, honorable fidelity to contracts, expressed and implied.

The American man of business has clearly grasped some at least of these primary conditions for industrial success, tho it remains to be seen whether in the long run high tariffs and trusts are making for the health of American industry. The American manufacturers and merchants believe in education, and, with conspicuous generosity, back their belief. They are convinced that it is necessary to the future welfare of American industry and commerce to have good education all along the line. One most remarkable thing in the democratic education of America is that Americans are not content with supplying floods of primary instruction, leaving the rest to rather desultory effort or to sectional interests; they have grasped the fact that for national welfare under modern conditions the highest and most costly types of technical and university training are as indispensable as the kindergarten and the primary school. That great Glasgow professor, Adam Smith, to whom modern industry owes so much, and whose individualistic philosophy has been on many sides so congenial to the American temper, had no doubt as to the wisdom of providing, by public effort, for the education of the common people: "An instructed and intelligent people are always more decent and orderly than an ignorant and stupid one." But he threw the weight of his great authority against the state organization, or public endowment, of secondary and university education. On this side, the influence of Adam Smith (in many respects invaluable) was, for two generations at least, a *damnosa hereditas* to British liberalism. But America, which followed Adam Smith's advice as to primary education, has had the good sense to go elsewhere for lessons in regard to higher education. It is Germany that has taught America that a great modern state must strain every nerve to provide the best, the most practical, and the most efficient training, in universities and technical high schools, not only for the older learned professions, but for all the new kinds of scientific calling brought into existence by the marvelous development of applied science, and by the consequent growth of industry, of commerce, and of scientific administration. This is the lesson which our own country has still to learn. It is possible we shall be more willing to learn it from America than from Germany. Canada is jogging our elbow, and Canada is largely Scotch. There are signs that we are beginning to learn the lesson, but we have not yet faced the necessity for spending largely on the higher and more costly development of modern technological education. The American business men have rendered their country a great service by insisting on the provision of the best kind of higher technical education. If the practical business men in Great Britain take the same view, and press as vigorously for the best and highest type of technical education, and for a modernized liberal secondary education as its only sure foundation—then our battle is won. The American organizer of industry believes, as a rule, in the college-bred man, but he insists that the college-bred man shall begin, as the American saying is, with his feet in the dirt. Modern industry and business need the products of the highest education, but they cannot afford to pay for, nor will they put up with, fine academic airs and fastidious nonsense, or unwillingness to do the rough work which everyone must learn to do who means, in truth and thru and thru, to learn a trade.

May we not therefore sum up the chief favorable characteristics of American education in some such words as these? America heartily believes in education. Rich and poor make sacrifices for education because they believe in it. The United States is organized as a democracy. Therefore Americans believe in developing, by means of education, individuality of aptitude and independence of

character. But America is in large measure an industrial and commercial democracy. Modern industry requires initiative, self-reliance, resource, imagination, and command of applied science, not to speak of deeper things. The American man of business realizes that schools and universities can help him by furnishing him with able assistants. He, therefore, encourages the leaders of American education to adapt their work to modern business needs. But he knows that this cannot be done without great expense, and he does not flinch from bearing his share of the cost. These new demands, however, are throwing a great strain on American schools and on American teachers. The latter feel that their work must be brought into gear with modern needs. Therefore, American teachers are experimenting in all directions, with a view to dropping nonessentials out of education, and to lessening the cost of production of active-minded, scientifically equipped men of business and affairs.

So far I have endeavored to follow David Hume's maxim, and, with a few interjections, to look on the favorable side of things. But, if I may presume on your patience for a short time longer, I desire to say a few words about what seem to me weaknesses of education in the United States. Every nation, and therefore every national system of education, has the defects of its qualities; and he would be an inexperienced and misleading critic who should represent American education as wholly worthy of praise, and should fail to indicate in a spirit of sympathy and of scientific truthfulness, what in his judgment are the dark sides of so bright a picture.

1. Americans use a striking phrase to describe certain inflated and unsubstantial forms of commercial enterprise. They say they are "built on wind." Some such thought must come into the mind of a cultivated American when he listens to some of the maxims which pass for political philosophy in many American schools. How, for instance, would an intelligent boy in South Carolina harmonize in his mind the truth of those words near the beginning of the Declaration of Independence, "We hold these truths to be self-evident, that all men are created equal"—how would he reconcile that maxim, I say, with the horrid lawlessness of such a case of lynching as we read of in yesterday morning's paper, or indeed with the normal attitude of the Southern white to the colored people? There seems to me a taint of unreality in many of the phrases

which are still current in American political democracy, and the close dependence of the majority of schools on the good will of public bodies must lead to a certain want of frankness in dealing with problems of popular government in that part of the school curriculum which aims at giving instruction in the duties of citizenship. It is a fact of evil significance that in America the word "politics" is generally used in a bad sense. It connotes undesirable forms of political influence. And it is notorious that, in some cases, municipal corruption has baleful results in the sphere of educational administration.

2. In the second place, there is grave doubt whether the stricter forms of intellectual discipline have not been unduly sacrificed in many American schools. The besetting sin of some modern methods of education is that they stimulate interest without laying correspondent stress on intellectual discipline. As it were, they feed the children on sweeties and plumcake, in a strenuous revolt against an austere tradition of too much oatmeal porridge. The American passion for candy and ice cream finds its counterpart in the schoolroom. Nor does home discipline restore the balance. There are complaints in well-informed quarters that the younger Americans find it difficult to focus their attention on uncongenial tasks. Part of the mischief is that parents at home listen far too readily to their children's criticism on their teachers. Sometimes the teachers flinch from giving rebukes for fear of incurring a bad name in influential places. But a more insidious evil is the tendency on the part of teachers to make lessons interesting by avoiding the harder, duller, and more disciplinary parts of the subject. Of course, this is all a reaction from the formality of the old tradition and from the dreary and somewhat heavy-handed dullness of an obsolete form of school discipline. And this reaction is again part of yet a larger one. The excessive desire for encouraging among young children what is called "self-realization," even occasionally to the point of impertinence, is a revolt from the repressive precision of the over-strict Puritan home.

3. Unreality and lack of severe discipline lead to a third weakness,—superficiality,— with its attendant evils, exaggeration in language and love of excitement. The Americans do not as yet sufficiently allow for the slow percolation of ideas into the mind. They make too many short cuts. They are too fond of the last new thing. They forget that a pupil gains true independence of taste and judgment, not by hastily absorbing the teacher's conclusions, or by listening to selections made for him, but by slowly and thoroly working his way, under guidance and with encouragement, thru masterpieces as a whole, and thru masses of work bearing on his subject of study. In fact, is it not one of the chief differences between professional work and work that is amateur that the professional learns his business by going thru masses of the same kind of work often against the grain, while the amateur picks and chooses the things which happen at the time to take his fancy and to please his taste. All true culture has in it an element of stubbornness and persistence, which must be acquired, chiefly thru the lessons of life, but also thru the lessons of the school, which ought to prepare for life.

4. A fourth danger in American education proceeds from the tendency of American men to become unduly concentrated in business pursuits. The last thing for which I wish to hold a brief is want of application to business duties. But many Americans admittedly overdo their devotion to business affairs. They sterilize part of their nature by too great absorption in the excitement and struggles of commercial life. In the northern parts of the United States there is too little of what the writer of the book *Wisdom,* called the "diligence of idleness." Not that the American business man is sordid or pettifogging. On the contrary, he often brings to his business a strong power of imagination and a large gift of idealism. What he wants is not so much money for the sake of personal enjoyment, as money because it means power. He wants the intellectual and social distinction which are earned by marked business success. He wants to be counted with those who are effective, and who can bring things to pass. It is a great mistake to regard American business effort as mere dollar hunting. The real objects of pursuit are the power and the consideration which are conferred by wealth and by a great business reputation. But the practical result of all this concentration in business affairs is that the strength and interest of thousands of the the strongest minds in America are drawn into the one channel of commercial competition. One is tempted to say that a special danger of American life is the pursuit of material success in the spirit of idealism, while the converse danger in English life is the pursuit of ideal aims in the spirit of materialism. A great nation needs variety

of interest, variety of culture, variety of type, and variety of standards of success. The number of the *Outlook* published in New York on December 13 contained a thoughtful article on this aspect of American life. "The country," it writes, "is full of men who are overworking, not because they care for money, but because they want to command the most comfortable conditions for their families, who, if they were told that they were shortening their lives ten years, would not hesitate to go on, accepting the sacrifice as part of their duty, and an opportunity to be welcomed rather than avoided. Those who know American men well know that there is a deep vein of idealism in the great majority of them in their attitude toward their families. It is here that they spend themselves lavishly; it is here that many give their lives without hesitation. But the American father does not always give wisely. The tragedy lies in the substitution in the family life of the material for the spiritual things, and for that exchange many men are unconsciously responsible. They are so eager to furnish comfort to their families that they forget to give life; they are so willing to surrender their strength and their time for those they love that they forget to share themselves."

This overzeal for business forms an atmosphere which cannot but affect educational ideals. Intense absorption in commercial enterprise is not an aim worthy to dominate the thoughts and lives of the rising generation of a great people. Robert Louis Stevenson wisely said that "perpetual devotion to what a man calls his business is only to be sustained by perpetual neglect of many other things. And it is by no means certain that a man's business is the most important thing he has to do." There often rang in Stevenson's ears that noble answer of the Shorter Catechism to the question "What is the chief end of man?"

This subtle spirit of commercialism has worked another injury in American education. The training given in the primary schools has, as a rule, been far too much in the direction of clerical work. "Is it possible," writes Miss Jane Addams, of Hull House, Chicago, "that the business men whom we

in America so tremendously admire, have really been dictating the curriculum of our public schools, in spite of the convention of educators and the suggestion of university professors? The business man, of course, has not said, 'I will have the public school train office boys and clerks, so that I may have them easily and cheaply.' But he has sometimes said, 'Teach the children to write legibly and to figure correctly; to acquire habits of punctuality and order; to be prompt to obey; and you will fit them to make their way in the world as I have made mine.'" "Has," she asks, "the American workingman so far shared our universal American optimism that he has really believed that his children would never need to go into industrial life at all, but that all of his sons would become bankers or merchants?"

These are the impressions of American education which I desire to submit to your consideration to-day. I have dealt on the good sides, and also on what seem to me the darker sides of the subject, because it is necessary that we in this country should try to get a balanced view of the merits and defects of the educational system of a country which is in many ways so nearly related to our own. Too much depends for the future of the world on the outcome of the great educational movement in America for it to be becoming for us to rest content either with indifference in regard to it or with indiscriminate praise. Of all the educational movements now going forward in the world, that in America seems to me at present the most forceful and the most pregnant in great issues. It is of deep importance to British civilization that the relations between our country and the United States should grow closer and more friendly as the years go by. Teachers on both sides of the Atlantic can do much to foster this spirit of mutual sympathy and regard. And the more we study American life and American ideals, the more shall we come to admire the earnestness of American belief in education; the more shall we respect the pluck and devotion with which American educators are addressing themselves to their stupendous task, and the more heartily shall we wish them Godspeed in their efforts and a happy issue to their labors.

Conclusion: The Twentieth Century

It is quite clear from the foregoing documentary collection that interest in the different aspects of international and comparative education increased more rapidly toward the end of the nineteenth century, in both Europe and America, than in previous periods. The results can be seen in the fact that systematic research and publication of comparative education studies became relatively common—not only by the Office of Special Inquiries and Reports in London (1895), the Musée Pédagogique in Paris (1879), and the Zentralinstitut für Erziehung und Unterricht in Berlin (1915), but also by the United States Bureau of Education (later the Office of Education, 1867). In 1897 Sir Robert Morant noted that the publications by the U.S. Bureau of Education

have probably done more than any other single agency to encourage the comparative study of education and the various systems of educational administration now in force in the different countries of the world.

This growing interest in international and comparative education also resulted in an increased number of students in these fields. In 1908 the young I. L. Kandel and Peter Sandiford decided to sail from Britain to study at Teachers College, Columbia University. This decision proved to be a momentous one for the development of comparative education in North America and later contributed to the promotion of the field in Europe and other parts of the world.

After World War I the interests of comparative education continued to be served by the older organizations. However, many new agencies—such as the Institute of International Education in New York (1919), the International Institute of Teachers College in Columbia University (1923), the International Bureau of Education in Geneva (1925), and the Institut International de Coopération Intellectuelle in Paris (1925)—began to make significant contributions.

The program of the Teachers College Institute, particularly its research publications and the *Educational Yearbook* edited by Professor Kandel between 1925 and 1944, had a worldwide impact in the areas of international and comparative education. Also of significance were the *Year Book of Education* (1932 to 1940 and 1948 to date) published by the University of London Institute of Education and Teachers College and the *Annuaire international de l'éducation et de l'enseignement* (later *International Yearbook of Education*) issued by the International Bureau of Education from 1933 to 1939. Of particular importance was the appearance in 1933 of Kandel's *Comparative Education*, a seminal, thoroughgoing, definitive, scholarly treatise, which encouraged research and instruction and which was later translated into several languages.

"Courses in comparative education proliferated greatly after 1920"[1] in the United States. On the initiative of the U.S. Office of Education, an Advisory Committee on Comparative Education was formed at a meeting in Washington on May 4, 1935. One year later this committee met again with sixteen members representing scholars interested specifically in "instruction and research" in comparative education. At that time Dr. James F. Abel of the U.S. Office of Education reported the results of a questionnaire which elicited responses from 468 institutions and which indicated that some fifty-six individuals claimed "a major interest in comparative education."[2] Since the participants recognized "the growing interest in comparative education,"[3] they recommended specific steps towards the expansion of the services in this

---

[1]Thomas Woody, "The Trend Toward International Education," *School and Society*, LXXXIII, (January 21, 1956), 20.

[2]I. L. Kandel, *Comparative Education Conference*, May 1-2, 1936, Circular No. 159 (Washington: U.S. Office of Education, 1936), p. 6.

[3]*Ibid.*, p. 7.

field by the U.S. Office of Education.

Although many organizations were unable to continue operations and many careers were interrupted during World War II, soldiers who returned from overseas brought with them observations, memories, and even documentary evidence of foreign culture and education. Many had had opportunities to visit educational institutions, talk with children and parents, and discuss problems with educators in several countries. To some extent at least, the revival of interest in the study of foreign languages, literatures, culture, and education is traceable to the wartime and postwar experiences of American and other servicemen. In any event, interest in international and comparative education grew rapidly during the decade following World War II. The Institute of International Education in New York and the International Bureau of Education in Geneva resumed work. Many new organizations and institutions were established, including UNESCO (established in 1946), the Institut für Vergleichende Erziehungswissenschaft (established by Professor Friedrich Schneider in Salzburg, 1946 to 1953), the Pädagogische Arbeitsstelle (first established in Wiesbaden and later in Bonn, 1947), the Hochschule (later Deutsches Institut) für Internationale Pädagogische Forschung in Frankfurt am Main (1949), UNESCO Institut für Pädagogik in Hamburg (1951), the Center of Comparative Education at the University of Ottawa (1954), and the Research Institute of Comparative Education and Culture at the University of Kyushu, Japan (1954).

Teaching and research in comparative education on the university level were strengthened through the establishment in 1947 of a chair at the University of London Institute of Education. Professor Joseph A. Lauwerys became the incumbent and his work led to the resumption of the student trips each spring to the various continental school systems. Together with Dr. Nicholas Hans and Professor Schneider, Lauwerys organized a comparative education conference in March 1951 in London. This was the forerunner of many subsequent conferences. After some three days of discussion of various problems, "the note of optimism seemed to bode well for the future development of this field."[4] Conferences were convened in 1955 and in subsequent years.

Professor Schneider resumed his teaching career in 1946 at the Catholic Theological Faculty of Salzburg and in 1949 at the University of Munich. He published *Triebkrafte der Pädagogik der Völker* in 1947 and *Vergleichende Erziehungswissenschaft* in 1961. These were notable contributions by a scholar of advanced age. In addition, he directed the Salzburg Institute of Comparative Education and revived in 1946 his *Internationale Zietschrift fur Erziehungswissenschaft*.

Another event of importance was the appointment of Professor Walther Merck in 1950 to the new chair of comparative education at the University of Hamburg. The late Professor Merck also served for several years as director of the UNESCO Institute in Hamburg and as the editor of the *Internationale Zeitschrift für Erziehungswissenschaft*, published under the Institute's auspices since 1955.

The last two decades have seen an abundance of major publications emanating from the International Bureau of Education and from UNESCO. The latter began in 1952 its valuable series of handbooks of data and statistics on educational systems throughout the world. The University of London resumed in 1948 its *Year Book of Education* under the editorship of Professor Lauwerys and various coeditors. Since 1953 this annual compilation has been published jointly by the University of London Institute of Education and Teachers College, Columbia University, ably represented by Professors Robert King Hall, George Z. F. Bereday, and David G. Scanlon. Other noteworthy European works in the field include Nicholas Hans, *Comparative Education* (1949); Erich Hylla and W. L. Wrinkle, *Die Schulen in Westeuropa* (1953); Hans Espe, *Marc-Antoine Jullien von Paris: Skizzen und Vorarbeiten zu einem Werk über die Vergleichende Erziehung* (1954); Helmut Goetz, *Marc-Antoine Jullien de Paris (1775–1848)* (also published in 1954 in German). During 1955 three useful bibliographical series were started: the *Annual Educational Bibliography* issued by the International Bureau of Education; the *Scientia Paedagogica*, edited by Professor R. L. Plancke of the University of Ghent; and *Pedagogika i narodnoe obrazovanie v zarubezhnikh stranakh*, an annual compilation of foreign educational works published by the Academy of Pedagogical Sciences in Moscow.

The American specialists also contributed to the literature. Adolphe E. Meyer's *The Development of Education in the Twentieth Century* (second edition, 1949) was well regarded

---

[4]William W. Brickman, "An International Conference on Comparative Education," *School and Society*, LXXIII (June 2, 1951), 345.

and widely used, both in the United States and abroad. *Comparative Education* (1952), edited by Arthur H. Moehlman and Joseph S. Roucek, contains chapters on major countries. In 1955 Professor Kandel published *The New Era of Education: A Comparative Study*, an abridged and updated version of his earlier classic work of 1933. A major reference work, the quality of which has still not been surpassed by later works, was compiled in 1950 by Professor M. M. Chambers for the American Council on Education under the title *Universities of the World Outside U.S.A.* Between 1954 and 1959 the School of Education at New York University issued the proceedings of the annual conference on comparative education, at one of which (1956) the Comparative Education Society was formed.

Many factors underlay the rising interest in international and comparative education as a field of scholarly research, both in the technical and applied senses of the term. With the aid of the United States government, American students enrolled in foreign universities and students from distant countries pursued higher education in the United States. Travel abroad became popular, and colleges and universities organized tours for credit. The various programs of aid to other countries resulted in a two-way traffic of specialists. These and other circumstances contributed to the greater attention in university and government circles to comparative education.

In November 1948 Columbia University organized a seminar on foreign education, at which Professor George S. Counts, Professor Robert King Hall (successor to Dr. Kandel), and other specialists discussed educational organization in different countries. The U.S. Office of Education organized in June 1950 a conference on graduate and post-doctoral research in comparative education and related fields. Most of the participants, representing universities, organizations, and the Office of Education, had not published any major research studies in this area. It may have been this circumstance, plus the fact that the available research generally lacked depth and was not relevant to the solution of world problems of education, that prompted Robert G. Templeton in 1954 to echo Dr. Kandel's critique of 1936. Templeton complained of the merely descriptive, limited, and superficial comparisons. He felt that "in this failure to be comparative much of the research endeavor is dispersive, wasteful, and even futile."[5] While many of the descriptive studies might have been of interest if they had been thorough, original, and analytical, they were rarely this way.

Although there was a rising interest in international and comparative education, it apparently had not been translated, in a meaningful way, into curricular terms. The subject was not being made available to prospective teachers and other students. There was a neglect of comparative education in the program of teacher preparation and in graduate curriculums, traceable as a rule to the lack of sufficient linguistic competency among the teachers of education. Professor Ulich of Harvard University deplored "the decline of comparative education in the United States and other nations, probably with the exception of England and Germany."[6] However, he also stated that "the study of comparative education requires an unusually long preparation; a knowledge of foreign languages, traveling, acquaintance with various cultures and their history, and an insight into the intellectual and spiritual forces which have shaped man's civilization."[7]

It is beyond dispute that during the past decade the student of international and comparative education has been better served than ever before by the quantity and quality of available textbooks. In addition, the number of institutions offering courses in his field has increased throughout the world. George Z. F. Bereday discussed the expanding resources for research and teaching in the United States and elsewhere in his substantive work, *Comparative Method in Education* (1964). It certainly would be advisable for the interested student to note the extensive list in Professor Bereday's book of primary printed sources available to him. In so doing, however, he would quickly notice an almost universal lack of attention to the historical and philosophical foundations of international and comparative education. He would also notice how quickly bibliographies and source works become out of date as the explosion and dissemination of information in international education continues. The various overlapping

---

[5] Robert G. Templeton, "The Study of Comparative Education in the United States," *Harvard Educational Review*, XXIV, Summer (1954), 157.

[6] Robert Ulich, "Some Observations Concerning the Study of Comparative Education in the Education of Teachers," in William W. Brickman, ed. *The Role of Comparative Education in the Education of Teachers* (New York: School of Education, New York University, 1954), p. 11.

[7] *Ibid.*, p. 14.

interests of professors, practitioners, and students connoted by the words *international, comparative, developmental, cross-cultural, polycultural,* and even *cosmo-cultural* education are indicative of the burgeoning subject areas for research, teaching, and action programs.

This is aptly revealed in a recent annual survey entitled *Research in International Education* (1966)[8] that categorizes research interest under such diverse headings as "Education Abroad," "Education and Development," "International Education: History and Commentary," "Overseas Activities of U.S. Universities," "Academic Achievement of Foreign Students," and "Teaching English As a Second Language." The time has at last arrived when international and comparative educators are being confronted with an overwhelming mass of information which they have to translate into "knowledge."

The origins of comparative studies, and certainly international ones, have been shown in the historical introduction to this book to be both ancient and extensive. But the first systematic studies in the field, with few notable exceptions, were developed principally during the nineteenth century. This has been illustrated, of course, in some depth by the preceding collection of documents. The scientific, systematic, and methodological study and practice of international and comparative education became more refined during the early part of the twentieth century. However, it is only during the last two decades that comparative educators have illustrated more fully their ability to approach and understand scientifically the universality of educational problems and the commonality of educational aspirations.

[8]Harold Epstein and Stewart Fraser, eds. *Research in International Education* (New York: Institute of International Education and National Association for Foreign Student Affairs, 1966). See also Stewart E. Fraser, "International and Comparative Education," *Review of Educational Research*, XXXVII (February 1967), 57-73.

Bibliography

Achelis, Thomas Otto. "Deutsche Studenten auf nordischen Universitäten während des Dreissigjährigen Krieges," *Archiv für Kulturgeschichte*, XXXIX (1957), 189–208.

Adams, Richard N., and Charles C. Cumberland. *United States University Cooperation in Latin America*. East Lansing: Michigan State University Press, 1960.

Adams, Walter, and John A. Garraty. *Is the World Our Campus?* East Lansing: Michigan State University Press, 1960.

Alexander, William M. *The Four Nations of Aberdeen University and Their European Background*. Aberdeen: Aberdeen University Press, 1934.

Allbee, Lewis. *Education As an Implement of U.S. Foreign Policy (1938–1948)*. Ph.D. thesis, Yale University. East Grand Rapids, Mich.: The Author, 1948.

Allen, Carleton K. *Forty Years of the Rhodes Scholarships*. London: Oxford University Press, 1944.

Analytical Bibliography on Comparative Education. Paris: UNESCO, 1964.

Arnold, Matthew. *Schools and Universities on the Continent*. London: Macmillan, 1868.

_____. *The Popular Education of France with Notices to That of Holland and Switzerland*. London: Longmans, 1861.

A Survey of Chinese Students in American Universities and Colleges in the Past One Hundred Years. New York: China Institute of America, 1954.

Atiya, Aziz S. *Crusade, Commerce and Culture*. Bloomington: Indiana University Press, 1962.

Aydelotte, Frank. *The American Rhodes Scholarships*. Princeton: Princeton University Press, 1946.

Bache, Alexander D. *Report on Education in Europe to the Trustees of the Girard College for Orphans*. Philadelphia: Bailey, 1839.

Barnard, Henry, ed. *American Journal of Education*. 1855–1881.

_____. *National Education in Europe*. Hartford: Case, Tiffany, 1854.

_____. *National Education: Systems, Institutions, and Statistics of Public Instruction in Different Countries*. 2 vols. New York: Steiger, 1872.

Basset, César-Auguste. *Essais sur l'éducation, et sur l'organisation de quelques parties de l'instruction publique*, 2nd ed. Paris, 1814.

_____. *Essais sur l'organisation de quelques parties d'instruction publique*. Paris, 1808.

Baudouin, J. M. *Rapport sur l'état actuel de l'enseignement spécial et de l'enseignement primaire en Belgique, en Allemagne et en Suisse*. Paris, 1865.

Baumeister, August. "Die Einrichtung und Verwaltung des höheren Schulwesens in den Kulturländern von Europa und in Nordamerika," Pt. 2 of *Handbuch der Erziehungs- und Unterrichtslehre für höhere Schulen*, Vol. I. Munich: Beck, 1897.

Beals, Ralph L., and Norman D. Humphrey. *No Frontier to Learning: The Mexican Student in the United States*. Minneapolis: University of Minnesota Press, 1957.

Becker, H. T. *Die Kolonialpädagogik der grossen Mächte: Ein Kapitel der Vergleichenden Erziehungswissenschaft der Gegenwart*. Hamburg: Kolonial-Institut der Universität Hamburg, 1939.

Beer, Adolf. *Die Fortschritte des Unterrichtswesens in den Culturstaaten Europa's*. 2 vols. Vienna, 1868.

Bell, Whitfield J., Jr. "Philadelphia Medical Students in Europe, 1750–1800," *Pennsylvania Magazine of History and Biography*, LXVII (1943), 1–29.

Benjamin, Harold R. W. *Higher Education in the American Republics*. New York: McGraw-Hill, 1965.

Bennett, John W., Herbert Passin, and Robert K. McKnight. *In Search of Identity: The Japanese Overseas Scholar in America and Japan*. Minneapolis: University of Minnesota Press, 1958.

Bentwich, Norman. *The Rescue and Achievement of Refugee Scholars: The Story of the Displaced Scholars and Scientists, 1933–1952*. The Hague: Nijhoff, 1953.

Bereday, George Z. F. *Comparative Method in Education*. New York: Holt, Rinehart and Winston, 1964.

_____, and Joseph A. Lauwerys, eds. *Education and International Life: Year Book of 1964*. New York: Harcourt, Brace, & World, 1964.

Bernstein, Harry. *Making an Inter-American Mind*. Gainesville: University of Florida Press, 1961.

Bersohn, Mathias. *Studenci Polacy na Uniwersytecie Bolońskim w XV i XVII wieku*. Cracow: Akademii Umiejetnosci, 1890.

Bird, Charles. *Higher Education in Germany and England*. London, 1884.

Bodenman, Paul S. *American Cooperation with Higher Education Abroad*. Bulletin 1957, No. 8,

U.S. Office of Education. Washington, D.C.:
U.S. Government Printing Office, 1957.

Bonner, Thomas N. *American Doctors and German
Universities*: *A Chapter in International Intellectual Relations, 1870–1914*. Lincoln: University of Nebraska Press, 1963.

Boyce, Gray C. *The English–German Nation in the
University of Paris During the Middle Ages*.
Bruges: Saint Catherine Press, 1927.

Bozeman, Adda B. *Politics and Culture in International History*. Princeton: Princeton University Press, 1960.

Brachmann, Botho. *Russische Sozialdemokraten
in Berlin, 1895–1914, mit Berücksichtigung der
Studentenbewegung in Preussen und Sachsen*.
Berlin: Akademie-Verlag, 1962.

Brereton, Cloudesley. *Studies in Foreign Education*. London, 1913.

Brickman, William W. "A Historical Introduction
to Comparative Education," *Comparative Education Review*, III (February 1960), 6–13.

_____. "An Historical Survey of Foreign Writings
on American Educational History," *Paedagogica Historica*, II, 1 (1962), 5–21.

_____. "Church, State, and School in International
Perspective," in William W. Brickman and
Stanley Lehrer, eds. *Religion, Government and
Education*, pp. 144–247. New York: Society for
the Advancement of Education, 1961.

_____. "Comparative Education," *School and So-
ciety*, LXV (February 22, 1947), 145–151.

_____. "Comparative Education," *Review of Ed-
ucational Research*, XXXIV (February 1964),
44–61.

_____. "Comparative Education," in Robert L.
Ebel, ed. *Encyclopedia of Educational Re-
search*. 4th ed. New York: Macmillan [1970?].
In press.

_____, ed. *Comparative Education and Foreign
Educational Service*. New York: School of Education, New York University, 1957.

_____. *Comparative Education in Theory and
Practice*. New York: Payne Educational Sociology Foundation, 1956. Reprinted from *Journal
of Educational Sociology*, XXX (November 1956).

_____, Claude A. Eggertsen, *et al. Comparative
Education*: *Key - Word - in - Context Index and
Bibliography*. Ann Arbor: Comparative Education Program, University of Michigan Press,
1964.

_____. "Education in Foreign Countries," *School
and Society*, LXXIV (November 24, 1951), 326–
333.

_____. "Education in Latin America," *School and
Society*, LXVII (June 26, 1948), 479–487.

_____. "Education in the Occupied Countries,"
School and Society, LXXV (January 26, 1952),
52–61.

_____. "Education under Totalitarianism and Re-
construction," *School and Society*, LXVI (December 27, 1947), 511–519.

_____. *Foreign Students in the United States*: *A
Selected and Annotated Bibliography*. New York:
College Entrance Examination Board, 1963.

_____. "Historical Background of International
Cooperation Among Universities," in William
W. Brickman, ed. *Educational Imperatives in a
Changing Culture*, pp. 164–179. Philadelphia:
University of Pennsylvania Press, 1967.

_____. "Historical Background of International
Cooperation Among Universities," *School and
Society*, XCIV (April 16–30, 1966), 227–234.

_____. "Historical Development of Governmental
Interest in International Higher Education," in
Stewart E. Fraser, ed. *Governmental Policy
and International Education*, pp. 17–46. New
York: Wiley & Sons, 1965.

_____. "I. L. Kandel—International Scholar and
Educator," *Educational Forum*, XV (May 1951),
389–412.

_____. "International Cultural Organizations,"
New Goliards, 4 (June 1965), 24–31.

_____. "International Education," in Walter S.
Monroe, ed. *Encyclopedia of Educational Research*, 2nd ed., pp. 612–627: New York: Macmillan, 1950.

_____. "International Educational Cooperation,"
School and Society, LXIV (November 30, 1946),
386–392.

_____. "International Educational Relations,"
School and Society, LXIX (April 30, 1949), 318–
325.

_____. "International Relations in Higher Educa-
tion, 1862–1962," in William W. Brickman and
Stanley Lehrer, eds. *A Century of Higher Education*, pp. 208–239. New York: Society for the
Advancement of Education, 1962.

_____. *Introduction to the History of International
Relations in Higher Education*. New York: Ford
Foundation, 1960.

_____. "John Dewey's Foreign Reputation as an
Educator," *School and Society*, LXX (October
22, 1949), 257–265.

_____. "Prehistory of Comparative Education to
the End of the Eighteenth Century," *Comparative Education Review*, X (February 1966), 30–
47.

_____. "Professional Education Outside the
U.S.A." in G. Lester Anderson, chm., *Educa-
tion for the Professions*. Pt. 2 of Sixty-first
Yearbook, pp. 68–100. National Society for the
Study of Education. Chicago: University of
Chicago Press, 1962.

_____, ed. *Research in Comparative Education*.
New York: School of Education, New York University, 1959.

_____. "Segregated Education in International
Perspective," in William W. Brickman and
Stanley Lehrer, eds. *The Countdown on Segregated Education*, pp. 95–103. New York: Society
for the Advancement of Education, 1960.

_____. "Selected Bibliography of the History of

International Relations in Higher Education,'' *Paedogagica Historica*, V, 1 (1965), 164–182.

_____. ''Soviet Attitudes Toward John Dewey as an Educator,'' in Douglas E. Lawson and Arthur E. Lean, eds. *John Dewey and the World View*, pp. 64–136, 140–149. Carbondale: Southern Illinois University Press, 1964.

_____. ''The Early Development of Comparative Education,'' *Educational Forum*, XXXI (May 1967), 403–410.

_____. ''Ten Years of the Comparative Education Society,'' *Comparative Education Review*, X (February 1966), 4-15.

_____. ''The Meeting of East and West in Educational History,'' *Comparative Education Review*, V (October 1961), 82–89.

_____, ed. *The Role of Comparative Education in the Education of Teachers*. New York: School of Education, New York University, 1954.

_____. *The Teaching of Comparative Education*. New York: School of Education, New York University, 1955.

_____. ''Thomas Woody— Educational Historian and International Educator,''*Educational Forum* (March 1964), 267–275.

_____. ''William Heard Kilpatrick and International Education,'' *Educational Theory*, XVI (January 1966), 4–33.

_____. ''Works of Historical Interest in Comparative Education,'' *Comparative Education Review*, VII (February 1964), 324–326.

Brinkmann, Johann Peter.*Vergleichung der Erziehung der Alten mit der heutigen, und Untersuchungen, welche von beyden mit der Natur am meister übereinstimme*. Dessau, 1784.

Bronfenbrenner, Martin. *Academic Encounter: The American University in Japan and Asia*. New York: Free Press of Glencoe, 1962.

Brown, John F. *The Training of Teachers for the Secondary Schools in Germany and the United States*. New York, 1911.

Budinszky, Alexander. *Die Universität Paris und die Fremden an derselben im Mittelalter*. Berlin: Hertz, 1876.

Campbell, D.*Mixed Education of Boys and Girls in England and America*. London, 1874.

Carnovsky, Leon, ed. *International Aspects of Librarianship*. Chicago: University of Chicago Press, 1954.

Castillero Reyes, Ernesto de Jesús. *La Universidad Interamericana: Historia de sus antecedentes y fundación*. Panama, 1943.

Chambers, M. M., ed. *Universities of the World Outside U.S.A.* Washington, D.C.: American Council on Education, 1950.

Cieslak, Edward C. *The Foreign Student in American Colleges*. Detroit: Wayne University Press, 1955.

Cleveland, Harlan, Gerard J. Mangone, and John C. Adams. *The Overseas American*. New York: McGraw-Hill, 1960.

Colenbrander, H. T. ''De herkomst der Leidsche Studenten,'' *Pallas Leidensis* (1925), 275–303.

Collège d'Europe. *Université Européene*. Leyden: Sythoff, 1960.

Connell, W. F. *The Educational Thought and Influence of Matthew Arnold*. London: Routledge and Kegan Paul, 1950.

Coombs, Philip H. *The Fourth Dimension of Foreign Policy: Educational and Cultural Affairs*. New York: Harper & Row, 1964.

Costa, Amélia Fernandes da. *O Ensino Público Primário na Itália, França e Bélgica*. Rio de Janeiro: Tip. Nacional, 1893.

Cotner, Thomas E. *International Educational Exchange: A Selected Bibliography*. Bulletin 1961, No. 27, U.S. Office of Education. Washington, D.C.: U.S. Government Printing Office, 1961.

Cousin, Victor. *Rapport sur l'état de l'instruction publique en Allemagne*. Paris, 1831.

Cowan, L. Gray. *A History of the School of International Affairs and Associated Area Institutes: Columbia University*. New York: Columbia University Press, 1954.

Curti, Merle. *American Philanthropy Abroad: A History*. New Brunswick: Rutgers University Press, 1963.

_____, and Kendall Birr. *Prelude to Point Four: American Technical Missions Overseas, 1838–1938*. Madison: University of Wisconsin Press, 1954.

Cuvier, Georges. *Rapports sur l'instruction publique en Allemagne, en Hollande, en Italie*. Paris, 1811.

Danton, G. H. *The Culture Contacts of the United States and China: The Earliest Sino-American Culture Contacts, 1784–1844*. New York: Columbia University Press, 1931.

DeHovre, Frans. *German and English Education: A Comparative Study*. New York, 1917.

Derie, L. *L'école et l'état: essai de législations comparées*. Brussels: Société Belge de Librarie, 1895.

Dewey, John. *Impressions of Soviet Russia and the Revolutionary World: Mexico—China—Turkey*. New York: New Republic, 1929. Republished in 1964 by the Bureau of Publications, Teachers College, Columbia University, New York, with introduction and notes by William W. Brickman.

Dibon, P. *Le Voyage en France des étudiants neerlandais au XVIIème siècle*. La Haye, 1963.

Dollot, Louis. *Les Relations culturelles internationales*. Paris: Presses Universitaires de France, 1964.

Dreyfus-Brisac, Edmond. *L'éducation nouvelle: études de pédagogie comparée*. 3 vols. Paris, 1882-1897.

Dubay, Thomas. *Philosophy of the State As Educator*. Milwaukee: Bruce, 1959.

DuBois, Cora. *Foreign Students and Higher Education in the United States*. Washington, D.C.: American Council on Education, 1956.

Ducpetiaux, Edouard. *De l'état de l'instruction et populaire en Belgique, comparé avec celui de l'instruction en Allemagne, en Prusse, en Suisse, en France, en Hollande et aux Etats-Unis.* Brussels, 1838.

———. *Etat actuel et statistique de l'instruction primaire en Europe et en Amérique*, Vol. III of *Des progrès et de l'état actuel de la reforme pénitentiaire et des institutions préventives, aux Etats-Unis, en France, en Suisse, en Angleterre et en Belgique.* Brussels, 1838.

Duggan, Stephen, and Betty Drury. *The Rescue of Science and Learning.* New York: Macmillan, 1948.

Eckelberry, R. H. "Comparative Education," in Walter S. Monroe, ed. *Encyclopedia of Educational Research*, pp. 345–353. New York: Macmillan, 1941.

———. "Comparative Education," in Walter S. Monroe, ed. *Encyclopedia of Educational Research*, 2nd ed., pp. 283–290. New York: Macmillan, 1950.

"Educational Research in Countries Other Than the United States," *Review of Educational Research*, XXXII (June 1962), 213–262.

"Educational Research in Countries Other Than the U.S.A.," *Review of Educational Research*, XXVII (February 1957), 1–159.

Educational Yearbook. Ed. I. L. Kandel. New York: International Institute, Teachers College, Columbia University, 1925–1944.

Eells, Walter C. *American Dissertations on Foreign Education.* Washington, D.C.: National Education Association, 1959.

Eijkman, P. H. *L'internationalisme scientifique (sciences pures et lettres).* The Hague: Bureau Préliminaire de la Fondation pour l'Internationalisme, 1911.

Elliott, Randle. *The Institute of International Education: 1919–1944.* New York: The Institute, 1944.

Elliott, William Y., ed. *Education and Training in the Developing Countries: The Role of U.S. Foreign Aid.* New York: Praeger, 1966.

Espe, Hans, ed. *Die Bedeutung der Vergleichenden Erziehungswissenschaft für Lehrerschaft und Schule.* Berlin: Orbis, 1956.

Evers, Ernst August. *Fragmente der aristotelischen Erziehungskunst, oder prüfende Vergleichung der antiken und modernen Pädagogik.* Zürich, 1806.

Feyl, Othmar. *Beiträge zur Geschichte der slawischen Verbindungen und internationalen Kontakte der Universität Jena.* Jena: Gustav Fischer Verlag, 1960.

Fischer, Ernst G. *Ueber die englischen Lehranstalten in Vergleichung mit den unsrigen.* Berlin, 1827.

Flexner, Abraham. *Medical Education in Europe.* New York, 1912.

———. *Medical Education in the United States and Canada.* New York, 1910.

———. *Universities: American, English, German.* New York: Oxford University Press, 1930.

Frankel, Charles. *The Neglected Aspect of Foreign Affairs: American Educational and Cultural Policy Abroad.* Washington: Brookings Institution, 1966.

Fraser, James. *Report on the Common School System of the United States and Canada.* London, 1867.

Fraser, Stewart E. *American Education in Foreign Perspective.* New York: Wiley & Sons, 1968.

———. "Americanism Versus Communism, 1873," *School and Society*, XCIV (October 29, 1966), 355–357.

———. *Chinese Communist Education: Records of the First Decade.* Nashville: Vanderbilt University Press, 1965, and New York: Wiley & Sons, 1968.

———. "Communist Education and Visiting Educators—Contrasts in Russian and Chinese Policy," *The 1966–1967 Jennings Scholar Lectures*, pp. 143–165. Cleveland: The Educational Research Council of Greater Cleveland, 1967.

———. "Count Leopold Berchtold: Eighteenth Century Educational Travel Counselor," *Peabody Journal of Education*, XL, 1 (July 1962), 4–11.

———. *The Evils of a Foreign Education: Or Birdsey Northrop on Education Abroad.* Nashville: Peabody International Center, 1966.

———. "Foreign Student Poetry: John Shaw, an American at Edinburgh, 1801–1803," *Peabody Journal of Education*, XLI, 5 (March 1964), 304–307.

———. *Governmental Policy and International Education.* New York: Wiley & Sons, 1965.

———. "International and Comparative Education," *Review of Educational Research*, XXXVII (February 1967), 57–73.

———. "Jullien de Paris: Nineteenth Century International and Comparative Education," *The Educational Forum*, XXVII, 2 (January 1963), 177–182.

———. *M. A. Jullien's Plan for Comparative Education.* New York: Teachers College, Columbia University, 1964.

———. "Notes on Educational Research in the U.S.S.R.," *Australian Journal of Education*, VI, 3 (June 1962).

———. "Notes on the Nature and Content of Comparative Education," *The Jamia Educational Quarterly* (Karachi, Pakistan: The Jamia Institute of Education), V, 1 (January 1964), 3–31.

———. "Residential Academic Centers for International Education; A Proposal for Their Establishment in the United States," *Peabody Journal of Education*, XLIII, 5 (March 1966), 265–270.

———. "Shattered Sino-Soviet Educational Relations," *Phi Delta Kappan* (February 1967), 288–293.

———. "Sino-Soviet Educational Cooperation, 1950–1960," in Stewart Fraser, ed. *Governmental Policy and International Education*, pp. 189–206. New York: Wiley & Sons, 1965.

———. "Some Aspects of University Cooperation

in International Education," *School and Society*, XCIV (April 16–30, 1966), 234–244.

_____. "U.S. International Education: The Chinese Communist View," *International Educational and Cultural Exchange* (Spring 1967), 74–81.

Frazao, Manuel J. P. *O Ensino Público Primário na Itália, Suíça, Bélgica, Inglaterra e Franca*. Rio de Janeiro: Tip. da Gazate de Notícias, 1893.

Friedel, V,-H. *La Pedagogie dans les pays etrangers*. Paris, 1910.

_____. *Traitements des instituteurs et des institutrices à l'étranger*. Paris, 1903.

Friedländer, Ernst, and Carlo Malagola, eds. *Acta nationis germanicae universitatis bononiensis ex archetypis Tabularii Malvezziani*. Berlin: Reimer, 1887.

Fück, Johann. *Die arabischen Studien in Europa bis in den Anfang des 20. Jahrhunderts*. Leipzig, 1955.

Garraty, John A., and Walter Adams. *From Main Street to the Left Bank: Students and Scholars Abroad*. East Lansing: Michigan State University Press, 1959.

Geanakoplos, Deno. *Greek Scholars in Venice: Studies in the Dissemination of Greek Learning from Byzantium to Western Europe*. Cambridge: Harvard University Press, 1962.

Goetz, Helmut. *M. A. Jullien de Paris (1775–1848): Der geistige Werdegang eines Revolutionärs*. Dornbirn, Switz.: Mayer, 1954.

Grasby, W. C. *Teaching in Three Continents*. London: Cassell, 1891.

Gray, George W. *Education on an International Scale: A History of the International Education Board, 1923–1938*. New York: Harcourt, Brace, 1941.

Green, F. C. *A Comparative View of French and British Civilization (1850–1870)*. London: Dent, 1965.

Gregory, Winifred, ed. *International Congresses and Conferences: 1840–1937*. New York: Wilson, 1938.

Griscom, John. *A Year in Europe*. 2 vols. New York, 1823.

Guilday, Peter. "The English Catholic Refugees on the Continent, 1588–1795," in *The English Colleges and Convents in the Catholic Low Countries, 1588–1795*, Vol. I. Doctor's thesis, University of Louvain. London: Longmans, Green, 1914.

Haines, George, IV. *German Influence upon English Education and Science, 1880–1866*. New London: Connecticut College, 1957.

Hans, Nicholas A. *Comparative Education*, 3rd ed. London: Routledge and Kegan Paul, 1958.

_____. *The Principles of Educational Policy: A Study in Comparative Education*, 2nd ed. London: King, 1933.

Hanson, Haldore. *The Cultural-Cooperation Program: 1938–1943*. Publication 2137, U.S. Department of State. Washington, D.C.: U.S. Government Printing Office, 1944.

Harley, John E. *International Understanding: Agencies Educating for a New World*. Stanford: Stanford University Press, 1931.

Hart, Henry. *Campus India: An Appraisal of American College Programs in India*. Minneapolis: University of Minnesota Press, 1961.

Hart, James M. *German Universities*. New York: Putnam, 1874.

Haskins, Charles H. *Studies in Mediaeval Culture*. Oxford: Clarendon, 1929.

_____. *The Renaissance of the Twelfth Century*. Cambridge: Harvard University Press, 1927.

Hazelton, M. W. *British and American Education: The Universities of the Two Countries Compared*. New York, 1880.

Hecht, Friedrich August. *De re scholastica Anglica cum Germanica comparata*. Freiburg, 1795.

Hessen, Sergius. "Kritische Vergleichung des Schulwesens der anderen Kulturstaaten," Sec. 3 of Herman Nohl and Ludwig Pallat, eds. *Handbuch der Pädagogik*, Vol. IV. Langensalza: Beltz, 1928.

Hevi, Emmanuel J. *An African Student in China*. New York: Praeger, 1963.

Hickson, William E. *Account of the Dutch and German Schools*. London, 1840.

Higginson, J. H. *Sadler's Studies of American Education*. Leeds: University of Leeds Institute of Education, 1955.

_____. "The Centenary of an English Pioneer in Comparative Education: Sir Michael Sadler (1851–1943)," *International Review of Education*, VII, 3 (1961), 286–296.

Hilker, Franz. *Vergleichende Pädagogik*. Munich: Hueber, 1962.

Hinsdale, B. A. "Notes on the History of Foreign Influences upon Education in the United States," in U.S. Bureau of Education, *Report of the Commissioner of Education, 1897–98*. pp. 591–629. Washington, D.C.: U.S. Government Printing Office, 1899.

Hirsch, Felix S. "The Migration of Scholars in History," *School and Society*, XLV (June 19, 1937), 832–839.

Hofler, Carl-Adolf-Constantin. *Magister Johann Hus und der Abzug der deutschen Professoren und Studenten von Prag, 1409*. Prague, 1864.

Holmes, B., and J. B. Robinsohn, eds. *Relevant Data in Comparative Education*. Hamburg: UNESCO Institute for Education, 1963.

Hughes, R. E. *The Making of Citizens: A Study in Comparative Education*. London, 1902.

Idenburg, Ph. J. *Inleiding tot de vergelijkende opvoedkunde*. Groningen: Wolters, 1959.

International Guide to Educational Documentation: 1955–1960. Paris: UNESCO, 1963.

International Yearbook of Education. Geneva: International Bureau of Education, 1933 to date. (Originally, *Annuaire international de l'education et de l'enseignement*.)

Internationales Jahrbuch für Geschichtsunterricht. Ed. Arbeitsgemeinschaft Deutscher Lehrer

Verbände. Braunschweig, 1952 to date.

Ivanov, S. V., and N. N. Iordanski, eds. *Novie sistemi obrazovatelnoi raboti v shkolakh Yevropi i S. Ameriki.* Moscow: "Rabotnik Prosveshcheniya," 1930.

Iyer, Raghavan, ed. *The Glass Curtain Between Asia and Europe.* London: Oxford University Press, 1965.

Jairazbhoy, R. A. *Foreign Influences in Ancient India.* New York: Asia Publishing House, 1963.

Jörgensen, E. "Nordiske studierejser i Middelalderen," *Dansk Historisk Tidsskrift* (1915–1917), 331–382.

Johnson, Walter, and Francis J. Colligan. *The Fulbright Program: A History.* Chicago: University of Chicago Press, 1965.

Jones, E. Alfred. *American Members of the Inns of Court.* London: Saint Catherine Press, 1924.

Jourdan, Edouard, and G. Dumont. *Etude sur les écoles de commerce en Allemagne, en Autriche-Hongrie, en Belgique, en Danemark, en Italie, en Roumanie, en Suède, en Suisse (L'Europe moins France), en Russie, et aux d'Amérique.* Paris, 1884.

Jullien, Marc-Antoine. "Esquisse et vues préliminaires d'un ouvrage sur l'éducation comparée," *Journal d'Education* (1816–1817). Issued as a pamphlet, Paris, 1817; Trans. in part, "M. A. Jullien's Questions on Comparative Education," in William Russell, ed. *American Journal of Education,* I (1826), 403–408, 481–485, 730–737.

Kandel, I. L. *Comparative Education.* Boston: Houghton Mifflin, 1933.

_____. "Comparative Education," *Review of Educational Research,* VI (October 1936), 400–416, 450–456.

_____. *Comparative Education Conference.* Washington, D.C., 1936.

_____. *Essays in Comparative Education.* New York: Teachers College, Columbia University, 1930.

_____. *The New Era in Education: A Comparative Study.* Boston: Houghton Mifflin, 1955.

_____. *United States Activities in International Cultural Relations.* Washington, D.C.: American Council on Education, 1945.

Kazamias, Andreas. "History, Science and Comparative Education: A Study in Methodology," *International Review of Education,* VIII, 3–4 (1963), 383–398.

Keene, Donald. *The Japanese Discovery of Europe: Hondo Toshiaki and Other Discoverers.* London: Routledge and Kegan Paul, 1952.

Keesing, Felix M. *Education in Pacific Countries.* London: Oxford University Press, 1938.

Keller, Franklin J. "Comparative Vocational Education and Guidance," *Review of Educational Research,* IX (October 1939), 408–411, 443–446.

Kellermann, Fritz. *The Effect of the World War on European Education.* Cambridge: Harvard University Press, 1928.

Kibre, Pearl. *The Nations in the Mediaeval Universities.* Cambridge: Mediaeval Academy of America, 1948.

King, Edmund J., ed. *Communist Education.* London: Methuen, 1963.

Klemm, Louis R. *European Schools.* New York, 1889.

Kneller, George F. "Comparative Education," in Chester W. Harris, ed. *Encyclopedia of Educational Research,* 3rd ed., pp. 316–323. New York: Macmillan, 1960.

Knight, Edgar W., ed. *Reports on European Education.* New York: McGraw-Hill, 1930.

Knod, Gustav C. *Deutsche Studenten in Bologna (1789–1862): Biographischer Index zu den Acta nationais germanicae Universitatis Bononiensis.* Berlin: Decker, 1899.

Konovalov, S. "Anglo-Russian Relations, 1620–4," in S. Konovalov, ed. *Oxford Slavonic Papers,* Vol. IV. Oxford: Clarendon, 1953.

_____. "Twenty Royal Russian Letters (1626–34)," in S. Konovalov, ed. *Oxford Slavonic Papers,* Vol. III. Oxford: Clarendon, 1952.

Kotschnig, Walter M. *Unemployment in the Learned Professions.* London: Oxford University Press, 1937.

Kraus, Michael. *The Atlantic Civilization: Eighteenth-Century Origins.* Ithaca, N.Y.: Cornell University Press, 1949.

Krumpelmann, John T. *Southern Scholars in Goethe's Germany.* Chapel Hill: University of North Carolina Press, 1965.

Kruse, C. A. W. *Betrachtungen über den Zustand der englischen Erziehungs- und Unterrichtsanstalten im Jahre 1836, veranlasst durch eine Reise nach England.* Elberfeld, 1837.

_____. *Vergleichende Bemerkungen über das französische Schulwesen.* Elberfeld, 1832.

LaFargue, Thomas E. *China's First Hundred.* Pullman: State College of Washington Press, 1942.

Laishley, R. *Report on the State of Education in Great Britain, France, Switzerland, Italy, Germany, Belgium, and the United States.* Wellington, N.Z., 1886.

Lambert, Richard D., and Marvin Bressler. *Indian Students on an American Campus.* Minneapolis: University of Minnesota Press, 1956.

Landreyt, Marie-Casimir. *L'instruction publique en France et les écoles américaines.* Paris, 1883.

Lange, Helene. *Higher Education of Women in Europe.* Trans. and accompanied by comparative statistics by L. R. Klemm. New York, 1890.

Laves, Walter H. C., and Charles A. Thomson. *UNESCO: Purpose, Progress, Prospects.* Bloomington: Indiana University Press, 1957.

Law, Narenda N. *Promotion of Learning in India by Early European Settlers (up to about 1800 A.D.).* London: Longmans, Green, 1915.

Learned, William S. *The Quality of the Educational Process in the United States and in Europe.*

New York: Carnegie Foundation for the Advancement of Teaching, 1927.

Levasseur, Pierre Emile. *L'ensignement primaire dans les pays civilisés*. Paris: Perger-Levrant, 1897.

Lindsay, Rao H. *Nineteenth Century American Schools in the Levant: A Study of Purposes*. Ann Arbor: School of Education, University of Michigan, 1965.

L'Institut International de Coopération Intellectuelle, 1925–1946. Paris: Institut Internationale de Coopération Intellectuelle [1946].

Lips, Julius E. *Die internationale Studentenbewegung nach dem Kriege*. Leipzig: Verlag Vivos Voco, 1921.

Long, Orie W. *Literary Pioneers: Early American Explorers of European Culture*. Cambridge: Harvard University Press, 1935.

Luchaire, Julien. "Principes de la coopération intellectuelle international," in *Académie de Droit International*, Donation Carnegie pour la Paix Internationale, Recueil des Cours, 1925, IV, 312–406. Paris: Hachette, 1926.

Luschin von Ebengreuth, A. "Quellen zur Geschichte deutscher Rechtshörer in Italien," in *Sitzungsberichte der Akademie der Wissenschaften, Philosophisch-historische Klasse*, Vols. CXIII, CXVIII, CXXIV. Wien, 1886–1891.

MacGregor, Gordon. *The Experiences of American Scholars in Countries of the Near East and South Asia*. Ithaca, N.Y.: Cornell University Press, 1962.

MacNair, H. F. *The Chinese Abroad*. Shanghai: Commercial Press, 1924.

Malagola, C. *I libri della nazione tedesca presso lo studio Bolognese*. Bologna, 1884.

Malkova, Zoya, compiler. *O vospitanii uchashchikhsya v stranakh sotsialisma*. Moscow: Uchpedgiz, 1961.

Mann, Horace. *Seventh Annual Report of the Secretary of the Board*. Boston: Dutton and Wentworth, 1844.

Matos, Luis de. *Les Portugais à l'Université de Paris entre 1500 et 1550*. Coimbra, 1950.

Matthews, Roderic D., and Matta Akrawi. *Education in Arab Countries of the Near East*. Washington, D.C.: American Council on Education, 1949.

Mayhew, Arthur. *Education in the Colonial Empires*. New York: Longmans, Green, 1938.

McMurry, C. A. *Die Organisation des höheren Schulwesens in den Vereinigten Staaten Amerikas und in England und die Stellung des Staates zu demselben*. Jena, 1888.

McMurry, Ruth E., and Muna Lee. *The Cultural Approach: Another Way in International Relations*. Chapel Hill. University of North Carolina Press, 1947.

Merriam, Charles E. *The Making of Citizens: A Comparative Study of Methods of Civic Training*. Chicago: University of Chicago Press, 1931.

Métraux, Guy S. *Exchange of Persons: The Evolution of Cross-Cultural Education*. New York: Social Science Research Council, 1952.

Meyer, Adolph E. *The Development of Education in the Twentieth Century*, 2nd ed. New York: Prentice-Hall, 1949.

Meyerhof, M. "Von Alexandrien nach Baghdad, ein Beitrag zur Geschichte des philosophischen und medizinischen Unterrichts bei den Arabern," in *Abhandlungen der preussischen Akademie der Wissenschaften* (Phil.-Hist. Kl.). Berlin, 1930.

Mitchell, R. J. "English Law Students at Bologna in the Fifteenth Century," *English Historical Review*, LI (April 1936), 270–287.

Molnár, Aladár. *Pädagogische Studien in der Schweiz und in Baiern: Im Auftrage des königlichen ungarischen Unterrichtsministeriums*. Budapest: Ludwig Aigner, 1874.

Monroe, Paul. *Essays in Comparative Education*. New York: Teachers College, Columbia University, 1927.

_____. *Essays in Comparative Education*. New York: Teachers College, Columbia University, 1932.

Morris, Richard T. *The Two-Way Mirror: National Status in Foreign Students' Adjustment*. Minneapolis: University of Minnesota Press, 1960.

Morsch, H. *Das höhere Lehramt in Deutschland und Oesterreich*. Leipzig, 1905, 1907.

Motylev, V. V., *et al. Sistema obrazovaniya v nekotorikh kapitalicheskikh stranakh*. Moscow: Vsesoyuzni Institut Nauchnoi Tekhnicheskoi Informatsii, 1960.

Mumford, W. Bryant, and John Williamson. "Comparative Colonial Education," *Review of Educational Research*, IX (October 1939), 395–400, 440–441.

Mumford, William B. *A Comparative Survey of Native Education in Various Dependencies*. London: Evans, 1937.

Murray, David. *The Use and Abuse of Examinations; with Sketches of Systems Now in Use in China, France, Germany, and England*. Syracuse, N.Y., 1880.

Nardi, Noah, ed. "Bayot ha-hinuch ha-ivri b'tfutzot Ha-golah," in *Problems of Diaspora Education*. Jerusalem: Department of Education and Culture, Jewish Agency, 1961.

_____. "Yesodot l'hinuch ha-ivri b'tfutzot ha-golah," in *Fundamental Principles for Diaspora Education*. Jerusalem: Department of Education and Culture, Jewish Agency, 1958.

Nash, Paul. *Culture and the State: Matthew Arnold and Continental Education*. New York: Teachers College Press, 1966.

Niemeyer, August Hermann. *Beobachtungen auf Reisen in und ausser Deutschland, nebst Erinnerungen an denkwürdige Lebenserfahrungen und Zeitgenossen in den letzten 50 Jahren*. Halle, 1924.

Northrop, F. S. C. *The Meeting of East and West*. New York: Macmillan, 1946.

Novie knigi po pedagogike i narodnomu obrazovaniyu zarubezhnikh stran. Moscow: Ushinskii Library. From 1956.

Novosti Press Agency. *Two Universities: An Account of the Life and Work of Lumumba Friendship University and Moscow State University*. London: Soviet Booklets, 1963.

O'Boyle, James. *The Irish Colleges on the Continent*. Dublin: Browne and Nolan, 1935.

O'Brien, Kenneth B., Jr. "The Cuban Educational Association: An Early Experiment in International Education," *Journal of Negro Education* (Winter 1963), 6–15.

Office of Inter-American Affairs. *History of the Office of the Coordinator of Inter-American Affairs*. Washington, D.C.: U.S. Government Printing Office, 1947.

Olde, Emanuel M., and Paul F. Watz. *De universitate Parisiensi a suecis medio aevo frequentata*. Ph.D. thesis, University of Uppsala. Uppsala: Regia Academia, 1830.

O'Leary, DeLacy. *Arabic Thought and Its Place in History*. London, 1954.

Open Doors. Annual Census of Foreign Students in the United States, issued by the Institute of International Education, New York City, since 1949.

Otlet, Paul. *L'Université Internationale: Documents relatifs à sa constitution. Rapport, Conférence, Statut. Session inaugurale*. Brussels: Palais Mondial, 1920.

_____. *Sur la création d'une université internationale*. Brussels: Lamberty, 1920.

Paludan, J. *Det høiere skolevaesten i Danmark, Norge og Sverig*. Copenhagen, 1885.

Parkin, George R. *The Rhodes Scholarships*. Boston: Houghton Mifflin, 1912.

Parsons, Edward A. *The Alexandrian Library*. Amsterdam: Elsevier, 1952.

Peacock, Edward. *Index to English Speaking Students Who Have Graduated at Leyden University*. London: Longmans, Green, 1883.

Pedagogika i narodnoe obrazovanie v zarubezhnikh stranakh. Moscow. Akademiya Pedagogicheskikh Nauk RSFSR, 1955 to date.

Persijn, Alexander. *Pfälzische Studenten und ihre Ausweichuniversitäten während des Dreissigjährigen Krieges. Studien zu einem pfälzischen Akademikerbuch*. Mainz, 1959.

Pfeiffer, Heinrich. *Ausländische Studenten an den wissenschaftlichen Hochschulen in der Bundesrepublik und West-Berlin: 1951–1961*. Wiesbaden: Steiner, 1962.

Pham-Tihi-Tu. *La coopération intellectuelle sous la Société des Nations*. Geneva: Droz, 1964.

Pochmann, Henry A. *German Culture in America, 1600–1900: Philosophical and Cultural Influences*. Madison: University of Wisconsin Press, 1957.

Porto-Carrero, Leopoldina T. *O Ensino Público Primário em França, Espanha e Portugal*. Rio de Janeiro: Of. do Instituto Profissional, 1896.

Pousson, Leon B. *The Totalitarian Philosophy of Education*. Ph.D. thesis. Washington: Catholic University of America Press, 1944.

Poznanski, Shmuel. "Anshei Kiruan," in D. V. Günzburg and I. Markon, eds. *Festschrift zu Ehren des Dr. A. Harkavy*, pp. 175–220. St. Petersburg, 1908.

Rapacz, Richard V., and Albert S. Kahn. "Comparative Education," *Review of Educational Research*, XXXI (February 1961), 57–69.

Rashdall, Hastings. *The Universities of Europe in the Middle Ages*. ed. F. M. Powicke and A. B. Emden. 3 vols. New York: Oxford University Press, 1936.

Rastoul, A. *L'internationale universitaire et la coopération intellectuelle au Moyen Age*. Paris: Les Editions Internationales, 1934.

Rawlinson, H. G. *Intercourse Between India and the Western World from the Earliest Times to the Fall of Rome*. Cambridge, England: University Press, 1916.

Rigg, James H. *National Education in Its Social Conditions and Aspects and Public Elementary Education, English and Foreign*. London, 1873.

Rivier, Alphons. "Die Schweizer auf der Hochschule Leiden 1575–1875," *Anzeiger für Schweizerische Geschichte*, N.F., 6 (1875), pp. 138–160.

Robinson, Arthur G. *The Senior Returned Students: A Brief Account of the Chinese Educational Mission under Dr. Yung Wing, 1872–1881*. Tientsin: Tientsin Press, 1932.

Rosen, Seymour M. *The People's Friendship University in the U.S.S.R.* Washington, D.C.: U.S. Office of Education, 1962.

Ross, George W. *Report on Compulsory Education in Canada, Great Britain, Germany, and the United States*. Toronto, 1891.

Rosselló, P. *Forerunners of the International Bureau of Education*. Abridged and trans. by Marie Butts. London: Evans, 1944.

_____. *Les Précurseurs du Bureau International d'Education*. Geneva: Bureau International d'Education, 1943.

Royal Commissioners of Great Britain. *Report on Technical Instruction*. 5 vols. London, 1884.

Ruge, Herman. *Skoletanker og skoleproblemer i det 20. århundre*. Oslo: Cappelen, 1961.

Sadler, John E. *J. A. Comenius and the Concept of Universal Education*. New York: Barnes & Noble, 1966.

Sadler, Michael E. *Contrasts between German and American Ideals in Education*. London, 1902.

_____. *How Far Can We Learn Anything of Practical Value from the Study of Foreign Systems of Education?* Guilford, England, 1900.

_____. *The Admission of Women to Universities*. London, 1897.

Sandys, J. E. "English Scholars of Paris and Franciscans of Oxford," in A. W. Ward and A. R.

Waller, eds. *The Cambridge History of English Literature.* Vol. I, pp. 183–216, Cambridge, England: University Press, 1920.

Sankalia, Hasmukh D. *The University of Nalanda.* Madras: Paul, 1934.

Sansom, G. B. *The Western World and Japan: A Study in the Interaction of European and Asiatic Cultures.* New York: Knopf, 1950.

Sarmiento, Domingo Faustino. *De la educación popular.* 1849.

Sarton, George. "The Unity and Diversity of the Mediterranean World," *Osiris*, II (1936), 406–463.

Scanlon, David G. *International Education: A Documentary History.* New York: Teachers College, Columbia University, 1960.

Schairer, Reinhold. *Die Studenten im internationalen Kulturleben: Beiträge zur Frage des Studiums im fremdem Lande.* Münster, Westfalen: Aschendorff, 1927.

Schleiden, Mathias I. *The Importance of the Jews for the Preservation and Revival of Learning During the Middle Ages.* (Trans. from the 4th ed.) London: Siegle, Hill, 1911.

Schmeckebier, Laurence F. *International Organizations in Which the United States Participates.* Washington, D.C.: Brookings Institution, 1935.

Schmidt, Steffi. *Die Niederlände und die Niederländer im Urteil deutscher Reisenden.* Siegburg: Schmidt, 1963.

Schneider, Friedrich. *Europäische Erziehung.* Freiburg i. Br.: Europa et Schola Editio, 1959.

_____. *Geltung und Einfluss der deutschen Pädagogik im Ausland.* Munich: Oldenbourg, 1943.

_____. *Triebkräfte der Pädagogik der Völker.* Salzburg: Müller, 1947.

_____. *Vergleichende Erziehungswissenschaft.* Heidelberg: Quelle & Meyer, 1961.

Schneppen, Heinz. *Niederländische Universitäten und deutsches Geistesleben: Von der Gründung der Universität Leiden bis ins späte 19. Jahrhundert.* Münster, Westfalen: Aschendorffsche Verlagsbuchhandlung, 1960.

Schools Inquiry Commission. *Report of the Commissioners, Presented to Parliament.* 4 vols. London, 1869.

Schwantes, Robert S. *Japanese and Americans: A Century of Cultural Relations.* New York: Harper, 1955.

Scigliano, Robert, and Guy H. Fox. *Technical Assistance in Vietnam.* New York: Praeger, 1965.

Scott, Franklin D. *The American Experience of Swedish Students.* Minneapolis: University of Minnesota Press, 1955.

Scott, Jonathan F. *Patriots in the Making. What America Can Learn from France and Germany.* London, 1916.

Scurla, Herbert. *Umfang und Richtung der zwischenstaatlichen Studentenwanderung.* Ph.D. thesis, University of Leipzig. Berlin: Deutscher Akademischer Austauschdienst, 1933.

Seebohm, Frederic. *The Oxford Reformers of 1498: Being a History of the Fellow-Work of John Colet, Erasmus, and Thomas More.* London: Longmans, Green, 1867.

Seeley, Levi. *The Common School System of Germany and Its Lessons to America.* New York, 1896.

Sewell, William H., and Oluf M. Davidson. *Scandinavian Students on an American Campus.* Minneapolis: University of Minnesota Press, 1961.

Singh, Amar Kumar. *Indian Students in Britain: A Survey of Their Adjustment and Attitudes.* London: Asia Publishing House, 1963.

Skard, Sigmund. *American Studies in Europe: Their History and Present Organization.* 2 vols. Philadelphia: University of Pennsylvania Press, 1958.

Smith, Bruce L. *Indonesian-American Cooperation in Higher Education.* East Lansing: Michigan State University Press, 1960.

Smith, Henry L. *Comparative Education.* Bloomington, Ind.: Educational Publications, 1941.

_____. and Harold Littell. *Education in Latin America.* New York: American Book Co., 1934.

Smith, R. W. Innes. *English-Speaking Students of Medicine at the University of Leyden.* Edinburgh: Oliver and Boyd, 1932.

Sonnenschein, A. *Educational Codes of Foreign Countries.* London: Sonnenschein, 1889.

Special Reports on Educational Subjects. Ed. Michael E. Sadler. Office of Special Inquiries and Reports, Privy Council on Education. 28 vols. London: Board of Education, 1897–1914.

Spindler, George W. *The Life of Karl Follen: A Study in German-American Cultural Relations.* Chicago, 1917.

Stein, Lorenz. "Das Elementar- und das Berufsbildungswesen in Deutschland, England, Frankreich, und anderen Ländern," *Verwaltungslehre,* V (1868).

Stelling-Michaud, S. *Etudiants Vaudois à l'Université de Bologne de 1265 à 1300.* Lausanne, 1944.

_____. *L'Université de Bologne et la pénétration des Droits Romains et Canoniques en Suisse aux XIIIe et XIVe siècles.* Geneva: Droz, 1955.

Stieda, Wilhelm. "Deutsche Gelehrte als Professoren an der Universität Moskau," *Abhandlungen der philologisch-historischen Klasse der sächsischen Akademie der Wissenschaften,* XL, 5 (1930), 1–127.

Stoker, Spencer. *The Schools and International Understanding.* Chapel Hill: University of North Carolina Press, 1933.

Stowe, Calvin E. *Report on Elementary Public Instruction in Europe.* Boston: Dutton and Wentworth, 1838.

Suter, H. *Die Araber als Vermittler der Wissenschaft und deren Uebergang vom Orient zum Occident.* 1897.

Swift, Fletcher H. *European Policies of Financing Public Educational Institutions.* 5 vols. Berkeley: University of California Press, 1933–1939.

Templeton, Robert G. "The Study of Comparative Education in the United States," *Harvard Educational Review*, XXIV (Summer 1958), 141–153.

Teng Ssu-Yu. "Chinese Influence on the Western Examination System," *Harvard Journal of Asiatic Studies*, VII (1943), 267–312.

Teutsch, Fritz. "Die Studirenden aus Ungarn und Siebenbürgen auf der Universität Leyden von 1575–1875," *Archiv des Vereins für siebenbürgische Landeskunde*, N.F., XVI (1881), 204–226.

The Institute of International Education: 1919–1944. New York: Institute of International Education, 1944.

Thiersch, Friedrich Wilhelm. *Ueber den gegenwärtigen Zustand des öffentlichen Unterrichts in den westlichen Staaten von Deutschland, in Holland, Frankreich und Belgien*. 3 vols. Stuttgart: Cotta, 1838.

Thomson, Charles A., and Walter H. C. Laves. *Cultural Relations and U.S. Foreign Policy*. Bloomington: Indiana University Press, 1963.

"Thoughts on Comparative Education. Festschrift for Pedro Rosselló," *International Review of Education*, V, 3 (1959).

Thurber, Charles H. *Principles of School Organization: A Comparative Study, Chiefly Based on the Systems of the United States, England, Germany, and France*. Worcester, Mass., 1899.

Thut, I. N., and Don Adams. *Educational Patterns in Contemporary Society*. New York: McGraw-Hill, 1964.

[Ticknor, George.] *Life, Letters and Journals of George Ticknor*. Ed. George S. Hillard. 2 vols. Boston: Osgood, 1876. 2nd ed., Boston: Houghton Mifflin, 1909.

Toulouse, Madeleine. *La nation anglaise-allemande de l'Université de Paris origines à la fin du XVᵉ siècle*. Paris: Recueil Sirey, 1939.

Tugwell, Rexford G., and Leon H. Keyserling, eds. *Redirecting Education*. 2 vols. New York: Columbia University Press, 1934–1935.

Turnbull, G. H. *Hartlib, Dury and Comenius*. Liverpool: University Press, 1947.

Ulich, Robert. *The Education of Nations: A Comparison in Historical Perspective*. Cambridge: Harvard University Press, 1961.

Ulrich, A. "Nierdersächsische Studenten auf fremden Universitäten" in *Zeitschrift des Historischen Vereins für Niedersachsen*, pp. 199–280. 1889.

University Exchanges in Europe, 2nd rev. ed. Paris: League of Nations Institute of Intellectual Cooperation, 1929.

Ushinskii, Konstantin D. Articles on comparative education in *Zhurnal dlya vospitaniya*. 1857–1858.

_____. *[Pedagogical Travels.]* 1862–1863.

_____. Writings on education in Great Britain, France, and Germany in *Zhurnal Ministerstva Narodnogo Prosveshcheniya*. 1860–1862.

Van Dorsten, J. A. *Poets, Patrons, and Professors: An Outline of Some Literary Connexions between England and the University of Leiden, 1575–1586*. Ph.D. thesis. Leiden: Universitaire Pers, 1962.

Veress, Andreas, ed. *Matricula et acta Hungarogrum in universitatibus Italiae studentium*. 2 vols. Kolozsvár: Fontes rerum Hungaricarum, 1915–1917.

Veress, E., ed. *Olasz egyetemeken járt magyarországi tanulók anyakönyve és iratai 1221–1864 (Matricula et acta Hungarorum in universitatibus Italiae studentium, 1221–1864)*, Vol. III of *Monumenta Hungariae Italica*. Budapest, 1941.

Villey, Pierre. *L'influence de Montaigne sur les idées pédagogiques de Locke et de Rousseau*. Paris: Hachette, 1911.

Vogel, J. Ph. *The Contribution of the University of Leiden to Oriental Research*. Leyden, 1954.

Voigt, Georg. *Die Wiederbelebung des classischen Alterthums*, 2nd ed. Berlin: Reimer, 1880–1881.

Walz, John A. *German Influence in American Education and Culture*. Philadelphia: Carl Schurz Memorial Foundation, 1936.

Wang, Y. C. *Chinese Intellectuals and the West, 1872–1929*. Chapel Hill: University of North Carolina Press, 1966.

Waterman, Richard, Jr. "Educational Exhibits at World's Fairs since 1851," *Educational Review*, V (February 1893), 120–139; (March 1893), 219–231.

Waxin, Marie. *Statut de l'étudiant étranger dans son développement historique*. Doctor's thesis, University of Paris. Amiens: Yvert, 1939.

[Weidner, Edward W., et al.] *The International Programs of American Universities*. East Lansing: Michigan State University Press, 1958.

Weidner, Edward W. *The World Role of Universities*. New York: McGraw-Hill, 1962.

Weigle, F., ed. *Die Matrikel der deutschen Nation in Perugia (1579–1727)*. Tübingen, 1956.

Weiss, R. *Humanism in England During the Fifteenth Century*, 2nd ed. Oxford: Blackwell, 1957.

Wheeler, W. Reginald, Henry H. King, and Alexander B. Davidson. *The Foreign Student in America*. New York: Association Press, 1925.

White, Lyman C. *International Non-Governmental Organizations*. New Brunswick: Rutgers University Press, 1951.

Wijnman, H. F. *Ethiopia and Western Europe: The Origins and Development of Ethiopic Studies and Printing in Western Europe in the 16th Century*. Leyden, 1964.

Wils, Joseph. *Les Étudiants des regions comprises dans la nation germanique à l'Université de Louvain*. 2 vols. Louvain: Smeetsters, 1909–1910.

Wilson, Howard E., and Florence H. *American Higher Education and World Affairs*. Washington, D.C.: American Council on Education, 1963.

Windakiewicz, Stanisław. *Informacje o akademiach uniwersytetu bolonskiego, Archiwum do dziejow literatury is oświaty w Polsce.* Cracow, 1892.

Wing, Yung. *My Life in China and America.* New York: Holt, 1909.

Winter, E., ed. *Die deutsch-russische Begegnung und Leonhard Euler: Beiträge zu den Beziehungen zwischen der deutschen und der russischen Wissenschaft und Kultur im 18. Jahrhundert.* Berlin: Akademie-Verlag, 1958.

Winter, Eduard. *Halle als Ausgangspunkt der deutschen Russlandkunde im 18. Jahrhundert.* Berlin: Akademie-Verlag, 1953.

Wischnitzer, Markus. *Die Universität Göttingen und die Entwicklung der liberalen Ideen in Russland im ersten Viertel des 19. Jahrhunderts.* Berlin: Ebering, 1907.

Wolf, Karl. "Altpreussische Studenten auf niederländischen Hochschulen im 17. Jahrhundert," *Ekkehard, Mitteilungsblatt deutscher genealogischer Abende,* XV, 1–3 (1939).

_____. "Pfälzische Studenten im 17. Jahrhundert auf niederländischen Universitäten," in *Mannheimer Geschichtsblätter* (1930).

Wooton, E. *A Guide to Degrees in Arts, Science, Literature, Law, Music, and Divinity, in the United Kingdom, the Colonies, the Continent, and the United States.* London, 1883.

World Handbook of Educational Organization and Statistics. Paris. UNESCO, 1952.

World Survey of Education: Handbook of Educational Organization and Statistics. Paris: UNESCO, 1955.

World Survey of Education II: Primary Education. Paris: UNESCO, 1958.

World Survey of Education III: Secondary Education. Paris: UNESCO, 1961.

World Survey of Education IV: Higher Education. Paris: UNESCO, 1966.

World Year Book of Education. University of London Institute of Education and Teachers College, Columbia University. 1932–1940, 1948 to date.

Wrangel, Ewert. *Sveriges litterära förbindelser med Holland särdeles under 1600-talet.* Lund, 1897.

Young, Robert F. "Bohemian Scholars and Students at the English Universities from 1347 to 1750," *English Historical Review,* XXXVIII (January 1923), 72–84.

Young, R. Fitzgibbon. *Comenius in England.* London: Oxford University Press, 1932.

Zimmer, H. *The Irish Element in Mediaeval Culture.* New York: Putnam, 1901.

Zimmern, Alfred. *Learning and Leadership: A Study of the Needs and Possibilities of International Intellectual Co-operation.* London: Oxford University Press, 1928.